AN INTRODUCTION TO Psychology

RALPH NORMAN HABER University of Rochester

AHARON H. FRIED John Jay College, The City University of New York

AN INTRODUCTION TO

Psychology

HOLT, RINEHART AND WINSTON, INC.

New York   Chicago   San Francisco   Atlanta
Dallas   Montreal   Toronto   London   Sydney

Library of Congress Cataloging in Publication Data

Haber, Ralph Norman
An Introduction to Psychology.
Includes bibliographical references and index.
1. Psychology. I. Fried, Aharon H., joint author.
II. Title. DNLM: 1. Psychology. BF121 H114i
BF121.H17   150   74-30068
ISBN: 0-03-007451-7

29875

Cover, frontispiece, and part opening photography by Jerry Weisburd

Acknowledgments

For permission to reprint from copyrighted materials the authors are indebted to the following:

Academic Press, for figures 1.2, 2.26, 2.27, 4.8, 4.10, 4.15, 4.17, 4.18, 7.4, 8.5, 12.2, 12.6, and table 8.2.

American Association for the Advancement of Science, for figure 5.6 from D. E. Berlyne. Copyright 1966 by the American Association for the Advancement of Science; for figure 7.8 from M. I. Posner and S. W. Keele. Copyright 1967 by the American Association for the Advancement of Science; for table 12.2 from S. Glucksberg and L. J. King. Copyright 1967 by the American Association for the Advancement of Science.

American Book Company, for figure 5.7, from J. W. Atkinson, 1964. Used by permission of the American Book Company.

American Institute of Physics, for figure 1.27.

American Psychological Association, for excerpts from the AAT from R. Alpert and R. N. Haber. Copyright 1960 by the APA; for the table 4.1a from E. J. Archer. Copyright 1960 by the APA; for figures 14.3, 14.4 from S. E. Asch. Copyright 1956 by the APA; for figure 2.9 from F. Attneave. Copyright 1954 by the APA; for figure 3.8 from P. E. Baer and M. J. Fuhrer. Copyright 1968 by the APA; for figure 3.15 from A. Bandura (a). Copyright 1965 by the APA; for 3.14 from A. Bandura and F. L. Menlove. Copyright 1968 by the APA; for figure 3.18 from L. E. Bourne and E. J. Archer. Copyright 1956 by the APA; for table 4.4 from R. Bugelski. Copyright 1938 by the APA; for figure 9.4 from W. Dement and N. Kleitman. Copyright 1957 by the APA; for figure 5.1 from B. Hillman, W. S. Hunter, and G. H. Kimble. Copyright 1953 by the APA; for figure 4.16 from W. C. F. Krueger. Copyright 1929 by the APA; for figure 9.3 from R. S. Lazarus and R. A. McCleary. Copyright 1951 by the APA; for figure 9.2 from E. McGinnies. Copyright 1949 by the APA; for figure 17.1 from S. A. Mednick. Copyright 1962 by the APA; for figures 5.3, 5.4 from N. Miller (a). Copyright 1948 by the APA; for figure 4.19 from B. B. Murdock, Jr. Copyright 1962 by the APA; for table 4.1b from C. E. Noble. Copyright 1952 by the APA; for figure 4.3 from C. E. Noble and D. A. McNeely. Copyright 1957 by the APA; for figure 8.1 from A. Paivio and K. Csapo. Copyright 1969 by the APA; for table 4.2 from A. Paivio, J. C. Yuille, and S. A. Madigan. Copyright 1968 by the APA; for figure 4.6 from L. R. Peterson and M. J. Peterson. Copyright 1959 by the APA; for table 17.3 from G. L. Paul. Copyright 1967 by the APA; for figure 7.6 from G. Sperling. Copyright 1960 by the APA; for figure 4.14 from B. J. Underwood. Copyright 1957 by the APA; for figure 4.9 from G. Wood and M. Bolt. Copyright 1968 by the APA; All reprinted by permission.

American Sociological Association, for excerpts from Guttman's Scale on pp. 694-695.

Archives de Psychologie, Geneva, for excerpts from Likert's Scale on p. 694.

British Psychological Society, for figure 9.6 from W. B. Webb, 1965. By permission of the British Psychological Society.

Cambridge University Press, for figure 2.4d.

Clarendon Press, for figures 3.4, 3.5; data adapted from *Conditioned Reflexes* by I. P. Pavlov (1927) by permission of the Clarendon Press, Oxford.

Clark University Press, for figure 1.12 from S. Hecht. Copyright 1934 by Clark University Press; reprinted by Russell and Russell, New York, 1969.

CRM Books, for figure 11.1 from R. Kellogg, 1967. Understanding children's art. In P. Cramer (ed.), *Readings in developmental psychology today*.

Children's Television Workshop, for figures 10.1, 10.2 from S. Ball and G. A. Bogatz. 1970. Copyright held by Children's Television Workshop, 1 Lincoln Plaza, New York, N.Y.

The Dryden Press, for figure 1.18 from *Psychology: Its Principles and Meanings* by Lyle E. Bourne, Jr. and Bruce R. Ekstrand. Copyright © 1973 by The Dryden Press. Reproduced by permission of The Dryden Press.

Grune & Stratton, Inc., for figure 6.20 from R. W. Sperry and M. S. Gazzaniga, 1967. Language following surgical disconnection of the hemispheres. In F. L. Darley (ed.), *Brain mechanisms underlying speech and language*; and figure 9.7 from B. T. Engel, 1973. Clinical applications of operant conditioning techniques in the control of cardiac arrhythmias, Part 1. *Seminars in Psychiatry*, vol. 5, no. 4 (November). By permission.

Harcourt Brace Jovanovich, Inc., for figures 1.28, 2.23, 3.6, and table 1.2; adapted by permission of the publishers from *Introduction to Psychology*, 5th edition, by Hilgard, Atkinson, and Atkinson, copyright © 1971 by Harcourt Brace Jovanovich, Inc.

Harper & Row, for the table on page 531.

Holt, Rinehart and Winston, Inc., for figure 3.19 from *A Time to Learn: A Guide to Academic and Personal Effectiveness* by Phillip L. Bandt, Naomi M. Meara, and Lyle D. Schmidt. Copyright © 1974 by Holt, Rinehart and Winston, Inc.; for figure 3.16 from *Social Learning and Personality Development* by Albert Bandura and Richard H. Walters. Copyright © 1963 by Holt, Rinehart and Winston, Inc.; for figure 12.1 from *Systems and Theories of Psychology*, Third Edition, by James P. Chaplin and

The past decade has seen increasing interest in psychology in every kind of college and university in the United States and Canada. Nearly every college student takes an introductory psychology course, and more students are choosing psychology as a major area of study than ever before. What is so special about psychology that can account for this growing attraction to it as a discipline and as a field of concentration?

Part of the answer lies in the perceived relevance of psychology to contemporary life, problems, and personal well-being. Living a satisfying life in today's world requires that we learn to know ourselves and to know others. The study of psychology makes it possible to learn how to solve new problems, not just understand old ones. The fact that psychology is a science of the study of human behavior rather than merely a storehouse of facts about such behavior accounts for much of its growing appeal.

A second reason for the appeal of psychology is more personal. As human beings, we are all psychologists. We have observed human behavior and have developed some general principles that have explanatory power, and even occasionally predictive power. Psychology is the only scientific discipline in which the scientist and the subject matter are the same—human beings. However, though we all may be psychologists at heart, we are not all scientists. This means that much of our knowledge is incomplete, inaccurate, biased, and even distorted. A course in psychology, then, offers each of us a chance to "test" ourselves against the experts.

A third appeal of psychology has to do with its direct application to fundamental problems facing us all. We hope that psychology may tell us how to equalize opportunities, reverse the effects of poverty and discrimination, make people honest with themselves and with others, and resolve a host of other real problems of individuals living in society.

Though there are other reasons for the appeal of psychology, the three reasons suggested are important ones and draw substantial attention throughout the text. All of the student's expectations may not be met, for some of them may turn out to be unreasonable or ill-founded on careful examination, but the examination is important.

Every new text must have a justification for its existence, especially one designed for a course that already has good textbooks available. Several features make *An Introduction to Psychology* a distinctive addition to the group.

1. Coverage is complete, including the full range of topics receiving the greatest attention in psychology today. I have not tried to write an encyclopedia, but have provided a range of coverage of sufficient depth so that the student will not have gaps in his knowledge or understanding of the discipline after using this text.

2. New topics that have come into their own within the past decade receive their due share of attention. Information processing analysis of perception, language, thinking, and memory is represented by an entire chapter in addition to significant parts of several others. The discussion of development is subdivided into those factors reflecting maturation and those that derive from an interaction between the individual and the world around him, a trend now permeating much of psychology beyond development. Consciousness as a topic is no longer taboo in scientific psychology, and an entire chapter is included. A revolution has been occurring in our concept of mental health, especially regarding treatment versus prevention, and the trend is reflected in the discussion of these topics.

3. Boxed material is included in every chapter to provide further discussion, illustrative experiments, more examples, an aside, or important information which is tangential to the content of the chapter at that point. The student may refer to the boxes while reading the text, turn to them after finishing the chapter, or omit them. They provide a mechanism for the better student to draw more from each chapter and be further challenged.

4. Introductory questions, marginal glossary terms, and substantial summaries are included throughout. The questions serve as an introductory guide to the important concepts in each chapter. The summaries are particularly helpful for review and as an aid in organizing what the student has understood from the chapter. Each of the marginal terms appears in the glossary along with a brief definition. The glossary is incorporated within the subject index so that the student may easily refer back to the text page where the terms appear.

5. The student is introduced to the scientific method. This is not a book on how to be a scientist, but is concerned with allowing the student to see the interplay of research, knowledge, and discovery. Research methods are discussed in the introduction as a set of principles to be applied and reapplied throughout the course.

6. A substantial appendix covers a rather full range of scaling and descriptive and inferential statistics. Although this text does not present results of experiments in great statistical detail, students have the opportunity to learn something about statistical methods. The instructor can refer the student to the chapter for independent study or it may be taught at any appropriate point within the semester.

7. The arrangement of chapters is flexible and may be reordered as the instructor wishes. The sequence in the text is from basic mechanisms (sensation, perception, learning, verbal processes, and biological bases) through more general cognitive processes (thinking, language, information processing, consciousness), on to personality, and finally to the influence of society upon the individual—that is, from building blocks to complete edifices.

8. A full range of ancillary materials is available. Most important is a study guide designed either for personalized study at the student's own rate or for more traditional study. It includes a summary and review of the content of each chapter and several sets of study and test questions. For the instructor there is a manual which provides lists of concepts introduced in each chapter, cross references to other parts of the text, suggested demonstrations, films and other audiovisual aids, and hints on effective means for presenting the content of each chapter.

In addition to my esteemed co-author, Aharon Fried, there are many people whom I wish to acknowledge for the contribution they have made to the writing and production of this book. Special appreciation goes to Nancy Schutz for her editorial advice and skill throughout the development of the manuscript, to Enid Klass for her photographic research, and to Robert Fendrich, Michael Friedman, Paul Richer, Ronald Scheff, and Vivian Shayne, who provided invaluable help with research, writing, and selection of illustrations. My secretary, Leslie Chopek, bore the brunt of the typing, filing, and general chaos in my office occasioned by so monumental a task as this one, and she did so with skill and ever-smiling warmth. Nearly every member of the staff of the college social sciences department at Holt, Rinehart and Winston participated in this project with typically superb professional skill. I could not have succeeded without their help.

Finally, I offer my love and thanks to my wife Lyn, who helped me survive the birth of this book with her understanding, patience, and love. For each of these, I dedicate the book to her.

Rochester, New York   R.N.H.
January 1975

Contents

PART 2 COGNITIVE PROCESSES 305

Introduction

What Psychology Is

Something in our human nature impels us to seek order out of confusion. We need to feel at home, surrounded by people and things about which we can make predictions and assumptions. We expect our friends to greet us with a smile; strangers to stay at a correct social distance; and our loved ones to remain affectionate.

There are two aspects of this human need to order our lives. On the one hand we share with our cousins the apes an irresistible drive of curiosity. We need to find out about the world around us, to understand and master our environment, both animate and inanimate. And when our assumptions fail us, when we learn that something is not what is seemed to be, we are confused and disturbed. If out of the blue a stranger greets us like an old friend or affection turns suddenly to hostility, we feel and behave as if we have "lost our bearings" —the world, or that part of it with which we are presently intimately involved, can no longer be understood.

A very important part of sanity is the ability to understand behavior. Psychologists have often remarked on the similarity of behavior of one who is suddenly confronted with the unexplainable and someone who is suffering from a serious mental disorder.

UNDERSTANDING BEHAVIOR

We start acquiring the ability to understand behavior in our first days of life. A face becomes familiar, becomes Mother, and then becomes particularly welcome when it smiles. We amass a collection of recognizable sights and sounds and learn to expect certain consequences from things we do or things other people do to us. We begin to map our world.

1

As our world widens, so does our search for significance in it. A toddler explores a new pattern of behavior just as he does a new toy: How does it feel to bang two pots together? What will Mother do if I bang them? Is banging pots good or bad? And gradually what had been initially an innate behavior—or behavior we are born with—becomes personally directed and verbal. We begin to articulate questions about people, things, and events around us; we acquire the ABC's of understanding behavior—we become, in a sense, psychologists.

There would seem to be a universe of difference between the tentative, exploratory approaches of a newcomer to a kindergarten class and the activities of a social psychologist studying a small group of people. Actually, the only real difference lies in the reasons for their behavior: the kindergartner has no choice —his mother has, so to speak, thrown him to the wolves, and he must learn about his classmates in order to survive; the psychologist has chosen to study the group and remains more or less aloof from it. For the toddler, attempting to order and understand other people's behavior is part of his life; for the psychologist it is part of his job as well. In both cases the experimenter, age 5 or 50, almost always arrives at an understanding of a particular type of behavior by moving from the general to the particular and back again. The baby does not say: "Smiles mean *good;* this face is smiling; this face is good," but something like that is going on inside its central nervous system. The kindergartner uses whatever he has learned about behavior in general to interpret the behavior of

Arthur Sirdofsky

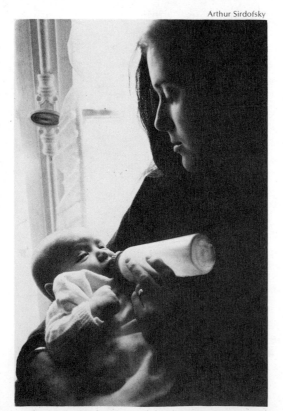

We start acquiring the ability to understand behavior in our first days of life.

the other toddlers, and in the light of his experience with them he modifies his general concepts about certain types of behaviors. The psychologist too selects some general statements about behavior, tests them in the light of specific behaviors he observes, and concludes that the general statements are right, wrong, or a bit of both. As we mature, our explanations of the world and of the people in it become more conscious. We move from direct and unreflective use of experience to speculation and enquiry. We begin to advance—to ourselves and others—"psychological theories," generalizations from what we have read, heard, or experienced, to explain why people act as they do.

But we soon realize that a statement explaining *why* somebody does something will satisfy some inquirers but not others, depending upon their ideas about the motives for the behavior. If, for example, we want to account for a good-looking and intelligent student who is nevertheless a loner, both in general campus activities and in terms of close friends of either sex, we can imagine at least two approaches to explaining the situation.

Understanding Jim

Psychologist One would take a careful history of the subject. What experiences have taught Jim to behave as he does? Consciously or unconsciously, people repeat the behaviors they have found to be rewarding. If Jim is a solitary sort of person, some past experiences must have either rewarded him for keeping apart from others or hurt him when he tried to be sociable. Perhaps his father was an Army officer who moved with his family from one military post to another throughout Jim's childhood and adolescence. An only child, Jim never had the chance to sink his roots into a community, either in school with his classmates or in a neighborhood with the other children. This isolation was perhaps aggravated by parents who were neither sociable nor very interested in Jim's loneliness and by the caste system of the Army, which limited even further the opportunities for socializing. Jim has never known what it is to be "one of the crowd"; to be a comparative loner is the only way of life he knows. And because the art of socializing is one of the most important and difficult childhood accomplishment, the verdict on Jim must be that he is merely undertrained; he just doesn't know how to behave as part of a closely knit peer group. The treatment must be to help him practice the social skills he lacks.

That is all very well, Psychologist Two may say, but not all Army children are loners, and Jim has certainly not lacked for peers who appreciate his good looks and are impressed by his grades. People are not the passive products of circumstance: Jim behaves the way he does because of the way he feels. What is important is not the objective world in which he has lived but the subjective world he experiences now—and apparently has always experienced. Jim spends several hours with Psychologist Two, taking tests and talking with him, until Jim's "personality profile" is ready.

Jim, Two reports, has the feeling of living in an alien universe. Other people are strangers, and strangers do not like you. For him the important thing is not to seek friendship and affection (both dangerous and futile) but to avert hostility. And one of the safest ways to do this is to avoid close contacts. Jim, Psychologist Two reports, has a very negative self-image. A postscript to the report, however, emphasizes that he is in no sense seriously ill emotionally; he is perfectly rational and well oriented, and his mild and apparently chronic depression does not prevent him from functioning efficiently, though in a somewhat limited fashion.

One thing, however, did concern Two. Whereas Jim did well on the psychological tests, just as he did on college tests, in conversation with him Two felt it hard to make adequate contact. Jim's answers sometimes didn't seem appropriate. It was almost as if Jim hadn't heard all that Two was saying. ... as if he hadn't heard. "Jim," the psychologist asked the next time they met, "have you ever had a hearing test?" Jim appeared surprisingly disturbed by the question, but replied that he had not.

The answer came back quickly from the audiologist. Jim definitely, though not acutely, had a hearing loss in both ears. It was clear that whatever else had contributed to Jim's sense of alienation, his inability to hear a good deal of what was going on, his difficulty in carrying on casual conversations, particularly in a group, and his frequent sense of social embarrassment were major factors.

The total Jim, then, lived in three worlds: the objective world of experience, the subjective world of feeling, and the sensory world of perception. None was unimportant, but was one more important than the others? Would Jim become able to live more satisfactorily in all three worlds by tackling his misfit in one? After considerable debate it was decided to attack all three problems. A simple hearing aid was able to bring Jim's hearing almost to normal. He was encouraged to join a couple of clubs concerned with his main scholastic interests and there learned the art of mixing freely and happily with others. And in group therapy he found that it was possible to be liked for his own sake and to exchange feelings and affection without fear or embarrassment. A new Jim began to emerge.

Is there an answer to the original debate? Was there a reason for Jim's behavior? We are all the products of our past; we are what we have become and we have become what we have learned. Regardless of anything else, Jim would have been a very different person if he had grown up in a stable and homogeneous community of lifelong friends and relatives. But at the same time behavior is motivated by the present, not the past. One cannot forecast a personality accurately by merely writing a biography. The main outlines may be the products of the past, but to understand a specific individual at a specific time the inner world—the personality, the self-image, the "feeling tone"—needs to be explored. And last but not least, we are creatures of flesh and bone—and nerves and hormones. We react by our bodily behavior to the stimuli our sense organs provide, and changed messages from either our sense organs or the rest of our body will result in changes in behavior.

Jim was helped by two different psychologists and a hearing specialist. Each probably contributed to his improvement; each may have taken full credit for it. And if they were typical of their specialties, they may have disagreed violently with each other about the theory and practice of psychology.

We should not be surprised at this. A discipline is not a set of answers and prescriptions for truth; it is a set of questions and some advice about how to go about answering them, based on the history of other such quests. Psychology is a relatively young discipline and its subject matter is the most complicated thing in the human universe—the behavior or organisms, including and particularly man. It is a mistake to think of psychology as being all of one piece. Psychology is whatever psychologists do, and they do a large number of very different things and they argue a great deal while doing them.

Such disagreement is a good thing, unless you are in dire need of certainties. One of the most realistic and therefore best ways to begin the study of a discipline is by considering its dilemmas: the important problems that are unsolved, either because nobody has found a plausible answer or because scientists have equally good but different answers. Now, what would psychologists argue about in considering the case of Jim?

The first point of disagreement would probably be over what makes Jim a "case" in the first place. Psychology is the science of behavior, so apparently Psychologist Two thought Jim's behavior, that is, being a loner, had something wrong with it. But is there then a right and wrong way of behaving? Shouldn't Jim be allowed to do his thing, so long as he doesn't feel sick or hurt himself or other people or break laws—and even then some people claim that the moral convictions of an individual may on occasion outweigh the laws.

Regardless of that, people, supposedly wise and interested in Jim, have decided that he would become a more fulfilled and happier person if he changed his way of life. They have compared his behavior with a picture they have in their minds of how the "normal" and reasonably happy student behaves, and the comparison has been unfavorable to Jim.

Jim may not agree with these people, however, and in that case they are stymied. He cannot be forced to receive professional help, and psychologists have long known that even if Jim were talked into trying therapy, it would be useless unless he was strongly motivated—unless he was unhappy in his present state ("felt sick") and wanted to change.

The important thing, then, appears to be not Jim's behavior but how he feels about it. We have moved from his objective world to his subjective one, from Psychologist One to Psychologist Two. Jim's feelings are the important thing behind his behavior. But do we know what they are? Does Jim, except in very general terms? We have two problems in exploring another person's subjective world: first, we never know it directly—it is, in a famous phrase, a "black box" we cannot open, and we must rely on the owner of the box to tell us about its contents; second, we know from our own experience that there are many ways in which we can misinterpret that report. Even assuming that Jim wants to reveal everything completely honestly, there may be things that he has pushed away from his consciousness, and there is always the problem of translating feelings into words.

Psychologist Two knows all this, and to a great extent Two goes about the job indirectly. Sets of questions, pictures, and other ways of testing Jim are standardized, and by comparing his responses with those of other persons a reasonably accurate, or at least systematic, idea of what's going on inside him can be formulated. Psychologist Two will, of course, never know for certain that this picture is accurate. The private world of the individual is, above all, private.

Psychologists One and Two represent the two main divisions of psychology today, particularly as it applies to the personal problems of individuals. Psychologist One relies on what we *know* about Jim, and what we know is what we see—his behavior. He would not dismiss feelings and emotions, but he would point out that these are, first, Jim's private possessions, and, second, that they are reflections of his behavior.

Jim, and unhappy people like him, have become entangled in bad habits. Untangle them, help them to learn more effective ways of acting, and their feelings about themselves will change. Psychologist One would contrast the methodical and scientific procedures of learning theory with the unsubstantiated guesses and "insights" of depth psychology, and the speed and effectiveness of his form of therapy with the lengthy treatment and doubtful outcome of his colleague's.

To this Psychologist Two would take great exception, asking whether his colleague believes that the most important thing about oneself is what one does or how one feels, and adding disparaging remarks about psychologists who behave like automobile mechanics, as if people were robots, with nothing inside them but the machinery of action. And Two would add, in a more serious tone, that judging behavior as healthy or unhealthy, as needing or not needing change, has its place in brainwashing and totalitarianism. Finally, Two would point to the many records of grateful clients in his or her files and say that nobody has a monopoly on effectiveness.

We can imagine Jim's hearing specialist, who had checked his hearing and improved it by a hearing aid, sitting in on the argument with a tolerant smile. The doctor would reflect that in general medical practice the great majority of emotional problems are handled perfectly satisfactorily by appropriate medical treatment, whether that be surgery or medication or a special diet. For the doctor the human body is a marvelous and mysterious thing that cannot be ignored, as the psychologists seemed to be doing. If concentration on anxiety or depression or ineffective behavior must result merely in interminable arguments, the doctor would be content with the prescriptions that had helped so many student patients through academic or personal crises. He would have in mind, too, the large number of hospitalized mental patients whose treatment with drugs and other modalities enabled them to return to the outside world.

You may very well be confused. If there is so little agreement about the application of psychological knowledge to real problems, psychology must be in a pretty bad way, and is it worth the time and trouble to take a course in it? But a rejection would be very unwise. Furious disagreement and debate is a sign of vitality in any discipline, and today's turmoil in no way invalidates the great progress that has been made. It is upon the foundation of this knowledge that the ability to solve what we have called the primary dilemmas is being erected.

NATURE OR NURTURE?

The discussion we have overheard has been between two clinical psychologists, whose job it is to help people lead happier and more successful lives. Behavior comes from what we have learned, says Psychologist One; behavior comes from how we feel, says Two. These two approaches to the *clinical* understanding of behavior—together with all their many variants—about cover the field.

But if we persist in our curiosity about the origins of behavior another problem emerges. It was stated in the first paragraphs of this introduction that we share with our cousins the apes an irresistible drive of curiosity. What else do we share with them?

Are we unformed lumps of human clay at birth, or, like complex computers, are we preprogrammed in various ways, with built-in reflexes, predispositions, abilities, and disabilities that our genes have set up for us? This question is a reflection of the old psychological and philosophical debate over nature versus nurture: do we behave as we do because we are members of the species *Homo sapiens* or because we are products of our culture?

The question is both broad and controversial, and we will discuss it in more detail in later chapters. But because it is so basic to the understanding

Harry F. Harlow, University of Wisconsin Primate Laboratory   Arthur Sirdofsky

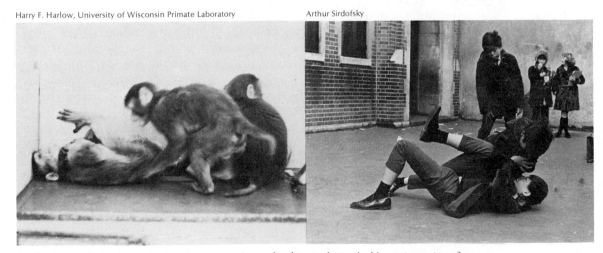

Are the innate behaviors inherited from our primate forebears of practical importance to us?

of behavior we need to learn something about it in this bird's-eye view of the discipline of psychology.

There are three aspects of nature—of this question of who we are. The first two will be dealt with only briefly here. First, as in the case of Jim, we are what sickness or health has made us. If we are deaf or blind or lame we are not like other people and will not behave as they do; if we are in very good health and bursting with energy we are also unusual; we are different when we are old from the way we were when we were young. These physical underpinnings of personality may have developed at any time, from the womb to the present day. Second, what we have inherited from our parents, grandparents, and our whole genealogical line makes us unique and provides us with individual advantages and disadvantages in the game of life.

Genetically we are unique—even if we are one of a pair of identical twins. But we are also members of a species; we are variations on a theme, which is *Homo sapiens.* Like everything else in the world, this theme has not remained, and cannot remain, constant. In fact, we might say that *Homo sapiens* is itself only the latest variation upon the great theme of Life, or organic, cellular existence, which has evolved from the Primeval one-celled organism to the miracle of man.

The central part of biology is evolution. More organisms are born than there is room or food for; the better equipped live and produce the next generation; the less fortunate do not, and their lines die out. Natural selection inexorably spreads the genes that provide success to the organisms possessing them and curtails those that do not. Genes change—or mutate—at random, and nature picks them over, throwing away those that are less useful. Every species moves over millennia toward greater and greater adaptation to its environment.

But environments change too, and some species, beautifully specialized for the old, perish, like the woolly mammoth, in the new. New species evolve, and as fortunate genetic changes succeed each other over almost endless time, organisms become more and more complex, through the primates to us.

These fortunate changes are of two kinds, with a considerable gray area between. Morphological changes provide new and better bodily equipment: the color of the skin shifts toward greater inconspicuousness; binocular vision, prehensile hands, and a swollen frontal cortex make a weak and naked ape the master of his environment.

But different and less visible changes are also wrought by the pressure of natural selection. The way an organism behaves is as much a product of its genetic equipment as is the make-up of its anatomy and physiology. A mallard duck does not decide—or learn from its fellow ducks—how to go about the complex courtship ritual. Its knowledge is built in, a product of the way its genes have dictated the development of its neural equipment.

All behavior of all animals is the product of evolution interacting with the experience the organism has in its environment throughout its life. Both parts of this combination are determinants of behavior. No organism is a robot, com-

Mike Levins   A. Devaney, Inc., N.Y.

James Foote, photographer; Courtesy Office of Economic Opportunity

We are products of our culture as well as our genealogy.

pletely preprogrammed without any reference to the environment; nor is any organism born a blank slate, motivated solely by experience. In the course of evolution, however, the relative importance of these two components of behavior has changed. The beautifully complex behavior of the social insects—bees and ants, for example—contains few options for the individual; bees learn the best places to gather honey but they learn very little else; the rest of behavior has largely been decided for them. And the equally complex social life of chimpanzees may look like a happy-go-lucky celebration of free will and anarchy, but bands of chimpanzees who have never met will behave in pretty much the same way. They do what their genes tell them to do, even though the pressures of natural selection have produced a successful way of life that allows a considerable role for learning and experience. No chimpanzee could be found that is monogamous; no gibbon would be as promiscuous as a chimpanzee.

The discipline of ethology, which is concerned with the biological, genetic components of behavior, is even younger than psychology, and its three great founders, Frisch, Lorenz, and Tinbergen, were alive and active in 1973 to share the Nobel Prize. Recently more and more attention has been paid to the implications of ethology in the study of human behavior, giving rise to a storm of debate and controversy. Here we have room for only a few general remarks concerning this issue. First, the genetic determinants of behavior exist in all organisms; we are not exempt. And what they are and how they operate in man is of enormous importance in our understanding of ourselves. Second, it has been reasonably well established that such *innate* behaviors—behaviors that we do not have to learn but know from birth—do exist and in some cases can be identified in man. All babies, even congenitally deaf and blind babies who are without any means of perceiving and learning from others, smile, frown, and weep under the appropriate circumstances. All flirting individuals in any culture so far investigated flick their eyebrows up and down as a part of their facial gestures. All cultures have a greeting gesture of flinging the arm up in the air. Our genes do tell us things about the way to behave.

Third, since man is preeminently a learning animal, are the innate behaviors he has inherited from his primate forebears and developed during his own evolution of any practical importance if all of them are submerged by his cultural conditioning? Can we assume that a useful solution to the problems of understanding behavior will be provided by a study of human innate behavior?

A practical and perhaps crucial problem immediately follows: how can we study innate behavior in human beings? Except in the rare and illuminating cases of the congenitally blind and deaf, we will never come across a human being who has not already modified to an almost infinite extent whatever innate behaviors he or she possesses. Finding innate behaviors in man is much more difficult than finding needles in haystacks, because in behavior the needles themselves turn into hay.

The example of Jim comes from the field of clinical psychology, which is concerned with the diagnosis and treatment of the emotional and behavioral problems of individuals. This is what most people think of when they hear the word "psychology," and to the layman it is undoubtedly the most interesting part of the discipline. But most psychologists are not clinicians, as evidenced by the fact that persons in this area represent only about 10 percent of the more than 40,000 psychologists in the American Psychological Association.

Photographer unknown

Marriage and the family are of continuing interest to psychologists. Three generations of the same family on their wedding day: Düsseldorf, 1908; New York City, 1943; Long Island, 1971.

Shulamith Stein   Catherine Noren

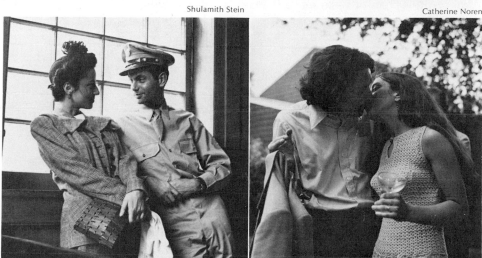

This is only one of the stereotypes people fall into about psychology. Even the clinical areas of psychology are by no means interested only in disorders, although it is true that early attention was focused on pathology. The meaning of mental health, the nature and nurturing of creativity, the ways in which gifted children can be stimulated, how learning can most effectively take place, all these offer as important opportunities for psychologists as do the problems of emotional illness, failure, and deviance.

Further, though no psychologist can possibly be an expert in all areas of the discipline, and nearly all psychologists specialize more or less narrowly, a psychologist is not a narrow problem-solver. He may specialize, but he needs to be broadly conversant with areas outside that specialty. Techniques are tools; his attention should be focused on what can be done with them rather than on narrow competence in their use. Psychology is more than a science, but the distinguishing characteristic of any psychologist is his ability to explore the problems of behavior scientifically, to know how to search.

Finally, in providing an outline of what psychology is—of what psychologists do—today, we should remind you that new interests, shifts of direction, and changes in priorities are happening all the time. The science and profession of psychology today is fluid, is as little specialized as possible, and frequently brings those specialties together for mutual assistance. A famous psychologist has said that "where behavior or thought or attitude or motivation is, there psychology is." And where are they not?

THE SCIENTIFIC METHOD

Earlier in the chapter we remarked that the distinguishing characteristic of any psychologist is his ability to explore the problems of psychology scientifically. Let us take a look at some of the important characteristics of the scientific method, and see how it and the psychologist's way of behaving interact.

First, science is *empirical*. It is an accumulation of facts, of descriptions of events, persons and relationships. One problem peculiar to psychology, as distinct from most other sciences, is that students approach the discipline with a wide range of preconceptions. While a physics or chemistry student has few predetermined ideas about the behavior of molecules or the difference between acids and bases, is there a man or woman alive, including psychologists, who has not a load of beliefs and prejudgments about human behavior and the nature of the self? To study behavior empirically—completely without prejudice—is essential; it is also extremely difficult.

Second, science is *systematic* and organized. The collection of facts about behavior is the brick-making of psychology, but we can learn to understand behavior only by putting those bricks together into explanatory structures. This is the process we talked about in the first part of the chapter—the process of "making sense" of behavior. Unfortunately, there are no rules or guarantees for this process. In going from collected facts to generalizations (the process of *induction*) or in the opposite direction, from generalizations to specific prediction *(deduction),* scientists use guesswork, hints from colleagues, ideas that come in dreams, hunches, and a multitude of other things—including, of course, logic.

This is the way the mind works. A scientist is not a computer that swallows a collection of data and prints out a theory. But to be able to work this way and at the same time to subject one's results to the criterion of empiricism is both intellectually difficult and emotionally demanding. The combination of empiricism and system-building leads to the central demand upon scientists: complete intellectual honesty.

Third, science is concerned with *measurable* quantities. An artist with words may be able to convey to a reader the essence of the difference between anxiety and depression, but the only way this can be expressed meaningfully in science is in terms of the difference between scores on tests designed to measure these two variables. Of course, two different kinds of physiological measures, or two different experimental manipulations, might very well produce different results. Most of the work of research scientists consists of comparing more of something with less of the same thing: more people behave in a certain way in this situation than in that; the rat reaches the goal of the maze measurably faster under these conditions than under those; this person scores x percent higher on a paper and pencil test than that person.

Fourth, science *defines precisely.* For one scientist to ensure that another will know exactly what he is talking about his definitions need not be eloquent, but they must be precise. One of the best ways of achieving this precision, particularly with abstract qualities such as intelligence or anxiety, is to define them *operationally,* to describe measurable (or at least concrete) activities or processes that produce or accompany them. For example, "intelligence" is defined as an ability to carry out certain specified tasks, particularly to make a certain score on an "intelligence test." Researchers in psychology depend upon three different tools to accumulate and check facts—natural observation, experiments, and correlational studies. Observation in the natural environment is often the only way one can collect information, and with appropriate care it can be an important source of facts and a means of validating those facts. But in general, since such circumstances leave too much uncontrolled, it is incredibly difficult

to determine the relationship between any of the facts, and especially to make any statements about what the causes of the behaviors in question might be. Therefore, natural observation is most often used as a source of ideas and hunches which then can be subjected to more controlled tests and verification by one of the other two methods. Before considering those, however, note should be made of one variety of observation that is often used in science—the case study. Most often used in personality and clinical research, it is a description of a person or an event, or of progress in therapy. A psychologist can take many such cases, each different in specifics, and examine them for similar patterns. From these similarities he can construct generalities that can then be used to predict and describe new instances of a particular behavior. He may also be able to develop ways to test his description experimentally.

The major scientific tool of the research psychologist is the experiment. If one of the characteristics of science is that it deals, whenever possible, with measurable quantities, then one of the preferred ways to find out how things work is to compare two of these measurable quantities and see whether their changes relate. We select one changeable quantity, one *variable* (such as light-dark), and do things to it so that at different times, under different circumstances, or with different people or animals (subjects) its values will be measurably different. This manipulated variable is called the *independent variable*. The subjects "possessing" this variable will have some other measurable characteristic (such as activity-sleep) whose relation to the first we wish to explore. As we vary the independent variable we measure the values of the *dependent variable* and come up with two sets of figures which are hopefully related. Rules exist for deciding how likely it is that they *are* related.

The rest of the experimental method consists of a series of precautions to ensure that the relationship we have searched out has not been *contaminated* by some unsuspected factors. This can become a complex and difficult task, and success in completing it is the distinguishing mark between a good and a bad experiment. Here we can mention only the most obvious of these precautions.

First, the experiment must be *replicable,* able to be repeated by anyone. Every relevant detail must be described. This is, in effect, saying that the experiment must be defined operationally, so that another can read the report of the experiment, repeat all of the manipulations on a comparable group of subjects, and duplicate the results. If he cannot produce the same results, and the original scientist made no error, then some relevant detail has been omitted from the report.

Second, the variables under study must be isolated by *controlling* all other variables. No person is identical to another (not even identical twins), and because persons do vary, precautions must be taken. The most frequent way of doing this is a four-step procedure. First, as many subjects as possible are involved, with the hope that the irrelevant differences among them will cancel out and the average result will become, so to speak, depersonalized. Second, subjects are chosen that are as like each other as possible on all variables except the ones being studied. Sex, age, intelligence, background, and personality are some of the factors that often are controlled, or made equal, depending on the nature of the experiment. Third, the subjects are divided into two groups, which are treated identically except that one group *(the experimental group)* is subjected to manipulations of the independent variable while the other *(the control group)* is not. This makes it possible to assume—or at least hope—that differences which show up between the two groups are caused only by the changes of the independent variable in one of them. Finally, whenever selections are made, such as who shall join the control group, they are made *at random,* by pure chance, again with the assumption that the differences among subjects will cancel out.

This experimental method has defects. For one thing, we cannot always use it, especially with human subjects, either because it is impossible—some behaviors are distorted by the mere act of measurement—or because it is unethical to conduct experiments in a particular area. In addition, the method is artificial. The selection and isolation of variables pares the complex totality of behavior down to what the experimenter thinks is important, and he then attempts to eliminate the others. This, in effect, involves a prejudgment that has to be based on the experimenter's guesses, hunches, and theoretical biases. The experimental method, in other words, attempts to be completely pragmatic, but it can never achieve this. Finally, even when we have found something that can be measured and manipulated and that we deem significant (this may be wishful thinking), the mere fact of the experimental situation must inevitably be a distorting factor. Maybe the subjects behave unnaturally because they want to please (or annoy) the experimenter. Too, they know that the situation is not real, so they cannot be expected to behave exactly as they would outside the laboratory. But we can admit these faults and perhaps others and still conclude that the above experimental method will have to do until something better comes along—and that is not likely.

Another method of conducting research is the *correlational approach.* The researcher chooses two measurable variables (such as height and weight) and records a score for each subject. The degree to which the two variables are related can be expressed statistically (see Appendix). A positive correlation is one in which high scores on one variable go with high ones on the other and low scores on one go with low scores on the other (as with height and weight); a negative correlation is one in which high scores on one variable go with low scores on the other and vice versa.

The disadvantage with correlational research is that is does not tell us anything about causation. If A and B are found to vary together, it is never certain that A causes B, or vice versa—or, to complicate matters, whether both A and B are both influenced by some other unexplored variable C. In an experiment we can be reasonably sure that at least some of the changes in the dependent variable are the results of the changes in the independent variable, but in correlational research all variables have the same status. Thus it is much more difficult to make meaningful analyses of correlational results, and there is a continual temptation to produce interesting interpretations of results when the factual backing is inadequate to support them.

The point we have just made can serve as an introduction to an important truth about science in general and experimental science in particular. One is never *told* anything in scientific research; a series of events are counted or measured by the researcher, who organizes and *interprets* these data to lead to certain conclusions on his part. And these conclusions are quantitative: no experimenter may say "A is caused by B"; all he can say is that "A is found more frequently (by a measurable extent) after B than without B; therefore it is probable that a given instance of A is caused by B," or that a given instance of B will be followed by A.

THE ETHICS OF PSYCHOLOGY

All of the behavioral sciences, as well as such professions as law and medicine, come into intimate contact with the more or less private lives of their subjects. Society values the contributions that psychology can make to the understanding of its collective and individual behavior through research and the diagnosis and treatment of maladjustment, but both the state and the American Psychological Association attempt to lay down ethical guidelines and to see that the privacy of the individuals involved is protected.

In psychological research, the guidelines are concerned with the relations of the researcher to his subjects with respect to privacy, honesty, and safety. The researcher observes (and may maniuplate) the behavior of his subject. This behavior may be very private, and whether it is observed directly or indirectly—through reports by the subject or record-searching—the research must observe all the principles of confidentiality that apply to legal and medical practice. In cases where the nature of the research makes it impossible for this confidentiality to be maintained in some degree, the American Psychological Association's *Ethical Principles of Psychologists* state that the situation must be explained to the subject, who must also be told of plans for protecting confidentiality as part of the procedure for obtaining his consent.

The subject must give his *voluntary consent* to the experiment after *full disclosure* of the experimental procedure. In practice, the two italicized terms raise many problems. For one thing, many experimental subjects are college students who are asked to volunteer for studies as part of their course work. In other cases subjects are institutionalized mental patients or retardates, prison inmates, schoolchildren, or other groups who are not entirely free to do as they wish. With regard to honesty, as you will discover from later chapters of this book, it is often necessary that subjects not have a full knowledge of what is ahead for them, so that the consent they give is not fully informed. For this

© 1965 United Feature Syndicate, Inc.

reason, the *Principles* state that after the data are collected the experimenter must explain to the subject the nature of the study and make an effort to remove any misunderstanding that may have arisen.

With regard to safety, the *Principles* say that where experimental procedures may have undesirable effects on the subject, it is essential for the investigator to detect, remove, or correct these consequences, even when they are long-term aftereffects.

Controversy and debate have existed regarding the classification of deviance and its treatment since there have been psychiatrists and clinical psychologists. For example, it has been observed that those diagnosed as retarded and mentally ill and institutionalized for their deviance come often from the lower socioeconomic groups. Cultural bias in assessment tests is considered a factor as is bias on the part of the diagnostician. In a healthy attempt at self-appraisal, psychologists from William James to the present have questioned and continue to question the discipline in a constructively critical way. In 1966 the American Psychological Association established ethical standards to be used in psychological testing, following a 1965 United States Congressional investigation into abuses in testing and invasion of privacy.

Unfortunately not all states have licensing requirements for psychologists in practice. However, in 1967 the American Psychological Association adopted guidelines for practicing psychologists designed to protect the client's welfare.

THE APPLICATIONS OF PSYCHOLOGY

For most of us our introduction to psychology is by way of one of its social applications. In school we are told that we are taking a test designed by psychologists in order to find out about our interests and abilities; we encounter an irresistibly persuasive ad and find out that it was created in consultation with motivational psychologists; like Jim we have problems in our relations with other people and seek help from a counselor or clinical psychologist. And so we may expect a text on psychology to deal mainly with its uses in "real life."

We are continually meeting problems in our day-to-day activities, and at some times we are more successful in finding solutions than at other times. When we hit on a satisfactory solution, it is usually because we have been able to eliminate—or at least reduce—the unknowns and unpredictables that created the problem in the first place. Using findings from the various areas of psychology, we can take much of the guesswork out of this process. From the following series of examples, it will become apparent that a knowledge of psychology can be applied to reduce the unknowns in a great many areas of human endeavor.

1. As a parent or teacher, how can you best help a child grow emotionally and intellectually? How will you face the introduction of increasingly complex tasks? When is he mentally able to learn to read?

2. How can mentally disturbed members of society be helped? Is there any way we can shape the social and emotional environment in which children grow to insure a good adjustment to later life?

3. What role should you play in dealing with someone who is depressed, anxious, or overexcited? How do you relate to someone who seems unable to make a rational decision? What do you do with a liar or a cheat, and how can you identify a liar?

4. Should drug addicts be jailed or treated as sick people? Is homosexuality or prostitution a sickness, a crime, or an individual moral decision?

5. Imagine that you are the personnel director of a large corporation. You have before you the applications of three capable candidates. How do you choose the most qualified? What tests can you give each to provide useful distinctions among them that are not the products of your personal bias?

The psychological effects of interior design are well recognized. Left, a cold, sterile interior; right, a warm and pleasing scene (office of the president of Lanvin–Charles of the Ritz, designed by Melanie Kahane).

Arthur Tress   Henry S. Fullerton, 3rd

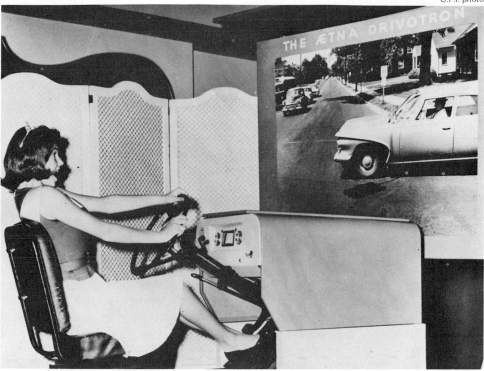

The findings of psychologists in the fields of sensation and perception contributed to the design of a driving simulator (above) and the 707 Astrojet cockpit (below left). The techniques of advertising have been developed through motivation research. Below right, advertising contributed for public good.

Give this card to someone you love.

I Love You & Wear your seat belt

Safety belts, when you think about it, it's a nice way to say I love you.

6. Once your man is on the job, how will you get optimal performance from him without lowering his morale? What incentives must be offered to make him want to do his best? How will you maintain his interest in boring and repetitious aspects of his job?

7. Your new worker will be using tools and machines of various sorts. Presumably they are efficient in doing what they are designed to do. But for this particular worker are they equally efficient in offering ease of control and adjustment? Do they tell him clearly and quickly what is happening? Are the dials and other forms of readout quickly legible and conveniently placed? Does the designer take into account the physical and psychological limitations of the operator? (In a broader context, how can the effective design of automobile controls and instrument panels contribute to road safety?)

8. Your company has spent five months hiring and training people to design and produce a new product. Management has picked what was thought to be the best design to motivate people to buy the product. Now, how does your company get people to choose its brand over another? What motivates the consumer to buy this product and how can that motivation be kept high?

9. In advertising your product, what is the best way to attract and hold people's attention? Should your selling message be emotional? rational? loud? subdued? What approach will appeal most to your consumers? What types of people are most likely to listen to your message? If part of your campaign is to put up billboards, how much should they try to say?

10. If a public-service organization, a political party, or a special interest group wishes to influence opinion or prejudice or stimulate action, can the techniques of advertising be used? What—if any—is the difference between "selling" a candidate, a cause, or a social campaign and selling a bar of soap?

11. What are the effects of "mood" drugs on the human being? Are they good for him? Can they produce harmful side effects? When—if ever—should they be used? Should they be illegal?

How can we best cope with any of these problems? Assistance in finding possible answers comes from the various areas of psychology. Psychologists work scientifically, drawing on available and existing theoretical knowledge, experimenting to test their hypotheses, and trying to adapt their findings to existing problems.

THE ORGANIZATION OF PSYCHOLOGY

No matter how we look at it, the end result of behavior is a series of movements—of muscles, of blood and hormones, of impulses along nerves—that taken together describe the actions of the individual. Because behavior is the subject matter of psychology, eventually the different areas of psychology should meld into a single unified statement of the origins and meaning of behavior.

But no discipline, including psychology, has achieved this unification of subject matter. There are, perhaps, two different reasons for this. First, to be able to assimilate all the partial theories into a single one without any internal contradictions implies a degree of maturity, of success in its task, that no science has ever attained or probably ever will attain. Second, to be able to understand a mass of data and the theoretical structures that are built up from them the scientist must "chunk" these data and theories into digestible portions and master them successively, before their interrelationships can be appreciated.

The way we have chunked the discipline of psychology in this book forms its table of contents, and the next part of this introduction will briefly outine these contents.

Principles of Behavior

As was pointed out at the beginning of this introduction, if we cannot react to and make sense out of the world around us, our behavior loses all coherence. The bridge between the person and the environment, the way the person uses the past in interpreting the present, and the forces, from within or without, that turn the passive recipient of stimuli into a behaving organism form the content of Part One of this book.

We stay in touch with the world through our sense organs—ears, eyes, nose, and the like. Certain kinds of energy in the environment are capable of stimulating these organs because of the specialization of the organs—the ears for vibration that constitutes sound, the eyes for electromotive radiation that constitutes light, and so forth.

We are always learning, and we are conscious of only a very small part of that continuing process. The past confronts the present in three ways, which almost always coexist in any example of learning. We are *conditioned* by previous experience to make certain behavioral choices, whether or not we are aware of why we do so; we can drive an automobile, play a role on the stage, or do well in a quiz because we have *practiced and memorized;* we fit in easily with our fellow group members because we have *modeled* our ways of behaving on those whose approval we desire.

Behavior, then, is shaped by the past and the present, by what has been learned and what is perceived. But what behavior? Just as we must consider behavior in time and place, so we must avoid thinking of behavior as merely a response to these factors; behavior is a positive thing, it is as much a statement as it is an answer.

Motivation is a very general term for all the determinants of behavior, for all the sources of energy that form, so to speak, the mainsprings of action. We can distinguish three general groups of motivating forces. First, the organism needs to keep in balance: it needs fuel—air, food, and liquid; it needs a certain operating temperature—protection against heat or cold; it needs to eliminate waste products. Second, evolution, as we have pointed out, has developed certain motives that have proved useful to the species: a desire to *do* things, to be active; curious, sexual, a need for sensory stimulation, for competence in manipulating the environment, and so on. Third, as a thinking animal, the human being makes decisions based on a coming together of needs and experience. A student is motivated to spend time and trouble to be trained to become a doctor in order to satisfy humanitarian motives or achieve status or a high income or whatever. Some levels of this pyramid of motives are rational decisions, others are more purely emotional and may not be fully conscious. And so, finally, the past shapes certain goals, needs, and drives in the individual that direct his behavior, motivate him, and about which he may rationalize but which are not themselves rational.

We have seen that each of these basic principles of behavior has an important physical component, and the concluding chapter of Part One considers aspects of neurophysiology that are important in behavior, as well as some pathological conditions that may account for behavioral abnormalities.

Cognitive Processes

In Part Two we focus on the activities of the monitor and guide of the organism-environment interaction. These activities are the cognitive processes, what may be described as the processing of sensory information, which uses a great deal of material available in the memory banks of the brain.

Information processing transforms the sensory input from the mental picture of something just seen that remains when we close our eyes into the short- and long-term memory. This memory store of symbols, including verbal symbols, forms the raw material of thinking.

Language is a medium of thought, both in the sense that we use language to communicate our thoughts and in the sense that we perceive our own thinking processes as verbal. The development of thinking and the development of language in the child are therefore closely related.

Although we all know of times when our brain functions, so to speak, by itself—as when we stop trying to remember a name or telephone number and are suddenly provided with it—most of the time we know at least most of what our brain is doing. We are aware of what we are perceiving, of what we think about it, and of what we intend to do. We are, in other words, *conscious*. There are, of course, many complicating factors to add to this simple description of consciousness. The use of "most of" in the definition recognizes the existence of the unconscious, particularly as expounded in the complex hypotheses of Sigmund Freud, and the strange activities of our brain during dreams and hypnosis, as well as the equally strange though very different state of consciousness during meditation. Finally, we must take account of the effect of drugs such as marijuana and LSD on our consciousness.

Development of Personality

So far our only mention of time has been in relation to the effect of learning on behavior. But a much broader behavioral effect of time is found in the maturation and development of the individual. We consider these topics in the first two chapters of Part Three, paying particular attention to cognitive development.

The fruit of this development—not only of cognition but of all the other behavioral principles we have discussed—is the personality of the individual, the characteristic way in which the individual behaves (and, we assume, thinks and feels) as he or she adapts to the environment. A completely satisfactory theory of personality would be able to account for the present in view of the physical and experiential past and forecast the future, at least in terms of probabilities. We have not yet even begun to have such a theory, but we have several competing partial theories, which will probably provide subsidiary insights to the unified one that is yet to come.

These theories differ chiefly in the attention they pay to one or the other hypothetical structure that is assumed to underlie the behavioral variable of the individual. Of these structural theories the Freudian is the best known and still the most influential. The structures or processes of the Id, Ego, and Superego are assumed to develop during infancy, childhood, and adolescence and to dictate the main features of adult personality. Almost all other structural theories of personality are revisions of or reactions against the Freudian.

Trait theories of personality enumerate many separate facets of the individual, calling the total his or her personality. The development of standardized questionnaires and other methods of assessment has been of great help in this approach. At the same time the development of computer methods of finding patterns in the mass of data that can be accumulated on any individual makes it possible that a new theory of personality structure will develop, this time statistical instead of philosophical.

The Social Context

We cannot understand the individual unless we recognize that behavior is always influenced by those with whom the individual has interacted or is interacting. It is, for example, doubtful that we could even conceive of the personality of someone who had always been completely solitary. Yet so far our attention has been focused on the origins of behavior of the individual, without paying much attention to the role of others in his or her life. Social psychology, then, has two important aspects. As usually considered, its subject matter is the interactions of individuals in a society, a community, or a group and the way in which that collectivity behaves as a whole. But the social context is also intimately involved in what is usually called abnormal psychology. Not only is disturbed behavior always disturbed because of or in relation to the behavior of others, but also anxiety and the sense of *dis*-ease of the disturbed individual arises in almost all cases from his perceptions of the behavior of others toward him. These two aspects of the social context of psychology are the subjects of Part Four.

Our interest is in the way in which we perceive others, not as amateur or professional psychologists but in our day-to-day working and playing lives,

Mike Levins   Arthur Sirdofsky

Mike Levins

The art of socializing, a significant and often difficult childhood accomplishment, is important throughout life.

and the way in which we achieve unified and consistent mental pictures of those with whom we come into contact. This process necessarily involves simplification and in many cases distortion as we extrapolate from the social glimpses we get of other persons.

One major reason our perceptions are biased has to do with our social motivation. We seek achievement, approval, friendship, and affection, and the emotional drives that activate us color our behaviors and perceptions. Just as others and our perceptions of them influence our behavior, so we influence others, and out of this mutual feedback the structure—both formal and informal —of the group or society develops.

An important part of social psychology is the attitudes we have toward social concepts, people, or groups of people. It is the structure of our attitudes that forms the cognitive steering mechanism of our social beliefs and actions, and therefore the assessment of attitudes is, perhaps, the most important part of social psychology.

The behavior of the individual in society, as we showed in our earlier example of Jim, can be judged from two points of view: by how it compares with other people's behavior or by how the individual himself feels about his behavior. An example of this double criterion of disturbed behavior is our changing attitude toward homosexuality. Homosexual behavior itself used to be viewed as a sign of disturbance; if you were homosexual you were "sick," regardless of how you felt about it. Now the "official" attitude of the American Psychiatric Association has shifted to regard homosexuality as a psychological disturbance only if it is accompanied by anxiety or depression: The treatment is aimed at the individual's feelings rather than his behavior. At the same time, of course, we should recognize that the attitude of society toward minority forms of behavior of any sort can cause neuroses in the minority member—society frequently creates neuroses by declaring some of its members to be neurotic.

The efficiency of the mechanisms by which we seek to protect ourselves from the stresses of coping with reality has been one criterion of "normalcy" or neurosis. If we become too unhappy or anxious to function properly, or if our efforts to cope with anxiety force us into ineffectual or self-destructive behavior, such as withdrawal or reliance on drugs, then we are candidates for psychotherapy. How we are treated will, of course, depend on the theory of neurosis that our psychotherapist accepts. These theories are, broadly speaking, of three kinds: those that emphasize the importance of how we have learned to behave, those that emphasize the importance of our structures of feelings and drives, and those that emphasize the complex mechanisms of our bodies, particularly our central nervous and hormonal systems. It is both puzzling and fortunate that each of these competing groups of theories produces successful treatments of neurosis.

Part 1

Principles of Behavior

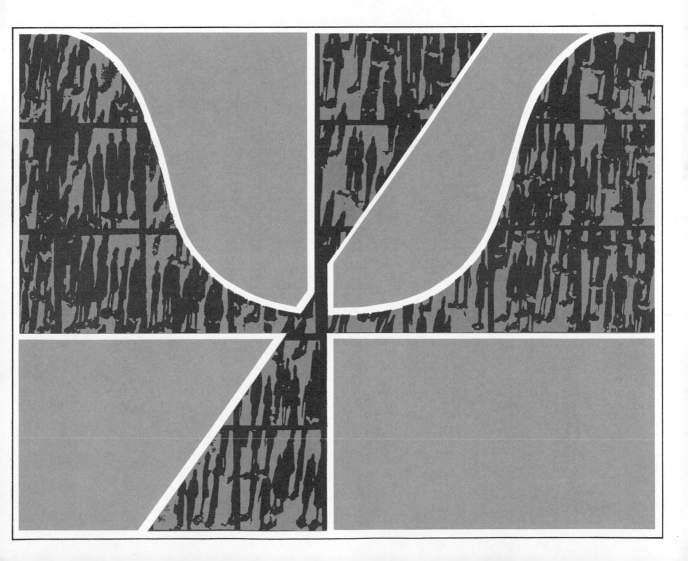

Chapter One

Sensation

What is the difference between sensory detection and
  discrimination?
How are sensations measured?
What is light?
How does the eye receive light and transmit it to the brain?
What is sensory coding?
How do we perceive color?
What is sound? How does the ear transmit it to the brain?
What factors influence our perception of smells?
What other senses does man have?

Every living being is in some way kept in touch with the external world. The bombardment of light, sound, temperature, pressure, and chemical stimulations on our senses offers us a never-ending array of information to use for maintaining our contact with the environment. During an afternoon at the beach, for example, our eyes are host to a succession of sights—sparkling water, boats in motion, shifting patterns of sunlight and shadow. We hear the cries of birds, the drone of passing planes, and the lapping of incoming waves. Our skin is stimulated by currents of air, the heat of the sun, and the shifting pressure of our clothing as we move our bodies. The smell of fish and suntan lotion mingles with the taste of sandwiches and salt water. In addition, we might feel hungry, tired, hot, or sleepy.

But even in these peaceful surroundings, many more sensations are available than we can possibly attend to. At times we are not aware of any of them. Or we can become so accustomed to a particular sensation—a steady humming noise, for example—that we no longer realize it is there. Yet, in order to function in our environment, we must receive information through sensory channels and we must organize and interpret that information in ways that are both efficient and beneficial to us. This chapter is primarily concerned with the reception of sensory information—with the ways in which our bodies are equipped to receive from the environment input that is vital to our survival. Chapter 2 will deal more directly with what we do with the sensations we receive—that is, with the subject of perception, the way we organize and interpret sensory information. Yet because these processes are very intimately connected, it is not always possible to consider them as separate entities; a certain amount of overlap between discussions of sensation and perception is inevitable.

Our perception of the world greatly affects how we behave in the situations we encounter. It is because we apply perceptions emanating from sensations received in one situation to other, similar situations that psychologists study sensations in detail.

The basic ways we interact with our environment are partly determined by the physical properties of that environment, which are conveyed to the brain in the form of stimuli. But our own senses—of sight, hearing, taste, smell, touch, and balance—also determine how much and what kinds of stimuli we receive. These sensory modalities serve as channels of information about the external world; what they do not transmit is lost. When there is an "overload" of stimuli, we may not receive the most important information—the fact, for example, that a dish with many ingredients and lots of seasoning contains mushrooms, to which we are allergic.

The senses, however, do not select but simply convey information. The selection process occurs in the brain after the information arrives there. The sensory channel does not serve the perceiver's expectations, wants, or needs. It simply picks up as much information as it can handle and passes it along to what are traditionally thought of as "higher" centers.

Each of our sense organs—eyes, ears, nose, skin, tongue—is a specialized receptor system geared to convert physical or chemical stimuli received from the environment into neural signals, or impulses. These impulses are transmitted by a network of connecting nerve cells to the brain, where they can be processed. Some processing begins even before the impulse reaches the brain. For example, vision includes both neural processes that modify signals from the receptors before they arrive at the brain and neural processes that transmit impulses by an independent channel directly to the brain. We will consider each of the major sensory systems separately in this chapter.

FOUR ASPECTS OF SENSATION

Imagine the predicament of a safecracker going about his business one night in a deserted office. He thinks he hears a noise outside in the hall. He stops to listen—has he only imagined it? His question is one of sensory detection—determining whether or not something is there. As he listens the sound is repeated;

Roy Berkeley

Eyes, ears, nose, and skin are specialized receptor systems which keep us in touch with the external world.

something is there. But what? Now his question is one of identification—what kind of sound is there? In this instance, the question isn't difficult; our safe-cracker correctly identifies the sound as that of approaching footsteps.

What should he do? If he makes a dash into the hall and down the fire escape whoever is out there may try to stop him. But his only alternative is to

31

risk a drop from the second-story window. His decision depends upon how he solves two further questions of sensation. First, there is the question of discrimination—determining how these footsteps differ from other footsteps. Do they sound like those of the cleaning woman? A policeman alerted to investigate? An executive ready to put in some late work? Our thief estimates that he could easily get past a woman; a man might be more difficult. But he is out of luck; the footsteps are definitely masculine. Still one more question remains to be solved before he gives up the easier escape route. The footsteps seem slow and heavy. Perhaps he can still make his dash provided only one man is out there. Determining how much of a thing is there is the sensory question of scaling. As the thief continues to listen to the approaching footsteps, he realizes that they belong to two men. That does it; he dives out the window.

Most sensory experiences are not as dramatic as those of the safecracker, but they all involve the four basic aspects of sensation—detection, discrimination, identification and recognition, and scaling. How human beings deal with these aspects of sensation, conceptualize them, and measure them is the core of psychophysics—the study of how stimulation from the environment is translated into usable psychological information by the senses.

Detection

detection

The first question we would ask if we thought we had sensed a stimulus in our environment would be, "Did something happen?" This would be the question of detection. Psychologists see detection as a matter of the amount of energy a stimulus must exert in order for us to determine that something happened. They attempt to measure the smallest amount of physical energy a person can distinguish through each sensory channel, and they define that smallest amount as a *threshold*.

threshold, absolute

threshold, differential

Sensory thresholds are of two kinds—absolute and differential. If we are talking about the amount of light that can be distinguished against a background of total darkness, or about the amount of noise that can be distinguished against a background of total silence, we are talking about an *absolute threshold*. The point at which a stimulus exerts enough energy to be detected against a background of zero stimulation of the sensory channel it impinges on is the absolute threshold for that stimulus (Table 1.1). But because for each kind of energy there is a range of intensity that a person will never detect, a range that he will always detect, and in the middle of these two a relatively narrow range that he sometimes can and sometimes cannot detect, our definition of absolute threshold needs to be further refined. Arbitrarily, psychologists consider the absolute threshold as the intensity of stimulation that can be detected 50 percent of the time.

Absolute thresholds are interesting to psychologists because studies of them help us to determine in part the nature of human sensory receptor systems. If an experimenter places a subject in a completely dark room and then flashes

Table 1.1 Some Approximate Values for Absolute Thresholds

Sense Modality	Threshold
Vision	A candle flame seen at 30 miles on a dark clear night
Hearing	The tick of a watch under quiet conditions at 20 feet
Taste	One teaspoon of sugar in two gallons of water
Smell	One drop of perfume diffused into the entire volume of a six-room apartment
Touch	Wing of a fly falling on your cheek from a distance of 1 centimeter

SOURCE: Galanter (1962)

a light of increasing intensity until it is seen on half of the flashes, then the intensity at which the light is seen by half the subjects on half the trials can be said to be the absolute threshold for the human detection of light. But in reality probably the only people who would ever have any experience of this absolute threshold are those who live in, work in, or visit caves! It is of interest primarily to learn about the processes in the receptors themselves.

Ordinarily, the environment contains some level of stimulation of each of our senses, called the adaptation level. Now, when we talk about the amount of energy a stimulus must exert in order to be detected against a background level of adaptation, we are talking about a *differential threshold*. The question here is: How much greater than the level of adaptation must the stimulus be in order to be detected? At night, when the level of light adaptation is very low we can see stars clearly—provided there is little atmospheric interference. Yet during the day we don't see any stars at all, although they are there and are emitting the same intensity of light as at night. The classic example of the relativity of the differential threshold is John Locke's demonstration that, if a person puts his left hand in a basin of cold water and his right hand in a basin of hot water, then plunges both hands in a basin of water at room temperature, his left hand will experience the tepid water as warm and his right hand will experience it as cool.

adaptation level

Discrimination

When two stimuli in the same sensory modality have been detected, we are faced with the necessity to discriminate, that is, to differentiate, between them. How much difference must there be in the energy exerted by two stimuli for a person to tell that they are different? Detection and discrimination are similar problems, for both of them deal with thresholds; however, detection is concerned with the difference between the presence and absence of a stimulus or between a heightened stimulation and an adaptation level, whereas discrimination is concerned with the difference between two heightened stimulations—a 25-watt and a 40-watt electric bulb. The discrimination threshold is usually defined as the *just noticeable difference* (j.n.d.); it varies with the base

discrimination

just noticeable difference (j.n.d.)

Signal Detection Theory

Our coverage of the threshold concept has assumed that when a subject says, "Yes, I see it" or "No, I don't see it," we can be certain that he did or did not see it. Early in their work psychophysicists began doubting this assumption. To check on the subject's "honesty" they instituted *catch trials,* in which no stimuli were presented. It soon became apparent that subjects often reported the signal present on some of these catch trials, though they were not trying to fool anybody. At the impoverished levels of stimulation they were working with, the subjects were very often not really sure whether or not they had seen the signal. They resorted to guessing, and what is more, their guessing was systematic. In order to accurately assess the subject's sensory capacities then, *signal detection theory* (or *decision theory* as it came to be called in psychology) appeared. This is a method of studying the process by which the subject decides whether or not he is confident enough that the stimulus is there to say, "Yes, I saw it."

In a classical psychophysical detection experiment, we present a signal of a specified intensity on some trials but not on others. The intensity chosen should be near threshold level. The subject may say either, "Yes, I see it" or, "No, I don't see it." He must give one of these responses; "I'm not sure" is unacceptable. On any given trial one of four things may happen: (1) The signal is present, and the subject responds yes; decision theory calls this a "hit." (2) The signal is not present, and the subject responds no; this is called a "correct rejection." (3) The signal is present, but the subject says "I don't see it"; this is a "miss." (4) The signal is not present, but the subject says, "Yes, I see it"; this is a "false alarm" (Fig. 1.1).

A fully "honest" subject would be expected to make only "hit" and "correct rejection" responses, or at worst only those two plus a few "miss" responses; we would not expect any "false alarms" from him. Thus in an experiment in which

level of the first stimulus presented. Adding one instrument to a string quartet will noticeably swell the ensemble sound, but an orchestral string section would have to be augmented by considerably more than one instrument for a difference in volume to be discriminated by the average human ear. (Most conductors, on the other hand, can probably make this discrimination. To that extent, we would say they have a smaller j.n.d.) The same principle operates when stimulation is diminished. Slowing a car from 20 to 10 miles an hour will be noticed immediately, but slowing from 80 to 70 probably will not.

A combination of physical factors has greatly simplified this problem for psychologists. It is an observed fact that the amounts of additional energy required to produce a j.n.d. are usually related to the base level of energy in a constant ratio. For example, a man carrying a 50-pound bag of cement will not notice an additional weight smaller than 1 pound. If the bag weighs only 25 pounds to begin with, he will notice the addition of only $\frac{1}{2}$ pound. On the other hand, a 100-pound bag must be increased by 2 additional pounds before he

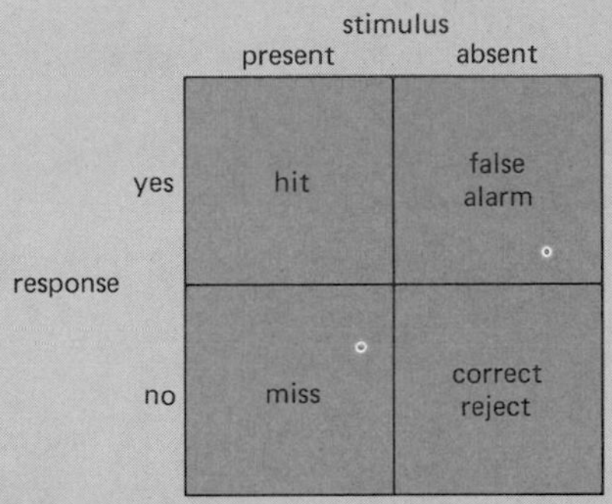

Fig. 1.1 A matrix which provides a classification of the four possible outcomes as a function of whether a stimulus or a blank was presented, and of whether the perceiver responded with a yes or no. (Haber and Hershenson, 1973)

the signal is presented on 50 percent of the trials, we might expect our subject to say the signal was present on approximately 75 percent of the trials when it is presented, and to miss it on about 25 percent of those trials. We would also expect, however, that he would say the signal was not present for fully 100 percent of the trials when it was indeed not presented.

In typical experiments, however, subjects usually give some false alarms; they say yes, they see the light, even when it was not presented. This is because the decision task—to decide whether the minimal stimulation they received really came from the stimulus or not—is difficult. The lower the intensity of the stimulus, the more difficult the decision.

If we find a subject who gives a lot of false alarms, we should also be aware that many of his "hits" should not be counted. He seems to be saying yes indiscriminately. What then should we call his threshold? What we need is a way of separating the subject's sensitivity to the stimulus intensity from the decisional processes that lead him to say yes.

will notice any difference. In each case the ratio of additional energy to base energy can be reduced to a single percentage: $\frac{1}{50} = \frac{2}{100} = \frac{4}{200} = .02$, which is the constant ratio of additional energy to base energy needed to produce a j.n.d. in the case of weight.

The constancy of this relationship for each sensory modality was first observed by Ernst Weber in the mid-19th century. It can be expressed in the formula $\Delta I / I = k$, in which I is the magnitude of the base energy (50 pounds of cement for example), ΔI is the amount of additional energy necessary to produce a j.n.d. (1 pound of cement), and k is the constant ratio (.02). This formula is known as *Weber's law,* and the constants are known as Weber fractions.

Weber fractions

Since Weber's day researchers have produced a long list of similar fractions or ratios for different kinds of stimulation. A comparison of these ratios (Table 1.2) reveals that the sound receptors are the most sensitive to changes in stimulus energy; they are capable of discriminating differences in pitch as small as .003. The taste buds are the least sensitive. The constancy of these ratios

Table 1.2 Weber's Constant

Sense Modality	Weber's Constant[a]
Pitch of a tone	1/333
Deep pressure, from skin and subcutaneous tissue	1/80
Visual brightness	1/60
Lifted weights	1/50
Loudness of a tone	1/10
Cutaneous pressure	1/7
Taste for saline solution	1/5

[a]Approximate values of Weber's constant for various sensory discriminations. The smaller the fraction, the greater the differential sensitivity.

SOURCE: Hilgard, Atkinson, and Atkinson (1971). Data are approximate, from various determinations.

tends to hold, however, only for the middle ranges of stimulus intensities. When the base levels of energy are very high or very low—particularly when they are very low—the ratios may deviate widely from the established constants. For weight, for example, the change needed to be just noticed when the base weight is 1 gram is much more than 20 milligrams, even though that is the size of the j.n.d. that the Weber fraction would indicate.

Identification and Recognition

identification   Like detection, identification is also subject to influences from the environment. Obviously, the safecracker has a better chance of identifying the footsteps correctly in a silent building than in one in which there is a great deal of noisy activity in the hallways. But influences can also be more subtle. If he is alert to the possibility of footsteps, he is much more likely to recognize them—or recognition   to recognize them more quickly—when they occur. The task of recognizing what a stimulus is, or classifying it in some way, will be discussed in Chapter 2.

Scaling

scaling   Scaling is the process of ordering different stimuli along some dimension, such as brightness or loudness. Once we have discriminated between several light intensities, for example, we may try to scale them, that is, to specify *how much* difference there is between them. Many sensory properties are difficult to scale, though we may try. "Sarah is twice as beautiful as Suzy" is a statement about the placement of two girls on a scale of beauty. Intuitively this differs from such a statement as, "This bag of cement is twice as heavy as that one." We have greater confidence in talking about a scale of weight than one of beauty.

But, in fact, psychologists have developed techniques to specify scales for any stimulus property you are interested in. Some of these are more useful than others, but all are possible. They all involve the assignment of numbers to stimuli. When we then relate the numbers to each other, we have a scale. These scales have different properties, depending upon how we assign numbers to stimuli.

The simplest scale is barely a scale at all. We can assign numbers to the members of a basketball team, but the fact that Jones is number 20 and Smith number 10 does not tell us anything about the relative heights, abilities, ages, or anything else about how Jones and Smith compare. House numbers are similar, though they at least tell us something about relative location of the houses on a particular street. These are examples of *nominal* scales, in which the number and the name are interchangeable, but the number has no arithmetical or mathematical significance. So a nominal scale is really not useful in measuring or scaling stimulus properties. nominal scale

The next most complex type of scale is an *ordinal* scale—one in which the stimuli are placed in order along the scale. Most college students can create an ordinal scale of the good looks of their classmates, or their intelligence, or creativity, or trustworthiness, etc. In the simplest procedure, all the stimuli (classmates) to be scaled are placed in order of ascending possession of the attribute being scaled. Tom is handsomer than Dick, who is handsomer than Harry. This is a scale. We have no idea by how much each boy differs from the next. Ordinal scales only give the rank order. In a horse race the order in which the horses pass the finish line is of utmost importance to the bettor. We use speed to rank the performance of each horse in relation to the others, but the actual differences in speed are secondary to the order in which they finish the race, and except for the record books, we ignore speed in determining the outcome, which is based entirely on the order of crossing the finish line. ordinal scale

Ordinal scales are acceptable for some types of scaling, but usually we want to know more, most particularly not only the order of stimuli, but also the distance between them on the scale. This means that the scale must have intervals with some specification and constancy. Such a scale is an *interval* scale. An instructor assigning grades on a quiz uses such a scale: the distance between a 90 and a 95 is the same as that between an 80 and an 85. interval scale

An interval scale is like a Fahrenheit or a Centigrade thermometer. Since it is divided into fixed intervals, it offers some precise means of measuring the difference between two stimuli. A temperature of 100° is 4 degrees higher than a temperature of 96°F. But an interval scale has no real zero point; zero on a Fahrenheit or Centigrade thermometer is an arbitrarily chosen temperature, meaning nothing more than 1 degree, or scale interval, less than 1°F or C. Therefore, it is not true that 100°F is twice as hot as 50°F; it is only 50° hotter.

Of greater relevance, nearly all psychological attributes can be specified on interval scales, but no more precisely. Thus, IQ scores, ratings on a personality test, and j.n.d.'s are all numbers that fall on an interval scale.

To see the contrast between the types of scales discussed so far and the most precise type of scale, a ratio scale, look what happens when you try to say that an exam grade of 40 is half as good as one of 80, or that Sarah has ratio scale half the personality of Suzy. Such statements are nonsense. But a 6-inch pencil is half the length of a 12-inch pencil. All physical measurements for which there is a true zero point fall on a ratio scale. Because we have no idea what a zero IQ is, a zero beauty, a zero personality, we cannot use ratio scales to measure such qualities. In the rest of this chapter, and in fact, in most of this book, the numbers we use to refer to attributes of stimuli or people belong to an interval scale at best. Sometimes we can only claim an ordinal scale—A is greater than B, but we have no idea how much greater.

This concludes our introductory discussion of stimulation in terms of detection, discrimination, identification, and scaling. In the remainder of this chapter, we will examine each of the sensory systems of man, and we will have to make reference to these concepts for each system.

In considering the major sensory systems, we will pay particular attention to vision, giving hearing and the other perceptual systems much briefer treatment. Our concerns here will not be with higher-order processing of sensations but with the nature of the stimuli that produce responses in these systems. How is the stimulus energy transduced into some kind of neural process, what kinds of sensory coding mechanisms are used, and how is this information transmitted to the brain? In Chapter 2 we will then examine some of the more general perceptual questions of recognition, identification, organization, selection, and the like. In both chapters we will emphasize vision because more is known about that system with respect to all of these questions than about the others, though a good deal is also known about hearing. The fact that we know so much more about vision and hearing probably reflects both the number of scientists working in these areas and the relative importance of these senses for human activities.

VISION

To understand how visual perception functions, we need to consider a number of processes and how they interact with physical energy, on the one hand, and the structure of the visual nervous system on the other. Thus, in this section, we will begin with the properties of electromagnetic radiation, which we call light, that are capable of producing sensations, and then we will look at the receptors in the eye that transform radiation into neural signals. This will lead us to a brief consideration of how various physiological characteristics of the perceiver and some of the physical properties of the stimulus affect vision.

The Stimulus: What Is Light?

light   There can be no vision without light. Anyone who has ever visited an underground cavern or mine where no daylight can penetrate knows the eerie feeling of the total absence of vision. As the minutes pass no shapes begin to emerge

The Physical Properties of Light

A knowledge of the physical properties of light is essential for an understanding of visual perception. The most essential of these properties are:

Intensity. In general we talk about the intensity of light in terms of the number of photons emitted from a light source in a given unit of time. But this is frequently not a useful approach since we are often more interested in the amount of light reflected from surfaces and the amount of light reaching and illuminating the eye than in the intensity of the light *source.* To measure the intensity of light reflected from a surface we take into account the intensity of the light source and the distance of the source from the surface. But even this measure of intensity is not practical for most perceptual phenomena, since we usually see light after it has been reflected from the surface, which absorbs some of the light it receives. How much light reaches the eye depends on how much light is reflected from the surface, which is known as the "luminance" of the surface.

Sometimes we want to know how much light actually enters the eye. This depends on the amount of light reaching the eye and the size of the pupil. As we open the pupil more light gets in.

Reflection. Most objects that photons encounter upon leaving a light source have relatively rough surfaces. A rough surface reflects light diffusely—that

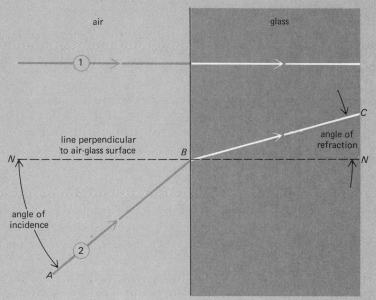

Fig. 1.2 Paths traveled by light incident upon an air-glass interface. (Cornsweet, 1970)

is, about equally in all directions (almost regardless of what direction the light came from). Very smooth surfaces reflect light in fewer directions.

Surfaces having high reflectance ratios (they absorb very little light and reflect most of the light incident on them) seem bright, while those with low reflectance seem dull or dark. Diffuse or rough surfaces look as if they might be emitting light rather than reflecting it, whereas the light reflected from smooth surfaces doesn't look as if it belongs to the surface; it is obviously reflected light. Because different wavelengths of light create different color impressions, surfaces that selectively reflect light of different wavelengths are seen as having the color corresponding to the reflected wavelength.

Refraction. As light travels, it moves from a medium of one optical density into a medium of a different optical density. With the change of optical density, generally both the speed and the direction of the light are changed. The magnitude of this change is a function of the difference in the densities of the two media. Fig. 1.2 traces the path of a photon of light passing from air into glass. Unless the light hits the glass straight on at a normal angle, as in the path labeled (1), the direction of motion will be changed as it enters the glass. The amount of this change depends on the angle of incidence of the light (angle *ABN* in the figure) and its change in velocity. Angle *CBN* in the figure is called the angle of refraction; it represents the angle of the newly bent path of the light.

Dispersion. The phenomenon of dispersion properly falls under the topic of refraction. Lights of different wavelengths travel at different velocities in a dense medium. It follows then that entering such a medium they will also be differentially refracted. White light entering a dense medium, since it contains all wavelengths, is dispersed in a number of directions. For example, a point of white light enters a glass prism and leaves it as a multicolored band of light.

in the darkness; after half an hour we still cannot see a hand moving before our eyes. Without some minimum stimulation in the form of light, our eyes cannot see. (Occasionally the experience of light can be artificially produced by pressure on the eyeball or by electric shock.) How does light energy act upon our visual apparatus to permit us to see?

photon   Physicists have had two concepts of light, one as bundles of energy called photons (quanta is the more general term) and the other as rays traveling in waves. We will have to use both concepts, the first to consider intensity of light and the second to understand the perception of color. We will be concerned only with intensity now, but will turn to wavelength later in the chapter, when we discuss color.

retina   To have any visual significance for us light must reach the photosensitive
photoreceptor   surface of the eye (the *retina*) and be absorbed by photoreceptors there. Photons flying around in the world have no visual resultants unless they enter someone's eye, reach the retina, and excite photoreceptors. Nearly all the light that reaches our eyes is reflected from surfaces of objects. We spend relatively little time looking at sources of light, such as the sun or a light bulb powered by some

form of man-controlled energy. The amount of light that actually reaches our photoreceptors depends upon (1) the amount of light, measured in candlepower, being radiated by the source; (2) the amount of light that illuminates the surfaces of objects around us, which is a function of the distance between these surfaces and the source; (3) the amount of light these surfaces reflect in relation to the amount they absorb, which has to do with reflectance; and (4) the amount of light that actually gets into the eye, which is a function of the size of the pupil, the opening in the iris (Fig. 1.3). Even then the story is not finished because not all the light that gets through the pupil is absorbed by the photoreceptors.

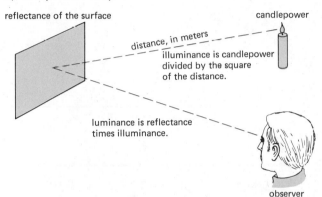

reflectance of the surface

candlepower

distance, in meters

illuminance is candlepower divided by the square of the distance.

luminance is reflectance times illuminance.

observer

Fig. 1.3 Measures to describe the intensity of light at the source, at a surface being illuminated, and as reflected from a surface to the eye. (Haber and Hershenson, 1973)

Visual stimulation—light reaching the eye—varies in wavelength, which we will discuss in the section on color; in intensity, the number of photons reaching the photoreceptors; and in distribution over the surface that reflects it. The different areas of a surface reflect different intensities of light, enabling us to apprehend the edges and contours of the surface. Finally, light energy can be exposed to the eye for varying durations, producing some of the effects of temporal coding, which we will talk about later.

The Receptor: How Does the Eye Receive Light?

Anatomy of the Eye The eye, like a camera, is structured so that light focuses on a specific area (see Fig. 1.4). When we examine an eye, we see a white, ball-shaped object with a colored circular area in the center and an apparently black area in the center of the colored part. The white area—the *sclera*—is a protective covering that allows light to enter only through the apparently black area, actually an opening—the *pupil*—which is covered by the *cornea*. The size of the pupil is controlled by the colored diaphragm in the center

sclera
pupil
cornea

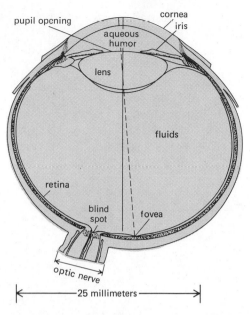

Fig. 1.4 The principal anatomical components of a human eye.

iris of the eye—the *iris*—which contracts or expands in response to the intensity of
lens light. Behind the pupil is a *lens,* which focuses the incoming light onto the light-sensitive back of the eye—the *retina.* Thus light enters the eye through the pupil and is focused by the lens on the retina in somewhat the same way a camera focuses light on film. Here, however, the analogy with a camera ends, for the retina corresponds in no way to camera film.

The retina is a light-sensitive surface, consisting of receptors and nerve cells that transform stimulation received in the form of physical energy (light) into neural (chemical) impulses that can be transmitted to the brain. The retina of each eye contains more than 125 million *photoreceptors*—about 120 million
rod, cone cylindrical cells called *rods* and more than 7 million *cones.*

The rods and cones are specialized nerve cells that respond only to light. Cones function primarily in daylight or other high illumination; they are distributed over the entire retina, with a heavy concentration in the *fovea,* a small area of the retina directly opposite the lens. Rods can function in dim light, whereas cones in dim light do not receive enough illumination to work at all. Rods are
fovea distributed over the entire retina *except* for the fovea; they are densest just outside the fovea.

From Photoreceptors to Brain If we now resume tracing the course of the photons admitted to the eye, we find that, once focused on the retina, they produce a reaction in the rods or cones that transforms their energy from a physical into a chemical form. The agents of this transformation are photopig-
rhodopsin ment molecules (chemicals) contained in the receptors—*rhodopsin* in the rods
iodopsin and *iodopsin* in the cones. Absorption of photons causes these pigment molecules to break down into their component parts and thereby to initiate a neural reaction (see Chapter 6 on neural function).

The neural impulses triggered by the photons are passed from the photoreceptors to the *bipolar cells* in the next layer of the retina and then to the *ganglion cells* (see Fig. 1.5). Although, as we have noted, there are approximately 127 million photoreceptors, there are only a few million bipolar cells and fewer than a million ganglion cells. The photoreceptors must therefore be grouped so that several can feed impulses into a single bipolar cell. Similar convergence occurs in the connections between bipolar and ganglion cells.

The cones in the fovea are an exception to these arrangements, however; each one connects to a single bipolar cell, which in turn connects to a single ganglion cell. The greater specificity of their connections is partly responsible for the functional difference between rods and cones. At lower levels of light energy, several rods connected to a single bipolar cell act simultaneously to excite the bipolar cell. The combination of smaller magnitudes of energy into a single magnitude sufficient to activate the next link in the neural chain is called *lateral summation*. Its advantage is that it permits us to see objects in fairly dim light—but not without some cost. Because the bipolar cell cannot discriminate among the many rods that feed to it—that is, it cannot code the spatial positions

bipolar cell
ganglion cell

lateral
summation

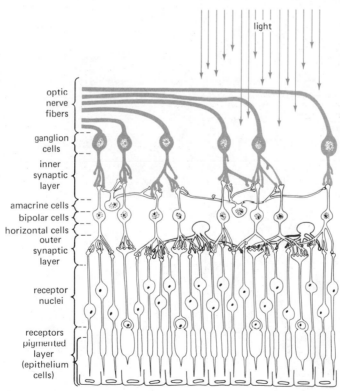

Fig. 1.5 Schematic diagram of the neural interconnections among receptors and bipolar, ganglion, horizontal, and amacrine cells. (Dowling and Boycott, 1966)

of the receptors that stimulate it—we see things less distinctly in dim than in bright light. The cones in the fovea, which are responsive only to relatively intense light, transmit sharper images because each one is connected to its own bipolar cell and from there to its own ganglion cell. Thus, a ganglion can code the position of the foveal receptors that have caused it to fire quite precisely.

The fibers of the ganglion cells are extremely long, extending all the way from the retina to the brain (see Fig. 1.6). They are clustered together in the *optic nerve,* which passes out of the eye through an opening in the retina. (Photons that fall on this opening, where there are no photoreceptors, are not, of course, "received," which accounts for the "blind spot" in each eye.) The

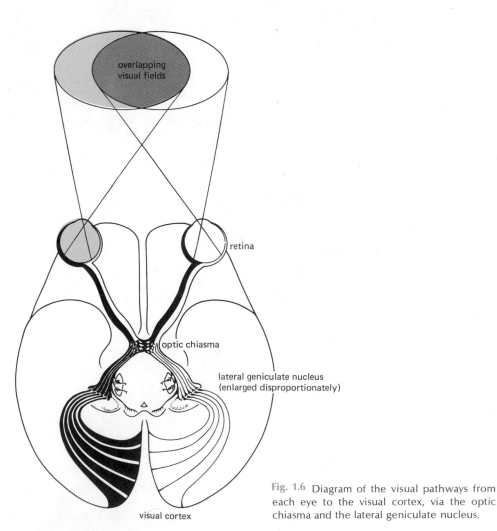

Fig. 1.6 Diagram of the visual pathways from each eye to the visual cortex, via the optic chiasma and the lateral geniculate nucleus.

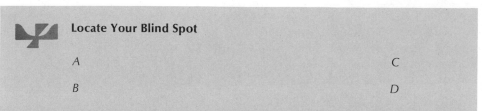

Locate Your Blind Spot

A   C

B   D

Close your left eye and with your right eye look at *A*. Move the book closer or farther from you until *C* disappears. It is now projected on your blind spot.

Shift your gaze from *A* to *B*. *C*, which has shifted from the blind spot, will now reappear as *D* disappears. This shows how eye movements shift objects on our retina. If you do this in reverse you will find your blind spot in the left eye.

optic nerves from both eyes come together in the optic *chiasma* at the base of the brain. There the ganglion-cell fibers are regrouped—those from the left sides of both retinas together and those from the right sides together—in new bundles called *optic tracts*. The optic tracts continue into the *lateral geniculate bodies* of the brain, the fibers from the right sides of the retinas going to the right side of the brain, the others going to the left side. In the lateral geniculate bodies the ganglion cells connect with a further set of neurons, which carry the impulses into the *visual cortex* of the brain.

We have now considered some of the characteristics of light, how it interacts with visual receptor systems, and the neuroanatomy of the visual system. We turn now to other factors affecting vision—some of the visual characteristics of the perceiver and some of the physical properties of light.

Factors Influencing Vision

Sensory Coding Our discussion so far has implied that the receptors originate impulses that are transmitted to the brain for further processing. But the story is more complex than that for two reasons. The first is implicit in the problems entailed in converging more than 100 million receptors onto fewer than 1 million fibers. Some kind of coding, which is essentially a concentration of information, has to occur or too much information will be lost. The second is somewhat the opposite. Despite the size and agility of the human brain, it would be overwhelmed by the amount of stimulation that even 1 million fibers from each eye could send to it, for each receptor is capable of receiving several thousand new stimulations a second. Therefore we should expect that before the neural impulses leave the retina via the ganglion fibers, a substantial amount of coding or information reduction will have occurred. We will briefly examine several of the more important coding mechanisms.

Steady-State Stimulation When a uniform patch of light stimulates part of the retina, the receptors the patch falls on are all stimulated equally. Similarly, the rest of the receptors, not being stimulated by the patch, are also in an equivalent though much less active state. In this example, there are only two excitation levels—high for those under the patch and low for all others. The coding procedure is very efficient. Instead of transmiting information to the cortex about the state of each receptor, it does so only for the receptors that differ in state from their neighbors—that is, only for those around the edge of the patch. The state of all other receptors is redundant; knowing one, you can predict the others. This coding process is rather like the work of the observer from a traffic helicopter. As long as cars are moving steadily along the highways below, the observer does not have to do much more than note that all is going smoothly. Only when there is an interruption in the flow—like the clotting of cars around an accident—does he zero in for closer attention. In the same way, if one photoreceptor registers a greater or lesser degree of excitement than is coming from receptors adjacent to it, the coding mechanism needs to signal that a change has occurred in the environment. Because steady-state stimulation is redundant, ignoring it does not involve the loss of important information. In fact, ignoring it is more efficient, for it means that fewer messages have to be sent over a particular channel per unit of time and also that fewer channels are needed.

lateral
inhibition

One mechanism by which the visual system is able to ignore steady-state stimulation is *lateral inhibition*. The photoreceptors are linked to bipolar cells by means of *synapses,* across which impulses can be transmitted (as will be discussed in Chapter 6). Some receptors, however, also form synapses with bipolar cells that inhibit the transmission of impulses. The inhibitory synapse prevents the bipolar cell from "firing" when a receptor connected to it is activated. Similarly inhibition can also occur between bipolar and ganglion cells.

H. K. Hartline, in his Nobel Prize-winning work with the horseshoe crab *(Limulus),* has shown how lateral inhibition eliminates redundant information from the coding process. To illustrate, suppose that two rods, *A* and *B,* are connected through bipolar cells to two ganglion cells, *A'* and *B'*, (Fig. 1.7). There are excitatory synapses between *A* and *A'* and between *B* and *B'*, but inhibitory synapses between the ganglion cells *A'* and *B'*. When photons stimulate only receptor *A,* the resulting impulse travels to ganglion cell *A'* and from there to the brain centers, at the same time triggering an inhibitory response at the synapse with *B'*. But when the photons stimulate *both* receptors *A* and *B,* the activity of each ganglion cell will effectively inhibit the other, and no impulse will be transmitted to the brain. When the stimulation falls uniformly on a large number of receptors, the excitations and inhibitions among the neural cells thus tend to cancel one another out (Hartline and Ratliff, 1957).

Inhibition generally occurs when the level of illumination is high. At low levels of stimulation the visual system must maximize its sensitivity in order to receive information, and therefore *summation* among receptors is more likely than inhibition. At high levels of illumination inhibition prevents the system from being engulfed in more information than it can handle.

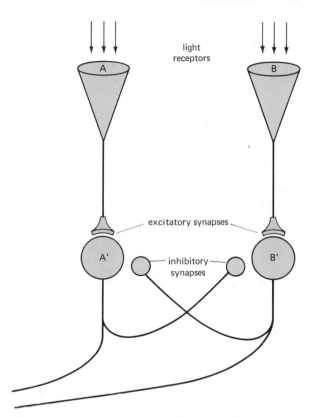

light
receptors

excitatory synapses

inhibitory
synapses

Fig. 1.7 Schematic representation of excitatory synapses between two pairs of receptors and ganglion cells and mutual inhibitory synapses between the two ganglion cells, as a description of the type of lateral inhibition found in *Limulus.* (Haber and Hershenson, 1973)

Edges and Contours But inhibition serves a much more important function than simply reducing the effects of overstimulation. It provides a mechanism for coding the presence of contours or other changes in the pattern of stimulation falling upon the retina. To see how this can be done, consider Fig. 1.8. We can see that the patch of light will produce more excitation than the surrounding background. Since each receptor both excites and inhibits bipolar cells it is connected to, the net effect will be in balance in the middle of the patch and in the background.

But look what happens at the edges of the patch. From the intense side, there is a lot of inhibition spreading out, which will tend to reduce the excitation from the background side. Therefore, just outside the patch there will be a lower net excitation than there will be well out into the background away from the patch. Similarly, since there is little inhibition spreading out from the background into the patch (because there is not much stimulation), the net excitation just at the edge of the patch will be greater than in the center of the patch. This will produce a brighter band just at the edge. Thus, as Fig. 1.9 shows, the edge is enhanced by this inhibition process, making it stand out more than the actual physical excitation would have predicted. These brighter and darker bands at

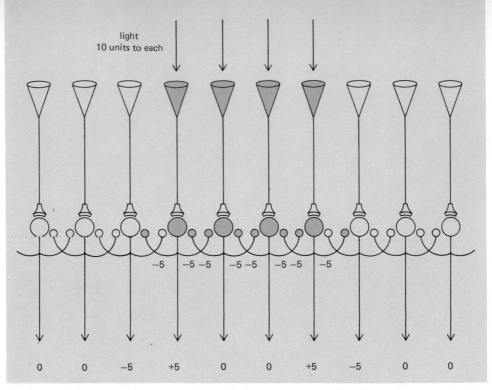

light
10 units to each

−5 −5 −5 −5 −5 −5 −5 −5

0   0   −5   +5   0   0   +5   −5   0   0

Fig. 1.8 To see how lateral inhibition can produce an involvement of edges, assume each of the middle receptors receives 10 units of excitation and that each stimulated ganglion cell provides −5 units of inhibition to its two neighbors. Compare the resulting excitation shown at the bottom of the figure with the input at the top. Only the edge of the patch of light is coded and sent to the brain.

Mach band

edges are called Mach bands, named after Ernst Mach who first investigated them in 1865. So, in addition to reducing the overall stimulation being transmitted to the brain, inhibition also provides a second coding mechanism to sharpen or enhance contours or edges of objects as they are projected onto the retina.

scotopic vision
photopic vision

Scotopic and Photopic Vision In general, it is possible to consider the retina as having two operating levels, one for daylight and one for night vision. With different parts of the retina specialized for each level, each type of vision can be handled more efficiently.

This specialization begins with the anatomical difference between the two types of receptors—cones and rods. The cones require relatively intense stimulation to excite them, and hence do not function at twilight or lower levels of light intensity. However, when light levels are high, cones are far more sensitive than rods to small changes in light intensity, and are capable of noticing far smaller details of objects than rods can. Further, it is the cones that respond differentially to different wavelengths of light, which as we shall see below is our basis for seeing colors.

These differences we have been describing are referred to as the photopic and the scotopic systems. Table 1.3 summarizes the specialization of each system. Evolution undoubtedly has had a lot to do with shaping these two systems. Since man rarely needs to perceive fine details of objects or colors at night, the

Fig. 1.9 Simultaneous brightness contrast. Each strip is actually of uniform luminance (*L*), as shown in the accompanying graph, but the distribution of perceived brightness (*B*) is such that the portion of each strip lying near a darker strip appears to be darker, and vice versa. (Kling and Riggs, 1972)

Table 1.3 Some Anatomical and Functional Differences between Scotopic and Photopic Processes

Scotopic		*Photopic*
Rods	versus	Cones
Night	versus	Day
Achromatic	versus	Color
Summative	versus	Discriminative
Low Acuity	versus	High Acuity

SOURCE: Haber and Hershenson, (1973)

night vision system does not have to cover those processes, leaving it free to develop maximum sensitivity to detecting the presence of small amounts of light. Conversely, the cones are specialized for fine detail perception and color discrimination, but never at low light levels.

We have been talking about eyes for several pages now without considering the implications of one of the most obvious facts about them. We have two eyes and they are placed slightly apart. Though their view of the world is similar, it is not identical, especially for objects that are nearby. This binocular characteristic allows us to be aware of more depth than a one-eyed creature would perceive; we will talk more about depth perception in Chapter 2.

Eye Movements Another obvious characteristic of our visual system is that our eyes are not still and passive. Rather, each eye can and does move, and rather frequently and quickly. This means that visual perception will always be a dynamic process. Eye movements give us a great advantage over animals whose eyes are fixed and who must therefore move their entire head or body in order to follow a moving object with their eyes or to search for something. Eye movements enable us to direct both eyes at an object of interest; to move the eyes about over the environment seeking out things of interest, importance, or danger; to track objects that are in motion; or when we are in motion, to keep an object—moving or stationary—temporarily in view by moving our eyes opposite to our body movement.

convergence
saccadic
movement

These circumstances define three major kinds of eye movements—convergence, saccadic movements, and pursuit movements. *Convergence* is the means by which we keep both eyes directed at the same object. *Saccadic movements* are used in searching; they involve a rapid shifting of the point of fixation, as when we are looking for targets, areas of interest, activities, motion, and so forth. The most familiar saccadic movements are the kinds our eyes make when we are reading; the eyes are stationary for about one-quarter of a second and then make a very rapid movement to a new position. We may feel that our eyes move continuously across a line of print, but in fact they make rapid jerks; if you doubt this, watch someone's eyes while he is reading. *Pursuit movements* are relatively smooth movements used to pursue an object moving across the visual field or to fixate an object when we are in motion.

pursuit movement

tremor
drift
microsaccade

In addition to these major kinds of eye movement, there are three very small types of movement—tremors, drifts, and microsaccades—that are also important to us (Fig. 1.10). A *tremor* is a small movement caused by tension of the muscle system that controls eye movements. A *drift* is a failure to hold a precise fixation. And a *microsaccade* is an attempt to bring the eye back to the point of fixation, thus correcting for the drift.

Fig. 1.10 Displacements of the retinal projection of a point source of light cause by a brief sequence of tremors, drifts, and microsaccades. Each number represents a fixation, the dotted lines are drifts imposed on tremors, and the solid lines are microsaccades. (Ditchburn, 1955)

typical intercone size

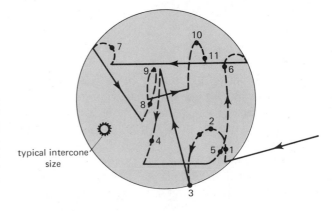

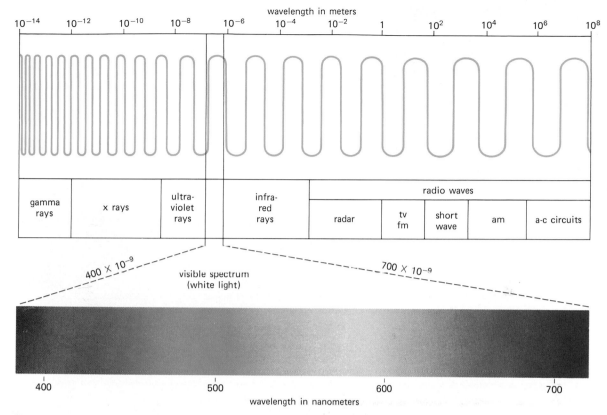

wavelength in meters

gamma rays	x rays	ultra-violet rays		infra-red rays	radio waves				
					radar	tv fm	short wave	am	a-c circuits

400×10^{-9}

700×10^{-9}

visible spectrum
(white light)

wavelength in nanometers

Fig. 1.18 The full spectrum of electromagnetic radiation, of which the human eye can see only the narrow band extending from 400 x 10^{-9} to 700 x 10^{-9} meters in wavelength. These very small units of length are called nanometers. Thus, the visual spectrum ranges from 400 to 700 nanometers. (Adapted from Bourne and Ekstrand, 1973, and McConnell, 1974)

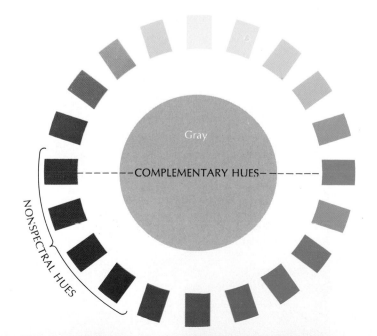

Gray

COMPLEMENTARY HUES

NONSPECTRAL HUES

Fig. 1.19 A color circle. The circle consists of spectral and nonspectral hues. The diameters of the circle connect complementary hues which, when mixed, produce gray. (Munsinger, 1971)

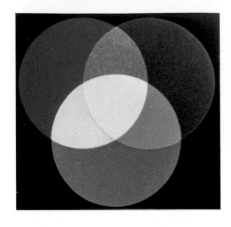

Fig. 1.20, Plate A Additive color mixture. In an additive color mixture light interacts with light to form other colors. The principal additive primaries in ths example are red, green, and blue (light).When mixed together in appropriate amounts as beams of light, they produce white light. The three circles left, represent beams of colored light. Yellow, magenta, and cyan result where each pair of additive primaries (red, green, and blue) overlap. Where they all overlap, white results. Color television is an example of this type of color mixing. (Inmont Corporation)

Fig. 1.20, Plate B In the demonstration right, red, green, and blue result where each pair of subtractive primaries (yellow, magenta, and cyan) overlap. Where all three overlap, black results. Color reproduction by photography or printing involves this type of color mixing. (Inmont Corporation)

Fig. 1.20, Plate C Seurat, Georges-Pierre, *Port-en-Bessin, Entrance to the Harbor*. (1888). Oil on canvas, 21⅝ x 25⅝". Collection, The Museum of Modern Art, New York. Lillie P. Bliss Collection. (See box, p. 59.)

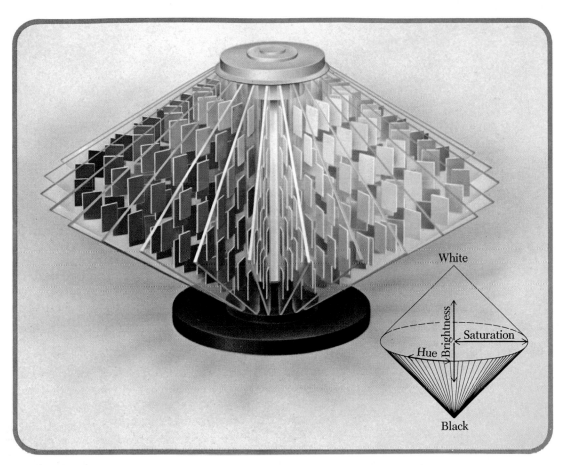

Fig. 1.22 A color solid showing the three dimensions of color sensitivity-hue, brightness, and saturation. The diagram in the lower-right corner illustrates the gradual change in brightness from black to white along the central axis. (Munsinger, 1971)

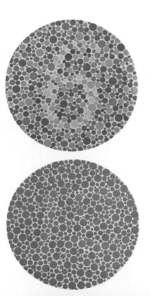

Fig. 1.23 These two illustrations are from a series of color-blindness tests. In the top plate, people with normal vision see a number 6, while those with red-green color blindness do not. Those with normal vision see a number 12 in the bottom plate; red-green blind people may see one number or none. These reproductions of color recognition tests cannot be used for actual testing. The examples are only representative of the total of 15 charts necessary for a complete color recognition examination. (American Optical Corporation from their AO Pseudo-Isochromatic Color Tests)

Fig. 1.24, Plate A Contrast stripe effect. Colors on a non-uniform background are subject to many unexpected changes. The blue areas in the pattern are printed with exactly the same color ink. Note how different they look. To observe heightened effects tilt the design or look at it from a distance. (Inmont Corporation)

Fig. 1.24, Plate B Simultaneous contrast. Although this is a continuous ring of the same color gray, you can change its color by placing your finger or a pencil along the line separating the red and blue. (Inmont Corporation)

Fig. 1.24, Plate C What the color-blind see. Many color-blind people cannot distinguish the colors red and green. To them they look like nearly identical grays, as shown on the right half of the demonstration. (Inmont Corporation)

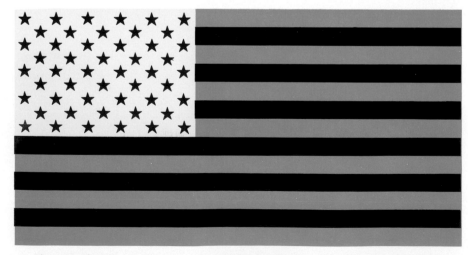

Fig. 1.24, Plate D Stare at the center of this flag for about 30 seconds. Then look at a white wall or sheet of paper. You will see a negative afterimage in the colors complementary to those shown here.

Saccadic movements best reveal the eyes' potential. From the time we decide to move the eye, or from the time the eye notices something moving or changing, about one-fifth of a second elapses before the eye actually moves. But, after this relatively long latency, saccadic movements are extremely fast, nearly 50 times as fast as the fastest pursuit movements the eye can make.

What with all these various types of movement, the eyes are virtually never still, and consequently the image on the retina is never stationary. The implications of the constant movements are considered in Chapter 2.

 Suppression During Eye Movements

It would be reasonable to expect that during eye movements the images we so quickly pass over should appear blurred on the retina (due to the high speed of our eye movements). Since we know also that our eyes are in constant motion, and almost constantly executing high-speed saccades we should expect to experience much blur or a hazy, blurred visual field much of the time. But we do not. Why?

Experiments by Latour (1962) and Volkman, Schick, and Riggs (1968) show that our visual system seems to actually suppress perception while saccadic movements are being made. Thus if we ask a subject to tell us whether or not a pulse of light came on while he was making a saccade, the path of which crossed the visual field of this light, he will probably say no. His sensitivity dropped from approximately 100 percent before beginning the saccade to approximately 10 percent for the period immediately preceding (about 50 milliseconds before), during, and immediately following (about 50 milliseconds after) the saccade (Fig. 1.11). Thus we are protected against the annoyance of blur. At the same time, of course, it should be remembered that we also lose some sensitivity to details.

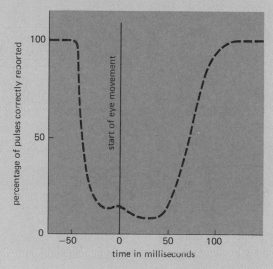

Fig. 1.11 Percent of light pulses detected as a function of the time of their occurrence in relation to the occurrence of a concomitant saccadic eye movement. (Latour, 1962)

intensity

Intensity of Light If would seem reasonable that if the intensity, or amount of energy, of a light source increases, the resulting light would appear to increase in brightness. While such a relationship between intensity and apparent brightness is generally found, a number of factors also produce other changes. Since the study of these factors has been useful in understanding how the visual system functions, we will examine a few of them. To do so, it is important to keep one aspect of labeling straight. We will refer to the *intensity* of light in terms of its physical energy, as measured with a meter for example,

brightness

and to the appearance of that light as its *brightness,* as measured by some psychophysical response given by a viewer. Thus, in general, more intense light appears brighter. This section will examine a few exceptions to this generalization, specifically conditions of adaptation, contrast, and temporal summation.

Dark and Light Adaptation Imagine walking into a movie theater on a sunny day. When you first enter you are unable even to see where the seats are, but after a few minutes you begin to make out shapes and in a short time you can see the person sitting next to you. When you leave the theater the

 Seeing in the Dark

If you have ever gone from a well-lit room to search for something in a dark closet, you have had the experience of being unable to see clearly for a few moments. Your eye required time to adjust to the change in light intensity. This time lag can present a problem to someone who must switch back and forth between light and dark.

Let us consider the case of the soldier on night patrol. In the darkness, he can see his path clearly. When he occasionally stops to look at his map under a flashlight, his eyes can adapt to the light almost immediately; however, once he turns off his flashlight, it takes several moments for him to be able to see clearly again. The same type of difficulty is encountered by the photographer who must walk in and out of his darkroom.

During World War II, it was discovered that the rod photoreceptors of the eye were not very sensitive to long wavelength light, which is red in appearance. This discovery provided the solution to the problem. If the soldier wears red goggles in the presence of light the rod photoreceptors of his eyes will not undergo light adaptation nor lose sensitivity. Thus, they will maintain a high degree of sensitivity in darkness.

reverse occurs. The intense sunlight is blinding, and you may have to shield your eyes from it. In a few seconds, though, you are once again able to see without squinting. These are examples of dark and light adaptation, respectively.

What these examples illustrate are changes in the sensitivity of the visual system to light intensity as a function of the overall light adaptation level. Dark adaptation is an increase in sensitivity to low amounts of light intensity, as typified by what happens when we enter a dark theater. It is a relatively slow process, as shown in Fig. 1.12. Once in a dark room for a while, our light sensitivity is very high, and we are overwhelmed if the lights are suddenly turned on. At high levels of light intensity we need to lose sensitivity, and light adaptation is a loss of light sensitivity. It occurs much more rapidly than dark adaptation. Two rather distinct mechanisms seem to account for adaptation.

One mechanism of adaptation is related to the amount of photochemical in each of the photopigment molecules in each receptor that is capable of absorbing photons. As the molecules of photochemical absorb photons of light they become bleached and hence incapable of absorbing more light for a short period of time. When the light is very intense, then, there is not enough photochemical to absorb all of it, and the eye is consequently insensitive to what is left over; in other words, it has reached an adaptation level. Thus, when we then enter a dark room, the receptors are not as sensitive, and we can't detect light. After we remain in the dark room, however, the photochemical unbleaches, thereby increasing sensitivity to light, as shown in Fig. 1.12.

But the amount of unbleached photochemical in the photoreceptor is not the only determiner of sensitivity. Very brief exposure to light that is not in excess of the amount the photochemical can absorb can also cause insensitivity to additional light. It is thought that this kind of adaptation must be due to a neural interaction between the bipolar and ganglion cells.

What is important here is that one of the variables affecting the sensitivity of the visual system is the adaptation state of the eye—that is, the amount of light to which the eye has been exposed. In fact, of all the things that change our sensitivity, transient adaptation changes are by far the most significant.

dark adaptation

light adaptation

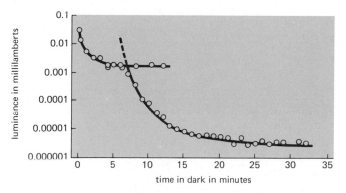

Fig. 1.12 The time course of dark adaptation as shown by the decrease in luminance threshold as a function of time after the exposure of a human eye to an intense light. The ordinate shows the intensity of a spot of light that is needed to be just visible. (Hecht, 1934)

Fig. 1.13 An example of simultaneous brightness contrast when looking at a gray square against backgrounds that differ in reflectance. (Haber and Hershenson, 1973)

brightness
contrast

Brightness Contrast Contrast refers to the effect the intensity of one object has upon the appearance of another object. The perceived brightness of an object is dependent upon the intensity of the background we see it against, or of the object we have looked at just before (Fig. 1.13). Thus white curtains will look brighter against a gray wall than against a white wall.

This effect of intensity is due to lateral inhibition. The more light received by the receptors recording the intensity of the background, the more the background receptors will inhibit the receptors receiving light from the central figure. Thus, the light from the white wall will inhibit the receptors receiving light from the white curtains to a greater degree than will light from the gray wall. The receptors receiving light from the white curtains can fire more when surrounded by receptors receiving light from a gray wall than they can when surrounded by receptors receiving light from a white wall, and so the curtains appear brighter against the gray wall. Similarly, if we look first at a dark object, then at a light one, the light one will appear brighter than if we had looked first at an equally intense object.

temporal
summation

Temporal Summation Although temporal coding of the duration of a light stimulus has more implications for perception than for sensation and will accordingly be talked about at greater length in Chapter 2, certain basic aspects of this discrimination variable are important for sensory processes also. If a brief flash of light is just below threshold, will extending its duration make it more detectable? In the visual system, it seems that up to a point, the effective brightness of a flash of light will increase if it is allowed to stay on longer. Suppose, for example, that in a given situation 100 photons of light are necessary to just detect the presence of a flash (the absolute threshold). If this is the case, then we could see a 1-millisecond flash of 100 photons *or* a 5-millisecond flash of 20 photons of light. In each case—20 × 5 or 100 × 1—the total amount of energy is 100 photons.

Bloch's law

This relationship between intensity and time is known as Bloch's law—the product of intensity and time is a constant. Thus up to a point, there is a trade-off between duration and intensity. The system adds up the total energy in that period of time, without regard to the relative amounts of intensity or duration that contribute to that total energy. This mechanism is known as temporal summation and is illustrated in Fig. 1.14.

But summation only occurs during a critical time interval that varies from about 100 milliseconds under scotopic conditions (very dim light) to about 20 milliseconds under photopic conditions (intense light). During this period total summation, without regard to the rate of intensity of the flash, occurs. All the system notes is the total energy.

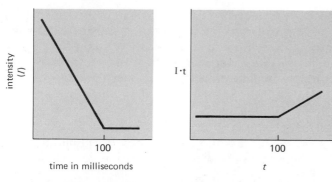

intensity (*I*)

time in milliseconds

I·t

t

Fig. 1.14 Two ways of illustrating Bloch's law showing the range over which time and intensity are reciprocally related. (Haber and Hershenson, 1973)

If the visual system cannot tell anything about a pulse of light during a given period of time other than its total energy, then it should also not be able to tell how many flashes were presented during the critical period. This is indeed the case, and the phenomenon is known as *temporal integration* (Fig. 1.15). Whether one, two, or even three flashes are presented during the critical period, only one flash is seen.

temporal integration

Although temporal summation and integration phenomena put a limitation on our ability to discriminate stimulus duration with great precision, in that we cannot tell exactly the duration of a light, they also allow us to see under conditions of lower illumination than would be possible without them. If a light is not quite intense enough to be seen in a flash, it may still be detected if it remains present long enough or is repeated several times.

We have considered three different reasons why brightness may not be a simple function of intensity, even though in general it is. Examining adaptation, contrast, and temporal summation has provided us with some further insight about the processing of sensory information.

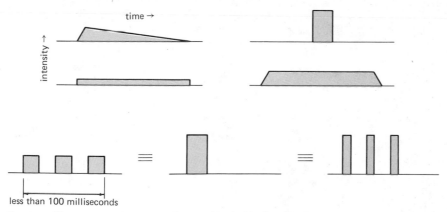

time →

intensity →

less than 100 milliseconds

Fig. 1.15 The top part illustrates that at threshold, the distribution of energy over time is irrelevant, as long as the duration does not exceed the critical duration. The bottom part illustrates temporal integration, in which the integration of time and intensity can encompass separate pulses as long as the total time does not exceed the critical duration. (Haber and Hershenson, 1973)

Acuity While all people are fairly similar in the extent to which they are influenced by sensory coding, eye movements, and intensity, there is a wide range of diversity in the aspect of vision known as acuity. Visual acuity is the ability to perceive fine details of the visual scene. The ability to find a small flaw in a piece of fabric would be an indication of detection acuity. Recognition acuity, on the other hand, is the ability to recognize familiar shapes. The familiar Snellen eye chart is a test of recognition acuity.

The finest visual acuity is an ability to detect the presence of a small detail, such as a fine black wire seen against a white background. If the illumination from the background is very high, then the wire can be as narrow as $\frac{1}{2}$ second

acuity

Snellen Recognition Acuity

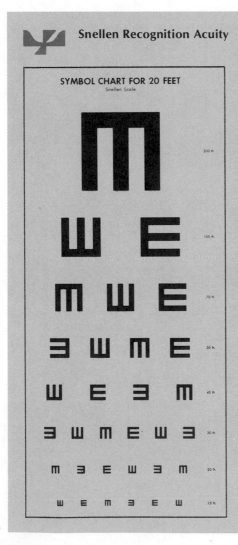

SYMBOL CHART FOR 20 FEET
Snellen Scale

The Snellen Chart is a measure of recognition acuity (Fig. 1.16). It is the standard clinical eye chart used to assess the need for eyeglasses. In this test a standard level of recognition acuity is used. This is the ability to recognize letters with lines that subtend an angle of 1 minute of arc at 20 feet. Acuity is specified by the ratio of this standard distance (20 feet) to the distance at which the same letters subtend an angle of 1 minute of arc for the subject. An acuity of 20/20 says that at 20 feet the subject recognizes letters with lines that project a retinal image of 1 minute at 10 feet or 1½ minute at 20 feet; this is a very good acuity. An acuity of 20/40 says that at 20 feet the subject can only recognize letters with lines that usually project a retinal image of 1 minute at 40 feet—in other words, letters that at 20 feet project an image of 2 minutes of arc. This is a somewhat poor acuity.

Fig. 1.16 Snellen eye chart. Courtesy of the National Society for the Prevention of Blindness, Inc., New York.

Visual Acuity in Combat

In combat conditions, truck convoys often must travel at night without the use of lights. Although the available starlight may provide the driver of the first truck with enough illumination to see the road, the drivers of the second and third trucks are at a serious disadvantage; they are confronted with the difficult task of maintaining proper distance between vehicles.

 To solve this problem, a simple visual acuity device has been developed. Three dim lights are installed in a horizontal row, about one inch apart, in the tail lights of each truck. These lights contain enough intensity to be seen from a distance as great as 40 feet. Now the task is simply a matter of resolving the number of lights.

 The number of lights a driver can see *increases* as the distance to the truck preceding him *decreases*. In other words, as the driver of a truck approaches the vehicle ahead of him, he is at first able to distinguish only one light, then two, and finally all three lights. Thus the drivers of the trucks are instructed to remain close enough so that they can distinctly see two lights, for then they are at a safe distance; being able to see all three indicates tailgating, while being able to see only one signifies too wide a gap between vehicles. By implementing this simple device, the number of collisions or lost trucks was substantially reduced.

of arc, which is about $\frac{1}{50}$ the width of a foveal cone, or the thickness of a telephone wire seen at 1.6 miles. Recognition acuity is not nearly so fine: the smallest details that can be resolved to distinguish among letters, such as in the Snellen Eye Test, are about $\frac{1}{2}$ minute of arc. For the average young adult, this is about 1 minute of arc (the size of a quarter at 250 feet).

 The major cause of poor acuity in humans is refractive error produced by a change in the shape of the lens with aging. This is usually compensated for by adding a corrective lens in front of the eyes, something that a substantial percentage of adults require eventually (Fig. 1.17).

 Color Perception Color is an impossibly large and complex topic, and we shall only consider a few aspects of it here. What is the stimulus for color? How do we describe colors? What receptors are responsible for color perception? How do these receptors and the retina encode information about color for later processing in the brain?

 Earlier we noted that light has been described as bundles of energy called photons and also as waves with differing wavelengths. Our focus up to this point

farsighted and nearsighted eyes

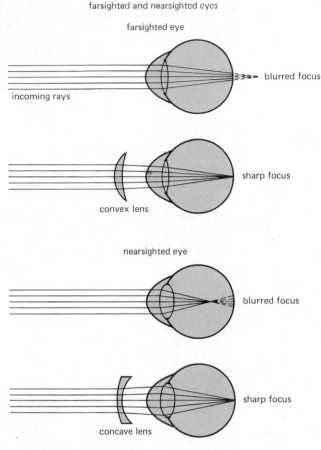

farsighted eye

blurred focus

incoming rays

sharp focus

convex lens

nearsighted eye

blurred focus

sharp focus

concave lens

Fig. 1.17 In the farsighted eye, the focal point falls behind the retina because the cornea and lens cannot bend the light ray enough to gather them together on the retina. Farsightedness is corrected by a convex lens (one that is thicker toward the center). Such a lens bends the light rays so that they focus sharply on the retina. In the near-sighted eye, the focal point falls in front of the retina and the rays have started to diverge by the time they reach the retina, causing a blurred image. Nearsightedness is corrected by a concave lens (one that is thicker toward the edges.) Such a lens spreads the incoming rays, making them strike the cornea at divergent angles to compensate for the greater distance to the retina.

in the chapter has been on light as photons. Now we have to concentrate on light as wavelengths because it is this property of light that is the stimulus for color perception.

Isaac Newton, in about 1600, discovered that when a narrow slit of intense sunlight shone on a prism, the light that passed through it was separated into a rainbow of colors—the spectral colors (see color insert, Fig. 1.18). We now know that Newton's prism was refracting or bending the light waves so that short wavelengths were bent more than long ones. In a simple sense, then, the

hue   color, or more technically the hue, that we see is simply a function of the wavelength of electromagnetic radiation. Long wavelengths appear red, short ones blue, and in-between lengths other colors.

spectrum   Fig. 1.18 shows the full electromagnetic spectrum, from gamma and x-rays at the short wavelength end to radio and TV waves at the long wavelength end. As you can see, only a tiny portion of the spectrum is visible. Our visual receptors absorb photons from only these wavelengths. Actually wavelengths shorter than 400 nanometers—the ultraviolet waves—cannot reach the retina because the cornea absorbs them to protect the retina from their harmful radiation and energy effects. Wavelengths longer than about 700 nanometers—those called infrared—are generally not intense enough to stimulate the receptors, though they can be felt as heat on the skin.

Certain wavelengths act as opposites, in that if you add equal amounts of each of them the result appears to be a cancellation of color—you get white light. These opposite wavelengths are called *complementary colors.* Further, the two ends of the visible spectrum are similar in appearance: both contain red, one bluish red and the other deep red. These two observations have suggested that the spectrum can be considered as a color circle, in which the two ends are joined and complementary colors fall opposite each other (Fig. 1.19). The

complementary
colors

 Mixing Colors in Light

The color circle (see Fig. 1.19) applies to mixing colors in light rather than in pigment. When paints are mixed, color is determined by absorption of all wavelengths except those which produce (reflect) the color. Because absorption is the main attribute of paint, the mixtures are called subtractive. Mixtures of colors in light are called additive (see Fig. 1.20).

Most people learn about mixing colors in pigments—the paints and enamels used in art classes, room decoration, and house painting. Mixing the same colors in light produces different results.

In paints, a mixture of blue and yellow with white light shining on the painted surface results in greens. The blue paint absorbs long wavelengths (yellows, oranges, and reds) while yellow absorbs the short wavelengths (blues and violets), leaving the intermediate wavelengths, or greens.

In light, when mixing blue light with yellow light on a white surface, both bounce off (are reflected) and the surface is seen as gray.

It is possible to apply the principles of mixing colors in light to mixing colors in paint to get the same final color. For example, a yellow in light can be created by mixing red and green lights. If red and green paints are mixed, it would come out a muddy color, probably reddish, but if the paints were equally distributed as individual dots cover the surface (not overlapping), the resulting impression from a distance where the dots could not be sorted out would be yellow. (See the Seurat reproduction, Fig. 1.20, Plate C.)

color circle indicates the appearance of colors that result from pure wavelengths and also from mixing two or more wavelengths in varying proportions.

If one of a pair of complementary colors is more intense than the other we see a color of the same hue as the intense one, but it looks as if it has more white in it. What we are talking about here is *saturation*. The more white light that is mixed with a pure spectral color, the less its saturation. Thus, proceeding outward from the center of the color circle, which is white, the saturation of a hue increases. Around the outside of the circle, the hues vary, but from the inside to the outside the saturation varies.

saturation

What happens if you mix two lights that are not complementary? You can see what the result will look like by drawing a line, *AB*, on the color circle between the two hues (Fig. 1.21). The color produced will be the color of any point along that line, except points *A* and *B* themselves, depending on the amounts of *A* and *B* used. If exactly equal amounts of *A* and *B* are mixed, the result will be *O'*. Now, to determine the hue of *O'*, draw line *WO* from the center of the circle, which is white, through *O'* to the circumference. The point at which *WO* meets the circumference is *O*, which is the hue of the new color. The saturation of *O'* is defined by its distance from *W*. Mixing any two spectral hues can result in a wide range of new colors, all of less saturation than the original hue. We cannot, however, mix *A* and *B* to get *O*. If we mix *A* with its complement, *C*, the result will be any point along line *AC*, and if we use equal amounts of *A* and *C*, the result will be white.

Besides varying in hue and saturation, colors can vary in brightness, according to their intensity as defined earlier in the chapter. To relate all these dimensions together, the color circle is expanded into a color solid (color insert, Fig. 1.22). Hue varies around the perimeter of the solid, saturation with distance from the center, and intensity vertically from top to bottom.

Color perception could be neatly explained if a different receptor were tuned to each wavelength of light, but this would require thousands of different color receptors. But if three colors relatively well spaced along the rim of the

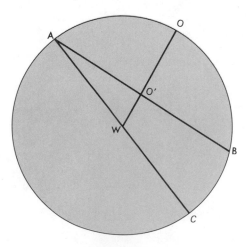

Fig. 1.21 See text for description.

color circle are mixed in varying amounts, all of the hues on the circle can be produced. This discovery, made around 1800, suggested that instead of thousands of different color receptors, each sensitive to a different wavelength, perhaps we have only three; if any color can be created by mixing only three wavelengths of light, then the outputs of three receptors, each sensitive to a different part of the spectrum, added together would give us all the hues around the color circle.

This notion was basically substantiated by the discovery of three types of cones, each maximally sensitive to a different range of the spectrum—one around 450, another about 530, and a third around 580 nanometers. For a while

 Color Blindness

Some people are unable to discriminate normally between certain pairs of complementary colors. In its most common form *color blindness* consists of the inability to distinguish red and green; loss of discrimation between blue and yellow with retention of red-green discrimination is, on the other hand, the rarest form of color blindness. Slightly more common is the inability to discriminate either pair, so that only black, white, and shades of gray are distinguishable. All three forms of color blindness together affect only about 7 percent of the population, mostly males.

Many color-blind people are able to discriminate colors by characteristics other than hue; in fact, some are so adept at using other cues that they may not know they are color blind. Many familiar objects can be distinguished by dimensions of color other than hue. For example, the person who cannot perceive the red and green of traffic lights can distinguish between the brightness of "on" and "off" (besides, the red light is almost always above the green one). In addition, as we noted before, the rods can distinguish different wavelengths as shades of gray, so that the color-blind person can perceive *differences* in the intensities of different wavelengths even though he does not perceive the colors themselves. Finally, some people who are blind to one pair of complementary colors, say red and green, can still perceive other colors. As the light waves reflected from most objects in our environment are seldom "pure," these people may be able to use the small amounts of yellow or blue wavelengths mixed with the predominant bands of red and green as an aid in discriminating the latter. Psychologists discovered this ability by observing people who are color blind in only one eye (Hsia and Graham, 1965); they can match the true experience of green in one eye with a particular tone of gray-yellow in the other and the true experience of red with a different tone of gray-yellow.

To detect color blindness the examiner tries to eliminate all the cues that normally help color-blind people to distinguish hues. The usual test involves a circle of colored dots in which is "buried" a figure composed of dots the same size but different colors (color insert, Fig. 1.23); colors are chosen to prevent the person from relying on the aids we have described. If the subject is color blind he will not recognize the figure.

it seemed that the outputs of the three cones were simply added together in the brain somewhere. Unfortunately, it has not turned out to be quite that simple. We now believe that the three types of cones do not add together, but in fact are combined in opposition to each other. The reason for this stems from what we know about color blindness—the inability of some people to discriminate all wavelengths. In red-green color blindness, the person cannot distinguish between red and green. If this were due to the absence of cones sensitive to medium and long wavelengths, hues between red and green should also be lost, since they are the result of mixtures of these two primaries. However, red-green color-blind persons usually have no difficulty seeing yellow.

Color-blindness therefore is evidently not caused by a deficiency of cones, but rather by some anomaly in how the outputs of the color-sensitive cones are combined together. It seems that for normal perceivers, the outputs from the three cones are combined to form two pairs of opposites, yellow-blue and red-green, and that it is these opposites that are sent to the cortex, not the separate activities of the three cones.

opponent
coding
component
addition

This is called *opponent* coding of color, as contrasted to *component* addition from three types of cones. Substantial evidence based on the appearance of colors is consistent with opponent coding. The fact that opposites on the color circle cancel each other suggests some type of opposition coding. Further, color contrast mechanisms work the same way. If you stare for 10 to 20 seconds at a patch of color and then look at a neutral gray or white surface, you should see the color on the circle that is opposite to that of the patch. Try this for the colors on Fig. 1.24, Plate D. Similarly, if you surround a color by a background of its complement, you will induce the strongest possible saturation in the appearance of the color, as is shown in Fig. 1.24, Plate B.

Many questions remain about how the brain processes color information. We are much more confident about the processing of color in the eye, and this discussion has been limited to these aspects of the initial coding of color stimulation.

This concludes our presentation of the sensory components of vision. We shall now turn to a much briefer discussion of man's other senses, focusing primarily on the nature of the stimuli for each, the receptor processes, and basic neural coding of the sensory information.

AUDITION

Man is unique, or nearly unique, among living creatures in his ability to use the sophisticated instrument of communication that we call language—the patterning of a relatively small number of spoken sounds to convey an unlimited variety of meaning. Actually, Chapter 8 will present some evidence that chimpanzees may also be capable of using language. While language is a product of highly developed mental capacities, it also depends upon a very efficient hearing apparatus.

In man the total range of sound energies that can be detected is not as great as it is in some animals; dogs, for example, can be trained to respond to whistles whose sound we cannot hear at all. But within our range of hearing we are capable of making extremely fine discriminations. Vocal sounds are only one category of sounds from which we draw information about our environment, but they make particularly strong demands on our ability to discriminate. Not only do we distinguish many small variations in the *quality* of vocal sounds —for example, between *p* and *b* or between *o* and *ow*—but we also note the slight rise in *pitch* that turns a statement into a question and the tiny increases in *intensity* that lend emphasis to certain words. In fact, we know from experiments with Weber's law (see p. 35) that hearing is the most sensitive of man's modes of interacting with his environment. We look now at the properties of energy and the physiological apparatus that make hearing, or *audition*, possible.

The Stimulus: What Is Sound?

The energy that we experience as sound is fundamentally different from light; it is a form of *mechanical* energy. Two physical elements are necessary for producing sound: a *source* that can be made to vibrate and a conducting *medium* through which the vibrations can be transmitted to receptors. When the sound source—for example, a piece of hide stretched tightly over a drum, a crystal bowl, or the thin diaphragm of a loudspeaker—is struck, the resulting vibrations cause alternating compressions and expansions among the neighboring molecules of the conducting medium. These changes in pressure cause similar changes in adjacent molecules, and a chain reaction is thus passed along through the medium. The most common medium for the transmission of sound is air.

The cycle of one compression and one expansion is called a *sound wave*   sound wave (Fig. 1.25). The number of waves generated by the sound source per second is

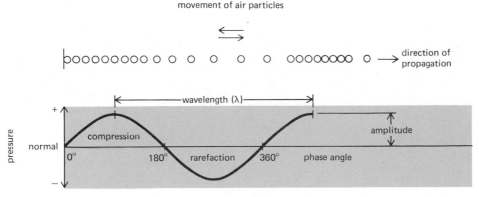

Fig. 1.25 A graphical representation of the instantaneous pressure changes in a simple acoustic wave as a function of time. (Corso, 1967)

frequency
amplitude

the *frequency* of the sound, which determines its pitch; the distance from the peak of a wave to its base line is the *amplitude,* which determines the loudness of a sound.

The Receptor: How Does the Ear Perceive Sound?

outer ear
middle ear
inner ear
auricle
ear drum

The sensory apparatus for hearing consists of three main divisions: the *outer ear, middle ear,* and *inner ear* (see Fig. 1.26). The visible portion of the outer ear, the *auricle,* is a shell-like structure designed to catch sound waves from the air and funnel them through the *ear canal* to the *ear drum,* a sensitive membrane separating the outer and middle ears. The captured sound waves strike this membrane and set it vibrating at the same frequency.

malleus, incus,

stapes, ossicles

In the middle ear, a chain of three tiny bones—the *malleus,* the *incus,* and the *stapes,* collectively called the *ossicles*—links the drum with another membrane, the *oval window,* which serves as a boundary between the middle and inner ears. When the ear drum is activated by sound waves, the vibrations are passed along through the ossicles to the oval window.

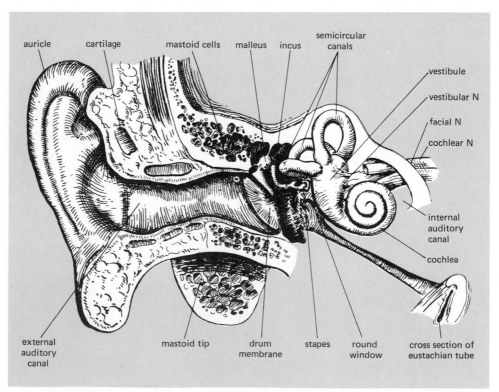

Fig. 1.26 A semidiagrammatic drawing of the ear. (Davis and Silverman, 1960)

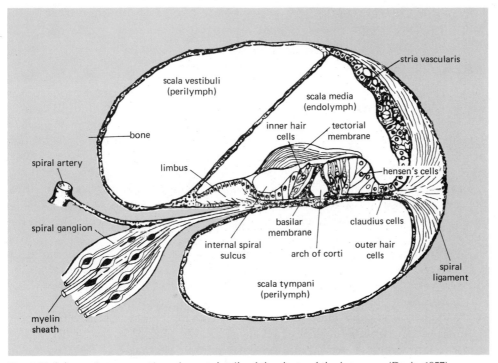

Fig. 1.27 Schematic cross section of some details of the ducts of the inner ear. (Davis, 1957)

The inner ear (Fig. 1.27) consists of two major organs: the vestibular apparatus, which will concern us later when we consider balance senses, and the
cochlea, a coiled tube filled with fluid, through the center of which runs a smaller
tube, the *cochlear duct.* The walls of this duct are lined with two membranes.
In the *basilar membrane* are rooted thousands of tiny *hair cells,* whose ends
are in contact with the *tectorial membrane.* These hair cells are the actual sound
receptors; their roots are intertwined in the basilar membrane with the *auditory
nerve* fibers. When sound vibrations from the oval window are passed along
to the cochlear fluid, they cause the walls of the tube to expand and contract.
These movements shift the two membranes of the cochlear duct in relation to
each other, so that the hair cells are distorted, setting up an electrical potential.
The electrical potential is translated into neural impulses by a mechanism similar
to the one we described in our discussion of the visual receptors. The hair cells
thus convert the mechanical energy of sound into neural energy that can be
transmitted to the brain by pathways similar to those for vision.

The auditory nerve cells pass out of the ear in bundles, but they synapse
with other sets of neurons at an earlier station than do the optic nerves, in the
cochlear nuclei at the base of the brain. From there the impulses travel through
the *olivary complex,* where some (but not all) fibers from each ear interact with

cochlea

basilar
membrane
tectorial
membrane

hair cell

fibers from the other, to the *medial geniculate bodies* of the brain, and finally to the *auditory cortex.*

Factors Influencing Audition

Frequency Frequency, or its reciprical, wavelength, determines pitch, which is perceived as "highness" or "lowness," much as the wavelength of light is perceived as color. The more sound waves per second, the higher the pitch. The human ear does not respond to an infinite range of pitch, however. Although human beings can detect pitches as low as 15 cycles per second (the very lowest notes on an organ), the upper limit is only 15,000–20,000 cycles per second (cps), compared, for example, to 70,000 cps for cats and 100,000 cps for porpoises. Human hearing is most acute for tones between 1,000 and 4,000 cps. Above or below these narrower limits greater amplitude is required for sound to be detected.

These thresholds are largely determined by the flexibility of the ear drum and the ossicles of the middle ear, which regulate the transmission of sound vibrations to the cochlea (Davis, 1959). The lighter and less resistant these structures are, the more susceptible they will be to very rapid vibrations. It makes sense, then, that small animals like mice have very high ranges of pitch reception, whereas elephants have one of the lowest ranges. Finally as one grows older, it is not surprising that sensitivity to higher pitches decreases.

Intensity The amount of energy in each sound wave, as represented by its amplitude, determines the loudness of the sound. Scientists have developed decibel | a unit for measuring physical sound pressure at the ear drum: the *decibel,* one tenth of a *bel,* named for Alexander Graham Bell. The zero point is arbitrarily established as the absolute threshold for detecting a tone of 1,000 cps. Normal conversation is centered in the region around 60 decibels; at about 120 decibels loudness becomes painful to the human ear. Fig. 1.28 shows where some common sounds fall on a decibel scale.

Auditory Sensitivity As we have already remarked, human hearing, within the ranges of sound energy that it can detect, is extraordinarily sensitive. It has been estimated that man can discriminate approximately 340,000 different tones on the basis of frequency and intensity. In terms of a difference threshold, some of these tones can differ in frequency by as little as .003. This means that after hearing a tone of 1,000 cycles, we could tell that a tone of 1,003 cycles was different in pitch.

When it comes to discriminating intensity, our auditory structures are equally finely tuned. In fact, it is probable that if they were any more sensitive we would actually hear less efficiently, for then it would be possible to detect even random movements of air molecules; the constant "static" resulting from these changes in pressure would interfere with our reception of significant sound energy.

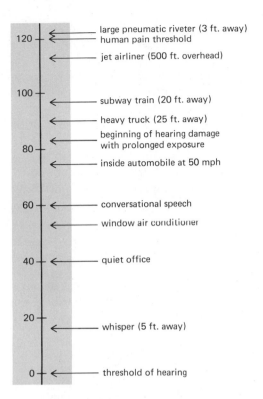

120 — large pneumatic riveter (3 ft. away)
human pain threshold

jet airliner (500 ft. overhead)

100 —

subway train (20 ft. away)

heavy truck (25 ft. away)

beginning of hearing damage
with prolonged exposure

80 —

inside automobile at 50 mph

60 — conversational speech

window air conditioner

40 — quiet office

20 —

whisper (5 ft. away)

0 — threshold of hearing

Fig. 1.28 Decibel scale. The loudness of various common sounds scaled in decibels. (Hilgard, Atkinson, and Atkinson, 1971)

It is clear, then, that in addition to the properties of sound energy itself, the very structure of our hearing apparatus is designed to maximize the amount of useful information that we receive from our environment.

Coding of Auditory Information The coding of intensity into loudness seems fairly straightforward—the greater the amplitude of the vibrations transmitted to the inner ear, the greater the frequency of firings of the fibers in the auditory nerve.

The coding of frequency into pitch is more complex, and appears to have two components, one for frequencies below about 3,000 cps and another for higher frequencies. Low frequency sounds set the hair cells in the cochlea vibrating in unison with the physical sound, which induces the same frequency of firing in the auditory nerve. This method of coding is limited by the fact that the hair cells apparently cannot be vibrated faster than several thousand cycles per second, so it can only work for lower frequencies. That it does work has been verified by direct electrical recording from the hair cells in the cochlea.

Higher frequencies are coded by means of a property of the medium through which sound travels. When the oval window is set in motion by a sound wave, that wave creates vibrations in different places along the cochlea, depending upon the frequency, much as will happen if you shake a rope at different rates. What this means is that different locations in the cochlea code different frequencies. Thus, higher frequencies are encoded by location or place rather than by the rate of vibration itself.

Although much more remains to be learned about the precise workings of the hearing apparatus, it appears that for low sound frequencies the rate at which nerve cells are fired is the coding mechanism that transmits information about pitch to the brain, whereas above the level of about 3,000 cps the location of the basilar membrane stimulation in the cochlea takes over this function.

There is, of course, much more to know about auditory perception. We have covered only the initial processing of sound waves into a neural code for intensity and frequency. These processes have some similarity to the comparable processes in vision, and as we shall see, also to the other senses.

THE CHEMICAL SENSES

Taste and smell—gustation and olfaction—are called the chemical senses because the stimulus energy comes from chemical substances in contact with the receptors.

Gustation

Volumes have been written on the orchestration of elegant meals. Among gourmets every detail of precise balance among flavors, variations in spicing, and selection of the proper wines to accompany them has been argued and defended with all the resources of philosophy and passion. Hamburger lovers, too, have their unshakable convictions. Some insist on combining beef with the sweetness of tomato ketchup; others will accept only the sharp, slightly sour flavor of mustard; the broad-minded prefer both ketchup and mustard.

What might astonish connoisseurs, whether of haute cuisine or the burger deluxe, is that they really have only four basic tastes to choose from—sweet, sour, bitter, and salty; the rest is all a matter of combinations and proportions. Once again, it is the highly developed discriminatory powers of our sensory apparatus that are responsible for the great variety of our taste experiences within such a seemingly small range.

The Gustatory Stimulus and Receptors The stimulus energy for taste is a variety of chemical substances, usually in the form of food or drink, which come into contact with sensory receptors in the mouth. The taste receptors, or *taste buds*, are clustered in little projections called *papillae*, which are scattered over the tongue but concentrated along its edges and back surface. Some parts of the tongue have no taste receptors; on the other hand, there are a few taste buds in the soft palate, the pharynx, and the larynx (see Chapter 6). Fig. 1.29 shows the distribution of taste sensitivity in the tongue. In human beings, each taste bud consists of several receptor cells arranged like the segments of an

taste bud
papillae

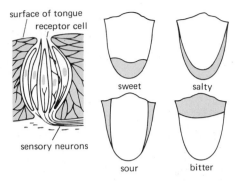

surface of tongue
receptor cell

sensory neurons

sweet   salty

sour   bitter

Fig. 1.29 Taste receptors are chemoreceptors. They are not neurons but specialized cells with hairlike processes at their ends. Sensory neurons lie close to them. When the receptor cells are stimulated, they generate nerve impulses in the sensory neurons. These receptor cells, grouped into structures of the tongue called taste buds, respond to four different tastes. Those on the tip detect sweetness and saltiness; those on the sides detect sourness, and those in back detect bitterness. (Ebert, Loewy, Miller, and Schneiderman, 1973)

orange. At the top of each cell slender, hairlike structures project into the taste pore, an opening to the outside surface of the tongue.

When a substance is taken into the mouth, it interacts with saliva to form a chemical solution that flows into the taste pore, stimulating the receptor cells. How this establishment of an electrical potential occurs is still a mystery; all we know is that certain substances are capable of firing the nerve fibers interwoven at the base of the receptor cells. The neural impulses are then carried to the brain by the same processes that function in the other senses we have discussed. Unlike vision and audition, however, gustation does not rely on a single, specialized nerve system connecting the receptors and the brain. Instead, the neural fibers from the taste buds travel through three different nerves, which also carry information from other kinds of sensory receptors, primarily those for touch. The impulses ultimately arrive at the cortex, though the specific cortical areas responsible for taste experience are still being mapped out.

Factors Influencing Taste: Quality Recognition of the quality of taste is, of course, fundamental to gustatory experience. We have mentioned that there are only four basic categories of taste. Researchers have frequently tried to extend this list, but have not been able to do so without including elements of smell and touch in their definitions of other tastes. It has not yet been possible to isolate the basic chemical components of these four taste categories. That is, no single chemical ingredient has yet been discovered to be present in all substances that yield the sensory experience of bitterness, and so on.

Nor is it certain how these different tastes are coded by the gustatory apparatus. It has been observed that sensitivity to sweetness is greatest at the tip of the tongue, to sourness along the sides, and to bitterness at the back, whereas sensitivity to saltiness is more evenly distributed over the tongue, with a slightly greater concentration at the tip. But there is still no satisfactory answer to the question whether or not individual papillae are specialized to single tastes or to specific combinations of tastes. Contradictory evidence on this question reflects the difficulty of isolating the tiny receptors for experimental purposes.

Experiments with single neural fibers in animals have suggested a new approach to the problem. Presumably, if the receptors are specialized to certain tastes, the connecting nerve fibers will reflect this pattern of responses. But studies of cats and other species have revealed no such specialization (Pfaffman, 1941, 1955). Rather, it appears that coding of taste quality depends upon the pattern of activity in a whole group of fibers. Information about specific taste qualities must then be coded at higher centers. Application of these conclusions to the coding of gustatory information in human beings is highly controversial, however.

Intensity A second taste phenomenon, *intensity,* reflects the concentration of the stimulus solution. The higher the percentage of sugar in solution, for example, the sweeter the taste will seem. There is some evidence, confirmed by a variety of experiments with rats, that the coding mechanism for taste intensity is the frequency of neural firing from the taste receptors (Pfaffman, 1960).

 Are Taste Receptors Specific?

Are the basic tastes limited to the familiar four—sweet, sour, bitter, and salty—or are there more? Early in the history of psychology this was a point of contention, and many longer lists were generated. But by the late 19th century, only the basic four remained. Another question, however, was whether the four tastes should be considered independent modalities. There was some evidence to support such a position. For example, different parts of the tongue are differentially sensitive to different tastes. Also some drugs have differential effects on the four tastes. Cocaine abolishes taste sensations in a particular order: bitter first, then sweet, then salty, and finally sour (Moncrieff, 1967).

Later research attempted to isolate four types of taste receptors corresponding to the four tastes. There are basically three ways of carrying out such research: (a) by chemically stimulating different papillae and obtaining subjective descriptions of what is experienced, (b) by electrically stimulating the papillae and noting whether stimulation of particular ones consistently produces the same taste experience, and (c) by chemically stimulating papillae by touching them with small drops of solutions and noting which papillae respond (by neural firing) to which solutions.

Békésy (1964, 1966) carried out experiments using both electrical and chemical stimulation. His results showed that when a given papilla was electrically stimulated with positive current, subjects reported tasting only one of the four tastes. Békésy could microscopically identify four different types of papillae and predict quite accurately what taste electrical stimulation of each type would produce. He also chemically stimulated papillae with small drops of solutions and found that most papillae responded to only one of the four tastes.

However, Harper (1966) using a slightly different technique got different results. By means of slight suction, individual papillae were pulled up into a small chamber containing solutions. Using higher concentrations of various solutions, he found, unlike Békésy, that individual papillae were responsive generally to more than one taste—that is, that they were not taste specific. Today the question of whether there are specific receptors for each taste remains unresolved.

Variations in intensity can be discriminated as j.n.d.'s (see p. 33), but they can also be measured directly. The unit for measurement of sweetness is the *gust,* arbitrarily defined as the perceived intensity of a 1 percent sucrose solution; similar scales have been constructed for some other chemicals.

Several factors influence the experience of taste intensity. One is the expanse of the tongue's surface that is stimulated. In general, for smaller areas the concentration of the solution must be higher to maintain a given level of intensity. Another factor influencing intensity is *contrast*—the heightening of sensitivity to a taste in one part of the tongue by stimulation of other parts of the tongue. Although this phenomenon is currently undergoing reexamination, it seems generally true that applying a low concentration of one substance—for example, a sucrose solution—to one area of the tongue will lower the threshold for another substance—in this instance salt—in another area; the experience of saltiness at the latter site will be correspondingly more intense. At concentrations higher than about 6 percent, however, the effect seems to be just the opposite: a rise in the threshold at the second area, with resulting *suppression* of sensitivity to saltiness.

Olfaction

Dogs, wolves, deer, and many other animals rely primarily on smell for vital information about possible danger, food, mates, and so on; in man this function is largely performed by vision and hearing. All the human senses, however, serve as sources of enjoyment, as well as of information, and this dimension especially dominates olfaction.

Many of our small daily pleasures and irritations result from odors in our environment. Few of us are totally indifferent to the smells of percolating coffee, exhaust fumes, perfume, cigar smoke, or charcoal-broiled steaks. Advertisers are well aware of the emotional, or affective, elements in our responses to odors. Try counting the number of commercials using the words "smells fresh" during a single evening of television or how many different kinds of products come irrelevantly "lemon-scented."

The Olfactory Stimulus and Receptors Whereas most senses can be differentiated by the kinds of stimulations to which they respond—light, sound waves, and so on—the stimulation for taste and smell appears to be about the same: molecules of chemical substance that enter the mouth or the nostrils and make contact with the sensory receptors (Fig. 1.30). That is probably why we sometimes have difficulty distinguishing these sensory experiences. Odors contribute as much to our enjoyment of a good meal as do the tastes themselves, which we can demonstrate by eating exactly the same dishes while suffering a bad cold.

The olfactory receptors are long bipolar cells that project through the lining (the *epithelium*) of the top and sides of the nasal cavity and into the mucous membrane; on their ends are delicate "hairs." There are probably also

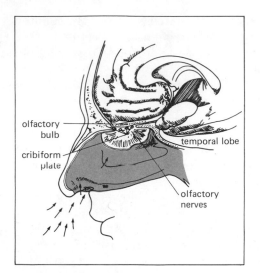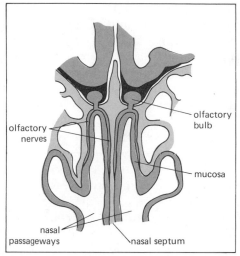

Fig. 1.30 Smell receptors. The olfactory epithelium in the upper nasal passages is a small area with slightly more than half a million olfactory cells. Although man's sense of smell is very weak compared to that of many animals, he is still able to recognize about 10,000 different scents. (Ebert, Loewy, Miller, and Schneiderman, 1973)

a few of these bipolar cells in the pharynx. They leave the nasal cavity in bundles and synapse with secondary cells in the *olfactory bulbs* at the base of the brain; regrouping of fibers also occurs at this station. The secondary cells then carry the impulses directly to the cortex. This system, with only two stations between the actual site of stimulation and the cortex, is the simplest of all man's senses, but because the upper nasal cavity is rather inaccessible, it is also the most difficult to study.

Factors Influencing Olfaction: *Concentration* A major factor influencing olfaction is the concentration of molecules in the odorant. Although the human nasal receptors are sensitive to quite low concentrations, we are not sure how low. The absolute thresholds for detection of a number of chemicals have been established, but their range is wide. For example, the concentration required for ether to reach threshold is more than 100,000 times greater than that required for artificial musk. Actually, the nose is probably sensitive to lower concentrations than we can measure with current laboratory techniques. Until more precise methods are devised, we cannot speak with certainty about absolute thresholds of olfactory detection.

Rate of Flow A second factor is the rate at which the odorant flows past the olfactory receptors. Although the volume of odorant at any given concentration does not seem to have perceptible effects on the absolute threshold, a greater rate of flow does lower it noticeably. One likely explanation is that the number of molecules required to produce the threshold response must flow past the receptors in a given period of time in order to permit temporal summation (see p. 54). It appears, then, that the absolute threshold for olfaction is determined by both the concentration of the odorant and its rate of flow.

The most striking feature of the olfactory apparatus in man is its poor ability to discriminate within the range of detectable odors. Engen (1961, 1964) and his colleagues discovered in the early 1960s that increasing the concentration of some odorants from that necessary for absolute threshold a hundredfold might only double the perceived intensity of the odor. In fact, successive equal increases in stimulus concentration yielded progressively smaller increases in perceived intensity. Often a very large increase in concentration of the stimulation was required before subjects could discriminate a single j.n.d.

This relative insensitivity of the olfactory receptors is reflected in the existence of two thresholds: one for detection of an odor and a second, higher one for recognizing the odor already detected. This difference has been demonstrated experimentally by Engen (1960), who asked two groups to smell substances in four test tubes, only one of which contained an odorant. One group was told to expect the contents of one tube only to smell "different"; the other was told to expect a specific odor. The thesholds for the former group were found to be considerably lower. These results raise the possibility that two different sets of receptors are involved in detection and recognition. Or must summation of detection responses be achieved at a higher center before recognition occurs? The answer awaits further research.

 How Do We Discriminate Odors?

It is difficult to study smell phenomena because odor discriminations are affected by many variables other than olfactory input. In order to circumvent the problem much research is done by looking at the neural discharges produced in the olfactory system by different odors. In this way odorants can be classified according to the neural discharges they produce rather than according to subjective reports.

Adrian (1953, 1954) conducted such an experiment. He recorded neural firing from second-order neurons in the olfactory bulb. All chemicals that excited a particular neuron were grouped together on the basis of these recordings. Adrian found that although in each of the resultant groupings of chemicals there was often one chemical that excited only that one neuron, most chemicals excited more than one neuron. Thus many chemicals fell into a number of groups. Each chemical excited different combinations of single units. Although most single bulbar units could be discharged by more than one odorant, the particular combination of neural firings among the single units was different for different odorants. Adrian postulated that olfactory discrimination depends on receptors that are selectively sensitive to overlapping groups of stimuli. These receptors respond in different ways when stimulated by different odorants and signal different odorant effects.

Quality Still another factor influencing olfaction is the quality of odors. There have been many attempts at classification, but none has been entirely satisfactory, partly because of difficulties in obtaining uniform responses to specific test substances. For example, in one such attempt four basic categories—fragrant, acidic, burnt, and caprylic (characteristic of animals)—were established (Crocker, 1947). Experimental subjects were asked to assign scale values for these qualities to different odors. The results, however, were unsatisfactory and difficult to reproduce in other experiments. One's own experience in the difficulty of describing odors reflects this same problem.

An effort to correlate the shapes of the molecules in specific odorants with the corresponding perceived qualities has met with rather more success (Amoore, 1963a, b). This approach has yielded close correlations between molecule shape and such odor qualities as ethereal, camphoraceous, musky, floral, and minty, but it has not yet been determined how these categories are discriminated by the sensory apparatus.

Still another approach is based on a process called *cross adaptation*. It is known that adaptation of the olfactory receptors to a high level of one substance will sometimes raise the threshold for detection of another substance, suggesting that the two have common characteristics. So far, however, no conclusive results have been obtained.

In fact, the scattered bits of evidence available suggest that odors should be classified on several different dimensions at once (Engen, 1962). One of these dimensions, on which little controlled experimentation has been done, is that of "pleasantness." Different people rank the same odorants in widely different ways, and this range of variation may reflect their individual affective associations growing out of past experiences. So strong are these associations that even when participants in an experiment are asked not to base their judgments on emotional reactions, they cannot help doing so. Furthermore, the ability to make distinctions in the pleasantness of odors is much greater than that for the dimension of odor intensity. It may very well be, then, that discrimination of odors depends more upon the affective responses that they arouse than on activity in the receptors.

CUTANEOUS SENSES

One whole group of sensory experiences—touch, pain, heat, cold—is conveyed through receptors in the skin. The importance of the cutaneous senses requires little comment. Not only does sensitivity to pain and to extreme temperatures enable us to avoid external dangers; it also alerts us to disorders within our bodies that require treatment. Aside from the many pleasures it affords us, our sense of touch can also be made to substitute for other senses on occasion. In a dark room we can sometimes feel our way where we cannot see. This

Braille

People communicate with their environment through their senses. Suppose one of the senses is damaged and you receive no information, no sensation through it. How would you relate to an environment that you could not see? Quite often people develop increased awareness of another sense. A blind person would depend on the sense of hearing or touch or smell or all of them.

In places where reading is a widespread means of communication, blind people are at a special disadvantage. To compensate for this, initially they learned to read raised-line lettering. Then in 1829, Louis Braille developed an improved system of reading, using dots in place of letters. The basic unit, or cell, of this system is a rectangular box consisting of six dots, two across and three down. Most people reading in Braille use the index fingers of both hands, moving them across the page in short up-and-down motions while exerting a slight pressure. Touch reading, though, is a time-consuming process, like reading letter by letter. In addition Braille books are larger and more cumbersome than printed books. A pocket dictionary transcribed into Braille would become six or seven thick volumes with larger than average-sized pages. Other problems include related educational and perceptual difficulties. It is hard to imagine something you have never seen.

There are three forms of Braille: grade 1, grade 2, and phonemic Braille. Grade 1, uncontracted Braille, is literal; each cell stands for a letter or a punctuation symbol. Contracted Braille, grade 2, utilizes one symbol or contraction for certain common letter groups (i.e., dis-, -ed, -ing) or words (i.e., of, the) in addition to the letter symbols. Phonemic Braille uses sound symbols instead of letters as the basic unit. In many cases, a Braille symbol has more than one meaning and is defined by its context.

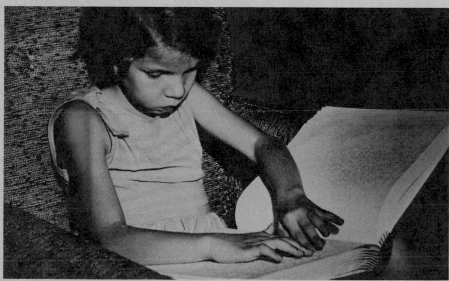

Photo courtesy of the New York Association for the Blind

adaptability has been refined to a high degree in many blind people who have learned to read Braille characters through their fingertips.

The Stimuli

Mechanical pressure on the skin receptors was long considered the source of energy for the perception of touch until experimenters noticed that only the *application* and *removal* of pressure causes neural responses. In fact, it is the gradient between the area of greater and lesser pressures that determines the perception of pressure (Meissner, 1859; Frey and Kiesow, 1899). We can demonstrate this gradient rather crudely by submerging ourselves up to the knees in a swimming pool. As long as we stand absolutely still we do not sense any differences in pressure on the part of our legs that is in the water (though we may at first sense a difference in temperature), but as soon as we begin to move we become aware of the different pressures above and below our knees. *Movement* of the skin receptors, rather than sustained tension, thus appears to stimulate tactile response.

The stimulus energy for sensation of heat and cold can also be mechanical, as in the application of an icepack to the forehead. Sometimes, however, radiant energy from the electromagnetic spectrum is responsible for the experience of heat. The main stimuli for pain seem to be extreme intensities of either mechanical or radiant energy.

 Acupuncture

Acupuncture is a science based on philosophy, a concept that most westerners find alien. Our philosophies emphasize the separation and distinction within the universe, whereas acupuncture and the philosophy it is based on are concerned with totality and interrelatedness. Therefore, acupuncture is not solely a form of medicine; it is a science of life, of health, and of nature. The central belief of this philosophy and science is the principle of polarity expressed by yin and yang, two inseparable parts understood in relation to each other and in constant change.

Acupuncture sees individual health as a balance to be maintained. The theoretical base of ancient Chinese medicine, of which acupuncture is one aspect, defines a medical problem as a fault in one's interaction with the universe, a disharmony between an individual and his or her environment. This definition makes no distinction between the physical and the psychological. Neither does it separate the body into autonomous systems. The individual is a totality; an ancient line of thought says that man is a microcosm of the universe.

Acupuncture is essentially a means of maintaining health. In acupuncture the disharmony that we call disease is treated with needles and herbal medicine.

The stainless stell needles work on the vital force—the life energy that runs through people and nature. The positioning of the needles is determined by pulse diagnosis along the 12 main meridians of the body. A meridian is a pathway of the vital energy. There are more than 300 acupuncture points. The effect of the needle is determined by its location, the depth to which it is inserted, how long it remains, and whether it is moved (twirled) after it is inserted. Another aspect of full treatment is discovering and altering the cause of the disharmony. This may mean a change of diet or attitude or what may be described as quality of life. Acupuncturists, or traditional doctors, believe that they are working with the disease in order to restore balance, that cure does not come from covering up the disease but from bringing it out. The law of cure states that a condition will worsen before it gets better and that symptoms will appear in reverse order until the body returns to balance. The job of the traditional doctor is to help one to be healthy.

In 1966, the western press "discovered" that acupuncture was being practiced in mainland China. Actually, this form of medicine had never been lost. It had been the least expensive and most effective form of health care for the masses in China. When the Maoist government began to organize health care, it was observed that the people were using acupuncture. In addition, there were not enough western-trained doctors to treat the population. The acupuncturists supplemented and eventually taught their knowledge to the western doctors. By the time the press discovered its use, acupuncture was being used for varieties of anesthesia. Chinese doctors are aware of certain problems involving acupuncture and anesthesia: sensations experienced in surgery and incompleteness of the anesthetic. It has since been used to treat deafness.

To practitioners of western medicine, acupuncture is a puzzle. They cannot see the meridians in the same way they see the circulatory system. Therefore some doctors believe it works because the patients believe in it, as a psychosomatic medicine. Another more scientific theory is that humans have two pain centers or gates. Insertion or twirling the needles causes an overwhelming amount of painless sensation. This prevents the pain of surgery from reaching the pain centers. This does not explain why acupuncture works in other kinds of treatment.

There are several contradictions between western medicine's use of acupuncture and modern acupuncture practiced by traditional doctors. Western doctors try to use acupuncture in pieces, as one part of their treatment. Traditional doctors see acupuncture as one aspect of their patient's lives. To them, acupuncture is not only a form of medicine; it is a way of life.

The Receptors

Fig. 1.31 is a diagram of some of the major skin receptors. In contrast to the chemical senses, which possess separate receptor systems but seem to be activated by similar kinds of energy, the cutaneous senses respond to several kinds of energy; it appears, however, that the skin receptors are not specific to different forms of energy, as was once thought.

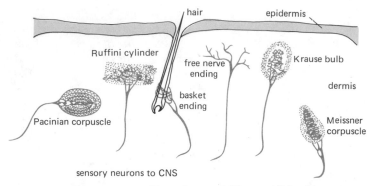

Fig. 1.31 Skin receptors. (Ebert, Loewy, Miller, and Schneiderman, 1973)

There are three basic types of receptors in the skin. The *hair follicles,* which are closely interwoven at their bases with nerve fibers, respond to even very light changes in pressure. The few areas of hairless skin on our bodies, for example, the fingertips, contain *corpuscles* that are probably very sensitive to touch. Finally, some nerve fibers have *free endings* in the skin—that is, they are not enclosed in protective structures—these receptors are particularly sensitive to pain.

All three kinds of receptors are attached to secondary nerve networks along which impulses are transmitted in ways with which we are familiar from our study of the other senses. The brain interprets the origin of a stimulus by where in the brain the nerve pathway from receptors ends. A good example of this is the "phantom limb phenomenon." Persons who have lost an arm or a leg may actually complain of sensation in the missing limb. Apparently many of these "phantom limb sensations" are due to the irritation of some of the remaining stumps of nerves that originally innervated the missing limb. These nerves send messages to the brain, which interprets them as real sensory events originating in the limb.

So far there is no satisfactory evidence that any of the cutaneous receptors is specialized to any of the four basic cutaneous sensations. It *is* possible to map points on the skin that are particularly sensitive to heat and cold, but the receptors in these areas show no difference in structure from other receptors that are not particularly sensitive to temperature.

Factors Influencing Cutaneous Thresholds

Experiments with hairs of graduated stiffness (measurable on a sensitive scale that registers how much pressure is required to bend them) have revealed that the absolute threshold for detection of touch varies in different parts of the body, probably because of variations in skin thickness and the density of nerve endings. Within a given area two thresholds can be isolated: the threshold for touch and another one for pain, the latter involving up to six times as much pressure on the same receptors.

The determination of thresholds for temperature change is very complex. Here we shall mention only that the main factors influencing these thresholds are skin temperature, the rate of change in the stimulus temperature (whether or not it is gradual enough to permit adaptation), and the size of the skin area stimulated.

THE EQUILIBRATORY SENSES AND KINESTHESIS

Still other senses provide us with information about the balance and orientation of the body and its separate parts, both in motion and at rest.

The Equilibratory System

The equilibratory system, which senses movement of the entire body, is centered in the *vestibular apparatus* of the inner ear (Fig. 1.32). One part of this system consists of three semicircular canals, each in a different plane; the canals are filled with fluid and lined with hair cells, which function as receptors. When the body rotates in any one of the three planes the fluid in the appropriate canal shifts, stimulating the hair cells, which fire associated neural fibers. The resulting impulses are transmitted through the *vestibular nerve* to the *vestibular nuclei* of the brain stem. From here they are dispatched both to the brain cortex and to the other body organs that must make rapid adjustments to the shift in position. If the body moves at an angle to the three planes, receptors in more than one canal respond.

vestibular apparatus

The other part of the vestibular system is the *vestibular sacs,* located between the canals and the cochlea. These structures are also lined with hair cell

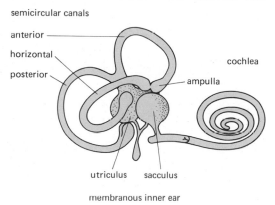

Fig. 1.32 The vestibular mechanism of the inner ear. (Johnson, Delanney, Cole, and Brooks, 1972)

semicircular canals

anterior

horizontal

posterior

cochlea

ampulla

utriculus   sacculus

membranous inner ear

Training Astronauts

A basic problem facing astronauts in space is adjusting to a state of weightlessness, or zero gravity. No ground device can simulate exactly what it is like without gravity, but a stone thrown in the air or a bullet at the top of its trajectory has an instant of weightlessness, as does the roller-coaster rider before he starts down from the peak of a curve.

Under zero gravity, blood and fluids normally kept in the legs and lower body by the force of gravity shift to the head and upper torso. Other physical effects include twice the normal amount of urinary discharge during the first days in space, and the loss of red blood cells, calcium, and potassium. The extra fluid being withdrawn from the tissues causes weight loss—one Skylab astronaut lost 4 inches around the waist. The weight is quickly regained on ground, and the body chemistry returns to normal.

Nausea is often an accompaniment of attaining zero gravity. Not all astronauts suffer this symptom, and to date no reliable test has been found to predetermine who will experience it. Aerospace physicains are not certain whether it is caused by the shift of body fluids or disturbance of the vestibular system.

Training for astronauts includes riding in airplanes that fly over an arc and into a steep dive. The occupants experience about 20 second of weightlessness on each flight. Other exercises are conducted under water to simulate the condition of weightlessness. Studies of persons confined to bed for long periods of time have contributed to information about the effects of lack of exercise on muscles.

It is necessary for astronauts to exercise while in space to avoid damage to the heart, blood vessels, and muscles. Special devices to lessen the physical effects of weightlessness include contour chairs with moving footrest and back that push against the astronaut so that he is forced to push back to avoid being doubled up. Pressure bands applied to legs and arms function as automatic tourniquets, suppressing and releasing the flow of blood.

receptors, but in this case they respond to the position of the resting body—whether it is upright or tilted at various angles.

Kinesthesis

The kinesthetic receptors are located in the joints between bones and in the muscles and tendons. They keep us informed of the shifting positions of our body parts, permitting us to coordinate our movements; they also control some of our involuntary reflexes. Kinesthetic receptors are nerve fibers that are connected to a complex network of neural pathways through the spinal cord to the brain.

In the beginning of this chapter we dealt with the ways in which our senses generally interact with the environment. We then explained the visual system and its physical and psychological relation to the perception of light. A short discussion of the other sense modalities and their relation to the environment followed. Basically, sensation in this chapter has been defined as the interaction between physical properties of the body and physical properties of the environment.

In Chapter 4, the brain's processing of information received from the senses will be discussed. How is sensory information acted upon? How is it stored? How is it used after it is in our memories? How are sensory inputs and outputs coordinated? In general, how are we able to convert simple neural impulses into complex mental processes?

SUMMARY

We are constantly kept in touch with changes in the environment through our senses. In fact, we are bombarded by sensory stimulations but can be aware only of some of them, since we are limited by the physical properties of both the environment and our own physiology. The senses do not select but merely transmit as much information as they can over neural pathways to the brain. There the information is processed (Chapter 4), though some processing begins during the receiving and transmitting stages.

Most sensory experiences involve four aspects of sensation—detection, discrimination, identification, and scaling. *Detection* asks the question, "Did something happen?" The point where stimulation is just intense enough to be noticed against a background of zero stimulation is the *absolute threshold*. This has arbitrarily been defined as the intensity of stimulation that is sensed 50 percent of the time. Usually, however, some stimulation is present in the environment, and the sense organs adjust to that level. This amount of stimulation is known as the *level of adaptation*, and the amount of extra stimulation that must occur in order to be noticed is the *differential threshold*. Detection depends upon sensory thresholds, which are influenced by physical states and most of all by adaptation levels.

Discrimination is a process of differentiating two different stimuli, both of which are above the differential threshold. Discrimination can be measured, since it asks, "How much is necessary to perceive a difference?" The minimum amount of energy change necessary to perceive a difference is the *just noticeable difference* (j.n.d.). This is also arbitrarily defined as the amount of energy change that is perceived 50 percent of the time, and it also varies with environmental and individual differences.

Weber's law mathematically describes the relation between the base energy and the change in energy that can be noticed; it is expressed as $\Delta I/I = k$, where I is the magnitude of the base energy, ΔI is the amount of additional energy needed to produce a j.n.d., and k is a constant. The constant for each sensory modality is called a Weber fraction.

Scaling is the process of ordering different stimuli along some dimension, such as brightness or loudness. In general there are four types of scales, all of which involve the assignment of numbers to stimuli. A *nominal scale* says nothing about the relationship of the numbers to each other. An *ordinal scale* puts the numbers in rank order (first, second, and so on) but says nothing about the intervals between them. An *interval scale* measures the difference between the numbers in terms of a fixed unit of measure. And a *ratio scale,* which has a fixed unit of measure and also an absolute zero, enables us to compare numbers in terms of ratios. Psychological measurement most often uses an interval scale.

The stimulus for vision is *light,* a form of electromagnetic energy that can be thought of as waves traveling from light sources or as bundles of energy called *photons.* To have any visual significance for us, light must reach the retina of the eye and be absorbed by photoreceptors there.

The eye, like a camera, is structured so that light entering it focuses on a specific light-sensitive area. Light enters the *pupil* and is focused by the *lens* on the *retina.* In the retina are receptors called *rods* and *cones,* which convert light energy into neural energy. Rods are specialized for night vision and cones for day vision. The rods and cones are connected by neural pathways to *bipolar cells,* which are, in turn, connected to *ganglion cells* in the retina. The ganglion-cell fibers form the *optic nerve,* which transmits information to the brain, where it is processed (see Chapters 2 and 6). Some of the receptors combine their impulses in this neural chain through a process known as *lateral summation.*

Several other factors have considerable bearing on the functioning of the visual system. *Sensory coding* is the process by which the flood of stimulation that constantly assaults us is reduced to as few salient facts as possible and conveyed to the brain. When stimulation is steady, *lateral inhibition* allows the system to "ignore" much of it. It also calls attention to certain features in the environment, such as edges and contours. Another coding mechanism permits us to function differently but effectively in both intense and dim light.

An important feature of the human visual system is that we can move our eyes independently of the rest of our body. *Convergence* is the movement that keeps both eyes focused on the same thing. *Saccadic movements* are used in searching, and *pursuit movements* in following. Tremors, drifts, and microsaccades are minor movements that mean that our eyes are in near-constant motion.

In general, brightness increases with light intensity, but a number of factors produce other changes. One is *adaptation,* which is the eye's characteristic of acclimating or adjusting to an amount of light that is present for a period of time. Our sensitivity to a new light stimulus depends on the adaptation state of the eye. It also depends on the *brightness contrast* between the stimulus and the background we view it against, and on the duration of exposure. Duration affects *temporal coding* in such a way that, within a limited time period, a light of a given intensity is more readily detected the longer it is present or the more frequently it is flashed.

Discrimination is also affected by *acuity,* the ability to perceive fine details of the visual scene. Detection acuity is the ability to detect small details of the visual scene. Recognition acuity is the ability to recognize familiar shapes such as letters of the alphabet.

The perception of color depends upon detection of the wavelength of electromagnetic radiation, not simply its energy. The appearance of color can be described as hue, which corresponds to the wavelength of light; brightness, which corresponds to intensity; and saturation, which corresponds to the amount of white light that has to be added to the hue to remove all color from it. These three attributes can be represented on a color solid.

Hearing is the most sensitive of man's modes of interacting with his environment. Sound is a form of mechanical energy that travels through a medium and is converted into neural impulses by the ear. The ear has three parts—the outer, middle, and inner ear, which contain physical structures to collect sound from the environment and transmit it to the interior of the ear, where it then is converted into neural impulses.

The frequency of a sound wave determines its pitch (highness or lowness); the amplitude determines its loudness. High-to-medium range frequencies are coded by receptors in particular locations of the basilar membrane. Low-frequency sounds are coded by the rate at which nerve cells are fired.

The chemical senses are the sense of *taste* and of *smell*—gustation and olfaction. Our taste experiences are made up of combinations of four basic tastes, *sweet, sour, bitter,* and *salty.* The stimulation for taste is usually food or drink that reacts chemically with the *taste buds,* our taste receptors, to create neural impulses. Taste phenomena of quality and intensity affect our sense of taste just as they do our sense of vision.

Olfaction is also triggered by chemical substances that react with receptors—in this case bipolar cells in the nasal cavity—to produce a neural impulse. Our sense of smell is closely linked to our sense of taste; we experience little taste when we have a cold. Factors influencing our sense of smell are concentration, rate of flow past the receptors, and quality.

Cutaneous sensations—touch, pain, heat, cold—are conveyed through receptors in the skin. These sense receptors respond to several kinds of stimuli and have several types of receptors to convert the stimuli into neural impulses. The stimuli can be either mechanical energy (touch, movement) or radiant energy (heat). There are three types of receptors in the skin—*hair follicles, corpuscles,* and *free nerve endings.* Cutaneous sensitivity varies in different parts of the body, and within a given area, it differs for touch and for pain.

The equilibratory senses and kinesthesis provide information about the balance and orientation of the body and its parts, both moving and at rest. The equilibrium system is located in the *vestibular apparatus* of the inner ear and is composed of fluids in the semicircular canals that signal changes in body movement.

The kinesthetic receptors are located in the joints between bones and in the muscles and tendons; they inform us of movement of body parts and aid in coordination.

SUGGESTED READINGS

Cain, W. S., and L. E. Marks, eds., *Stimulus and Sensation: Readings in Sensory Psychology.* Boston, Little, Brown, 1971.
A collection of articles, many of them classics, on historical and current problems of sensation.
Montagu, Ashley, *Touching.* New York, Columbia University Press, 1971.
Montagu discusses the importance of skin to human beings.
Mueller, G. G., and Mae Rudolph, *Light and Vision.* New York, Time-Life Books, 1968.
An illustrated, easily read treatment of the physiology of vision.
Proust, Marcel, *Remembrance of Things Past* (many editions; originally published between 1922 and 1931).

This long and somewhat difficult novel moves backward and forward in time as the narrator encounters incidental sensory stimuli that trigger his memory of past experiences and their meaning in terms of his whole life.

Stevens, S. S., and Fred Warshofsky, *Sound and Hearing*. New York, Time-Life Books, 1968.

A treatment of audition, in the same series as *Light and Vision*.

Chapter Two

Perception

Why do things look the way they do?
Do we always see things as they really are?
What are "good figures"?
What is a texture-density gradient?
What is the advantage of having two eyes?
How do we perceive motion?
What happens if you wear goggles that turn everything upside down?
Does an infant have to learn distance and depth perception from experience?

"Look, there's a duck on the other side of the lake. Let's row over and see it."
"Save your strength—it's a rock, not a duck."

We react to situations in our environment on the basis of how we interpret the messages we receive through our senses. If you're interested in waterfowl, on spotting the bird you reel in your fishing line and start to row as fast as you can to identify what kind of duck it is before it takes off. But when you find out that the "duck" is only a rock, you cast out again and resume your leisurely fishing.

HOW DO WE PERCEIVE THE WORLD AROUND US?

Our perceptions guide some of our most important inner thoughts and outward actions, but what we perceive is not a simple reflection of the environment. *Why do things look as they do?* This basic question has plagued man for cen turies. At various times in history the following answers have been put forward: (1) because things are what they are; (2) because things are what our nerves tell us they are; (3) because things are what we are.

Things Are What They Are

Wilhelm Wundt

analytic
introspection

In 1790, Thomas Reid attempted to explain the apparent discrepancy between what is and what seems to be by differentiating between what he termed sensation and perception (Boring, 1942). *Sensation,* Reid proposed, is the registration of the physical stimulus on the sense organ. *Perception* is the interpretation or meaning the person gives the sensation. Thus sensations are objective representations of the physical world, while perceptions involve subjective judgments human beings make about that world.

Until the late 19th century research in perception was largely aimed at reducing sensation to its basic elements. The German psychologist Wilhelm Wundt established a laboratory in which he sought to analyze the discrete elements that he believed made sensation. Wundt (1902) developed a method of *analytic introspection* by which he studied visual sensation with a reduction screen in terms of (1) intensity, (2) extensity, and (3) quality. A reduction screen is simply a piece of paper with a hole in it. If we look at the world through this hole, we can identify only blotches of color, which we can classify according to their intensity, extensity, and quality. But the analysis of sensation into presumably elementary attributes fails to tell the whole story of perception. How can we identify the following configurations through a reduction screen?

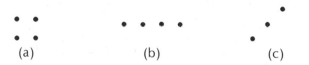

(a)   (b)   (c)

According to Wundt's theory, our conclusions about these configurations would be identical; in each case we would see four equally spaced black dots. But what we actually perceive are (a) a square, (b) a horizontal line, and (c) a diagonal. Wundt erroneously assumed that the whole can be understood solely as the sum of its parts. He failed to take into account form and organization in the visual field. *Perception is a function of the relation of elements to one another in forming a whole.* When a familiar tune is played in a new key we still recognize it. Even though all of the notes, or elementary components, are different when *Jingle Bells* is played in F major instead of C major, we can identify the organizational, or configurational, relation between tones; we may not even know that the notes are different. What we perceive cannot be explained simply in terms of the isolated attributes of physical objects. Clearly, things are not perceived solely as what they are.

J. Weisburd

Things Are What Our Nerves Tell Us They Are

Nineteenth-century physiologists proposed that the nerves act as intermediaries between the brain and the environment. According to Johannes Müller's doctrine of *specific nerve energies,* each nerve channel carries its own perceptual quality and is excited by certain specific stimuli. Light, for example, excites the visual channel and sends a visual message. (If the visual channel is excited by other stimuli, however, it still carries a visual message. When you poke your finger in your eye, in addition to feeling pain, you usually see a flash of light; that is, the nerves carry visual messages although there are no visual stimuli.) Müller postulated, therefore, that what we perceive is not the direct registration of stimuli on our sense organs but the message relayed by our nerves.

specific nerve energies

Radio Times Hulton Picture Library

Johannes Müller

The way we perceive objects and people in the world around us is incredibly consistent. Yet there are countless instances when this consistency breaks down and what we perceive is an inaccurate representation of the environment. The examples in Fig. 2.1 point up some key problems that perception theory must explain.

It is true that the length of the retinal sensations representing lines *A* and *B* in the Mueller-Lyer illusion would have to be the same, but the neural coding of the two lines does not necessarily represent them identically. In fact, we do not fully understand the coding of some of these line figures, particularly those that give rise to illusions. But we know that the retina does not simply provide the brain with an isomorphic or one-to-one representation. As we have seen in Chapter 1, extensive coding occurs at the retinal level and dramatically influences the kind of information the brain receives. Further on in the information referral process, additional coding may render our perceptions even more removed from the characteristics of the sensations projected on the retina.

Things Are What We Are

Our perception of objects in the environment is influenced by our past experience and by our present attitudes and motivations. What we hear others say can predispose us to misperceive an object. If you are shown a luminous globe in a dark room you will judge it as farther away from you if you are told the object is a beach ball than if you are told it is a golf ball.

Fig. 2.1 Examples of Inconsistent or Illusory Perception

(a) The Phi Phenomenon   When two spots of light spaced somewhat apart are illuminated consecutively, we seem to see a single spot of light that moves from a to b.

$$\frac{a}{0} \qquad\qquad \frac{b}{0}$$

Why do the two lights, flashed on and off in rapid succession, appear to be a single light moving through space? Our perception of motion clearly depends on more than just the stimulation of certain neural structures.

(b) Reversible Figures

As you look at the accompanying reversible figure, you can see either a white vase against a black background or two black profiles against a white background. Can you see both figures at the same time?

(c) Sander Parallelogram

Which line is longer, *AY* or *AX*?

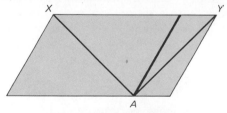

(d) Concentric Circles Appearing as Spiral

Why do the concentric circles appear as a moving spiral?

(*Fig. 2-1 continued*)

(e) Titchener's Circles

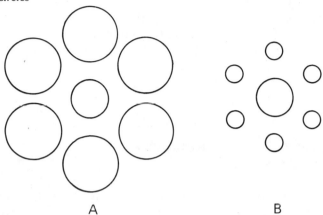

A   B

Why do the surrounding circles in (A) make the circle in the center appear much smaller than the central circle in (B)?

(f) The Mueller-Lyer Illusion

Which line segment is longer, *A* or *B?* A ruler will show that they are the same length, and therefore must evoke the same sensations in our eyes. Yet why do we perceive *B* as longer?

Carmichael, Hogan, and Walter (1932), showed subjects two circles connected by a line and asked them to draw what they saw. Those who were told the circles were eyeglasses drew something quite different from those who were told the circles represented a barbell.

In everyday life we are apt to evaluate a guest lecturer more negatively if we have been forewarned that this is his first appearance before a group than if we have heard that the speaker is a distinguished professor.

Finally, then, perception depends on all three—(1) what things are; (2) what our nerves tell us things are; and (3) what we are—that is, our past experience and our present attitudes and needs. It is a process that involves a continual interaction between the physical properties of objects, the information we receive from our nerves, and our state of mind at the time we receive the information. The information we extract from stimuli determines our behavior in the environment; to understand why things are perceived in the way they are is to understand why man acts as he does. But to understand perception we need to know (1) how the organism receives and transfers (transduces) information, (2) how it modifies the input (information), and (3) how it converts stimuli into organized perceptions. Thus the psychophysical relation between objects and self, the physiological bases of sensation, and the psychological processes that influence perception must all be taken into account if we are to explain fully why we perceive the world around us as we do.

Since to a considerable extent the principles of perception are the same for all the senses, for the sake of simplicity we will discuss only visual perception in this chapter. It must also be noted that our concern here will be with the psychophysics of vision. The physiology of the sensory processes was treated in Chapter 1, and psychological influences will be the subject of much of the rest of this book.

ORGANIZATION OF FORMS AND PATTERNS

As we have seen, perception does not consist merely of points of sensory stimulation impinging on a sense organ. We as perceivers take an active part in perception. As Müller stated, what we perceive are messages relayed to the brain by our neural system. In the case of sight, we take the light waves that strike the retina of the eye and organize them into meaningful patterns, forms, and shapes.

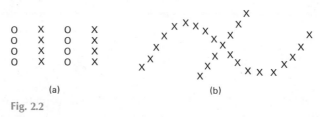

(a)   (b)

Fig. 2.2

When we see configurations like those in Fig. 2.2, we perceive them in ways that make sense to us. In (a) we note vertical rows of O's and X's rather than horizontal rows of OXOX. We think of (b) as a wavy line intersected by a straight line, not as the two isomorphic projections in Fig. 2.3.

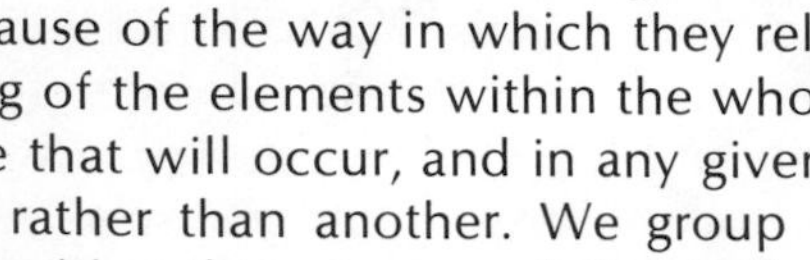

Fig. 2.3

Within a specific context we perceive elements as occupying positions relative to one another. When we look at a configuration we tend to group two elements together because of the way in which they relate to form the whole. The relative positioning of the elements within the whole determines the type of perceptual response that will occur, and in any given situation one type of perception will result rather than another. We group the O's in Fig. 2.2 (a) together because the position they occupy relative to the X's causes us to do so.

The basic principles that govern how objects are organized and perceived were formulated in the early part of this century and are known as the *Gestalt laws* (Koffka, 1935). These laws enable us to describe with a good deal of accuracy how we organize stimulus elements to construct a representation of the visual field. But they still do not explain *why* we see what we do. What underlying mechanisms enable us to organize the visual field in such an orderly, predictable manner? Nevertheless, the basic principles of perception stated in the Gestalt laws are the cornerstones of contemporary theories of perception.

Gestalt laws

 Gestalt Laws of Organization

The Gestalt principles of perceptual organization are concerned with structural or organizational arrangements of elements that permit us to see things as we do. They describe how certain features are grouped together into larger units.

Fig. 2.4 illustrates the ways in which we relate stimuli according to the Gestalt laws of proximity, similarity, continuity, common fate, and closure.

Fig. 2.4 A number of examples of Gestalt laws of perceptual organization.

```
  O   O   O      ●   ●   ●
  O   O   O      O   O   O
  O   O   O      ●   ●   ●
  O   O   O      O   O   O
      (a)            (b)
```

a. *Proximity* Elements that are closer to one another tend to be grouped with each other rather than with similar elements that seem spatially or temporally farther away. The dots are seen as vertical rows because their spatial proximity is closer vertically than horizontally.

b. *Similarity* Elements that are similar tend to be seen as a unit. The dots here are spaced equally but we group them horizontally because the vertical rows are less similar.

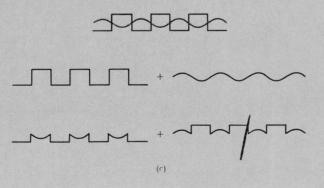

(c)

c. *Continuity* Stimuli are grouped together when they are seen as a continuation of the direction established by previous elements. We see configuration (c) as a curved line crossing through right angles rather than as the other logically possible perception illustrated.

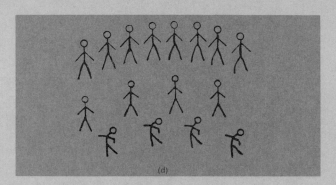

(d)

d. *Common Fate* This law is essentially the principle of similarity applied to moving objects. When elements move or change in the same direction, they are seen as belonging together or sharing a common fate. Our tendency to see elements in this way enables us to enjoy the changing formations executed by a band at a football game. (Hanson, 1958)

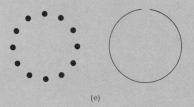

(e)

e. *Closure* This is the tendency to close an incomplete figure by filling in the missing parts.

Some other determinants of what is seen as a figure are shown in Fig. 2.5.

a. *Area* As a closed area is made smaller it is more likely to be seen as figure. The smaller fins in a and b are seen as figure, the wider ones as ground, regardless of orientation.

b. *Orientation* When the sizes of the fins in the same ambiguous figure are equal, their orientation determines which is figure and which ground. Thus in c and d it is the cross with horizontal and vertical limbs that is seen as figure.

c. *Symmetry* In e and f the symmetrical areas are seen as figure regardless of color or shading. In one case we have black figures on a white background, and in the other white figures on a black background.

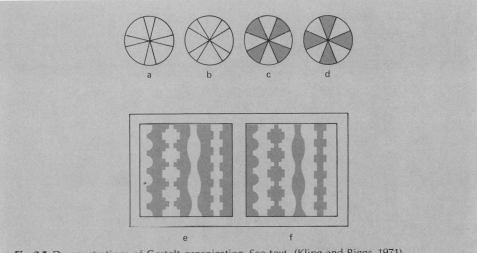

Fig. 2.5 Demonstrations of Gestalt organization. See text. (Kling and Riggs, 1971)

One aspect of the Gestalt laws that needs study is their interaction. For example, we may sometimes find two laws of organization theoretically working against each other. Another basic problem with these laws is that there are not adequate criteria for measuring why they work. They are descriptive statements of organizational properties that seem intuitively reasonable. The strength of the Gestalt laws lies in their making us aware that perceptions are lawful; even the perception and organization of ambiguous figures, as fleeting as they may be, are not haphazard but lawful. Future work must attempt to reach a better understanding of these laws.

Figure-Ground Separation

We see objects or patterns around us against surfaces or backgrounds. We see a painting hanging on a wall, not a wall behind a painting. The painting has form because its contours are defined against the wall, while the properties of the wall are only vaguely perceived. So too we identify the objects or designs in the painting itself because we see them as standing out against the background of the picture.

The Gestalt laws of organization begin with a distinction between what is seen as *figure* and what is seen as *ground* in the visual field. The laws of organization are really a list of the determinants of figure-ground organization. **figure, ground**

The figure-ground distinction was first made by Rubin (1915), who noted some striking differences between what is seen as figure and what remains in the background, or ground. He noted that figures have shape while ground is shapeless—thus the figure is a "thing" while the ground is a shapeless mass. Further, the ground seems to lie behind the figure and its area is seen as extend-

An impossible figure in art (M. C. Escher's "Reptiles").

ing beyond the figure's edges. In addition, the figure is more impressive and more meaningful, and it should be more easily remembered. Fig. 2.1b illustrates these observations well. Regardless of which configuration we see in this ambiguous figure—the vase or the two faces—the "other" becomes a shapeless, meaningless mass of *background* lying behind the figure.

      Objects do not have to be identifiable to be perceived as figures. Whatever is seen as the figure seems closer and more distinct than the ground, whether the ground has form properties or not. We must, however, have some kind of contour to see a figure-ground, or to segregate figures from grounds. This is shown by an experiment in which subjects wore halves of ping-pong balls over their eyes (Hochberg, Triebel, and Seaman, 1951). This produced a **Ganzfeld** *Ganzfeld,* or completely homogeneous visual field, because light was distributed evenly over the entire visual area. When light was first focused on the visual field through a red filter, the subjects reported seeing a hazy fog of red color. But as they continued to look at the red-light stimulation, the color seemed to disappear. Within 3 minutes the entire visual field was perceived as a dark gray

Fig. 2.6 Do you see the young wife or the mother-in-law? Can you see both at once?

area. A similar effect can be produced by simply closing the eyes: perception ceases rather quickly because there is no stimulus patterning on the retina even though there is still light. Before figure-ground segregation can even occur, then, our visual nervous system must pick up inhomogeneities in the visual field.

Hochberg (1968, 1970) has made an important distinction between what is seen on a first impression and what is perceived after several glances. It is difficult to integrate all the components of a figure against a ground immediately unless we are looking at something rather far away. We must often look at a pattern several times before we can clearly discern a unified figure. This involves integrating the information that is picked up in a series of successive eye movements. What is seen at first glance may well determine the direction in which the eye will travel on subsequent viewings. On the basis of our initial impression, we look further until we have gleaned from a stimulus pattern enough information to segregate the visual field into figure and ground. This process suggests that figure and ground separation is not always an immediate response, as the "impossible figures" in Fig. 2.7 make clear.

Julian Hochberg

Figure-ground separation underlies all of the more complex perceptual tendencies described by the Gestalt laws. It is basic to perception because an object cannot be identified until this segregation occurs. The separation of the visual field into figure and ground, then, provides the substrata for all our perceptions.

The MAR-LUN Project

Drawings by Jesse Hathaway

With the successful completion of the recent Apollo missions, the Mathematics Department of Compton College released details of the MAR-LUN Project which played an important role in our space missions. The project was the outgrowth of the casual discovery by a team member of a drawing, reproduced right (a), which was found to be a sketch of an experimental sensor. The subsequent designs of the sensor reflect the steps taken to develop means of landing this equipment on planets in outer-space. The final sleek modern design includes built-in motion to achieve stability in space.

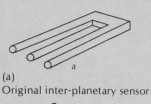

(a)
Original inter-planetary sensor

(b)
The Lunar Probe proved to be effective but developed severe oscillations and became unstable in weak gravitational fields.

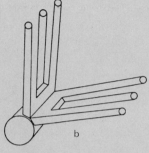

(c)
Two-dimensional stable platform for the support of the lunar-space probe.

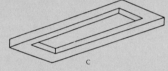
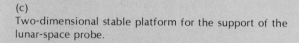

(d)
Duplexed stable Platform which replaces earlier single base. Increased stability makes this design more attractive.

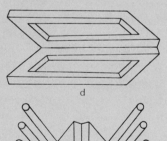

(e)
Final MAR-LUN Sensor. A highly stable yet flexible device.

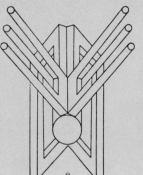

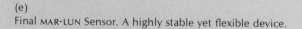

Fig. 2.7 Several examples of two-dimensional drawings of impossible forms.

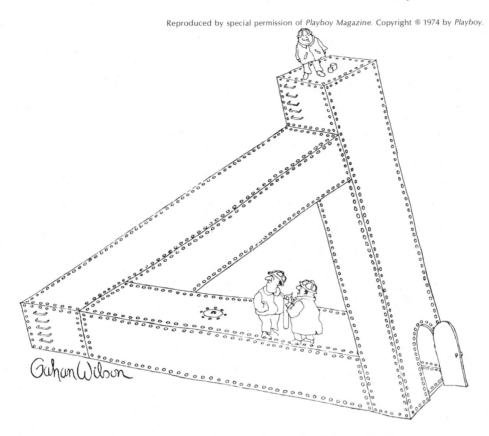

"Let's have another look at the blueprint."

Measurement of Grouping Principles

In recent years several attempts have been made to devise a criterion of measurement that would enable us to predict particular perceptions on the basis of properties inherent in the relations among elements. Important research into the variables that determine our perception of similarity has focused on the measurement of the angles, turns, and slopes in a figure. Other attempts to quantify complex aspects of perceptual organization have applied information theory to the stimulus properties of elements. Information theory is the attempt to understand psychological processes by comparing them to physical communications systems, such as digital computers.

Perhaps the most puzzling of the grouping principles are the concepts of good figure. How can we measure and define the "goodness" of a figure? Why is one perception good as opposed to another? Two noted psychologists, Hochberg and Attneave, have provided some important insights into these

Fred Attneave

An artistic perceptual illusion (M. C. Escher's "Ascending and Descending").

 ### Determinants of Perceptual Groupings

A recent seemingly fruitful approach to the study of figural "goodness" has been made by Beck (1972). Beck set out to study perceptual organization and groupings in an attempt to determine what properties of perceptual stimuli favor and facilitate one particular organization over the many others possible.

Using relatively simple stimuli, such as those shown in Fig. 2.8, he searched for any process that would facilitate a subject's differentiating between legitimate U shapes in the bottom of the figure or V shapes in the top of the figure and the rotated shapes. Subjects were asked to count the number of V's or U's in each set of figures and the time taken was noted. Beck assumed that the speed of counting indicated the relative facility of grouping; thus any stimulus manipulation that was shown to facilitate counting did so by making each item more discriminable—that is by reducing its being grouped with other items.

Beck found that speed of counting was fastest for the stimuli on the left of the figure (A and D) and slowest for those on the right (C and F). Analysis

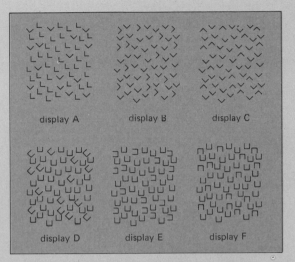

Fig. 2.8 An example of a stimulus display to study the role of form similarity. (Beck, 1972)

shows that the shapes on the left have the greatest difference between the slopes of the lines of the legitimate V's and U's and the slopes of the rotated figures. In the stimuli on the right the slopes of the lines of legitimate and rotated figures are identical; in addition, the rotated figures are rotated 180° instead of 90° as in B and E. It seems then that to a great extent, organization is a function of similarity of slopes of the line elements.

Beck further demonstrated that slope differences are picked up in peripheral as well as central vision. If a subject is asked to discriminate differences between figures in his perceptual field prior to a narrowing of visual attention, he will notice figures with a different orientation from the other elements in the field first. In one experiment, four forms at each of the corners of an imaginary square were presented. The perceiver's task was to pick out the form that was different from the others. This was best done when the odd form differed in slope from the other three. No differences in accuracy of description were seen, however, where only one form was presented at any one of the four locations. Orientation, here, had no relation to accuracy of description. Beck argues that it is not orientation per se but orientation differences that enhance grouping. He notes further that grouping occurs over the entire retina to the extent that there are differences in the stimulus elements that can be noticed before any detailed analysis of them is carried out. Perceptual grouping is thus primarily an acuity task.

questions. Attneave (1954) defines a good figure as one with a high degree of internal redundancy; that is, we can predict what we will see next from what we have already seen. We group the portions of the field that are redundant because they give us the same visual information. The greater the degree of internal redundancy, the faster we can group stimulus elements on the basis of partial information. This process, of course, implies that we perceive form in the simplest way possible. A similar conclusion was reached by Hochberg (Hochberg and McAlister, 1953). Hochberg's *minimum principle* determines what organizations will be perceived. The principle states that we organize in whatever ways require the least amount of visual information. Thus we see two overlapping rectangles in Fig. 2.9 because this perception requires less information than the perception of five squares. Fig. 2.10 illustrates the minimum principle for depth cues.

minimum principle

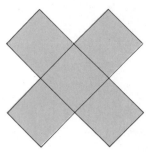

Fig. 2.9   Fives squares or overlapping rectangles.

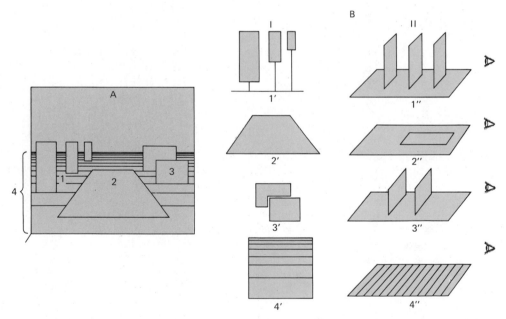

Fig. 2.10   The depth cues as cases of organizational simplicity. (A) A simple picture using four monocular depth cues: (1) relative size; (2) linear perspective; (3) interposition; and (4) texture-density gradient. (B) Compare each cue as a flat pattern in an upright plane (column I) and as the tridimensional arrangement it represents (column II). Which seems simpler in each case, the arrangement in (I) or (II)? If organizational simplicity were an innate operating characteristic of the nervous system, what would this figure imply about depth perception? (Hochberg, 1964)

Redundancy and Perception

Although the Gestalt laws may be interesting, it soon became apparent that they would not further understanding in their qualitatively stated form. A method of quantifying the laws was needed. Attneave (1954) applied the concepts and techniques of information theory to an analysis of the visual system. Information theory is an approach to the precise quantification of the *amount* of information contained in a communication. In this paradigm information is defined as the amount of uncertainty reduced by a communication. Such a reduction of uncertainty can be quantified. If you tried to guess what number from 1 to 4 your friend was thinking of, you would need to ask only two questions: (1) Is it above 2? and if the answer to question (1) is yes, (2) Is it 3? These two questions are sufficient to reduce all uncertainty in all situations where there are four alternatives. Since the answers to two questions are all that is needed, such a situation is said to have two bits of information.

To be sure, you could ask other questions about the number your friend is thinking of—for example, if it is an odd number, if it is written with curved lines, if it is double one of the other numbers in consideration, and so on. Such information is unnecessary, however, for knowing which number your friend is thinking of, and it is said to be redundant.

Attneave applied this analysis to the perception of figures as a way of understanding their stimulus qualities. He sees perception as an information-processing system, and he notes that much of the information received is redundant.

information theory

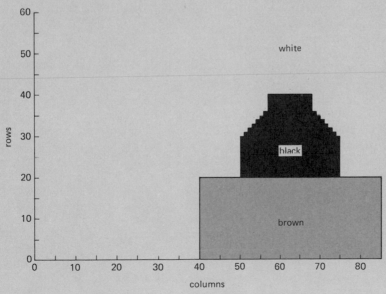

Fig. 2.11 An example of redundancy in pictures (Attneave, 1954)

Consider a picture of a black ink bottle on a corner of a brown desk in front of a white background. Suppose we divided this picture into a large number of cells, as graph paper is divided. In principle any scene can be duplicated by coloring (or not coloring) or shading the different cells in a given pattern, provided the mosaic of cells is fine enough. We can now think of information in this graph as the certainty of the color of a particular cell. If we know that all the cells in the matrix are of one of two possible colors, we require only one bit of information for the entire matrix. If, however, we are told that the color of a particular cell is completely independent of the color of any other cell, the matrix is then maximally uncertain and we require one bit of information for each cell in the matrix. The more cells in a pattern that one is uncertain of, the more information he has to remember.

Attneave demonstrated, with the use of the ink-bottle-on-desk picture in Fig. 2.11, that most visual scenes are not maximally uncertain and in fact we can know much about an entire visual field with information from only a very small part of it. Suppose an observer who is trying to guess the color of each of the cells in the matrix in Fig. 2.11 starts with cell 1, in the lower lefthand corner, and works his way across the bottom row to the right, after which he will proceed up to the next row. The first guess is of course going to be completely by chance and we expect a few wrong guesses before he hits on white. Finding that white is correct, he will probably assume that white is correct for the next cell. After again finding that he is correct he will continue guessing white and be correct until he reaches the first brown cell, where he is told white is wrong. He will now again have to engage in some random guessing until he hits on the correct color, brown. He will then continue to say brown and be correct until the end of the first row. Continuing in this way the perceiver can correctly guess the color of the cells until he reaches the top of the desk, where the white-to-brown transition is replaced by a white-to-black transition farther to the right in the row of cells. The perceiver will make some errors here, but soon he will have learned the pattern.

Attneave found that indeed perceivers guessed in this manner and did not require all of the information present in a pattern. All that was really required was information about changes from an area of homogeneous color or brightness or changes from a contour of homogeneous direction or slope. Areas without such changes contain redundant information. Even where such changes occur but are repetitious or mirror images of known changes in the visual pattern, the information is redundant.

Attneave argued that certain Gestalt laws may be reducible to the more general principles of information theory. A "good figure" in this paradigm would be one for which a minimum of information needs to be remembered. Thus a "good figure" is one that contains a high degree of internal redundancy. For example, the Gestalt laws of continuity and symmetry are both demonstrated in the experiment described as reducing uncertainty. The Gestalt laws, according to this analysis, might be renamed "the laws of information redundancy."

The Basic Unit of Analysis for the Perception of Form

What is the unit of analysis used by the visual system? Do we have some sort of representation of figures in our head to which we attempt to match forms we perceive? When we look at the letter *A*, for example, in order to identify it, do we compare the perceived letter with every form stored in our brain until the proper match is obtained? Neisser (1967) argued convincingly that such a template-matching model was naive and inadequate, especially for explaining our ability to identify forms that have undergone many variations. How do the same forms retain their identity under different variations? How do all retain the same identity? Or better yet we might ask, what makes them the same?

A, *𝒜*, 𝔄, and *A*

To answer this question a number of so-called visual feature models (for example, E. J. Gibson, 1969) have been introduced. Such models see perception as an analytic process. As a first step in perception, all forms are analyzed into their basic components or features. Thus for example an *A* may consist of two vertically tilted lines and a horizontal line. These features are then stored in memory, possibly in list form. As we develop perceptually and experience and analyze many forms, the list of features grows longer. New incoming stimulation or percepts are now analyzed into their basic component features and then compared with the stored list of basic visual features. A match occurs and a stimulus is identified when there is close correspondence between the features of a new stimulus and those of a particular list previously identified with a particular form.

Gibson has applied this analysis to the visual recognition of letters of the alphabet. She suggests that 12 basic visual features (for example, vertical line segments, horizontal line segments, closed loops) can be used to describe all the letters of the alphabet. According to this analysis, the first step in form perception is the analysis of any form into its basic visual feature components. In the second step, these features are compared with the stored lists for all of the 26 letters until the best match is found.

Thus, a feature testing approach to recognition of form seems to work better than a template approach, though we still need to know more about how the latter would work in practice.

ORGANIZATION OF SPACE: DEPTH PERCEPTION

One approach to perception argues that retinal projections are a sufficient source of information for nearly all our perceptions of the visual world. If, alternatively, perception were the product of past experience, how could we ever agree about what we see in the visual world? No two people have the same life experiences. How can they share the same perceptual experience? There must be some *psy-*

chophysical correlates between the physical dimensions of objects and the perceptual experience that results.

As we have seen, when we isolate the components of a stimulus, they do not add up to what we actually see. However, we do not arrive at our knowledge about the organization of space from an isolated feature in an object or its retinal projection. Rather, we consider all the information on the retina so that we can see the relation between the different sources of information from all the objects in our visual field. Thus if we simply concentrate on the retinal projection of one object, such as a door as we walk past it, that projection becomes variously shaped trapezoids, depending on the orientation of the door with respect to the viewer. When we consider the entire retinal projection, however, the irregularities in the shape of the door are perfectly correlated with the other irregularities in the retina. For example, all the objects on the wall the door is on are transformed in the same way. Further, the texture of the wall is also transformed, so that the parts of the wall close to us have a coarser texture than the parts farther away. When this information is correlated with the shape of the retinal projection of the door, then it is not quite so difficult to understand how we might come to have object constancy, that is, how we might see the door as a rectangle all the time, regardless of our orientation. A critical factor in this view of perception, therefore, is to consider all the information rather than simply the part the perceiver is attempting to judge or perceive.

Stationary Retinal Projections: Texture-Density Gradients

J. J. Gibson (1950) has been responsible for some major developments in research on perception using the approach we have just discussed. His analysis of visual space perception focuses on the transformations that take place in the continuous, but constantly changing, visual world. Perceptions are rarely, if ever, the result of only what we see in a single glance. Even the initial separation of the visual field into figure and ground usually occurs after a series of glances. We integrate the information received from a succession of continuously changing retinal images into a single perception. Yet, a single retinal pattern has visual field variations which convey spatial information. If we look first at the information in a single projection and then at the various transformations it undergoes as we shift perspective, we can explain perception in terms of the way in which these successive stimulations of the retina are integrated by the visual nervous system.

texture   The ground, or surface, against which we see objects is usually of reasonably uniform *texture*. Square tiles on a kitchen floor repeat the same pattern over the entire surface area. If we could look straight toward each tile, the retinal projections would all be the same. In the real world, however, we have to look down to see the floor, and the surface area is at a slant to our line of sight. The squares decrease in retinal size as they extend away from us, and the change in size occurs along with a change in projected shape.

Photo, right, by Arthur Tress

⊌ Empiricist Approach to Perception

The empiricist view of perception, which dominated the field for many years, holds that since retinal projections are virtually two-dimensional, our information about spatial arrangements must come from some other source.

According to the 18th-century British philosopher George Berkeley (1709), generally considered the founder of the empiricist school of thought, our memories of past experiences give us the ability to judge the distance and depth of objects. The ability to perceive distance is not innate, Berkeley argued, but learned from childhood as our perceptual experiences increase in number and complexity. Babies learn depth perception as they learn to associate different visual impressions of objects with how far they have to reach to touch these objects. In Berkeley's view most of our perception of constancy of the visual world is due to the fact that we know what the real sizes, shapes, locations, and so forth, of objects are, and, consequently, we correct, by means of our knowledge, the sense impressions we receive. Therefore, these impressions result in a perceptual organization that we know corresponds to the real world. As we will see later in the chapter, however, substantial evidence has accumulated to indicate that a child is born with the ability to perceive depth and distance.

A theory related to Berkeley's was developed by Hermann von Helmholtz (1867), a physicist and physiologist. He proposed that our perception of distance is unconsciously inferred from two distinct sources of information: (1) the size of the retinal projection itself and (2) our memory of the size of an object. When we see a chair, for example, we compare the size projected on the retina to the familiar size we remember and then compute the actual size and our distance from the chair.

The view of perception as a learned process is frequently referred to as the *empiricist* approach, since it rests on the assumption that perception is based on experience. To test the validity of this assumption, empiricists today generally begin with an analysis of stimulus properties. Using the physical dimensions of either the object or its retinal projection as a starting point, they seek to determine the possible perceptions that could result from the information at hand. Then they compare these possibilities with the actual perception that results. What do they find? The perception reported by a perceiver invariably requires more information than can be found in the retinal projection. The isolated components of an object broken down in the laboratory do not add up to the total perceptual experience. Some other source of information—memory, according to the empiricists—must enable us to organize visual stimuli into three-dimensional objects seen in space. We have not followed this position in the chapter. Our analysis has argued rather that if the complete retinal projection is used, and if the changing perspectives produced by a moving observer are included, more than enough information is available from visual sources alone, to arrive at an accurate visual perception. Thus, reference to past experiences or knowledge or logic is not necessary.

Hermann von Helmholtz

Fig. 2.12   Alinari—Art Reference Bureau

Leonardo da Vinci explained visual perspective by noting how a painter would look at a scene through a plate of glass and then sketch out the scene on the glass so that his painting corresponded with the view the eye got. Clearly, the painter would place far objects at the top of the glass and near objects at the bottom; he would make far objects much smaller than near ones; he would show near objects as having a "coarser" texture than those far away; and so forth. To get organization and appropriate depth into his picture the painter would use all the perspective cues the visual system presumably uses in the real world to decode depth. In the sketch on the glass the projection of object dimensions changes at a constant rate from foreground to background (Fig. 2.12). This change can be thought of as a change in the *density* of the projected texture. The rate at which texture changes is called the *texture-density gradient.*

visual perspective

This texture-density gradient gives us information about spatial arrangements. Normally we see books on tables and people on floors; in short, we see objects on surfaces. The size, shape, and distance of an object on a surface can be determined by the rate at which the texture-density of the object changes with respect to the surface gradient. Fig. 2.13 shows five textured figures on a textured surface. Shape A appears to be standing at right angles to the surface. This is because it has no texture gradient; all the elements that make up square A are effectively equidistant from us. Shape E, on the other hand, has a texture gradient that is changing at the same rate as the texture gradient of the surface; for this reason it is seen as lying on top of the surface. Texture-density gradients apparently provide us with a perceptual scale for visual space. The texture-density of a surface or object at any given slant always changes at precisely the same rate. The squares in Fig. 2.13 all appear to be the same distance from us because they all intersect the surface at a point where object and surface texture-density gradients are equal. We see them all as the same size and shape

texture-density gradient

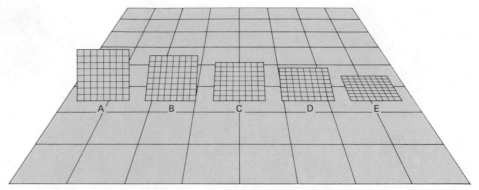

Fig. 2.13 Textured shapes on a textured ground. (Haber and Hershenson, 1973)

because they all cover the same number of texture surface units. Our perception of object slant, however, varies with each square because the texture-density gradient of each object changes at a different rate with respect to the surface gradient.

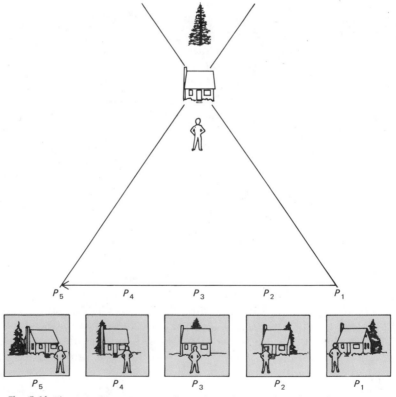

Fig. 2.14 The transformations on the retina when moving through a sequence of positions while fixating a point of intermediate distance. (Haber and Hershenson, 1973)

Measure with a ruler the distance between tracks at bottom and top of picture.

The concept of texture-density gradient gives us a scale for visual space that seems to hold true for everything we see. Whether we are standing directly in front of a house or passing it, our perception of the house results from the changing texture-density relations between the house and the surface on which it is seen as these multiple stimuli flow over the retina.

Moving Retinal Projections

As we move past a scene laterally, the objects in it project moving patterns on the retina, giving us information about distance. This information is called *motion parallax*. The objects appear to switch positions relative to our line of sight. The change in position for each object depends upon whether it is in front of, behind, or precisely at our point of fixation. Objects behind our point of visual fixation appear to move with us, objects at the fixation point remain stationary, and those in front seem to move in the direction opposite to our travel.

Fig. 2.14 shows the transformations in the retinal projection as an observer passes a typical outdoor scene. At point P_1, all three objects are lined up along

motion parallax

109

a single line of vision. There is not yet any flow of stimulation on the retina. Now, assuming the observer fixes his eyes on the house, what happens as he moves from right to left? The house continues to stimulate the same spot on the retina, so its position relative to the man and the tree stays the same as the observer walks by. The near object, the man, moves from left to right against the direction in which the observer is moving. However, the tree moves with the observer.

These effects result because we perceive moving retinal patterns in a direction opposite to the one in which they occur. When we look ahead, retinal patterns flow downward and outward, to the right if we are looking right and to the left if we are looking left. When we look back the flow is upward, and objects are displaced according to their positions relative to the point of fixation and the direction in which the eye of the observer is moving. These different displacements give us important information about distance. Since the tree is displaced at a slower rate, it is seen as farther away.

As moving patterns flow across our line of vision, there is a gradual change in the angle from which they are viewed (Fig. 2.15). This change, we have seen, is produced by a gradual change in the texture-density gradient. When we are moving, objects can be perceived as near or far by the rate at which their texture elements are displaced on the retina. This gradient is called *motion perspective*. Since the rate at which a stimulus flows over the retina decreases proportionately with its distance from the eye, objects that shift pattern the least are seen as farthest away. For the same reason, more distant objects seem closer together than near ones when we are moving. For example, when we drive down a country road looking at the horizon straight ahead, the trees in the distance seem bunched closer together than those that are near to us (see Fig. 2.16). And the distant trees do not seem to be moving as fast as those in the foreground.

motion perspective

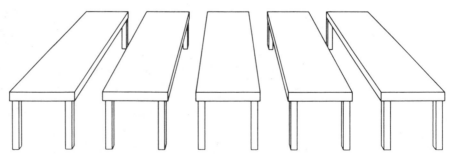

Fig. 2.15 Five momentary views of a table showing the perspective transformations which would occur in the retinal projection when an observer walks by. (Haber and Hershenson, 1973)

Fig. 2.16 Motion perspective for a perceiver moving straight ahead down a country road and fixating at the horizon. (Haber and Hershenson, 1973)

Other Monocular Sources of Information

The texture-density gradient is accepted by many perceptual theorists as the scale by which we measure size, shape, and distance. However, perception is seldom the result of a single visual cue. Other information besides texture-density gradients is available on a retinal projection, and we tend to use it in the perceptual process. Monocular visual cues, those given to either eye alone, also include interposition or overlap, aerial perspective, and light and shade patterning. Each of these produces an impact with respect to texture characteristics. Of course, because perception is a dynamic process, visual cues are not perceived in a static manner, nor are they treated by the visual nervous system as distinct aspects of a retinal image. The visual information projected on the retina changes constantly, and we integrate this changing information over time in order to construct accurate perceptions of the world around us.

Interposition refers to the fact that when the outline of one object interrupts the outline of another object, the object with a continuous border is seen as closer and in front of the other (Fig. 2.17). This source of information is

interposition

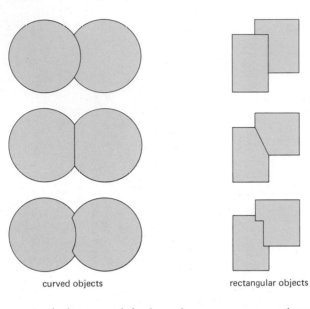

curved objects   rectangular objects

Fig. 2.17 The relative positions of the borders of figures in the retinal projection is a strong cue for relative depth. The figure with the continuous border is perceived to be in front of the other object. (Haber and Hershenson, 1973)

aerial perspective
light and shade
patterning

particularly powerful when the eye moves, and especially when the head moves. Here, the object that is in front actually covers and uncovers the far object as one moves in space. Interposition is much more relevant to the moving than to the static retina, though, in fact, it can be used during a single fixation. *Aerial perspective* and *light and shade patterning* are illumination cues that give us information about the relative depths of objects. *Aerial perspective* adds a further gradient to texture that is particularly relevant to distance perception. The retinal projections of distant objects are less sharp and less saturated in color than those of near objects because light coming from them is more diffracted in the atmosphere. *Light and shade patterning* is the highlights and shadows cast on an object by a source of light (Fig. 2.18). These patterns help us to define contours in objects and to see them as three-dimensional.

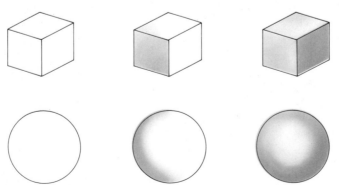

Fig. 2.18 Rectilinear and spherical objects showing the impression of solidity resulting from gradients of illumination (shading). (Haber and Hershenson, 1973)

Binocular Sources of Information

All of the cues just described can be apprehended by one eye. When we move in relation to objects, or when objects move in relation to us, the flow of information on the retina enables us to form stable perceptions. Our perception of depth and distance, however, is enhanced by two cues that depend on the functioning of both eyes: *convergence* and *retinal disparity*. These two sources of information are often called *binocular cues*.

binocular cues

Since the two eyes are separated, they must turn toward each other, or *converge*, to fixate on near objects. The degree of convergence of the eyes gives us information about distance because the eye muscles are in different states of tension when we view near and far objects. However, because muscle control systems are slow in comparison to the speed with which we see objects in space, convergence on its own doesn't seem to be an important source of information (Ogle, 1962).

convergence

A more important cue to depth, also dependent on binocular vision, is *retinal disparity*. For nearby visual scenes, the $2\frac{1}{2}$-inch separation of the two eyes in our head means that each eye receives a slightly different view of each object in the scene. The right eye can see farther around the right side of a solid object then can the left eye, for example. It is the differences in the retinal projection received by the two eyes that provide a source of information about depth, since these differences can only arise when some of the objects in the scene are not all at the same distance from the perceiver. Rather then see a scene that is slightly different, the two retinal projections are fused into a single perception in which the different objects are seen at different distances from us.

retinal disparity

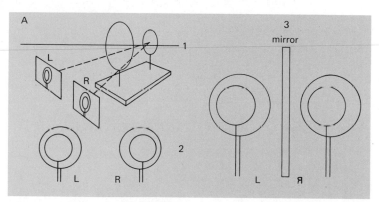

Fig. 2.19 Stereograms: three dimensions from two views. In (A) each eye receives a slightly different view of the two rings at (1). Although neither the left view (L) nor the right view (R), as shown at (2), contains any depth cue to indicate which ring is nearer, if you present each view to the appropriate eye using the stereogram at (3) (in which the right view has been reversed), the correct spatial arrangement will appear after a moment's viewing. (Hochberg, 1964)

The fact that the two eyes work together to produce perceptions of depth and distance can be demonstrated with a stereoscope (Fig. 2.19). Two still photographs, taken at least $2\frac{1}{2}$ inches apart laterally, are placed in the instrument to correspond with the two images received by the eyes. A special lens system in the stereoscope allows each eye to see only one of the flat pictures. When a viewer looks into the stereoscope he perceives a single scene in three-dimensional depth. The objects seem real enough to touch because they appear to be standing in space rather than pictured flat against the background of a photograph. Stereoscopic vision is possible only when each eye receives a different retinal image of the same scene. When both eyes look at only one of the pictures, or when one eye views both photographs simultaneously, the perception of depth disappears.

How To Construct a Stereoscope

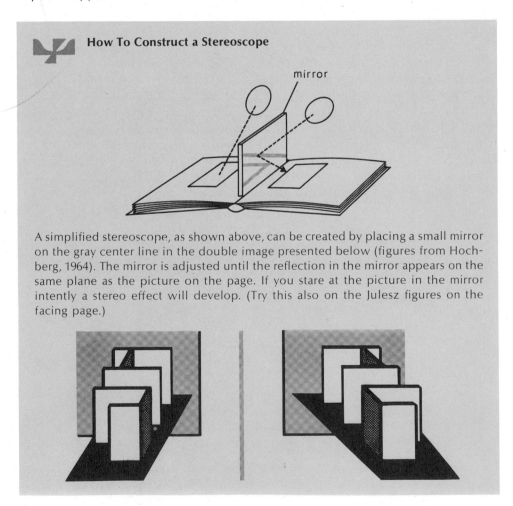

A simplified stereoscope, as shown above, can be created by placing a small mirror on the gray center line in the double image presented below (figures from Hochberg, 1964). The mirror is adjusted until the reflection in the mirror appears on the same plane as the picture on the page. If you stare at the picture in the mirror intently a stereo effect will develop. (Try this also on the Julesz figures on the facing page.)

Julesz Patterns

In "normal" stereoscopic vision, when we displace images to one eye relative to the other eye we experience stereoscopic depth. But disparity is not the only cue to depth available to the viewer. Any picture contains other visual depth cues. It would thus be ideal if we could create a situation in which disparity is the only cue available.

Such a situation was created by Julesz (1960, 1964), who prepared a set of two stereograms that consisted of identical random dot patterns. (These random patterns were generated by a computer.)

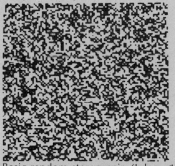 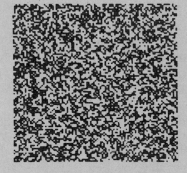

Basic random stereo pair. (Julesz, 1964)

However, in one of these patterns an entire middle region was displaced horizontally relative to the other pattern. This displacement cannot be detected by looking at the patterns monocularly or looking at both patterns with both eyes. But when one of the patterns is viewed by one eye and the other by the second eye, the displaced region then becomes visible, floating in space at a different distance from the rest of the pattern.

In this case then we have created an impression of depth with only disparity cues.

STABILITY OF PERCEPTION

The concept of stability underlies the Gestalt principles of perception. We perceive a car as the same size and shape whether it is in front of us or down the road. When a door swings open we continue to see it as a rectangle even though our retinal image is a trapezoid. A black cow does not seem to change color as she moves from under a shady tree into the bright sun. A plane taking off does not appear to shrink as it flies off into empty space. Our perception of the plane's size and shape remains constant in spite of changes in the retinal image. The way things look remains incredibly stable, regardless of the movement of either the object or the perceiver. How do our perceptions of objects and people remain so stable?

Size, Shape, and Other Constancies

size constancy

The most obvious explanation for the visual phenomenon of *size constancy* is that though objects do look smaller at a distance, they don't look as small as their retinal projection indicates. We rely on memory to give us the actual size of the object and then compute the difference between the retinal size and the familiar size. An alternative explanation is concerned with the relation between texture gradients and surface slant. Surfaces, as we have seen, have texture-density gradients. If we base our size judgments on the number of surface-texture elements an object covers, we can conclude that a friend appears to remain a constant size as he moves away from us because he continues to cover relatively the same number of surface-texture elements. Another kind of size constancy is seen in Fig. 2.20. This will hold true whether he walks away up a hill or down a slope or moves sideways out of our line of sight.

shape constancy

Shape constancy is maintained by the same information that allows for size constancy. We can recognize the actual shape of an object even when its dimensions are distorted on a retinal projection. We judge the outline shape

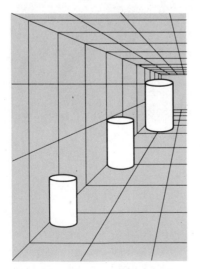
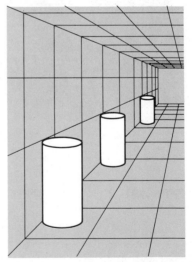

Fig. 2.20 (Left) The size illusion showing the role of the scale provided by gradients of texture, size, and perspective in determining perceived size of three objects subtending the same visual angle. (J. J. Gibson, 1950) (Right) Perceptual constancy resulting from objects projecting different sizes onto retinal surfaces, but intersecting the ground plane at different levels and thereby scaled differently. (Haber and Hershenson, 1973)

of an object by its relation to the texture-density of the surface it is standing on. Fig. 2.21 illustrates what happens when a perceiver is asked to draw a picture of a circular plate on a table. The retinal projection he receives is more like an ellipse than a circle, yet he perceives a circular object on a table and he draws a circle. Because of *brightness and color constancy* a black cat will look black whether scurrying down a dark alley or snoozing in the sun. We appear to take account of the ratio between the light being reflected from the object and the light reflected from the background. If the total illumination is changed, that ratio remains constant. Thus a light object will always reflect more light than a dark object, whether there is a lot of light falling on the scene or only a little. In this sense, then, the constancy of the ratio appears to be what provides us with constancy of perceptual organization and with brightness constancy. The same is true of color constancy.

The information we receive on a retinal projection about the size, shape, and color of an object depends on the fact that we see things in a given *context*. Forms can be twisted and turned so the retinal images they project are quite different from their familiar appearance. Still, they are perceived as the same form when we see them in relation to other objects and backgrounds. Fig. 2.22 shows two rectangles at different distances from us on a textured surface. The retinal image of the far figure is smaller than that of the nearer one. But the fact that the figures are shown in the same context enables us to compare their texture-density gradients and thus suggests that they are probably identical in size.

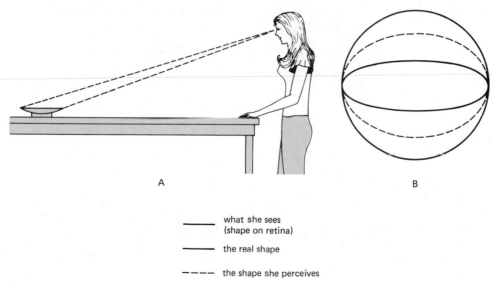

A   B

—————— what she sees
                   (shape on retina)

—————— the real shape

— — — — the shape she perceives

Fig. 2.21 When a subject observes a circular plate as in (A), she perceives a shape more like the real circle than like the ellipse that actually falls on her retina. See (B). (Her perception is determined by asking her to "draw what she sees.")

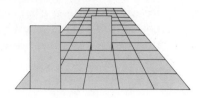

Fig. 2.22 From J. J. Gibson (1950)

In part, perceptions are also the product of our motivations. What we find in the visual world is influenced by what we are looking for, whether or not we are aware of our anticipations. We may more likely perceive the background rumblings we hear while camping out on a remote island as thunder than as reverberations of jet engines because of the setting in which the sound occurs. In the wilderness we may expect to hear sounds of nature rather than those of man.

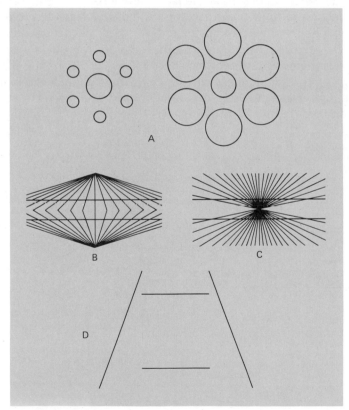

Fig. 2.23 A. Illusion based on relative size. The center circles are the same size, but the one to the left looks larger. B. and C. Illusions based on intersecting lines. The horizontal lines in B and C are parallel. D. Ponzo illusion. The two horizontal lines are the same length, but the upper one appears longer. (Hilgard, Atkinson, and Atkinson, 1971)

Context, then, is an important aspect of perception. It can lend stability to our perceptions by providing a framework within which we can accurately judge size, shape, and color; or it can fool us. Identical objects can appear to be different because of the settings in which we see them. This is due to the *contrast effect.* The center circles in Fig. 2.23 are the same size, but the one on the left looks larger because of the context in which it is seen. Large objects stand out when they are surrounded by smaller ones; small objects look even smaller in relation to large ones. When a woman of 4 feet 9 inches stands next to a man 6 feet tall, both her shortness and his height are accentuated. Colors too seem more vivid when seen in contrast, and our perceptions of hue change with the background it is seen against. A gray tie looks darker against a white shirt than against a blue shirt because of the contrast effect. These effects, then, depend directly on the context in which objects are viewed.

Our perceptions of object size, shape, color, and location remain essentially stable as we scan the world around us. We organize the light patterns impinging on the retina into meaningful messages. Visual cues are the building blocks with which we construct our perceptions. However, they are not added together like bricks one on top of the next. The information available on a continuous but changing retinal pattern is integrated over time. Our total impression of a scene results from the way the stimuli flowing over the retina have been organized. Textureless objects seen in textureless space have no meaning. However, this is not the way we look at the real world. We do not see objects and people in a vacuum. Everything occupies a place relative to other things. For this reason we can organize what we see in time and space, and what we perceive remains constant as we move.

PERCEPTION OF MOTION

We have discussed why a person appears to remain the same size as he moves away from us. However, how can we tell he is moving? And if he accelerates his walk as he hurries down the street, how can we perceive that he is moving faster?

Motion-Detection System

Successive Stimulation of Adjacent Retinal Points Contemporary theory and research indicate that perception of motion uses three different sources of information. One source is the successive stimulation of adjacent retinal points, which evidently is coded as movement by the visual nervous system. Thus, if a spot of light is moved across the retina, it will first stimulate one area, then the area next to the first one, and so on. It seems reasonable that there could be a sensory coding system that would take patterns of successive stimulation of adjacent retinal locations and code them as the result of an inhomogeneity of light moving across the retina. Such a motion-detection system has been documented in cats by Hubel and Wiesel (1962), who found selectivity cells in the cortex that are responsive to movement. The best evidence for the same kind of motion-coding system in human beings is based on what happens to the threshold for detecting movement of a particular pattern in a given direction after concentrated exposure to that movement. Sekuler and Ganz (1963) had perceivers view stripes that moved in one direction for 5 seconds and then assessed the threshold for movement detection when the stripes moved in the same direction or in the reverse direction. Their finding that the threshold for detecting movement in the same direction was elevated after the experimental situation is strong evidence that the sensitivities of human motion-detecting systems are temporarily changed after stimulation—that is, that adaptation affects our ability to detect motion.

Such a motion-detection system is probably also responsible for what happens when we view "motion" pictures, which are really a series of separate, slightly displaced still scenes flashed in rapid succession. The visual system fills in the gaps between the scenes, and we perceive continuous motion even though, in fact, nothing is actually moving.

Other evidence for a human motion-detection system based on successive stimulation of adjacent receptors is found in *motion aftereffects*. After prolonged viewing of something in motion—a good example is a waterfall—stationary objects in the background scenery will appear to move in the opposite direction—upwards, in the waterfall illusion. After prolonged exposure to a given motion the motion detector that is keyed to that motion becomes insensitive, so that when the motion stops or we look away from it stationary objects appear to move in the opposite direction. This is the same kind of phenomenon that occurs when, after staring at something red for a while, we can close our eyes and see green (see Chapter 1).

Relative Retinal Transformations But while a motion-detection system sensitive to successive stimulation of adjacent retinal points is sufficient for the perception of movement per se, it would not be able to differentiate between object motion and motion of the eyes or body of the perceiver himself. Therefore, we evidently have another source of information about motion, and that is a relative transformation in the retinal projection, a shifting of one part of the projection relative to another part. Keeping your eyes, head, and body motionless, look at the wall of your room and whatever intervenes between it and you. Now move your eyes to the left, without moving your head or body. The entire pattern will shift to the right, the righthand edge of it will disappear, and a new part of the scene will come into view on the left. Returning to your original position, pick up a pencil and move it across the scene in front of you to the right. The pencil moves, but everything else remains stationary. Now, with your head turned toward the scene, or even better toward a window in the room, and your body at a right angle to your head, walk parallel to the scene from right to left. The entire pattern shifts to the right, but some components, specif-

motion
aftereffects

ically those in the foreground, move faster than others. In each of these situations, no pattern of physical movement except the one described can produce the specific visual result obtained, and every change in the relationship of elements in the retinal projection can have only one cause—a specific eye movement, or movement of something in the visual world, or body movement. Of course two such causes can operate at once; something in the visual world, for example, may be moving at the same time as we ourselves are moving. We are able to distinguish our own motions from motions in the visual world on the basis of transformations within the retinal projection.

Some very interesting evidence that relative transformations on the retina help us to distinguish between eye movements and object movements is a phenomenon known as *autokinetic movement*. If a small stationary light is viewed in an otherwise dark room, the light will appear to move about, usually in an unpredictable and erratic fashion. What has happened here is that because we can see nothing but the light itself, we have no frame of reference, nothing against which to compare it and the eye movements that we constantly make (see Chapter 1). The result is that we attribute some of the movements of our own eyes to the stationary light.

autokinetic movement

What happens when we move in relation to a moving object? New visual information is introduced that can be correlated with our own movements. As we saw in our discussion of space perception, a continuous flow of stimulation tells us in what direction we are looking; for example, if we look ahead, the flow is downward. This same flow of stimulation over the retinal surface tells us when we are moving, because the flow changes in very systematic ways as we move. When we go forward there is a downward expansion of the visual field. If we walk toward a closed door in the middle of a hall, the distance between the walls on either side of the door seems to widen as we approach the door. If the door is open, the doorway will expand to reveal objects in the room as we approach it. This phenomenon helps us to see stationary objects remaining in fixed positions as we shift perspective (Fig. 2.24). The change in the angle from which we view them produces a relative displacement of near and far objects depending on our point of fixation. Yet the fixed objects continue to intersect the surface at the same points and their locations remain constant. How can we tell when other objects are moving? Because they progressively cover and uncover surface-texture elements.

Self-Initiated Movement A third source of information that could be especially useful in telling us whether we moved or something out there moved would be feedback from our own movements themselves. Such feedback, however, is usually too slow, especially with respect to vision. The eye muscles do not seem to have accurate means of reporting their positions. But an even better source of information has been discovered—not feedback for the body's position, but the instruction sent by the brain to produce the movement in the first place. Thus, if the brain signals the eye to move, and *then* the visual scene changes in a corresponding manner, these two changes can cancel and no mo-

Fig. 2.24 The optical transitions when moving from one vista to another. (J. J. Gibson, 1966)

tion is perceived. This can be seen when you wink your eye. When you do so directly, the visual scene remains stable. But poke your eye on the side with your finger—now the world jumps around. In the latter case, there is no signal from the brain to the eye to move (the signal went to the finger instead), so no cancellation, and the motion on the retina is attributed to the world, not your eye.

What this implies is that active self-initiated motion is critical for accurate perception. One technique used to study this has been to rearrange the retinal projection through the use of special glasses worn by the viewer. Kohler (1951) conducted a series of experiments using mirrors attached to a subject's forehead which reversed the normal up-down (or left-right) orientation of objects in the field of view.

Kohler and his subjects report that at the beginning they were completely disoriented. The world seemed strange—walking people seemed to move mechanically, and when the subject moved his head the world seemed to move about wildly.

As they continued to wear the glasses, the subjects began to adapt to the change in their view of the world. Things began to look stable, and soon the subjects could engage in even complicated behavior such as bicycling, skiing, and fencing. However, adaptation to the point that things appeared in their normal (pre-spectacles) orientations proceeded in a slow and piecemeal manner. Some parts of the visual field often appeared in their correct orientation while other parts continued to be reversed. A car might have been perceived

Integration of Visual and Motor Information

Whether motion is perceived on the basis of successive stimulation of adjacent retinal points or of a relative transformation in the retinal projection, its perception rests on purely visual information, something that takes place in the retina. But in certain situations at least we evidently make use of nonvisual information, specifically, of the *results of signals from the brain that control the eye*. Knowing what these *efferent* signals (see Chaper 6) are may influence us to perceive motion as emanating from objects in the visual world or from ourselves.

Von Holst (1954) paralyzed the eye muscles of a perceiver so that the eye could not move to the right and then instructed the perceiver to move his eye to the right; the perceiver reported that the visual world moved to the right. When von Holst moved the paralyzed eye mechanically to the right, the perceiver reported, as one would expect, that the visual world moved to the left. But when von Holst instructed the perceiver to move his eye to the right and at the same time moved the eye mechanically in that direction, the perceiver reported, as he would have if he had voluntarily moved his unparalyzed eye, that the visual world was stationary. These results indicate that there is some integration between perceptual and motor information.

Brindley and Merton (1960) report a direct attempt at settling the question of whether we have feedback from our eye muscles or whether what we might have is information that the brain has ordered our eyes to move. They anesthetized the surface of the eyes and the inner surface of the eyelids of subjects, but not the eye muscles. They then covered the corneas with opaque caps so that the subjects could not see whether their eyes had moved. Then, using forceps they mechanically moved the subjects' eyeballs. The subjects could not tell when their eyes had been moved even though they were sometimes moved back and forth quite rapidly. It should be noted that since the eye muscles had been left intact, they should have signaled the subject that his eye had moved. But no such information was forthcoming. Brindley and Merton conclude that what was lacking here was an *order from the brain to the eyes to move;* therefore there was no knowledge of movement. Eye muscles cannot tell us whether or not our eyes have moved.

as riding on the "right" side of the road while the numbers on its license plate were seen reversed as in a mirror image. Only after a longer time with the spectacles would the numbers appear in their normal orientation.

Kohler noted a number of interesting points. Adaptation, that is veridical perception, was observed when the subject was permitted to reach for and touch the object he was looking at, as when a subject held a pendulum in his hand. In the latter case, the subject perceived the orientation of the pendulum veridically and was able to generalize from it to the orientation of other objects in his visual field. Thus where the modified perceptual system met conflicting cues

Adaptation to Altered Visual Environments

Why and how does adaptation occur? Held (1963) argued that it occurs as a result of a rearrangement of the correlation between the subject's efferent neural commands to action on the one hand and the visual changes that occur as a result of these actions (or reafference) on the other.

If, for example, I am wearing glasses that displace the visual field 10° to the right, and I reach for an object and notice that I miss it by 10° (I didn't go far enough to the right), then the next time I sense an object 10° to the right of me, I will now perceive the stimulation coming from that direction as really being 10° to the right or in other words "straight in front of me." I will now reach for it straight in front of me. I have recalibrated the relationship between my sensations and the sensory responses I will make to them.

If Held is right, then adaptation should not occur if no voluntary motor movements (involving efferent commands from the brain) are engaged in. Held did a series of experiments in which some subjects were allowed to engage in voluntary motor movements while wearing distorting prisms while others, who also wore the prisms, were either not allowed to move or were moved by others. The latter showed no adaptation.

In one such experiment, for example, one subject walked around on his own while another was wheeled in a wheelchair over the same area. Although the subject in the wheelchair was exposed to the same visual environment as the active subject, the two subjects did not show the same aftereffects to having worn the prisms. Adaptation was much greater for the active subject.

from a different sensory system—for example, touch—it changed its perception in accordance with the veridical. In this case a conflict between the cues from two senses resulted in modification of one of them.

Furthermore very familiar objects that could not possibly occur in a reversed orientation were seen correctly. For example, if the subject looked at a candle with reversing glasses he would see it upside-down. But if the candle was lighted, the subject saw it in its right-side-up orientation. It is impossible for a flame to rise downward.

If the glasses were worn long enough for adaptation to occur, removing them resulted in an aftereffect. Things now looked upside-down without the glasses on! Such aftereffects would seem to argue strongly that what occurs in adaptation is an actual perceptual change, not merely an intellectual recalibration of the stimulus and sensory inputs. If the latter were true, no aftereffect should occur. The subject has no reason to change his calibrations when he is not wearing the glasses.

The human nervous system, then, is equipped with a number of mechanisms for perceiving motion. At the simplest level is a motion-detection system based on the successive stimulation of adjacent retinal receptors that occurs when something in the retinal projection moves. This system, however, is not able to differentiate motion due to eye movements or to body movement from motion in the visual world. Such a differentiation is made by identification of the relational transformations in the retinal projection. In other situations non-visual cues help us to perceive motion—we seem to integrate visual information with internally originating information.

PERCEPTION IN INFANTS

Is perception innate or learned? Must an infant both see and touch a ball at arm's length to know in the future how far he must extend his arm to grasp the ball when it is the same distance away from him? Recent studies have shown that newborn babies may have all the necessary equipment for perception, without needing to specifically learn how to do it.

Eye Movements of Newborns and Infants

A 5-day-old baby can follow a moving object with his eyes, and his visual system is probably developed to the point where he can bring an object into reasonable focus. When newborn babies are awake their eyes frequently appear to cross and otherwise aimlessly scan the world. However, experiments have demonstrated that babies can and do fixate on specific stimuli once their attention is captured. Infants, like adults, move their eyes more frequently horizontally across the visual field than up and down. In the absence of a specific stimulus, they move their eyes predominantly in horizontal directions.

Infants 4 to 10 weeks old look at the outline of a geometrical figure rather than at its center (Salapatek, 1969). The younger ones concentrate on only a limited portion of the outline, while the older ones explore some of the lines and angles within the outline shape as well. When can an infant correlate internal features of a figure with an outline shape? At what age does this correlation produce a meaningful perception? Can they recognize their own mothers' faces? Studies have shown that this does not happen before the age of about 2 months. The very young infant, evidently, is capable of responding to stimulus elements; however, he does not yet have the ability to attach specific meanings to many configurational patterns.

Philip Salapatek

Can he coordinate his eye and head movements, or does he turn his head in one direction while his eyes roll off the other way? Infants 3 to 15 weeks old integrate head and eye motions adeptly, yet if they are shown gaily colored moving objects, the older children fixate on more aspects of the visual pattern than the younger ones. The important point in all these studies is that the difference in what younger and older infants look at is quantitative rather than qualitative. They can all fixate on stimulus elements, and they can all coordinate head and eye motion. With increased age, however, they become more adept at seeking information about what they see.

Recording and Scoring Eye Movements in Infants

The study of infants and their patterns of looking has made it necessary to develop methods for obtaining precise information about where the infant is looking. We will here briefly describe two such methods.

Kessen, Salapatek, and Haith (1972) place the baby in a prone position on a mattress and, with a head rest, hold his head at a steady "forward" position (see Fig. 2.25a). Directly above the infant, where he is looking, is a stimulus display board on which stimuli can be placed. A hole in the center of the display board permits a camera lens to photograph the infant's eyes. In the visual field is placed a "marker lamp," which is reflected off the cornea. By observing where on the eyeball the marker light is reflected at a particular moment in time one can obtain

William Kessen

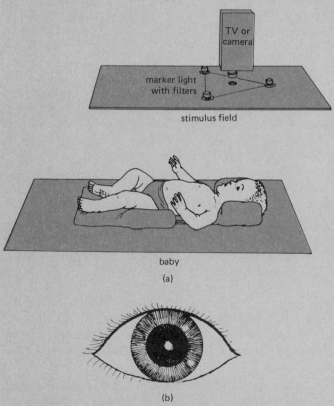

Fig. 2.25 Schematic representation of method for obtaining pictures of the eyes of infants looking at forms on a screen and of the type of pictures obtained. (a) Typical apparatus for observing the corneal reflex of infants. (b) Typical photo frame showing eye directed at one angle of a triangular stimulus, indicated by light reflected from marker lamps. (Haber and Hershenson, 1973)

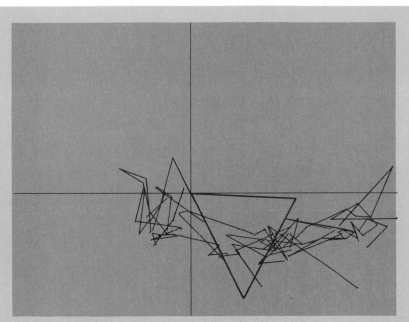

Fig. 2.26 Visual scanning pattern of human newborn of a homogeneous field. Each dot represents one time sample of eye orientation. (Salapatek and Kessen, 1966)

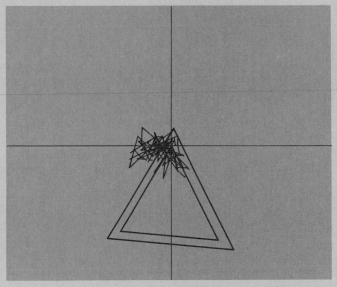

Fig. 2.27 Visual scanning of human newborn of large black equilateral triangle. Each represents one time sample of eye orientation. (Salapatek and Kessen, 1966)

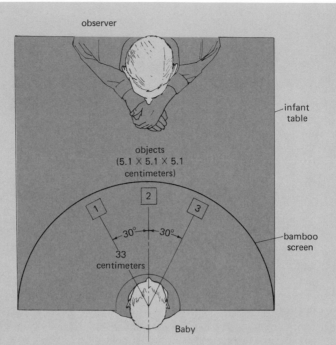

observer

infant table

objects
(5.1 × 5.1 × 5.1
centimeters)

2

1   3

30° 30°

33
centimeters

bamboo screen

Baby

Fig. 2.28 Apparatus used by Tronick and Clanton (1971) to study infant looking patterns. (Haber and Hershenson, 1973)

quite precise measures of where in the stimulus field the child is looking. For example, if the photograph shows the marker light reflected from the center of the fovea (see Fig. 2.25b), we know the infant is looking straight at that marker light. If the marker lights is reflected from a position off the fovea, we can calculate the distance and direction of the marker from the fovea and thus discover where the infant is looking. When many such samples of eye position are obtained we can plot a graph of where the eye has been looking as a function of the stimulus presented. Figs. 2.26 and 2.27 show the eye movement patterns under two conditions: (a) when no stimulus is present, and (b) when the stimulus is a black equilateral triangle. When no stimulus is present eye position is random, but when the triangle is presented, the eyes look mostly at one vertex of the triangle.

Tronick and Clanton (1971) use a method which they feel gives them a more natural picture of the child's patterns of looking. The child is seated at a table with three brightly colored objects in front of him and is allowed free head movements. The experimenters are interested primarily in how the child looks at or scans the objects in front of him. A light, free-moving gimballed harness is attached to the child's head, and measurements of its displacements provide records of the child's head movements. Eye movements are recorded by electrooculograph. Electrodes are attached, generally on the two sides of the head, at the temples, immediately adjacent to the eyes, or on top of or beneath the eyes. These electrodes record the movements of muscles that control the eye, and hence eye movements. Generally movement is represented by the deflections of a pen writing on graph paper. The eye movements are recorded as positive or negative electrical deflections, which are in turn translated to the pen, which has been calibrated so that when it is at a certain position the eyes are looking straight ahead. Deflections of the pen to either side of that position are read as eye movements to the left or right. The magnitude of the pen's deflections can also be calibrated to reflect the magnitude of eye movement. By combining these eye movement records with the head movement records, Tronick and Clanton can obtain a good idea of where the child was looking at a given moment in time and what his general pattern of looking was. Fig. 2.28 shows their apparatus.

Infant Space Perception

How much can infants do? How much do they have to learn? Do we actually have to move about in visual space and see and touch things simultaneously before we can estimate how far they are from our line of sight? To answer this question Bower (1965) trained a group of 6-week-old infants to turn their heads toward a 30-centimeter cube positioned almost 1 meter from their eyes. The infants had had no previous tactile experience with the cube and were not yet mature enough to crawl. When the infant, who was placed in an infant seat, turned his head toward the cube, a smiling experimenter popped up and said, "Peek-a-boo" (see Fig. 2.29). In this manner the head-turning response to this particular object was reinforced.

Once the response to the cube was established, the infants' perception of size, shape, and distance was tested. To do this Bower used both the 30-cen-

T. G. R. Bower

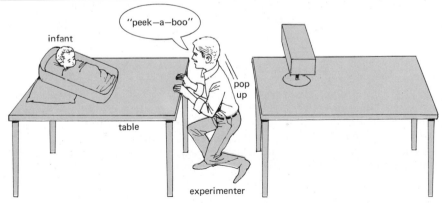

Fig. 2.29 Arrangements in Bower's (1965) experiment with different sized objects in which experimenter pops up to say "peek-a-boo." (Haber and Hershenson, 1973)

timeter cube and another cube three times larger and positioned them alternately 1 and 3 meters from the infants. When the 30-centimeter cube was 3 meters away, the retinal image of it was smaller than when it was 1 meter away. When the 90-centimeter cube was 1 meter away, both the object itself and the projected image of it were larger than the 30-centimeter cube at 1 meter. However, when the 90-centimeter cube was placed 3 meters away, the greater distance annulled the effect of the greater size of the larger cube, and the retinal image projected was identical to that of the original stimulus. If the infants were unable to perceive distance, they should respond to this retinal image as frequently as they had responded to the image of the 30-centimeter cube 1 meter away. But in fact, the 90-centimeter cube at the 3-meter distance elicited the fewest responses. Bower concluded that the infants must have been using at least some of the visual information that was available for judging size at a distance, since they responded to absolute size and distance rather than to the projected retinal size. The results of this experiment strongly indicate that we do not have to move about in space in order to perceive objects in depth.

Practice and experience obviously enhance the accuracy of our perceptions. Infants extract increasingly more information from their visual environment as they mature. Their perceptions become meaningful in the light of additional visual information that becomes available to them. We shall return to some other examples of this in Chapters 10 and 11.

Summary

Why do things look as they do? Three answers have been proposed during various times in history: (1) because things are what they are; (2) because things are what our nerves tell us they are; and (3) because things are what we are. If we assume that things are what they are, then by reducing physical objects to their basic components we can understand what we are perceiving. But perception is a function of the relation of elements to one another in forming a whole; what we perceive cannot be explained simply in terms of the isolated attributes of physical objects.

Nineteenth-century psychologists approached perception with the idea that our nerves act as intermediaries between the brain and the outside world. The way we perceive objects in our environment is incredibly consistent, but at times what we perceive is an inaccurate representation of the environment. Numerous visual illusions demonstrate that the environment is not always perceived as it is.

Our perception of objects in a particular environment is influenced by our past experiences and our present attitudes and motivations. Perception therefore involves a continual interaction between the physical properties of objects, the information we receive from our nerves, and our state of mind at the time we receive the information. To understand perception we must know (1) how the organism receives and transfers information; (2) how it modifies information; and (3) how it converts stimuli into organized perceptions.

Neural coding processes enable us to organize our visual field into patterns, forms, and shapes that are meaningful to us. Within a specific context we perceive elements as occupying positions relative to one another. The Gestalt laws are the basic principles governing how objects are organized and perceived. We see objects or patterns against surfaces or backgrounds. This separation of the visual field, called figure-ground segregation, is basic to perception because an object cannot be identified until it occurs. Some kind of contour must segregate figures from grounds, but objects do not have to be identifiable to be perceived as figures.

Recently attempts have been made to provide some criterion of measurement to enable us to predict particular perceptions on the basis of properties inherent in the relations among elements. In examining what constitutes a good figure, Attneave has contributed the principle of internal redundancy—the greater the repetition of pattern within a figure, the faster we perceive it. Related to this is Hochberg's minimum principle, according to which we organize visual sensations in whatever ways require the least amount of information.

Retinal projections are a sufficient source of information for nearly all our perceptions of the visual world. However, we do not consider isolated features of a projection, but instead all the information on the retina. Gibson postulated that successive stimulations of the retina are integrated by the visual nervous system in a way to produce perceptions.

Texture is a uniformity in the retinal projection, but changes appear to occur in it according to the angle from which we view it. This change can be thought of as a change in the density of the projected texture, and the rate at which this change occurs is called the texture-density gradient. It gives us a scale for visual space that appears to hold true for everything we see.

Motion parallax provides information about distance by means of moving patterns on the retina. As we move, objects behind our point of visual fixation appear to move with us, objects at the fixation point remain stationary, and those in front of the fixation point seem to move in the direction opposite to our own. Motion perspective enables us, when we are moving, to perceive objects as near or far according to the rate at which their texture elements are displaced on the retina.

Other monocular retinal cues include interposition (or overlap), aerial perspective, and light and shade patterning. Interposition refers to the fact that an object which partially overlaps another is seen as closer than and in front of the other. Aerial perspective and light and shade patternings are illumination cues that give information about the relative depths of objects.

Binocular sources of information, or cues that depend on the functioning of both eyes, include convergence and retinal disparity. Convergence refers to the turning inward of both eyes to focus on a nearby point. Retinal disparity refers to the fact that the two eyes receive slightly different images, which they fuse into a single perception that includes depth.

In spite of changes in the retinal image, we perceive certain constancies of fixed objects. Size and shape constancy are a result of a relation between texture gradient and surface slant. Brightness and color constancies are probably related to the constancy of the ratio between the luminance of an object and the luminance of the background, regardless of the intensity of the light source.

Our perceptions of objects are influenced by the context in which they appear. For example, identical objects can appear to be different because of the settings they are in; this is the contrast effect.

Motion perception is based on three sources of information: a retinal motion-detection system, relative retinal transformations, and a comparison of self-initiated motion with retinal changes. The simplest source is the motion-detection system, in which cortical cells respond to successive stimulation of adjacent retinal points. It is this system that causes us both to perceive movement when two stationary objects are alternately illuminated (the phi phenomenon) and to become insensitive to patterned motion in a given direction (the waterfall illusion, for example).

To distinguish between object motion and motion of our own eyes or body we need information from the relative transformation of elements in the retinal projection. This is a shifting of one part of a projection relative to another part. Each change in the relationship of these elements can have only one particular combination of causes—an eye movement, a body movement, or movement of something in the visual field. When we are deprived of some of the information relative transformations usually supply, we perceive autokinetic movements.

The results of self-initiated movements allows us to adapt to grossly distorted visual environments, such as those produced by goggles that turn everything backwards or upside down. In such situations, we integrate motor and visual information to perceive motion and respond to it appropriately.

Newborn babies seem to have the necessary equipment for perception and can bring an object into reasonable focus. The very young infant is capable of responding to visual stimuli, but does not have the ability to attach specific meanings to many configurations. Infants from 3 weeks on are able to coordinate head and eye movements, though older infants explore more features of a stimulus than younger ones. Visual-tactile associations are evidently not necessary for accurate judgment of depth and distance; visual information alone seems sufficient. Infants derive more and more information from their visual environment as they mature.

SUGGESTED READINGS

Köhler, W., *Gestalt Psychology,* rev. ed. New York, Mentor, 1947.
  A classic presentation of the Gestalt approach to perception.
Gombrich, E. H., *Art and Illusion,* 2d ed. Princeton University Press, 1961.
  How illusion is used in the creation of art.
Trevor-Roper, P., *The World through Blunted Sight.* Indianapolis, Bobbs-Merrill, 1970.
  The author suggests that many great works of art were produced as a result of visual disorders on the part of the artist.
Bester, A., *The Demolished Man.* New York, New American Library, 1970.
  The characters in this science fiction tale are able to perceive thoughts.
Vernon, M. D., ed., *Experiments in Visual Perception.* Baltimore, Penguin Books, 1966.
  Includes classic papers on perception and Piaget's ideas concerning perceptual development in infancy.
Keller, Helen, *The Story of My Life* (many editions; originally published in 1902).
  Totally blind and deaf from early infancy, Helen Keller learned about the world through her fingertips with the help of a great teacher.

Chapter Three

Learning

What is learning?
What is the difference between classical and operant conditioning?
Why does practice make perfect?
What kinds of relationships can exist between stimuli and responses?
What is learning by modeling?
How are skills learned?
What is the best way to study?

Learning is a process that occurs almost without our being aware of it. Finding the mailbox in a new neighborhood, memorizing a poem for a homework assignment, or discovering how to withdraw from a course without penalty are but a few common examples. As you read the next few pages and are introduced to a number of new terms—operant conditioning, reinforcement, extinction—you will even be learning about learning.

Although common sense leads us to believe that all of these situations constitute learning because they involve the acquisition of new skills or information, psychologists seek to go beyond common sense. They attempt to discover what else learning activities have in common, and also ways in which they are unique, because learning is the means by which we acquire both adaptive and maladaptive behaviors. Since learning is such a significant part of life, psychologists strive to define and analyze the principles of learning so that they may better understand and predict human behavior.

DEFINITION OF LEARNING

Psychologists have defined learning as *a relatively permanent change in behavior resulting from the effects of practice;* they generally rule out changes that are

learning

temporary or easily reversible and those that happen without practice. To help make clear what learning is, we will briefly consider some of the things it is not. Because learning is so variable and pervasive, and because it extends to changes in expectancies, which are not observable, it is sometimes extremely difficult to recognize. It thus becomes helpful to specify as nearly as possible what learning is *not*.

Adaptation to darkness, a sensory response (discussed in Chapter 1), is reversed by exposure to light regardless of how many times it occurs. Therefore this adaptation is not a learned change. Learning consists of phenomena with extended effects on behavior.

Other native response tendencies—unlearned behaviors—include reflexes (the knee jerk, the contraction of the pupils when exposed to light), tropisms (the cockroach's scurrying from sources of light, the moth's flying toward them), and instincts (the nest building of birds, bird and fish migration patterns). Maturation, the development of bodily and mental faculties as a result of growth, accounts for such behaviors as the flying of birds and the swimming of tadpoles. These activities do not have to be "taught" to the animal; they simply occur in the course of development. In humans, maturation is seldom if ever the sole cause of a behavior, but it is frequently a necessary condition for the learning of a behavior.

Disease, injury, or fatigue may produce alterations in behavior. For example, if you had little or no sleep last night, you will undoubtedly have trouble reading this text, even though you learned to read years ago. Your ability to read is not permanently impaired, but it is temporarily altered by your state of fatigue.

As we move up the ranks of the animal kingdom learned behavior becomes increasingly predominant over unlearned, or instinctive, behavior. As lower organisms develop they instinctively display certain behaviors that are specific to their species. Some of their behaviors, such as the nest building of many birds, are quite complex, but they are not learned. The problems and situations that confront human beings, however, far surpass in number and complexity those faced by other members of the animal kingdom. Instinctive responses would seldom be adequate to the human situation. Learning must therefore play an immense role in human behavior.

A distinction is often made between learning and performance. Learning is the acquisition of an *expectancy* that a certain behavior will produce, perhaps

performance   under certain conditions, a particular response. Performance is the translation of learning into a behavior. Psychologists are interested in learning, but their observations must necessarily be confined to performance.

Hillman, Hunter, and Kimble (1953) studied the effects of varying drive levels upon performance and learning. Rats that performed poorly in maze learning over a period of trials suddenly improved their performance if their degree of hunger or thirst—their drive level—was increased and a reward of food or drink was given for correct responses. Even though learning occurred during each trial, it was not displayed until drive and thus performance was increased.

Distinction between Learning and Performance

We know from common experience that we do not always display what we know, even in situations that call for the known behavior. For example, a rat who has had extensive experience in running a maze under conditions of great hunger may not move from the starting point when he is not hungry. Thus we are forced to recognize a distinction between learning and performance—the fact that learning may not always manifest itself in overt performance.

This distinction between learning and performance has been a useful concept in explaining the phenomenon of latent learning and the effects of certain reinforcement variables upon the development and maintenance of a habit.

The learning-performance distinction was introduced by Tolman (1932) as a consequence of his latent learning theory. One of the principal ideas of this theory was that reinforcement or reward affects performance but has little to do with learning. Blodgett (1929) designed one of the earliest experiments to test the notion of latent learning. He allowed one group of hungry rats to explore a maze that did not have food in the goal box. The rats were therefore thought to be in a nonreinforcing situation. The rats in the second group received a conventional reward, namely food, at the end of the maze. As might be expected the rats in the reinforcement condition learned the maze rapidly while the nonreinforced rats continued to make errors. However, when Blodgett introduced food into the goal box of the nonreinforced rats, their performance suddenly improved dramatically, so that they immediately made as few errors as the rats that had been reinforced throughout the experiment. This finding indicated that, although the nonreinforced group did not perform the maze, they had nonetheless learned it. But the results of their learning were not apparent until a reward was provided (Fig. 3.1).

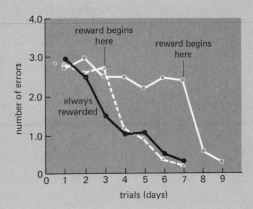

Fig. 3.1 Number of errors during reinforced and nonreinforced trials in maze learning. When reinforcement is introduced, errors drop to a level comparable to that of animals reinforced from the beginning of training. (Deese and Hulse, 1967; data from Blodgett, 1929)

Reward therefore does not always affect learning. It affects performance, however, and internal states are important when discussing what is displayed. Performance fluctuates with the temporary state of the organism, while learning usually does not.

Any definition of learning must inevitably have some difficulty accounting for all manifestations that have been considered as learning because they are so diverse. It comes as no surprise, then, that some investigative techniques have succeeded in establishing as learning phenomena a few events that are excluded by our definition. For instance, short-term memory studies, as we will see in Chapter 4, are considered learning experiments though the behavioral changes observed generally last only a few seconds and occur without practice. In such studies, the subject is usually shown an arbitrary set of letters or numbers; after several seconds, during which he is prevented from practicing by a requirement to attend to something else, he is asked to recall the set. Retention decreases rapidly as the length of time increases. Clearly, "relatively permanent" changes are not involved here, but learning of a sort is.

Psychologists have resolved the problem of classifying learned behaviors in two ways: (1) by stressing the adaptive nature of learning processes in general, and (2) by relying on the guidelines offered by theoretical paradigms of learning. These will be the material of the remainder of this chapter.

THE ADAPTIVE NATURE OF LEARNING

Radio Times Hulton
Picture Library

Charles Darwin

In 1859 Charles Darwin published *The Origin of Species,* in which he set forth his theory of evolution. According to his thesis, all living organisms from the first moment of life are faced with the problem of surviving in the environment they are born into. Because of genetic variation within the different species, some members are endowed with capacities or physical traits that better enable them to adjust to the rigors of climate, terrain, food supply, and other conditions. These organisms are more likely to survive to reproductive age, to multiply their kind, and thus to preserve their own characteristics. The environment, then, presents situations that only the best adapted can overcome; the rest do not survive.

The capacity to learn is reflected in Darwin's principle of natural selection. Obviously, if an organism is able to learn to avoid potentially dangerous situations and to find or produce necessary commodities—food or water—its survival potential increases.

Learning is essential to survival, as most newcomers to urban communities realize. They must learn the art of self-preservation from veterans. Stories of neighbors' misfortunes are told and retold, details are examined, and suggestions on how to protect oneself are offered.

Let us imagine the situation of a reclusive soul who doesn't read the daily

Norman Myers/F.P.G.

Adaptation means survival. The speed of the cheetah and the long neck of the giraffe have enabled them to cope with their environment.

newspaper and discourages the rumors of neighbors and co-workers. Soon after arriving in New York City this person sets out for a stroll at 5 A.M. along the East River and gets "mugged." He (or she) makes a mental note to avoid rivers before sunrise. Fond of crickets, he frequents Central Park after sunset and gets mugged. This time he resolves to stay away from dark parks. Disliking noisy, crowded streets, he walks along quieter side streets. He gets mugged again and makes another mental note.

Gradually the newcomer begins to notice a high correlation between certain areas of the city at certain hours and high crime rates. Once he has learned that this association occurs with regularity, he can then begin to regard one situation as a forewarning for the other. He has, in other words, established a basis for prediction with reasonable accuracy.

This conclusion by itself, however, is not enough to increase our newcomer's chances of survival. He must discover what response will effectively eliminate the attacks. One solution is to adopt various offensive tactics. He may carry a legal weapon, or learn judo. Such responses may incapacitate the attacker long enough to permit escape.

But is this an optimal solution to the problem? The attacker may himself have the rank of black belt or may carry a more deadly weapon. Avoidance of the situation is a better solution. To this end, the newcomer begins to carry a

map of the city around in his mind, with various areas labeled: "fine until sundown," "safe," "never enter," and so on. By adopting this series of responses, he gains effective control over his environment and, simultaneously, his own survival.

For most people, of course, such an education is more easily acquired. Through language, others communicate their experiences so that mistakes need not be repeated. They explain how external events are related and how best to control them. All such pieces of information add to the body of learning that is passed from one person to another.

The information that allows you to see relationships and build expectancies about them can come from personal experience, seeing the results of the behavior of others, being told by others without actually observing them, or figuring it out for yourself. Each of these methods will result in slightly different strengths of learning, or confidence in your expectations, but the general principle underlying the acquisition of knowledge should be the same. Thus, in this chapter, we shall encounter all of these methods, and in most cases, not carefully distinguish among them.

The Learning of Significant Relations

The learning process involves two relations: (1) the relation of environmental events to each other and (2) the relation between behavior and the environment.

Learning that one event in the environment almost always signals another event permits us to anticipate the course of future events. If the first event should occur, we may respond to it before the second event occurs. When we react to the first event as we would react to the second, we are exhibiting *classical conditioning*. Of course, this statement is an oversimplification; other factors involved are discussed in the next section. But when a cook chops onions for his recipe tears will probably form in his eyes. If he experiences this reaction to onions several times, eventually he may begin to tear at the mere sight of unpeeled onions in a plastic bag—that is, he will react to the first event—the sealed onion—instead of to the second—the unsealed and fuming onion. This is an example of how we perceive and anticipate connections between events in our environment.

We also learn how our behaviors can affect environmental events. By trying out various responses we can learn which ones produce the greatest control of events. This type of learning is known as *operant conditioning*. For example, present a small child with an apparatus that has two buttons. Pressing the orange button releases a piece of candy; pressing the blue one has no result. After pressing the buttons at random for a while, the child learns that only the orange button gives candy. He soon presses it exclusively and ignores the blue button. The child has learned that he can effectively control the amount of candy by pressing a button. In general, he has learned how to elicit events from his environment.

Human beings have a great ability to acquire knowledge about the relations between environmental events and behavioral responses. They can make decisions that shape events. Do I press the orange or blue button? Do I accept the known results? Can I change the results? Can I change myself to adapt to the results?

Darwin's startling assertion of the continuity of development from lower forms of life to human beings implied that animals should hold the process of learning in common with man, but to a lesser degree. Thompson and McConnell (1955) demonstrated with a light-shock situation that animals as low on the phylogenetic scale as the planarian (flatworm) could be classically conditioned. At first the expected response—the unconditioned response—occurred. When shocked, the flatworm turned its head slightly and contracted its entire body. Then, in each successive trial, a light was turned on just before the flatworm was shocked. The worm soon responded to the light in the same way it had responded to the shock.

It is possible to talk about learning in terms of the kinds of things learned. We can consider the learning of a sequence of actions, such as following a route to a destination or hitting a baseball; or the learning of expectancies capable of generating predictions about the environment, such as if I do A, B will result; or the learning of specific associations, such as the meanings of words in a language or of causes of the American Civil War. But it is equally possible to talk about learning in terms of general principles, in the hope that these principles will apply to all kinds of learning. We will take the latter course to some extent in this chapter, focusing on the two general models of learning, those of classical and operant conditioning. For each of these we will examine how the model works, what affects the kind of learning that takes place, and how these principles are applied to specific learning situations. At the end of the chapter we will look briefly at the learning of skills, saving a more general discussion of learning of verbal processes, including language, for Chapters 6 and 9.

CLASSICAL CONDITIONING

One of the great difficulties in studying learning in complex organisms is that they often learn new relationships by simply being told them or by figuring them out. When this happens it is often impossible to examine the role of practice, or the process of association or pairing, because it all happens so fast, or in only one apparent trial. One solution to this scientific problem has been to work with subjects for whom language is not available and who are not adept at reasoning or figuring. This has meant that basic learning research has mostly

 Classical Conditioning in Humans

Although the initial work on classical conditioning was done with dogs, and much of what we know about it has emerged from other animal studies, many experiments in this field use human subjects. In fact, one psychologist successfully conditioned human fetuses during the last two months of gestation (Spelt, 1948).

Spelt conditioned fetal movements by pairing a vibrator (CS) applied to the maternal abdomen with a loud noise (US), which naturally elicits fetal movements. He found that from 15 to 20 paired stimulations were necessary before three or four successive responses would be given to the vibrator (CS) alone. The fetuses also demonstrated such processes as experimental extinction, spontaneous recovery, and retention of the response over a 3-week interval.

Probably the most popular classically conditioned response with humans is eyeblinking. In the typical *eyeblink conditioning* experiment a puff of air (US) is applied to the cornea, eliciting a blinking reflex. When a neutral stimulus such as a light (CS) is paired with the air puff, the eyelid response can become conditioned to the light.

GSR conditioning involves reaction of the autonomic nervous system (see Chapter 6). The galvanic skin response (GSR) is a measure of the skin's resistance to electrical conduction, which decreases when sweating increases. Electric shock is usually the US and a wide range of conditioned stimuli may be employed, such as a light, a noise or even verbal items (words and nonsense syllables).

Although it is not possible to discuss all the different types of conditioning done with humans, others deserving mention are electroencephalographic conditioning, pupillary conditioning, and the conditioning of heart rate.

used animals. But even in human beings, it has turned out that some of the simple processes of learning can be observed and studied. And these processes seem to be relevant to the more complex ones.

For example, one of the simplest is a kind of expectancy learning called classical conditioning. Here, a signal, originally without special meaning or significance, can create an expectancy simply by being paired or presented together with another signal that already has a particular meaning or significance. Food in the mouth leads to salivation, an unlearned reflexive response. If a dinner bell is always rung just before food is eaten, the bell creates an expectancy of food and therefore itself produces salivation. The learning process then is one of associating the neutral bell with the food. Given the potential importance of this type of learning or conditioning, let us examine it in more detail.

classical conditioning

Certain stimuli elicit biological and behavioral responses that are unlearned, and those that repeatedly elicit reflexes fall into this category. The biological process of salivation, for example, occurs naturally when food is placed in the mouth, and it occurs without prior experience and without thinking about it. This unlearned process of salivation is considered an *unconditioned response* (UR). Food, a stimulus for salivation, is considered an *unconditioned stimulus* (US).

unconditioned response
unconditioned stimulus

While studying the salivary reflex of dogs, Ivan Pavlov, a Russian physiologist, noted that the dog's salivary flow was elicited by the mere sight of food. He began experimenting with such neutral stimuli as a bell, a light, and a metronome to see what effects they would produce if they were presented just before or with food.

Radio Times Hulton
Picture Library

Ivan Pavlov

Prior to the experiment one of the animal's salivary glands was exposed by means of a simple operation so that the saliva would flow into a measuring device. The dog, already trained to stand calmly, was then placed in a harness on a table in front of a window through which it could see whatever stimuli were presented (Fig. 3.2). All possible distractions were eliminated in the experi-

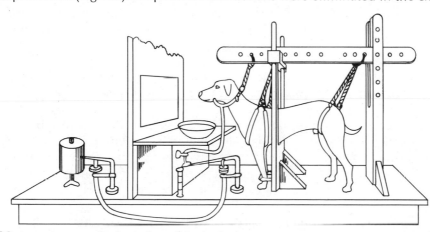

Fig. 3.2 Apparatus to study classical conditioning in dogs.

mental room, and the animal was left alone. First a light (or some other netural stimulus) appeared. Then meat powder (US) was delivered. The dog, being hungry, ate, at which time salivation (UR) occurred. After several such trials Pavlov found the the dog salivated upon seeing the light. The dog somehow made a correlation between the light and the food, so we can say the light produced an expectancy of food. We call the light (or any neutral stimulus eliciting salivation) a *conditioned stimulus* (CS). Salivation to a previously neutral stimulus is called a *conditioned response* (CR). Pavlov knew that learning had occurred because the dog would salivate upon seeing the light even though no food followed. In brief, salivation (UR) to food (US) occurs naturally. When a light (CS) preceding food causes salivation (CR), the response is learned.

conditioned
stimulus
conditioned
response

To avoid confusion it should be noted that basically the CR and UR appear to be the same. It is the nature of the stimulus (natural or neutral) that indicates the type of response displayed. Two views of the CR have been taken. One view holds that it is not a duplicate of the UR but a fractional component of it. Thus, salivation to a light produces a smaller quantity of saliva than salivation to food. Another view is that the CR is a preparatory response for the coming of the US. The general behavior of the animal seems to indicate an "expectation," which is different from the dog's response to the US alone.

The variables in conditioning situations must possess certain properties in order for conditioning to take place. First, the unconditioned stimulus must be able to elicit the unconditioned response with high frequency. Then the conditioned stimulus must fulfill three requirements. First, the learner must be capable of sensing it and therefore of responding to it. The experimenter can determine whether this is the case by testing for an *orienting reflex* (OR). The organism turns toward the source of the stimulus and experiences a number of physiological changes. Generally, stimuli that elicit such orientation are those that are new or complex, conflicting, or particularly significant.

orienting reflex

Second, the CS, prior to the conditioning procedure, must not elicit a response identical to that of the US. If the light made the dog salivate from the beginning, we would not be able to determine the effectiveness of our conditioning procedure. This problem is unavoidable, however, with learners for which we are able to observe only one response to all stimuli, with very immature organisms, and in certain experiments with human beings. We will see later that delayed and trace conditioning somewhat overcome a potential for this kind of confusion.

Third, the CS must not be too strong. The animal must be able to habituate to the stimulus that originally elicited an orienting reflex; that is, after a certain number of stimulations, generally 10 to 30, the learner must demonstrate that it has ceased responding as though the stimulus represented something unique or significant. Unless this happens the OR persists and learning will not occur.

Classical conditioning occurs when the pairings of the CS with the US produce nearly identical responses to both stimuli. The CS thus essentially substitutes for the US. For this reason classical conditioning is sometimes spoken of as learning through *stimulus substitution*. The neural changes that occur are not yet well understood, either for classical conditioning or any of the other forms of learning. Some of our present partial knowledge is discussed in Chapter 6.

Parameters of Classical Conditioning

Pavlov also investigated the important parameters of classical conditioning: acquisition, extinction, spontaneous recovery, generalization, discrimination, and higher-order conditioning.

    Acquisition Every pairing of the CS with the US constitutes a trial. The phase of classical conditioning in which this stimulus association is learned is called *acquisition*. The timing of the presentations of the CS and US has important effects on acquisition (Fig. 3.3). In general, learning is fastest with *delayed conditioning,* in which the CS begins several seconds or more before the US occurs and is then contemporaneous with it until the response is elicited. In *simultaneous conditioning* the CS appears only a fraction of a second before the US and then is contemporaneous with it. The third type, *trace conditioning,* is so named because the CS is terminated before the onset of the US; thus, only a *neural trace* is left. Pavlov also tried reversing the order of stimulus presentation *(backward conditioning)* but found little evidence of learning in these trials.

    The occurrence of a CR provides the only indication that acquisition has been successful. In delayed and trace conditioning enough time exists after the onset of the CS and before the onset of the US for the CR to occur on every

acquisition

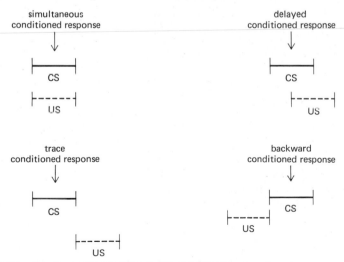

Fig. 3.3 Four temporal patterns frequently used in conditioning experiments.

trial. In simultaneous conditioning, however, because there isn't time enough for the CR to occur before the US is presented, the experimenter must omit the US after a number of acquisition trials. If a CR is then elicited by the CS alone, conditioning can be said to have taken place.

reinforcement   Pairing the CS with the US, which is automatically followed by the UR, constitutes *reinforcement* of the CR. Reinforcement is the presentation of any event that increases the probability that a response will occur. Thus, continuously following the CS with the US increases the probability that the CR will occur. The experimenter can determine the effectiveness of the reinforcement by measuring the strength of the CR over a number of trials. In the Pavlovian paradigm, he can count the drops of saliva upon presentation of the CS. When salivation is plotted on a graph against the number of acquisition trials, the result is a learning curve that increases rapidly over the first several trials, then flattens out at a stable level that represents the maximum strength of the CR (Fig. 3.4).

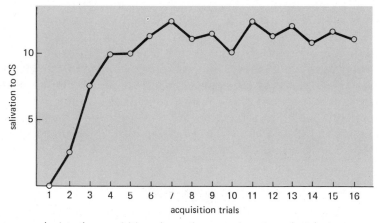

Fig. 3.4 The curve depicts the acquisition phase of an experiment employing the trace-conditioning procedure. Drops of salivation to the conditioned stimulus (prior to the onset of the US) are plotted on the ordinate and trials on the abscissa. The conditioned response gradually increases over trials and approaches an asymptotic level of about 11 to 12 drops of salivation. (Data from Pavlov, 1927)

The amount of salivation in Pavlov's experiment is a measure of the *amplitude* of the CR and hence of the effectiveness of the conditioning procedure. Other indicators of the strength of the CR include *latency,* the time that elapses between CS and CR; *number of trials to criterion,* the amount of reinforcement necessary to produce the first signs of conditioning or some specific number of CR's; and *probability,* the percentage of trials eliciting a CR. Usually these four indices of learning yield similar results, but frequently, depending upon the task, some of them are easier to measure than others.

Extinction When reinforcement of the CS is terminated—that is, when the US is no longer regularly paired with it—the CR slowly weakens until it disappears altogether. This process is called *extinction*. In a Pavlovian experiment, plotting salivation against extinction trials would yield a curve essentially the reverse of the acquisition curve (Fig. 3.5). It would decrease rapidly in the first few trials, then more slowly until it reached zero. Obviously, extinction means that the expectancy formed during acquisition is no longer predictive, and the association therefore weakens.

extinction

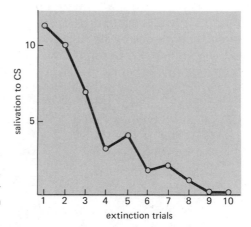

Fig. 3.5 The conditioned response gradually decreases when food reinforcement is no longer paired with the conditioned stimulus. (Data from Pavlov, 1927)

Spontaneous Recovery Following extinction, if the animal has been allowed to rest for a time, he may demonstrate the CR once again, though not at its former maximum level of strength. Such a reappearance of the CR after a period without reinforcement is termed *spontaneous recovery*. In Pavlov's view, this phenomenon revealed that the result of extinction was not forgetting or unlearning the CR but inhibition of it. He assumed that inhibition dissipated during the rest period after extinction. But if extinction is prolonged, eventually no spontaneous recovery occurs. The expectancy is in fact unlearned (Fig. 3.6).

spontaneous recovery

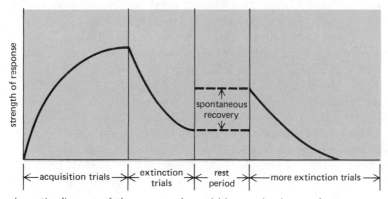

Fig. 3.6 A schematic diagram of the course of acquisition, extinction, and spontaneous recovery. Within limits, the longer the rest period, the greater the degree of spontaneous recovery. (Hilgard, Atkinson, and Atkinson, 1971)

Generalization   Once a conditioned response has been learned, the same response can be made to follow stimuli similar to the conditioned stimulus without additional conditioning. Such behavior is known as *generalization*. An early study now considered classic (Hovland, 1937) demonstrated specifically that the amount of generalization decreases consistently as the secondary stimulus becomes less like the primary one. Subjects were given a mild shock (US) that was paired with a tone of a particular frequency (CS). The emotional reaction (UR) was measured by means of the galvanic skin response (GSR), which provides an index of sweating. Once a GSR was conditioned to the tone, the experimenter tried sounding tones of higher and lower frequency. He found that the amplitude of the GSR was greatest when the subjects heard the original CS; the farther away from this frequency the other tones were, whether higher or lower, the lower was the GSR. When this relationship is graphed, amplitude of GSR against stimulus frequency, the resulting curve (Fig. 3.7) is highest in the middle, marking the GSR to the CS; it slopes off on either side as frequency increases or decreases. Such a curve is called the *gradient of generalization*.

generalization (margin)

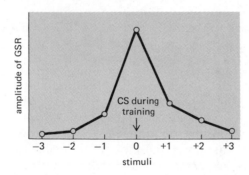

Fig. 3.7 Gradient of generalization. Stimulus O denotes the tone to which the galvanic skin response (GSR) was originally conditioned. Stimuli +1, +2, and +3 represent test tones of increasingly higher pitch; stimuli -1, -2, and -3 represent tones of lower pitch. Note that the amount of generalization decreases as the difference between the test tone and the training tone increases. (After Hovland, 1937)

John Watson demonstrated generalization in an experiment. Watson and Raynor (1920) found a small boy, Albert, who had no fear of rats, dogs, and many other things that children frequently fear but who was frightened by loud noises. They conditioned him to fear a white rat by banging a metal bar right after showing him the rat. At first, Albert was frightened by the loud sound, but eventually he exhibited the same fear toward the white rat. He then generalized his fear to other furry objects, including even a wad of cotton.

Discrimination   The converse of generalization, *discrimination* is a process of responding to the differences between stimuli. Once a particular stimulus has been identified as the most reliable signal of significant consequences, it would be unproductive to respond to less important stimuli. Gradually, a subject can be conditioned to respond only to the CS and to inhibit responses to irrelevant stimuli. This process is facilitated if the CS differs in some noticeable way from the other stimuli.

Discriminative training is also facilitated if it is combined with extinction (Fig. 3.8). Thus, if the signal to be learned is always reinforced, but no other one is, the correct expectancies will develop more rapidly.

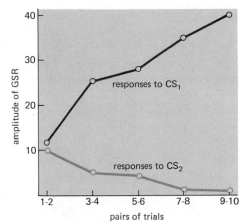

Fig. 3.8 The course of conditioned discrimination in man. The discriminative stimuli were two tones of clearly different pitch (CS$_1$ = 700 cps and CS$_2$ = 3500 cps). The unconditioned stimulus, an electric shock applied to the left forefinger, occurred only on trials when CS$_1$ was presented. The strength of the conditioned response, which in this case was the GSR, gradually increased following CS$_1$ and extinguished following CS$_2$. (After Baer and Fuhrer, 1968)

Generalization and discrimination occur in everyday life as well as in the laboratory. When a baby is born, he is fed almost entirely by his mother. Originally he salivates to the nipple placed in his mouth. Eventually, the mere sight of the mother causes salivation. Then a generalization to all women occurs, but the feeding process does not follow the sight of all women. The generalization is extinguished and the baby learns to discriminate the mother from other women he sees. Such a procedure would also underlie how Albert would unlearn his fear of white furry animals and objects like them. If the US (loud bang) no longer follows the sight or handling of the rat or bunny, exinction would occur. If you wanted him to remain afraid of the rat but not of any of the other white furry objects, this discrimination would require that the sight of the rat (CS) be followed by the US (bang), but the sight of the other objects (CS) never be followed by the bang. Eventually, the fear of the latter should dissipate.

Occasionally, conditioning experiments subject animals to such severe stress that a phenomenon known as experimental neurosis occurs. A Pavlovian discrimination study first revealed this reaction in a dog conditioned to salivate to the sight of a circle. The dog learned to differentiate between the circle and an ellipse. Then the experimenter began little by little to make the ellipse more like a circle. The final test was a discrimination between a circle and a figure identical to it except for a slightly depressed side. The dog salivated correctly until the last discrimination, when performance began to decrease abruptly. Not only could the animal no longer differentiate between the circle and the original ellipse, but its general behavior also deteriorated: it became fearful, barked, struggled in its harness, and showed other signs of distress. This is by no means unique to classical conditioning, and is, in fact, not a direct outcome of the conditioning process. We are merely asking for a higher level of discrimination than the dog can give.

Higher-Order Conditioning Through regular association of the CS with the US in conditioning training, the CS eventually serves as the US itself; a neutral stimulus preceding it then becomes the CS, which, in turn, elicits the CR, and so on. This phenomenon, termed *higher-order conditioning*, was also noted in

experimental
neurosis

higher-order
conditioning

a Pavlovian experiment. An animal reacting to an injection of morphine (US) with nausea and vomiting in time gave a similar response to the sight of the needle (CS_1) before the injection. Moreover, the rubbing of alcohol on the skin (CS_2) soon elicited vomiting. Then the container for the needle (CS_3) and finally the experimental room itself (CS_4) elicited the nausea. Even though in none of these cases was the CS-CR unit physiologically associated, it was sufficiently established to condition new learning. Some aspects of psychological addiction are probably caused by this type of higher-order conditioning.

In general, psychologists have had trouble going beyond second-order conditioning ($CS_2 \rightarrow CS_1 \rightarrow US$). Even here, success is not guaranteed unless the UR is strong and the CR is reinforced by the original CS-US trials from time to time.

Higher-order conditioning has thus posed a problem, especially because some of the great potential of classical conditioning as expectancy learning seems to depend upon it. Expecting what leads to what should not be limited to only one or two steps. Perhaps the difficulties encountered in the laboratory, however, are due to using animals that cannot remember complex chains of expectancies.

The Role of Classical Conditioning in the Development of Behavior Theory

John B. Watson

Classical conditioning was recognized by John Watson as the cornerstone of a behaviorist theory of psychology. Challenging the Freudians and the structural psychologists, on the one hand, and the instinct theorists, on the other, Watson maintained that behavior consists exclusively of overt physiological responses to particular stimuli. He considered Pavlov's conditioned response to be what he called habit. He therefore concerned himself with exploring the dynamics of these relationships and regarded conjectures about mental processes that could not be observed as unscientific. He hoped that in the absence of an empirical means of investigating cognition, or thinking, stimulus-response (S–R) theory would adequately explain behavior.

In the knowledge of S–R associations, Watson thought, lay the means for predicting and controlling human behavior. He was convinced that scientific manipulation of the environment—the stimuli that people react to—would make it possible to determine the course of people's lives, whether for good or ill and regardless of individual will or genetic makeup.

Although subsequent investigations have established that heredity and cognition do in reality contribute to the shaping of human beings, the implications of Pavlovian theory for the science of behavior remain enormous. Presumably, this significance will grow as more is learned about the role of the cerebral cortex in conditioning, an avenue of inquiry that Pavlov himself opened up.

Aversive Counterconditioning

Behavioral modification is a method of therapy employing principles of classical and operant conditioning to change behavior that may be personally or socially objectionable. One type of behavioral therapy, *aversive counterconditioning,* pairs a noxious stimulus, such as a nausea-producing drug, with the undesired but highly reinforcing behavior. Alcoholism has been treated in this manner with varying degrees of success. In one procedure developed by Voegtlin (1940) the alcoholic is given emetine, a drug that causes nausea upon the sight, smell, taste, or thought of alcohol, in four to seven brief sessions distributed over a period of about 10 days. Voegtlin reports (Lemere and Voegtlin, 1950) that he has treated over 4,000 alcoholics in this manner and has obtained a complete abstinence rate of 51 percent for patients up to 10 years.

    Another means of treating compulsive behavior such as alcoholism or obesity is with aversive therapy using self-control rather than drugs or electric shock. The patient is taught to relax, then imagine the stimulus, food or liquor; just before the stimulus is about to reach the patient's mouth, he is told to imagine that he is vomiting all over the food or drink, and himself. After several more trials, the patient is directed not to take the stimulus, and as a result feels calm and relaxed.

OPERANT CONDITIONING

As we have seen, classical conditioning serves an adaptive purpose in letting the person learn how environmental events are related. The CS comes to act as a signal that the US is about to occur, and the CR can be seen as a preparatory adjustment for the forthcoming US. In classical conditioning the learner remains passive in that it cannot itself determine how its actions and the environment are connected. Such an opportunity is, however, provided in the *operant* or *instrumental* conditioning paradigm, which allows the learner to discover what consequences its behavior has on its environment and to change its be-

operant
conditioning
instrumental
conditioning

havior or the environment on the basis of these consequences. It also involves expectancies, specifically those relating to the consequences of the learner's actions.

In studies of operant conditioning it is usually necessary to use subjects who do not possess language and high levels of reasoning powers in order to isolate the principles of learning. This is not to say that human beings do not *learn* the consequences of their actions. Rather, some of that learning takes place in one or two trials or exposures; it may even be accomplished by someone telling the learner what will happen, thereby saving him the trouble of having to practice the behavior himself. After looking at some of the operant conditioning processes, we will examine the relationship between how something was learned and the retention of that learning.

Thorndike's Puzzle Boxes

At the turn of the century, E. L. Thorndike, an American psychologist, conducted a series of experiments that illustrated what he termed instrumental conditioning. He placed hungry cats in puzzle boxes (Fig. 3.9) from which they could emerge only by performing some action such as pushing a button or pulling a string. The correct action released a weight and thereby opened the door. Food was set outside the box, within sight of the cat.

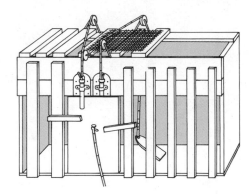

Fig. 3.9 Thorndike's cats were confined in boxes like this one and food was placed outside of the box. To get out, the animal had to loosen a bolt, bar, or loop in order to release a weight which would then pull the door open. (Thorndike, 1898)

The animal's reaction to confinement was generally an attempt to escape by random means. It clawed at everything in the box, tried to squeeze through the bars, stretched its paws outside the box, scratched at any object nearby, and so forth. Sooner or later, the cat managed to operate the proper mechanism and effect its escape. Over numerous trials, it began to learn which of its many responses to confinement succeeded in freeing it—that is, which was *instrumental* in its release. Thereafter, the cat performed the correct action as soon as it was placed in the box. Food was the reward on each trial.

Thorndike inferred that the animal's observable behavior must have been motivated by internal rather than external stimuli, and he termed it *emitted* behavior. He conceived that these internal stimuli created strong *drive states* that aroused the animal and urged it into action.

The form these actions took depended, Thorndike thought, partly on the cat's innate characteristics and partly on its prior learning. Thus, it had a range of possible responses to the internal stimuli. Through a process of trying out these various responses, what Thorndike called *trial-and-error learning*, it slowly narrowed down the possibilities. Thorndike hypothesized that external cues aided in this response selection; for example, if light served as a dependable signal that food was present and the absence of light that food was not there, then the cat soon began to attempt escape only when the light was on.

On the basis of these observations, Thorndike constructed what he called the *law of effect*. It took particular account of the tendency of the cats to retain actions that were instrumental to their escape and to take less and less time to initiate them. Essentially, Thorndike explained this by postulating that actions bringing an animal satisfaction—those, in other words, having a desirable effect on its environment—become associated with a particular situation and are, therefore, more likely to be repeated in that situation; those, however, bringing discomfort do not become associated with the situation and are much less likely to be repeated. What Thorndike regarded as a satisfying state of affairs—the cats' escape and their food reward—functioned essentially as reinforcement in his law of effect.

We made a distinction early in this chapter between learning and performance that is particularly relevant here. Taken literally, the law of effect has implied that some motivating circumstance must be operating in the organism for learning to occur or else no stimulus event in the environment could be reinforcing to him. But we know from many experiments that even animals will learn when they are not hungry, thirsty, sexy, or what not. As we will see in Chapter 5, learning theorists have differed substantially on how they describe the motivational properties of underlying states. Some talk about bodily needs, others about arousal of drives, and still others, wishing to avoid unobservable internal circumstances altogether, simply talk about the number of hours since the subject has been allowed to eat or drink. But whatever the role they ascribe to the underlying motivational state, all agree that food will not serve as reinforcement unless the animal is hungry, and subjects may not perform what they have learned unless some internal state renders the environmental events rewarding or reinforcing. So again the law of effect, as an operational statement, is acceptable to most psychologists, even though we know little about what happens neurologically when reinforcement occurs. Thus, we are reluctant to define the process of reinforcement.

The most systematic studies of operative learning have been carried out by B. F. Skinner, whose name is most associated with this type of learning.

trial-and-error learning

law of effect

Skinner's Operant Conditioning

An apparatus constructed by Skinner, called a Skinner box (Fig. 3.10), has frequently been used in experiments to illustrate operant conditioning. The box is equipped with a tray and spigot (for delivery of food and water), a lever, and a light protected by a screen. Before a subject (any animal, including a human) is placed inside, it is deprived of food or water for a time.

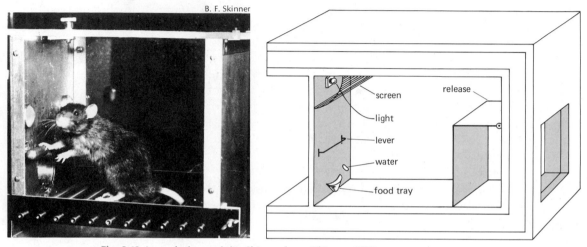

B. F. Skinner

Fig. 3.10 An early form of the Skinner box. (Skinner, 1938)

operant level

Once in the box, the subject wanders about, touching various places from time to time, including the lever. A record is made of the frequency of this random bar pressing prior to conditioning; this is known as the *operant level* of the emitted behavior. Once this level has been ascertained, conditioning is initiated by the automatic delivery of a food pellet to the tray each time the subject presses the bar. The subject soon begins to press the bar more often, which results in his obtaining more pellets, and a record of this new frequency of bar pressing is kept (Fig. 3.11). The food acts as reinforcement of the bar pressing. The subject's increased bar pressing is termed *operant behavior* because it operates on the environment to produce a desired result.

operant behavior

In a variation of this experiment, the subject learns to press the bar only when a particular external stimulus is present. For example, if food is delivered only when the light in the box is on, then the subject limits its response to these times. The light, in other words, serves as a *discriminative stimulus* by signaling that the reinforcing stimulus is available if the conditioned response is emitted.

discriminative stimulus

Measuring Operant Strength One of the primary measures of operant strength is the rate of response since, in the Skinner box, the subject is free to emit reinforced behavior (behavior that causes food to appear, for example) at any time. Every response is recorded directly on a constantly revolving drum by a pen attached to the bar. Whenever the subject presses the bar, the pen moves up a fixed distance, then continues horizontally across the paper until the next response occurs. The result is a cumulative curve that records the number of responses over time.

B. F. Skinner

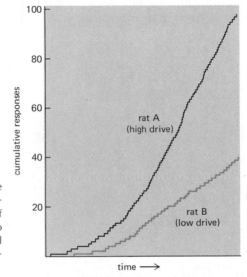

Fig. 3.11 A comparison of the cumulative response curves for two rats during acquisition of a bar-pressing response. Rat A had been deprived of food for 30 hours and Rat B for 10 hours prior to the experiment. This difference in the drive level of the two rats is reflected in the rate of responding. (Data from Skinner, 1938)

Comparison of Operant and Classical Conditioning

Operant conditioning reveals many of the same phenomena as classical conditioning:

1. *Extinction.* The rate of response declines upon the withdrawal of reinforcement. For example, if a food pellet no longer appears when a bar is pressed, the subject will stop pressing the bar (Fig. 3.12).

2. *Spontaneous recovery.* If there is a rest period after extinction, the subject will start emitting the operant behavior spontaneously; that is, he will begin to press the bar.

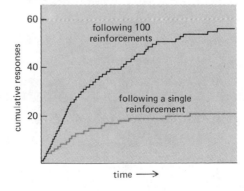

Fig. 3.12 Curves of extinction of operant responses in the rat are plotted following a single reinforcement and following 100 reinforcements. The plot shows the cumulative number of bar-pressing responses: every response raises the height of the curve, and the curve levels off when responses cease. (Data from Skinner, 1938)

Teaching Machines

One of the most innovative teaching devices to be used in recent years—programmed instruction—has been made possible by advanced research on learning theory. Programmed instruction uses learning materials that enable the student to work at his own pace. The device may be a simple book or a complex computer, but they operate on similar learning principles. The material is presented in the form of short-answer questions to which the student must respond. The student answers the question and then compares his response to the correct answer given by the machine. If he is wrong he is bypassed to a review of the material just presented; if he is correct he goes forward. In this manner, he goes through the material only as fast as he can absorb it. Instruction is thus tailored to the needs of the individual student.

Programmed instruction is not limited to classroom instruction. Skills and techniques can also be learned by following programmed procedures. For example, typing can be taught by using a combination of a record and a book in which instructions and examples are given. The student works on his own, progressing to more difficult tasks as his skills improve.

RCA

Teaching machine.

3. *Generalization* (in this case, to a discriminative stimulus). If, for example, a 1,000-cycles-per-second tone serves as the discriminative stimulus, the subject will also emit operant behavior in response to a 500-cycles-per-second tone, though not as strongly.

4. *Higher-order conditioning,* called in this case *secondary reinforcement.* In a representative experiment, a pigeon pecks at a dark window to obtain a reward of food. At each peck, a light appears in the window as the food pellet is presented. After a number of trials the light itself becomes a reinforcement for the pecking response through constant association with the primary reinforcement of food. The bird will now peck when even the briefest glimmer of light appears at the window, even though the food reward might not follow. The light is considered a secondary reinforcement.

secondary reinforcement

B. F. Skinner

After the pigeon learns to associate a gleam of light with food, he will peck when a light appears even if no food follows.

We can better appreciate the differences between classical and operant conditioning by examining how the same response may be acquired in both paradigms. In classical conditioning we might pair the sound of a bell (CS) with a mild electric shock (US) delivered by means of an electrode attached to the subject's leg. The onset of the US causes the subject to flex its leg involuntarily, but no action it may perform has any effect on when or how long the shock is administered. In an operant design, however, the electrical apparatus might be set up to deliver the shock through an electrified grid. By voluntarily flexing its leg, the subject could terminate the US or, following the onset of some discriminative stimulus such as a bell, avoid it.

In the former procedure the response is *gotten from* the subject; in the latter the response is *given by* the subject. In addition, classical conditioning is concerned with the *antecedents* of behavior, while operant conditioning is concerned with the *consequences.* In the laboratory, then, the qualities of the two paradigms can easily be made distinct. However, human behavior in daily life cannot be compartmentalized as conveniently. Since we are all constantly attending to different cues from the environment, often the two types of conditioning are superimposed on one another. What further complicates the matter is that certain operant responses are built on unlearned behavior. In feeding oneself, for example, first the musculature involved in eating must be sufficiently developed to carry out the necessary motor movements. This is an unlearned, maturational process. Second, the body prepares itself for digestion. The sight of food induces salivation and other anticipatory responses. These are classically conditioned responses—antecedents of eating. Or a dinner bell may elicit them and concurrently serve as a discriminative stimulus signaling that if one goes into the dining room, one will be rewarded with food.

Chaining, Shaping, and the Stimulus Control of Behavior

Some forms of operant conditioning can be quite complex, particularly when humans are involved. Consider learning how to bake a cake. The reinforcement in this situation is obvious but the act itself is not so simple or unitary. What is involved is really a series of discrete responses such as (1) learning what ingredients to buy, (2) what temperature to set the oven, (3) how long to bake the cake, and so on. A series of responses in which each response leads to the next is called *chaining*.

chaining

Learning the words to a song is an example of the chaining of responses. We may learn one line, and then the next. In this sequence the termination of one line, together with the melody, serves as a stimulus for the next line. In this way, the sequence of responses becomes very important as you can find out for yourself by trying to start in the middle of the "Star-Spangled Banner."

The chaining of responses is possible only when each link in the chain is available. If this is not the case, each response must be established independently. To accomplish this, *shaping* or the method of *successive approximations* is often used. Consider as an example, teaching a dog to fetch a stick. In the beginning the trainer may reward the dog just for going near the stick. Then the reinforcement may be contingent on picking up the stick, and then later, a reward may be given only for carrying the stick toward the trainer. In this way the given behavior is shaped gradually until it reaches the desired form.

shaping

Much, if not all, of our behavior is controlled by discriminative stimuli. The ringing of a telephone is a discriminative stimulus for the response of answering and being reinforced by hearing another voice. Similarly, a green light at an intersection tells us that we are able to cross. Stimuli that tell us when and what reinforcers are available to us exert a large influence on our behavior.

Kimble (1961) makes this point clear in discussing normal and neurotic sexual responses. A normal sexual response is under the control of an available, attractive partner. The other person acts as a discriminative stimulus, in this case, for a sexual response. A neurotic sexual response, however, may be under the control of internal and response-produced stimuli. This means that the neurotic person may be sexually aroused by responses that occur in the absence of an appropriate stimulus and furthermore may fail to be aroused by appropriate stimuli. He thus carries around a conflict that the nonneurotic person doesn't have.

Schedules of Reinforcement

In the laboratory it is possible for the subject, whether it be rat or man, to receive reinforcement every time the required response occurs. However, in the everyday world such *continuous reinforcement* would be rare. The gambler does not win every time he plays, nor do we get paid for every correct response at work or at school. Operant conditioning studies have therefore extensively investigated *partial reinforcement* of behavior. Many different schedules of partial reinforcement are possible, but they can be broadly classified according to whether the period between reinforcements is regular or irregular and whether it is defined in terms of elapsed time between reinforcements or in terms of

partial
reinforcement

the ratio of reinforced to nonreinforced correct responses. Within this classification four types of schedules have been devised: fixed ratio, fixed interval, variable ratio, and variable interval.

In a *fixed ratio* schedule, the subject receives a reward only after a fixed number of correct responses *without* reinforcement. For example, a rat receives a food pellet only on every fifth correct response, or a dog may receive a "yummy" every third time he fetches a newspaper. The fixed ratio may be small (approaching continuous reinforcement) or quite large.

fixed ratio reinforcement

A *fixed interval* schedule sets a specific time interval as the criterion for reinforcement. Most people get paid once a week or once every two weeks regardless of the amount of work done in any given work period. That is, reinforcement is dependent on the amount of time that passes since the last reinforcement and is not contingent on the amount or kind of responses occurring in the interval. We are reinforced the same for a hard work-week as for an easy work-week. The person who receives Social Security checks is also on a fixed interval schedule.

fixed interval reinforcement

A *variable ratio* schedule is similar to the fixed ratio schedule in that reinforcement is given only after a certain number of correct responses. The difference is that the number of correct responses necessary for reinforcement varies, so that a reward may be contingent on three correct responses at one time and on five the next time. The gambler who plays the slot machines is on a variable ratio schedule.

variable ratio reinforcement

The *variable interval* schedule, like the fixed interval, delivers the reinforcement after a specific length of time, but, in this case, the time span between reinforcements changes. The fisherman is rewarded in varying intervals. He may wait hours to get his first catch and thereupon may catch two or three fish in the next few minutes.

variable interval reinforcement

Fig. 3.13 shows typical, idealized views of the various types of reinforcement schedules. These curves reveal some important facts. Because reinforcement is partial a subject learns to be highly sensitive to discriminative stimuli in its environment and emits operant behavior according to the dependability of these cues as signals for reinforcement.

Four distinct response patterns emerge on the four different reinforcement schedules. A subject accustomed to either the fixed or variable ratio schedule responds at a fairly steady, rapid rate. It appears to learn that reinforcement is contingent upon the number of correct responses.

On the interval schedules, however, the subject seems to be aware that time rather than number of responses is the significant factor. Thus, on the fixed interval schedule the subject ceases responding almost entirely for a time after reinforcement and then begins again, and at an increased rate, as the interval draws to a close. The subject on the variable-interval schedule, on the other hand, cannot be certain of the length of intervening time, so its responses predictably come much more regularly, though in the end less often.

Partial reinforcement leads to great resistance to extinction. This *partial*

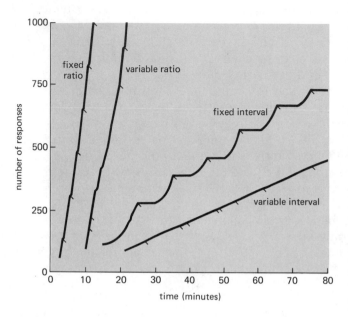

Fig. 3.13 Typical, "idealized" curves that have come to be identified with the main kinds of reinforcement schedules. Thousands of studies have found that interval schedules generally maintain a moderate rate of responding (shown in the gradual slope of the cumulative record curve). The fixed interval schedule typically yields the "scalloped" curve shown here, reflecting the fact that the subject virtually stops responding after a reinforcement and waits till near the next scheduled reinforcement before responding actively again. Both the ratio schedules typically maintain a high level of responding, as shown in the steepness of the curves. These records are characteristic whether the subject is a rat or a pigeon or a child. (Adapted from "Teaching Machines" by B. F. Skinner. Copyright © 1961 by Scientific American, Inc. All rights reserved)

partial reinforcement effect

reinforcement effect seems to be produced because the subject does not really know when extinction begins. If a response is reinforced on a continuous schedule, as soon as one reinforcement is missed extinction is apt to begin. But on a partial reinforcement schedule, particularly the variable ones, an unreinforced response may mean little to the subject. A slot machine player would have to drop a lot of quarters in order to determine that the machine was broken and that he was not just having a streak of "bad luck."

Stimulus-Response Relationships

As conditioning progresses, relationships between stimuli and responses slowly develop. What was once a neutral stimulus might now lead to a specific behavior, just as one response might trigger the start of another event. The relationships between the variables usually strengthen with repetition, so that learning occurs over a number of trials. Four basic stimuli and response relationships are the

S→S, S→R, R→S, and R→R relationships. We will briefly examine each of these here.

S→S Relationships The investigation of S→S relationships yields information about the environment. We have encountered this type of association chiefly in classical conditioning experiments, where an unconditioned stimulus is paired with a conditioned stimulus. Through this repeated association, the subject discovers what kind of stimulus the US is and how strong it is; how it and the CS are related in time; and how the CS functions as a signal. Stimuli may become associated in operant conditioning if, for instance, a discriminative stimulus signals the availability of the reinforcing stimulus, or if a pleasant or unpleasant stimulus occurs after the reinforcing stimulus. Thus, an association is made between two previously unrelated stimuli due to their presentation at the same, or nearly the same, time.

S→R Relationships The observation of the high consistency with which certain responses follow certain stimuli has led psychologists to isolate specific S→R relationships. Reflexes, such as pupillary constriction in light, are primary examples of this type of association. We have seen that inhibition of a response, which in itself is a behavior, may also be regularly produced by certain stimuli, such as, for instance, the word "no" spoken to a small child. In both cases, the stimulus is said to elicit the response.

More specifically, the S→R relationship is held to be the model of classical conditioning and of all learning by some theorists (notably Guthrie, 1952). Operant conditioning is also sometimes conceived in terms of S→R, since a discriminative stimulus S_0 signals the animal to respond, and the response elicits a reinforcing stimulus S_1. Therefore, $S_0 \rightarrow R \rightarrow S_1$.

R→S Relationships The R→S relationship is considered more typical of operant conditioning. The subject learns to control certain aspects of its environment through its own actions. Certain stimulus events, you observe, are absolutely dependent on your actions. You turn the faucet with the certainty that you will see and feel the flow of water. The elevator moves when you press one of the buttons. The green light at a highway toll booth goes on after you deposit your quarter. In such situations you expect that the S will always follow the R. When it doesn't, you call the plumber, the elevator company, or the toll collector in order to restore the proper relationship.

Certain other events can be affected by your actions, although they are not as directly produced by them. Because these stimuli do not depend on you, they may not always follow your responses. If you are bent on growing tomatoes in the backyard and adhere faithfully to all the instructions on the seed package regarding soil, light, and so on, it is likely, but not certain, that you will eventually harvest a crop. The occurrence of the stimulus is, in other words, contingent upon your response but also upon other conditions, such as the amount of rainfall, which are beyond your control.

If you were a successful tomato grower one year, you would probably

Operant Conditioning of the Autonomic Nervous System

Psychologists have tried to demonstrate that classical and operant conditioning are two distinct phenomena by showing that learning occurs under different conditions in the two situations, and also that they are governed by two distinctly different neurophysiological mechanisms. The traditional belief has been that involuntary visceral responses—those controlled by the autonomic nervous system—can be modified only by classical conditioning and that voluntary skeletal muscle responses, which are controlled by the central nervous system, can be modified only by operant conditioning.

Neal Miller (1969), a learning theorist, has held that classical and operant conditioning are not two distinct phenomena but rather two manifestations of the same phenomenon under different conditions. To support such a position he had to show that operant training could produce learning of any visceral response that could be acquired through classical conditioning—that is, that visceral responses could, through operant conditioning, be brought under the voluntary control of the cental nervous system.

Operant modification of visceral responses had to overcome one basic problem: most visceral responses can be affected by such skeletal activities as tension of muscles or changes in rate or pattern of breathing. Therefore it would be difficult to prove that the desired visceral response had been acquired directly rather than as a by-product of some subtle undetectable skeletal response. For example, a yoga can stop his heart sound by controlling his rib cage and diaphragm muscles so that the pressure within the chest is increased to the point where venous return of blood is considerably retarded.

To guard against this artifact, paralysis of skeletal muscles was induced by the drug curare. But now, because the experimental animals were paralyzed, they had to be maintained on a mechanical respirator, and the possibility of rewards was limited. Food, for example, could not be used. Two methods of reinforcement were devised: electrical stimulation of a center in the brain that is known to control pleasure, and avoidance or escape from mildly unpleasant electric shock.

With these techniques, Miller and DiCara (1965) showed that curarized rats could learn visceral responses in the same way they learned skeletal responses. More specifically, they demonstrated that increases or decreases in heart rate could be obtained when pleasurable stimulation ensued. First, small changes in the desired direction were rewarded during the time periods (signified by a light) when the reward was available. Then only larger changes were rewarded. Miller and DiCara were thus able to shape rats to increase or decrease their heart rates by about 20 percent, from a baseline measure, in a 90-minute period.

This experiment was repeated with electric shock in order to be sure there was nothing unique about brain stimulation as a reward for visceral responses. A shock signal was presented to a rat. After it had been on for 5 seconds a brief pulse of mild electric shock was delivered to the rat's tail. During the first 5 seconds the animal could turn off the shock by making a correct heartbeat response, thus avoiding shock. Rats clearly learned to make this discrimination.

These experiments showed that operant conditioning of visceral responses follows the laws of skeletal operant conditioning and that it is not limited to a particular kind of reward. They also opened up the possibility of training human beings to control such visceral responses as heart rate, intestinal contractions, and blood pressure, which have important effects on physical health. Studies such as these also have implications for the understanding of psychosomatic disease: perhaps Jane's fainting spells are conditioned reactions to situations she wishes to avoid.

use the same methods the next and expect similar success. However, situations in which the contingencies are determined by other people cannot be handled in so stereotyped a fashion. Your responses must differ according to the person involved. Getting a raise from one boss may be contingent upon your independence and creativity, whereas from another, it may depend on punctuality and short lunch hours.

In operant conditioning the experimenter can influence the subject's behavior by manipulating the relationship between it and the reinforcing stimulus—by changing the contingencies. In daily life, too, such manipulation is everywhere in evidence. The knowledge of the probable penalties to follow upon doing 60 mph in a 50-mph zone deters most would-be speeders. Parental praise for sharing toys encourages a little boy to repeat his behavior. A bonus for perfect attendance succeeds in cutting down the absentee rate at a large company.

We have seen that in operant conditioning any reinforced behavior is likely to be repeated. But in some situations the relationship between the response and the reinforcing stimulus is purely *coincidental*. In an experiment, for example, the subject may be given a food pellet every 30 seconds, no matter what it does. Eventually, it begins to repeat the action it happened to be performing when it was rewarded. Although in actuality the response has absolutely nothing to do with the reinforcement, the subject behaves as if it did.

In human beings this phenomenon is manifested as superstition. Accidentally, certain good or bad consequences become associated with certain actions. For example, imagine that a boy on a Little League baseball team gets a brand new cap to replace the one he has lost and thereafter manages to hit a home run three games in a row. On the day of the next game he forgets his cap and not only does not hit a home run but does not even make it to first base once in nine innings. His conclusion: his new cap endows him with superior abilities.

R→R Relationships Just as we learn more about the workings of the environment through observing what stimuli occur together, so, too, we can better understand the dynamics of behavior by noting what responses follow upon one another. A psychotherapist seeking an explanation for a patient's neurosis,

superstition

for example, must first observe his entire repertoire of responses over a period of time before he can make an informed analysis. In attempting to draw inferences from such observation, however, one must beware of mistaking a response that regularly precedes or accompanies another response for the cause of the second behavior. A child may consistently follow a pattern of doing poorly on tests and being truant from school, but one behavior does not necessarily produce the other. They may both be caused by a third factor, perhaps some emotional problem. The chief advantage to be gained from establishing such reliable correlations of responses is a basis for the prediction of behavior. One can begin to be fairly certain that, given one action, another will occur. Then we can look for the stimuli that must be mediating these response correlations.

LEARNING BY MODELING

modeling   We learn a great deal through watching other people. This is known as *imitation* or learning by modeling. The advantages of this type of learning should be obvious. If each of us had to directly experience a situation, such as diapering a baby, without the advantage of watching someone else do it first, learning would be tedious and would often proceed by trial and error. However, by watching another person perform an act, we pick out relevant approaches to performing that act without having to discover them from scratch.

Two psychologists, Albert Bandura and the late Richard Walters, have used imitation learning to explain personality development and particularly the learning and maintenance of deviant behavior. Bandura and Walters point out that past learning theories have been inadequate in explaining what they call *social learning.*

> During the past half century, learning theory approaches to personality development, deviant behavior, and psychotherapy have suffered from the fact that they have relied heavily on a limited range of principles based on . . . studies of animal learning or human learning in one-person situations. . . . It is necessary to extend and modify these principles and to introduce new principles that have been established and confirmed through studies of dyadic [two-person] and group situations. (Bandura and Walters, 1963a, p. 1)

Modeling Behavior

In a typical study investigating modeling behavior, an observer watches a model perform a certain act or series of acts and then the observer is given an opportunity to imitate the model. The observer's behavior is compared with that of a control group who did not observe the model. A study by Bandura, Ross, and Ross (1963) illustrates the technique. Observers watched aggressive or nonaggressive models, while controls were not exposed to a model. Subsequently all the subjects—observers and controls—were given an opportunity to display aggressive or nonaggressive behavior in a similar situation to the one in which the models performed. Judges' ratings of the responses were then compared to see if the observers and controls differed to a significant degree, and whether the two groups of observers—those who watched an aggressive model and those who watched a nonaggressive model—differed significantly.

As Flanders (1968) explains, an observer is said to imitate a model when observation of the behavior of that model affects the observer so that the observer's behavior becomes more similar to the model's behavior than it was. According to this formulation, the study of imitative behavior is concerned with *causal* relationships between M's (the model) behavior (or alleged behavior) and O's (the observer) behavior (Flanders, 1968, p. 316).

Fig. 3.14 shows a girl who was initially afraid of dogs engaging in fearless

Fig. 3.14 A girl who was afraid of dogs engaged in fearless interactions with them after exposure to a series of films in which a peer model displayed progressively threatening interactions with dogs. (Bandura and Menlove, 1968)

interactions with a dog after watching a series of movies in which a young boy played with a dog (Bandura and Menlove, 1968).

Vicarious Reinforcement We have seen how important reinforcement is for operant conditioning. Vicarious reinforcement, that is, observing a model being reinforced, is equally important for imitative learning. Fig. 3.15 shows the results of an experiment by Bandura (1965a) in which children watched a film of an aggressive model being rewarded, punished, or experiencing no consequences for his actions. Note the effect that watching a punished model had in suppressing aggressive behavior. In vicarious reinforcement, observers learn what the consequences of a given act are by observing others being rewarded or punished after performing that act.

vicarious
reinforcement

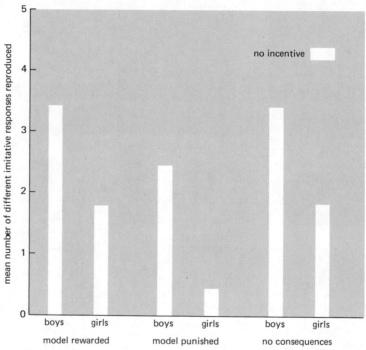

Fig. 3.15 Mean number of different matching responses reproduced by children as a function of response consequences to the model and positive incentives. (Adapted from Bandura, 1965a)

Inhibition and Disinhibition Effects Each of us has been in a situation where we would like to do something such as ask a woman to dance or even whistle a song on the street but do not do it because we are afraid of rejection or social disapproval. If we see another person doing the very thing we feel like doing, it suddenly becomes much easier to do.

Walters, Bowen, and Parke (1963) investigated the inhibiting or disinhibiting effects of imitative learning. Subjects (observers) looked at movies of nude males and females engaging in erotic poses. Each subject was told that a spot of light that also appeared in the film indicated the eye movements of the last subject. For approximately half the subjects the spot of light was concentrated on the breasts and genital areas, while for the other half the light appeared in the background, as if avoiding erotic areas. The subjects were then shown slides of nude people and the subject's own eye movements were recorded. Subjects that had been exposed to the supposedly uninhibited models spent more time watching the breasts and genital areas of the nudes on the slides than did subjects who were exposed to "inhibited" models (Fig. 3.16).

Fig. 3.16 A spot of light, seen in the background in the pictures on the left, on the left breast of the female figure on the top right, and in the genital area of the male figure on the bottom right, indicates where the subject is looking. (Bandura and Walters, 1963a)

Punishment

We saw in Fig. 3.16 how observing a model being punished *suppressed* imitation of the modeled behavior. However, this does not mean that punishment eliminates a behavior, but only that it suppresses it in a particular situation (Skinner, 1938). Experiments with rats show that conditioned bar pressing was not extinguished by punishment with electric shock. One group of rats received the standard extinction treatment—they were no longer reinforced with food for bar pressing—while the experimental group was given a shock for each bar press. Bar pressing was suppressed for a while in the experimental group, but it later resumed at the same rate it had attained previous to the shock; the standard extinction group, however, made fewer and fewer responses (Mussen and Rosenzweig, 1973).

Does this mean that humans should not use punishment, especially in child rearing? Yes and no. Punishment may be useful if alternative responses are available and these responses are positively reinforced. For example, children who throw rocks at cars will not benefit from punishment unless alternative, desirable behavior such as playing baseball is available.

Punishment by itself can have highly negative effects. Through such learning principles as stimulus generalization and imitative learning, a child who is punished in the home may imitate his parents' treatment of him when someone outside the home does not comply with his wishes; his aggressiveness may get him in a lot of fights. This behavior may be strengthened all the more if the child gets his way (is reinforced) in certain situations (Dollard and Miller, 1950; Bandura, 1969).

Up to this point, our discussion of learning has been confined primarily to developing expectancies about what follows what. We will now give some consideration to a quite different type of learning: how we learn to perform a smooth sequence of actions, as in such skills as hitting a baseball or driving a car.

THE LEARNING OF SKILLS

The principles of operant and classical conditioning, and also those of modeling, play a significant role in the learning of skills. Out of both necessity and desire, people learn numerous kinds of skills, all of which obviously involve vastly different levels of difficulty. Some of the earliest ones acquired are verbal: speaking, reading, and writing. Such activities as bowling or pole vaulting are athletic; operating a linotype machine or a switchboard is mechanical. Others—painting, playing the oboe, or ballet dancing—are artistic. And these by no means exhaust the categories. Despite their manifest differences, however, all these

skill   activities conform to the definition of what a skill is, namely, a well-integrated sequence of perceptual-motor activities. Some factors involved in learning various skills are listed in Table 3.1.

Table 3.1 Some Important Factors Which Occur in Various Perceptual-Motor Tasks

Factor	Description	Some Tasks
Control precision	Highly controlled adjustments of large muscles	Rudder control, lathe
Multilimb coordination	Coordinating the movements of more than one limb	Shifting gears
Response orientation	Fast visual discrimination with appropriate movement	Any task demanding the rapid choice of a response
Reaction time	Speed of response to stimulus	Any simple response to a single stimulus
Arm movement speed	Rapidity of gross arm movement	Hitting two plates about 6 inches apart alternately
Rate control	Following a moving target	Controlling the movement of a steel ball by tilting a board
Manual dexterity	Skilled rapid arm movements	Wrapping packages
Finger dexterity	Controlling tiny objects with the fingers	Repairing watches
Arm-hand steadiness	Moving an object slowly and steadily	Threading a needle
Wrist-finger speed	Tapping rapidly with pencil	Filling in a circle with dots
Aiming	Hitting small circles accurately with a pencil	Making check marks

SOURCE: Deese and Hulse, (1967), after Fleishman, (1962)

The Process of Learning

Let us examine the process of learning to type in order to illustrate the steps involved in acquiring a skill. When a novice sits down at a typewriter, he first becomes familiar with the locations of the different letter-keys. This task is largely perceptual. Then he must associate each key with a particular finger. Some schools now paint the fingernails of the students four different colors and color code each key to correspond to the correct finger. As he begins typing, the student's main concern is to hit the correct keys. He sees words in terms of their individual letters, which he types one at a time. As practice brings proficiency, a reorganization occurs. The typist becomes concerned with the patterning of separate responses in which words are now the new units. With further practice greater integration occurs, and whole phrases become of prime importance.

As more proficiency is gained, a third phenomenon takes place: automation. As we become highly skilled at a task, we perform swiftly and with minimal error, paying little or no attention to our actions. A proficient driver can talk to a passenger or listen to the radio and simultaneously watch the road. Only

The Talking Typewriter

One of the skills that is acquired at an early age is reading. Omar Khayyam Moore has been one of a group of psychologist educators that have been concerned with what types of environments best support acquisition of this skill. Moore's concept of environment, however, goes beyond the idea of general surroundings to include an interaction between general educational philosophy and machines that accelerate reading. Moore calls this approach the *responsive environment* (Moore and Anderson, 1968).

Ackerman (1971, pp. 424–425) describes Moore's concept of responsive environment in this manner:

1. It permits the learner to explore freely.
2. It informs the learner immediately about the consequences of his actions.
3. It is self-pacing; that is, events happen within the environment at a rate determined by the learner.
4. It permits the learner to make full use of his capacities for discovering relations of various kinds.
5. Its structure is such that the learner is likely to make a series of interconnected discoveries about the physical, cultural, and social world.

In order to study the general notion of a responsive environment, Moore took the acquisition of language as a starting point and developed a machine called the "talking typewriter" to accelerate this process. It was designed to teach

World Wide Photos

A six-year-old listens to a "talking typewriter," which spells and pronounces words.

both the written and spoken forms of a language. Suppose someone wishes to learn Russian. These are roughly the steps the learner would go through:

Step 1. The machine is set so that the user may strike any key, after which the keyboard locks until the voice-box gives the user the name and/or the phonetic value of the character. Repeated explorations of the keyboard lead to both visual and auditory command of the alphabet.

Step 2. The machine is reset so that the voice-box names a letter, and the user is to find the corresponding character and strike the appropriate key. Arrangements can be made such that if the machine names a letter—or gives its phonetic value, or both—only the appropriate key can be activated, the rest of the keyboard being locked.

Step 3. The machine is reset so as to display some word, perhaps with an appropriate picture on a screen to the right of the keyboard. A typical sequence of events at this stage might run as follows:

(a) The projection screen displays a picture of a table and directly above the paper carriage there is displayed the Russian word for "table."

(b) The keyboard is locked so that only the keys for the letters of a word in order can be depressed, so that the user may strike the operable keys, and the voice-box will give the phonetic value of each in turn.

(c) The voice-box repeats the spelling, pronounces the word, and allows the user time to repeat and record the word.

(d) The voice-box may make additional remarks about some words, calling attention to irregularities, etc. (Moore and Anderson, 1968, pp. 177–178.)

The "talking typewriter" has been used in teaching adults and children both a second language and their own language. Moore emphasizes, however, that the activity must be "autotelic," performed solely for its own sake and not for extrinsic rewards and punishments. He maintains that the curiosity or competence drive is all-important, and that the sooner the learner is put in a position to fulfill this drive the greater and more lasting the effects will be (Dallman et al., 1974).

if something unexpected happens does he feel it necessary to break off his conversation or turn off the radio in order to give the situation the same degree of attention he gave the initial acquisition of the skill.

Fitts (1962, 1964) has described the learning of a skill as including three stages: *cognition, fixation,* and *automation.* Initially, cognition, the perceptual function involved in becoming familiar with a task, is of great importance. The person readies himself for performance by determining where the different typewriter keys are. But, of course, this is not enough. Along with cognition must come *kinesthetic feedback,* or information from our muscles, as we physically carry out the task. This occurs during the fixation phase, when perceptual-cognitive processes begin to be dominated by the process of gaining perceptual-motor coordination. Because reaching this point necessitates repeated practice sessions, the second phase lasts the longest. Finally, as perceptual and

Paul M. Fitts

kinesthetic information become associated, or coupled, automation, as already described, takes place.

The major determinant in skill learning is practice, even more so than in the kinds of expectancy learning we have been discussing. You cannot be told how to hit a home run or bowl a strike. You have to actually carry out the motions many times, integrating each of the separate actions. Knowledge, understanding, and even observation are not adequate by themselves, though they greatly help the learning process.

Distribution of Practice

massed practice
spaced practice

When learning a skill, is it better to train continuously, using the *massed-practice* method, or to take breaks between sessions, using the *spaced-practice* method? Psychologists long interested in this question have sought the answer through studying the effects of both regimens in numerous studies. In one (Fig. 3.17), subjects were assigned a "pursuit rotor" task, which involved keeping the tip of a stylus, held in one hand, in touch with a small circular target near the edge of a turntable as both the target and turntable rotated (Digman, 1959). The results from such experiments as this have in general determined that performance under spaced conditions is better than under massed conditions (Fig. 3.18). Further, performance under spaced conditions shows a *reminiscence effect:* that is, after the subject has rested, his performance starts off at a level higher than it had attained at the end of the previous session.

Massed practice seems to create a great amount of inhibition or fatigue, almost as if the subject got tired. This happens less if the trials are spaced out in time. The reminiscence effect results then from the dissipation of the inhibition during the break, so that performance can start off without the suppressive effects of fatigue. In a practical sense, then, you will acquire a skill more efficiently if you space out the learning experiences.

Retention of a Skill

One of the most startling of experiences is getting on a bicycle after not having ridden one for 10 years and finding that most of the skill has been retained. In fact, subjects in most studies have shown so little evidence of forgetting motor activities that it is impossible to know what factors contribute to these results. In one representative experiment subjects practiced a difficult perceptual-motor task over a period of 7 weeks (Fleishman and Parker, 1962). Subsequently, they were checked at different intervals, lasting up to 2 years, for skill retention. The results showed that, no matter what the duration of the interval was, almost no loss of skill occurred. Two reasons are generally given for this phenomenon: (1) because the skill is so well learned in the first place, it is also well retained;

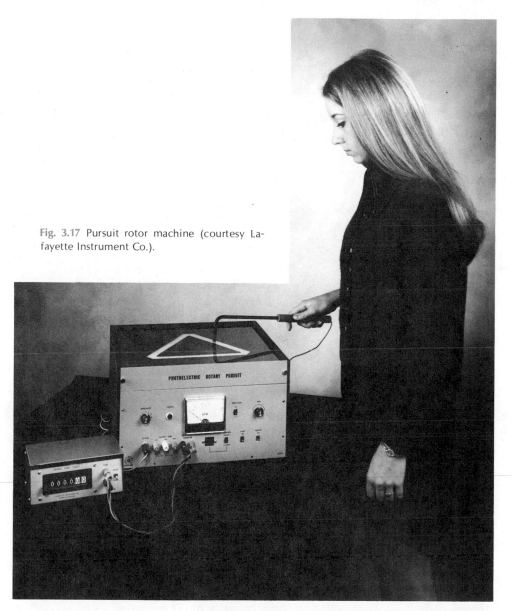

Fig. 3.17 Pursuit rotor machine (courtesy Lafayette Instrument Co.).

and (2) very little interference from other tasks occurs during the intervals between exercise of the skill.

The latter is quite important. Once the perceptual-motor sequence is well integrated and automated, even learning a similar skill cannot create much interference. Although some specific step may be the same, the entire sequence is different and so is not affected. Even such a seemingly difficult transfer of

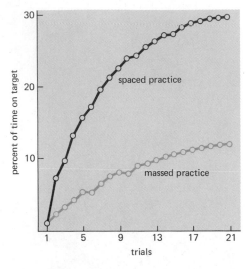

Fig. 3.18 Learning curves for pursuit rotor. Each trial lasts for 30 seconds, with some subjects having a 15-second rest period between trials (massed practice) and others a 45-second rest period (spaced practice). The dependent variable is percentage of time on target per trial. (Hilgard, Atkinson, and Atkinson, 1971; data from Bourne and Archer, 1956)

skills as driving a car on the left side of the road, as in England, after driving for many years on the right side is easy for most drivers. Only a few minutes of difficulty are reported, and thereafter only an occasional lapse.

HOW TO STUDY

The perennial problem of the student is how to do better in courses and on exams, and of course how to use studying time more efficiently. Maybe you have told your professor upon receiving a bad grade on an exam, "Well, I studied but the material did not sink in."

The first step in coming to grips with this problem is being *honest* with yourself. Do not fool yourself. Some material is easy and may only take a few hours to master; however, a lot of college course material is quite difficult and requires extended amounts of time. Get to know the level of difficulty of the material and plan accordingly. However, sometimes spending time on studying is not enough. Often students approach examinations and papers in ways that are self-defeating, frustrating, and nonproductive. In these cases three approaches, which apply principles of learning discussed earlier in the chapter, might help.

1. *Learn to reduce apprehensiveness associated with exams.* Often competitive (nonproductive) avoidance behavior has become conditioned to examination situations. Learning to recognize these avoidance tendencies is the first step in dealing with them.

2. *Find a successful student and try modeling your studying behavior after this person's.* In the section on imitation learning we saw how effective models can be in learning new responses.

3. *Plan an enjoyable event after an evening of study.* Self-reinforcement is important in studying. Of course, getting an A on a paper is reinforcing, but

in changing approaches to studying you may have to provide your own reinforcement for a while.

Sometimes getting hold of a book on how to study can be quite effective
in learning new approaches. Many of these study guides are available, and one
that is enjoyable as well as effective is *A Time To Learn* by Bandt, Meara, and
Schmidt (1974). These authors use a graphic device called the "learning pyramid"
(Fig. 3.19) that highlights both level of learning, which is a quantitative dimension,
and depth of learning, which is qualitative. ·

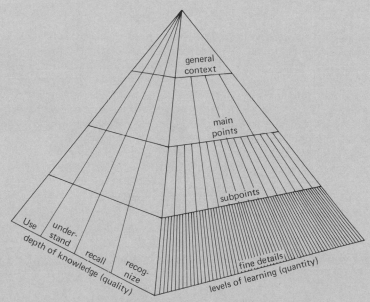

Fig. 3.19 Learning pyramid. (Brandt, Meara, and Schmidt, 1974)

Bandt and his co-workers describe different styles of learning that do not
work. You may recognize yourself in one of these descriptions. For example, the
"cognitive prisoner" learns details very well but cannot integrate his knowledge
into a sound understanding of what he is studying. They also give helpful hints
for taking examinations. Some of their tips are:

1. Reduce "panic" before exams by eliminating certain behaviors (these can even be
   self-defeating thoughts) which arouse anxiety.
2. Avoid all-night studying—cramming—unless you have a good understanding of the
   material in the first place and wish to work on minor detailed points.
3. Follow directions on the test.
4. Organize your answers before putting them down on the exam sheet. Often a bad
   start produces more of the same because the student is aware that it is not going
   well but feels compelled to continue because of limited time.
5. Do not guess wildly, but educated guesses are more often than not correct.
6. Develop a legible handwriting. Often professors or their assistants have many papers
   to mark and their impatience with a difficult handwriting can cost precious points.

In this chapter we have discussed the principles of learning as set down in operant and classical conditioning. We have sought to understand their application to various learning situations and various acquired skills. In the next chapter, we will be primarily concerned with verbal learning and memory and how those principles also contribute to our overall knowledge of our environment.

Summary

Learning is defined as a relatively permanent change in behavior resulting from the effects of practice. Changes that are temporary, such as reflexes and tropisms, instinctive, or caused by temporary states of the subject are usually not considered learning. *Performance* is the translation of a learned expectancy into displayed behavior. Peformance fluctuates with the temporary state of the subject; learning does not.

Learning is a process of adapting to the environment. It involves two processes: (1) learning how environmental events are related to each other and (2) learning how behavior affects environment. *Classical conditioning* occurs when one event in a specific way elicits a response similar to one previously given to another event. *Operant conditioning* occurs when we learn to make responses that are maximally capable of controlling environmental events.

Classical conditioning involves four basic variables: An *unconditioned stimulus* (US), which naturally elicits an *unconditioned response* (UR), and *conditioned stimulus* (CS), which if paired frequently enough with the US, elicits a conditioned response (CR).

These variables must possess certain properties in order for classical conditioning to occur. The US must elicit the UR with a high degree of frequency. The CS must be able to be sensed by the subject, which is indicated by an *orienting reflex* (attentiveness). The CS must not elicit a response identical to the US, and it must not be so strong that the subject cannot habituate to it.

The parameters of classical conditioning are acquisition, extinction, spontaneous recovery, generalization, discrimination, and higher-order conditioning. *Acquisition* is the phase in which the association between the CS and the US is learned. Different methods of timing this pairing produce different results. Timing can be delayed, simultaneous, trace, and backward. By reinforcing the CS with the US, we increase the probability that the CR will occur. When the CS is no longer paired with the US, *extinction* occurs, which means that the CR disappears. *Spontaneous recovery* is the reappearance of the CR after it has been extinguished. Dissipation of inhibition might explain why the CR reappears. *Generalization* occurs when the CR is given to stimuli similar to the CS; it decreases as the stimuli presented become less like the CS. *Discrimination* is a process of responding to differences in the stimuli presented.

When the conditioned stimulus becomes the US, and another neutral stimulus becomes the CS, we have *higher-order conditioning*. Although theoretically, this chain of events can continue indefinitely, it usually does not go beyond second-order conditioning.

Operant (or *instrumental*) *conditioning* provides the subject with a process of discovering the consequences of its behavior upon environmental events and how to change its behavior or the environment on the basis of those consequences.

Thorndike demonstrated instrumental conditioning by placing a cat in a puzzle box with food outside. The animal learned how to escape from the box by *trial-and-error learning*. Thorndike's *law of effect* stated that actions that aided the animal in escape would be repeated more and more, while actions that had no effect on escape would not be repeated as often.

Skinner constructed a box (called a Skinner box) in which a subject is required to press a lever or a button to effect a change in its environment. Skinner labeled this "operant conditioning," since the subject is "operating" on his environment. (Note that "operant" and "instrumental" are interchangeable terms.) An external stimulus that must be present in order for bar pressing to be effective is a *discriminative stimulus*.

Operant conditioning displays many of the same phenomena as classical conditioning: extinction, spontaneous recovery, generalization, and higher-order conditioning (secondary reinforcement). But in classical conditioning a response is *gotten from* the subject, whereas in operant conditioning the response is *given by* the subject. In real life, the two can seldom be separated.

Learning a series of operant responses in which each response serves as a stimulus for the next is called *chaining*. A behavior that cannot be broken down into successive responses is conditioned by *shaping* or the method of successive approximations, where at first rewards are given for anything approaching a correct response but later only for closer and closer approximations to the desired response and, finally, only for the precise response.

Schedules of partial reinforcement include: fixed ratio, fixed interval, variable ratio, and variable interval. A *fixed ratio* schedule rewards the subject only after it has made a fixed number of correct responses. A *fixed interval* schedule rewards the subject at specific intervals regardless of the desirability of exhibited behavior. A *variable ratio* schedule is similar to a fixed ratio schedule except that the number of unrewarded correct responses varies from reinforcement to reinforcement. A *variable interval* schedule varies the time between reinforcements. Ratio schedules are dependent upon the number of responses, and interval schedules are dependent upon a time period. Partial reinforcement leads to great resistance to extinction.

Various relationships between stimuli and responses can be established during conditioning trials. S→S relationships associate two previously unrelated stimuli by pairing them in time (classical conditioning) or by using one to indicate the availability of the other (operant conditioning). In S→R relationships, certain stimuli almost always elicit certain responses. These are the basis of classical conditioning, but they can be said to exist in operant conditioning too, insofar as the discriminative stimulus is a signal for the operant response. R→S relationships are typical of operant conditioning, where a response is made in order to obtain or activate a reinforcing stimulus. If the response-stimulus relationship is purely coincidental, the result is likely to be superstitious behavior. The R→R relationship is the pairing of one response with or right after another. Such relationships are carefully studied by, for example, psychotherapists, in attempts to predict behavior. When response relationships are known, stimuli that mediate them can be sought out.

Learning acquired by watching other people is known as imitation or *modeling*. It is extremely advantageous to us in that it permits us to avoid tedious trial-and-error procedures in many learning situations. Studies of modeling have shown that rein-forcement, both negative and positive, can operate vicariously—that is, that an observer may be influenced by the consequences the model experiences. Inhibitions can also be strengthened or decreased by the behavior we observe in others.

The learning of skills entails classical and operant conditioning, and frequently also modeling. A skill is a well-integrated sequence of perceptual-motor activities. The process of learning a skill entails *cognition, fixation,* and *automation.* Fixation is the longest stage because it includes *kinesthetic feedback,* or information from our muscles, which is only obtained by repeated practice.

Practice may be either *massed* or *spaced.* Spaced practice, which includes periods of rest, is far more effective than massed practice. Once learned, skills are retained even without practice over a long period of time.

SUGGESTED READINGS

Ardrey, Robert, *African Genesis.* New York, Atheneum, 1961.
   In Ardrey's view man's nature is aggressive, determined by innate fighting instincts passed down from his primate ancestors.
Bandura, Albert, *Principles of Behavior Modification.* New York, Holt, Rinehart and Winston, 1969.
   A comprehensive analysis of basic psychological principles governing human behavior within a social learning framework.
Burgess, Anthony, *A Clockwork Orange,* New York, Norton, 1963; Ballantine, 1971.
   The personality of a young offender is totally altered through operant techniques in prison.
Gagné, Robert M., *The Conditions of Learning,* 3d ed. New York, Holt, Rinehart and Winston, 1974.
   An analysis of the circumstances under which learning takes place and proposals of principles for classroom application.
Guillaume, Paul, *Imitation in Children.* University of Chicago Press, 1971.
   An examination of the factors that lead to the development of learning as imitation of others.
Montagu, Ashley, ed., *Man and Aggression.* New York, Oxford, 1968.
   Fourteen experts consider the view of man as a creature driven by primitive instincts and an in-born aggressive drive.
Skinner, B. F., *About Behaviorism.* New York, Knopf, 1974.
   In his most recent book, the psychologist whose earlier work in operant conditioning led directly to the development of programmed instruction elaborates on his ideas concerning the nature of human behavior, thinking and knowing, emotion, and the question of the Self.
Skinner, B. F., *Beyond Freedom and Dignity.* New York, Knopf, 1971.
   Skinner suggests that certain ideas we have concerning freedom and dignity are "out-worn illusions" and that human behavior is not governed by free will but by responses to environmental stimuli.
Skinner, B. F., *Walden Two.* New York, Macmillan, 1960.
   This novel, perhaps Skinner's best-known work, concerns a behaviorally controlled community.

Chapter Four

Verbal Learning and Memory

What is the difference between learning and remembering?
Why do we forget things?
Why do some people fail to remember names but "never forget a face"?
Does WIS mean more than JYC? Why?
What are short-term memory and long-term memory?
How can you improve your studying?

We saw in Chapter 3 how the principles of classical and operant conditioning contribute to our knowledge of the environment and our interactions with that environment. These principles apply not only to humans but also to birds, rats, lemurs, and many other organisms. *Verbal learning,* however, is all ours. It is distinctly human and, with some exceptions, cannot be studied in other organisms. That is not to say, however, that classical and operant conditioning have nothing to contribute to our understanding of verbal behavior. In fact some psychologists (for example, Skinner, 1957) have used these principles in an attempt to explain one of the most puzzling phenomena—how we acquire our native language.

Language acquisition is really the province of linguists and developmental psychologists (see Chapters 8 and 11). In this chapter we will concentrate on verbal tasks that confront us after we have acquired a language. How do we memorize a poem or learn a grocery list? When someone we meet at a party gives us a telephone number what do we do with it, before we write it down, in order to remember it? In French class, how do the at first meaningless words *la plume* come to mean "the pen"?

The preceding examples raise a number of further questions that must be dealt with and that have perhaps already occurred to you. First, what is the distinction between verbal learning and memory? When we discover that we did not pick up eggs or a carton of milk at the market does this mean that we did not learn the grocery list in the first place or merely that we forgot a few items on the list? The distinction between memory and learning is a tricky one that actually matters more in theory than in practice. In order for learning to occur what is learned must be stored in some form; that is, it must be remembered. Therefore when learning is not demonstrated, one of two things might have happened: (1) the material was not learned in the first place, or (2) there was a failure to retrieve what was learned. In practice, psychologists generally are concerned with learning itself when they concentrate on changes in behavior over different trials, regardless of the time interval between trials. Retention, or memory, is the variable of interest when psychologists are concerned with the interval between trials or with the events that occur during this interval.

Another question that may have crossed your mind is related to the learning of telephone numbers. When someone gives you a telephone number, you repeat it a number of times to yourself until you have an opportunity to write it down. We will see later in the chapter what this type of rehearsal means for transferring what we've learned from a short, temporary type of storage, called *short-term memory,* to a more lasting type of storage, *long-term memory.* Already, it can be seen that verbal learning and memory are not simple processes but complex phenomena that bear on everyday experience. This chapter will concentrate first on the acquisition of verbal materials—how we get information into our heads—and then go on to discuss retrieval of that information—how we get the information out again.

short-term memory
long-term memory

MATERIALS AND METHODS FOR STUDYING ACQUISITION

nonsense syllable

The materials and methods used in verbal learning research vary from experiment to experiment. Verbal materials range from paragraphs to words to nonsense syllables. In this way units of varying meaning can be manipulated.

The nonsense syllable has had a prominent place in the history of verbal learning. Hermann Ebbinghaus, who published the first study of human memory in 1885, invented the nonsense syllable because he did not want prior learning—real words—to contaminate his measure of retention. He reasoned that real words carry previously learned associations that affect the learning of the material and its subsequent recall. He assumed that nonsense syllables are free of such associations and therefore are of uniform difficulty to the learner. They generally take one of two forms: (1) the CVC, or consonant-vowel-consonant (BUJ, RAV, GOX) and (2) the CCC, consisting of three consonants (BKT, RND, CPZ).

Although Ebbinghaus' assumptions about the meaninglessness of nonsense syllables proved not to be completely correct (see p. 181), he did provide

The Bettmann Archive, Inc.

Hermann Ebbinghaus

important information about the nature of serial learning. He learned lists of nonsense syllables by spreading the material out in front of him and reading each syllable once to the beat of a metronome, so that each syllable would be allotted the same amount of attention. He attempted to form mental associations among the syllables on the list. He would then read through the list, attempting with each syllable to anticipate what the next one would be. The complete presentation is known as *serial anticipation learning* and is one of the most commonly used procedures in verbal learning. *Paired-associate learning* and *free recall* are two others that will be discussed in this section.

serial anticipation learning
paired-associate learning
free recall

It should be remembered that procedures using nonsense syllables have been devised for experimental convenience. The kinds of verbal tasks that we perform in everyday life, of course, use quite different materials, but the tasks themselves are essentially the same.

Methods of Verbal Learning

Serial Anticipation Serial anticipation learning is not confined to the laboratory. George Johnson uses the same shopping list each week when he goes to the supermarket. This week, he has forgotten his list. As he goes up and down the aisles, he remembers to buy bread, eggs, milk, cereal, but can't remember what comes next. Is it sugar, or is there something between cereal and sugar that he has forgotten? He tries to think of what he might have used up at home, or he scans the shelves in hopes of seeing the missing item. He then repeats the list mentally. Somehow cereal, beginning with a *c*, has been associated with cheese, which also begins with *c*. He remembers the item and continues his shopping.

In studies of serial anticipation learning the subject is shown a list of words or nonsense syllables, one item at a time, by means of an apparatus called a memory drum (Fig. 4.1). As each item appears in the window of the drum, the apparatus pauses for a preset time. The subject views the entire list once in this manner. On subsequent trials, upon seeing each item, he tries to anticipate what the next item will be before it is presented. Each item serves both as a response to the one preceding it and as a stimulus for the one following it. This process continues until some criterion of learning is reached, usually one or two perfect trials.

Fig. 4.2 illustrates the number of anticipation failures for both words and nonsense syllables as a function of list position (Postman and Rau, 1957). The resulting curves, typical of serial learning, illustrate two important points: (1) words are more easily learned than nonsense syllables; and (2) in both cases, items at the beginning and end of the list are learned more easily than items in the middle. This second point is known as the *serial position effect*.

serial position effect

Paired-Associate Learning The main principle behind paired-associate learning is to establish a relationship between two elements. The first element becomes the stimulus for the second element, which is the response. For ex-

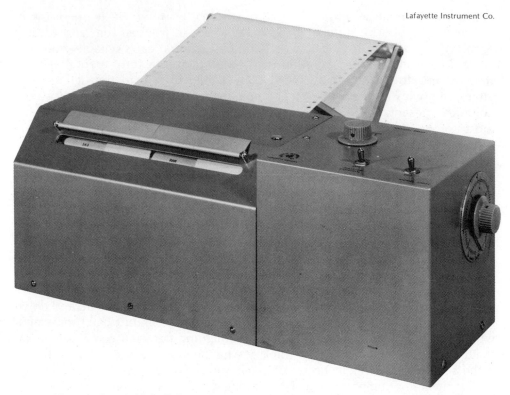

Lafayette Instrument Co.

Fig. 4.1 Memory drum with built-in programmer.

ample, when our French instructor says "the pen" and asks what the French equivalent is, we learn to answer "la plume." When she says "the book," we respond, "le livre." Then we go home and study these words by repeating "the pen—la plume, the book—le livre," in each case trying to build an association between the English word and the French one.

We also learn English synonyms in this manner. For example the word *credence* is a synonym for *belief*. We first learn *credence* by associating it with the word *belief*. Later, as *credence* takes on more and more of its own meaning, we can integrate it into our vocabularies.

In studies employing the paired-associate method, subjects view the material to be learned—words, nonsense syllables, numbers, or some other symbols —in pairs. If the memory drum is used, the sequence of presentation usually is as follows: The first half of the pair is shown alone, then the complete unit; the first half of the next unit, then the full unit; and so on. In a later trial, the subject sees the first half alone and must give the second half before he is shown the full pair.

Free Recall Let us suppose that George Johnson's shopping list contained the following items:

cheese	apples	cookies
grapes	pork	yoghurt
steak	peas	paper towels
milk	lettuce	mustard

He might be able to remember the items by grouping them in categories such as dairy products, meats, and fruits rather than in the order he originally wrote them down.

When free recall is used in the laboratory, the experimenter shows the subject a list of words or reads the list to him, then asks him to try to recall as many items as possible, but not necessarily in the order of presentation. Usually the subjects seek some principle of organization. This procedure therefore usually employs more meaningful material than nonsense syllables. Although free recall does not permit the experimenter to know what stimulus prompted a response, it does shed light on how learned responses are organized (see p. 205).

Ebbinghaus worked within the theoretical framework of stimulus–response association. He therefore designed methods of isolating individual stimulus–response pairs, in order to study how the two constituents are related, and he attempted to eliminate the influence of meaning, mediation, and other factors that might obscure this relationship. Meaning and mediation are, however, properties of most human learning outside the laboratory, and therefore psychologists today are very much concerned with studying them. Some researchers still use Ebbinghaus' methods, but more and more often their conclusions are inadequate just because they have failed to allow for the subject's use of mediators, reorganization of material, and free rehearsal in everyday learning, in which the only correct response is exact reproduction of the learned material.

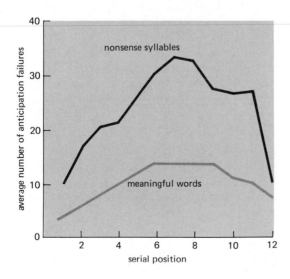

Fig. 4.2 Serial position effect, showing more errors for the middle items in the list to be learned. (Postman and Rau, 1957)

But most verbal learning in everyday life is not literal; we need only to be able to grasp the gist of new material. Psychologists are turning more and more to techniques for studying this kind of learning. Some of the most effective techniques are already familiar to anyone who has taken comprehension examinations: you are asked to *paraphrase* material, to show that you understand concepts well enough to *transfer* them to different situations, and so on.

Characteristics of Verbal Materials

A number of characteristics, such as meaningfulness, similarity, frequency, and concreteness, influence how effectively verbal materials are learned, as does ability to transfer earlier learning to the new learning task.

meaningfulness

Meaningfulness As noted in Fig. 4.2, words are learned more readily than nonsense syllables. Since Ebbinghaus' time, however, researchers have discovered that this is not because nonsense syllables are completely lacking in meaning, as he had believed. Subsequent research has shown that nonsense syllables do, in fact, suggest varying degrees of meaning.

The reader, at this point, should have three questions in mind: How is meaningfulness defined? How is it measured? Why does it have such a great import? Experimenters must answer these questions before they can test the generalization that the more meaningful the items, the quicker they will be learned and the more readily they will be retained.

In most cases, psychologists proceed on the assumption that the meaningfulness of a stimulus word or syllable can be measured by how promptly it suggests an association or by how many associations it suggests. The number of associations is an operational definition of meaningfulness based on the theoretical view that the more connotations, dimensions, and uses a word has, the more meaningful it has become.

Measures of meaningfulness are usually taken in one of two ways: (1) by asking subjects to give as many associations as they can to a word or nonsense syllable in a stipulated period of time, or (2) by asking subjects whether the stem evokes an association or not. In the first method, for example, Noble (1952) printed words on each line of a response sheet. The subject was instructed to write his responses on the same line as the printed word. A time limit of 1 minute was set. These responses are free association responses in that the experimenter has placed no restrictions on the types of responses given. Whether the subjects themselves place restrictions on their responses and if so, what kind of restrictions, is not known.

In the second method, the experimenter tries to determine the association value of nonsense syllables. As he shows each syllable to a subject, he spells it, and the subject indicates either (1) what the syllable means, (2) that it has a meaning that cannot be verbalized, or (3) that it has no meaning. JYC, for example, is usually found meaningless, while FAC and WIS are considered meaningful syllables.

Table 4.1 (A) Association Value or Meaningfulness
for Selected CVC Trigrams[a]

Trigram	% S's	Trigram	% S's	Trigram	% S's
XYF	3	DUJ	13	BUP	34
YEQ	4	BIW	15	LOZ	40
MYV	5	RUV	16	VOX	46
QEJ	6	TIW	18	QIN	50
NIJ	7	QED	20	MYR	58
WUQ	8	HOJ	22	BEK	66
GEX	9	BIQ	24	VIK	74
PYB	10	SIW	26	NEV	80
ZOF	11	DYT	28	DAT	90
NYV	12	TAZ	32	TEX	100

(B) List of Disyllables and the Meaningfulness
Values for them[b]

Disyllable	M value	Disyllable	M value
GOJEY	0.99	BODICE	2.80
NEGLAN	1.04	JITNEY	3.51
BELAP	1.22	PALLET	3.62
XYLEM	1.24	ORDEAL	3.91
QUIPSON	1.26	YEOMAN	4.60
BODKIN	1.39	KENNEL	5.52
ATTAR	1.71	INCOME	6.24
MAELSTROM	1.84	ZEBRA	7.12
ROMPIN	1.90	JELLY	7.70
JETSAM	2.54	ARMY	9.43

[a] The numbers are the percent of subjects indicating that a given syllable is meaningful to them. (Data from Archer, 1960)
[b] The meaningfulness value is defined as the average number of associations given to each disyllable in one minute. (Data from Noble, 1952)
SOURCE: Deese and Hulse (1967)

The resulting meaningfulness values, examples of which are given in Table 4.1, serve as predictors of the rate at which the various items will be learned. It seems that as the meaningfulness of the elements on a list increases, the less time it takes to learn the list. Also, in a paired-associate task, if the stimulus and response items are equated for meaningfulness, fewer errors are made for associates that are high in scaled meaningfulness (Noble and McNeely, 1957) (Fig. 4.3). This generalization also holds for free recall learning. McGeoch (1930) found that subjects could recall more items that were scaled high on the association-value scale.

Why does meaningfulness have such an impact? While psychologists do not agree on the answer to this question, it is known that any variable that makes an item or a response, in the case of paired-associate learning, more *available* increases the chance that that item will be learned and correctly recalled. Availability clearly refers to the distinctiveness of an item.

Pronounceability is a potentially important, yet little understood, relative of meaningfulness. Intuitively, it makes sense that if an item (such as CAT) can

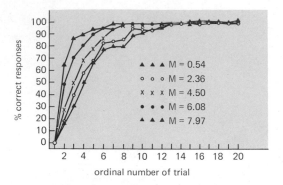

Fig. 4.3 Acquisition curves for single stimu-lus-response pairs as a function of mean-ingfulness ($\overline{m}$). (Noble and McNeely, 1957)

be pronounced, it will be more easily learned than an unpronounceable item (TCA). Underwood and Postman (1960) constructed two lists of high-frequency trigrams (three-letter combinations) that were either words or nonwords and two lists of low-frequency trigrams, either words or nonwords. Each of the 48 items was rated for pronounceability. The researchers found a moderately high correlation of .46 for the pronounceability ratings and the total number of correct anticipations in a serial learning task. Thus pronounceability facilitates mean-ingfulness, probably because it too increases an item's availability.

The differentiation hypothesis states that the characteristics or informa-tion we gain from a given stimulus is used to discriminate it from similar stimuli and thus to increase its availability. Meaningfulness provides some of these characteristics. The more meaningful an item, the more easily we can differen-tiate it from its neighbors in a list. That is why the next variable we will discuss, *similarity,* has an important effect.

Similarity Similarity, though it sounds like a single variable, actually en-compasses four variables. Verbal units may be similar in that they look or sound alike, have the same meaning, belong to the same category, or are associated by someone for his own reasons.

The effect of manipulating similarity depends on the type of similarity and the type of task. The following are some generalizations that can be made about experiments manipulating similarity.

Underwood and Good (1951) used lists of adjectives and found that a list containing the items *elated, gleeful, carefree, jolly, laughing, happy, pleasant, festive, sunny, blissful, genial, smiling, cheerful,* and *hearty* was much more difficult to learn than a list of adjectives that were not synonymous. For serial learning, a list of items becomes more difficult as the similarity in meaning of its items increases. The same occurs when similarity in appearance increases (Underwood and Schultz, 1959).

Paired-associate learning situations provide an opportunity to manipulate similarity either of the stimulus items, the response items, or both concurrently. Most studies find that similarity, either in appearance, meaning, or category, inhibits paired-associate learning. However, similarity has a greater inhibiting

effect on the stimulus side than on the response side. Other studies (Hall, 1971) have shown that similarity between stimulus and response seems to hinder the association of the two, rather than the learning of the discrete responses.

    Frequency The mere frequency with which particular words are encountered also determines how easily they will be learned and retained. Fig. 4.4 shows that in one study subjects were better able to recall words that are frequently seen or heard (Hall, 1954). The experimenter's procedure was to present subjects with a list of 20 words once, then ask them to freely recall as many of the words as possible. While the accuracy with which words were recalled within any one list was uniform, it varied from list to list.

Allen U. Paivio

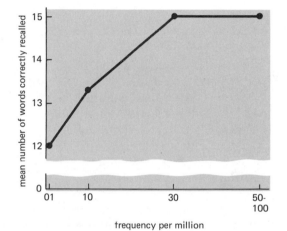

Fig. 4.4 The mean number of words re-called in free recall as a function of the relative frequency (Thorndike-Lorge) of the words presented. (Data from Hall, 1954)

    Frequency, while conceptually different from meaningfulness, seems to act in the same way. We seem to be better able to differentiate the acquired characteristics of frequently seen words so that they are, again, more available to us. Incidentally, word frequency also affects recognition time in tachistoscopic presentations. Generally, the more frequent, or familiar, a word is, the more quickly it is recognized during brief presentations (Solomon and Howes, 1951).

    Concreteness and Imagery The variables concreteness and imagery have gained increasing importance in the study of verbal learning. Concreteness refers to where a verbal item lies on a concrete-abstract dimension. For example, *banana* is more concrete than *fruit*. Paivio, Yuille, and Madigan (1968) have developed a 7-point scale for rating verbal items for concreteness and also for imagery. The study found that these variables are highly related, which means that the more concrete a noun is the better able it is to elicit a mental image. Table 4.2 presents imagery and concreteness ratings for some of the 925 nouns used in the Paivio study (1968).

    Epstein, Rock, and Zuckerman (1960) conducted a paired-associate experiment in which they presented pairs of either (1) pictures of concrete nouns,

concreteness

Table 4.2 Imagery and Concreteness[a]

	Imagery	Concreteness		Imagery	Concreteness
Accordian	6.5	7.0	Glory	4.1	1.8
Afterlife	2.4	1.8	Pride	4.2	1.5
Belief	2.7	1.6	Prison	6.2	6.6
Bird	6.7	7.0	Simile	2.9	4.0
Chance	2.5	1.5	Soul	2.1	1.9
Debacle	2.1	4.0	Surtax	1.6	4.1
Determination	3.6	1.7	String	6.2	6.9
Devotion	3.9	1.5	Unreality	2.1	1.2
Elbow	6.3	6.9	Workhouse	4.0	6.3
Encephalon	2.2	5.1	Yacht	6.8	7.0

[a] Each noun is rated on a 7-point scale, where 7 is maxium imagery (or concreteness) and 1 is minium.
SOURCE: Paivio, Yuille, and Madigan (1968)

(2) concrete nouns, (3) verbs, or (4) abstract nouns. They found that facility of learning declined in that order. A number of studies have found that the concreteness of the stimulus term is more important, in paired-associate learning, than that of the response term. Paivio (1969) has suggested that this is because images elicited by concrete nouns act as "pegs" on which other items may be "hung." We do not know how this process works, but the results suggest that concrete images provide more associations between items. We will discuss such *mediation* in detail shortly.

transfer of training

Transfer The type and amount of past learning we have done also affects our acquisition of new material. Let us consider how this *transfer of training* works in light of the hypothetical case of a traveling cosmetics salesman. He succeeds in selling one woman $50 worth of lotions, essences, and creams by begging her pardon for disturbing her since she obviously has no need of his wares. Flattered, she confesses to having a few minor problems with her skin, though they're not visible to the naked eye, and ends up giving him a generous order. He tries the same strategy on his next prospective customer, and—lo and behold!—it works again. He reaps the benefits of a *positive transfer* of learning from the first situation. By now highly assured, he approaches a third woman with the same comment and is told he is absolutely right—the lady has no need of his wares—and has the door slammed in his face. This represents a *negative transfer*.

What is learned in one situation, then, is sometimes appropriate to another and sometimes not. When it facilitates later learning or performance, it transfers positively; when, on the other hand, it interferes, it transfers negatively.

In the laboratory, paired-associate learning has been used to study the variables affecting transfer. The experimental design is usually in this form:

Experimental group:	Learn Task 1	Learn Task 2
Control group:	Rest	Learn Task 2

Table 4.3 Sample Stimulus-Response Items from the Bruce Experiment on Transfer

Experimental Condition	Relation of S-R Items in the Two Tasks	Task 1		Task 2		Direction of Transfer
		Stimulus	Response	Stimulus	Response	
1	Stimuli dissimilar— responses identical	LAN	QIP	FIS	QIP	Slightly positive
2	Stimuli identical responses dissimilar	REQ	KIV	REQ	ZAM	Negative
3	Stimuli similar— responses identical	BES	YOR	BEF	YOR	Very strongly positive
4	Stimuli identical— responses similar	TEC	ZOX	TEC	ZOP	Slightly positive

SOURCE: Morgan and King (1971); modified from Bruce (1933)

If positive transfer occurs, then the experimental group will do better on Task 2 than the control group; if, however, negative transfer takes place, the experimental group will do less well on Task 2.

Psychologists have found that it is possible to predict whether positive or negative transfer will occur on the basis of how similar the stimulus and response items of paired associates are. Table 4.3 gives the four types of relations between stimulus and response items that were tested for transfer in a well-known study (Bruce, 1933). In this case, the items in both tasks consisted of lists of paired nonsense syllables. From this study and others, the following generalizations about transfer can be made:

1. Positive transfer occurs when one learns to make identical responses to new stimuli (Conditions 1 and 3 of Table 4.3).
2. Negative transfer occurs when one learns to make new (dissimilar) responses to similar or identical stimuli (Condition 2).
3. The degree of transfer, be it positive or negative, depends on stimulus similarity between Tasks 1 and 2; that is, as the stimulus similarity increases, so does the degree of transfer.
4. The direction of the transfer—that is, whether it is positive or negative—depends on response similarity.

The predictive function of these observations is of considerable, even critical, importance. The overall generalizations that similarity of stimuli and of responses produces positive transfer and that dissimilarity of responses produces negative transfer have implications for learning of all kinds. Classroom learning of different materials can be facilitated by emphasizing their similarities. For example, a knowledge of Latin facilitates acquisition of an English vocabulary, or for that matter of a vocabulary in any of the Romance languages, if stress is placed on common roots and word derivation. If you know that the Latin word *atavus* means *ancestor* and you are confronted with the unfamiliar word *atavism,* you may assume that its meaning is related to *ancestor* because of its similarity to the Latin. We will return to discussion of transfer tasks in our section on retrieval.

It is clear from this discussion that learning new verbal material is quicker and easier when that material is meaningful to the subject, sharply distinct from other material to be learned, presented more frequently and in concrete images, and related to earlier learning. All these variables are associated with the material to be learned.

VARIABLES AFFECTING VERBAL LEARNING

Here we will examine some of the variables involved in the way we go about learning verbal materials—that is, the task itself. But first a note of caution. In the introduction to this chapter we discussed the difference between learning— that is, acquisition—and memory, implying that these processes were different sides of the same coin. The reader shold keep this in mind when we examine such concepts as *rehearsal* and *verbal mediation*. These variables also affect memory or retrieval, which is stressed in the next section.

rehearsal
verbal mediation

  Incremental versus Single-Trial Learning

Let us look at a controversy in verbal learning that concerns just how verbal associations are formed. Take, for example, the paired associate *bottle–radio*. According to the incremental learning theory, each time the learner sees the response *radio* paired with the stimulus, *bottle,* the association is strengthened by small increments until finally the correct response is given when the stimulus item is presented alone. However, this view is not accepted by all psychologists. Some, notably Rock (1957), contend that a verbal association is learned on one trial or not learned at all. This view has been called the *all-or-none* theory of verbal learning, and a look at Fig. 4.5 will illustrate the conflicting theories.

Rock (1957) gave a paired-associate task to two groups of subjects and counted the number of trials each group needed to give one perfect recitation of a complete list. The control group always saw the same list, but for the experimental group, every time an error was made a new paired associate replaced the one that was not responded to correctly. Rock reasoned that if no incremental learning occurred the experimental group should need no more trials to learn a complete list than the control group, and this is what he found.

Fig. 4.5 Schematic representation of the learning of a single paired associate as explained by an incremental theory and by an all-or-none theory. The response was first given correctly after the fourth trial. At that point, according to the incremental theory, the strength of the association between the two members of the pair had become great enough to control the verbal response. According to the all-or-none theory, all the learning takes place on the fourth trial. Note that the exact shape of the incremental curve may be different from the one here, which is used for illustrative purposes.

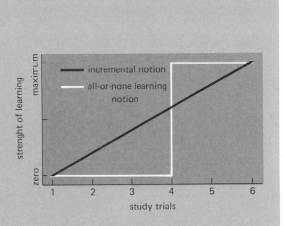

Rock's study has been highly criticized, however. It has been pointed out that the experimental group and the control group received different instructions (Sultz, 1971). And when new items were substituted in the experimental list, they were apparently not controlled for difficulty (Underwood, Rebula, and Keppel, 1962). Martin (1965) solved the problem of list difficulty by having both an experimental group and a control group learn the same final list. However, on the first two trials, for three critical paired associates, the experimental group saw the same stimulus and response terms as the control group but they were paired differently on each trial. After two trials the three critical items were the same as those on the control list. Martin found that the control group learned the three pairs significantly more quickly than the experimental group and concluded that there must have been some incremental learning.

The theoretical controversy has waned on this question, in part because no technique appears to offer an unambiguous test between the two approaches. In this sense, it can be argued that there is no controversy, even if the theories appear to differ intuitively.

Rehearsal

In general, whenever it is necessary to remember a telephone number, a book title, or any other newly acquired information, we consciously repeat that information over and over again. This silent, inner, repetitive speech is called *rehearsal.*

The classic experiment on short-term memory was performed by Peterson and Peterson (1959), who gave subjects a three-consonant trigram followed by a number and asked the subjects to count backwards by threes from that number

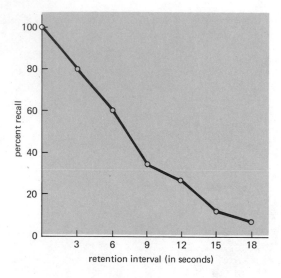

Fig. 4.6 Retention curve for short-term memory   When rehearsal is prevented, recall of information stored in short-term memory decays rapidly. (Peterson and Peterson, 1959)

until a signal was given and then to recall the trigram. The number task was designed to prevent rehearsal of the trigram. Fig. 4.6 shows the effect of preventing rehearsal when subjects were asked to recall the nonsense syllable after 3, 6, 9, 12, 15, and 18 seconds.

If we assume that acquisition of a single nonsense syllable is perfect and could not be affected by interference (the counting task), the Peterson task is one affecting retrieval. On the other hand, even though only a single item is to be learned in this task, if the subject is given no opportunity to rehearse it, we may just as reasonably state that the learning process was never completed.

Rehearsal appears to serve two functions. First, it allows items in short-term memory to be retained indefinitely. Secondly, it seems to aid in transferring material from short-term to long-term memory (see p. 178). Fig. 4.7 is a schematic representation of this process.

Rehearsal or silent speech takes place at about the same rate as spoken speech (Lindsay and Norman, 1972). You can measure your own rate of silent

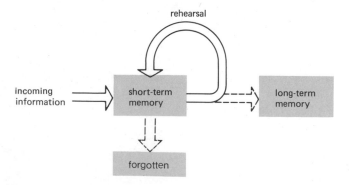

Fig. 4.7 Short- and long-term memory diagram.

speech by counting from 1 to 10 silently, and then starting over again, each time making a scratch mark on a piece of paper. Do this for 10 seconds and then count the marks plus whatever number you just passed. A score of 78 means that you rehearse 7.8 digits per second.

When studying a French lesson is it better to spend 3 seconds on each new word, go over the list once, or 1 second on each item and go over it three times? In each case the total *presentation time* is the same, but is one method better than the other?

Most studies have shown that within certain limits, it doesn't matter which method you use, that it is the *total* learning time that is important. Bugelski (1962), for example, gave subjects a paired-associate task (CVC's) in which items were presented for 6, 8, 10, 12, or 19 seconds. The subjects had to learn the list until they could name each response item twice correctly. As Table 4.4 shows, even though the shorter presentation time required more trials, the total expo-sure time (trials × presentation time) remained almost constant.

Murdock (1962) got similar results in a free recall experiment in which the number of words recalled was studied in relation to presentation time. Mur-dock presented lists of 10, 15, and 20 words at a rate of 2 seconds per word; he also presented other lists of 20, 30, and 40 words at 1 second per word. This generated three comparable total time conditions: 10–2 and 20–1, 15–2 and 30–1, and 20–2 and 40–1. The mean number of words recalled varied only as a function of total time and not of individual presentation rate.

Why is total time spent learning so important as opposed to individual presentation rate and number of trials? While this question has not been fully answered, the invariance in total learning time may be due to rehearsal. That is, it may be the amount of time spent in rehearsing a given item that is impor-tant. But even if this is so, presentation rate must not be too fast or too slow. If one looks at a French verb and its English equivalent too fast, no time is allowed for rehearsal. Too long a time on each item, on the other hand, allows lapses in attention with a resultant loss in rehearsal.

The idea that rehearsal may be responsible for the invariance of total presentation time, no matter how it is divided up, is an inference, since silent speech cannot be observed. However, Rundus and Atkinson (1970) have con-

Table 4.4 Memory Trials and Total Time To Learn
Lists (In seconds)

Presentation Time per Item To Be learned	Trials Needed To Learn List	Total Exposure Time of Each Item on List
6	10.2	61.2
8	8.8	70.1
10	5.8	57.9
12	4.7	56.1
19	3.3	62.2

SOURCE: Bugelski (1962)

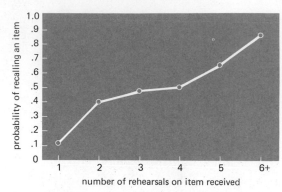

Fig. 4.8 The probability of recalling an item as a function of the number of rehearsals of the item. (Rundus and Atkinson, 1970)

ducted a study in which they attempted to directly observe the rehearsal process and its effects on retention in a free recall experiment. Lists of 20 nouns were given to subjects at the rate of one every 5 seconds. Subjects were instructed to study the items aloud during the 5-second intervals, and a tape recording was made to count the number of rehearsals each item received. Fig. 4.8 shows the probability of recalling an item as a function of the number of rehearsals it got.

Is rehearsal necessary for learning? There is no absolute answer to this question, but in most contexts it is. The few exceptions seem to be for highly dramatic material, such as the deadly insults screamed in a quarrel, or for material that is well organized to begin with, such as stories or nursery rhymes. We do not know how such learning occurs. One possibility connected with dramatic material is that the subject continues to think about it, a form of rehearsal. Perhaps also high doses of emotion cause transfer from short-term to long-term memory without further rehearsal. We will come to this problem again on p. 197 in the discussion of incremental versus all-or-none learning.

Mediation

We are fairly certain that simple stimulus–response associations do not account for most verbal learning. For one reason, such associations do not seem to be unitary; for example, a stimulus such as "ball" can call up several different responses. Which response is actually given must therefore be determined by factors that occur *between* the stimulus and the particular response. The stimulus–response association is thus more complex than Ebbinghaus and others have assumed. The *mediating* factors, some of which arise in the learning situation itself and some of which are transferred from previous learning, are crucial in the organization of learning, as we will see later in this chapter.

Given the problem of associating the words *dog* and *nine,* is there some third term that will help to build this association? What is involved in this question is the principle of mediation, that is, using a third, implicit term in order

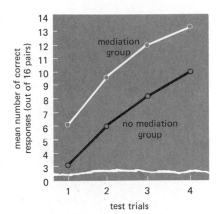

Fig. 4.9 Mean number of pairs learned correctly over four trials as a function of whether a mediator was suggested to the learner. Having a mediator available increased learning by about three items. (Wood and Bolt, 1968)

to associate two other items. "Cat" would be an appropriate mediator in the above example, just as "party" can serve as a mediator for *democratic* and *birthday*. Mediators are usually subjectively generated items that have something in common with both original terms.

Jenkins (1963) illustrates three ways in which mediation can work in a paired-associate task. Let us say that the association *pipe-leaves* is to be learned. The response can be *chained* so that *pipe* (A) elicits *fire* (B), which in turn elicits *leaves* (C). This is the paradigm used in studying idiosyncratic mediators called *natural language mediators. Stimulus equivalence* results when A and C elicit the same response, as *democratic* and *birthday* both elicit *party*, while *responsive equivalence* occurs when the mediator elicits both A and C terms, as *record* might for the paired associate *stop-hop*.

natural language mediator

A study by Wood and Bolt (1968) illustrates the facilitative effects on learning of the use of mediators in a paired-associate task. The stimuli (A terms) were letters while the responses (C terms) were high-frequency words. An experimental group was given a mediator that started with the same letter as the stimulus term and in addition was highly associated with the response term,

Natural Language Mediators
Memory Trials and Total Time To Learn Lists (In Seconds)

In the experiment by Wood and Bolt (1968) subjects were supplied mediators to help them learn a paired-associate task. However, we often generate our own, subjective, idiosyncratic mediators that are often bizarre and frequently unique. Adams and his colleagues (Adams, 1967; Adams and Montague, 1967; Montague, Adams, and Kriess, 1966) have labeled these self-imposed mediators natural language mediators (NLM's) because they are generated from the person's rich lan-

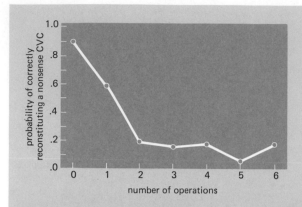

Fig. 4.10 From Prytulak (1971).

guage habits. As an example, suppose you are given the pair *cat–rat* to learn. You might impose your own mediational device to remember the pair; for example, you may note that they have two letters in common, or that they rhyme, or you may imbed them in a sentence such as "Cat eats rat" (Adams, 1967).

Prytulak (1971) has developed a theory of how natural language mediation works. Let us say a subject is shown the nonsense syllable PYN. This is known as the nominal stimulus, that which the subject is shown in the laboratory. The nominal stimulus is then encoded into a functional stimulus such as "PIN-with-a-Y." According to Prytulak the subject remembers the natural language mediator PIN along with a decoding instruction "with-a-Y," which allows the mediator PIN to be transformed back into the nominal stimulus PYN. The theory goes on to state that the success of decoding the NLM is a function of the complexity of the transformations (T's) or in other words the number of "operations" that have to be performed on the nominal stimulus to convert it into an NLM. Changing the nonsense syllable FET to PET would involve one operation—"Change F to P"—while changing LYV to LIVE would involve two operations—"Change Y to I and add E." In a test of this model, Prytulak gave subjects a list of nonsense syllables and had them write down their NLM's. It was found that the probability of recalling a CVC was dependent, as can be seen in Fig. 4.10, on the number of operations in the transformation.

for example T(table)–chair; K(king)–queen. A control group was not given the mediators, and of course test trials, in which the subjects had to provide the responses to the stimulus letters, omitted mediators. Fig. 4.9 shows how powerful the use of mediators can be.

Mediators in verbal learning do not themselves have to be verbal. Paivio and Foth (1970) compared a group of subjects who were required to draw a mediational picture for noun pairs to a group who used verbal mediators. Subjects who used imagery (pictures) recalled more noun pairs when the paired associates were "concrete," while the subjects who used verbal mediators re-called more items when the terms were "abstract." This seems to indicate that imagery is a better mediational device when an image is evoked, as in the case of concrete-noun paired associates. However, when an image is not easily evoked, as in the case of abstract words, then verbal mediators are more facilita-tive.

RETRIEVAL OR REMEMBERING

Just about everyone has had the experience of taking a test and not being able to remember the answer to one or more questions. You might say to yourself that you studied the material and know just where in your notes the answer is, but still no answer comes to mind. What happened? One of two things may have occurred: either (1) the answer was not learned or (2) the answer cannot be retrieved from memory.

So far, we have discussed how verbal information is acquired or learned, and the factors that affect that acquisition. Variables such as meaningfulness, similarity, and imagery of verbal materials have been discussed and their effects on the acquisition process noted. When we talk about memory rather than learning, the acquisition process is called *encoding*. A second mnemonic process is *storage*. After a new poem is learned or encoded, how and where is it stored? *Retrieval* is the utilization of stored information.

retrieval

When information is stored in memory it is said to be *available*. A distinc-tion must be made, however, between availability and *accessibility,* which is important in the retrieval process, or getting at the stored information. Mandler (1967) has made this distinction by means of an analogy. Think of words in a person's vocabulary, writes Mandler, as equivalent to books in a library. Now, obviously, any book in the library may be available, but it is only accessible if one knows where to find it. This is the problem of retrieval—how to find what's already there.

Forgetting, then, is a failure of retrieval. In terms of Mandler's analogy, it is the inability to find the desired book in the library. But why does retrieval fail? Is it because learning was inadequate; that is, did we not learn the material well enough to retrieve it, even though it may be in storage? Can retrieval fail even with adequate learning? What does the structure of the memory system have to do with retrieval failure? We have noted earlier that there are actually two storage facilities, a limited capacity, short-duration *short-term memory* and a storage system with supposedly unlimited capacity called *long-term memory*. Does retrieval fail because material failed to get into long-term memory, or can there be failure also for items in long-term memory? These are some current questions that psychologists working in the field of memory are asking, and we will see how they are going about answering them. But first let us look at how we can measure what is in storage.

Measures of Retention

Empirically, retention has been assessed in three ways: by recall, recognition, and relearning.

recall

Recall The measure of retention most easily produced in the laboratory is recall. Typically, a subject learns some material—for instance, a list of nonsense syllables—then, after a specified period of time, tries to reproduce it. The percentage of responses accurately remembered yields the *recall score*. Recall may be *rote* (verbatim), in which case the reproduction of the material learned is precise. This is typical of the kind of memory required for verbal learning tasks in the laboratory and for such material as algebraic formulas or lines in a play to be produced.

The more usual type of recall, however, is *reconstruction,* which is a partial, often abstracted, but very sensitive reproduction of the information. If you were to be tested tomorrow on the material you are now reading, you would be expected to summarize the essential ideas presented, not to reproduce the exact wording of it (unless you had a very unreasonable instructor). Similarly, when testifying in a court of law, you are asked to remember occurrences of major importance. You are not suspected of perjury if you cannot recall every minute detail of past events.

If we measure the information retained by rote recall or reconstruction, we find that people generally do not remember very much. Recall is not as sensitive a measure as recognition and relearning; however, sometimes it is the only appropriate method. Grocery shopping is not considered successful unless all the desired items are retrieved. Similarly, reciting a poem cannot be accomplished by merely recognizing that poem, but is only successful if all the words are recalled in the right sequence. So, while we can talk about the comparative sensitivity of different measures of retention, it is important to recognize that only certain measures may be appropriate for a given situation.

Recognition A measure of retention that is commonly relied upon in everyday life and that is more sensitive than recall is recognition. Many a student has breathed a sigh of relief when given multiple-choice rather than essay questions on a final exam in such subjects as history and biology, which require extensive memorization. He knows he has stored up a good deal of information that he can recognize as accurately represented if he sees it but that he cannot recall it at will. Although a child lost at a crowded beach may not be able to tell the lifeguard where his mother is encamped, he will probably recognize familiar landmarks when he is taken back over the terrain.

The psychologist measures a subject's recognition by asking him if a particular stimulus item is one he has learned on a previous trial or one he has never seen before. In a variation of this technique, the subject views a number of items at once and picks out any he remembers from earlier presentations. In the same way, we might meet an acquaintance on the street, recognize him as someone we know, perhaps by his unique hairstyle or manner of walk, yet not recall his name, although we have been introduced to him before. Thus, even if we are unable to recall something, we still can recognize it.

Relearning Another sensitive, although more indirect, measure of retention is relearning. It is based on the assumption that one needs less time to learn material on a second try, after an intervening period of time, than one needed to learn it originally. Most people who think they have entirely forgotten a language they once knew well, for instance, are pleasantly surprised at the comparative ease with which they are able to relearn it.

The experimental procedure for testing relearning is to record how long a subject takes to meet some standard of performance on a verbal task—say, two consecutive recalls without errors. After a specific interval, the subject relearns the material until he can meet the same standard again. The *saving*—that is, the time saved on the second trial—is then converted into a percentage by means of a formula:

$$\text{Saving score} = 100 \left[\frac{\text{Original trials} - \text{Relearning trials}}{\text{Original trials}} \right]$$

relearning

saving score

This was the measure Ebbinghaus used to test for retention of his lists of nonsense syllables. In one study, he learned seven lists until he could recite them twice perfectly. In each case, he waited for a different length of time—ranging from a minimum of 20 minutes to a maximum of 31 days—before relearning the list to the same criterion. As indicated in Fig 4.11, his retention diminished rapidly. After 20 minutes, the saving score was already only about 60 percent, and, at the end of 2 hours, it had declined to below 30 percent.

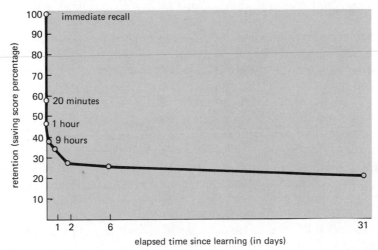

Fig. 4.11 Retention curve Retention of lists of nonsense syllables was measured by relearning. The dependent variable is the saving score percentage. (Ebbinghaus, 1885)

A study by Burtt (1941) furnishes an extreme example of the sensitivity of relearning as a measure of retention. Burtt read the same three selections of Greek literature (in Greek) to a boy about 1 year old every day for 3 months. Then he read the boy three new selections daily for another 3 months. He maintained this regimen until he had read 21 selections in all. At the ages of 8, 14, and 18 the boy memorized selections from the original material, in addition to similar passages that were completely new to him. At no time did the boy actually study Greek. Burtt found that at 8 the boy needed 30 percent fewer repetitions to relearn the old material than to learn the new; by the age of 14 there was only an 8 percent saving; and at 18 there was no saving at all. The relearning measure showed that as long as 5 years after the boy's first acquaintance with the literature the effects of the early learning were still sufficiently retained to facilitate memorization.

Factors Affecting Retrieval

We will now look at some of the variables that may affect retrieval of items from memory. A lot of empirical work has attempted to discover why there are failures in retrieving certain information. After we have looked at the major factors in forgetting, we will discuss what we can do to improve the chance of retrieval.

decay

Decay   According to the theory of decay, we forget what we have learned because it falls into disuse. This view regards forgetting as an organic process that is a function of the passage of time. The memory "tract" physically changes, with the result that it is no longer available for retrieval.

You may find corroboration for this explanation in your experience. You read a newspaper article, vowing to get the international monetary situation straight once and for all; but even as you are putting the paper aside, you find that already you cannot remember the major points. In a similar vein, how many times have you looked up the same word in the dictionary and found minutes later that you have forgotten the definition? Such common occurrences as these seem to lend credence to the decay theory.

Certain objections to this view have been raised, however. To begin with, the decay theory presents a logical problem: time in and of itself does not have causal properties. That is, processes occur *in* a given time period but not *because* of that time period. For example, it is not time that causes a pipe to rust, but oxidation. However, a certain amount of time must pass before oxidation can occur. Empirically, time may be a useful variable when the causal process (that which happens in time) is unknown. Another objection to the decay theory is based on the fact that long-lost memories from childhood are often recovered, for example, by people growing senile or by those in delirium. Despite their "disuse," then, such memories have not disappeared.

On the other hand, some evidence supports the decay theory. For one thing, experiments dealing with storage of sensory information (sensory register)

Penfield's Work with Epileptics

Epilepsy was until recently a little understood disease that had fascinated men for centuries. Hippocrates speculated about its origin, Julius Caesar was subject to its seizures, and Doestoevsky (himself an epileptic) described it vividly, through his character Prince Mishkin, in *The Idiot.*

Epilepsy is now understood to be a disease caused by an electrical disturbance in the cerebral cortex of the brain. The cerebral cortex is composed of *gray matter,* consisting of collections of cell bodies, and *white matter,* the nerve fibers which conduct electrical impulses. As long as the gray matter is normal, the electrical energy is used in a functional, coordinated, way. But if the gray matter is damaged by injury or disease, the regulating mechanisms which normally control electrical discharge becomes inhibited in some way. (Penfield and Roberts, 1959). The area affected (called an *epileptogenic focus*) becomes a self-discharging electrochemical unit. In such an area excess electrical energy is formed, and from time to time mass discharges of electrical energy may be released, resulting in an *epileptic fit* or seizure. The energy is propagated along the nerve fibers and in that way involves other areas of the brain. When the electrical disturbances are limited, the seizure may be small, hence the term *petit seizure.* When extensive, a *grand mal* fit results in convulsions and unconsciousness. Sometimes a visual aura occurs in which the epileptic may see lights of different shapes. The case of R. S. N., described by Penfield and Jasper, 1954, is illustrative of this.

> Each attack was ushered in by an awareness of a light which was cone-shaped. The wide part of the cone was well out to his left in the field of vision and the small end of the cone was directly in front of him. He said the light looked like a shaft of sunlight in which small particles of dust were moving.
>
> One such attack was as follows: The patient became aware of the usual visual aura. He remembered that following this, he went to the bathroom and that he found himself breathing deeply but had no further memory of the incident. Nurse Ann Johnson followed as he left his bed and observed that he staggered. In the bathroom, he voided in normal fashion and then sat down on a chair where he remained for 2 or 3 minutes. During this time he told Miss Johnson that he had the headache which ordinarily preceded an attack. She asked if he was seeing the "lights." He replied, "No."
>
> Following this, Miss Johnson observed trembling of the right arm and right leg. "The hand trembled like a leaf." During this trembling he still appeared to be conscious. Finally, the left arm was raised, the head and eyes turned to the left, and he fell from his chair in a generalized tonic and clonic convulsive seizure. (p. 122)

Wilder Penfield, a neurosurgeon at the Montreal Neurological Institute, and his colleagues have performed over a thousand operations to relieve epileptic seizures when the use of anticonvulsant drugs, the usual method of treatment, has failed to arrest the symptoms. The usual procedure is to open the skull, which exposes the brain, and surgically remove the affected area. In order to do this, however, Penfield uses a stimulating electrode to map out the epileptogenic focus. The patient remains conscious during the operation (through the use of a local anesthetic) and reports any reaction to the stimulating electrode. During the course of these many operations Penfield became aware that when the focus was in the temporal lobe, the electrode would evoke memories from the recent as well as the more remote past of his patients. Penfield's cases J. T. and G. F. are illustrations of what happens:

> When the current was switched on, the patient cried out in great surprise: "Yes, Doctor, yes Doctor. Now I hear people laughing—my friends in South Africa." He was asked if he could recognize who these friends were and he replied, "Yes, they are two cousins, Bessie and Ann Wheliaw." (p. 137)

> During the course of operation upon this woman's right temporal lobe, stimulation of the superior temporal cortex as it lay upon the insula was carried out. It caused her to say, "I just heard one of my children speaking." She added that it was "Frank" and that she could hear the "neighborhood noises" as well—by which she meant automobiles passing her house, and other children. When the same point was restimulated, she said she heard the neighborhood noises but not Frank. (p. 137)

Though this exploitation of a rare research opportunity, Penfield has provided evidence for what he calls a "permanent memory record." Penfield believes that, "Whenever a normal individual is paying conscious attention to something he is simultaneously recording it in the temporal cortex of each hemisphere." (Penfield, 1951, p. 23–24). What is more, Penfield believes that an intrinsic permanent memory record exists even when forgetting, or to paraphrase Penfield, in more recent terms, a failure at retrieving the record, occurs.

The idea of a permanent memory record, if true, means that there is a relatively large discrepancy between recall and stored events. This has led psychologists to speculate (e.g., Adams, 1967) that the barrier might be broken down through as yet undeveloped techniques, giving us virtually unlimited recall.

have shown that such information does decay (see discussions of perception and information processing in Chapters 2 and 7). Other experiments concerning short-term memory also support this notion. We will turn to these later in the chapter in the section on memory. However, the relevance to later storage of these early processes in acquisition has not been established, and it should be kept in mind that time is often evoked as an explanation when the real processes are unknown. In general, then, there does not appear to be very much evidence for the decay theory, even though it has a certain common-sense appeal.

interference

Interference The variable that has received the most attention in studies concerned with forgetting or failure of retrieval has been interference. Briefly the interference theory states that when we are unsuccessful in our attempt to retrieve something from memory, other information—stored either before or after the sought information—has interfered. The interference factor is actually a dual factor, including both *retroactive inhibition,* the interference of new learning with old, and *proactive inhibition,* the interference of material learned earlier with what is learned later. Fig. 4.12 shows the experimental designs used to investigate both phenomena.

retroactive
inhibition

Retroactive Inhibition Retroactive inhibition is the interference of new learning in the retrieval of old learning. Studying this evening for a chemistry

Proactive Inhibition   *Retroactive Inhibition*

EXPERIMENTAL GROUP   EXPERIMENTAL GROUP

Learn B ⟶ Learn A ⟶ Recall A   Learn A ⟶ Learn B ⟶ Recall A

CONTROL GROUP   CONTROL GROUP

Learn A ⟶ Recall A   Learn A ⟶ Recall A

Fig. 4.12 Experimental designs used to investigate proactive and retroactive inhibition.

exam may interfere with your ability to recall tomorrow the history you studied yesterday.

In order to determine whether retroactive inhibition is taking place, we compare for recall of List A a control group that has studied nothing since List A (Fig. 4.12) with an experimental group that has studied something in the interval.

Besides formal interpolated activity, the commonplace activities of everyday waking life also have adverse effects upon retention. Jenkins and Dallenbach (1924) tested subjects for recall after both a normal waking regimen and a period of sleep. They asked two students to learn a list of 10 nonsense syllables so that they could recite them once perfectly. The students were tested 1, 2, 4, and 8 hours after learning the syllables, and they spent the intervals either sleeping or in daily activity. While some forgetting occurred during the first hour or two of sleep, very little took place throughout the rest of the sleep period. When awake, however, the students forgot considerably more (Fig. 4.13).

Proactive Inhibition When psychologists test for proactive inhibition, they ask the experimental group to learn List B *before* List A, while the control learns only the latter. Both groups are then asked to recall List A. A superior performance by the control group would indicate that learning List B proactively interfered with the retention of List A.

proactive inhibition

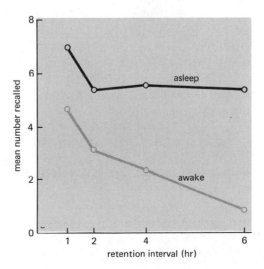

Fig. 4.13 Recall after intervals of sleep or waking. (Data from Jenkins and Dallenbach, 1924)

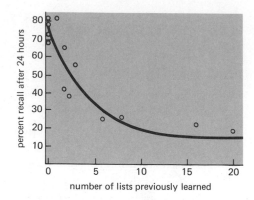

Fig. 4.14 Proactive inhibition Each dot represents results from one experiment. For those experiments in which the subject had less previous experience in list-learning, the amount retained after an interval of a day was greater than in those in which the subject had learned many prior lists. (Underwood, 1957)

Underwood (1957) has shown that proactive inhibition can have major effects on the learning of verbal materials in the laboratory. Fig. 4.14, in fact, shows that the number of lists a subject learned prior to the material he was asked to recall directly influenced forgetting; that is, as the number of lists learned earlier increased, so did forgetting of the succeeding material.

Proactive and retroactive inhibition can occur in our studies as well as in the laboratory. Memorizing a list of Spanish words either before or after learning a list of French words might interfere with retention of the French words.

tip-of-the-tongue state (TOT)

Momentary Failures of Accessibility: Tip-of-the-Tongue Phenomenon Sometimes when we are trying to recall a familiar name or place, we have the feeling that we know the word but cannot recall it. This phenomenon has been called the tip-of-the-tongue (TOT) state. It is an appropriate name for a sometimes tormenting and frustrating feeling.

Brown and McNeill (1966), in an investigation of the TOT state, found that the words that come to mind during a frustrated search for a target word have certain characteristics in common with the target word. They read definitions of infrequently used English words (*cloaca, ambergris, sampan*) to college students. A TOT state was said to occur when the subject felt he knew the word being defined but was unable to recall it.

The majority of words that came to mind during the TOT state were similar in sound to the target word (*Siam* or *sarong* for *sampan*). An analysis of these words also revealed that the subject can often specify the number of syllables in the target word and the initial letter.

This study is one of many attempts to find out more about the retrieval process and how words are stored. Long-term memory for words and their meanings is known as *semantic memory*, and is covered in more detail in Chapter 7.

repression

Repression Repression is a concept of "motivated forgetting" that was first proposed by Freud, who noted that people often unconsciously prevent the recall of certain painful memories in order to avoid the anxiety associated with them. In psychoanalytic terms, repression is a defense mechanism of the

Free Association as an Aid to Memory

Sometimes we register more than we realize. A frequent experience that illustrates this is trying to recall for a friend who was present at a party. You may rattle off nine or ten names and then be unable to recall more, though you know you knew more people at the party. But if you remember a political issue that was discussed at the party, you may immediately remember two or three more people. Here the information (names) was registered but was not conscious; that is, you could not recall the last two or three names.

Haber and Erdelyi (1967) conducted an experiment that demonstrates the recovery of previously unavailable information by the use of free association.

Subjects (40 male undergraduates at Yale) were shown the picture at the top of Fig. 4-15. It depicts a cotton gin in the South and was chosen because the scene was thought to be unfamiliar to most of the subjects. The picture includes such things as a loading platform, a suction pipe, a wagon, a horse, workers, bales of cotton, several buildings, roads, trees, and the like. This picture was flashed on a screen for 100 milliseconds. Thirty of the 40 subjects were shown the stimulus picture and were then asked to produce the general kind of drawing of the picture that is shown in the middle of the figure. The experimenters urged the subjects not to leave out any detail. Then the 30 subjects were divided into a group of 20 (the experimental group) and another of 10. Each subject in the experimental group was told to look at the blank screen and, concentrating on what he had just seen, to free associate in the form of single discrete words. The first 12 words called out in this way were recorded and each of those words was in turn pre-

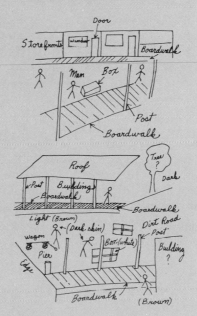

Fig. 4.15 The stimulus (top) and the recall drawings for one selected experimental subject. (Haber and Erdelyi, 1967)

sented to the subject, who associated 10 more words to each of the original 12, making 132 associations in all. The control group played darts with the experimenter for a comparable length of time without free associating. Another group of 10 was called a "yoked-control" group because each subject was "yoked" to an experimental subject. These subjects viewed the drawings that their yoked partners had produced, but not the original photograph. They were asked to copy the drawing and then were given the same free association task as the experimental subjects.

Finally, all 40 subjects were asked to draw the scene again, and the experimenters scored the drawings (which allowed a comparison between the first and second drawings) for content. The drawing at the bottom of the figure is what one of the experimental subjects produced. Only the experimental group showed a significant improvement in recovering information (Table 4.5). The dart-control group did less well on the second drawing than on the first, and while the yoked-control group improved, the difference is not of the same magnitude as the difference the experimental subjects showed. The latter result seems to indicate that initial exposure to the stimulus is necessary for recovery of correct, and not merely probable, information.

Table 4.5 Mean Recall Scores for the Experimental Dart-Control and Yoked-Control Groups on Three Scoring Indices

	Overall Rating		
Group	Average Score for 1st Drawing	Average Score for 2nd Drawing	Difference or Recovery Score
Experimental	36.0	51.8	15.8
Dart-Control	38.5	32.0	−6.5
Yoked-Control	25.5	31.5	6.0

ego, which prevents painful memories from passing from the unconscious into consciousness. The main point is that repression is clearly a block in retrieval of painful memories; it is not simply forgetting. Sometimes repressed events can only be recalled with the aid of intensive psychotherapy using free association or hypnosis. Repressing may block out neutral events that happen to be associated in some way with the main event.

How To Improve Retrieval

Between interference, decay, repression, and so on, how is it that we retain anything at all? Is it hopeless to study French now because *that* learning will

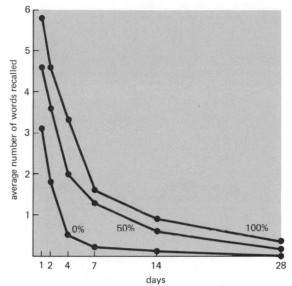

Fig. 4.16 Subjects who had already memorized a group of words were divided into groups which either practiced the words again for the same amount of time it had taken them to learn the words originally (100%), practiced the words for half the time it took to learn them originally (50%), or did not practice at all (0%). The 100% group recalled about twice as many words on each of six later tests, though by the 28th day, recall was very low for all groups. (Ruch and Zimbardo, 1971; data from Krueger (1929)

be interfered with, or repressed, later by something else? The answer is a qualified no—qualified because certain things can be done to aid the process of retrieval.

Overlearning The first and most important way to avoid interference is to overlearn the material in the first place. The better something is learned—and overlearning involves rehearsing material over and over—the more resistant that information is to interference. Or, in other words, the better something is learned, the more accessible it is. Fig. 4.16 illustrates the effect of *overlearning* as it was demonstrated in a classic study done by Krueger (1929). It can be seen that both the group that spent the same amount of time overlearning as they spent on original learning (100 percent) and the group that spent one-half the original time on overlearning (50 percent) had considerably higher recall scores than the group that spent no time overlearning (0 percent).

Organization Another helpful way to resist the effects of interference is to organize the material learned in some way, so that it is unified and at the same time segregated from competing elements. If one studies Spanish verbs connected with sports and French nouns connected with cooking, the different organizations of the two word lists should help deter interference of one with the other.

In a series of verbal learning studies, Bousfield and his associates presented subjects with lists of words for free recall (Bousfield, 1953; Bousfield, Cohen, and Whitmarsh, 1958). Typically, the lists contained 64 items, which fell evenly into four conceptual categories, 16 items to a category. The four categories might be, for example, names of animals, professions, vegetables, and minerals. In order to test whether organization influenced recall, the experi-

overlearning

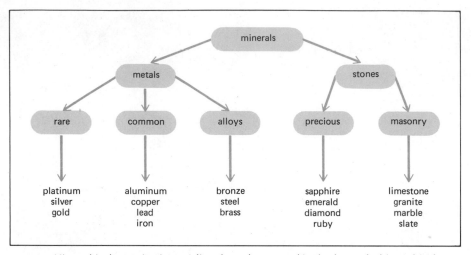

Fig. 4.17 **Hierarchical organization**   A list of words arranged in the form of a hierarchical tree. Trees of this sort have a simple construction rule; all items below a node are included in the class whose label is appended to the node. The same rule for constructing the tree also serves as an effective retrieval plan when a person is trying to remember the list of words. (Bower, 1970)

menters presented the items randomly—the members of the four categories were thus intermixed—and then asked subjects to recall as many items as they could in any order they wished. The subjects tended to cluster the items together in their original categories.

Recall, then, can be facilitated by any organization the learner can impose on the material. In fact, the greater the organization, the greater the recall. Bower (1970) asked subjects to learn four separate lists of words that could be arranged in a hierarchical order. Some subjects viewed the items in hierarchical order (Fig. 4.17), while others saw them for the same amount of time in random order. The recall score for the subjects exposed to the hierarchical slides averaged 65 percent, as compared with only 19 percent for subjects exposed to the random-order lists.

chunking

Chunking When confronted with the task of memorizing verbal material, we tend to break it down into *chunks,* that is, already familiar units. Miller (1956), among other psychologists, has determined that people have relatively fixed capacities for short-term memory—generally seven chunks plus or minus about two chunks depending upon the test. Although these numbers remain relatively constant, the chunks themselves can vary a great deal in complexity and length. Thus, if presented with a list of unrelated letters, and asked to recall them after a few moments of study, we should expect to be able to remember about seven of them, regardless of how many had been presented. However, if the letters are arranged to spell familiar words, then we will remember up to about seven of the words, even though these seven words may now contain from 25 to 50

George A. Miller

letters in total. If the words are arranged so as to form meaningful sentences, we should be able to remember up to about seven of them, even though they may total up to 50 words, made up of several hundred letters. If the sentences form paragraphs, each of which contain a different and unrelated cosmic idea,

Table 4.6 Some Sample Approximations to English[a]

Zero-order Approximation

OUTFLOW FESTOON SHEAVES CANNOT LUMINOUS VELVET TRACTION DETESTABLE MUSLIN INTERPOLATION CENTAUR AMAZINGLY VICINITY WOBBLE PRECLUDE MISCHANCE RECIPROCAL BANDBOX FRITTER BEAMING DIFFI-CULTY UNWILLING COOKBOOK BUFFER PLENARY TROUT VULTURE BARK STROKE NECKWEAR UNATTENDED BREACH WORTHLESS HELPMATE BLOT ARROW EXIST BLINKER CAPE PLOTTER EARNEST PRETTY PLAYFULNESS GREW GOSH PERICLES IDENTIFICATION SUBSTANTIALLY OCCUPANCY FORTITUDE

First-order Approximation

THE THEN IS LAST LAKE THERE WHETHER INSURANCE BE THE IS INTO CLOSED WENT SIGHT HAD ORDER IN DUST COULD WHAT TERMS FRIENDS BOY A GOVERNMENT NIGHT OUR STUDYING SINCE DEEDS IT CAME A FIRE WHEN BALL SWIM AT WE WILL SHE WHEN THE OF IS TO CLOSED BE CAR

Second-order Approximation

IS THIS IS THERE THEY WENT TO GO BACK HOME TO SEE THE DOG IS A BOY GOES THE PICTURE WAS IS GOING TO GO TO CLASS IS THAT IS THAT IS THAT WHICH ONE DAY IS THIS COURSE OF MICE ARE THEY SKY FOR HER FRIEND OF MARYLAND WILL

Third-order Approximation

ARE SOMETIMES PROBLEMS OVERCOME ARE THE COLTS ARE A GROUP CAN DO ONLY WHAT IS THEY BOY MOUNTED HIS HORSE WAS A BOY JOE AND SAM CAME TOO WHICH IS THE GLEE WAS NOT THERE BUT I THOUGHT HE WOULD NOT BE HOME IN THE DRAWER STICKS IN DAMP WEATHER

Fourth-order Approximation

BELL WAS RINGING TOO LOUD THE NOISE DISTURBED THE MEN BECAUSE THEY HAVE NO LAWS IS NOT THE CORRECT METHOD TO DO THIS HE HAD LAST WORKED TUESDAY BUT NOT WEDNESDAY BECAUSE I HAD A NICKEL BUT THAT IS NOT RIGHT IN THE FIRST DIVISION SPLIT INTO TWO PIECES AND

Fifth-order Approximation

GREAT PEOPLE ARE HUMBLE BECAUSE THEY HAVE NO ELECTRICITY BUT WE MADE IT IS TOO AND ALWAYS WILL BE IN HIS ROOM BY HIMSELF SO HE HAD A COLD BUT WENT AFTER THE BALL AFTER DINNER WAS TOO LATE LAST TIME SO DON'T MISS WHAT IS BEING SAID ABOUT ME

Sixth-order Approximation

HOMES FOR PEOPLE ARE A NECESSITY CAN YOU DO THE JOB IF YOU ARE CAPABLE IS THE PHRASE SAID WHEN YOU WRITE ENCLOSE THREE DOLLARS BEFORE YOU REMIT THE BOOK READ THE RULES TWICE THEN BEGIN THE PRO-CEDURE AGAIN HE SAID SLOWLY SO ALL THE WORDS COULD BE LISTED IN

Eighth-order Approximation

AN AUTOMOBILE WHEN THE VALVES GET STICKY NEEDS THE PROPER TREATMENT IS OUT OF THE SCOPE OF OUR IMAGINATION COME OUR NIGHTMARES WHICH ARE OFTEN REALITY CONFUSED CAN INDICATE A LIVING INSE-CURITY FOR WE WILL BASE HIS SALARY ON OTHER FACTORS IF WE FIND IT TO BE IMPORTANT WE SAID

[a] Each list is 50 words in length.
SOURCE: Deese and Hulse (1967)

we should be able to remember up to seven of these ideas, and so forth. These examples show that the chunk is the largest unit of meaningful organizations available. The value of chunks that can be held in short-term memory seems to be fixed, even though the size of each chunk can vary dramatically. Thus, an important way to improve memory is to find a way to reorganize the material into larger chunk sizes.

Miller illustrates this principle with the Morse code student. At first, the student is concerned with identifying separate letters. Later in his training, letters become grouped into words, and as learning progresses phrases might become the important units. The point is that the number of chunks or cognitive units remains relatively fixed, even though the complexity of each unit may increase immensely.

The phenomenon of chunking has been demonstrated empirically. In one study, subjects listened to a taped reading of lists of words whose organization resembled that of natural English sentences to various degrees (Table 4.6 gives some sample approximations) (Miller and Selfridge, 1950). They were then instructed to free-recall as much as they could from each level. Not surprisingly, the number of words recalled increased as the resemblance of the word sequence to English increased. The greater syntactical familiarity the word order had, the larger and fewer were the chunks.

In a similar study these results were not only confirmed but also further refined (Tulving and Patkau, 1962). The experimenters examined what the subjects recalled and picked out what they termed *recall chunks*—sequences of words remembered in their original order. They discovered that the average length of these chunks increased for higher-order approximations to English, while their number stayed roughly the same.

Memory: Two Processes

We have said that memory seems to have two stages—short-term and long-term memory—and we have a great deal of evidence on how they differ. We have discussed some of these differences, but what do they tell us about how imperfect memory actually works—and fails to work? Does material recorded by the human brain undergo organic decay (through interference or the passage of time) and hence become permanently irretrievable? Or is all of it stored forever in memory, though portions of it are occasionally unavailable (because of repression or, again, interference) but will deliver themselves up if we find the proper "open sesame"? The theories of forgetting we discussed in the preceding section produce a conflicting picture of the mechanisms affecting loss of memory. Since none appears to account for all empirical findings thus far, some psychologists have concluded that an explanation lies in the difference between short- and long-term memory.

Insight into short-term memory was provided by the Peterson and Peterson study (1959) in which subjects attempted to recall a single CCC trigram (for

▼ A Model of Memory

Lately theories of memory have been replaced by models of memory. They are plans which describe how information flows from the environment to a storage system within the organism. The most reacted to model (and the one best received) was put forth by two psychologists from Stanford, R. C. Atkinson and R. M. Shiffrin (1968, 1971). Their model is pictured below. Information flows from the environment to the sensory register. This is a perceptual process. What is attended to from the sensory register or what is called by Atkinson and Shiffrin the *sensory store,* is transferred to a *short-term store* (STS) which is identical with what other psychologists call short-term memory. That information in the sensory register which is not attended to decays in a quarter of a second or less.

Once in the *short-term store* the information may go straight into being encoded into a form acceptable to storage in the *long-term store* (that is it starts being worked on right away) or it may be shuttled into one of the slots in the *rehearsal buffer.* Here the item (chunk of information) may be kept alive through rehearsal and eventually be encoded into the long-term store (LTS). However, if the item is not valued enough or if for a number of other idiosyncratic reasons it is not rehearsed, it then decays and is lost. Or our chunk of information may meet an equally ignoble fate: it may be pushed out because of new (more recent) information and the limited number of slots in the buffer. Once in the LTS information does not decay, but there may be trouble in retrieving it (given the fact there is no physical change in the brain).

One of the reasons the model has been so widely accepted is because it divides structural processes from control processes. A structural process is the existence of the storage mechanisms themselves. The control processes (which can be conscious but are not necessarily so) direct the flow of information. Attention is a control process which decides what will be accepted in the STS. Other control processes direct what items will be rehearsed. These control processes

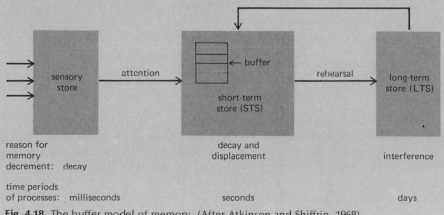

Fig. 4.18 The buffer model of memory. (After Atkinson and Shiffrin, 1968)

give the model a more active and constructive flavor than some of the more passive "flow charts." These guiding controls are based on sex, expectation, and experience, and the specific characteristics are unique from individual to individual (Cermak, 1972).

However, like all models, the buffer model fails to account for everything. There is a lot of evidence that interference, especially between acoustically similar items, is also responsible for forgetting in STS. Atkinson and Shiffrin handle this by noting that information in the sensory register must be identified by contact with the LTS before it is admitted into the short-term store. That is, something from LTS must direct the attentional control process. Experiments revealing interference in the STS are really confounding STS and LTS because of the initial contact with the sensory register (Cermak, 1972).

example, QTX) after counting backwards by threes from an arbitrary number. Thus prevented from rehearsing, very few of the subjects could accomplish the task after 18 seconds had elapsed.

As we have already learned, the storage mechanism for STM has a limited capacity—sufficient to retain only approximately seven (plus or minus two) chunks of information (Miller, 1956) for a few seconds at a time. This aggravatingly brief memory span is familiar to anyone who has ever asked for directions in a new place. You search for a native, who obliges by telling you to take the next left for half a mile, then turn right at the gas station until you reach the third light; turn right again and look for an overpass. . . . If, by the end of this you still remember the first instruction, you carry that out and promptly begin hunting for another native. Names of people at parties and pearls of wisdom from your favorite professor are similarly elusive. Unless such information is deliberately rehearsed, it is soon forgotten.

By contrast, LTM is thought to be capable of holding a huge amount of material. Although its actual capacity must be finite, it is nevertheless so vast that no one could hope to approach its limits within his lifetime. All information that is remembered for more than a few seconds—the learning that you rely on every day—is stored in LTM, retrieved from it for use, then stored there again: grammatical knowledge, vocabulary, your birthdate, your Social Security number, and so on.

When incoming information, especially visually presented material, is first received from the sensory register, it is encoded in an acoustic form in short-term memory. Evidence for this is the finding that errors made during memorization are in the form of acoustic confusion. For instance, a subject who makes a mistake in an attempt to recall a hard C will probably remember it as K rather than as O, even though C and O have common visual features.

Extensive evidence supports the theory that short-term and long-term memory involve different physiological processes, as we will see in greater detail

The Case of H. M. and N. A.

Clinical cases often yield valuable insights into psychological phenomena. Two such cases, concerned with memory deficit, are that of H. M. and N. A. These two men both are unable to transfer information from short-term to long-term memory. They can carry on a conversation, but if interrupted, can no longer remember what was said before the interruption. They both suffer from anterograde amnesia.

H. M. suffered a minor head injury at the age of 7 which was accompanied by a loss of consciousness. Three years later epileptic seizures began. At first, they were confined to the *petit mal* variety, but by age 16 H. M. was experiencing *grand mal* seizures on the average of once a week. The episodes were accompanied by a loss of consciousness, convulsions, and resulting injuries from falling. Although diagnostic tests revealed no epileptogenic focus, there were abnormalities in the EEG readings from both temporal lobes. Since anticonvulsant drugs had failed to arrest the seizures, his doctors decided to operate (Scoville, 1968). They removed both temporal lobes and what was then (1953) a little understood part of the brain called the hippoconepus.

After H. M. recovered from the operation the doctors realized that he had anterograde amnesia. While he showed a dramatic reduction in seizure frequency, he appeared to have almost a complete loss of recent memory. Fourteen years after the operation H. M. stills fails to recognize family friends or neighbors who got to know him only after the operation. H. M. has normal preoperational recall but recalls very little since the operation. He recalls the names of recent presidents and recognizes his immediate vicinity. (Milner, Corkin, and Teuber, 1968). He seems to learn only very gross, general changes in his environment that are constant enough to keep supporting that learning process. When H. M.'s father died it took him a few months to learn about the change (learning in a permanent sense), but compared to his usual learning rate this was quite remarkable.

In 1966 H. M. spent three nights in a hospital. He kept ringing the night nurse for an explanation of how he got there and what he was doing there. Milner, Corkin, and Teuber (1968) are three of the many people who have studied H. M. This is how they describe the state of his life:

> On another occasion he (H. M.) remarked, "Every day is alone in itself, whatever enjoyment I've had and whatever sorrow I've had!" Our own impression is that many events fade for him long before the day is over. He often volunteers stereotyped descriptions of his own state by saying it is "like working from a dream." His experience seems to be that of a person who is just becoming aware of his surroundings without fully comprehending the situation, because he does not remember what went before. (p. 211)

N. A. became amnesiac in quite a different manner. A gruesome fencing accident resulted in a foil entering his nostril and piercing the base of the brain. Several months after the incident N. A. appeared completely normal except for one thing: he was not able to retain any new knowledge for more than a short time. Lindsay and Norman (1972) report a conversation that psychologist Wayne Wickelgren had with N. A. After being introduced to Wickelgren, N. A. replied:

"Wickelgren, that's a German name, isn't it?"
I said, "No."
"Irish?"
"No."
"Scandinavian?"
"Yes, it's Scandinavian."
After having about a five-minute conversation with him, I left to go to my office for perhaps another five minutes. When I returned, he looked at me as if he had never seen me before in his life, and I was introduced to him again. Whereupon he said:
"Wickelgren, that's a German name, isn't it?"
"No."
"Irish?"
"No."
"Scandinavian?"
"Yes."
Exactly the same sequence as before. [Wickelgren, personal communication] (p. 310)

While N. A. has shown gradual improvement, he still has trouble recalling events that have happened about the incident. When questioned about the movie he watched the previous evening, N. A. could only recall fragments. (Teuber, Milner and Vaughan, 1968). N. A. also complained that he forgets the story-line of a television show when it is interrupted by commercials.

The cases of H. M. and N. A. are supportive of the view that there are two memory systems: a short-term, immediate memory and a long-term more lasting storage system. Cases of anterograde amnesia, where new information cannot be held for long periods of time, are revealing of the duality of memory.

in Chapter 6. Here we are able to review only a fraction of it. One frequently cited phenomenon is the serial position effect, which shows evidence of both short-term and long-term memory. A subject asked to free-recall as many items from a list as possible generally remembers best the several that were given most recently, that is, those at the end. These are the items "dumped" from STM. The subject then attempts to dredge up from LTM any others he may have retained. Hence, when the percentage of recall is plotted against the serial position of each item, the resulting curve has two distinct parts. The upward-pointing end of the curve represents the latter items in the list, which are usually recalled relatively accurately. The lower first part of the curve represents the beginning and middle items. (Fig. 4.19 shows that although the length and speed of presentation of lists may differ, the STM component is the same for all curves, indicating again its fixed capacity, while the LTM sections differ. Longer presentation times presumably enable subjects to store more information in LTM, its capacity being considerably larger. Clinical evidence of amnesia and certain cases of brain damage also tend to support the two-process theory.

In this chapter we have discussed the principles that govern verbal learning and memory. The student of French relies on a combination of factors when

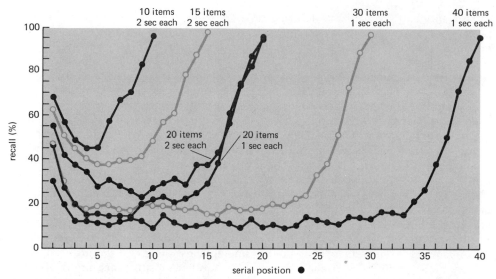

Fig. 4.19 Serial position curves each showing a similar STM component for the last item presented, but somewhat differing LTM components for the early and middle items of the lists. (Data from Murdock, 1962)

learning a new language, as we all do every day in our own learning situations. But what is it that makes a student want to do well? Why does one student study harder than another? The next chapter will discuss what it is that makes us want to learn—or not to learn—and to do other things; it will discuss the principles governing motivation.

SUMMARY

Verbal learning and memory are distinctly human phenomena. They are pervasive in everyday experience, yet they are complex processes. The distinction between them is more important in theory than in practice; learning studies are concerned with changes over different trials, whereas memory studies are concerned with the interval between trials.

In the laboratory—and in everyday experience—verbal materials are learned in several ways. In *serial anticipation learning*, each item in a list serves as a stimulus for the following item. An effect of this method is that items at the beginning and end of a list are more easily learned than items in the middle. In *paired-associate learning*, we establish a relationship between two elements such that one is the stimulus for the other. *Free recall learning* is interesting mostly as a means of studying how people naturally organize verbal material.

A number of factors influence the ease with which verbal materials are learned. *Meaningfulness*, which is measured by the promptness with which a stimulus evokes an association or by the number of associations it evokes, has a positive impact on learning, probably because it increases the distinctiveness of an item. *Similarity*, however, seems to have a mostly inhibiting effect, though its influence varies with the kind of similarity and the particular learning task. *Frequency* of occurrence, like meaning-fulness, enhances learning. *Concreteness* and *imagery*, which are closely related, also enhance learning. Finally, ease of learning is promoted by *transfer* of old learning to new situations.

The two principal ways in which we facilitate learning of any kind of verbal material by any method are rehearsal and mediation. *Rehearsal* allows items in short-term memory to be retained indefinitely and aids in transferring material from short-term to long-term memory. It is probably the explanation for the fact that total learning time is a far more significant factor in learning than either time spent on each item or number of trials. *Mediation* is the use of extraneous material to facilitate an association between stimulus and response. A mediator may chain a response, as is $A \longrightarrow B \longrightarrow C$, where B is in the mediator. It may be elicited by both terms. Or it may elicit both terms.

To use learned (encoded) information, we must remember, or *retrieve* it. We can measure what is stored in memory by noting how much can be *recalled* after a specified interval. Recall may be either rote (verbatim) or reconstructed memory. It is not the most sensitive means of retrieval but is often the only appropriate one. *Recognition* is more sensitive than recall but considerably less precise. It requires only a yes (recognition) or no (nonrecognition) response. Another sensitive measure of retrieval is *relearning* time, which is based on the assumption that it is easier to learn partially remembered material than never learned or totally forgotten material.

Retrieval may fail because the stored information has *decayed,* as a function of disuse over time, or has been *interfered* with, by either newer or older learning. The interference of new learning with old is *retroactive inhibition;* of old learning with new, *proactive inhibition.* Momentary failures of retrieval may be due to the *tip-of-the-tongue phenomenon,* in which we feel we know the word but cannot bring it forth, or to *repression,* in which we unconsciously suppress the word to spare ourselves the pain of its associations.

Retrieval may be improved by *overlearning,* or rehearsing longer than necessary for immediate recall, by *organizing* material to be learned in any way that is meaningful to the learner, and by *chunking,* or breaking the material down into already familiar units.

Memory seems to consist of two processes: short-term memory with a relatively brief capacity—seven chunks plus or minus two over a brief duration—and long-term memory with a virtually unlimited capacity over a lifetime.

SUGGESTED READINGS

Ausubel, D. P., *The Psychology of Meaningful Verbal Learning.* New York, Grune & Stratton, 1963.
    Presents a cognitive view of verbal learning.
Bruner, Jerome S., *Toward a Theory of Instruction.* Cambridge, Mass., Harvard University Press, 1966.
    Essays, all by Bruner, concerned with the learning process and the art of teaching.
Furth, Hans G., and Harry Wachs, *Thinking Goes to School, Piaget's Theory in Practice.* New York, Oxford, 1974.
    The authors have devised 179 games for classroom use based on Piaget's principles.

Honig, W. K., and P. H. R. James, *Animal Memory*. New York, Academic Press, 1971.
A collection of articles on learning and memory.

Meenes, M., *Studying and Learning*. New York, Random House, 1954.
A guide to applying learning principles to the task of studying.

Piaget, Jean, *The Language and Thought of the Child,* 3d ed. New York, Humanities Press, 1959.
A detailed presentation of the idea that children's thinking develops in an orderly, sequential way.

Postman, L., "Transfer, Interference, and Forgetting," in J. W. Kling and L. A. Riggs, eds., *Woodworth and Schlosberg's Experimental Psychology*. New York, Holt, Rinehart and Winston, 1971.
A brief introduction to some important aspects of human learning.

Toffler, Alvin, *Learning for Tomorrow: The Role of the Future in Education*. New York, Random House, 1974.
In this book the author of *Future Shock* presents his ideas for educational reforms.

Chapter Five

Motivation

What are motives?
Are we ruled by biological needs or by reason?
Why does a reinforcer reinforce?
What are secondary reinforcers?
What are id, ego, and superego?
What is repression?
Why do we dream?
Do we learn if not rewarded for doing so?

When two infants of the same age are given some brightly colored toys to play with, why does one child attentively investigate them, while the other, crawling restlessly about, evinces no interest whatsoever? Why did Van Gogh, alone and periodically mad, repeatedly face an empty canvas and continue to paint? What inspired him? You read that a man has stepped out of a crowd and shot a public figure. What possessed him?

Implicit in such questions is the recognition that not all people behave similarly under similar conditions. The two infants, although of the same age and of normal development, are not equally inspired by the same toys. The stimulus situation may be the same, but the responses are different. Lay and professional observers alike assume that the crucial factors differentiating behaviors in identical situations lie within the individual. These internal unknowns are what "possesses" or "inspires" a person to do something. In other times and places inhabitation by devils or angels, bad spirits or good spirits, has explained conspicuous deviations from expected behavior.

We also have our own personal motivational theories. For example, "Redheads have a greater temper than brunettes" or "Fat people are jolly." Are these valid statements? The man in the street may well argue that his own personal experience "proves" their validity. But psychology today requires much

Vivian Duncan

more, both in terms of empirical evidence and, even before that, in the definition of motivation.

WHAT IS MOTIVATION?

motivation   The modern term for these posited inner unknowns is *motivation*. Today, psychologists who study motivation are concerned not only with the extraordinary manifestations of human behavior but also with the ordinary. They recognize that all behavior—from lifting a spoon to scaling a mountain—has a cause. Because their study is scientific, what answers they arrive at are obtained not from dogma but from observation under controlled experimental conditions. It is important to keep in mind, however, that motivation itself, being something that takes place inside a person, is inferred, not directly observed. The concept of motive provides the clarifying link between a stimulus and a response.

Psychologists define motivation as the *immediate* forces that act to energize, direct, sustain, and stop a behavior. Past experience, momentary perceptions, environmental variables, and other factors may affect the direction and strength of an action, but they are considered distinct from motivation itself. Yet it is recognized that the strengths of various motives differ from person to person and, within any one person, from time to time.

The motivational puzzles posed at the beginning of our discussion—and those that we usually find most intriguing—involve highly complex behavior. How, for instance, do we go about determining what motivates an archaeologist to spend years patiently restoring artifacts? No doubt many factors are involved: curiosity about the past, the desire to achieve, the need to support himself and his family, and so forth. Each of these motives is a major study in itself. Clearly, then, to begin to understand complex behavior we must first work with simple behavioral sequences, studying the way motivation affects and guides them and the ways in which different psychologists have approached the problem.

The Nature of Man

All motivation theories reflect larger philosophical biases about the "nature" of man. The theorists whom we will examine in this chapter—Clark Hull, Sigmund Freud, Edward Tolman and other cognitive theorists—can be identified with four major conceptual frameworks.

Man, the Machine; Man, the Animal Clark Hull was influenced by the conception of man as a machine and by Charles Darwin's theories of man as an animal.

Certain reflexive aspects of human behavior, such as the knee jerk, led some observers to liken man to a machine. A stimulus triggers a response, which acts as the stimulus for another response, and so on. Neither thought nor purpose is necessary to account for such behavior. Pavlov's work on the conditioned reflex was necessary, however, to provide a plausible explanation for more complex, learned behavior. Pavlov demonstrated convincingly that new, formerly neutral stimuli can be made to elicit responses not naturally, or reflexively, associated with them.

A somewhat akin but far more complicated view was Darwin's theory of evolution. According to Darwin, man is an animal; he has evolved from the lower animals through a long process of natural selection of the fittest for sur-

THE PROFESSOR TAKES A PILL AND DOPES OUT A DEVICE FOR CLOSING THE WINDOW IF IT STARTS TO RAIN WHILE YOU'RE AWAY.

PET BULL FROG (A), HOMESICK FOR WATER, HEARS RAIN STORM AND JUMPS FOR JOY, PULLING STRING (B) WHICH OPENS CATCH (C) AND RELEASES HOT WATER BAG (D) ALLOWING IT TO SLIDE UNDER CHAIR (E). HEAT RAISES YEAST (F) LIFTING DISK (G) WHICH CAUSES HOOK (H) TO RELEASE SPRING (I) TOY.

AUTOMOBILE-BUMPER (J) SOCKS MONKEY (K) IN THE NECK PUTTING HIM DOWN FOR THE COUNT ON TABLE (L). HE STAGGERS TO HIS FEET AND SLIPS ON BANANA PEEL (M). HE INSTINCTIVELY REACHES FOR FLYING RINGS (N) TO AVOID FURTHER DISASTER AND HIS WEIGHT PULLS ROPE (O) CLOSING WINDOW (P), STOPPING THE RAIN FROM LEAKING THROUGH ON THE FAMILY DOWNSTAIRS AND THINNING THEIR SOUP.

vival. Consequently, man has in common with other animals certain biological drives whose function is to spur the behavior necessary for sustaining life: the search for food and water, propagation of the species, avoidance of pain, and so on.

Unconscious Man Freud's conception of unconscious man is also part of the legacy of Darwin. In Freud's view, man, as animal, also shares with lower organisms certain irrational impulses that are socially threatening and are therefore repressed in the young child. Because they cannot, however, be completely repressed, they continue to influence behavior in ways not readily discernible to the conscious mind. Conscious explanations are in fact facades that obscure the underlying reality. Unconscious man cannot therefore hope to arrive at an understanding of his motives except through exhaustive analysis.

Rational Man Before the advent of the theory of evolution, philosophers believed that man alone among the creatures of the world was ruled by reason; his will was thought to be in control of instinctual impulses and his behavior was therefore voluntary. Later, in the 20th century, after the major impact of evolution had died down, Edward Tolman and other cognitive theorists believed that man, by virtue of his capacity for reason, makes conscious decisions about

United Press International Photo

Independence.

Mike Levins

Dependence.

goals, estimating the probable outcome of each course of action, considering all relevant factors, then acting or not acting, accordingly. Motives thus derive from rational processes.

Social Man Also represented to a certain extent in cognitive theories is the idea that man's behavior reflects the expectations of his social group, what his society approves, prohibits, and idealizes. The particular values of a society are shaped by its relationship with its environment. For instance, in the early days of this country when a vast land lay uncharted, self-reliance and fearlessness were among the virtues necessary to ensure the growth and protection of the original settlements.

From anthropological studies we have the idea of cultural relativism, the notion that human behavior cannot be appreciated apart from its cultural context. For example, the achievement motive plays a dominant role in Western society, but by no means everywhere, and should therefore not be regarded as a fixed part of human nature. In fact, probably the most important conclusion from the study of other cultures has been that man's "nature" is variable.

The idea that human behavior can be influenced by society is sometimes expanded into the belief that man is completely subject to social, historical, and economic forces—that his behavior is determined so that he satisfies the needs of society at large before his own. By understanding how these forces work, however, man can manipulate them to satisfy human needs and ultimately to change the ways in which social forces shape human behavior. Laws ensuring equality of opportunity to all, for example, have had far-reaching effects on behavior over the years. Through such indirect methods we slowly change the value systems that motivate people.

These broad theories of the nature of man contain the seeds of motivation theories. Three important theories of motivation will be discussed in this chapter. Social determination of motivation will be postponed until Chapter 14, since it requires substantial elaboration of some general concepts in social psychology.

BIOLOGICAL DRIVE THEORY: HULL

Clark L. Hull

The biological drive theory of motivation reflects the concept of man as animal. Clark L. Hull began developing this theory in order to explain data that had been accumulating from the study of learning. It had become increasingly obvious that the basis of complex behavior remained unexplained by psychologists of the stimulus-response persuasion.

Traditionally, in learning experiments with animals the acquisition of new responses is reinforced by the delivery of a food reward after each correctly performed trial (for Pavlov's classic research on the conditioned response, see Chapter 3). But why does a reinforcer reinforce? And what determines the variability of performance strength?

Hull's Basic Theory

Hull's theory of behavior had to account for both these questions. Of specific relevance for his study of behavior was Darwin's belief that evolution affects not only bodily structures but also predispositions to particular actions.

drive

Hull's initial formulation of the theory of reinforcement applied solely to the primary biological predispositions, or drives, such as hunger, thirst, sex, and pain. A physiological need is created by homeostatic imbalance (the deprivation of something necessary to the organism, for example, water); this imbalance produces a drive (thirst) to initiate a behavior (looking for a drinking fountain or doing whatever the subject has learned will make water available) that results in the reduction of the drive and, simultaneously, the end of the need state (through consumption of water). Variability in performance strength is due to differences in the strength of the drive state, which, in turn, depends on the degree of deprivation. Further, rewards reinforce new behavior because they reduce the drive and restore homeostatic balance.

The symbolic representation of this process is Performance = Drive × Habit. Performance depends upon two factors: existence of a learned association or habit and the organism's drive or need state. A rat must be thirsty before it will activate a habit, knowledge of the maze pattern, and run the maze.

The major biological drives that Hull considered were the appetitive drives of hunger, thirst, and sex, and the aversive drive of pain avoidance. He was not concerned in his initial formulations with the physiological mechanisms underlying each, but defined their properties by antecedent and consequent conditions. The antecedent condition for arousal of appetitive drives was deprivation. For the aversive drive, it was injury—in the form of electrical shock in most experiments.

 Measures of Drive Strength

Four different measures have been commonly applied to drives: general activity level, performance rate, acceptance of punishment, and goal selection. According to Hull, these measures should be in principle at least equally applicable to all the biological drives.

General activity level of the person or animal is expected to increase whenever a drive is present. We have all occasionally experienced nervous restlessness when we have been forced to put off eating for a long time. Activity is not a uniformly reliable indicator, however. One experiment demonstrated that food-deprived rats were more active than those that had been fed only when a noise or some other jarring stimulus was introduced (Campbell and Sheffield, 1953). Apparently it was their sensitivity to stimuli that was heightened, affecting their activity level only secondarily.

A second measure of drive strength is performance rate. A worker who is given a bonus for putting extra time and effort into his job continues to increase his efficiency in the hope of future rewards. A hungry rat presses a lever with increasing speed and frequency as its hunger increases. It has been shown, however, that the frequency with which a water-deprived rat presses a lever and the amount of water it consumes after each bar press may not be equal indicators of the strength of its thirst (Miller, 1961).

A third measure is acceptance of punishment. A commuter who lives in the suburbs decides that he is through fighting traffic for 3 hours a day, so he quits his high-paying city job and settles for a job with a small company nearer home. The degree of punishment a subject is willing to suffer in order to reach its goal, then, provides an additional gauge of drive strength. Experimenters with animals commonly measure this factor by placing a heated or electrified grid between a rat and some goal-object and recording how often it is willing to undergo pain in order to obtain the goal.

A fourth measure of drive strength concerns selection among goals. A hungry, thirsty, lonely young man at the beach watching a hot dog man go in one direction, a soda vendor in another, and a pretty girl in a third has to choose. Presumably, he acts on the dominant drive first, factors such as attainability being equal. In animals, too, it is possible to determine which drive is the strongest by observing which goal is selected first. This method measures comparative rather than absolute drive strength.

What Determines the Variability of Performance Strength?

In a study of rats running a 10-unit T-maze, Hillman, Hunter, and Kimble (1953) recorded the time taken by four groups of animals to run 15 trials after being deprived of water for different lengths of time. One group (2–22) ran Trials 1 through 10 after 2 hours of deprivation and 11 through 15 after 22 hours, while a second group (22–2) ran the first 10 after 22 hours without water and the last five after 2 hours; of the two remaining groups, the controls, one (22–22) ran all trials after 22 hours of deprivation, and the other (2–2) ran them all after 2 hours. The result was that Groups 2–22 and 22–2, both of which underwent abrupt changes in degree of deprivation on the 11th trial, demonstrated correspondingly abrupt changes in performance: specifically, running time for Group 22–2, which had been steadily increasing, suddenly dropped, whereas the time for Group 2–22 increased considerably with Trial 12 (Fig. 5.1). Since nowhere else in the results were such fluctuations in evidence, they obviously represented something more than just changes in the strength of S–R bonds, or learning. Motivation must have been involved. When rats accustomed to severe deprivation (22–2) suddenly experienced a decreased need for water, their motivation to run also decreased. Exactly the reverse occurred with Group 2–22: When their need for water increased, their motivation likewise increased, with the result that they ran much more quickly. Moreover, even though the control groups both produced gradually decreasing running times, the trials of the severely deprived rats (22–22) from the outset were consistently faster than those of the less deprived rats.

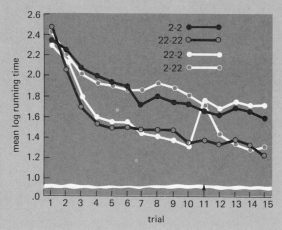

Fig. 5.1 Learning curves showing the results of an experiment to determine whether motivation affects learning or just performance. (Hillman, Hunter, and Kimble 1953)

Secondary Reinforcers Most people are motivated to spend most of their lives working for money, which does not reduce any primary drives; it does, however, help to obtain commodities that do satisfy them. It has, in other words, become a *secondary reinforcer*. Hull needed a way to show how an object might acquire reinforcing properties without being food, water, or a reciprocating sex object.

Secondary Reinforcement

In one experiment, monkeys learned to obtain food by putting tokens into a slot machine (Cowles, 1937). Gradually, the tokens acquired value in themselves for the monkeys, who began working for and often hoarding them. They even learned new tasks in order to get them. In a second experiment two groups of rats learned to press a bar for a food reward (Bugelski, 1938). Following this, the reward was eliminated, and the bar-pressing response was gradually extinguished. During this period after the elimination of the reward, one group of animals continued to hear the clicking noise that had formerly accompanied the delivery of food, while the other group did not. The result was that the click group pressed the bar 30 percent more than the nonclick group before terminating the response altogether. In both studies, then, neutral stumulus objects, the tokens and the click, had become secondary reinforcers through association with the primary reward of food. Moreover, as indicated by the latter study, this reinforcing power ceases when the association ceases.

He had precedent for such a concept in Pavlov's work on higher-order conditioning (see Chapter 3). Pavlov discovered that when a neutral stimulus (such as a light) was paired with an unconditioned stimulus (food), it came to elicit the response (salivation) originally elicited by the unconditioned stimulus.

Hull built heavily on the notion of secondary reinforcement to explain the more complex aspects of human behavior; this notion permitted the belief that all motivation derived ultimately from the primary biological drives, no matter how complex the behavior or how seemingly removed from hunger, thirst, sex, or pain avoidance it seemed to be.

The motive to achieve, for example, was interpreted in the following way: From the first day of an infant's life, his needs for food are met by his mother. Because feeding also involves physical closeness and interaction, the mother is also the child's earliest and most consistent source of social contact. He learns to associate her attention or approval with food and reduction of the hunger drive (as well as with pain avoidance). Her attention acquires the power of a secondary reinforcer. As certain responses are rewarded with her attention, the infant strengthens and maintains those responses. He gradually becomes motivated to perform activities that have mother's approval, from building with blocks to achieving high grades in school. Eventually, striving for success assumes a permanent role in his motivational system. (We will consider a quite different interpretation of achievement motivation later in this chapter.)

Earlier we said that motives both energize and direct behavior. Hull framed this distinction in terms of *generalized drive* and *habit*: drive energizes and arouses an organism, but behavior is directed by whatever habit happens to be dominant in a given situation. Drives are additive: the more drives operating at once, the greater is the general level of arousal. If a subject is not only

generalized drive

Increases in Stimulation Can Be Pleasurable

In Hull's formulation (and for that matter in Freud's) any increase in stimulation is defined as painful to the subject. Pleasure is the decrease in stimulation to some optimal state of rest or homeostasis.

Olds and Milner (1954) discovered that an increase in direct electrical stimulation of certain areas in a rat's brain may be pleasurable. They used a technique by which they could directly implant an electrode into different parts of the brain, leaving the animal free to behave. In the course of their studies they found that stimulation at certain electrode cites had the effect of a positive reinforcer.

For example, in a later study the rats were placed in a Skinner-box apparatus rigged up so that the rat could send an electric current through its own brain by pressing the bar. The rate of bar pressing, when reinforced by direct stimulation of the brain, increased far beyond what had been observed with famished rats rewarded with food for pressing a bar. When the current was turned off, the rats virtually stopped bar pressing.

These findings question the notion that in order for reinforcement to occur an increase in stimulation—or drive—must be removed or reduced. Here an excitation of the brain is found to be positively reinforcing and pleasurable.

very hungry but also somewhat thirsty, it will run faster to food than if it were only hungry. We will come back to the concept of arousal in Chapter 6. The important point here is that Hull considered drives pretty much interchangeable in their effects on motivation.

Modifications of Hull's Basic Theory

Although at first Hull held strongly to his original theory, in which drives were the primary biological drives only, reinforcers were elements that reduced primary drives, and incentive was governed only by drive strength, he later changed his view. Specifically, he introduced goal incentives and acquired drives.

goal incentives

Goal Incentives   The addition of goal incentives was important. Hull came to believe that biological need state alone is not enough to explain motivation; the attractiveness of the goal object being sought to reduce the need state must also be considered. Specifically, the more attractive the goal, the greater the likelihood that the behavior, or habit, would be performed.

This introduced an important change. Habit strength was now gauged solely by the number of rewarded trials, and incentive became what directs motivation, though the incentive value of an object differs according to the particular drive state of the subject. A sirloin steak has high incentive value

The Activating Function of Generalized Drive

Drive in motivation theory is thought of as an activating, energizing force. It acts much like the fuel in an automobile; it does not give the vehicle direction—the steering wheel does that—but it supplies the energy necessary to activity. Drive creates a state of restlessness.

The relationship between drive and activity level has been demonstrated in a number of experiments in which the restless activity of rats was correlated with the number of hours during which they had been deprived of food. For example, rats were placed in a running wheel (Fig. 5.2) and their activity level was observed just before they were fed. In most experiments this activity level is directly related to the number of hours since the last feeding. Thus it would seem that an increased hunger drive results in greater restless activity.

Campbell and Sheffield (1953) point out, however, that there is no difference between the activity levels of hungry and satiated rats unless some external stimulation, such as a disturbing noise, occurs. Still, the overt activity serves as a useful measure of generalized drive.

In Hull's framework, drive is seen as being nonspecific and generalized. Thus drive doesn't care what its source is—hunger, fear, sex, and so on. It is an energizer and it will energize all behavior. It follows from this theory that if the energy component of drive is not specific, an increased hunger drive, for example, should facilitate a response for a fear-producing stimulus and vice versa. Meryman (1952) showed that at least for rats this occurs in a very marked way.

Fig. 5.2 As the rat runs in the cage, the distance is recorded; the longer he is without food, the greater the distance. (Photo courtesy Lafayette Instrument Co.)

Rats were shocked after every presentation of a loud noise. Thus they were made fearful of the noise, and their startle response to the noise was increased. Half of the rats were deprived of food for 46 hours, and the other half for only 1 hour. Then the noise was presented. The resulting startle response of the rats that had been hungry for 46 hours was much greater than the startle response of the rats that had been hungry for only 1 hour.

This demonstrates the generalized and nonspecific properties of drive. In this case the hunger drive energized an activity that is not at all related to the satisfaction of hunger.

only if the hunger drive is aroused. Thus, Hull significantly increased the importance of directive properties in his motivational theory (direction had previously been a function of habit strength alone). Cognitive theorists, such as Tolman (see p. 240), attributed even more significance to the directive properties of motives and played down their generalized arousal properties.

aquired drive

Acquired Drives   Just as a neutral stimulus acquires reinforcing properties through association, so, according to Hull, does a neutral stimulus associated with a drive acquire drive properties.

 Atypical Results in Conditioning

Pavlov, in his work on conditioning, noticed that under some conditions it is virtually impossible to obtain a conditioned reflex, no matter how many times the combination of stimuli is repeated. For example: (a) "If the dog is drowsy during the experiments, the establishment of a conditioned reflex becomes a long and tedious process and in extreme cases is virtually impossible to accomplish." (b) "In a dog which has not long ago been fed . . . conditioned reflexes either are not formed at all or are established very slowly" (Pavlov, 1927).

Perhaps the most striking example of the momentary or temporary nature of goal seeking is the following account by Pavlov: "In one case an experiment may be running smoothly and suddenly all conditioned reflexes begin to fail and finally disappear altogether. The dog is taken out to urinate, and then all the reflexes return to normal. . . . Another example may be chosen in the season when the females are in heat. If the males have been housed near the females before the experiment, it is found that all their conditioned relexes are inhibited in greater or lesser degree" (Pavlov, 1927).

Those who believed that stimulus-response connections are the underlying mechanism of all learning and behavior looked upon these "atypical" cases where no conditioning occurred as anomalies or extraneous (stimuli) reflexes that had to be controlled. To those who noted that ordinary behavior was highly purposive in nature these "anomalies" served to highlight the importance of motivation in human learning. Obviously mere stimulus-response repetitions were not sufficient for learning to occur.

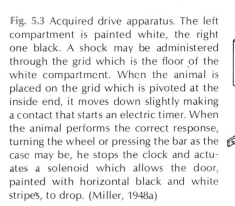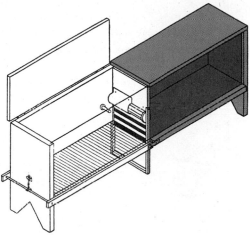

Fig. 5.3 Acquired drive apparatus. The left compartment is painted white, the right one black. A shock may be administered through the grid which is the floor of the white compartment. When the animal is placed on the grid which is pivoted at the inside end, it moves down slightly making a contact that starts an electric timer. When the animal performs the correct response, turning the wheel or pressing the bar as the case may be, he stops the clock and actuates a solenoid which allows the door, painted with horizontal black and white stripes, to drop. (Miller, 1948a)

Thus, in theory, a neutral stimulus paired with food deprivation should after enough pairings be capable of energizing behavior by itself. In this sense, then, it would produce an acquired drive. However, in practice, no one has been able to demonstrate acquired appetitive drives.

But acquired aversive drives or pain avoidance drives are easily demonstrated. A neutral stimulus paired with shock is capable of arousing the pain avoidance drive even when shock is absent. This acquired drive is usually called fear, though perhaps the term anxiety is more appropriate.

Fear as an *acquired drive* was illustrated by a well-known experiment with rats (Miller, 1948a). The animals were placed in a box consisting of two compartments—one white, one black—separated by a door (Fig. 5.3). An electric shock was administered in the white compartment, from which they were able to escape by running through the door to the black compartment. When they received the shock, the rats showed typical signs of pain and took less and less time to escape. Soon, however, they began fleeing the white compartment *before* the shock occurred, thus avoiding the shock instead of simply escaping it.

In a second phase of the experiment, the door between the compartments was shut so that the rats had to learn to open it in order to escape. The shock, however, was not administered. In spite of this, the animals continued to demonstrate fear and quickly learned to escape from the white compartment. When a new device for opening the door was substituted for the old one, they again learned with surprising speed to manipulate it (Fig. 5.4).

The implications of acquired anxiety are obvious. Experiencing the environment in which a noxious stimulus once occurred can arouse it. The resulting behavior—typically that of flight—will reduce the pain-avoidance drive and thus provide reinforcement.

When the stimulus associated with pain is perceived, we try to get away from it. Getting away is thus reinforcing, and we tend to avoid that stimulus

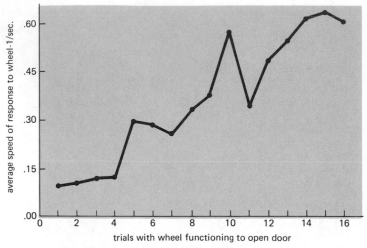

Fig. 5.4 Learning the first new habit, turning the wheel, during trials without primary drive. With mild pain produced by an electric shock as a primary drive, the animals have learned to run from the white compartment, through the open door, into the black compartment. Then they were given trials without any electric shock during which the door was closed but could be opened by turning a little wheel. Under these conditions the 13 out of the 25 animals which turned the wheel enough to drop the door on four or more of the first eight trials learned to turn it. This figure shows the progressive increase in the average speed with which these 13 animals ran up to the wheel and turned it enough to drop the door during the 16 non-shock trials. (Miller, 1948a)

in the future, even though it no longer is paired with actual pain. The rat runs out of the white compartment without waiting for the shock. The shock can be turned off, but the rat never finds that out. Avoidance drives generated by anxiety about anticipated harm are extremely difficult to extinguish.

Even though anxiety is the only acquired drive that has been demonstrated, it is a critical motivating factor in behavior. We shall consider some of its human manifestations in Chapter 16.

Are All Drives Biologically Based?

A major challenge to theories like Hull's has been the notion that unlearned drives are not limited to hunger, thirst, sex, and pain. Other kinds of drives that have been proposed all seem to be based on something like activity or curiosity. We will look at these briefly here (for further material see Chapter 8).

All young children and animals indulge in active play. This apparent need for activity has been termed a motivation for competence (White, 1959). An experiment demonstrates the force of the activity drive (Hill, 1956). After rats

"Treadmills! Mazes! There must be more to life than this."

had been confined for a period of time, it was discovered that the opportunity to engage in activity could be used as an effective reinforcer of new learning.

The manipulation of objects also seems satisfying in its own right (Fig. 5.5). In one study, monkeys took locks and other devices apart without being induced to do so in any way (Harlow, Harlow, and Meyer, 1950). In another, they were given a mechanical puzzle to take apart, again without being offered any inducements (Butler, 1954). The monkeys not only mastered the puzzle but continued taking it apart as fast as it could be reassembled, one monkey even persisting for as long as 10 hours. Because it is difficult to imagine what biological drive might be reduced by this activity, some theorists have suggested that there must be a manipulation drive.

In the same vein, a curiosity drive has been invented to explain exploratory behavior. This drive is manifested in locomotor explorations of new surroundings. For instance, rats that had learned to select one branch of a Y-maze for a food reward chose to explore a new passageway when it was opened to them on the 81st trial (Thiessen and McGaugh, 1958). In another study, rats spent more time investigating new figures on walls behind empty goal boxes than familiar ones (Berlyne and Slater, 1957). There may be a tendency to seek out complexity. For example, rats stayed in complex rooms longer than in simple ones, whether they were familiar with the rooms or not (Walker, 1964); infants, too, have proved more attracted to complex designs than simple ones (Berlyne, 1966) (Fig. 5.6).

Investigatory responses also consist of manipulating objects, but with the added goal of learning something about them. For instance, an infant confronted with a new object will put it in its mouth, bang it on the floor, shake it, or engage in some other such exploratory behavior.

The stages in the development of investigatory responses in children have been described in great detail by Jean Piaget (see Chapter 11). Briefly, he believes that as curiosity impels the young child to learn more and more about his world, his cognitive growth spirals upward; new ways of thinking, gained through the pursuit of curiosity satisfaction, in turn inspire curiosity on a higher level, and so on. The infant's first tentative probings of his environment are the initial steps in this growth.

We have considered the biological drive theory of motivation in some detail, and have found it remote from the complexities of much known behavior, even for most animals, let alone for man. Yet theories like Hull's have been very appealing in their postulation that complex processes can be understood in terms of only a few basic principles and mechanisms. Such an approach has by no means been proved wrong. Rather, it seems to underplay processes of great importance, especially in human motivation. Nonbiological drives seem more important than Hull permits. Further, to define all acquired motivation as

Fig. 5.5 The monkey takes the latches apart, even though there is no reward except that of the manipulation itself. (Harry F. Harlow, University of Wisconsin Primate Laboratory)

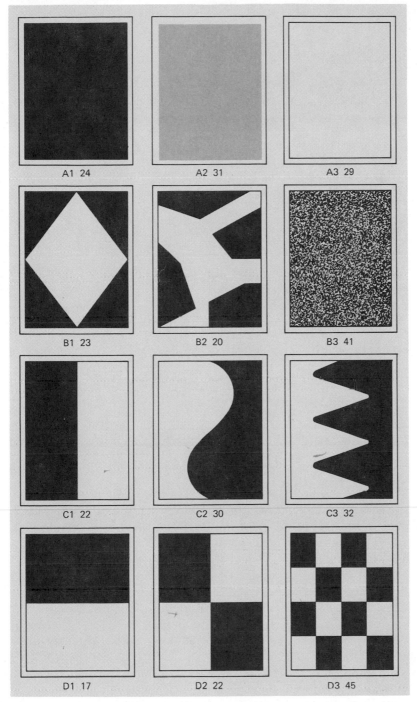

A1 24   A2 31   A3 29

B1 23   B2 20   B3 41

C1 22   C2 30   C3 32

D1 17   D2 22   D3 45

Fig. 5.6 Four sets of three visual patterns used in experiments with 3- to 9-month old infants. The patterns of a set were presented in pairs, and the member of each pair that first attracted the subject's gaze was noted. The numeral under each pattern denotes the number of times out of 56 presentations (four with each of 14 subjects) that the pattern was fixated first. (Berlyne, 1966)

Curiosity impels the young child to learn more and more about his world.

based upon pain avoidance seems to do violence to all but the most negative conceptions of man's nature.

We turn next to Freud's approach to motivation. This is not much more cognitive than Hull's, but it does provide a very different picture of man and why he behaves the way he does.

PSYCHOANALYTIC THEORY: FREUD

Perhaps the best-known theory of motivation is the one developed by Sigmund Freud. Together with his theory of the origin and treatment of the neuroses it forms the essence of psychoanalytic theory.

Sigmund Freud

Its distinctive qualities reflect the scientific climate of Freud's day. The theory of evolution, the beginning of psychophysics, and theories of the conservation and exchange of energy together led Freud to a belief that psychology was a part of biology, subject to the scientific laws of causality.

When Freud began his work on psychopathology and the unconscious he had already earned a respectable reputation as a neurologist; his clinical experience led him to believe, as many 19th century scientists did, that careful observation and analysis rather than experimentation were the key to the secrets of psychology.

Psychology in Freud's day was primarily concerned with consciousness, which was explored through systematic introspection. Partly as an extension of that interest and partly in reaction against it—he did not believe that consciousness could adequately explain the forces that motivate behavior—Freud focused his attention on the role of the unconscious in motivation. He postulated a *psychic energy* that did the psychological work of the organism. He did not conceive of this as a vitalistic or supernatural force, but as a force analogous to the energy that supplied power to the skelatomuscular system.

Freud believed that all behavior is motivated by the tendency to approach pleasure and avoid pain. He felt that this tendency, which he called the *pleasure principle,* governed even the physiological responses to basic drives or instincts —hunger, thirst, and sex. An instinct, or drive, is a strong internal stimulus that, unlike an external stimulus, one can neither escape nor avoid. As such a drive increases, stimulation increases, causing the person psychological pain. The function of the nervous system, as Freud saw it, is to reduce excitation to the lowest possible level. The person is consequently compelled to obtain the object of the instinct and thereby eliminate the source conditions of the stimulus. Only when the need is satisfied in a suitable manner does pleasure finally result.

pleasure principle

The domain of the instinctual impulses is the unconscious. As a young physician, Freud saw many demonstrations of the unconscious through hypnosis. In a typical session a physician instructed someone in a hypnotic state to perform some action at a specific time—for example, to open an umbrella 5 minutes after awakening—then told him not to remember what had occurred during the trance. Upon being awakened, the subject behaved normally until the appointed time, when he suddenly carried out the physician's instructions without being able to explain why. Freud concluded that the impulse to open the umbrella must have lain buried in the unconscious as a result of the physician's admonition not to remember the events of the trance. The subject's inability to explain his behavior Freud later termed *resistance,* refusal to admit certain ideas to consciousness. He discovered ways to infer these unconscious processes from errors, dreams, and additional activity that cannot otherwise be explained.

resistance

Freud felt that the child's upbringing and training determine how he will gratify his needs. Early training determines what is repressed into the unconscious and how strongly it is repressed; it therefore shapes the motivational systems that guide behavior throughout life.

Freud eventually came to believe that early childhood is the source of neurotic anxiety, which causes repression. The original source of threat in which anxiety arises, Freud felt, is the birth trauma. The newborn infant suddenly finds himself at the mercy of external and internal stimuli over which he has no control. He is therefore absolutely dependent on his mother for gratification of his basic needs and must be reassured that he will not experience nongratification. Later, when the young child is chastised by his parents for giving free rein to sexual and aggressive impulses, he experiences anxiety over the possible withdrawal of their love. He therefore represses the impulses that cause their displeasure rather than suffer such a loss. In adult life, anxiety reappears whenever these repressed feelings are in danger of surfacing again. Because its object remains unconscious, anxiety takes on the character of a generalized dread of something unknown.

The Structure of the Mind

The innate needs of the individual are satisfied by its behavior, which is mediated by its mental apparatus. Freud conceived of this as the result of a three-stage id   developmental process. First, at birth, is the *id*, the reservoir of instinctual energy. It is unorganized, illogical (or, perhaps more accurately, alogical), and without regard to time. It discharges instinctual energy as fast as it can, without regard to reality, by means of the *primary process*. This is evidenced in such acts as the spontaneous urination and defecation of the infant or the blind aggression of rage, and also, when no immediate discharge is available, by images of the desired object, which the id cannot distinguish from reality.

The id and its primary process is not a very effective provider of gratification, and after repeated experience, a "portion" of the id, so to speak, be-ego   comes organized into the *ego*, which has the same goals of pleasure and tension reduction as the id, but which can negotiate with reality to attain them. As Freud said, the ego "interpolates between desire and action the procrastinating factor of thought"; it performs the *secondary process* of reality testing. Freud believed that the ego received its energy from the id by the "trick" of identifying itself with the desired object and so obtaining the psychic energies that these objects would ordinarily receive from the id.

In the course of identifying with the desired objects of the instincts within the social bounds of reality, the ego tends more and more to identify with models of significant others—usually the parents or parent figures—and from them receives guidelines of behavior, criteria of the good and bad, reasons for rewarding itself with praise or blame. This becomes the source of the third stage superego   of development—the creation of the *superego*.

Behavior or potential behavior thus becomes screened in three ways: the id discriminates the pleasant and unpleasant; the ego, the real and unreal; and the superego—that part of the ego that has incorporated the values of the social environment—the good and bad.

Freud distinguishes three types of anxiety: real anxiety, the response to a danger from outside "in real life"; neurotic anxiety, when the ego is threatened by excessive stimulation from the id and the prospect of punishment for discharge of this libidinal energy; and moral anxiety, the result of "reprimands" from the superego because of acts or impulses that violate the internalized moral code.

This uneasy and shifting alliance between the three regulating agencies of the psyche is the source of all motivation. The effectiveness of this alliance, and particularly the ability of the ego to mediate between its source, the id, and its derivative, the superego, determines the mental health of the person.

(We will see the details of this model much more in Chapter 12 on personality, and in Chapters 16 and 17 on disturbed behavior and its treatment.)

The ego cannot take effective action against the internal demands from the id, which are unconscious. Consequently the ego adopts various strategies of defense, the most important of which is *repression,* preventing the threatening impulse from becoming conscious. Other mechanisms of defense, which will be discussed in Chapter 16, have similar functions and characteristics: they are unconscious, and they deny, distort, or falsify the ego's perception of threat from within or without.

repression

The pattern of a person's defense mechanisms creates the unconscious sources of his behavior—the nature and strength of his motivation. Cues to the person's psychic structure are disclosed in slips and errors of everyday life and in dreams and daydreams.

Freud's Methods of Studying Motivation

Sigmund Freud's methods of studying human motivation actually pointed the way for others, such as Hull, to follow. He thought that one must begin with an analogy. For example, Freud compared mispronouncing a name by mistake with the intentional distortion of a name for the purpose of ridiculing someone. Next, one must consider all available knowledge about the person's state prior to his actions—his mental situation, character, and feelings. One must realize that the first two steps may not be sufficient to establish the motive; an unsubstantiated hypothesis may have to suffice until subsequent events either bear it out or disprove it.

Freud believed that all behavior is motivated, that is, has antecedents. He persisted in believing that so-called accidents—which are usually ascribed to fatigue, excitement, distraction, or illness—are in fact unconsciously motivated. The significance of such actions and other seemingly trivial occurrences is readily denied because the mental stuff comprising the antecedents of behavior is not necessarily available to consciousness. Freud was thus content to begin piecing together the picture of a person's underlying motivation from the merest scraps of his daily life.

Slips and Errors The intent behind printed and spoken slips and errors is often transparent. Thus, a newspaper article about a war-correspondent's interview with a general, who was notorious for certain foibles, reads "this battle-scared veteran"; and the apology in the following day's edition amends the text to "this bottle-scarred veteran" (Freud, 1920).

Freud also found hidden motives in the accidental distortion of names. For instance, a student who, in private, has repeatedly scorned the intellectual capabilities of a Professor Whitmore one day addresses him in class as Professor Whit*less.*

Even seemingly unintelligible slips, the varieties of which are endless, can, under scrutiny, reveal motive. For example, a man and his wife have entertained a rather dull couple all evening; but the hostess feels compelled to be polite and says to them on leaving, "We must make it a boresome again some time."

The task of any analysis of motivation is to bring the hidden motive to light through interpreting these bits of behavior. Excitement, fatigue, illness, and distraction can only be contributing influences, factors that increase the possibility of errors but are not their causes.

Dreams   Dreams, according to Freud, also represent a compromise between conflicting motives. He gave three observations in support of this interpretation.

The first was based on the experience that probably everyone has had, the incorporation of some persistent external stimulus such as the buzzing of an alarm clock or the ringing of the doorbell into a dream. One may even dream of silencing the noise by shutting off the buzzer or going to see who is at the door. The practical result of such a dream is to reduce the impact of the stimulus so that sleep may continue undisturbed. Freud's initial conclusion, therefore, was that dreams express the motive to preserve sleep.

Daydreams provided Freud with a second indication of the motivational function of dreams. While daydreams occur during a wakeful state and are not hallucinatory, they nevertheless have fantastic content. Freud believed that

women's fantasies are primarily erotic while men's are primarily egoistic, though often influenced by the erotic since their imagined exploits are meant ultimately for the eyes of women. The obvious longings expressed in daydreams confirmed in Freud's mind the general function of dreams to fulfill wishes.

The third observation came from Freud's study of the nocturnal dreams of young children, which he found devoid of the distortion evident in the dreams of adults. For example, a little boy was asked to give someone a basket of cherries; he carried out the instructions obediently but grudgingly, despite the promise of some of the fruit for himself. That night he dreamed that he had eaten all of the cherries himself. Apparently the earlier events of the day had resulted in an unfulfilled wish that reemerged in the child's dream. The dream removed an internal stimulus threatening to disturb the child and thus preserved sleep. Freud saw the dream in its simplest and most uncensored form, then, as a compromise between the motives of preserving sleep and fulfilling a wish.

This is by no means a complete description of Freud's motivational theory, or of his sources of evidence in its support. What is presented here is his concept of the source of motivation, the way motivation leads to behavior, and the kinds of evidence that he noted in supporting his ideas. Hull worked out his theory with animals as subjects, and motor responses were the only behaviors he attempted to explain. Freud dealt exclusively with human beings and was much more interested in their verbal processes, and especially their feelings, which

often had not even reached consciousness in the person himself. Nevertheless, the two theories share one underlying principle: the biological origin of motivation. In both, the primary motive is tension reduction.

Both Hull and Freud can now be contrasted with a third concept of motivation, which we have called cognitive because of its focus on decision-making processes. Its principal exponent was Edward C. Tolman, although there are many more recent adherents, and we will look at several of them as well.

COGNITIVE MODELS OF MOTIVATION

Edward C. Tolman

Unlike both Hull and Freud, Edward C. Tolman's philosophical bias goes back to the pre-Darwinian idea of man as a rational being. His theory was an attempt to translate concepts of "mind" or "thought" into more objective, behavioristically oriented language.

Man: Cognitive or Biological?

Are we motivated and ruled by biological-physiological variables or by cognition? Although it seems that for lower organisms biological drives are the prime determinants of behavior, this becomes less and less so the higher an organism is on the phylogenetic scale. For example, the sex act for lower animals is limited to certain seasons and times when the female is in heat. Sex behavior is predictable, stereotyped. This is not the case for humans. Both men and women are roughly equivalent in being potentially receptive all of the time. Here, however, social pressures and determinants usually impose limitations. The biological drive is not all-powerful, then, but is channeled by cognition.

Even more striking evidence of this phenomenon appears in studies in which feelings of hunger, thirst, and fear are controlled by cognition. In one experiment of this kind, subjects were asked to skip breakfast and lunch, for the ostensible purpose of assessing how deprivation affects intellectual and motor functioning (Brehm, 1962). The subjects rated how hungry they were before carrying out some task. Upon finishing it, they were again asked to go without food and to return later for another test. One group of subjects received $5.00 as an inducement to remain in the study, while the other group received nothing. After both groups had agreed to continue, they rated their degree of hunger for a second time. The results showed that those who had received money, and who therefore presumably had a substantial justification for continuing to deprive themselves of food, reported being hungrier after the agreement to remain in the study; those, however, who had been given no inducement reported feeling less hungry. Apparently, the latter group, having insufficient justification for prolonging their hunger, changed their cognition of their physical state and thereby reduced the inconsistency between their discomfort and their behavior (see the discussion of "cognitive dissonance" in Chapters 15 and 17).

In a variation of this experiment, subjects went without water instead of food. All procedures were identical with the addition that after subjects gave their second thirst rating, they were given water to drink. As was expected, those in the insufficient justification group drank less water.

In this experiment the subjects' behavior was evidently determined by their cognition of their physiological state. The conditions of hunger and thirst differentially affected consequent behavior according to the degree to which they had cognitive representation.

Tolman was much more interested in knowledge than in drives. Empirical studies had suggested to him that cognition, knowledge, and understanding are present in animals, and he came to conceive of knowledge, in both man and animals, as a kind of "cognitive map" of the world. Tolman thus approached motivation from the vantage point of two different concepts: *expectation,* the **expectation** estimate of the probability that a given behavior will have a particular result, and *value,* the worth of the expected result. Whether or not an act is performed **value**

Imprinting

An important class of behavior attributed in part to maturation is the "imprinting" behavior of certain birds, notably geese and ducks. When they are several hours old, these birds instinctively follow the mother bird. If the real mother is not available, however, the young bird will follow, not only another animal, but any moving object that is present. Konrad Lorenz raised a flock of geese who followed him, and other birds have followed decoy ducks and even footballs. Moreover, they continue to follow the originally imprinted "mother," even if the real mother is subsequently available. Lorenz and his associates eventually taught the geese to fly by running in front of them and flapping their arms; the birds took off while the models remained earthbound.

Nina Leen, photographer, Life Magazine. © 1972, Time, Inc. Reprinted by permission.

Konrad Lorenz and his geese.

thus depends on what outcome is expected and what value is attributed to that outcome: Performance = Expectation × Value.

Most research into human motivation today follows the approach developed by Tolman, though often without acknowledging his contribution. We will consider his theories in general first and then examine a couple of specific motivations in greater detail. Tolman's emphasis on decisions guided by expectations and values means that his focus is primarily on incentives, rather than on internal states, or drives. In his view, drives may determine when a person will act in a particular way, but they have nothing to do with the enduring *disposition* toward action that we call "motivation." For example, in order for the achievement need to influence behavior at all, a situation must first make the need salient. When there is no possibility for achievement or its evaluation, the achievement motive has no effect on behavior. But once an achievement situation has occurred, a person with a high need for achievement will react one way, whereas a person with a low achievement need will react differently. Tolman was particularly concerned to show that learning can occur in the relative absence of internal drive states; he called this "latent learning." He thus introduced the distinction between learning (or acquisition) and performance.

"Oh, go away!"

Distinction between Learning and Performance

Tolman pointed out the necessity of distinguishing between an animal's "knowledge" of a particular behavior and its "desire" to demonstrate it. Earlier many had assumed that learning was simply a matter of practicing the association between a stimulus and a response, and that overt performance was the measure of learning. Considerable time elapsed before psychologists finally worked out the experimental techniques for separating the variables of knowledge and the demonstration of that knowledge.

For earlier theorists, variations in performance produced by different kinds and amounts of rewards resulted from the degree of satisfaction the rewards offered. But what about changes in learned behavior that occurred in the total absence of a reward?

Clearly, a way had to be found to account for the dramatic changes in performance from one trial to the next. The question to be answered was how past learning merged with immediate factors to direct behavior during a particular trial.

Tolman believed that learning is a matter of building up expectancies about the outcomes of various responses; by no means is a particular response *automatically* elicited by a given stimulus. In trial-and-error learning, the subject begins to recognize at the different choice points what the consequences of the alternative responses will be as a result of having tried them all out. Once it has acquainted itself with all the consequences, it can determine whether or not to engage in the given activity.

Latent Learning

In the earliest study of latent learning, now regarded as a classic, three groups of hungry rats ran a multiple T-maze for food (Blodgett, 1929). The first group was rewarded on each trial; the second, from the third trial on; and the third, from the seventh trial on. The second and third groups both showed a marked decrease in errors immediately after introduction of the reward.

A subsequent experiment was similar in all respects except that it varied the reward pattern somewhat (Tolman and Honzig, 1930a). One group continued to receive food on every run, while a second group received none at all, and the third received food beginning with the 11th trial. Here, too, an abrupt improvement in performance occurred in the third group once it had been rewarded. In both of these experiments the groups who were not rewarded until later caught up with the continuously rewarded group. To have done so means that even when not rewarded, they must have been learning.

In the third experiment two groups of rats were used (Crespi, 1942). In order to test whether a change in the amount of food would show similar results, one group was shifted from a small reward to a larger one, and the other, from a large reward to a smaller one. Directly after the shift, the group receiving the increased reward greatly improved its performance, while the group receiving the smaller reward diminished its performance.

Further studies, which focused on manipulating the quality rather than the quantity of the incentive, expanded the understanding of the latent learning phenomenon. For instance, slightly hungry but very thirsty animals ran a maze poorly when rewarded on the first nine daily trials with only bran mash. After the introduction of water on the 10th trial, however, performance suddenly increased (Elliott, 1929).

Two other experiments demonstrated what Tolman later called *demand strength* for a goal object by using different kinds of incentives. In the first (Simmons, 1924), hungry animals were given a taste of either sunflower seeds or bread and milk (a preferred diet) before starting through a maze and another taste when they had reached the goal box. Although all of the animals steadily reduced their errors and running time, those fed bread and milk improved at a much faster rate. Animals fed sunflower seeds improved more rapidly than animals fed nothing at all. Both phases of the experiment, then, showed that the animals' performance depended on the kind of incentive they were given.

The experiment of Tolman and Honzig (1930a) provided further illustrations of cognition by demonstrating the effects of substituting, in his words, *more-* or *less-demanded* incentives. Thus, the group of hungry rats rewarded for the first time on the 11th daily run through a maze dramatically improved its performance from the 12th trial on, surpassing the performance of hungry rats that had been rewarded from the beginning. The switch from a less- to a more-demanded incentive increased performance. In another phase of the experiment, one group of hungry rats received food at the end of each daily run through a maze until the 11th trial, when the reward was terminated. Performance suffered immediately following the switch from a more- to a less-demanded incentive.

The basis of its decision is the expected outcome of a behavior (which determines the action) and the value of the expectancy (the subject's desire for the expected outcome). Thus, in order to predict behavior we must understand the decision-making process that goes into it.

Tolman based his research primarily on animals, but the most important applications of the cognitive approaches to motivation have come from research with human beings, both children and adults. Further, since most of the developments in research on decision processes have been limited to human beings, the best studies in this approach to motivation have used human subjects.

In many studies motivated behavior is conceptualized pretty much without regard to antecedent drives or internal needs. However, as the application to humans has developed, it has become clear to cognition theorists that some kinds of motivational predispositions must be built up inside the person. David C. McClelland has been most responsible for developing this idea, and we will consider several important aspects of his research, which is still considered within the framework of the cognitive approach because of its greater emphasis on incentives than on internal drives. But the focus is on the antecedent learning conditions and consequent behavior surrounding each of a number of motives, rather than on motivation in general. We turn now to some examples of the way in which a cognitive theorist conceptualizes human motives.

David C. McClelland

Specification of Motives

A person might be described as having a strong achievement motive. In what way is this a useful description? If we are talking only about his behavior, rather than his motives, then we might talk about what he has learned—to work hard at school and so forth. But the concept of motive refers to more than simply the person's habits. The notion that motive refers to a disposition to act, not necessarily just the actions themselves, is also crucial.

achievement motive

How does one acquire such a generalized predisposition? Not by learning specific habits, because they could not generalize broadly enough. What has to be learned is that successful competition against a standard of excellence produces pleasure or rewards, regardless of the particular standards or behavior. Therefore, the learning experiences have to be pretty general, too, and must concentrate most on a kind of diffuse relationship between reward and action—diffuse enough so that it will not extinguish in circumstances in which competition is unsuccessful. One quality of a motive then should be that once acquired, it sustains itself independently of the success of the behavior in producing rewards. We will consider the achievement motive in greater detail.

Achievement Motivation McClelland defined the achievement motive as a predisposition to compete against an internalized standard of excellence. Thus, a person with such a motive will work hard, do a "good" job, try for good grades, records, and the like, whenever standards for performance are available, and he will provide his own standards when none exist.

Expectancy and Value of Incentives

Following Tolman's work on incentives, other investigators have explored other variables, further refining the role of cognition in motivation.

In one study (Atkinson, 1958), college students were informed that they would compete for a prize against other members of groups to which they had been randomly assigned. The groups consisted of twenty, four, three, or two persons, and the prize was either $2.50 or $1.25. Subjects assigned to the twenty-, three-, and two-person groups were told that only one prize would be awarded; those assigned to the four-person group were told that three prizes would be awarded. Each subject knew the size of her group, the amount of the prize, and the number of prizes to be awarded to the group. Thus, the probability of winning for each subject was 1/20, 1/3, 1/2 or 3/4, and the incentive value was either $2.50 or $1.25. Each subject performed two 20-minute tasks: marking X's inside circles on numerous pages of circles, and solving an extensive list of three-step arithmetic problems. Predictably, the amount of the incentive influenced the level of performance: subjects did better when the incentive was $2.50 than when it was $1.25 (Fig. 5.7). What was not predictable, however, was that for both incentives the performance was best when the probability of winning was 1/2. One might have expected the best performance with a probability of 3/4 since this offered a better chance to win. The added factor of satisfaction in attainment seemed also to have influenced the results. Subjects did best when there was a 50–50 chance of winning—not too low, but not too high either.

Similar findings emerged from a study in which the experimenter asked young children to toss a ring at a peg from a distance of their own choosing (McClelland, 1958). Children regarded as strongly motivated to achieve tended to throw more often from an intermediate distance, as if they received little satisfaction from a sure thing by standing very close.

Another experimenter presented boys with the dilemma of choosing which of two different kinds of candy they would rather win by trying their luck with

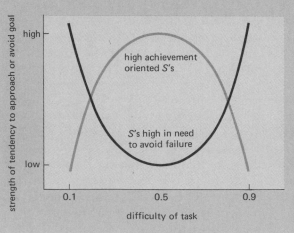

Fig. 5.7 High achievement oriented subjects typically choose tasks of intermediate difficulty, since they have a reasonable (.5) chance of being accomplished and also have incentive value. Subjects, high in the need to avoid failure, typically choose task of either low (.1) difficulty or high (.9) difficulty. If the task is very easy, the probability of failure is small. If the task is very hard the probability of failure is high but the degree of unpleasantness associated with failure at a difficult task is not very high. (Atkinson, 1964)

a lottery box (Feather, 1959). The box contained 15 red marbles and five blue ones and was constructed so that a gate at the bottom allowed only one marble to pass through at a time. The boys were told that they would win one kind of candy if they managed to roll a red marble out of the box; for the other candy, they would have to roll a blue marble out. The boys obviously had a better chance of winning the red-marble candy since the red marbles were more numerous. Having outlined the conditions, the experimenter next asked the boys which candy they would feel more pleased about winning. The question did not entail an actual decision to try for one or the other candy but simply an indication of preference for winning one over the other. The boys were divided into two groups before being asked the question; one group thought the situation was a test, and the other thought it was a game, the assumption being that in a test of skill the feeling of success increases with the difficulty of the task.

The results indeed showed that those boys who regarded the task as a game demonstrated a roughly equal preference for both candies. Those, however, who regarded it as a test showed a greater preference for the candy that was harder to obtain. The value of the outcome of a decision depended on the conditions surrounding the choice. In one instance the value rested simply on the attractiveness of the object, while in the other it rested also on the attractiveness of *attaining* the object.

For example, someone with a strong motive to achieve may not work hard when the odds of success are very small, as there is little hope of achieving anything, including the pleasure of accomplishment. On the other hand, neither will he work hard if the task is too easy, for while the reward is almost assured, the feeling of accomplishment will be hollow. This accounts for the finding that strong achievers work best when the chances of success are intermediate, neither too high nor too low. Translated into the terms we have already used, the *expectancy of success* and the *incentive value of success* are related to each other.

It seems reasonable that early learning experiences would be ones in which parents encouraged the child to try, in which they pointed out external standards and suggested internal ones to him, and in which they provided rewards for accomplishments. A number of studies have shown exactly these relationships. In one (Rosen and D'Andrade, 1959), 9- to 11-year-old boys were asked to complete several tasks, including building a tower out of blocks while blindfolded. The parents were present during the tasks. Boys independently rated high in achievement motivations were more often urged to set higher goals by their parents, and were more often given hints, especially by the mothers.

Encouragement is not the only antecedent, however. It has been shown (Winterbottom, 1958) that sons of mothers who provide independence training develop stronger achievement motives. Such mothers create situations in which the child has an opportunity to accomplish something, and then they reward that accomplishment. They do not indulge the child, or encourage dependency.

Motivation to achieve is high as college students of a few years ago took examinations which helped their draft boards decide whether they would stay in school or be drafted into the armed forces.

In this sense, the child knows that in any situation, if he adopts some standard of excellence, and then works hard to compete with it, he will be rewarded. Gradually he comes to internalize the reward too, to anticipate feeling good over the success even if no one else knows about it.

Achievement-related behaviors have other motivational aspects. Where behavior is to be evaluated, the motive to succeed exists simultaneously with the motive to avoid failure, characterized by anxiety, which inhibits action rather than exciting it. Like the motive to succeed, the motive to avoid failure is strongest when there is a 50–50 chance of failing.

A person who is highly motivated to avoid failure feels safer performing either a very easy or a very difficult task; he is almost certain to pass the easy task and will assuredly not be censured for failing a difficult one. Theoretically, then, a person's actual performance represents some resolution of the conflict between the tendencies to approach success and avoid failure (Atkinson, 1964).

The motivation to avoid failure was shown in an early study of goal setting in children (Sears, 1940). Children accustomed to success set reasonable performance goals for themselves, whereas those whose records revealed repeated failure avoided any real challenge by setting goals that were either very low or very high.

Another experiment investigated situations in which cues demanding competition with a standard of excellence were particularly salient (Raphelson, 1957). It was found that in a significant number of college-age subjects, the greater their motive to succeed, the lower was their anxiety level. As circumstances grow increasingly competitive, persons highly motivated to achieve perform better than those who are highly anxious over the possibility of failure or are little motivated to succeed.

In an achievement-oriented activity, then, the goal, or level of aspiration, is not constant. When a person performs a task successfully, he does not necessarily experience a feeling of success, nor upon failing does he necessarily feel like a failure. The subjective experience of success or failure depends on whether the difficulty of the task falls within the person's range of aspiration.

level of aspiration

Murray's Motives

Need	Brief Definition
Abasement	To submit passively to external force. To accept injury, blame, criticism, punishment. To surrender. To become resigned to fate. To admit inferiority, error, wrongdoing, or defeat. To confess and atone. To blame, belittle, or mutilate the self. To seek and enjoy pain, punishment, illness, and misfortune.
Achievement	To accomplish something difficult. To master, manipulate, or organize physical objects, human beings, or ideas. To do this as rapidly and as independently as possible. To overcome obstacles and attain a high standard. To excel oneself. To rival and surpass others. To increase self-regard by the successful exercise of talent.
Affiliation	To draw near and enjoyably co-operate or reciprocate with an allied other (an other who resembles the subject or who likes the subject). To please and win affection of a cathected object. To adhere and remain loyal to a friend.
Aggression	To overcome opposition forcefully. To fight. To revenge an injury. To attack, injure, or kill another. To oppose forcefully or punish another.
Autonomy	To get free, shake off restraint, break out of confinement. To resist coercion and restriction. To avoid or quit activities prescribed by domineering authorities. To be independent and free to act according to impulse. To be unattached, irresponsible. To defy convention.

Need	Brief Definition
Counteraction	To master or make up for a failure by restriving. To obliterate a humiliation by resumed action. To overcome weaknesses, to repress fear. To efface a dishonor by action. To search for obstacles and difficulties to overcome. To maintain self-respect and pride on a high level.
Defendance	To defend the self against assault, criticism, and blame. To conceal or justify a misdeed, failure, or humiliation. To vindicate the ego.
Deference	To admire and support a superior. To praise, honor, or eulogize. To yield eagerly to the influence of an allied other. To emulate an exemplar. To conform to custom.
Dominance	To control one's human environment. To influence or direct the behavior of others by suggestion, seduction, persuasion, or command. To dissuade, restrain, or prohibit.
Exhibition	To make an impression. To be seen and heard. To excite, amaze, fascinate, entertain, shock, intrigue, amuse, or entice others.
Harmavoidance	To avoid pain, physical injury, illness, and death. To escape from a dangerous situation. To take precautionary measures.
Infavoidance	To avoid humiliation. To quit embarrassing situations or to avoid conditions which may lead to belittlement: the scorn, derision, or indifference of others. To refrain from action because of the fear of failure.
Nurturance	To give sympathy and gratify the needs of a helpless object: an infant or any object that is weak, disabled, tired, inexperienced, infirm, defeated, humiliated, lonely, dejected, sick, mentally confused. To assist an object in danger. To feed, help, support, console, protect, comfort, nurse, heal.
Order	To put things in order. To achieve cleanliness, arrangement, organization, balance, neatness, tidiness, and precision.
Play	To act for "fun" without further purpose. To like to laugh and make jokes. To seek enjoyable relaxation of stress. To participate in games, sports, dancing, drinking parties, cards.
Rejection	To separate oneself from a negatively cathected object. To exclude, abandon, expel, or remain indifferent to an inferior object. To snub or jilt an object.
Sentience	To seek and enjoy sensuous impressions.
Sex	To form and further an erotic relationship. To have sexual intercourse.
Succorance	To have one's needs gratified by the sympathetic aid of an allied object. To be nursed, supported, sustained, surrounded, protected, loved, advised, guided, indulged, forgiven, consoled. To remain close to a devoted protector. To always have a supporter.
Understanding	To ask or answer general questions. To be interested in theory. To speculate, formulate, analyze, and generalize.

SOURCE: Hall and Lindsay (1970); data from Murray (1938)

Task difficulty also influences the goal a person sets for himself. If, for instance, a high school wrestler pits himself against someone in a much higher weight class, he will not feel threatened by defeat; nor will beating someone in a lower weight class bring him much satisfaction. Wrestling an opponent within his own class, however, does afford a real test of his ability, so the outcome of this contest will engender feelings of success or failure. He is, in other words, ego-involved.

Group standards also influence level of aspiration. Experimenters observed this effect when they placed college students in small groups to solve simple arithmetic problems (Hilgard, Sait, and Magaret, 1940). Everyone's score was

 Affiliation and Power Motives

Besides the achievement motive, studies have experimentally aroused and then measured other kinds of motivation.

For example, Shipley and Veroff (1952) and Atkinson, Heyns, and Veroff (1954) have produced a scoring system for affiliation motivation. In their study members of a group first rated each other in a group setting. This was done to arouse concern in the subjects over how likable or acceptable they were to other people. Immediately after this rating session, the subjects were asked to write whatever stories were suggested to them by particular pictures. These stories were then compared with stories written in a relaxed, neutral condition where no affiliative needs had been aroused. The stories in the aroused condition showed significantly more "concern over establishing, maintaining, and restoring positive relations with others."

These stories were then further tested for validity. People who knew the subjects rated them as to whether or not they were approval seekers. The subjects who had yielded high affiliation-need scores were also more often described by their friends as needers of approval than were subjects who had low affiliation-need scores.

Obviously, then, the affiliation-need test is identifying a motive that manifests itself in behavior.

Veroff (1957) designed a study to measure a power motive, defined as "concern over controlling the means of influencing the behavior of another person." He also compared stories subjects wrote under relaxed and aroused conditions. He had subjects who were running for high student offices write stories on the night of the election and compared them with stories written by a relaxed control group. As expected the students in the former group told stories in which a concern for controlling others was much more manifest than it was in the stories of the second group. The students who showed high power-need scores were also more frequently described by their professors as being argumentative in class and spending much time trying to convince others.

Similar studies have been able to elicit aggressive tendencies and fear in stories written under arousal conditions.

announced to the group, after which each student privately noted the score he expected to make on the following test. The results showed that students whose scores were below the rest of the group's usually raised their level of aspiration, whereas those who scored above the group usually lowered theirs.

Other Motives Achievement is not the only human motive, although it has been studied most because it seems important to mid-20th-century Western man. Murray (1938) drew up a list of several dozen motives that are acquired, but only the affiliation motive and the power motive have been extensively investigated. As for the achievement motive, particular early learning experiences have been identified in the acquisition of affiliation and power motives.

How do these various motives relate to each other? Do some go together more than others? Do we acquire them in any order or hierarchy? Abraham Maslow, whom we will consider in more detail in Chapter 12 on personality, proposed a hierarchical organization of motives. In his view, man had five levels of motives (which he called needs): physiological, safety, belongingness and love, esteem, and self-actualization needs. The ascending order in which he places them symbolizes his idea that motivating forces do not remain static but develop. A need that is "lower" in the hierarchy is of a more biological nature, begins earlier, and must be sufficiently satisfied before a higher need can be met. Not that one cannot *begin* to fulfill a higher need until a lower one is completely satisfied; one simply cannot be primarily concerned with it until then. One must have enough to eat and drink, for instance, before fulfilling the need for security and stability.

SUMMARY

Not all people behave similarly under similar conditions. Laymen and psychologists alike attribute differences of this sort to inner factors, which psychologists term more specifically *motives*. Although motivation today is studied under highly controlled experimental conditions, it remains something that is inferred, not directly observed. It is the immediate forces that act to energize, direct, sustain, and stop a behavior.

Philosophically man has been viewed within four major conceptual frameworks, basic to the different theories of motivation existing today. Man as machine, whose responses are automatically triggered by stimuli, and man as animal, ruled by biological drives, are relevant to biological theories of motivation. Freudian theory, in which the unconscious rules but is not totally inaccessible, is close to the biological theories. Rational man, in whom reason rules the passions, is most relevant to cognitive theories of motivation. Social and cultural theories of human behavior play some part in cognitive theories of motivation.

Clark Hull's drive theory of motivation attempted to answer two questions posed by learning theory: Why does a reinforcer reinforce? What determines the variability of performance strength? His answer to the first was that a physiological need created by homeostatic imbalance produces a drive to initiate a behavior to reduce the drive and, simultaneously, the need. Hull's answer to the second question was that variability is due to differences in the strength of the drive state, which depends on the degree of deprivation or pain.

For Hull, activation of any of the biological drives (hunger, thirst, sex, pain) should result in increased general activity level, performance rate, acceptance of punishment, and appropriate goal selection.

He later made significant modifications of this rather primitive model of motivation, first admitting the existence of incentives as additional determiners of the performance of a behavior. Then, still on the basis of animal research but with broad implications for humans, he recognized secondary reinforcers: objects, such as money, that in themselves do not reduce any primary biological drive. For Hull, however, primary drive reduction remained at the center of motivation. Finally, Hull recognized acquired drives, specifically the drive to avoid pain, which in humans is the basis of anxiety.

As biologically based as Hull's theory but more specifically human is Freud's psychoanalytic theory of motivation, which attributes most causation to the unconscious and its psychic energy. All behavior, Freud said, is motivated by the pleasure principle, but it is mediated by a mental apparatus, including an Id, the reservoir of instinctual energy; an Ego, or reality tester, which mediates between the demands of the Id and environmental limitations; and a Superego, or conscience.

The precarious alliance of these three forces is subject to many threats, which produce anxiety—real, neurotic, or moral. The Ego's characteristic response to anxiety is a defense mechanism, most specifically repression.

For Freud, all behavior is motivated or caused. He found particularly significant evidence of causation in accidents, such as slips of the tongue and forgetfulness, and in dreams, where, with or without disguise, we fulfill our wishes.

A third and very different approach to motivation is represented by Tolman's cognitive model of behavior. Even in animals, Tolman found evidence of cognition, specifically of *expectancy,* the animal's estimate of the probability that a known behavior will produce a desired result, and of *value,* the worth of the result. Behavior results from a decision process that considers the goal objects or incentives in a central role. In emphasizing the importance of incentive, Tolman pointed to the phenomenon of latent learning—evidence that a behavior had been learned though it wasn't performed until there was a significant incentive for doing so.

Following Tolman, whose research was largely confined to animals, other cognitive theorists have made valid applications of his theories in experiments with humans. They found that the amount of an incentive and the satisfaction in attainment could influence the level of performance.

McClelland has been interested in the antecedent learning conditions and consequent behavior that surround a number of motives, especially the achievement motive. A generalized predisposition to achieve is usually learned in early childhood from parents who encourage trying, who suggest both external and internal standards, and who reward accomplishment. Even more important may be independence training.

Other components of achievement-related behavior are fear of failure and level of expectation. As circumstances grow increasingly competitive, persons highly motivated to achieve perform better than those who are highly anxious about failing or are little motivated to succeed. Both personal and group standards influence one's level of aspiration.

Other motives that have been extensively investigated are the affiliation motive and the power motive. Maslow has proposed a hierarchical organization of motives in which the highest need is self-actualization, but this can only be pursued when needs lower on the scale have been fulfilled.

Suggested Readings

Bartoshuk, A. K., "Motivation," in J. W. Kling and L. A. Riggs, eds., *Woodworth and Schlosberg's Experimental Psychology*, 3d ed. New York, Holt, Rinehart and Winston, 1971.
  A brief introduction to current motivation research.
Conrad, Joseph, *Heart of Darkness* (many editions).
  A novel about a powerful European who reverts to savagery in an isolated African trading post.
Fest, Joachim C., *Hitler*, trans. by Richard and Clara Winston. New York, Harcourt Brace Jovanovich, 1974.
  In this book about Hitler's rise to power the author examines the factors in the Fuehrer's personality as well as those in society that made possible the era of Nazi Germany.
Lorenz, Konrad, *Evolution and Modification of Behavior*. Chicago, University of Chicago Press, 1966.
  A somewhat technical examination of the whole question of innate versus learned behavior by the author of the popular *King Solomon's Ring*.
Montagu, Ashley, *Man and Aggression*. New York, Oxford, 1968.
  Montagu refutes the notion of some behavior theorists that man is merely an instinct-driven beast, contending instead that our problems are of our own making.
Osborne, John, *Luther*. New York, New American Library, 1961.
  In this play the conflicts of the young Martin Luther are portrayed in neo-Freudian terms.
Wells, H. G., *The Island of Dr. Moreau* (originally published in 1856). New York, Lancer, 1934.
  The theme of this novel is the animal nature of man.

Chapter Six

The Biology of Behavior

What is a cell?
What is the function of the human nervous system?
What is a synapse?
What is the difference between afferent and efferent nerves?
  Between sympathetic and parasympathetic nerves?
How many cells does the human brain contain?
What is the function of the human endocrine system?
What are hormones?
Is sex physiological?
What effects do drugs have on the brain?

In preceding chapters, we have discussed some of the ways in which man perceives things, learns, remembers, and is motivated. In other words we have discussed ways in which man interacts with his surroundings. In this chapter we examine the physiological mechanisms for these interactions or behaviors.

Man, like other animals and like plants, is biologically a multicellular organism. The fact that animals and plants function so well even though they are communities of millions of separate cells shows that the individual lives of these vast populations of cells are coordinated. The activity of cells in one part of the organism is coordinated or *integrated* with the activity of cells in another part. Integration is brought about by two distinct mechanisms, *chemical control mechanisms* and *nervous control mechanisms*.

The principal chemical control mechanisms for integrating the activities of different cells are *hormones*. These are "chemical messengers" produced by certain specialized cells of the body that exert specific effects on certain other tissues of the body. In animals, hormones are produced by special groups of cells called *endocrine glands*. Animal hormones are transported to all parts of the body by the blood or other body fluids. Animals use hormones to integrate many activities where speed is not required—digestion, reproduction, and growth.

When speed is essential, animals use their nervous systems, and not hormones. When you inadvertently put your hand on a hot stove, a speedy response is important. Nerve impulses fly from pain receptors in your hand along nerves to the spinal cord. The spinal cord sends nerve impulses immediately to the muscles of the arm, which withdraws your hand. Animals have evolved both muscles and nervous systems to make such rapid movements possible.

The nervous system can act so quickly for two reasons. First, all the muscles of the body are connected to the spinal cord and brain by nerves. Second, nerve impulses travel over nerves far more rapidly than the blood circulates hormones. In addition the nervous system can act selectively and can exert far more localized effects than any circulating hormone, because the nerve endings release transmitter chemicals "locally," that is, only a few microns away from the cell to be stimulated. (A micron is one-thousandth of a millimeter.)

All multicellular animals more complex than hydra have both a slow (endocrine or hormonal) and a fast (nervous) control system. To guarantee that these two control systems do not conflict with one another, they are closely integrated, usually by the brain. We will consider the nervous system in some detail here, and then the endocrine system more briefly.

NERVE CELLS

cell   All cells in a multicelled animal have the basic life apparatus in common: a nucleus, cytoplasm, and an outer membrane. However, each cell is specialized in its function.

Among the simplest of multicelled animals is the sponge. Like one-celled animals, the sponge lacks a nervous system but responds to stimulation. In the sponge, cells influence each other by means of muscle fibers. Without nerve connections among its cells, the sponge is capable of only a very limited range of behavior.

In higher forms of life, nerve connections begin to take shape in the form of a nerve ring. Yet, it is only in still higher life forms that actual nerve cell connections occur. It is in these that we have the start of a nervous system, with cells specially designed for conducting information to and from various parts of the animal.

The simplest nervous systems like that of hydra contain only a few hundred or thousand nerve cells. A bee's nervous system may contain half a million cells. The most complex nervous system—man's—contains more than 10^{10} nerve cells. Fortunately all nervous systems, whether simple or complex, are composed of the same basic kinds of cells—nerve cells. As far as we know nerve cells function in much the same way wherever they are found—in a hydra, a boy, or a man. The nerve cell is where we begin our examination of the nervous system.

Structure of Nerve Cells

Nerve cells or *neurons* carry messages, and they do this in two ways.

Messages may be sent from one part of the nerve cell to another part, that is, intracellularly. Such intracellular messages, called *nerve impulses,* are electrical changes in the cell membrane. Nerve impulses are not electric currents in the sense of electrons moving down a wire, and therefore they do not move with the speed of light. They are movements of electric charges in and out of the cell membrane and are conducted very rapidly from one part of a nerve cell to another part.

Messages may be sent between cells, that is, intercellularly. Such intercellular messages are transmitted usually in the form of a *transmitter chemical.* As might be expected, neurons are specialized for sending and receiving these messages.

nerve impulse

transmitter chemical

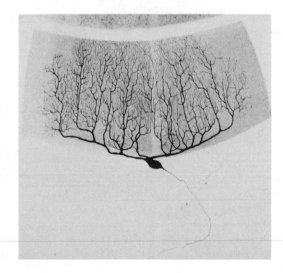

Fig. 6.1 A neuron from a region of the human brain called the dentate gyrus. This drawing was prepared in 1886 by Camillo Golgi, a brilliant Italian neuroanatomist who developed a technique in which only a few of the nerve cells in a piece of tissue are stained. Moreover, these few cells are stained in their entirety. This method opened the way for a detailed analysis of the anatomy of the brain which has continued actively to this day. Note the faintly stained fine axon leaving the cell body and the hundreds of branching dendrites from this single cell. (Ebert et al., 1973)

A human nerve cell (Fig. 6.1) is about 0.1 millimeter in diameter, and it contains many ribosomes—protein synthesis centers. This should not be surprising, for nerve cells are very active in synthesizing proteins. There are also many structures in the cell that we usually associate with secretion. Some of these structures may play a role in making transmitter chemicals.

Unlike the cell body of most other cells, the cell body of a neuron has branches. Most of the branches are short, very thin, and have a spiny look. They are called *dendrites.* Dendrites act as "antennae," receiving incoming messages in the form of transmitter chemicals from other nerve cells. When enough of the dendrites of a receiving cell get excited by transmitter chemicals, the electrical charges spread to the cell body. Most nerve cells also have a single long branch, the *axon,* which conducts nerve impulses away from the cell body. Some axons, such as one running from the spinal cord to the big toe, may be extremely long. The axon of some neurons, however, may be only a few microns long.

dendrite

axon

The Methods of Physiological Psychology: Anatomical Procedures

Much of the material presented in this chapter may have a "magical" quality to it, urging you to ask in amazement, "How do you know?" In fact, this material has required much painstaking reasearch, a lot of it directed at the question, "How can we study the brain and nervous system?" Over several centuries a number of ingenious techniques have been developed. Some of the material in boxes throughout this chapter will focus on the methods of study developed. A detailed discussion of the methodology and an example of research done with each technique will be presented. Here we will be concerned with anatomical procedures.

In studying any object, we should be able to identify its different structures, for only in this way can we hope to understand their function and, in turn, the function of the entire object. With the brain, however, it is not always easy to identify individual structures. Many of them are so complex and minute that it is very difficult and, with the naked eye impossible, to pull apart the many intertwined fibers, thus to identify the different structures of this seemingly amorphous mass. However, with the help of microscopes and some ingenious techniques, much anatomical identification has been possible.

When a peripheral nerve is sectioned, there is a gradual degeneration of the fiber that connects to it. By watching the course of this degeneration we can follow the path of the fiber and identify its central locus of control and the pathways leading to it.

Staining procedures are also useful in identification. A stain is simply a dye that is applied to brain tissue. Because different tissues are of different chemical composition, dyes color them differently. Thus a dye might color one tissue but not another. In this way under a microscope the different parts of the nerve cells and structures become "visible." In many instances the two methods we have described—peripheral nerve section and staining—are used in conjunction. Because degenerating myelin (the material that covers many nerve fibers) differs chemically from normal myelin, it stains differently. This principle allowed an early worker in physiological psychology, Vittorio Marchi (1851–1908), to trace degenerating fibers in microscopic sections.

When the nerve impulse reaches the end of the axon, a transmitter is released onto a neighboring cell's dendrites, and the whole process starts again in the neighboring cell. In man the diameter of axons ranges from less than 1 to about 100 microns. Although axons and dendrites usually look different, the basic distinction between them is in how they work. Dendrites are excited by other cells, whereas axons usually are not. Also axons can excite other cells by releasing transmitters, whereas dendrites cannot. Although neurons have many, many dendrites, they usually have only one axon, but the axon may be branched.

Like the rest of the nerve cell, the axon is covered by the nerve cell membrane. The axon of many neurons is also covered by layers of a fatty substance called *myelin,* which is composed of the cell membranes of special cells, called sheath cells, which are wrapped tightly around the axon like a jellyroll. There are gaps in the myelin covering called nodes; at these gaps the axon is bathed by body fluids. As we will see later these gaps in the myelin greatly speed up the conduction of impulses in myelinated axons.

Axons usually branch, and the branches end in tiny buttonlike structures called *synaptic knobs*. Synaptic knobs almost, but do not quite, touch other cells. The regions where the knobs come so near other cells are the *synapses*. If the knobs end near a skeletal muscle cell, the synapse is called the neuromuscular junction. Within the synaptic knobs are tiny sacs, called synaptic vesicles, containing the transmitter chemical (Fig. 6.2). It is here that the chemical transmitter is released.

synapse

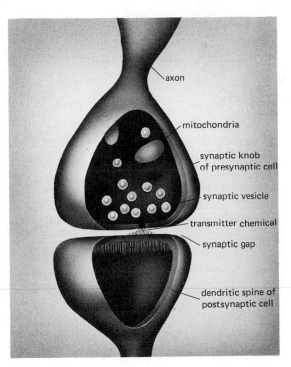

axon

mitochondria

synaptic knob of presynaptic cell

synaptic vesicle

transmitter chemical

synaptic gap

dendritic spine of postsynaptic cell

Fig. 6.2 Structure of a synapse. The cell before the synapse (presynaptic cell) does not actually touch the cell after the synapse (postsynaptic cell). There is a gap of about 20 millimicrons (millionths of a millimeter) between the two cells into which the transmitter chemical is released by the presynaptic cell. (Ebert et al., 1973)

Most biologists believe that neurons have become so specialized that they do not even divide. Parts of a damaged nerve cell may regenerate if the cell body is still healthy, but nerve cells do not divide to produce new ones. If, as many biologists believe, learning and memory are tied up with the structure of nerve cells, it may be essential that they *not* divide. If they did, our memory might change even more than it does! Most biologists believe that very shortly after we are born we have all the nerve cells we will ever have. In fact several thousand nerve cells die each day of our life, especially as we grow older. This may be one reason why some people become senile.

How Nerve Cells Function

Conduction of Nerve Impulses Biologists have determined what happens during the passage of a nerve impulse and the crucial role the cell membrane plays in conducting impulses. Their studies focused on the giant nerve cells of squids (Fig. 6.3). The axon of these neurons is about 1 millimeter in diameter—large enough to poke electrodes into (in order to measure electrical changes) and large enough to be able to follow the movement of radioactively labeled substances through it.

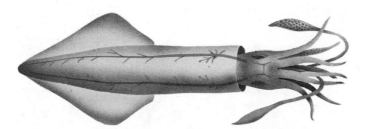

Fig. 6.3 Giant nerve cells of a squid. (Ebert et al., 1973)

By inserting tiny electrodes into these giant axons, it was confirmed that the inside of a resting nerve cell—one that is not conducting impulses—has a negative charge compared to the outside of the nerve cell. This is true of the entire surface membrane of the cell, including the axon and the cell body. When the axon is stimulated, a nerve impulse is rapidly conducted down it. When a nerve impulse reaches the electrodes, the inside of the axon becomes positively charged; as the impulse moves on past the electrodes the inside of the axon recovers its original negative charge (Fig. 6.4). Further work has shown that the electrical changes across a nerve cell membrane are caused by changes in the permeability of the membrane to sodium, potassium, and calcium ions. The electrical and ionic changes that travel down an axon are the nerve impulse.

In resting nerve calls, sodium (NA^+) ions are pumped out and potassium ions (K^+) are pumped in. This sodium-potassium exchange pump mechanism causes a redistribution of potassium and chloride (Cl^-) ions and results in an excess of negative ions inside the cell. But when the axon is stimulated, it becomes leaky to Na^+, which then enters faster than it can be pumped out. As a result, an action potential is initiated. An instant later, K^+ diffuses out of the axon. During repolarization the cell becomes less permeable to Na^+, and the Na^+–K^+ exchange pump can once again pump excess Na^+ out and K^+ in.

Many different stimuli—heat, touch, electricity, chemicals, for example—will excite a neuron. These stimuli change the permeability of the membrane in a way that we do not yet understand. In an intact animal, of course, it is usually the transmitter chemical arriving from other cells that excites a nerve cell and triggers impulses. The impulses conducted by the nerve cell membrane stimulate the synaptic knobs at the tips of the axons to release transmitter chemicals.

Nerve cells can conduct several hundred or up to a thousand impulses each second. Yet the cell still has time for an incredibly brief rest after the passage of each impulse.

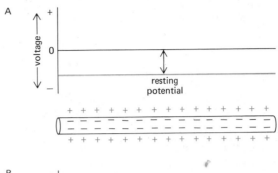

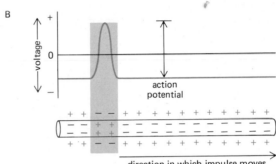

Fig. 6.4 Conduction of a nerve impulse. The curves represent electrical changes, and the cylinders represent an axon and the electrical charges inside and outside its membrane. An impulse is conducted in the following way. A. In a resting nerve cell (one that is not conducting an impulse) the inside of the cell is negative to the outside. Thus a voltage difference exists which is referred to as the resting potential (electrical potential = voltage). B. When the axon is stimulated the inside becomes positive or depolarizes at the point of stimulation. This increased voltage difference is called the action potential. Although the excited region quickly recovers its original negativity or repolarizes, the impulse does not disappear. C. Instead it moves forward along the axon. At the same time that the original excited region repolarizes, the region in front of it depolarizes. D. These events are repeated down the length of the axon, which in this way conducts an impulse. (Ebert et al., 1973)

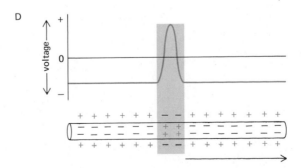

Neural Language Although the normal stimulus to a nerve cell is a transmitter chemical, biologists usually use electrical stimuli in their experiments with nerve cells. The reasons for this are that the size and duration of the electrical stimulus can be controlled easily, and gentle electrical stimuli do not damage neurons. If a neuron is stimulated with a weak electrical stimulus, nothing happens. If the strength of the stimulus is increased, a point will be reached at which the nerve cell conducts an impulse. The weakest current or other stimulus that excites a neuron is the *threshold stimulus* of that neuron. Each neuron has its own threshold.

When a neuron is excited, the size, or voltage, and the duration of the impulses it conducts can be measured by simple electronic recording devices. When this is done you discover that all the impulses generated by a given neuron have the same size and the same duration. Increasing the strength of a stimulus beyond the threshold does not increase the size or duration of the nerve impulse. The transmission of a nerve impulse is an *all-or-none reaction*. It either goes completely or not at all.

all-or-none
reaction

If all nerve impulses are just alike, how does a neuron send different messages? This question can be answered by a simple experiment. Suppose you stimulate a neuron for 2 seconds with a threshold stimulus. You find that the neuron conducts only a few impulses per second for 2 seconds. Now stimulate the neuron for 2 seconds with a much stronger stimulus. The neuron now conducts many more impulses per second for 2 seconds. In both cases the neuron starts conducting nerve impulses when you stimulate it, and stops conducting when the stimulus stops (Fig. 6.5). Thus the neuron sends information about the *intensity* of the stimulus by varying the frequency of nerve impulses. Under normal conditions (not experimental electrical stimulation), a neuron sends information about the intensity of a stimulus not only by varying the frequency of impulses, but also by varying the pattern of grouping of impulses. The start and stop of these impulses tell the duration of the stimulus.

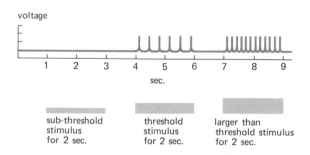

Fig. 6.5 Effect of varying the intensity of a stimulus on the size and frequency of nerve impulses. Stimuli of varying strengths (but lasting 2 seconds) affect the frequency but not the size of impulses. (Ebert et al., 1973)

Synapses Impulses are conducted away from the cell body along an axon toward the synapse. At the synapse they trigger the release of a transmitter chemical from the sacs in the synaptic knobs of the *presynaptic cell* (cell before the synapse). The transmitter chemical diffuses across the tiny gap next to the presynaptic neuron and reaches the *postsynaptic cell* (cell after the synapse).

It combines with receptor molecules on the membrane of the postsynaptic cell, changing the permeability of the membrane. In this way messages are sent from a nerve cell to the postsynaptic cell, which may be another neuron, a muscle cell, a gland cell, or some other effector.

Transmitter chemicals are promptly destroyed by specific enzymes after they have been released and have transmitted their signal across the synapse. This destruction is necessary for the control function of the nervous system. If a transmitter persisted, then the postsynaptic cell could no longer be controlled.

A synapse may be either *excitatory* or *inhibitory,* depending on whether the transmitter chemical released by the presynaptic cell excites or inhibits the postsynaptic cell. An individual neuron apparently synthesizes only one type of transmitter chemical. Several transmitter chemicals have been identified in man and other animals. The excitatory transmitter chemical released at neuromuscular junctions between neurons and skeletal muscle in vertebrates and many invertebrates is acetylcholine. It is also the excitatory transmitter chemical for synapses between certain neurons. The chemical nature of the inhibitory transmitters of vertebrates is not yet known. All excitatory transmitter chemicals make the inside of the postsynaptic cell more positive than usual. On the other hand, inhibitory transmitter chemicals make the inside of the postsynaptic cell more negative than usual.

excitatory synapse

inhibitory synapse

Anyone who drives knows that he can regulate the movement of a car more accurately by using both an accelerator and a brake. In a similar way, having both excitatory and inhibitory synapses permits much more precise control of nervous activity than is possible with just one kind of synapse.

Usually a postsynaptic neuron synapses with many presynaptic neurons. Some of the presynaptic neurons release an excitatory transmitter, whereas others release an inhibitory transmitter. What a postsynaptic neuron does depends on the amounts of these excitatory and inhibitory transmitters that are released by the cells that synapse with it. A postsynaptic neuron will conduct impulses only when it receives enough of an excitatory transmitter chemical to overcome any inhibitory transmitter chemical released at the inhibitory synapses.

The firing of a nerve cell in response to excitatory transmitters released by one group of cells can be blocked by the inhibitory transmitters released by another group of cells. This interplay and balancing of excitation and inhibition are nervous integration. See Chapter 1 for a discussion of inhibition as a means of coding sensory messages in the retina.

THE HUMAN NERVOUS SYSTEM

The neurons of almost all animals including man occur in four characteristic arrangements. (1) Some neurons form an interconnecting nerve net. (2) Neurons may become concentrated into *nerve cords* containing cell bodies, synapses, and axons. (3) Neurons also become aggregated into clusters known as *ganglia,* which, like nerve cords, consist of many interconnecting nerve cells. (4) Nerve cells form *nerves,* which are bundles of axons that run from nerve cords and ganglia to effectors and from sense organs back to nerve cords and ganglia.

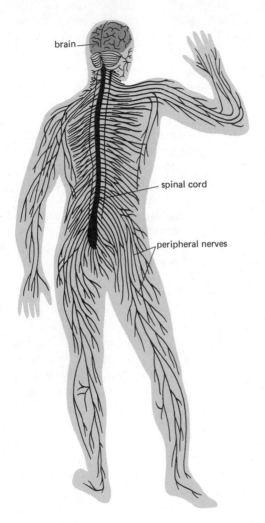

brain

spinal cord

peripheral nerves

Fig. 6.6 Human nervous system. (Ebert et al., 1973)

central nervous system

In humans the brain and spinal cord make up the *central nervous system.* Information about the environment is fed into the central nervous system in the form of nerve impulses from receptors in all parts of the body (Fig. 6.6). The neurons that relay these sensory impulses to the central nervous system are called sensory neurons. They make up the *afferent* (from Latin words meaning "to carry to") nervous system. Sensory neurons usually synapse with one or many *interneurons* in the central nervous system. An interneuron is a nerve cell that acts as an intermediary between other nerve cells. Interneurons synapse with many other interneurons. Indeed, about 99 percent of human nerve cells are interneurons. They are "managerial" cells. Together they sort, integrate, balance, and sharpen all of the sensory input and finally send out nerve impulses to neurons that innervate muscles and other effectors. The neurons that relay these nerve impulses to effectors make up the *efferent* (from Latin words meaning "to carry away") nervous system. Some nerve impulses go by way of *motor neurons* to skeletal muscles. Other efferent neurons called *autonomic neurons* conduct nerve impulses to other effectors, such as the heart, smooth muscles, and glands. We will have more to say about autonomic neurons later.

efferent nervous system

The Spinal Cord

Our spinal cord is like a rope no larger in diameter than a little finger. Fig. 6.7 shows how the cord looks in cross section. The H-shaped *gray matter* is made up of the cell bodies of interneurons and motor neurons, as well as their dendrites and synapses, and of glial cells. The cell bodies of sensory neurons are

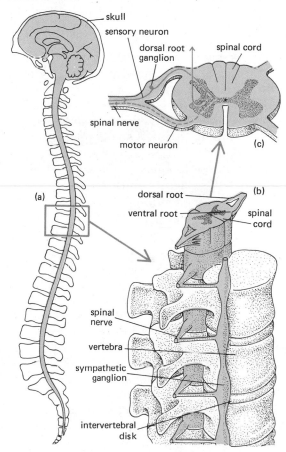

Fig. 6.7 (a) The human spinal cord and brain (central nervous system) are housed in the vertebrae and skull, respectively. Nerves running from the spinal cord in spaces between the vertebrae connect the central nervous system with all parts of the body. (b) How the spinal cord is protected by vertebrae. Adjacent vertebrae are separated by an intervertebral disk, a cartilaginous structure that cushions the vertebrae and further protects the spinal cord. When one of these disks gets out of place (a "slipped disk") it exerts pressure on a spinal nerve, thus causing an extremely painful condition known as a "pinched nerve." (c) Cross section of the spinal cord. (Ebert et al., 1973)

aggregated in clusters of nerve cell bodies known as the *dorsal root ganglia,* which lie just outside the spinal cord. The surrounding *white matter* is composed of bundles of axons called *fiber tracts,* which conduct impulses between different levels of the spinal cord and between the spinal cord and the brain. Sensory axons extend from the dorsal root ganglia and motor axons from the ventral root of the spinal cord. A short distance from the cord itself, the axons from both roots join to form a *spinal nerve.*

A nerve is composed of thousands of separate axons bound together, each able to transmit a separate message, just as a telephone cable is composed of many telephone wires bound together. Each nerve contains both motor and sensory axons. There are no synapses in nerves, just axons. Synapses occur in the gray matter of the spinal cord, in dorsal root ganglia, and at the endings of motor nerves. There are 31 pairs of spinal nerves entering and emerging from the spinal cord through spaces between the vertebrae. Each pair of nerves innervates a different area of the body. They branch and rebranch until at last they extend into almost every part of the body below the head. They are the major means of communication between the central nervous system and most of the body. There are also 12 pairs of cranial nerves, which carry neural messages directly to the brain.

Journey of a Nerve Impulse Where does an impulse go after it arrives in the spinal cord by way of a sensory neuron? It may follow millions of possible pathways. Some of these are complex, involving many neurons, and therefore are difficult to trace. We can, however, get some idea of how the nervous system works by following an impulse along routes that involve only a few neurons.

spinal reflex   The simplest such pathways in man and other vertebrates are called spinal reflexes, and the simplest spinal reflex is the knee jerk reflex.

Spinal Reflexes When you have a physical examination the doctor tests your response to a tap on the knee (Fig. 6.8). The tap stretches the tendon that attaches the extensor muscle above the knee to the knee and excites stretch receptors in the tendon. These stretch receptors in turn excite a sensory neuron that conducts nerve impulses to the spinal cord. Within the spinal cord the sensory neuron synapses with a motor neuron to the extensor muscle. This is an excitatory synapse; the motor neuron conducts impulses to the extensor muscle, which contracts, causing the leg to jerk. This knee-jerk reflex is the simplest nervous pathway in our body because it involves only two neurons, sensory and motor, and only a single synapse in the central nervous system. Most reflexes involve hundreds or even thousands of neurons.

So far we have considered the reflex activity of only the muscle that was stretched. This is only half of the story. Most skeletal muscles are arranged in antagonistic pairs. The knee-jerk reflex depends not only on the contraction of the extensor muscle but also on the relaxation of its antagonist, the flexor muscle in the back of the thigh. Its relaxation is accomplished in the following way. The same sensory neuron that excited the motor neuron to the extensor muscle also synapses with an interneuron. This particular interneuron makes an inhibitory synapse with the motor neuron that goes to the flexor muscle. Consequently

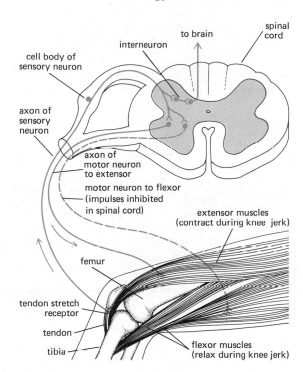

cell body of
sensory neuron

axon of
sensory
neuron

interneuron

to brain

spinal
cord

axon of
motor neuron
to extensor

motor neuron to flexor
(impulses inhibited
in spinal cord)

extensor muscles
(contract during knee jerk)

femur

tendon stretch
receptor

tendon

tibia

flexor muscles
(relax during knee jerk)

Fig. 6.8 Pathway of the knee-jerk reflex.
(Ebert et al., 1973)

this motor neuron does not fire, and the flexor muscle relaxes. Thus the reflex contraction of the extensor muscle is accompanied by the reflex relaxation of the flexor muscle. Most antagonistic muscles are "wired up" this way. In daily life the knee-jerk reflex helps us to remain upright when we stand. Should the leg start to buckle, the reflex would again extend the leg.

The Emerging Importance
of the Brain

The nerve pathway of a spinal reflex generally includes neurons that synapse and interconnect with other parts of the nervous system, including the brain. For this reason "simple" reflexes often become quite complex, especially in man. Spinal reflexes are automatic and need not involve the brain, but the brain can modify or even override a spinal reflex. For example, consider what may happen when a doctor tests a small boy's knee-jerk reflex. The child is probably frightened—he remembers the last time he visited the doctor and received an injection. He is wary and tense, and stiffens his knee. As a result there is no knee-jerk when the doctor taps the boy's knee.

The child can inhibit his knee-jerk reflex for the following reason: the sensory neuron conducting impulses from the stretch receptors in the extensor muscle also synapses with a number of interneurons in the spinal cord. Some of these interneurons eventually channel the impulses to the child's brain. His

Evolutionary Studies

Since for most experimental purposes we do not use the human brain, it becomes necessary to study animal brains and nervous systems. From parallels in structure found between the brains of man and lower animals inferences are made about the function of the human brain.

Although usually the standard laboratory animals—dogs, cats, and monkeys—are studied, often other animals who by nature are especially well equipped for a particular study are substituted. We have seen in the text that the invertebrate squid is useful because it has large enough axons to allow the insertion of experimental equipment. And we saw in Chapter 3 that the horseshoe crab (Limulus) is good for research because its light receptor system is easily accessible.

Obviously a certain amount of caution must be exercised in the application of animal findings to human phenomena, but the danger of misapplication is not so great as it might seem. As Bishop (cited in Livingston, 1962) has pointed out, although in the evolutionary process "ganglionic masses have gotten larger [and] axons have been stretched to greater length, the fundamental neuronal mechanisms seem to be the same."

brain blocks the reflex by sending out impulses to his flexor muscles, which cause him to stiffen his knee. (The doctor's way around this problem is to tell the child to twiddle his thumbs or spell his name. The boy then concentrates on the task, and he will usually forget to stiffen his knee.)

Our brain can do more than alter spinal reflexes; in man, as in other mammals, it takes over jobs that the spinal cord or nerve cord performs in less complex animals. For example, if the brain of an insect or even a frog is destroyed, each of these animals can still make coordinated movements. A spinal frog (one without a brain but with the spinal cord intact) can jump about when stimulated. However, a spinal mammal cannot even stand. In the course of vertebrate evolution the brain became increasingly important at the expense of the spinal cord; movements once controlled by the spinal cord came under the ever-increasing control of the brain.

Autonomic Nerves

Animals are at the mercy of two environments, the outside world and the world inside themselves. Let us now see how the nervous system helps to regulate the internal environment.

Internal organs are innervated by sensory nerve fibers that send input to the central nervous system. The central nervous system responds to this input by means of two sets of motor nerves, which innervate and control the activities of internal organs. These motor nerves are called *autonomic nerves*. They are further divided into a *sympathetic* and a *parasympathetic* branch. The autonomic nerves and some of the tissues they control are shown in Fig. 6.9.

autonomic nerves
sympathetic
parasympathetic

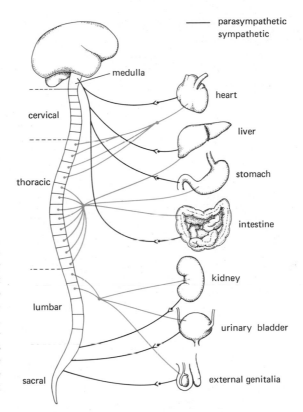

parasympathetic
sympathetic

medulla

heart

cervical

liver

stomach

thoracic

intestine

lumbar

kidney

urinary bladder

sacral

external genitalia

Fig. 6.9 The autonomic nervous system, and some of the organs that it innervates. Most large organs are served by both sympathetic and parasympathetic nerves which function in opposition to each other. If, as is usually the case, the sympathetic nerve excites an organ, then the parasympathetic nerve produces the opposite effect and inhibits the activity. The balance between these two systems produces the normal state of activity of the various organs. (Ebert et al., 1973)

What autonomic nerves do can be seen when we consider how they control the rate at which the heart beats. When a man asleep on the beach awakens in response to a cry for help, his heart immediately begins to pump blood faster than before. It does so because the heart-accelerating center in the medulla of the brain sends impulses over a sympathetic nerve to the pacemaker of the heart. The pacemaker then increases its rhythm, and the rate at which the heart beats increases. On the other hand, impulses over the vagus nerve, the parasympathetic nerve, to the heart originate in the heart-inhibiting center in the medulla and slow down the rate at which the heart beats.

Thus sympathetic and parasympathetic nerves have opposite effects on the tissues they innervate. These nerves offset and balance each other's effects. For example, if one autonomic nerve stimulates the smooth muscle of the gut to contract, the other autonomic nerve inhibits the muscle from contracting. Each type of autonomic nerve releases a different transmitter chemical. Acetylcholine is released at the synapses of parasympathetic neurons and the tissues they innervate. Noradrenalin is the transmitter chemical released at the synapses between sympathetic neurons and the tissues they innervate.

The autonomic nervous system was so named because we usually have little control over its activities. In addition to regulating the rate at which the heart beats, it controls respiration, excretion, reproduction, the diameter of blood vessels, digestion, secretion by the sweat glands, and the release of hormones from many endocrine glands. These processes go on without our even being aware of them.

It now seems likely, however, that autonomic processes can be learned in much the same way that acts involving motor neurons and skeletal muscles can be learned. We all know people who become genuinely ill when faced with an unpleasant task. It has been suggested that such a person learned to bring on illness when as a child his mother allowed him to stay home from school when he "developed" a headache. No doubt as we learn more about how the autonomic nervous system functions, we will uncover the roots of many similar psychosomatic illnesses.

THE CENTRAL NERVOUS SYSTEM—THE BRAIN

The human brain is a dense jungle of 10 billion nerve cells. It is the most complex single structure in the known universe. Analyzing its structure and function seems almost impossible. Yet the rewards are immense, for within the brain lie

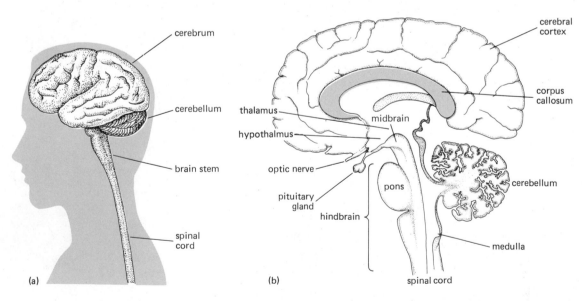

Fig. 6.10 The human brain. (A) External surface of brain. (B) Longitudinal section through the midline of brain, showing the inside of the right hemisphere. (Ebert et al., 1973)

Studying the Effects of Missing, Diseased, or Injured Parts of the Brain

A purely anatomical description of the brain and nervous system does not, of course, tell us the function of each part of the brain. One way to obtain a functional anatomy of the brain is to study the effect of injury of a circumscribed area on behavior or psychological functions. In this way we may infer the functional role of that area of the brain. Many studies of this sort have been done with people who have suffered brain injuries. Goldstein (1939), for example, showed how brain-damaged patients (cortical damaged) lose their capacity for abstraction.

Scientists, however, do not sit around waiting for chance to supply them with such experiments. They have developed methods by which parts or areas of the brain of experimental animals can be extirpated surgically. In very rare instances these procedures are used in humans when, for medical reasons, parts of the brain may be removed. Some classical studies of this sort were carried out by Goltz (1892), who removed the cortex from one or both hemispheres of dogs and described how this procedure limited the animals' behavioral capacities. One study, for example, focused on the part played by the lower brainstem in the emotional behavior of animals. The dog whose brainstem had been transected showed very clear and coherent rage responses, sometimes to stimuli that before surgery had not elicited rage at all. However, during the 18-month period that the animal lived, it showed no other emotional responses. Using the same methodology, Goltz studied the effects of ablations on other functions, including sexual activity.

In studies using ablation, when the animal dies the brain is removed and stained to ascertain that only the intended specific area had been removed and that it had been entirely removed. Without this confirmation nothing certain can be concluded from such studies.

reason, memory, creative talent, and consciousness itself. What makes the human brain even more challenging is that each one is different from every other. One human kidney works pretty much like every other human kidney, but the brain of a man is the man himself.

Despite its complexity, the human brain can be analyzed. This section describes briefly the basic way the brain is put together and how we believe it works. For convenience we will consider separately the *hindbrain,* the *midbrain,* and the *forebrain* (Fig. 6.10). Do not get the idea that specific functions are precisely localized in each of these regions. In most activities the brain functions as a unit with many parts of the brain participating.

Another feature of the brain is its flexibility or plasticity in terms of where various functions are performed by the brain. Normally movement of the left foot is controlled by a specific region of the brain. However, if that region is damaged, another part of the brain takes over that function. This plasticity makes the brain immensely adaptable.

The brain communicates with the body by two main routes. The major route is the spinal cord, which extends from the hindbrain to the last vertebra of the backbone. Its 31 pairs of spinal nerves provide inflow and outflow paths for the brain and the part of the body below the neck. The brain also communicates directly with the organs and tissues of the head and neck by 12 pairs of cranial nerves.

Hindbrain

The lower part of the hindbrain is the *medulla,* which controls respiration and heartbeat. In addition it is the region through which nerve impulses must pass in both directions between the spinal cord and the rest of the brain.

reticular formation

Running through the medulla and on into the midbrain and part of the forebrain is a complex organization of nerve cells called the *reticular formation* (Fig. 6.11). This alerts and arouses other regions of the brain, especially the *cerebral cortex* and *thalamus,* which we shall discuss. For example, if someone knocks on your door, sensory nerve impulses set up by the knocking reach the cortex of your brain. However, you will not react to the knock unless the reticular formation is excited and unless it simultaneously excites the cortex. Fortunately the reticular formation is choosy and does not make the cortex aware of every stimulus bombarding our body. If it did and we tried to respond to them all, we would be overwhelmed. The reticular formation is very efficient; for example, all of us at some time have become so engrossed in a book or a television program that all movements and noises around us were completely blocked out. This example of *selective attention* illustrates the reticular formation at work.

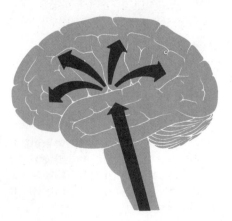

Fig. 6.11 The reticular formation is a network of neurons that runs through the medulla and on into parts of the forebrain, including the thalamus and cortex. Since it is a network and not a discrete structure, it is represented by arrows in the diagram. (Ebert et al., 1973)

Located on the surface of the brainstem between the medulla and the midbrain is the *pons.* Like the medulla, the pons is a passageway through which nerve impulses to and from the higher parts of the brain must pass. The pons also controls sleep and has the reticular formation running through it.

Lying above the medulla on the back surface of the brainstem is the

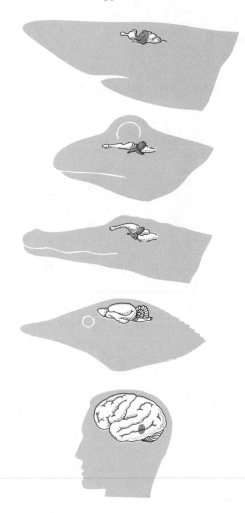

Fig. 6.12 Relative size of major regions of the brain in fish, frog, alligator, shrew (a primitive mammal), and man. Notice that in the series from fish to man, the relative size of the midbrain (in color) decreases whereas the forebrain (white) expands enormously. (Ebert et al., 1973)

baseball-sized *cerebellum,* which has a wrinkled cover. The cerebellum seems to be larger in relation to the rest of the brain in animals that move in a three-dimensional world (fish and birds) than in animals that live mostly on the surface of the earth. Surprisingly, perhaps, man's cerebellum is quite large relative to the rest of his brain even though he is biologically a surface creature (Fig. 6.12). His large cerebellum makes sense when we learn that the cerebellum coordinates skeletal muscle movement. Certainly no other animal has as large a repertoire of voluntary movements as man.

However, the cerebellum does not initiate movements. A man whose cerebellum is damaged can move, but he may reel and stagger as though he were drunk. It is the cerebral cortex that initiates movements. We might say, then, that it is the cerebral cortex that makes the policy but the cerebellum that sees that the policy is carried out efficiently.

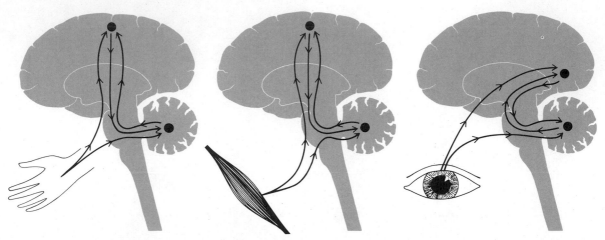

Fig. 6.13 Some sources of input to the cerebellum. If one turns a page, for example, input enters the cerebellum from the cerebral cortex, the fingers, muscles of the hand and arm, and the eyes. (Ebert et al., 1973)

The events that go on within the cerebellum illustrate especially well how a group of neurons within the brain works (Fig. 6.13). Basically these groups of neurons do three things:

1. They receive input in the form of nerve impulses from receptors and from other parts of the nervous system.
2. They sort out all this input. This is the real decision-making process, the summing up of all the things going on at the synapses within the cerebellum. We begin to understand why there are so many cells in the brain; it receives so many messages that one of its biggest jobs is "talking to itself"—sorting out these messages and deciding what is important.
3. On the basis of this sorting out, the cerebellum sends output in the form of nerve impulses to other parts of the brain, and may send nerve impulses by way of the spinal cord and efferent neurons to effectors.

Suppose you wish to turn this page. Out go commands from the cerebral cortex to the skeletal muscles involved in the act; at the same time the cortex tells the cerebellum that it should expect certain sensory input from stretch receptors in the hand and arm, touch receptors in the fingers, and photoreceptors in the eyes. That is, the cerebral cortex tells the cerebellum what these muscles are supposed to be doing. Receptor cells in the fingertips, muscles of the hand and arm, and eyes send nerve impulses to the cerebellum and keep it informed of what is happening. Should your fingers miss the edge of the page the cerebellum would send impulses to the cortex to the effect that the original commands must be changed to correct for the error. In other words, the cerebellum compares what *is* happening with what *should be* happening. In this way it coordinates the movement.

Midbrain

During the long evolution of vertebrates the midbrain became smaller and less important in the higher vertebrates than in the lower ones (Fig. 6.12). It was in effect sacrificed to permit the huge forebrain of mammals to develop. However, even in man the midbrain is still important. It is not only a connecting link between the hind- and forebrain, but it also receives some impulses from light receptors in the eyes and is primarily responsible for controlling movements of the eye muscles. But most of the functions (primarily sensory) that the midbrain performed in our vertebrate ancestors have been taken over by our forebrain.

Forebrain

Man has the largest forebrain of any animal, almost exclusively caused by the enormous growth of the *cerebral cortex*. It is the cortex that really makes us what we are.

    The gray matter covering the cerebrum is made up of the cell bodies of neurons. In fact most of the nerve cells in the brain are in the cortex. And yet this covering is only about 2 millimeters thick. It is, however, very wrinkled or convoluted. These convolutions provide for an increase in the surface area of the forebrain without requiring a larger skull. The cerebrum is split down the middle into a right and a left hemisphere. The two halves are actually connected by the *corpus callosum,* a tract of myelinated axons from one hemisphere crossing to the other hemisphere. As we will see when we discuss memory, this axon tract is a freeway over which impulses move between the two hemispheres. Lying at the base of the cerebrum and above the midbrain is the *thalamus,* and beneath it the *hypothalamus.* Wedged between these areas and the cerebral cortex is the *limbic system.*

forebrain

cerebral cortex

cerebrum

corpus callosum

 Chemical Stimulation

The direct injection of chemicals into the brain has also been used to study neural function and control centers. Thus in the Andersson studies on thirst, it was also found that the injection of a hypertonic sodium chloride solution into the hypothalamus of goats resulted in drinking behavior. (See p. 276.)

    Often the effect of a hormone or chemical on behavior is studied. Much work has been done in particular with the injection of sex hormones into animals. Ball (1937) reported male sexual responses in female rats following injections of testosterone propionate. Further research showed that the injection of hormones of the opposite sex frequently induces bisexual behavior, the direction of which is determined primarily by environmental stimuli. Androgen-treated females act like males in the company of normal females, but revert to a female behavior pattern if they are confronted by a sexually aggressive male.

Electrical Stimulation and Measurement

Another way of studying the functions of different parts of the brain in behavior is to apply mild electric currents to parts of the brain. It is assumed that stimulation of this sort results in the same behavioral effects that normal "biological" stimulation of these parts of the brain results in.

One such study was carried out by Andersson in 1951. Andersson was actually interested in the hormonal regulation of lactation, but in stimulating various regions of the hypothalamus, he noticed rumination and licking responses in his animals. This led to a concentrated experimental attack on the role of hypothalamic mechanisms in the regulation of thirst.

In a subsequent study Andersson and McCann (1955) electrically stimulated the hypothalamus of goats. They found that such stimulation time after time reliably produced drinking behavior. The drinking began within seconds after the onset of electrical stimulation and continued without interruption as long as the current flow was maintained. Three to four seconds after the cessation of electrical stimulation, drinking stopped.

This initial work was subsequently replicated and carried further. It was strongly instrumental in identifying the locus of control for drinking behavior.

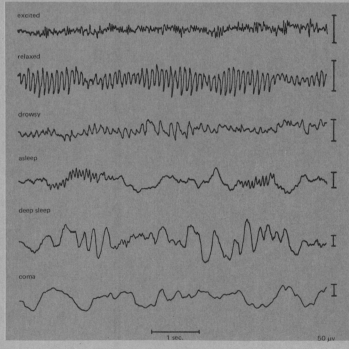

Fig. 6.14 Typical EEG records from normal subjects in different states of arousal and from a comatose subject. (Jasper, in Penfield and Jasper, 1954.)

In the experimental work we have discussed up to now, something was generally done to the nervous system; it was cut or stimulated electrically or chemically, and the effect on behavior was observed. Much experimental work, however, has been done in the reverse manner. Behavioral events or stimuli of the senses are initiated, and their effect on the nervous system is noted.

One way of doing this is by noting changes in the spontaneous electrical activity of the brain during behavior. Although it is not clear as yet what causes and maintains the rhythm of this electrical activity, much research has attempted to correlate changes in electrical activity with behavioral and functional changes. The clearest example of such a correlation is the relationship between different levels or states of relaxation and excitation. During relaxation there is a preponderance of high-voltage, slow (8 to 12 cycles per second) waves. In excitation, these are replaced by fast (30 to 60 cycles per second), low-amplitude wave patterns. Different stages of sleep have also been identified on the basis of changes in the EEG (electroencephalogram). Fig. 6.14 illustrates typical EEG readings for different levels of arousal.

The EEG is generally obtained by connecting recording electrodes to an ink writer. The ink writer amplifies the difference between the recording potentials of two adjacent electrodes in the brain and plots the difference on a drum.

Hypothalamus The hypothalamus controls eating and body temperature and produces the antidiuretic hormone. It is also involved in regulating thirst, pleasure, pain, and sexual and reproductive activity. In fact, all the nervous mechanisms involved in holding the internal environment constant and in determining the use that is made of the resources of the body are in some way related to the hypothalamus. Yet this critically important area constitutes less than 1 percent of the human brain.

Hunger One of the most important functions of the hypothalmus is the regulation of hunger and thirst. Generally we become aware that we are hungry when we experience what we call hunger pangs, usually the strongest indication that the body's food supply has been depleted. Does the hunger drive originate in the stomach?

The contemporary view is that the chain of internal events culminating in the hunger drive actually begins with the depletion of chemicals vital to the blood. This signals the hypothalamus to trigger the conscious experience of hunger. When the organism responds by eating, the hypothalamus then terminates these sensations, and a feeling of fullness and decreased taste-sensitivity result. These regulatory functions—the stimulation and depression of appetite—are controlled by separate centers in the hypothalamus.

The theory that hunger originates in the bloodstream explains why a man whose stomach had been removed continued to experience hunger, and why food-deprived rats whose stomachs were removed experimentally demonstrated food-seeking behavior similar to that of normal rats. The condition of depriva-

hypothalamus

© 1965 United Feature Syndicate, Inc.

tion in the blood signals the hypothalamus, which initiates symptoms of hunger other than stomach contractions.

Thirst   Thirst is usually consciously experienced as a parched feeling in the mouth and throat and, after extreme deprivation, as weakness, nausea, and breathing difficulty. Like hunger, the sensation of thirst is not confined to specific areas of the body. It arises when the body's tissues become deficient in water, which every cell requires for growth and proper functioning. Evidence for this was provided by a study in which the experimenter put water directly into the stomach of a water-deprived dog through a surgical opening or a tube down its throat; its mouth and throat thus remained dry (Adolph, 1941). The amount of water the dog was given equalled the amount that had been withheld from it. When it was permitted to drink immediately afterward, it consumed water as though it were still thirsty; but when it was forced to wait until the water in its stomach had been absorbed by the body tissues, it drank nothing at all. The animal's thirst had subsided although its mouth and throat had been bypassed by the water.

Each organism not only needs water but needs to maintain it in proper proportion to the other substances in the tissues. Thus, besides actual deprivation, disturbing this balance by injecting strong salt solutions, for instance, also produces thirst.

The thrist drive is regulated by the hypothalamus. This is demonstrated by a study in which a minute amount of a salt solution injected directly into the hypothalamus stimulated an animal to drink, while an injection of water caused it to stop drinking (Miller, 1958). In another experiment, electrical excitation of the hypothalamus of a goat induced the animal to drink (Andersson and McCann, 1955).

Reproduction and Sex   The hypothalamus plays a major role in reproductive activity because it controls and adjusts various chemical environments in the body. The female reproductive cycle is triggered primarily by hypothalamic secretions interacting with the pituitary and the ovaries to produce the hormones estrogen and progesterone, which regulate the menstrual cycle. In males, the hypothalamus stimulates the pituitary and the testes to produce testosterone, which brings about the development of genital organs and secondary sex characteristics (beard, deep voice, and so on).

Human sexual relations are for the most part independent of hormone levels. But in other species, the female under natural conditions will engage in sexual intercourse only when she is biologically able to conceive. We will consider other aspects of sexual behavior later in this chapter.

Thalamus   The thalamus, a pair of oval bodies, is the region of the brain through which most sensory nerve impulses finally travel on their way to the cortex. Impulses are integrated in the thalamus and then relayed to other areas in the cortex. The thalamus is very much like a giant relay through which the body and the rest of the brain are able to reach the cerebral cortex. With the single exception of smell, all sensory systems funnel through it.

The Limbic System   It is in the limbic system (Fig. 6.15) that emotion is organized. If, for example, an electric current stimulates part of the limbic system of your affectionate house cat, she will suddenly go into a fit of rage—clawing, spitting, and yowling. She will have nothing to do with you. Stimulate nearby cells in the limbic system, and she becomes affectionate once more, purring and rubbing against you.

Fig. 6.15 Various parts of the forebrain. The hypothalamus lies at the base of the cerebral hemispheres close to the pituitary gland. It is of special importance in regulating the internal environment and processes such as eating, drinking, and sleeping. It interconnects with many regions of the brain including the limbic system. The limbic system is an integrated network that includes the hippocampus, the septal area, the amygdala, parts of the reticular formation, and the hypothalamus itself. These structures seem to be important in aspects of behavior such as emotion and motivation. For instance, the amygdala become active whenever we encounter anything new or unexpected, whereas the septal area depresses emotional reactions. The thalamus is located just above the midbrain. It relays sensory information to the cerebral cortex from specific sensory pathways. It also plays a role in processes such as sleep and wakefulness, and closely interacts with the limbic system. (Ebert et al., 1973)

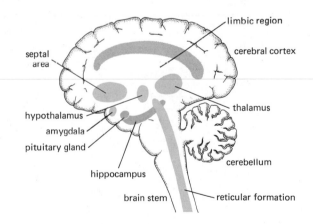

The Hippocampus Another section of the limbic system has long puzzled brain scientists, because it had no known functions. However, in 1958 a possible function for the hippocampus was discovered in a dramatic and unexpected fashion. The first human being without a hippocampus was found that year and psychological studies revealed that this lack produced only one clear-cut effect: the man was unable to transfer information about his surroundings into long-term memory.

Cerebral Cortex If you surgically remove the cortex of a rat, the animal can still do many things that a normal rat does—even walk about and drink—but it moves sluggishly. However, removing the cerebrum from a monkey leaves the animal helpless, and it will soon die. The cortex of a newborn baby is not functional, but those tragic infants born without a cortex, anencephalic babies, never live very long.

We can get some idea of how a decorticated man (the equivalent of one without a cerebral cortex) would act simply by observing a man after he has had several drinks. An intoxicated person is in effect a partly decorticated animal. This is discussed again later in the chapter when we consider drugs and the brain. Thus one role of the cortex is to regulate the rest of the brain. It stops us from eating until dinner; it allows us to suppress our temper and to organize behavior so that we can carry on social life. But even this monumental task is not the totality of its function.

Sensory and Motor Areas As a result of various experiments it is possible to map the sensory and motor areas of the cortex (Fig. 6.16). Studies reveal that parts of the cortex will respond to only one kind of sensory input. For example, a cell in the so-called visual area of the cortex will respond only to input from the optic nerve but not to input from the auditory nerve.

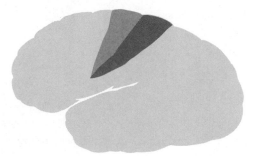

Fig. 6.16 Sensory and motor areas of the cerebral cortex. Sensory cortex is darker. (Ebert et al., 1973)

A part of the cortex is also associated with bodily sensations such as touch. There is a spot in this somatic sensory cortex, as it is called, for each part of the body. Just as you can find Chicago at a certain place on a map of the United States, so you can find a spot on the somatic sensory cortex that receives sensory impulses from touch receptors in the left big toe. If we were to draw a picture of the different parts of the body as they are represented on

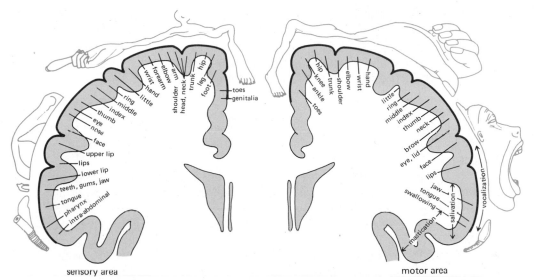

sensory area   **motor area**

Fig. 6.17 Map of the surface of part of the human cerebral cortex indicating areas associated with movement (motor cortex) and bodily sensations (somatic sensory cortex). Stimulation of a specific area in the motor cortex causes a movement in the corresponding part of the body. Stimulation of various parts of the body evokes electrical activity in corresponding parts of the somatic sensory cortex. Notice that the area of cortex devoted to each part of the body is proportional to the extent of motor activities and the sensory capabilities of that part, not to its size. In man the mouth and the thumb occupy a huge area of the cortex. As you might expect when you map the brain of a pig, the snout occupies a large area of the cortex whereas in a spider monkey, the tail occupies a large area of the cortex. (Ebert et al., 1973)

the map of the sensory cortex, we would see a grotesque, dismembered little man (Fig. 6.17). He is so oddly shaped because the amount of cortical surface related to a specific body part such as the lips is proportional to the number of receptors the part of the body has, not to the actual size of the part. For example, a man's lips have many touch receptors that send messages to a large area of the sensory cortex, whereas a man's back has only a few touch receptors and they send messages to a small area of the sensory cortex.

The motor cortex is arranged in a similar way. Its specific parts control the movement of specific body parts such as the hand and the thumb. Man's hands take up a larger area of the motor cortex than his back, because he can move his hands much more than his back.

Association Areas Three-fourths of man's cortex is neither motor nor sensory. These areas of the cortex have been called *association areas*. Presumably they are places where different kinds of inputs are integrated. Evidence comes from the discovery that some individual cells in the association cortex will respond to three kinds of sensory input: touch, sound, and light. In this respect the cells in these association areas behave differently from individual cells in the sensory cortex, which respond to only one kind of sensory input.

association areas

There are also individual cells in the association area of the cortex that appear to "count." If you present a series of stimuli to an anesthetized cat (sounds to the ear, light flashes to the eye, mild electric shock to a paw), certain individual association cells respond by discharging after a specific number of stimuli. For instance, a "number 7" cell will respond after 7 stimuli, but not after 5 stimuli. The response of the "counting" cell has little to do with the intensity or rate of presentation of the stimuli. Nor does it matter whether the stimulus is sound, light, or electric shock. These cells seem to be responding to the number of stimuli presented. About 1 percent of the cells in the association areas of a cat appear to be "counting" cells.

Other association cells respond to no sensory stimuli. What they are doing no one knows, but presumably they are involved in putting together and evaluating the complex stimuli the animal receives.

The more complex the brain of a mammal, the larger is the association area. The association area of man is the most complex of all. Most psychophysiologists believe the association area of the cortex is the part of the brain that enables us to interpret, remember, learn, and reason. How these particular kinds of behavior take place is largely unknown.

ENDOCRINE SYSTEM

hormone

Our discussion so far has largely focused on the nervous system, but it is only one of the two systems used to integrate all aspects of function. The other is the endocrine system, which uses relatively slow-acting hormones to communicate and to effect changes throughout the body. Because of the vast scope of this system, we will concentrate on only one area of function, that concerned with sexual behavior.

Let us examine the monthly cycle in the human female, looking first at events withing the ovary—the female gonad—itself. As an egg-bearing follicle matures it produces the primary female sex hormones or *estrogens,* which maintain the uterus and vagina, play a role in the development of the breasts and the feminine form, and regulate the distribution of hair. After shedding the egg, the follicle is transformed in appearance and function; the cells are laden with fat. In animals whose fat is yellow, the transformed follicles are bright yellow, which is why they were originally named corpora lutea, or yellow bodies. They have the appearance of secretory glands, as indeed they are, producing the second major female hormone, *progesterone,* whose role is to prepare the uterus for implantation and nourishment of the embryo. Progesterone acts on the uterine lining, where it stimulates glandular activity, without which implantation cannot occur. Progesterone is, then, the hormone of pregnancy.

The ovary does not act alone; it functions in concert with the *anterior pituitary gland.* The monthly cycle is dependent on the release by the anterior pituitary of two hormones, follicle-stimulating hormone (FSH) and luteinizing hormone (LH). The release of these gonadotropins is in turn dependent on

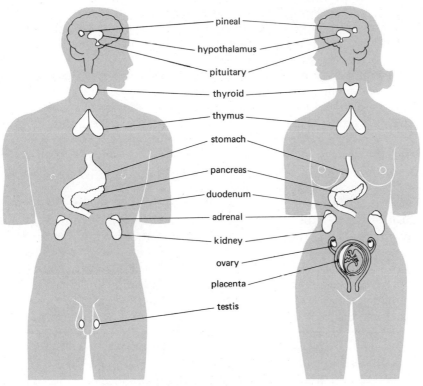

Fig. 6.18 The major endocrine glands in man and woman. (Ebert et al., 1973)

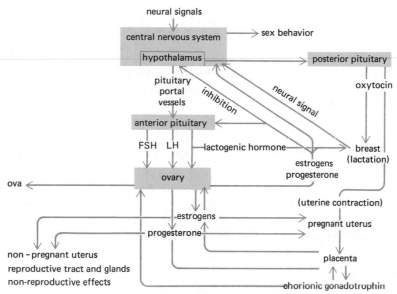

Fig. 6.19 An outline of the neuroendocrine control of reproduction in a female mammal. (Ebert et al., 1973)

signals from the closely related part of the brain, the hypothalamus. This pattern involving the interaction of hypothalamus, anterior pituitary, and gonad is not an uncommon one. It is representative of the pattern exhibited by many of the endocrine glands (Figs. 6.18 and 6.19).

FSH stimulates some of the primary follicles of the ovary to begin growing each month, promoting proliferation of the cells surrounding the egg. These cells then begin to secrete estrogens. Thus the two functions of the follicle-stimulating hormone are to stimulate proliferation of the ovarian follicular cells and to stimulate secretory activity by these cells. As the follicles approach their maximum size, the anterior pituitary begins to produce LH. It is LH that influences the mass of follicle cells to undergo their transformation into a corpus luteum and to begin producing progesterone.

How does the cyclic pattern of release of pituitary and ovarian hormones begin? The cycle is established by the ovary. The developing hypothalamus and pituitary are noncyclic; they become cyclic only after estrogen is produced by the ovary.

The testes of the male produce billions of spermatozoa (sperm), which elaborate the androgens or male hormones androsterone and testosterone. The production of these hormones is in turn controlled by the pituitary hormones FSH and LH. In the male, FSH and LH are released at the onset of puberty, and secretion continues throughout most of life. Both are necessary for continuous sperm production. In the male, release of the gonadotropic hormone is continuous, rather than cyclic as in the female. FSH causes proliferation of spermatozoa. LH stimulates production of male hormones by the interstitial cells of the testis.

Sex Hormones and Human Behavior

Development does not end at birth but continues throughout life. Nowhere is this statement illustrated more clearly than in the delayed action of the hypothalamus-pituitary-gonad axis. In humans the reproductive functions of the gonads do not begin until puberty, some 11 to 16 years after birth. We do not know what signals the release of FSH at puberty. We know only that once released it brings about maturation in both males and females.

In males, the second pituitary hormone, LH, is also released at puberty, which usually occurs somewhat later in males than in females. It is the release of testosterone, stimulated by LH, that profoundly influences the sexual maturation and behavior of the male at puberty. A growth spurt, production of hair, change in voice (caused by changes in the larynx) are all evidence of systemic changes in the male at puberty, as is his heightened aggressiveness. Puberty runs its course in about two years, after which the male becomes adjusted to the testosterone level, which ordinarily remains rather constant over many years because of feedback controls on the pituitary-hypothalamus.

Puberty usually begins earlier in the female, at about 11 years. Under the influence of FSH, eggs begin to mature, and the female hormone ("the hormone of preparation of the uterus") estrogen is produced. Estrogen causes widespread systemic changes, resulting in the characteristic female form and behavior. The vagina, into which the male penis is inserted during copulation, and the uterus mature rapidly, the breasts grow and differentiate secretory cells for milk production, and the hips widen, providing an opening in the pelvic arch. In addition to estrogen small quantities of male hormones, androgens, are also produced in the female at puberty in the adrenal gland. These hormones act in initiating the appearance of pubic hair and in growth regulation. Adrenal tumors and other abnormal conditions may result in increased production of androgens, leading to disturbances in secondary sex characteristics.

In the female, LH, the hormone of gestation, is produced only after the first cycle is under way, with the production of the corpus luteum. During ovulation a woman is ordinarily highly receptive to the male. After ovulation, when progesterone is produced (and the egg is not fertilized) and the menstrual period approaches, many women are less receptive, even increasingly irritable and aggressive. How much of this behavior can be attributed to progesterone is unclear, but its high level is surely a factor. Since variation in sexual arousal over women's cycles is found, some psychological factors must be involved.

The emotional stress associated with the *menopause* is also well known. This period of a year or two at the end of a woman's reproductive life (in the absence of an outside source of hormones) may be attributed to the failure of the pituitary to secrete LH and to the subsequent dropping off of the ovary's ability to produce estrogen and progesterone. The withdrawal of these hormones, to which the body has been accustomed for 35 to 40 years, can cause physiological and psychological disturbances until a new balance is established.

Mechanism of Sex Hormone Action

Tissues associated with the reproductive process, such as the uterus and vagina, are unable to grow and function optimally without sex hormones. Either they have lost some vital capacity, which these hormones restore, or they have gained an inhibitor or some mechanism of growth restraint, which the hormone relieves. The actual mechanism is still obscure, but enough is now known to indicate which directions may warrant closer scrutiny. The most promising lead has come through studies of the distribution of estrogens in the tissues of the body. These hormones circulate throughout the body, but only the "target" tissues—the uterus, vagina, and oviduct plus the interacting organs, anterior pituitary and hypothalamus—possess a striking affinity for them. This was learned by administering highly radioactive estrogens. The target cells contain specific estrogen-binding substances, generally believed to be proteins. Thus when an estrogen encounters the cell, it is coupled in some manner to a *receptor* protein. The hormone appears not to be metabolized or modified in any way. However, as a result of the binding, the protein may undergo a transformation in shape (conformation) that permits it and its attached hormone to move from the cell's cytoplasm into the nucleus. There the protein may be modified further and, interacting with the genes, regulate the synthesis of ribonucleic acids (leading in turn to the synthesis of cellular protein and growth). Thus the mechanism has two steps.

Hormones, according to the classic definition, are chemical agents that are released from one group of cells and travel via the bloodstream to affect one or more different groups of cells. Another definition focuses less on their mode of travel and more on their function; it states that hormones are information-transferring molecules, whose essential function is to transfer information from one set of cells to another. This definition is valuable for several reasons. (1) Since it includes neurotransmitter substances released from nerve endings, it emphasizes the similarities instead of the differences between the endocrine and nervous systems. (2) It is broad enough to include agents released from unicellular organisms; these agents may play a role similar to that of hormones in multicellular organisms and may also act similarly at the biochemical level. (3) It helps to distinguish hormones from other classes of biologically active compounds. Vitamins, for example, are concerned primarily with energy metabolism and not with the transfer of information.

Does this definition include all of the chemical agents included in the classic definition of hormones? It is not entirely clear that it does.

Today we usually recognize at least two very distinct types of hormones. One type includes epinephrine, glucagon, insulin, gastrin, secretin, parathyroid hormone, calcitonin, and many of the hormones released from the anterior and posterior lobes of the pituitary gland. These and certain other hormones, together with the neurotransmitter substances released from nerve endings, seem clearly to play an *information-transferring role*. Cells respond to these hormones more or less rapidly, and the response is very often of short duration, or at least the magnitude of the response at any given instant is closely related to the amount of the hormone present.

The second class of hormones includes the steroid hormones, thyroid hormone, and at least one of the hormones produced by the anterior pituitary, namely growth hormone. These hormones play an important maintenance role, and in their prolonged absence cells may become incapable of responding to other hormones. Consequently they have been referred to as *permissive hormones*. Since cells and tissues do not develop properly in their absence, they have also been called developmental hormones.

Biologists have designated the hormones of the first group as *messengers* and those of the second group as *maintenance engineers*. It is difficult to draw hard and fast lines, but in general despite some overlapping in functions, the distinction is a useful one.

Although hormones regulate much more than just sexual behavior, this overview can give some picture of how they function. We will now turn our attention to some behavioral processes, especially in man, to see how these physiological mechanisms operate.

PSYCHOPHYSIOLOGICAL FUNCTIONS

As is obvious, the nervous system and the endocrine system are involved in every aspect of behavior. For some behaviors, we have learned a substantial amount about how these systems function, but for many little knowledge is available. We will select only a few topics to illustrate what has already been learned about the physiological control of complex behavior—specifically sleep, arousal, emotion, pain, fear, learning, memory, thinking, and sex.

Sleep and Arousal

Sleep is one of the necessities of living organisms; lack of sleep can affect perceptions, thinking, and personality. It is believed that sleep occurs because of chemical changes in the body. A daily build-up of toxins must somehow be destroyed, and the sleeping process in some way does just that.

Electroencephalogram (EEG) changes are an indication of drowsiness and sleep. As sleep becomes deeper, large, slow waves are recorded. Physiological signs of sleep are lowered body temperature and blood pressure, and regular breathing.

After the subject has been asleep for a while, the slow waves change and come to resemble those of a waking state. But the sleeper is not awake. In fact, it is difficult to wake him in this state. This sleep is known as paradoxical sleep. An important part of paradoxical sleep is the occurrence of rapid eye movements (REM), and it is during this period that dreams take place. External stimuli are very often incorporated into the dream at this time. Deprivation of REM sleep can cause marked physiological and behavioral changes.

REM

Arousal, or generalized drive (see Chapter 5), is manifested through various physiological symptoms, according to the particular drive involved, and fluctuates in degree from very high to very low, depending on the activity. An athlete before competition is alert and keyed up, ready to react speedily to any eventuality. Once the competition is over, he gradually winds down until he reaches a needed state of rest, during which his attentiveness and reaction time are considerably diminished. Some psychologists find the idea of general arousal and the study of its fluctuations of greater benefit than the idea of particular drives; they believe that a person naturally tends to move from a condition of low arousal to high arousal and vice versa.

The *reticular activating system* of the brain, which stretches from the brainstem to the region of the thalamus and hypothalamus, is considered to be vital to the process of arousal. In one experiment it was demonstrated that monkeys were more efficient in performing a discrimination task when their reticular activating systems were stimulated electrically than when they received no stimulation.

Before the game, an athlete is keyed up to react quickly; when the game is over, the state of arousal lowers.

The level of arousal necessary to perform a task efficiently varies with the nature of the task. High arousal is not by any means uniformly productive. Reaction time is usually at its peak with an intermediate level of arousal and begins to fall off when arousal increases beyond that point. Experiments in which animals and human beings are tested on different degrees of task difficulty have shown that high arousal is most instrumental in the performance of easier tasks, but becomes detrimental as tasks become more difficult. We shall return to the psychological study of sleep again in Chapter 9.

Emotion and Fear

Emotion and physiological changes are linked together. Physiological responses to situations include changes in heart rate, blood pressure, skin conductance, and muscle tension. Chemically, changes in the adrenal hormones seem to be related to different emotions.

Noradrenalin is very similar to the hormone released by the adrenal gland sitting atop each kidney. In danger or stress, the sympathetic nerves to the adrenal glands stimulate them to release *adrenalin* in greater amounts than usual. Together adrenalin and noradrenalin bring about several changes. Consider a mouse being chased by a cat. These chemicals cause the blood vessels of the mouse to constrict. As a result much of the blood is rerouted from the internal organs and is sent to the brain, heart, and skeletal muscles. Adrenalin and noradrenalin cause the heart to pump blood faster than before and increase the blood pressure. They relax the bronchioles, thus permitting a greater exchange of air in the lungs. They stimulate the liver to release glucose, which is used to refuel the mouse's skeletal muscles as it scampers away. They cause the pupils of its eyes to widen, enabling it to see in the dim light under the furniture. And if the mouse is lucky enough to escape with just a scratch, adrenalin and noradrenalin speed up the clotting time of the mouse's blood. In short these two chemicals prepare the mouse for "fight or flight." An animal without its adrenal glands can also get prepared for "fight or flight," but the massive release of adrenalin from the adrenal glands helps greatly.

Pain

Hunger and thirst are cyclic drives; we always know that we will be hungry and thirsty again. Pain, on the other hand, is episodic; most of us at least do not *know* that we will feel pain again on a regular schedule.

Unlike hunger and thirst, however, pain is an aversive stimulus; the drive is to stop it. Sometimes, of course, hunger and thirst can be described as types of pain—we talk of hunger pangs—in their higher levels of drive.

The avoidance of pain is extremely important, for pain is a warning signal that the organism may be damaged if it does not separate itself from the source of pain. The rare animal or human that is constitutionally insensitive to pain is often injured because of this deficiency in his nervous system; he must be constantly on guard instead of trusting to the defenses supplied by his nerves. The danger of biting one's lip or inside cheek after being given novocain by a dentist is quite serious, and often severe lacerations occur.

Whether the complete absence of pain represents one end of a physiological continuum of sensitivity to pain is not known. That humans and animals vary considerably in their reactions to pain is, of course, a matter of common observation, but measurement of this reaction is not the same as measurement of the basic sensitivity uncontaminated by the many other factors that influence the report of pain.

We do know that the response to pain varies in the same individual over time. Analgesics, hypnosis, even placebos and states of extreme emotion can raise either the threshold of pain tolerance or the threshold of the actual perception of pain; experimentally it is difficult if not impossible to distinguish between the two thresholds. We do know, however, that after prefrontal lobotomies for intractable pain, the pain remains but the patients are less responsive to it.

The influence of the social or cultural situation is of considerable importance in the response to pain. This influence may include a tradition of stoicism, of toleration of a certain degree of pain and discomfort, and this attitude may interact with experience to reduce the pain sensation itself. Children or adults who are frequently punished physically appear to achieve a growing tolerance of pain, quite apart from any stoicism they may demonstrate. Pavlov, after using shocks as conditioned stimuli for food, found that after training dogs did not react in the normal way to a painful stimulus, either behaviorally or physiologically.

The role of learning in response to pain is, however, even broader than this. Dogs in isolation, with limited sensory experience, from puppyhood to maturity do not respond with avoidance to such stimuli as pinpricks or shock, and sometimes do not even display an emotional response to pain. We are reminded of the explanations of the origin of masochism—a sexual pleasure in the experience of pain—that trace it to early experiences of pain or physical punishment associated with sexual gratification. Apparently a large part of the response to pain is a nonspecific state of arousal, which under normal circumstances becomes a cue for avoidance behavior but may be a conditioned cue for other behavior. We have described some studies demonstrating the existence of pain and pleasure centers in the brain in a box in Chapter 5 (p. 226).

Sex

Unlike food and water, sex is not vital to individual members of a species but rather to the species as a whole. Among mammals, both males and females can continue to function without sexual activity.

For this reason and others, Beach (1956) prefers to call sexual behavior an appetite rather than a primary drive, such as hunger and thirst. He points out that sexual activity, unlike primary drives, tends to be exhausting and needs a period of recovery. In addition, external stimuli are more important to sexual activity than they are to eating and drinking.

The sex drive is manifested only when the organism's sex glands have matured enough to produce sex hormones—androgens in the male and estrogens in the female. The relationship of the hormonal level to the strength of the sex drive in rats has been demonstrated in a study of the female rat, whose reproductive or estrus cycle peaks every 4 to 5 days (Wang, 1923). At the peak of an estrus cycle both the rat's general physical activity and its specifically sexual activity reached their greatest intensity. Males of most species are not subject to a cyclical hormonal flow and are therefore always ready for copulation.

Sterilization does not have as predictable an effect on human beings as it does on the lower mammals. The sex drive and ability to engage in sexual intercourse may remain largely unimpaired in sterile males and females, although the sexual interest of the castrated male may decline over a period of time.

The effects of castration provide another example of the increasing freedom from hormonal control as we go up the evolutionary ladder. Lower mammals cease sexual activity after the female's ovaries or the male's testes are removed, though not necessarily immediately. Female monkeys and apes reduce but do not eliminate their sexual behavior after removal of the ovaries. In the human female a lowering of sexual drive after surgical or natural menopause is apparently psychological rather than hormonal in origin, since many women report no diminution or even, with the chance of pregnancy gone, an increase in sexual drive.

In both males and females these observations apply to removal of the gonads (sex glands) after puberty and sexual experience. Sterilization before puberty produces an essentially neuter adult—the typical eunuch of history.

Physiological Processes in Sexual Behavior In the male there is normally a supply of sperm in the testes and ducts, awaiting a signal from the nervous system. Sensory receptors (visual, touch, olfactory) are stimulated by interaction with a female. As a result of such stimuli in sexual foreplay, sperm move into the *epididymis* and *vas deferens,* the tubes and canal that connect to the urinary canal of the penis. The sperm remain inactive until they are discharged into the vagina during copulation, as a result of stimulation of sensory receptors in the head of the penis. At *orgasm,* a massive neuromuscular reaction, sperm move through the vas deferens into and out of the urethra; with them in the ejaculate flows the seminal fluid, provided by the seminal vesicles and prostate gland. This fluid contains substances that nourish and activate the sperm.

When sperm accumulate in the passages without discharge, muscle tension results in pain in the groin, which can be relieved by masturbation, a self-induced emission of sperm, or by spontaneous emission during sleep ("wet dream") as frequently occurs in adolescent males.

For the male the "essentials" are an erect penis, erection being the result of the filling of *cavernous bodies* with blood during foreplay, and copulatory movements resulting in orgasm, with release of sperm. Although females generally enjoy stimulation of the vaginal walls and the tip of the uterine cervix by the penis, the female orgasm results primarily from stimulation of the *clitoris* during movements of copulation. The clitoris is analogous to the glans penis of the male, becoming erect due to increased blood pressure. The female orgasm is similar to that of the male, with three exceptions: (1) it may be longer than in the male; (2) there may be multiple orgasms; and (3) there is no discharge.

Sperm, moving partly under their own power, but assisted by muscular movements of the uterus, traverse the cervix, the uterus, and the fallopian tube to reach the egg. If the male has a normal sperm count of 100 million or more (in an ejaculate of 3.5 milliliters), a few thousand will reach the egg. If the male has been hyperactive sexually (more than once every 24 hours) or inactive (less often than every 5 days), his sperm count may be low, thereby reducing the probability of fertilization.

The "Safe Period" There is evidence from many mammalian species, including humans, that eggs can be fertilized only while in the oviduct, some 2 to 4 days after their discharge from the ovary. We know, too, that in humans sperm cells can survive only about 36 hours in the female reproductive tract. Since ovulation usually occurs about midway between menstrual periods, it is sometimes thought that the fertile period can be safely charted, and that if

Determination of Heredity

The zygote receives half its genetic material from the father and half from the mother. Each parent thus supplies half the genes that determine such features as hair color, body proportions, and so on. What happens when the "instructions" from the two genes controlling a particular feature are contradictory?

The basic research on this question was conducted in the mid-19th century by Gregor Mendel, an Austrian monk who determined from his observations of flowering pea plants that certain traits dominate others. More particularly, he found that crossing plants with red flowers and plants with white flowers produced only plants with red flowers. But when he crossed these second-generation red-flowered plants, he found that approximately one-quarter of their "offspring" had white flowers. Since that time other geneticists have conducted a variety of parallel experiments with both plants and animals and have succeeded in confirming and elaborating the laws of inheritance originally formulated by Mendel.

The occurrence of blue and brown eyes offers an excellent example of how these laws work. Every gene in a chromosome has a "partner" in the paired chromosome. If the maternal and paternal genes both specify blue eyes, the child will have blue eyes. If both specify brown eyes, the child will have brown eyes. But when one gene says blue eyes and the other says brown, the child will have brown eyes. The gene for brown eyes is *dominant*. But the gene for blue eyes remains a part of the child's chromosome structure, a *recessive* gene. When he grows up and his body begins to manufacture reproductive cells, half his gametes will receive the recessive gene for blue eyes and half will receive the dominant gene for brown eyes when the chromosome pairs are divided through meiosis. Let us suppose that he mates with a person who has a similar combination of genes for eye color. Four possible gene combinations can occur in the zygote. Three of them (brown eyes from both parents, blue eyes from the father and brown eyes from the mother, brown eyes from the father and blue eyes from the mother) will produce brown eyes in the child. The fourth possibility is that the recessive genes for blue eyes from both father and mother will combine and produce blue eyes in the child. There is thus a 25 percent chance that a child will inherit a recessive trait that both parents carry.

The child's sex is determined somewhat differently. One of the 23 pairs of chromosomes in the zygote is specifically responsible for this characteristic. There are two kinds of sex chromosomes: a large one with many genes (the X chromosome) and a small one with few genes (the Y chromosome). Female cells contain pairs of X chromosomes, and thus a woman's contribution to the zygote will always be one X chromosome. The cell of the normal male, on the other hand, carries one X chromosome and one Y chromosome; when meiosis occurs, half the resulting sperm cells will thus carry X and half will carry Y chromosomes. If one of the former fertilizes the ovum, the result will be a pair of X chromosomes, and the offspring will be a girl. On the other hand, if a Y chromosome combines with the mother's X chromosome, a boy will be born. It is important to note that the X chromosome is not recessive in males; *both* an X and a Y chromosome are necessary to determine male sex. No matter what the combination, it is always the male's contribution that determines the sex of an offspring.

copulation is avoided for 5 days preceding and 5 days following this midpoint, the possibility of fertilization can be eliminated. This is the theoretical basis of the so-called safe period or rhythm system of birth control. If all women had regular cycles, and things never happened out of turn, it would be an effective method. Irregularity and human error make it much less than certain. In addition, it now appears that copulation infrequently may start a cycle in the alternate ovary. Thus any calculation of a safe period is thrown into doubt. While speaking of the "unsafeness" of safe periods, now is a good time to dispel the myth that pregnancy cannot occur during lactation, the period after pregnancy when the breasts secrete milk. Ovulation, and thus fertilization, may occur within a month after childbirth.

Birth Control Methods An effective and acceptable way of controlling fertility is one of man's primary needs. The fight to gain acceptance of this concept by the medical profession and the laws of the land is one of our most striking examples not only of how science contributes to the solution of societal problems but also of how social innovators influence the course of science.

Abstinence—the complete elimination of sexual contact (celibacy)—is even more difficult to achieve than the rhythm system, except for those rare instances where religious vows (and isolation) are strong enough to ensure separation of the sexes.

Surgical ligature of the vas deferens or fallopian tubes achieves infertility without affecting sexual drive. However, they are not "harmless" techniques for precluding conception. Although vasectomy is a simple office procedure, it is accepted by only about 40,000 American males annually. Sterilization of women requires hospitalization, but is nevertheless elected by about 100,000 women each year. The surgical procedures are being simplified; however, the problem is the very limited reversibility of the procedures in both males and females.

Sperm blocking and killing methods include a condom or rubber sheath worn over the penis; a rubber diaphragm, blocking the cervical opening; and spermicidal creams to kill sperm in the vagina. These methods may be used singly or in combination. Singly they may be 95 percent effective.

Intrauterine devices (IUDs), which are 98 to 99 percent effective, consist of a plastic or plastic plus metal (copper, zinc) coil inserted into the uterus by a physician. Normal fertility is restored upon removal of the loop. We do not know precisely how it works, but presumably it maintains the uterus in a "motile" state, thereby preventing implantation of the fertilized egg.

The "Pill" contains a mixture of estrogens and progesterone in a balance designed to reproduce the hormonal level in the body during the period between ovulation and implantation. If properly used, the Pill inhibits ovulation. When its use is discontinued, pregnancy may occur promptly, unless other methods are employed, for by regulating the cycle fertility is enhanced. Should pregnancy occur, owing to a lapse in using the Pill or its rare failure, its further use should be stopped at once, for it stimulates excessive production of male hormone, which may bring about the masculinization of female embryos.

There are other difficulties. The Pill is not medically safe enough for use by a substantial fraction of the population. For obscure reasons calcium balance is upset, leading to the formation of blood clots inside blood vessels (*thrombosis*). The incidence of thrombosis is high enough to preclude the use of the Pill by anyone with a history of vascular disease. In addition the relations between the Pill and mammary cancer have not been clarified. Many physicians and patients find it unacceptable. Thus the search for other chemical means must be continued.

Sterility and Venereal Disease   About one male out of every 30 is sterile, the most frequent cause being previous infection in the male genital ducts, although occasionally the seminiferous tubules of the testes may have been destroyed by mumps, typhus, or X-rays. Or congenital defects may result in the production of abnormal sperm that cannot fertilize an ovum.

About one female in 15 is sterile. Although sterility may result from congenital defects or from dysfunction of the anterior pituitary (or other steps in the reproductive process), the most common cause is previous infection, blocking the oviducts or enclosing the ovaries in scar tissue.

The most common infection causing both male and female sterility is gonorrhea. Venereal disease, including both gonorrhea and syphilis, is on the rise. There have been many positive consequences of the ready availability of IUDs and the Pill and of the changing attitudes throughout the world leading to increased sexual freedom. However, there has been at least one unfortunate consequence—the rapid spread of "VD," especially among young people who are reluctant to seek prompt, responsible medical care. The importance of immediate attention to these infections to avoid the prospect of permanent damage is critical.

Homosexuality and Transvestism   There are many forms of homosexuality; it is no more precise to speak of homosexuality than it is to speak of cancer, for in neither case is one dealing with a single circumstance. There are few overt "exclusive" homosexuals, the incidence being under 5 percent in both men and women.

It is especially important to distinguish between the purely erotic aspect of sexual behavior and the gender role (or preferred sex role), a term used to denote aspects of attitudes and behavior that serve to disclose the person as having the status of boy or man, girl or woman.

Homosexuality may be incidental—adolescents get involved "for kicks"—or situational—in prisoners isolated from heterosexual possibilities. Some, but not all, homosexuals display varying degrees of reversal of preferred sex role. Thus one can identify effeminate (or passive) male homosexuals or masculine (or active) female homosexuals. The only common denominator in homosexuality is the use of, or preference for, a sexual partner of the same biologic sex.

Transvestism ("cross-dressing") is the term used to refer broadly to people who dress, or intensely desire to dress, in the clothes of the opposite biologic sex in a search for psychosexual comfort and satisfaction. Again, like homosexuality, transvestism is not a uniform behavioral condition, but occurs in varying degrees and with sundry implications.

The term "transsexualist" has been used to distinguish transvestites who earnestly desire and often actively seek as a possible solution to their dilemma surgical removal or "correction" of what they consider to be inappropriate genital equipment. These people seek acceptance as members of the opposite biologic sex, because it seems to them vastly more natural to behave and think like members of the opposite biologic sex.

The human habit of labeling any given sex practice as emotionally sick, abnormal, or perverted is largely a judgment reflecting the consensus of attitudes about sexual behavior in the society. Flourishing societies exist where homosexuality is a normal and accepted part of the communities' sex life. Such societal differences appear to be the result of differing influences on social learning within the culture itself; genetic differences have never been found to be sufficient to account for the diversity of ethnic customs. It seems both inaccurate and unnecessary to regard psychosexual variations as manifestations of illness, unless the term is to be narrowly defined as any deviation from the cultural mode.

What evidence we now have tells us that "homosexuals are made, not born." There is no clear or compelling evidence of chromosomal or hormonal differences between homosexual and heterosexual populations. It appears that sexual behavior in humans, both typical and atypical, is the product of learning and experience in the social context.

In our culture, most homosexuals live "against the grain"; when their behavior and life styles conflict with the cultural mode, their resulting emotional stress may be intense. Psychotherapeutic techniques can effect improvements in a person's social adjustment and personal comfort. Looking toward the future, however, what are most needed are (1) public acceptance and a legal code that does not penalize homosexuality per se; and (2) greater emphasis on the detection of inversions in gender-role learning during a child's growing years, for it is then, if ever, that remedial intervention can take place.

Learning and Memory

Some physiologists believe that memory involves some permanent change in the neuron's structure. Other theorists speculate that an increase in the number of synapses is responsible for memory, and still others view it as a series of chemical changes. Perhaps extra protein is used in some way to form memories, or perhaps ribonucleic acid (RNA) in the cytoplasm, which stores genetic information, also stores memory. It has been found that protein synthesis is responsible for long-term memory but not for short-term memory.

Memory is not stored in any one place in the brain, but is a combination of many small memory traces. Lashley (1942) taught rats to run a maze and then removed various parts of the cerebral cortex to see the effects. He found that maze memory was based on the total amount of brain matter removed and not upon the specific areas removed.

Memory can be stored in duplicate and triplicate. Monkeys were trained to perform tasks and then their brain was split into two halves, cutting the cerebral connections. An uninjured hemisphere still remembers and the animal's behavior was not markedly affected, indicating that memory traces must be on both sides of the brain. (This in no way indicates that each hemisphere duplicates the function of the other—they each have their own functions.)

Retrograde amnesia, the loss of memory caused by head injury or concussion, might be due in part to incomplete consolidation of disrupted memory traces. Following severe injury to the head, there usually is a period of complete loss of memory for a few seconds or minutes, followed by a period of transient amnesia. Russell and Nathan in 1946 studied 1,000 head-injured patients and found that 700 had suffered amnesia from a few seconds to a half hour after the injury, 130 suffered amnesia for longer than a half hour, and about the same number suffered no amnesia at all. The differences in injuries probably account for the differences in amnesia, but this still gives insight into the time it takes to form a memory trace.

Thinking

Thinking is one of the many physiological functions that physiologists do not completely understand. Does thinking involve the entire brain or only specified areas?

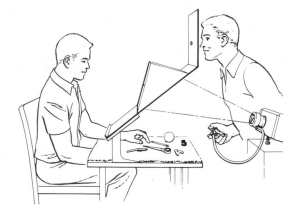

Fig. 6.20 Apparatus for testing patients with sectioned corpus callosum. (Sperry and Gazzaniga, 1967)

In 1967 Sperry and Gazzaniga designed experiments for patients in whom the corpus callosum—the bundle of nerve fibers connecting the two hemispheres of the brain—had been partially split as a treatment for epilepsy. The results are of interest in speech-location studies.

Anatomically, visual stimuli are transmitted to each hemisphere so that the right visual field is projected only on the left occipital lobe and the left visual field is projected on the right occipital lobe. Similarly, tactual information from the left hand goes to the right hemisphere and tactual information from the right hand goes to the left hemisphere. Sperry and Gazzaniga used these anatomical facts and devised an apparatus whereby words or pictures were flashed on either the left or right side of a screen and objects were placed on a table under the screen out of the patient's view (Fig. 6.20). When a picture was flashed on the right side of the screen, the patient was able to say what it was. However, the patient could not verbalize what he had seen on the left side of the screen except to say that there was a flash. Similarly, he was able to tell what object had been placed in his right hand but was unable to verbalize what the object was that was placed in his left hand. The right hemisphere has no speech mechanisms but "knows" intuitively what it has seen or felt. Only when the right hemisphere is provided with a means of communication, that is, with intact brain connections, can it communicate the sensations it is receiving.

Although our thinking process manipulates symbols in the absence of a sensation, it is necessary to compare our thoughts with reality and to be able to change our ideas when sensory inputs contradict them.

BRAIN MALFUNCTIONS

An organism's early environment plays an important part in shaping its future behavior. When rats were reared for 80 days in either enriched or impoverished environments, the enriched rats surpassed the impoverished rats in maze learning (Bennett, Diamond, Krech, and Rosenzweig, 1964). In addition, physiological differences in the nervous system were observed (Rosenzweig and others, 1969). The brain of an enriched rat and the brain of an impoverished rat differed in weight and chemical activity. The enriched rat brain was heavier and had a thicker cortex. Chemically, the enriched rat brain showed more activity of acetylcholine esterase (a transmitter substance) and choline esterase (an enzyme).

Differences between the rats' brains appeared to be greatest in the occipital cortex. One would suppose, then, that the increased visual stimulation of the enriched environment was the cause. However, rats reared in enriched but totally dark environments exhibit the same physiological signs. This could suggest that the occipital cortex is the center for more than just visual input.

Mental Deficiencies

Intelligence measurements (see Chapter 13) attempt to establish a criterion for judging and classifying mental deficiencies. Typically the mentally deficient have been categorized as morons, imbeciles, or idiots.

Moronism, like average or high intelligence, seems to be the product of an interplay between heredity and environment; usually no evidence of damage to the nervous system is found. These people may simply be at the lower end of the distribution curve of intelligence. Imbeciles and idiots, however, almost always show evidence of structural defects in the nervous system and other organs.

Mongolism, an extreme form of mental deficiency, is actually a form of general developmental arrest. The body is distorted; there are an odd-shaped head, a large tongue, and small hands, feet, and general stature. The brain cells show structural abnormalities that are the result of a chronic deficiency of oxygen and sugar. Genetic studies have shown that mongoloids have an extra chromosome, which interferes in some way with cellular metabolism and organ development.

Epilepsy

Epilepsy is a disorder of the brain that causes periodic seizures accompanied by a temporary loss of consciousness and motor and autonomic disturbances. Between seizures, the person functions normally.

Epileptic seizures are classified into three varieties—*grand mal* attacks, *petit mal* attacks, and a third unlabeled variety. Each has its own physiological characteristics. If an electroencephalogram (EEG) is used to register neural disturbances during an epileptic seizure, the readouts become extremely abnormal. Each variety of the disorder has its own unique EEG pattern.

Epilepsy is sometimes caused by brain injuries or tumors. In the case of focal epilepsy, where a specific point of origin, usually associated with an injury, can be detected, excessive neuronal firing spreads throughout the cerebrum, producing seizures. This type of epilepsy can be treated surgically. Other types are often treatable by drug therapy.

Old Age

As treatment of disease becomes more successful, more people will be experiencing the physiological and psychological effects of reaching 60 or 70 years of age. The overall deterioration of cells with age causes a general impairment of body functions in which the nervous system is no exception.

Senile psychosis, a chronic mental disorder of the aged, is characterized by a slow loss of contact with reality. It is basically caused by an inadequate blood supply to cerebral tissues. The cerebral cortex becomes altered, the brain shrinks, and the number of nerve cells is reduced.

Arteriosclerosis can cause a much more severe psychosis than that brought about by old age alone. The hardening and thickening of both large and small blood vessels reduce the blood supply to the brain, causing serious brain injuries.

Other Brain Disorders

Anoxia Anoxia, a deficiency of oxygen reaching the cells of the body, causes irreparable damage to nerve cells, primarily to those of the brain. Brain cells must oxidize glucose to function properly. A shortage of either oxygen or glucose produces a state of unconsciousness, and a severe shortage causes death. Prenatal anoxia can result in brain injuries at birth.

Localized Brain Injuries Depending upon the area affected, a local brain injury may produce various physiological effects. When the parietotemporal area is injured, for example, language skills are affected, resulting in the condition known as aphasia. Speech, writing, and understanding are in various degrees impaired. Sometimes an aphasic person can be retrained in his lost skills. A neurologist is often able to diagnose the area of injury by the nature of the abnormality in behavior it produces.

DRUGS AND THE BRAIN

In many cases the symptoms of mental illness and brain disease are all too well known, but the physiological basis of these symptoms is poorly understood, if it is known at all.

There is hope, however, that certain drugs not only will buy us a little time until research shows us why and how things go wrong in the brain, but also will give us clues as to how the brain works. Certain drugs frequently help relieve the distress and suffering that accompany mental illness and brain damage. Several years ago mental patients received electric shock, or, even worse, part of the association area of their brain was removed (prefrontal lobotomy). These drastic treatments usually achieved only one positive result: quieting a difficult or violent patient and making it easier for overworked staffs of mental institutions to care for him. Often the patient's personality changed and his mental ability decreased. Now drugs such as *reserpine* can quiet upset patients and help them to lead more productive lives. The symptoms of Parkinson's disease in which certain cells that work with the cerebellum in coordinating movements are damaged can now be relieved temporarily by drugs such as L-DOPA (dihydroxyphenylalanine). Scientists today are at work trying to develop drugs to help the slow learner.

However, other drugs that affect the brain have kicked up a storm of controversy. When more alcohol is consumed than the liver can handle, the excess goes to the brain, the direct target of alcohol. Alcohol depresses—it does not stimulate—the activity of the brain. The first part to be affected is the reticular formation; as a result a stimulus such as a "stop sign" will take an unusually long time to be properly registered by the cortex. If still more alcohol is drunk, the function of the cortex itself is affected; one becomes emotional, giddy, and his tongue trips up. He is emotional because the limbic system centers that control emotion are no longer held in check by the cortex. His speech is slurred and his steps are unsteady because the alcohol depresses the areas of the cortex that control these functions.

What do drugs such as LSD do to the brain? Some evidence suggests that

LSD (lysergic acid diethylamide) blocks the activity of certain nerve cells that form serotonin, a transmitter substance in the brain. On the other hand, other evidence indicates that LSD can "fool" nerve cells into accepting it in the place of serotonin. Certainly the chemical structure of LSD and several other "hallucinogens" or "psychedelics"—mescaline, peyote, psilocybin, psilocin—is very similar to that of serotonin. However, LSD cannot transmit messages in the same way that serotonin can; as a result the message becomes "garbled" as it crosses the synapse between two nerve cells. This may explain the wildly exaggerated sensations that one experiences on a "trip." In addition LSD may overstimulate the reticular formation, which in turn alerts the cortex more than it usually does; this may account for the "heightened awareness" that LSD users often report (see Fig. 6.21).

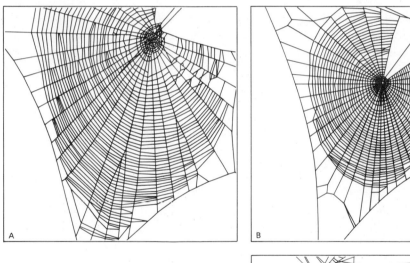

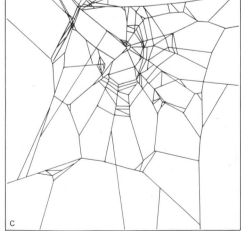

Fig. 6.21 The nervous system of many animals besides mammals is affected by various stimulatory and hallucinogenic drugs. These drawings show the webs spun by spiders which were drugged by pharmacologist Peter Witt. The normal web (A) has the familiar precision of spider architecture and is surely one of the most effective snares in nature. However it has numerous flaws such as branching radii and unequal spacing between the concentric circles. LSD (B) causes the spider to produce a nearly perfect web, as if it were "totally concentrating." Caffeine (C) gives the spider the equivalent of "coffee nerves" and the web is a disorganized tangle. (Ebert et al., 1973)

We do not know exactly how marijuana affects the brain. Much seems to depend on the purity of the drug and the person using it. Many users report feelings of well-being and elation—a "high." Marijuana may, like alcohol, do this by depressing the activity of the cortex, which normally holds a tight rein on the emotional centers of the brain. There is good evidence that it interferes with skills such as driving a car.

What dangers do marijuana and the hallucinogens pose to the brain and the rest of the body? Unfortunately we do not know the answer to this question. Although there is evidence that LSD can lead to mental illness, there is not enough evidence at present to show that marijuana is physiologically dangerous. Further research and careful follow-ups on long-term marijuana users are clearly necessary.

It is said that neither marijuana nor any of the hallucinogens is physiologically addictive; that is, the cells do not change their metabolism so that their functions depend on the drug. These substances, however, may well be psychologically addictive; that is, a user may feel that he simply cannot face his world and its problems without his drug. We do not understand the physiological functions of the brain that lead to psychological addiction.

There is no doubt that narcotics such as opium and its derivatives (morphine, heroin), alcohol in immoderate amounts, amphetamines, and barbiturates are physiologically addictive.

The body does increase its tolerance to LSD and the other hallucinogens; this simply means that with continued use of a drug, larger doses are needed to get the same effects. However, a user who suddenly stops taking a hallucinogen need not experience the agonizing "withdrawal symptoms" that a narcotic addict endures when he comes off his drug. There is no increased tolerance to marijuana, whereas an alcoholic does have increased tolerance to alcohol.

The amphetamines, generally known as speed or pep pills, have a chemical structure that resembles adrenalin. When amphetamine or adrenalin is released in the bloodstream, it gives a sudden burst of energy such as would be needed for a flight, fight, or fright response. They appear to act partly by stimulating the sensory cortex and partly by causing the release of noradrenaline and other stimulatory chemicals within the body. When used in low doses, amphetamines produce a general increase in alertness, a sense of well-being, and decreased feelings of fatigue. They suppress appetite, increase heart rate and blood pressure, and change sleep patterns. When taken for prolonged periods, increased tolerance develops, as in the case of LSD, and increased doses are required to induce desired effects. These gradually increasing doses of amphetamine can lead to highly abnormal behavior manifested by unfounded suspiciousness, hostility, hallucinations, and persecutory delusions—in other words, what we commonly term paranoid behavior. Another pattern of amphetamine use is the "speed binge," which involves repeated intravenous injections. This use of amphetamines is associated with aggressive and assaultive behavior, exaggerated self-confidence, increased tendencies to take physical action quickly without consideration of consequences, hostility, and distrust. The evidence indicates clearly that chronic amphetamine use does serious harm to the user and to those around him.

It appears almost certain that man will continue to use various chemicals such as drugs, alcohol, and tobacco to change his behavior. It is hoped that further research may make it possible to avoid many of the dangers of drug and other chemical use and yet obtain particular behavioral effects that may be desired under certain circumstances.

SUMMARY

Physiological psychology studies the biological bases of psychological functioning. Man, the most complex of animals, is made of the same building block as other living things—the cell. The cell consists of a nucleus, cytoplasm, and an outer membrane.

Coordination and integration of the activity of the multitude of cells in our bodies is achieved by chemical and nervous control mechanisms. The nervous system is a complex structure of nerve cells, called neurons. The neurons are responsible for transporting information among the body parts. When neurons are stimulated, nerve impulses—electrical changes in the cell's membrane—are propagated through the cell. Neurons are stimulated by excitations of their dendrites. If enough excitation is present, the neuron fires a nerve impulse down its axon, which releases a transmitter chemical when it reaches a synapse at the end of the axon. These transmitter substances work to stimulate the dendrites and cell bodies of neighboring neurons, and the process is repeated in them. This is how nerve impulses travel through the body. Axons of neurons may be coated with a fatty substance called myelin, which speeds the conduction of impulses.

The transmitter chemicals of one neuron might excite or inhibit the firing of a nerve impulse in a neighboring neuron. Transmitter chemicals achieve excitation or inhibition by adjusting the levels of sodium, potassium, and chloride ions at the postsynaptic cell's membrane. The fact that neuronal firing can either be excited or inhibited affords much more precise control of nervous activity than would be possible with just one kind of synapsing.

In animal nervous systems neurons are arranged in nerve nets, nerve cords, such as the spinal cord, nerve bundles, called ganglia, and nerves, or bundles of axons. In man, the brain and spinal cord make up the central nervous system, which handles information about the environment received from receptors throughout the body. Sensory neurons relay sensory impulses to the central nervous system; they make up our *afferent* nervous system. The *efferent* nervous system relays information from the brain and spinal cord by way of motor neurons to the skeletal muscles. Other efferent neurons, called autonomic neurons, conduct nerve impulses to the heart, smooth muscles, and glands.

The gray matter of the spinal cord contains sensory neurons in the dorsal root ganglia. The white matter is composed of fiber tracts, which conduct impulses between the spinal cord and the brain. Some idea of how the spinal cord works can be obtained by considering such spinal reflexes as the knee jerk.

The internal adjustments of body organs are regulated to a large extent by the autonomic nerves, which are divided into sympathetic and parasympathetic branches. Sympathetic and parasympathetic nerves have opposite effects on the tissues they innervate; sympathetic nerves excite the organ, and parasympathetic nerves slow its functioning.

The brain is a dense jungle of 10 billion nerve cells. It has been functionally divided and subdivided. The lower part of the hindbrain is the medulla, which controls respiration and heartbeat and through which all nerve impulses from the spinal cord to the brain must pass. Located in front of the medulla is the pons, above and behind which is the cerebellum. The cerebellum coordinates skeletal muscle movements but does not initiate these movements.

The midbrain is proportionately smaller in man than in other animals because of the increasing dominance of the forebrain in highly evolved animals. Besides being a connecting link between hindbrain and forebrain, the midbrain also receives sensory input from the eyes and is responsible for the control of eye movements.

Running through the medulla and on into the midbrain and part of the forebrain is a complex nerve cell organization called the reticular formation. This organization alerts and arouses other regions of the brain such as the cerebral cortex and the thalamus and is thus responsible for allocating our attention.

The forebrain, the cerebrum, is by far the dominant part of man's brain. At the base of the cerebrum is the thalamus, which processes all sensory input to the brain except olfactory sensations. Beneath it is the hypothalamus, which controls hunger and body temperature, as well as thirst, pleasure, pain, and sexual activity.

Wedged between the thalamus, hypothalamus, and cerebral cortex is a system of structural connections called the limbic system, which is responsible for much of our emotional experience. One part of the limbic system, the hippocampus, probably is responsible for the formation of long-term memory.

The cerebral cortex is the area of the brain in which the highest level of brain functions occur. The cortex can be mapped into sensory and motor areas, but most of it, the association areas, is involved in the integration of all the inputs into the brain.

Like the nervous system, the endocrine system also helps to integrate behavior. This system is responsible for the production of the hormones that regulate sexual behavior—progesterone and estrogen in the female and testosterone in the male—as well as other kinds of behavior.

All the functions we perform have a physiological basis. In the case of the more complex activities involved in sleeping, waking, fearing, experiencing emotion, feeling pain, engaging in sex, learning, remembering, thinking, and so on, physiological psychologists are continually performing experiments to determine the precise processes involved.

Much of the knowledge of the brain and its workings is gained by studying the effects of mental deficiencies, diseases, injuries, the aging process, and so on. Likewise, studies of the effects of drugs—depressants and stimulants—with their associated psychological and physiological effects are adding more links to our chain of knowledge of the human nervous system.

Suggested Readings

Aaronson, Bernard, and Humphrey Osmond, eds., *Psychedelics: The Uses and Implications of Hallucinogenic Drugs.* New York, Doubleday Anchor Books, 1950.
  Twenty-nine articles examine psychedelic drugs from a variety of points of view, from

their physiological effects through their social implications and the part they play in therapy.

Chorover, Stephan L., "Big Brother and Psychotechnology II: The Pacification of the Brain," *Psychology Today,* May 1974.
Using evidence from monkeys, a neuroscientist reports on the potentially disastrous effects of employing brain surgery to treat human behavioral disorders.

Darwin, Charles, *The Expression of the Emotions in Man and Animals* (originally published in 1872). Chicago: University of Chicago Press, 1965.
Darwin's classic investigation of the link between mental states and their manifestation in physiological behavior.

Faraday, Ann, *Dream Power.* New York: Coward, McCann and Geohegan, 1972.
The author presents physiological research concerned with sleeping and dreaming, and maintains that anyone can, without professional help, learn to decode his dreams and thereby gain valuable insights into his feelings and attitudes.

Friedman, Meyer, and Ray H. Rosenmann, *Type A Behavior and Your Heart.* New York, Knopf, 1974.
Based on studies over a number of years, the authors (both medical doctors) believe that Type A behavior, a particular complex of personality traits which can be found in persons at all socioeconomic levels, is a major factor causing coronary heart disease.

Hjortsberg, William, *Gray Matters.* New York, Simon and Schuster, 1971.
The possibility of the brain living outside a human body is explored in this science fiction novel as a possible cure for overpopulation.

Huxley, Aldous, *The Doors of Perception.* New York, Harper & Row, 1970.
The well-known novelist describes his mescaline trip.

Jackson, Charles, *The Lost Weekend.* New York: Holt, Rinehart and Winston, 1948.
This famous novel vividly describes what it is like to be an alcoholic.

Kesey, Ken, *One Flew over the Cuckoo's Nest.* New York, Viking Press, 1962.
The heroic struggles of a mental hospital patient are stopped forever by a lobotomy.

Wooldridge, Dean E., *The Machinery of the Brain.* New York: McGraw-Hill, 1963.
A highly readable treatment of the mechanisms of the brain.

Part 2
Cognitive Processes

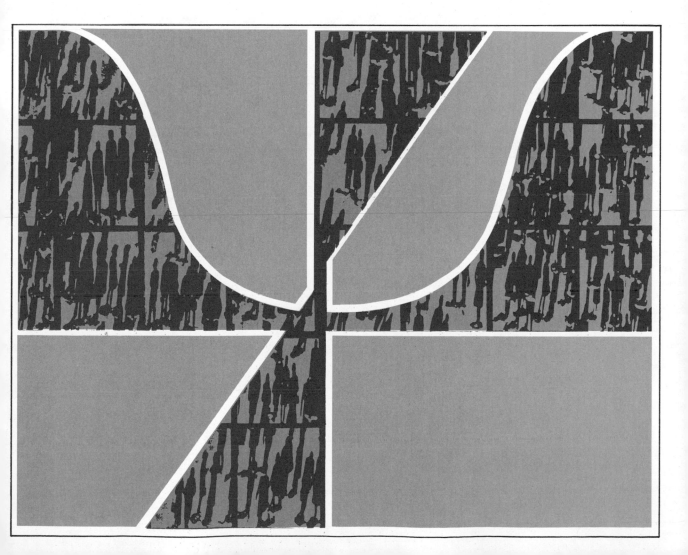

Chapter Seven

Information Processing

What is meant by "information processing"?
What is a flow diagram?
What are the origins of the information processing approach
   to psychology?
What is iconic storage?
Which is superior—visual or verbal memory?
How can you improve your memory?
What is the role of selectivity in information processing?
How do we translate wiggles on the page into meaning when we
   read?

As human beings we constantly interact with the world as it exists both outside us and within us. We continuously register, process, and respond to images, sounds, and other stimuli. Try to imagine an instant during your waking day when you are not seeing, hearing, thinking, or using your other senses to relate to the world. While munching your cereal in the morning you may be searching the paper for news of the most recent political events or listening to last night's ball scores on the radio. While waiting in line at the cafeteria, you may check to see if the lasagna looks appetizing, seek out a friend, or frantically attempt to read half of *Moby Dick* for your next class.

We do more than merely gather information from the world we live in. We actively sort out this information and act on it. In previous chapters we have discussed sensation (Chapter 1) and perception (Chapter 2). With a little thought, it is easy to realize that a great deal must go on between our act of sensing an object and our act of responding to it. What goes on during this interval is actually a complex series of events that we are hardly aware of. Our experience suggests that from the onset of stimulation to the onset of awareness, no time has passed, and that awareness must be immediate. However, careful experiments have shown that it takes time for the perceptual processing of events, even though we are usually not aware of it. We will call the series of processes that intervenes between sensation and perception "information processing."

We may think of information processing as the events by which "raw" physical data gathered by our senses are converted into meaningful perceptions. For example, light reflected from the environment and reaching the retinas of our eyes consists of energy of various wavelengths. But we do not speak in terms of wavelengths but rather in terms of colors. You don't say to a friend, "What a nice 474-nanometer sweater you have!" but you may say, "Your blue sweater is very nice." In other words, we perceive objects that are familiar, or related to familiar things, in our environment. We see things we expect to see; we do not, in fact, see the elements of stimulation described in Chapter 1. Thus, we do not describe experience in terms of its intensity, wavelength, contours, homogeneity, or other sensations. Instead, we talk of sweaters, figures inside the sweaters, chairs, people, and the like. Yet it is obvious that we must have started at some time with sensations. This chapter aims at explaining the transition from

A recently invented information processing machine, courtesy of Dr. Seuss.

© 1962 by Dr. Seuss

Counting up sleepers..?
Just how do we do it..?
Really quite simple. There's nothing much to it.
We find out how many, we learn the amount
By an Audio-Telly-o-Tally-o Count.
On a mountain, halfway between Reno and Rome,
We have a machine in a plexiglass dome
Which listens and looks into everyone's home.
And whenever it sees a new sleeper go flop,
It jiggles and lets a new Biggel-Ball drop.
Our chap counts these balls as they plup in a cup.
And that's how we know who is down and who's up.

the physical sensation to the psychological perception of the sensation as information.

WHAT IS INFORMATION PROCESSING?

Information processing is a coherent and orderly way of studying the cognitive tasks performed by human beings. Perception, knowing, and memory may be examined from this viewpoint. Information processing aids us in understanding how we experience the perceptual world, how we recognize objects and patterns, how we understand pictures, how we use and understand language, how we interpret ideas.

information processing

The information processing approach rests on several basic and very important assumptions. The first is that the operations of perception, cognition, memory, and so on, are not the immediate and direct outcome of stimulation but the consequences of a series of processes. Each of these processes takes up an interval of time. These time intervals, measured in milliseconds (thousandths of a second) usually are too brief for us to be aware of them. Yet we must remember that they are discrete time intervals that actually exist and that can be carefully and exactly measured. In studying a complex psychological task such as visual recognition, for example, the time interval between the onset of the stimulus and the occurrence of a response is divided into a number of stages or processes. These processes correspond to a series of transformations performed upon our internal representations of the information gathered from the outside world.

The information processing approach assumes that experimental procedures can be designed to examine the contents of our internal representation of the stimulus information at every point in the sequence of processes that we perform. Comparing the samples of this content at various stages of processing with the original projection of the stimulus provides psychologists with a basis for making inferences about the characteristics and nature of the processes involved. A simplified but useful analogy of this kind of investigation is the following: Assume a bank robbery has taken place. Fortunately, the entire series of events that composes the robbery has been recorded on the bank's closed circuit television. In order to catch the culprits, the investigating detective wishes to learn all he can of the criminals' method of operation. He plays the tape over and over, studying the criminals' actions at every stage of the robbery until he can build up an idea of just how these particular thieves work.

Actually, the work of the psychologist is much harder than the work of this hypothetical police detective. In the first place, the psychologist does not have a tape but must try to devise experimental strategies to stop or tap the processes while they are actually occurring. And in the second place, the psychologist does not work with pictures or recordings of the actual processes, but

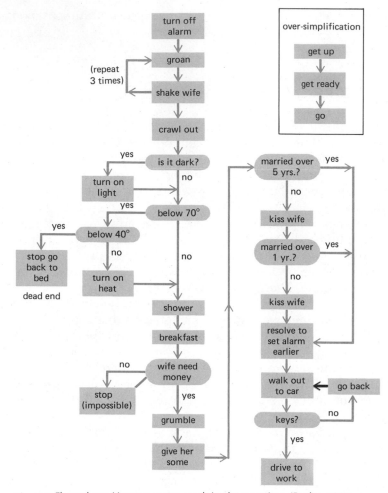

Fig. 7.1 Flow chart: How to get to work in the morning. (Borko, 1962)

with *reports* of the processes at various stages. From these reports—such as reported perceptions, recognitions, and memories—the psychologist must infer the nature and characteristics of the process.

Several corollary assumptions follow from the assumption that information processing consists of a series of discrete stages. It is assumed that the total time from the onset of the stimulus to the occurrence of a response can be divided into separate time intervals of a definite duration, each characterized by a different operation. For purposes of study, the juxtapositions of these various processes are sketched on a chart or *flow diagram* (an example is given in Fig. 7.1). Blocks are drawn to represent processes occurring at various time periods. Each block is labeled according to its specific process. The blocks are

flow diagram

connected by lines in order to represent the sequence in which the operations are thought to occur. Thus, the information processing approach attempts to delineate the operations that occur between stimulation and response.

Another assumption is that there is a continuity between input and output. In other words, sensation and perception are parts of a continuous process, which we arbitrarily divide for study purposes. Each stage can be further subdivided, and the resulting substages both influence and are influenced by the preceding and following stages. Thus, the flow of information from one stage to another is continuous.

The processes composing the information processing chain are generally believed to be limited in the amount of information they can contain or process in a given time period. The amount of information that can be handled by each process must be determined by experimental research. The capacity of each operation in the chain must be considered separately. In some situations only a few items of information can be processed at once. In others, the amount of information processed appears to be unlimited.

It is believed that capacity limitations within the information processing system lead to selectivity. Since not all information can be processed to the same degree in the time period available, the system makes some kind of selection. Selectivity is a method of ordering priorities. If you have a large number of things to do on a given afternoon and not enough time to do them all, you will select some things to do completely, some things to do partially, and some things that you will not do at all. Selectivity in information processing may be thought of in a similar manner. A great deal of work in information processing analysis is devoted to identifying the determinants and mechanisms of selectivity.

WHY DO WE USE THE INFORMATION PROCESSING APPROACH?

In what ways is the information processing approach especially useful? What does it tell us that other approaches are not able to tell us? How does it help us to open up new areas of research? What developments have preceded it?

To answer these questions we will consider first how the information processing approach originated and second why we use this approach here.

Origins of Information Processing

Information processing emerged from several new conceptualizations and techniques that other sciences began to use in the late 1940s and that psychologists soon adopted. Three distinct developments led to the establishment of the information processing approach. The first is the mathematical model of communication or "communication theory," originated by Shannon and Wiener

Norbert Wiener

(1948). These innovative researchers presented a model of communication in which senders transmit messages over channels to receivers. Originally developed for application to telephone switchboard engineering, their theory can be applied to any communication system. The significance to psychology of this model is that it may be easily applied to human perceptual systems, which are then viewed as communication channels.

The second development that fostered the establishment of the information processing approach also derives from the work of Shannon and Wiener on information content. These investigators developed a way of measuring the information content of a message completely independently of any measurements of either the stimulus or the response. The method rests on the idea that the amount of information in a message is equivalent to the reduction of uncertainty the message brings about. Thus it is possible to measure information content in and of itself, without reference to either the events being communicated or the mode of communication. All information, then, whether in words, Morse code, picture patterns, or the like, can be defined by uncertainty reduction—the amount we learn about the event that enables us to distinguish it from other events.

The concept of measuring information in this way provided a crucial ingredient for information processing. It made possible a means of comparing the content of different stimuli in different situations and hence of formulating generalized statements about the nature of information processing.

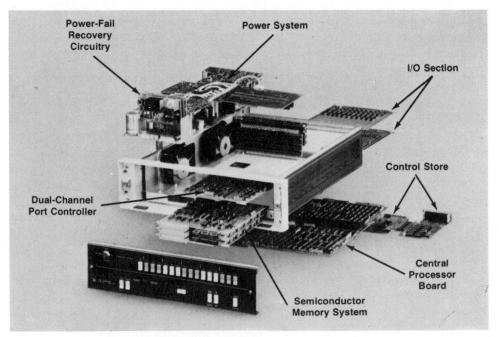

Fig. 7.2 A digital computer (photograph courtesy Hewlett-Packard Company).

A third development that speeded the adoption of an information processing approach has been the increasingly widespread use of digital computers (Fig. 7.2). As psychologists became aware of the capabilities of these computers, they began to notice a number of similarities between computer operations and human behavior, notably in tasks such as perceptual learning, problem solving, recognition, thinking, and game playing. Soon models of human behavior were being based on computer operation. As an aside, let us say that although perceptual and cognitive functioning has been explained in terms of computer models, no one has yet been able to program a computer to perform some of the operations that humans perform routinely and almost perfectly. For example, a computer has yet to be built that can recognize and distinguish between a potentially infinite number of human voices—a task that we all perform during the course of our lives.

Why Information Processing?

In previous chapters we have studied sensation, perception, and learning. Why are we now looking at these same activities again from the point of view of information processing? The reasons for doing so are many. We will outline them here, and they will become clearer as we proceed with our analysis.

The information processing approach gives us a way of understanding many problems that might otherwise remain unclear. For example, how are perception and memory related? Everyday experience tells us that there is a connection between these activities. What we remember has obviously been perceived at some point. An information processing approach allows us to view perception and memory as being on opposite ends of a continuum, linked by a series of complex but empirically researchable processes.

Another reason for adopting the information processing approach is that it enables us to view the perceiver as an active processor, not just the passive recipient, of information which he stores and responds to. From this perspective, we must speak about stimulation in terms of units that have some relevance to the perceiver, that underline the fact that the perceiver is an active processor. The term "information" conveys this meaning much more effectively than the term "stimulus."

A further reason for employing the information processing approach is that it allows us to compare the ways in which different aspects of perception are established in memory, so that we can talk about the properties they have in common. Recognition, reading, auditory functioning—all represent various aspects of perception whose relation to memory may be profitably studied by the information processing approach.

Finally, we use the information processing approach because it provides a means to describe as precisely as possible the many separate steps, stages, storages, processes, and analyses that an active processor of information goes through. At this time the identification of specific stages or processes with specific neurological activities is only beginning. However, this area of vagueness does not impede our ability to conceptualize and understand various functions from an information processing perspective.

WHAT KINDS OF PROBLEMS DOES INFORMATION PROCESSING CONSIDER?

The information processing approach enables us to probe a variety of issues and topics of current concern. The following are examples of the types of problems we will examine in this chapter:

pattern recognition

1. *Pattern recognition.* How is it that when we see the letter *B* we recognize it as *B*? It may appear in different sizes, at different angles, in different styles of lettering, or even in barely legible handwriting, but it is *B* to us. The phenomenon of pattern recognition is something we perform rapidly and automatically. Viewed by the psychologist, however, it is a complex operation, requiring a complicated (and still unperfected) explanation.

selective attention

2. *Selective attention.* Suppose you spend a day in the country. You are in a beautiful field of wildflowers. Fascinating cloud configurations pass overhead. Your attention is directed toward perceiving and enjoying the natural features of the landscape. Now suppose you are playing baseball in the same field. Your attention will be directed toward very different things: who has the ball, whether a hit has been made, who's on first. You may not notice the features of the landscape because you are concentrating on the game. Thus attention may be directed toward very different things and may at different times shift from one aspect of a scene to another. Psychologists refer to several theories in attempting to explain the complex phenomenon of selective attention.

3. *Fading memory.* Have you ever found, after just looking up a phone number, that you could not remember the number as you started to dial it? You have probably discovered the solution to this problem: if you repeat the number over and over until you dial it, you will remember it. What is going on in this situation? How does the number get "lost"? How could your memory fail you in such a short time? Perhaps studies in information processing can suggest some answers.

familiarity

4. *Familiarity.* Perceivers respond differently to stimuli they have never seen before than they do to familiar stimuli. For example, it is easier to recognize non-English words whose letter sequences are similar to those that occur in English words than to recognize non-English words whose letter sequences are unlike those of English. This effect is not true only for words, though it may appear to be most prominent with them. We are much more likely to recognize something we have seen before as compared to something new, because we will have an easier time figuring out what the object is. This has been shown

for recognition of words, sentences, faces, and so forth. In addition, things in familiar orientation are easier to recognize. An upside-down face, for example, is usually difficult to identify. All of these phenomena have been attributed to familiarity.

5. *Information retrieval.* The human brain contains an incredibly efficient data storing system. Stored data are useless, however, unless they can be retrieved and used. Thus, the human brain also contains an incredibly efficient information retrieval system. Suppose that someone asks you what you were doing on July 4, 1973, at 3:30 P.M. At first you might say, "How can I possibly remember what I was doing then?" But if you consider the question further, some surprising things will begin to happen. Your thinking might go something like this: "Let's see . . . in 1972 I was a high school sophomore. That summer I was a counselor at Camp Hiawatha. On the Fourth of July we took the kids on a trip. We took them to, to, let me see. . . . We took them to Lake Quaboag. We had a barbecue on the lake shore . . . and at 3:30 P.M. we were just about getting ready to leave. I can answer your question! On July 4, 1973, at 3:30 P.M., I was getting ready to return to Camp Hiawatha from Lake Quaboag." If you think this is a made-up example, try it yourself with any date supplied by a friend.

WHAT IS THE SEQUENCE OF INFORMATION PROCESSING STAGES?

A Description of Operations

Before we present a model of information processing, we will first point out the general properties of several of the operations and processes included in the model. While most of the discussion in this chapter refers to visual information processing, because sight is the sense that we know the most about, hearing and other sensations are processed in similar ways.

Information may be deposited and kept at various points along the way in the sequence of processing. This property of an operation is called storage or memory. It is possible for different types of storage to be distinguished on the basis of their comparative duration in time, as we will see with both short- and long-term memory. As the chapter proceeds, a number of questions will arise about the characteristics of the contents of different storages. Images from the outside world reach us via light projected onto the retina. Since light projection can't get "into" the brain, a representation of it, which we call information, is the content that we will be speaking of in our theories. We will be concerned with the relationship between the stored form of information and the original information in the retinal projection of the stimulus. Is the stored information in the same form as the original information or has it been transformed? And how can information be removed from storage?

The transformation of information is at the heart of the concept of information processing. Information that is deposited in storage becomes involved in two processes: a read-in process, which puts it there, and a read-out process, which takes it out. One example of a read-out process is scanning. This is an organized procedure of going from one part of an information field to the next, **scanning** treating each item in turn. Scanning is an example of serial processing. Another method of processing is parallel processing, in which all items are processed at once. As we shall see, this becomes an important distinction in solving various problems that arise in the analysis of information processing.

Read-in and read-out processes transfer information from one place to another in the information processing chain. Transfer usually occurs between separate storage points. The transfer processes can handle information arbitrarily or according to some predetermined pattern of transfer. Not infrequently, some information is lost during transfer. Some information is ignored and not processed at all. We lose other information because we do not have enough time to process it before its current storage fails either by decaying or by being inter-

Another information processing device, courtesy of Dr. Seuss.

Now the news has arrived
From the Valley of Vail
That a Chippendale Mupp has just bitten his tail,
Which he does every night before shutting his eyes.
Such nipping sounds silly. But, really, it's wise.

He has no alarm clock. So this is the way
He makes sure that he'll wake at the right time of day.
His tail is so long, he won't feel any pain
'Til the nip makes the trip and gets up to his brain.
In exactly eight hours, the Chippendale Mupp
Will, at last, feel the bite and yell "Ouch!" and wake up.

fered with. Still other information is lost because something else comes in on top of it and covers it over, or because it is recoded in a form that does not allow retrieval. All of this entails a process of selection. Transfer may involve coding processes in which portions of the information are preserved in more efficient forms. In our study we shall see many examples of these processes.

A Model of Information Processing

A number of information processing models have been developed to explain various psychological tasks. The model we will use here is a more generalized version of these previous models. It performs several functions. First, it provides an illustration of various perceptual and cognitive tasks. It also provides us with a framework with which to guide our discussion of issues and problems in perception and cognition. This model (see Fig. 7.3) shows many of the elements belonging to the information processing sequence: stages, processes, storages, channels, and the interdependence of these elements.

The total model may be broken down into three major sections: (1) the patterns of light projected onto the retinas of the eyes at any given moment in time; (2) the nonobservable internal processes, which form the part of the model in which we are most interested; (3) the observable, behavioral response

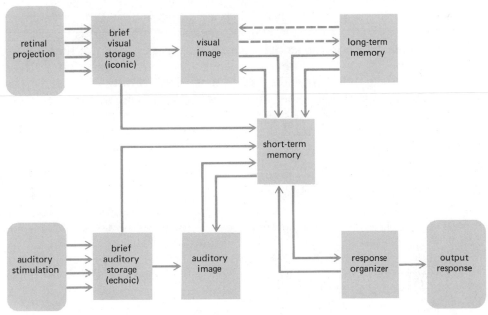

Fig. 7.3 An information-processing model illustrating the more important stages, storage processes, and channels. (Haber and Hershenson, 1973)

made by the perceiver. Many, if not most, models combine the first two sections of the model we are using, assuming that the difference between observable and nonobservable events is intuitively understood. Our model, however, clearly delineates the difference between the projection of light on the retina and the immediately constructed internal representation of this projection. Our model also draws a distinction between the internal organizing processes required in order to produce overt responses and the responses themselves. We shall examine several stages of the middle part of this model, the internal process.

Stage One: Iconic Storage   The first stage in the visual information processing system that we will discuss is iconic storage, also known as brief visual storage. It should be remembered that Chapter 1 has already discussed the input part of this system and Chapter 4 has dealt with one aspect of the output side. Here we examine the processes that occur in the middle, that is, the internal parts of the process. In iconic storage the information received when light hits the retinas is represented internally, most probably in some central location. For now, it is sufficient to say that in iconic storage information is registered in visual codes.

iconic storage

The content of the iconic store is closely related to the rapid and brief eye movements we use in viewing the world. These movements, called saccades, are discrete jumps that occur three or four times per second. They automatically shift our attention from one part of a scene to another. During the fixation time between saccades, about 250 milliseconds (or one quarter of a second), visual representations may be registered in the iconic store. When a saccadic movement occurs, the representations from the last fixation are lost. Even if the image viewed lasts for less than 250 milliseconds, persistence mechanisms function to keep its representation in the iconic store for the usual amount of time, which is again 250 milliseconds. This phenomenon is very useful in situations such as television or movie viewing, where an image is exposed only very briefly. The representation in the iconic store deteriorates rapidly over this time and has pretty much faded away after a quarter of a second. Therefore, a perceiver has only about a quarter of a second in which to process the content of this stage so that the information may be transferred to a more stable or long-lasting storage.

Stage Two: Visual Image Representation   Very soon after exposure to visual stimulation, we construct visual representations of the stimulus. At this stage we experience a conscious awareness of perceiving. A number of perceptual theorists propose that such a process occurs after the original iconic storage. Accordingly, we have inserted this stage in our information processing model following the iconic store. This visual image representation may be thought of as a constructed representation built upon the content of the icon. Some researchers do not differentiate this stage from the iconic processes, but the question of whether it is a separate stage has yet to be settled. If a visual representation is constructed, we would suppose that it is built up over time. As successive eye movements (saccades) introduce new visual components, the

visual image
representation

new components are combined with previous ones to form a coherent image. The information of this image follows the rules of perceptual organization, and it is not limited by the quarter of a second time duration of the iconic store.

Stage Three: Short-Term Memory In the short-term memory stage visual information is encoded into linguistic or conceptual representations. This process is thought to occur at the same time as, but independently of, the construction of a visual image. It is in this stage that we apply names to the information we are processing.

Short-term memory is not a permanent storage. It lasts only a few seconds. Remember the case of the telephone number. Between the time you looked it up and the time you began to dial it, you forgot some or all of the seven digits. However, when you repeated the number over and over, you were able to remember it. This repetition is called "rehearsal." Rehearsal can greatly increase the duration of short-term memory.

Stage Four: Long-Term Memory The last stage we are concerned with is the most important and most complex of the memory systems involved in human information processing. As its name implies, long-term memory is also the longest lasting of the memory systems. Unlike short-term memory, which has quite a small capacity, long-term memory has a very large, perhaps limitless, capacity. All learned experience and knowledge are stored in long-term memory. The procedures for brushing your teeth, the rules for constructing an English sentence, the meanings of the words you are reading, the year in which Columbus discovered America, all are stored in long-term memory. Long-term memory stores so much information that the major problem for researchers in this area is to discover how any particular portion of the information in it becomes available to us when we need it.

The content of long-term memory may be words, letters, or images, but it is most probably some form of semantic representation that is structured so as to include meaningfulness as one of its attributes. We will explore these and other problems related to long-term memory later in the chapter.

Before leaving the discussion of our model of information processing, we should note that most of the research this model is based on employs stimuli that we ordinarily label with words or names. Linguistic operations are a central feature of this model. Later in the chapter we will consider the processing of pictures and scenes, stimuli that are not labeled or represented by words.

We have, so far, introduced the concept of information processing, given a number of reasons for its development and use, and outlined the crucial steps in the information processing sequence. In the sections that follow, we will examine these stages in more detail. We will also consider how information is transferred from one stage to another. Much of our discussion in the following pages will be based on the experimental studies that knowledge of information processing is derived from.

A human information processing system has, in addition to visual inputs, also auditory ones coming in through the ears. Present evidence points to a very brief sensory storage for auditory information, and it has been named echoic storage. Echoic storage appears to last longer than iconic storage, perhaps as long as a second or two. Just like iconic storage, however, echoic storage evidently fades and is irretrievable unless its contents have been processed and transferred to a subsequent store. But again like iconic storage, echoic storage must be capable of entering long-term memory, for we can continue to hear a tune long after it has been presented to us. We also can recreate a tune from noncurrent stimulation: if someone asks you to hear-image *Yankee Doodle,* you can do it without having to physically hear the tune.

There is also a connection between echoic storage and the short-term memory representations we talked about for vision. This is particularly important for language, but also for any auditory input for which we have a name. For example, a particular sound in the forest has an auditory representation, but it also is called a cuckoo. While little research has been done comparing visual and auditory input in short-term memory, it seems reasonable to expect that there is no difference; once information reaches this stage it is probably treated alike, no matter what its source.

ICONIC STORAGE

As the first central stage in processing of visual information, the iconic store serves a very important function. Its job is to accurately register a representation of everything that arrives at the visual sense organs. The input for iconic storage derives from the receptive-field coding mechanisms of the retinal projection. The inhibitory and excitatory responses of the on-off cells of the retina are carried by the optic nerve to the brain, where information processing can occur (see Chapter 3).

Much of the evidence for the existence of the iconic store comes from visual persistence studies. Visual persistence refers to the fact that extremely brief visual presentations have been experimentally found to last, or persist, in

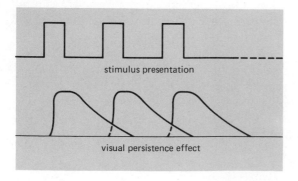

Fig. 7.4 Schematic representation of a hypothetical persistence resulting from repeated stimulus presentations. (Haber and Standing, 1969)

the visual system for periods exceeding their actual length. The results of a number of studies point to a persistence, or a duration, of approximately 250 milliseconds before the stimulus appears to fade out. Investigations by Haber and Standing (1969, 1970) of visual persistence suggest that there is a store or "reception room" where information is kept until it can be adequately processed (Fig. 7.4).

Ralph Norman Haber

Studying the Iconic Store

At this point we are ready to entertain questions about the content of the iconic storage. Several researchers have devised a technique for finding answers to such questions. They hypothesized that if they could stop the processing procedures immediately after the iconic stage, subjects could report what they perceived of a test visual field—and the report would contain information available from the iconic store alone. In order to prevent further processing of the test stimulus, these researchers presented a visual noise mask to their subjects very soon after the presentation of the stimulus. They proposed that in this way it would be possible to let the information reach iconic storage, but that the information would be somehow destroyed or made ineffective before it could be transformed into either images or names. Other researchers performed experiments using this method to examine the contents of iconic storage. The results of their work show that if a visual noise mask immediately follows the test display, subjects report that they reached a visual impression of the display but are not able to describe any of its characteristics. Apparently nothing remains of the representation after the mask is introduced. However, if the mask is delayed somewhat, the subjects are able to describe the general layout of the display, or to name some of the items in it.

How Is Information Extracted from the Iconic Store?

An important area of study for researchers in information processing is information extraction from the icon. Most of the work in this area concerns the extraction, or transfer, of information from the icon into short-term memory. We will again note that most of the stimulus material used in these studies is linguistic material—letters or words. As we will make clearer as we proceed, this reliance on linguistic material causes the route from the icon to short-term memory to become the most studied transit route.

Several questions come up in our examination of information extraction from the icon: How fast does it occur? Is there a spatial sequence or pattern to the processing? Is this processing serial (one item at a time) or parallel (many items at one time)? Are familiar items processed faster than unfamiliar items?

If information is processed serially in the icon, we would expect that it would take a certain fixed amount of time to process each of similar items. The greater the amount of time allowed for processing, the greater the number of items that could be processed.

Sperling (1963) developed an ingenious method for measuring the rate of information processing in the iconic store. For this work he used a technique entailing masking by visual noise (Fig. 7.5). A stimulus light pulse containing a particular pattern was flashed to a subject on a tachistoscope. Very quickly afterwards, a pattern of visual noise was flashed. Sperling explained the masking effect of visual noise by proposing that it disrupted the processing of the internal representation of the retinal light patterns some time after they had reached the cortex of the brain. He theorized that the representation of the second stimulus pattern (the noise) somehow interferes with the representation of the original stimulus pattern (the icon). It may either replace it, combine with it, or in another way cause it to become ineffective. The representation of the original stimulus may be processed until the second pattern arrives.

visual noise

 Duration of Iconic Storage

Sperling (1960) judged the amount of information received by an initial visual display with the use of a partial report method, though only after he had first tried a complete report experiment. He devised a display of 12 letters in three rows of four letters each, which he showed to subjects for brief intervals. When asked to recall all the letters, most subjects could not recall more than four. The complete report method raised a lot of questions: Did the subject fail to report all the letters because he failed to perceive them all or because he failed to process them all, or did he in fact perceive and process them, but was unable to remember them or to get them organized into a response? The partial report method attempted to answer these questions. In different trials, subjects were asked to report only the letters on one of the three rows. The row to be reported was indicated by a high, medium, or low tone, according to whether the requested row was the top, middle, or bottom row. The tone either followed directly after the display was shown, or several seconds later (see Fig. 7.5). Sperling found that

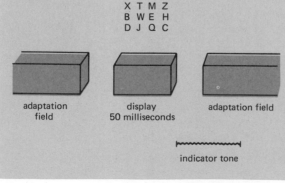

Fig. 7.5 Schematic representation of the stimulus sequence in the Sperling (1960) poststimulus indicator experiment. (Haber and Hershenson, 1973)

the subjects were able to repeat an indicated row when the interval between the display and the tone was not greater than one-quarter of a second, and he therefore concluded that this was the duration of the iconic storage. The viewer had actually perceived every part of the display; having no advance knowledge of which row he would be asked to repeat, he had to have perceived it all in order to repeat any part of it. But he was either unable to remember every letter or to get them organized into a response. Fig. 7.6 shows the number of letters correctly reported as a function of the delay of the poststimulus indicator. The shaded area in the figure represents the direction of availability of information from the stimulus after stimulation had terminated.

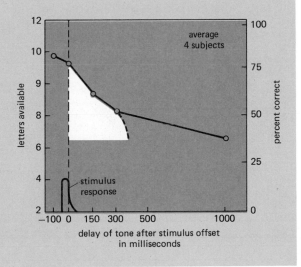

Fig. 7.6 Number of letters correctly reported as a function of the delay of the poststimulus indicator (Sperling, 1960)

Sperling presented a test stimulus containing a display of letters. In different trials he varied the number of letters in the display from two to six. This display was followed by a noise pattern and the intervals between the two patterns were varied from 20 to 60 milliseconds. After seeing both patterns, the subjects were asked to report the initial letters. Sperling found that for each 10 milliseconds that the noise pattern was delayed past the beginning of the test stimulus, the subject could report one more letter. This led Sperling to conclude that the presence of visual noise controlled the amount of time that the test stimulus was available for information processing, and the time data suggest that it takes about 10 milliseconds for each letter to be extracted and transferred out of the icon into a later storage.

The results of these experiments suggest that visual noise prevents the transfer of information from the icon by erasing, covering over, or somehow preventing further processing of it. While there is enough time for a visual representation to develop so that a subject can make out its general form against a background, that iconic representation is not available long enough for the extraction of the names of forms to occur. These results provide evidence to the effect that the formulation of a visual image begins before, or faster than, the naming of the items.

In Sperling's experiment, as the visual noise mask was delayed, thereby increasing the duration of the display, this provided more time for processing the content of the icon, and the subjects could report more letters correctly. Sperling found the rate of extraction to be one letter every 10 milliseconds. From a mathematical analysis of the results of his experiment, Sperling suggested that the letters were processed serially. According to this model, the perceiver scans the internal visual representations, naming the first letter, then the second, and so on until he runs out of processing time. If a parallel processing model were

 Extracting Information from Familiar and Unfamiliar Material

In the English language, certain letters are more likely to appear together than others. In our reading we come to expect certain combinations of letters and not to expect others. Thus, if you saw the combination *st--* or *--ion* on this page, you would not be surprised. But if you saw the combination *gox---*, you would check it twice and probably suspect a typographical error.

Evidence indicates that words can be recognized even when we cannot identify all the letters they contain. This suggests that words are perceived as wholes rather than as collections of single units or individual letters; that is, we grasp them in accordance with a template-matching theory. But a major reason for rejecting this theory lies in the fact that the word apprehension effect is not limited to real words. Certain kinds of meaningless combinations of letters are more easily perceived than others, even though there is no overall template for them.

Since a template theory of word recognition is therefore not tenable, some kind of feature analysis of spelling pattern or overall shape of words must take place. The classical demonstration of this phenomenon was performed by Miller, Bruner, and Postman (1954), who used strings of letters or "pseudowords" that vary in the degree to which they approximate the naturally occurring sequence of letters in English. Zero-order approximations were strings of letters drawn entirely at random, without regard to the frequency with which letters occur naturally in English. An example of a zero-order letter string is HHJHUFSW. First- and higher-order strings come successively closer to approximating the letter sequences that naturally occur in English. RSEMPOIN is a first-order string, WALLYLOF, a second-order string, and OTATIONS a third-order string. OTATIONS looks somewhat familiar—as though we might have seen it, or something very similar, somewhere before.

Miller and his co-workers found that high-order approximations were the most easily identifiable under conditions of tachistoscopic presentation. It took more time to identify ZQRM than PARMA. This finding is important because it rules out the possibility that a template theory is applicable in word recognition.

These investigators interpreted their results in a slightly different theoretical framework, however. They reasoned that information as a quantity, measured in bits, is the same at threshold for all orders of approximation; that is, NERNALT contained less information than, for example, ZQMPXLA, since it was redundant. Because of this redundancy, one had a better chance of guessing the succession of letters without having seen them. Using an appropriate estimate of the redundancies involved, Miller, Bruner, and Postman succeeded in showing that the amount of information transmitted to a subject at any given exposure duration was roughly constant. The implication was that, although more letters were reported at higher-order approximations, each letter represented correspondingly fewer bits of information.

A significant experiment to test for the effect of familiarity on information extraction was performed by Mewhort (1967). He presented to his subjects two sets of letter strings, one a first-order approximation and the other a fourth-order approximation to English. Immediately after the brief presentation, he sounded one of two tones. A high tone signified that the subject was to report the string appearing on the top row of the presentation card; a low tone signified that the letter string from the bottom row should be reported. Mewhort found that subjects were more successful in correctly reporting fourth-order letter strings than first-order letter strings (Fig. 7.7).

All of these experimenters have interpreted the results of their investigations as evidence that information from familiar material is extracted more quickly than information from unfamiliar material.

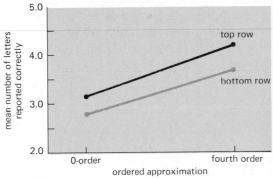

Fig. 7.7 Mean number of letters reported as a function of the order of approximation of the sequence to be reported and whether the row to be reported was on top or bottom. Both effects are significant— more letters are reported from sequences which more closely resemble English spelling sequence and more letters are reported from the top as compared to the bottom row. The latter finding suggests that subjects begin to process the top row first. (Mewhort, 1967) Right: D. J. K. Mewhort

correct, it should have been found that more letters were reported per unit of time for larger than for smaller letter displays. Sperling's findings do not support this type of model; rather they support a model of serial processing, or scanning.

Scanning the Icon Now that we know something of the time sequence involved in serial processing of information out of the icon, we may investigate the spatial sequence involved in this information extraction. It is logical to suppose that the order of processing follows a direction. Since we read from left to right, it is also logical to ask whether we process the contents of the internal visual representation in a left-to-right sequence. When Sperling repeated his experiment in 1967, he found evidence for just such a left-to-right model of scanning. When subjects did not have enough time to report all of the letters in the display correctly, they showed more success in reporting the letters on the lefthand side of the display as compared to those on the righthand side (Sperling, 1967). His results imply that the perceiver encodes the letter names following a left-to-right scan of the internal visual representation stored in the icon.

VERBAL SHORT-TERM MEMORY

We have seen that after information is processed in the iconic store, it may enter short-term memory. Here information which may have also been coded in a visual form is encoded in a linguistic, or named, form. In our discussion of information extraction from the icon, we referred to the naming, or reporting, of various test stimuli. This process of naming is the work of the short-term memory store.

Short-term memory has quite a limited capacity and also a rather short duration, though it lasts much longer than iconic storage. As we indicated in Chapter 6, its capacity is thought to be seven items, give or take a couple, and its duration is in the area of 20 seconds.

We have stated that in the short-term memory information is coded in linguistic form. To be more specific, it appears that in this store, information is coded in an acoustic representation. The evidence for this is shown in a simple experiment, which you can do yourself with a little help from a friend. Visually present a sequence of letters to your subject. Ask him to write down all of the letters he can recall. An analysis of his mistakes will be surprising. If, for example, there is an error in remembering a "C," it is likely to be noted as a "T," rather than as an "O." "C" and "T" do not look at all alike. They do, however, sound alike. In the same way, an "F" is more likely to be remembered as an "X" than as an "E"; "F" and "X" have the same beginning sound. You will observe that when the subject makes a mistake in attempting to remember the letters, it is most likely to be by producing a letter that sounds like the test letter, rather than a letter that looks like the test letter. On the face of it, these results are rather strange. Nowhere in the course of the experiment is there a verbal recitation of the test letters. Both the test stimulus letters and the responses are presented in writing. However, the errors that occur represent acoustic, rather than visual, confusions. These errors reveal that in the process of encoding the visually presented information into short-term memory, it has been converted into an acoustic representation.

Rehearsal

Rehearsal is the repetition of material that is to be stored in short-term memory. Often, it is an inner, mental form of speech, but we have all experienced whispered, or even audible, instances of rehearsal. In trying to remember a telephone number, we repeat the necessary information over and over again. Rehearsal plays an important role in remembering. Unless conscious repetition, or rehearsal, takes place, information cannot be retained for more than just a few seconds. Rehearsal serves two major functions. First, it permits information to be kept in the short-term memory for an indefinite time period. Second, rehearsal is thought to facilitate the transfer of information from short- to long-term memory.

Loss of Information

A more common term for the phenomenon of loss of information is forgetting. There are two possible explanations to account for why information is lost or forgotten. First, loss of information may result from interference from the arrival of other information. Alternatively, the loss may simply be a result of the passage of time. All of our evidence suggests that loss of information in the *icon* is due to both decay and interference. Decay is suggested by the fact that a brief flash that is not followed by anything else persists for only a quarter of a second. The interference effect is shown in that if you follow a presentation with another one within a quarter of a second, further processing is effectively prevented. However, this is a different kind of interference than the ones that occur in short-term memory, since it seems to be a visual overlay covering up the information and thereby preventing further processing.

When we consider forgetting in short-term memory, the two explanations—interference and decay—both seem to apply, with a greater effect being due to interference. The interference effect arises because of the limited capacity of short-term memory. Only a few items can be held at any one time. The representation of an item in the memory store is its memory trace. We will consider relative strengths of memory traces as a function of the number of items present in the store at a given time. Let us call the particular memory trace we are concerned with the *signal*. Other memory traces in the store will be called *noise*. The ratio of signal level to noise level will determine the ability to understand the signal. This situation is somewhat similar to what happens when you try to listen to a speaker in a noisy room. Unless the speaker's voice is significantly louder and clearer than the surrounding noise, you can neither hear nor understand it. Similarly, the stronger the memory trace, the easier it is to retain and remember. As the memory is crowded by other memories it begins to fade away until its trace is so weak as to be undecipherable. In this situation, how would a memory trace become weaker? A possible explanation is that each time a new item of information is introduced into the short-term memory, all of the trace strengths of previously entered items are reduced by a certain percentage of their previous value. After enough new items are introduced, some trace strengths will be so weakened as to become undecipherable. Thus, forgetting becomes a function of the number of items in the store and results from the arrival of new information, thus an interference effect.

According to our second model of forgetting, the strength of a memory of a particular item depends upon the length of time it has been in the store. With the passage of time a memory in the short-term store gradually gets weaker until it totally disappears. According to this explanation, each moment in time causes the memory trace to become weaker, much like the decay process of radioactive materals.

How can we test these two theories to see which is the more accurate? One way of doing this would be to present a subject with a test stimulus and then have him do nothing until he is asked to recall the test information. According to the interference theory, there would be no loss of memory. According to the time decay theory, there would be a loss of memory.

There are several methodological problems involved in such an experiment. If the subject has nothing to do, he will rehearse the material and consequently show a perfect memory. However, if he is given a task to perform that inhibits rehearsal, the task can cause interference. Thus, great care has to be used in choosing the task that will prevent rehearsal but will not interfere with memory.

Reitman (1971) has suggested that some combination of the two theoretical explanations is correct. Subjects presented with a series of letters to learn were then asked to detect a weak sound signal from a background of noise. The auditory detection task probably meets the requirements of preventing rehearsal without harming memory. Thirty seconds later, they were asked to recall the original test letters. They could recall the letters quite perfectly. This would seem to indicate that forgetting would be due to interference. However, the memory at this point was very delicate; the least bit of interference could destroy it. Thus, although the ability to remember items remained strong after 30 seconds, there was a change, or increase, in the susceptibility to interference after this interval. Thus, both decay and interference are thought to be involved in the loss of information from short-term memory.

Perceptual Defense

McGinnies (1949) has found that words with emotional connotations (in this case "dirty" words) have a higher threshold for recognition than neutral words. McGinnies called this effect "perceptual defense." In his experiment dealing with this phenomenon he presented socially taboo words (like *whore* or *Kotex*—remember, this research was done in the 1940s) and ordinary words tachistoscopically. The stimuli were first presented at a very rapid rate and then with increased duration until the subject correctly identified the words presented. McGinnies also recorded GSR responses during the stimulus presentation. He reported two major findings. First, the threshold for correct identification of taboo words was consistently higher than the threshold for identification of neutral words. Second, the GSR responses to the taboo words were higher than those for the neutral words even before the taboo words were consciously recognized. McGinnies argued that these two findings implied that subjects were aware of the taboo words but by some defensive process blocked their access to consciousness.

Lazarus and McCleary (1951) designed a study to demonstrate discrimination without awareness that would get around some of the problems encountered in the McGinnies study. For example, subjects might be aware that a taboo word was presented but perhaps for reasons of embarrassment chose not to report that they saw it. Therefore, Lazarus and McCleary used 10 nonsense syllables in their tachistoscopic presentations. Five of these nonsense syllables were initially paired at random with shock. They then presented all 10 nonsense syllables tachistoscopically, at ascending durations, until the subjects correctly identified the syllables. They also obtained GSR readings for the stimuli. They found that the average GSR response to a stimulus that was not identified correctly was larger when the stimulus was a syllable that had been paired with shock than with a nonshock syllable. This difference defined the "subception effect," which was taken as evidence of discrimination without awareness.

Eriksen (1958) has criticized the discrimination without awareness hypothesis on methodological grounds and has proposed an alternative hypothesis. He starts with the proposition that the "subception effect" is defined in terms of a discrepancy between two different response systems that is indicative of the subject's perception. The GSR response is a continuous indicator, permitting the recording of a range of magnitudes of response to the stimuli, while the verbal report allows only a dichotomous response—correct recognition or incorrect recognition. The difference between these two response indicators raises the possibility that the verbal report may be artificially constrained. For example, in a brief presentation, the subject may be uncertain as to which of two stimuli were presented. Hence, his first response may be a nonshock syllable that is incorrect. However, the second verbal response to the same stimulus presentation may have been a shock syllable and the correct response, but because no provision is made for this second response, it goes unrecorded. The GSR, on the other hand, registers the subject's uncertainty and possible awareness of a shock syllable.

Do We Select What Gets into Short-Term Memory?

The problems of perceptual defense and perceptual vigilance have bothered psychologists for quite some time (see Chapters 3 and 9). Various schools of psychology have offered different solutions to these perplexing problems, but none have been entirely satisfactory. Neither have experimental studies solved these problems.

One of the most troublesome aspects of the perceptual defense problem has been that the statement of the problem itself appears to contain a logical paradox. If the perceptual defense is truly a phenomenon of perception, how can a perceiver selectively defend himself against a specific stimulus unless he first perceives just that stimulus against which he should defend himself?

In a recent analysis, Erdelyi (1974) shows how an application of the information processing approach puts the perceptual defense issue into a reasonable light and offers a solution to it. A major premise of information processing is that input is sequentially subjected to various transformations and storages. It is therefore logical to assume, and experimental research has supported this idea, that cognitive selectivity might operate at each of the different levels of processing. Perceptual defense may be just such a process of selectivity or bias, operating at various points along the information processing continuum.

As a visual example of selectivity in viewers, it can be observed that some members of an audience watching a horror movie may hide their eyes at unpleasant parts. Thus, the expectations of the viewers and what they select to see comes into play. They select not to view what from experience they know to be unpleasant but instead might look at another person for those few seconds.

Physically, there is evidence that in vision pupil diameter, accommodation, and occlusion by the eyelids play a part in what is perceived, according to the attitudes and needs of the observer.

The horror movie example shows selectivity before the information reaches the retina. Erdelyi continued his analysis to show how selection would occur during later stages of processing. All evidence to date suggests that no cognitive selection occurs behind the retina and the iconic storage stage. While the sensory coding processes do produce changes in the content of the information relayed from the eye to the brain, none of these changes is the result of the expectation or prior experience of the perceiver. However, once the information is represented in the icon, decisions have to be taken about which parts to process further, the order in which the processing should occur, and how much processing in each item should be done.

With respect to perceptual defense against potential anxiety-producing stimuli, many aspects of selection are likely. If the inputs are words, the reader might process them sufficiently to determine that they have emotional tones he does not like without actually having completed enough to identify each word completely. In this way, the arousal of emotion could be used to turn off further processing, so that if the reader were asked to name the words he could not do so, but he could still have been made anxious by them.

VISUAL SHORT-TERM MEMORY

We have seen from our original model of the information processing system that after information leaves the iconic store, it may enter verbal short-term memory or the visual image store, or perhaps both in parallel. The visual image store, or visual short-term memory, is relatively unimportant in the processing of linguistic material. It is, however, of great importance in the processing of pictures, scenes, and photographs and in the construction of an organized visual representation of the world around us, which we see as stable configurations of people and things (see Chapter 2).

To discuss visual short-term memory, we must first explain how our eyes construct a visual image. In most situations and under most conditions, the eye remains fixed for only about a quarter of a second and then saccades to a new fixation. When the eye moves on, it usually moves to a nearby location on the same picture or scene. Yet our experience of seeing is not an experience of this jumping effect. We do not see the world as though we were looking through a kaleidoscope. Instead, we see the world as a stable and integrated structure, various parts of which we may sample with our eyes. We use the information gained from each visual fixation to form an integrated image, but we do not limit ourselves to that bit of information. New information is combined with information from previous fixations.

Integrating Successive Looks

Hochberg (1968, 1970) has suggested that the information that can be obtained from a single glance or fixation is quite different from the information that can be obtained by successive integrated looks. The difference can be explained by the fact that visual acuity falls off very rapidly from the central fovea. As a result, complete information about visual space cannot be extracted from a single fixation, since not enough visual information can be gained if the stimulus includes a large area. For example, in order to see each corner of a large cross clearly, the eye must make at least four successive glances or fixations. In addition, these four fixations must somehow be integrated so that the cross can be distinguished from any other figure that might be built upon perpendicular corners. This implies that our perceptual systems must be able to register and store the relative location of each corner.

Hochberg (1968) has demonstrated that if the outline of a large cross is presented so that successive parts of the cross appeared through a stationary peephole, the subject is still able to recognize the whole shape. Some type of postretinal storage in the form of schematic maps must be operating, Hochberg has postulated, since no complete pattern could be made by eye movements. This is very similar, we will see, to Neisser's concept of figural synthesis, where incoming information is cognitively reconstructed.

Gibson (1950) believed that an important amount of potential visual information was gained when an observer moved through space. The visual input changes as the characteristics of the world around him change. The geometric relationship of the perception is such that the relative movement of objects as the observer moves in space is proportional to their relative distance from the observer. Thus, all the stationary objects perceived at a given distance change at the same rate as the observer moves through space. For Gibson, this way of getting information produced a scale of the visual world as long as the elements remained constant with respect to each other as the observer moved. In addition, self-produced movements cause a change on the retinal projection different from changes caused by moving objects, so that what is moving can be detected also.

This type of representation, forming an integration based upon successive looks that go beyond what is on the return at any given moment, is probably the most important function of the visual short-term memory. What is constructed in it is not the source of any single retinal projection, and this would be so even if the eye did not move so frequently. This image is a construction, not a photograph, and its organization is the result of a combination of the stimulus properties on the retina with the perceiver's expectation of and prior experiences with the visual world around him.

Comparison of Visual and Verbal Short-Term Memory

Posner originated an interesting series of experiments (Posner and Mitchell, 1967; Posner and Taylor, 1969) that compare rates of processing for information from the visual short-term memory with rates for information from verbal short-term memory. If you ask an observer to tell you if two shapes are identical, he should be able to do that from a visual representation alone, without having to name anything. However, frequently two shapes that are not the same have the same name, as, for example, an upper and lower case pair of letters (A a). It would be necessary to go through a naming process in order to say that they are similar. For this type of experiment, Posner asked his subjects to indicate by pressing a key whether both members of a pair of letters were the same or different. The subjects were told to make their decision as quickly as possible. Comparisons were made between the time needed to match the letters for their physical characteristics (whether they were visually the same) and the time needed to match the letters on the basis of their letter names.

The responses based on physical identity were made approximately 75 milliseconds faster than the responses based on letter-name matching (Fig. 7.8). The time necessary for processing under these conditions supports the idea that

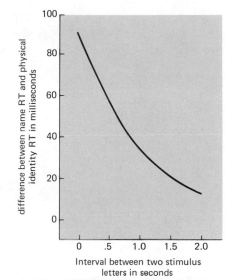

Fig. 7.8 Difference in reaction time for a name versus a physical match as a function of the time interval between the presentation of the two letters. (Posner and Keele, 1967)

different levels of processing are involved in responding to the two sets of instructions.

These results suggest that when a physical match is required, it is made on the basis of the contents of the visual representation alone. When classification by name is required, processing in the verbal short-term memory must take place. The 75-millisecond delay is believed to reflect faster transfer of information from the icon to the visual representation than from the icon to verbal short-term memory.

What Is the Capacity of Visual Memory?

Our visual memory capacity is phenomenally high. Standing, Conezio, and Haber (1970) showed subjects 2,560 photographic slides over a period of several days. An hour after viewing the last of these slides, 280 pairs of photographic slides were shown. One member of each pair was a slide the subject had already seen. The subjects were asked to identify which of the two slides they had seen before. In this task, correct choices were made more than 90 percent of the time! And when the subjects were shown mirror reversals of slides they had already seen, their performance was not reduced at all.

This experiment suggests that our memory for pictures is almost perfect. It is certainly much higher than our memory capacity for verbal or linguistic material. Haber (1970) suggests that in addition to being nearly perfect, recognition memory for pictures lasts indefinitely and is not produced through verbal coding or by labeling the contents of pictures. It appears that contents of the

Eye Movements in Reading

Interesting data about the way in which we build up visual representations is gained from studying the eye movements that occur in reading. It has been found that eye fixations do not proceed in an entirely straight left-to-right line, but include backward, or regressive, fixations. The number of these regressive movements has been found to decrease with age and reading experience, although this decrease cannot fully account for the great increase in reading speed between first-graders and college students. The presence of regressive movements in reading poses a problem for models that describe reading as a smooth left-to-right process, picking up information from the text in the order in which it is presented. Kolers notes several theoretical problems in this area. It is known that saccadic eye movements must be programed several hundred milliseconds before they occur. Thus, a regressive saccade is made on the basis of a previous fixation, not on the basis of a fixation that is currently being made. The programing of regressive saccades, then, is made not because of an awareness of difficulty of understanding, but because of information that is not yet in awareness.

visual short-term memory seem to get transferred into some kind of longer-term store without much difficulty, and are maintained in many cases indefinitely.

The high retention rate for pictorial information suggests to researchers in this field that effective organizing principles are at work in our construction of visual images. If a person looks at an organized picture, such as a face, his chances of remembering it are much greater. If the image is not organized, the viewer has to remember a lot more information—that is, the location in space of a number of meaningless splotches. Organization reduces the amount of information needed and leads to an improvement in memory.

We may conclude that the probability that a picture will be remembered is not based entirely on its visual characteristics, but also depends on the perceiver's ability to construct a meaningful visual image.

LONG-TERM MEMORY

In our discussion of verbal short-term memory, we noted that memory traces in that storage system may last, without rehearsal, for about 20 seconds. We are all aware that many memories last for much longer periods. They may last for days, weeks, years, or even a lifetime. It is clear that in addition to verbal and visual short-term memory, another memory store exists. This last store is long-term memory.

The existence of long-term memory is significant in shaping our lives. Try to imagine what it would be like if you could not remember information you have learned, your past experiences, images of people and things you are familiar with. Researchers have worked with people who suffer memory disturbances to various degrees. The following is a description (Milner, Corkin, and Teuber, 1968) of a subject who apparently has no way of introducing new information into the long-term memory store:

> During three of the nights at the Clinical Research Center, the patient rang for the night nurse, asking her, with many apologies, if she would tell him where he was and how he came to be there. He clearly recognized that he was in a hospital, but seemed unable to reconstruct any of the events of the previous day. . . . After his father's death, H. M. was given protected employment in a state rehabilitation center, where he spends weekdays participating in rather monotonous work programmed for severely retarded patients. A typical task is the mounting of cigarette lighters on cardboard frames for display. It is characteristic that he cannot give us any description of his place of work, the nature of his job, or the route along which he is driven each day to and from the center [this after 6 months on the job]. (p. 217)

The type of damage suffered by this person presents some interesting implications about the functioning of the memory systems. His memory systems work well except for one procedure—that is, the entry of information into the long-term store. In this case, entry and extraction of information from short-term memory occur without disruption. And the fact that the patient can conduct conversations shows that he is able to retrieve word meanings from their permanent store in long-term memory. Both memory systems function, but the long-

 Memory Training

The art of memory or mnemonics has been practiced for centuries. A few people have always known special techniques that make memorizing seem easy. These techniques have tended to be looked upon as mere tricks, used mainly by entertainers to amuse and astound audiences. However, if we examine these techniques we see that they rest on principles that are quite familiar to psychologists. A study of popular systems of memory training reveals that they all teach the user to pay attention and to organize the material.

A mnemonic device that we are all familiar with is the use of rhymes. Rhymes let us connect separate items in ordered relationships and any deviation from this order destroys the rhythm. For example, "*I* before *E*, except after *C*, or when sounded as *A*, as in *neighbor* or *weigh*." Another popular technique is the method of loci, in which the person imagines that the items to be learned are located in different physical locations (loci). Recall is accomplished by retrieving the location, which facilitates retrieving the object. Analytical substitution, a favorite technique for learning lists of items or numbers, is accomplished by changing numbers or words into sounds, sounds into words, or words into sentences.

What do these techniques have in common? For one thing, they all attempt

to organize arbitrary material according to three rules that conform to what is known about human memory. First, the material must be categorized into small groups, because short-term memory has a limited capacity. Second, sentences, categories, and so on must be ordered logically because order relationships are learned only with great difficulty. Third, rich associations to previously learned material seem to be necessary in the retrieval process, for a well-linked association provides the starting place for the search of memory, in much the same way that a card catalog in a library provides the starting place for retrieval of a particular book.

In very rare instances, certain persons apparently don't have the restrictions of memory that afflict most of us. One such person was closely studied by Luria (1968). His subject had acute synesthesia; that is, he saw, felt, and tasted each sound he heard instead of merely hearing it. He reported transformations of sound into lines, blurs, and splashes of color. Of particular interest in the analysis of his exceptional memory and the role it played in shaping his personality was this transformation of words into visual imagery and the effect it had on his recall and understanding of these words. Because each word was able to summon up a graphic image for him, he was able to perform remarkable feats of memory. For example, after a few minutes of study he could memorize a list of 50 numbers and could recall them, by the vertical columns, the rows, the diagonals, or in any square pattern. Although as a professional mnemonist he had been presented with hundreds of lists to be reproduced, he could recall any particular list 16 years later.

Besides the obvious advantages of such a talent there were many disadvantages. The style of thought that dominated the subject's awareness was associative chains of images; therefore, one word would trigger off associations with tangential connection to the original word. These associations made comprehension of books, for example, difficult and chaotic, because irrelevant details obstructed a more general understanding of the material. Also, abstract concepts were particularly confusing to the subject, for they had to be translated into images to be grasped. As a result he found it difficult to follow conversations because his mind became overloaded with images of concrete objects and a variety of shapes, colors, sounds, and textures.

term memory is not able to assimilate new information. (Memory loss and amnesia are also discussed in Chapters 6 and 16).

People have always been concerned with the problem of transfer from short- to long-term memory, though they certainly haven't always thought about the problem in those terms. More often, even today, it is thought of simply as the problem of committing something to memory—be it a speech, the multiplication table, the names of a group of people, or an admired poem. These are the kinds of things we usually think of having to make a concerted effort to remember; they are all verbal things. But we also remember, usually without conscious effort, a lot of visual things—houses we have lived in, houses we have visited, paintings we've admired, faces we've seen.

Mnemonic Systems

The general superiority of our memory for visual rather than verbal things lies behind the most ancient, as well as many modern, systems for memorizing verbal material. As long ago as the fifth century B.C., when poetry was circulated orally and rhetoric was the principal subject of learning, the Greek poet Simonides invented a mnemonic system based on the conversion of words and ideas into images. The basis of his system is not much different from that taught by Dale Carnegie, today's popular public-speaking instructor, or for that matter from methods that research psychologists have found empirical support for.

Simonides' and other ancient mnemonic systems taught the student to visualize a place such as a large, preferably real, building with many variegated rooms and then to associate an idea with each room, proceeding in an orderly direction through the building, and also of course through the verbal material being memorized. If specific words were also to be memorized, images of other things could be made to represent the words and could be placed inside the rooms. The two most significant principles behind this kind of mnemonic system are (1) the importance of an orderly arrangement in memory and (2) the recognition that visual representation can be used to supplement verbal memory.

More modern techniques, such as Carnegie's, involve the principles of order and visual imagery but combine them with the verbal device of rhyming. Specifically they suggest finding words that rhyme with numbers (whose logical progression supplants the logical progression of rooms in a house), associating images with those words, and then associating the ideas or facts we want to remember with the images. Carnegie suggests, for example, *one-run, two-zoo, three-tree, four-door, five-beehive.* Then for *run,* we might picture a horse running, and we might pick some concrete object from the first fact or idea to be remembered and picture it riding on the horse's back. For the second item, we might picture our object being sniffed by a bear in a cage in a zoo.

Modern researchers have showed that mnemonic training works, though no one system has emerged as clearly superior to others. Once mastered, however, these systems can be used over and over again for memorizing different things. Moreover, systems based on visual imagery can be used to learn complex associations consisting of more than two items. A given visual image can serve as a "hook" on which to hang up to 20 items to be remembered (Bower, 1969).

The study of long-term memory involves consideration of the organization of the store itself, retrieval processes, loss of information, the structure that gives semantic organization to the content of the memory store, and the transfer of information from short-term to long-term stores. For a discussion of these topics, see Chapter 4.

In the remainder of this chapter we will discuss several problems that cut across the boundaries of the stages of information processing discussed above. These topics will include recognition of visual patterns, selective attention, visual search, and reading.

RECOGNITION OF VISUAL PATTERNS

It should be clear by now that pattern recognition plays an important role in information processing. Pattern recognition is the process by which we convert the various lines, squiggles, blobs, and colors that we perceive into meaningful forms. Among other things, our ability to see patterns in the world around us enables us to reduce the amount of information we must work with and thus to process information much more efficiently. In fact, without pattern recognition, information processing would probably be a hopeless effort.

Theories of Pattern Recognition

Pattern recognition is complex, and an entire book can be devoted to its explication. In addition, the theories about it we have at present are somewhat inadequate. Here, we shall briefly and simply discuss the three leading theories of pattern recognition.

template matching model

Template Matching Model Template matching is the simplest of all possible systems for classifying and recognizing patterns. This model assumes an internal representation of a pattern that is structurally identical to the stimulus pattern. Pattern recognition, then, consists of matching the pattern of an external stimulus to an internal template. The internal template that best matches the pattern of the stimulus identifies the pattern.

There are many problems with this model of pattern recognition. First, we can recognize a certain pattern, for example the letter "A," in different sizes and colors, at different angles, and at different places in our visual field. This effect cannot be explained by the template matching model. Each different presentation would require its own template. The system would become very large and cumbersome. Also, this model offers no means of recognizing new patterns, for which there would be no template. Furthermore, the number of patterns we handle in the course of our daily lives is gigantic. The number of templates required to do the work of recognition would be prohibitive.

visual feature model

Visual Feature Model A second explanation of pattern recognition is offered by the visual feature model. According to this model, a form or pattern is analyzed into specific features of the same kinds that are present in the icon. These features are stored, perhaps in a list form. With increasing perceptual experience, this list of known features becomes larger. The features of incoming patterns represented in the icon are compared with the features on the list. When there is a relatively complete correspondence between the features of an incoming stimulus and the features on the list, a match is made, and the pattern is identified. Specific features for the recognition of letters might include the existence and number of straight lines and the existence and number of open or closed curved lines.

The visual feature model is more successful than the template model in accounting for pattern recognition and was discussed in Chapter 2. Its most serious problem is that it lacks a way of describing the relationships between the various features in a given pattern.

Constructive Model   A third model of pattern recognition is a constructive model, or analysis by synthesis (Neisser, 1967). This model incorporates feature analysis, but makes provisions for the relationships between features. It also takes into account the context in which a pattern occurs and the fact that we

constructive model

 Pandemonium: A Model for Pattern Recognition

Suppose we wanted to write a program, or in non-computer terms, construct a model for identifying letters of the alphabet. Probably the simplest thing we could do would be to store all the possible letters (A through Z) and identify any new letters through a matching process with the stored template. Our model would identify *W* merely by matching this input with a stored representation of that letter. At first glance the template matching process seems to solve our problem but our problems have just begun. There is a wide variety of patterns associated with any given letter. Any handprinted letter would have to be standardized before the template matching process could be done. Nor is variation in letters the only problem of template matching. Changes in size, position, and orientation also present difficulties.

Another approach, known as *feature analyzing,* is illustrated by Oliver Selfridge's (1959) *pandemonium* model. This is a hierarchically organized, multilevel program with each level of processing represented by a type of *demon,* each performing a different job.

The first level of demons, known as *image demons,* have the simplest job. They merely record the input for further processing. The image then goes to a set of *feature demons,* who analyze the pattern for particular characteristics. They look for the presence of certain types of angles, the orientation of certain lines (horizontal or vertical), or whether there are discontinuous or continuous curves present. *Cognitive demons* are stored representations of the alphabetic characters. Each cognitive demon represents a different letter and "watches" the feature demons to signal qualities that may be attributes of the letter they represent. For example, the cognitive demon representing the letter *C* would be sensitive to any feature analysis indicating a discontinuous curve, but for that matter so would the demon representing *R*. When a cognitive demon finds an appropriate feature, it begins yelling. The job of the *decision demon* is to listen to the pandemonium (hence the name of the model) caused by all the sensitized cognitive demons and decide which cognitive demon is yelling loudest. In this way a specific letter is identified. Models such as *pandemonium* are designed to simulate human perception.

utilize expectations in recognizing patterns. Proponents of this model propose that the perceiver initially forms an abstract representation of the stimulus pattern, guided by the rules of perceptual organization (see Chapter 2). He then formulates hypotheses based on expectations about what the stimulus might be ("This is probably a square, because . . ."). These hypotheses arise from the rules of similarity, redundancy (repetition), and probability, which the perceiver has learned from past experience. In the synthesis process, one part of a pattern might be tried and rejected if it results in an inconsistent, incomplete, or unlikely representation. A square with one curved side would be an example of an inconsistent and unlikely pattern. If one hypothesis is rejected, another is constructed, and then another, until one is found that matches the incoming information. The hypothesis or combination of hypotheses that works best will be stored as a representation of the stimulus.

None of these models provides the last word on pattern recognition, although some of them appear to work better than others. Much more research is needed in this area before our knowledge of pattern recognition can be considered adequate.

SELECTIVE ATTENTION

The visual environment in which we live is immensely rich and complex. Objects, surfaces, colors, textures, movements exist in great abundance. Obviously, we cannot process information from all of the sources available to us. We pick and choose to process information from only a relatively small part of the world around us. Our choices vary, according to the meaning and importance that particular stimuli hold for us as individuals. Choice, then, governs where we look and what we notice in each glance.

In this discussion of selective attention we will concentrate on the idea of selectivity, or choice. The major selective device appears to concentrate on what information is processed and what is ignored; some information simply drops out before we have chosen either to use it or ignore it. Thus, given limited channel capacities, fading traces, and interference, anything the perceiver decides he wants to process first is likely to get through, and anything he saves until later or puts at the end will probably be lost. In discussing selectivity in the information processing sequence we will be primarily concerned with the movements our eyes use to locate objects of potential interest, and also the selectivity that occurs within a single fixation of the eyes. (See also p. 401.)

Central versus Peripheral Attention

cental attention
peripheral attention

The surface of the retina of the eye is not equally sensitive in all areas. Its central area, the fovea, is much more sensitive than the peripheral areas around it. Visual acuity is significantly greater in the fovea than in the periphery.

The difference between these two types of vision, foveal and peripheral, is significant in the process of searching to find a chosen visual target. The objects in central, foveal vision can be identified in detail. It is this central vision that is used to determine whether the object under observation is the target object, since what you see in central vision is clear and available for identification. What you see in peripheral vision is usually not clear, but is identifiable enough so that you can decide whether it is of interest to look at more clearly, in which case you can direct an eye movement toward it.

Preattentive versus Focal Attentive Processes

There are two parts ot the visual search process that occur at the same time: an identification process of the parts of the retinal projection, which fall on the fovea, and a decision process regarding the direction of the next eye movement, based on information from the periphery. How can these tasks take place at the same time, and how are they interrelated?

preattentive process
focal attentive
process

Neisser (1967) proposes that objects cannot be visually identified until they are segmented, until the entire visual field is broken down into a figure-ground organization (see Chapter 2). He refers to this segmentation as a preattentive process, implying that it is a primary and automatic process. Later, after this process occurs, other processes may focus on specific aspects of the figure and proceed with further analysis. The preattentive process would serve as a forerunner to focal attention. Preattentive processes also serve another function:

 Tunnel Vision

It is possible to measure the size of the visual field of attention. Mackworth (1965) accomplished this by locating several targets in various parts of the periphery of the visual field. He then asked his subjects to indicate whether or not all the targets were the same. For one trial of this experiment, he flashed three letters for 100 milliseconds. One of these letters was located on the center of fixation (the center of the fovea). The other two letters were located at equal distances to either side of the central letter. Under this arrangement, accuracy was almost perfect when the two side letters were as far apart as 10 degrees of visual angle. However, when 14 irrelevant, or visual noise, letters were added on the line formed by the original three letters, the success rate decreased very sharply. The same results occurred when 20 other lines, each containing 17 letters, were added. When all three targets to be matched were contained within the foveal area, an interesting effect occurred. When no additional targets were present, accuracy of matching was 99 percent. However, when either a line or a page of irrelevant letters was added, reports dropped to 70 percent accuracy (Fig. 7.9). When the original targets were located across an area larger than the fovea, the introduction of extra letters caused the accuracy of report to fall from 95 percent to about 10 percent.

Mackworth concluded from these results that the size of the useful visual field, the area surrounding the fixation point from which information can be briefly stored and processed during one fixation, changes. When there is too much information in the immediate environment, the visual field becomes smaller to prevent an overloading of the visual processing system. The addition of visual noise or irrelevant signals can narrow the visual field of attention, creating a phenomenon Mackworth called *tunnel vision*. In tunnel vision, top priority is given to targets located in the fovea, even though under this condition there is some loss of foveal recognition. Tunnel vision occurs in the presence of information overload, but also when we are under great stress, or when the circumstances of perception are made very important. In driving, for example, when any thing suddenly increases the driver's stress, tunnel vision may narrow the range of peripheral vision just at a time when it is most needed.

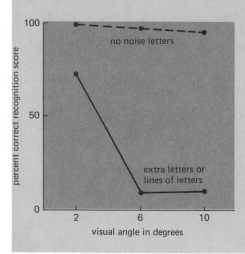

Fig. 7.9 Percent of correct matches between central and peripheral letters as a function of visual angle and the presence of noise letters. (Mackworth, 1965)

they may directly guide bodily movements. For example, when we drive a car, we often do not pay detailed attention to the visual environment. We respond to objects, such as other cars, directly, without aware recognition. In this situation, preattentive processes are at work. The preattentive processes, being primary and automatic, probably occur in the icon itself. Undoubtedly some kind of grouping of visual features or segmentation into figure and ground occurs in the icon. Some of this may also occur in visual short-term memory, before there has been any identification or naming process, but it is much more likely to occur in the icon.

When a significant aspect of the visual field is segmented, focal attention goes to work. At this point, attention is focused on only one aspect of stimulus information at a time. As a result, a feature may be analyzed, or a construction may be built, on the basis of information previously extracted.

Visual Search Tasks

Psychologists have studied a variety of visual search tasks. Many of them are similar to activities that we perform every day. In one type of task, subjects are asked to locate a target in a large, often cluttered, field of similar stimuli. This is very much like the process we go through when we search for a friend in a dense crowd, for example, at a department store sale. Often in this type of task, there is little concern for objects other than the target. You don't care who is at the sale, as long as you find your friend. This task requires the selection of one stimulus and the dismissal of others.

visual search task

Neisser, beginning in 1963, has given a clear example of the operation of selectivity during the processing of the contents of the iconic storage. These experiments are often referred to as visual search tasks.

In this type of experiment, lists containing 50 rows of letters have hidden within them a target letter. Subjects must search each list as fast as possible and signal when they find the target letter. Neisser then computes the processing time required for each list of letters by dividing the time needed to complete the search by the number of letters in the list preceding the target. Reaction time is plotted as a function of the row in which the target letter appeared. This relationship is always found to be a straight line increase in search time with target position; that is, the farther down the list the target letter is located, the longer the search time. (See Vigilance, p. 400.)

  Neisser's Search Experiments

In experiments studying pattern recognition, decision time, and visual search, the subject must make *n* different responses depending on which of *n* stimuli have appeared. A sequential processing theory would predict longer reaction times with more alternatives. Hick (1952) showed that if he doubled the number of alternatives the reaction time was increased by a fixed amount. Doubling the number of alternatives would mean that one more binary feature was needed to distinguish them. This result lends support to the notion of sequential processing.

However, sequential processing fails to apply when letters, numbers, or words are the stimuli and their names the responses. The time needed to respond does not depend on how many numbers are used or the range of the vocabulary. Neisser believes that some form of feature or attribution theory seems to be necessary in cases where the number of alternatives is of no importance.

Neisser (1963), Neisser and Lazar (1964), and Neisser and Beller (1965) report evidence confirming this hypothesis. The stimuli were 5-line lists. Each

Ulric Neisser

contained a single target letter at some random position. As soon as the list appeared the subject was instructed to begin scanning down from the top of the list looking for the target letter. When he found it he turned a switch, which stopped a clock, and the search time was recorded.

A template theory would suggest that subjects compared each letter on the list with a template and stopped only if there was a match. This seems extremely unlikely since the subjects' phenomenological reports indicate that they did not see individual letters. The time involved in locating a target stimulus suggests that subjects take in several lines in a glance. Further, search times do not increase linearly with the width of the column. Interestingly enough, Neisser found that multiple search takes no longer than a simple search provided that some prepractice is permitted. Subjects can look for 10 targets as rapidly as one.

In another of Neisser's visual search experiments, subjects had to look down through a list of words 3 to 6 letters in length in search of the one word that denoted an animal or, in another condition, a proper first name. This task required a subject to examine each word and establish its meaning at least well enough to make the required discrimination. Yet with practiced subjects scanning rates exceeded 5 words per minute. Hence, we can be sure that the words were not read by the identification of component letters.

These findings suggest some sort of parallel processing of separate features simultaneously. In addition, since his subjects report hardly seeing the irrelevant letters during the search task, this would indicate that preattentive analyzers, sensitive to the features of the display as a whole and spontaneous in their recognition, were operating.

The most interesting issue in this type of experiment is the time required to determine whether any of the letters in the current fixation is the target letter. Neisser assumed that the time taken for each row would reflect the complexity of the information extraction process for the letters of that particular row. If this task allowed the subject to test specific visual features of the shapes of the letters, without having to name them, processing should be a good deal faster.

Another type of visual search process occurs when we view pictures. Although there is less research in this area than in some other areas related to visual search techniques, several interesting studies have been made of the ways in which we look at pictures. Mackworth and Morandi (1967) used a television camera to measure and record eye fixation choices that occurred as subjects examined two unfamiliar pictures (Fig. 7.10).

This experiment produced clear-cut findings. An impressive observation about these findings is that the fixations are not distributed evenly around the picture. There is, instead, a great concentration of fixations in a few areas of the picture. These areas contain relatively great variation, unpredictability, or a high rate of change. Also impressive is the fact that the subject appears to know where to look before he has even given the picture a once-over look.

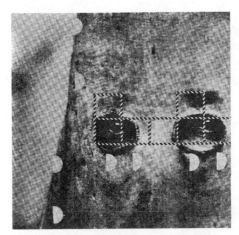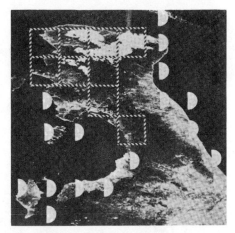

Fig. 7.10 Eye fixations made while looking at a map picture. (Mackworth and Morandi, 1967)

Peripheral cues must be adequate to direct fixation choices to the more unusual areas of the picture.

Another interesting observation is the lack of a regular pattern in searching the pictures, even in the relatively dull areas. No natural order of viewing a picture has been found. Kolers (1972) pointed out that in the area of picture searching, theory must come up with an explanation of how so many different input sequences can be used to produce so standard a perceptual experience.

Once more, we should note the difference between our eye movement patterns and our experience while looking at pictures. Within about a second of first viewing a picture, we have the feeling that we've seen it all, and all at the same time. However, records of our eye movements show a discontinuous jumping back and forth with some areas never looked at at all (Fig. 7.11).

Reading

Reading may be regarded as our most common visual search task. However, reading differs a great deal from most other visual search tasks. In reading, we make a search for meaning during which we must locate many targets and at the same time construct an integrated story. It is, after all, the story that we are looking for, rather than the words or the letters. In order to construct the story, however, we must pick up some of the letters and some of the words along the way. Accordingly, we will discuss the eye movements involved in reading.

The eye movement patterns that occur while reading a Shakespearean sonnet are shown in Fig. 7.12. Notice that the reader of this sonnet fixates on nearly every word once. There are few regressive movements. The last word of each line is fixated for a longer period. This is most probably a pattern peculiar to poetry and may reflect time used for gaining an understanding of the line or for checking its rhyme. Except for the last fixation on each line, the average

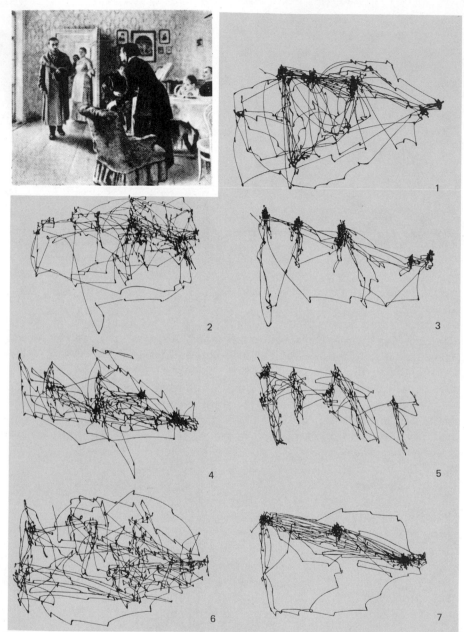

Fig. 7.11 Different eye-fixation patterns made to the same picture as a function of the instructions to the perceiver (from Yarbus, 1967). (1) Free examination of the picture. Before the subsequent recording sessions, the subject was asked to: (2) estimate the material circumstances of the family in the picture; (3) give the ages of the people; (4) surmise what the family had been doing before the arrival of the "unexpected visitor"; (5) remember the clothes worn by the people; (6) remember the position of the people and objects in the room; (7) estimate how long the "unexpected visitor" had been away from the family.

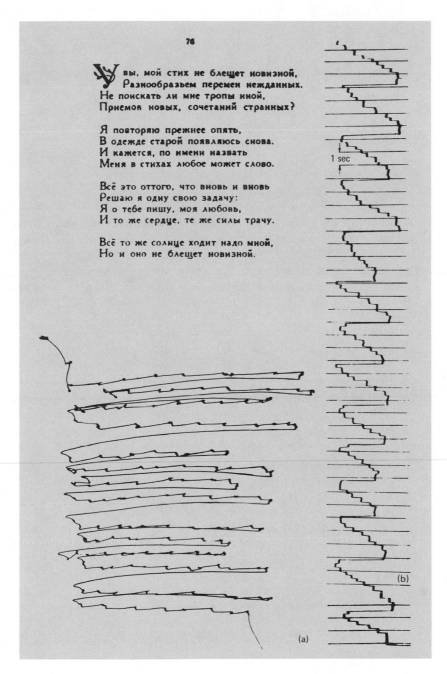

Fig. 7.12 Two different ways to record eye movements made while a perceiver is reading a poem. (Yarbus, 1967)

number of words per fixation here is 1.2. The average duration of each fixation is almost 300 milliseconds. The average time needed to shift the eyes from one fixation to the next is 35 milliseconds, approximately. These three factors are the important characteristics of eye pattern movements.

In the reading of prose, research has shown that the average fixation lasts 250–300 milliseconds. The average speed of eye movements is between 25 and 50 milliseconds, independent of individual reading speed, difficulty of the material, or the ability of the reader. Reading speed actually depends on how far apart each fixation is, both in time and space, rather than on how long each fixation lasts or on how long it takes to move the eyes. The point of most speed-reading programs is to teach the reader to make fewer fixations, by covering more words during each fixation.

At the beginning of a paragraph, fixations are close together, and there may be a couple of regressive movements, or refixations of a word. However, once the context of a paragraph becomes clear to a reader, he picks up a pattern of reading based on the difficulty or familiarity of the material.

A problem posed by regressive eye movements in reading is that their occurrence would seem to present to a reader a sequence of text that would be a word jumble. Models of reading have yet to account for the fact that they don't.

Kolers (1970) points out that in the course of reading research, almost all efforts to classify fixation choices by either the syntactic or the semantic content of the reading material have failed to show any pattern. This is in line with the distinction between preattention and focal attention presented earlier. Peripheral cues are used to guide fixation, and these cues are sensitive to physical properties, such as shape and spatial position, rather than to semantic properties. Research is now attempting to discover how word shape and word length act as peripheral clues.

Information processing occurs all the time. We use it to gather data from our surroundings and to interpret sensations in a cognitive way. Information processing is a continuous process consisting of many stages of selection and integration of the information around us. Without such a system, physical sensations received from the environment would be practically meaningless.

Summary

As human beings, we actively process information gathered from our environment and act on the basis of our processing. From the time we sense a stimulus to the time we respond, a whole series of steps occurs so rapidly that we are hardly aware of it.

Information processing is a coherent and orderly way of studying a variety of cognitive tasks performed by human beings, such as perception, cognitive processing, and memory. These operations are the consequences of a series of processes. Experimental procedures can be designed to examine the contents of our internal representation of stimulus information at every point in the sequence of processes we perform. In addition, information processing consists of a series of arbitrary discrete stages or processes. Flow diagrams are drawn to visually describe each operation and the sequence of operations. There is a continuity between input and output such that processing is a continuous operation whose stages cannot in reality be separated.

Each operation in information processing is believed to be limited in the amount of information it can handle or contain in a given time period, and this limitation leads to selectivity. Selectivity is a system of ordering priorities.

Information processing came to psychology from new concepts and techniques that arose from other sciences. These developments were the following: mathematical model of communication, definition of information content as uncertainty reduction, and the use of digital computers.

We use the information processing approach for many reasons: it gives us a way to understand many problems that might otherwise remain unclear; it allows us to view perception and memory as being on opposite ends of a continuum linked by a series of complex processes; it enables us to view the perceiver as an active processor; it allows us to compare how different aspects of perception are established in memory; and it provides a way of describing the many separate operations by which we assimilate information.

In studying information processing, we examine the following problems: pattern recognition, selective attention, fading memory, familiarity, and information retrieval.

Storage or memory keeps information deposited at various points along the processing route, and transfer of information from one point to another is an important operation. A model of visual information processing can be broken down into three major sections: (1) the pattern of light projected onto the retina; (2) the nonobservable internal processes; and (3) the observable behavioral response. This chapter has concentrated on the second of these.

In vision, the first stage of information processing is iconic storage, which is characterized by a large capacity but a brief time duration. Its job is to accurately register everything that is seen, almost like a nondiscriminating, catch-all system. It registers a great deal more than is extracted from it.

In stage two, a visual image, following the rules of perceptual organization, is formed. This is a conscious process not limited to the very brief duration of the iconic store.

In stage three, short-term memory, visual information is encoded in a linguistic or conceptual form. The process of naming is the operation of short-term memory. This stage also has a limited capacity and a fairly short duration, although longer than that of iconic storage. Rehearsal seems to aid in keeping things in short-term memory for an indefinite period of time and helps to transfer information from short-term memory to long-term memory.

Stage four, long-term memory, is the most important and complex of the memory systems. It is also the longest lasting, and it has the largest capacity.

The iconic store is studied by following a visual presentation with visual noise to prevent processing of information in the presentation. While there is enough time for a visual representation to develop so that a subject can make out its general form against a background, there is not enough time to extract a name for the form. The formation of a visual representation thus apparently begins before, or happens faster than, the naming of the items in the image. The processing method used is evidently serial—a scanning method—rather than parallel, and it proceeds from left to right.

Verbal short-term memory has a limited capacity (about seven items) and duration (about 20 seconds). It encodes material in an acoustic rather than a visual form. Rehearsal helps to keep material in verbal short-term memory and also to transfer it to long-term memory. Material is lost from this store both by decay with time and by interference from other material. Selectivity seems to occur at this and other stages of information processing.

The visual image store or visual short-term memory comes into use in the processing of purely visual, as opposed to verbal, material—pictures, scenes, photographs. It helps us to see the world as a stable and integrated structure. Information is processed more rapidly in visual than in verbal short-term memory, and visual memory has an almost infinite capacity. The high retention rate for pictorial information is in part due to the perceiver's ability to organize visual material into a meaningful image.

A number of mnemonic systems have been devised to facilitate the transfer of material from short- to long-term memory. Most of these rely on the superiority of our visual over our verbal memory. Some combine a visual device with the verbal device of rhyming.

Pattern recognition enables us to recognize and identify visual information we must work with and thus to process information more efficiently. The best theory of pattern recognition allows for analysis of both individual features and relationships between features. It also allows for the influence of context and of the viewer's expectations.

We select information for processing from only a relatively small part of the world around us. Factors influencing selection are the superiority of central over peripheral vision and the simultaneous occurrence of preattentive and focal attentive processes. In selecting information for processing we perform visual search tasks. When the information is purely visual, fixations are confined to high-content areas and the search pattern is highly irregular. Eye movements in reading are very much more regular.

Suggested Readings

Luria, A. R., *The Mind of a Mnemonist*. New York, Basic Books, 1968.
  The famous Russian psychologist's account of his experimental work with a man who could remember anything for any length of time.
Neisser, Ulrich, "Experimental Mentalism," *Science,* May 12, 1972.
  A brief look at the work of contemporary information-processing psychologists.
Norman, D. A., *Models of Human Memory*. New York, Academic Press, 1970.
  Describes current research in information processing.
Smith, Frank, *Understanding Reading*. New York, Holt, Rinehart and Winston, 1971.
  Reading is examined in terms of concepts from information processing, neurophysiology, and psycholinguistics.
Young, M. N., and W. B. Gibson, *How To Develop an Exceptional Memory*. Philadelphia, Chilton, 1962.
  The authors present a system of conceptual pegs to aid memory.

Chapter Eight

Language and Thought

What is the relationship of language to thought?
Why are concepts useful in thinking?
Can a stimulus-response model account for language learning?
What are phonemes and morphemes?
How can identical sentences have different meanings?
Does logical thinking develop in a fixed sequence?
What is the best way to go about solving a problem?
What can computers tell us about human thinking?

You are driving with a companion along a country road, on the way to a mutual friend's house. You haven't visited him before and are following his directions. But although the road is strange to you it is straight and there is no traffic, and you allow your mind to wander briefly, thinking of your friend and looking forward to the visit.

Then you catch sight of a bunch of trees ahead on the left. Your daydream abruptly ends, and you slow down slightly. What did your friend say? "A stand of dogwood"? What does dogwood look like, and do these trees fit the description? "Think that's the dogwood Fred mentioned?" you ask your companion. He leans forward and looks: "If I know dogwood, yes," he says.

You near the left turn by the trees, slow down, check the rear-view mirror, and swing into the side road. As you settle down for the last 5 miles, and as the silence has been broken, you and your companion begin to chat idly.

In these few moments almost every aspect of language and thought that this chapter will discuss has been exemplified. If we could explain the psychological mechanisms that enabled you and your companion to carry out this series of everyday behaviors we would have solved the crucial problem of what it is that makes *Homo sapiens*—"knowing" or "wise" man—different from his fellow creatures. You may find it interesting after reading this chapter to reexamine these paragraphs in light of the material that has been discussed.

We cannot yet explain precisely how humans use language and thought. But a lot of important things are known, and this chapter will attempt to introduce them to you. One of the first things you must understand is that language and thought are inextricably mingled. Accordingly, we will begin with a very brief discussion of the cognitive processes that are the basis of all thinking and all language. From there we will consider images and concepts, and how we manipulate these in language to order our thoughts.

We cannot understand the way we build concepts until we have explored the ways by which we attain the power to speak, the routes by which we acquire language; and we will discuss the development of language in the young child and various theories of the structure of language.

That discussion will prepare us to understand in a richer way what we might say language is for—thinking; as with language, we will discuss thinking in terms both of its development in the young child and of its nature in the adult. Finally, we will examine two crucial aspects of thinking, problem solving and creative thinking.

WHAT IS THINKING?

thinking Thinking is defined as a process in which we manipulate representations of the world. That is, we examine them from many different angles, combine them in more or less elaborate ways—or "take them apart"—and test them against one another. But what are these representations? A better term for our purposes is symbol "symbols." A symbol is a stimulus that can be substituted for an actual object or event. Very often the symbols we think with are words. Even in a very simple sentence such as "I like chewing rubber bands" we are using words to symbolize a person (I), a feeling (like), an action (chewing), and a kind of object (rubber bands). People, feelings, actions, and objects are only a few aspects of our world that we can symbolize. (See Implicit Speech, p. 398.)

language All the word symbols available to us, as well as the rules for relating them to one another, form a structure that we call language. With language we can explore actual or potential relations among the parts of our world that the words symbolize: we can think about them. Thinking frees us from the limitations of our physical environment in many ways. For one thing, we can think about the possible consequences of various actions and decide which ones seem most promising without having to try them all out in direct experience. If we had to test every alternative by "living" it before making a choice, life would be much more difficult than it is now—and a lot shorter.

The processes involved in thinking are called *cognitive processes*. In Chapter 3 we discovered that learning can be viewed as the acquisition of patterned stimulus-response associations. Thinking is a more complex activity in

Fred Weiss

Beginning very early in life, language and thinking are inextricably mingled.

which we are released from the requirement of a specific stimulus to produce the correct response and are free to marshal what we already know from earlier learning, as well as our current perceptions, in the service of a variety of purposes. The psychologist who studies cognitive processes is interested in how symbols of objects and events are related to one another in the thinking of human beings. He therefore concentrates on stimulus-stimulus, rather than on stimulus-response, relations (see Chapter 5).

In human thinking the types of symbols used are images and concepts.

Images

We can experience two kinds of pictures: percepts and images. A *percept* is the internal picture of a fragment of reality; it is bound in a stimulus-response fashion to the sensations impinging upon the person at the moment it occurs, although it may be transformed and distorted by the person's past experiences, sets, and expectations. But the present is continually flowing into the past, and as it does so percepts become *images*, internal pictures that are not directly dependent upon the incoming flow of stimulation. They do so via icons, which were introduced in Chapter 7. An icon is a very "percept-like" persistence of

percept

image

353

sensory stimulation. You can isolate an icon in yourself by glancing quickly at the face of a stranger or some other novel object and immediately closing your eyes. You will be able to "see," as if against your eyelids, a more or less vivid reproduction of the object you have glimpsed. But this reproduction, though vivid, fades rapidly.

Images are stored representations of sensory information that can be recalled in almost "unprocessed" form, very close to their previous manifestations as percepts. For instance, when any one of us thinks of his room, he can "see" a picture of it in his mind. Although this picture is not as clear or as vivid as the sight of the room itself, it is much closer to the objective reality than any verbal description of it could be.

 Memory and Images

What role do mental images play in remembering? Does memory operate primarily by means of pictures or words—or both? One psychologist, Allan Paivio, has argued that there are two independent memory systems, a visual system and a verbal system. The visual system works via the recall of stimulus names; in any given memory task, either or both may be operating. Paivio has argued that various stimulus conditions naturally favor the use of one of these systems over the other; the visual system is better suited to the recall of pictures than the verbal system, while the verbal system is better suited to the recall of nonsense syllables and abstract words—items that are difficult to visualize. When both systems can function effectively, as in cases where objects easily imaged are named or objects easily named are pictorially represented, recall is most efficient. In addition, Paivio has argued that in tasks involving the sequential learning and recall of lists of items, the verbal mode of recall is more effective than the visual.

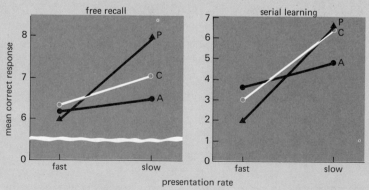

Fig. 8.1 Mean number of correct responses in four memory tasks for pictures (P) concrete words (C), and abstract words (A) at two presentation rates. (Paivio and Csapo, 1969)

Paivio and his associates have performed a considerable number of experiments designed to support their hypotheses. (A comprehensive overview of them is available in Paivio, 1971.) In one experiment (Paivio and Csapo, 1969) two sets of nine words each, one set composed of concrete words *(piano, snake, pencil)* and one set composed of abstract words *(ability, ego, theory)*, and a set of nine pictures representing the objects named in the concrete word list, were presented to subjects for memorization. Each subject was required to memorize only one of the lists. The items were presented sequentially at one of two presentation rates: 5.3 items per second or 2 items per second. In the recall task, some subjects were allowed "free" recall of the items memorized and some were required to recall the stimuli in the serial order in which they had been presented.

On the basis of previous research, the experimenters were able to make the following specific predictions. With the free recall memory task, pictures, abstract words, and concrete words presented at the fast presentation rate would all be recalled with equal efficiency, since each would be recalled by the use of only one of the two memory systems. With the slow presentation rate, however, pictures and concrete words would be recalled through the use of both the verbal and the visual memory systems, and would therefore be recalled more efficiently. Abstract words, however, limited at both presentation rates to recall by verbal memory alone, would not be recalled significantly better at the slow presentation rate than at the fast rate.

In the case of the serial-order recall task, on the other hand, the relative ineffectiveness of visual memory relative to verbal with respect to serial recall was expected to produce a marked deficit in the recall of pictures relative to concrete and abstract words at the fast stimulus presentation rate. With the slow presentation rate, the ability of subjects to use verbal labels to facilitate recall of the pictorial items was expected to overcome this disadvantage, resulting in a marked improvement in the recall of the pictorial stimuli. Since even in the serial recall task visual memory would be of some value, however, the availability of both the verbal and visual systems for the memorization of pictures and concrete words presented at the slower rate was expected to result in the better recall of those items than of abstract words presented at the faster rate. The experimental outcomes confirmed the experimental predictions (Fig. 8.1).

Pictures are not the only form images can take, however. Any sensory modality can produce images, though by no means all people experience all of them. People differ also in the form of image they most frequently experience: most people seem to experience visual images most frequently; second are the predominantly auditory imagers who *hear* images; a small minority most frequently experience smell, taste, or neuromuscular images. Images are not perfectly stored replicas of percepts. Our experiences, interests, motivations produce more or less subtle changes in the images we carry with us. The image of a pretty girl in her mother's and in her boyfriend's minds will not be identical.

Concepts

concept

Thinking also utilizes another set of symbols: concepts, or representations in language of *connections* among two or more objects or events. Concepts help us to reduce an overwhelming mass of stimuli to manageable proportions and permit us to think at high levels of complexity.

One way to accomplish a significant reduction in the quantity of stimuli that must be dealt with is to classify objects and events, so that we can think of them in groups rather than one at a time. Bananas, watermelons, and grapefruit look and taste very different, yet we can isolate a set of features common to all three that permits us to classify them as "fruit."

Concepts also enable us to select objects or events that have only one or a few properties from a larger set of properties that define the category. In baseball, for example, a strike is called when the batter misses the ball *or* hits a foul ball *or* lets a ball pass over the plate in the strike zone. The rules of the game define a strike as any event that exhibits *one* of this group of properties.

We also use concepts to sort out relations among objects and events in order to find underlying unities or differences. In this case concepts enable us to contrast and compare. The concept "loud noise," for example, conveys something about relations among different amounts of sound; the concept "sweet wine" conveys something about relations among different taste perceptions.

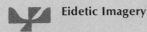

Eidetic Imagery

A very small percentage of human beings are capable of *eidetic imagery*—the ability to produce very clear visual images that can be scanned for details. Haber and Haber (1964) found in a study of 151 children that 12 could, after looking at a picture of 10 Indians for only a few seconds, summon up an image so clear that they were able to report details as minute as the number of feathers in each Indian's headdress and the different colors in a multicolored blanket.

    Eidetic imagery is a report by a perceiver that even though he is no longer looking at the stimulus, he can vividly see it before his eyes roughly where it had been presented to him. He can move his eyes over it and he can report details of it. Since the perceiver clearly admits to the impression that there is something out there, we refer to it as an image, and eidetic imagery really represents an inability to tell the difference between images and percepts. A distinction should be made, however, between eidetic imagery and the notion of "photographic memory." When memory is said to be photographic, we generally imply great accuracy of memory, which may be available to a person because he has very vivid imagery or simply because his memory is extremely good. In theory, a photographic memory could involve no images at all. Clearly, however, some people who have photographic memory do have very good images.

    A curious feature of eidetic imagery is that it is much less common in American adults than in children. There is also some evidence from Africa that rural adults are more frequently capable of such imagery than are urban adults (Doob, 1964). Psychologists have yet to explain these differences satisfactorily.

    Eidetic imagery is a mixed blessing. For example, you and I have a clear but fairly abstract "image" of an apple; we also have, or can have, a clear and specific image of the particular apple we ate for lunch. This continuum of imagery from abstract to concrete is not so easy (and may even be impossible) for those with eidetic memory. One of the most famous possessors of eidetic imagery, studied by the Russian psychologist Luria (1968), was unable to understand simple abstract ideas because he attempted to visualize them in concrete images.

eidetic imagery

Concept Attainment Our ability to use language permits us to deal with concepts on many different levels, from such concrete notions as "cat" to such highly abstract ideas as "justice." Much experimental evidence indicates that concrete concepts are more easily acquired than abstract ones and are thus the first to be learned (see "Development of Thinking" later in this chapter). Apparently even adults learn concrete concepts more quickly.

    Heidbreder (1947) demonstrated these varying levels of difficulty with selected concepts ranging from the concrete "tree" and "building" to the more abstract "circle" and "five." She gave these concepts names that were nonsense syllables: "tree" became "molp," "circle" became "fard," "five" became "dilt," and so on (Fig. 8.2). Subjects were shown pictures of one representative of each of the concepts to be learned; as the picture was shown its nonsense label was

Edna Heidbreder

Fig. 8.2 These pictures were shown one at a time, starting on each trial from the top of the column and proceeding to the bottom. As each picture was shown, the subject tried to anticipate the nonsense word paired with it. After the subject made his response the experimenter called out the correct nonsense word, which is listed below each picture. On the first trial the subject had no way of knowing what word was paired with a picture, but over the course of several trials he gradually learned to anticipate correctly on all pictures. Note that none of the pictures are ever repeated, so it is not a question of learning a specific response to a specific stimulus, but rather learning a response to a concept. In this example the concept of face = relf, building = leth, tree = molf, circle = fard, the number two = ling, and the number five = pilt. (Heidbreder, 1947)

repeated. The subjects in this study learned the names of concrete concepts such as "tree" and "building" more quickly than those for spatial forms such as "circle"; number concepts were the most difficult for them to acquire.

How do we acquire concepts? One way is by attaching labels to objects and events, so that we gradually abstract the common properties that define categories. This is the usual process by which children form concepts; they extract the common properties of trees, houses, and other objects.

We also acquire new concepts by means of the *contexts* in which they appear. Sometimes we are able to grasp the meaning of a word by the way in which it is used in a sentence. Other elements in the sentence (and perhaps in adjacent ones as well) may demand that the word have certain properties if the whole utterance is to make sense. The force of these demands may be such that we are compelled to recognize the one concept that will fit, even if we do not know the word for it, as in the following example:

The cowboy uncoiled his _____ from his saddle horn, swung the loop three times above his head, and let it fly; it settled around the bull's neck, stretched taut, then brought him crashing to the ground.

On the other hand, hearing the same unfamiliar term in a number of different contexts permits us to "zero in" on its meaning in a way that a single context may not be "powerful" enough to do. Werner and Kaplan (1950) have demonstrated how this process works. At what point in the following sentences are you absolutely sure that you know what a "corplum" is?

A corplum may be used for support.
Corplums may be used to close off an open place.
A corplum may be long or short, thick or thin, strong or weak.
A wet corplum does not burn.
You can make a corplum smooth with sandpaper.
The painter used a corplum to mix his paints.

Definition is a third way of acquiring concepts, and it is perhaps the most important method for learning complex concepts. Basically, the definition of a concept is the description of it in other words; this book is full of examples.

Yet another form of concept learning, analogous to computer programing, will be discussed later in this chapter.

It should be clear from this discussion that the development of concepts is dependent upon the acquisition of language, as well as upon cognitive development in general. This is an example of the close relationship, which we have pointed out, between language and thinking. The two processes go hand in hand.

Attainment of concepts represents the process of creating the building blocks of thinking; it is logical from here to move to a consideration of the development of the building blocks of language.

ACQUISITION OF LANGUAGE

Babbling

The first vocalization of an infant is normally the "birth cry," and in the first month of life the baby is restricted to cries and grunts. By about the second month his parents begin to recognize differences in the cries that he utters for various kinds of discomfort—hunger, pain, wetness, and so on.

In about the third month the infant begins to exercise his vocal apparatus in an unorganized way—producing *spontaneous babbling*, which progresses over a period of about 4 months from simple gurgling to coos, gutteral noises, and even vowel sounds. Some investigations have revealed that infants at this stage are capable of making almost all the sounds the human vocal apparatus can produce. A general outline of the development of language in the child is given in Table 8.1.

Spontaneous babbling has two primary functions. The first is to exercise and strengthen the muscles of the vocal apparatus, as well as those associated

Table 8.1 Development of Language in the Infant

Language Behavior	Average Age, Months after Birth
Cries, grunts, and makes other respirant sounds	0
Makes different sounds for discomfort, hunger, and pain	1
Makes vowel sounds like *ah, uh, ay*	1–2
Looks toward sound of human voice	2–4
Babbles and coos	3–4
Talks to himself, using sounds like *ma, mu, do, na*	4–6
Makes sounds of pleasure and displeasure	5–6
"Sounds off" when he hears a familiar voice	6–7
Puts sounds together and repeats them over and over like *mamama-mama, booboo, dadada*	6–9
Imitates sounds made by others	9–10
Understands gestures (can wave bye-bye and often can say it)	9–12
Understands and responds to simple commands ("Hold the spoon," "Look at the doll baby")	11–15
Imitates syllables and simple words (the first word?)	11–15
Says two different words	12
Says three to five different words	13–18
Understands and responds to the "don'ts" (Don't touch that," "Don't spit it out")	16–20
Names one object or picture in book (cup, ball, doggy, baby, etc.)	17–24
Combines words into phrases ("Go out," "Give me milk," "Where ball?")	18–24
Identifies three to five familiar objects or pictures	24
Uses phrases and simple sentences	23–24

SOURCE: *Introduction to Psychology* by C. T. Morgan and R. A. King. Copyright 1971 by McGraw-Hill, Inc. Used with permission of McGraw-Hill Book Company; after McCarthy (1946)

with the jaw. The second is to provide a kind of feedback about the results of various sounds. By means of such feedback the infant gradually learns which sounds are likely to produce which results; he thus begins to produce sounds purposefully. This kind of control is obviously prerequisite to acquisition of meaningful speech.

Between 6 and 10 months, the child can begin to modify his vocalizations in response to influences from his environment. For one thing, he is able to repeat syllables ("ma-ma-ma-ma"); in *syllabic babbling* he frequently changes the sound of the syllable slightly with each repetition, thus gradually extending the range of sounds that he can control. He also begins to imitate the sounds he hears, particularly the vocalizations of his parents. He thus begins to acquire the patterns of pronunciation and intonation characteristic of his native language and culture.

Some time between 12 and 18 months the first word usually appears, but it is likely to be used in several different contexts. "Mama" may be used for mother or for another woman in the house, as a demand or simply as an identification, and so on. The child has begun to differentiate words but not yet their precise meanings, or *referents*. From here on he makes rapid strides in both vocabulary and understanding.

Interestingly, all children, regardless of nationality, first use "words" beginning with a front consonant (one produced in the front of the mouth)—*p, m, b,* or *t*—followed by a back vowel—*a* or *ah*. This fact may very well be the reason for the similarity of *mama* and *papa* in so many languages (McNeill, 1970). At the same time, consonants such as *k* and hard *g* will be used in vocal play. Difficulty in pronouncing them appears to arise only when they are used volitionally (Jakobson, 1968).

Development of Grammar

As the child learns to put two and three words together, he begins to develop the *grammar* of his language, the rules for combining words to convey meaning. This stage lasts from about 1 to about 5 years of age (Fig. 8.3).

     grammar

The infant begins using simple two-word "sentences" when he is about 18 months old. The main grammatical rule acquired at this age determines the construction of such sentences from *pivot* and *open* words (McNeill, 1966). Pivot words make up the small class of words the child uses most frequently; they have achieved relatively stable positions in his utterances and can be combined with any number of other words. For example, the pivot word *allgone* may be used to express a single, unvarying idea, which always initiates a sentence (Braine, 1963): "allgone sock"; "allgone milk." Some pivot words always appear at the ends of sentences (Braine, 1963): "do *it*"; "push *it*." Pivot words rarely appear alone or in combination with other pivot words at this stage of development.

     pivot words

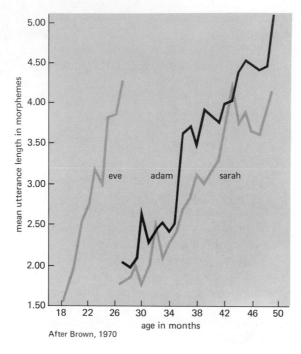

Fig. 8.3 The graph plots mean utterance length of each child in morphemes (meaningful segments) rather than words in order to give credit for the use of inflections such as plural word endings. (Ruch and Zimbardo, 1971)

open words

Open words constitute a rapidly growing body of words that appear less frequently in the child's speech; they can appear alone, as well as in combination with pivot words. "Sock" and "milk" in the sentences with "allgone" are open words. Specific pivot and open words vary with each child.

Two-word sentences are usually limited to certain kinds of words, mainly simple forms of nouns and verbs. The child's speech at this stage is like the economical language of a telegram, in which all the small, connecting words are left out: "Home Friday; meet plane."

The comparative ease of communication achieved between a mother and her child should not make us forget the grammatical ambiguity of the child's speech. As the child's utterances expand, the mother uses the context to interpret the meaning. Brown and Bellugi (1964) illustrate this. A little girl said "Eve lunch" while her mother was preparing the meal. "Yes, mummy is going to fix Eve's lunch," replied the mother. Thirty minutes later, while eating, Eve repeated "Eve lunch." "Yes, Eve is eating lunch," said the mother.

Until about age 2 the child's use of language is based on meaning rather than on linguistic structure. Speech reflects the level of understanding of the world, the conceptual level, he has achieved. This is another example of the need to study the development of language and of thinking together.

Anywhere between 22 and 32 months of age the child begins to use many pronouns, some articles and modifiers, and occasional prepositions. He also begins to use inflected forms of nouns and verbs, notably plurals and the past tense.

Ursula Bellugi

Children at this age "play" with language a great deal, practicing their rapidly expanding vocabularies and trying out new words and combinations even when alone. Such frequent practice no doubt speeds up the consolidation of grammatical rules already acquired, but probably more important in the learning of new rules are the child's efforts to imitate his parents' speech.

We must not overestimate the importance of parental correction, however. Brown and Hanlon (1970) analyzed many child-parent exchanges and found that correction of grammatical errors was far too infrequent to account for the acquisition of grammar.

Between about 25 and 48 months of age the child's grammar begins to be a recognizable, though simpler, edition of adult grammar. He can now use a wide variety of auxiliary verbs in many different contexts: "Mommy will come home," "Tommy won't play." Certain grammatical rules have yet to be mastered, however.

In acquiring language, then, the infant is limited in the beginning to cries and grunts. But these sounds help strengthen his vocal muscles so that he can produce new sounds. Soon he is producing syllables and even a few words, though he doesn't know, or even have any interest in, what they mean. The feedback he receives from those around him teaches him that some of the sounds he is making have meaning for others, and because people respond to those sounds he makes them more frequently than sounds that elicit no response. The most dramatic moment in the child's acquisition of language occurs when he begins to imitate, for then he progresses rapidly toward a grammatical command of his language. He begins with 2-word sentences and then moves gradually to longer and longer, and more formally correct, sentences.

 Acquisition of Plurals and Irregular Past Tenses

Young children have difficulty mastering the formation of certain plurals and of irregular past tenses. The regular sound patterns of English noun plurals take three basic forms: "s" ("hawks"), "z" ("doves"), and "ez" ("albatrosses"). Jean Berko (1958) conducted a study with kindergarten and first-grade children to explore their mastery of the grammatical rules for forming plurals. In order to rule out the possibility of a child's already knowing particular plural nouns, she used nonsense syllables presented with pictures of imaginary animals. Fig. 8.4 shows the most famous example from her study; the sentence was designed to lead children to complete it with a plural, and 91 percent of those in her sample correctly responded "wugz." (This was an oral, not a written, exercise.) In fact, the percentages of correct responses were uniformly high (79–91 percent) for all the examples that required "s" and "z" plural endings. It is clear that the children had achieved a high degree of mastery of the rules for these formations. The rule for applying the "ez" ending had still not been firmly grasped, however, for the correct responses on the related presentations ranged between only 28 and 36 percent.

This is a wug.

Now there is another one.
There are two of them.
There are two _____.

Fig. 8.4

In the same study Berko identified another area of difficulty for children at this stage: forming the correct past tenses of irregular verbs. Some of the most commonly used verbs in English are irregular in the past tense: "do-did," "come-came," "see-saw," "go-went," "make-made." The forms of each of these verbs must be learned separately. The 5- or 6-year-old child is familiar with the rule for constructing the past tense of regular verbs—adding the sound "d" ("smelled"), "t" ("liked"), or "ed" ("wanted") to each. But confronted with an irregular verb, he is likely to *overgeneralize* the rule he already knows, producing such forms as "goed," "comed," "maked." It is almost certain that the child is applying a grammatical rule in such instances, for he is not likely to have heard such forms in adult speech.

WHY DO WE LEARN A LANGUAGE?

Traditional learning theories, based on classical or operant conditioning (see Chapter 3), have been put forward to explain the processes by which children acquire their native language. These explanations, however, for reasons we will consider in this section, seem inadequate to account for most aspects of language acquisition.

Stimulus-Response Learning of Language Unlikely

Critics have pointed out a number of flaws in conditioning theories of language acquisition. For one thing, these theories do not account for the uniformity of language patterns in a single culture in spite of enormous variety in kinds and degrees of reinforcement. Even among different cultures there is a surprising similarity in patterns of language development. Lenneberg's work (1969) with children of deaf parents, who were unable to repeat (and thus to reinforce) the vocalizations of their children, has provided striking confirmation of this criticism. He recorded the vocalizations of six infants of deaf parents and six infants of normal parents from before they were 10 days old until they were just over 3 months old and found no differences in the crying and babbling sounds the infants made. It appears, then, that at least in the earliest phase of development the acquisition of sounds necessary for language is independent of parental reinforcement.

A second criticism of learning theories stems from their assumption that language is learned in part by associating certain sounds with certain objects. Acquisition of language by means of associations implies a continuous and regular process, a gradual expansion of the linguistic repertoire through imitation. Learning theorists point to evidence that in the babbling stage there is a standard sequence of development from predominantly vowel sounds to predominantly consonant sounds and then to combinations of the two, which ultimately take on rhythm and intonations resembling those of language. However, other investigators claim that the production of sounds in the babbling stage is not systematic and that therefore the transition from random production of sounds to purposeful imitation represents a sharp break in behavior. If babies babble at random yet learn the same speech patterns in the end, it does not seem that language development can depend upon regularities in learning experiences.

Still another argument against learning theories is the demonstrable ability of children to use familiar language in novel ways that do not reflect prior associations or reinforcement patterns. From the time that children begin to utter primitive sentences, at an age of 18 to 24 months, a process of experimentation with new combinations of known words begins. Many of the pivot-open combinations that Braine recorded, McNeil (1966) notes in a discussion of this work, "are very unlikely to be imitations or reductions of adult sentences." Consider, for example, "see cold," "byebye dirty," "allgone sticky," "no down," "more high," "more car," "other fix," "allgone outside." All of these are meaningful utterances, though their meaning may not be clear out of context, and are fully "grammatical" within the child's system. One child observed by Braine made use of "the" as a pivot word, producing sentences like "the byebye" and "the up." McNeil makes particular note that a number of "allgone" sentences recorded by Braine—for example, "allgone shoe," "allgone egg," and "allgone lettuce"—are in fact *inversions* of the normal pattern of adult speech; an adult would say, "The lettuce is all gone." Thus, the research of Braine and others (Brown and Bellugi, 1964; Ervin, 1964) suggests that while the child acquires quite early in life a set of rules for relating the words in his utterances, his grammar is not identical to the grammar of the adults surrounding him.

If novelty is common in the verbalizations of children, it is a paramount characteristic in the speech of adults. We endlessly produce sentences that we have never uttered or heard before, and we do this as a matter of course. The linguist Noam Chomsky (1957) has written:

> The central fact to which any significant linguistic theory must address itself is this: a mature speaker can produce a new sentence of his language on the appropriate occasion and other speakers can understand it immediately, though it is equally new to them. . . . It is evident that rote recall is a factor of minute importance in ordinary use of language. . . . It is clear that a theory of language that neglects this "creative" aspect of language is of only marginal interest. (p. 55)

All these criticisms of the learning theories, particularly those based on the observation that standard language patterns seem to develop out of a complex variety of learning experiences, have led some psychologists to propose a genetic basis for the acquisition of language, an *innate* capacity for acquiring the grammatical relations that are fundamental to all languages.

Acquisition of Language as Rule—Structural Theory

structural theory of language

The foremost proponent of the genetic, or *structural,* approach is Chomsky (1957; Chomsky and Halle, 1968; Chomsky, 1969), who argues that language learning is based on certain innate principles of mental organization that provide the basic structure for all cognitive processes—perceiving, learning, and thinking. Such principles may account for the similarity in patterns of language development common to the entire human species. The notion of innate capacity for language development receives apparent confirmation from the fact that once the child has reached a specific stage of physical maturity, his acquisition of language seems to be quite consistently correlated with his motor development (Lenneberg, 1969).

Structuralists consider that what the child learns are rules that permit him to produce and understand an unlimited variety of utterances he has not heard before. Clearly, given the speed at which language is acquired, the argument can be made that a rule strategy is a far more likely route for the acquisition

Noam Chomsky

of language than is the rote learning of new sentences. The number of different words recorded from one of Braine's (1963) children in successive months was 14, 24, 54, 89, 350, 1400, 2500+. Any theory of language acquisition that takes the position that new utterances are learned one at a time from adult models is rendered questionable by these numbers.

Evidence of the early development of rules by which words are sorted into "pivot" and "open" classes has already been cited. How do the "rules" of early speech develop into the more complex rules that characterize adult grammars? Brown and Bellugi (1964), among others, have made longitudinal observations of the development of children's speech that suggest that the initial "pivot-open" system is developed into a more advanced grammar by a process of "differentiation," in which groups of words originally belonging to the "pivot" class are set off from that class by virtue of the fact that special sets of rules are adopted for their use. In this way pivot words, which originally serve simply as "generalized modifiers," subdivide into groups of "articles," "possessive pronouns," and so forth. From their observations, Brown and Bellugi are led to conclude the very intricate simultaneous differentiation and integration by which the noun phrase is evolved resembles the acquisition of a conditioned reflex less than it does the biological development of an embryo.

The set of rules that determine how a particular language is structured may be taken to constitute the "generative grammar" of that language. Chomsky (1957) has attempted to specify the grammar underlying the structure of English. These rules, set out in a formal way, are extremely complex. However, the structuralist approach does not hold that the generative grammar of a language is learned in the same way that the proscriptive and restrictive "rules of English" taught in the grade school classroom are learned (or not learned). Rather, the generative rules are thought to be spontaneously incorporated into the child's mental structure during the early years of verbal development because the human brain has evolved in such a way as to make the incorporation of linguistic rules one of its natural functions. We acquire these rules and use them because our brains are designed to do so, just as the brains of other organisms are built to facilitate the acquisition of various species-specific behaviors. Asked, however, to state the rules by which we speak, we are likely to stand mute.

generative grammar

While the nature of innate language-acquiring abilities in human beings is still a matter widely debated by psychologists, the idea that an understanding of the underlying rules and structure of a language plays a vital role in enabling a child to learn to speak the language has now gained wide acceptance.

STRUCTURE OF LANGUAGE

Units of Language

The smallest units of sound are called *phonemes*, which constitute the different vowel and consonant sounds that are *recognized* in any given language. English

phoneme

has 45 phonemes; some languages have far fewer and some a great many more. Arabic, for instance, has a sound halfway between the English "k" and hard "g" sounds, but it does not recognize the English phonemes "p" or "v" at all. From the point of view of the English speaker, another peculiarity of Arabic is that in it differentiation of vowel sounds has relatively little importance; sounds corresponding to short English "a," "i," and "u" are often interchanged without altering the meanings of words.

morpheme

Phonemes can be combined into *morphemes,* the smallest units of meaning in a given language. In English these units can be whole words ("house," "frog," "cope"), prefixes ("pre-," "anti-," "de-"), or suffixes ("-ed," "-ing," "-ness"). There are more than 100,000 morphemes in the English language, yet all the possible combinations of the 45 phonemes have by no means been exhausted.

The number of morphemes is limited, in English as in all languages, by certain rules restricting the combination of phonemes. In English, for example, we never begin a phoneme with more than three consonant sounds, and even the number of such permissible triads is quite small ("spl," "str," and a few others). Russian, on the other hand, permits initial "zdr," "stch," and other combinations that do not occur in English. The Slavic languages in general also permit many two-phoneme beginnings—such as "zb" and "vg"—that are excluded in English.

Restriction on phoneme combinations is highly functional, for if the possibilities were unlimited, every change in a single phoneme would produce a new morpheme, and errors in communication would be even greater than they are now.

Surface and Deep Structures

Language is the system by which patterns of meaning are communicated through patterns of sounds or symbols. There is an important difference between spoken and written sentences and the ideas underlying them. The only language behavior that can be observed and measured is actual spoken or written material;

surface structure of language

we call such productions the *surface structure* of language. The corresponding patterns of meaning are composed of elements and according to rules that are stored in memory and thus cannot be observed directly. These patterns consti-

deep structure of language

tute the *deep structure* of language. An example will help to clarify this distinction. Consider the following sentences:

Roger threw the ball.
The ball was thrown by Roger.

The observable surface structures are quite different, but the sentences mean the same thing; that is, they have the same deep structure. On the other hand, consider these two sentences (Neisser, 1967):

They are eating apples.
They are eating apples.

In this example the surface structures are identical, but the two sentences may represent quite different deep structures, which can also be represented by these sentences:

Apples are being eaten by them.
They are apples for eating.

 Research Using Chomsky's Structuralist Notions

If we accept Chomsky's generative theory of language as a psychological theory, then we must be able to delineate psychological correlates that act in accordance with generative grammar in an abstract way. A number of experiments have been done to test the adequacy of generative theory as a theory of human cognition. It is realized, of course, that other cognitive factors such as attitude and emotional state must be taken into account.

Perhaps the first relevant experiment testing Chomsky's claim that sentences are interpreted in terms of deep structure as well as surface structure was done by Mehler (1963). Mehler's subjects were to memorize sentences. One of these was the kernel sentence—for example, *the secretary has typed the paper*—but the others incorporated one or more optional transformations. Only three transformations were used—passive voice, negation, and question. However some sentences used combinations of these transformations. *Hasn't the paper been typed by the secretary?* employs all three transformations.

The subjects were given five practice trials to learn the sentences. Mehler's results show that there tended to be a shift toward the kernel sentence. This shift expressed itself in several aspects of the data. Kernel sentences were easiest to learn. Subjects frequently made errors by changing a transformed sentence back to its kernel, but rarely in the other direction. Even errors that did not involve the kernel tended to move in that direction so that fewer transformations were presented in the recalled version. Mehler interpreted his results as involving memory capacity, or more specifically, span of apprehension. He felt that grammatical transformations represented additional information that had to be stored along with the raw kernel information in the sentence.

To further test the notion that grammatical transformations take up space in memory, Savin and Perchonock (1965) devised an "overflow" method. They reasoned that the volume of an irregular object can be determined by dropping it into a full container of water and measuring the overflow. The analog of water in this experiment was a set of unrelated words that the subject had to recall in addition to the sentence. Thus, the subject might be asked to remember, "Has the boy hit the ball? truck, tree, cat, month, lamp, rain, shirt, blue." It was predicted that the greater the transformational complexity of the sentence, the fewer the

kernel sentence

number of additional words the subject would subsequently be able to recall along with it, or the greater the number of words that would "overflow" out of memory.

The results conformed to the prediction (Table 8.2). Kernel sentences (in which surface structure and deep structure were the most similar) produced less interference than transformed sentences since they took up less storage space.

Table 8.2 Mean Number of Words Recalled after Each Sentence Type

Sentence Type Words Recalled	Example	Mean No. Words Recalled
Active Declarative	The boy has hit the ball.	5.27
Wh-Question	What has the boy hit?	4.78
Question	Has the boy hit the ball?	4.67
Passive	The ball has been hit by the boy.	4.55
Negative	The boy has not hit the ball.	4.44
Negative Question	Has the boy not hit the ball?	4.39
Emphatic	The boy *has* hit the ball.	4.30
Negative Passive	The ball has not been hit by the boy.	3.48
Passive Question	Has the ball been hit by the boy?	4.02
Negative Passive Question	Has the ball not been hit by the boy?	3.85
Emphatic Passive	The ball *has* been hit by the boy.	3.74

SOURCE: Savin and Perchonock (1965)

The results of these experiments are impressive but still indirect. It is necessary to infer the effect of deep structure from its influence on another task. Another experiment by Mehler and Carey (1967) provides more direct evidence.

The experiment presented a series of 11 sentences in which the first 10 were identical in either surface or deep structure and the last was different in both respects. Each subject listened to and tried to identify these sentences superimposed upon a noisy background. In the critical condition, the first 10 sentences were all of one deep structure type, while the 11th was of a different type. The subjects were prepared for a particular syntactic structure and, as predicted, had difficulty identifying the last sentence correctly, thus providing direct evidence that the ability to learn a sentence accurately depends upon the perception of its deep structure.

Chomsky (1957) was one of the first to recognize the distinction between surface and deep structures, and he has built his theory of *transformational grammar* on this foundation. He believes that deep structure is represented by a *kernel* in surface structure—the basic declarative sentence such as:

John frightens Mary.

This basic structure can be *transformed* into seven other surface structures, all representing the same kernel:

Mary is frightened by John.
John doesn't frighten Mary.
Does John frighten Mary?
Mary isn't frightened by John.
Doesn't John frighten Mary?
Is Mary frightened by John?
Isn't Mary frightened by John?

These eight transformations, including the original sentence, constitute the basic patterns of English surface structure.

Semantics

Because deep structure cannot be observed directly, it is difficult to discover precisely how meanings are combined into sentences and again how sentences are "decoded" for meaning by the listener. This problem of relating meaning to surface structure is the problem of *semantics*.

semantics

Several psychologists have devised ingenious methods for demonstrating how we infer deep structure from surface structure. Collins and Quillian (1969) conducted a study based on the notion that certain concepts are stored in memory along with some of their most salient properties, called *markers*. Their approach was to measure the times respondents required to search their memories for answers to different kinds of questions (see Fig. 8.5). Here is one sequence of such questions:

Is a canary yellow?
Does a canary have wings?
Does a canary breathe?

The time required to answer questions such as the first one in this sequence was about 1.1 second. As the experimenters had already determined that it takes about 1 second simply to read the question and press a response button, they concluded that it took only about .1 second for respondents to scan their memories for the answer "yes" to the first question.

The participants took about 1.18 seconds to answer questions such as "Does a canary have wings?"—almost twice as much time for "memory search" as they had required for the first question. Collins and Quillian had thus correctly hypothesized that the marker "yellow" is stored with "canary" in memory and thus can be recovered almost immediately. The marker "wings," however, appears to be stored with the more general concept "bird." Respondents had first to search their memories for markers stored with "canary"; having failed to find

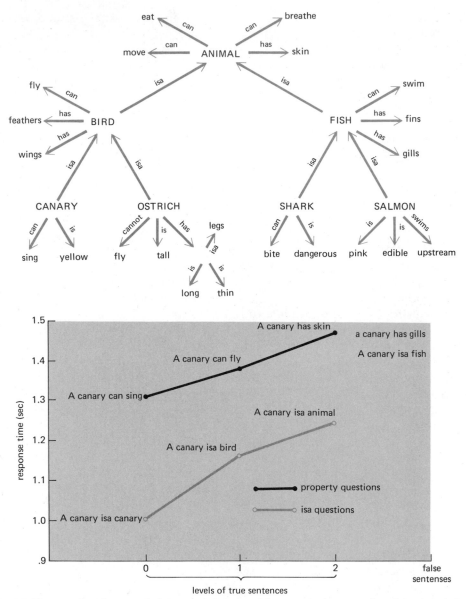

Fig. 8.5 The reaction time needed to respond true or false to questions as a function of their level of storage in memory. (Collins and Quillian, 1969)

the correct one, they then moved to the next level of generality, "bird." The necessity for searching two memory levels accounts for the additional time required.

The third type of question required respondents to search still a third level of memory, for "breathing" does not seem to be stored with either "canary" or "bird"; rather, it is stored with the broader concept "animal." Again subjects apparently scanned the lower two memory levels first, for answers to this kind of question required the most time of all. The experimenters found, in fact, that each level of memory searched adds about .1 second to the total response time.

A whole series of experiments of this kind is helping to fill in our picture of how concepts are semantically organized.

Language, then, has both form and meaning—a surface and a deep structure. To get from the one to the other requires certain cognitive operations, certain thought processes, which we are only just beginning to document. What is certain, however, is that language cannot exist without thought and so it is appropriate now to turn our attention to a brief survey of cognitive processes.

THE DEVELOPMENT OF THINKING

Brown Brothers

Plato

We have examined briefly how language is developed and structured, and we have taken a look at some of the ways in which "meaning" is studied. Now we turn to the larger question of cognitive development, of which acquiring and using language are only one part.

In recent decades the leading figure in the exploration of cognitive development has been the Swiss psychologist Jean Piaget. Through a long series of experimental studies, Piaget has developed an elaborate body of theory to explain how the basic thought processes evolve in children. We will examine only a few of his basic principles here; his ideas are developed at greater length in Chapter 11.

General Principles

D. Smith Collection, Columbia University

Rene Descartes

The nature of "mind" and of thought has been a matter of philosophical speculation and debate almost from the beginnings of recorded history. One line of thought, known as *nativism* and extending from the Greek philosopher Plato in the fourth century B.C. through the brilliant 17th century thinker Descartes, has tended to consider "ideas" as having an independent existence of their own. They are viewed as universals, "born" into every man and gradually revealed to him through the medium of critical experiences during his lifetime. Another line of thought—*empiricism*—whose foremost exponent was another 17th century figure, the Englishman John Locke, assumes that at birth the human mind is a *tabula rasa,* a blank tablet on which ideas are subsequently imprinted by life experiences. Distant echoes of these two traditions can still be recognized in modern psychological thought.

Almost 50 years ago Piaget undertook to resolve this question by means of detailed empirical studies of mental development in children. His interests

The Bettmann Archive, Inc.

John Locke

Jean Piaget

have led him to probe every aspect of mental development: intelligence, language, grasp of causation, acquisition of morality, and so on.

Piaget began with the fundamental assumption that mental growth results inevitably from the child's continuous interaction with his physical world. This interaction enables him progressively to increase his ability to handle the demands the world makes of him: each level of competence he achieves permits him to interact at a higher level than before and thus prepares him to take the next step. We have already seen an example of this kind of adaptation in our discussion of the acquisition of language. In an early developmental stage the child's interaction with his environment is reflected in his ability to imitate sounds made by others, which in turn prepares him to strive for a higher level of interaction: employing his ability to imitate, he learns the names of objects, which permits him to acquire concepts.

schema

The mechanism through which such continuous adaptation is manifest is the *schema*. Schemata are organized patterns of thought and activity that mediate the child's interactions with his world. They are highly flexible, continuously changing in scope, structure, and complexity as the child adapts to new environmental demands.

Although our discussion so far suggests that Piaget's thinking belongs to the empiricist tradition, in fact it is not purely empiricist, for he finds evidence for inherent elements in cognitive development. The power that "drives" the adaptation process is one of these elements; he believes that the motivation to think and act at ever higher levels of complexity is "born" into human beings and that it functions in its "own right," rather than merely reflecting biological drives such as hunger, self-preservation, and sex.

The parallel between Chomsky's deep structure in language and Piaget's schemata underlying behavior is striking; in fact, much of Piaget's work and that of other students of cognitive development is based on a structural approach similar to that of the psycholinguists.

Developmental Stages

Piaget has found that different types of schemata dominate the child's thinking at different stages of development. A detailed description of these stages and the accompanying schemata is presented in Chapter 11, as part of a general treatment of cognitive development. Here we are concerned only with a very broad view of Piaget's notions about how thinking develops.

sensorimotor
period

Sensorimotor Period   At birth and for some time afterward the infant's mental organization consists only of some inborn reflex responses such as sucking and grasping. Gradually, throughout the first 2 years of life, these responses bring aspects of his environment to his attention. For example, in grasping his rattle he may notice that it makes an interesting noise. He begins to seek out such new and interesting stimulation, playing with anything he can reach and with his own body.

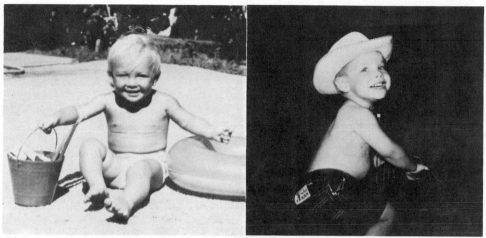

In the sensorimotor period the child explores and plays with all objects within his reach. By the time he is 2 or 3, in the period of preoperational thought, he likes to "make believe."

At this stage the infant learns the boundaries of his own body and comes to recognize that he is separate from his environment and the objects in it. He also comes to understand the integrity of objects; that is, he learns that his teddy bear is the same object whether he sees it upside down or right-side up, beside him in his crib or across the room. At the same time, the child learns that his teddy bear continues to exist even when he cannot see it, thus making it possible for him to look for it and for other objects that are out of sight when he wants them.

Preoperational Thought The period of preoperational thought consists of two phases, lasting approximately from 2 to 4 and 4 to 7 years of age respectively. This entire stage is notable for the child's rapid development in symbolic activities. We have already seen that one aspect of this rapid growth is the child's great strides in the acquisition of grammatical rules, beginning at about 2 years of age. But the child also plays with symbols other than words, "making believe" that one object is another, for example. He may crawl under a table and pretend that it is his "house." Many children imagine playmates, with whom they carry on lively conversations. But the child recognizes the difference between symbol and object.

preoperational thought

Characteristic of this period is the egocentric quality of the child's view of his world. He can understand objects and events only in relation to himself. He knows his teddy bear is a single, unchanging object, but when he looks at it from the front, he is unable to describe its profile. To him any object *is* what *he* sees at that moment.

The main accomplishment of the second phase in the preoperational period is acquisition of the principle of *conservation*. The best illustration of this principle is Piaget's famous "lemonade study." When a 5-year-old child is

conservation

Pedestrians have the right of way as schoolchildren in Helsinki, Finland, learn the symbols that give them the rules of the road.

shown two identical tumblers containing equal amounts of lemonade, he recognizes that each glass contains the same amount. But when the lemonade from one tumbler is poured into a taller, thinner tumbler, the 5-year-old will say that the taller one holds more lemonade, even though he has watched the pouring operation. He is relying solely on the perceptual cue of height as a criterion for what is "more" and what is "less." At 6 years of age he will be uncertain about which glass holds more, but by the age of 7 he will have grasped the principle of conservation as it applies to this problem: when a change in the tumbler's height is compensated for by a change in its width, the volume of liquid is *conserved*. The child will recognize that the amounts of lemonade in the two tumblers are equal, that the underlying reality has not changed. He does not yet apply the conservation principle to all problems, however. The conservation of weight is the most difficult for him to master. Even an 8-year-old will probably fail to realize that changing the shape of a piece of clay from a long cylinder to a compact ball does not make it heavier.

concrete operation

Concrete Operations Mastery of conservation forms the bridge between the periods of preoperational and concrete operational thought. The concrete operational child knows in advance that water will be higher in a narrower vessel and also realizes that it *has* to be; he has grasped the principle of "necessary truth."

Another example of the child's progress is his new-found ability to add and multiply classes of objects. If he is shown a collection of stuffed animals with two groups of dogs and one group of kittens, he will not only be able to report the number of animals in each subgroup but he can also give the total number of dogs and the total number of animals.

Yet the child at this stage is still limited in his ability to cope with the world. He can deal only with specific, concrete situations and objects. While he can classify blocks according to shape and color and follow the rules for childhood games, he cannot apply the principles he has mastered from these situations to tackle new problems. Every situation he meets is separate and distinct from all others.

Formal Operations With adolescence the final stage of cognitive development arrives. The child begins to be able to think hypothetically, to imagine principles of operation.

formal operation

With this mastery of the formal level of abstraction the ability to experiment and think scientifically appears. The arena for much of this kind of thinking is, of course, the school. It is in the late elementary-school years that more advanced mathematical operations, dependent upon clear understanding of certain abstract numerical relations, can be introduced.

The Sequence of Stages

The actual ages at which individual children pass through these developmental stages vary widely, but Piaget is convinced that the stages themselves always follow the sequence we have outlined. A considerable body of experimental evidence supports his conviction, as far as Western societies are concerned. But in some non-Western societies it appears that, though the basic stages of cognitive development follow this pattern, the order in which schemata are acquired *within* a given stage may be somewhat different (Hyde, cited in Flavell, 1963).

Psychologists, noting both the apparent stability of the developmental sequence and the wide variation in ages at which the successive stages are attained, have been led to ask whether or not cognitive development can be speeded up by means of special training. A number of studies have been designed to explore this possibility, but so far the results have been inconclusive.

Several points in the development of thinking and language are often forgotten. First, as Piaget emphasized, the cognitive development of the child reflects *both* a process of neurological maturation characteristic of all human beings *and* a continuous interaction with a specific environment. Failure to fulfill the child's potential may come from either an impoverished environment, which will impair the child's cognitive development, or from mental retardation, which even the most stimulating environment cannot completely compensate for.

Second, Piaget is describing the *capacities,* not the *abilities,* of children within a broad framework. What it is within the child to do is not necessarily

Research on Piaget's Concepts

Much research has been concerned with the best known of Piaget's theories, that of the inevitably successive stages of cognitive development. An early study (Piaget and Inhelder, 1941) established the generality of the developmental transition from nonconservation to conservation of substance and weight. Furthermore, these data seem to indicate that conservation of substance invariably precedes conservation of weight. When sugar was melted in a glass of water, children with conservation of substance but not of weight asserted that the melted sugar was still there (conservation of substance), but that the glass with sugar would have the same weight as a glass of pure water.

Piaget (1950, 1957) holds that a child's thinking is not at first logical, but that logic develops as a function of the child's activity and experiences. This point of view differs sharply from learning theory, in that it attributes learning not to external reinforcement but to the mutual influence of the child's activities on one another. Logical inferences are not derived from the characteristics of the external world but from a reformulation of the previous activities of the subject so that they are seen in a different way.

Smedslund (1959) designed a study to examine Piaget's theory of the development of logic by showing the effects of direct external reinforcement on acquisition of conservation and transitivity of weight. Three groups of nonconservers (children who had not yet mastered conservation of weight) were treated differently: (1) group A witnessed a series of 30 empirical demonstrations with a scale, permitting direct observation that objects do not change weight with changes in shape; (2) group B also witnessed 30 demonstrations with the scale, but 11 of the deformed items were exchanged for items to which material was added or subtracted; (3) group C, the controls, were given no practice sessions.

It was thought that if the learning theory interpretation was correct group A should learn faster than group B since A experienced only direct reinforcement of a single response. On the other hand, if Piaget was correct group B could be expected to do better since it had experienced the operations of addition and subtraction, which are assumed to lie beneath the concept of conservation.

No significant difference was found between groups A and B, but group A did slightly better. This result would seem to favor a learning explanation—that the concept of conservation of weight may be acquired as a function of external reinforcement. Smedslund, however, reasoned that pseudoconservation had taken place: the children had learned a response in a particular situation that they would not be able to apply in a different situation.

what the child can do, unless he has learned the necessary skills. A seesaw can be used to test for concrete operational and formal operational stages of development only if the child is familiar with a seesaw.

Finally, though the general principles of Piaget's thought have been validated, we still know too little about the relative importance of innate and environmental elements in cognitive development. An example that has been too little explored is the curious similarity of Piaget's stages to current Western concepts of child rearing, a cultural habit that is certainly not the same for all cultures and periods. We cannot know, for example, how Piaget's stages of cognitive development would apply to an Elizabethan child, who was treated as a "little adult." As we have seen and will see time and time again, like fish in the sea we cannot "see" the element, watery or cultural, in which we swim. What is innate—a part of human nature—to us or to Piaget may be, to a visitor from a different civilization, a product of the peculiar culture we live in.

And so, having looked briefly at the development of language and of thinking, let us go on to consider the nature of mature thinking and problem solving.

PROBLEM SOLVING AND CREATIVE THINKING

Often when we encounter a problem we rely on our memories of how we have handled similar situations in the past. But for some problems there are no precedents in our experience; solutions depend upon *creative,* or *productive,* thinking (Wertheimer, 1945). Both kinds of problem solving reflect *realistic thinking,* reasoning guided largely by the demands of the objective situation. In contrast to this kind of reasoning is *autistic thinking,* which is determined primarily by our subjective needs and wishes. (We will see a similar division of thinking in Freud's distinction between the *primary* and *secondary processes* in Chapter 12.) Of course, realistic and autistic thinking rarely occur in pure form; most thinking contains elements of both, though one or the other usually predominates. In this section we will be concerned only with the kind of realistic thinking that is responsible for innovative problem solving.

Experience, of course, has a positive effect upon our ability to solve problems when we can draw directly upon it to find similar problems in our past. But when innovative thinking is required, experience may be a hindrance more than a help. Our *habits*—products of experience—may prevent us from finding new and better solutions to problems, Hammering, for example, is done by using hammers—our habits tell us so. But if delicate work is required and all we have is a large household hammer, we will be well-advised to break out of our habit and recognize that a smaller object will better produce the light taps that are required.

An aspect of habit is *set* (or in German, *Einstellung*), which describes the way the individual prepares to receive a particular stimulus. A simple example of set would be to spell the following words aloud to a friend and ask him each time to pronounce them: MacBeth, MacDonald, MacTavish, machine. The way he will almost certainly pronounce the last word is obvious.

An allied effect of experience—indeed, some psychologists regard it as a type of set—is *functional fixedness,* which prevents us from perceiving new

productive thinking

autistic thinking

set

functional fixedness

Wertheimer's Productive Thinking Problems

On the basis of his experiments with young children, Wertheimer (1945, 1959) asserts that productive thinking is the exception rather than the rule. Wertheimer believes that the deficiency in productive thinking is mainly the product of poor teaching methods that have sought to ensure "correct thinking" by insisting on precise definitions, exact judgment, and carefully formulated concepts. Wertheimer finds this approach limited and empty because it fosters blind repetition of sets of rules. When the child is faced with a variation of a problem studied under such a system, he is unable to solve it even though it involves the same basic procedures.

To exemplify his argument Wertheimer investigated the technique employed to teach students how to find the area of a parallelogram. The procedure was as follows: (1) the teacher reviewed the process for finding the area of a rectangle (base × altitude), (2) a parallelogram was drawn, (3) perpendicular lines AB and CD and the extension BE were drawn,

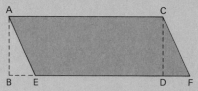

and (4) it was shown that the area of a parallelogram AEFC is equal to the area of the rectangle ABCD. The parallelogram had been transformed into a rectangle.

Following this demonstration, students had no difficulty in solving a variety of similar problems. But when a new situation such as the following

was presented, many of them refused to attempt a solution, saying that they had never been exposed to this sort of problem; others attempted illogical or incorrect solutions such as

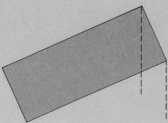

Wertheimer argues that what is lacking is a knowledge of the inner relationship between the size of the area and the form of the figure. If we take a rectangle and subdivide it into squares, the squares are immediately organized into an integrated whole. Wertheimer points out that the solution becomes meaningful in terms of the relationship between area and form. The student can now find the area by totaling the number of squares.

Wertheimer found that children with no training in geometry were able, after learning the squares method of obtaining the area of a rectangle, to find the areas of parallelograms and trapezoids with little difficulty. He noted that all the geometric solutions arrived at involved structural changes or transformations of the original figure.

As a result of his investigation Wertheimer formulated a theory of productive thinking. He began by summarizing his general finding. First, productive thinking is a natural way to think that has been discouraged by the pedagogic methods used in most schools. Second, the processes employed by his subjects, such as "grouping," "centering," and "reorganization," had not been recognized by logicians and associationists in their analysis of thought processes. Third, productive solutions were not perceived as a group of part solutions but were grasped as wholes with a "structural truth."

Wertheimer emphasizes that thinking cannot be a purely intellectual process but is rather a process in which feeling, attitude, and emotion play a significant role. There must be a willingness to adopt an honest and sincere attitude and to take cognizance of the demands of the situation rather than a blind egocentric view.

In summary, then, productive thinking involves a grasp of the inner structural relationship of the problem, followed by a grouping of the parts into a dynamic whole.

and useful ways of using objects to which a specific function has been attached by habit and tradition. Adamson (1952) showed this effect. He provided his subjects with candles, thumbtacks, and matches, which were in small cardboard boxes. The subjects were asked to mount the candles on a vertical screen, using only what he had given them.

Only 41 percent of the subjects were able to solve the problem by breaking out of the functional fixedness of perceiving the boxes as containers only, instead of potential stands, which could be attached to the screen by the thumbtacks and upon which the candles could be mounted by melted wax. If, however, the items were displayed separately, and the boxes were not presented as containers for the other items, the percentage of successful solutions went up to 86 percent. Thus with some direction, subjects were able to structure the problem in their own minds and start thinking along lines that would lead to a solution.

Insight

Wolfgang Köhler

As we saw in Chapter 3, Thorndike's experimental cats managed to escape from their box only after a long process of trial and error. Thorndike nevertheless concluded that they had "solved" their "problem." Gestalt psychologist Wolfgang Köhler objected to Thorndike's conclusion, on grounds that true problem solving cannot be said to have occurred without the kind of planning and foresight characteristic of realistic thinking. As Thorndike's experiments were designed so that the cats could not see the release mechanism that would have opened the doors for them, they could not "figure out" a solution but had to go through a long period of random activity before they finally stumbled on the means of escape.

Köhler himself designed a series of experiments with chimpanzees (1926) in which all the elements necessary for solution to the problem were in full view of the animals. His findings confirmed his argument that the arrangement of elements necessary to a solution largely determines whether or not that solution will be reached (Fig. 8.6).

After experience with sticks as play tools, the chimpanzee is able to solve the problem of how to get the food within reach. (Photo courtesy Yerkes Primate Center of Emory University.)

We cannot, however, dismiss learning entirely from the achievement of insight. This was demonstrated by Birch (1945), who placed food beyond the reach of chimpanzees, and a hoe, with which they could rake in the food, inside the cage. Apes who had played with short sticks and were familiar with their use as play tools for digging, pushing, and so on, solved the problem fairly easily but animals without this experience found it too difficult. We are reminded of Harlow's experiments in which monkeys "learned to learn" (Chapter 5).

insight

The experience of sudden insight is also familiar to human beings; it is frequently called the *"aha" experience,* for obvious reasons. But some psychologists have doubted that *all* creative problem solving is necessarily as sudden as some experiments imply. Karl Duncker (1945) concluded that problem solving most frequently consists of a series of progressively more specific formulations of the problem, each arising from the one before it and partly shaped by it. Such

 Duncker's Tumor Problem

Karl Duncker's (1945) studies of problem solving sought to reveal the essential nature of the thought process. His most noted study posed the following question: Given an inoperable stomach tumor and a ray that at high intensities would destroy both healthy and diseased tissue, how can the tumor be destroyed without damaging the surrounding tissue?

He presented this problem to college students and found that their responses fell into a number of stages. First was the discovery of the "general or essential properties of a solution." At this stage, the problem is reformulated in a goal-oriented direction. One response made at this level of problem solving was: desensitize the healthy tissue or decrease the intensity of the rays on the way to the tumor. Since proposals at this stage are generally impractical, the subject continues to formulate solutions that are still broad but are more in the realm of genuine solutions as opposed to mere reformulations of the problem. These solutions Duncker classified as "solutions with functional value." Then out of the functional solutions the subject develops specific solutions, one of which is acceptable—for example, focusing the rays on the tumor by means of a lens. (This idea is only correct in principle, however, because X-rays are not deflected by lenses.) Another is to use several weaker ray beams converging on the tumor from different directions. They would be intense where they intersected but elsewhere weak enough not to harm healthy tissue.

Of course not every student clearly progressed through all three stages during the course of problem solving, nor did each come up with the same functional and specific solutions. But Duncker argues that however primitive the solutions offered, they were not given "in terms of meaningless blind trial and error reactions."

Problem solving consists of related but progressively more specific solutions to reformulations of the problem. A key word here is *reformulations,* for every meaningful answer is a response to a reformulation of the original problem.

a series can be considered to have three main parts. In the first stage, or *general range,* the person reformulates the problem in such a way as to suggest the direction in which a solution might lie. In the next stage a *functional solution* is achieved. The person narrows the range to the point at which he can say: when *X* is achieved the problem will be solved. Finally, in the *specific solution,* the person hits on a way to achieve *X* and thus has solved the problem. If this solution is not satisfactory, he returns to one of the two earlier stages and resumes the process until finally he hits upon a solution that is satisfactory.

Creative Thinking

Creativity can be defined as the production of something which is novel and which is evaluated by recognized judges to be socially desirable and significant. Psychologists are generally agreed that a solution is novel if it is new to the person who arrives at it; it does not matter that other people may have already reached the same solution, as long as the person arrives at it independently. There is less agreement, however, on how creativity can be measured in precise terms. And unless we can measure creativity and compare the scores obtained, we can draw few scientifically valid conclusions about it.

One of the most satisfactory tests of creativity that has been developed so far is Mednick's Remote Associations Test (1962), which is based on the notion that the unique or unusual (novel) response that also fulfills specific criteria imposed by the problem (appropriateness) is an index of creativity.

Another way to approach creativity is to study the characteristics of people who are considered to be creative. This kind of research is based on the

Sarnoff A. Mednick

   Chimpanzees and Language Development

In the last 40 years several attempts have been made to teach language to animals. There is no doubt that animals are able to communicate to each other, for example, about the distance and direction of food and about mating and danger situations by inborn, unlearned signals emitted either vocally or nonvocally. But this kind of communication is not to be confused with language, which is an arbitrary set of symbols that occurs in an order specified by certain rules. Furthermore, language can be used without any specific reference to the immediate environment. It may also be inappropriate or wrong, in that the communication may be misunderstood. Animals, on the other hand, do not make mistakes in their mating signals and do not communicate about yesterday's food or all of the dangers that may lie ahead. Communication is one of the uses of language, and language is one of the media through which communication may take place; but language and communication are not identical.

One effort to teach language to an animal was made by Hayes and Hayes (1951), who attempted to develop language ability in an infant chimpanzee named

Vicki. This couple focused on speech training, actually shaping the chimp's lips in an attempt to get her to produce the appropriate sounds. After three years, Vicki could utter only three recognizable words—*Mama, Papa,* and *cup.*

The most successful attempt to date has been made by another husband and wife team, Gardner and Gardner (1969). This couple started with the premise that previous attempts had failed because the chimpanzee's vocal apparatus is not well adapted to the production of human speech patterns. They reasoned that American Sign Language, a language taught to deaf people, might be more appropriate since chimpanzees are dexterous with their hands. Training was begun when Washoe, a female chimp, was 1 year old, and it has continued now for 8 years. Washoe lives in a pleasant environment equipped with children's toys and an outdoor play area. In her presence, only sign language is used. At age 4, when the Gardners published their report, Washoe could use about 85 signs; she had learned such concepts as *dog, cat, open* (as a command or request), *sweet,* and many others.

At first these signs were taught by shaping natural responses the chimp made into a useful sign. For example, when Washoe wanted to get through a door she would pound on it with open palms. When she put her open palms on the door, the Gardners would take her hands and position them, palms down, side by side, then move them apart while turning the palms up. This is the sign for *open.* Washoe was able to generalize the *open* sign to other doors and even to various kinds of containers and to faucets. What she could not do, however, was initiate language behavior herself. Most 2-year-old infants show an active interest in objects in their environment and continually demand to know, "What's that?" Washoe did not show this kind of behavior at age 4. She also was not able to combine signs in any sort of consistent sequence, though she did combine signs meaningfully. A 2-year-old child is able to use correct noun-verb order consistently, but Washoe was just as likely to say "Open you" as "You open."

Comparisons are difficult because word order is less fixed in sign language than in English and because Washoe's "parents," though they know sign language well, cannot consider it their first language. Washoe's abilities may have improved considerably since she was 4 years old, and if they haven't, another chimp raised solely with deaf-mutes might master sign language as well as his human companions. Obviously this is an area for much broader investigation and one that would combine great pleasure, at least for animal lovers, with a very real scientific contribution: information about the peculiarly human aspect of human language development.

assumption that creative people share certain consistent patterns of personality traits. One characteristic that we might suppose to be important in creativity is intelligence, but surprisingly, there is considerable evidence that, within fairly high-intelligence groups, there is very little apparent correlation between intelligence and creativity.

Independence of mind is a characteristic widely believed to distinguish creative people. Being less concerned about what others think of him, the creative person feels freer to let his thinking range over a wider field of possibilities

How Some Famous People Solve Problems

Since our understanding of the creative process is still somewhat limited, we must bring to bear any data that are available. One interesting source of information is firsthand accounts of creative people. Here are often-quoted statements made by three famous and highly creative people: Poincaré, a mathematician; Mozart, a musician; and A. E. Housman, a poet (see Ghiselin, 1952).

It is time to penetrate deeper and to see what goes on in the very soul of the mathematician. For this, I believe, I can do best by recalling memories of my own. But I shall limit myself to telling how I wrote my first memoir on Fuchsian functions.... This theorem will have a barbarous name, unfamiliar to many, but that is unimportant; what is of interest for the psychologist is not the theorem but the circumstances.

For fifteen days I strove to prove that there could not be any functions like those I have since called Fuchsian functions. I was then very ignorant; every day I seated myself at my work table, stayed an hour or two, tried a great number of combinations and reached no results. One evening, contrary to my custom, I drank black coffee and could not sleep. Ideas rose in crowds; I felt them collide until pairs interlocked, so to speak, making a stable combination. By the next morning I had established the existence of a class of Fuchsian functions, those which come from the hypergeometric series; I had only to write out the results, which took but a few hours. (p. 25)

When I am, as it were, completely myself, entirely alone, and of good cheer—say, traveling in a carriage, or walking after a good meal, or during the night when I cannot sleep; it is such occasions that my ideas flow best and most abundantly. Whence and how they come, I know not; nor can I force them. Those ideas that please me I retain in memory, and am accustomed, as I have been told, to hum them to myself. If I continue in this way, it soon occurs to me how I may turn this or that morsel to account, so as to make a good dish of it, that is to say, agreeably to the rules of counterpoint, to the peculiarities of the various instruments, etc.

All this fires my soul, and provided I am not disturbed, my subject enlarges itself, becomes methodised and defined, and the whole, though it be long, stands almost complete and finished in my mind, so that I can survey it, like a fine picture or a beautiful statue, at a glance. Nor do I hear in my imagination the parts successively, but I hear them, as it were, all at once....

When I proceed to write down my ideas, I take out of the bag of my memory, if I may use that phrase, what has been previously collected into it in the way I have mentioned. (pp. 34–35)

Having drunk a pint of beer at luncheon—beer is a sedative to the brain, and my afternoons are the least intellectual portion of my life—I would go out for a walk of two or three hours. As I went along, thinking of nothing in particular, only looking at things around me and following the progress of the seasons, there would flow into my mind, with a sudden and unaccountable emotion, sometimes a line or two of verse, sometimes a whole stanza at once, accompanied, not preceded, by a vague notion of the poem which they were destined to form part of. Then there would usually be a lull of an hour or so, then perhaps the spring would bubble up again. I say bubble up, because, so far as I could make out, the source of the suggestions thus proffered to the brain was an abyss which have I already had occasion to mention, the pit of the stomach. When I got home I wrote them down, leaving gaps, and hoping that further inspiration might be forthcoming another day. (Housman, 1933, p. 48–49)

(including some that are "taboo") and to put forward original ideas, even when they are unpopular or seem ridiculous to other people.

Recently Dellas and Gaier (1970) have shown that interest, attitudes, and drives seem to be more consistent predictors of creativity than is intelligence.

Wallach and Kogan (1965) make a strong case for considering creativity as an aspect of thinking that is quite different from general intelligence. They point out that if tests of creativity are removed from the timed, classroom atmosphere of the group intelligence test, the scores of different creativity "tests" correlate more closely with each other than with intelligence tests.

INFORMATION PROCESSING AND THINKING—COMPUTER MODELS

So far most efforts to explain complex cognitive processes such as problem solving and creativity have been unsatisfactory. Theories based on learned associations and stimulus-response patterns do not account for the highly integrated nature of cognitive processes, with their subtle cross connections, multiple levels, and flexibility. Such theories are especially weak in that they offer no sound explanations of innovative thinking, which departs from previously learned associations.

Other theories are more descriptive than explanatory. Köhler observed subjects experiencing insight, but was not able to explain how and why it happens. Nor did Duncker isolate the basic cognitive processes underlying his three-stage model of problem solving.

A recent approach, based on a computer model of information processing, is generating a great deal of exciting new research on human thinking. This new approach is the direct outgrowth of the boom in computer processing that began in the early 1950s. A computer is used to solve problems; a *program* directs it to retrieve certain information stored in its memory bank and how to manipulate this and new information in order to reach solutions to specified problems.

Psychologists were quick to recognize the similarities between certain elements in this kind of information processing and in human thinking. The outcome has been many information processing models of human behavior, on the assumption that a machine that can accurately simulate the important aspects of a person's behavior provides a genuine explanation of that behavior. If we can program a computer so that it solves problems just as we would, then we can say that the program embodies the principles of human problem solving. This assumption is not acceptable by itself. Achieving the same answers from the same input as a human being would does not prove that the computer and the human arrived at the answers by the same steps, yet such agreement is often a good starting place.

Concepts

From our description of the computer it is clear that its performance as a problem solver depends heavily upon the program that "instructs" it. Information—stimuli, data, instructions for processing—constitutes the input of the computer; it is generally fed into the system in the form of punched cards. The person who devises the program must thus first break down the problem into its smallest components, in order to overlook no area in which confusion might arise. One of the best ways to design a program is to begin by constructing a *flow chart*. Fig. 8.7 is an example of the kind of flow chart that might be used when the problem is to calculate the average of a series of numbers. Once the problem has been broken down in this way, the programer writes a set of detailed instructions for the handling of each component. These instructions constitute the actual program.

The input to the computer is then processed through a series of steps corresponding to the "stations" shown on the flow chart. The *output* of the computer, usually printed on paper or displayed on a cathode-ray tube, is a solution to the problem.

Inspection of the flow chart will show one important characteristic of computers: each step—particularly each decision step—is extremely simple, and it is the addition of these steps and the speed with which they operate that

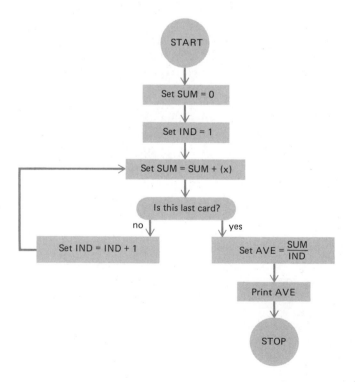

Fig. 8.7 A flow chart depicting the steps in a hypothetical computer program designed to calculate the average of a series of numbers. Each number to be processed is presented on a keypunched card. SUM stands for a memory cell of the computer which is being used as a temporary working space. IND stands for the index number which tells how many cards have been added. The computer is instructed to read the number (x) from each card in the stack, increasing IND by 1 each time it does so. When the last card in the series has been processed, the computer averages the numbers (dividing SUM by IND) and prints out the result (AVE). (Ruch and Zimbardo, 1971)

makes the computer valuable. Someone has defined a computer as "a crowd of very quick idiots with good memories"; this facetious definition captures one aspect of these instruments.

Computer "Intelligence"?

Since the Logic Theorist (LT) many other simulation models have been constructed to duplicate such aspects of human cognitive behavior as attitude change, verbal learning, and even neurotic personality processes. But all these models are limited to simulating only certain aspects of such behavior. Simon and Newell (1964), observing that all the models nevertheless have a great many component processes in common, incorporated these processes into the design of their General Problem Solver (GPS). As a single model designed to simulate the entire apparatus of human intelligence, the GPS incorporates a great many concepts, heuristics, and strategies that are believed to underlie human problem solving and other cognitive processes. The most exciting implication of this model is that, to the degree that it approximates the total complex of human cognitive behavior, the GPS provides a *general theory* of such behavior.

Herbert A. Simon

The GPS treats each problem it deals with as a difference between two states, which may be designated A and B. State B is the desired goal and state A is what actually exists. To solve the problem, A must be made identical to B. To accomplish this end, the *features* of the two states are analyzed and the *differences* between them are detected by a matching procedure. If A is not identical to B, a series of transformation procedures, called *operators,* alters the features of A. Each new state of A is checked against B until all the differences have been removed. A "solution" to the problem therefore consists of a sequence of operators that render the existing state identical to the goal state.

To show the analogy between the operation of the GPS and real-life human problem-solving situations, Newell, Shaw, and Simon (1960) cite the following illustration.

> I want to take my son to nursery school. What's the difference between what I have and what I want? One of distance. What changes distance? My automobile. My automobile won't work. What's needed to make it work? A new battery. What has new batteries? An auto repair shop. I want the repair shop to put in a new battery; but the shop doesn't know I need one. What is the difficulty? One of communication. What allows communication? A telephone. . . . And so on. (p. 259)

The steps involved in solving the problem "getting the son to nursery school" are categorized by the authors as follows:

> 1. If an object is given that is not the desired one, differences will be detectable between the available object and the desired object.
> 2. Operators affect some features of their operands and leave others unchanged. Hence operators can be characterized by the changes they produce and can be used to try to eliminate differences between the objects to which they are applied and desired objects.

3. Some differences will prove more difficult to affect than others. It is profitable, therefore, to try to eliminate "difficult" differences, even at the cost of introducing new differences of lesser difficulty. This process can be repeated as long as progress is being made toward eliminating the more difficult differences. (p. 259)

To the extent that this analysis reflects the true structure of human problem solving, the GPS mimics the human course of action.

One interesting and possibly important recent development in computer simulation is a program for chess playing that can "take advice" (Zobrist and Carlson, 1973). Patterns of chess pieces not tied to a particular place on the board (except when the place—for example, near the edge—is important) have negative or positive values attached to them, describing their usefulness or danger to the computer's game. These represent the bits of "advice," and each bit can be taught to the computer in about 5 minutes. The computer, whenever it has to move, takes a series of "snapshots" of the board, compares them with the bits of advice, and evaluates alternative moves. After each game the computer plays, it is analyzed by a chess master and more bits of advice are given to the machine, thereby improving its subsequent games. There is apparently no limit to the advice it can be given, and of course its memory for the advice is infallible.

How much have simulation models actually contributed to our understanding of complex cognitive processes? The best answer to this question has been supplied by Newell and Simon (1963), the builders of both LT and GPS:

The first thing we have learned—and the evidence is by now quite substantial—is that we can explain many of the processes of human thinking without postulating mechanisms at subconscious levels which are different from those that are partly conscious and partly verbalized. The processes of problem solving, it is turning out, are the familiar processes of noticing, searching, modifying the search direction on the basis of clues, and so on. The same symbol-manipulating processes that participate in these functions are also sufficient for such problem-solving techniques as abstracting and using imagery. It looks more and more as if problem solving is accomplished through complex structures of familiar simple elements. The growing proof is that we can simulate problem solving in a number of situations using no more than these simple elements as the building blocks of our programs. (p. 402)

Allen Newell

Simulation Models

simulation model Information processing systems designed to duplicate aspects of the cognitive activities of human beings are called *simulation models.* The first major program of this type, the Logic Theorist (LT), was developed by Newell and Simon in 1958. The task was to find proofs for logical theorems; in one test the LT was able to prove 38 of the first 52 theorems in Whitehead and Russell's *Principia Mathematica* (1925).

heuristics Besides instructions for problem solving, the LT incorporated several *heuristics.* Heuristics are shortcuts, gimmicks, rules of thumb, and the like, commonly used by human beings to cut down the amount of material they must scan in order to find appropriate answers. For example, a chess player does not have to consider all possible moves; rather, he need choose only among those that satisfy certain criteria determined by his own "game strategy" and his opponent's attack. Another common heuristic, also incorporated into the LT, is "working backward," from what seem likely alternative answers (perhaps chosen intuitively) to the problem itself, then determining whether or not any of the alternatives can be deduced from the initial information given. This procedure involves considerably less effort than might be required in the laborious working through of all the theoretical possibilities that arise at each stage in the chain of deduction.

The LT was so successful a simulation that it even exhibited sudden "insights" and could also apply the solution of one theorem to subsequent problems. This success in simulating one aspect of intelligent human behavior has naturally raised the question whether or not computers themselves are "intelligent," a question that has aroused a great deal of controversy.

SUMMARY

Language and thought cannot be treated separately because, as humans, once we have language, most of our thinking makes use of it. Words, the basic units of language, and concepts, the basic units of thought, are indistinguishable. Both language and thought consist essentially of the manipulation of symbols.

The symbols human beings use in thinking are images and concepts. Images are most frequently pictures, or visual inputs, but they may come from other sensory channels as well. Images play a very much smaller role in most people's thinking than does language, which permits us to think at higher levels of complexity and abstraction.

Language also permits us to think in terms of concepts, or representations of connections among things or events. Concepts enable us to reduce stimuli to categories. Concrete concepts, for adults as for children, are more easily acquired than abstract ones. We acquire concepts by abstracting the properties common to a given class of items, by analyzing what the concept must be from the context or contexts in which it is used, and by defining the concept in other words.

The acquisition of concepts is dependent upon the acquisition of language and on cognitive development in general. The infant is restricted to cries and grunts, which are not "language" at all, until, by means of exercising it, he develops his vocal apparatus to the point where he can babble. Babbling is first spontaneous, then syllabic; later, words begin to be uttered, though without regard for their meanings. When the child begins to imitate, he also begins to acquire the basic grammatical rules of his language. In this stage of language development, he proceeds from two-word sentences to more and more complex and mature statements.

Learning theories of language acquisition fail to account for the uniformity of language patterns in a culture, for the sharp break between the babbling stage and the purposeful imitation of sounds, and for the ability to use familiar language in novel and meaningful ways.

Opposed to learning theories of language acquisition are structural theories, which argue that the capacity for linguistic structure—like the capacities for other cognitive processes—is innate. Structuralists contend that what the child learns or acquires are rules for generating sentences in his language.

The basic units of language are the *phoneme,* the smallest recognizable unit of sound, and the *morpheme,* the smallest recognizable unit of meaning. Phonemes combine in certain limited ways to produce the morphemes of any given language, and, according to completely different sets of rules, morphemes combine to produce words, and words, sentences. Sentences that we actually speak or write have both a surface structure—what we hear or see—and a deep structure—a meaning, or what we understand. Chomsky's transformational grammar recognizes, for English, eight possible transformations of any given kernel sentence.

Semantics addresses the question of how we get from the surface to the deep structure of a sentence. One theory is that concepts are stored in memory along with their most salient properties, called markers. *Canary,* for example, is stored with the marker *yellow,* but to get to the marker *wings,* we have to call up the concept *bird,* and further, to get to the marker *breathing,* we must call up the concept *animal.*

In this century Jean Piaget has attempted to resolve the long-standing controversy between nativists and empiricists about the nature of "mind." Piaget's method has been to closely observe mental development in children. His results lead him to the belief that the child learns by interacting with his environment (empiricism), but that his motivation to do so is innate (nativism).

More important, however, than Piaget's general concept of the nature of mind is his finding of a fixed developmental sequence in all children: a sensorimotor stage, in which reflexes are fused into meaningful behavior patterns; a stage of preoperational thought, in which the capacity for symbolic activity develops; a stage of concrete operations, in which the concept of conservation is mastered and a number of operations are represented internally; and a stage of formal operations, in which the child learns to think hypothetically.

Problem solving frequently requires creative, realistic thinking. Sometimes past experience is helpful in finding the solution to a problem, but frequently the habits of thought—or sets—it has produced inhibit us. An example of a set is functional fixedness, which prevents us from finding new ways of using familiar objects.

The experience of "seeing" the solution to a problem is called insight, which does not always occur suddenly or even all at once. Problem solving is frequently a series of progressively more specific formulations of the question.

Most efforts to study creativity—the production of something novel that is also significant and valuable—use tests that attempt to measure this elusive quality. One test assumes that the ability to produce an unusual associative response that fulfills certain imposed criteria is an index of creativity. Another approach is to study creative people, assuming that they must share some consistent pattern of traits.

Recent information processing models of problem solving and creativity have seemed to offer better explanations of these aspects of complex thinking than earlier models. Information processing models are based on the breaking down of a problem to its smallest units of information and the devising of instructions for handling each piece of information.

SUGGESTED READINGS

Blumenthal, A. L., *Language and Psychology: Historial Aspects of Psycholinguistics*. New York, Wiley, 1970.
An historical view of the application of psychology to the understanding of language development.

Chomsky, Noam, *Language and Mind*. New York, Harcourt Brace Jovanovich, 1968.
A general introduction to Chomsky's transformational grammar.

Clarke, Arthur C., *2001: A Space Odyssey*.
A science fiction novel about a computer that is able to outperform most human feats of intellectual activity.

"Computer Helps Chimpanzees Learn To Read, Write and 'Talk' to Humans," *The New York Times*, May 29, 1974.
A report on the remarkable results obtained in recent efforts to teach chimps language skills with the aid of computers.

Farb, Peter, *Word Play*. New York, Knopf, 1974.
An entertaining introductory book on language and what happens when people talk.

Ferguson, Charles A., and Dan Isaac Slobin, *Studies of Child Language Development*. New York, Holt, Rinehart and Winston, 1972.
A collection of readings that investigate the ways in which children acquire speech.

Gardner, B. T., and R. A. Gardner, "Two-way Communication with an Infant Chimpanzee," in A. Schrier and F. Stollnitz, eds., *Behavior in Nonhuman Primates*. New York, Academic Press, 1971.
Describes the Gardners' efforts in communicating with a chimp.

Lenneberg, Eric H., *Biological Foundations of Language*. New York, Wiley, 1967.
A look at language from the point of view of biological and physiological functioning.

"TICIT and PLATO," *Science*, June 9, 1972.
A comparison of two quite different technical and social approaches to computer-assisted instruction.

Vygotsky, L. S., *Thought and Language*. Cambridge, Mass., MIT Press, 1969.
A classic treatment of the origins of thinking and language in children.

Chapter Nine

States of Consciousness

Are we ruled by the mind or by the body?
What is consciousness?
What is the unconscious?
Why do we dream?
What is the meaning of dreams?
What is it like to be hypnotized?
How can meditation produce an altered state of
    consciousness?
What are psychedelic drugs?

Crossing campus you are so preoccupied with thoughts about an imminent exam that you fail to notice that you are walking dangerously close to an active baseball game. The batter connects with the ball, and, as the runner takes third, the ball connects with your head. After a yowl that registers surprise and pain, you angrily throw the ball back to the players and hurry on your way.

Ordinary as this experience may seem, it represents a problem that has puzzled psychologists and philosophers alike for many years. The ball that hit you on the head was most definitely a physical object. In striking you, the ball produced feelings and emotions: surprise, pain, anger. These feelings and emotions do not seem to be either physical or material, yet they were caused by physical, material objects and may, in turn, affect physical objects—for example, your head.

THE MIND-BODY PROBLEM

Any discussion of the nature of consciousness inevitably leads to a consideration of the mind-body problem. Psychology has inherited this dilemma from the fields of natural science and philosophy, in which investigators have been grappling with it for more than 2500 years. Philosophers as early as Plato (fourth century B.C.) divided man into psychic and physical components and pondered the relationship between the two.

As well as being a legacy from other fields of study, the mind-body problem becomes a legitimate issue for psychology insofar as psychology proposes to be a science. As with any other science, psychology must establish concepts both about the physical nature of reality and the nature of causal relationships. In addressing itself to the mind-body problem psychology attempts to fulfill these epistemological obligations.

No one single solution to the mind-body problem is accepted as psychological fiat, and at this time there is no scientific method for choosing among the various solutions. Yet, the question is one that has stimulated much valuable thinking and that continues to ignite controversies among psychologists today.

The Introspectionists' Solution

Pioneer research psychologists Wundt and Titchener saw the work of psychology as analogous to the work of chemistry. Whereas the job of the chemist is to break down complex compounds into their basic elements, the work of the psychologists is to break down the human mind into elementary conscious experiences. For their laboratory the psychologists would have the human mind; for their subject matter, immediate experience; for their tools, they would use the methodology of introspective analysis. Once the nature of the basic elements of conscious experience was discovered, psychologists would explore, under controlled experimental conditions, the interconnections between these basic elements and attempt to state the laws regulating their interconnections (Titchener, 1899).

For their approach to a solution of the mind-body problem the introspectionists adopted the view of psychophysical parallelism. This position, originated by the philosopher Spinoza in 1665, maintains that mind and body are independent but parallel systems that do not directly interact. Thus, the mind is not dependent on the body and can be studied directly. This position was quite handy for the introspectionists because their method of research, as we have seen, depended on the direct and immediate study of mental processes.

The Behaviorists' Solution

Other psychologists, in particular the behaviorists, differed from the introspectionists both in their approach to, and their solution of, the mind-body problem. Led by the school's founder, J. B. Watson, the behaviorists concentrated their studies and observations on behavior, the observable actions and words of people. They did not concern themselves with introspective accounts of the contents of consciousness, finding them a poor basis on which to construct a science of psychology. In treating the mind-body problem the behaviorists maintained that the mental referent (or mind) did not really exist, but was merely a description of physical events. In this way, they reduced the mind-body dilemma to physical monism.

An example of this way of thinking is shown in Watson's idea that thought is reducible to fine motor movements of the vocal apparatus called "implicit" speech. While implicit speech has been shown to occur, the question of whether thought is totally reducible to these minute muscular contractions or whether these observed contractions are merely correlates of thought, is still under debate.

The Gestalt Psychologists' Solution

The Gestalt psychologists brought a new perspective to the field of psychology. Rather than breaking down processes and phenomena into constituent elements, the Gestaltists stubbornly insisted on looking at all things as wholes.

A central idea in Gestalt theory is the concept of isomorphism, a one-to-one relationship between two objects or processes: an identity of pattern between two objects or events. An example of isomorphism is the relationship between a road map and a road. An interstate highway may be designated on the map by a wide yellow line, distinguishing it from a country road, which is a thin pink line. In fact the interstate highway is wide, but it is not yellow. Similarly, the country road may be narrow, but it is not pink. The road and the road map have an isomorphic relationship to each other. While they are clearly not the same thing, the characteristics of one (such as turnings and width) may be read from the other.

For their solution to the mind-body problem the Gestalt psychologists adopted the principle of psychological isomorphism. According to this principle, an isomorphic relationship exists between subjective experience (particularly perceptual experience) and the chemical-electrical processes going on in the brain. Given this correspondence, it should be possible to take information learned about conscious experience (for the Gestaltists, specifically perceptual experience) and project it, forming a "map" of actual neurological processes.

psychological isomorphism

Semantic Solutions

Two other treatments of the mind-body problem are of special interest to psychology. The solutions used in both these approaches revolve around our use of language.

Gilbert Ryle and B. F. Skinner have suggested that the mind-body problem isn't a problem at all—it's a "pseudoproblem" created entirely through our use of language. Terms referring to mental states ("subjective" terms) are acquired

Gilbert Ryle

Implicit Speech

implicit speech

To explain thought, John B. Watson, the founder of behaviorism, reduced thinking to muscle movements. Thinking is merely implicit speech, involving the same muscle movements as explicit, overt speech, but to a lesser degree. "The behaviorist advances the view that what the psychologists have hitherto called thought is in short nothing but talking to ourselves. . . . My theory does hold that the muscular habits learned in overt speech are responsible for implicit or internal speech (thought)," hypothesized Watson (1930).

In order to test this notion a number of experiments have attempted to record muscle movements during relaxed thought. Jacobson (1932), for example, first trained subjects to relax and then took electromyographic readings (electrical recordings from muscle movements) of the right elbow while they were imagining performing certain tasks. Fig. 9.1 shows for one subject the contrast in muscle movements between imagining lifting a weight with his right arm and imagining lifting it with his left arm.

Another interesting experiment in this realm was performed by Edfelt (1960) who took electromyographic (EMG) recordings of laryngeal movements from college students who were given either difficult or easy prose to read. Edfelt also classified his subjects into "good," "medium," or "poor" readers by preexperimental testing. He found that the "good" readers engaged in less implicit vocal movements than did the "poor" readers but surprisingly, more implicit speech occurred while reading a difficult passage than an easy passage. It had been thought that implicit speech interfered with reading, but the conclusion drawn from this experiment was that "silent speech," as Edfelt labeled it, "actually constituted an aid toward better reading comprehension. . . ." And McGuigon (1970) even suggests that implicit speech both facilitates the reception of external language stimuli and the internal processing of information.

Do these findings prove Watson's hypothesis? Studies show that implicit speech is correlated with mental activity (thinking), but is it necessary for thinking? What is involved here is the old adage in psychology: "Correlation is not causation." In order to support the behaviorist position that the mental can be reduced to the physical it is not enough to show that physical correlates exist; they must be proved both necessary and sufficient evidence of thinking.

Relevant to this question are a number of studies done with the drug curare. This drug, used as an arrow poison by South American Indians, produces

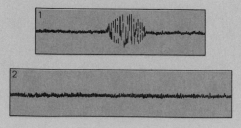

Fig. 9.1 In an early experiment, action potentials at the right elbow were recorded while the subject imagined performing certain actions. (1) When the subject imagined lifting a ten-pound weight with his right arm, there was a sharp rise in electrical activity. (2) When he imagined lifting the weight with his left arm, there was no such response in the right arm. (Jacobson, 1932)

paralysis by acting at the junction of the motor axon and the muscle cell. If Watson's hypothesis that thinking consists of small motor movements is correct, then the completely paralyzed person should not be able to think. Smith et al. (1947) conducted an experiment in which Smith, as the subject, was given enough curare so that complete paralysis occurred and artificial respiration had to be maintained. From both subjective and objective reports consciousness and memory were unimpaired. Even when completely paralyzed Smith understood every question put to him as was later tested when the effects of the drug wore off. Other experiments using dogs as subjects (for example, Solomon and Turner, 1962) have shown that discrimination tasks can be learned while under curare paralysis.

The conclusion from these experiments seems to be that, although muscle movements may accompany thought and even aid in processing information, they are not necessary for thought. Thinking may occur independently of implicit speech.

as part of the process of acquiring language. Being a medium of communication, language is by its nature intersubjective rather than subjective. A mother may observe her child and say, "Johnny, you are tired," "Johnny, you are angry," or "Johnny, you have a stomachache." Soon Johnny will learn to say, "I am tired," "I am angry," "I have a stomachache." But perhaps Johnny is not reporting the result of an introspective examination, but ascribing to himself terms that were initially applied to him on the basis of cues (symptoms, behavior situations) observed by his mother. This approach takes the "mind" out of the mind-body problem.

Rather than semantically maneuvering the mind-body problem out of existence, Herbert Feigl carefully examines our use of terms to provide a new solution to the old puzzle. He proposes an *identity theory* of the mental and the physical. The reasoning behind this theory is that certain neurophysiological terms and certain phenomenal terms (terms alluding to subjective experience) refer to the same events. These terms differ in the sense in which they are used, but they have identical referents. When we say, "I was scared," we are using a phenomenal term to describe a certain event. A physiologist may describe the same event, but he will use different terms. He might say, for example, that your body produced a great deal of adrenalin, or that your heart rate accelerated to so many beats per minute.

Herbert Feigl

Using this approach to the mind-body problem, the scientist does not have to refer to entities such as "soul" (something scientists never like to do anyway). Instead, he is able to direct his discussion toward events and processes and the organization and integration of these events and processes. Rather than dividing the world into two realms, the mental and the physical, this solution focuses on one reality, though it may be described by two different conceptual systems.

In this chapter, we will largely follow this last approach to consciousness, although we will not be very much concerned with its philosophical implications. Our approach will be to accept and examine subjective states in the terms in which they are presented to us. Such states clearly belong to psychology, even though for much of its experimental history psychology has ignored them.

THE NATURE OF CONSCIOUSNESS

What Do We Mean When We Say We Are Conscious?

For most of us consciousness is something we take for granted. We are conscious until we go to sleep or sustain a particularly hard knock on the head, and then we are unconscious. Actually, consciousness is not such a simple matter. It is not an all or nothing affair, but rather is graded into a number of states. These states range from coma, which occurs in situations of severe bodily injury, through dreaming, which we all experience, to wakefulness, alertness, full activity and creative thinking, and hyperactivity. We experience all but the most extreme of these states frequently in our everyday lives.

At the beginning of a class we think will be dull, we may find ourselves fighting the temptation to drop our pencil and fall asleep in our chair. But as we become aware that the professor is asking questions, we become more wake-

 Vigilance

Vigilance research has grown out of the necessity to maintain performance under monotonous conditions, a situation regularly encountered, for example, by radar operators, who have to maintain attention to a screen for long periods of time.

A vigilance task is one in which a subject must respond over an extended period of time to a specified small change in stimulation, which occurs sporadically at random intervals.

Mackworth (1950) designed a test of vigilance using a clocklike apparatus. A pointer rotated around the face of the clock, making a small jump every second. Occasionally, and at irregular intervals, the pointer made a double jump. The subject was told to pay close attention to the movement of the pointer and to report each double jump by pressing a key. After about half an hour subjects began missing double jumps. After that point errors increased steadily. Mackworth discovered that errors could be reduced by telling the subject when he signaled correctly, or by telling him when he had made a mistake. Improvement was also noted when the experimenter called the subject up on a special telephone and asked him to do better.

Selective Attention

As we stand in a crowded, noisy room, how is it that we are able to selectively attend to one particular conversation and effectively block out another that we do not wish to listen to? Cherry (1953) was the first to address himself to this problem of selective attention or, as he put it, the cocktail party phenomenon.

Couched in information processing terms this question can be stated in two parts: (1) What is our selective ability? (2) How are we able to select the voice we wish to attend to? The technique Cherry used to investigate this phenomenon is called *shadowing*. The subject is required to repeat a message while other material is simultaneously presented. Cherry noted that subjects did not find the shadowing task particularly difficult, but they began to speak in a monotone and they very often had little idea of the content of the repeated message. He also found that the nature of the selected material was critical to the subject's ability to perform the shadowing task. For example, narrative prose was easier to shadow than a passage from a technical work. Even in the absence of physical cues, two speeches mixed together could be distinguished from one another if sufficient semantic constraints were involved.

Broadbent (1958), a British psychologist, developed the first complete theory of selective attention. In his filter model he suggests that our ability to discriminate between competing messages is perceptual. Since we are only able to analyze a limited amount of the information that arrives at our sensory receptors, a selective filter can be tuned to accept the desired message (or channel) and to block competing messages. Broadbent proposes that human perceivers select among various sources of information on the basis of the physical characteristics of the stimuli. When desired, attention may be switched among the various input sources. A short-term memory system serves to prevent loss of the immediate information from the unattended channel. Broadbent's theory makes strong assumptions, some of which have been shown to conflict with empirical evidence.

A critical experiment was done by two undergraduates at Oxford, Grey and Wedderburn (1960), who rejected the notion that attention is based on the physical attributes of the sensory channel. They suggested that psychological attributes play an important role in the selection process. They reasoned as follows: Suppose we listen to a word divided in syllables so that successive syllables are presented to alternating ears. At the same time, a second word of a similar form is presented to the complementary ear. Would not attention switch from ear to ear, thus synthesizing each word correctly rather than sticking to one physical channel—that is, one ear—and getting a meaningless mixture of syllables? If so, then the attention mechanism is able to extract the meaning of information and use it in order to choose among input sources. The difference between their theory and Broadbent's is that in Broadbent's attention is directed at an early stage of processing, before meaning can be extracted.

Treisman (1961) examined the role of verbal and linguistic features in subjects' ability to select one message from among several. She studied selective attention to competing messages presented binaurally. The messages were created by systematically varying a number of attributes. Irrelevant material was sometimes read by the same voice that read relevant material. The irrelevant material also varied in nature: sometimes it was technical, other times it consisted of passages from a novel or from the same novel as the relevant material. Finally the passages of the irrelevant material varied from English, Latin, French, German, Czech (with a deliberate English accent) to English played backwards on a tape recorder. The subject's job was to shadow the relevant channel and ignore the irrelevant material.

As we can predict from the Cherry study, when the voices and material were similar in nature the shadowing task was difficult; when there was a distinct difference between the relevant and irrelevant channels, subjects had little difficulty shadowing the required message. When the irrelevant material was in a foreign language, the better the subject knew the language of the irrelevant channel, the more interference it caused. The most difficult task was to shadow the relevant message when both channels were read in the same language by the same voice.

To explain these results, Treisman postulated an anlytical mechanism that performs a series of tests on incoming messages. The first tests distinguish between sensory inputs on the basis of physical attributes; the later tests distinguish among syllabic patterns, specific sounds, individual words, and grammatical structure and meaning. (If channels have physical differences, then it will be easier to separate them at an earlier stage of processing. This is done by attenuating the signal of the irrelevant channel.)

Treisman's contribution lies in her specification of the level at which selection of material occurs and the sequence in which these operations take place. She has been criticized, however, for the complicated nature of her model.

ful, and as we see him looking in our direction, we rouse ourselves to alertness. At a dinner party our date's father delivers a monologue about his favorite method of fly casting. After the first 15 minutes, we realize that we are staring into the knot of his necktie. In a frantic effort to regain alertness, we scratch a knee, smooth down our hair, sink our fork into the chicken Maryland, and politely ask someone to pass the Brussels sprouts. Such actions keep us from becoming inattentive and falling asleep.

In addition to being either attentive or inattentive during waking states of consciousness, we perform a wide variety of activities. We may talk, listen, look, think, plan, or do several of these things at the same time. While listening to our mother as she asks us to take out the garbage, we may be formulating a reply containing all 17 reasons why we can't comply. At a party we may be talking to the host about the merits of his quadraphonic stereo system, listening with one ear to a nearby conversation about the exam grades in our psych course, and all the while keeping an eye on the good-looking guy we want to meet. At some point, however, we reach a limit to the number of things we can pay attention to (see Chapter 7). Listening to a rock album and watching TV while trying to read a difficult class assignment can become a chaotic and confusing experience.

One further aspect of consciousness concerns an activity that goes on "inside our heads" during most of our waking hours: talking to ourselves. We keep up a constant monologue to ourselves, commenting silently on what is going on, making plans, thinking through problems. "If I cut this class again, will the professor notice it and lower my grade?" "Shall I buy the outrageous purple bell bottoms or stick with the conservative blue ones?" "This movie is a bore."

In defining consciousness Davis (1962) lists three things we must be aware of in order to be considered conscious:

1. Self. Recognition of self as distinguished from the environment.
2. Time. Recognition of *now* as opposed to the past and the future.
3. Location in space. A sense of where we are located in the external world.

Consider what happens in the morning when we wake up. First, we are aware of ourselves. We are able to distinguish what is "me" from what is "not me." Without giving it a thought we are able to distinguish self from the furniture in the room, the light coming in the window, the sound of a radio. If we stub our toe on the bureau while racing to turn off the alarm clock, we know that the toe is part of "me" and hurts. The bureau isn't part of "me" and doesn't hurt. The alarm reminds us that it is 7:30 A.M. We are *aware* of *now* and can separate it from yesterday. We know it is Monday morning and we have a 9 o'clock class. Finally, we are aware of where we are: sprawled out on the bed or tripping over a shoe left in the middle of the floor. We know we aren't walking on the ceiling, floating over the roof of city hall, or digging for rocks on the moon.

Consciousness and Awareness

During our usual waking state, we may be conscious of many things without being explicitly aware of them. We may, however, become aware of any of them that our attention is directed toward. If a friend asks us if we think it will rain, we may look at the sky and reply, "Hmmm . . . it looks like a thunderstorm is coming on." If asked a question in psychology class, we may direct our attention toward that. William James remarked on this quality of awareness when he said, "Consciousness is at all times primarily *a selecting agency*. . . . We find it always doing one thing, choosing one out of several of the materials so presented to its notice, emphasizing and accentuating that and suppressing as far as possible all the rest . . ." (1890).

Automatic Behavior   Automatic behavior illustrates the difference between consciousness and awareness. A familiar example of automatic behavior

consciousness

awareness

Alice Boughton

William James

is driving a car. We generally do not expend much effort or concentration on driving. We may talk to friends in the car or tap out a song playing on the radio. Actually, we are perceiving a large number of stimuli and reacting to them by performing a complex series of operations. Yet we have little awareness of those processes; they have become automatic. If we were to be aware of all that we were doing while driving, our interior monologue might sound like this: I am putting my right foot on the gas pedal and exerting pressure until the speedometer reaches the numeral 45 because I saw a sign indicating that the speed limit here is 45 miles per hour and I don't want to get a ticket. I am turning and adjusting the steering wheel so that the car remains in the center of the lane. Because my car is getting close to the car in front of me, I shift my right foot to the brake pedal and exert pressure until I compute that the distance between us appears to be greater than my stopping distance. Every 30 seconds I glance into the rear view mirror. . . .

But such a monologue does not occur because we have highly automated the processes of driving. However, unregistered stimuli may suddenly leap into our awareness. We may not have noticed a group of children playing ball on the sidewalk. If, however, a child darts into the road after a ball, the specifics of this scene are immediately registered in awareness. Our motor responses are still performed automatically, however; we overlearned these responses when we learned how to drive a car, and though the stimuli that call them into action have jumped suddenly into immediate awareness, we do not need to think about what motor responses to make.

perception without
awareness

Perception without Awareness Another instance in which we are conscious but not aware of stimuli occurs in "incidental memory." In this phenomenon though we are apparently not aware of an event when it happens, later recall of the event reveals that in fact we did perceive it. This phenomenon, which we all experience, was the subject of an experiment by Belbin (1956). Posters illustrating driving safety practices were hung on the walls of a waiting room in which experimental subjects sat for 3 minutes before going to another room to be tested. When questioned, the subjects noted that there were posters in the waiting room, but they could not recall the content of the posters with any accuracy. Later they were tested to see if they could apply the specific safety messages contained in the posters to practical situations. It was found that the drivers among the subjects in this task succeeded in significantly larger numbers than did the nondrivers. A control group who had not seen the posters did not exhibit this difference. The drivers in the experimental group, set by their experience to assimilate safety warnings, did so even though they were not conscious of perceiving the messages.

subliminal
perception
(subception)

Another case in which there is an apparently unconscious assimilation of information has been studied by researchers of subliminal perception—subception. Subliminal refers to stimuli presented below threshold, that is, at a speed or intensity that is insufficient for the person to recognize the word. In the late 1950s, a public stir was created when a commercial enterprise claimed to have used subception as an advertising technique (McConnell, Cutler, and McNeil, 1958). Newspapers reported that the messages, "Eat popcorn" and "Drink Coca-Cola" were flashed alternately, at subliminal threshold speeds, during the showing of motion pictures. Although the sponsors claimed an increase in the sales of soda and popcorn, no carefully controlled evaluations were performed, so that we do not know whether in fact the technique had any results.

The Federal Communications Commission reported that a television station in Bangor, Maine, experimented with the broadcast of public service announcements at subliminal levels (Lessler, 1957). "Negative results" were reported. As you might expect from its obviously controversial nature, subliminal advertising has been quite thoroughly investigated. None of the studies has found any evidence that it is effective. There appears to be no serious threat that human behavior can be changed in this way.

Perceptual Defense Subliminal advertising was designed to change behavior. Quite separate is the question of whether we can assimilate information when we are not aware of doing so, or conversely, block information when it is threatening. Closely related to subliminal perception is the phenomenon of perceptual defense (see also Chapter 2). Freud suggested that anxiety-arousing events and stimuli might be totally or partially blocked from awareness. One way of demonstrating this phenomenon would be to show that perceptual thresholds for such stimuli are higher when anxiety is present than when it is not.   *perceptual defense*

McGinnies (1949) attempted such a demonstration by presenting a series of words, some of them taboo, to his subjects (see Perceptual Defense box, p. 329). Two major findings emerged from this experiment (Fig. 9.2). First, it took subjects longer to identify taboo words than neutral words. Second, at the subliminal level of presentation, that is, when the person could not correctly repeat the word, GSR responses to taboo words were higher (showing more emotional shock) than GSR responses to neutral words. From these results McGinnies concluded that the subjects were aware of the taboo words, but for a time used

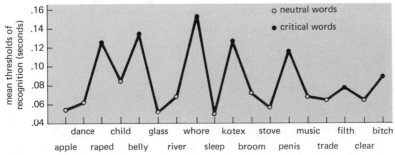

Fig. 9.2 Mean thresholds of recognition of neutral and emotion-charged words. (McGinnies, 1949)

some defensive process to keep them out of consciousness. He believed that a process of discrimination without awareness was at work.

McGinnies' experiment was attacked from several quarters. Howes and Solomon (1950) criticized both his experimental design and his interpretation of its results. They noted that the more frequently a word occurs in the language, the more quickly it can be perceived. Taboo words, by the very fact of being taboo, occur less frequently than neutral words and so take longer to recognize. They also pointed out the possibility that the subjects were as quickly aware of the taboo words as the neutral ones but hesitated before uttering them to the psychologist. "What, say that word? It's too embarrassing!" or, "I must have seen wrong. No college professor would ask me to say *that!*"

Richard S. Lazarus

Two other researchers designed a study to show discrimination without awareness, or perceptual defense, that would avoid the defects of McGinnies' study. Lazarus and McCleary (1951) presented 10 nonsense syllables to their subjects at subliminal speeds. By using nonsense syllables they avoided the confounding effects of word familiarity; all items were equally unfamiliar. They also avoided the response-suppression effect; there is nothing wrong with saying nonsense syllables. Five of the syllables were first accompanied by mild electric shock during an earlier training stage of the experiment. The syllables were then presented at slower and slower speeds until they could be identified correctly. GSR responses were recorded. Syllables that had originally been associated with shock later caused higher GSR responses than unshocked syllables. Further, Lazarus and McCleary found that even before subjects were able to identify any of the syllables, they registered higher GSR responses to previously shocked syllables (Fig. 9.3). Lazarus and McCleary interpreted these results as evidence for discrimination without awareness. We are able to selectively respond to stimuli before we consciously recognize them.

Matthew H. Erdelyi

Since these early studies of subception and perceptual defense, researchers have been trying to discover whether subception is a real phenomenon or an artifact created through experimental design. A central issue in this question is whether subception is a perceptual phenomenon or a response phenomenon. Erdelyi (1974) has used an information processing approach to resolve this problem. According to him, information processing is selective at many

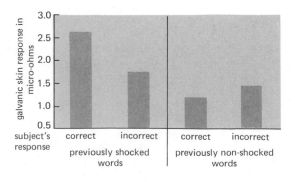

Fig. 9.3 The height of each bar indicates the amount of sweating. When subjects incorrectly identified a previously shocked word, they sweated more than when they misidentified a previously non-shocked word. This is the discrimination without awareness effect. (Lazarus and McCleary, 1951)

points along its route (see Chapter 7). From the time the stimulus first hits the receptor until a response is made to that stimulus, information selectivity (in this case, perceptual defense) can occur. Thus, we can be selective by where we choose to look. Turning away from an accident, or not watching a violent scene is a perceptually defensive act. This aspect of selectivity is perhaps the most common and typical. But we can also look at and "see" something yet not save it. Most have had the experience of reading a paragraph and realizing at the end that you have no idea at all of what it is you read. Presumably here the words were seen, in the sense of registered in a brief iconic storage (see Chapter 7), but you were paying attention to something else and so they were never encoded into short-term memory, rehearsed, or processed further for meaning. Here then is another kind of selectivity, where you chose to select something else for processing, allowing the text you were reading to get no further than the icon.

Similarly, the selectivity could occur at any of the subsequent stages of information processing. By noting the multistage processing, Erdelyi has recognized the many possible ways in which selection, enhancement, inhibition, vigilance, or defensiveness can occur. This makes the process of perceptual defense far less mysterious and far more reasonable than it had once been considered.

THE UNCONSCIOUS

Our discussion of consciousness and awareness has led us to examine automatic behavior, subception, and perceptual defense. In all of these cases we have observed that stimuli and processes that we have not consciously perceived or experienced have exerted an influence on behavior. These and similar phenomena have led some psychologists to posit the existence of an entity called "the unconscious," though they have not reached an agreement about what is meant by the unconscious.

Freud, Psychoanalysis, and the Unconscious

The unconscious is the basis for Freud's psychology and his therapeutic technique, psychoanalysis. Freud divided the mind into three territories: the conscious, the preconscious, and the unconscious. The preconscious contains thoughts, memories, and so on that can be made conscious by an effort of attention, while the unconscious contains psychic events that are actively buried from consciousness and can only be made conscious with considerable effort. The preceding section on consciousness and awareness was concerned with the preconscious. Repression is the term originated by psychoanalysis to describe the primary means by which we keep a painful or anxiety-producing idea out

unconscious

preconscious

of consciousness. Repression is the most extreme form of "taking our mind off things." In emphasizing the role of the unconscious Freud presented a great challenge to the everyday view that behavior can be explained in terms of a conscious act of will that precedes it. According to Freud's system and thought the unconscious plays a very significant role in motivation. This is true not only in cases of neuroses, but in common events of everyday life as well. Errors, slips of the tongue, and dreams are evidence of unconscious wishes "breaking through" into consciousness. When we mishear or misread a word, forget something or "accidentally" destroy something, unconscious motivations are liable to be at work.

Freud pointed out the similarity between errors and dreams. Through the imagery of dreams we express unconscious wishes and impulses. Often, these elements are expressed in dream form because they would be extremely painful and cause anxiety if they were revealed in the conscious waking state.

Although Freud introduced the idea of the unconscious 75 years ago, a number of psychologists do not accept it as fact. It is, however, a useful concept, in explaining the phenomena of slips, errors, and dreams and in explaining many issues in motivation. Phenomena such as automatic behavior, subception, and perceptual defense also suggest the existence of mental processes that occur at levels other than the level of immediate, conscious awareness.

We turn now to an examination of a number of states that represent borderlines between normal consciousness and other, more or less unconscious states.

ALTERED STATES OF CONSCIOUSNESS

For any person the normal state of consciousness is the one in which he spends most of his time. We all experience the waking state of consciousness, know its feel, and take it to be normal. We also assume that the normal state of consciousness of others is similar to our own. Although this normal state of consciousness is our relatively constant mental habitat, much of our knowledge about consciousness has come from the study of altered states of consciousness. An altered state of consciousness for a particular person is one in which he clearly feels a qualitative change in his basic patterns of mental functioning. He experiences more than just a quantitative change, such as a difference in degree of alertness, more or less visual imagery, sharper or duller focus. In an altered state of consciousness a person experiences the qualities of his mental processes as being radically different. Entirely new mental functions may operate, totally new perceptual qualities may appear.

We will discuss the following altered states of consciousness: sleeping, sensory deprivation, hypnosis, meditation, and drug-induced altered states of consciousness.

SLEEPING

The most frequently experienced altered state of consciousness is sleep. Most of us make the "trip" between waking and sleeping twice a day. Although sleep has been around as long as man has, only recently have scientists been able to gather factual data on the nature of sleep. The technological breakthrough that made the scientific study of sleep possible was the development of the electroencephalograph (EEG), a machine that measures and records electrical activity of the brain. In 1937 Loomis and his co-workers made the important discovery that "brain waves," the brain's recurrent electrical patterns, change in form as sleep begins and exhibit further changes as sleep progresses. Although a student may not know exactly when his state of drowsiness turned to sleep as he nodded over his book, researchers can use the EEG to determine the exact beginning and end of sleep.

electro-encephalograph

      The study of EEG recordings reveals four distinct stages of sleep (Dement and Kleitman, 1957) as shown in Fig. 9.4. A wave pattern of 10 cycles per second, called an *alpha rhythm,* is found during the relaxed waking state. As a person begins to fall asleep, the alpha rhythm disappears and is replaced by the low amplitude, fast, irregular rhythm of stage 1. The stage 1 pattern is similar to the EEG pattern found in an active, waking person. As sleep progresses to stage 2, the person is more soundly asleep and his EEG pattern shows sleep spindles, or sharply pointed waves. Stages 3 and 4 exhibit delta waves, which are slow and have a high amplitude.

alpha rhythm

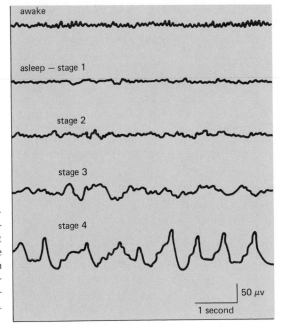

Fig. 9.4 The four stages of sleep, as indicated by EEG records   Stage 1 sleep is characterized by low voltage and relatively fast patterns of change; Stage 2 is recognizable by the presence of sleep spindles, with some complex responses with a low-voltage background; Stages 3 and 4 are identified by slow waves known as delta waves. (Dement and Kleitman, 1957)

Fred Weiss

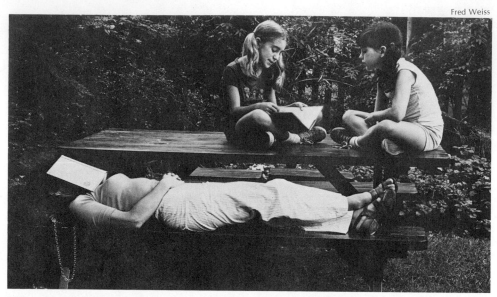

The most frequently experienced altered state of consciousness is sleep.

 Biological Clocks

Humans, like all organisms, have certain biological rhythms which coincide with environmental events. For example, most of us are diurnal—we sleep at night and are active during the period of daylight. This sleep–wakefulness cycle tends to be relatively constant, that is, we tend to sleep about the same amount of time each day and we tend to go to sleep and to get up about the same time. After frequent alternations of sleeping and waking as children, one period of sleep is gradually lengthened and we arrive at the wake-sleep patterns of human adults.

Biological rhythms that continue with a period of about a day (18–33 hours) have been given the term circadian (circa—about; dian—a day) (Halberg, 1959). There are generally two types of circadian rhythms, depending upon the environment in which an organism lives. Diurnal and nocturnal animals and plants follow a solar-day circadian rhythm of about 24 hours. Other organisms follow the lunar tidal periods of 24.8 hours in the natural seashore environment (Brown, 1972).

The figure on the top right shows the activity cycles for diurnal and nocturnal animals (Brown, 1972). Days A and B show activity lines of a 24-hour light–dark regime. However, if these animals are put in constant illumination (days B to C) the activity cycles become "free-running." These cycles either advance for diurnal animals (such as birds and lizards) or are delayed for nocturnal animals (such as rats and mice). However, the cycles remain relatively unchanged; the same ratio of activity to rest is present. This has given rise to the idea of the "biological clock," an independent, internal mechanism which keeps the organism on its own circadian rhythm even in the absence of external cues.

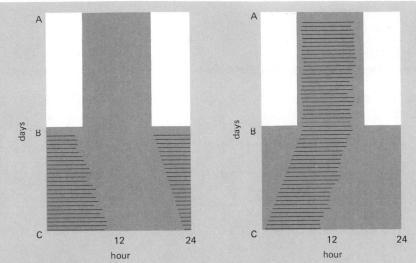

Activity cycles for nocturnal animals (left) and diurnal animals (right). Shaded areas indicate times of darkness. Horizontal lines show times of activity. (Brown, 1972)

What happens if we put man in a constant environment with no cues as to time? Early experiments showed that people are able to judge time, in the absence of any temporal referent, to within a few minutes, even after 86 hours. Yet this was still a relatively short time. Klectman (1939) reported a study in which two men lived in Monmouth cave for a month on a 28-hour day. One of the men was able to adopt to this new 6-day week while the other's body (as judged by body temperature changes) continued on a 7-day week (24 hours per day).

In 1966 a group of French psychologists (Fraisse et al., 1968) conducted a study in which a 24-year-old male subject lived in a cave for 174 days. Thus, the young man went 6 months without any idea of what time it was and was free to set his own wake–sleep rhythm in accord with his biological clock. The findings were surprising. For the first 10 days (bar 1) a circadian rhythm was retained (25 hours 9 minutes), but then the subject abruptly went into a bicircadian

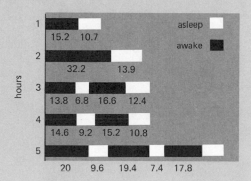

Wake-sleep rhythm for subject who lived in a cave for 174 days. (Oléron et al., 1970)

rhythm which lasted from the twelfth day to the forty-second day. Bar 2 shows the long periods of sleeplessness which the subject maintained. The third, fourth, and fifth periods of the experiment show increasingly longer rhythms, although they remained consistent. Undoubtably boredom and fatigue contributed greatly to upsetting the subject's circadian cycle. (Oléron et al., 1970.)

While the cave experiments are inconclusive, since only a few subjects have lived in this type of environment, they cast doubt on the idea of a completely independent "biological clock." Brown (1972) has suggested that there is no such thing as a completely constant environment, and even when organisms are kept in a constant state of illumination they may be responding to subtle electromagnetic changes resulting from the earth's rotation and the lunar orbit about the earth.

There is another, very significant, stage of sleep called *stage 1—REM*. This stage shows the same EEG pattern as stage 1, but in addition rapid eye movements (REM's) occur. REM's are jerky movements of the eyes beneath the lids. If you place your finger very lightly over your closed eyelid and move your eyeball, you can feel a similar movement. REM's are detected and measured by another electrical recording device, the electro-oculogram (EOG). It is during stage 1–REM that dreaming takes place (Aserinsky and Kleitman, 1953). Although the EEG pattern during this stage is similar to the pattern of an alert, waking person, this is a period of deep sleep. It is difficult to wake someone out of this stage of sleep. For this reason stage 1–REM has been called "paradoxical sleep" (Fig. 9.5).

REM's

EOG

paradoxical sleep

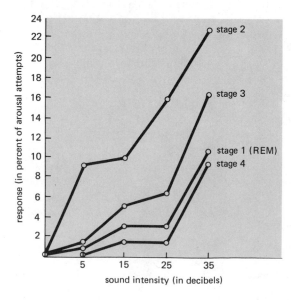

Fig. 9.5 Sound intensity requisite for arousal from sleep. The subject was asked to press a key attached to a finger when he heard a loud sound. It is interesting that this response can be made at all depths of sleep and is more frequent to louder sounds at all stages. The impressive finding in this experiment is that it is difficult to waken the subject at Stage 1 when this stage is accompanied by rapid eye movement (REM's). (Williams, 1967)

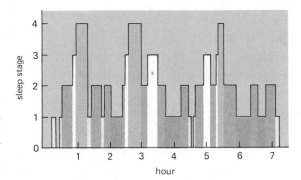

Fig. 9.6 The graph shows an individual's progression through various stages during seven hours of sleep. The solid color bars indicate periods of Stage 1-REM. (After Webb, 1965)

During the course of a night we drift from one stage of sleep to another (Fig. 9.6). The amount of time spent in the different stages of sleep varies from person to person, but is relatively constant for any given person night after night. One study has shown that on the average we spend about 5 percent of our night's sleep in stage 1, 25 percent in stage 1-REM, 50 percent in stage 2, and 20 percent in stages 3 and 4 combined (Williams, Agnew, and Webb, 1964).

REM's and Dreaming

Although early EEG studies told researchers a good deal about the stages of sleep, they yielded no information about dreaming. While scientists suspected that dreaming occurred only in certain stages of sleep, they had no evidence to support this suspicion. A lucky "accident" opened up the field of dream research. While studying sleeping subjects, Aserinsky and Kleitman noticed quick, jerky movements of the eyelids, indicating eye movements. Measurements revealed that during the periods of eye movement both heart rate and breathing rate increased. Speculating that these increases indicated emotional responses and that REM activity was associated with dreaming, the experimenters woke their subjects during REM periods. At these times subjects almost always reported that they had been dreaming. When awakened at other times, they rarely reported dreaming (Aserinsky and Kleitman, 1953). Physiological changes, including large, irregular fluctuations in heart rate and blood pressure, have also been found to occur during REM sleep. Although we are lying still in our beds, physiologically speaking, our nervous system is very active.

In our dreams we may be extremely active, climbing mountains, running, doing any number of things, but while pursuing these dream adventures, our bodies are relatively motionless. During REM sleep a good deal of spontaneous muscular twitching occurs, but all in all, once in our beds, we tend to stay put. What keeps us from acting out our dreams? Scientists have found a special, protective mechanism in the brain that functions during REM sleep to inhibit motor activity (Dement, 1969). By blocking nerve impulses to the muscles, this mechanism causes our bodies to go into deep relaxation during REM sleep and

Somnambulism

Sleepwalking is not a rare nocturnal disturbance. It has been estimated to occur in 1 to 5 percent of the population, predominantly in males, and to be more common in children than in adults. Sleepwalkers have a significantly higher than average incidence of enuresis (bedwetting) and a family history of somnambulism (Jacobson and Kales, 1965).

There has been some disagreement about the somnambulistic state. It has been described both as a state in which the person is not awake, and as a condition in which the person is not asleep. Many disagreements have concerned the degree of motor performance and dexterity of the sleepwalker and his ability to carry out difficult tasks. There is general agreement, however, that the episodes last 15 to 30 minutes and that there is total amnesia for the entire incident.

Sleepwalking has been regarded as a symptom of an epileptic state. Researchers have found a significantly greater frequency of electroencephalographic (EEG) abnormalities among sleepwalkers than among controls and a strong correlation between the frequency and severity of sleepwalking and EEG abnormalities.

Sleepwalking is generally thought to be an immature habit pattern, but if it persists into adolescence or adulthood a more severe, sometimes organic diagnosis is implied. Psychological explanations range from regarding sleepwalking as a dissociative state involving a memory disturbance and loss of awareness of personal identity to considering it a dreamlike disturbance of consciousness.

saves us from duplicating the actions in our dreams with real movements. When experimenters destroyed this inhibitory mechanism in the brains of cats, the animals jumped around, spat, and hissed during REM periods, although they were deeply asleep and unaware of their environment (Jouvet and Delormé, 1965). It is a widely held conception that sleepwalking occurs during dreaming ("I dreamed I went to the kitchen to make a sandwich and woke up when I dropped the mayonnaise"), but experimental evidence has shown that sleepwalking occurs during stages 3 and 4 of sleep, when we are not dreaming.

An interesting effect was observed when experimenters deprived volunteer subjects of REM sleep. The subjects were allowed to sleep until they began to go into REM periods; then they were awakened and allowed to go back to sleep until another REM period began. Subjects in a control group were awakened the same number of times per night, but only during non-REM periods. A number of differences between the two groups were observed. The REM-deprived subjects began more REM periods each successive night of the experiment. And during the day they were more tense, irritable, and anxious and had difficulty concentrating and remembering. When allowed to resume undisturbed sleeping patterns, the REM-deprived subjects made up for their deprivation by dreaming 60 percent more than they usually did. Dement labeled this compensatory mechanism "REM rebound." This attempt to dream more when we have been deprived of REM sleep seems to indicate a psychological need to dream.

© 1962 by Dr. Seuss

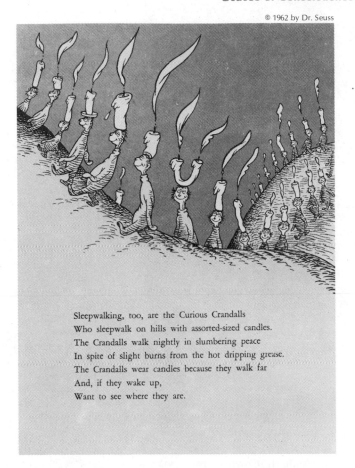

Sleepwalking, too, are the Curious Crandalls
Who sleepwalk on hills with assorted-sized candles.
The Crandalls walk nightly in slumbering peace
In spite of slight burns from the hot dripping grease.
The Crandalls wear candles because they walk far
And, if they wake up,
Want to see where they are.

Since dreaming seems to be important to us, we may ask what biologically adaptive role it plays. While this question can't be fully answered at this time, a possible clue can be found in the fact that infants spend 50 percent of their sleep time in REM sleep—twice as much as adults. Several psychologists have theorized that the REM mechanism stimulates the higher centers of the brain and thereby perhaps helps important sensory and motor areas of the central nervous system to develop. As a child grows older and relates more to the outside world there is less need for this self-stimulation, and the amount of REM sleep decreases (Roffwarg, Muzio, and Dement, 1966).

The Psychology of Dreaming

The exact function of dreaming is not yet fully understood by sleep researchers. Since REM patterns occur in subhuman species as well as man, it is possible that this aspect of sleep and dreaming itself may serve some important biological function. The psychoanalysts have proposed that dreaming acts as a "safety valve," providing a mechanism for the discharge of instinctual pressure. Others

Sleep Deprivation

In a study at UCLA (Pasnau et al., 1968) four subjects were deprived of sleep for 205 consecutive hours. After 168 hours of deprivation, one of the subjects suddenly went berserk during a psychomotor training task. He screamed in terror, pulled the electrodes off, and fell to the floor crying and muttering incoherently about a gorilla vision he was experiencing.

Behavioral changes noted after sleep deprivation ranged from simple irritability to dramatic and bizarre behavior such as the gorilla hallucination. The changes were found to be transitory. Sleep loss itself does not necessarily provoke a psychotic state. In studies where more psychotic-like behavior developed in subjects after 220 hours of sleep deprivation, it was noted that the subjects had had traumatic childhoods and other neurotic and work disturbances.

Many physiological changes have also been noted after prolonged sleep loss. Among them are a decrease in alpha wave abundance and a tendency toward a low voltage EEG similar to that seen in activated alert subjects as well as in drowsy subjects, so that the interpretation of this phenomenon differs widely. One group maintains that the decrease in alpha is a reflection of increased activation and a second group interprets the alpha decrement as an indication of a drift toward sleep and decreased activation.

have suggested that dreaming acts as a homeostatic device, serving a binding, synthesizing, or restorative function. While prolonged REM deprivation has been shown to cause personality aberrations (Dement, 1960, 1966), it has not been proved physiologically harmful to the dreamer.

Because the psychology of dreams occupies such an important place in psychoanalytic theory, we will briefly review it here. No other phenomenon offers us such direct access to the richness of unconscious mental life. Dreams lead not only to a general understanding of unconscious mental processes but to specific mental contents that have been repressed from consciousness. As Freud so aptly put it, "Dreams are the royal road to the unconscious."

We have already said that the psychoanalysts consider dreaming a process of discharging unconscious instinctual energy. Freud (1949) states that this fanciful release of instinctual tension serves essentially the purpose of maintaining sleep.

As the sleeper regresses from the external world, the walls separating fact from fantasy seem to melt. Hence, repressed material is allowed a certain degree of freedom. Our dreams represent the demands of unconscious repressed forces seeking expression. What we consciously experience during sleep is referred to as the *manifest dream;* this is what we remember on awakening. It is often thought of as the dream proper, but it is only the end product of unconscious

manifest dream

Drawing by Dana Fradon; © 1973 The New Yorker Magazine, Inc.

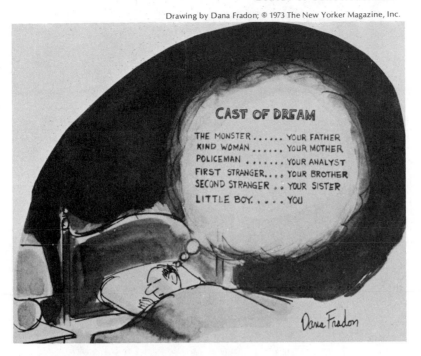

mental action (Freud, 1949). The unconscious thoughts and wishes that threaten to awaken the dreamer are known as the *latent dream*. The latent dream content may be divided into three categories, depending upon the nature of the stimulus that gave rise to it.

Latent Dream Categories The first category of latent dream, nocturnal sensory impressions, consists of stimuli that impinge upon the sleeper. They may be the sound of an alarm clock or some internal biological state such as hunger, thirst, or the need to urinate.

The second category consists of thoughts, fears, or aspirations that the dreamer experiences in a conflictive way in waking life. When these conflicts are not resolved adequately in reality, dreaming may provide a solution, at least in fantasy.

The third and most important category of latent dream content consists of instinctual impulses that are at least infantile in nature but may go back to ancestral origins. Because censorship is relaxed during sleep, these impulses may slip into consciousness. What the dream ends up satisfying however is not the raw impulse, which may be horrifying, but essentially a compromise. Defensive mechanisms transform latent content into manifest content through a process called dreamwork. The purpose of dreamwork is to obscure by distorting unacceptable wish-impulses so that they appear innocuous to the dreamer and thus allow him to continue sleeping. Freud (1949) described this process as a compromise between opposing forces—the impulse and the desire to sleep—vying for simultaneous expression.

latent dream

dreamwork

Dreamwork Dreamwork makes use of a number of devices. There is a tendency toward *condensation,* toward collapsing into a single unit experiences that in waking life are separate or unique. A single image in a dream may represent a number of disparate impulses. Another result of dreamwork is *displacement.* Something that is of no consequence to the dreamer may replace an important item. Dreams also make use of a vast number of *symbols* that can only be described as archaic. They too hinder our recognition of unacceptable, unconscious wish-impulses.

The number of things that are represented in dreams is not great. The human body, parents, children, brothers and sisters, birth, death, and nakedness are typical dream subjects. According to Freud (1916), the sexual organs are represented in dreams in many ways. For example the number three symbolizes the male genitalia. The penis is symbolized primarily by objects that resemble it in form, such as sticks, trees, poles, or pointed objects, and also by objects that have a penetrating quality such as knives and guns. The female genitalia are symbolically represented by objects that share the property of enclosing

Freud's Analysis of a Dream

Freud (1923) reports that a young, unmarried man told him the following dream:

The dreamer . . . was sitting in the restaurant at which he usually ate. . . . Several people then appeared, in order to fetch him away, and one of them wanted to arrest him. He said to his companions at table: "I'll pay later; I'll come back." But they exclaimed with derisive smiles: "We know all about that; that's what they all say!" One of the guests called out after him: "There goes another one!" He was then led into a narrow room in which he found a female figure carrying a child. One of the people accompanying him said: "This is Herr Müller." A police inspector, or some such official, was turning over a bundle of cards or papers and as he did so repeated "Müller, Müller, Müller." Finally he asked the dreamer a question, which he answered with an "I will." He then turned round to look at the female figure and observed that she was now wearing a big beard. (p. 494)

    In this dream, Freud finds "two different and opposing phantasies which coincide with each other at a few points and of which one is superficial while the second is, as it were, an interpretation of the first." Analysis of the manifest content leads us quite easily to a possible latent dream, but a closer look reveals that another latent dream—the real content of the dream—lies beneath this first distortion. Freud says:

There is no difficulty in separating the two components. The superficial one was a *phantasy of arrest* which appears as though it had been freshly constructed by the dream-work. But behind it some material is visible which had been only slightly re-shaped by the dream-work: *a phantasy of marriage*. Those features which were common to both phantasies emerge with special clarity. . . . The promise made by the young man (who up till then had been a bachelor) that he would come back and join his fellow-diners at their table, the scepticism of his boon-companions (whom experience had taught better), the exclamation "there goes another one (to get married)"—all of these features fitted in easily with the alternative interpretation. So, too, did the "I will" with which he replied to the official's question. The turning over the bundle of papers, with the constant repetition of the same name, corresponded to a less important but recognizable feature of wedding festivities, namely the reading out of a bundle of telegrams of congratulation, all of them with addresses bearing the same names. The phantasy of marriage actually scored a victory over the covering phantasy of arrest in the fact of the bride's making a personal appearance in the dream. I was able to discover . . . why it was that at the end of it the bride wore a beard. On the previous day the dreamer had been walking in the street with a friend who was as shy of marrying as he was himself, and he had drawn his friend's attention to a dark-haired beauty who had passed them. "Yes," his friend had remarked, "if only women like that didn't grow beards like their fathers' in a few years' time." This dream did not, of course, lack elements in which dream-distortion had been carried deeper. It may well be, for instance, that the words "I'll pay later" referred to what he feared might be his father-in-law's attitude on the subject of a dowry. In fact, all kinds of qualms were evidently preventing the dreamer from throwing himself into the phantasy of marriage with any enjoyment. One of these qualms, a fear that marriage might cost him his freedom, was embodied in the transformation into a scene of arrest. (pp. 494–495)

space or are capable of acting as receptacles. These include pits, caves, jars, bottles, and most frequently, rooms. With all the distortion of latent content imposed by censorship there is little wonder that the dreamer often experiences his dreams as incomprehensible or just plain meaningless. Occasionally, however, the dream may appear to the dreamer in its undisguised form. In this case, the dreamer awakens, and we say he has had a nightmare, whether he wakes up laughing or in terror.

Dream Analysis In analyzing dreams we must work our way back from the manifest dream to the latent content. This can be done by a number of techniques. Some therapists have the patient give spontaneous free associations to the dream content while others make tentative formulations of the dream dynamics by attempting to connect established symbolism with the patient's impressions.

Daydreams Daydreams are sometimes mistakenly identified with dreaming though in fact they have little to do with the universal characteristics of dreams. They are more reality-oriented than dreams are, and their content is more acceptable and more like reality. They are actually fantasies, which are commonly experienced by healthy as well as disturbed people. We simply imagine something that we recognize is the work of fantasy. The content of these fantasies is particularly transparent. Daydreams are conjured up images of scenes or events that gratify egoistic cravings for power or for ambitions or erotic pleasures.

Not everyone agrees with Freud's interpretation of the purpose and meaning of dreams, but no other theory rivals his in insightfulness or in acceptance. The major accomplishment of Freud's theory was the abandonment of all notion that dreams predict the future, an idea that originated in ancient Greece. In Freud's day, and even occasionally today, it is given credence by some scientists. For Freud, dreams were products of the present and the past, but they had absolutely nothing to do with the future. Some laymen still find it difficult to accept the idea that dreams are not prophetic.

SENSORY DEPRIVATION

sensory deprivation

In our daily lives we constantly perceive, process, and react to a great variety of information and stimuli. What happens when the supply of external stimuli is greatly reduced? This condition or situation is known as sensory deprivation. Prisoners held in isolation, explorers, pilots, and writers have described experiences of sensory and social deprivation. They relate many instances in which enforced solitude and restriction of bodily movement have led to severe changes in thinking, strong feelings of loneliness, and hallucinations. Such experiences have aroused curiosity for a long time, but it is only relatively recently that research psychologists have become interested in sensory deprivation.

Experimental Studies of Sensory Deprivation

Research on human sensory deprivation attempts to reduce or distort the sensory input available to the subject. Of course, it is impossible to remove all external stimuli. Even in the most soundproof room, the subject will be able to hear the surge of blood through the vessels near his ears and the sounds he makes while breathing; he will be able to detect changes in body temperature and body moisture and odors. However, several major techniques are able to reduce external stimuli greatly.

One kind of experiment attempts to reduce sensory stimulation as much as possible. The subject may be immersed nude in a water tank, where he breathes through a tube attached to a blacked-out face mask. Or he may be placed in a dark, soundproof chamber. Ear-muffed to prevent him from hearing his own sounds, he lies still on a mattress and is asked not to move or talk.

A second approach to the study of sensory deprivation has been to change the nature or pattern of sensory input available to the subject. In one experiment of this type (Heron, 1961), the subjects wore translucent goggles that admitted light but prevented the perception of visual patterns. In addition, a constant buzzing noise blocked out the sounds of the environment.

In a third approach to sensory deprivation, experimenters create highly structured or monotonous sensory environments. Wexler and his co-workers (1958) placed subjects in tanks of the type used to treat polio patients. The subjects' arms and legs were placed in rigid cylinders that minimized both movement and tactile stimulation.

Research has shown that sensory deprivation affects perception, cognitive processing, problem solving, and learning processes. It has also been shown to cause hallucinatory behavior. Before we discuss the effects in each of these areas, we should make note of a problem in methodology in these studies. Different experimental conditions were used, inputs to different sense modalities were altered, and different tests of problem solving and learning ability were used. As a consequence, it has been difficult to come up with widely generalized findings and to duplicate experimental results. We will, however, note some types of effects that have been observed.

Several varieties of disturbance in visual perception have been observed as a result of sensory deprivation. When translucent goggles were removed from the eyes of subjects, objects in the visual field appeared to be moving, the walls of the room undulated, and flat surfaces appeared to be curved.

Subjects who experienced sensory deprivation for long periods have reported trouble thinking clearly and concentrating. Some found it difficult to count beyond 20 or 30. After the first day of sensory deprivation, many subjects experienced a disorganization of thought processes. When this happened, the subjects frequently turned to extensive daydreaming.

Arthur Tress

In a dream, one may find himself caught in mazes or glass corridors.

One experiment found that isolation and sensory deprivation produced changes in scores on intellectual functioning tests. Short-term memory was increased, but decreases appeared in arithmetical reasoning, reasoning ability, and in the ability to abstract and generalize (Cohen and co-workers, 1961). It has been proposed that tasks requiring logical reasoning are the most likely to be affected by sensory deprivation, but tasks such as simple arithmetic, which involve overlearned processes, are not as likely to be affected (Goldberger and Holt, 1961).

hallucinations ## Hallucinations

Hallucinatory behavior is the most dramatic effect of sensory deprivation and has been reported in a great number of studies. In one study utilizing translucent goggles (Bexton, Heron, and Scott, 1954), 14 of 22 subjects reported visual hallucinations. Images seen included spots of light, geometric patterns, visual scenes, and cartoons. They tended to disappear when subjects were engaged in difficult tasks, such as multiplying 3-digit numbers in their heads.

Of 16 subjects confined to soundproof chambers 11 experienced hallucinations (Zubeck and co-workers, 1961). Visual hallucinations consisted of glowing, flashing, or flickering lights in the periphery of vision. Auditory hallucinations included dogs howling, bells ringing, and typewriters typing. Two subjects reported kinesthetic hallucinations. One felt cold steel pressing on his forehead and cheeks; the other felt the mattress being pulled out from under him.

In a study employing translucent goggles, subjects experienced a great deal of hallucination (Heron, 1961). They saw geometric figures and patterns, movies playing in their goggles, and objects flying toward them. They became confused to the point that they didn't know whether they were awake or sleeping.

Freedman, Grunebaum, and Greenblatt (1961) suggested that such hallucinations result from the subjects' efforts to place any available stimuli into meaningful patterns in order to satisfy a need for meaning in the environment.

In some cases, the hallucinations that occur during sensory deprivation appear to be similar to the hallucinations common in schizophrenia. These apparent similarities have interested a number of psychiatrists and clinical psychologists. It has been proposed that schizophrenia may involve processes related to those that occur in a severely reduced sensory environment.

Rosenzweig (1959) suggested that in schizophrenia the internal organization and processing of sensory and perceptual inputs is disrupted, making the input unavailable for cognitive or other processing. In sensory deprivation a similar situation is held to occur, except that the disruptions are external rather than internal. When the natural environment is changed so as to greatly reduce or distort stimuli, the available stimuli lose their meaning. Since they have no relevance for further internal processing, schizophrenia-like behavior results.

Sensory Deprivation in a Social Setting

While ethical and humanitarian considerations prohibit researchers from exposing infants and young children to prolonged sensory or social deprivation, such situations may arise when children are raised in impersonal institutions. Spitz (1945) compared the development of children raised in an orphanage with the development of children raised in a nursing home. In both institutions the children received good food and medical care and lived in a sanitary environment. In the nursing home all of the children were taken care of by their own mothers. In the orphanage six nurses cared for 45 babies. Further, in the nursing home the babies were able to watch the activities in the ward, but in the orphanage, sheets had been draped over the bars of the babies' cribs. The effect was similar to that produced by wearing translucent goggles; an undifferentiated stimulus field was created, leading to a condition of sensory deprivation.

During the first 4 months of their lives the orphanage babies matched or exceeded the nursing home babies on tests of development. However, by the last 4 months of the first year, the orphanage babies tested far below the nursing home babies. Also, the orphanage babies fell into a weakened physical and mental state, which led to a high mortality rate. At the ages of 2 and 3, the nursing home babies were walking and talking. At the same time, only two of the 26 orphanage-raised babies could walk and talk. Spitz's work suggests that sensory and social deprivation in early life leads to serious problems in the development of normal functioning. We will consider this research with infants again in some detail in Chapter 12, when we look at the personality needs that are affected.

These studies indicate that a certain amount of sensory stimulation is necessary for proper functioning. Hallucinations and distortions of time and space seem to be an attempt on the part of the person to structure his perceptual situation and to provide himself with "meaning" (however bizarre) in the absence of stimulation.

HYPNOSIS

hypnosis   The term "hypnosis" comes from the Greek word *Hypnos,* the name of the ancient Greek god of sleep. Although to early observers, persons in hypnotic trances may have appeared to be sleeping, hypnosis is not actually a form of sleep. The EEG of a hypnotic state is not the EEG of any of the four stages of sleep; rather, it is similar to the EEG of the waking, active state.

Although its exact nature is not yet known, hypnosis has intrigued the popular imagination since it was "discovered" in 1843. In the public view hypnosis partakes of the magical, and we often imagine the hypnotist as a sinister, powerful figure who makes people do things against their will. Unfortunately, this conception has been strengthened by the somewhat unethical use of hypnosis for public entertainment. An audience seems to enjoy the spectacle of watching a grown man or woman barking like a dog at the suggestion of a show-business hypnotist. Entertainment and skeptics aside, scientific experiments have indicated that hypnosis is a true altered state of consciousness.

Hypnotic Induction

Hypnosis can be induced by a variety of techniques, but all of them are aimed at getting the subject to relax, let his imagination go, allow his mind and body to operate involuntarily, accept perceptual and causal distortions of reality, and accept suggestions from the hypnotist.

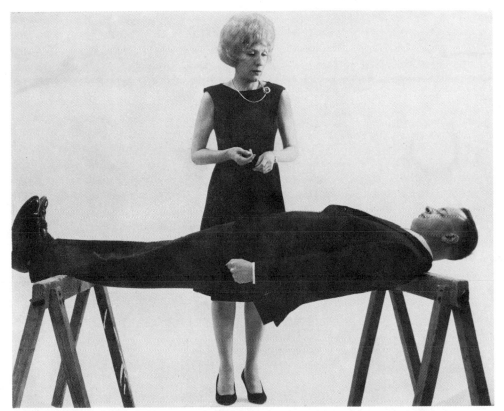

Subject in state of rigid catalepsy after hypnotic suggestion. (Photo courtesy Lynne Gordon, Hypnotherapist, Executive Director of the Autosuggestions and Hypnosis Center of New York, 160 West 73rd St., New York, N.Y. 10023)

 ### The Hypnosis of Aldous Huxley

Early in 1950, the novelist Aldous Huxley and the psychologist Milton Erikson planned a joint investigation into various states of psychological awareness (Erikson, 1956).

Huxley suggested an investigation of hypnotic states of awareness, using himself as a subject. He wanted first to experience a light trance to permit an exploration of his subjective experience. He found several repetitions of the light trance interesting but as he put it, "too easily conceptualized—a simple withdrawal of interest from the outside world." That is, one gave less and less attention to the outside world and more and more attention to inner subjective sensations. In this state of balance, he remarked, one could "reach out and seize upon reality." In the light trance state he found that anesthesia, amnesia, time distortion, and hyperamnesia were possible.

In experimenting with medium-deep trances, Huxley experienced much more difficulty in maintaining a fairly constant trance level. He found he had a subjective need to go deeper in the trance and an intellectual need to stay at the medium level. As a result, he found himself trying to "reach out for awareness of his environment."

For both types of trance, experiments were designed to discover what hypnotic phenomena could be elicited in both light and medium trances. The most important finding seemed to be the need for subjects in both trance states to maintain at least some grasp upon external reality. Huxley described the medium-deep trance as primarily a subjective sense of comfort and a vague sense of the existence of an external reality.

Huxley was able to experience hallucinatory effects in both the light and medium-deep trances. He achieved this by enjoying his subjective state of physical relaxation and adding to his enjoyment an additional subjective quality, a pleasant gustatory sensation. He found it quite easy to hallucinate various taste sensations and finally kinesthetic, proprioceptive, and tactile sensations also. It was much more difficult for him to achieve auditory and, particularly, visual hallucinations. His first visual hallucinations were a flowing of vivid pastel colors. He then attempted to visualize a flower. Since movement had helped him finally to experience auditory hallucinations, he began turning his head from side to side and up and down in barely visible rhythmic movements. Very shortly a giant rose became visible, perhaps 3 feet in diameter. He was able to add to this hallucination by imagining a sickeningly sweet odor.

In Huxley's investigation of the deep trance, he found that he was completely disoriented as to time and place. He was able to open his eyes but described his field of vision as "a well of light" that included Erikson, the chair in which Erikson sat, and himself and his chair. Careful questioning by Erikson revealed that Huxley had amnesia for preceding events. In other deep trances Huxley was able to develop partial, selective, and posthypnotic amnesia.

In one particular deep hypnotic trance, Huxley experienced catalepsy, a phenomenon not unusual in deep trance states. He had been comfortably positioned in a chair and then commanded to move a book from a table to a nearby desk. Huxley, unable to rise from the chair, sat there extremely puzzled. The comfortable arrangement of his body had resulted in a positioning that would have to be corrected before he could arise from the chair; and no suggestions for repositioning had been made. Huxley was amazed at his loss of mobility and became even more surprized when he discovered a loss of orientation to the lower part of his body and a corresponding total anesthesia. He did not relate the comfortable positioning of his body to the cataleptic state, which had disturbed his sense of body awareness.

Susceptibility to hypnosis varies widely. Some people apparently cannot be hypnotized at all or achieve a trance only after hundreds of trials. Usually, an experienced and professional hypnotist can determine his subject's susceptibility during the first attempt at induction (Hilgard, 1965).

In a random sampling of university students (Table 9.1) approximately one quarter achieved a satisfactory level of hypnotic responsiveness (Hilgard, 1965).

Table 9.1 Items of the Stanford Hypnotic Susceptibility Scale, Form A

Ernest R. Hilgard

Suggested Behavior	Criterion of Passing (Yielding Score of +)
1. Postural sway	Falls without forcing
2. Eye closure	Closes eyes without forcing
3. Hand lowering (left)	Lowers at least six inches by end of 10 seconds
4. Immobilization (right arm)	Arm rises less than one inch in 10 seconds
5. Finger lock	Incomplete separation of fingers at end of 10 seconds
6. Arm rigidity (left arm)	Less than two inches of arm bending in 10 seconds
7. Hands moving together	Hands at least as close as six inches after 10 seconds
8. Verbal inhibition (name)	Name unspoken in 10 seconds
9. Hallucination (fly)	Any movement, grimacing, acknowledgment of effect
10. Eye catalepsy	Eyes remain closed at end of 10 seconds
11. Posthypnotic (changes chairs)	Any partial movement response
12. Amnesia test	Three or fewer items recalled

SOURCE: Weitzenhoffer and Hilgard (1959)

Characteristics of the Hypnotic State

The following characteristics typify the behavior of a person in the hypnotic state:

1. *The subject does not initiate activity.* Typically, the hypnotized person is passive; he waits for suggestions from the hypnotist.
2. *Attention narrows.* Under hypnosis attention is extremely selective. If the subject is told to pay attention to a particular object, he will do so with great concentration.
3. *Distortion of reality is accepted.* If a subject under hypnosis is told that a friendly puppy is at his side, he will willingly play with it. If told that the room has suddenly become extremely warm, he may start perspiring.
4. *There is a great increase in suggestibility.*
5. *Role playing is facilitated.* At the suggestion of the hypnotist the subject easily plays at being someone else. He may take on the characteristics of the other, and he can carry out complex activities related to that role. At the hypnotist's suggestion, the subject may play himself as he was at a younger age—for instance, as a child of 8. The subject is able to reproduce his own behavior as it apparently was at that age and may restage specific situations or incidents.
6. *Hypnotic amnesia may be induced.* On the suggestion of the hypnotist the subject may forget an event that occurred during the session or he may forget the entire session. Later he may recall the forgotten material on a prearranged signal from the hypnotist.

Applications of Hypnosis

Hypnosis has been used for medical purposes in dentistry, obstetrics, and psychotherapy. It is of special use in these areas because it is a relaxed state and as such functions to reduce anxiety. Moreover, it can relieve or reduce pain.

In an experiment designed to test the "pain-killing" effect of hypnosis, a series of painful electric shocks was administered to a student subject. His GSR (a measure of arousal) was found to be quite high. He was then hypnotized and told that the shocks would not hurt as much. The suggestion was successful as measured by his GSR after hypnosis. The response to the inital shock following the suggestion was only a tenth the size of the initial shock in the unhypnotized situation. After seven more shocks the pain response was entirely eliminated (Zimbardo, Rapaport, and Baron, 1969).

This pain-killing or, more accurately, pain-controlling power of hypnosis has been used in the treatment of terminal cancer patients. Through hypnosis the severe pain of this disease can be brought under control to the extent that morphine is no longer necessary (Sacerdote, 1966).

A number of people who have experienced the hypnotic state report it to be very pleasant. An acquaintance of the author had this to say about her experience with hypnosis: "It was quite a pleasurable experience. I felt very relaxed and happy. At one point the hypnotist suggested that I would count to ten, but forget the number seven. I remember thinking to myself, 'That's silly, I know how to count, I know that seven comes after six.' However, when I reached the number six, I felt a very strong urge not to say seven. I giggled and went on to eight."

In recent years hypnosis has moved out of magic and pseudoscience into scientific inquiry. At present several theories attempt to explain hypnosis, and we have yet to develop any unified account. Although much remains to be discovered about this altered state of consciousness, it presents a striking illustration of the amount of cognitive control potentially available to us.

MEDITATION

meditation   Meditation is a state in which subjects report a new, radically altered form of consciousness. At the outset we are at a disadvantage in trying to describe meditation, because the language we must use belongs to another state of consciousness. We are in the position of someone who must explain color to someone who has been blind from birth.

One investigator has said, "Meditation is first of all a deep passivity, combined with awareness" (Maupin, 1972). In meditation a concentrated effort is made to empty the mind of all usual concerns, thought processes, and perceptions. When these are gone, radically new phenomena can presumably arise.

Meditation has long been used as a technique for reaching states of mystical union or transcendence. Although we usually think of meditation in connection with Eastern religions, it has been used by Western sects of Christianity, particularly Roman Catholicism.

Inducing Meditation

Typically meditation is induced through special exercises—Yoga (from the Hindu tradition) or Zen (from the Buddhist tradition). The meditator usually sits or kneels on the floor in a position that is conducive to relaxation but not sleep. The surroundings are simple so that there are few distractions. The meditator focuses his attention on breathing, a part of his body, or, in the case of contemplative meditation, an object. Contemplative meditation, the form of meditation we will discuss here, requires that the subject relinquish his usual mode of thinking and perceiving and contemplate the object in a totally nonanalytical and nonintellectual manner. The following instructions, taken from the principles of Yoga and Zen, were given to the subjects of an experimental study of meditation:

> The purpose of these sessions is to learn about concentration. Your aim is to concentrate on the blue vase. By concentration I do not mean analyzing the different parts of the vase, or thinking a series of thoughts about the vase, or associating ideas to the vase, but rather trying to see the vase as it exists in itself, without any connection to other things. Exclude all other thoughts or feelings or sounds or body sensations. Do not let them distract you but keep them out so that you can concentrate all your attention, all your awareness on the vase itself. Let the perception of the vase fill your entire mind. (Deikman, 1966 p. 330)

The subjects in this experiment had had no previous experience with meditation. Given these instructions, with additional explanations as required, they were asked to meditate during 12 sessions spread over a period of 3 weeks. The initial sessions lasted 5 minutes; subsequent sessions lasted 15 minutes, though in several cases subjects wished to prolong the sessions to approximately half an hour. All of the subjects achieved a state of meditation. In reports of their experiences, all noted the following phenomena:

1. Perception of the vase changed. The blue became more intense; a number of subjects described it as "luminous." The shape of the vase changed. Its boundaries dissolved. For one subject the vase appeared as a film of blue.

2. Sense of time was distorted. Most subjects felt the sessions were shorter than they actually were.

3. Conflicting perceptions existed. One subject said the vase filled his entire visual field, and then said it didn't completely fill his visual field. Many subjects felt these conflicts couldn't be described in words.

4. Distracting stimuli were effectively ignored. Though tapes of music and spoken words were played, the subjects had little or no awareness of them.

5. Subjects developed a personal attachment to the vase. In a 13th session the vase was removed. Subjects looked for it, asked for it, and generally exhibited a sense of loss at its absence. One subject became mildly depressed.

6. The sessions were deemed pleasurable. All subjects reported they found the sessions pleasurable, valuable and rewarding. (p. 331)

A Theory Explaining Meditation

Deikman (1963, 1966) has offered an interesting explanation of contemplative meditation. Earlier in this chapter we discussed automatic behavior and perception without awareness. Deikman hypothesizes that what happens in contemplative meditation is a *deautomatization,* an undoing of these automatic processes. Deautomatization is brought about by "reinvesting action and percepts with attention." An intense amount of attention is given to perception, while none is given to abstract categorization or thought. Thus, our usual form of perception and cognition is totally changed, our usual mode of organizing the environment is disarranged. Radically new cognitive and perceptual experiences arise. "Deautomatization is here conceived as permitting the adult to attain a new, fresh perception of the world by freeing him from a stereotyped organization built up over the years and by allowing adult synthetic and associative functions access to fresh materials, to create with them in a new way that represents an advance in mental functioning" (Deikman, 1963).

Presumably physiological processes, such as alpha, can be controlled if the person can find some way of monitoring that process. Kamiya gives his subjects such a way. Perhaps in Yoga or Zen, the meditative process permits the person to become aware of his body and its activity in ways that are not possible under typical attention, and in this manner he can bring such processes under control.

Control over Physiological Processes

The popular press often carries stories of Indian mystics who have been buried alive or submerged in tanks of water for hours on end. For centuries it has been reported that Yogis (those who practice Yoga) can gain remarkable control over physiological processes not usually under voluntary control, such as heart rate (Wenger and Bagchi, 1961). While scientists do not completely understand how these feats are accomplished, similar phenomena (though on a much smaller scale) have been produced in the laboratory.

In the section on sleep we mentioned that the EEG wave characteristic of the relaxed, waking state is known as an alpha rhythm. When a person becomes more alert, the alpha rhythm disappears as the EEG becomes desynchronized. By hooking special equipment up to the EEG, Kamiya (1969) showed that it was possible to convert the presence of alpha to an audible tone. When alpha disappears, the tone turns off. By listening for this tone, the subject can tell whether or not his brain is emitting alpha waves. Using this information as feedback, a subject can learn to control his alpha state (that is, maintain it or prevent it) in as little as 30 minutes. Fig. 9.7 shows how 10 subjects gained

Biofeedback

"Once upon a time . . ." as the story goes, autonomic responses such as heart rate, blood pressure, and body temperature were thought to be automatic and involuntary. One man, Neal Miller, more than any other person is responsible for changing that view. Along with Leo Di Cara, Miller trained rats to control their heart rate by as much as 20 percent through the use of operant conditioning techniques (Di Cara and Miller, 1968).

Researchers, seeing the medical applications of voluntary control of autonomic processes, began applying this technique to humans. They found the key ingredient was *feedback*. A patient with an irregular heartbeat, for example, can be trained to regulate his heart rate if he can be made aware of the irregularities. This can be done by using a "traffic signal" device, such as the one in Fig. 9.7, which provides information concerning the patient's heart. A green light signals the patient to increase his heart rate, a red light to lower it, and a yellow light to maintain the present rate.

Baltimore City Hospital

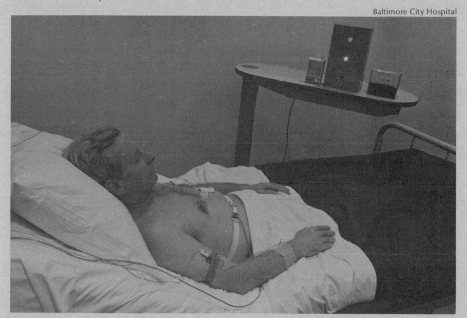

Fig. 9.7 A subject during a typical training session. The devices attached to the subject record his EEG and his breathing. (Engel, 1973)

Biofeedback (the term comes from feedback of biological information) can also be used to control "brain waves." Alpha waves are the EEG (electroencephalographic) pattern produced by the brain in the relaxed, waking state. Researchers have found that beta waves are the characteristic electrical activity for most persons during everyday business life, including the stress of commuting. Through the use of biofeedback people may learn how to maintain an alpha state even under pressure. In doing this, a person is given auditory information about his EEG. For example, a soft sound may indicate when alpha waves are present and a loud, shrill sound may indicate other electrical activity. Gradually, the person learns to control the brain's electrical activity and hence to relax more.

Biofeedback can also be useful in treating problems of old age. The dominant alpha frequency in young adults is between 10 and 12 cycles per second, but in the elderly (about 70 years) it drops to 7 or 8 cycles (Cherry and Cherry, 1974). Some psychologists see this drop in frequency as responsible for the slow movements and lengthened reaction time that accompany old age. Woodruff and Birren (1972) have trained older people to increase the frequency of their alpha waves and report that both movements and reaction times are quicker.

No one knows exactly how biofeedback works, least of all the patients and subjects involved in the research. Some psychologists see the process as analogous to learning a skill, such as riding a bicycle. Certainly it involves making fine, subtle discriminations based upon both bodily feelings and sensations and the external feedback information of the biofeedback machines. Through this association of external and internal signals we learn, first, which internal signals are desired, and second, how to get more of these desired internal signals.

alpha control. Subjects using this operant feedback technique report reaching a state of calm detachment similar to states reported by meditators.

DRUGS THAT ALTER CONSCIOUSNESS

Although the term "drugs" has developed strong emotional connotations in the last few years, most people don't realize how common drug-related altered states of consciousness are in our society. Alcohol, tranquilizers, barbiturates, nitrous oxide (the gas the dentist uses) are a few of the accepted, legal, widely available, and widely used drugs that are capable of altering consciousness. Although literally scores of drugs can produce altered states of consciousness, here we will discuss only two of the most controversial ones—marijuana and LSD.

Marijuana

Marijuana comes from the Indian hemp plant. Used for the making of rope, this plant was formerly cultivated in the United States. Today it still grows wild in many areas, but government officials make special efforts to destroy the wild fields that can be located. Several years ago it was noticed that birds in an area near a major highway in New Jersey flew in crazy, zig-zag patterns. Upon investigation, it was found that these birds were feeding on a field of wild marijuana. Newspapers carried the story and the field was quickly burned.

The leaves and flowering tops of this plant provide the cannabis, also known as marijuana, "pot," or "grass." The resin and pollen of the plant contain high concentrates of the active ingredient and are the source of "hashish."

Many myths have been propagated about marijuana, as a result of both public hysteria about the subject and a lack of well-controlled scientific investigations. We thus have few facts about the drug, though the following statements (Tart, 1971) are generally considered to be true:

1. *Marijuana is not a narcotic.* It is pharmacologically distant from opium-derived drugs such as heroin.
2. *Marijuana probably is not detrimental to the user's health.* Although extensive research is lacking, studies to date have not shown any harmful effects.
3. *Marijuana does not release aggressive behavior.* Instead, it seems usually to act in the opposite direction to inhibit aggression.

 Effects of Marijuana

Tart (1971) provides a detailed analysis of reports given by experienced marijuana users concerning the effects that are commonly experienced during marijuana intoxication. His study also provides data indicating which effects are associated with low, medium, or high levels of intoxication.

Tart first carefully prepared a questionnaire containing 220 items that described the various potential effects of marijuana. The items pertained to the effects of marijuana on such processes as vision, hearing, touch, smell, taste, sexuality, memory, thinking, and emotion. The respondents were asked to rate each item for frequency during marijuana intoxication and how "stoned" one had to be in order to experience it. The questionnaire also contained items that asked for evaluative judgments—for example, how does marijuana intoxication compare with experiences produced by LSD or other psychedelic drugs?

Tart gave 750 of these questionnaires to his students and acquaintances whom he thought used marijuana or had friends who might use it. Of these 750 questionnaires, 150 (20 percent) were returned in usable form. Generally speaking, the following effects were reported: (1) a euphoric sense of well-being; (2) enhanced perception: brightness and quality of colors, subtleties of sound and taste are more intensely perceived; (3) a change in time perception: time seems to pass more slowly; (4) a lowering of social inhibitions; (5) an enhancement of sexual pleasure; (6) changes in thought processes such as entertaining contradictory ideas more readily than usual.

The major problem in drawing conclusions from this study is that it was based on a rather special population sample. Each of the 150 respondents had used marijuana more than a dozen times; the sample does not include people who had used marijuana only a few times or people who had stopped using it. Thus, this sample is biased in the direction of reporting more pleasant and desirable effects than would a broader sample of the population.

Despite the widespread use of marijuana, there is little clearcut scientific data confirming its effects. All drugs, including marijuana, have multiple effects, none of which are completely reliable or predictable. They vary from person to person and from time to time for the same person. Since reaction to marijuana is at least in part determined by the person's unique psychological and physiological constitution, no research program can provide definitive answers. The number of variables and the interaction among them is simply too vast to incorporate into a controlled research design.

LSD

The consciousness-altering effects of lysergic acid diethylamide-25 were first discovered in 1943, when a Swiss research chemist accidentally ingested a minute amount of this recently developed chemical compound. Within a short time very strange things began happening to him. He experienced marked perceptual changes, intense fantasies, and severe cognitive changes. Inadvertently, this chemist had discovered the most powerful mind-altering drug yet known. As little as 100 micrograms can produce an extremely altered state of consciousness (Tart, 1972). Along with mescaline and several other substances, LSD-25 is classified as a "psychedelic" drug. "Psychedelic" literally means "mind manifesting."

 LSD and Mystical Experiences

Reports of mystical consciousness stemming from the use of LSD mark the presence of the following phenomena (Pahnke and Richards, 1966):

1. *Unity.* Unity may be internal or external. In the experience of internal unity, the usual sensory impressions seem to fade away while a feeling of pure consciousness of what is being experienced paradoxically remains. This feeling expands as a vast, new inner world is encountered and explored. Awareness of one's ego disappears and there is a feeling of mergence with all being. This mergence is felt to be an ultimate reality. In the experience of external unity, the subject-object relationship is transcended. Awareness of sensory impressions may grow in intensity to the point that the object of perception and the ego seem to cease to exist as separate entities, and seem to melt into each other. This process may be accompanied by the insight that truly "all is One." The subject-object transcendence may include the ego and another person, the ego and an object, or the ego and an auditory object such as music.

2. *Objectivity and reality.* There are two components to this category. First, insightful knowledge or enlightenment about existence in general is experienced in an intuitive, nonintellectual, and nonrational way. Second, in this experience there is a certainty that such knowledge or enlightenment is truly and ultimately real, as opposed to the feeling that this experience is a subjective delusion. People having experienced this state may report that they have found the answer to the

riddle of existence, have intuited the harmonious nature of the universe, have experienced the true brotherhood of man, or have realized the transcendent quality of life.

3. *Transcendence of time and space.* This refers both to the loss of a person's usual ability to locate himself in time and space, and the feeling that he is outside of time, in eternity, beyond past and future.

4. *Sense of sacredness.* There is often a feeling of profound holiness or sacredness, experienced at a very basic level. Feelings of awe, reverence, and humility may accompany this sensation.

5. *Deeply felt positive mood.* Feelings of joy, love, and peace are involved in the mystical consciousness. Emotions of tenderness and spiritual love may be extended to encompass the entire cosmos.

6. *Paradoxicality.* Various aspects of the mystical, psychedelic experience are felt to be true, even though they violate the ordinary laws of logic. For example, a subject may claim that he has died, but he is obviously alive as he speaks or writes of this experience. These paradoxical qualities are accepted in a suspension of reality-testing.

7. *Alleged ineffability.* When a subject attempts to verbally transmit explanations of his experiences, he usually claims that language is inadequate to this task. This may arise because of the paradoxical nature of many of the experiences, or because these experiences are so unique that the subject has not learned any language with which to describe them. The task of explaining these experiences has been likened to the task of explanation facing a caveman who had been instantly transported to the middle of Manhattan and then returned to his caveman friends. "What was it like, Og?" "Well, there were these . . . uhn. . . ."

8. *Positive changes in attitude or behavior.* Some people who have experienced the phenomena listed above reported changes in their lives as a result of these experiences. Changed attitudes included attitudes toward themselves, toward others, toward life, and toward the mystical consciousness itself. (pp. 177–183)

The state of our scientific knowledge about LSD-25 is difficult to determine, not for lack of experimental studies, but because the effects of the drug (as with other major psychedelic drugs) are very much influenced by personal psychological factors. Mogar (1965) notes some of the problems facing the researcher: "Systematic study of human reactions to LSD poses unique problems associated with greater organic complexity [of the drug], the ubiquity of individual differences, lack of an adequate theoretical model, and the influence of nondrug variables such as set and setting. In addition to these experimental obstacles, LSD has until recently been the center of a complicated medico-legal-social controversy. This has tended to obscure the relevant empirical questions and inhibit investigations which are both imaginative and objective."

The use of LSD-25 can promote two varieties of psychedelic experience: an experience of mystical consciousness, and a nonmystical form of altered consciousness. The major phenomena of LSD-induced states of consciousness are vivid perceptual distortions or hallucinations, including changed spatial relationships; apparent flexibility of solid masses; intensification of color; sharpening of contours; synesthesia, in which sound, usually music, is accompanied by rich visual imagery.

Some of the difficulties involved in LSD-25 research have been mentioned. It is particularly hard to obtain objective reports of the effects of this drug. However, several relatively objective accounts are available from investigators who have administered LSD to subjects under experimental conditions. Cohen (1964) reports that intellectual functioning is impaired, though subjects frequently believe their thinking processes are accelerated. He attributes the impairment to reduced motivation and attention. Ego boundaries tend to dissolve and the separation between self and the world is tenuous and sometimes nonexistent.

In a review of a number of experimental studies Jarvik (1967) notes that ingestion of LSD is followed by very unpleasant symptoms—nausea, sometimes vomiting, headache, sweating, and so on. Insomnia the night after taking LSD is almost inevitable. Marked changes in mood and extreme emotionality occur. There are also perceptual changes, particularly visual and tactile distortions and hallucinations.

If such effects were obtained in carefully selected and prepared subjects under controlled conditions and with drugs obtained through reputable channels, it is no wonder that naive users of LSD have experienced even more severe symptoms. Psychotic reactions, convulsions, and suicide have been reported to follow ingestion of LSD.

CONCLUSION

Our normal waking consciousness . . . is but one special type of consciousness, whilst all about it, parted from it by the flimsiest of screens, there lie potential forms of consciousness entirely different. We may go through life without suspecting their existence; but apply the requisite stimulus, and at a touch they are all there in all their completeness, definite types of mentality which probably somewhere have their field of application and adaptation. No account of the universe in its totality can be final which leaves these other forms of consciousness quite disregarded. How to regard them is the question—for they are so discontinuous with ordinary consciousness. Yet they may determine attitudes though they cannot furnish formulas, and open a region though they fail to give a map. At any rate, they forbid a premature closing of our accounts with reality. (James, 1929 pp. 378–379)

In this poetic paragraph psychologist and philosopher William James speaks of the roles altered states of consciousness may play in our lives. In the previous sections of the chapter we have discussed sleeping, sensory deprivation, hypnosis, meditation, and drug-induced altered states of consciousness. Some of these states, such as sleeping, we may experience quite frequently in our lives. Others, such as the use of psychedelic drugs, we may never experience. Throughout history, altered states of consciousness have been used by different cultures for a variety of purposes: for healing, in religious ceremonies, as a means of gaining new knowledge and experience, and in group settings to fulfill social needs. Only recently have altered states of consciousness become an area of interest to Western scientists and psychologists. However our culture may come to regard them, and whatever roles they may assume in our lives, they provide alternative ways of experiencing the self and the world.

Summary

Discussions of consciousness lead inevitably to the historic mind-body problem of philosophy and, subsequently, of psychology. In psychology, introspectionists adopted a solution called psychophysical parallelism: mind and body are independent, parallel systems that do not directly interact. Behaviorists solved the problem by physical monism, a denial of the reality of mind. The solution for Gestalt psychologists was psychological isomorphism between subjective experience and the purely physical processes of the brain. Two other solutions are semantic in nature. One, a behaviorist approach, denies subjectivity; subjective language, like all language, is acquired through conditioning. Another approach, the one adopted here, proposes that mind and body are the same referent; the only difference is in the way we talk about them.

Consciousness exists in a number of states ranging from coma to hyperactivity. To be considered conscious we must be aware of self, time, and location in space. We may be conscious of many things without being explicitly aware of them. For example, we perform overlearned behavior automatically. We also perceive some stimuli without awareness as we reveal when we incidentally recall them. Sometimes stimuli are perceived at subliminal levels of exposure (subception). Similarly we are capable of blocking from awareness certain anxiety-arousing stimuli; this is known as perceptual defense.

Beyond peripheral consciousness, as exemplified by automatic behavior, subception, and perceptual defense, psychologists of the psychoanalytic school posit a powerful unconscious, which contains psychic events that are repressed from consciousness. The concept of an unconscious is useful in explaining errors, dreams, and many issues in motivation.

An altered state of consciousness produces a qualitative change in basic patterns of mental functioning.

Sleep is an altered state of consciousness. EEG recordings have revealed four stages of sleep, each characterized by clearly different electrical activity in the brain. The first stage has a substage characterized by rapid eye movements (REM's); dreaming occurs during this stage of sleep. Distinct physiological changes occur during dreams, though a mechanism in the brain inhibits actual motor activity. We evidently have a psychological and perhaps a biological need to dream.

Freud believes that the principal purpose of dreams is to maintain sleep by allowing instinctual impulses to find symbolic, nonthreatening expression. The remembered dream is the manifest dream; the repressed material underlying this is the latent dream. Latent dream material may be sensory impressions, conflicting thoughts or aspirations, or, most importantly, instinctual impulses. Dreamwork, the process of converting latent into manifest dream, uses condensation, displacement, and symbolization to disguise unacceptable impulses. Dreams are analyzed by working backwards from manifest to latent content. Daydreams are not true dreams, but relatively transparent fantasies. The major contribution of Freud's interpretation of dreams is a rejection of all prophetic interpretations.

Sensory deprivation is a condition in which external stimuli are greatly reduced or altered. The condition is now scientifically studied by putting people in deprived environments or by distorting their perceptual input. Sensory deprivation may disturb visual perception, thinking, concentration, and intellectual functioning. It may also cause hallucinations, sometimes similar to the hallucinations of schizophrenia, which may involve processes similar to those of sensory deprivation. Sensory deprivation in infancy disrupts the development of normal functioning.

Hypnosis is induced by persuading the subject to relax, concentrate, imagine freely, and open himself to suggestions. Susceptibility to hypnosis varies widely. Hypnosis has been used in medicine to promote relaxation, reduce anxiety, and relieve pain. The state is generally considered very pleasant.

Meditation can produce a radically altered state of consciousness. In contemplative meditation, the subject contemplates an object in a nonanalytical, nonintellectual manner. It produces altered perceptions, a distorted sense of time, conflicting perceptions, avoidance of distracting stimuli, a personal attachment to the contemplated object, and a pleasurable state. Meditation may be a deautomatization of normal perceptual activity. It has been used to control electrical activity of the brain.

Marijuana and LSD are drugs that alter consciousness. Marijuana is probably not a narcotic and is probably not injurious to health. LSD promotes two varieties of psychedelic experience, one mystical and one nonmystical. Its effects include impaired intellectual functioning, reduced motivation and attention, depersonalization, unpleasant physical symptoms, and marked mood changes and emotionality. There are also perceptual changes, including hallucinations. Psychotic reactions, convulsions, and suicides have been associated with LSD.

SUGGESTED READINGS

Barber, T. X., *Hypnosis: A Scientific Approach.* New York, Van Nostrand, 1969.
An attempt to examine the phenomenon of hypnosis from a scientific point of view.
Caldwell, W. V., *LSD Psychotherapy: An Exploration of Psychedelic and Psycholytic Therapy.* New York, Grove Press, 1968.
A popular book on therapeutic aspects of psychedelics.
Curtis, David, *Sleep and Learn.* New York, Lancer Books, 1972.
A description of procedures for learning while asleep through the subconscious mind.
Hartmann, E., ed., *Sleep and Dreaming.* Boston, Little, Brown, 1970.
An overview, in question and answer format, of the last 15 years of research in the area.
Jung, C. G., *Memories, Dreams and Reflections,* Aniela Jaffe, ed. New York, Random House, 1965.
Contains Jung's ideas concerning dreaming (as well as his thoughts about life after death and the meaning of life).

Needleman, Jacob, *The New Religions*. New York, Doubleday, 1970.
     A readable overview of eastern religions, which includes interviews with many major teachers.
Ornstein, Robert E., ed., *The Nature of Human Consciousness*. New York, Viking Press, 1974.
     A book of readings on the intuitive mode of consciousness.
Schmeidler, G. R., ed., *Extrasensory Perception*. New York, Atherton, 1969.
     A reference work on parapsychology.

Part 3
Development of Personality

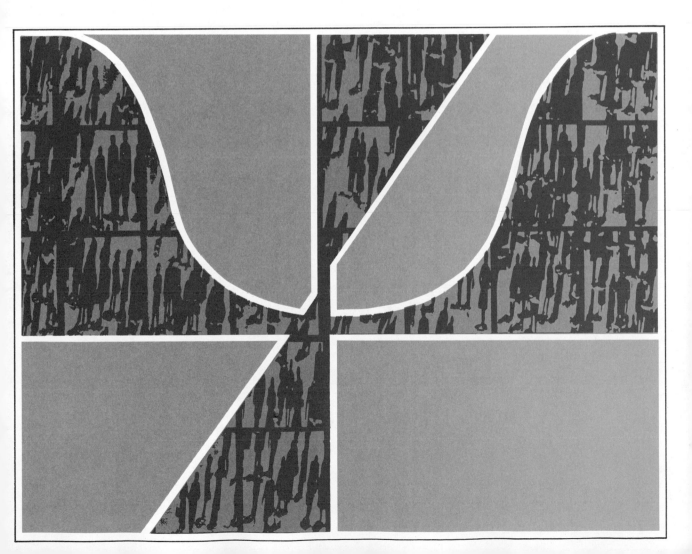

Chapter Ten

Maturation

How does rate of maturation affect learning?
Is maturation determined by heredity or by environment?
What are the prenatal periods of maturation?
What is the significance to maturation of the prenatal
    environment?
What are the major maturational events of infancy, childhood,
    and adolescence?
What processes influence the adoption of a sex role?
What are some of the difficulties we face in the quest for
    autonomy?

The study of man is not limited to the study of adults. Indeed, it must start even before birth—with conception—for that is the beginning of the developmental process that ultimately shapes each person. At every stage from conception to adolescence constellations of forces affect the direction and pace of the march toward adulthood. Cultural and individual experiences and expectations play an important part in determining the course and rhythm of a child's development, but certain patterns of growth and change appear to be universal. Developmental or child psychology is the study of all the processes that shape the human being.

Child psychology has practical implications for many people who are not psychologists. Those who expect to become parents or to work with children in some capacity are eager to keep abreast of scientific discoveries about development so that they can more effectively guide the children in their care. The continuing popularity of books such as those by Arnold Gesell (1940) and Benjamin Spock (1946), which attempt to convert the principles of human development into practical advice for everyday dealings with children, is evidence of this concern. The views presented by Haim Ginott (1965) and Lee Salk (1972) have

443

also made a substantial splash. Controversies arising from differences in the practical applications of developmental principles have come from various groups, but particularly from those representing women's liberation views, which are discussed later in this chapter.

The study of development is still young, and psychologists have not yet achieved a unified explanation of exactly what happens—or when and how it happens—as the child progresses toward adulthood. A great deal of exciting research is currently being conducted on ways in which the child participates actively in his own development. We will look at some of this material in Chapter 11. In the present chapter, however, we will concentrate on processes of development that seem to occur in every child, regardless of his individual personality and the specifics of his culture. Although these processes appear to be relatively invariable, the timing of their appearance and the rate at which they evolve often are subject to environmental influences. It will not always be possible to keep the topics in these two chapters completely separate; some topics will come up more than once.

 Changing Advice to Parents

Traditionally, child feeding has been the occasion of bafflement, anxiety, some humor, but little agreement. Opinion has ranged from strict regularity, brooking no disagreement, to virtual self-demand feeding and faith in the child's sense of his own needs.

Dr. Arnold Gesell, main author of *First Five Years of Life* (1940), was aware of the revolutionary change in the child's status in society. Above all, he says, there is the child's need for the mother's guidance through the course of maturation. As regards feeding, liberal allowance is made for individual deviation from the norm, but there is no attention paid to the causes or specific solutions of problem eating. Children who experience feeding difficulties—refusal to eat, gagging, vomiting—are seen merely as being particularly "sensitive" to the eating situation. The nature of this problem is not examined, but nonetheless it is the duty of the mother to successfully "manage" the situation: She must keep in mind the prescribed developmental sequences and yet be alert to the cues of the child's own differences. No great understanding is shown for the parents' own worries, no specific solutions are offered, and the mother is left with an incomplete, though rational, approach to what are not always rational problems.

Then came Dr. Benjamin Spock, by far the most well-known parent adviser. The paternal tone of Spock's best seller, *Common Sense Book of Baby and Child Care* (1946), and its detailed helpful hints distinguish it from Gesell's previous scientific tome designed for an educated audience. Diagrams, recipes for formulas, and a chapter devoted to vitamins were part of the new approach of encouraging the parent. Much greater emphasis was placed on each baby's individuality. Naturalness and flexibility are encouraged, for feeding is the source of the baby's initial

Arnold Gesell

Benjamin Spock

impressions about the world and its ability to satisfy him. The mother is urged to also think of her own convenience and sanity in feeding matters. The baby can be trusted to take as much as he needs, and the mother is not to worry over apparent lack of appetite. Breast feeding and gradual weaning are promoted for their physical and emotional benefits to both mother and child. Spock's book was revolutionary, then, in its concern for parental anxiety and its clarity and depth of detail and prescription.

Dr. Haim Ginott, author of *Between Parent and Child* (1965), starts out with a psychological bias and stresses the need for parents and children to share an atmosphere of mutual respect and dignity. The feeding situation is not treated as such, but falls into the area of the child's responsibility for his actions. The child has a right to indicate a choice in the feeding situation, and it is the duty of the parents to develop decision-making ability by creating such choices. Ginott follows the more permissive trend, urging parents to trust the child's ability to select the amount of food eaten. The emphasis is on humanistic relations, but once again specific solutions are not included.

Dr. Lee Salk, in his book *What Every Child Would Like His Parents To Know* (1972), is analytical in his correlation between the emotional problems of early childhood and later personality disorders. He tells of the later consequences of improper breast-feeding habits (insecurity and emotional instability) and poor weaning (smoking and alcoholism). The feeding situation itself is viewed primarily as a period of sensory stimulation and social interaction. The book's tone is not reassuring and "permissive" as in Ginott's and Spock's books; rather it emphasizes the socializing responsibility of parents to use preventative measures to ensure healthy emotional development.

Haim Ginott

Lee Salk

GENERAL PRINCIPLES

The maturation process—the fundamental process of child development—is both orderly and discontinuous. In all children, regardless of background and environment, there is a common process within the mother's womb. And immediately after birth, similarly universal processes are reflected in the variety of reflex responses that constitute almost the whole of the newborn's behavior. Environmental forces affect only the timing and rapidity of certain advances; opportunity and encouragement may lead some babies to walk earlier than others, but these factors are of no effect until the requisite muscle strength and coordination have developed.

In the early years of life, the role of maturation is proportionally very great, but as the child grows older, maturation is increasingly supplemented by active involvement with the environment, and the child exerts an ever-increasing influence on his own development (see Chapter 11).

After early childhood, it is difficult to predict when a child will achieve each new level of development. Some advances arrive "on schedule," others are precocious, and still others lag behind and then appear in a sudden spurt. When development seems stalled, or rapid progress is being made, it sometimes seems that energy is drawn away from previous gains, that the child is actually regressing. Frequently, a child who has begun to talk will temporarily fall off in language ability when he becomes occupied with walking.

Within broad categories, maturation tends to follow several fundamental directions. First, physical growth seems to center in the head; the head grows rapidly immediately after conception and may reach as much as 60 percent of its adult size by the time the baby is born. After birth, the rate of head growth declines, and it is the torso's turn to grow—by the age of 2, the torso has usually reached half its adult size.

Motor skills also develop from the head downward. In the first few weeks after birth, sucking is the infant's best-organized behavior, and he early gains a measure of control over eye movements and learns to tilt his head at will. Later he learns to sit up, jiggle, and roll over—to control the torso.

Development also follows a *proximodistal* (near to far) direction; the central part of the body is controlled before the fingers and toes. A third tendency is to progress from broad, generalized movements to controlled gestures, especially in the hands. The infant goes from uncoordinated grasping to simple clutching to more varied and active manipulation of objects.

Maturation and Learning

maturation   We have already defined maturation as those processes that occur relatively independently of environment and experience, in a fairly fixed sequence, although at uneven rates, and in certain predictable directions. Learning has been defined as a relatively permanent change in behavior as a result of practice (Chapter 3). As the outgrowth of new associations, learning occurs at many levels. When the infant grasps his foot and realizes for the first time that it is *his,* he has learned the relationship between a part of his body and himself. Later he finds, as he crawls about the floor, that putting his finger in an electric outlet is associated with a sharp reaction from his mother; that is, he learns that the outlet is a "no-no." When he goes to school he learns to associate certain shapes on a page with sounds he already knows.

In this chapter we are interested in learning mainly as it relates to maturation. Most learning depends primarily upon the child's *readiness* to learn. It is impossible to train an infant of 3 months to associate letters on a printed page with sounds, for he has not yet developed the ability to differentiate such small figures with his eyes or to correctly differentiate sounds with his ears or his vocal chords. While maturation thus defines readiness to learn, it has little effect on the learning process or the content of what is learned. For example, many children who are mature enough for language-play have little opportunity for it; one of the goals of television's *Sesame Street,* therefore, is to encourage children to recognize and manipulate the basic units of language.

Latest Follow-up of Terman's Gifted Children

Oden in 1960 sent out a questionnaire to the surviving members of the original group of high-intelligence people first tested by Terman. Six-hundred and sixty-four men and 524 women responded to this questionnaire. The basic question Oden was interested in was "is the promise of youth fullfilled?" That is, do people who are deemed to be "bright" at a young age fulfill their promise? Do they accomplish more than this?

The findings of this study reported by Oden in 1968 corroborate earlier follow-up studies of 1940, 1945, and 1955. As Oden puts it, "All the evidence indicates that with few exceptions the superior child becomes the superior adult."

The superior child maintains his high intellectual ability; his physical health is good to very good. People with superior intelligence rank higher than the general population in educational and vocational achievements. They publish more papers, make more scientific discoveries, and are awarded more honors. They are also more involved in community activities, 95 percent of them vote "always" or "usually," and they have wide-ranging interests and activities. To dispel the popular myth of geniuses being half-crazy, Oden reports "the incidence of serious mental illness and personality problems appears to be no greater, and perhaps less, than that found in the general population."

These findings were true for women as well as for men, although the women were less interested in vocational careers and achievements. Those who had embarked on such careers were extremely successful and well placed in prestigious positions. Also, practically none of the "housewives" confined their activities to their homes. They were all involved in community and civic affairs.

Both men and women expressed satisfaction with having achieved their potential, and 80 percent of the men and 84 percent of the women picked "work itself" as the aspect of life from which the greatest satisfaction is derived. (Married men chose their work second only to marriage as a source of satisfaction.)

Genetic Inheritance

The influence of heredity on human behavior has long been a matter of scientific controversy. Many scientists, particularly biologists, once believed that most of our important characteristics are determined genetically. Even criminal types were said to be "born," and skull shape was once studied as an index of criminality and other traits.

In reaction to nativistic explanations such as this, social scientists (and behavioral psychologists in particular) began to insist on the influence of environmental forces. In the extreme, this produced an equally mechanical view of man as a passive being, controlled by environmental influences.

This issue, called the *nature-nurture controversy*, has not been resolved; a combination of both nature and nuture is generally thought to be the most likely determinant of human characteristics. More recently, research has begun

nature-nurture controversy

Sesame Street: First Year Report Card

What is the impact of *Sesame Street?* The producers of the television show asked Educational Testing Service (ETS), a nonprofit educational measurement service in Princeton, New Jersey, to conduct an evaluation of the program and its impact during its first year on television (Ball and Bogatz, 1970).

ETS gathered data from a sample of 943 children from five different locales. The sample included disadvantaged children from the inner city, advantaged children from the suburbs, children from rural areas, and disadvantaged Spanish-speaking children. Most of the children were 4 years old, but some were 3 and some were 5.

At the beginning of the study all of the children were tested on eight major tasks. After the show had run for a year, they were retested on the same tests, and their pretest and posttest scores were compared.

The children were separated into four groups, or quartiles, on the basis of how frequently they watched the show. Q1 children rarely or never watched it, Q2 watched it two or three times a week, Q3 watched it four or five times a week, and Q4 watched more than five times weekly.

The overall results showed simply that "the more you watched the more you learned." Q1 children gained 19 points between the pretest and the posttest;

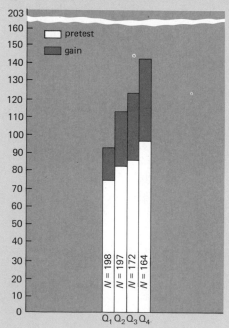

Fig. 10.1 Pretest and gain on total test score for all disadvantaged children (by viewing quartiles), *N* = 73l. (Ball and Bogatz, 1970)

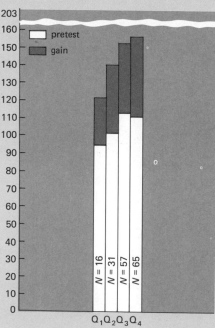

Fig. 10.2 Pretest and gain on total test score for all advantaged children (by viewing quartiles), *N* = 169. (Ball and Bogatz, 1970)

Q2 gained 29 points; Q3, 38 points; and Q4, 47 points. Thus although all children gained between the two tests, the basic gain—that shown by the Q1 group—was due to maturation. The extra gain in points by those frequently exposed to *Sesame Street* was due to the impact of the program.

Fig. 10.1 shows pretest scores and posttest gains for disadvantaged children in all quartiles, and Fig. 10.2 shows this comparison for advantaged children in all quartiles. It is apparent that children who watched most, especially in the disadvantaged groups, started with higher scores. A special study (an age cohorts study) was conducted to isolate the effects of viewing time. A group of children aged 53 to 58 months at the time of pretesting, before they could have watched the show, were matched for mental age, previous attainments, and home background with a group of children aged 53 to 58 months at the posttest. When the pretest scores of Group 1 were compared with the posttest scores of Group 2, gains on the test again increased as a function of frequency of viewing. This study eliminates the effects of both previous viewing and maturation.

The advantaged children in the survey showed the greatest gains, and they also tended to be among the most frequent viewers of the program. This may be related to another finding—that children who watched *Sesame Street* most tended to have mothers who watched the show with them and talked to them about it. Such mothers also tended to have higher expectations of their children.

Overall the study showed *Sesame Street* to be a highly successful way to teach children basic skills without supervision. Perhaps even more important was the finding that 3-year-olds can learn many skills that are generally not introduced until the child is 5 or 6 years old.

to discover just how genetic and environmental influences interact to determine specific kinds of behavior. We will begin our study of maturation with a discussion of heredity, as it is modified by environmental factors.

Certain traits are largely determined by "instructions" coded in the cells. Eye color, pigmentation, and the shape of ears and noses probably are determined exclusively by heredity. More abstractly, heredity is responsible for a high potential for muscular coordination, physical endurance, and timing of reactions. Without training, none of these capacities may be developed, but without an inherited capacity, practice, training, and discipline will produce no more than a mediocre level of skill in these endeavors.

Weakness too can be genetically influenced, as predispositions to disease are passed from one generation to the next, or in some cases, to every third or fourth generation or to a certain percentage of a generation. Diabetes occurs in family lines, in no clear pattern. Sickle-cell anemia usually affects only those of African descent. The ethnic specificity of this disease may, however, be evidence of an ultimate environmental origin; sickle-cell anemia probably first appeared as an immunological defense against malaria—indicating the complexity of nature-nurture interaction.

Mechanisms of Heredity

chromosome

The human body has two main kinds of cells. By far the most numerous are the cells that compose bones, muscles, and other body tissues; each of these body cells contains 23 pairs of *chromosomes,* the carriers of genetic inheritance, which we shall discuss shortly. This type of cell reproduces itself by a process of subdivision called *mitosis.* First, the chromosomes duplicate themselves within the cell; then the two identical groups of chromosomes cluster on opposite sides of the cell, which splits down the middle. The result is two cells identical in every respect to the "parent" cell, each containing 46 (or 23 pairs of) chromosomes. Mitosis occurs rapidly during the years of a child's growth, for cells must multiply at a great pace in order to increase the sizes of the various body parts. The process continues more slowly in adulthood, for, though little further growth typically occurs, dead cells must constantly be replaced.

A second, specialized kind of cell are the *gametes,* or reproductive cells. The gametes of males are called *spermatozoa,* or *sperm cells;* those of females *ova,* or *egg cells.* These gametes have in common certain special properties that distinguish them from body cells in general.

One basic difference is the way in which the gametes are produced. We have already noted how in mitosis each body cell duplicates itself exactly. In a contrasting process called *meiosis,* the chromosomes are first duplicated as we have described, and the cell splits into two cells of 23 pairs each. But then each of these cells splits again, resulting in four gametes, each containing only 23 single chromosomes—one half of each of the original 23 pairs. Which member of each pair of chromosomes goes into a particular gamete appears to be a purely random matter.

Thus gametes have a different structure from that of body cells. When a spermatozoon from the father unites with an ovum from the mother, the single chromosomes form pairs in a new cell called the *zygote,* the first body cell of the new human being. Conception has occurred, and it is clear that the offspring receives his entire genetic inheritance from both parents at that moment.

gene

We have mentioned that the chromosomes are the carriers of this genetic inheritance. Each chromosome is a tiny hairlike structure that contains approximately 20,000 genes, which embody the instructions for specific features of the new human being—the color of his hair, the ultimate size of his brain, the shapes of his hands and feet, and so on. Actually, groups of genes usually combine to determine the ultimate conformation and characteristics of specific organs and traits.

It is clear that all the hereditary components of the child are already present and complete in the first cell, the zygote. This cell proceeds to duplicate itself exactly by mitosis, the resulting cells subdivide again, and this process continues throughout the development of the child. Because the process of mitosis results in precise duplicates of the original zygote, the hereditary components contributed through that first union of gametes are thus present and complete in all the body cells, which eventually total many trillions.

The power of hereditary factors has been confirmed by studies of identical twins living in different environments. Because these twins come from the division of a single zygote, their genetic instructions are identical. This research shows that certain physical similarities persist. One study of identical twins over 60 years old showed that despite quite different life experiences, patterns of skin wrinkles, changes in hair and teeth, especially declines in mental and physical agility—and even the life-span—were very similar (Kallman and Sander, 1949).

THE PRENATAL PERIOD

Development

Conception Fertilization of the ovum by the sperm cell results in a zygote that, within 24 hours, has already mitotically subdivided into two identical cells. As cells continue to divide and cluster on the wall of the uterus—a process that takes perhaps 2 weeks—they begin to differentiate. An "envelope," which will protect and nourish the developing being, forms around this new cell cluster, the *blastocyst,* which attaches itself to the uterine wall and becomes the embryo.

Wide World Photos

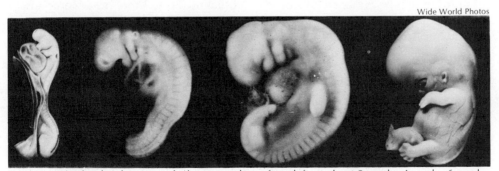

Four stages in the development of a human embryo; from left, at about 2 weeks, 4 weeks, 6 weeks, and 8 weeks.

The Embryo Between the second and eighth weeks after conception, the outer envelope of cells becomes further differentiated. Part becomes the amniotic sac, a fluid-filled membrane that protects the embryo and maintains a stable environment. Later, the cells of the embryo differentiate according to function.

The Fetus The fetal stage lasts from 8 weeks after conception to birth. Size increases enormously during this period, and the muscles develop. As the fetus begins to move in the womb, it becomes capable of grasping and sucking movements. In the last 3 months in the womb, the fetus moves around a great deal, and the brain gains increasing control over respiration and temperature regulation.

Effects of the Prenatal Environment

We tend to think of after-birth factors when we speak of the environment, but in fact, the fetus is subject to environmental influences during the course of its development in the womb. Certain elements of the prenatal environment are particularly likely to have effects, and we will examine a few of them here.

Mother's Age One of the most crucial factors—and one of the most difficult to explain—is the age of the mother. A higher than average proportion of children born to women younger than 21 or older than 29 have birth defects. One study has shown that mothers under 20 or over 35 are more likely than other mothers to give birth to mentally retarded children (Pasamanick and Lilienfeld, 1955). Mongolism is especially frequent among the offspring of older mothers.

Diseases and Disorders The child is especially vulnerable to injury during the embryonic period, while most of the vital systems are still in the process of formation. German measles affecting the mother during this time, for example, may wreak havoc on the embryo. Yet if the mother is exposed to German measles after the third month of pregnancy, the child rarely suffers damage. Syphilis, however, poses the greatest threat after the fifth month of uterine life.

Chronic disorders of the mother also harm the child's health. Diabetes is a prominent example; if it is treated and diagnosed in time, however, damage to the fetus can be minimized.

Emotional States Extreme anger or fear causes increased concentration of glandular secretions such as adrenaline in the mother's bloodstream, and in that of the fetus as well. In the early stages of pregnancy, the mother's emotional reactions may cause physical damage to her child. Later, emotional stress of the mother is more likely to affect the behavior of the fetus rather than his body. One manifestation is excessive movement in the uterus. Anxious mothers seem likely to have irritable and restless infants. It is not clear, however, that the infant's behavior can be traced to uterine life; it may well be caused by maternal tension after birth. (See the discussion of Ader's study of stress, Chapter 5.)

Stress and Body Size

Although most research on child-rearing practices and size has been concerned with severe reductions in stimulation, some work has been done on the effects of increases in stimulation, or stress, on infants.

Landauer and Whiting (1963) conducted a cross-cultural study comparing societies that apply differing degrees of stressful procedures in the normal process of infant rearing. The different societies and their stress levels were taken from the Human Relations Files, a cross-cultural index of practices in different cultures assembled from the work of many researchers. Landauer and Whiting picked out societies whose child-rearing practices included pain, shaping (of the limbs, for example, by tying them at birth), exposure to extreme cold or heat, intense stimulation such as subjection to loud noises, and other stressful events. They found that adult males in such stressful societies were on the average 2 inches taller than adult males from nonstressful societies. Furthermore the effects on adult stature seemed to be produced maximally by stresses occurring before the infant had reached the age of 2.

Although Landauer and Whiting made attempts to control for genetic, climatic, and nutritional variables in their study, their results are at best only suggestive. The correlation found between stress and body size in particular societies might be due to the fact that societies in which stressful child-rearing practices are common may be societies in which hardship and stress are generally common. The hardships of life in such environments might result in natural selection of largeness and physical strength. Although research with animals indicates that too much stress ought to be harmful, no such effects have been reported in human societies.

Nutrition Because the pregnant mother is feeding her unborn infant as well as herself, any vitamin deficiency will be passed along to the fetus. Insufficient vitamin B seems to retard mental activity, whereas shortages of C and D stunt growth and cause various physical deficiencies, as well as slowness in learning. On the other hand, excessive vitamin A early in the gestation period causes physical abnormalities and later in pregnancy may produce poor motivation and limited attention span in the offspring. Most of our evidence is with sub-human animals, though many scientists feel the generalizations are appropriate to human beings. Children of well-nourished mothers grow taller than those whose mothers are vitamin-deficient.

Drugs When, in 1961, the use of thalidomide caused pregnant women to give birth to armless and legless infants, public attention focused for the first time on the necessity of controlling drug use by expectant mothers. Some research has taken a more futuristic direction, with the aim of determining the infant's sex through the administration of hormones.

Addictive drugs also seem to have serious effects on unborn children. A heroin addict passes her addiction to the child, who experiences withdrawal symptoms at birth. Some have suggested that LSD may cause abnormalities in infants' chromosomes. The destructive effects of nicotine, a drug consumed by all who smoke, have only recently been widely recognized. Heavy smokers are twice as likely to give birth prematurely, and their babies tend to weigh less. The effects of smoking may be indirect, however; the mother's need to smoke and the premature delivery of her child may be connected to still another factor.

Socioeconomic Status Nutrition and prenatal care for women of poor backgrounds are often inadequate. Illnesses are more common in this group, and the incidence of premature births is higher. Socioeconomic status is a good predictor of health at birth because it is correlated with other factors: nutrition, mental attitude, and medical care.

Birth When labor is particularly painful, the administering physician may give the mother a sedative or anesthetic; a heavy dose just before childbirth may reduce the infant's oxygen supply, causing a loss of mental alertness, slow weight gain, and initial nursing difficulties.

A long and difficult labor in itself may seriously damage the infant's brain. Heavy pressure on the baby's head can rupture the blood vessels that carry oxygen to the brain.

INFANCY: 0—2 YEARS

The newborn infant is not, as we have seen, a neutral being ready to be shaped by the forces around him. He is capable of some complex behavior. With the exception of taste, all his senses are in full operation. He follows moving lights with his eyes, turns his head in response to a touch, and withdraws from contact with sharp objects and other painful stimuli.

The reflexes of the newborn infant reflect the complex level of development the nervous system has reached. Unlike sucking and withdrawal, however, not all these reflexes are clearly related to survival. When he is surprised by being suddenly moved, the infant exhibits the *Moro reflex,* in which he flings his arms wide, then clasps them across his chest. When the sole of his foot is touched, he spreads his toes in the *Bibinski reflex.* In the first months, the brain stem alone controls these reflexes; later, the cerebral cortex becomes operative, blocking or modifying many reflex signals.

At first, sleeping and eating are the major behaviors of the infant. He may sleep up to 20 hours a day, tapering off to 12 hours by the end of the first year. In his diet, the infant is soon eating semisolid foods on a regular schedule. Bowel and urinary movements remain under reflexive control until the child is 2 or 3 years old.

The satisfaction of basic needs is the first requirement for the infant's physical growth and development, but the *manner* in which they are satisfied has great impact on the course of his social development. In the following discussion of development during infancy, we will trace first the child's physical growth from birth to 2 years, then the maturation of his motor abilities, and finally his social development. It is important to keep in mind during this discussion that our use of the word "normal" does not imply that any child *should* conform precisely to the pattern we describe. Healthy, active children vary enormously in their rates of development, yet most grow into competent and productive adults. We use the term "normal" here to refer only to a *statistically average* age at which a given feature or ability makes its appearance.

Physical Maturation

The first 2 years of the child's life are a time of rapid and extensive physical growth. In the first year especially his length increases by a third, and his weight triples. An infant who is 21 inches long and weighs 8 pounds at birth will be approximately 28 inches tall and weigh 24 pounds at the age of 1 year. While male babies tend to be larger, girl infants seem to grow at a steadier rate.

The overall growth rate is actually a composite of the varying growth rates of different parts of the body, which result in major changes in the body *proportions* of the infant. Whereas at birth his head is quite large in relation to the length of his body—perhaps one-quarter of the total—the ensuing rapid enlargement of his torso means that by the age of 2 he will have assumed overall body proportions close to those of an adult (see Fig. 10.3).

These changes partly reflect the growth of his skeleton. Many portions of the infant's skeleton cannot accurately be called bones. Instead they are flexible cartilage tissue, which can absorb the shock of falls and other bumps and thus help to prevent injury. Through a proper concentration of minerals

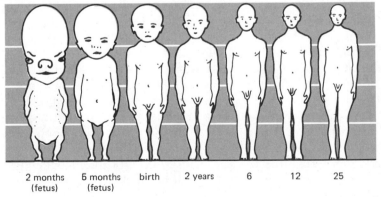

| 2 months (fetus) | 5 months (fetus) | birth | 2 years | 6 | 12 | 25 |

Fig. 10.3 Changes in body proportions during human fetal and postnatal growth. The head grows proportionately much more slowly than the limbs. (Modified from *Morris' Human Anatomy*, ed. by C. M. Jackson, © Blakiston, 1925. Used by permission of McGraw Hill Book Company.)

in the infant's diet, the soft cartilage gradually hardens into bone; this ossification process continues at very uneven rates in different parts of the body.

By the age of 2, the head no longer accounts for a large proportion of the infant's total length. Nevertheless, the fastest-growing anatomical structure in the early development period is the brain, which increases from about 12 ounces to 2½ pounds. Teeth begin to form early in the fetal period; calcium deposits have begun to build up by the fifth month of pregnancy. The first calcified tooth appears about 7 months after birth, but for many children, no teeth are cut for an entire year. Teeth do not seem to be correlated with other aspects of development. Girls tend to have teeth earlier, and black and Oriental children usually have their first teeth before Caucasians.

Motor Development

The maturation of the child's neuromuscular system has a direct impact on the development of his motor behavior. As his muscles become stronger, his ability to coordinate movement increases, and greater coordination is reflected in his moving about, in more varied manipulative activities, and in more effective eye functioning.

At first the child's neck and back muscles are not strong enough to allow him to sit up, but by the age of 3 or 4 months he can sit with some help. In another 3 or 4 months he not only can sit up alone; he also can stay in that position for longer stretches of time—for as long as 10 minutes by the age of 9 months.

At about 7 months the child begins to make uncoordinated kicking motions while lying on his stomach, and in another 6 weeks or so he is able to wriggle and drag himself along on his stomach. At 10 months his arm and leg muscles are strong enough to support his body's weight, and he begins to crawl on his hands and knees. Finally, at about a year he can propel himself on his hands and feet with his back arched.

Once he has learned to use his feet in crawling, it is only a short time before he discovers that by holding onto a chair he can pull himself up to a standing position. By the age of 14 months he can stand alone without support, and in another month he can launch himself rather unsteadily into space. Although the statistical norm for the age at which walking begins for American children is 15 months, some children walk alone at 10 months, others only at 2 years, and many at all the ages between. There is absolutely no evidence that the age at which a child first walks or makes any comparable advance in motor activity is correlated with sex, social background, or intelligence. It appears to be mainly a function of the maturation of his skeletal and neuromuscular systems.

Once the necessary level of maturation has been achieved, environmental influences can play a decisive role in the rapidity with which specific motor skills appear and are consolidated, as Dennis (1960) has shown in a series of studies conducted among children in institutions. In two institutions babies were not permitted to sit up or to lie on their stomachs while playing; these babies learned to walk significantly later than did children raised in the less restrictive atmosphere of a third institution, where they were given some opportunity to move around.

A related study was conducted in an infant home in Lebanon, with two control groups drawn from Lebanese and American infants reared in their own homes. The institutionalized infants were largely confined to their beds and received even solid foods lying down; the overworked staff had time for only perfunctory attention of feeding and changing these babies and rarely paused for more affectionate handling or chatter. This hurried treatment was reflected in serious lags in the children's motor activities up to the age of 12 months. The lags were noticeable in both their locomotive and manual behavior and appear to have resulted from lack of opportunities for practice (Dennis and Najarian, 1957).

Object manipulation develops simultaneously with locomotion. We have noted that the child's reflexes undergo a period of transition, when control shifts from the brain stem to the cerebral cortex. During this period, the child is unable to grasp objects firmly, but he begins to try to coordinate movements of eye and hand. By 6 months, he may be able to pick up an object by grabbing it with both hands; by 9 months, he has learned to secure his hold by curling his fingers around the object. Later he coordinates thumb and forefinger until, by 15 months, he can grasp a block as well as any adult.

Perceptual Development

Gaining control of eye muscles is an important development in the process of motor coordination. The newborn infant sees a clear image only when an object is a foot or two in front of him; if it is farther away, or much closer, the image is out of focus because he is not yet able to make accommodative changes of the lens. He can also move his eyes together so that each is converging on the same object. It also appears that he can begin to perceive depth, as the prerequisite for the successful manipulation of depth. By two months, he can notice the internal details of figures, and begins to attend to the eyes and mouths of faces, rather than just the outer perimeter. This would seem to be a prerequisite for the recognition of faces and objects.

The most graphic demonstration of the infant's ability to perceive depth, however, is his performance on the "visual cliff," a platform consisting of a central strip covered with a checkerboard pattern and flanked by two heavy glass plates (Fig. 10.4). On one side the checkerboard pattern continues several feet below the glass surface, creating the illusion of a sheer drop (Walk and Gibson, 1961). Despite heavy coaxing, infants of 6 months placed on the central strip refuse to crawl over the visual cliff, even though they can touch the heavy glass surface that would prevent them from falling.   visual cliff

Fig. 10.4 The "visual cliff."

To some extent we can follow the maturation of the child's visual motor skills by observing the kinds of visual stimuli he pays attention to. The newborn infant is most strongly attracted during his first months by objects that move, by sharp contours, by bold contrasts between dark and light colors. Almost all his eye movements can be accounted for by such stimuli.

In the fourth month, however, his eyes begin to respond to other kinds of stimuli. He begins to be attracted by greater complexity in the number and variety of objects. For example, his preference shifts from a checkerboard of four squares to one of 64 squares, and at the age of 14 months he is fascinated by a board of 576 squares! Experimenters have also found that, whereas very young infants pay most attention to a circle containing nine triangles, older infants attend most to a circle containing three triangles, three squares, and three stars (Brennan, Ames, and Moore, 1966).

Infants between 4 and 6 months seem to be strongly attracted by *familiar* objects and people. Haaf and Bell (1967) presented four oval pictures, each bearing some resemblance to a human face, to infants at varying ages (Fig. 10.5). All the babies paid more attention to the oval that most closely approximated a face; their attention to each of the other ovals was directly related to the degree of resemblance to a face.

The fact that infants prefer familiar objects and people suggests that some sort of "memory" processes are at work. Psychologists call the infant's mental

schema representations *schemata*. A marked preference has been observed for objects that resemble the infant's schemata generally while differing in small ways. For instance, the picture of a face with only one eye where his schema demands two will rivet the infant's attention for considerable periods of time.

stimulus	degree of faceness	amount of detail	percent fixation time
	1	3	.33
	2	1	.28
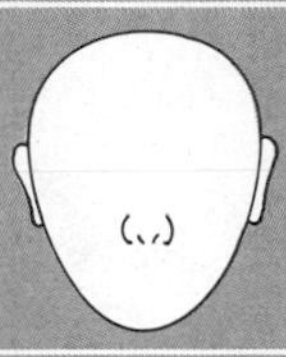	3	4	.19
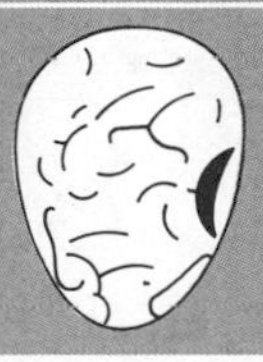	4	2	.20

Fig. 10.5 Differences in fixation time for four different facial stimuli. (Haaf and Bell, 1967)

Perceptual Abilities in Infants

To test perceptual abilities in infants requires some ingenuity, and it has not been lacking. Several researchers have done a series of experiments whose ingenuity is surpassed only by the clarity and portent of their findings.

Bower, Broughton, and Moore (1970) set out to determine whether infants 10 to 20 days old could respond appropriately to objects changing with respect to real or apparent spatial position. The responses they were looking for were the adaptive ones generally exhibited when we are faced with approaching objects: the head moves backwards, and both hands come up between the object and the face.

Because the approach of real objects very much upset the infants, real objects were abandoned. Instead the shadow of an object was projected onto a screen in front of the infant. This shadow was made to expand, so that it seemed to move closer to the child, or to contract, so that it seemed to move farther away. Eight of the nine infants showed avoidance responses to the expansion pattern.

These responses were not as fully developed as the responses to the approach of actual objects, but it should be kept in mind that real objects approaching give more cues, such as binocular parallax, which is not present with shadows. It is significant that any responses were elicited.

In a later experiment with infants aged 2 to 11 weeks Ball and Tronick (1971) clearly demonstrated the adaptive response to approaching objects. They noted avoidance responses and signs of being "upset" in infants viewing symmetrically expanding shadows, an optical stimulus that signifies approaching objects. The same infants did not respond in this way to asymmetrically approaching shadows, optical patterns that signify an object approaching, but on a "miss path" that will not hit the observer. Neither did the response occur for contracting shadows, an optical stimulus signifying a receding object. Apparently these infants were able to detect the direction and relative depth of approach and also to differentiate between a collision and a "miss" path, purely on the basis of the visual input available. Infants can perceive objects in depth, even at these very early ages.

 ## Environmental Influences

The effects on motor development of deprivation—the absence of appropriate stimuli from the environment—have been suggested by animal studies. Dogs raised in environments that permitted no exploration did not develop entirely normal behavior once they were released into a more stimulating setting. Neither pricking them with pins nor stepping on their tails aroused any response indicating pain. Furthermore, the dogs repeatedly poked their noses into the flame of a match (Scott, 1968). In fact, animals raised under conditions of severe stimulus deprivation are seldom able later in life to learn new tasks as quickly as animals raised under ordinary conditions.

Enriched environments, on the other hand, have beneficial effects on motor development, at least up to a point. Gerbils raised together in a cage filled with all kinds of toys, ramps, and other stimulating equipment were found to have both heavier brains and greater concentrations of some chemicals associated with learning than did gerbils raised singly in bare cages (Rosenzweig and Bennett, 1970).

Parallel results have been found in studies conducted among children. White (1969) found that the rates at which hospitalized infants learn to coordinate eye and hand muscles in order to grasp objects can be accelerated by increasing the amount of overall stimulation in the environment. White's enrichment program included more frequent physical handling of the babies by the staff, opportunities to watch what was going on in the ward, patterned crib sheets, and mobiles constructed of contrasting colors and shapes. Babies put in this environment learned to coordinate hands and eyes approximately 5 weeks earlier than did babies reared entirely in routine hospital conditions. It should be noted, however, that a great deal of stimulation seems to distress infants younger than 2 months. A simple bright crib toy seems to be about all that such a small baby can tolerate; later his sensory environment can be gradually enriched.

Mark Haven   Vivian Duncan

The social development of the child has its beginnings in his relationship with his parents.

Social Development

Ordinarily the newborn infant's main channel of human contact is with his mother. She provides food, pleasure, attention, and play. As he matures, the greater variety of his reactions to her elicits a greater variety of responses, and the bond between them becomes sufficiently complex to constitute a "social" relationship. The specific terms of this relationship serve as a model for the infant, although his social contacts are generally limited to his immediate family until the age of 2.

Many psychologists have considered the mother's satisfaction of her child's hunger to be the core of this first social bond. But this explanation is too simple, as Harlow's experiments with monkeys have shown (see Chapters 5 and 12). If attachment to the mother were based solely on satisfaction of hunger, then the monkeys should have preferred the "mothers" from whom they received nourishment. But in fact, between feeding times as well as when they felt afraid, *all* the infant monkeys preferred to huddle against the cuddly mother. Human infants seem to show a similar fundamental need for close physical contact and clinging (Bowlby, 1958). Bowlby's work on the significance of the infant's relationship with its mother is treated at greater length in Chapter 12.

Despite the long-standing controversy between proponents of breast and bottle feeding, the controlling factor in the child's social development appears to be the quality of his physical contact with his mother during feeding, rather than the manner in which he is fed. By holding him close in her lap, and cuddling and fondling him, and speaking to him softly and warmly, she strengthens the

461

bond of love and trust between them. The infant's nutritional needs can be met perfectly well in a matter-of-fact and hurried silence, but this treatment denies him pleasure in being fed and thus disrupts the formation of a bond with his mother and, later, with others.

separation anxiety

The strength of the attachment between child and mother can be measured by the intensity of the *separation anxiety*—the fear he experiences when his mother leaves him alone even momentarily. In American society, the infant is often left alone to play in his crib, and this anxiety appears relatively late, at around 10 months. It increases in intensity until the child is about a year old, and then declines.

By the age of 2, the child is fairly competent in his ability to move about and manipulate objects. He is starting to use language, and through his attachment to his mother, he has laid some foundation for later social relationships. He now enters the stage of childhood proper, a stage characterized particularly by advances in cognitive and social skills.

CHILDHOOD: 2–12 YEARS

Physical and Motor Development

Between 2 and 12 years of age growth continues to follow the trends we described earlier in this chapter. We saw that the head grows most in the prenatal period and is then overtaken by the torso, which reaches half its adult size by the age of 2. Although the torso continues to grow, it is now the arms and legs that lengthen most rapidly, in keeping with the *proximodistal* tendency of maturation. At 6 years of age the proportions of the child's head, torso, and legs are similar to those of an adult. His body continues to increase in size throughout childhood, but not until adolescence will he again experience an intense spurt of physical growth.

As part of this overall growth pattern, the child's bones and muscles also mature. Besides increasing in size, many of his soft, flexible bones harden in this period. He has a complete set of baby teeth, which begin to fall out and to be replaced by permanent teeth at about the age of 6. At about 4 years, his muscles quickly gain in size and strength, although the fine muscles are slower to mature. This lag shows in his motor skills: the typical 6-year-old still finds pulling a wagon much easier than writing small characters in an even line.

The brain expands from 75 to 90 percent of its adult weight between the ages of 2 and 6 years. The formation of protective myelin sheathing (see Chapter 6) around the nerve fibers accelerates, helping to speed transmission of nerve impulses to and from the brain, so that the child's reactions to stimuli become quicker and better organized.

Along with increasing size and muscular strength comes a sharp upswing in the variety and duration of motor activities. The child is capable of sustained expenditure of energy in running, jumping, climbing, and so forth. He is much better coordinated and more sure-footed than before. His manual skills also improve, although, as we have already noted, fine manipulations are still frequently beyond him. Nevertheless, many 4-year-olds can make quite recognizable images with crayons.

The major accomplishment of these childhood years is social development. The child's individual personality plays a decisive role in this development, but we have reserved discussion of that aspect for Chapter 11. Here we are concerned mainly with the forces that act to shape him as a social being. Although the environment has a more prominent part in this process than in most of those we have described so far, it is important to remember that maturation is still a determinant of the child's readiness to expand his social interactions.

The young child spends most of his time in and near his home. It is not surprising then that the behavior and attitudes of the people in his home are critical in determining his ability to form satisfactory social relationships.

Independence

Dependence is the basis of the close bond that links mother and child. As the child matures, his dependence naturally lessens. He learns to do for himself a great many things that had previously been done for him. When he is old enough to move around, he launches into active exploration of his environment, often disregarding parental warnings and admonitions.

One of the main dimensions determining the degree and persistence of the child's dependence is the restrictiveness or permissiveness of his mother. The mother who imposes a host of rigid rules and exacts strict obedience to them tends to discourage independent behavior. Such behavior is unpredictable and therefore makes greater demands on her attention and is more likely to disrupt her routine. It is clearly more convenient for a mother who may be overburdened with household duties and responsibilities to reward behavior that tends to follow a safe, prescribed pattern. She thus encourages her children to remain highly dependent. At about the age of 10 years boys begin to break away from such a confining relationship, but girls generally do not attempt to become more self-reliant during childhood. Since overdependent children are accustomed to having their behavior prescribed for them, they may be rather timid and tentative in their social interactions, especially when there are few reassuring rules to guide them.

Permissive mothers, who are willing to grant considerable freedom of action within clearly established guidelines, seem to raise more independent children. Their expectations of their children are often quite high but are expressed in terms of reason within a context of confidence and warm affection. Permissiveness is quite different from neglect. Some mothers simply do not pay much attention to their offspring. They make few demands and show little warmth. Their children, too, are often highly dependent, though their dependence tends to center on other children, perhaps somewhat older than themselves, instead of on adults.

Identification

identification

A central element in the child's efforts to become independent is the process of *identification,* in which he strives to become *like* another person. In early infancy the child gradually comes to distinguish himself from the world around him and to recognize other people in it. He also becomes aware of his own smallness and helplessness in relation to the world. At first his only resource for coping with his helplessness is his relationship with his parents; as he grows older he begins to recognize that they have many powers he lacks. He therefore strives to become more and more like his parents.

At 2 or 3 years this striving takes the form of imitating the parents' behavior. He copies their gestures and typical expressions with almost uncanny fidelity. Many a mother has been startled to overhear her child scolding his dog in the same intonations and phrases that she uses to scold the child himself.

The child's parents are his most consistently available models, and it is on them that his most sustained identifications are centered. These identifications are strengthened when his relationships with both parents are warm and nurturing. If one of them is cold, aloof, and uninterested in him, the child may

Vivian Duncan

The process of identification begins with imitation of parental behavior.

never develop a real attachment to him, and his efforts at identification will be correspondingly limited.

Gradually, as the child matures, imitative behavior gives way to internalization of his parents' values and attitudes. The normal age at which this development occurs varies widely, but from that point on the child considers his parents' attitudes part of *himself.*

The attitudes that the child internalizes cover a vast territory; they extend from behavioral idiosyncrasies to personality characteristics, motivations, and moral standards. Perhaps most significant of all aspects of identification is self-concept. The child tends to view himself in the same way that his parents—and especially his same-sex parent—view themselves. Generally speaking, if the parent feels secure and adequate in his world, the child will feel secure and adequate in his. Conversely, parental feelings of inadequacy are passed on to the child.

Besides their parents, children also identify with the ethnic, social, and religious groups they belong to. By the time he is about 5 years old, the child stops identifying himself and others solely by names. If his environment includes them, he begins to understand concepts such as poor, rich, black, white, Jewish, Catholic, Protestant, Polish, Puerto Rican, and American, and he frequently attaches the same value to these concepts that most of the people around him attach to them.

Perhaps the most significant determiner of the adaptability of the child's identification process is the kind of authority he is exposed to, both at home and at school. Excessive discipline and restrictive and punitive attitudes appear to disrupt the identification process on all levels. Children subjected to such treatment conform to expectations only externally; internally they are full of rebellion. They don't want to accept either the sex roles or the moral standards forced upon them, and they tend to have very poor self-concepts and low tolerance of people different in class or race from themselves.

Where the home and the school environments are intimate and accepting of the child, where he is invited to participate in the rule-making procedures, and helped to understand the necessity for rules, above all where the adults he has an opportunity to identify with are tolerant and affectionate among themselves as well as toward him, his chances of making an appropriate and adaptive identification are very good.

Conscience

Identification appears to be a determinant of several other important aspects of the child's socialization, for example, the evolution of a set of personal moral standards and ethics that will guide his behavior. We have noted that internalization of parents' values and beliefs is one of the phases in identification. Some of these standards help the child to decide what behavior is "right" and "wrong" when there is no adult around to assist him.

conscience Conscience, like most of the child's other achievements, evolves gradually through a series of stages. At first he refrains from certain undesirable behavior mainly out of fear of punishment. Later on he will feel that some behavior is

 The Development of Conscience or Morality

Research on the development of morality has focused on many different aspects of this very complex problem. For meaningful research to be done specific measures of "moral development" had to be formulated. A popular method used in laboratory investigations is "resistance to temptation" in a cheating situation. In such studies generally a child is prohibited from playing with or touching a particular toy. The experimenter then leaves the room and watches the child by means of a one-way vision screen so that the child doesn't know he is being seen. The experimenter notes how long the child resists before deviating and how often he deviates.

Generally research of this sort is done to test the effectiveness of differing child-rearing methods on moral development. Children may be disciplined in a number of different ways and the relative effectiveness with which each resists temptation is attributed to the teaching method employed.

One such study was carried out by Parke and Walters (1965) to investigate the effects of differing levels of punishment intensity on moral behavior. Six- to 8-year-old boys were allowed to choose among several toys a number of times. They had previously been told that some of the toys were for another boy. Whenever a child started to reach for or touched one of the "forbidden" toys he was punished. Punishment consisted of being told, "No, that's for the other boy," and was accompanied by a noise. In the high-intensity punishment situation, the noise was very loud. In the low-intensity situation, the noise was soft.

The children were then left alone for 15 minutes in the room with the same toys. An experimenter seated behind a one-way vision screen noted for each child: (a) the number of times he touched a forbidden toy; (b) how long he waited before "cheating" the first time; and (c) how much time he spent playing with the forbidden toys.

They found that children in the high-punishment condition took longer before deviating, deviated less often, and spent less time with the forbidden toys than children in the mild-punishment situation.

Further studies of the relation between intensity of punishment and resistance to temptation by Freedman (1965) seem to suggest, however, that the relation is not that simple. Freedman's findings suggest that although higher intensities of punishment seem to contribute to resistance to temptation immediately following punishment, this may not be the case at a later date. It seems that those who experience mild punishment tend to resist temptation over longer periods of time.

This is consistent with the general finding that strong parental assertion of power is not effective in producing resistance to temptation in children (Hoffman, 1970).

"wrong" and will experience guilt over transgressions against his conscience. Ultimately he will even experience positive satisfaction at having done "the right thing." (See also p. 236 and pp. 550–551.)

Although some form of punishment is necessary in the inculcation of moral standards, and even of good or desirable behavior, physical punishment or the threat of it seems to be the least effective sort, though perhaps it should not be totally discarded. What works best is simply disapproval, which carries with it the threat of a withdrawal of love. Of course, there must be a warm and affectionate relationship between parents and child for disapproval to be an effective punishment, but where it is the child quickly accepts the parents' standards and even "punishes" himself verbally when he violates them, just as he shows obvious self-satisfaction when he manages, despite temptations, to adhere to them.

The degree to which a child's conscience has developed can be gauged by the intensity of his guilt feelings, by his resistance to temptation, and by his spontaneous confession of transgressions. High scores on all these measures seem to be correlated with the parents' use of reasonable explanations as part of their approach to discipline and with their warmth and supportiveness (Hoffman, 1954). A cold or hostile parent who relies on physical punishment to ensure that his child conforms to his standards of right and wrong apparently provides little encouragement for the child to develop a conscience of his own (Hoffman and Saltzstein, 1967). Curiously, verbal punishment administered in an affectionate atmosphere appears to contribute to the development of a firm conscience. From our examination of the development of independence, identification, and conscience, it seems that parental affection is the most pervasive factor shaping the child's socialization.

Aggression

Identification seems also to play an important role in determining how the child learns to handle his own aggression, which can be defined broadly as "attack behavior," either physical, verbal, or even covert. We have seen that the child typically models his behavior after that of his parents. Whether they indulge fairly freely in aggression toward him, toward each other, and toward people outside the family or whether they inhibit their expression of aggressive impulses, he is likely to follow their lead.

A number of other factors have also been identified as contributing to aggression. For example, it has recently become fashionable to claim that man is a natural-born aggressor, a notion arising from studies of innate aggression in other animal species. For example, Eibl-Eibesfeldt (1961) reared wild Norway rats in isolation. During that time, no aggressive behavior was observed. But when he placed two male rats together, they began to fight "spontaneously."

Scott (1970) has argued convincingly, however, that such findings cannot be generalized to man without further study; he thinks it more probable that

aggression

Bowling Green State University Photo

J. P. Scott

human aggressive behavior has persisted for so long because it has been suc-cessful in bringing rewards and eliminating obstacles more quickly and deci-sively than have other forms of available behavior. Scott's suggestion that the rewards of aggression reinforce the behavior has been partly confirmed in re-search with small children. Bandura and Walters (1963) attribute much of chil-dren's aggressiveness to the behavior of aggressive models such as parents and other significant persons (see Chapter 3). If the aggressive behavior a child wit-nesses in adults is rewarded—that is, if it gets the adult what he wanted or visibly releases some tension in him and does not have adverse consequences—the child is especially likely to adopt the behavior for himself. Parental disapproval, especially when expressed in rational terms in warmly supportive relationships, seems, however, to curb aggressive behavior effectively, especially if the parents control their own aggressive impulses.

Sex Roles

sex role
Still another aspect of socialization in which the identification process is influ-ential is the adoption of a sex role. As part of establishing his overall identifica-tion, the child imitates the behavior of his parents, and much of this behavior reflects social expectations about the activities appropriate to men and women. The small boy may trail about after his father while he trims hedges or piles wood in the fireplace, learning activities that are frequently associated with masculinity. A girl meanwhile may work beside her mother, making motions of pushing a vacuum cleaner, or she may decide to put her doll to bed.

Identification behavior is not usually neatly associated with sex roles, however. Especially in a home where both parents take an affectionate interest in their children, a boy may clamor to help his mother mix cake batter, and a girl may delight in washing the car with her father.

Apparently sex-role identifications are stronger when the adult model is perceived as powerful. The child, who feels himself relatively helpless in his world, will try to pattern his behavior after an adult who seems able to control that world—and him. If that person is someone with whom the child also shares a close and loving relationship, then his identification will be doubly strength-ened.

The primary influence on sex-role identification of preschoolers is the parents, but as they get older, children begin to be influenced by other adults and by their own peers, who represent an increasingly larger cultural group. Havighurst, Robinson, and Dorr (1946) asked children aged 8 to 18 to write an essay on "the person I would like to be." Children younger than age 10 chose their parents, while older children wrote about real or imaginary glamorous adults. As the child matures, heroes from other sectors of the community be-come increasingly important. The child can be found playing doctor, fireman, spaceman, or another identification game. The model a child picks depends upon prior parent-child relationships and the child's specific skills.

Social sex-role concepts become internalized as the child grows older. These concepts become standards for actions and goals. Proper goals and attitudes are reinforced, while attitudes that do not conform to society's concepts of the proper sex role are negatively reinforced.

By age 5 or 6 children see males as physically more powerful and invulnerable than females. However, sexual physiology is not yet in the child's concept of sexual identity. Katcher (1955) asked children to assemble and identify cut-out figures of heads, trunks, and leg sections. The cut-outs were of clothed and unclothed males and females. Children between 3 and 6 had little trouble assembling the clothed figures but had some difficulty assembling the unclothed figures. Even children whose parents have attempted to acquaint them with genital differences between the sexes do not form clear genital concepts much before age 7.

 Toward Human Liberation

"Me man, the hunter. You woman, the childbearer."

With these words, prehistoric man established the traditional division of labor according to sex. Encumbered with childbearing, the female was forced to stay near the cave caring for the young and foraging for food among nearby vegetation. In the meanwhile, the male was free to venture far with the pack to hunt for meat.

Society has long perpetuated these original job assignments by developing certain "sex specific" characteristics. Men were proclaimed to be aggressive, independent, unemotional, competitive, logical, ambitious, and achievement-oriented. Women were supposed to be submissive, passive, dependent, emotional, illogical, indecisive, and hearth-oriented.

Children are taught the appropriate "masculine" or "feminine" traits as part of their self-identity. Little girls are not expected to achieve more than little boys of the same age, although girls are known to have a faster maturation rate. They must play nurse to the boys' doctor.

As children grow older, boys are given independence much sooner than girls—they are free to roam about the neighborhood while girls must find their fun in the yard. In adolesence, pressure increases to conform to what society considers sex-appropriate behavior. The 12-year-old boy who likes to help with kitchen tasks is called a sissy and a girl of that age who enjoys playing baseball is branded a tomboy. Teen-age girls are permitted to be weak and helpless around boys, who must appear strong and confident.

For centuries education was available for males only. They were forced to learn a trade with which to support their families. Girls could be taught at home the requisite skills for their roles as wives and mothers. For fear of being thought "unmasculine" or "unfeminine," few voiced their dissatisfaction with the duty of providing for wife and children or the sentence of life in the kitchen or laundry room.

When society became more affluent, women were allowed to attend school and, more recently, college. However, the training most women received was related to the homemaker role: nursing, teaching, home economics. As the general public became more enlightened, females began to study social work and humanities because of their ascribed qualities of gentleness and sensitivity. Powerful opposition faced the young woman who wanted to become an electronic engineer and the young man who wished to be an interior decorator.

Gradually women gained entry into the world of business, but they were generally considered temporaries, working only until marriage. Therefore females were given jobs related to homemaking and jobs with less prestige and lower pay (than a man filling the same position). Most women who chose to make a career in industry were denied administrative jobs and continued the helpmate role by being secretaries to men. Those women who worked to supplement family income were often poorly educated and consequently had to take unskilled, dead-end employment.

On the other hand, men were encouraged to choose careers of high esteem and great reward, requiring aggressive and analytical abilities. They were urged to be ambitious and climb to the top. Society has tended to look down on males who pursue vocations which it has labeled "woman's work," such as teaching young children or designing clothes.

In recent years as women received more extensive educations, they came to realize that they could be independent and assertive in a full-time business career and still be successful wives and mothers. Today some married women are choosing not to have children and others are deciding not to marry. Females are becoming a vigorous and important part of every area of the work force. Spurred by the consciousness-raising efforts of the women's liberation movement, many males are questioning their traditional roles as the sole, aggressive family breadwinner. When both sexes come to recognize that the archaic reasons for defining occupational roles by sex no longer hold true, there may be an emancipation of humankind. Men will no longer fear being called "unmanly" if they take seriously their roles as husbands and fathers—they can feel free to assume jobs as nursery teachers or house workers. And females will feel no guilt when they leave their homes every morning for their vocations as lawyers or neurosurgeons.

Walter Mischel

Behavioral characteristics are very much subject to sex-typing in our culture. Mischel (1966) showed that sex-type behavior patterns are divided into aggressive and dependent behaviors. Boys are expected by society to be strong, courageous, assertive, and ambitious, while girls are expected to be sociable, well-mannered, and neat. These social expectations are fulfilled even in young children. Sears, Maccoby, and Levin (1957) found that parents made the largest distinctions between methods of rearing boys and girls in the aggressive and dependent behavior patterns they encouraged. Boys were permitted to express aggression and were encouraged to "fight back." In contrast, girls were subjected to withdrawal of love for aggressive behavior. Girls are more rewarded for dependency, passivity, and conformity.

Leslie Berkeley   F.P.G.

By the age of 5, the child engages in many cooperative activities with his peers.

These sex-role standards are being challenged by women's liberation groups, and advocates of "gay liberation" have questioned what really constitutes "normal" sexual persuasions. It is as yet uncertain what impact either of these movements is making on typical sex-role concepts.

Peers

During infancy the child's social interactions are almost completely limited to members of his family, but at about age 3 he begins to enjoy group play and to display interest in other children. Social participation, like other developmental processes, evolves through several phases. The child begins by simply watching other children at play; then he begins to play alongside them without interacting. Eventually he begins to interact with other children, and finally he is ready to share in the kind of organized cooperation necessary for games. By the age of 5 or 6 years the child is actively engaging in a great deal of cooperative play and actively seeks attention and approval from his peers.

At about age 4, a time when most children prefer to play in small groups, social hierarchies begin to be formed. Leaders emerge, based somewhat on physical strength and somewhat on a genuine ability to give encouragement and attention to others for a common goal. The effect of peer group participation—whatever the child's role within the group—involves the discovery that outside the family circle fantasies and will often must conflict with those of others. This broadening contact with the realities of group interaction reinforces

peer group

471

socially oriented behavior—sharing, for example—that the child has already learned at home.

Peers also serve as behavioral models at this age. Once a child sees another rewarded for a certain behavior, he is likely to imitate that behavior whether or not he earns the same reward. This process is intensified when the child begins schooling, for at about the age of 6 or 7, the sexes begin to separate in play situations. The exclusion of the opposite sex in play is the first step, especially for boys, in confirming sexual identity. As groups become sex-exclusive, they also become age-exclusive, further intensifying the possibilities for identifying with peer-group models.

ADOLESCENCE

puberty

Puberty is initiated by maturation of the reproductive apparatus (see Chapter 6), which is generally heralded by a final surge of overall physical growth. The physical changes are accompanied by new, and often confusing, emotional responses and a broadening of social awareness and functioning, yet most of these events occur in such diffuse fashion and so unevenly that it is difficult to define the precise beginning and ending of this last developmental stage.

adolescence

Indeed, until quite recently, *adolescence* was not recognized as a distinct stage at all. At most puberty was viewed as a brief transitional phase between childhood and the assumption of adult responsibilities. Even today this view prevails outside the industrialized West.

In western societies, on the other hand, generally high standards of nutrition have resulted in a gradual lowering of the age at which puberty begins; at the same time an extension of the average span of years spent in school has postponed assumption of financial and professional independence for a large proportion of young people. The result is a fairly long period in which the boy or girl is in a sort of limbo, no longer a child but not yet a full-fledged member of adult society. This period has come to be recognized as a distinct developmental phase, characterized by specific needs and patterns of change, a few of which we will discuss here.

Physical Maturation

At about 11 years for girls and 13 years for boys physical growth suddenly accelerates. It continues at a high level for several years, then tapers off as the adolescent approaches his adult height and weight. There is very wide variation in the age at which this growth spurt begins; many children experience it earlier or much later than the statistical averages suggest (Fig. 10.6). And for some this phase lasts a relatively long time, whereas others finish growing in a year or two.

Furthermore, different parts of the body grow at different rates, so that many adolescents are temporarily afflicted with awkward body proportions—

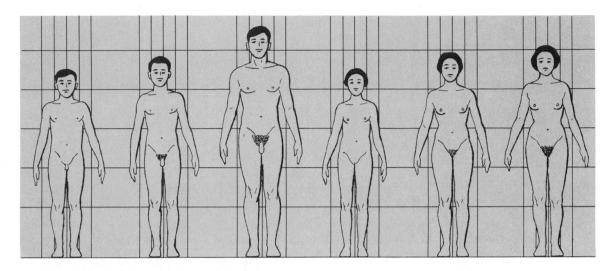

Fig. 10.6 Different levels of maturation at the same chronological age. Left, three boys aged 14½; right, three girsl aged 12½.

with enormous feet or long, dangling arms, for example. Frequently the adolescent does not have time to become accustomed to his new proportions before they have altered again. As a result it is not uncommon for the teen-ager to seem less coordinated than the child he was. Yet for some the transition to an adult body occurs smoothly and without even temporary discomforts.

By far the most significant physical change in adolescence is the maturation of the sexual and reproductive system. Again, the ages at which puberty begins vary considerably, but the maturation process itself follows a fairly fixed sequence. In a girl puberty is announced by the first swelling of her breasts, followed shortly by the appearance of pubic hair. At the same time the uterus and vagina begin to develop, and the external sex organs (the labia and the clitoris) become enlarged. When the uterus is fully developed, perhaps two or three years later, her first menstrual period, called *menarche,* occurs. The average age for menarche is 13 years, but it can appear at any time between 10 and 17 years.

menarche

The first sign of puberty in a boy is acceleration in the growth of the testes and scrotum, which is also followed shortly by the appearance of pubic hair. About a year later the penis begins to grow more rapidly and the prostate to expand. At the end of about 2 years the boy is capable of ejaculation. As this phase of development nears completion, the secondary sex characteristics begin to make their appearance. Hair grows on the face and armpits, although its full density may not be achieved for several years more. One of the last changes is in the voice, which gradually lowers in pitch until adult masculine timbre is established.

Sexual Relationships

Physical maturity brings with it changes in the predominant modes of social interaction. In preadolescence the child and his friends had segregated themselves by sex during most play activities. Now the adolescent shows a new interest in heterosexual social relations. Initially boys and girls may get together in groups, but soon they begin to see each other in pairs.

The emergence of the adolescent's sexual apparatus is accompanied by new sexual urges and fantasies, especially in boys. These feelings and sensations lead to sexual experimentation, both alone and with partners. During the last few years sexual attitudes and behavior in the United States and other western societies have changed so fundamentally that it is difficult to determine just what the predominant patterns of adolescent sexuality are now. Sexual activity in our society seems to be characterized by greater freedom and perhaps also by demands for deeper emotional involvement than was common a decade or two ago. In a 1966 survey by *Look* Magazine of 550 adolescents aged 13 to 20, 75 percent believed a new sexual morality was developing, but they did not think there was a lowering of morals; 82 percent of the survey said their morals were "no lower than their parents'." One girl said, "Adults are just plain phonies about sex." The new morality, then, entails a greater openness and honesty about sex.

The Kinsey Reports It is quite questionable, however, that the new morality entails any significant change in standards over those of the preceding

Dick Swift

Early adolescent heterosexual social relations begin in groups; pairing off comes later.

Alfred C. Kinsey

generation or two. According to the best-documented information available—that of the Kinsey Reports (Kinsey, Pomeroy, and Martin, 1948; Kinsey, Pomeroy, Martin, and Gebhard, 1953)—the most significant change in actual sexual behavior in recent years occurred in the 1920s and 1930s. The incidence of petting, which we may define as any affectional heterosexual contact exclusive of coitus, in adolescence was 66 percent for women born before 1900; for those born between 1900 and 1909, it jumped to 81 percent. Among the mothers of today's adolescents, the incidence was about 94 percent (Reevy, 1961). The figures for premarital sexual intercourse show similar differences: the incidence before age 20 among women born before 1900 was only 8 percent and 14 percent before age 25; among women born after 1900, the incidence before age 20 was 21 percent and before age 25, 37 percent. Data about today's young women are inadequate, but what they seem to indicate is an incidence of premarital intercourse before age 20 at somewhere between 25 and 30 percent, and before age 25, between 30 and 40 percent (Blaine, 1967; Lake, 1967). Insofar as these data are reliable—and even Kinsey's very well-documented studies are not impeccable—they show virtually no difference between the sexual behavior of girls today and that of their mothers. (We have limited this discussion of premarital intercourse to women because there are no current studies of its incidence among men. The Kinsey Reports showed it to be consistently higher among men than among women and did not find the same generational difference among men.)

What has changed between the present generation and the preceding one is attitude toward sexual matters. Young people today feel far freer to talk about sex and to be honest about their sexual feelings and their sexual behavior. This is largely because their parents and grandparents laid the groundwork for them by rebelling against *their* parents' standards.

The Pill and Liberation   Today, in spite of the wide availability of the Pill   the Pill
and the move, especially among educated women, toward liberation in sexual as well as other realms, there apparently has been no increase in promiscuity (Simon, Carnes, and Gagnon, 1972). Girls feel freer to masturbate than they once did, but they increasingly limit premarital sexual intercourse to relationships in which there is some sort of mutual commitment and love. Even the widespread fear that coeducational dormitories would lead to unrestrained and indiscriminate sexual relationships has evidently proved unfounded. If anything the almost familial atmosphere that develops in these dormitories has inhibited sexual relationships and most residents seek dating partners outside the "family."

Social Influences   Having said this much about adolescent and premarital sexual experiences, we must qualify it all by emphasizing that the range of experiences is extremely wide, so that generalization becomes almost meaningless. Influences are exerted by individual temperament and, most importantly, by religious and socioeconomic background. Kinsey reported consistently greater sexual activity, both before and after marriage, among people of all religious backgrounds (that is, Protestant, Catholic, and Jewish) who did not attend church regularly than among both moderately active and devout church members. Variations related to socioeconomic background, though they apparently pertain only to men, are equally great. Masturbation and petting are far more common among higher social-class boys than among lower-class ones, who are more likely to consider these practices abnormal. Hence they are more likely to engage in actual intercourse. Kinsey reported that by age 15 nearly half of lower-class boys but only 10 percent of higher-class boys had engaged in intercourse.

Friendship Relationships

A related aspect of social development in the adolescent period is the changing nature of friendships. Whereas children tend to relate to their friends in groups centered around play activities, in adolescence there is greater emphasis on close personal ties, particularly among girls under 16 years old. Boys persist longer in the old childhood patterns and seem to feel less need for intimacy with their friends. On the other hand, girls' close friendships often do not last very long; apparently they do not hold up well under pressure of demands for total loyalty at a time when the girls' personalities are undergoing rapid alterations.

Paradoxically, just when new kinds of individual relations are making their appearance among adolescents, group membership takes on even more importance than before, to the point that exclusion from a particular group or clique

Ron Benvenisti

Adolescent boys continue to relate to friends in groups; girls normally form close personal ties at an earlier age.

can often cause painful self-doubt. Coleman (1961) found low self-esteem in students who were not part of the "in" crowd but wanted to be. Boys in particular seem to rely on groups as channels for assertion of their independence. Although membership in the group requires a certain amount of conformity to group values, those values themselves may be in conflict with the accepted notions of parents, school authorities, and the larger community. The adolescent boy is thus afforded a secure base among his peers from which to challenge established values: he does not yet have to "go it alone."

Autonomy

autonomy

Adolescence is clearly a time of fundamental reorientation in social functioning. The teen-ager is inducted into modes of social contact that will increasingly characterize his adult life, heterosexual relationships of varying intensities, intimate friendships, and meaningful group participation. The other side of this coin is the necessity for breaking the bonds of dependence upon his parents. Whether this separation is accomplished smoothly or becomes an area of major conflict between the generations is largely a function of the predominant pattern of discipline and identification in the family. The adolescent who has been reared in an atmosphere of reasoned explanation, measured autonomy, and parental warmth already possesses a measure of self-reliance and independent identity that should help him through this crisis.

In contrast, the adolescent whose parents have always demanded strict obedience to authority faces greater problems. First, his parents are less likely to adjust their patterns voluntarily or to make concessions to his demands for autonomy. Second, he has very likely reached adolescence without having experienced any meaningful degree of independence. He must now bridge the developmental gap between dependence and autonomy in a single leap and without any real preparation for the task. He may thus be forced to adopt a posture of extreme defiance, which by its very nature is likely to stiffen the opposition of his authoritarian parents.

Regardless of family background, the problem of gaining autonomy seems to be somewhat greater for boys—not because parents are more willing to grant freedom to girls but because girls are less likely to demand as much freedom as boys do. One factor in this difference between the sexes appears to be the boy's need to live up to society's expectations that a man will adopt a forcible and dominant attitude in most of his dealings and, conversely, the girl's need to fulfill societal expectations that she will adopt a passive attitude. Passivity is a "destiny imposed upon [the girl] by her teachers and by society" (de Beauvoir, 1949).

Sometimes the adolescent is unable to resolve the conflicts arising from his striving for autonomy and the simultaneous demands of a broader network of relations with his peers. His resulting frustration may lead him to reject adult society in any of several different ways.

Delinquency One alternative is delinquency. Delinquency among teenagers, especially boys, is a serious social problem, frequently involving a complex of causes related to low socioeconomic status: poverty, overcrowding, broken homes, inadequate education, and so on. Among other causes that have been cited is the failure of some fathers to function as models for identification.

Failure to resolve the autonomy crisis may result in general alienation from society—a common characteristic among adolescent users of heroin and other "hard" drugs. Habitual drug users typically report strong feelings of isolation, poor communication with parents, and a sense of powerlessness. One group of adolescents being treated for drug use appeared unusually passive in personal relationships (Kuehn, 1970), which suggests failure to break the bonds of childhood dependence.

Activism So far we have been discussing antisocial reactions associated with cold, harsh, disinterested, or authoritarian family backgrounds. There is one group of adolescents who also reject much of adult society yet who seem to be drawn primarily from homes characterized by permissiveness, flexibility, and warmth. They are the student activists, the supporters of radical social and politcal causes. Findings at Berkeley and San Francisco State College have revealed that activists, though they constituted only a small minority of the student body on either campus, ranked much higher in such qualities as autonomy, flexibility, individualism, and social commitment than their fellow students (Heist, 1965; Somers, 1965; Watts and Whittaker, 1966; Haan, Smith, and Block, 1968; Haan and Block, 1969). Most of the committed students had been encouraged from childhood to develop independent minds and strong consciences.

Although political activism, like delinquency and drug use, is a complex phenomenon that cannot be analyzed in detail here, it seems generally true that activists have been so successful in developing personal moral standards independent of the claims of social convention that they find themselves compelled to try to close the gap between their ideals and the disillusioning realities of government policies and institutional behavior.

Rick Smolan

Women have special difficulties in seeking and developing autonomy.

Women and Autonomy In spite of the "consciousness raising" and general popularity of the Women's Liberation Movement, women are still far less successful at developing—and frequently at seeking to develop—a sense of autonomy. Although superficial changes in education have been instigated—girls are allowed to play softball and to learn about the workings of an automobile, while boys may be taught how to bake a cake and perhaps even to sew on buttons—there has been no revolution in the essence of the traditional sex roles taught to young men and women. Girls are expected to be passive, to renounce their desires for autonomy, and to learn instead to please others, whereas boys are taught to seek self-realization by *doing* things and to expect members of the opposite sex to help them in their realization struggles.

While the young boy expects to find self-fulfillment in work of some kind, the young girl, recognizing early in life that the world is controlled by men and not by women, looks to a man for fulfillment and escape. The incapacity of young girls "to be self-sufficient engenders a timidity that extends over their entire lives and is marked even in their work. They believe that outstanding success is reserved for men; they are afraid to aim too high" (de Beauvoir, 1949).

For the woman who, in spite of this kind of discouragement, elects independence and autonomy, the principal problem is maintaining and fulfilling her sexuality. As de Beauvoir (1949) points out, "Man is a human being with sexuality; woman is a complete individual, equal to the male, only if she too is a human being with sexuality. To renounce her femininity is to renounce a part of her humanity." Yet it continues to be difficult for a woman to maintain both a professional career and a sense of female sexuality.

With the adoption in 1970 of the Equal Rights Amendment to the U.S. Constitution, and the consequent increase in employment opportunities available to women, it is possible that autonomy will come to be an accepted part of the American female sex role. As women fill positions that demand autonomy, perhaps they will develop it, offering themselves also as models of autonomous women for the next generation of young women.

CONCLUSIONS

In tracing the course of maturation from conception to adolescence, we have avoided the presentation of a single unified theory of development—largely because none seems ultimately satisfactory. Attempts at global explanations that have been offered generally fall into three categories: mechanistic, organismic, and psychoanalytic.

Mechanistic explanations, the outgrowth of the thinking of John Locke and David Hume, view the developing human being as passive. Here, the central concern is to measure the behavioral effects of environmental causes. Controlled laboratory experimentation, the "scientific method," is the preferred approach.

organismic
theory

Organismic theory focuses on the qualitative differences among emerging structures within the human being and on the implications of these differences for development. Jean Piaget (whose theories are discussed in Chapter 11) is the most noted contemporary exponent of this school of thought.

Psychoanalytic theory originated with Sigmund Freud, and although it has been highly modified by his successors, certain assumptions are still basic to all psychoanalytic theories. The importance of the sexual and aggressive drives in particular is crucial in the Freudian model of development. In this sense, the Freudians offer a compromise between the first two models, for they focus on internal development while giving almost equal importance to the impact of environmental forces on developing internal structures. Freud based his original formulations on clinical observations of abnormal behavior, and these reports of patients' thoughts and feelings are still the basic research materials.

Our approach in this chapter has most closely approximated the mechanistic model, in that we have considered the child mainly as a passive being, acted upon by biological and environmental forces. In Chapter 11, we will consider these same aspects of development from an organismic point of view, focusing on the child as an active force in his development, a participant in a chain of influences that shape his development. In Chapter 12 on personality, we will spend much more time considering Freud's approach to development.

Summary

Developmental psychology is the study of all processes that shape the human being during his early years. The process of maturation seems to follow a sequential pattern in all children, regardless of background or environment. Another important characteristic of maturation is its unevenness and discontinuity; sometimes rapid growth in one area seems to draw energy away from other areas for a time.

Maturation tends to follow several fundamental directions. Growth occurs from the top of the body to the bottom and from the center to the extremities. It also develops from gross movements to more finely controlled movements.

Learning seems to depend upon the child's readiness to learn—that is, his level of maturation. Once he is mature enough to learn, his experience will determine what and how much he learns.

The extent to which the environment as opposed to biological inheritance influences development raises the nature-nurture issue. Certain human tendencies are determined by hereditary factors but full development of these tendencies might need environmental encouragement. On the other hand, some hereditary traits cannot be changed no matter what the environmental factors are.

The prenatal period progresses through the conception, embryonic, and fetal stages. Conception occurs when the male sperm cell penetrates the female egg cell, causing division of cells and formation of a blastocyst. This differentiated cell structure attaches itself to the wall of the uterus, and the embryonic stage begins. The amniotic sac forms a protection for the growing organism, and development continues to the fetal stage, which is the last stage before delivery.

Prenatal effects on the growing person are as important as postnatal effects. The age of the mother is a crucial factor, as well as diseases or disorders that she might have. Her emotional state and her diet affect the unborn child. Use of drugs can impair fetal growth. A factor that is highly correlated with the incidence of many prenatal adverse conditions is the mother's socioeconomic status; low status is associated with high incidence of prenatal disorders. A final factor influencing the health of the unborn baby are the conditions of delivery. A difficult birth or shortage of oxygen can cause severe damages.

The infant is born with a complex array of behaviors. His reflexes and senses are constantly working to keep him in touch with his world. The infant, like all human beings, has a set of needs that must be met if he is to survive. Sleep and a balanced diet are just two of them.

The infant's physical growth proceeds rapidly in the first 2 years. His body proportions change and his bones begin to harden through a process of ossification. Teeth begin to form and voluntary muscle control is increased. As his muscles become stronger, he experiences greater coordination; environmental influences affect what skills are developed. Deprivation of affection and social contact can retard development. Object manipulation develops at the same time as locomotion and entails hand-eye coordination. Maturation of visual motor skills can be followed by observing what the child likes to look at. Usually he is most fascinated by things that are familiar but offer some new and challenging aspect.

The first social contact the infant experiences is with his mother, who cares for him and holds him. This is the strongest social relationship of infancy. The amount of feeding and attention the baby receives influences his development.

Childhood (ages 2–12) is a period in which growth continues and social development increases. Social interactions help to form the child's personality. The child becomes increasingly less dependent upon his parents and more interested in his peers. The degree to which the parents permit the child to express his independence is an important variable in the child's growth.

As the child matures, he begins to identify with significant people around him. At first, identification is primarily with his parents, and especially with his same-sex parent, but later it encompasses others in his social situation. The identification process is important in the development of personal moral standards that will guide future behavior. Conscience evolves through stages. First, fear guides the child. Then guilt takes over. Finally a feeling of positive satisfaction at having done "right" will guide him. Identification also plays an important role in the expression of aggression. If the child identifies with an aggressive adult, he will probably model his behavior on that of the adult.

The adoption of a sex role is the result of both social reinforcement and identification. Socially acceptable views of sex roles are rewarded, while unacceptable views are discouraged. Generally boys are encouraged to be aggressive and girls to be dependent.

Social participation develops through several phases. First, the child watches other children at play; then he begins to play alongside them without interacting with them. Eventually, he begins to interact and then becomes a full participant in the game. Groups form hierarchies of dominant and submissive members. Peers act as strong models for future behavior.

Puberty initiates the maturation of the reproductive process, but with this come changes in social interactions. Though premarital sexual intercourse is becoming more widespread and a socially acceptable behavior, there appears to be no increase in promiscuity. In adolescence, both friendships and group relationships take on increased importance. Probably the most difficult aspect of adolescence is the problem of attaining autonomy. At opposite ends of success in this quest are delinquency and activism. Women face a special problem in attaining autonomy in that society has made it difficult for them to achieve fulfillment in both work and sex.

SUGGESTED READINGS

Bettelheim, Bruno, *Dialogues with Mothers.* New York, Free Press, 1962.
   Most of the book consists of verbatim parent education sessions, focusing on children under 6, led by the author.
Bock, Richard, and Abigail English, *Got Me on the Run: A Study of Runaways.* Boston, Beacon Press, 1973.
   This readable report offers some fresh insights into why teen-agers run away from home.
Cohen, Albert K., *Delinquent Boys, The Culture of the Gang.* New York, Free Press, 1955.
   An examination of how the different standards of working-class and middle-class society affect the behavior of youth.
Dickens, Charles, *Great Expectations.*
   A classic novel about a young man's growth into manhood.
Faber, Adele, and Elaine Mazlish, *Liberated Parents, Liberated Children.* New York, Grosset & Dunlap, 1974.
   Two disciples of the late Haim Ginott, author of *Between Parent and Child,* apply Ginott principles to raising children without guilt.
Friedenberg, Edgar Z., *The Vanishing Adolescent.* New York, Dell, 1962.
   A Freudian view of adolescence as the conflict between the individual and society.
Havighurst, Robert J., and Hilda Taba, eds., *Adolescent Character and Personality.* New York, Wiley, 1967.
   Though based on a 1942 study of a small Midwestern town, the book is current in what it says about adolescent behavior and thinking.
Maccoby, Eleanor, ed., *The Development of Sex Differences.* Stanford, Calif., Stanford University Press, 1966.
   The readings in this collection, including articles by Kohlberg, emphasize the causes of sex differences.
Mead, Margaret, *Coming of Age in Samoa* (many editions; first published in 1928).
   The famous anthropologist's study of adolescents on a South Sea island.
Millett, Kate, *Sexual Politics.* New York, Doubleday, 1970.
   Review of the societal influences and pressures on women, and a discussion of the representation of male and female roles in literature.
Piaget, Jean, and B. Inhelder, *The Psychology of the Child.* New York, Basic Books, 1969.
   A brief but complete introduction to Piaget's theory on the development of human intelligence.
Schreiber, Daniel, ed., *Profile of the School Dropout.* New York, Random House, 1968.
   A study of the large group of American students who fail to finish high school.

Chapter Eleven

Cognitive Development

What is the difference between intelligence and cognition?
What is the best indicator of intelligence in infants?
What are the different ways in which cognitive development
  can be viewed?
What are the major periods of cognitive development?
How does cognitive development affect perception?
Is there a relationship between cognition and moral
  development?
Is adolescence a time of identity crisis?

We said at the end of Chapter 10 that there are three ways of looking at human development: the mechanistic view regards the person as an essentially passive being who is shaped by his environment, the organismic view sees the person as an active shaper of his own being, and the psychoanalytic view falls somewhere in between the others in that it sees man essentially as shaped by the conflict between environmental demands and his instinctual needs and wishes. It can be said further that mechanistic and organismic views share with each other, and not with the psychoanalytic view, an idea of man as intellectual and rational. While the psychoanalytic view does not deny human intelligence, it has little interest in it; its concern is rather with the health or effectiveness of the individual personality. We have paid some attention to this view of human nature in Chapter 5 on motivation, and we will examine it at greater length in Chapter 12 on personality; it will also be the basis of much that we say about disturbed behavior and its treatment in Chapters 16 and 17.

INTELLIGENCE OR COGNITION?

The mechanistic view of development was the foundation of our approach to maturation in Chapter 10. What we did not talk about there was a mechanistic view of intelligence. Our omission was purposeful because it seems to us that mechanistic views no longer offer a satisfactory explanation of the complex intellectual development of the human being. As we will see, mechanistic views have given us a wide variety of intelligence tests, but useful as these instruments are, they cannot tell us anything about what is actually in the mind. The organismic view alone seems to offer a description and an explanation of intelligence in which intelligence is regarded as autonomous and self-generating. Its view of intelligence is in fact so different from the mechanistic view that it has become standard practice to use the term *intelligence* only when we are con-

cognition

cerned with mechanistic views of mentality and to speak of *cognition* instead when our approach is organismic. We will follow that practice in this chapter.

Intelligence tests, unfortunately, do not take account of the cognitive stages of development the child passes through as he learns to deal with his environment. Piaget and other researchers, as we will see, believe these stages or levels of cognitive development are critically important and have attempted to explain them. They are not as much interested in the *content* of a child's mind, or in his repertoire of behaviors, as in how the child's mind *functions*. Before turning our attention to this organismic approach to cognitive development, however, we will discuss how intelligence tests are used to measure mental capacity, and we will see that they are subject to several limitations, especially as they are used for testing infant intelligence.

The Mechanistic Approach— Intelligence Tests and Measurements

Modern scientific interest in the intelligence of infants began with Charles Darwin, who compiled detailed infant "biographies" in an attempt to measure intellectual development. At the turn of the century, the French psychologist Alfred Binet devised the first comprehensive infant intelligence test. The test consisted of an extensive series of tasks, and the child's score was based on the number of tasks he completed within a fixed period of time.

In the United States, the basic concept of the intelligence test has been broadened and refined with the development of standardization. A standardized test provides not only a raw score of correct answers but also a comparative rating. The comparison reflects the child's performance relative to national norms, which are based on the scores of a broad sample of children of the same age. Today, there are literally dozens of such tests—among them the Minnesota Preschool Scale, the Gesell Development Schedules, and Bayley's Scales of Infant Development. These tests all present the infant with a large number of tasks

Nancy Bayley

selected to measure several different aspects of intellectual development: sensorimotor activity, manual dexterity, and often a rudimentary grasp of language. They have also proved useful in the early detection of mental retardation.

Infant intelligence tests, however, have not proved to be accurate predictors of a child's intelligence several years later. In fact, studies have established that intelligence tests begin to show predictive power only when they are administered later than 2 years of age. The reason for this limitation has to do with the skills infant tests measure. Manual dexterity and sensorimotor acts—muscular activity stimulated by sensory contact—are the most advanced skills the infant possesses. But they are quite different from the skills measured by intelligence tests for older children: reasoning, memory, and the ability to apply abstract concepts.

Most recently, a new type of infant intelligence test has been developed that measures attentiveness rather than sensorimotor abilities. The most successful of these tests gauges the infant's ability to distribute his attention and to switch his attention from familiar stimuli to novel ones. The results of this test given at 1 year of age have been shown to correlate closely with IQ scores at age 4. Lewis (1971) has explained the apparent predictive power of these tests

Table 11.1 Items from Bayley's Scale of Mental Development

Task	Age in Months (when 50% of infants could perform the activity)
Blinks at shadow of hand	1.9
Head follows vanishing spoon	3.2
Recovers rattle, in crib	4.9
Picks up cube deftly and directly	5.7
Manipulates bell; interest in detail	6.5
Fingers holes in pegboard	8.9
Stirs with spoon in imitation	9.7
Imitates words	12.5
Builds tower of two cubes	13.8
Says two words	14.2
Uses gestures to make wants known	14.6
Attains toy with stick	17.0
Imitates crayon stroke	17.8
Places two round and two square blocks in a board	19.3
Follows directions in pointing to parts of a doll	19.5
Points to three pictures	21.9
Names three pictures	22.1
Builds tower of six cubes	23.0
Names three objects	24.0
Names five pictures	25.0

SOURCE: Bayley (1969)

as follows: "Attention is most necessary for any subsequent intellectual functioning, and individual differences in it will be predictive of differences in other learning phenomena."

In general, most tests attempt to measure intelligence—like blood pressure or weight—on a single scale. They fail to account for the large variety of ways in which the growing child can actively participate in and intelligently interact with his environment. For example, in one test, the child's ability to build a pyramid with blocks is tested. If the child doesn't build with the blocks it is assumed that he can't. But perhaps he is turning the blocks to discover what occurs when they are moved, or maybe he wants to push them off the edge of the table. The test considers such activities to indicate a lack of intelligence because the infant did not build the specified pyramid. However, active exploration of the blocks is as valid an indication of intelligence as successfully building a pyramid.

Organismic Theories

By far the dominant figure in organismic notions of cognitive development is Jean Piaget, whose meticulous observations of children have resulted in a comprehensive theory for the development of intelligence. We have already seen a brief overview of Piaget's notions of cognitive development in Chapter 8. Other organismic approaches emphasize substantially different ways of viewing child development. They are not necessarily opposed to the ideas of Piaget, but they deal with the problems of cognitive development on different levels. Here, we will lean heavily on Piaget's research and ideas, but at appropriate places we will tie his work to that of other organismic theories of development. Piaget has proposed a sequence of stages by which intelligence progresses from an undifferentiated thought system into a highly organized facility for abstraction. The person, in Piaget's view, interacts with his environment. As he assimilates it, he reorganizes his ideas and concepts about the world and the objects in it—including himself—and in this manner accommodates himself to the world. Intelligence, then, is the result of the organism's interaction with his environment and his adaptation to it.

Piaget's Concepts of Cognitive Development   The living organism, in Piaget's scheme, has two basic biological functions: organization and adaptation. *organization*   Organization reflects an inclination on the part of all species to order their processes, both physical and psychological. A good example of physical organization is the infant's breathing apparatus—mouth, nose, larynx, trachea, and lungs. These structures are closely related and coordinated into an efficient system for supplying oxygen to the blood. Similarly, on the psychological level, the infant's experience of reality prompts him to integrate his behavioral structures into systems. Among the behavioral structures of the newborn infant, for example, are separate structures for grasping and for looking. He will sometimes grasp at a toy, and at other times he will simply look at it. But the newborn has not yet integrated the two structures in order to grasp the toy and look at it more closely. By 4 months, however, he is able to organize the looking and grasping structures into a single, more complex structure. This new structure enables him to hold the toy and look at it simultaneously. Organization, then, is the biological tendency to integrate separate structures into higher-order systems.

Adaptation is the dynamic aspect of organization. It is the organism's capacity to develop in diverse ways, depending on the circumstances of the environment. All organisms tend to adapt to their environments, though the methods of adaptation vary widely from one species to another, and from one individual to another within a species. The process of adaptation, according to Piaget, consists of two complementary subprocesses: *assimilation* and *accommodation.*

In the case of infants, *assimilation* is the child's expansion of his cognitive categories to include a greater number of objects or events. A newborn infant will only suck on a human breast or something that closely resembles a breast—such as the nipple of a baby bottle. Within a few months, however, he begins to treat a wide variety of objects as "suckable": fingers, toys, crackers, fabric, and so on. He assimilates these new objects into a previously existing category: things to suck. In addition, when a child hears the people around him talking, he starts to babble sounds vaguely resembling the speech he hears. Eventually, "da-da" and "ma-ma"—and a host of more or less meaningful sounds—are assimilated into the child's small but growing vocabulary. As the child grows older, most of his learning experiences entail assimilating new ideas and concepts into already existing categories. Assimilation, then, is the adaptive process by which an increased number of objects or events are subsumed under, and trigger, the exercise of a particular behavioral schema. Piaget defines *schema* as an organized pattern of behavior. It can refer to reflexes, such as nursing, or to patterns of behavior learned from experience, such as thumb-sucking. Each infant has his own unique scheme of nursing and of thumb-sucking.

Accommodation is the adaptive process complementary to assimilation. In it the child alters a behavioral scheme or creates a new one in response to conditions he finds in the outside world. To continue with the example of sucking, during the first few weeks of life the infant becomes increasingly adept at this activity. Soon he is able to modify his sucking action to suit environmental conditions. Thus, sucking may proceed in a slightly modified way, depending on the angle at which the child is held, the shape of the nipple, the amount of fluid desired, the degree of pressure required to get the fluid at a desirable rate, and so on. And, later on, sounds assimilated into the child's vocabulary are changed so that they become coherent speech. Thus, the child accommodates to the language of his surroundings. Piaget calls the balance between what

adaptation

assimilation

accommodation

Table 11.2 Piaget's Outline of Cognitive Development

I. Sensorimotor Period

Stage	General Development	Object Concept
1. Reflex (birth to 1 month)	Engages basically in reflex activity, especially sucking.	Has none, cannot differentiate self from other objects.
2. Primary circular reactions (1–4 mos.)	Begins to build repertoire of behaviors: bringing hand to mouth to suck on thumb. Repeats what he finds pleasurable.	No differentiation between movement of self and movement of other objects. Disappearance of an object elicits no reaction.
3. Secondary circular reactions (4–8 mos.)	Begins crawling and can reproduce interesting events—pulling a string to shake a rattle; perceives relationship between his actions and their results.	Anticipates positions of moving objects.
4. Coordination of secondary schemes (8–12 mos.)	Learns to apply previously learned responses (or behavioral schemes) to new situations; will lift pillow to find object under it.	Develops object permanence; searches for vanished objects.
5. Tertiary circular reactions (12–18 mos.)	Begins to search for novelty—a period of experimentation. Uses trial and error behavior to attain goals and invents new ways to do things.	Searches for vanished object and takes into account the sequence of places it disappeared to.
6. Internalization of thought (18–24 mos.)	Real beginning of thought. Invents new ways of doing things, not only through actual trial and error but by mental trial and error—by thinking. Can have mental images and think of objects not immediately present.	Can have mental images of objects and their displacements.

II. The Conceptual Period of Intelligence

Stage	Phase	Development
1. Preoperational (2–7 yrs.)	a. Preconceptual (18 mos.–4 yrs.)	First use of representational thought and symbols, such as words, for objects; classification of objects.
	b. Intuitive thought (4–7 yrs.)	Beginning of reasoning, but thinking is fragmented, centered on parts of things, rigid, and based wholly on appearances.
2. Concrete operations (7–11 yrs.)		Can perform mental operations and reverse them. Can add up "all the marbles" and subtract all the black marbles. Operations are however confined to concrete and tangible objects that are immediately present.
3. Formal operations (12–15 yrs.)		Can form hypotheses, can go beyond appearances to deal with the truth or falsity of propositions.

is taken in (assimilated) and what is changed (accommodated) *equilibration,*   equilibration
and it is this that enables the child to maintain a coordination between the two. •
Equilibration is the mechanism for growth and change in cognitive development.

Sequences of Cognitive Development From a lifetime of close observation and experimentation with children, Piaget has divided intellectual development into two major periods: sensorimotor and conceptual. Although he specifies the average age at which these developments occur, he also points out that there is wide variation among children in the rate of development. His primary concern is with the sequence of stages through which development takes place. The same sequence, he says, occurs in all children. Each stage is a prerequisite for the next; each level of cognitive operation sets the stage for another. We will give first an overview of these stages and then a discussion of each in detail. Table 11.2 provides a quick overview of the different periods, stages, and phases of development. It may help in the following discussion to turn back to this table for quick reference and orientation.

During the *sensorimotor period of intelligence,* which occupies the infant's first 2 years, the child gains increasing mastery of his actions in a world   sensorimotor period
of objects. The infant is unable to use images, ideas, or words in his thinking. Rather, his developing intelligence expresses itself solely through action. By the end of the period the child demonstrates—through his interactions with objects and with other people—that he has an elementary sense of space, time, and causality, and that he is able to negotiate his way successfully around the environment.

The second major period of intellectual development is known as *conceptual intelligence* and is characterized by the increasing use of language and symbols. This period extends broadly from the middle of the second year to the age of 12 or 15 and actually consists of three subperiods. In the *preoperational stage,* which spans the years from 2 to 7, language emerges and becomes quite sophisticated. The child also makes enormous strides toward intellectual autonomy—toward independence from the world of objects. By the end of this period, he no longer has to perform a given piece of behavior in order to discover its probable result; he can manipulate concepts and symbols in his head and thereby "imagine" the result without actually going through the motions.

The next subperiod is called the *stage of concrete operations;* it extends from 7 to 11 years. During this time the child's comprehension of ordinary physical reality increases to the point where he understands many systematic cause-and-effect relationships among objects and events. He has a solid grasp of the concepts of number, weight, volume, measurement, and perspective. The term *concrete* implies that the child is continuing to deal with concrete materials—things, physical states, persons, and so on. The *operational* aspect suggests that the child is capable of manipulating these objects intellectually.

The final broad phase of mental development is the stage of *formal operations,* which is usually attained between the ages of 12 and 15. The child has perfected his ability to understand and express his reality in terms of ideas and abstractions. He can think deductively, conduct mental "experiments" in which he varies one factor at a time, and reach a reasoned judgment about causal factors.

This, then, is the basic scheme of Piaget's concept of cognitive development. However, a brief description is not enough. The details of these periods are developed in the next sections of the chapter.

SENSORIMOTOR PERIOD

Piaget has described six stages the infant passes through during the 2 years of the sensorimotor period. Each stage is characterized by a new mode of behavior—and each new mode is a prerequisite for the next phase of the series. Overall, the child moves from simple reflexes to a practical mastery of the world of persons and objects around him.

1. Use of Reflexes

During the first month of life the newborn's activity is mostly confined to innate reflexes—principally sucking, crying, swallowing, and gross bodily movements—though he learns to modify them somewhat through the processes of accommodation and assimilation. He is able, to some extent, to discriminate among stimuli; when he is hungry, for example, he can recognize the specific stimulus (the nipple) that will provide food.

2. Primary Circular Reactions

primary circular
reactions

During the second stage of sensorimotor development, from 1 to 4 months, the child begins to undertake systematic coordinations between behavioral patterns. For example, he is capable of reaching out to grasp something. Piaget calls these coordinations "primary circular reactions." They are random behaviors that may cause something interesting or pleasurable to happen in the infant's immediate vicinity. When it does, the infant immediately tries to discover which of his behaviors produced the result, and after a series of attempts, he usually succeeds in reproducing the act.

3. Secondary Circular Reactions

secondary circular
reactions

Between the ages of 4 and 8 months the infant's developing sensory and motor abilities permit him to crawl and to manipulate objects in the environment that interest him. During this third phase, secondary circular reactions begin to occur in which the infant's primary, earlier developed behaviors are amalgamated. They are repetitive and are thus called circular. When the infant notices that something works, he will repeat it. In particular, he discovers procedures for making interesting events last. Thus a child may discover that shaking a rattle produces a fascinating noise. He will then repeatedly shake the rattle in order to get the noise. This is his first intentional behavior displaying a rudimentary understanding of a means-end relationship.

During this stage Piaget has also discerned behavior indicating that the infant is forming a *concept of objects*. Until this point, he has made no sharp distinction between himself and the outside world. The world existed only as a function of his immediate perception. He is now capable of understanding that objects have an existence independent of himself, and he begins to explore the connections between his actions and their consequences in the outside world.

At this stage the infant learns that his mother always returns to him after leaving his sight, though not necessarily when he might want her to appear, as she would do if she were an extension of himself. After several months, evidence begins to accumulate that she continues to exist even when he cannot see her. From the concept of person permanence it is only a very short jump to the concept of object permanence—the idea that an object continues to exist when it is out of sight.

An early indication of the infant's progress to this stage is his ability to anticipate where a dropped object will land, even if he is unable to follow the descent with his eyes. At first, the infant can only anticipate where a ball will land if *he* drops it. Later, he can predict the landing spot regardless of who drops the ball. In addition, if the child reaches for a toy but the toy drops out of sight, he will reach in the correct direction for the toy. If, however, the toy should drop when the infant was not reaching for it, he will not search for it. The toy exists for the child only when he is actively relating to it.

During this stage, the child also learns to recognize a partially covered object. He reconstructs the whole object from the parts that are visible. For example, Piaget (1952) describes his son Laurent at 9½ months:

> . . . Laurent lifts a cushion in order to look for a cigar case. When the object is entirely hidden the child lifts the screen with hesitation, but when one end of the case appears Laurent removes the cushion with one hand and with the other tries to extricate the objective. (p. 219)

4. Coordination of Secondary Schemata

In this phrase, which extends from 8 to 12 months, the infant begins to adapt past sensorimotor patterns (or schemata) to new situations. For the first time the child is able to adapt to new situations through the systematic use and combination of familiar schemata. A good example of this new level of capability is the setting aside of one object in order to reach a more desirable object behind

coordination of
secondary schemata

it. Such a sequence of behavior requires not only a clearly established intention but also the capacity to execute a plan so that the two behaviors will occur in the proper sequence.

tertiary circular
reactions

5. Tertiary Circular Reactions

Vivian Duncan

This stage occupies the period from 12 to 18 months. The essential process of this stage is the same as that of stage 3, but it is at a higher level. Here too the infant repeats activities that produce interesting results. But rather than simply repeating the action, the infant now, of his own volition, varies his action slightly and observes the altered result. Piaget (1952) has described an example of these tertiary reactions from his observation of his son Laurent:

> [At 10 months, 5 days] Laurent discovered in "exploring" a cake of soap, the possibility of throwing this object and letting it fall. What interested him at first was not the objective phenomenon of the fall, but the very act of letting it go. He observed fortuitously, which still constitutes a "secondary" reaction. . . .
>
> [At 10 months, 10 days, however] . . . Laurent manipulates a small piece of bread . . . and lets it go continually. He even breaks off fragments, which he lets drop. Now, in contradistinction to what has happened on the preceding days, he pays no attention to the act of letting go, whereas he watches with great interest the body in motion; in particular he looks at it for a long time when it has fallen, and picks it up when he can. (p. 268–272)

The child at this stage is continually experimenting with new combinations of responses. Despite his remarkable facility with objects, however, he is still restricted to the world of objects that are present. Objects do not yet have full permanence for him, and when something disappears from view, unless he has been actively pursuing it, he still behaves as if the object had ceased to exist.

internalization of
thought

6. Internalization of Thought

The sixth and final phase of sensorimotor development spans the ages from 18 to 24 months and marks a decisive point in the child's development. For the first time, he is able to devise means of solving problems through internal or mental coordination. He is capable of entirely novel sequences that he devises in his head—with no trial-and-error experimentation. This, then, is the beginning of abstract thought—an awesome moment that Piaget (1952) has recorded in the life of Laurent.

> [At 14 months, 25 days] I give him [a] stick. . . . Laurent grasps the stick and immediately strikes the floor with it, then strikes various objects placed on the floor. He displaces them gently, but it does not occur to him to utilize this result systematically. . . . I put various desirable objectives 50 cm. or 1 meter away from Laurent, but he does not realize the virtue of the instruments he holds. . . . If I had repeated

such experiments at this period, Laurent . . . would have discovered the use of the stick through groping and apprenticeship. But I broke off the attempt and only resumed it during the sixth stage.

At 16 months, 5 days, Laurent is seated before a table, and I place a bread crust in front of him, well out of reach. Also to his right I place a stick 25 cm. long. At first Laurent tries to grasp the bread without paying any attention to the instrument, and then he gives up. I then put the stick between him and the bread; it does not touch the bread but nevertheless carries with it an indeniable visual suggestion. Laurent again looks at the bread, without moving, looks very briefly at the stick, then suddenly grasps it and directs it toward the bread. But he grasped it toward the middle, and not at one of its ends, so that it was too short to attain the objective. Laurent then puts it down and resumes stretching out his hand toward the bread. Then, without spending much time on this movement, he takes up the stick again, this time at one of its ends (chance or intention?), and draws the bread to him. He begins by simply touching it, as though contact of the stick with the objective were sufficient to see the latter in motion, but after 1 or 2 seconds at most he pushes the crust with real intention. He displaces it gently at first, but then draws it to him without difficulty. Two successive attempts yield the same results. . . . An hour later, I place a toy in front of Laurent (out of his reach) and a new stick next to him. He does not even try to catch the object with his hand; he immediately grasps the stick and draws the toy to him. (p. 33–36)

Clearly, Laurent has internalized actions he would previously have acted out. He now thinks about the problem—and cognitively solves it—before he acts. This capacity for representation forms the basis for all later forms of abstract and symbolic thinking.

By the end of the sixth stage, with the ability for at least basic thought and the retention of images, the child can now store away a behavior he has seen somebody else do and reproduce it later. Now he can actually imitate something.

Overview of Sensorimotor Development

In the first 2 years of life the child makes rapid strides in acquiring many of the tools necessary to further cognitive development. The principal changes that occur during the sensorimotor period involve imitation, classification, relations, space and time, and causality.

Imitation Early in the sensorimotor period the infant imitates only himself, replicating behaviors he has already performed. During later stages he becomes progressively more proficient at imitation, so that by stage 6 he is capable of *deferred imitation,* or reproducing behavior from memory.

deferred imitation

Piaget first noted deferred imitation in his daughter Jacqueline at 1 year, 4 months. Jacqueline was playing with a neighboring boy of about her own age. The boy threw a temper tantrum—screaming, stamping his feet, and shaking the playpen bars. Jacqueline merely looked on. But the next day, when her mother put her in the playpen, she threw a temper tantrum—screaming, stamping her feet, and shaking the bars just as the boy had done.

Classification The infant's ability to recognize objects and their distinct properties begins to develop quite early; Piaget has noted an instance of it as early as 6 months:

> Lucienne perceives from a distance two celluloid parrots attached to a chandelier and which she had sometimes had in her basket. As soon as she sees them, she definitely but briefly shakes her legs without trying to act upon them from a distance. (Piaget, 1952, p. 186)

Here the child's little kick signifies that the objects are familiar. She has classified the parrots as objects she has already experienced.

Relations During stages 2 and 3 the infant acquires a primitive understanding of relations. He may shake the bars of his crib vigorously, producing movement of the crib and a loud noise, then shake them more slowly, recognizing that the gentle rocking and softer sound are results of less vigorous shaking. These perceptions of differences in volume and intensity are the source of the infant's later quantitative thinking. By stage 6, the child is able to pull toward himself one object in order to reach another object that he otherwise could not have reached. This behavior demonstrates an understanding of the relation between two objects.

Space and Time Until the infant is about 3 months old, he cannot differentiate between the positions of objects and the movements he must make to perceive those objects. Yet at this age, he has a *practical* concept of space because he knows, for example, how to carry an object he cannot see to his mouth and adjust it for sucking. He also has a practical concept of time: he turns his head in the direction of a sound he has heard. At this practical level of conceptualization, his movements are spatially and temporally correctly ordered, but they do not reveal a specific awareness of space or of time. These movements are not very far removed from reflexes.

By the end of the sensorimotor period, the child sees himself and his movements as separate from other objects and their movements. And he recognizes the impermanence of positions of things. Just as an object is the same whether he can see it or not, or whether it is in one place or another, so it has the possibility of moving or being moved from one place to another and then back again. As the child's concept of time develops, he begins to search for hidden objects and then to recognize that a hidden object may move sequentially from one place to another; these attainments depend on the development of memory. Finally, the child is able to represent time symbolically—to talk and to think about it.

Causality In the early months of life the infant, according to Piaget, is probably aware only that effort must be exerted if something is to happen—if, for example, he is to get his thumb into his mouth. But he doesn't know which movement accomplishes the objective, or how it works. The child's first associations of cause with effect are weak and imprecise. He behaves as if his movements alone could produce results, shaking his own leg, for example, in an attempt to produce movement in a doll that is at a distance. Piaget calls this the "magico-phenomenalistic" stage of causal reasoning because, he contends, even when the child knows that, for example, by pulling a string he can make a toy rattle, he doesn't understand that there is an intermediary between his action and its effect. The child gradually comes to realize that many causes are completely external to his own activity. Finally he is able, through representation, to recognize causes that he cannot perceive; he is able to reconstruct causes—from memory—in the presence of their effects alone.

CONCEPTUAL PERIOD OF INTELLIGENCE

Preoperational Stage

In Piaget's view, the emergence of symbolic thought at about the age of 18 months signifies a major transition from sensorimotor intelligence to the beginnings of mature conceptual intelligence. This stage of intellectual development is known as the preoperational stage, and it lasts until the age of about 6 or 7 years. It occurs in two phases: the preconceptual phase (18 months to 4 years) and the phase of intuitive thought (4 to 7 years).

preoperational stage
preconceptual phase
intuitive thought

Preconceptual Phase During this phase the child begins to use representational thought and symbols. New levels of reality are now opened to him, for he is no longer so closely tied to the immediate physical world. Two examples of early symbolic thought on the part of a toddler are apparent in his ability to defer imitation and to search for lost or hidden objects; as we have noted, these abilities begin to appear toward the end of the sensorimotor period. A child of 2 years may observe his father lighting a pipe and then, several days later, pick up a stick and pretend to light it like a pipe. The child must have formed some mental image of the pipe-lighting procedure and based his delayed imitation on it. Similarly, a deliberate search for a hidden object, which Piaget reports as early as 18 months, also entails the ability to represent objects in the form of a mental symbol.

Imitation is also the basis of *visual imagery* in Piaget's view. He argues that when a child looks at an object—for example, a fire engine—his eyes scan the object, following its contours, noting the color, and focusing in order to fix the object in space. When the engine is gone, the child will go through this same scanning process in his head—imitating his own previous physical activity. This shortened version of the original perception constitutes the child's visual image of the car. Alternatively, the child's principal image of the car may not be visual at all, but auditory (the sound of the motor) or tactile (the "feel" of riding in a car).

symbolic play

Once the ability to symbolize occurs, the child begins to spend an enormous amount of time in symbolic play. Piaget defines symbolic play as the use of one concrete object in place of another that the child encounters in his daily life.

> At 21 months Jacqueline saw a shell and said "cup." After saying this, she picked it up and pretended to drink. (She had often pretended to drink with various objects; but in these instances the object was assimilated to the drinking schema. Here the identification of the shell with the cup preceded the action.) The next day, seeing the same shell, she said "glass," then "cup," then "hat," and she took an empty box and moved it to and fro saying "motycar".... (Piaget, 1951, p. 124)

A final cognitive ability that begins to develop between 1½ and 4 years of age is the power to classify objects into categories. At this stage, however, the ability remains quite primitive. The child often perceives two separate objects from the same class as being the same object. Similarly, he may exclude an object from its appropriate class for a superficial reason. A likely explanation for these mistakes, according to Piaget, is the child's limited memory capacity. He will often quickly forget the defining property he was using to build a class of objects. When he does, his attempt to classify will go awry.

The Phase of Intuitive Thought Up until now, we have been labeling various stages and periods as if they began and ended on specific days of the child's life. While it is possible to define these stages according to the significant problems the child is confronted with and the concepts he acquires, the discontinuities often seem larger than they really are because of the theoretical divisions imposed on them. In reality, of course, cognitive development is a continuous process of growth, and this point needs to be kept in mind.

The years from 4 to 7 represent a transition from the fragmented illogical thinking of the toddler to the systematic, practical thinking of the 7-year-old. In Piaget's scheme they represent the second half of the preoperational stage—the *phase of intuitive thought*. The major observable changes during this period involve vocabulary, learning, memory, and imagery. Piaget regards these new activities as manifestations of new cognitive structures and abilities.

Although this period represents a great step forward from the sensorimotor stage, it is still marked by traits that make it fall far short of adult thinking. Specifically the child between 4 and 7 has not developed the concepts of conservation and reversibility. Nor can he pay attention to more than one aspect of a thing at a time. He thinks in terms of the parts of a given situation, but he cannot integrate these parts into a satisfactory whole at the same time. Similarly, his thinking is irreversible. Once he has divided an object in two, he loses the ability to think of the object as a whole. Piaget showed some children a tray of wooden beads, most of them brown and a few white. He then asked them which would be longer—a necklace made of all the brown beads or a necklace made of all the beads, both brown and white ones. Most of the children said the necklace made of brown beads would be longer. Children at this stage cannot reason about the whole (all the beads) and a part of it (the brown beads) at once. Asked to make a comparison, they compared the brown to the white beads rather than the brown beads to all the beads.

The child's thinking at this stage also tends to be static. He thinks of objects as having permanent states, and he has no way to conceptualize the process of transformation. If a ball of clay is shaped into a donut, the child will be able to conceptualize the two shapes, but he will be unable to form a mental image of the change of form that occurred. He will thus lose the relationship of the quantity of clay to its shape. He will not be certain that the amount of clay remains the same even as its shape is transformed.

Classification Some time between the ages of 4 and 7 the child becomes able to use simple classifying schemes fairly accurately. He can comprehend states of classes but remains incapable of understanding the relationship between classes. Once he has divided an entity into two subclasses, he is unable to hold in his mind both the original whole entity and the divisions into which he has separated it.

For example, present a child with 2 red squares, 2 blue squares, and 5 blue circles and ask him, "Are all the blue things circles?" He will usually answer correctly, "No." If, however, the child is then asked, "Are all the circles blue?" he will again say, "No." Children at this stage cannot understand how *all* of one thing (all the circles) can be *some* of another thing (some of the blue shapes). Their classification skills are not fully developed.

Seriation During the period of intuitive thought the child makes enormous strides in his ability to conceptualize the relations between objects. At 4 years, the child who is given a set of 10 sticks of varying lengths will be unable to order them in terms of length. He will have no understanding of what the problem calls for or any way to analyze its details. His attempt to solve the problem will amount to no more than a haphazard manipulation of objects. Some time between the ages of 5 and 6 the child will be capable of solving the problem correctly, but he will rely on trial and error and visual judgment rather than a full cognitive understanding of the relation between the objects. But by the age of 6 or 7 he will have no difficulty in ordering the sticks or in inserting new sticks in an existing series. He no longer relies on trial and error, and he has a full conceptual understanding of the relation between the sticks. This represents the beginnings of a major new cognitive stage: the stage of concrete operations.

Numbers Once the concepts of classification and seriation have been developed, the child can begin to understand numbers. Piaget calls the most basic element of this concept "one-to-one correspondence"—the ability to create numerical equivalence in two sets of objects. If a child of 4 is shown a row of 7 cups and is asked to select the same number of eggs from a basket, he will be unable to do so. He may make a very dense row of 10 eggs or a very sparse row of only 4 eggs. For him, the length of the row is the important variable—the concept of number is not yet available to him. By the age of 5 or 6 the child will have no difficulty in creating two numerically equal sets by placing one egg in each cup. But if these sets are rearranged, he will be unsure of how to restore their equivalence. He is still likely to confuse the concepts of length (or size) and number and seems unable to concentrate on both of these dimensions at the same time. By the age of 7 he has mastered these concepts fully and can coordinate the two dimensions in his head. In this respect, as well, he is on the threshold of the stage of concrete operations.

stage of
concrete
operations

Stage of Concrete Operations

As was noted earlier, Piaget has identified a major shift in cognitive operations at about the age of 7 or 8. He refers to the new level of ability as *concrete operationalism*. Before looking at the specific new kinds of competence this level of operations allows it will be helpful to mention two of the general cognitive trends that Piaget has identified during this period. One of these pivotal developments is *decentration*—the child's increasing ability to focus on more than one facet of an object, situation, or event. With decentration the child also becomes more flexible and realistic in his responses to external reality. Another general trend is the increase in ability for *categorization*. The child becomes capable of isolating smaller phenomena and of detecting more subtle kinds of similarities and differences between them.

decentration

Concrete operationalism refers to the child's ability to perform mental acts or operations in response to environmental changes. And these acts are also reversible. That is, the child can mentally add up the members of his class and then subtract the children who are absent. However, he is able to perform these operations only on tangible objects. He is not yet able to deal with hypothetical situations. He cannot, however, be fooled by appearance as he could in the preoperational stage. In the eggs and cups experiment, if you took all the eggs out of the cups and put them in a cluster and then asked the child whether there were more eggs than cups, he would say something like, "Of course not. There was an egg in each cup before you took them out; there must still be an egg for each cup."

The 7- to 11-year-old is able to match a row of pennies with an equal number of candies, regardless of the density or length of the row. The child at the stage of concrete operations recognizes how the two dimensions of length and density relate—that density compensates for length in the *conservation* of number.

conservation

Similarly, the child at this stage is capable of new kinds of mental images. He is capable of both kinetic and transformational imagery—unlike the preoperational child who is limited to static imagery. He can represent (in his head, or on paper) the movement of two objects in relation to each other (the displacement of two blocks described earlier) as well as the process by which a substance (a ball of clay) is transformed from one shape into another.

In the area of social development Piaget maintains that the growth of decentration leads to new levels of awareness in perceiving the motives and emotional states of others. These abilities lend themselves to much more com-

Conservation

One of the most important cognitive concepts that a child has to master is that of conservation—or the notion that things have a permanence even though they may change in shape or organization.

Two types of conservation that Piaget discusses at some length are the conservation of quantity and the conservation of number. Children in the preoperational stage of development—which lasts until about the age of 7—judge size, quantity, and other physical characteristics entirely by appearances. Milk in a tall, thin glass is judged to be "more" than the same amount of milk in a shallow bowl. In an experiment Piaget poured the milk from the tall glass into the shallow bowl right in front of the child, without spilling a drop, but the child was convinced that there was less milk in the bowl than there had been in the glass. In a related experiment Piaget made a ball of clay and asked a child to make another ball the same size with the same amount of clay. When the child had done this and was satisfied that the two balls of clay were indeed the same, Piaget took one of the balls of clay and, in front of the child, rolled it into a long, sausage-like shape. Children in the preoperational stage maintain that the sausage-shaped piece of clay contains more clay—because it looks longer. These children have not learned the concept of conservation of quantity. They do not understand that amounts remain the same even as appearances change.

Conservation of number, the notion that the number of objects in a group remains the same even if they are arranged in a different way, is another concept that preoperational children don't understand. Piaget observed, for example, that children in the preoperational stage judge a row of eight objects spread out over a large space as being more than eight objects grouped together in a small space. Such children are obviously not ready to learn numbers. They do not understand the property of "eightness," for example. Numbers to them are like names, and for them learning to count is the same as reciting a nursery rhyme.

Piaget believes that the concept of conservation depends on the concept of reversibility. The milk can be poured back from the shallow bowl into the tall glass, and the clay can be reshaped into a ball. A preoperational child cannot visualize these reversals, but if he actually plays with the materials and physically carries out the reversals he can learn the notion of conservation.

plex and selfless kinds of social relationships—with both peers and adults. The child is able to *decenter* from his own narrow perspective and fully appreciate the immediate circumstances of another person.

Stage of Formal Operations: 11—15 Years

In Piaget's theoretical formulation adolescence marks the change from concrete operationalism to *formal operational thought*. The concrete operational child can deal rather successfully with the immediate world of sensory experience.

formal operational thought

During adolescence, however, new cognitive capacities develop that permit assessment of the truth or falsity of abstract propositions and mental compensation for *possible* changes in reality. The adolescent also develops the ability to analyze complex phenomena in terms of cause and effect—using the *hypothetico-deductive method* of modern science. He is able to imagine hypothetical situations, deduce their consequences, and devise a test to see if the consequences hold true. He has the capability of analyzing a problem situation, thinking of all the possible variables that may affect the outcome, controlling for them, and reaching a solution. In short he can think logically about abstract problems.

hypothetico-deductive method

A good example of the formal operational thought that the adolescent becomes capable of is the law of floating bodies. The young person who has attained this stage of cognitive development is capable of thinking at the same time about both the weight and the volume of two different quantities—an object in water and the water itself.

 Problem Solving Processes: An Alternate Approach to Cognition

Piaget approaches cognitive development by identifying a sequence of fundamental cognitive operations. An alternative approach is to study the component processes of cognition rather than the fundamental operations. This approach is favored by many American psychologists, who assume that the child must progress through a variety of levels of competence in each cognitive process and then integrate them into a larger and more general cognitive ability. Let us consider the component process theory of cognitive development as it relates to problem solving, one of the major abilities the child acquires during the period from 4 to 7 years.

Problem-oriented thought is highly directed mental activity which has as its goal the solution to a problem. A child's success in arriving at solutions to problems is thought to depend on his mastery of five distinct mental processes: encoding, memory, hypothesis generation, evaluation, and deduction.

Encoding refers to the comprehension and labeling of stimuli. In infants and young children all stimuli are encoded as images. Once language is acquired, however, words become the primary mechanism for encoding the elements of the child's experience. Successful problem solving depends on flexible encoding—the ability to abandon inappropriate labels until the problem is successfully encoded and a solution is found.

Memory is the next step in the problem-solving process. A child's ability to register and retain encoded experience affects the store of information and knowledge he has to draw on in solving problems. Studies have found that memory increases dramatically with language facility—suggesting that vocabulary is an important memory tool. However, the child who wants to retain information must actively use words to reinforce and even rehearse his recent memories. Flavell,

J. H. Flavell

Beach, and Chinsky (1966) assembled groups of children in three age groups (kindergarten, second grade, and fifth grade) and showed each of them a series of pictures. The pictures were shown several times—each time in a different order —and then the children were asked to reassemble the pictures in their original sequence. The older children did much better at this task—repeating the names of the pictures to themselves as they worked (Table 11.3). The 5-year-olds, although they knew the names of the pictures, did not use this information in solving the problem. The experimenters then *taught* the children to use words in performing the task—and their scores improved remarkably.

A child may possess all the cognitive abilities and information required to solve a problem and still fail to do so. The ability to combine these elements in uniquely constructive ways also requires *creativity,* an attribute which depends partly on the child's freedom to generate ideas and his lack of concern about the possibility of making mistakes. Creativity blossoms in an atmosphere where the child feels free to take chances and risk unusual ideas—where he can be "playful."

Table 11.3 Number of Children Showing 0, 1-2, and 3+
Verbalization Instances

	Number of Instances		
Grade	0	1–2	3+
K	18	1	1
2	8	7	5
5	3	4	13
Total	29	12	19

SOURCE: Flavell, Beach, and Chinsky (1966)

Evaluation is the next step in the problem solving process: Is the hypothesis that has been generated correct? As early as age 2 a child may already exhibit a marked individuality in the manner and degree to which he evaluates his thinking. One child acts impulsively, making a decision on the basis of his first hypothesis. Another will pause and proceed cautiously, reflecting on the relative value of several hypotheses. These early trends seem to persist in later life although, through training, most children seem able to reverse either tendency. The capacity to consider a hypothesis before acting on it increases steadily between the ages of 5 and 12.

Deduction and hypothesis generation are complementary processes. The hypothesis that building blocks and dominoes, for example, are similar because both can be used to construct a large structure may lead to the deduction that a group of identically shaped blocks may be put together meaningfully. Thus, the child's store of hypotheses (for example, that blocks can be used as building elements) determines his deductive ability. Piaget believes that the child's ability to use hypotheses deductively improves significantly between the ages of 4 and 12, as new cognitive operations come into play. Other investigators contend that deductive ability improves continuously as new rules are absorbed, but that no fundamental change occurs in reasoning skill.

Mediation is a cognitive process involved in problem solving that stands apart from the other five processes. It is an internal middle step and is somewhat broader and more inclusive than the other processes that have been described. Mediators are any of several types of internal processing phenomena: words, concepts, images, and other mental realities.

The ability to use mediators is vital to the solution of a special class of problems known as *reversal-shift* problems. The child's basic task in such an exercise is to shift his responses and do the opposite of what he did earlier in the identical circumstance. For example, he may be shown two blocks—one black and one white—and asked to pick the larger of the two. In several trials, sometimes the black block is larger and sometimes the white block is. When the child has learned to pick the larger block regardless of color, he will then be asked to pick the *smaller* block. A child with good verbal mediation skills will have no trouble with this reversal shift. He will use words as a mediator—in effect coaching himself by saying, "Look for the small block this time." Empirical studies of this process suggest that verbal mediation develops into an effective cognitive tool some time between the ages of 5 and 7.

David Elkind

The cognitive changes that appear in the adolescent years open up new capacities for thinking about oneself and one's behavior in relation to other people and the physical environment. The adolescent is more aware of personal alternatives, and he is capable of imagining an ideal self that differs from his present real self. One possible result is that the adolescent becomes preoccupied with moral principles, introspection, and self-criticism. Elkind (1968) has suggested that many of the extreme emotional phenomena of adolescence, such as identity crises, may be the result of the new capacity for abstract and hypothetical thought. Formal operationalism also carries with it a changed time perspective. The adolescent is capable of transcending present reality and becomes aware of future possibilities and adult roles. Of course, all of these new cognitive abilities emerge slowly, at various times and rates, and the adolescent frequently falls back on earlier modes of thinking.

COROLLARIES OF COGNITIVE DEVELOPMENT

Up to now we have been discussing Piaget's views of the development of cognition alone. But while cognition is developing, certain other traits and concepts that may be seen as corollaries of cognition are also developing. We will now discuss these aspects of development. And in our discussion we will introduce the work and thinking of a number of other researchers besides Piaget. Specifically we will discuss the concepts of egocentricity, imagining and perceiving, language and cognition, play and mental imagery, and moral development.

Egocentricity

One of the chief characteristics of the child during the preoperational period (18 months to 6 or 7 years) is his *egocentricity*. He assumes that everyone literally sees things as he does and thinks as he does and that the world was made for him. In one experiment a preoperational child was shown pictures of a lamp from several different views and was asked to choose the one that represented the way someone on the opposite side of the room from himself would see it. The child consistently selected the view that represented his own view of the lamp.

egocentricity

    Piaget believes that egocentricity begins to break down toward the end of the stage of intuitive thought through interaction with other children—especially through communication conflicts (arguments). In such conflicts the child is forced to pay attention to another child's viewpoint and maintain that perspective for the sake of argument. Murray (1972) has studied the role of social conflict in cognitive growth by means of an ingenious experiment with a group of 6½-year-old children, some of whom understood the concept of numerical equivalence and some of whom did not. He gave them a problem involving this concept and told them that the group as a whole must arrive at a single answer. Needless to say, a vigorous debate occurred. Later, Murray tested the members of the group individually and found that they all showed significant gains in their understanding of the numerical equivalence concept. His results clearly demonstrate the importance of social interaction as an agent of cognitive growth. In fact, one researcher (Smedslund, 1966) argues that the most important interaction leading to intellectual development during the years between 1½ and 7 is between the child and those about him—rather than interaction with the physical environment. Conflicts between the child and his peers are necessary for a transition from egocentric to operational thought.

Imagining and Perceiving

According to Piaget, by the age of 4 the child's imagery is fairly well developed. He can readily represent events and objects that are not actually present (static imagery). The 4-year-old, however, does not have the capacity for *kinetic imagery*—the mental representation of objects in motion. If he is first shown two blocks, the second of which is resting squarely on top of the first, he is able to draw a recognizably accurate picture of them. If the top block is then moved off center he can draw another accurate picture. But if the blocks are realigned, he is unable to draw a picture of the second position from memory. Moreover, he is unable to select the proper drawing from among a series drawn by an adult. Piaget's experiments suggest that kinetic imagery becomes available to the child at about age 7. As in the case of numerical relations, children under 7 seem to form a "global" impression of what has occurred. They know the blocks have changed position, but how they have changed eludes them.

Other researchers have emphasized the specific tasks involved in the act of perception and have studied the child's gradual acquisition of these skills during the period from 4 to 7. In general, they argue that the child makes steady, unspectacular progress in two important areas: (1) his ability to *differentiate* stimuli—to make precise distinctions between objects on the basis of their appearance; and (2) his ability to recognize the details of a particular stimulus *and* the whole stimulus when he integrates these details.

Theories of Perceptual Development   Broadly speaking, there are two important—and contradictory—theories that attempt to explain how children achieve the ability to distinguish between visual stimuli. Neither theory has been conclusively proved, but experimental evidence exists to support both. Clearly, further research will be required before the issue can be firmly resolved.

The first theory contends that children first perceive select geometrical features of objects—corners, curves, and lines intersecting at various angles. Through experience, these distinctive features are compiled into a "dictionary" of translations in which every specific object translates into a unique combination of these features (Gibson, 1969). Gibson's idea has been tested by determining whether children could easily identify letter-like but meaningless forms. Line drawings resembling printed letters were formed and showed to children of post- and prereading age. Errors were found to decrease from age 4 to age 8. The biggest decline in errors was found in children aged 5 to 6 who were first learning to read. These results seem to support the theory that perception is based upon a building-up process of recognition of distinctive features of shapes.

Heinz Werner

The second theory contends that children are first able to percieve *gestalts* or "wholes"—shapes such as squares, circles, and triangles. With experience, however, the child learns to refine his perceptions and is able to differentiate a whole object on the basis of its parts. Simultaneously, he begins to be able to reintegrate the parts into new kinds of perceptions in which the parts are separate yet related to the "wholes" (Werner, 1957). This second theory is more closely allied to Piaget's approach in the sense that the development proceeds from global undifferentiated perception to differentiated and integrated perception.

One of the most intriguing though still unconfirmed pieces of evidence for this view is Kellogg's studies of children's drawings from all over the world (Fig. 11.1). All children, Kellogg found, go through four sequential stages in the drawings they produce. First they make random scribbles that demonstrate an awareness of figure-background relationships. Second, they produce simple overall *gestalts* or shapes (circles, rectangles). Third, these shapes are combined to produce designs. And finally, between the ages of 4 and 5, most children begin to produce designs that resemble real objects, such as houses and people (Kellogg, 1967).

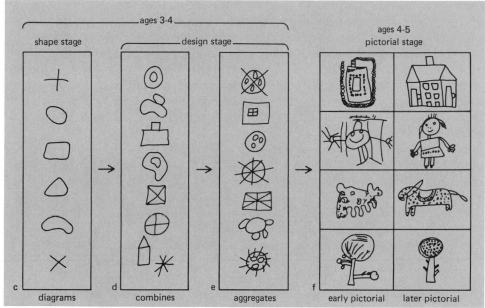

ages 3-4

shape stage   design stage   ages 4-5
                                                    pictorial stage

c diagrams   d combines   e aggregates   f early pictorial later pictorial

Fig. 11.1 The sequential stages in children's drawing. (Reprinted from May 1967, *Psychology Today*. Copyright © 1967 Ziff-Davis Publishing Company. All rights reserved.)

These two theories of perceptual development attack the problem from opposite points of view. One theory sees it microscopically while the other sees it macroscopically. The question of whether things are seen as a whole or as a compilation of their parts is an issue in many aspects of psychology. Perhaps the theories are indeed different, or perhaps they are just various ways of describing the same thing.

Interpersonal Perception A final area of perceptual growth is interpersonal perception—the ability to empathize with others, to put oneself in another person's shoes. Piaget found that at an early age a child's speech is not "social" or communicative. The child merely verbalizes what he is thinking without realizing that the other person cannot understand. He thus leaves out bits of information, assuming that the other person "sees his thoughts." Borke (1971) has given children of various ages the opportunity to articulate an emotional response to the feelings of other children. Her conclusion is that by 3 years of age children have begun to be aware of other people's feelings (particularly happiness) and are able to respond in an appropriate way. Interestingly enough, the ability to recognize fear in another person does not emerge until the age of 4 or 5.

Language and Cognition

The broad question of the relationship between language and cognition, as we saw in Chapter 8, is the subject of lively debate among psychologists. Which of the two powers develops first? Does one exert a primary influence over the other? Those who believe that language influences cognition have contended that only with the development of language is the child capable of complex learning, thinking, concept formation, reasoning, and problem solving. Furthermore, they see the acquisition of language as the beginning of a lifelong period of self-control through words. Luria (1957) has argued that the child internalizes speech in much the same way he internalizes his imitations of actions or events. Once internalized, language serves to organize the child's experience and to guide and control his behavior.

Piaget and others disagree strongly—maintaining that language development is dependent on cognitive operations that precede speech in time. These operations (or schemata) begin forming early in infancy as a result of the infant's sensory and motor activities. Toward the end of the second year of life, the child begins to apply words to these schemata—a process that accelerates rapidly and continues at a rapid pace through the fourth year.

Evidence for this view consists of numerous studies of deaf children to determine whether their deficiency in language had interfered with their cognitive development (Furth, 1971). These studies compared the performance of deaf children with that of normal children in a number of tasks involving cognition, memory, and perception. The results showed that deaf children performed at the same level as normal children in almost every case. Furth concluded that language played an indirect role in cognitive development. Language can increase cognitive development by acting as a pathway for additional information and experience. It facilitates quick and easy communication through the use of already learned symbols.

Hans Furth (left)
James Yauniss (right)

Language influences our perception of the world and our responses to the environment. Our nationality and culture determine the language we will be taught. Benjamin Whorf believes that different languages have different effects upon thought, and Edward Sapir, Whorf's teacher, sees language as influencing all experience—seeing, hearing, and so on. However, the concern of some psycholinguists, such as Noam Chomsky, is to find linguistic and cultural universals so that the underlying cognitive process of learning a language—any language—might be better understood. Thus, instead of viewing language and cognition as two opposing forces in psychological studies, they should be viewed as two important and interacting variables in the mental development of the child.

 The Whorf Hypothesis of Linguistic Relativity

Language is one of the more obvious differences displayed by a culture or sub-culture. It is also the outward aspect of thought. Benjamin Lee Whorf (1956) formulated a hypothesis of "linguistic relativity," correlating language and thought. According to Whorf, our perception and interpretation of our environment is largely determined by our language. As a symbol for our ideas and attitudes, the unstated aspect of language is reflected in our thoughts. The contrast between English and the languages of North American Indians illustrates his thesis. In English, the grammar classifies words into nouns and verbs. Corresponding to this, we tend to think in terms of "things" and "events." Whereas in the Hopi language, words that we would classify as nouns, such as "lightning, flame, wave," are verbs because they last a short time. Another language, spoken on Vancouver Island, makes no distinction between nouns and verbs; "a house occurs" or "it houses" is the same as our meaning for "house." Whorf understands these varying distinctions to express one way in which language shapes our thinking. The Hopi and Vancouver Island people think more in terms of activity than English-speakers do.

Another support for Whorf's hypothesis is based on languages that have many words for a single English word. In the Eskimo language, there are several words for snow. Whorf maintains that the existence of this variety of words meaning snow leads to a way of thinking about snow different from that of people who speak a language that uses one word for snow. Whorf believes that language structures the way we see the world, and that view influences the way we think.

The question Whorf is attempting to answer is as complex as the chicken and the egg riddle. His research breeds as many questions as it answers. Do Eskimos experience snow differently because they have many other words for it? Does our single word snow prevent us from understanding the Eskimo meanings? Are all languages capable of expressing all thoughts, though one may use one word and another many? Or is the relationship between thought and language in the process of continual change?

Play and Mental Imagery

The development of imagining and perceiving, as well as of language, as we have said before, is largely dependent on imitation, especially the kind of imitation that occurs in children's play.

voluntary behavior

Jerome Bruner

We have seen that as the child begins to develop concepts, he also begins to engage in voluntary behavior. Bruner (1968) has identified five characteristics of voluntary behavior: anticipation of a goal and selection of means for reaching that goal; freedom from domination by immediate sensory stimuli; the ability to maintain a behavior beyond a single response; the ability to order responses sequentially; and possession of the necessary skills to make the desired response. The newborn is deficient in all five of these capabilities. And yet, in the space of a few months, his abilities develop at an astounding rate, and he soon exhibits true voluntary behavior.

Given that voluntary behavior is ubiquitous at an early age, psychologists have recently begun to consider the question of its motivation. The traditional biological motives—hunger, thirst, and pain—are inadequate to explain the infant's substantial capacity for initiative. Berlyne (1960) has suggested that the actual motive may be curiosity or a drive to explore and that this drive emerges out of the simultaneous arousal of two conflicting responses. (See Chapter 5 for a more detailed examination of this and other motives.) For example, a large stuffed dog that barks when it is wound up will probably elicit incompatible and conflicting responses. On the one hand, the infant will want to hold the furry toy; on the other, he will have an impulse to retreat from the loud noise. Berlyne proposes that the infant resolves this conflict by cautiously exploring the novel object. According to Berlyne, complexity, uncertainty, surprisingness, and incongruity usually elicit exploratory responses.

D. E. Berlyne

One of the most familiar kinds of voluntary behavior among infants and children is *play*. In the sensorimotor period (the first 2 years of life) play is essentially a matter of assimilation winning out over accommodation. It begins in the third sensorimotor stage, when a few behaviors begin to be performed for their own sakes rather than for their usefulness or instructiveness (squeezing a rubber duck in order to hear it squeak). It continues through the use of means as ends in their own right (slapping the side of the crib without any attempt to attract attention) and ritualization (repeatedly dropping an object from the crib in exactly the same place on the floor). Finally the child becomes capable of symbolic representation and begins imaginary play—treating one thing as if it were something else (pretending the area under the kitchen table is a house) or going through the motions of doing a thing without actually doing it.

Brian Sutton-Smith

Play seems to have an important role in increasing the infant's range of responses and cognitive operations. Sutton-Smith (1967) analyzes play as the working through of novel responses and operations. It thereby provides the child with a mechanism for the *socialization of novelty*. Children who are given many

Follow the leader—imitation is an important part of play in early childhood.

opportunities for spontaneous, unstructured play have more experience in dealing with novelty and unfamiliar situations than those whose play is restricted, and the former are thus better prepared to give a novel response in a new social situation.

Play during childhood bears a theoretical relationship to later creativity. When the child playfully varies his responses to objects, he increases the range of his associations for those objects and discovers many new uses for them.

Childhood play may be a private adventure.

Sometimes the new uses are completely private inventions—fantastic, absurd, amusing, preposterous, of no use except as an expressive, rewarding exercise. It is also likely, however, that the child's repertoire of responses and cognitions will have been increased by such play. When he is again faced with a novel situation involving even a slightly similar object, he is more likely to be able to make a unique or creative response. Thus, play increases the child's repertoire of responses, an increase that has potential value for later responses in different situations.

PERSONALITY AND SOCIAL DEVELOPMENT

As the child develops cognitively he begins to perceive himself as an entity and builds schemata that include himself in relation to others. We turn our attention now to the social development of the growing child. Most of the concepts that we will consider only briefly in this section are examined in greater detail in the next chapter. They are mentioned here, however, because many of them tie in with the notions of development that we have been considering throughout this chapter.

Self-Concept Development

Early Childhood As the child develops a clear understanding of his own separateness form other people and from the physical world, he begins to demonstrate a desire to be like one or both of his parents. This desire goes far beyond mere imitation; rather, the child is impelled toward *identification* in quite a

Steven Berkowitz

The child develops through social play.

complete sense. Usually the child chooses the parent of the same sex as his or her own as a behavior model. This is because in order to identify with another person the child must be able to detect some physical or emotional similarity between himself and the adult.

Gradually the child's own individuality comes into sharper focus as his motor and cognitive abilities develop. He begins to display identifiable personality traits and behaviors that are uniquely his own. At first this uniqueness is more apparent to his mother and father and to his friends than it is to the child himself. The responses of others to the child begin to take his individuality into account—creating a kind of feedback that enhances the child's growing self-awareness and autonomy.

 Sex Typing: Freudian, Social Learning, and Cognitive Theories

One of the most significant examples of identification that occurs during childhood is sex typing—the process by which the child comes to identify himself as male or female. Different theories account for this process in different ways.

The Freudian view (see Chapter 12) holds that gender identity develops out of the Oedipal conflict, which all children between 3 and 6 experience in relation to their parents. In the case of boys, Freud proposed that the child initially assumes that his mother will meet his need for genital gratification—just as she met his oral needs earlier. He also begins to perceive that his mother and father have a unique relationship that prevents gratification of his sexual needs. He finds himself rivaling his father for his mother's affection and is, at the same time, fearful that his father might retaliate. In order to handle his anxiety, according to Freud, the child *identifies* with the father—thus reducing the threat and allowing for some vicarious participation in the father's relationship with the mother. This process also lays the groundwork for the child's internalization of many cultural values and norms.

The controversy between social learning and cognitive theories of acquiring sex-appropriate behavior is primarily conceptual. Still the implications of the respective positions are interesting and should be considered.

The social learning model begins with the notion of identification. A boy, perceiving his father as attractive and as similar to himself, will imitate his father's behavior and mannerisms. As a result, he will begin to adopt many characteristics that are considered specific to the male personality. His concept of his own maleness will be the end product of his identification with his father. Imitation of sex-appropriate behavior is enhanced by the approval or disapproval a child receives for his activities. Little boys are praised for helping their fathers shovel snow or put up storm windows, and little girls are encouraged to help set the table or wipe the dishes. Most boys are rewarded for "manly" rough-tough behavior, while most girls are rewarded for being sweet and polite.

In this paradigm a sex-typed identity emerges only after and as a result of the child's having acquired a set of sex-appropriate behaviors. It is as if one were to say, "If a child behaves like a boy he must be a boy."

In this social learning view, the role of the adult model is very important. Some adults may enhance sex-appropriate identification more than others. Identification results from dependency on the adult. Thus a nurturant parent will have more dependent children who will identify more thoroughly with the parent. More positive sex-role identifications are also formed if the same-sex parent is perceived as powerful. An habitually submissive husband is unlikely to be an attractive model for a young boy.

The cognitive theory of sex-role identification (Kohlberg, 1966) begins where social learning theory ends and in fact turns the tables. Instead of seeing sex typing as the end result of a process beginning with identification, identification (or attachment to the same-sex parent) is seen as the end result of a process beginning with a sex-typed identity. Kohlberg maintains that the child first develops an idea of himself as a boy or girl. He then notices that, in his society, certain behaviors and attitudes are categorized by sex type and as a result adopts those traits that are associated with his sex. Identification with the parent of the same sex results from the child's growing interest in the activities and the qualities of his own sex. The child says, "I am a boy; therefore I want to do boy things." It then becomes rewarding to adopt the traits of his own sex.

The original sex-type identity develops gradually. The child hears his parents and others refer to him as a boy or girl and begins slowly to develop the concepts of boy and girl. Eventually he can sort out people on the basis of their sex traits. At first the toddler's usage of the words boy and girl depends on superficial traits, clothes, hairstyles, and so on. Until they are about school age children are uncertain about the stability of sex-type identities. In one study 4- to 8-year-olds were shown a picture of a girl and were asked whether she could become a boy by wearing boys' clothes, playing boys' games, or cutting her hair short. The majority of the 4-year-olds said the girl could become a boy. The 6- and 7-year-old children disagreed. The older children, Kohlberg argues, had formed stable mental categories based on intrinsic rather than superficial traits.

At about 6 or 7 years, having solidified his sex-type concepts, the child begins to add more abstract and more complicated distinctions to his male-female concepts. Thus he may see the male as strong and the female as passive and weak.

Looking at the research, one would have to conclude that both the internal cognitive structure and the external parental reward and modeling have a strong influence on sex typing. There is no evidence as yet to show which is the more important. At present all of these theories have adherents.

This development is accelerated by the child's emerging cognitive ability to make comparisons. Concepts of size, color, weight, and shape all contribute to his ability to distinguish between himself and others in these respects. The toddler's emerging self-awareness is apparent in numerous characteristic activities. For one thing, he can now recognize his image in a mirror, though he is often confused about what the image actually represents. For another, he now refers to himself as *I*—a symbol of significant identification and individuation. Finally, a sharpened self-concept is apparent in the toddler's insistence on choosing for himself in every area of life. This behavior is often characterized as "negativism" and is marked by the child's endless use of the word "no." He opposes almost any suggestion his parents make—thereby asserting his sense of independence and separateness from them.

Adolescence The development of a self-concept is not completed in early childhood. The adolescent is faced with the sometimes difficult task of forming and maintaining a coherent sense of who he is and what purpose he will ultimately serve in his world.

Adolescent thinking is characterized by increased differentiation and articulation. For one thing, the individual becomes capable of finer psychological distinctions, and he applies them not only to others but also to himself. He is engaged in a perpetual cycle of self-definition, personal change, and redefinition from which his self-concept emerges. The self-concept is also affected by social expectations and the increasing reality of future possibilities.

A corollary development is that the adolescent begins to seek a sense of independence from his parents and to develop a feeling of personal autonomy. Douvan and Gold (1966) have distinguished between two types of personal autonomy: behavioral autonomy and emotional autonomy. Their studies have shown that behavioral autonomy—for example, dating, employment, financial independence, and choice of companions outside the family—increases markedly during adolescence. They found little increase, however, in emotional autonomy—valuing friendships over family relationships, willingness to seek personal advice outside the family, and disagreeing significantly with parental opinons or ideals. It appears that emotional autonomy develops later than behavioral autonomy—conceivably during the period of postadolescence (the early 20s).

There is considerable debate among psychologists about how much change in roles and role expectations takes place in adolescence and the effect of these changes on the individual. The psychoanalyst Erik Erikson is one of the main proponents of the *crisis* view of adolescence, and he has coined the term *identity crisis* to refer to the changes in emotional structure and self-conception that take place during this period. In Erikson's view (1950) the adolescent is involved in a continuing struggle to redefine his sense of himself (his identity)—incorporating new elements while trying not to relinquish the feeling that he is the same person he has always felt himself to be. A third element in this process is the changing expectations and perceptions of the adolescent on the part of peers and family.

Erik H. Erikson

Other theorists contend that the severity of the emotional changes during adolescence has been exaggerated by Erikson and other neo-Freudians. The *noncrisis* view holds that there is no sharp emotional discontinuity between adolescence and adulthood (Douvan and Gold, 1966). Gergen (1972) has even questioned whether the formation of a stable, coherent identity is a normal healthy process. He proposes that the healthy personality is actually multidimensional, that adolescence marks the beginning of this mature circumstance, and that identity crises represent a rare pathological form of this process.

Paul Mussen

A final issue related to the development of the adolescent's self-concept is his sexual identification and sex-role development. Mussen (1961) found that adolescent boys exhibiting highly masculine interests on the Strong Vocational Interest Test tended to have more self-confidence and more positive self-concepts than boys with more feminine interests. In a follow-up study (1962) Mussen found some interesting developments. He tested the same subjects, then in their 30s, and found that those who had shown highly masculine interests as adolescents continued to express those interests. But he also found that these men tended to lack the qualities of leadership, self-acceptance, and self-confidence. Conversely, those who had shown more feminine interests as adolescents now demonstrated more positive signs of leadership, self-confidence, and self-esteem. In order to account for these results Mussen theorized that many respected and well-rewarded adult attributes and vocations require a combination of the stereotyped "masculine" and "feminine" characteristics. For example, doctors and teachers must be dominant and aggressive (masculine) as well as sensitive and receptive (feminine). Thus, extremely masculine characteristics may have a "prestige" value during adolescence and may contribute to the teen-age boy's self-esteem. But these same characteristics may also inhibit the development of other abilities and characteristics that will be important to him as an adult—in terms of both vocation and personal fulfillment.

Adulthood The adult's question of identity centers on the establishment of reciprocal relationships among others in his social situation—family, friends, co-workers, members of organizations. He is usually what he sees himself to be in these interactions. The ultimate concept of self, however, is faced when the adult ponders the meaning of his own death—the meaning of not being. Thus, the conception of the self from birth till death is a continuous, ever-changing process.

Moral Development

As the child begins to experience more complex and differentiated kinds of social relationships his sense of morality also becomes more complex and differentiated. According to Piaget, moral development accompanies the acquisition of autonomy and grows out of the need to operate with peers in social situations. The most intense period of moral development occurs around age 7. At this time the child's cognitive powers have recently expanded—facilitating a new level of social relations—and he is ready for greater physical and emotional independence from his parents.

Moral Development

The moral development of the child is a complicated process. Piaget (1932) tells us that the child progresses from absolute to relative kinds of moral judgments. Initially rules appear to be perceived as inviolate and absolute; the wrongness of a deviation is measured in terms of the amount of harm done. In time the child realizes that the rules of a culture, like those of a game, are made to serve the participants and that they can be modified by mutual consent.

The progression from absolute to relative conceptualizations about morality has been elaborated by Kohlberg (1968, 1969), who built his theory of the development of moral judgment on research done with children of different ages and from many different cultures (Swiss, Belgian, Chinese, Mexican, Israeli, Hopi, Zuni, Sioux, Papago). His methodology generally was to give children a story presenting a moral dilemma and note the responses and moral judgments of the situation given by children of different ages. One of his stories appears below (from an unpublished doctoral dissertation by J. Rest, in Kohlberg, 1969).

Lawrence Kohlberg

> In Europe a woman was near death from cancer. One drug might save her, a form of radium that a druggist in the same town had recently discovered. The druggist was charging $2,000, ten times what the drug cost him to make. The sick woman's husband, Heinz, went to everyone he knew to borrow the money, but he could only get together about half of what it cost. He told the druggist that his wife was dying, and asked him to sell it cheaper or let him pay later. But the druggist said no. The husband got desperate and broke into the man's store to steal the drug for his wife. Should the husband have done that? Why? (p. 379)

The experimenter analyzed the responses given, not for content, but rather for the type of reasoning used.

The results for all cultures showed a regular sequence of development. Most 10-year-olds gave responses at the first or premoral (preconventional) level. For these children the act could be justified if it satisfied the self's needs. (Occasionally there is also reference to satisfying the needs of the other, with an orientation toward exchange and reciprocity.) For example, one 10-year-old responded:

> He should steal the drug. It isn't really bad to take it. It isn't like he didn't ask to pay for it first. The drug he'd take is only worth $200, he's not really taking a $2,000 drug. (p. 379)

At age 13 most children gave conventional responses showing a concern for approval and for pleasing and helping others. At this age, there is also a strong conformity to stereotyped images of natural role behavior and an emphasis on the intentions of the doer. An example of such a response follows.

> He should steal the drug. He was only doing something that was natural for a good husband to do. You can't blame him for doing something out of love for his wife, you'd blame him if he didn't love his wife enough to save her. (p. 380)

Most American 16-year-olds gave responses of the principled morality sort. They viewed morality in terms of contractual obligations and democratically accepted law. Thus a typical answer might be:

The law wasn't set up for the circumstances. Taking the drug in this situation isn't really right, but it's justified to do it. (p. 380)

From this data it would seem then that like cognitive development, moral judgment develops in a regular and predictable order.

Kohlberg's elaboration of moral development into six progressive stages (see Table 11.4) represents a kind of resolution of Freudian and Piagetian constructs that transcends both theories. For Kohlberg the chief motive for moral behavior is less social than an attempt to satisfy one's own conscience, to avoid self-condemnation. Typically the child is seen as having learned to anticipate punishment for transgression. Subsequently anxiety becomes associated with the transgression itself and is manifest even in cases where there is no objective reason to fear punishment. For Kohlberg, the manifestation of guilt is less a function of such learning and more a matter of the resolution and integration of a moral decision into the child's complex moral construct system. The child is thus considered a "moral philosopher" in his own right.

Table 11.4 Moral Levels and Developmental Stages According to Kohlberg

Preconventional Level	STAGE 1: Orientation toward punishment. Deference to superior power. Goodness or badness is determined by the physical consequences of action.
	STAGE 2: Right actions are those that satisfy needs (mainly one's own needs). People share but in a pragmatic way, not out of a sense of justice or loyalty.
Conventional Level	STAGE 3: "Good boy-good girl orientation." Behavior that pleases or helps others and is approved by them is good behavior. Emphasis on conformity and on being "nice" to gain approval.
	STAGE 4: Focus on Authority, fixed rules, and the social order. Right behavior consists of maintaining the given social order for its own sake. Respect is earned by performing dutifully.
Postconventional Level	STAGE 5: "Social contract orientation"— legalistic, utilitarian. Standards that have been agreed upon by the whole society define right action. Emphasis upon procedural (legal) rules for reaching consensus. Awareness of the relativism of personal values.
	STAGE 6: Emphasis on decisions of conscience and self-chosen, abstract ethical principles that are "logical, comprehensive, universal, and consistent." These abstract ethical principles are universal principles of justice, of reciprocity and equality of human rights, and of respect for the dignity of human beings as individuals.

SOURCE: Kohlberg (1963, 1967)

Mike Levins

As the child approaches adolescence, the expectations of his peers become increasingly important.

During the period from 7 to 12 the child steadily moves away from authoritarian prohibitions (usually parental) against specific behaviors. Instead, he begins to see morality as based on the need for harmony between persons rather than conformity to an iron and arbitrary law. His sense of morality begins to acquire a social base—relativism replaces absolutism. Mutual accommodation becomes the primary consideration (Piaget, 1932).

Piaget has also related morality to the child's new concern with the intentions of others and with the consequences of actions. The ability to realize that other people have intentions depends almost exclusively on the child's ability to decenter. Decentration also allows the child to "theorize" about his peers' expectations of him—and these expectations, in turn, become an important element in the child's emerging moral sense.

In Piaget's view, moral reasoning undergoes profound changes during adolescence as a result of the new ability for hypothetical thought. The adolescent appeals less to arbitrary authority and relies increasingly on his capacity to imagine the social and personal consequences of any given behavior or action.

Kohlberg (1970) has amplified and extended Piaget's ideas and has proposed a three-stage sequence to account for moral development. During the *preconventional* stage of early childhood—up to about age 7 or 8—the child will do whatever leads to personal gratification unless he is physically stopped or consistently punished. During the second or *conventional* stage—age 7 or 8 to adolescence—the child bases his morality on the expectations and rules of peers and parents. Finally, during the *postconventional* stage, he develops personal principles that are often abstract and may conflict with the conventional morality of his society. Kohlberg's moral stages correspond very closely to Piaget's cognitive stages. In fact, Kohlberg contends that each new stage of moral development is dependent upon the emergence of major new cognitive abilities.

Keniston (1970) has isolated three factors that are present in adolescent experience to varying degrees and that promote the development of postconventional morality. The first factor is a prolonged period of disengagement from adult institutions, such as attendance at a college away from home. Under these circumstances the adolescent begins to evolve his own sense of moral priorities and to question standards and practices that he had previously accepted uncritically. A second variable is the opportunity for exposure to alternative points of view. This variable, like the first, is highly dependent on economic and social-class factors. The final variable is the extent to which the adolescent discovers corruption and hypocrisy in the conventional society around him. Keniston has explained the wave of student protests and political initiatives during the late 1960s in terms of the increasing prevalence of these three variables; his work on "Young Radicals" is examined further in a box in Chapter 14.

In the next chapter, we will discuss theories of personality. It is well to keep in mind that the early cognitive development of the person plays a significant part in the formation of personality and the way problems confronted are resolved.

Alburtus—Yale News Bureau

Kenneith Keniston

Summary

Standardized intelligence tests to measure mental capacity present a series of tasks designed to assess different aspects of intelligence—for example, sensorimotor activity, manual dexterity, and language. The child's total score on the entire series reflects his overall intelligence relative to established national norms.

Infant intelligence tests have limited value as predictors of intelligence several years later because they cannot measure the same skills as tests of intelligence developed for older children. Tests for infants are also limited by the fact that they do not take into account the many ways in which a child can interact with his environment.

Piaget's organismic notions of cognitive development rest on the assumption that the child moves through a sequence of developmental stages as he grows. Each stage rests on the cognitive abilities and behavior acquired in the preceding one, and intelligence progresses gradually and systematically from an undifferentiated thought system into a highly integrated capacity for abstract thinking. Piaget divides cognitive development into two major periods: the sensorimotor and the conceptual.

During the sensorimotor period, which spans the first 2 years of life, the infant progresses from simple reflex activity, such as sucking and crying, to acquisition of the basic tools necessary for dealing practically with the world of objects and persons around him. Piaget has described six distinct stages within the sensorimotor period: use of reflexes, primary circular reactions, secondary circular reactions, coordination of secondary schemes, tertiary circular reactions, and internalization of thought. By the end of these stages the infant has acquired deferred imitation, or the capacity to reproduce another person's behavior in mental form; the ability to recognize objects and their properties, or rudimentary classification; a primitive understanding of relations between objects; an objective concept of space and time; and a grasp of causes in terms of their effects.

From the middle of the second year until about the age of 12 or 15 the child is in the period of conceptual development, which Piaget has divided into three stages. By the end of the first stage—the preoperational (2 to 7 years)—the child has made great strides in the use of language and symbols and in the further development of systematic, practical thinking. He has learned, for example, to use simple classifying schemes with a fair degree of accuracy, he has acquired a conceptual understanding of the relation between objects, and he has learned the basic component of the concept of numbers—one-to-one correspondence, or the ability to create numerical equivalence in two sets of objects.   •

The second stage of conceptual development—concrete operations (7 to 11 years)—is characterized by two major cognitive developments: decentration, the child's progress in being able to deal with more than one aspect of an object or event; and categorization, his increasing ability to see subtle relations between phenomena. By the end of this stage the child can perform mental operations in response to changes in what he sees around him, but he cannot yet deal with hypothetical situations.

With approaching adolescence the child enters the final broad stage of conceptual development—formal operations (11 to 15 years)—during which he develops a full range of cognitive abilities that enable him to think abstractly and to solve problems on the basis of deductive reasoning. At this time too the person becomes concerned with himself in relation to others and begins to give thought to the future and to his role as an adult in society.

As the child interacts with other children during the preoperational stage, his egocentricity—the tendency to see everything in terms of himself—breaks down and he becomes more capable of seeing another's point of view. This social interaction is seen as a necessary corollary to his intellectual development.

During the same stage children grow rapidly in their powers of perception. Two contradictory theories have been put forward to explain how children learn to differentiate between visual stimuli, and experimental studies support both. One theory proposes that children first perceive geometrical features of objects, such as lines. The second holds that objects are first perceived as wholes—shapes such as squares. Research indicates that by age 3 children have acquired some interpersonal perception, or the capacity to respond to the feelings of others.

Psychologists are not in agreement concerning the relation between language and cognition. One group maintains that language development is the foundation of all complex learning. For Piaget and others, language is dependent on the acquisition of certain cognitive operations. Some psycholinguists such as Chomsky believe that language and cognition are not separate forces but interacting variables in the child's mental growth.

Play is seen as the child's opportunity to experiment with novel responses, the avenue by which he increases his repertoire of cognitions as he discovers for himself new ways of seeing and using objects and situations. There is thus a theoretical link between childhood play and creative expression later in life.

Moral development proceeds as the child gains independence from his parents and experiences more complex social relationships. Between the ages of 7 and 12 he comes to see morality in terms of the need to get along with others rather than to adhere strictly to parental rules. Kohlberg sees three stages in moral development—the preconventional, the stage of self-gratification; the conventional, the stage of obedience to rules; and the postconventional, the stage of abstract moral reasoning. Keniston explains postconventional moral development in terms of three variables: removal from adult authority, exposure to points of view other than his own, and the recognition of corruption in conventional society.

At the same time that the child is acquiring more complex cognitive behavior, he is also growing socially, and his concept of himself gradually takes form. At first the young child identifies with his parent of the same sex, modeling his own behavior on that parent's in every way that he can. But as his cognitive abilities grow, so does his self-awareness, and he is increasingly able to see himself in relation to others. He comes to recognize clearly the physical differences between himself and other people and responds in terms of his own uniqueness.

Growth in the concept of self continues in the adolescent years as the young person becomes capable of seeing subtle psychological distinctions between himself and others. Some psychologists view adolescence as a period of preoccupation with defining and redefining the self; Erikson has called this time of emotional turmoil the identity crisis. Other theorists maintain that there is no sharp emotional break between adolescence and adulthood.

Related to the development of self-concept is the development of the adolescent's sexual identification and sex role. At this time the person acquires the attributes and characteristics that are stereotypically masculine or feminine, and these may exert a lifelong influence on performance in certain areas and vocations.

In adulthood, self-concept is important in terms of how the individual sees himself in his relationships with those around him. To consider one's own death is to face the ultimate concept of self.

SUGGESTED READINGS

Anderson, Poul, *Brain Wave*. New York, Walker, 1959.
   In this science fiction novel, human intellectual capacities are fantastically increased, with almost limitless implications for the individual and society.
Beard, Ruth M., *An Outline of Piaget's Developmental Psychology*. New York, Basic Books, 1970.
   An introductory overview of Piaget's theory and research findings.
Bettelheim, Bruno, *Children of the Dream*. New York, Macmillan, 1969.
   About the effects of communal child-rearing on an Israeli kibbutz.
Dittmann, Laura L., ed., *Early Child Care: The New Perspectives*. New York, Atherton, 1969.
   Various authors discuss the intellectual development of the very young child.

Erikson, Erik, *Young Man Luther.* New York, Norton, 1958.

   Erikson's work is a psychoanalytic study of the identity crisis not only of the young Martin Luther but of emerging Protestantism itself.

Hoppe, R. A., G. A. Milton, and E. C. Simmel, eds., *Early Experiences and the Processes of Socialization.* New York, Academic Press, 1970.

   A collection of readings on how the process of socialization is influenced by a child's experiences in his immediate environment.

Knowles, John, *A Separate Peace.* New York, Macmillan, 1960.

   A novel that probes the deep feelings of two adolescent schoolboys at the outbreak of World War II.

Kramer, Cheris, "Folk Linguistics: Wishy-Washy Mommy Talk," *Psychology Today,* June 1974.

   Male and female stereotypical roles are still with us, as the author illustrates using contemporary cartoons.

Offer, Daniel G., *The Psychological World of the Teenager.* New York, Basic Books, 1969.

   A study of adolescent boys.

Piaget, Jean, *Play, Dreams, and Imitation in Childhood.* New York, Norton, 1962.

   Piaget's own somewhat difficult presentation of his theory of cognitive development.

Salzman-Webb, Marilyn, "Woman as Secretary, Sexpot, Spender, Sow, Civic Actor, Sickie," in Michele H. Garskoff, ed., *Roles Women Play: Readings Toward Women's Liberation.* Monterey, Calif., Brooks-Cole, 1971.

   Women's occupations are still determined, the author contends, by the traditional female nurture role that was once required of women in order to insure the survival of the family in an economic and social sense.

Chapter Twelve

Personality

Why do children "take after" their parents?
How may a child's rate of growth affect his personality?
What is the most important environmental influence on the
    infant's development?
What role does the father play in personality development?
Who are the adolescent's chief models?
Are you an extrovert or an introvert?
What is at the center of Freud's personality theory?
What is learning by modeling?
How can you become self-actualized?

Personality is probably the most widely appealing area of psychology because it is concerned with two questions that have occupied men's thoughts since the dawn of consciousness: Who am I? How did I become what I am?

We perceive ourselves as unique, yet we are aware that we have traits in common with people we interact with. As a consequence we are also curious about the personalities of others. We are quick to label them in a word or two, using adjectives that we believe synthesize the characteristics they display most consistently—such words as warm, honest, narrow-minded, vulnerable. In doing this, we attribute a basic core to personality; we assume that it is a centralized organization of behavior. We do this quite naturally as a means of ordering and predicting our world.

But because personality is the integration of many characteristics, the psychologist, as a scientist, must make a constant effort to avoid fitting people into neat categories. Like other human beings, he is subject to the natural tendency to perceive consistency in people and events. He too would like personality to be organized around a basic core. But whether there is in fact such a

personality

Photos by Theresa O'Reilly

Personality is the integration of many characteristics.

recognizable and describable core or whether the descriptive terms that imply such a core are simply a convenient means of classifying a complex world is a debatable issue.

In this chapter we will discuss theories involved in this issue. We will also show that descriptions may vary from viewer to viewer. Each of us perceives the world slightly differently from everyone else; psychologists too differ in how they view the world and, specifically, in how they view personality. In the Freudian view, for example, human behavior stems from unconscious, instinctive urges; to Freud, the unconscious is the core of personality. Behaviorists such as B. F. Skinner, however, reject the core concept altogether and see personality as a series of learned habits based on individual experiences.

Regardless of theoretical differences in approaches, personality description serves an important function to both layman and psychologist. In our everyday life, personality descriptions help us to interpret and predict the behavior of other people as well as to evaluate ourselves and predict our own actions. For example, you need someone to take care of your dog while you are away on vacation. In deciding which of your friends to ask, you would probably think in terms of such personality characteristics as friendly, helpful, and compassionate. It would be a mistake to leave the dog with an inconsiderate or careless person.

For the psychologist, personality description is a crucial starting point, for he must be able to describe his subject before he can study his development. Similarly, if he is concerned about changing someone's personality characteristics, he must first be able to describe those characteristics to determine the nature of the changes he would like to bring about.

Many personality theorists are involved with therapeutic applications of their ideas—that is, with changing or modifying the behavior of sick, unhappy, or disturbed people. Freud based most of his thinking, even about normal people, on his studies of neurotic patients. And learning theorists, such as Dollard and Miller, and Bandura, use their theories as much to modify as to understand behavior.

Fundamental to the theories of personality discussed in this chapter is a concern with the similarities and differences among people. Some of them emphasize the uniqueness of each person and try to account for it. Others focus on the dynamics and innate drives that are common to all human beings and seek to discover general laws that govern the nature and development of personality.

Contrary to popular usage of the term, personality is not something we may have a little of or a lot of, or something that is "great" or "terrible." It is, rather, the way in which people behave, and a comprehensive description of any personality requires a vast number of categories. In our zeal to categorize and explain, however, we run the risk of reducing the person to a passive conglomeration of traits, a tool of irresistible external forces, or a victim of his own overpowering impulses. These dangers can be avoided if we bear in mind the distinction between theory and reality. Descriptions of personality and theories of personality development are not the same thing as personalities themselves. A theory that may offer a valid explanation of the behavior of large groups of people may not prove to be very helpful in arriving at the real meaning of the behavior of a particular person. All scientific enquiries encounter differences between the general and the specific, and these differences are especially evident in the study of personality.

The human personality is formed and modified by the interaction between biological man and his environment, or between the entities known in psychology as nature and nurture (see Introduction). In the section that follows the effects of genetic and somatic, parental, peer-group, and cultural factors on the development of the personality, and their interaction, are discussed.

The remainder of the chapter is concerned with theories of personality—type and trait, Freud and neo-Freudian views, learning and social learning, and phenomenological theories. These theories are concerned with different aspects of personality and are useful for different purposes. Some emphasize developmental phenomena; others look at day-to-day behavior; still others are concerned primarily with the person's image of himself. But while theorists may differ in approach, they have a common goal—to shed light on human personality.

ANTECEDENTS TO PERSONALITY

Genetic and Somatic Factors

Children often have many of the personality characteristics of their parents. To what extent are these similarities the result of genetic inheritance? This is a difficult question since parents also create a social environment that influences the personalities of their children. Therefore, it is usually impossible to determine

whether a given personality trait shared by a parent and a child has been genetically inherited or imparted by the parents to the child through social interaction.

Several studies of fraternal and identical twins have shed light on this
experimental problem, suggesting that heredity plays an important role in determining personality. Identical twins have an identical genetic make-up. Gottesman (1963) found that a large sample of identical twins were more alike on
several scales of the Minnesota Multiphasic Personality Inventory (MMPI), which
will be described in the next chapter, than were fraternal twins. These results
appear to support the case for heredity, but Gottesman was unable to control
for the fact that the social environment of identical twins is usually more similar
than that of fraternal twins: because identical twins usually *look* more alike than
fraternal twins, they are usually *treated* more alike.

Shields (1962) realized that if identical twins were reared by different
families the effects of heredity and environment could be separated. A search
conducted through BBC television turned up 44 pairs of identical twins who
had been reared apart for most of their childhood. Shields also assembled 44
pairs of identical twins who had been raised in the same household, and 32
pairs of fraternal twins, ranging in age from 8 to 59. Both groups of identical
twins were subjected to a battery of tests, including physical examinations,
questionnaires, interviews, and intelligence tests.

The results of the Shields study (Table 12.1) strongly suggest that heredity
has an important influence on many personality traits. For example, 78 percent
of the separated identical twins shared the same smoking habits—that is, they
were both either smokers or nonsmokers—and 71 percent of the identical twins
raised together had similar smoking habits. By contrast, only 50 percent of the
fraternal twins were alike in this respect. Similarly, Shields found that intelligence, extroversion, neuroticism, and body weight—traits that are closely related
to personality—showed a correlation with heredity.

In evaluating these results, we should bear in mind that the separated
twins were subjected to many of the same environmental influences. For example, the families in which each of a pair of twins was reared were generally
in the same social class, and in all pairs both twins were exposed to the same
national culture.

Identical twins are likely to have many of the same personality traits throughout life.
Schneider, F.P.G.   F.P.G.

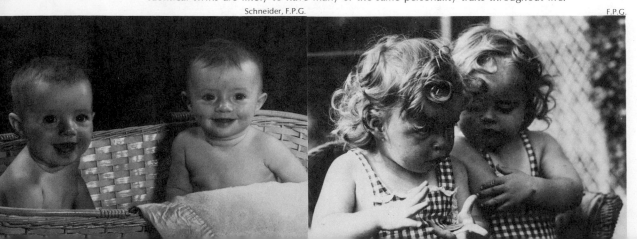

The question of the relative influence on personality of heredity and environment is complicated by the interaction of these influences and its tendency to intensify certain traits. A quiet, placid baby, for example, tends to be treated quietly and placidly by his parents. An active baby, on the other hand, tends to elicit vigorous responses and energetic handling. Similarly, a child's achievement bears a close relation to both his environment and his heredity. A child who scores high on intelligence tends to strive for achievement, and vice versa.

Table 12.1 Comparisons of Physical and Psychological Characteristics in Various Sets of Twins

Trait	Percentage of Pairs Much Alike		
	Identical, Raised Together	Identical, Separated	Fraternal
Height	42	21	4
Weight	43	43	28
Intelligence	44	32	14
Self-rating questionnaire: extroversion	49	45	28
Neuroticism	35	33	36
Author's rating: personality resemblance	55	36	9

SOURCE: Shields (1962)

Environmental factors can either strengthen or weaken the innate ability to achieve. The logical, competitive, skillful child receives positive reinforcement (verbal praise or tangible rewards) from his environment, and he is motivated by the reinforcements he receives. In a social environment in which achievement is not recognized and reinforced, the child is less likely to develop his innate ability to achieve. An environment that provides the right stimulation can thus substantially increase the likelihood of achievement. Thus, even in later stages of life, the social environment tends to magnify and reinforce personality traits that may be hereditary in origin.

Some studies of the influence of heredity on personality characteristics have focused on somatic factors, or physiological traits—physique, hormonal balance, and how the sense organs function. Inherited somatic factors may play an indirect role in the shaping of personality. The personality of a very short person, for example, is likely to be affected by his stature.

Again, psychologists studying somatic factors have found it difficult to isolate traits that are purely hereditary. The influence of the environment begins even before birth, while the infant is still in the uterus. Whether the mother is active or inactive during pregnancy, whether her diet is adequate for the needs of the fetus, and whether she is in good emotional health during this period, all affect the characteristics of her infant. Stott (1957) noticed, for example, that anxiety and stress, especially during the last trimester of pregnancy, seemed to

Robert Ader

Ader and Conklin's Research on Emotionality

Ader and Conklin (1963) conducted an experiment to test the effect of handling of pregnant rats on their offspring. Earlier research had shown that pregnant rats who had gone through conditioning procedures which were anxiety-provoking produced highly emotional and withdrawn offspring. Ader and Conklin wanted to test the effects of more handling on emotionality.

Two groups of pregnant female rats were separately treated. One group was allowed to stay in the cages and was not manipulated during pregnancy. The second group was handled for 10 minutes three times daily. Handling consisted of picking up the animal and holding it loosely in one hand.

The offspring were tested for emotionality at 45 and 120 days after birth. Three indices of emotionality were used. Two tests were in an open field situation. Rats placed in an open field (an open cage 5 ft. in diameter) were observed. Rats are generally uncomfortable in such a situation, some more than others. A very emotional rat will generally cower in one spot in the field, squeal, and defecate. The more a rat moves about in the field the less emotional he is said to be. The more emotional the rat is the more he is likely to defecate. The results of the Ader and Conklin experiment showed that the offspring of the "handled" rats were less emotional in that they moved about more in the open field and defecated less.

The third test for emotionality was the use of an emergence-from-cage test. In this test the time required for a rat to emerge from the home cage is recorded. Emotional or timid rats take longer to emerge. In the Ader and Conklin study the offspring of handled rats emerged sooner from their cages.

Ader and Conklin conclude by noting that the effects of handling are not simple—it is important to note what kind of handling occurs. In their study, the handling was beneficial in that it reduced emotionality.

produce offspring showing signs of mental retardation and behavioral disturbances, though without physical impairment.

A partially somatic factor that has been found to have a close link to personality is hormonal functioning. *Hyper*thyroidism, a fairly common malfunction of the thyroid gland, is physiologically detected by an elevated metabolic rate and high levels of pulse, blood pressure, and respiration. It is frequently accompanied by the psychological symptoms of irritability, difficulty in sleeping, frantic activity, and some degree of emotional instability. Over a period of time the afflicted person may become physically exhausted, lethargic, and depressed. Extreme hyperthyroidism *before birth* or during early childhood causes *cretinism,* a condition in which the infant is dwarfed, abnormally formed in several respects, and mentally retarded. Drugs are now available that reduce the output of the thyroid hormone and usually restore normal physical growth; they are less successful at averting mental retardation.

The close relation between the body and the mind is seen in psycho-somatic disorders, in which real physical symptoms are experienced, but the cause of the disorder is psychological. Stomach ulcers, for example, are ascribed to tension and anxiety. (Psychosomatic disorders are discussed at greater length in Chapter 16.)

 Physique and Personality

W. H. Sheldon (1942), an American physician, has developed a sophisticated classification of personality on the basis of somatic characteristics. After inspecting some four thousand photographs of male college students, Sheldon and several other judges were able to isolate three primary components of physique (Fig. 12.1).

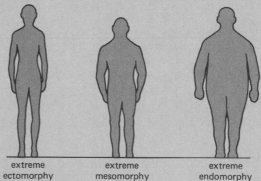

Fig. 12.1 A diagrammatic representation of Sheldon's three fundamental somatotypes. (Chaplin and Krawiec, 1968)

extreme ectomorphy   extreme mesomorphy   extreme endomorphy

endomorphy—a rounded, soft, spherical body with comparatively underdeveloped bone and muscle and highly developed digestive viscera. Endomorphs float well in water.

mesomorphy—a hard, rectangular body with a preponderance of bone and muscle. This tendency to strength and toughness enables the mesomorph to resist injury and to meet strenuous, exacting physical demands.

ectomorphy—a delicate, linear body with a flat chest. Unusual leanness and light muscu-lature are coupled with a relatively large skin surface and a large brain and central nervous system.

Sheldon then extracted from the current personality literature lists of personality traits, which he redefined and reduced by statistical correlationary methods to a single list of 50 traits. Using this list, he and his colleagues rated 32 subjects—graduate students and instructors whom they had studied for a year—and Sheldon analyzed the results statistically. He was able to isolate three major temperament components:

viscerotonia—relaxed posture, love of eating, high sociability.

somatotonia—assertive posture, energetic manner, high courage.

cerebrotonia—restraint in posture, fearfulness, introversion, artistic nature.

When he subsequently scored these same subjects for somatic tendencies,

Sheldon found some quite dramatic correlations:

Somatotype	Viscerotonia	Somatotonia	Cerebrotonia
Endomorphy	+.79	−.29	−.32
Mesomorphy	−.23	+.82	−.58
Ectomorphy	−.40	−.53	+.83

He thus concluded that physique and temperament are highly related, and specifically that endomorphy tends to be accompanied by viscerotonia, mesomorphy by somatotonia, and ectomorphy by cerebrotonia—that is, that fat people seek comfort, food, and other people; athletic people seek physical activity; and lean people seek mental activity and solitude. What is frequently overlooked in discussions of Sheldon's theory is his premise that very few people are clearcut examples of either his physique or his temperament categories, which in fact are not classes but tendencies. Sheldon himself uses scales to rate people on all three tendencies within both measures.

Nonetheless his belief that temperament can be *predicted* from physique, and physique from temperament, has met a good deal of well-founded criticism. Others have pointed out that his technique is subject to rater bias (one person rates both physique and temperament), that he has assumed without proof that a person's somatic type does not change, and that his research has been limited to male subjects.

Other somatic factors affect personality in accordance with the reaction to them of the social environment. A blind person's personality, for example, is affected not only by his inability to see but also by the way his family and friends treat him. The feeling of inferiority that accompanies blindness is heightened by reactions of pity, unnecessary helpfulness, and condescension.

The process of growing into adulthood involves an interaction between somatic and social factors that also influences personality. According to studies of the maturation rate of adolescent boys, the age at which puberty begins can vary by as much as 5 years. During puberty, enormous physical changes take place, including a complete hormonal reorganization, and the teen-age boy finds that the way people react to him depends on his physical appearance. His height, build, voice, and beard usually determine whether they regard him as essentially a man or a boy. Two grown men who are very much alike in physique and general appearance may in adolescence have matured at vastly different rates. Consequently they were probably treated quite differently during some of the most important years of their lives if one of them looked like a young man and the other like a boy. Several scientific studies have examined this phenomenon in search of answers to two questions: What effects do differing rates of maturation have upon the personality of the mature adult? And do these effects stem directly from a pattern of abnormal development or are they related to the reactions of others, including family?

Dick Owen

Adolescent boys of the same age may be at vastly different stages of maturation.

Jones (1963) has summarized the results of a number of such studies. He has concluded that males who matured early tend to be poised, somewhat conventional "solid citizens" who take their responsibilities seriously and generally accommodate themselves to the roles society habitually rewards. The early maturers tend to present these characteristics in both adolescence and adulthood. Late maturing males, on the other hand, during adolescence tend to be socially ill at ease but highly expressive and often creative. In adulthood the late maturers tend to be more self-reliant and broad-minded and to exhibit greater intellectual interests and achievements. Jones attributes the personality differences to differences in the young men's "social stimulus value" during adolescence. He concludes that early maturers, since they were treated as adults from an earlier age, adopted adult roles earlier—and adopted them in a more rigid, less adaptable form.

Peskin (1967) has interpreted the findings from a somewhat different vantage point. For instance, growing at a slower rate, the late maturer has more time to gain emotional maturity at each stage of development and is therefore better prepared for the onslaught of the massive hormonal change of puberty. As an adult his conception of himself is more flexible and less bound by the conventional models seized upon by his early-maturing counterpart. Both Peskin and Jones, however, stress that the maturation rate is only one part of the complex determination of personality.

Hormonal changes in adolescent girls seem to have far less effect on social reactions. This is almost certainly because our society has less precise standards of maturity—both physical and emotional—for women than for men. Smallness in a woman is accepted and may even be praised, as is dependent behavior very often.

Biological factors are only a part of the spectrum of influences on personality development. Other factors are parents, peers, and culture.

Parental Factors

While a child's ultimate behavior as an adult is fixed up to a point by his genetic makeup, it is influenced considerably by two separate environmental factors that at times operate in combination. These are (1) early childhood experiences, particularly the interaction between the child and his mother—a subject that will be explored in this section—and (2) influences from the society at large, which will be discussed in the sections that follow. Each of these factors is extraordinarily complex and multidimensional, presenting enormous difficulties for scientific investigation.

Importance of Mother Studies of early childhood experiences have generally indicated that the person's relationship with his mother in his early years is probably the single most important environmental influence in his life. Because ethical considerations forbid experimentation with this relationship in human beings, research in this area has used monkeys as subjects. In one of the most famous of such studies, Harry and Margaret Harlow (1966) placed newborn monkeys in total isolation and kept them there for periods of up to 12 months. When the infant monkeys were removed from isolation they showed extremely abnormal social development. They crouched down on the floor, avoided all social contact with other monkeys, and seemed highly anxious and fearful, and the damage tended to be irreversible. Monkeys removed from isolation before 6 months were generally able to recover and exhibited fairly normal

Harry F. Harlow, University of Wisconsin Primate Laboratory

Monkeys reared in total isolation for more than 6 months show abnormal social behavior from which they are unable to recover.

Harry F. Harlow

behavior after a period of adjustment. The animals kept in isolation for a longer period, however, continued to exhibit abnormal social and sexual behavior.

These results supported those of an earlier study, which showed that monkeys reared in isolation or near isolation made poor mothers when they had offspring of their own (Seay, Alexander, and Harlow, 1964). In general they avoided their children and refused to nurse them, and they were often abusive to the point of endangering the lives of their offspring.

Studies of human infants reared in orphanages tend to confirm the findings of the Harlows. Spitz (1949) studied a group of children who were institutionalized from birth and had received no sustained mothering of any kind. He found them markedly retarded in both emotional and intellectual development and attributed these deficiencies to the absence of normal mother-child interaction.

Further evidence of the importance of the mother-child relationship was provided by Yarrow (1963), who studied a group of infants raised by their natural mothers. The level of the child's emotional and intellectual development was directly related to the amount and quality of his interaction with his mother. Moreover, the effects of the relationship were observable as early as 6 months of age. For example, Yarrow found a high correlation of .65 between the infants' IQ at 6 months and a direct-observation rating of the amount of social stimulation that took place between mother and child.

Clearly, then, the mother-child relationship is crucial to normal personality development—but why? The studies by the Harlows, Spitz, and Yarrow are empirical; they demonstrate the importance of the relationship but say little about the dynamics of the child's tie to his mother.

Instinctual Attachment Using the results of experimental studies and his own direct observation of infants and young children, Bowlby (1958) has formulated a theory that accounts for the data and provides an explanation of the importance of the mother-child tie. Bowlby proposes that the child's attachment to his mother is related to five instinctual responses—sucking, crying, smiling, clinging, and following. (Freud also attached great importance to the development of the instinctual responses, as we will see.) Together these responses serve the function of binding the child to the mother, and the mother to the child. From an evolutionary point of view this reciprocal tie is necessary for the survival of the species. Human infants are totally helpless at birth and require a longer period of postnatal care than any other species. For man to have survived, the tie between mother and child had to be an especially strong one. Bowlby proposes that the five infantile instincts he has identified were bred into the species by natural selection.

instinctual
attachment

John Bowlby

At birth only the crying and sucking instincts are present. In the course of the first 6 months the smiling, clinging, and following instincts become apparent as the child's motor abilities and nervous system mature. Proper emotional and intellectual development can occur only if the responses become integrated into a complex but unitary behavior, which Bowlby calls *attachment*.

Cross-cultural Study of Child Rearing

Whiting and Child (1953) have made wide-ranging studies of child training practices in a large number of primitive cultures and in a group of middle-class Americans. They have concluded that "child training the world over is in certain important respects identical. . . . In all societies the helpless infant, getting his food by nursing at his mother's breast and, having digested it, freely evacuating the waste products, exploring his genitals, biting and kicking at will, must be changed into a responsible adult obeying the rules of society." On the other hand, there are important differences among cultures in the *character of the rules* children are taught to conform to and in the *techniques* of enforcing conformity.

Whiting and Child stress the importance of the cross-cultural method for studying child rearing practices and their effects. They point out that scientists cannot usually experimentally alter the ways in which children are reared and then look at their differential effects. One way of approaching this problem is to study training practices across several different cultures and to relate these to personality variables in these different cultures.

To illustrate this point Whiting relates a number of examples of research which would have remained short-sighted if not for cross-cultural data. Thus Sears and Wise in a study of 80 children in Kansas City found that there was a positive relationship between the age of weaning and emotional disturbance. That is, the later a child was weaned the more disturbance he revealed. Can we apply this finding to the entire human race? Not so, said the anthropologists. Blackwood in a separate study on Hurtachi children of the Solomon Islands found although they were weaned very late they showed no emotional disturbance. What then is the truth or is there no rule relating the two variables? Whiting and Child in a study of 37 societies from all over the world found that children from societies that weaned children at 2 years or less showed more emotional disturbance than children in societies that weaned their children later than 2 years. This would seem to say that the findings with the Hurtachi were no exception, but what then was going on in Kansas City? Were there different psychological processes working there than in the rest of the world? The answer to this question required a closer analysis of all of the cross-cultural data, including that of Kansas City. It was found that the ages at which infants in Kansas City were weaned were from less than a month to 7 months, whereas for the other cultures it was from 12 months to 6 years. This indicated that at a very early age, up to about one year, the later the weaning occurred the greater was the emotional disturbance, but beyond 12 months the later the weaning occurred the less was the emotional disturbance. This relationship and the theoretical formulations to explain it would have been impossible without cross-cultural study.

John W. M. Whiting

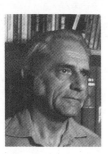

Irving L. Child

Disturbances in this behavior caused by the mother's absence or neglect will result in abnormal development. Thus, the child's tie to his mother initially develops out of her reactions to her infant's basic instinctual responses. During the first year of life, her response or failure to respond to his needs determines

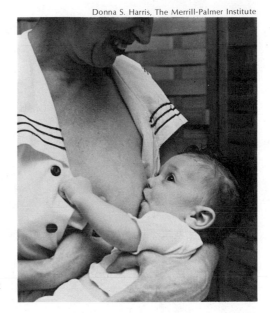

Donna S. Harris, The Merrill-Palmer Institute

Proper emotional and intellectual development begins with the mother-child tie.

whether the child will form a favorable or an unfavorable conception of himself and of the outside world.

Bowlby further suggests that clinging and following may be even more important than feeding, or the sucking response, which can be easily satisfied by a bottle. Clinging and following, however, require the physical presence of the mother.

> This view is strengthened by clinical observation. My impression in taking the histories of many disturbed children is that there is little if any relationship between form and degree of disturbance and whether or not the child has been breast-fed. The association which constantly impresses itself upon me is that between form and degree of disturbance and the extent to which the mother has permitted cling-ing and following, and all the behavior associated with them, or has refused them. In my experience a mother's acceptance of clinging and following is consistent with favorable development even in the absence of breast feeding, while rejection of clinging and following is apt to lead to emotional disturbance even in the presence of breast feeding. (Bowlby, 1958, p. 370)

Empirical evidence for the primary importance of clinging and following, as opposed to sucking and feeding, is provided by another experiment with monkeys (Harlow and Zimmerman, 1959). Infant monkeys were reared in isola-tion from their mothers and were supplied with two surrogate-mother objects. One surrogate mother was made of wire mesh that could be clung to with the fingers, while the other was made of soft cloth that was much more "cuddly." In the course of the experiment food was made available from a bottle attached to first one and then the other of the surrogate mothers. The infant monkeys

Harry F. Harlow, University of Wisconsin Primate Laboratory

Infant monkeys isolated from their mothers instinctively prefer a cuddly surrogate mother.

demonstrated a decided preference for the softer dummy—even if the one made of wire had a bottle attached to it. It was also noted that proximity to the cloth mother gave the infants a sense of security; they seemed much less fearful and more willing to explore and play when they were within reach of the softer object. Although they occasionally ran to the wire surrogate mother for food, they immediately returned to the soft surrogate mother for cuddling—confirming Bowlby's theory.

But what if the child's instinctual responses are not satisfied—what if attachment behavior does not satisfactorily occur? According to Bowlby (1960), the deprived child experiences *separation anxiety*. This is an emotional state that, in its extreme form, is almost totally incapacitating to the child and makes normal development later in life almost impossible. Through direct observation Bowlby has identified three stages of separation anxiety, depending on the length of time the child's instinctual responses were frustrated. The initial phase, *protest,* may last from a few hours to a week or more. During this stage the child appears acutely distressed at having lost his mother and will often cry loudly, shake his crib, and look eagerly toward any sight or sound that might possibly be his missing parent. During the stage of *despair* his preoccupation with his mother's absence is still apparent, but his behavior increasingly suggests hopelessness. He is withdrawn and inactive, he makes no demands on the environment, and he appears to be in a state of deep mourning. If the separation persists, the stage of *detachment* soon follows. Superficially, the child appears more sociable, but he has become increasingly self-centered and is no longer willing to risk attaching himself to anyone. Instead of showing interest in people, he becomes preoccupied with material things such as sweets, toys, and food. In this stage, the child has suffered irreversible damage to his cognitive and emotional development.

Parents and Personality Problems There is evidence that parents who are inconsistent in their behavior toward children cause personality problems. Bateson and his associates (1956) found that a stress-producing situation is created when a parent communicates first one message to the child and then a contradictory one. A child might find himself in a "double bind" if, for example, his mother verbalizes her love for him but physically rejects him when he tries to hug her.

Other research has concerned the effects of parental influence on schizophrenics. Lidz and his associates (1957, 1958, 1960) found that mutual understanding and cooperation were absent in the marital relationships of the parents of schizophrenics they studied. Children who grow up in disturbed families may interact with their environment in abnormal ways.

Conversely, a series of studies performed by Bell (1968) has demonstrated that children can exert a significant influence on the personality of their parents. Bell found that schizophrenic, brain-damaged, and physically impaired children can create a pathogenic mother who aggravates mental illness by overprotectiveness.

Significance of Father Much has been said about the role of the mother in the personality development of the child, but how significant is the father? The influence—or lack of influence—of the father is a factor in personality development. His absence has a notable effect upon the growing child. Mischel (1958) found that children of two cultures—Negro and East Indian—living together in Trinidad were equally inclined, in the absence of a father, to insist on smaller, immediate rewards rather than to choose larger, delayed gratification. But when a father was present, children of the East Indian culture were twice as likely as those of the Negro group to choose a larger, delayed reward. This study, which attempts to control culture, an antecedent to personality that we will discuss later in this chapter, suggests that, in any culture, absence of the father may be related to an inability in the children to trust and thus to become adequately socialized. Nash (1965) points out that the absent father syndrome crosses economic and racial lines and produces the same effects in both ghetto children and affluent suburban children. However, it is apparent that among the poor, absence of the father usually creates an economically deprived environment in which rewards truly cannot be depended upon; the child in this situation grabs at any material object when he has the chance.

The influence of the father is probably most important in connection with the child's sexual development. Greenstein (1966) investigated the effects of the father-son relationship on sexual development. Fathers rated as closest to their sons seemed to have had sons who exhibited the greatest homosexual tendencies. Freud would argue, however, that it is the lack of close father-son relationships that leads to homosexuality.

The presence of the father appears to decrease in importance as the child grows older and comes more under the influence of peer pressures and less dependent on his home environment. In addition, Greenstein (1960) has indicated that the father-son relationship is not as crucial to the older child with respect to the development of homosexuality, since the child now responds more to extrafamilial factors. Let us therefore consider the influence of the peer group on personality.

School and Peers

What we value and place worth upon is determined to a large extent by the opinions of other people. We see ourselves as others see us. One aspect of the theory of personality advanced by Carl Rogers (see p. 569) is the notion that a person's opinion of himself depends on how others of importance to him (significant others) see him. The developing person comes to learn that he is accepted either in accordance with certain "conditions of worth," or unconditionally, for what he is despite his actions. The person develops ideally, according to Rogers, when he experiences unconditional positive regard from significant others—that is, in an environment in which people accept him in spite of what he does or does not do.

When the child goes to school, he meets academic success or failure. Depending on the particular educational system and the child's own psychological adjustment, these experiences can be either beneficial or destructive to his developing personality. A secure child can accept failure as a learning experience, while one who has been rejected may not be able to deal with failure.

The primary rewards of learning are the learner's satisfaction in learning and the approval of the group. Classmates wield a tremendous influence on each others' intellectual, emotional, and social development. Coleman (1966) found, for example, that when minority group children were integrated into relatively affluent, primarily white schools, their level of school achievement rose significantly. But his most surprising finding grew out of an analysis of what specific factors contributed to this rise in achievement. Three school characteristics were

Mike Levins   Fred Weiss

Interaction with peers is a principal means of overcoming the young child's egocentrism.

considered: the facilities and curriculum of the schools involved, the teaching staff, and the student body. Coleman's central finding, in his own words, was that "attributes of other students account for far more variation in the achievement of minority group children than do any attributes of school facilities and slightly more than do attributes of staff." Further analysis indicated that an advantaged student body has its greatest effect on students from educationally deficient backgrounds, and that "the apparent beneficial effect of a student body with a high proportion of white students comes not from racial composition per se, but from the better educational background and higher educational aspirations that are, on the average, found among white students."

Maria Montessori, the educator, and Jean Piaget (see Chapter 11) emphasize interaction with peers as the principal means of overcoming the child's egocentrism in learning. Both see socialization as the major goal to achieve.

Glasser (1969) has criticized the schools for the role they play in blocking the achievements of students who are unable to compete. Educational institutions, by and large, reward only students who perform well. Their emphasis, Glasser points out, is on academic performance, with little attention to other kinds of learning experiences. Such an atmosphere can only hinder true personality development.

The school years are a prime period of social development in a child's life. School is the institution that expresses and attempts to enforce the social norms of society. If a child is unable to assimilate the social ideals his education is supposed to reflect, he will invariably find it difficult to be accepted in the larger society.

A major influence in a child's educational experience is the teachers he meets along the way. Davidson and Lang (1960) found a significant correlation during elementary school years between a child's perception of himself and the

539

reaction to himself he perceives on the part of the teacher. Academic achievement was greater and behavior was more desirable among children who saw themselves as adequate in the eyes of the teacher.

As a child grows older, particularly as he enters adolescence, the role of the peer group usually becomes extremely important in his social development. Young people have a need for group organization and social structure beyond what is provided by the family. Partly through peer recognition they acquire a sense of belonging in the larger world and of personal identity. But though peers usually come to take precedence over parents in the adolescent's interests, it is doubtful that they often exert a stronger influence on the developing personality.

Social interaction with peers rapidly merges with cultural influences on personality. We examine now the cultural factors that affect both the person and the groups he is a part of.

Cultural Factors

Besides the influence of parents and of peers and school, the culture in which he grows up also has a deep effect upon the child's personality development. Cultural differences, of course, vary greatly among nations, but even within a single country there may be several subcultures in which child rearing occurs in vastly different ways.

Urie Bronfenbrenner

Bronfenbrenner (1958) found that middle-class children in the United States were likely to have been breast-fed, to have been on a self-demand feeding schedule, and to have been weaned and toilet-trained at a later age than working class children, In addition, middle-class mothers were more permissive toward their children with respect to language use, toilet accidents, dependency, sex, aggressiveness, and freedom of movement outside the home.

Working-class parents were more likely to use physical punishment to discipline, while middle-class families relied more on reasoning, isolation, appeals to guilt, and other methods involving the threat of loss of love. Disciplinary techniques favored by the middle class tended to result in the internalization of values and controls in children, Bronfenbrenner found, whereas lower-class children obeyed without necessarily accepting the standards enforced by their parents. In general, he concluded that parent-child relationships in the middle class were more acceptant and egalitarian, while those in the working class were oriented toward maintaining order and obedience.

In a later study Bronfenbrenner (1970) compared child-rearing practices in the United States with those in the Soviet Union. In Russia, the state plays a much larger role by providing advice and instruction to parents as well as an extensive system of state-supported nurseries and schools in which the child spends a great deal of his time. In general, the family's role has been de-emphasized in an effort to foster "collective consciousness."

Specifically, Bronfenbrenner found that Russian babies receive substantially more physical handling than American infants, but that they are given little opportunity for freedom of movement or individual initiative. Another striking finding was the prevalence, among Soviet parents, of the withholding of love as a disciplinary method. This technique is given strong encouragement by the state, as the following quotation from a Soviet child-rearing manual suggests:

> A "talking-to" involves a brief but short evaluation of the behavior of the disobedient child including an expression of one's own indignation at such behavior. Moreover, after giving the reprimand, one should not permit himself to resume his usual affectionate manner with the child, even when the parent feels that the youngster has genuinely repented. For a period of time it is necessary to remain pointedly reserved with the child and somewhat cold, thereby showing him that his disobedience has hurt the adult. This measure turns out to be very effective and in most instances gives a palpable result. (Quoted in Bronfenbrenner, 1970, p. 13)

This approach is designed to produce children with high levels of internal control—children who are obedient, conscientious, industrious. As one might expect, however, the children do not exhibit much creative, innovative, or impulsive behavior.

Another feature of Soviet child rearing is the emphasis on collective play and work in the state nurseries and schools. Toys are designed, for example,

Mike Levins   Arthur Tress

The culture in which a child is reared has a deep effect on the development of personality.

to require two or three children to make them work. Gradually the adult teacher withdraws from his role of leader in order to forge a "self-reliant collective" in which the children cooperate in disciplining themselves.

In accounting for this pattern Bronfenbrenner points out that Soviet children are confronted with fewer divergent views, both within and outside the family, than their American counterparts and, in consequence, are more conformist.

Our discussion of the major forces that contribute to the development of personality has shown that neither somatic factors nor parental, peer, and cultural factors operate on the individual in isolation. Rather, there is a subtle interplay that accounts for the infinite range of personalities among the human race.

In the remainder of this chapter, we consider several of the most significant theories of personality and its development. Some of these theories emphasize hereditary factors while others are more concerned with cultural influences. Some contradict others, while many overlap; no single theory is comprehensive and complete in itself. All are significant, however, for the light they shed on personality and because they have stimulated research and further theoretical development. Many also have important implications for other areas of psychology such as learning and memory, maturation and cognitive development, perception, and abnormal behavior. Indeed, many of the theorists we discuss arrived at a personality theory in an effort to understand and to treat abnormal behavior.

PERSONALITY THEORIES

Type Theories

The oldest approach to personality study categorizes people according to type. A primitive type theory was first proposed about 400 B.C. by the Greek physician Hippocrates, who believed that there were four main types of temperament or personality—sanguine (optimistic), melancholic (sad), choleric (irritable), and phlegmatic (apathetic). One's temperament was biologically determined by the balance of four body fluids or "humors"—blood, black bile, yellow bile, and phlegm. Of course, modern physiology has discredited this theory, but the impulse to classify personalities according to type persists.

The best known of the modern typologies was proposed by the Swiss psychiatrist Carl Jung (1923), an early follower of Freud. The basic elements of introversion Jung's typology are two opposed characteristics, which he called *introversion* extroversion and *extroversion*. Jung saw the introvert as a basically shy person who is often withdrawn into himself, especially during periods of emotional stress, and is often highly imaginative and intellectual. The extrovert, on the other hand, tends to be outgoing and sociable and prefers to deal with people rather than with ideas.

The terms *introversion* and *extroversion* have since become part of our everyday language, and they are often used carelessly to label people. But Jung's typology was a complex one; he did not propose that people could be neatly classified as one type or the other. A study of senior medical students and clinic patients (Neymann and Yacorzynski, 1942) found that most people scored midway between introversion and extroversion and that very few scored at either extreme.

Carl Gustav Jung

The main limitation of type theory is that it tends to categorize people into static types. Implicitly, it views personality as genetically determined, ignoring the fact that behavior changes and develops over a lifetime under the influence of personal and social experiences. Another limitation of type theory is that it tells us little about the immediate environmental factors that influence behavior. All of us behave differently in different situations, as the theories of the social behaviorists (p. 559) will explain. For such reasons, trait theory has emerged as the more important source of personality description.

Trait Theories

Trait theory like type theory developed out of one of the most basic human impulses—to categorize and label the behavior of others. Imagine yourself mentioning the name of someone a friend doesn't know. "What's he like?" your friend asks. You would almost certainly describe the person in terms of his traits. "Well, he's a friendly guy, bright, not very assertive. He's fun to be with, but you always have to coax him to do anything." This is by no means a complete picture, but it gives your friend some idea of what the other person is like. And if he asked others about this person, he would probably get similar kinds of answers.

Categorizing people in terms of their traits is useful; the problem is that a list of possible traits is likely to be endless and to have many duplications and a high degree of imprecision. In fact, Allport and Odbert (1936) compiled a list of 17,953 adjectives in the English language that could be used to describe a person's behavior, attitudes, and moods. For scientific purposes, of course, a list of this length is highly impractical. Moreover, a mere list has no principle of order and therefore does not permit an analysis or generalization about personality. Trait theory studies have attempted to introduce order into the description of human behavior.

Cattell's Surface and Source Traits Probably the most influential of the trait theorists has been Raymond B. Cattell. Cattell devised a system of using behavior observations and ratings, laboratory studies, and personality inventories to isolate a small number of fundamental traits that could account for an individual's behavior. In his view, traits explain why a person behaves consistently and why people differ in their responses to the same stimulus. For Cattell, traits are more than descriptive epithets; they are basic components of personality, in much the same way that molecules are components of matter.

trait

Cattell's Analysis of Personality Traits

Cattell uses three sources of personality data: life records obtained from people who know the subject well; questionnaires the subjects themselves complete on the basis of self-observation and introspection; and objective tests, miniature situations designed to test some aspect of the subject's behavior without his awareness.

The source traits Cattell tests for, in order of their statistical significance, are:

Factor	+	vs.	—
A	Outgoing		Reserved
B	More intelligent		Less intelligent
C	Stable		Emotional
E	Assertive		Humble
F	Happy-go-lucky		Sober
G	Conscientious		Expedient
H	Venturesome		Shy
I	Tender-minded		Tough-minded
L	Suspicious		Trusting
M	Imaginative		Practical
N	Shrewd		Forthright
O	Apprehensive		Placid
Q_1	Experimenting		Conservative
Q_2	Self-sufficient		Group-tied
Q_3	Controlled		Casual
Q_4	Tense		Relaxed

Personality factor A is the most significant factor contributing to individual differences; it accounts for most of the person's uniqueness. Factors further down the list contribute progressively less to individual differences.

The following table, from Cattell (1965), indicates what surface traits are correlated with + (outgoing) and − (reserved) ratings on factor A:

A +	vs.	A −
Good-natured, easy-going		Critical, grasping
Cooperative		Obstructive
Attentive to people		Cool, aloof
Soft-hearted		Hard, precise
Trustful		Suspicious
Adaptable		Rigid

And here, also from Cattell (1965), are some sample questionnaire items with responses typically chosen by A + (outgoing) people printed in italics:

(1) I would rather work as:

    (a) an engineer   (b) *a social science teacher*

(2) I could stand being a hermit.
    (a) True   (b) *False*

(3) I am careful to turn up when someone expects me.
    (a) *True*   (b) False

(4) I would prefer to marry someone who is:
    (a) a thoughtful companion   (b) *effective in a social group*

(5) I would prefer to read a book on:
    (a) *national social service*   (b) new scientific weapons

(6) I trust strangers:
    (a) sometimes   (b) *practically always*

The person who is highly positive in factor A is likely to be a good salesman or club manager. Good electricians and researchers turn out to be well to the negative side on Factor A.

Cattell has identified source trait C with the psychoanalytic concept of ego strength. Here are some typical observer ratings for factor C:

C+	vs.	C−
Mature		Unable to tolerate frustration
Steady, persistent		Changeable
Emotionally calm		Impulsively emotional
Realistic about problems		Evasive, avoids necessary decisions
Absence of neurotic fatigue		Neurotically fatigued (with no real effort)

Sample questionnaire items concerning source trait C, with positive responses in italics, are:

Do you find it difficult to take no for an answer even when what you want to do is obviously impossible?
    (a) yes   (b) *no*

If you had your life to live over again, would you
    (a) *want it to be essentially the same?*   (b) plan it very differently?

Do you often have really disturbing dreams?
    (a) yes   (b) *no*

Do your moods sometimes make you seem unreasonable even to yourself?
    (a) yes   (b) *no*

Do you feel tired when you've done nothing to justify it?
    (a) *rarely*   (b) often

Can you change old habits, without relapse, when you decide to?
    (a) yes   (b) no

Cattell (1946) first reduced Allport and Odbert's list of trait variables to 171 terms that, he believed, described the entire "personality sphere." Most of these trait descriptions were expressed in terms of opposing tendencies—cheerful versus gloomy, for example. In subsequent studies using a statistical technique called cluster analysis (see the box on p. 604), he was able to further prune his list to 35 trait clusters, which he called surface traits (1950) because they are easily defined and readily observable and because no process of inference is required to determine their underlying uniformity.

Raymond B. Cattell

With the development of factor analysis (also described in the box on p. 603), a sophisticated statistical technique, Cattell found correlations among surface-trait ratings and further refined the list to only 12 variables, which he termed source traits (1965). Source traits presumably are the most basic variables of personality. According to Cattell, they are the building blocks of personality, and they determine the more familiar surface traits through some complex process that remains to be discovered. Standardized tests have been designed to measure individual personality in terms of Cattell's source traits.

Criticisms of trait theory have been made on both empirical and method-ological grounds. For one thing it has not been demonstrated that Cattell's source traits are present in children as well as adults. And if they are not, a major question is whether these traits are really fundamental. Moreover, efforts to confirm Cattell's findings using different groups of people have not been entirely successful; the correlations Cattell found among surface traits do not always reproduce themselves exactly. Another criticism has been that Cattell's subjects, out of a need for approval, may have given answers they thought the experi-menter was looking for. Others have pointed out that the initial reduction of the list of 17,953 traits to 171, done without mathematical analysis, must have reflected Cattell's own attitudes and biases. While all of these criticisms have some merit, none of them discredits the total theory.

Cattell and his followers have made a major contribution by providing a simplified and structured method of describing human behavior. As long as the traits they isolated are viewed as descriptions of personality rather than as components of personality, their ideas are highly useful.

Barr

H. J. E. Eysenck

Eysenck's Correlation of Types and Traits   The British psychologist Hans J. Eysenck used Jung's personality type model as a starting point in devising a more rigorous typological theory of his own that he was able to relate to trait theories. In addition to the extroversion-introversion dimension, Eysenck, using factor-analytic methods, determined a second fundamental dimension of per-sonality—stability-instability. Empirically, this dimension simply indicates the degree to which a person's emotions are controlled and not easily aroused. Stability implies calmness, thoughtfulness, and dependability. Instability charac-terizes people who are "moody, touchy, anxious, restless" (Eysenck and Rach-man, 1965).

In conjunction with each other the dimensions of extroversion-introver-sion and stability-instability imply the existence of four basic personality types—stable extrovert, unstable extrovert, stable introvert, unstable introvert. Curiously these four personality types are strikingly similar to the four types Hippocrates proposed almost 2,500 years earlier; the stable extrovert is sanguine, the unstable extrovert choleric, the stable introvert is phlegmatic, the unstable introvert mel-ancholic. Eysenck has been able to relate his model to modern trait theories by demonstrating how his two fundamental personality dimensions can be used to account for a large number of specific character traits. Beyond that he has used factor analysis to devise a personality inventory that will locate any given

Physiological Arousal and Personality

Eysenck has conducted laboratory studies of the physiological basis of extroversion and introversion, and his results are highly intriguing. He found that this personality dimension is directly related to the person's characteristic level of cortical arousal, as well as to the ease with which cortical arousal can be increased. Arousal is a physiological state closely associated with drive and energy; it is measured by brain-wave patterns. Eysenck found that introverts as compared to extroverts produced relatively more brain-wave patterns characteristic of arousal and that they required much less stimulation to increase their level of arousal (Fig. 12.2). These findings have many interesting implications concerning the circumstances under which introverts and extroverts are most likely to achieve high levels of performance.

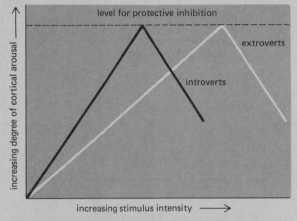

Fig. 12.2 The relationship between stimulus intensity and excitatory processes in introverts and extraverts. (adapted from Brody, 1972)

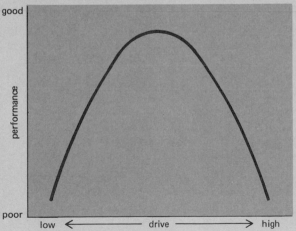

Fig. 12.3 Inverse-U relationship between performance and drive indicates that optional performance occurs under conditions of moderate drive.

Yerkes and Dodson (1908) had proposed that the relation between arousal and performance could be simply depicted as an upside-down U (Fig. 12.3). As shown in the figure, when arousal is at a low level, there is little interest in the task at hand and performance tends to be low. Up to a point (top of the inverted U), additional arousal increases performance, but beyond this point performance deteriorates because the person is overstimulated and therefore disorganized. The highest levels of performance, then, are induced by moderate arousal, a condition in which the person is alert and motivated but not overwhelmed.

person in terms of his model. This approach has been highly useful in identifying latent or manifest problems. Unstable introverts, for example, are characterized by such personality problems as depression, feelings of inferiority, and emotional instability. Unstable extroverts, on the other hand, more frequently manifest conduct problems such as delinquency, destructive behavior, and temper tantrums (Eysenck, 1960). Some of the correlations Eysenck found between types and traits are shown in Fig. 12.4.

Trait and type theories aim for the same goal—the description and understanding of personality. Trait theory takes a microscopic approach to the problem, while type theory views personality macroscopically. They differ in viewpoint, just as other theories differ according to whether they emphasize ways in which people are alike or individual differences.

FREUD

The Bettmann Archive, Inc.

Sigmund Freud

psychoanalysis

Of all the theorists of human behavior, Sigmund Freud (1856–1939) has had by far the most profound influence, not only within psychology but in the development of modern ideas concerning the nature of man. Before Freud no one seriously argued that the events of childhood might have a bearing on adult behavior and consciousness. Rather, human nature was thought to be the result of some interaction among heredity, chance, and will. By means of intense self-observation and deep involvement with middle-class emotionally disturbed patients in Vienna at the turn of the century, Freud started a revolution in thought with reverberations that are still being felt today.

Working as a physician, Freud staggered the neo-Victorian world with his theory of personality that saw all human behavior as unconsciously motivated by the sexual urge. In his own time his revolutionary ideas were greeted with outrage, embarrassment, and vehement denial.

The movement Freud established—known as psychoanalysis—is both a complex school of thought and a therapeutic procedure for treating emotional disturbances. Freud attracted numbers of disciples, some of whom amplified and extended his own ideas, while others broke away and established systematic theoretical formulations of their own.

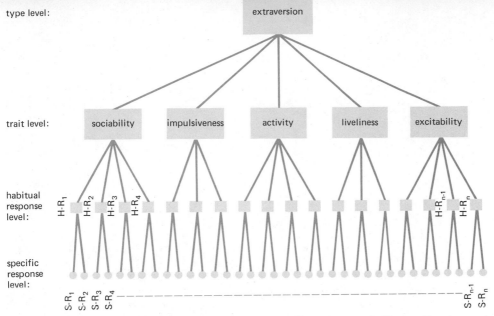

type level: extraversion

trait level: sociability | impulsiveness | activity | liveliness | excitability

habitual response level: $H\text{-}R_1$ $H\text{-}R_2$ $H\text{-}R_3$ $H\text{-}R_4$ ... $H\text{-}R_{n-1}$ $H\text{-}R_n$

specific response level: $S\text{-}R_1$ $S\text{-}R_2$ $S\text{-}R_3$ $S\text{-}R_4$ — — — — — — — — — — — — — — $S\text{-}R_{n-1}$ $S\text{-}R_n$

Fig. 12.4 Hierarchial model of personality. Types are supraordinate concepts built up on the observed intercorrelations between traits. (From Eysenck, H. J., The Biological Basis of Personality, 1967. Courtesy of Charles C Thomas, Publisher, Springfield, Illinois.)

The Unconscious

The key to Freud's work is his concept of the unconscious. Freud believed that the thoughts and feelings of which a person is aware represent only a fraction of his actual mental experience. A far larger portion of what goes on inside him takes place without his conscious knowledge of it. Suppose you are walking down the street, deep in conversation with a friend. You stop talking for a moment and suddenly find yourself whistling a familiar tune such as "Strangers in the Night." Your friend laughs and asks what made you choose that song. You are genuinely surprised and tell him you haven't the faintest idea. Your friend takes you back up the block where a man is waiting in his car with the radio on, listening to "Strangers in the Night." What happened? The first time you passed the car all your conscious mental activity was concerned with the conversation. And yet your brain was receiving sensory impressions that you were not conscious of—among them the tune. Later, when the conversation stopped for a moment, the unconscious memory of the tune surfaced into consciousness (see Chapter 7, the section on attention).

Freud introduced two types of unconscious drives, or instincts, which he believed are present in each person at birth. The two drives are sexuality (eros) and aggressiveness (thanatos). Arousal or activation of these two drives produces tension, which leads to action to in some way satisfy the unconscious drive. Freud believed that most of human behavior is motivated by an attempt to reduce the tension created by these unconscious drives. Eros and thanatos, moreover, can never be separated; they work in tandem, and in all instinctual manifestations both are present. As a hypothesis, this view of the impulses underlying behavior allowed Freud to develop a comprehensive theory of personality development that accounts for a great deal of human behavior, and

549

Freud on Slips of the Tongue

Believing that in the psychological realm pathology is no different in kind from normality—though it does differ in degree—Freud (1915) maintained that we do nothing accidentally. In *The Psychopathology of Everyday Life,* he analyzes many "human errors," revealing the frequently humorous—and embarrassing—unconscious thoughts or wishes that prompted them. Slips of the tongue are particularly frequent, probably because in speaking we have so little time to edit, or censor, what we say. Freud enjoyed recording these errors.

He relates that the President of the Lower House of the Austrian Parliament opened a session from which little good, from his point of view, was to be expected by saying: "Gentlemen I take notice that a full quorum of members is present and herewith declare the sitting *closed.*"

Freud also reports slips of the tongue passed on to him by his colleagues. For example, from a Dr. Stekel:

> I was to give a lecture to a woman. Her husband, upon whose request this was done, stood leaning behind the door listening. At the end of my sermonizing, which had made a visible impression, I said: "Goodbye sir." To the experienced person I thus betrayed that the words were directed toward the husband; that I had spoken to him. (p. 89)

From a Dr. Brill:

> While writing a prescription for a woman who was especially weighted down by the financial burden of the treatment, I was interested in her saying: "Please do not give me any *big bills,* because I cannot swallow them." Of course she meant to say pills. (p. 103)

Freud cites another example:

> A similar mechanism is shown in the mistake of another patient whose memory deserted her in the midst of a long-forgotten childish reminiscence. Her memory failed to inform her on what part of her body the prying and lustful hand of another had touched her. Soon thereafter she visited one of her friends, with whom she discussed summer homes. Asked where her cottage in M was located, she answered, "Near the mountain loin" instead of mountain lane. (p. 83)

parts of this theory have been experimentally confirmed. Most studies of Freud's ideas have concentrated on the sex drives.

Id, Ego, and Superego

For Freud (1927), personality has three parts, which he calls the id, the ego, and the superego. In this scheme, the unconscious is represented by the *id,* a primary, instinctual core that seeks immediate gratification of impulses. The id is ruled by the pleasure principle. Over this "cauldron of seething excitement" stands the *ego,* which attempts to mediate between the instinctual demands of the id and the demands of the outer world, reality. The ego must subjugate the id to reality, but it can accomplish this purpose only with the consent of the id, which must be kept at least minimally satisfied. At the same time that it must deal with the demands of the id and of reality, the ego must also answer to, and in part control, the *superego,* a repository of ideals and morals that is, in its way, every bit as demanding as the id. Thus the ego, though it is the decision maker, is also the servant of three demanding masters: the id, the superego, and reality.

From an evolutionary and a developmental point of view, the id exists first but because, as a formless, completely unordered mass of impulses, it is unable to meet the demands of reality—that is, to survive in the environment—it permits a part of itself to develop specialized abilities—mostly to interpret or test reality and to control the organism's responses to reality. Thus, part of the id becomes the ego. Sometime later in his development, man learns that he cannot survive simply by dealing with things as they are but must have some notion of how things ought to be and must attempt to order both himself and his environment according to that notion. To meet this need, part of the ego becomes further specialized into a policy maker—a superego. The superego is, in part, passed on from generation to generation because, Freud maintained, the child in the process of identifying with his parents, acquires not so much their actual behavior as their ideals and morals, their superegos.

Freud did not think of these parts of the personality as real things that could be located in the body or even as disembodied forces that control the person. They are, like personality itself, abstractions. The id, ego, and superego are three different directions in which every personality is pulled. We have instinctual needs and desires, we have a need and a desire to cope with and to understand the world we live in, and we have goals to pursue and standards for pursuing them—these are our id, ego, and superego.

Psychosexual Development

psychosexual development

Freud's theory of personality development is based on the person's successive attempts to reduce the tension created by the sex drive (1927). Bodily pleasure, which reduces this tension, is obtained from different zones of the body (mouth, anus, genitals) as physical development proceeds. Thus, there are three psychosexual stages of development, in each one of which a different erogenous zone provides a unique potential for physical gratification or pleasure. Freud believed that experiences during each of these stages shape the development of the adult personality.

Oral Stage During the first 18 months of life the mouth, lips, and tongue are the chief organs of gratification as the infant derives pleasure from sucking, biting, and chewing. According to Freud's theory, an excess of either gratification or frustration at any psychosexual stage of development results in an unconscious fixation at that level which does not permit the child to progress to the next stage of development. Fixation at the oral stage, according to Freud, may be responsible for such adult personality characteristics and habits as drug addiction, smoking, compulsive eating, and even such verbal traits as sarcasm and glibness. A fixation, if it occurs, is the result of the interplay between the child's inborn drive and the environmental forces that shape and limit the expression of that drive.

Anal Stage   The next stage in the Freudian schema is the anal stage, in which the other end of the alimentary canal, the anus, becomes the most important site of sexual tensions and gratifications. It is during this period that the child meets his first external conflicts as toilet training is imposed upon him. The way in which the parents conduct toilet training affects later traits and values. Internal conflicts in adulthood about giving and withholding of love, for example, as well as personality characteristics such as sadism, masochism, stubbornness, punctuality, cleanliness, and orderliness can result from fixation at this stage.

Phallic Stage   Toward the end of the third year the leading source of pleasure begins to be the genitalia. This stage of development is known as the phallic stage and is characterized by masturbation and curiosity about the anatomical differences between the sexes—impulses often discouraged by parents. In extreme cases parental restrictions may result in the child's inability to achieve the transition to full adult sexual activity later on. As in the previous two stages, repressed impulses from childhood may remain in the unconscious and express themselves in indirect and disruptive ways.

During the phallic stage another important mechanism comes into play, the Oedipus complex, named after the Greek legend of Oedipus, who unknowingly killed his father and married his mother. This complex is the combination of unconscious fantasies of incest with the parent of the opposite sex with jealousy and a death wish directed at the same-sex parent. According to Freud, the Oedipus complex, though modified and repressed during later childhood, remains a vital force in adult personality.

Vestiges of the stage of oral gratification may linger throughout life.

Steve Hurwitz   Bob Fitch, Black Star   Fred Weiss

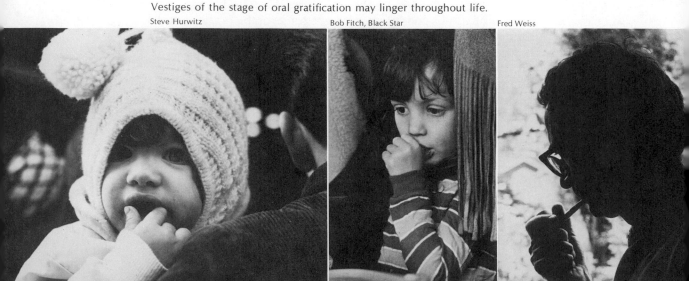

In boys these sexual desires for the mother and the death wish toward the father are accompanied by fears of punishment by the father in the form of castration. In time the male child overcomes these conflicts and anxieties by abandoning or repressing his fantasies about his mother. One mechanism for doing this is to identify with or try to become like the father. This allows the boy some vicarious satisfaction of his sexual impulses toward the mother and also results in his internalizing the values and standards of society, which his father represents. The extent to which identification is a possible and constructive step depends upon a number of environmental factors, chiefly the personality of the father.

In girls, of course, the Oedipal situation is different. According to Freud, the initial impulse for a genital relationship with the mother, to whom both girls and boys are most strongly attached, comes to grief with the little girl's realization that she does not have a penis. This discovery results in a complex set of feelings that Freud called penis envy—shame, inferiority, jealousy, and rage against the mother. The female child next turns to her father in search of a love relationship, but of course, she is thwarted here too. She too must abandon and repress her wishes, and in the process she identifies with the mother. In both boys and girls unresolved conflicts from the phallic stage may result in homosexuality, authority problems, and an inadequate sense of gender identity.

 ### Defense Mechanisms

When we do or feel things that are offensive to the superego, the ego suffers a great deal of anxiety, which it must defend itself against (the ego and superego are defined in Chapter 5). Freud (1933) suggested that the ego characteristically uses particular defense mechanisms in stressful situations. Foremost among these and really the first step in all the other defense mechanisms is *repression*. Repression operates in two ways, or on two different kinds of material. It causes us to "forget," or to banish from consciousness, painful or shameful experiences, and it also prompts us to deny, or suppress from consciousness, our unacceptable impulses and desires. Maintaining a repression requires a great deal of energy that the ego would otherwise be using in its reality-testing function, and the more unacceptable the material repressed, the more energy the ego must spend repressing it. If the ego is entirely diverted from its appropriate function in this manner, the person develops a neurosis or psychosis, which can only be cured by removing the repression.

Other defense mechanisms operate on repressed material in some way. *Denial,* the simplest one of all, is merely the refusal to believe that the unwanted behavior or impulse ever occurred. This mechanism is frequently used by very young children.

denial

Reaction formation replaces an anxiety-arousing impulse by its opposite. A woman who feels hostile toward an unwanted child may replace her hostility

reaction formation

with overprotective behavior toward the child, interfering with his development by preventing him from playing with his peers. She tells the child and herself that she is motivated by love and concern for the child, but she manages to hurt him nonetheless.

regression

Regression is the substitution of satisfaction appropriate to an earlier level of development for present desires that are repressed. A child may regress to an earlier level of language achievement upon the arrival of a new baby in his family. He is using a devious means of attracting his mother's attention because to ask for it directly would mean acknowledging his jealousy, which is unacceptable to him.

rationalization

Rationalization is substituting acceptable reasons for conduct that is in fact motivated by unacceptable impulses or desires. Perhaps the most commonly used of the defense mechanisms, rationalization is probably used by everyone to some degree. Everyone occasionally invents reasons for not doing what he believes he ought to be doing at a particular time.

fantasy

Fantasy is probably as common as rationalization. It is the substitution of imaginary satisfactions for real ones. Fantasy is a very necessary form of ego defense, for no one can have everything he wants; yet it, too, if it becomes a substitute for attainable real satisfactions, can be indicative of maladjustment.

sublimation

Sublimation is the redirection of sexual impulses to socially accepted activities. Freud believed that all creativity was a result of sublimation, which was therefore a normal and desirable defense mechanism. Many later psychologists have disagreed with Freud, maintaining that creative endeavors are rewarding in their own right and not only as substitutes for sexual satisfaction.

projection

Projection is the attribution of one's own unacceptable feelings or traits to others. In the Oedipal situation, a young boy may temporarily believe that his father wants to hurt him because he cannot accept his own desire to hurt his father. In adults, however, projection is usually an indication of emotional imbalance.

identification

Identification is a means of satisfying unacceptable or practically unrealizable desires by imagining oneself in another's place. We use it appropriately and healthfully in the theater and in reading novels but inappropriately in substituting vicariously experienced emotions for real ones.

conversion

Conversion is the attempt to deal with anxiety by converting it into a physiological disorder. The result is psychosomatic illness.

For a further discussion of defense mechanisms, see pp. 711–717.

Latency and Adolescence   During the latency stage, beginning as early as the age of 5 in some children and lasting until adolescence, the child is no longer overtly preoccupied with sexual matters. With the onset of puberty, however, as physical changes take place in his body, he experiences an awakening of adult sexuality and enters the final period of psychosexual development. In Freud's view, it is here that the person becomes able to give and receive mature love. If he has been unsuccessful in resolving conflicts inherent in earlier stages, however, he finds himself unprepared to handle the problems he meets at this

Bradford Hess   Fred Weiss

Identification with same-sex parent or parent substitute helps a child resolve the Oedipal situation.

stage of development. (Other aspects of Freudian theory are discussed in Chapters 5, 9, and 16.)

Evaluation of Freudian Theory

Freud built most of his theory on *clinical evidence,* relying on what his patients told him about their fantasies and experiences. He maintained that in the realm of the unconscious, imagined experiences are as important as real ones. This means that it is difficult to test or verify his conclusions. Another problem is that his concepts are often metaphoric rather than precise and thus do not lend themselves to quantitative measurement. What objective observations are required, for example, to conclude that an individual is fixated at the oral stage? What kind of evidence would indicate that he is not fixated at that stage? How can we measure the *degree* of fixation? Is a college student who organizes a protest against the way his college invests its endowment money acting out unconscious emotional conflicts with authority figures stemming from an unresolved Oedipus complex? Or is he motivated by a sense of social justice? A true Freudian would say the question cannot be answered without a series of clinical interviews with the student. But even then the answer would be based only on the psychoanalyst's trained intuition, and once again we have results that do not satisfy rigorous scientific requirements.

It is also important to bear in mind that Freud based his theory on his experience with emotionally disturbed people rather than on a cross-section of society. Thus, although he sought to describe the developmental process as it unfolds in the life of everyone, he theorized on the basis of clinical observations and generalized to society as a whole. In addition, Freud assumed that he could distinguish between normal and abnormal behavior, but his theories were based on behavior within a rather narrowly circumscribed society—early 20th century, middle-class Vienna. Conceivably, a more diverse society would admit some of the behavior Freud found abnormal into the realm of normality. Freud's assumptions are not necessarily wrong, but they are open to question and very difficult to confirm. Is it true, for example, that the two instinctual drives (sex and aggression) that Freud postulated are present at birth and persist unchanging throughout life? To what extent are oral, anal, and phallic stages of development culturally determined; that is, do they exist in other cultures besides our own? Again, we face important questions that are very difficult to answer.

But while their being based on so many unverified assumptions has limited the credibility of Freud's theories, the importance of his contribution to the study of personality cannot be ignored. Freud's contribution falls into three main areas. First, his concept of the importance of the unconscious made it possible to consider human personality as a consistent underlying structure in which nothing happens by chance or in a random way. Mistakes, slips of the tongue, forgetfulness, and misperceptions all have roots in the psyche. They represent unconscious needs and wishes coming to the surface and affecting conscious thoughts and behavior. Second, Freud made sexuality a legitimate subject for scientific study as well as a legitimate subject of discussion for society as a whole. Whether or not sexuality has as broad an influence as he believed, it is basic to the nature of man and occupies a central place in our behavior and thoughts. Third, Freud was the first theorist to concern himself with developmental aspects of personality. His emphasis on the events of early childhood has had a tremendous influence on the subsequent history of psychology.

NEO-FREUDIAN DEVELOPMENTS

Many later personality theorists retained Freud's basic approach while making important modifications of some of his concepts. Almost all of these neo-Freudians have questioned Freud's emphasis on the sex drive as well as his view that personality is largely shaped by the age of 5. In general, they tend to place greater emphasis on social forces than on instinctual drives.

Jung: The Collective Unconscious

collective unconscious

Carl Jung's enduring contribution was a unique concept of the unconscious (1931). He argued that there are two kinds of unconscious material: the personal unconscious, which, as Freud proposed, contains memories, sensory impressions, and repressed wishes; and the collective unconscious, which contains elements of personality that are inherited from ancestors. He called the contents of the collective unconscious, "archetypes," emphasizing their universality, at

Laboratory Analogy of Repression

Although the concept of repression has intuitive plausibility, it, like most Freudian concepts, is hard to test experimentally. One of the more successful attempts at this was conducted by two psychologists from Princeton, Tom Glucksberg and Lloyd King.

To do this Glucksberg and King (1967) adopted work done by other psychologists (Russell and Storms, 1966) on mediation. In the Russell and Storms study subjects first learned an *A-B* paired-associates list. Association *B-C* and *C-D* were inferred from word association norms. For example, if the *A-B* pair were *cef-stem,* then the *B-C* pair association would be *stem-flower,* and the *C-D* association would be *flower-smell.* Thus by way of the implicit *B-C* and *C-D* mediated associations *A* and *D* become linked. Russell and Storms found that the learning of the *A-B* pair facilitated the learning of a related *A-D* pair, as opposed to the learning of an unrelated neutral *A-D* pair. It should be noted that in the paradigm the *C* term was never given but always inferred.

Glucksberg and King had 16 subjects learn the *A-B* list of paired associates as shown in Table 12.2 by the method of anticipation until all the pairs were correctly anticipated. Then electrodes were hooked up to the third and fourth fingers of the left hand and a buzzer placed by the right hand. The subjects then began learning the *A-D* list. For one-half the subjects the *D* terms *smell, war* and *tree* were followed by an electric shock. The rest of the subjects were shocked following the items *brain, good* and *take.* The subjects were told to press the buzzer after each shock, which served to insure that they knew which words were followed by shock. They learned the *A-D* list, again, to one perfect anticipation.

The experimenters reasoned that if the subjects were employing implicit mediators to learn the *A-D* list and if the *D* word is associated with the unpleasantness of an electric shock, then the likelihood of saying, or thinking of, the associated *B* word should be reduced, because the *B* term has become associated with the fear-eliciting *D* word. In other words, subjects should "repress" the *B* words.

The results supported the reasoning. For the subjects with *smell, war,* and *tree* as the shocked *D* words, 20.8 percent of the associated *A-B* pairs were not correctly anticipated on a relearning trial, as opposed to 3.6 percent of the control pairs forgotten. Similarly, the other group of subjects forgot 37.5 percent of the experimental pairs, and 8.9 percent of the control pairs.

Glucksberg and King replicated this study in order to deal with the objection that maybe the shock caused differential retroactive interference that is, maybe the shocked terms were learned better than the control words, thereby causing more forgetting of their associated *B* terms. If this were the case the type of motivation involved would be irrelevant.

A group of 40 subjects was used in the replication. Half of them received shock associated with the experimental *D* words while the rest of them received a money reward. Differential forgetting as a function of shock was similar to the data obtained in the first experiment. Fifteen percent of the experimental (shocked)

A-B pairs were forgotten as compared to 5 percent of the control pairs. In contrast, no significant difference was obtained between the experimental and control pairs in the money-reward condition (10 and 11 percent, respectively).

Table 12.2

List 1		Inferred Chained Word	List 2	
A	B	C	D	
CEF	stem	flower	smell	(1)
DAX	memory	mind	brain	(2)
YOV	soldier	army	navy	
VUX	trouble	bad	good	(2)
WUB	wish	want	need	
GEX	justice	peace	war	(1)
JID	thief	steal	take	(2)
ZIL	ocean	water	drink	
LAJ	command	order	disorder	
MYV	fruit	apple	tree	(1)

least within a single culture, and sought to prove their existence by means of an exhaustive study of myths, folklore, and literature from many cultures.

Jung rejected Freud's emphasis on early childhood influences and on the sex drive, which he replaced with the will to live. He also rejected the almost tyrannical position Freud attributed to the unconscious, emphasizing instead the possibility of cooperation between the conscious and the unconscious.

Adler: Compensation and the Inferiority Complex

The Granger Collection

Alfred Adler

For Alfred Adler (1930) all of human motivation represents a striving for superiority, and everyone's principal goal is to perfect himself in an effort Adler called compensation. Children become aware early in life of some weakness or deficiency in themselves. Once the inadequacy is perceived, efforts to overcome or compensate for it are initiated. Often a person ultimately distinguishes himself, directly or indirectly, in the area in which he felt the greatest weakness as a child. Thus a child who was tyrannized by his father may become a lawyer and devote himself to defending the poor and helpless. Adler found the social environment all-important in individual development. Severe personality problems arise only when feelings of inferiority are strongly reinforced by the social environment or when efforts to compensate are continually frustrated. When this occurs the individual may develop an inferiority complex. But under optimal conditions, Adler believed, strivings for superiority manifest themselves in co-operative relationships and efforts to change society in a humane direction.

Horney: The Importance of Early Childhood

Karen Horney

Like Adler, Karen Horney (1937) believed that the social environment plays a larger role in personality development than innate tendencies. Horney stressed the effects of anxiety on the individual, in particular the feelings of insecurity the child experiences in relation to his parents. If the stress is prolonged or espe-cially severe—such as that caused by parental neglect, domination, or extreme overprotectiveness, or by intense conflicts between parents—the child's efforts to cope with it may permanently affect his motivational patterns and result in neurotic needs, such as the need to exploit others or to restrict his life within narrow limits, or the need for absolute dependency or for power and unassail-ability.

Erikson: Psychosocial Development

Possibly the most complete and influential neo-Freudian theory is that devel-oped by Erik Erikson, who synthesized the Freudian concepts of developmental stages and instinctual drives with the emphasis placed on the social environment by Adler, Horney, and others. According to Erikson (1963), the person passes through eight "psychosocial" stages as he develops from a newborn infant into a mature adult, at each stage facing what Erikson terms "crisis." The success

---

 Erikson's Stages of Development

Erikson's (1963) notion of development differs from Freud's in two ways: he em-phasizes the significance of social interaction, and he sees development as a lifelong process rather than as something that is completed by adolescence. He postulates the following stages and crises:

   1. First year of life: oral-sensory stage; the crisis is trust versus mistrust. The significance of this stage for Erikson is that it either evokes or stifles the child's ability to trust others, according to whether he receives sufficient nurturance and love from his mother. If all goes reasonably well, the infant learns to trust his environment and to see it as orderly and predictable. If his needs are frustrated during this period, he learns to be suspicious, fearful, and ill at ease in a world that seems to him to be all chaos and unpredictability.

   2. Second year: muscular-anal stage; the crisis is autonomy versus doubt. With the development of motor and mental abilities, if the child has the opportu-

nity to explore and manipulate he acquires a sense of autonomy, adequacy, and self-control. If his attempts to explore and manipulate are limited or curtailed, however, he may come to feel shame and may doubt his adequacy.

3. Third to fifth year: locomotor-genital stage; the crisis is initiative versus guilt. If the child's self-initiated motor and mental activities are reinforced, he emerges from this period with a sense of purpose and goal directedness. Failure to resolve the conflicts engendered at this time may cause the child to feel like an inept intruder in an adult world.

4. Sixth year to start of puberty: latency; the crisis is industry versus inferiority. The relatively sexually unpreoccupied child here busies himself in learning how things work, in formulating rules, and in general industriousness. A sense of inferiority may develop, however, if the child is rebuffed or rebuked, or if his efforts are deemed silly, mischievous, or irritating.

5. Puberty and adolescence; the crisis is identity versus role confusion. This is a time for exploration and experimentation. The person plays a number of different roles and consequently acquires many different perspectives. It is a time for developing an integrated sense of identity, a feeling of being distinct from others and personally acceptable. Failure to resolve the identity crisis can lead to confusion about one's role in life, or perhaps the adoption of an uncomfortable, negative identity—a "loser," a "speed freak," a "class clown."

6. Early adulthood; the crisis is intimacy versus isolation. At this time the person's reaching out toward others can result in commitment to those others on a moral, sexual, and emotional level. If his efforts are dispelled, he may feel isolated and unable to form close personal relationships.

7. Young and middle adulthood; the crisis is generativity versus self-absorption. The person's concerns for others are expanded as he thinks about family, society, and posterity. But if he has not resolved earlier crises satisfactorily, he may choose to preoccupy himself with his own material and physical well-being.

8. Mature adulthood; the crisis is integrity versus despair. At this last stage in life, the person takes a long look back at what his life has been about. He may feel a sense of fulfillment or gratification or he may suffer a sense of despair in the realization that it was all wasted, his energy was misdirected and there is nothing now to be done about it.

with which he resolves the conflicts inherent in each stage is a measure of his ultimate psychological functioning. Erikson believes that development of the human personality is governed by the person's readiness to develop—that is, to interact with an increasing number and variety of other people.

Fromm: Society and Personality

For Erich Fromm (1941), personality is the result of society's success or failure in providing what the growing person needs. The crucial stage of personality development is not the first years but the period from 5 years on when the child is gradually widening his social contacts beyond the home and finally breaking away from it altogether. The freedom he wins in late adolescence brings with it a certain loneliness and a natural need to establish connections with others. Man's other basic needs, according to Fromm, are a sense of personal identity, an opportunity for creativity, a stable view of the world, and security. Human personality is the result of the interplay among these needs and the degree to which society provides for their fulfillment. Thus, from Fromm's point of view, abnormal or neurotic development is at least in part the product of an abnormal society.

Liss Goldring

Eric Fromm

As we can see, the neo-Freudians moved away from Freud's emphasis on instinctual drives and concentrated more and more on social and cultural factors in personality development. We turn now to another approach to personality theory that in major ways is in sharp contrast to the orientation of Freud and the neo-Freudians. We will see, however, that the insights of Freud play a major role in the formulations of at least some of the behaviorally oriented psychologists.

LEARNING THEORISTS

A large group of psychologists known as learning theorists focuses on learning experiences (see Chapter 3) as the main determinants of personality. These investigators share a rigorous commitment to experimental methodology.

Dollard and Miller: Reinforcement Theory

Yale University News Bureau

John Dollard

Among the earliest learning theorists to be concerned with personality were John Dollard and Neal Miller at Yale University. Both men had a deep appreciation of Freudian theory as well as a strong belief in the importance of laboratory research. Dollard and Miller's accomplishment was to translate many of Freud's concepts into hypotheses that were amenable to experimental verification (1950). They retained Freud's basic notion of drives as mechanisms demanding tension reduction, but unlike Freud, they emphasized drives that the individual learns as he develops rather than innate ones. With the Freudians they maintained that early childhood experiences are crucial in shaping the later adult personality. Again like Freud, but unlike other behaviorists, such as John Watson, Dollard and Miller accept unconscious factors as critically important determinants of behavior, and they too give anxiety, or learned fear, a central place in personality dynamics.

Dollard and Miller's theory begins with the primary physiological needs of the infant—food, water, oxygen, and warmth. Although these needs and some of the rudimentary behaviors that help to satisfy them are innate, generally the innate behavior does not remain sufficient; a more complex response has to be

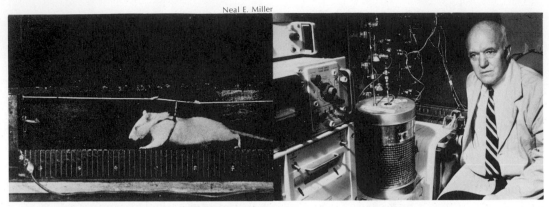

Neal E. Miller

The harness attached to the rat makes it possible to measure the amount of pull exerted.

Neal E. Miller

learned. For example the infant must learn to suck more efficiently than he does at birth. According to Dollard and Miller, the four important ingredients of the learning process are *drive* (motivation), *cue* (stimulus), *response* (the behavior itself), and *reinforcement* (reward). Stated simply, their idea is that "in order to learn one must want something, notice something, do something, and get something" (1941, p. 2). For example, suppose that a hungry rat is placed in a box that is empty except for a small lever. Because he is hungry, the animal anxiously scurries around the box. He notices the lever (cue) and brushes against it (response). Food is released and the animal eats it at once, thereby reducing the tension of his hunger drive (reinforcement). The next time the rat is put in the box, he proceeds directly to the lever and presses it, for he has learned that this is the way to obtain what he wants.

 Approach-Avoidance Conflicts

approach-avoidance conflict

According to Dollard and Miller, some of the most difficult human conflicts involve goals that we have "mixed" attitudes about. A young man may desire the income and status of a professional career but not the hard work and commitment involved; or a dieter may strongly want a piece of chocolate cake but also a slender figure. Dollard and Miller termed these situations approach-avoidance conflicts and built their learning theory on the basis of experimental situations like the following: A hungry rat learned to run down a passageway in order to get food at a specific point in a maze. To generate "ambivalence" (approach-avoidance tendencies) an experimenter gave the rat a brief electric shock while he was eating. Now when the rat was placed in the passageway he started toward the food but hesitated before reaching it. The distance from the food at which he stopped could be changed by manipulating (modifying) either the amount of his hunger or the strength of the electric shock. To analyze the conflict further, the experimenters applied the concept of goal gradients. Goal gradients are changes in the strength of a response as a function of distance from a goal. They have been measured by placing a rat in a light harness by means of which the strength of his pull toward the food or away from the shock could be measured (Brown, 1948).

On the basis of this and similar experiments Dollard and Miller derived four principles that govern conflict situations (Miller, 1944).

1. The tendency to approach a desired goal becomes stronger the nearer the individual is to the goal.

2. The tendency to avoid a negative stimulus becomes stronger the nearer the individual is to the stimulus.

3. The strength of the avoidance tendency increases more quickly with nearness than does the strength of the approach tendency.

4. The strength of both tendencies varies with the strength of the drive they are based on.

The first three of these principles are graphically represented in Fig. 12.5.

Dollard and Miller's model allows for predictions about behavior in approach-avoidance situations once something is known about the strength of the opposing tendencies. Within this general framework many of Freud's postulates about intrapsychic conflicts between drives have been analyzed and reformulated on a more solid methodological basis.

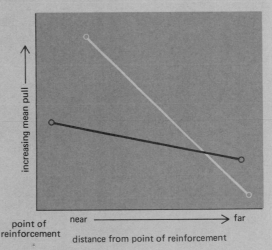

Fig. 12.5 Approach-avoidance gradients. (adapted from Miller, *Studies of Conflict,* in Hunt, 1944)

In Chapter 5 we discussed Miller's work on learned fear, and especially the difficulty one has in unlearning or extinguishing such an anxiety. This is the prototype of the reinforcement model, for it provides a clear mechanism to account for the strength of early learning and motivation, and explains why it can continue throughout life and persist even in the face of attempts to get rid of it.

Most of the criticism directed at the work of Dollard and Miller has questioned the legitimacy of theorizing about human behavior on the basis of experiments with rats. In particular, the attempt to quantify and verify Freudian theory on the basis of rat behavior has been sharply questioned by Freudians and non-Freudians alike. Another line of criticism argues that it is essential to study behavior in a social setting rather than in isolation and that Dollard and Miller's work completely ignores this point. Nevertheless, their work has generated several important conceptual advances and has laid the groundwork for more comprehensive learning theories.

Skinner: Operant Conditioning of Personality

The work of B. F. Skinner has had enormous influence in many areas of modern psychology (see Chapters 3 and 4), including personality theory. His approach has been to completely reject "motives" as a useful explanation of behavior; it thus represents a total break with both Freudian theory and Dollard and Miller. Instead of focusing on underlying drives or needs that may cause a particular behavior, Skinner seeks the conditions that strengthen it.

Skinner's theoretical model (1953), which is based on the principles of operant conditioning, views behavior as essentially random until it is either positively or negatively reinforced by the environment. After reinforcement, the frequency of a particular behavior either increases or decreases depending upon the *valence* of the reinforcement: reward is positive reinforcement; punishment

 Behavior Modification

Behavior modification entails therapeutic techniques based on fundamental concepts of learning theory (see Chapter 3). Notable among such techniques is the systematic desensitization technique of Joseph Wolpe, based on principles of classical conditioning. Wolpe, disillusioned with the reluctance of psychoanalytic theory to treat symptoms, reasoned that "if a response antagonistic to anxiety can be made to occur in the presence of the anxiety-evoking stimuli so that it is accompanied by a complete or partial suppression of the anxiety responses, the bond between these stimuli and the anxiety responses will be weakened" (Wolpe, 1958).

Wolpe ascertains in detail what emotionally arousing situations evoke avoidance. Various areas of anxiety, such as fear of failure, guilt about sex, fear of authority, and so on, are treated separately. For each theme the person ranks provoking stimuli in their order of severity. Thus someone who is afraid of snakes may fear the actual snake most, a film of the moving snake next, a still picture of the snake, and finally the word "snake" on a written page.

In the next step the person is taught how to relax and then to associate relaxation with the anxiety-arousing stimuli. Working from the least aversive stimulus in a given area upward, the person gradually learns how to relax in the presence of each item in the hierarchy.

Another method of behavior modification is the observation learning or modeling technique of Albert Bandura. In one use of this method preschool children who were intensely afraid of dogs observed a fearless model playing with a dog. The model made progressively bolder approaches to the dog while the children watched from a safe distance. These children later showed far less fear than a group of fearful controls who did not watch the model (Bandura, Grusec, and Menlove, 1967). (See p. 163.)

Conditioned aversion is yet another behavior modification technique. It is used to reverse pleasurable arousal to stimuli the culture deems aversive, as in fetishism (sexual arousal to underwear or to feet, for example), alcoholism, homosexuality, and so on. The positively valued stimulus may be neutralized by counterconditioning if it is presented contiguously with stimuli that evoke extremely unpleasant reactions. Gradually, as a result of repeated pairings, the positive stimulus acquires some aversive emotional properties from its association with noxious events. Smokers, for example, may shock themselves when they feel a desire for a cigarette. Fetishists and transvestites have been treated with nausea-inducing drugs administered contiguously with the pleasurable sensations derived from their unacceptable behaviors. Typically aversion therapies are used only as a last resort. They are rarely imposed without the client's consent. (See p. 149.)

Finally a large number of therapeutic procedures focus on changing the consequences of behavior. Such procedures rest on the theory that the maladaptive behavior was acquired in the first place because it was in some way rewarded. The modification usually entails positive reinforcement for desirable behavior only; the undesirable behavior is ignored. Tantrums in some children may have been inadvertently reinforced by attention or acquiescence to unreasonable demands. But in aversion therapy the attempt is to avoid reinforcement of the deviant behavior and to reward the subject for more desirable behaviors.

is negative reinforcement. In Skinner's research, the subject behaves freely, but the experimenter decides in advance to reward or punish a particular kind of response. For example, he may reward by indicating approval—by saying "good" or "fine" or by smiling—each time the subject uses a personal pronoun such as "I" or "me." Skinner found that in this way subjects could be conditioned to change their speech patterns without being aware that they were doing so. Studies have shown that a wide range of other human behaviors can be modified in this way, including psychotic talk, delinquency, sexual aberrations, and patterns of social interaction. We shall see some examples of these in Chapters 16 and 17.

Skinnerian theory also provides a powerful explanation of superstitious and other kinds of inappropriate behavior. Skinner points to the fact that an inappropriate response may be *accidentally* rewarded. For example, an experimenter gives a confined pigeon a small amount of food at fixed intervals. The pigeon is likely to continuously repeat whatever it was doing when the food was first given, for this behavior has been accidentally reinforced by the receipt of food. Thus a strong likelihood develops that the irrelevant behavior will be in progress when the food is given again—if not the very next time, then the time after that. Eventually the behavior is almost always in progress when food is given and at that point it becomes a permanent behavior pattern of the bird. Inappropriate responses that have been conditioned in pigeons in this way include turning to one side, hopping from one foot to the other, bowing and scraping, and strutting.

In a similar way neurotic behavior in human beings may be accidentally reinforced. A child whose profuse crying at a slight mishap attracts his mother's elaborate attention may well continue to be a "cry baby" in later life.

Social Learning Theory

social learning
theory

Gene's Studio

Albert Bandura

The Chevron

R. H. Walters

Both of the learning theories we have considered so far emphasize the role of reinforcement in the shaping of behavior and personality. More recently, however, some psychologists have been interested in social learning, or observational learning, in which reinforcement or reward plays no prominent or even obvious part. Rather, social learning takes place through observing other people, called *models,* or symbols, such as events, words, and pictures. Social learning theory, although it concentrates on the direct stimulus, is also concerned with cognition, the processing and interpretation of information in the learning experience.

Bandura and Walters (1963), leading social learning theorists, make a sharp distinction between the acquisition and the performance of a behavior. Although almost everyone in our culture knows how to primp in front of a mirror and to use lipstick and face powder, men and women do not do these things with equal frequency. While many behaviors can be learned through observation, which of these behaviors a person chooses to perform in a given situation depends upon which behaviors have been rewarded or reinforced in the past. Thus social learning theory incorporates many of Skinner's ideas in its analysis of the effects of reinforcement on behavioral performance but goes beyond Skinner in its analysis of how behavior is acquired.

Bandura (1965b) reports an experiment that clarifies many of these ideas. In this study children watched a film of an adult who displayed strong aggressive behavior—such as kicking and hitting a Bobo doll. The film had three endings, only one of which was shown to each child. In one ending the adult's aggressive behavior was punished; in a second his behavior was rewarded; and in a third there were no consequences at all. After seeing the film, the children were placed in a room with a similar doll and their behavior was observed. Those who saw the version in which the aggressive behavior was punished imitated the behavior far less than those who had seen it rewarded or ignored. Yet when the children

Imitation in Learning

Although the role of imitation in learning may have been obvious to the common-sense layman, it was not until Bandura shone the spotlight of research on it that it came to occupy a theoretically central position. Bandura pointed out that the vast array of behaviors that we learn to perform in a short span of life cannot all be learned by direct experience. It must be then that we learn vicariously—by observing others and imitating their behavior.

Bandura conducted a series of research projects to demonstrate empirically the phenomenon of learning by imitation. Most of this research revolves around the acquisition of novel aggressive responses, and it demonstrates that whether children observe live adults or films, they learn by observation. To be sure, this learning is to some degree dependent on whether the model is rewarded or punished for his behavior. Fig. 12.6 shows the results for the experiment described in the text.

Bandura cites examples of imitative learning by children in many cultures. For example, Nash (1958) describes the social training of children in a Cantelense subculture of Guatemala.

The young Cantelense girl is provided with a water jar, a broom, and a grinding stone, which are miniature versions of those used by her mother. Through constantly observing and imitating the domestic activities of the mother, who provides little or no direct tuition, the child readily acquires a repertory of sex-appropriate responses. Similarly, small Cantalense boys accompany their fathers while the latter are engaged in occupational activities and reproduce their fathers' actions with the aid of smaller versions of adult implements. (pp. 47–48)

Ford and Beach (1951) describe the acquisition of sexual behavior among Seniang children.

Young Seniang children publicly simulate adult copulation without being reproved; older boys masturbate freely and play sexual games with little girls, but the boys are warned not to copulate on the grounds that this behavior would weaken them. Lesu children playing on the beach give imitations of adult sexual intercourse, and adults in this society regard this to be a natural and normal game. (p. 189)

Evidence for imitative learning is avialable even from animals. Thus Bandura cites a case from Kellog and Kellog (1933)

Each [Donald, the human child, and Gua, the ape] was much interested in typewriters, and during the last few months would go to one whenever it was within reach and pound the keys with his fingers, in this case demonstrating a common tendency for its manipulation. It is impossible to say which of the two first exhibited this behavior, since they were originally observed going to it within a few moments of one another. Gua would even climb on the typewriter stool and seat herself properly before the machine, moving her hands simultaneously up and down upon the keyboard. According to our records, they first imitated the motions of a typist at the respective ages of 13 and 15 months. At that time they had both seen a typewriter operated from time to time for more than five months. (pp. 140–141)

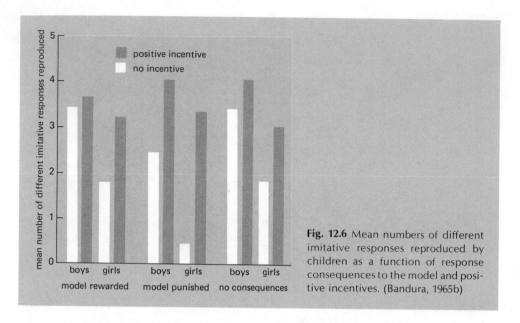

Fig. 12.6 Mean numbers of different imitative responses reproduced by children as a function of response consequences to the model and positive incentives. (Bandura, 1965b)

were offered an attractive incentive to imitate the aggressive behavior, those in all three groups performed equally well. Clearly, then, all the children had acquired the behavior through observation, but some of them were inhibited in their performance of the behavior by negative reinforcement, which they had also only observed, not experienced.

According to social learning theory, both direct and observed learning experiences determine what behaviors are available to us. Each person's choice among behavioral alternatives depends on the probable consequences (reinforcements) of each alternative in a particular situation. The implication is that a person will behave consistently in many different situations only if he thinks the behavior will lead to similar consequences in all those situations. Of course, it frequently does not. For example, while boisterous singing is expected on the part of students in the cheering section at a football game, it is not treated as acceptable (reinforced) when the students are part of a church choir. We learn, then, to behave one way in some situations and another way in others. Unlike trait or type theories of personality, social learning theory emphasizes behavioral specificity—that is, the idea that most behaviors are specific to the situation in which they occur—rather than consistency. It provides a powerful explanation for the wide range of behaviors we all exhibit in our daily lives, including changed behaviors in response to changed stimuli.

It should be kept in mind that social learning theory is almost exclusively concerned with environmental influences on behavior; it does not take into account any of the hereditary factors that have been shown to operate. Moreover, the concept of man implicit in the social behavior view is that of a rather passive and malleable creature. It sees man as primarily reactive rather than active—as easily influenced by outside forces and constraints. On the other hand, a social learning theorist might argue that his model of human behavior includes responsiveness to subtle changes in the environment and thus allows for man's adaptiveness and flexibility. But the criticism that social learning theory fails to account for human creativity and novelty has yet to be answered.

PHENOMENOLOGICAL THEORIES

Phenomenological theories of personality stress the uniqueness of each person and the significance to his behavior of his current life situation as opposed to his past history. They are also more interested in the conscious than the unconscious mind, and they put special emphasis on the person's view of himself and of the world, on his subjective experience. Most of their theories attribute considerable significance to man's desire for self-actualization.

phenomenology

The phenomenological approach has been strongly influenced by the work of **Gordon Allport** (1961), who presented a holistic view of man as an integrated biological and social organism rather than as a bundle of traits, motives, and responses. Allport also denied the idea of motivational continuity throughout life, arguing instead that the motives of infancy are totally different from those of adulthood. Although he accepted sex and aggression as motives, he believed that with maturity the human being can control those and other instinctual motives. The independence of mature motives from instinctual underpinnings is frequently called "functional autonomy."

Gordon Willard Allport

functional autonomy

Functional autonomy is the idea that an originally instrumental behavior may become an expressive behavior; that is, it may become autonomous and detached from the motivation that originally gave rise to it. For example, an insurance salesman might learn golf in order to meet customers but then come to like playing golf for its own sake, quite apart from the business it helps him generate. Allport suggested that the more mature a person is, the more autonomous are his motives.

The uniqueness of each person, the significance of the desire for self-actualization, and a holistic view of man are central also to the personality theory of **Carl Rogers**, one of the best known of the phenomenologists. To these concepts, Rogers (1959, 1963) added two others: the self-concept and the importance of positive regard. The self-concept is the view one has of himself in the world—what kind of person he is and, most importantly, how effective (strong or weak) he is. The self-concept, according to Rogers, is so pervasive that it affects one's perceptions of the world and one's behavior, or responses to the world. It is for this reason that positive regard, particularly from the self but also from significant others, becomes important. The ideal state is one of unconditional positive regard—genuine liking with no strings attached. When positive

Carl Rogers

self-concept

regard is conditional upon our doing something or being a particular kind of person, we are thrown into a state of anxiety each time we do not do, or even wish not to do, the thing required or when we have feelings that are inconsistent with the kind of person we are required to be. The only solution to this sort of situation is to get rid of the conditions—whether they are our own or someone else's—placed on our having positive regard, to revise our self-concept so that it includes what we in fact really are.

self-actualization

The drive toward self-actualization has been further elaborated by **Abraham Maslow** (1954), who held that man has five basic needs that fall in a particular order from lower to higher:

1. Physiological needs—for example, food and drink
2. Safety needs—for example, security, stability
3. Belongingness and love needs—for example, affection, identification
4. Esteem needs—for example, prestige, self-respect
5. The need for self-actualization

"Lower" needs, according to Maslow, manifest themselves earlier in life; they are more closely related to biological necessity and are narrower in scope. Moreover, a lower need must be adequately satisfied before the next higher need may come into play. Self-actualization, man's highest need, is possible only if all the preceding levels of need have been satisfied. The "natural" course of development can go wrong when there is insufficient gratification of needs at any given level. The ideal physical and social environment, then, is one that facilitates gratification of each level of need as it manifests itself in the course of development.

Abraham Maslow

Maslow specified the characteristics of self-actualization more precisely than any of his colleagues (1954). He derived these characteristics from a study of outstanding historical and contemporary persons—among them Lincoln, Einstein, Beethoven, and Eleanor Roosevelt. The most important characteristics he identified include: the ability to perceive reality more effectively than most people do and to be able to tolerate ambiguity or uncertainty; acceptance of oneself and one's various characteristics with little feeling of guilt or anxiety; the capacity for spontaneity in both thought and behavior; relative independence of the culture and the environment; the capacity for mystic experiences such as ecstasy, wonder, power, and helplessness; and "primary creativeness," which comes directly out of the unconscious and produces truly original discoveries.

Phenomenological theorists, then, stress the basic drive toward self-actualization as the organizer of all the diverse forces out of which the person creates himself and his experience. Their primary emphasis is on ways in which the person perceives himself and his world and on the processes of health and growth. In these respects phenomenological theory overcomes some of the limitations of previous theories discussed in this chapter. It is not without limitations of its own, however. For one thing, the concept of self-actualization, as developed so far, is still too imprecise to meet the requirements of rigorous

Abraham Maslow's Whole Characteristics of Self-actualizing People

They have more efficient perceptions of reality and are more comfortable with it.

They accept themselves and their own natures almost without thinking about it.

Their behavior is marked by simplicity and naturalness and by lack of artificiality or straining for effect.

They focus on problems outside themselves; they are concerned with basic issues and eternal questions.

They like privacy and tend to be detached.

They have relative independence of their physical and social environments; they rely on their own development and continued growth.

They do not take blessings for granted, but appreciate again and again the basic pleasures of life.

They experience limitless horizons and the intensification of any unself-conscious experience often of a mystical type.

They have a deep feeling of kinship with others.

They develop deep ties with a few other self-actualizing individuals.

They are democratic in a deep sense; although not indiscriminate, they are not really aware of differences.

They are strongly ethical, with definite moral standards, though their attitudes are conventional; they relate to ends rather than means.

Their humor is real and related to philosophy, not hostility; they are spontaneous less often than others, and tend to be more serious and thoughtful.

They are original and inventive, less constricted and fresher than others.

While they tend toward the conventional and exist well within the culture, they live by the laws of their own characters rather than those of society.

They experience imperfections and have ordinary feelings, like others.

(Condensed from "Self-Actualizing People: A Study of Psychological Health" in *Motivation and Personality* 2nd ed., by Abraham H. Maslow, Copyright 1954 by Harper & Row, Publishers, Inc.; Copyright © 1970 by Abraham H. Maslow. By permission of the publishers.)

scientific inquiry. Furthermore, phenomenological theorists have not demonstrated that the drive toward self-actualization is inborn rather than socially acquired. And, finally, the theory does not provide for any behavioral predictions, nor does it account for individual differences in any systematic way.

In this chapter we have looked at some significant attempts to understand the nature and development of personality. None of the theories discussed is definitive—each has its shortcomings and limitations; the subject of personality is so wide-ranging and complex, that at this stage in the development of psychology it is probably unreasonable to expect a general theory of personality to have emerged. In fact, the theorists we have discussed, with the possible exception of Freud, have not attempted to account for every aspect of personality development but only for a limited sphere—behaviors that are learned by observation or modeling, behaviors that can be conditioned, the nature of personality traits, and so on. The theories, however, complement one another, each one compensating for the limitations of the others. And since each of the theories is relatively reliable in terms of its own limited objectives, taken together they account for most of the important dynamics in personality development. The fact that no single theory is broad enough to account for all of the data may simply suggest that the questions we are asking are too large. No one would expect a biologist to come up with a single answer to the question, "What is the nature of living things?" In the same way we may be asking too much of the psychologist if we look for a single answer to the question, "What is the nature of personality and how does it develop?"

Unquestionably, understanding of personality dynamics will continue to advance. Perhaps it will account for much of the unexplained variability that today's theories stumble over. If so, the theories we have examined in this chapter will have laid the groundwork for the future's more comprehensive understanding of personality.

SUMMARY

Personality studies ask two universal questions: Who am I? How did I become what I am? They are also concerned with the validity of descriptive categories and of the concept that personality is organized around a central core.

Personality descriptions help the layman interpret and predict his own and others' behavior. For the psychologist they are also the first step in studying personality development and behavior modification.

Personality is shaped by the interacting influences of genetic and somatic, parental, peer, and cultural factors. Genetic and somatic factors have to do with the influence of inheritance and of physiology on personality. Studies done with fraternal and identical twins have found that heredity is an important influence on personality. Physiological influences on personality, both before and after birth, include the emotional and physical state of the mother during pregnancy, the level of hormonal functioning, and the rate of maturation during adolescence.

The most important environmental influence on personality is the infant's relationship to his mother in the early years. Infant monkeys reared in isolation develop neurotic traits, and human infants reared in orphanages are often retarded in development. Both emotional and intellectual development are directly related to the amount and quality of interaction with the mother.

Bowlby proposes that the child's attachment to his mother is a result of five instinctual responses—sucking, crying, smiling, clinging, and following. The primary importance in this sequence of clinging and following seems to be supported by the preference of infant monkeys for a cloth over a wire surrogate mother, even when the wire mother dispensed food. Frustration of the attachment instinct causes severe separation anxiety.

Disturbing home environments can lead to disturbed behavior in the child. On the other hand, impaired children can provoke neurotic responses from their parents.

Absence of the father may be related to an inability in the children to trust and thus to become adequately socialized. The father also plays an important role in sexual identification.

In school, the child encounters other significant personality influences: his own academic success or failure and his relationships with both peers and teachers. Eventually, peers usually get more of the child's interest and attention than parents, but they seldom exert a stronger influence.

Cultural influences on personality differ from nation to nation and also from one socioeconomic class to another. Parent-child relationships in the middle class are more acceptant and egalitarian, while those in the working class are oriented toward maintaining order and obedience. A study comparing Soviet and American child rearing found that Soviet child rearing stresses obedience, collective play and work, and conformity.

Type theories of personality represent the oldest known method of labeling and categorizing personality. The best-known modern typology is Jung's complex extroversion-introversion continuum.

Trait theories have been more valuable than type theories in the description of personality. Cattell reduced a list of nearly 18,000 traits to 171 terms, then to 35 surface traits and finally to 12 source traits, and he devised tests that measure personality in terms of source-trait variables. Eysenck found four basic personality types—stable extrovert, unstable extrovert, stable introvert, unstable introvert—and correlated them with personality traits.

Basic to Freud's theory of personality is the importance of the unconscious, and especially of unconscious sexuality and aggressiveness. Freud thought of personality as having three aspects—the id, or pure unconscious instinct; the ego, or reality priciple; and the superego, or conscience. The ego is charged with monitoring the demands of the id, the superego, and reality.

Freud divided personality development into five stages of sexuality—oral, anal, phallic, latent, and adolescent—each associated with a particular erogenous zone and carrying with it particular needs. In the phallic stage, desire to possess the mother sexually leads to the Oedipus complex, which is resolved by identification with the same-sex parent.

The neo-Freudians questioned Freud's emphasis on the sex drive and gave more importance to social forces that shape personality. Jung proposed two kinds of unconscious, the personal unconscious and the collective unconscious; the latter is inherited from one's ancestors. Adler stressed the importance of the social environment and introduced the concepts of compensation and inferiority complex. Horney was concerned with the effects of anxiety, especially childhood feelings of insecurity, on the personality. Erickson synthesized Freud's developmental stages and the social influences of Adler, Horney, and others. He postulates eight psychosocial stages of development. For Fromm, personality is the result of society's success or failure in providing what the growing person needs.

Dollard and Miller translated Freud's concepts into hypotheses that could be experimentally tested with rats and other animals. They viewed drives as learned rather than innate mechanisms for tension reduction, and found four important ingredients in the learning process—drive, cue, response, and reinforcement.

Skinner ignores the motivation behind behavior and concerns himself with the conditions that positively or negatively reinforce particular behaviors. His theories attempt to explain both appropriate or logical behavior and inappropriate, "superstitious" behavior.

Social learning theorists such as Bandura and Walters postulate the acquisition of behaviors through observation of others, or modeling, without direct reinforcement. They emphasize the difference between acquiring and performing a behavior and the idea that behavior is specific to the situation in which it occurs.

Phenomenological theories stress the uniqueness of each person and the subjective nature of his experience. Allport proposed a holistic view of man and the idea of functional autonomy—the notion that mature motives have no instinctual underpinnings. Carl Rogers postulated the significance of the self-concept and of positive regard. Maslow held that man has a hierarchy of needs, and that self-actualization is the highest. Each level of needs can be satisfied only if lower levels have been met.

These widely different personality theories complement and interact with each other. Each one is relatively reliable in terms of its own limited objectives.

Suggested Readings

Adorno, T. W., E. Frenkel-Brunswik, and D. J. Levinson, *The Authoritarian Personality.* New York, Norton, 1969.
  An examination of the complex of traits that make this personality type.
Bowlby, John, *Child Care and the Growth of Love.*
  Bowlby is concerned with the effects of maternal deprivation on the mental health of children.
Erikson, Erik, *Identity: Youth and Crisis.* New York, Norton, 1968.
  The theory behind Erikson's identification of the eight stages of psychosocial development.
Eysenck, H. J., *Crime and Personality.* Boston, Houghton Mifflin, 1964.
  Eysenck believes that the genetic make-up of certain individuals may make them likelier followers of crime than others, and that society can take certain measures to prevent the development of criminality in such persons.
Ferguson, L. R., *Personality Development.* Monterey, Calif., Brooks-Cole, 1970.
  A readable study of personality from a developmental point of view.
Horney, Karen, *Feminine Psychology.* New York, Norton, 1973.
  A collection of papers by a pioneer psychoanalyst who questioned many of Freud's ideas concerning the psychosexual development of women.
Laing, R. D., "The Ghost of the Weed Garden," in *The Divided Self.* New York, Pantheon, 1969.
  An analysis of a schizophrenic young woman, with insights into the behavior of the mother as an ultimate cause of the daughter's psychosis.
Solzhenitsyn, Aleksandr I., *Cancer Ward.* New York, Bantam Books, 1971.
  The novel centers on a group of men who have cancer, all of whom lived under Stalin and responded in different ways to that era of brutality.
Oedipus Rex. Sophocles.
  The classic Greek tragedy from which Freud derived the name Oedipus complex for the phallic stage in the development of the male child.

Chapter Thirteen

Assessment

What is the principal objective of psychological assessment?
In assessment, what do we mean by reliability and validity?
What is intelligence?
What do interests have to do with aptitudes?
How would you go about assessing someone's personality?
What is a personality inventory?
Why do some psychologists ask people to interpret inkblots or
  pictures?

A friend moves to your town, where he knows no one but you, and asks you for the names of some girls he might date. Instead of giving him a list of all the girls you know, you probably select only those you think he will like. You look for girls who share some of your friend's interests, whose social and cultural backgrounds are somewhat similar to his—perhaps above all, girls you think he will find attractive. In the process of sorting out names to give him, you assess characteristics of both your friend and the girls you are considering. We all engage in these informal kinds of appraisal throughout life as we relate to others in our families, jobs, schools, and social settings. We try to understand others by identifying their characteristics and from these estimations to predict what our relations with them in the future will be.

Early in life we learn, however, that quick assessments frequently backfire. You may introduce your movie-buff friend to a gorgeous redhead who loves movies and can talk about all of them. But it turns out that your friend can't stand redheads. People are always defying analysis and prediction—not completely, of course—but often enough to keep us in continual suspense. Serious, plain Sally turns out to be a perfect model because she photographs well. George, who seemed very well put together and destined for a good life, comes so unglued that he needs a respite in a mental hospital. Frank, a dedicated and successful professional football player, quits the team at the height of his career to teach high school mathematics.

How do we explain such seemingly incongruent behavior? We need first to gather a great deal of information about the person, but even then it isn't always easy to uncover the factors that prompt his behavior. Because of the increasing importance of accurate character assessment—in the fields of mental health, education, and career counseling, for example—psychologists have given much time and effort to the development of formal assessment techniques that are systematic and objective. This chapter deals with several of the more successful of these techniques.

THE WHAT, WHY, AND HOW OF ASSESSMENT

Psychological assessment is the measurement and evaluation of human characteristics and behavior. Its broad purpose is to predict future behavior on the basis of some current characteristics that are measured. Prediction of course, assumes consistency between present and future characteristics and behavior.

Psychologists have several reasons for wanting to predict behavior. Perhaps the primary one is to help people find settings in which they will be successful. In this function, various psychological assessment procedures—achievement and aptitude tests, interviews, past histories, and personality measurements—are used by educational institutions in the selection of students.

Louise Bates Ames testing a child at the Gesell Institute, New Haven, Conn.

Later in their school careers, students may take more tests to help them decide on specific occupations. Business and industry also rely heavily on assessment procedures in hiring and placing personnel. On the basis of the outcome of such tests, applicants who do not show promise of succeeding in a specific school or job are advised to consider other alternatives.

Assessment techniques are also important to clinical psychologists and to psychotherapists. Psychological tests help to detect and diagnose mental and emotional problems and to determine methods of therapy. Alternate forms of the same tests used in detection and diagnosis are usually administered to patients throughout treatment to see if the desired behavioral change has been obtained. In this function, assessment techniques have had varying amounts of success beyond psychiatric hospitals and private psychiatric treatment. In schools they have often identified, and led to help for, mentally or emotionally problematic children. Parole boards and courts, too, use them in prescribing and measuring rehabilitation of the criminal.

Assessment is, in the third place, a major part of the continuous research and theory-making that goes on in psychology. Applied in this way, assessment procedures attempt to determine and define more precisely various concepts about such complex traits and behaviors as creativity, perceptual judgment, intelligence, and authoritarianism. They are also used in the devising and refining of still other assessment techniques. As research generates further research, psychologists hope to develop procedures with yet greater ability to predict success and behavior change. In this function, assessment procedures contribute to their own improvement and to the efficacy of the clinical psychologist.

To be most effective, assessment of a given trait or behavior should entail many methods and tests applied in a variety of situations. Numerous choices are available to the psychologist; among them are interviews, rating scales such as adjective checklists, psychometric inventories of personality and intelligence, behavior sampling in standardized test situations, and such projective stimuli as inkblots and ambiguous pictures. In all these procedures, the evaluations can be made by an observer, and in some they can be made by the subject himself. The results are analyzed and interpreted in standardized ways, often with the aid of computers. Each of these methods will be discussed more fully in later sections of the chapter.

EVALUATING ASSESSMENT TECHNIQUES

The worth of an assessment technique rests on two firmly established criteria. It must be reproducible or *reliable;* that is, it must consistently produce the same result. It must also be *valid;* that is, it must measure the characteristics it claims to measure.

reliability
validity

Reliability

Several methods have been developed to assess reliability. The principal means of measuring the reliability of an entire test is to administer it twice to the same people, with sufficient time between testings to assure that most of the original responses will be forgotten. The extent to which the separate scores correlate helps to gauge the test's reliability. Other methods are more concerned with a test's *internal consistency*—the extent to which all items or parts measure the same thing. A test can be administered in two or more alternate forms, or it can be divided into sections. The consistency with which scores on different forms or sections correlate measures internal reliability. For example, different parts or forms of a test designed to reveal schizophrenia can be given to a group of diagnosed schizophrenics; if the test is internally consistent, all parts of the test should provide the same indication of schizophrenia.

internal consistency

 Some Largely Discredited Methods of Assessment

Some assessment studies have attempted to link characteristics and behavior to physical traits. Who has not, for example, tried to "size up" a person by his face? But formal, controlled experiments have found little relation between facial appearance and behavioral traits, though it is often easy to gauge a person's emotional state by the expression on his face.

Other studies have tested the relationship of behavior to body type, or somatotype. In 1936 the German psychiatrist Kretschmer suggested a classification of his patients into two types of physiques. Schizophrenics, he proposed, were generally tall and thin, and manic-depressives short and somewhat fat. Although later tests of Kretschmer's classification did not bear him out, other studies have developed along similar lines. Sheldon's somatotype theory is discussed in a box in Chapter 12 (see page 529). Test conditions for the results from Sheldon's classifications have varied, and few psychologists support the concept fully. But many feel there is some significant relationship between body type and behavior yet to be assessed.

Graphology, assessment based on handwriting, is another method with a few strong advocates. Unfortunately much of what is theorized about handwriting tends to be subjective, and few objective procedures have yet been developed to uphold its usefulness as an indicator of personality.

Those who support the validity of handwriting analysis argue that although writing is a physical act, it requires the full cooperation and attention of our minds—and accordingly that the way we form our letters is a reflection to some extent of our state of mind. The experts also maintain that while handwriting can reflect the mood of the moment, basic constancies in a person's writing permit us to make some sort of personality assessment of him.

Among the first things considered in a handwriting analysis is size of the letters. Large handwriting may suggest a rather extroverted type who enjoys activity and achievement, seeing and being seen, who is enthusiastic, holistic, and impatient. Those with a medium-sized hand are simply like most of us. Those with a small writing are more patient, and they concentrate more; small writing suggests a person is thorough, concise, interested in details, someone who thinks things through. A scientist, philosopher, psychologist, or student is likely to acquire or to have a small handwriting. These people may also be more objective and observant. And they may sometimes be stingy. Some handwriting varies in size according to the person's mood.

Hey, there's a fly in my soup!

Hey, There's a fly in my soup!

Hey, there's a fly in my soup!

Optimism or pessimism may be revealed by the baseline of a person's handwriting. Writing that runs uphill is said to indicate a cheerful, optimistic, ambitious person. Downhill writing may suggest depression, pessimism—someone who feels down. Even handwriting suggests that the person runs on an even keel.

Let's all go to the movies

Let's all go to the movies

Let's all go to The movies

The graphologist looks to many more aspects of handwriting than those mentioned here. He bases his personality assessment on all of the characteristics he observes—including slant, speed, distance between lines and between words, thickness of the writing, and the kinds of finishing strokes at the ends of words. The validity of these interpretations has not been tested, and most personality theorists dismiss assessments based on graphology as unfounded. Whether this is a premature judgment remains to be seen.

Another kind of reliability measure is concerned with *scoring consistency* —the extent to which different, equally qualified interpreters will read the test the same way. This kind of reliability comes into question only when the interpreter must use some degree of subjectivity in making his evaluation; projective tests such as the Rorschach and the TAT, which we will discuss later in the chapter, are examples of tests for which scoring consistency must be measured. To measure scoring consistency, one simply has several qualified examiners interpret data from the same test. If the results are widely divergent, the test apparently cannot be scored reliably by different examiners, though conceivably it still might work well enough for one particular examiner, especially if it is reliable in other respects.

 Use of the Correlation Coefficient To Specify Reliability

The correlation coefficient is a statistical index of the degree to which two variables may be related and the nature of that relationship. The strength of the relationship may be expressed by a number varying from −1.00 to 1.00. Two variables are perfectly correlated if for every increase (or decrease) in one variable there is a corresponding increase (or decrease) in the other. Thus, for example, two plastic 12-inch rulers may be perfectly correlated. If you measure the length of an object with one of the rulers and then with the other, the measure you get will be exactly the same. The age of a child and his grade in school are (if all goes well) perfectly correlated. For every one-year increase in age (after age 6) there is a corresponding increase of 1 in the grade number. Such a perfect correlation is expressed by the correlation coefficient of 1.00.

But perfect correlations are the exception rather than the rule. Thus if one of two 12-inch rulers was wooden and warped, it would not correspond perfectly with measurements made with a new plastic 12-inch ruler. If the ruler is warped around the middle and something measured one inch long, there would be no difference between the rulers, but at 6 inches, ⅛ of an inch difference would occur. Or in the case of schoolchildren, some children may have failed a grade or started school a year early or late and thus age and grade will not be perfectly correlated. In both cases however, the two variables are still very strongly related and by looking at one variable an accurate prediction can be made of the other. Thus if a child is 8 years old one can fairly assume he is in the third grade. Such a correlation, although not perfect, is still quite good. When two variables are not at all related they have a correlation coefficient of 0. Two such variables may be the color of your eyes and your grade point average in school. It would hardly be likely that one could be predicted from the other.

The correlation coefficient is very useful for testing the reliability of assessment measures as they are being developed. If a test is to be checked to see whether it really measures intelligence, presumably a stable trait for individuals, and not some other performance which may vary, the same person may be tested twice in a short period of time and then the correlations between the two tests checked. Such test-retest correlation coefficients, if they are high, may help establish the reliability of a test.

A test that presumably measures a personality trait should do so equally well on the first and second halves of the test, or on any two different parts of the test. Often correlation coefficients relating scores on one part of the test with scores on the second part of the test are computed as a reliability check (split-half correlation).

Tests that have more than one version are also checked for reliability by testing the same people on different versions of the tests and computing the strength of the relationship between them. To the extent that the different versions are related they may be said to be measuring the same thing.

Correlation coefficients are also computed on the relationship between different scorers scoring the same tests (intra-scorer reliability) or alternately the same scorer scoring the same test at different times (inter-scorer reliability). To the extent that the relationships are strong the test may be said to be reliable.

The long-range stability of a trait and/or its measure may also be checked by computing the correlation coefficient relating scores on tests taken at different times with a long period between them.

The criterion of reliability is most often met when a procedure is clear and unambiguous and when the items of the test are clearly and simply worded. Ambiguous items must be eliminated, since responses to them vary from person to person and from time to time. Even those who evaluate the test results can make different interpretations of responses from ambiguous items. The tools for obtaining results must also be precise in order to be consistent. Consider the difficulty of establishing the precise length of a long piece of lumber measured several times with an ordinary 12-inch ruler. You would probably find that no two of the measurements were exactly the same; each would deviate half an inch or more one way or the other from each other. Thus the ruler would not have proved a reliable tool for obtaining an exact measurement, and you would have to find a more consistent measure.

Validity

Validity is usually an even more difficult criterion to meet. Weekly quizzes in a history class might be a reliable measure in that the items correlate highly with each other. But is the quiz also a valid measure of anything—of the ability, or willingness, to memorize material on a weekly basis, or of comprehension of history information?

Part of the problem of ascertaining that a test really measures what it purports to measure is obtaining agreement on the conceptual definitions of the characteristics being tested. What is anxiety, or intelligence, or creativity? Many people disagree with the definition of intelligence that IQ tests seem to assume, believing that people who do not score well on such tests are frequently quite intelligent. Does this disbelief imply that the intelligence test is invalid?

To establish the validity of an assessment procedure we must compare the results it produces with those of some other, clearly defined criterion. Suppose our test is intended to measure anxiety. We might begin to test its validity by asking a subject it designates as anxious if he would rate himself as anxious. Then we might ask several people who know our subject fairly well, and whose judgment we have some reason to respect (for example, we know they have some experience in assessing others; clergymen, medical doctors, schoolteachers, work supervisors generally fall into this category) whether they would judge our subject as anxious. If both the subject and most of the experienced observers agree with the test results, we have at least an indication of *face validity*.

face validity

But some anxious people take great pains to conceal their anxiety, particularly if they suspect that its underlying causes might be socially unacceptable. A person who is ashamed of his anxiety may not rate himself as anxious, and he may also be so adept at concealing his inner state that even an experienced observer may be tricked into judging him secure and relatively serene.

So we really need some other, more objective, criterion of well-established validity to measure our test against. In the case of anxiety, we have several good objective criteria. Anxiety usually produces certain physiological symptoms: heart palpitations, high blood pressure, breathlessness, diarrhea, nausea, sleeplessness, perspiration, muscular tensions, and so on. It is also likely to cause a disturbance of cognitive behavior. An anxious person frequently has difficulty thinking clearly and remembering correctly. If we can establish a correlation between our test results and some of these behavioral indexes of anxiety, we will have a better validation of our test. Of course, the more criteria we use, of both subjective and objective types, the better our validation procedure will be.

If a test is designed to predict future behavior, we need to test its validity in an entirely different way. We must have an established criterion of the behavior that we can apply in the future. For example, if a test is to predict success in learning to play the piano, we must have a criterion of such success by which we can measure subjects in a year or two. A test, of course, may have predictive validity without any other kind of validity; that is, it may predict success in learning to play the piano and yet be unrelated to any other measure at the time of administration.

No psychological test has perfect reliability or validity. As you will see when we look at the projective tests particularly, some of the best-known and most frequently used are rather poor in both reliability and validity. Yet we go on using them and probably will continue to use them for a long time to come. This is not because we are lazy, but because we are often so convinced of the validity of a test, even without good evidence, that we will tolerate less than adequate reliability. We work the test over and over, trying to refine and improve it, but we go on using it until someone comes up with a better test for the same thing.

Considerations in Evaluating Assessment Procedures

We can examine assessment procedures from a number of points of view. We can look at their goals and we can identify the characteristics and behavior the assessing psychologists want to study. Then we can proceed to weigh goals against results.

We can also examine assessment in terms of the concepts the investigators support. As we saw in Chapter 12, some psychologists work on the broad assumption that personality can be conceived of as a unified and consistent whole. They regard behavior as highly predictable, because it stems from a unitary organization of common traits. A more current approach defines personality as less predictable. It views personality as a composite of behavior and abilities, which are sometimes considered to be quite independent of each other. This newer view of personality also does not assume that behavior is consistent. It is seen rather as highly modifiable, often a reaction to the specifics of a situation or environment. Each approach employs procedures and identifies goals consistent with its theoretical predisposition.

Obsolescence and bias are other factors that we must be alert for in evaluating assessment methods. Many tests eventually become obsolete, some of them more quickly than others. Verbal tests are extremely susceptible to obsolescence because, especially in today's world of technology and television once-infrequent words such as *submarine* and *atomic* quickly become familiar and therefore less indicative of superior knowledge. Tests of this nature must be evaluated and updated continuously.

Tests using pictures, such as the Thematic Apperception Test (TAT), also become obsolete, though less rapidly than verbal tests. As fashions in clothing, hairstyles, and furniture change—and even more important, as certain life situations and relationships change—the original pictures may be rendered meaningless. We must add, however, that a change in the interpretation of a picture does not of itself affect the usefulness of the picture.

Bias is a more complex problem. Cultural bias has been repeatedly unmasked in both intelligence and personality tests administered to groups who experience difficulty with the language or who are unfamiliar with objects the tests use as stimuli. Minority-group children have been classified as retarded because English is not their primary language or because their homes do not offer the stimuli used by the test to assess them. Bias is also a danger for assessors who work with tests that rely heavily on their subjective analysis of results. In these cases, testers are apt to see what they want or expect to see, rather than what is actually there.

culture-fair tests

Attempts to avoid cultural bias have resulted in so-called *culture-fair tests*. The classic example is the Goodenough Draw-a-Person Test, which simply asks the subject to draw the best picture of a person that he can. This test has been used to assess both intelligence and personality—intelligence according to the correctness of proportions and completeness of detail and personality according to what, if anything, the drawing may reveal about the subject's relationship with his parents. Artistic ability is not considered in the evaluation of the drawing. Though presumably children of all cultures would be equally prepared to draw a person, in fact Hopi Indian children consistently score better than non-Indian children on the test (Table 13.1).

Table 13.1 Percentage of Subjects Depicting Hair, Profile, and Heel[a]

	Age				
	6	7	8	9	10
Hair					
Hopi subjects	41	75	88	75	86
Goodenough's subjects	16	22	45	45	58
Profile					
Hopi subjects	11	11	35	46	53
Goodenough's subjects	1	2	7	20	28
Heel					
Hopi subjects	15	19	31	33	33
Goodenough's subjects	10	18	37	52	66

[a] The fact that older Hopi children depict the heel less frequently than other subjects is explained by the fact that Hopi shoes do not have elevated heels; the heel is most often represented by the heel of the shoe in children's drawings.
SOURCE: Dennis (1942)

We shall see later that most intelligence tests today include performance as well as verbal items, largely in an attempt to avoid the cultural bias that favors use of standard middle-class American English. This attempt is partly successful, but other aspects of the test situation besides language are also stumbling blocks to certain cultural groups. One group may be unaccustomed to the extensive use of paper and pencil that most tests require, another may not have learned the motivation to do well in a testing situation, another may be intimidated by the test administrator.

Assessment procedures are apt to be invalidated by test-takers as well as by test-makers. Certain behavior patterns have been observed in test-taking situations, especially among people rating themselves on personality inventories. Subjects have been found to distort their responses, even to lie outright, in an effort to appear more intelligent or creative or socially acceptable. Others always agree with or always reject statements regardless of their content. Fairly successful attempts to eliminate these tendencies have asked subjects to select from among two or more equally desirable statements. Some psychologists, however, regard set behavior patterns as indicative of characteristics that in themselves can be assessed. We will see many examples of these problems throughout this chapter, along with some solutions to them.

TESTING FOR INTELLIGENCE

A general tendency in talking about assessment procedures is to consider them all assessments of personality. A great percentage of them are, personality being the most pervasive and perhaps the most difficult aspect of psychology. But although we detect some overlap, we cannot really consider personality to include such cognitive behaviors as intelligence, aptitude, and creativity. Assessment, therefore, is concerned with several kinds of characteristics and behavior, and as such it has somewhat varying goals. Procedures testing for intelligence, aptitude, creativity, and similar abilities are administered mainly in order to predict educational or vocational success. Personality assessment, as we will see later in the chapter, is used in part to predict, but also as a step in the clinical process of producing behavior change and as a tool for the development of theories.

Intelligence and IQ

Intelligence is sometimes described as the ability to learn quickly and to retain learning. Other definitions stress the application of learning and describe intelligence as the ability to apply possessed knowledge in adapting to new situations or in dealing with the abstract. In actuality, the only definition of intelligence that psychologists have accepted is that intelligence is what is measured by intelligence tests.

Development of the Stanford-Binet IQ Test

Alfred Binet's first intelligence test, published in 1905, consisted of 30 tests covering a wide range of difficulty and content. The 30 tests were arranged in order of difficulty, beginning with the lowest intellectual level that Binet could recognize and ending with average intelligence.

The innovative aspect of this test was that it attempted to measure the individual child's general or average level of performance rather than to measure each of his abilities separately. Another important innovation was the use of a large number of diverse but quite short tasks, recognizing the comparatively short attention span of very young children.

Binet revised his test in 1908 and 1911, but he retained the important concepts of the 1905 test. The new tests, however, were classified by level, according to the age at which a majority of children could pass them. A test classed at a given age level was passed by 50 to 90 percent of normal children at that age. This arrangement introduced the concept of *mental age*, which Binet considered as the age level at which a child, regardless of his chronological age, passed all except one test.

The major weakness of the Binet test was that it remained dependent on actual age. A child of 12 scoring at 12 was not differentiated from a child of 10 who scored at 12. This very real fault was corrected by Lewis M. Terman at Stanford University, who published the first Stanford-Binet test in 1916.

Terman's principal contribution was a new scoring procedure by which he obtained an *intelligence quotient*—the relation of mental growth to actual age. This IQ rate was found by dividing the mental age by the chronological age and multiplying by 100:

$$IQ = \frac{MA}{CA} \times 100$$

With this system, an IQ of 115 meant the same thing regardless of the actual age of the subject.

The Stanford-Binet was revised in 1937 (Terman and Merrill, 1937), essentially to extend its age limits. Eventually, however, it became evident that IQ was still somewhat bound to chronological age. In 1960 another revision of the Stanford-Binet was designed to correct this difficulty (Terman and Merrill, 1960). The result is that IQ is no longer computed from a formula but is located on a table instead. This table forces the average IQ at each age to be 100 with a standard deviation (see the appendix) of 16 points. With this revision the term intelligence *quotient* has become meaningless, though it is still used; the IQ now is simply a test score adjusted, or "corrected," for the age of the subject.

IQ   The best-known intelligence tests are those that score intelligence quotient, or IQ. Items for a standardized IQ test are selected in terms of their proved reliability and validity when administered to a representative sample of schoolchildren or of adults under standardized conditions. IQ items for schoolchildren

Alfred Binet

must prove less difficult with age. Whether for children or adults, they must also be relatively free of bias and test for reasoning ability as well as knowledge, and they must be culturally appropriate for the test-takers and consistently related to increased intelligence when compared to performance on the rest of the test. Many of the procedures that are used to select and arrange IQ tests have grown out of the work of Alfred Binet.

Binet, a French physician working on the problem of retardation at the turn of the 20th century, assumed that intelligence normally increases with age and that the older children are, the more items they should be able to deal with on a test. The dull and retarded, accordingly, are those who do not perform as well on a test as the mean for their age group. They score instead with children younger than they, and the more the retardation, the younger the age group they fall into. From there it was a short step for Binet to formulate the concept of mental age as a measurement of intelligence. Binet reasoned that 10-year-olds of average intelligence should be able to pass all items passed by a majority of other 10-year-olds tested. Children who pass fewer items are scored at lower mental ages, and those who answer more items are scored at higher mental ages.

Binet's tests were revised in 1916 by L. M. Terman at Stanford University, who produced the standard Stanford-Binet Test. The Stanford-Binet is arranged by age levels, each level containing six items that measure general intelligence. A child's mental age is established at the level at which he passes all six items, no matter what his chronological age is. For every item passed which is assigned to a higher age level, he earns 2 additional months. A child who passes all the items for 8-year-olds and one item for 9-year-olds and one for 10-year-olds would have a mental age of 8 years, 4 months.

Terman (1916) also adopted a ratio for relating mental age to chronological age as a means of summarizing and interpreting the results of intelligence tests. According to this IQ ratio, a mental age of 8 years, 1 month (8.1) divided by the chronological age of 9 (9.0), for example, yields .9, which multiplied by 100 designates an IQ of 90.

Lewis M. Terman

What is the nature of the intelligence that the Stanford-Binet and other intelligence tests measure? Is it a single ability or a group of specific abilities? Charles Spearman in 1904 postulated that intelligence is both kinds of abilities; general ability is necessary to the performance of all mental tasks, and a specific ability is necessary to the performance of each kind of mental task. General ability explains the high correlation among all tests of intellectual skills, but specific ability accounts for individual differences in abilities among people with the same IQ.

L. L. Thurstone (1935) divided intelligence into group factors, which he thought of as midway between specific and general abilities. The factors he differentiated were verbal, number, spatial, perceptual, memory, reasoning, and word fluency. Reasoning, for example, is measured by tests requiring logical inferences, such as whether a particular syllogism is logically sound. One syllogism the test asks subjects to evaluate is: "Some radishes are rumble seats, and some rumble seats sing soprano; therefore some radishes sing soprano." But when he devised tests of these abilities and correlated the results, he had to admit at least a small amount of general ability. Specifically, he found that in adults correlations among the abilities are postive but low, while in grade-school children they are considerably higher. Evidently we specialize as we mature and as our interests develop.

Since any printed test requires the subject to read, no matter what kinds of questions it asks, it is to some extent a test of verbal skills. It is thus subject to cultural bias, because it is usually more difficult for people whose native language is not the one in which the test is administered. Printed tests may also be biased against the deaf and possibly also others whose intelligence may not be reflected primarily in verbal skills. David Wechsler sought to compensate for this difficulty, which characterized almost all intelligence tests, by devising a combination of verbal and performance tests. He published the Wechsler Intelligence Scale for Children (WISC) in 1949 and the Wechsler Adult Intelligence Scale (WAIS) in 1955. Table 13.2 indicates how WAIS scores are interpreted. These tests are similar, but the WAIS is intended for people 16 years and older. The performance part of the tests includes problems in picture completion, block design, picture arrangement, and object assembly. The block design test involves reproducing patterns of blocks shown on cards by arranging actual blocks each of whose sides is a different color. Picture arrangement requires placing a series of pictures in a storytelling sequence.

Some typical items from the WISC are:

How many wings does a bird have?
What should you do if you see someone forget his book when he leaves his seat in a restaurant?
Sam had three pieces of candy and Joe gave him four more. How many pieces of candy did Sam have altogether?
In what way are a lion and tiger alike?

Some typical items from the WAIS are:

Who wrote "Paradise Lost"?
What is the advantage of keeping money in the bank?
Why is copper often used in electrical wires?
What is the Kremlin?

Today most tests for intelligence, even if they do not include a performance section, have both verbal and nonverbal items. While verbal and performance measures are partially correlated, they assess different aspects of intellectual ability.

We have examined the origins of most of the intelligence tests in use today, and we have looked at theories about the nature of intelligence that they are based on. It seems safe to conclude that intelligence, at least as our tests measure it, consists of both a general intellectual ability and more specific abilities. We turn now to the relationships between measured intelligence and some other personality factors.

Table 13.2 Distribution of Intelligence Scores on the Wechsler Adult Intelligence Scale

IQ	Verbal Description	Percentage of Adult Population
130 or above	Very superior	2.2
120–129	Superior	6.7
110–119	Bright normal	16.1
90–109	Average	50.0
80–89	Dull normal	16.1
70–79	Borderline	6.7
Below 70	Mentally retarded	2.2

IQ and Mental Retardation

mental retardation

Terman's original formulation of IQ was based on the concept that a score of 100 indicated average intelligence. Not very far beneath that, at scores of 80 to 90, were people he classified as "dull" and, at scores of 70 to 80, "feebleminded." One would hardly aspire to dullness or feeblemindedness, but in the early days of psychological testing, anyone who could score 70 on an IQ test was at least considered normal. Below that score were the patently deficient: the morons (50–70), the imbeciles (20–50), and the idiots (below 20).

Today, happily, retardation is no longer so absolutely, or so psychometrically, defined. It is one of the most assiduously studied and treated conditions of the 20th century. Once it became apparent that poor academic performance, and even a very low IQ score, was not necessarily associated with unsatisfactory life adjustment after the school years, the concept of retardation was reexamined. The latest definition of the American Association of Mental Deficiency (Heber, 1959) specifies only that retardation, a "subaverage general intellectual functioning," must originate during the developmental period and must be associated with maladaptive behavior in maturation, learning, or social adjustment. It can be either constitutional or accidental in origin, and it cannot be diagnosed by an intelligence test. Most important, the new definition assumes that the functionally retarded are capable of achieving typical functioning. With special schooling, most retarded people are able to achieve a satisfactory life adjustment, and in some instances, these people are even able to increase their measured IQ, though usually not beyond 80 or 90.

IQ and Genius

Just as a low IQ score does not mean lifelong maladjustment and incompetence, a high one does not necessarily mean instant, or even eventual, genius. Nevertheless, high IQ is necessary to genius, which may be defined as outstanding achievement.

genius

Our best current knowledge about genius comes essentially from one cross-sectional and one longitudinal study. The former, undertaken by Cox in

The Identification of Genius

Sir Francis Galton

An eminent British scientist, Sir Francis Galton, published the first systematic study of genius in 1869. Appearing on the scene before the introduction of IQ tests or any other means of measuring human abilities, Galton selected eminent persons to study on the basis of their widely accepted reputations as leaders. He arbitrarily decided that only one in 4,000 people would be eligible for eminence and then proceeded to find 1,000 eminent men in only 300 families. Of the 1,000 men he identified as eminent, he was able to make extensive studies of 977. He found that these men had a total of 739 eminent relatives. Thus, the entire force of Galton's work—and in a sense its prejudice, for this was undeniably what he set out to prove—was that genius, indeed all natural ability, is inherited. Galton spent the rest of his life devising methods of measuring human perceptual and cognitive abilities in an attempt to identify genius early in life. His ultimate hope, of course, was that people so identified would be encouraged to choose spouses with similar levels of ability and in procreating would improve the human race, or at least produce a large "family" of extraordinary achievers.

1926, studied the backgrounds and accomplishments of 301 people who were rated as eminent according to a set of objective criteria. The consensus was that superior mental ability characterized *all* of the people studied. Most of them were attributed an IQ of 160 or above. Other findings were that most of the subjects had fathers with a high occupational level and that most of them as children had exhibited broader, more intense, and different kinds of interests than their peers. Moreover, when Cox and his colleagues rated the character and personality traits of their subjects, they agreed that geniuses were once again considerably higher than average.

The longitudinal study of genius was undertaken by Terman and his colleagues in 1925, using California schoolchildren who demonstrated a very high order of ability. Information was collected about these children and follow-up studies have been conducted every few years. The latest of these studies was reported in 1968 by Oden, who assumed leadership of the project after Terman's death.

The initial study revealed some interesting, though not startling, findings about gifted children as a group. On the whole, their fathers have a high occupational level; both parents have a higher than average educational level; the frequency of insanity in the family is lower than average; their parents are likely to have had good health and to have been in the prime of life (that is, older than usual) at the time of the gifted child's birth; they are more likely to be the first-born than a later-born child; they are superior to their peers in physical and developmental characteristics; and they evidence good personality development.

Follow-up studies of Terman's gifted children have revealed that in every case the intelligence remains high. In spite of a few failures and many mediocre records, the group as a whole has been outstandingly successful, both in occupational status and in personal happiness. (See box on page 445.)

In comparing subgroups of these gifted children—those with IQ's above 170 and the others—Terman and Oden (1947) found no essential difference between the extremely gifted group and the entire group. They concluded that there is no particular advantage in an IQ greater than 140.

Both the cross-sectional and the longitudinal studies of genius have led investigators to conclude that intellectual ability is likely to be accompanied by superiority in other areas as well—in physical and mental health, in personality and character development, in development of interests. The findings also agree that gifted people are more likely to have parents whose educational and occupational achievements are above average. Moreover, gifted people are likely to maintain their intellectual superiority throughout life.

IQ and Creativity

We might define creativity as a unique organization of characteristics and behavior that can be measured against norms and other standardized criteria. Creativity is not, however, to be confused with idiosyncratic behavior. Both are original, but creativity is meaningful originality. Several studies have attempted to isolate the factors that make up creativity in order to assign it its own place within the total realm of intellectual behavior. Based on the work of Guilford (1957), for example, researchers have tried to rank creativity according to the number of possible answers a subject can give on tests that ask for word association, alternate story endings, suggested uses for objects, and possible consequences of different events. Creativity is determined then by the number and variety of responses.

creativity

J. P. Guilford

 Creativity

A number of psychologists have made detailed investigations of creativity, which in psychological research is often synonymous with divergent-production ability. Psychologists here are interested in fluency, flexibility, and originality of thought. These qualities are correlated but not necessarily synonymous with IQ ratings. Similarly the ideas of creative children are often difficult for teachers to evaluate. Children scoring high on tests of divergent production are frequently characterized as having wild, silly, and even naughty ideas. Yet these children, when placed in problem-solving groups with children who score comparatively low on divergent production, typically initiate ideas far out of proportion to the rest of the group.

Barron (1955) has given much attention to the validation of a number of tests designed to measure originality. He has correlated scores from divergent-production tests (these ask the subject to list unusual uses for a number of objects, to invent clever or remote consequences that might follow if certain changes were to take place, and to suggest a number of unusual titles for some given story plots) with various other scores of originality in a sample of 100 Air Force captains. The tests correlated .30, .32, and .36 respectively with the assessment-staff ratings of originality, and the multiple correlation was .55. In view of the elusiveness of creativity, these correlations are rather strong.

Of course, creativity is evasive enough a quality to be dealt with by itself. Certainly there are different types of creativity. Writers, scientists, and planners may draw heavily on semantic resources, while inventors and those in the visual arts may depend on visual, figural resources. Translation would probably be an important resource for mathematicians, who depend on symbolic information. There is evidence for the importance of considering content categories (Guilford, 1957; Welch, 1946).

Perhaps such considerations enabled Elliot (1964) to provide some of the strongest predictive validities for semantic divergent-production tests. Elliot worked with public relations personnel and advertising copywriters. He asked supervisors to rate his subjects in terms of their creativity, and then divided the subjects into more creative and less creative groups. Divergent-production tests successfully discriminated between the two groups.

Creative potential is sometimes viewed (Guilford, 1967) as a complex mélange of many variables. Creative performance in daily life may be enormously variable in terms of the kinds and amounts of demand made on one's intellectual resources. It is difficult to determine if in fact the divergent-production categories that have been singled out by researchers do in fact figure significantly in the creative act. And so once again it may be said that the term creative potential is in need of further qualification.

Personality inventories also supply data on creativity. They have shown that creative people tend to be more individualistic, inventive, artistic, persevering, open-minded, self-perceptive, and emotional than the rest of the population. While these characteristics cannot always be used to differentiate between creative and noncreative people, they seem to be more frequent among the former.

Getzels and Jackson (1962) made a study of children who were very high in either creativity or intelligence, but not in both. The average IQ in the High Creativity group was 127, and in the High Intelligence group 150, but the groups were equally superior in academic achievement. Differences between the groups were in the realms of motivation, values, personality, and family background. The High Creativity children were less oriented toward success and more toward self-expression; they were from less well-educated families and had had less supervision from their mothers. These investigators have found very low correlations between creative abilities and intelligence. Torrance (1962, 1964) reached the same conclusion but added that correlations were higher at the lower levels of ability than at the higher. He proposed that above an IQ of about 120, further increments bear no relationship to creativity. Tyler (1965) suggests that "the most favorable combination for achievement may be an IQ of at least 120 along with a considerable development of the creative thinking abilities that are independent of intelligence."

Summarizing the effectiveness of IQ as a predictor of outstanding achievement, we may say that intelligence is necessary but not sufficient. Other requirements are special talent and powerful motivation.

IQ and Age

Do we grow more intelligent as we mature physically and emotionally? What happens to intelligence when the body stops growing? What happens to it when physical stamina declines?

Finding answers to such questions is made extremely difficult by the fact that intelligence doesn't grow unless it is fed. We are once again confronted with the interaction of nature or heredity—which accounts for natural intelligence—and nurture or environment—which accounts for the amount and kinds of education we receive (see Introduction). After the age of 14, measured intelligence tends to decline if schooling is discontinued, but Thorndike (1948) has shown that it increases consistently up to 21 years for people who continue schooling.

David Wechsler

Studies of the effect of advancing age on intelligence have been inconclusive, even contradictory. Cross-sectional studies have indicated a decline in measured IQ with age, though the rate of decline appears to be different for different kinds of mental ability. Vocabulary and retention of information seem to remain constant, and in some cases to increase, up to age 60, but the ability to perceive analogies and to grasp numerical symbols appears to decline quite rapidly. Wechsler (1958) similarly found relative stability of verbal abilities but a decline in performance skills with age (see Fig. 13.1).

Longitudinal studies, on the other hand, have found a significant growth in IQ at least until age 60. One study (Bradway and Thompson, 1962) found evidence of such a growth in a non-college-level population, though it did not follow its subjects beyond their 30th year. In view of the fact that most of the cross-sectional studies date back to the earlier years of the century, Tyler (1965) speculates that the intellectual decline they find in early adulthood may have been a product of the paucity of intellectual stimulation in the lives people lived rather than of biological changes.

At least one study, however, has found essential agreement between cross-sectional and longitudinal studies. Schaie and Strother (1968) tested 50 people in each 5-year age group from 20 to 70 years and, 7 years later, retested as many of them as they could locate. The longitudinal results of such a study are, of course, inferential but probably valid. In any event, both approaches

average decline (verbal and performance tests combined).

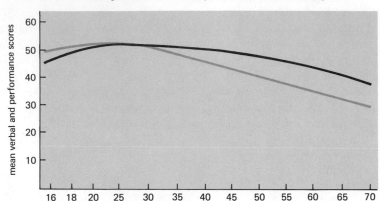

Fig. 13.1 Comparative decline of verbal and performance subtests on WAIS with age. Ages 16–75 and over, 2052 cases. Black line, Verbal; colored line, Performance. (Wechsler, 1958)

yielded the same result: mental abilities appear to reach their height at about age 35 and to decline fairly rapidly after age 50.

Yet because of the very wide range of individual differences within all these studies (there are always a few 60-year-olds who outperform most of the 30-year-olds), we are thrown back time and again on the interaction of native intelligence and educational stimulation. Doubtless at some point—perhaps after age 70—mental abilities decline, but they don't need to decline very much before that if the environment remains stimulating. Many world leaders today, after all, are over 65 and still going strong.

IQ and Race

In 1969 as the Head Start Program, aimed at compensating for the deprived environments of underprivileged children, appeared to be failing, psychologist Arthur Jensen wrote an evaluation of it. One very small part of his paper burst into the news like a bombshell, for Jensen claimed that heredity accounts for about 80 percent of the variation in IQ and strongly suggested that the widely observed 15-point inferiority of black Americans to white Americans on all known IQ scales was evidence of an inherited and therefore uncorrectable racial deficit in intelligence.

Jensen defined two levels of intellectual ability: level I is associative learning, where blacks and whites show no appreciable differences; level II is abstract reasoning, which is what IQ tests largely measure, and here is where the racial difference shows up. Jensen did not consider the question of why blacks should be inferior to whites in abstract reasoning, but argued that because they are, they should be encouraged to pursue only level I learning—the learning of specific skills.

Arguments refuting Jensen have pointed mainly to evidence that environmental factors account for far more of intellectual functioning than Jensen gives them credit for. Hunt (1969) cited a number of studies showing that socioeconomic improvements led to immense increases in IQ within only a few years. Skodak and Skeels (1949) found that 100 adopted children had substantially higher IQ's (20 points) than their natural mothers, even though the correlation with their natural mothers' was greater than with their adoptive mothers' IQ's. Deutsch (1969), tabulating IQ differences between monozygotic (identical) twins reared apart, found *mean* differences of 6 to 14 points but a *range* of differences as great as 30 points. He also cited the contribution of his own program of compensatory education in improving reading scores as long as 3 years after completion of the program.

As is occasionally the case, one of the most clearcut and convincing arguments came from animal psychology. In 1958, Cooper and Zubek had conducted an experiment with the 13th generation of Tryon's maze-bright and maze-dull rats. Testing the influence of various environments on the maze-learning abilities of the two strains, they subjected a number of young rats from each group to (1) an "enriched" environment (increased perceptual stimuli), (2) a normal laboratory environment, and (3) a perceptually restricted environment. Both strains of rats raised in the restricted environment had more difficulty learning the maze than the dull rats raised in a normal laboratory environment. Most surprisingly, in the enriched environment, dull rats learned almost as quickly as bright ones and significantly more quickly than dull rats raised in the normal environment.

Kaufmann (1973) argues that *even if* American blacks do not reason abstractly as well as American whites, and *even if* it is true that intelligence is inherited, it is still quite plausible that the difference is not racially innate but due instead to selective reproduction. Only those blacks who were willing to do laborious, monotonous work may have been in a position to reproduce. Those who were more intelligent would naturally have been rebellious and, lacking economic and social stability, would have been less desirous of producing offspring. He takes particular issue with Jensen's implication that any child should, on the basis of race alone, be channeled into a particular educational program.

This debate is an ancient one, and particularly difficult to evaluate when the social and political consequences of the various outcomes drown the possibility of objective discourse and research. The issues are not settled, nor are the methodologies even completely adequate to the tasks of distinguishing nature from nurture. Nowhere is this more true than in the area of intelligence and race.

APTITUDE

So far we have considered tests that deal with intelligence as an intellectual ability. But need often arises, particularly in vocational placement and training, for assessment of nonintellectual and perhaps undeveloped abilities or aptitudes aptitude tests with which to predict future performance. Aptitude tests measure potential ability to perform a specific task. They are distinct from achievement tests and other forms of intellectual assessment, which measure what can be accomplished at the time of taking the test.

Perhaps the most widely used and successful "aptitude test" is not a test of aptitudes at all, but of vocational interests. It is the Strong Vocational Interest Blank, first developed by E. K. Strong in 1927. The test has been expanded and refined over the years to include more than 50 occupations for men and at least 25 for women.

Strong assumed that people in a particular occupation are likely to enjoy similar kinds of activities, and he suggested that a young person having similar interests to, say, the interests of engineers might consider engineering as a vocation, while students with interest patterns deviating from the engineer norms would do well to consider another vocation.

The response pattern for a profession is determined by tabulating the item responses of satisfied members of that profession. This pattern is then compared with a pool of "people in general." Items that significantly distinguish between the two samples of the population are retained as test items. The subject is asked to indicate whether he likes, is indifferent to, or dislikes certain tasks, academic subjects, amusements, personality characteristics, and so on; to rank some activities in order of preference; to indicate which of certain paired activities he prefers; and to rate his own abilities and characteristics.

Reliable predictions of success in a particular endeavor are usually not based on a single aptitude or interests test, but on a battery of tests that includes assessments of both interests and specific aptitudes. A student debating between medical school and an engineering career might use such tests to help him with his choice. They would measure his potential ability in mechanical and scientific areas and his talents, such as his drawing ability. There would also be tests of dexterity, perceptual judgment, and other specific characteristics. The results of the total assessment battery would finally be viewed in conjunction with personality and other factors.

In addition to intellectual ability, we sometimes need assessments of more particular abilities or aptitudes, particularly in evaluating a person's potential success in a given profession or craft. Interests are sometimes a reliable, though indirect, indicator of aptitude. We turn now to a consideration of personality assessment.

PERSONALITY APPRAISAL

Personality is the most studied area of psychological assessment. In this section we will consider the diversity of approaches to the enormous task of assembling accurate information about persons. We will see that data about personality can come from several sources—the observations of trained researchers, the ratings or estimations given by peers, friends, and family, and the self-ratings of the person himself. Whatever the source, the assembled data are evaluated by a judge—or, if possible, by two or more judges—who examines samples of data collected over a period of time.

We will see that some approaches to personality appraisal reflect the methodological orientations we have already considered in Chapter 12, such as the carefully controlled methods of the trait personality theorists or the far less structured projective procedures of theorists in the Freudian tradition. Other methods represent a combination of orientations and predispositions.

Structure, of course, is relative. The highly structured type of test relies on prepared materials, such as printed questionnaires and standardized interview schedules, which attempt to eliminate irrelevant topics and direct the assessment toward the particular behavior under consideration. In this category is the widely used Minnesota Multiphasic Personality Inventory (MMPI). Here the choice of answers is limited to a few that are easy to score, and the judges can evaluate the responses with relative objectivity. There are also less structured methods, such as the well-known inkblot tests, that rely on prepared materials but give the respondent much greater latitude in his answers. The least structured type of appraisal is the open-ended interview.

Every method of psychological assessment, of course, is subject to some degree of error, no matter how sound its design. As we examine each of the various approaches to personality appraisal in this section we will also consider the major limitations of each with respect to reliability, validity, and other sources of inaccurate or erroneous data.

The Interview

The most basic kind of rating situation is the interview, which is a purposeful conversation. The participants usually are two people who meet in an office and talk—most often about the interviewee. The interview is the most widely used procedure of assessment, probably because it is extraordinarily flexible. Interviews are systematically part of educational recruitment, vocational placement, and clinical treatment. Researchers use them extensively as a measure of validity, to ascertain whether the subjects clearly understood the procedures of an experiment.

Structured interviews use standardized schedules that impose controls on what questions are asked by the interviewer, and usually also on the kinds of answers available to the interviewee. They are most valuable in research settings where exact quantifications are desired and also in job placement, where unstructured, open-ended interviews have been quite unreliable. The unstructured interview, on the other hand, allows the person being interviewed to determine its content. The interviewer guides the conversation only by aptly placed questions that either elicit more detailed information or channel ideas in a specific direction. Such open-ended interviews have been most useful in counseling and clinical situations.

Criteria for College Admission

What factors determine who is admitted to college? The answer to some extent depends on the particular college, but a few general statements can be made. Under normal circumstances one may assume that the major question a college admissions officer is concerned with is, "What is the likelihood that this student will successfully complete the academic program at this college?" (A nonnormal circumstance might result in the question, "What can he contribute to our football team?") The most reliable predictor of academic success in college has been found to be past academic performance as indicated by a student's high school record. In a very large body of studies directed to this point, an average correlation coefficient of about .50 has been found between college grade point averages in the first year and high school class rank. Standardized test scores are a second factor of major predictive significance. Correlations between freshman grade point averages and scores on a number of standardized academic aptitude or achievement tests, such as the *Scholastic Aptitude Test,* average about .47. Thus, high school performance and standardized aptitude test scores, in that order, are the two best predictors of college success. When high school rank and standardized test scores are combined, the resulting index of intellective competence has been found to correlate with freshman grade point averages with a median value of about .63. Most colleges therefore use such an index in choosing students.

A wide variety of other measures may be used by individual colleges in attempts to further predict which students will succeed. Personality tests and special interest, attitude, and biographical inventories may be used. None of these measures has been found to consistently yield significant amounts of predictive information. A number of nontest factors may be considered: extracurricular skills, economic status, parental education levels, home location, and physical attractiveness are some of these. While demonstrably useful in particular situations, the general applicability of such criteria is limited, and the use of some of them is ethically questionable. Interviews have been widely employed, but predictions of success based on them have been shown to have little relation to the actual probability of success (Mayhew, 1965).

It appears then that after a student's academic record and aptitude and achievement test scores have been taken into account, further selection procedures are apt to proceed in a somewhat idiosyncratic basis. Some investigators have proposed that the role of chance in college selection procedures should be made truly equitable by the use of formal random selection techniques.

The popularity of the interview is not a reliable measure of its validity for behavior prediction. Many unrelated stimuli can influence both its course and its usefulness. For example, such conditions as time of day, setting, and manner of the interviewer can affect the outcome. Interferences such as murmurs, nods, and interruptions, or failure of the interviewer to respond can greatly alter a subject's behavior. Since its results can be conditioned by so many uncontrollable variables, the interview is best used in conjunction with other assessment procedures.

Rating Scales

Rating scales designate the traits to be assessed and provide the means for measuring those traits. The basis for rating can be an interview or series of interviews, or it can be observation, usually in a fairly natural situation. The rater evaluates a subject according to the degree to which he exhibits the traits in question, and the results of the ratings are assigned numerical scores. There are several variations within the overall rating technique. A trait such as shyness can be scored along a continuum that includes the extremes of the trait and several middle points. For example, a rater might have five points to choose from along a shyness continuum: either a scale of numbers 1 through 5 to show increase, or a verbal scale such as *very, above average, average, below average,* and *not at all.* For each subject, the rater would check the rating that most applied. Such ratings, however, have often been found to require explanations detailing the specifics of the characteristic. One person may be extremely shy in all situations, another only when faced by a large group or by only one other person. Finer distinctions encourage more specific interpretation of the data. Rating scales are often used by an interviewer after the interview is completed. In this way the rater uses information he gathered during the entire interview.

rating scale

Another kind of rating scale is the adjective checklist, on which the rater marks off words that best describe the subject. Sometimes, for each adjective the rater must select from such gradations as *always, frequently, occasionally,* and *never.*

Still another rating variation, the Q-sort technique, makes use of a number of cards, each stating a characteristic. The rater—either the interviewer or the subject himself—sorts the cards into piles that are numerically scaled to indicate the degree to which the subject reveals each of the characteristics. For example, if the rater is allowed six categories (the first being for characteristics that most apply to the subject and the sixth for those that least apply), he might sort eight of the cards as follows: Group 1: is affectionate, is liked by his peers; Group 2: likes to converse, is honest; Group 3: participates in group activities; Group 4: is moody; Group 5: likes intellectual pursuits; Group 6: enjoys solitude. With this sorting, we can gain some insight into how the rater views the subject. The Q-sort technique has been used in a wide variety of situations. In a therapeutic situation, the patient may be asked to rate himself as he thinks he actually is at the moment and also, by means of the same printed cards, to describe his ideal self—what he would like to be. Later therapeutic sessions attempt to bring the self-report and the ideal closer together either by improving the patient's self-image or by influencing him to adopt more realistic ideals.

Ratings are subject to several kinds of misuse, stemming mostly from the difficulty of establishing rater objectivity. First, the rater must understand scale use—both the total purpose and the specific conceptual definitions of the traits being measured. Ratings should be made wherever possible by several observers and on successive occasions. And the raters should summarize their findings in detailed descriptions rather than in brief, ambiguous evaluations, so that others can use the descriptions in treating the subject or in making further evaluations.

halo effect

Another problem has to do with what is called the halo effect, a tendency on the part of some raters to score a person high on all traits because he does well on one or two, or to score him low because he does poorly on a few. Raters also fall into stereotyping, judging subjects by preconceived ideas of what to expect from certain kinds of people rather than by the way the person actually behaves. Halo effects are possible with many other kinds of evaluation ratings. Professors often give a student higher marks on subsequent essays because he did exceptionally well on an earlier one, rather than on the basis of the actual performance on the later papers.

Self-Ratings

Assessment based on self-rating occurs when a subject provides information about himself by scoring himself on one or more characteristics. The kinds of responses elicited by self-rating techniques range from likes and dislikes to descriptions of psychological reactions to selected stimuli. When the subject does not fake answers or fall into a set pattern (such as acquiescing to almost all suggestions, or almost none, or consistently denigrating or exalting himself), self-rating can be valuable in guiding him toward successful educational and job placement and in uncovering disorders for therapy.

Self-reports have been utilized increasingly by the phenomenologists (see Chapter 12), who seek an understanding of a person's perception of himself and his experiences around which to predict behavior or to build therapy. The phenomenologists consider such distortions as equivocation, acquiescence, and limited perspective, if the subject introduces them, not as errors but as integral factors in the subject's personality. Distortions reflect how the person sees himself and how he wishes to be seen. In this approach what matters is not the accuracy of a self-rating but what the self-rating reveals about the person. The Q-sort technique is one frequently used.

Self-ratings so interpreted are deemed the most reliable source of a subject's self-perception. In addition, they have proved repeatedly to be as dependable, or more so, for predicting future behavior than objective assessment by others. People who fake answers on a projective test in order to appear better qualified as often as not will do well on the task for having to try harder to match their ratings of themselves. It has been found, for instance, that students can predict their own grades as accurately as other measures used. The comparative success of many kinds of self-rating indicates that the best way to find out something about someone may be simply to ask him.

Phenomenological Approaches to Assessment

In addition to self-ratings, phenomenologists are interested in a number of other primarily subjective assessments of character, or assessments that attempt to tap the person's subjective experience. What keeps the phenomenological approach scientifically valid is its insistence on using objective measurements, even though what is measured is subjective. For example, a phenomenologist may score a person's self-references in a series of therapeutic interviews according to whether they are predominantly positive, negative, ambivalent, or ambiguous. He is interested in measuring any change in self-evaluation that may occur during the therapy, and of course if he finds the change toward a positive self-image he will conclude that the therapy has been successful.

Another phenomenological type of assessment is known as the "semantic differential." The subject is asked to rate a number of concepts on a series of 7-point polar-adjective scales. The 7 points are not defined but are understood as gradations between two extremes. For example, one might rate "self," "mother," "father," and several other concepts on such scales as strong-weak, masculine-feminine, active-passive. The test opens the door to the person's subjective state and tells the examiner quite a lot about how the subject thinks.

A less specific but still revealing phenomenological key to personality is nonverbal communication. Eye contact, posture, hand movements—all give the perceptive and knowledgeable examiner strong clues about the person's self-image.

A final attempt at examining the inner life is the use of "consciousness-expanding" drugs, such as LSD-25 and psilocybin. There has been a good deal of speculation about both the effectiveness and the harmfulness of such drugs, and not very much is known about either (see Chapter 9). Though a number of people have reported beneficial subjective results, drugs tend to be used less and less frequently because of their suspected harmfulness.

Personality Inventories— Psychometric Methods

In our discussion of intelligence and other ability tests, we have already talked about psychometric methods, which include the IQ tests, the vocational interest and aptitude tests, and many of the personality tests that we will talk about here. Psychometric methods attempt to measure individual differences on particular traits. They are the primary assessment techniques of the type and trait personality theorists (see Chapter 12).

psychometric methods

Personality inventories are based on psychometric methods. They can assess either one trait, a wide range of traits, or a range of variables known to characterize certain personality types. For many of the single-trait inventories, the scoring is direct and simple: the number of yeses is taken as the measure of the amount of the trait being assessed. The broader inventories are more complicated to score. A response for one item must be correlated with those for other items assessing the same trait within the total personality.

Personality inventories were developed following the introduction of intelligence tests. Those who devised them hoped to be able to measure traits in standardized ways, much as intelligence was being measured. But personality traits proved far more difficult to isolate and to test. They have to be more precisely defined and related, and test items have to be more carefully tailored. Two methods aimed at overcoming these difficulties of design have been to devise empirical constructs and to find intercorrelations among the items by cluster and factor analysis, which are sophisticated statistical procedures.

empirical construct

criterion group

Empirical Construct An empirical construct is derived by testing many items repeatedly with criterion groups known to exhibit various degrees of specific traits or personality disorders. Items shown to correlate highly with either strong or weak displays of a trait are retained for the final test. The responses of those who are later tested are scored on scales based on the responses of the criterion group.

The most widely studied personality inventory constructed empirically is the Minnesota Multiphasic Personality Inventory (MMPI). It is a self-rating test designed originally to assess for 10 psychiatric disorders, including depression, paranoia, hypochondria, hysteria, and schizophrenia. Some of the newer scales that have been developed permit the test to be used as an assessment of personality type among "normal" people. The MMPI has been used extensively with hospitalized patients and with the population at large—students, employees, delinquents.

The MMPI includes some 500 statements to which the respondent must answer *true* or *false*. The items deal with attitudes and emotional adjustments and reactions, as well as with bodily complaints and other topics that could disclose symptoms of pathological conditions. Sometimes the statements are quite clear about what they are assessing. More often they are indirect. Some are short, some long, some general, some specific. Typical MMPI items are:

I am easily awakened by noise.
I get mad easily and then get over it soon.
What others think of me doesn't bother me.
I am sure I am being talked about.
I wish I could be happy as others seem to be.

Endorsement of a statement indicates that the person may be suffering from symptoms of the illness it is designed to measure, especially if he endorses most of the other items on that scale.

Scoring, as expected, is based on an absolute scale. A respondent's score in depression, for example, is scaled against the test results from criterion groups of known depressives. The MMPI with its great variety of questions has provided material for innumerable scales and many more are still being constructed. These scales have been collated and coded and are quickly available for comparison purposes and other information. The MMPI has also proved invaluable as a model and source for designing other personality inventories.

Factor Analysis Factor analysis is a mathematical method used by psychologists to attempt to simplify the interpretation of trait assessment procedures. It is a means of grouping together answers that are correlated into a single "factor." On 10 questionnaires consisting of 50 items each, presumably not every item indicates a different trait or factor. Some, even within a single questionnaire, are related to others. If we ask 20 people to answer the 10 questionnaires, then we have 10,000 items to submit to factor analysis, which may tell us that in fact our battery of 10 tests is assessing a much smaller or perhaps larger number of factors, or traits.

Factor analysis is not a means of arriving at any kind of truth except statistical relationships. When test responses are reduced to a number of factors, we have learned that the items within each factor are related or correlated and the items in different factors are not correlated. This information is useful in refining the traits being measured. It permits the test-maker to select items that relate to each other in ways that he wants. Further, it helps him identify what

factor analysis

 Factor Analysis

If one assumes, as do trait and type psychologists, that certain basic personality dimensions are common to all people and that personality is best described in terms of these dimensions, then an immediate task will be to determine just what these basic dimensions of personality are. A technique that has been widely employed in recent times in attempts to accomplish this task is *factor analysis,* a mathematical technique that enables one to isolate from a wide array of test results a relatively small set of variables that many tests appear to be measuring in common.

How is factor analysis used to derive a set of personality dimensions? First, it is necessary to decide on a set of personality measures that are likely to reveal the relevant features of personality. To be as certain as possible that no crucial attributes are missed, this battery of measures must be made as comprehensive as possible; the measures must reveal a broad spectrum of attitudes, feelings, beliefs, motives, values, and physical and psychological modes of responding to many situations. These measures would be administered to a sample group of people, and for each person tested the information obtained would be recorded as a battery of numerical test scores.

Now among the many different sets of test scores thus obtained, some will be *correlated,* either *positively* or *negatively,* with others. Two sets of test scores are positively correlated if high scores on one of the tests tend to be regularly associated with high scores on the other; they are negatively correlated if high scores on one are regularly associated with low scores on the other. If two tests are *perfectly* correlated, the score on one *exactly predicts* the score on the other, but perfect correlation between tests rarely occurs in real life, at least not in the domain of the social sciences. From the correlations that are obtained, it is possible to estimate the *probable* score on one test from the score on the other. The stronger the correlation between two tests, the more dependably this estimate can be made. With a moment's thought you will see that if two tests are strongly correlated, it is not necessary to give both tests, since the score on either one will predict the score on the other. Similarly, if 10 tests are strongly correlated, then any one of them will predict the scores on the other nine.

Returning to the battery of personality test scores we have obtained, some will be correlated with others. Envision inspecting a matrix of all the correlations existing between the various sets of tests and *sorting the total battery of test scores into clearly correlated groups.* This sorting procedure is a simple *cluster factor analysis* by the *inspection method.* Each of the correlated groups formed constitutes one *factor,* and the tests in each group can be assumed to measure some *common underlying attribute* in personality. By considering the nature of the correlated groups of tests, a judgment as to the nature of that underlying attribute can be made and a name can be assigned to the attribute. Each personality factor thus labeled could then be regarded as a fundamental personality dimension. Having completed the cluster analysis, and labeled each of the factors, one might as a final step pick a representative test from each of the correlated groups to serve as a measure of that particular factor; a personality profile can then be obtained by administering this select group of tests, rather than the entire battery originally used.

Unfortunately, such a simple method of cluster analysis is not likely to be practical. In the original battery of tests many, and probably most, will turn out to be a measure of *several different factors* at once. That is to say, many of the tests will belong to various degrees simultaneously to several different groups, and the pattern of correlations obtained among the multitude of tests administered will be highly complex and not divisible into clear groups in any obvious fashion. In this situation, it becomes necessary to resort to one of several complex mathematical procedures designed to extract from the overall pattern of correlations the *major sources of variability,* which, by acting simultaneously on many different tests, are causing those tests to correlate in part with each other. The technique of *factor analysis* consists of these complex procedures.

The outcome of a factor analysis is a set of hypothetical *factors,* each of which consists of a source of variability that is acting in common on many of the administered tests, and a set of numerical values indicating the extent to which the score on each of the tests appears to be determined by each of these factors; these values are said to show the *loading* of each test on each factor. The factors thus obtained may be interpreted, in the manner previously described, as the various dimensions of personality, and tests that load almost exclusively on one particular factor may be used as relatively pure measures of those personality dimensions.

the separate traits might be, though in this he obviously will be affected by the items he selected in the first place to subject to factor analysis.

Problems with Psychometric Tests Set patterns of test behavior, we have seen, are a continuing difficulty in psychometric personality research. Subjects frequently fall into patterns, called response sets, of always agreeing, or always disagreeing, or of having no opinion. Checks must therefore he made to ascertain whether a subject is answering each item in relation to its content or is just being positive or negative. Test-makers also have to beware of respondents who always mark answers on the right or left side of an answer sheet. This can be

 Test Anxiety

Many students have had occasion to say, "If I hadn't been so nervous, I could have done better on that exam." But what objective evidence is there that anxiety actually can interfere with good performance on a test? Is it possible for anxiety actually to improve a person's test performance?

S. B. Sarason and his co-workers addressed themselves to these questions in the 1950s. They hypothesized that anxiety could have either a *facilitating* or a *debilitating* effect on test performance. More specifically, they hypothesized that when anxiety simply arouses the test-taker and increases his drive, it will result in an improved test performance. However, when anxiety evokes a set of responses that are likely to interfere and compete with the test-taking behavior, it will have a disruptive effect and result in a poorer test score.

To test these hypotheses, Sarason developed a questionnaire he called the Test Anxiety Scale (TAS), which was designed to measure the degree to which test situations evoked anxiety responses that were likely to interfere with efficient test taking (Sarason and Mandler, 1952). The items on this questionnaire are of the following nature.

[Before a test] how often do you think of ways of avoiding the test?
While taking a course exam, to what extent do you worry?

Subjects scoring high on the questionnaire were taken to be persons who suffered from debilitating anxiety symptoms in test situations; subjects scoring low were assumed to be those for whom anxiety had a primarily facilitating effect. In an attempt to check the validity of the TAS as a measure of debilitating anxiety, Mandler and Sarason (1952) observed subjects as they worked on a complex task and noted various task-irrelevant behaviors characteristic of anxiety, such as perspiration, excessive movements, and inappropriate laughter and exclamations. They found that subjects scoring high on the TAS were those who tended to manifest such symptoms.

In a subsequent experiment (Sarason, Mandler, and Craighill, 1952), subjects who had been tested on the TAS were given a stylus maze task to perform. One group of subjects was given an "ego-involving" (EI) set of instructions in which they were told that the task was an intelligence test; a second group of subjects was given a "non-ego-involving" (NEI) set of instructions in which they were told that the task was *not* an intelligence test. It was assumed that the EI subjects would be more likely to feel anxiety about their performance on the task than the NEI subjects. Among subjects who had rated high on the TAS, those given the ego-involving instructions performed worse than those who had been given the non-ego-involving instructions. Among subjects who had rated low on the TAS, the reverse was true. The experimental hypotheses cited above were thus supported: under conditions designed to produce anxiety subjects performed either better or worse than under conditions designed not to produce anxiety, depending on whether or not they reported having task-irrelevent anxiety symptoms. As might be expected from the experimental hypotheses, the difference between high TAS scoring subjects and low TAS scoring subjects was greatest under high anxiety conditions, when low TAS subjects performed significantly better than high TAS subjects.

Sarason and his co-workers postulate two forms of anxiety, facilitating and debilitating, but the TAS was designed to measure only the latter. They assumed that subjects scoring low on the TAS would be subject only to anxiety of the facilitating kind and, moreover, that *subjects scoring high on the TAS would not be in any way facilitated by anxiety.* Alpert and Haber (1960) objected to this assumption, arguing that in a single subject *both facilitating and debilitating* anxiety might occur. They therefore developed a questionnaire, the Achievement Anxiety Test (AAT), which is composed of two parts, one designed to test for facilitative anxiety and the other for debilitative anxiety.

Some sample items from the facilitating anxiety scale (AAT+) are:

Nervousness while taking a test helps me to do better.
I work most effectively under pressure, as when the task is very important.

Some sample items from the debilitating anxiety scale (AAT−) are:

Time pressure on an exam causes me to do worse than the rest of the group under similar conditions.
I find my mind goes blank at the beginning of an exam, and it takes me a few minutes before I can function.

For each item, persons filling out the questionnaire are required to indicate whether or not the item is true of them.

To determine whether these two test scales appeared to be valid measures of facilitating and debilitating anxiety, Alpert and Haber correlated the grade point averages (GPA) of a number of college freshmen with their scores on these two scales. It was found, as anticipated, that the AAT− scale correlated negatively with the GPA and that the AAT+ scale correlated positively with the TAS. Finally, combining the two AAT scales produced a joint anxiety measure that correlated significantly better with the GPA than did either scale of the AAT alone, suggesting that the two scales were testing different traits, and were not merely the opposites of the same thing.

detected if the statements are carefully worded and arranged so that the most desirable answers fall randomly into both columns.

Other behavior patterns of test-takers are a reflection of response style as well as of response sets. Because many people will lie to avoid social disapproval, scores on tests like the MMPI may relfect, more than anything else, the respondent's willingness to confess socially undesirable qualities. Subjects may distort their answers in both directions. Some people, because they fear disapproval, will always give what seems to them the most desirable answer; others, because they have an extremely poor opinion of themselves—or sometimes of "society"—will always give what they think is the least desirable answer. Complicating this matter is the fact that even to tell the truth about oneself, in the case of idiosyncratic behavior, requires a willingness to confess socially undesirable qualities.

Situational Tests

situational test

Situational testing involves observing, recording, and analyzing behavior responses in standardized contexts that resemble real-life settings. The types of behavior it measures include verbal and nonverbal as well as physiological changes. Variously referred to as behavior sampling, behavior observation, and behavioral assessment, it is the method most consistent with the ideas of behaviorists and social learning theorists, such as Albert Bandura, who stress the role of subject observation in behavior analysis.

In a situational test, the subject should be unaware of being observed. In fact, as far as possible he should not even realize that he is being tested or know for what he is being assessed, since such knowledge can inhibit or change his natural responses. A test can be administered to one person alone or to groups when the investigator is interested in examining interpersonal reactions. Many of the standard tests are designed to measure response in stress situations. And some work has been done to estimate the effects of stress conditions in normal living patterns. Marriage, for example, is a stress situation requiring great behavior changes and personality adjustments. What then is the correlation between divorce rates and the stress that often accompanies the early period of marriage?

A recent study (Cronbach, 1970) calculated that situational tests are successful in predicting job success when three conditions exist. First, a candidate's situational behavior should be rated by peers, as opposed to judges from outside the job setting who know less about the job requirements. Second, tests are best when conditions of the performance test replicate real-life conditions, that is, when the task assigned is similar to the work the job would require and the situation repeats most of the conditions of the work situation. And third, the tests prove most valid when the observers have fully assessed the psychological demands of the job.

Examples of Situational Tests Situational testing is predicated on the belief that behavior in structured situations will resemble behavior in actual situations. Early work based on this assumption attempted to measure honesty (MacKinnon, 1938). Subjects were instructed to solve several problems without using the answer books provided them. Observers noted the extent of cheating when the subjects thought they were alone.

During World War II, the Office of Strategic Services developed situational tests for assessing potential candidates for critical and dangerous assignments. Of the different measures used in a short period of intensive evaluation, the construction test was the most unusual. A subject was assigned a construction task, such as building a bridge in simulated field conditions. As part of the experiment, a group of workers under the subject's supervision had been instructed to frustrate his efforts in several ways. His behavior in these stress conditions was observed and analyzed to determine his suitability for OSS work. Though the subject didn't know it, what he was being tested for was not his ability to build a bridge, but his ability to cope with stress conditions.

A test designed to measure fear of snakes used subjects who expressed fear of snakes (Lana and Lazovik, 1963). The subjects first were requested to look into a topless case containing a large but nonpoisonous black snake. Those who did this were instructed to touch the snake, then to pick it up. Subjects were scored on their progressive reactions to each step of the experiment. In Chapter 12, we mentioned similar work done with children who were afraid of dogs. Scores indicating least fear were given to the children who proceeded step by step until they climbed into the dog's pen and played with the animal. This kind of situational test has been used, according to the principles of behavioral conditioning, to overcome specific fears as well as to assess their strength.

Criticisms of Situational Tests Evaluations have indicated that situational techniques are not highly reliable. Some theorists attribute the difficulty to faulty theories about personality. Predictions based on situational tests assume that behavior is consistent over time and independent of minor variables in the situation. In this view an honest person is always honest—even when you give him the answer book, make him think he is not being observed, and tell him his course grade depends on the test he is taking. Those who disagree say that behavior is, instead, "situation specific," that it varies with situational changes. Behavior, for example, can be modified by the personalities of other people involved in a test, both subjects and examiners. Place, time, physical conditions that change can also have considerable impact on behavioral response.

Accordingly, situational tests are best used to assess present behavior, rather than to predict future behavior, or to isolate the variables responsible for behavior change. Suppose we want to identify the situational variables that affect Jane's studying behavior, for example. We may vary the amount and kinds of noises in her studying environment, the material she must study, the ventilation in the room, the neatness and attractiveness of things in the room, the position of her desk (even her use of it), and so on, until we find the optimal conditions for her studying.

Projective Techniques

Personality theorists and test administrators who follow the psychoanalytic tra- projective
technique
dition of Freud frequently use projective techniques as major procedures for
diagnosis and therapy. Projective procedures are far less structured than psychometric methods. The subject is not limited to prescribed answers, but is asked
to interpret freely what he sees. Free association of this nature is thought to
reveal deeper and more complex dimensions of personality, on the theory that
the subject projects into the stimulus material his needs and attitudes. The
rationale underlying projective approaches reflects the psychoanalytic theory of
behavior with its emphasis on unconscious motivation and the notion of a
central unchanging personality organization.

Projective techniques tend to pose ambiguous and unobvious tasks.
In this manner the clinician hopes to tap aspects of the subject's personality
that the subject himself deems unacceptable and therefore must not be aware
that he is revealing. The tests often evoke seemingly extraneous ideas, which are
taken as clues to unconscious perceptions.

In administering projective tests, it is important to record the emotional
reaction of the person being assessed. The tester notes whether or not the subject clearly avoids responses, whether he seems anxious upon presentation of
the test stimulus, and whether his responses are disrupted. Ideally, fixed meanings are not attached to the test stimuli. There is a difference between a creative
interpretation of test materials and a reaction that stems from mobilization of
defenses against an anxiety-arousing stimulus; the latter symbolizes some underlying repressed conflict. This difference is ascertained by examination of the
subject's emotional reaction. The results of projective tests are not merely translated; they must be interpreted in light of the patient's situation—his immediate
context.

Projective techniques have the advantage over more structured tests in
allowing the respondent the opportunity to qualify and refine answers. But at
the same time they are more liable to rater bias, even when objective measurements are available. The clinician scoring these tests must be well trained and
experienced, and even then the margin for error is considerable.

The two most popular projective tests are the Rorschach Inkblot Test and
the Thematic Apperception Test (TAT). The Rorschach, among the oldest of the
projective techniques, was published in 1921 by the Swiss psychiatrist Hermann
Rorschach. The TAT was developed in the mid-1930s by researchers at Harvard
(Morgan and Murray, 1935).

The Rorschach Inkblot Test The Rorschach test uses 10 cards, each carry- Rorschach test
ing a symmetrical inkblot, sometimes in color. Because they vary in complexity,
some being more difficult for the subject to organize perceptually, the cards are
administered in an arranged order. The subject is instructed to describe everything he sees in each inkblot, either in parts or as a whole.

Rorschach responses are scored on several counts. Content analysis considers the form of the projections—whether the subject tends to see human

Scoring the Rorschach

Scoring the Rorschach is a somewhat standardized but quite intricate process. The first judgment category used is concerned with what area of the blot the subject gives his attention to—the whole blot or parts of it. Subjects who react to the whole figure as a unit—in Rorschach terminology, instant whole—are scored W. Typical W responses to the first Rorschach blot, which resembles Fig. 13.2, are "bat" and "butterfly."

Fig. 13.2 Inkblot similar to one used in the Rorschach Test.

A subject who responds to some select portion of the entire figure is scored D, detail, or Dd, rare detail. D responses are readily identifiable; they relate to fairly prominent portions of each blot. Some of these include for the first blot seeing the center as a woman's body, seeing the side as a witch or bear, seeing the upper third of the center as a crab. D's are typically larger than the less frequently produced Dd's. Fairly typical Dd responses to the first blot are to see the uppermost details as heads, to see the lower side as a woman's head, to see the bottom projection as feet.

Such a scoring category is an attempt to assess organizational activity. The number of W responses is an index of the energy at the subject's disposal for the organizational drive. Other varieties of organizational activity are indicated by adjacent details and distant details. An example of an adjacent detail: For the first blot if a subject perceived two wolves with sticks in their paws, the sticks would be an adjacent detail.

Another category on which responses are scored is perception of movement. Rorschach has interpreted the response as being, on one level, a reproduction of movement or activity the subject carries in his mental life. Movement associations are scored M, whereas forms perceived without activity or signs of life are scored F. M responses are seen as representing wish-fulfilling activities, the fibers of our fantasy life. Perceptions of human body parts in motion—lips kissing, teeth biting, arms and legs in movement, the eyes or face expressing emotion, and rarely the male genital in erection or in the process of penetrating a vagina—are scored as movement. Scores of M may also be given for interaction between two perceived forms, as in the perception of two birds talking, or a lobster's claw tickling the back of a man's neck. Perception of emotion is also scored in this category; for example, someone might see a caterpillar with a sense of humor smiling at him. The attribution of human activity to animals is scored M, whereas behavior not anatomically available to humans, such as flying, might be given an F score.

Color perceptions are scored primarily in terms of their relationship to form perception. It is of special concern to determine whether color contributes to the perception of form. Scores are C (color without form), CF (color dominant over form), FC (form dominant over color).

A 21-year-old schizoid male made the following responses to Rorschach Plate I:

1. A woman with a toad head conducting an orchestra, with a see-through dress.
2. Two large-nosed devil-like [female] figures with warts on their lips. Their necks have been cut and are dripping blood.
3. A man with nose, hat, and chin, scary and suspicious looking.

Typical responses made by a 24-year-old normal male to the same plate are:

1. A bat.
2. An angel in the middle.
3. Two wings on either side.

or animal figures, imaginary characters, or objects. Location of what is seen is another factor of response style. Where on the cards does the subject focus? Does he generally see the cards as assemblages of separate parts or as a whole? The examiner can also determine what physical aspects of the stimuli the subject stresses—shape, color, movement, shading, or texture. Originality of response is still another source of information.

The frequency of certain kinds of responses is used as an index for diagnosis, since frequency is equated with tendency. Certain interpretations of Rorschach scores have become fairly standardized over the half century of the test's wide use. Perceiving the inkblots as a whole is interpreted as a tendency toward abstraction, while concentration on small parts indicates preoccupation with details. Color and movement are related to emotional behavior: a predominance of color answers is seen to show a tendency toward uncontrollable emotionality, and high movement scores are said to signal introversion.

Such scoring standards, however, do not eliminate the problems the clinician faces in correlating the scores from all the cards to form an overall estimation of personality patterns, conflicts, and disorders. Thus, the same test results can elicit quite different interpretations from different examiners.

The Thematic Apperception Test (TAT) Apperception is conscious perception, the inclination to see something new in a way that is unique to one's personal experience. The TAT, therefore, tests for themes a person perceives in

Henry A. Murray

Thematic Apperception Test (TAT)

Fig. 13.3 Reprinted by permission of the publishers from Henry A. Murray, *Thematic Apperception Test.* Cambridge, Mass.: Harvard University Press, Copyright 1943 by the President and Fellows of Harvard College, 1971, by Henry A. Murray.

Terry's story: The young man has decided to enter the army and fight in the war. But he realizes he may never come back, as his two brothers were lost before him. He can only think of his mother now, and her weariness with the war. He can remember her wrinkled face and slouched shoulders as she mourns her dead sons. But he knows he must fight and die. Her face will remain with him to the grave.

Susan's story: The old lady is the younger lady's great aunt, who has come to visit. The aunt has just told her niece that she is going to live with her and her family because the woman she was living with just died, and she has no place to go. The young woman is upset by this because they don't have enough room. She tries to explain this, but her aunt does not seem to understand. She finally convinces her it would be best to live with another relative who has a big house.

ambiguous pictures and the way the themes are related to his personality needs, such as the need for affiliation, achievement, autonomy, or understanding. The TAT consists of several sets of cards, each set applicable to different groups of subjects—that is, young or adult, male or female groups. Each card contains a simple scene, neutral in content and context. The subject is requested to tell a story about each picture, including the events that have led up to the moment of the picture, what is happening at the moment illustrated, how the characters are feeling, and what will happen later. It is expected, as in the Rorschach test, that the subject will project himself into the stimulus material and develop stories that manifest his own self-conception, emotional conflicts, and pathologies. Fig. 13.3 shows a TAT card with subject responses.

TAT responses are scored according to predominant themes and their frequency. Several more objective scales have been constructed, such as the one

Experimental Uses of the TAT

The TAT is used not only for assessment purposes, but very often in research. Some of the best known research in this area is that done in the use of the TAT to measure needs like achievement, affiliation, and power.

Generally the procedure calls for separating two groups of subjects based on their TAT responses on some variable (such as need achievement.) Predictions are then made as to how a subject should act if he indeed was a high need achiever. The subjects are then thrown into a situation where this need is aroused and their behavior is observed.

The TAT is also used to measure the existence of a need as a result of some experimental manipulations. Thus, for example, in some research carried out by Festinger to test the effects of cognitive dissonance (see Chapter 14) on hunger, thirst, and pain wherein some subjects would be expected to feel more (or less) hunger, thirst or pain than others, the TAT is used to determine whether this is indeed so. Often the TAT shows that a subject reporting no hunger when asked, "Are you hungry?" may show himself to be quite hungry by his TAT responses.

The TAT may also be used as an adjunct to an experiment manipulation. For example, if an experimenter wants to look at the effect of frustration on behavior, he may introduce manipulation designed to frustrate his subject. He may, however, be more certain that his manipulations worked if the subject's TAT responses show frustration as being highly salient in his stories.

The TAT may thus be used both as a check or a measure of the independent variable and a check on the effects of the independent variable or the dependent variable.

for achievement (McClelland, 1953). Besides recurrent themes, scales compute such other response elements as the characteristics ascribed to the people in the stories, the way in which the subject resolves the outcome of the story situations, and the extent and type of fantasy imagery. The best of the scales then correlate these elements, according to highly detailed and objective procedures, with various personality traits. The TAT is a widely used instrument of assessment. In testing a single individual it is most meaningfully used in combination with other procedures, such as psychometric tests and the clinical interview. In the study of groups, it has provided valuable data related to such broad variables as age, sex, ethnic and cultural background, economic status, and social orientation.

Like the Rorschach, however, the TAT does not always have very high score reliability and different scorers are likely to disagree about its interpretation. In addition to problems regarding the reliability of projective test evaluations across different examiners, there are also problems concerning their validity—that is, the extent to which evaluations of patients based on these techniques agree with evaluations based on other techniques. Silverman (1959) gave a group of clinicians the results from a Rorschach, a TAT, and several other projective tests for a number of psychiatric patients. On the basis of this information, they were asked to evaluate the patients by means of a Q sort. They sorted a deck of cards containing various descriptive statements into two piles, one applicable to a particular patient and one not applicable. Their Q sorts were compared with Q sorts provided by the patient's therapists. With respect to defenses, diagnoses and symptoms, character traits, and a number of other scoring categories, little evidence could be found of successful prediction of the patients' traits from the projective tests. The relatively small correlations that did occur between the clinicians' appraisals and those of the therapists were further reduced when the "Barnum effect," a tendency to ascribe to particular persons very general characteristics widely applicable to people in general, was controlled for. Such findings cast serious doubt on the diagnostic value of projective techniques such as the Rorschach and the TAT, but despite this fact, they continue to be widely employed.

INTERPRETING PERSONALITY DATA

The preceding sections have dealt with numerous methods of collecting data about personality. We have suggested that no one of them has proved adequate by itself for appraisal and prediction. Yet each of them has shown sufficient validity to be considered a potential source of information. An understanding of these limitations, reinforced by a public outcry in the past few decades against the use and misuse of single personality assessments, has convinced most psychologists of the necessity to use several techniques in combination, that is, to use batteries of tests.

Statistical versus Philosophical Approach

Having thus amassed a large amount of information about a subject or group of subjects, how does the psychologist proceed to arrange and interpret it for the purposes of diagnosing disorders and predicting behavior? His first step is to choose between the two general approaches available—the statistical or empirical approach and the philosophical or intuitive approach.

The psychologist using a statistical approach relies on precise observations and methods of analysis based on accepted definitions in proceeding toward an objective interpretation, often with the aid of computer analysis. Statistical interpretation is empirical inasmuch as it observes and mathematically measures present behavior as a means of predicting future behavior or of analyzing personality factors.

A psychologist approaching test results philosophically, on the other hand, reviews them in terms of his particular theories, concepts, and intuitions to derive an interpretation of the total personality. His observations rest on an underlying belief that each person has an overall value structure or philosophy of life that shapes and unifies him. A classic example of this approach is seen in the work of Eduard Spranger (1928), who classified people into six dominant value-personality types: theoretical, economic, aesthetic, social, political, and religious. A person can thus be typed according to the value that predominates in him. Spranger's theory generated an inventory of attitudes and preferences called the Study of Values (Allport, Vernon, and Lindzey, 1960), which measures the incidence of these six values, and their importance to personality.

Philosophical interpretation, obviously, tends to be more based in subjective evaluation and inference than statistical analysis. For example, a psychologist who depends on intuition and personal theory in studying a subject for pathological problems may talk to his subject repeatedly and, without the benefit of objective assessment, judge him as not deviant. The examiner's observations might lead him to determine that problems the person faces are those faced by many normal people; although perhaps eccentric, the subject is lucid and sane. But another psychologist viewing the same person may administer tests on which we know that people who are pathological perform in certain ways, that, for instance, hundreds of hospitalized schizophrenics answer specific items in a distinct manner. The results of the subject's testing, correlated with these sample or criterion answers, might reveal schizophrenic or other pathological tendencies not detected in the interviews. Such tests are relatively quick, economical, and objective. And the subjective standards and morals of the examiner are far less likely to color the final scoring.

Studies have been made to evaluate the superiority of one approach over the other as a more reliable predictor. Gough (1962), in a review of the evidence he had collected, favored the statistical approach as being more often correct, although he and others admit that more evaluation is needed for a definitive conclusion. What is perhaps more meaningful, however, than establishing such a comparative rating of the two approaches is to recognize the increased usefulness of both in combination. For just as intuitive assessments are more valuable tools when supported by objective measures, so statistical results should be weighed against the psychologist's intuitive perception of less measurable factors that can influence behavior.

Status of Psychological Assessment

Psychological assessment has come under widespread attack from both public and professional critics. The public has been especially concerned about ethical matters, such as the invasion of privacy these tests might constitute and, especially in the case of ability tests, their unfairness to minority culture groups. Critics in the field have pointed to the questionable reliability of assessment data for predicting behavior in specific nontest situations. Resolving such criticisms is a complex problem that entails redefinition of assessment goals and refining of methods. It also requires that the public be educated to understand the advantages of assessment procedures in helping people to pursue realistic goals and to find recognition and treatment of their psychopathological problems. Of course, they must also understand the limitations of the tests; none of them are perfectly reliable or valid, and any of them used alone, or without reference to the opinion of competent judges, can be extremely misleading.

At best, assessment provides limited predictors. Its success has been shown to be slightly better than chance would predict, which probably indicates that the techniques are indeed measuring real characteristics but that definitional concepts and methods of testing are not yet precise enough. At this point, assessment can be ranked as most successful when used for experimental research—that is, as a means of generating theories of personality and behavior—but less so when used for the diagnosis of disorders and the prediction of behavior or of success of therapy.

Assessment, nonetheless, provides one of the most valuable quantitative operations available to psychology at the present, and as an aid to research, it has become essential to the field. First, assessment enables psychologists to formulate operational definitions or objectives. Second, it furnishes a means of delineating the relevant processes involved in behavior. Tests that ascertain to some extent who is, for example, more intelligent, more stable, or more imaginative are tools psychologists employ in studying the processes of these specific behaviors in selected individuals.

Assessment, third, enables psychologists to broaden their theoretical concepts and perspectives. Theorizing, indeed, goes hand in hand with assessment, each stimulating the other. Seen this way, assessment is more than a mere tool for classification. It requires thorough understanding of the theoretical nature of the characteristics being studied. And theory, for its part, must go beyond generalized abstraction and relate the concrete raw material supplied by assessment to its concepts. A theory of intelligence, for example, might begin with the concept that intelligence consists of some large number of both verbal and nonverbal skills. But a factor analysis of performance on intelligence tests, based on many different tests administered to a large number of culturally diverse people over a considerable period of time, may reveal that the skills being tested define only a small number of independent factors. Theories of intelligence are accordingly modified, and attention is now turned toward defining the intellective skills more precisely. Some theorists may remain convinced that intelligence includes more, or fewer, than the number of factors produced by the factor analysis and may attempt to devise valid tests that reliably measure the skills they have in mind. When, and if, they produce such tests, and their tests prove to be better able than others to predict "intelligent behavior" (according to a generally agreed upon definition), we have not only a superior *measure* of intelligence but also a better *theory* of intelligence.

And so, there is a great demand for better tests to prove or disprove the continuous outpouring of theories. It is almost axiomatic to say that new assessment techniques designed for new theories will establish new horizons in the understanding of human characteristics and behavior. Assessment, thus, is an area of constant change and growth, and its achievements must be evaluated and re-evaluated again and again.

SUMMARY

Psychological assessment is the measurement and evaluation of human characteristics and behavior. It is used in career advisement, in detection and diagnosis of psychological abnormalities, in research, and in the formation of theories.

Criteria for establishing the worth of an assessment procedure are *reliability* and *validity*. A test is reliable if it consistently produces the same result, if all parts of it test for the same thing, and if all qualified users consistently interpret it similarly. A test is valid if it truly measures what it sets out to measure.

Tests that are otherwise reliable and valid are subject to the hazards of obsolescence and bias, especially cultural bias. Culture-fair tests attempt to minimize cultural bias by reducing verbal content to a minimum. Occasionally tests that are otherwise valid are invalidated by tendencies on the part of test-takers to respond in certain ways, for example, to put themselves in a socially desirable light.

Intelligence is generally measured by obtaining an intelligence quotient or IQ. This is the ratio of the subject's mental age to his chronological age, multiplied by 100. Intelligence tests measure both verbal and nonverbal abilities, which, at least in grade-school children, are highly correlated and therefore together are considered to indicate general intelligence. For teen-age children and adults, the concept of general intelligence is less useful.

Today mental retardation is not judged solely by poor performance on intelligence tests, or even in school, but also by poor adaptation. With appropriate schooling, many people who score very low on IQ tests are able to achieve a satisfactory life adjustment.

In the case of genius, or outstanding achievement, studies indicate that high IQ is a necessary but not sufficient condition for it. Gifted children are likely to come from successful, contented parents and to be superior in physical, personality, and intellectual development.

Tests of creativity look for nonidiosyncratic uniqueness. Children who are very high in creativity are also high in intelligence; their academic achievement is usually equal to that of children who attain higher IQ scores but lower creativity ratings.

Individual differences make it difficult to estimate the relationship of IQ to age. Most likely, however, if the intellectual environment is stimulating IQ continues to grow until about age 35. In the absence of stimulation it may begin to decline at age 14. It usually declines after age 50 (though certain mental abilities may remain stronger than others).

Examination of the relationship between IQ and race has centered on the relative contributions to intelligence of heredity and environment. Jensen's recent argument that heredity accounts for most of measured IQ, with its implication that IQ is a function of race, has sparked widespread controversy. Many psychologists maintain that intelligence is the result of complex interactions between heredity and environment; others say it may be inherited, but if so, racial peculiarities are due to selective choice of mates rather than to innate genetic differences.

Aptitude tests assess specific talents and potential abilities. They are used in vocational counseling and recruitment,for example. The Strong Vocational Interest Blank measures potential ability to perform certain tasks on the basis of present abilities and interests.

A wide variety of techinques, some highly controlled, others far less structured, are used to derive data about personality. Several of these methods represent particular psychological orientations, while others reflect a combination of theoretical views. Sources of information about personality are ratings by trained observers; ratings by peers and family; and self-ratings. All measures of personality are subject to errors imposed by the difficulties of establishing test reliability and validity.

The interview, either structured or open-ended, is a frequently used method of personality appraisal. Interview results are usually indicated on rating scales, which ask the interviewer to rate the subject on a number of traits according to whether he is high, low, or at one of several intermediate points in the trait. The Q-sort technique is a highly adaptable and useful rating procedure.

Relative rating scales render a subject's position on a given trait with respect to others with whom he is compared. Absolute scales render his position with respect to a group of people carefully selected to include all degrees of the trait in question.

Sometimes a person is asked to rate himself on one or more rating scales. Self-ratings are relatively good predictors of future behavior, particularly of success or failure in a particular job.

Personality inventories ask subjects to respond to printed items selected either empirically or by factor analysis. Empirically constructed inventories, such as the Minnesota Multiphasic Personality Inventory (MMPI), consist of items with known correlations to the trait in question. Inventories constructed by factor analysis attempt to set a limit on the number of traits that contribute to personality. To counteract the tendency to respond to questionnaires in a set pattern, especially to choose only socially acceptable answers, some procedures offer only equally desirable responses.

Another kind of personality test is the situational test, in which a person is observed in a natural context. Such a test might be used to determine how a job applicant behaves in a situation analogous to the actual work situation or to measure a specific fear. Situational tests have been more successful in assessing present behavior than in predicting future behavior.

Projective assessment techniques attempt to tap the unconscious by asking the subject to interpret ambiguous stimuli, on the theory that he will project his innermost needs and attitudes into the stimulus materials. The Rorschach inkblot test asks the subject to interpret 10 inkblots, and the Thematic Apperception Test asks for stories suggested by a series of pictures. Projective tests tend to yield low levels of correlation.

In general, no one kind of personality test should be used in exclusion of others. The best assessments are based on a battery of representative tests. Similarly, the collection of data obtained should be viewed from two points of view: the statistical, empirical view and the philosophical, intuitive view.

Psychological assessment is under broad attack today for its frequent use of procedures of questionable reliability and validity. Yet the measures it employs are the best available, and as an aid to psychological research, it is invaluable. It helps in the formulation of definitions, the delineation of behavioral processes, and the evolution of theories.

Suggested Readings

Burdock, E. I., and A. S. Hadest, *Structured Clinical Interviews.* New York, Springer, 1969.
An analysis of how interviews are conducted and their outcomes evaluated.

Cheever, John, *The Wapshot Chronicle.* New York, Harper & Row, 1957.
The hero of Cheever's novel has to face a battery of baffling psychological tests when he applies for a job.

Crow, Lester D., Walter I. Murray, and Hugh H. Smythe, *Educating the Disadvantaged Child: Principles and Programs.* New York, David McKay, 1966.

Garcia, John, "IQ: The Conspiracy," *Psychology Today,* September 1972.
A critical report on some of the biases inherent in standardized IQ tests and the devastating effects of the misuse of IQ data.

Gross, Martin, *The Brain Watchers.* New York, Random House, 1962.
A sharp attack on practically all kinds of tests and testing on several grounds.

Grost, A., *Genius in Residence.* Englewood Cliffs, N.J., Prentice-Hall, 1970.
Children with superior cognitive abilities are the subject of this study.

Holmen, Milton G., and Richard F. Docter, *Educational and Psychological Testing.* New York, Russell Sage, 1972.
An examination of current practices in educational measurement.

Koestler, Arthur, *The Act of Creation.* New York, Dell, 1966.
Koestler believes that creative activity in all areas of human endeavor has a basic common pattern.

Langer, Walter, *The Mind of Adolf Hitler,* New York, Basic Books, 1972.
The psychoanalytic profile of Hitler by the American psychiatrist commissioned to do the study by the OSS in 1943.

Mercer, J. R., "The Meaning of Mental Retardation," in R. Koch and J. C. Dobson, eds., *The Mentally Retarded Child and His Family.* New York, Brunner-Mazel, 1971.

Rosenthal, Robert, and Lenore Jacobson, *Pygmalion in the Classroom: Teacher Expectation and Pupils' Intellectual Development.* New York, Holt, Rinehart and Winston, 1968.
Two educators describe how teachers' preconceived impressions of students affect their development.

Wallach, Michael A., and Cliff W. Wing, Jr., *The Talented Student: A Validation of the Creativity-Intelligence Distinction.* New York, Holt, Rinehart and Winston, 1969.
The authors question the usefulness of the concept of intelligence in understanding creativity.

Williams, Robert L., "Stimulus-Response: Scientific Racism and IQ—The Silent Mugging of the Black Community," *Psychology Today,* May 1974.
A psychologist contends that IQ tests are perpetrators of racism.

Wolf, Theta H., *Alfred Binet*. Chicago, University of Chicago Press, 1973.
A study of Binet's pioneering work in the measurement of intelligence (as well as of his other concerns).
Yeats, W. B., "The Tower," *Collected Poems*. New York, Macmillan, 1928.
Yeats's poem has much to say about the creative vision of the artist.

Part |4|
The Social Context

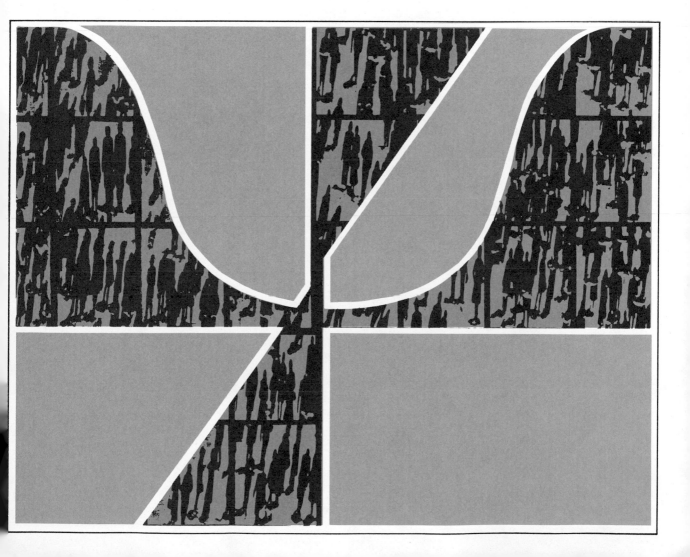

Chapter Fourteen

The Individual in Society

How do we react to contradictory information?
How do social factors affect achievement motivation?
What circumstances cause us to seek the companionship of others?
Is there a difference between liking and loving?
Is it possible to predict what kind of person we are apt to like?
Do you run because you are afraid, or are you afraid because you run?
Do we really adjust our behavior and thoughts according to the norms of groups we are in?
How influential are group pressures?
How are leaders chosen?

That man is a social animal hardly needs remarking; in fact it is very difficult to distinguish people from their groups. Though warm bodies move about separately, not even touching, each one's mind is occupied with visions of others, sounds of their voices, recollections of encounters with them, and with things they do and make. Even in their solitary moments, people soliloquize in languages they learned from their groups, wear clothes developed by group culture, and eat or drink what and as their groups have taught them.

The general observation that people are much occupied with and influenced by one another does not preclude the possibility of an independent life. The hermit and the religious solitary attempt to relate exclusively to nonhuman things. The hermit may choose the woods, a lake, the sky, and their creatures; the religious solitary may choose a dark room, the desert, or the top of a pillar in the sun where he attempts to free his mind of all distractions and directly know the One.

Cy Tetenman

Easter Sunday on Fifth Avenue.

It can be argued that the person who chooses the life of the hermit, or of the mystic, does so for social reasons—that withdrawal is in fact a negative relationship to the group, or an attempt to achieve a new relationship with the group. Perhaps a person chooses the monastery because of the way his mother or father responded to him when he was a baby. On the other hand, though the individual, like a drop of water, is part of something much larger than himself, again like a drop of water, he is more fundamental than the sea of social influence he moves in; in many ways, he may exist without that sea.

Somewhat less ambiguous is the case of the child lost or abandoned early in life who survives in the wilderness and grows up without human associations.

Mike Levins

We need not be alone to be solitary, and even in solitude one's thoughts may be with others.

Ron Benvenisti

If such a child is found in the company of wolves and in many ways behaves like a wolf (running on all fours and barking or howling), but in some ways is different and displays "human" characteristics, one may assume (provisionally) that a tendency to develop certain human ways of behaving is inherited. We may say that some of the child's behavioral characteristics are a part of "human nature," unless, of course, we know that before being lost or abandoned, the child was exposed to human beings long enough to be influenced by them. A fascinating instance of this sort was reported by Singh and Zingg, 1942. Two girls found living in a den with wolves were removed to an orphanage, where the younger, estimated to be about a year and a half old, survived for 10 months and the older, Kamala, who was about 8, survived and developed until her death at the age of 16. Kamala at first moved on all fours, grimaced, growled, and howled like a wolf. At 8, her teachers felt she had the human characteristics of a child of 3 or 4.

One might interpret Kamala's backwardness in terms of her having passed the optimal period for learning to walk and talk. Or one might consider that she had already been socialized by wolves and had the problem of unlearning wolf ways before she could replace them with human ways. Whether Kamala had developed any distinctive human characteristics during her years with the pack we cannot say; to find that out, we would have had to observe her, without influencing her, in the wild state in which she was living. Did she do anything the wolves didn't do? Did she have any interests that were different from theirs? Many interesting and subtle aspects of her behavior might have been observed in this situation, in which she was thoroughly rooted. Taking her away destroyed her psychic root system and created a new situation where, homeless and among strangers, she found very little that was familiar, comforting, or comprehensible. It must have been very difficult at this point for either Kamala or anyone else to know who or what she was, and it is difficult now to interpret her adventures and her development, or to draw any firm social psychological conclusions.

Even so, we do have in social psychology a considerable accumulation of controlled observations and a respectable repertoire of working hypotheses. The subject of these observations and hypotheses is, broadly, interpersonal behavior: how we perceive other people, social aspects of motivation, social determinants of emotion, and the influence of social groups on behavior. Interpersonal behavior may occur in face-to-face encounters, as when a motorist rolls down a window to face a policeman, or through various media, as when a shopper is stopped by a display in a supermarket, or a mountain climber reads graffiti on the wall of a shelter. The presence of a sidewalk causes people to take the long way around a grassy square; the presence of others may deter someone from picking up a coin he sees in a gutter.

When we talk about people in groups, we are talking about two quite distinct phenomena—the individual and the group—and a thorough social psychological analysis must be concerned with both phenomena. We cannot pretend to be thorough in this chapter, however, and so we will adopt the more

Human Aggression

H. Kacher

Konrad Lorenz

Irenäus Eibl-Eibesfeldt

We have spoken of the nature–nurture controversy frequently in these pages. On the one side, representing nature and biological character, has stood Konrad Lorenz, whose theories of aggression have received much publicity. According to Lorenz man is doomed to violence because he has somehow failed to inherit from his animal ancestors the instincts that inhibit violence among members of the same species.

A countertheory is attracting attention, however. Its main proponent is Irenäus Eibl-Eibesfeldt, a prominent German researcher and head of the human ethology division of the celebrated Max Planck Institute for Behavioral Physiology in Munich. Taking exception to such biologically deterministic views, Dr. Eibl-Eibesfeldt believes that man actually has evolved the same kind of control of violent behavior that animals have. But the shortcomings of human cultures and the accessibility of deadly weapons have foiled instinctive control of aggression among humans.

Research has seemed to confirm Eibl-Eibesfeldt's theory. Working with thalidomide babies, he studied the inborn behavior of infants lacking both sight and hearing. These babies showed normal violence-averting techniques—the standard behaviors of smiling and crying—which like certain animal behaviors, are thought to be universal pity-releasing cues among members of the same species. But though in nature such mechanisms are sufficient to avert violence, they are virtually useless in human society.

The flightless cormorant in the Galapagos must signal friendship when approaching his mate's nest by offering food. Neglecting this gesture will cause attack. Chimpanzees signal submissiveness with such gestures as pressing the lips together in what looks to us like a kiss and by extending an upturned hand to a dominant member of the group.

Such data, for Eibl-Eibesfeldt, indicate that animal species inhibit aggression more effectively than human societies, though we apparently have the same instinctive aggression-inhibiting mechanisms that other animals have. The problem is that we have not ritualized the control of aggression as effectively as most animal species have.

Members of the scientific establishment see Eibl-Eibesfeldt's approach as a hopeful synthesis of nature and nurture. What was once a battleground is now opening up to new discussions of the complex interaction between externals such as cultural influence and the biological givens. It is to cultural development that man must look for survival, to ritualized forms of controlling aggression such as negotiations and moratoriums. The logical conclusion, Dr. Eibl-Eibesfeldt feels, will ultimately be an effective worldwide parliament in which issues can be debated without recourse to weapons.

A further contribution to the debate on man's aggressiveness has been offered by Erich Fromm. Fromm points out that the aggressiveness we associate with animals—particularly the predators—is of a very different nature from the sadism, violence, and brutality that have been characteristic of so much of man's history. The first is both adaptive—it helps the species—and comparatively emotionless (the predator does not hate its prey); the second is a product of culture and its defects, and of the emotional disorders that result from man's inability to cope with that culture. The "aggression" of a forceful salesman and the "aggression" of one country invading another or of a bully and his victim are very different things.

It is ironic that Fromm's argument evokes a favorite point of the ethologists, who point out that "true" behavior cannot be found among animals in laboratories or zoos. Perhaps the "true" nature of man cannot emerge in the zoos that most contemporary cultures resemble.

classic psychological approach: we will look at groups from the point of view of the individual. What is it, inside the individual, that causes him to seek out other people, to perceive them in certain ways, to aspire to be like them or different from them, to be influenced by them in a wide variety of ways? It seems likely that forces outside the individual, emanating from the group at large, also affect these social phenomena. For example, perhaps we seek out others because they expect us and teach us to do so. But for the purposes of this introduction to psychology, it seems more profitable to talk about what happens inside the individual.

HOW DO WE PERCEIVE OTHERS?

The test of a good brain, F. Scott Fitzgerald once told himself, is the ability to hold two opposed ideas in mind and still take action. This feat is particularly difficult in interpersonal perception, where people seem quite averse to ambiguity. If you see a new neighbor as possibly friendly or possibly hostile, possibly either honest or devious, either attractive or repulsive, you experience considerable unwillingness to interact with him—probably far more reluctance, in fact, than if you knew for sure that he is hostile, devious, *and* repulsive. People seek to form a unified impression and to affirm it, even in the face of disconfirming evidence, rather than continue in a state of suspended judgment. One may say, "I think she's really my friend even though sometimes she doesn't act like it." Or, "He's honest enough about some things, but deep down I don't trust him." These judgments, of course, could be weighted the other way: "She seems friendly enough but I think she's out to get me." Or, "I know he lies now and then and takes paper home from the office, but I think fundamentally he's honest."

One might see this tendency as an aversion to the unknown. Contradictory ideas of what a person is leave us with an unknown. We can eliminate this unknown by forming an hypothesis that takes account of the opposites but makes an affirmation, as in the examples above. We can then act as if our hypothesis were correct. If sufficient evidence contradicting the hypothesis piles up, we may, either because we love the truth or because we are becoming uncomfortable, reevaluate our hypothesis and perhaps modify it. But if we have anything at stake in the issue, we are likely to hold onto our original hypothesis all the more firmly when we are faced with disconfirming evidence. Consider the fact that the cigarette industry continues to flourish in spite of strong warnings from the medical profession that smoking is injurious to health. In 1954, the *Minneapolis Sunday Tribune* polled its readers on their acceptance of the findings that cigarette smoking is linked with lung cancer. Disbelief was directly related to the smoking behavior of the respondent: nonsmokers accepted the linkage most readily, and heavy smokers were most inclined to reject it (Festinger, 1957).

Leon Festinger

One study of interpersonal perception asked subjects to judge, on the basis of case histories, whether welfare applicants were entitled to receive payments. The information provided was intentionally distorted to show the applicants in an unfavorable light. Later, after the judgments had been made, the subjects were given some very favorable information about the applicants, including some data that discredited the original information. Subjects who were told that their judgments would not be used in any practical way readily modified their opinions after receiving the new, contradictory information; in fact, they tended to overcompensate for the harshness of their original judgments. But subjects who were told that their first judgment had been acted upon by a caseworker tended to maintain that judgment unequivocally even after receiving strong disconfirming evidence. Evidently for this second group of subjects discomfort would have been greater if they accepted the contradictory evidence that they had denied a worthy person what was entitled to him. For the former group, who didn't have to live with the consequences of their actions, discomfort would have been greater if they had rejected the contradictory information. These people, for whom nothing was at stake, could "afford" to accept more objective facts.

Resolving Contradictions: Cognitive Dissonance

cognitive
dissonance

Such findings as the ones just described have led Festinger (1957) to a theory of cognitive dissonance. Dissonance and consonance, according to Festinger, are relations among a person's cognitions—which include beliefs, attitudes, knowledge of one's world, and of one's own behavior and feelings. When two of these elements are inconsistent or contradictory, they are dissonant. When a person perceives dissonance of this sort, he will become uncomfortable and try to reduce or eliminate it. He may try to change one of the dissonant elements, such as one of his attitudes. Or he may seek to reinforce whatever consonance he feels by acquiring new information about the matter in question. Or he may try to ignore the dissonant elements. Most attempts to reduce dissonance, and thereby discomfort, are successful only if they are backed by some form of support in the environment.

Perhaps the clearest illustration of cognitive dissonance is what happens to our perception of members of an alien nation during a war that we support. Our enemies become cruel aggressors. The principle of cognitive dissonance causes us to reason: "We are killing them; therefore they must be bad." In this way we resolve the highly dissonant contradiction between "We are killing them" and "They are people like us."

Sometimes dissonance cannot be dispelled simply by changing one of our cognitions, especially when our cognitions are inconsistent with our knowledge about what *other people* feel, think, or do. In some cases attempts to reduce cognitive dissonance lead to social action. In the 1960s people who believed very strongly that the racial doctrine of separate but equal was wrong were likely to participate in marches, sit-ins, and other social demonstrations designed to call the attention of the larger society to the injustices it was inflicting on a minority group. Similarly, people who believe that the way to eternal salvation is through pursuing a particular lifestyle are likely not only to follow that lifestyle themselves but also to make a widespread effort to convert others to their way.

 When Prophecy Fails

Imagine the elation of researchers who discover that a real event of the sort they have been studying on the basis of evidence from laboratory experiments or from history is actually going to happen and that they may witness the event! This is what happened to social psychologists Festinger, Riecken, and Schachter (1956), who had concerned themselves for many years with the question of why, when people are confronted with evidence that incontrovertibly contradicts their convictions, they are likely to proclaim those convictions with increased fervor, especially if they have strong support from a social group who believes as they do and experiences with them the same contradictory evidence.

One fine September day, Festinger and his colleagues discovered that a Mrs. Marion Keech in a place called Lake City was proclaiming the destruction by flood of that city and of the entire world on the coming December 21. Mrs. Keech had been receiving messages from a planet called "Clarion" which she recorded in automatic writing. Mrs. Keech had made very little effort to spread word of the coming disaster to others; she had, it turned out, been warned by a visitor from Clarion not to try to convince others but to tell what she knew only to those who sought her out, for only such people would be guided by the right spirit.

Eventually a group of believers, including several students attending the college in Lake City, was formed. For several days preceding the cataclysm, the group remained together at Marion Keech's house, waiting to be picked up by a flying saucer that Mrs. Keech's spiritual informer had promised would transport them to safety. Only a few of the student members were missing; they had gone home for the Christmas holidays. When the saucer failed to arrive and, worse, the cataclysm failed to occur, the believers were thrown into confusion—but not disbelief. After a long struggle to find an explanation, Mrs. Keech finally received a message that satisfied everyone. The earth had been saved because of the faith of those who who believed! The group was ecstatic; now even those who previously had had some reservations accepted the "truth" unstintingly. Mrs. Keech herself picked up the telephone to inform the press, whom she had previously avoided, of her good news, and a fervent proselytizing effort was launched. Now it became of the utmost importance to tell the world what had happened, whereas it had not been important to seek believers *before* the event.

Only the few members of the group who were not at Mrs. Keech's house during those days of anguished waiting failed to take up the banner. These people, unfortified by the social support of the group during the crucial hours, lost faith and abandoned the cause.

The following are the conditions under what we would expect to observe increased proselytizing follow the disconformation of a belief:

1. A belief is held with deep conviction and the person holding the belief must have committed himself to it. That is, he must have taken some important action which is difficult to undo.
2. The belief must be sufficiently specific and sufficiently concerned with the real world so that events may unequivocally refute the belief. Such undeniable disconformation must occur and be recognized by the individual holding the belief.
3. The individual must have social support. It is unlikely that one individual could withstand the above mentioned disconformation by himself.
4. If the believer is a member of a group of convinced persons who can support one another, it would be expected that the belief would be maintained and proselytizing would ensue, trying to convince nonmembers that the belief is correct.

Since some kinds of cognitive dissonance lead us into social behavior, it is not surprising that much of the work in dissonance theory has been done by researchers who have been trained in social psychology. Thus, this chapter on social psychology and the following one on attitudes contain many examples of dissonance and dissonance reduction, although such processes are not restricted to social phenomena.

Another way of reducing the unknowns in our lives, and thereby reducing our cognitive efforts, is by inferring unknown characteristics of people from a few known ones. What is known may be as little as the person's ethnic background or nationality. Is he English? He's polite and stuffy. Is she Polynesian? She's cheerful, affectionate, and a graceful dancer. This practice is known as stereotyping, and we will encounter it again in this chapter and the next as we examine the processes we use to try to understand other people. Sometimes amusing, stereotyping can also be sinister—a technique seized upon by greed- or hate-possessed people to justify, for example, their robbery of the farms of thousands of Japanese-Americans during World War II ("No Japanese can be trusted to be loyal to the U.S."), their subjugation of a minority group ("All blacks are stupid and dirty"), their denial of jobs to ex-convicts ("Once a criminal, always a criminal").

Interpersonal perception, then, may be shaped more by the mind of the perceiver than by what is perceived. Since so much in human life depends upon interpersonal perception, small wonder that psychologists have explored its mechanisms. We will look very briefly here at a few of these investigations.

Forming a Unified Impression

Solomon E. Asch

Asch (1946) offered his students a series of descriptive terms: energetic, assured, talkative, cold, ironical, inquisitive, persuasive. These terms, he told them, all described a single person who was not further identified. Could they write down their impression of this person? They could and did—quite readily producing descriptions of full and rich personalities in which they not only interpreted, weighted, and fitted together the suggested traits to form a unified impression but also added new traits to serve as bridges and fill in gaps.

Gollin (1954) presented a group of students with a slightly different task. Here the raw material was scenes from a motion picture in which a young woman displayed different characteristics. In one scene she gave money to a beggar; in another she helped a woman who had fallen down. In another scene she appeared to be offering herself sexually with a generosity that might be called promiscuous.

Asked to give their impression of this young woman, half of the students simply ignored one of the characteristics and reported the other. This suggests that they found the implied traits conflicting (even though the "whore with a heart of gold" has been a legendary figure for hundreds of years). Unable to integrate them, they were not willing to retain both, and to ignore one trait was their way of achieving a unified impression.

About a quarter of the students described the woman as both helpful and promiscuous. These students apparently found no conflict between the traits they inferred from the woman's behaviors and hence no need for a unifying interpretation of them. Or perhaps these students had a greater tolerance for cognitive dissonance than the others. Another quarter of Gollins' subjects related the two traits to achieve a higher-order, unified impression of the young woman's behavior, seeing them all as manifestations of a fundamental sympathy, affectionateness, or generosity.

Why do people tend to form unified impressions? We can suggest various explanations, each having a certain validity. (1) Unification is a help to memory; in fact, many mnemonic devices are based on this phenomenon. Since memory is a practical matter and vital to survival, it should not be surprising that people have adopted unification as a standard way to help them remember what people are like. (2) Unification is a help to prediction. We may not know what a four-legged animal that runs without barking may do, but we have a good idea what a mistreated and enraged German shepherd may do. (3) Unification reduces cognitive dissonance. We tend to be more comfortable if we like, or dislike, virtually everything about a person, to the extent that we frequently change our own opinions and behavior to conform with those of an admired person or to disconform with those of a disliked person. Evidently, we make such changes out of a cognitive need for agreement among our perceptions or attitudes toward others. (4) Unification simplifies thinking and makes thinking easier.

 Choice of a Romantic Partner: A Computer Study

Elaine Walster

Elliot Aronson

The reason behind one's romantic choices is often not apparent to others, sometimes not even to one's self. Several researchers have speculated that individuals may decide whom to date after a careful assessment of their own desirability, thus the criterion used in choosing a romantic partner is influenced by one's perception of whom he can get. As Fromm (1956) has said, "Two persons fall in love when they have found the best object available on the market considering the limitations of their own exchange values."

A number of experiments have investigated this proposition. The data suggest that while there may be a very slight tendency for individuals to try to date individuals of approximately their own "social desirability," this tendency is not very pronounced. Several studies found no evidence that individuals take into account their own attractiveness when deciding whether or not to approach a date. Only one study demonstrates a tendency for individuals to be objective in their level of aspiration when making a romantic choice.

Walster, Aronson, Abrahams, and Rottman (1966) proposed the following specific hypotheses: (1) individuals who are themselves very socially desirable (physically attractive, personable, possessing great social recognition or material assets) will require a romantic partner more socially desirable than will a less desirable individual; (2) if couples varying in social desirability meet in a social situation, those couples who are similar in social desirability will most often attempt to date one another, after actual experience with potential dates of various desirability; (3) an individual will express the most liking for a partner of approximately his own desirability.

These hypotheses were tested in a field study of 752 college students who were recruited to attend a freshman dance, for which partners were matched by computer. When the freshman students arrived to purchase tickets to the dance their physical attractiveness was secretly rated by a group of college sophomores. Although one's social desirability is made up of many things besides physical attractiveness, the authors choose this criterion as an indication of the subject's social desirability because it could be quickly assessed under standard conditions. Freshman filled out questionnaires which provided a great deal of information, including age, height, race, and religious preference. Also assessed were the students' popularity (a self-report), their expectations in a computer date (in how physically attractive and how considerate they expected their date to be), and their self-esteem. In addition, several objective measures were used, including the student's high school academic percentile rank, his Minnesota Scholastic Aptitude Test score, his MMPI score and Minnesota Counseling Inventory score. Two days after the student completed his questionnaire, he was randomly assigned to a date. The couples arrived at the dance at 8:00 P.M., and danced and talked until the 10:30 P.M. intermission. During the intermission students' impressions of their dates were assessed. How often the couples actually dated following the dance was determined six months later.

The data confirmed the first hypothesis, that subjects who were very attractive expected that a "suitable date" be more physically attractive and personable and also more considerate than a less attractive subject. The data however, did not confirm the second and third hypotheses. Subjects did not tend to choose partners of approximately their own attractiveness, nor did they only date partners of approximately their own social desirability.

The experiment secured additional information which deserves mention. Physical attractiveness was just as important an asset for men as for women, and was by far the most important determinant of how much a date would be liked by the partner. However Terman (1959) has pointed out that intelligence, physical attractiveness, creativity, and certain personality traits tend to go together. Thus one might argue that it is really not physical attractiveness per se that is of critical importance in affecting liking but that it is one of the correlates of attractiveness.

Notice that in (4) we did not say "Unification simplifies thinking and makes *life* easier." Many kinds of simplified thinking embody errors and lead to further errors, such that life is made more difficult both for ourselves and for others. For example, some persons, finding "promiscuous" and "loving" incompatible, may drop the latter entirely.

Another aspect of the simplification problem was illuminated by Cohen (1961). Cohen gave his students a list of traits, some of which were contradictory. He told half the students they would be required to communicate to others their impressions of the persons these traits described. The remaining students were told both that they should consider these traits and that they would later be given further information about the people in question. The students who expected further information tended to form complex impressions that attempted to rationalize and integrate the contradictory traits. The students who were preparing to communicate, however, tended to form impressions that were either consistently good or consistently poor.

The "communicators" apparently found a simplified impression more satisfactory for their purposes. They tended to organize around the simplifying theme of goodness or badness, reflecting their greater concern with communicating effectively than with representing the subjects accurately. We might

Interpersonal Attractiveness

What makes people like each other is a question that has occupied social psychologists for many years. It has been noted that we appear to like people who are close to us better than those who are distant, people who agree with us better than those who disagree, people with similar personality traits to our own, and under certain conditions, people whose characteristics make it easy for them to satisfy our needs—and whose needs we can easily satisfy. We like competent people Better than incompetent people, and finally we like people who like us.

Much of the above seems obvious—so obvious that intuitively one might sense that things aren't that simple. And sure enough, many of these generalities have their own qualifiers, as Elliot Aronson and his associates are quick to point out. Aronson has undertaken a systematic investigation of "interpersonal attractiveness." He reports (1969) that we are particularly likely to be attracted to highly competent people who prove to be vulnerable in some sense. According to a Gallup poll, John Kennedy's personal popularity, for example, increased immediately after the Bay of Pigs fiasco. Aronson notes that the president was "young, handsome, witty, a war hero, superwealthy, charming, athletic, a voracious reader, a master political strategist, an uncomplaining endurer of physical pain—with a perfect wife (who spoke several foreign languages), two cute kids (one boy, one girl), and a talented close-knit extended family." Evidence of fallibility probably served to make him more human, and hence more likable.

Aronson, Willerman, and Floyd (1966) investigated this issue in the laboratory, where they compared persons with superior abilities who either blundered or did not blunder with persons with average abilities who either blundered or did not blunder. The most attractive people were those with superior abilities who committed a blunder, while the least attractive were those of average ability who committed a blunder.

Aronson and Finker (1965) have found evidence indicating that we prefer people who initially did not like us and then changed to those who liked us from the start and conversely, that we dislike those who having once liked us subsequently changed their minds more than we dislike people who always disliked us.

Finally, Mills and Aronson (1965) in a similar vein found that a male subject likes a beautiful woman who evaluates him positively better than a homely woman who evaluates him positively. However, he dislikes the beautiful woman more than the homely one when both evaluate him negatively.

Actually even though subjects reported a great dislike for a beautiful woman who negatively evaluated them, they still professed a greater desire to be in another experiment with the same person. The experimenters interpreted this as a desire to change the beautiful woman's impression of the subject, who apparently didn't care about the impression he made on the homely woman.

liken this process to caricature, which distorts certain facial features and omits others in order to achieve a quick, strong, unequivocal effect.

The students who expected further information rather than a test of their ability to communicate had a reason to suspend judgment, because "making up their minds" might cost them further effort later if the new data did not readily fit their overall impression. Whether it was largely this motive, or simply the absence of pressure to formulate an impression for communication, Cohen's experiment does not precisely tell us. It does indicate clearly, however, that in organizing an impression the demands of the situation influence the choice of criteria and the mode and method of organization. We may infer that the same person using the same data may, in different circumstances, come up with sharply different interpretations of the data.

Inferring a Lot from a Little

One may form a wide-ranging picture of a person's personality on the basis of very little evidence. We have observed that we tend to do so, because uncertainty makes us uncomfortable; we might say that the mind abhors a vacuum and tends to fill it up, if not with fact, then with inference, or speculation, or mere fiction. In the matter of rounding out our impressions of people, certain common procedures come to our aid.

For one thing, each of us has an "implicit theory of personality." From observation of people or from other influences, such as reading fiction or watching movies, one comes to believe that certain clusters of traits go together. If we see a powerfully built man with steely gray eyes snap to attention as the flag goes by, we do not expect him to cry over stepping on an ant. If we see a gaunt youth with long slender fingers weeping over an ant he has just stepped on, we do not expect him to snap to attention when the flag goes by.

The effect of first impressions—sometimes called the "primacy effect"—has been investigated by a number of researchers. One method used was to present a list of traits to two groups of subjects. For one group the list began with the good traits, for example, idealistic and intelligent, then went on to the bad traits. For the other group the list began with the bad traits. Those to whom the good traits were given first formed a more favorable impression of the person in question and were likely to attribute other good traits to him. But we might ask, What made the difference? Was it the mere fact that a trait came first, or the inference that because a trait came first it was the dominant one in the mind of the observer who made up the list?

Luchins (1957) found a similar primacy effect when subjects were given extended descriptions of hypothetical persons. The person was depicted moving through a number of situations in ways that suggested either loneliness, gloom, and introversion or conviviality, sunshine, and extroversion. When the material suggesting introversion came first, the majority of respondents envisioned an introverted personality; when the same material was presented in reverse order, so that the material suggesting extroversion came first, the majority formed an impression of an extroverted personality.

primacy effect

Abraham Luchins

Pursuing his study further, Luchins discovered that if he warned his subjects not to make hasty judgments, they ceased to display the primacy effect. In fact, they might reverse it, forming an impression more strongly influenced by the later than the earlier materials. We note here again the intriguing possibility that when verbal material is presented, the listener in our culture anticipates that the important material will come first; what he shows is a mental set effect. When cautioned to avoid hasty judgment, he deliberately sets his mind to weight all evidence equally, and he may overcompensate by weighting more heavily what he habitually underweights.

Similar to the effect of first impressions is the "halo effect," or the tendency to perceive a person as consistently good or consistently bad on the basis of the first impression he makes. We then ascribe to that person a whole spectrum, or halo, of traits that bear out our initial assumption. A student who gets all A's on his first two report cards may continue to receive superior grades even though his work is falling off because the teacher first saw him as an "A student" and evaluates everything he does in that light.

The ways in which we perceive others, then, are greatly influenced by what we ourselves bring to our interactions with other people. We attempt to resolve our own conflicting behavior, attitudes, and feelings by seeking some unified view of the people who come into our lives. In an effort to see things consistently and so to reduce the incongruities we might otherwise see, we may fall prey to stereotyping or to the "halo" and primacy effects. We establish a mental set, or bias, that makes us more ready to see things in one way than in another.

SOCIAL ASPECTS OF MOTIVATION

A sixth-grade boy decides to see how long he can hold his breath. He takes a deep breath and begins watching the big school clock. Fifteen seconds, 30 seconds—not bad. One minute. He feels a pull at his throat. Another 10 seconds. Twitching in his chair, he feels his lungs about to burst.

"Edward, is something the matter?"

He shakes his head no. Now at a minute and 30 seconds it begins to get strangely easy, even as Miss Segovia walks toward his desk. Confound her, she's going to interrupt what might be a world record. Little gray fish wriggle on the rim of his world and he sees the eyes of all his classmates turned on him just before everything goes blank.

Achievement

Much of our behavior is oriented toward achieving certain relationships with others. But we are also oriented toward achieving certain relationships with ourselves and with inanimate things.

If asked what was behind Edward's behavior, we might reasonably say: "The achievement motive." We should note, as we have before in similar circumstances, that in applying this term we are not advancing our knowledge. If we ask what makes a moth fly toward the light, we may answer, "positive phototropism," but if we ask what positive phototropism is, the answer is, "It is what makes a moth fly toward the light."

The achievement Edward sought by holding his breath was not necessarily socially oriented. Instead, he might have been attempting to maximize his performance on a physical task that was privately chosen and, he thought, privately performed to gain a private satisfaction.

One might argue that what Edward really wants to achieve is not, ultimately, encompassed by his ostensible goals; his deeper purpose is to alter his relationship with himself or, we might say, his concept of himself. He may set tests and ordeals for himself in order to "prove himself," to establish a basis for more favorable self-evaluation: How far can I jump? How deep can I dive? Can I crumple a tin can in my hands? Can I climb Mt. Aconcagua? Or he may have no psychic axe to grind; his goal might simply be self-knowledge.

If Edward announces to a group of friends in the schoolyard, "I bet I can hold my breath for a minute and a half," his motive is no longer self-evaluation or self-knowledge but the display of achievement. He may be looking for social approval. Or if he challenges his peers to a breath-holding contest, his goal is social comparison. And if he were to find himself in a situation where holding his breath became crucial, and where he felt anxiety about the outcome, he might tend to seek affiliation with others who were similarly distressed: "Two minutes? How can anyone hold his breath 2 minutes? I'm getting a little scared." "Me too."

We see here that the achievement motive, while it is not in fact a social motive, has a social component. We achieve partly in order to enjoy the rewards for achievement (recognition, praise) that others bestow on us. Probably no one

 Achievement and Needs of Society

McClelland and his co-workers (1953; see also McClelland, 1965a) have hypothesized that achievement needs are related to the economic and technological growth of a society.

In McClelland's view such growth depends on individual striving and risk-taking with successful performance as the goal—an orientation characteristic of people with high achievement need and uncharacteristic of people with low achievement need. McClelland compared the level of achievement need revealed by an analysis of children's readers in a number of nations with the rate of economic growth in those nations and found that a high level of achievement need tended to be a predictor of an unusually high rate of national economic growth in subsequent years.

The question arises whether the correlation is causal. More specifically, we may ask whether the need for achievement—the achievement motivation—may not in fact be a natural phenomenon from which man is discouraged by conditions that make achievement an unrealistic and unrealizable aim. Madigan (1967) and Guthrie (1970) have studied the (to our eyes) strangely limited goals of Filipino farmers who persist in seeking social equality above all else, viewing individual enterprise as wrong, since it sets some people above or ahead of their neighbors. This group of farmers, though current political and economic conditions freely permit it, refuse to "better themselves," turn down offers of government aid, and decline responsibility for the successful running of business ventures.

Their purpose is to avoid excelling, and those who stray from this purpose are chastened by their neighbors. Among the consequences of this aversion to enterprise are inadequate nutrition and poor health—entirely unnecessary conditions from our point of view, but a price the Filipinos willingly pay in support of their philosophy. In the past, when they were relatively helpless to change economic conditions, this philosophy eased their anguish; today its persistence prolongs that anguish, at least so far as inadequate food, health, and material well-being are concerned. Possibly as younger generations look around and see with fresh eyes that progress is possible, that children need not be undernourished and stunted, that their parents could live much longer, they may develop a higher achievement need. As time passes, succeeding generations may manifest these needs more broadly and intensely—and so the shuttlebox of subsistence living may give way to the shuttlebox of living in order to "get ahead." Whether this is progress the reader must decide for himself.

At this point another interesting question arises. If high achievement motivation is conducive to successful enterprise, and if we consider successful enterprise a good thing, can we do anything to increase achievement motivation in people who are suffering for lack of it? McClelland (1965b) and McClelland and Winter (1969) investigated the effects of a 10-day achievement-motivation training program on businessmen in both America and India. These men were taught to organize their thinking in terms of achievement and to distinguish this motive clearly from others. It was found that not only their achievement need scores but also their entrepreneurial activity and their business success increased after they had completed this program.

wants to write the great American novel only to publish it anonymously or under a pseudonym. Many people seem to be moved to achieve only when they know they will be rewarded by others. In some people, however, achievement motivation is highly internalized, or personalized, and does not require external rewards in order to operate. Such people reward themselves, as it were, with the personal satisfaction of achieving.

Why do some people develop a higher achievement need than others? One group of researchers found that children tend to develop a high need to achieve if they have parents who set high standards for them, reward them for success, punish them for failure, and express considerable affection for them (McClelland, Atkinson, Clark, and Lowell, 1953). A child is more likely to have low achievement needs if his parents, especially his father, are highly restrictive or authoritarian. Achievement motivation is discussed at greater length in Chapter 5 on motivation. Its assessment is covered in a box in Chapter 13 (p. 613).

Social Approval

Edward, we have seen, may try to set a breath-holding record to win the social approval of his classmates. A boy stunts on a bike for a favored girl's approval, a girl cooks a gourmet meal for her boyfriend's approval, a man writes plays for the approval of audiences of strangers.

People seek social approval—from individuals and from small and large groups—not only by achieving but by wearing certain styles of clothing, driving certain automobiles, practicing certain social graces, and in hundreds of other ways. They also seek to keep approval by what they do not do: the man on the assembly line refrains from working faster or harder or better than his co-workers. Social approval may reduce one's uncertainty. It may pacify anxiety. It may comfort insecurity. It may prop a tottering self-esteem. We will briefly consider a few of these sources of approval.

Social Comparison

We have seen that if Edward challenges his buddies to a breath-holding contest, he may be engaging in social comparison—testing the limits of his own endur-   social comparison

Mike Levins   Arthur Sirdofsky

We seek social approval by conforming to the customs and fashions of our group.

ance against those of his peers. Thus the purpose of social comparison is not self-knowledge per se but relative self-knowledge.

Relative self-knowledge can have some strange effects. Edward's time of a minute and a half may be very good in absolute terms, but one or several of his friends may be able to hold their breath for even longer periods. The result is that Edward feels better or worse about himself, depending on his performance relative to his friends'. The man who has been unable to pay his income tax may feel acutely apprehensive and inferior until he receives the dreaded notice from the IRS and finds it is a printed form letter: he is not the only one!

Festinger (1954) has proposed that we want to evaluate our opinions and abilities and that, where objective or physical standards do not exist, we compare ourselves with other people, especially with others who belong to the same groups as we do.

Social comparison can be instrumental in the reduction of cognitive dissonance. If we voted for a political candidate in the belief that he was an honest man and then discovered that his honesty is open to question, we are potentially in a state of cognitive dissonance. If our dissonance is great enough to demand resolution, one means we might pursue is to attempt to discover what our friends who also voted for him are thinking. (If we voted for this candidate, it is likely that most of our friends also voted for him, for friends are largely chosen from among people who share our attitudes and beliefs.) Are our friends excusing his questionable campaign practices on the grounds that he had to be reelected at all costs, or that politics has always been a dirty business for both parties? Or are they condemning him or his associates for breaking faith with the people? Chances are that the members of our group will line up pretty much on one side or the other of this issue and that we will adopt the opinion of the majority. At least that's what we are likely to do if we resort to social comparison to resolve

    Student Radicalism

The eruption of political activism on American campuses stimulated a quantity of psychological research. Concern with student violence has fostered many theories as to what kind of people become radicals. Kenneth Keniston, a psychologist whose central interest is young radicals, synthesized much of the research done in the late sixties.

The studies dealt with generalities made about student radicals. Were the student activists angry, violent nihilists or idealistic, former civil rights workers? Were they immoral, irresponsible troublemakers? Were male protesters merely acting out their feelings of Oedipal rebellion? Were student activists mainly the children of former radicals? Was there a relationship between parental permissiveness and politcal beliefs of students? Did radical beliefs lead to radical action?

Based on many studies from all parts of the country, Keniston concluded that: (1) student radicals comprised an elite group; (2) moral issues were important to radical thought; (3) the male radicals studied came to their beliefs through identification or rejection of identification with their fathers; and (4) many students held radical beliefs without acting on them.

While doing his own research, Keniston realized how quickly the radical political scene was changing. (This article was written in 1969, before further changes occurred after the bombing of Cambodia. So essentially his findings apply to the radical students of the 1960s.) His attitude toward the movement was positive. In terms of events, he saw the student movement as an extension of the Civil Rights movement. The change incorporated movement from the South to the North, from initially nonviolent pacifism to angry violence.

Before making any definitive statements, Keniston noted the essential ambivalence found in human nature. No one is good or bad, wrong or right, but good and bad, wrong and right. He reminded the reader that this must be kept in mind when dealing with groups of people. So statements labeling radicals as idealistic or nihilistic, violent or nonviolent were examined in light of the likelihood of students, or for that matter anyone, being capable of either depending upon circumstances.

A study in San Francisco contrasted students who had taken part in protests with those who had not. The students were categorized according to definitions of moral development distinguished by Lawrence Kohlberg: pre-conventional, morality defined by one's ego; conventional, defined by society; post-conventional, defined by one's own sense of right and wrong. This study found most protesters to be at the post-conventional stage and most non-protesters to be at the conventional stage. Noticing that many protesters were at the pre-conventional stage, the researchers realized that this stage was intermediary between the others, leading to post-conventional morality. The moral concern of the protesters was in marked contrast to that of the non-protesters.

Another issue that researchers aimed at was the relationship between student radicals and their parents. Keniston's article primarily reflected an interest in the father-son relationship. Either there is no research on women in the student movement or he chose to ignore it. One study cited showed evidence that radicals were not acting out Oedipal feelings, but they were responding to either identification or rejection of identification with their fathers. Those who identified with their fathers were more likely to be political activists, whereas those who did not were more likely to take on a hippie life-style.

our dissonance in this instance. There would be people, of course, who felt they had strong enough internal standards of honesty and responsibility—plus, if it should become necessary, the ability to admit a mistake—to resolve the dissonance on their own.

Aesthetic disputes offer a different kind of example of the use of social comparison. Since few aesthetic dicta are accepted as absolute today, most people—probably even established critics—feel compelled to compare their reactions to a startling new painting, book, or movie with those of others whose aesthetic judgments they at least respect.

People tend to form their opinions and develop their abilities along the lines of those of the majority of members of their group. A Future Farmer of America studies agriculture and probably expresses conservative Republican political opinions and traditional moral values. A Weatherman adopts revolutionary political opinions and learns militant persuasive tactics, even some forms of guerilla warfare. A feminist expresses Women's Liberation views and develops abilities that will permit her to compete with men in the job market. By making clear what it is for, the group helps the person who needs it to clarify what he is for.

Affiliation

affiliation Some psychologists have claimed that the need to affiliate is innate. Others say that it is not innate, but appears early in life; they speculate that the need is fostered by the very young child's helplessness and dependence on others for the receipt of rewards and reinforcements. In the normal course of development, at least in most societies, affiliation continues to be fostered and thus remains a strong need. For the most part, social psychology has assumed that affiliation is a universal need, and instead of asking why it occurs, has asked what circumstances are particularly likely to give rise to it. Underlying this approach is the recognition that in many of the circumstances of life, individual needs can best be satisfied by the presence of others.

If Edward in our old example finds himself in a circumstance where holding his breath is vitally important—perhaps to his survival in a burning building—he seeks to establish some relation with others who are in the same life-or-death situation. His own fears and anxieties are reduced because others are sharing them. Social psychologists have examined the specifics of the social setting that arouse affiliative needs and also the motivational circumstances of particular persons and how specific pressures are likely to modify them.

Does affiliation serve any purpose other than alleviation of anxiety? We have said that people seek others, and hence affiliate, when they are uncertain about something. We mentioned the same desire to reduce uncertainty in our discussion of how we perceive others. Indeed, it is possible that the reduction of uncertainty is man's prime social motive—that the real reason behind our affiliating with others is to remove ambiguity from our lives—to learn what is expected of us in certain situations, what attitudes and beliefs we can most comfortably live with, what our own real abilities and opinions are.

It should come as no surprise that we choose to affiliate with people who are very much like ourselves, especially people who share our attitudes and beliefs. It is both self-affirming and rewarding to make friends with people who think pretty much as we do. Again unsurprisingly, by and large we choose friends who live near us or work with us; in this respect we seem to operate on an economic principle of proximity—why travel across town to see a friend if there's someone in our block who will do just as well? It seems equally possible, though, that we may make friends with those who are near us because there is some

Affiliation and Fear

The observation that people seek each other out in times of duress is an old one. In this connection Schachter (1959) conducted a colorful experiment with overtones of gothic science fantasy and Dr. Frankenstein.

Schachter took his college-women subjects to an experimental room where they met a man called Dr. Zilstein, wearing a white lab coat and surrounded by elaborate scientific equipment. Dr. Zilstein explained his interest in investigating the effects of electric shock.

He described the procedure he would use in two ways to two different groups. One description was designed to arouse a high degree of fear. Subjects were told that the shock would be painful and intense but would not result in permanent damage. In the low-fear condition every attempt was made to relax and reassure the subjects, who were told they would feel no more than a tingle.

Subjects were questioned in order to determine the degree of fear they anticipated. Then a 10-minute delay for preparation of the equipment was announced, and the subjects were offered the alternatives of waiting alone in a comfortable room with armchairs and magazines or with other participants in a classroom. They were also given a chance to leave the experiment altogether.

About a third of the subjects who anticipated painful electric shock chose to leave; none of the subjects left who expected only mild shock. Of the subjects remaining in the severe-shock group, about two thirds chose to wait with others; of those in the mild-shock group, about two-thirds chose to wait alone (Table 14.1).

The conclusion was that anxiety increases the tendency or need to affiliate—or at least it did with these subjects under all the conditions, known and unknown, of this experiment.

Stanley Schachter

Table 14.1 Effect of Fear on Affiliation

| | Percentage Choosing | | | Strength of |
Condition	Together	Don't Care	Alone	Affiliation[a]
High fear	62.5	28.1	9.4	.88
Low fear	33.0	60.0	7.0	.35

[a] Figures are ratings on a scale from -2 to $+2$.
SOURCE: Adapted from Schachter (1959)

In order to find out more directly that affiliation could be prompted by fear, Schachter conducted another study just like the first one except that during the waiting period subjects were either forbidden to talk or were required to talk only about things not pertaining to the study. This, it was assumed, would make it more difficult for subjects to reduce fear by reassuring each other. Indeed, under these conditions, subjects were less inclined to wait with others.

One interesting supplementary finding of these studies was that birth order appeared to be an important determinant of a person's desire to affiliate (Fig. 14.1). First-born and only children were most likely to affiliate in fear; and there was a progressive decline in tendency to affiliate with birth order. This relation remained constant despite family size; the second-born in a family of two seemed to show the same degree of affiliation as the second-born in a family of six.

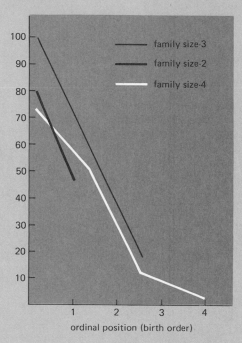

ordinal position (birth order)

Fig. 14.1 The need for affiliation with respect to birth order of siblings. (Schachter, 1959)

The most widely accepted interpretation of this finding is that first and only children are brought up to be more dependent; their parents show more concern, give them more attention, and think (at least initially) more about how to bring them up. With later-born children, parents have in general less time and attention to devote to them and so give them less comfort as they meet the difficulties of growing up. The child, in this case, does not learn that in affiliation he can obtain reassurance and comfort to combat his fears.

It has been suggested by MacDonald (1970) that some of the birth order differences reported in the literature are a result of different levels of socialization operating among first- and later-born children. That is, first-borns are more highly socialized than later-borns in the sense that they feel more obligated to conform to the expectations of adults or authority figures.

To test his socialization hypothesis, MacDonald designed an anxiety-affiliation experiment in which birth order, sex, waiting preference (alone or with another), and volunteering behavior were the independent variables focused upon.

Threat of painful shock was used to induce anxiety in 180 (81 males, 99 females) volunteer college students.

It was found that first-borns and later-born females reduced their anxiety by affiliation, later-born males more in social isolation than in affiliation.

As predicted, first-borns were more responsible about keeping their appointments and were less likely to indicate that the experiment was not as the experimenter had represented it to be. It is further observed that first-born males were less likely than later-born males to express a desire to withdraw from the experiment before the administration of shocks. However, first-born females were most likely to withdraw.

The result can be summarized as indicating a pronounced link between anxiety and affiliation, and between first-born males and later-born females.

security in doing so. We also tend to seek out people of our own race, religion, and nationality, though with somewhat less perseverance than we seek out those with similar attitudes and values. Some people learn to prize diversity among their friends, but usually only after they have perceived their basic similarity with a wide variety of people. True belief in the brotherhood of man depends on the understanding that all people share certain important and fundamental characteristics. It is also possible to arrive at that belief "by the back door," however—by the perception that one has more in common with a Ugandan tribesman one 'strikes up a conversation with on an airplane than with one's nextdoor neighbor, whose racial and social identity matches one's own. People of different backgrounds or races living in close proximity sometimes eventually become friends, after they have come to see that they hold some important values in common or after they have shared a meaningful experience, such as a flood or work on a community improvement project.

One aspect of affiliation has received much more attention from poets, novelists, and other laymen than from psychologists. This is the tendency to seek out others whom we like, or even love. Unfortunately psychologists have largely focused on affiliation as a means of solving such needs as anxiety reduction and ambiguity reduction; but affiliation is also a means of enriching ourselves and of enhancing the pleasures of life. One joyful exception in psychology is the work of Zick Rubin, who has been interested in affiliation, loving, liking, and romanticism.

Rubin (1973) succeeded in developing and validating both a love scale and a liking scale (Table 14.2). The love scale includes items that seem to assess attachment ("If I were lonely, my first thought would be to seek _____ out"), caring ("If _____ were feeling bad, my first duty would be to cheer him [her] up"), and intimacy ("I feel that I can confide in _____ about virtually everything"). Items on the liking scale, on the other hand, assess evaluation of the other person's adjustment, maturity, judgment, and intelligence and also the tendency to view the other person as similar to oneself. Rubin had 182 dating couples of college age complete these scales both for their dating partner and

Zick Rubin

Table 14.2 Love-Scale and Liking-Scale Items

Love Scale

1. If _____ were feeling bad, my first duty would be to cheer him (her) up.
2. I feel that I can confide in _____ about virtually everything.
3. I find it easy to ignore _____'s faults.
4. I would do almost anything for _____.
5. I feel very possessive toward _____.
6. If I could never be with _____, I would feel miserable.
7. If I were lonely, my first thought would be to seek _____ out.
8. One of my primary concerns is _____'s welfare.
9. I would forgive _____ for practically anything.
10. I feel responsible for _____'s well-being.
11. When I am with _____, I spend a good deal of time just looking at him (her).
12. I would greatly enjoy being confided in by _____.
13. It would be hard for me to get along without _____.

Liking Scale

1. When I am with _____, we almost always are in the same mood.
2. I think that _____ is unusually well-adjusted.
3. I would highly recommend _____ for a responsible job.
4. In my opinion, _____ is an exceptionally mature person.
5. I have great confidence in _____'s good judgment.
6. Most people would react favorably to _____ after a brief acquaintance.
7. I think that _____ and I are quite similar to one another.
8. I would vote for _____ in a class or group election.
9. I think that _____ is one of those people who quickly wins respect.
10. I feel that _____ is an extremely intelligent person.
11. _____ is one of the most likable people I know.
12. _____ is the sort of person whom I myself would like to be.
13. It seems to me that it is very easy for _____ to gain admiration.

SOURCE: Rubin (1973)

for a friend of the same sex as their dating partner. The subjects also completed a romanticism scale assessing their adherence to romantic ideas of love. Both men and women unsurprisingly reported loving their partners considerably more than their friends, though women loved their friends appreciably more than men did. Love and liking for one's dating partner were only moderately correlated, indicating that there is some difference between them. Men, however, seem to make the distinction less succinctly than women do, but—what is probably far more significant—women like their dating partners considerably more than they are liked in return. This is almost certainly a result of masculine notions of supremacy rather than of any greater likability of men over women (in the ratings of same-sex friends, there was no tendency for men to be liked more than women). Insofar as the liking scale asked for judgments of characteristics traditionally ascribed to males—maturity, intelligence, good judgment—the results seem to show that dating relationships perpetuate the stereotypical differences between the sexes. The men felt it inappropriate for their partners to have the characteristics suggested. Most important, for both sexes, love—but not liking—was highly correlated with estimates of being in love and of the probability of marriage.

Six months later, Rubin had his subjects complete a brief questionnaire assessing the progress of the couples' relationships over the intervening months. Somewhat surprisingly, the correlation between love scores and progress was relatively small. But for subjects who had scored high on the romanticism scale, the correlation between love and progress was substantial, especially when both partners were romantic. "The pattern of correlations indicated that love indeed predicts progress in dating relationships, but only for those people who subscribe to the ideology that this is the way things ought to be." Liking, however, was almost as highly correlated with progress as love was.

If we examine who actually marries whom, we see that whether love is present or absent (which we really don't know), the patterns are very much the same as those for other affiliations. We choose spouses who are nearby, who are similar to us in social, economic, educational, religious, and racial background, and who share our attitudes and values. We also select people who are physically attractive to us, though there is an interesting difference between the sexes here. Physical attraction is far more important to men than to women; for men it dominates all the other desirable characteristics, while for women it falls at the bottom of the scale. But when we consider that traditionally in marriage the woman assumes the social and economic status of her husband, rather than vice versa, this difference between them seems quite logical. Marriage might be the only business venture a woman engages in in her entire life, but she seems on the whole to be prepared to negotiate it to her advantage.

We have seen in this section that one of the central questions of social psychology has to do with motivation: Why do we seek the company of others? What draws us to other people? Probably the best answer we have is that others help to reduce uncertainty, especially ambiguity. "Although most of us can comfortably live with a great deal of ignorance, few of us can tolerate much ambiguity" (Rubin, 1973). We are frequently uncertain about the quality of our achievements—sometimes to the extent that we wonder if they aren't failures instead—until someone else has seen them. We constantly compare ourselves to others on a wide variety of dimensions—abilities, attitudes, beliefs, appearance, and so on and on—not only to find out how good or bad we are in a given respect, but far more importantly to approach the truth about ourselves. It is only by comparing ourselves with other people that all of the elements that make up our own personality take on meaning. Finally, largely on the basis of achievement, social approval, and social comparison, we affiliate with others whom we perceive to be similar to us in the ways we consider important. And of all the similarities that might be important to us, probably the most important one is a similarity of attitudes and values. This is true whether we are considering a business association, friendship, or marriage.

SOCIAL BEHAVIOR AND EMOTION

What Is Emotion?

The role our feelings and emotions play in shaping our social behavior has been the focus of extensive psychological investigation. Research in this area has been concerned with such questions as: Do you tremble because you are angry, or are you angry because you tremble? Do you run because you are afraid, or are you afraid because you run?

The commonsense, everyday view of emotion is that first something happens, *then* we experience an emotional reaction, and *then* our body responds in various ways. William James (1884), however, proposed a different order of events: something happens, then our body responds, and then we experience our body's response, which we call emotion. The emotions of fear, elation, anger, sympathy, and love are nothing but our experiences of bodily changes.

James-Lange theory

This James-Lange theory (Carl Lange had advanced similar ideas) was disputed by Walter Cannon (1927). Cannon noted that essentially similar physiological changes accompanied quite different emotions, so that the bodily changes in themselves were insufficient to account for the range of human feelings.

Maranon (1924) had found that direct injection of epinephrine (adrenaline) produced pseudo or "as if" emotional responses. The subject might say, "I feel as if I were angry" but not, "I am angry."

Bachrach

Walter B. Cannon

From these starting points, researchers have explored emotions through various avenues. Some have attempted to analyze physiological responses to external events to establish whether they are indeed subtly differentiated: Does the response for fear differ from the one for anger? Others have attempted to map the path of responses from the senses through the thalamus, hypothalamus, cortex, muscles, and viscera. A less physiological approach was taken by Schachter and Singer (1962), who asked whether a social situation could influence the emotional state of a person who had been artificially and inexplicably aroused. These experimenters injected some of their subjects with epinephrine and some (the control group) with an inactive solution (salt water). Epinephrine usually produces an increase in heart rate and respiration, trembling, and a feeling of warmth and flushing. Some of the subjects injected with epinephrine were told to expect these effects and some were told to expect only itching, headache, or numbness; the remainder were not informed about effects. All were told that the drug injected was "Suproxin" and that the experiment concerned its effect upon vision.

After the injection, each subject was paired with a confederate of the experimenters in a separate room, ostensibly to wait for the Suproxin to take effect. The true prupose was to find out how the subject would respond to the confederate, who pretended to be a participant in the experiment. For half of the subjects the confederate displayed irritation, then anger, at the nature of a questionnaire the experimenters had supplied—finally ripping it to pieces and stomping out of the room. For the other subjects the confederate twirled a hula hoop, threw paper airplanes, and indulged in other antics that expressed euphoric exuberance.

The experimenters found that the epinephrine-aroused subjects who had the least information about the cause of their physiological arousal tended most to assume the mood of the confederate; they reported that they were either happy or angry, depending on the behavior of the confederate. The subjects who had been correctly informed of the drug's effects and those who did not receive it did not adopt the mood of the confederate. These people already had an explanation of their arousal, or else did not experience an arousal. The others, however, experienced an arousal for which they had no explanation and therefore adopted the one that was offered them by the confederate. In other words, as Schachter and Singer put it, "Emotional states may be considered a function of a state of physiological arousal and of a cognition appropriate to this state of arousal"—and the cognition may be supplied by evironmental influences. This study, which strongly supports the James-Lange theory of emotion, helps us to see how people in different cultural and social situations learn different interpretations of what they are feeling. Even more interestingly, when a mother labels her child's feelings for him, it is easy to see why the child accepts these labels so readily. Therefore, if the labels are in fact inappropriate, the child is caught in a vicious circle which can lead to severe disturbance. The process will be examined in a bit more detail in Chapter 16.

 Eye Contact

Eye contact is a significant aspect of social interaction. Coss (1965) found evidence   eye contact
that a response to eyes may be innate. Pairs of circular stimuli placed side by side, so that they resembled a pair of eyes, produced more arousal in infant subjects than one or three circular stimuli and more than one circle positioned above another. Arousal was increased even further when solid black circles resembling pupils were placed inside the pairs of circular stimuli.

Social interaction between two people often begins with a period of eye contact that seems to indicate each person's readiness to interact with the other. Goffman (1963) observed that once interaction is under way, each person looks at the other in the region of the eyes intermittently, in glances of varying length usually between 1 and 10 seconds. The proportion of time one person may spend looking at the other may vary from 0 to 100 percent; typically it lies between 25 and 75 percent. The proportion of time spent in eye contact is much smaller. The person listening gives longer glances than the one talking and tends to look more frequently.

Argyle and Dean (1965) have observed eye contact equilibriums in action and report that they appear to be a function of physical proximity and other aspects of intimacy. Eye contact is reduced when two people are positioned closer together.

Exline and Winters (1965) found that a person looks more at another whom he likes than at someone he dislikes or is indifferent to. In addition, Exline (1963) and Exline, Gray and Schuette (1965) found that people high in affiliation motivation look at an interlocutor more frequently when the interview or discussion is nonthreatening and less often when intimate topics are broached. Affiliation motivation appears to call for eye contact accompanied by a smile.

Eye contact is involved in the establishment of a variety of relationships. It may be friendly, designed to establish a closer relationship. Yet a person who excessively seeks eye contact with another may create anxiety. Eye contact may be sexual, as suggested by the phrase "making eyes." In this instance eye contact is usually accompanied by a softened smile and slightly dilated pupils. Eye contact may also signal a threat, as it frequently does in primates and other animals, and it may be used to establish dominance. Strongman and Champness (1968) used frequency of looking away first from eye contact as a measure of submission. They caution, however, that the person who talks first (an indication of dominance) is also typically likely to look away first.

When animals are threatened, one mode of defense that may be resorted to is to cut off the aggressor from view (Chance, 1962). Humans may do the same, in an effort to lower their level of arousal. An extreme form of this behavior is seen in autistic children and other mental patients.

Eye contact also serves a more cognitive function in interaction. It enables both speaker and listener to obtain feedback; a speaker, for example, looks at his listener's eyes to determine whether he is really listening or not. Eye contact also enables the speaker to know how his message is received—whether it is understood and accepted, for example. People actually do look up at, or just before, the end of long utterances at the point at which they need feedback (Kendon, 1967).

Martin Gonzalez   Steve Hurwitz

Words are not essential to the expression of emotion.

Words or Actions as Sources of Emotional Information

In the experiment we have just discussed, the subjects took emotional cues from other people, but the cues did not consist simply of what the other people said. We interpret other people's emotions by what they do as well as by what they say.

"Now you're getting angry."

"No I'm not."

"Yes you are—I can tell. You're drumming your fingers the way you always do when you're angry."

Actually, it has been found that people rely least on a person's words in judging his emotions. This is not hard to understand: words are easily formed and readily reversed ("talk is cheap") and often are mere labels for policy. But actions are substantial; they are the policy itself. Moreover, the physical accompaniments to human action—tone of voice, facial expression, bodily posture—are considered expressive of genuine emotion since it is assumed that they are not readily controlled or falsified. When, in responding to the emotions of others, we find that their verbal and nonverbal cues conflict, we tend to give more weight to the nonverbal evidence. There is probably some evolutionary support for this as well. Animals are dependent primarily on nonverbal communication, and even man in his early history had much more limited communication processes, and so had to rely on action. Thus, the adage "Sticks and stones may break my bones, but names can never harm me" seems still to underlie much of human communication.

SOCIAL INFLUENCE

Our interactions with other people are shaped by social influences that operate on us in a variety of ways, both obvious and subtle. We are to a certain extent influenced by the happenstance proximity to us of an individual or group. But more subtle and more complex matters, such as acceptance of group norms or deviation from those norms, are also important factors that guide our behavior in relation to others. In considering deviation, we naturally ask: Do those who are isolated deviate, or do those who deviate become isolated? Isolation does not inevitably lead to deviation, for the isolate may try all the harder to conform in order to be accepted. Nor does deviation lead inevitably to isolation, for those who have deviated may be wooed—or threatened—by the group to conform and "come back home." Where deviation continues or is extreme, the group may exclude the deviant—but a certain degree of deviation is often tolerated or even welcomed. Eccentric people may be prized members of a group, provided their eccentricity does not seem threatening. If we engage in the activities of the members of a particular group and take on the obligations expected of members

norm

of that group, how far will we go in carrying out what is expected of us? Or perhaps we reject the norms of certain groups, and in the very fact of doing so take on other sets of norms representing different standards. What does acceptance of group norms entail in terms of helping us decide what to do in particular situations? We will explore such questions in this section as a further means of understanding our social role.

The Effect of Proximity

Some groups we choose to join; others we simply find surrounding us. Do the people among whom we just happen to be exert any influence upon our standards? Do group standards develop among people who are thrown together? Do the members tend to conform to these standards, and does the group tend to enforce them against deviance?

Some interesting answers were obtained by Festinger, Schachter, and Back (1950), who studied social life in two sets of buildings, called Westgate and Westgate West, in a housing project for married college students. Because these buildings were physically isolated from the rest of the town, the residents tended to find their social life within the project. It was found, first, that these people tended to choose their friends from among those who lived very close to them or who used the same stairwell. Proximity, physical or functional, was a major factor predisposing to friendship choices.

It was found too that in Westgate, which at the time of the study had been occupied for 15 months, social norms had developed, whereas in Westgate West, occupied only a few months, they had not. The norms concerned participation in and attitudes toward a tenants' council. What one did or felt about this council in Westgate West was of no particular concern to others, but in Westgate there was a marked tendency to reject those who deviated from the norms that had developed among the residents of each court. Moreover, among the subcommunities in Westgate, higher social cohesiveness was associated with lower deviation rates. Even those who were planning to move kept up their activities in the tenants' council.

It must be noted, however, that all of the findings of this study rest on a condition that does not always obtain among people living in close proximity. That condition is an interaction among the people living in the housing project. In mid-Manhattan, for example, where people live in as close or closer proximity as in the college buildings, there is considerably less—sometimes almost no—interaction. The probable reason for high interaction in Westgate and Westgate West is the pronounced similarity of the occupants: they had life situation, family status, even a degree of social status, in common. In addition, they were isolated from other interactions.

Perhaps, then, the conclusions of this study on social influence might better be stated: *Where there is significant interaction in a community,* people tend to choose their friends among those who live closest to them, to develop a set of common social norms, and to reject those who deviate from the norms.

Bradford Hess

Contrasting kinds of entertainment in the small town and the city.

Louis Mélancon

Group Recognition

Group membership requires group recognition. Just as the person identifies himself to some extent with the group, the group identifies itself to some extent with him, and it does so by recognizing and welcoming his personal identity. Though groups are often condemned as inimical to personal uniqueness, they are in fact a primary means of individuation. The group that cares most about a person, such as his family or club, and that best appreciates his skills and accomplishments, such as fellow-workers at a job, is the source of his most unique and personal recognition. It is in the light and warmth of this recognition that the person is likely to realize himself most constructively, as well as make the greatest efforts to contribute.

A complaint often heard about small-town life is that the individual is overrecognized, overidentified, and overinfluenced (pressured) to conform to group norms. The modern city frees the individual from this pervasive social inspection; here he enjoys a kind of generalized privacy. Even in a crowded restaurant or a public museum he is remote from his fellows. This may be just what he wants as he moves between places and groups where he is known. On the other hand, he may lack such places and groups. He may in fact become anonymous and, as a consequence, deindividuated. The influence of societal norms on such a person is tenuous. His relationship with society tends to deteriorate further; he grows less responsible and often more aggressive.

deindividuation

Group Norms

Norms are the behavioral guidelines that may be inferred from common, average, or standard performance of members of groups. Norms are different from ideals, in that ideals are guidelines that may diverge widely from average behavior. A norm among college students might be stated: "You don't hurt nice people for no good reason"; or, "When your team is out there playing, you are out there cheering"; or, "Nobody in this dorm steals from anybody else in this dorm." Norms describe acceptable and approved things that people in a group actually do and ways in which they do them; they also describe what is unacceptable and disapproved. Norms, thus, are group value judgments.

norms

Deindividuation

Zimbardo (1969) tested the tendency of deindividuated people to become aggressive by rendering a group of coeds anonymous: they were never referred to by name, they wore baggy coats and hoods that covered their faces, and they operated in the dark. A second group worked with uncovered faces in the light, wore name tags, and were repeatedly referred to by name.

The students then took part in an experiment involving electric shock. Each was to administer a series of shocks to a victim, ostensibly to see whether the subjects felt more empathy when watching or when shocking. Before administering any shocks, however, each subject listened to a supposed recorded interview with the victim, which made her appear either nice or nasty. She then proceeded to administer the shocks, to which the victim (a confederate of the experimenter and actually disconnected from the shock apparatus) responded by squirming, jumping, and writhing.

The individuated subjects, as they progressed through the series, administered shocks of decreasing length to the "nice" girl and of increasing length to the "nasty" girl (Fig. 14.2). The deindividuated students began by shocking each victim twice as long (close to 1 second) as did the individuated students, and they administered shocks of increasing length to both victims; the aggressive behavior of these hooded subjects appeared to feed upon itself.

Philip G. Zimbardo

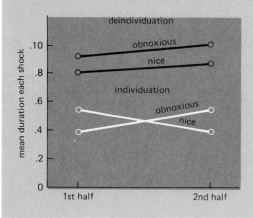

Fig. 14.2 The human choice. (Zimbardo, 1969)

internalization   People may "internalize" or make a part of themselves the norms of a given group and carry them into other groups that have different norms. A European explorer who finds himself among the headhunters of the upper Amazon may, out of curiosity or the wish to ensure his safety, become friendly with the tribe and perhaps even join its expeditions. Probably, however, he will continue to judge his hosts not by their own norms but by those of his own group, even though that group is thousands of miles away. On the other hand,

Social Class and Stratification

One of the basic facts which characterizes the nature of human associaton is the existence of rank differences between individuals and groups in all human societies. We cannot fully understand social life in humans unless we take into account these rank differences and their interrelations and patterns in social relationships.

In our society, the ranking system takes the form of a class structure which constitutes one of the essential elements in determining social relationships and other class factors which enter into almost every aspect of our life. From them stem variations in health, income, and knowledge. Class distinction also influences our choice of marriage partners, the number of children we have, and the age at which we marry. They largely determine the kind of education we receive, the occupation we enter, the kind of books we read, the way we dress, and the level of power, prestige, and authority that we attain in society.

While ranking is universal, we find that most, though not all, societies elaborate the process of ranking further in arranging certain social positions in a graded hierarchy of socially superior and inferior ranks. Whenever a society displays this graded series of ranks, we say that it is stratified. Social stratification is a special type of social differentiation, signifying the existence of a systemized hierarchy of social position whose occupants are treated as superior, inferior, or equal, relative to one another, in socially important respects.

if he has not internalized his own group's norms, he may "go native," embracing the norms of the new group. He cannot really be a member of the group without adhering to the norms, just as the group itself cannot exist until norms emerge. A functioning social group, as distinguished from a merely statistical

Joe Molnar   Cy Tetenman

Dancing partners—in the city one need not travel far to encounter contrasting group norms.

or spatial grouping, is defined by its norms. One need not travel across continents or national boundary lines to encounter alien norms; they can be as close as the "hippies" (or the "squares") next door. People often move from group to group and fully support the norms of each. At college, your roommate lies nude on the floor attempting to play the guitar with his toes—but he probably doesn't behave like that in your parents' living room.

    Brainstorming

Do people solve problems better working alone or in active participation with others? Research has found both negative and positive effects of groups on an individual person's problem-solving capacities. The impetus for research of this sort has come mostly from business and government, and its implications extend more to those groups than to others. Business and governmental agencies have been interested in exploring the problem-solving possibilities of "brainstorming" sessions, in which an unstructured, free-association, group-participation approach is used.

brainstorming

Credit for this procedure is usually given to Osborn (1963), though it may be considered analogous to W. J. J. Gordon's (1961) synergic method. Both these men maintained that group thinking is superior to individual thinking, that it can accomplish in hours what might take a single person months. Group activity is said to encourage a kind of irrational creativity and to set the stage for daring, competition, and a broadening scope for the search for ideas.

The question psychologists have been asking is: Can a group of people working together think better and more effectively than a group of people working in isolation? Is it better to work in groups or alone?

Taylor, Berry, and Block (1958) found that five people working alone produced about twice as many solutions and unique ideas as five people working together. They concluded that the mutual stimulation of a group was offset by interfering and distracting effects. However the people involved in group projects worked together for a comparatively short time and had not been preselected to be especially compatible or trained to work together. At least one study (Cohen, Whitmyre, and Funk, 1960) suggests that such considerations play an important role in group thinking.

Dunnette, Campbell, and Jaastad (1963) used research scientists and advertising personnel as subjects who worked in teams or alone on four problems. The production of people working alone was about 30 percent greater in terms of quantity with no reduction in quality. Thus group interaction appeared to inhibit these people.

That a great deal more can be learned from a greater consideration of the people involved in brainstorming research is an idea forwarded by Guilford (1967), who noted that creative persons known for their originality and competence and a comparative lack of sociability and who seem to adhere to their own set of values

Alex F. Osborn

are not likely to flourish in group projects in contrast to more sociable people of lesser creative and intellectual talents.

People seem to be all too easily or at least just as easily inhibited as stimulated, distracted as involved, by other group members. Possibly the use of less artificial groups would result in a decrease of error and an increase in efficiency. Possibly the nature of the problem itself has to be given more consideration, especially with respect to its interaction with specific personality types. Certain problems might best be solved by people who are naturally unsocial and consequently uncomfortable in group projects.

Portrayals of brainstorming groups as highly pressured, highly competitive think tanks are not entirely accurate. Yet pressure and competition undoubtedly contribute to the effectiveness of these groups, when they are effective. Without pressure and competition brainstorming would deteriorate to the level of creativity of the production assembly line, where productivity is frequently restrained at a kind of median pace and those who exceed that pace are pressured to conform. Group pressure works in many ways that have not yet been systematically delineated.

Norms are useful. They reduce the confusion, uncertainty, and anxiety of social confrontations by helping us to know what to do and what to expect. By reducing the mechanisms of social interaction to habit, they allow us to concentrate on refinements, on the "important things." When a person feels that norms unduly cramp his style, he may complain of "restrictive social norms," as if norms as such caused the problem. But investigation usually shows that he would continue to embrace many norms and would not dream of giving them (or society) up—it is a select few norms that he objects to.

Obedience to Norms

Whether one volunteers for a group or is simply born into it, the group will attempt to impose conformity to its norms. The member may either experience the pressure or apply it, and he is likely to do a lot of both.

Groups influence their members not only to behave but also to interpret evidence and sense data in expected ways. The first of these influences is called normative and the second informational.

Hood and Sherif (1962), to test social informational influence, devised an experiment involving the autokinetic effect. This effect (see Chapter 2) is the tendency to see a pinpoint light move in the dark, even though the light source is in fact motionless. The subjects were told that their visual acuity would be tested and that they would wait briefly in the dark so that their eyes could adapt. Each subject, while waiting alone, overheard another subject (a confederate of the experimenter) describing his own perceptions of the movement of the light. Half the subjects overheard that the range of movement had been from 1 to 5 inches; the others, from 6 to 10 inches. When the real subjects later reported their own observations, the estimates of the first group ranged around a median of 4 inches; those of the second group, around a median of 7 inches.

Asch (1956) studied a less ambiguous situation—in fact, one involving no ambiguity at all. He projected on a screen a picture of three lines, one of which was equal in length to a fourth projected line, and asked his subjects to identify the equal line (Fig. 14.3). The experiment was arranged so that from one to 15 confederates consistently gave an answer so obviously incorrect that the subject would never make that mistake unaided. The subject gave his own answer last, after all the confederates had given theirs. Would the "pressure" of their judgments influence him to conform?

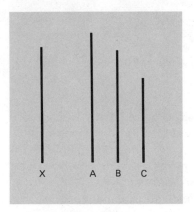

Fig. 14.3 A representative stimulus in the Asch conformity study. Subjects were shown four lines simultaneously and asked which line was most similar in length to that of line X. (Asch, 1956)

About one out of three subjects was in fact influenced to give an incorrect answer (Fig. 14.4). The influence of a single confederate was nil, but the influence of two was appreciable. Three confederates in unanimous agreement had a

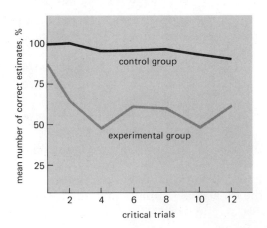

Fig. 14.4 The influence of group pressure on conformity. (Asch, 1956)

strong influence that the addition of more confederates did not increase. However, a reduction of the difference in length between the reference line and the line wrongly chosen as equal to it increased the subject's conformity to the group judgment. On the other hand, the true subject was almost entirely freed of group influence when one of the confederates consistently gave the correct answer.

Among the most famous and fascinating studies of the effects of group norms have been those of Stanley Milgram (1963, 1964, 1965). Milgram's series of experiments asked the question: To what extent will a person be obedient to authority and social pressure in inflicting pain and injury upon another person? The experimental situation ostensibly was set up to test the effect of punishment on memory. The subject was to take the role of "teacher" and inflict electrical shocks whenever the "student" gave a wrong answer. The "student" (more properly called a victim) was strapped into an "electric chair." The subject was set up in another room before a potent-looking "shock generator"; he could no longer see the victim and could infer what was happening only by the sound of the victim's voice, broadcast over an intercom. What he actually heard was a tape recording, which played responses that were keyed to the level of shock he administered.

Thirty shock levels were indicated on the control panel, ranging from "Slight Shock—15 volts" to "Danger: Severe Shock—450 volts." The victim's responses began with a grunt at 75 volts. At 150 volts he complained of a heart disturbance (he had mentioned a mild heart condition while being strapped into the chair), cried out and asked to be released from the experiment; at 180 volts he exclaimed that he couldn't stand the pain. Later he screamed in agony, and after 300 volts he no longer responded.

Left to exercise their own judgment as to how much shock to administer, a group of control subjects averaged about 50 volts over a series of 30 incorrect answers. Only two of 40 subjects administered shocks greater than 150 volts.

Urged on by two confederates of the experimenter, ostensibly fellow "teachers" in the experiment who gave their opinions first, subjects in a second group administered progressively greater shocks. The confederates urged that the shock be increased one level after each error, so that at the 30th error the highest possible shock, 450 volts, would be administered. Although the mean shock level chosen by the subjects lagged behind the confederates' recommendations, 27 of the 40 subjects administered greater shocks even after the "victim" had cried out (150 volts) that he had heart trouble and wanted to be released; seven went all the way to administer 450 volts. The experimental subjects' internalized norms of sympathy and consideration for another person's well-being, when subjected to conflicting counterpressure by a small group (two other persons), proved to be relatively feeble and ineffective—shockingly ineffective.

This experiment casts into stark relief one of the worst consequences of modern, mobile, decentralized social structures. Few people belong to a norm-perpetuating group for a sufficient length of time to truly internalize the group's

Ethical Considerations in Research

In doing research, the investigator must first narrow down a psychological problem to a testable proposition (a hypothesis); his next task is to design the methodolgy (how to do it). In designing any research, especially when people are involved, ethical considerations must be taken into account. Because the social psychologist wants to find out how people behave in varied social situations, he must first expose subjects to certain manipulative conditions and observe how they respond. But he must be sure in doing this that no extreme discomfort or ill effect to his subjects occur as a result of his experimentation.

The social psychologist must therefore set down certain guidelines and limitations. First, subjects should be informed of the nature of the experiment to the extent that it is consistent with the objectives of the study. However, it is often impossible to tell subjects everything about the experiments without biasing the results. Second, it should be made clear that compliance in the experimental situation is voluntary. Before placing the individual in a well-controlled, experimental situation, in which everything is structured to make noncompliance difficult, the subject should be told that he is free to refuse any directive given by the experimentor.

Third, the experimenter must give careful consideration to whether the conditions produced in the laboratory are similar to those found in a real life setting or if they are unique conditions. Being threatened with a situation found in everyday life in contrast to an uncommon or unusual situation (for example, being isolated for many hours) can determine whether a subject has the ability to adequately cope with the experience. In many cases the real life setting will provoke less anxiety. It also has the advantage of producing results which are more widely generalizable in the real world. And finally and perhaps most obvious, the experimenter should not do anything which may possibly cause the subject harm. This encompasses exposing subjects to drugs, or other objects which could cause considerable harm, as well as respecting the individual's right to privacy.

The issue of violation of ethical conduct was raised by the American Psychological Association in connection with the well-known Milgram (1963) experiment (in which electric shocks were supposedly delivered in an alleged learning experiment—see text for more detailed explanation). It was argued that the pressure of the situation and the urging of the experimenter made refusal of delivery of supposedly severe shocks difficult. Under these circumstances a large number of subjects (about half) dutifully delivered alleged shocks labeled "danger level," although the confederates to whom they were being delivered screamed for mercy. It is hard to assess what psychological damage was suffered by those who dutifully obeyed the experimenter's direction. It is clear however, that if any long-range discomfort or anxiety was experienced by subjects as a result of this experimental procedure, the experiment was unwarranted.

norms. In fact, few groups today serve a norm-perpetuating function. So many traditional norms have been called into question that even groups that continue to function, including the family, are frequently unwilling or unable to enforce more than the most basic of social norms; some families are barely able to do more than toilet train their children. When we add to that the high mobility that prevails today, with people moving from group to group, and hence from one set of norms to another, we see that most people are quite honestly confused about what is expected of them, even of what they expect of themselves, in a given situation.

In this respect, we might recall the Zimbardo deindividuation experiment, where the point was made that deindividuation increases hostility and aggression. But from the point of view of norm internalization, we might find the behavior of even the "individuated" students a bit strange. Norms of consideration for others would seem to forbid participating in an experiment where someone else is hurt simply to find out whether it costs you more pain to watch him being hurt or to actually do the hurting yourself. The excuse for the experiment would not seem to be a sufficient reason for performing it. Yet even the individuated students had no trouble administering shocks when they didn't particularly like their victim.

Milgram's work raises a different specter for contemporary man. Nice typical American citizens are quite capable of causing apparent bodily harm to others just like themselves, without suffering any physical coercion to do so. This is one of the standard defenses offered at virtually every war crime trial: I was only following orders, I am a nice guy, not a psychopathic brute. Results from experiments like the ones just reported suggest that the defense may have some "psychological" validity.

Who Goes Along?

A good case can be made that most of the "harm" done in the world (however one may define harm) is not by self-starting evildoers but by others who "go along." A similar case might be made for the "good" that is done in the world. Why do people go along?

Some research has linked tendency to conform with particular personality characteristics. The ability to maintain independent judgment in opposition to group pressure has been correlated with intelligence, originality, ego strength, and self-confidence. However, it has also been found to be related to the specific situation and to considerations of expediency. A person may sometimes go along with the group judgment while he is with the group and yet privately believe it to be wrong. In this case, his inner cognitions remain unaffected, but they also remain ineffective; as far as everyone else is concerned, he agrees with the group.

Individual Differences in Conforming and Nonconforming

The results of experiments are often reported in terms of numerical relationships that give us only an incomplete insight into the reality of a situation. We may, for example, learn from the Milgram (1963) and Asch (1956) experiments that typically one-third of a given population is likely to conform. But what constitutes conformity—how the individual subjects reacted as they conformed—is rarely disclosed.

Fortunately Asch has given us a detailed account of the climate of his experiment. He has specified not only the nature of his subjects' response but their manner of responding as well. He has thus given us a description of individual differences.

Few of Asch's subjects suspected the genuineness of the confederates. General agreement with the group was established by a number of trials in which the confederates gave the correct response. One of the results of this agreement was that the subjects became confident of their own perceptions and judgments. But suddenly, for certain critical trials, the subject found himself in radical opposition to the group. He found himself in a state of conflict. Asch notes that even subjects who remained firmly independent in their judgments seemed a bit shaken.

Many subjects expressed their discomfort in half-hearted attempts at resolution. Some noted that a few of the confederates wore glasses, or that each person looked at the lines from a different position in the room; they also expressed notions that the others might be basing their judgments on some property of the lines other than length. Some subjects became more scrupulous in their observations and comparisons. They frequently asked to see the lines again, and some tried to approach the lines and measure them. Some began to experience self-doubt. For example, one said, "I'd probably take [the opinion] of the people here [if this were a practical situation]. I'd figure my judgment was faulty. I feel puzzled. . . . In all the years I've lived I haven't had any trouble like that."

Opinions fluctuated rapidly: "Probably I'm wrong. . . . No, I don't mean that. If everybody saw it the other way I guess I'm wrong, but I think I'm right."

Subjects expressed a genuine longing to agree with the majority: "I felt disturbed, puzzled, separated like an outcast from the rest. Every time I disagreed I was beginning to wonder if I wasn't beginning to look funny."

Asch classified yielding behavior into three types. The rarest type was a change in actual perception of the lines. "They made me reconsider," one said. He maintained that he had answered honestly. "Otherwise it would defeat the purpose of the experiment."

In another kind of yielding subjects distorted their judgments. They said, "I am wrong; they are right." Asch observed that primary doubt sapped both confidence and energy to resist; disagreement with the others was a sign of personal defect. These subjects often confessed to reacting out of fear of ridicule. "I probably wanted my own ideas, but it was easiest to give in."

Other subjects in yielding distorted their action. They lost sight of the task and became relatively unconcerned with correctness; they wanted merely not to appear different and consequently suppressed judgment. "I did not want to be apart from the group; I did not want to look like a fool." One subject, whom Asch noted was an attractive, bright man, said, "I have a horror of being a solitary individual socially—a horror of being an outcast. I have a basic feeling of insecurity."

Subjects who remained independent often appeared to manifest unshakable conviction. Nonverbally they appeared to say, "I will not be moved." Uncertainty was resolved by holding on to their judgment. One said, "Looking at it logically I must say that I am wrong, since the others disagree. But looking at it subjectively I must say I'm right." Another said, "Inasmuch as I saw the lines I will believe that I am right until I am proved wrong. . . . Measure them and prove empirically that I am wrong."

Some independent subjects reported their perceptions without confidence. They differed from yielders only in terms of their overriding sense of obligation to report what they actually saw, whether their perceptions were correct or not.

How do bystanders react when someone is mugged on a busy metropolitan thoroughfare? Evidently, most of us look to our fellows for information about how to respond. Latané and Darley (1970) had a female researcher administer a questionnaire-type test to a naive subject alone or to a naive subject and a stooge. The researcher left the room and, in an adjoining room, played a tape recording of a loud crash. She then cried out in pain. When the naive subject was alone, in about 70 percent of instances he rushed to the woman's aid. When the subject was with a stooge who rushed to her aid, he followed suit in the same percentage of instances. But when the stooge ignored the researcher's scream, the subject rarely responded to it.

When those around us fail to respond, we tend to reinterpret the situation. If we see someone attacked on the street and others around us fail to respond, we try to find some benign cause for the attack. Perhaps a movie is being filmed, or the people involved are merely acting for some private reason of their own. Perhaps the attacker is justified; he has been wronged by his victim in some way. The bystander in a sea of indifferent bystanders becomes afraid of appearing foolish. Perhaps the others know something he doesn't know.

Moscovici, Lage, and Raffrechonx (1969) have shown that a consistent minority of two could influence four other members of a group to call a blue light "green." About one out of three of the subjects was susceptible to such influence. Thus, when a consistent minority remains firm, either out of conviction, stubbornness, or special circumstances (as where the consistent minority are confederates of the experimenter), a situation is created in the group that resembles the situation in which there is a consistent majority. In either event, the individual's unified impression is disrupted.

We noted earlier in this chapter that people seek to form a unified impression and affirm it, even in the face of disconfirming evidence, rather than continue in a state of suspended judgment. Once the state of suspended judgment comes into existence, we see now that neither the weight of the evidence nor the numerical balance of opinion, nor both together, will consistently determine how the person goes along.

In value-judgment terms, we might infer that neither the "good" nor the "evil" majority in a society is safe from upset by a determined minority, and neither the "evil" nor the "good" minority, no matter how small, is without hope of gaining support and beginning to roll.

Leadership

The question of going along is related to the question of leadership, for when we join a group it is likely that we will go along, at least temporarily, with the people in power—the leaders. More or less consciously, we surrender some of our autonomy, our control over our own lives or at least our thinking, to the group and, within the group, to the leader or leaders. Why are we willing to make this kind of sacrifice? The best answer, once again, probably lies in the motive we have posited to underlie all social behavior—to reduce uncertainty or ambiguity. If this is so, then the leaders we as members of the group choose or accept must be those people who are best able to reduce the uncertainty that brings that particular group together.

It is very difficult to discern a pattern of traits that characterize leaders. In fact, examination of leadership trait research done before 1940 reveals that only about 5 percent of named traits were common to four or more studies. More recently, certain traits seem to appear more frequently. These include intelligence, adjustment, extroversion, dominance, masculinity, and interpersonal sensitivity, but the correlations among these traits are very low (Mann, 1959).

One very good indication of who will be the leader in any given group is to observe who does the most talking. Leaders talk more than others, and among a group of total strangers, the person who talks most is typically—at least initially—perceived as the leader.

The difficulty of establishing a universal pattern of leadership traits becomes quite clear if we consider the many different kinds of groups that require leaders—states, corporations, college faculties, militant revolutionary groups such as the Weathermen and the Black Panthers, religious sects and congregations, even families. The abilities and styles of the leaders of these groups must be geared to the needs, goals, and values of their followers. The very power of a leader may in fact be limited by the wishes of those who follow, and leaders in some cases are simply those who best realize the groups' values.

Lewin, Lippitt, and White (1959) attempted to compare autocratic, democratic, and laissez-faire leadership styles. They demonstrated that the same person had a different impact when he employed one style as opposed to another. The autocratic leader maintains complete control, determining policy, dictating techniques and activities, and curbing individual initiative by withholding certain information as to procedure and planning. The democratic leader encourages and assists group decision-making, gives general plans that allow for individual variation and decision-making, and offers constructive criticism. The laissez-faire leader provides virtually no structure; he supplies only the needed materials and information and offers criticism only when it is requested.

In this experiment, the democratic style of leadership was considerably more effective than the others. It resulted in higher motivation and interest and permitted the group members to function in the absence of the leader. The democratic groups were also more friendly and reciprocative toward each other. Autocratic groups did somewhat more work but were more hostile, aggressive, and likely to engage in scapegoating. They were more dependent and less individualistic than the democratic groups. The laissez-faire groups did far less work and spent much more time playing than either of the others.

The curious fact, in view of this study, is that autocratic leaders continue to arise and to stay in power. We have noted that leaders typically realize the demands or needs of their followings. Perhaps autocratic leaders appear, then, when a group wants them, when the members relinquish their control over their activities. On the other hand, perhaps the autocratic leader persuades his following to relinquish control. Such leaders typically have a great deal of "charisma"; they are able to mesmerize people, to captivate an audience by appealing to values that are deemed sacred. But possibly the followers of such a leader want to be captivated.

Machiavellianism Quite aside from, and yet frequently related to, the question of who will lead people is the matter of who will prevail. While this is in large degree determined by the situation, it is also true that certain people are adept at prevailing, at having their way with life, often at others' expense, often in fact by manipulating others. This trait is frequently called Machiavellianism, after Niccolo Machiavelli, the 16th century Italian political philosopher who wrote *The Prince*, a treatise instructing the power-hungry how to obtain their goal by manipulating others.

Christie and Geis (1970) have constructed a questionnaire scale to measure Machiavellianism. The scale defines a subject as either High Mach, Low Mach, or Moderate Mach, according to the kinds of statements he endorses. High Machs endorse statements indicating relative standards of behavior ("A white lie is often a good thing"), whereas Low Machs have absolute standards ("Honesty is always the best policy"). Beyond that, High Machs are pragmatic; they are more inclined toward behavior that works than toward behavior that is principled, toward the assumption that the end justifies the means. In experimental situations, High Machs are adept at cheating and lying, at disrupting the

Machiavellianism

performance of competitors. Moreover, they can tolerate cognitive dissonance far better than Low or Moderate Machs; they feel little need to change an attitude in order to justify their behavior.

In this section, we have examined some of the ways in which social influence works. We have observed that, given a group of people who interact with each other, influence is related to proximity. We are more likely to conform to the social norms of those with whom we have frequent interaction than with the norms of more distant members of the group. We have seen, incidentally, that norms do not develop overnight, but only gradually, probably coincidentally with the group's success in defining itself. We have looked very briefly at deviation from group norms and have seen that a certain amount of it is not only tolerated but even welcomed. The amount of deviation the group accepts is probably proportional to the amount of dissonance the deviation introduces; in a classroom, for example, good-humored disagreement with the instructor and nonconformist attire may be accepted, but violent disagreement and disruptive behavior will probably not be tolerated because they interfere with the task the group has gathered to perform. We have seen, too, that group recognition, which is necessary to a feeling of membership, bestows certain rewards—most importantly and perhaps paradoxically, a greater sense of individuation and identity. In a state of deindividuation, people tend to become undiscriminatingly hostile and aggressive toward others. We have examined group norms, or actually practiced standards of behavior within groups, and have seen that committed membership in a group entails internalization, or personalization, of its norms. We have also looked at the current difficulty of internalizing norms and, to a degree, of finding norms to internalize. We have seen that people are quite highly subject to the influence of others in endorsing both ethical and informational norms. In view of the foregoing, it is not surprising that we should find the phenomenon of "going along"—of looking to others in ambiguous situations to help us decide what to do. But we have also seen that some people are able to maintain an independence of judgment and that a consistent minority can wield an overwhelming influence. Lastly, we have looked at leaders and have determined that they derive their power from the group whose members choose (or at least get) the leaders who best answer the needs that have brought them together.

We chose, early in this chapter, to look at social psychology from the point of view of the individual rather than the group. We said then that there may be forces outside the individual as well as within him that cause him to seek out others and to form certain relationships with them. But now that we have made a brief excursion through most of the concerns of social psychology, looking at them always from the point of view of the individual, we think it appropriate to suggest the possibility that human interaction is perhaps always due to some need or motivational state of individuals rather than to some force operating from without. Perhaps our perceptions of others can always be explained better in terms of our own needs, especially our need to dispel uncertainty or ambiguity rather than in terms of the needs of others to impose certain perceptions on us. Similarly, perhaps we seek out other people more because of motivating forces existing within us than because "society" expects us to form relationships with our fellow man, and perhaps we form the particular relationships we form because those are the ones that satisfy our transient or permanent needs rather than because those are the only ones available to us or because of some external factor such as a zodiacal affinity of stars or planets. Finally, when we are influenced by others, perhaps it is as much or even more because we are open to their influence as because they desire to exercise some kind of control over us. There can be no definitive statement about what causes human interaction at present, but we think it entirely possible that all of it might be understood in terms of individual need or motivational state.

Summary

Whether people choose to live in society or alone, as hermits, they are very much concerned with other people. Social psychology is the study of interpersonal behavior: how we perceive other people, the social aspects of human motivation, social determinants of emotion, and the influence of social groups on behavior.

Perception of other people is governed in part by the desire to avoid ambiguity, which results in cognitive dissonance. Tolerance of cognitive dissonance is particularly low when perception of others entails a judgment with consequences for the perceiver, or when the perceiver has some need to act on his perception, for example, when he must communicate his impression to someone else. Sometimes the desire to avoid ambiguity leads us to the formation of racial or other stereotypes.

One method of dissonance reduction is to form unified impressions, which we sometimes do by ignoring dissonant, or contradictory, information. Sometimes, however, we are able to integrate such information into a higher-order general impression.

Inferring a lot from a little is another method of dissonance reduction. We act on our own implicit theories of personality, which cause us to assume that certain clusters of traits always go together. We form first impressions, assuming that what we discover first is more important than later information. And, in the "halo effect," we extend the favorableness or unfavorableness of the first impression to our perception of someone's entire behavior.

Certain behavioral motivations have social components. While the achievement motive is not, in itself, a social motive, it is largely influenced by social factors—parental standards, the economic goals of one's society, the social mores one lives with.

The need for approval is satisfied by achieving approved goals, purchasing approved clothing, behaving according to approved standards. When we are uncertain about our own abilities, attitudes, and beliefs, we frequently are motivated to compare ourselves with others and to adopt the prevalent attitude or evaluation of our group. We also tend to form our opinions and develop our abilities along the lines of the opinions and abilities expressed by the majority of members of our group.

The affiliation motive, though it varies widely from one person to another, causes most people to seek the presence of others in certain life situations. People in anxiety-arousing situations and people who are by nature anxious are particularly likely to be affiliative. But some people, who might otherwise be affiliative, turn away from others in moments of anxiety. Affiliation may also be related to efforts to reduce uncertainty, and certain affiliations, such as marriages, are related to sexual needs and, we are just beginning to see, to romantic needs.

We affiliate largely with people who seem to us to be like ourselves, especially to have similar values and attitudes, but also to have similar social, economic, educational, religious, and racial status. Some evidence points to a difference between liking and loving, but apparently only for people who firmly believe in the difference. Affiliation patterns in the vast majority of marriages are the same as those in other interpersonal relationships.

Emotion is more a perception of a physical state than a physical reaction to a perception. Fast heartbeat and sweating palms precede the thought, "I am afraid," and if these physical signs arise without explanation or with conflicting explanations, we may very well think something other than, "I am afraid." Emotions, in other words, are largely learned rather than innate, and they are learned mostly from the social contexts we find ourselves in. Moreover, we tend to interpret others' emotions far more by their behavior than by their words.

The groups we belong to, whether by choice or by circumstance, influence our behavior in quite far-reaching ways. Within an interacting group, we tend to choose our friends among people who live near us, and our attitudes toward and participation in community activities tend to follow the dominant attitudes and participation trends of the community. Pressures to conform, for some people in some communities, may be too great. The individual may need to deviate, even to leave the community. But most people find some kind of group membership rewarding.

The isolated person becomes deindividuated and increasingly aggressive, gratuitously hurting other people. He has failed to internalize group norms, which are descriptive standards of things that people in a group actually do and ways in which they do them. Norms are not absolute standards of behavior, for we readily adopt the conflicting norms of the many different groups we temporarily belong to. The Milgram experiments indicate that people can be influenced to abandon norms that, in most middle-class American social groups, we would expect to be quite firmly internalized. Under the influence of other people, we also deny our own perceptions and say that we see, hear, taste, etc., what others claim to have perceived, especially if the others are consistent in what they claim. The influencing group does not have to be a majority; a consistent minority can be very powerful. But not everyone always conforms to group pressure. Those who do not usually are higher in traits of intelligence, originality, ego strength, and self-confidence.

Leaders attain their status because they best fulfill the group's needs and expectations. Democratic leaders generally prove more effective than autocratic or laissez-faire leaders, but again, the group usually gets the kind of leader it wants or deserves.

Groups also have manipulators, who may or may not be leaders. The manipulator usually has relative rather than absolute moral standards, is pragmatic rather than principled. He has a high tolerance of cognitive dissonance.

Suggested Readings

Bales, Robert F., *Personality and Interpersonal Behavior*. New York, Holt, Rinehart and Winston, 1970.
A nontechnical study, though based on technical research, of the interaction of personalities.

Berne, Eric, *Games People Play: The Psychology of Human Relationships*. New York, Grove, 1964.
A popular book about the unconscious ways in which people use duplicity in their social relations with others.

Brown, Claude, *Manchild in the Promised Land*. New York, Crowell Collier and Macmillan, 1965.
A firsthand description of what it is like to grow up in a black slum.

Byrd, Richard E., *Alone*. New York, Putnam's, 1938.
The Antarctic explorer's description of his several months spent alone in a remote polar region illustrates how much a person depends on human contacts.

Clark, Charles H., *Brainstorming*. New York, Doubleday, 1958.
Discusses the principles, procedures, and problems of brainstorming.

Fromm, Erich, *The Art of Loving: An Enquiry into the Nature of Love*. New York, Harper & Row, 1956.
For Fromm the sociocultural environment of the individual is the critical factor that determines whether a person will grow in his ability to give and accept love.

Hersey, John, *Hiroshima*. New York, Bantam, 1946.
An account of six people in the hours before the dropping of the bomb and the days immediately following.

Hersh, Seymour M., *My Lai 4: A Report on the Massacre and Its Aftermath*. New York, Random House, 1970.
This report, based largely on interviews with those who took part in the massacre, depicts the reactions of those involved and of the world at large.

Huxley, Aldous, *Brave New World* (originally published in 1932). New York, Harper & Row.
Huxley's world-famous novel about a barren, drug-controlled future where morality no longer has a place.

Huxley, Aldous, *Brave New World Revisited*. New York, Harper & Row, 1958.
Huxley looks at the world today in the light of his original novel and does not believe that his earlier prophecies were fantastic.

Lifton, Robert Jay, *Death in Life: The Survivors of Hiroshima*. New York, Random House, 1968.
The author examines the immediate and long-term psychological effects on those who lived through the blast.

Lindgren, H. C., *An Introduction to Social Psychology*. New York, Wiley, 1969.
A recent basic textbook in the area.

Milgram, Stanley, *Obedience to Authority*. New York, Harper & Row, 1974.
Milgram reports his findings from 10 years of research on the conditions that foster or hinder obedience.

Mills, C. Wright, *The Power Elite*. New York, Oxford, 1956.
The well-known sociologist's readable study of those who make the crucial decisions in contemporary American society.

Packard, Vance, *A Nation of Strangers.* New York, McKay, 1972.

Packard studies the effects on people of the extensive mobility in American society today.

Read, Piers Paul, *Alive.* Philadelphia, Lippincott, 1974.

The story of the survivors of the Andes plane crash who had to choose between using their dead companions for food or perishing in the remote mountains.

Shaw, M. E., and P. R. Constanzo, *Theories of Social Psychology.* New York, McGraw-Hill, 1970.

Considers some of the major theories in this area of psychology.

Tavris, Carol, "The Frozen World of the Familiar Stranger," *Psychology Today,* June 1974.

An interview with Stanley Milgram about his current work on life in the city.

Wright, Richard, "The Ethics of Living Jim Crow," in *Uncle Tom's Children* (originally published in 1936). New York, Harper & Row, 1969.

Wright tells about his cruel education in discrimination while growing up in the Deep South of the 1920s.

Chapter Fifteen

Attitudes

What are attitudes?
How are attitudes formed and changed?
Are attitudes in general comparatively stable or comparatively changeable?
Are our attitudes influenced by the groups we belong to? By our own personalities?
How are attitudes detected and measured?

In Chapter 14 we explored ways in which individual people and society interact, how the groups we belong to influence us and how we influence them. We have seen that certain generalizations about these relationships are possible, and that as a result we can to some extent make predictions about the outcomes of encounters between the person and his social environment.

In Chapter 14, however, we did not consider one of the most important determiners of what happens between the person and the social environment. This component is the usually fairly stable set of *attitudes* toward other people and toward events, places, and things that each of us carries around with him. Obviously, attitudes are not entirely *social* phenomena. We have attitudes toward ourselves and others as well as toward a host of objects that are at least partially nonsocial; we have preferences among automobiles, literary genres, china patterns, cat and dog breeds, even the foods we eat. Yet attitudes have come to be the province of social psychology more than any other division of psychology. This is essentially because social forces play a larger part than any other factor in the formation of attitudes, and consequently in the changing of attitudes.

WHAT ARE ATTITUDES?

Provisionally, let us say that attitudes are predispositions to respond, favorably or unfavorably, to a more or less predictable degree, to particular situations on the basis of ideas and feelings we bring to these situations. This is a complex definition with many elements that need elaboration.

Notice first that an attitude is a predisposition to respond, not a response or behavior per se. Many of our attitudes are not acted on consistently. We may fail to act for many reasons: the action may be inappropriate to the circumstances, it may carry a threat of punishment, it may be unrewarding, or it may contradict stronger attitudes. We may find kittens irresistible, yet we would not arrive at a formal reception at the college president's home with a little ball of fur we found abandoned on the way. We also exhibit no behavior toward kittens when none is present. We may agree that diamonds are a girl's best friend, but we probably manage to resist the ones displayed in Tiffany's, especially when we notice an armed guard patrolling the store. Though we may have a positive attitude toward social justice, we very likely refrain from interfering when we overhear our hostess giving her maid an undeserved tongue-lashing. And while our neighbor's political opinions may be anathema to us, we might ardently defend his right to hold them.

Many attitudes may never lead to any action at all. We have feelings and beliefs about hosts of things that we never *do* anything about—except perhaps voice our attitudes. We may like a person without ever doing anything to increase our contacts with him.

Notice also in our definition that the response toward which an attitude predisposes us is "more or less" predictable. This means that attitudes are measurable. Some are stronger than others, and of course, the strongest ones are the ones most likely to lead to action.

An interesting illustration of the relative strengths of attitudes is contained in a poll taken in 1944 by the American Institute of Public Opinion (Cantril, 1944). Two questions were asked:

Do you believe in freedom of speech?
Yes   97%
No   1%
Don't know   2%

If "yes," do you believe in it to the extent of allowing Fascists and Communists to hold meetings and express their views in this community?
Yes   23%
No   72%
No opinion   5%

The first question asks whether the respondent accepts the Bill of Rights. The second has to do with the respondent's beliefs regarding Communists and Fascists and with his resulting attitudes toward these groups. This question involves attitudes because a person's predisposition to act (forbid meetings) goes along with his evaluative judgment (of Fascists and Communists) and, presumably, his emotional attitude. In addition, the poll demonstrates an aspect of attitude-holding that we will discuss at some length later in the chapter—the consistency of different attitudes. Although the second question is posed in terms of strength of belief, it is really asking whether the respondent is able to hold two contradictory beliefs at the same time—"People should be allowed freedom of speech" and "Some people should not be allowed freedom of speech"—without feeling discomfort.

Finally, notice that, according to our definition, attitudes are based on both ideas and feelings. That is, they are the result of both cognitive and affective components. Our idea (cognition) of a person may be that he is warm, intelligent, generous; our feeling (affect) is "I like him." Especially if the person is of the opposite sex, our sensory response has certain physiological correlates: our pupils dilate, our heartbeat increases, we have an elevated galvanic skin response. Our attitude is favorable. Or our idea of a person may be that he is selfish and cruel; our feeling is "I don't like him," and our attitude is unfavorable. Either the idea or the feeling component may exist independently of the other. We may dislike a person without knowing—or caring—why. And we may voice attitudes that we have never really felt.

Another characteristic of attitudes is not stated explicitly in our proposed definition. Most attitudes are based on cognitive stereotypes. They have to be, because we don't have time and we aren't able to make a scientific analysis of everything and everyone even in our own small world. Anyone who approached his world in this way would never be able to accomplish anything. He would die of starvation, his first meal sitting before him waiting for him to decide whether steak and potatoes would make a wholesome and satisfying dinner.

The much-maligned hippie with his long hair is obviously stereotyped. Any recognizable characteristic of a category of people—long hair, dark skin, employment as a college teacher, Italian origin, even age—triggers a series of

Can you tell which group of students is German? British? Swedish? (See credit lines at end of chapter to check your answers.)

assumptions about the personality and life-style of that person. If she is a red-head, she is quick-tempered and volatile; if he speaks with an Italian accent or has an Italian-sounding name, he is family-loving, demonstrative, voluble, and quite possibly apt to break the law.

A stereotype is unjustified even if it is based on personal experience: the fact that one has met a quick-tempered redhead is not an adequate basis to equate red hair with quick temper. In practice, however, stereotypes are usually without even that inadequate justification; they are passed around by word of mouth and occasionally by the media. Stereotypes usually display the kind of generalization claimed by the ethnographer who, upon returning from a field trip, stated: "All Indians walk single-file; at least the one I saw did."

Stereotypes are not always negative. We make favorable assumptions just as superficially and just as erroneously: fat people are not necessarily jolly; pretty girls with impressive figures are not necessarily sexy—or somewhat stupid; intelligent people are not necessarily wise, well balanced, or successful.

Yet, in spite of the generally undesirable and frequently quite incorrect nature of stereotypes, they seem to be necessary for our survival. Perhaps what the psychology of attitudes can contribute in this respect is to heighten our awareness of our tendency toward stereotyping, in the hope that before acting on these biases in situations with serious consequences, we may be aware of their insubstantiality. Attitudes seem to serve a very important function, as we will see; the important thing is to recognize them for what they are and not confuse them with descriptions of reality.

Why Do We Have Attitudes?

If we do not necessarily act in accordance with our attitudes, if in fact we sometimes act in contradiction of them, what function do they serve? Why do we say, "I like redheads" or "I don't like Italians" or "John Smith is disgusting" if much of the time such statements have little effect on how we live our lives?

Cognitive Purpose Most psychologists today would agree that the primary function of attitudes is to provide some kind of *cognitive* organization of the world we live in. We have noted elsewhere in this book that man is a cognitive creature, a being who is to some extent driven toward an intellectual mastery of his environment. Obviously some of us are smarter or more curious than others, but we all seem to want to have notions and feelings about the things in our world, and even the most intelligent of us has attitudes toward objects and people he knows nothing about. Attitudes thus provide us with a cognitive structure, a simplified grammar of behavior that tells us how to act in our social world. As soon as we meet a new person we form an attitude toward him. If his clothes are nondescript and his racial origin isn't immediately apparent, we may have nothing to go on initially, but in short order we categorize him—as well-to-do, as intelligent, as a political liberal, as a Jew—and we respond to him according to our pre-existing attitudes toward people in these categories.

Attitudes, Stereotypes, Prejudice, Opinion

Attitudes are relatively stable and enduring predisposition to behave or react in a certain way toward persons, objects, institutions, or issues. Attitudes typically imply a tendency to classify or categorize. Thus one with a favorable attitude toward liberal politicians is likely to react favorably to all politicians of that persuasion, regardless of their unique characteristics as individuals. The sources of attitudes are cultural, familial, and personal.

Stereotypes are rigid, biased perceptions. Most stereotypes tend to be somewhat inaccurate and are usually not very helpful in identifying members of a particular group.

The concept of *prejudice* has no consensual meaning. In its most common usage, prejudice is defined as "an unfavorable ethnic attitude" (*Dictionary of Social Sciences*, 1964; *Handbook of Social Psychology*, 1954). Krech, Crutchfield, and Ballachey (1962), have said that "prejudice is an unfavorable attitude toward an object which tends to be highly stereotyped, emotionally charged, and not easily charged by contrary information."

An *opinion* is a belief, particularly one that is tentative and still open to modification.

David Krech

Instrumental Purpose Just as attitudes help us to know what to do in situations and thus indirectly help us to satisfy our primary needs, they may also be more directly instrumental in attaining secondary goals. Thus attitudes have a *utilitarian* function. We may adopt an attitude because it is held by a social group we wish to belong to. If the members of the local country club are outspokenly anti-Semitic but nonetheless attractive to us, we may find ourselves voicing anti-Semitic sentiments though perhaps we have never experienced such feelings.

Utilitarian attitudes such as the one just described can serve as tickets of admission—or sometimes as leaves of absence. If a rebellious son wants to break his middle-class family ties he may reflect negative attitudes toward the clothes, the educational and job objectives, and other aspects of his parents' life-styles to demonstrate that he is no longer a part of their world.

Both positive and negative utilitarian attitudes frequently start by being bogus; the individual adopts them in public for a purpose, not because he believes in them. But more often than not they end up being internalized, in a manner similar to the process of *functional autonomy* (Chapter 12). The insurance salesman who professes enthusiasm for golf in the hope he will meet prospective customers on the links may well end up an avid golfer.

If a person has high affiliative needs—if he desires close and affective contact with his peers—any group or institution that supplies that contact will be valued by him, and he will be predisposed to join it and to continue as a member of it. He will also, of course, be predisposed to have a favorable attitude toward it. At the same time, the typical isolation and anonymity of big-city life will deprive him of opportunities for close personal contact, and he will tend to have a negative attitude toward life in New York City, Chicago, or San Francisco. Thus attitudes are engendered toward social objects because these objects are instrumental or utilitarian in satisfying the individual's needs.

Self-Protecting Purpose Attitudes may offer us a means of solving problems that would normally be beyond our control or that threaten to overwhelm us. Prejudice is frequently explained on this basis. A person who sees his own social situation as precarious, or who is insecure emotionally, may take some comfort in expressing hostile attitudes toward members of another race or class. For example, in the United States it is probably true that no group is so prejudiced against black people as whites in the lowest socioeconomic categories, regardless of their own social ancestry. In this function, attitudes serve an *ego-defensive* purpose.

Self-defensive attitudes may provide a means of externalizing unacceptable inner states. Feelings that I perceive as offensive to society or to my own code of behavior are continual sources of discomfort to me, but I can alleviate this discomfort in two ways. For example, if I have strong erotic drives, I may find relief by indulging in erotic fantasies by means of daydreams or appropriate literature. On the other hand, if my discomfort stems not so much from the fact that I may not act out these drives as it does from my feelings of guilt and self-condemnation, I may assuage my discomfort by condemning others who act out these feelings. I may even become an advocate of censorship and a leader of "anti-smut" campaigns. In this case my attitude will actually be ambivalent: I am condemning pornography because it mirrors my own "wicked" drives, yet unconsciously I find it devilishly attractive. Whether or not it is true that sincere censors of erotica have extensive libraries of pornography "for research purposes," it is psychologically plausible that they should have.

Attitudes play self-defensive roles in many aspects of behavior less obvious than the example given above. For instance, if I feel inferior to someone, I will be uncomfortable and annoyed with myself for feeling that way. It is a simple and psychologically logical step to externalize that uncomfortable self-perception into a dislike of the perceived superior person. I dislike feeling inferior, so I dislike the person I feel inferior to.

scapegoat   One of the least attractive and best-known self-defensive uses of attitudes has to do with the making of a *scapegoat*. If things have gone wrong we need to know why; if we can put the blame on a person—the mayor, the governor, the president, or on a minority group, such as the Jews in Hitler's Germany—we have provided ourselves with a means of organizing the chaos around us and of venting our frustration. It is obvious that this kind of attitude also serves a cognitive function, as do most attitudes. But in the scapegoat situation the cognitive element plays a larger role than in many other attitudes. I am willing—perhaps even eager—to explain how the whole mess originated with some person or group, and I may very well cite elaborate theories or bits of history to back myself up. To the possessor of purely self-defensive attitudes—those with only a small cognitive element—no such explanatory scaffolding is necessary. It is obvious to him that sexual license, or permissive child-rearing, or softness on communism are evil things; and disagreement with him is almost as bad as supporting the evil. The purely self-defensive attitude is generated from within as a means of protecting oneself from some real or imagined threat. But attitudes toward scapegoats arise from a need to explain a situation and to lay the blame for it on someone.

Another self-defensive role of attitudes, the authoritarian personality as defined by Adorno and his colleagues, will be discussed later in the chapter (p. 681).

authoritarian personality

How Are Attitudes Related to Each Other?

If the major function of attitudes is to provide a cognitive structure, then that structure must be discernible and describable. Psychologists who have examined the structure of attitudes have decided that its most significant characteristic is consistency, sometimes called balance or harmony. We described Leon Festinger's theory of cognitive dissonance at some length in Chapter 14, though there we were concerned more with its application to overt behavior than to attitudes. Yet the structure of attitudes for a given person seems also to obey the tendency toward consonance or consistency. The perception that a particular attitude is inconsistent with other attitudes we have tends to cause us internal discomfort, so that we feel some pressure to change either the new attitude or a few of the old ones enough to bring them into harmony. Later in the chapter we will examine some research on cognitive dissonance and attitude structure.

Generally, the members of any group share the same set of attitudes, at least toward issues central to the group. Conservationists will see pollution in the same way, though of course the intensity of their attitudes will vary. But because each member's personality and past is unique, this consensus on central attitudes will be accompanied by differences in attitudes toward other objects and situations. We can expect both Republicans and Democrats to be interested in conservation, and we can therefore expect conflict, or at least debate, within the consensus, depending on the extent to which members perceive attitudes toward noncentral subjects to be related. And this conflict will occur not only between members but within them. I may be both an ardent conservationist and a supporter of the state governor, but if the state enacts a law that is unfavorable to conservation and the governor signs it, somehow I will have to reconcile these two contradictory attitudes.

Situations such as these, in which the individual seeks consistency among his own attitudes and between his set and the different sets of the groups to which he belongs, are both the commonest and the most complex examples of the social role of attitudes. Attitudes are long-lived and resistant to change, but they are also continually subject to pressures toward change. It is this dynamic aspect of attitudes that is the main concern of social psychologists.

Why Do We Utter Attitude Statements?

Though we did not include it in our definition and we have not mentioned it so far, one of the most distinct characteristics of attitudes is that they are spoken. Though presumably it is possible to hold an attitude without speaking it, such a state of affairs is extremely rare. We vocalize our attitudes all the time, for a number of reasons. We speak out on matters to tell others how we feel and what we are all about. Probably subsidiary to the broad function of communication are two perhaps more important functions of speaking our attitudes. One is to influence others. We seek to make others feel as we do, either because our attitude may lead to some action we desire, such as a vote for a particular candidate, or simply because our own ego is bolstered when others, especially admired others, share our attitude. A second subsidiary function of speaking our attitudes is self-confirmation or self-realization. Expressing an attitude can be a means of creating or affirming an identity. Self-confirmation and influence work hand in hand in the expression of attitudes: if by speaking a particular attitude I influence someone else to change his mind, I may take up that attitude all the more strongly myself. Human beings seem to have a great need not only to share their attitudes with others but also to influence others to adopt their attitudes and to convince themselves that the attitudes they hold are correct. We will see that people frequently test the validity of their attitudes not by collecting data or observations that would tend to support or refute their position, but by attempting to influence others to adopt the same attitudes, even in the absence of any relevant data.

Why do we speak our attitudes, which are predispositions to action, rather than act them out directly? In discussing our definition of attitude, we gave many reasons why action is frequently omitted, but the principal reason we don't act is that we don't need to. The function of an attitude is not primarily to guide our behavior but rather to let us know what we think about a particular object or person in the world around us. Further, our attitude structure gives us a set of relationships among various objects in our world; it links them together in particular ways and also links each of them to us. A set of attitudes provides us with a way of organizing the world and understanding our place in it. Presumably in a situation that demanded action we would behave in accordance with our stated attitudes, but the fact is that most of our attitudes never get put to that kind of test.

HOW ARE ATTITUDES FORMED
AND CHANGED?

In the preceding chapter we explored the nature and varieties of social influence. We defined norms as "the behavioral guidelines that may be inferred from common, average, or standard performance of members of groups." Attitudes—at least those held in common with other group members—may be regarded as the internalized equivalents of norms. If I belong to a group whose norms include the strict avoidance of pollution, my behavior, and my expressed attitudes, will certainly tend to coincide with those of other members. And even if I originally subscribed to their norms only to gain entry into the group, I will

 Classical Conditioning of Attitudes

Staats and Staats (1958) demonstrated classical conditioning (see Chapters 3 and 4) of attitudes experimentally. Two groups of subjects were told that they would take part in a verbal learning experiment and were given groups of words containing, together with many other words, names of six nationalities: Dutch, French, German, Greek, Italian and Swedish. For half of the subjects the word *Dutch* was always followed by favorable words and *Swedish* was always followed by unfavorable words; for the other half *Swedish* was followed by favorable words and *Dutch* by unfavorable ones. Later the subjects were asked to rate single words, including *Dutch* and *Swedish* in terms of pleasantness and unpleasantness. The subjects who had learned groups of words in which *Dutch* was associated with favorable words and *Swedish* with unfavorable words rated *Dutch* "pleasant" and *Swedish* "unpleasant"; the opposite occurred when *Dutch* was associated with unfavorable words and *Swedish* with favorable ones. The study was repeated using two masculine names (Table 15.1).

Table 15.1 Evaluative Ratings (on 7-point scale)[a]

	Names (Exp. 1)		Names (Exp. 2)	
	Dutch	Swedish	Tom	Bill
Unfavorable following words	2.67	3.42	3.42	4.12
Favorable following words	2.67	1.83	2.71	1.79

[a] 1 is pleasant and 7 is unpleasant.

There was, in other words, nothing intrinsic about *Dutch* or *Swedish* or the masculine names that generated the attitudes. In each case "irrelevant" aspects of the total situation *conditioned* an attitude toward what was originally a neutral social object; in some cases, the "irrelevant" factors may even have changed an attitude that previously existed. It would be interesting to know how stable attitudes formed in this manner might be.

After President Nixon visited China in 1972, a change took place in our political attitudes toward that country, as evidenced in the press. Left, in 1962 Chinese men, women, and children were pictured rummaging through a refuse pile in the hope of finding something to eat. Right, in 1972, it looks as if there's plenty of meat available at a Chinese market.

probably end up believing in the norm and acquiring a genuinely unfavorable attitude toward pollution.

Not all attitudes, of course, are internalized norms. Some attitudes, as we have noted, may be created or changed outside the influence of a group. They may be the result of a person's individual experiences or needs, such as in response to a challenge to his ego. Or they may be the result of the degree to which a person reacts to fear. In other cases attitudes are created or changed on the basis of how we perceive people, objects, and events in the world.

Despite their general tenacity, some attitudes are only provisional—adopted to meet the needs of a particular situation, perhaps, and lasting no longer than the situation itself. Attitudes can be formed in one way and changed in another, with or without the influence of the groups to which the person belongs. No one theory of attitude formation and change can explain all that happens when a person acquires, changes, or relinquishes an attitude.

Whatever the forces are that lead to the creation of an attitude or to its change, they operate in the same way. Usually a new attitude involves the change or relinquishment of an old one, if only indirectly. After President Nixon visited China in 1972, a considerable *change* took place in the political attitudes of many Americans toward that country. At the same time, museums, stores, and the media reflected a *new* interest in and favorable attitude toward the culture and life of historic China, and even of Communist China. Here and elsewhere it is more realistic to explore the forces that *shape* attitudes than to divide our discussion into the ways in which attitudes are formed and the ways in which they are changed.

How Does Ego Defense Affect Attitudes?

Just as attitudes may serve an ego-defensive function, they may also be formed or changed as a person responds to an assault on his ego. The ego-defensive role of attitudes was explored at length by Adorno and his colleagues in their classic *Authoritarian Personality* (1950). By a series of tests—particularly the California F ("Fascism") Test—these investigators isolated a personality type whose main characteristics are a rigid adherence to "middle-class" morality, deference to authority, a dominating attitude toward inferiors, and stereotyped perceptions of and prejudice against minority groups. These people seem to think they are nearly always right, unless someone with authority contradicts them; instead of recognizing their faults they project them onto defenseless others. Adorno and his colleagues traced the origin of this personality type to dominating, harsh, and punitive parental treatment. On the one hand the enforced submissiveness to parental authority generalized to all figures of authority; on the other hand, the hostility the child felt but could not express to his parents was repressed and then displaced onto comparatively defenseless others.

The anti-Semitism and other antiminority prejudices of the authoritarian personality have very little if anything to do with real experiences. Hostility toward others serves as a means of venting impermissible drives against the parents and eventually other authority figures whom the person slavishly obeys. If a scapegoat did not exist, such a person would have to invent one.

 Authoritarianism

In 1950, not many years after the fall of Nazi Germany, Adorno and his associates at the University of California devised a scale for detecting potentially fascistic or authoritarian personalities. It is known as the California F Scale (Adorno, Frenkel-Brunswîk, Levinson, and Sanford, 1950). F here represents Fascism. The test asks subjects whether they agree or disagree with such statements as:

The most important thing to teach is absolute obedience to their parents.
There are two kinds of people in the world, the weak and the strong.
No decent man can respect a woman who has had sex relations before marriage.

Agreement with many statements of this sort results in a high F scale or authoritarianism score.

Some characteristics appear to be typical of people who score high on the F scale. Authoritarian persons tend to be highly conscious of belonging to some ethnic group and are suspicious of persons outside that group. This makes them likely to be racist, anti-Semitic, or otherwise prejudiced. They believe in a rigid adherence to conventional middle-class values and are on the lookout for persons they believe to be violating those values. These persons they condemn, reject, and desire to see punished. They are outwardly submissive to authority and tend to idealize authority figures uncritically. They believe in mystical determinants of a person's fate. They tend to think in terms of stereotypes and oversimplified categories. They believe in strength and toughness, as opposed to "tender-mind-edness," and are often antiintellectual. They express feelings of pessimism and cynicism, believing the world to be filled with "evil forces . . . with plots and conspiracies, germs, sexual excesses." They are particularly concerned with viola-tors of their sexual mores.

In seeking an explanation of how the authoritarian personality develops, Adorno and his co-workers made use of the Freudian concept of the superego—the rigid, internalized, rule-enforcing and punishing parent Freud believed we carry within us (see p. 236). In authoritarian persons, they argue, the superego has seized control of the total personality and dominates it. Impulses alien to the superego are violently repressed, and they seek release through the psychological mechanism of "projection." That is, these impulses are denied within the person and attributed to alien persons and groups; thus externally localized, they can be safely attacked by the superego with a self-righteous vehemence.

What conditions can lead to such an overdevelopment of the superego? Researchers on authoritarianism have stressed the causative role of strictly rule-enforcing, overly disciplinarian parents. They argue that children of such parents develop strong feelings of hostility toward their parents—feelings they do not dare express and are fearful of even harboring. They resolve this conflict by identifying with the parental rule enforcers and displacing their hostile feelings onto outside persons, who are treated as surrogates of their own rebellious selves. Underlying the veneration for authority figures, who eventually replace the parents, then, is a fundamental aggression, which is overcompensated for by veneration.

Researchers on authoritarianism have attempted to produce experimental evidence in support of these hypotheses. Parents of high F-score students have been tested on the F scale (Byrne, 1965), the dreams of high F scorers have been analyzed for signs of repressed hostility toward parental and authority figures (Meer, 1955), and attempts have been made to demonstrate a greater than normal use of repression in authoritarian persons (Kogan, 1956). Such studies have claimed some success, but the significance of the F scale is by no means undisputed.

Irving Janis

What Part Does Fear Play in Attitude Formation?

The effect of fear on attitude formation and change has been explored by several workers, with some contradictory results. Janis and Feshbach (1953), who ini-tiated the research, claimed that fear arousal effectively induced compliance with a message if the fear aroused was low, while high fear arousal had less of an effect. This finding was confirmed later by Janis and Terwilliger (1963) in a classic experiment with subjects who were given high- or low-fear messages about the effects of smoking. In the later experiment, low fear arousal produced greater attitude changes, that is, greater acceptance of the message that smoking is injurious to health.

These findings were contradicted by Lowenthal and Niles (1964), who found that subjects with a higher fear of lung cancer showed greater agreement with a message to stop smoking, and by Berkowitz and Cuttingham (1960), who obtained similar results with messages about the safety features of automobile seat belts. McGuire (1966), after an exhaustive review of the literature, concluded that "there have been a few findings of a negative relationship, but predominantly findings of a positive relationship, between fear arousal and amount of attitude change." He added the suggestion that the subject's intitial level of concern over the issue was important: those with no alarm or with high alarm would tend to react less than those with moderate initial fear; the former subjects would either not be particularly interested or would be so frightened that they would, in effect, run away.

William McGuire

The effect of fear on attitude formation and change has been the subject of several studies.

How Does Perception Influence Attitudes?

The relation of perception to attitude formation and change was considered by Asch, Black, and Hertzman (1940). Subjects were told that other groups had rated such broad categories as businessmen, lawyers, and politicians as high or low in intelligence and in social usefulness. They were then asked to rate these professions themselves. The information they had been given about other groups' ratings proved effective in influencing their own. The interesting point in this experiment was that when the subjects were asked what, for example, they meant by "politician" the low raters cited "ward heeler" or "machine boss," while the high raters mentioned national political figures or statesmen.

Persuasion (which in this case took the form of "information" regarding other groups' ratings) involves, according to Asch and his colleagues, not so much changing the believer's opinion about a given object as changing his perception of which object he is giving his opinion about. "Politician = statesman" takes the place of "politician = ward heeler"; the subject has, so to speak, perceived a politician as a different person rather than changed his attitude toward the persons he originally identified as "politicians." He started with, and still has, a favorable attitude toward statesmen and an unfavorable attitude toward ward heelers.

A similar situation is seen in many experiments that have asked for judgments about a statement ascribed for one group to a high-prestige historical figure such as Jefferson or Churchill and for another to a low-prestige figure such as Stalin or Hitler. Subjects judge the quotation differently according to the category ("sayings of Jefferson" or "sayings of Stalin") in which they perceive it to belong.

How Does Cognitive Dissonance Shape Attitudes?

It must be apparent by now that attitudes are formed and changed in complex ways. If a set of rules concerning attitude formation can be stated at all, it will be a rather long set with many exceptions and extenuations. One reason for the complexity of attitudes is that virtually none of them exist in isolation; all are part of a cognitive system whose predominant characteristic is consistency. In our attempts to maintain consistency, or really to avoid dissonance, we are forced to adopt favorable attitudes toward certain people and things and unfavorable attitudes toward other people and things. As we become aware of new information about some of the objects of these attitudes or about new feelings on our part (or on the part of important people in our lives) toward these objects, we are sometimes forced to change some of our attitudes.

The individual strives for a state of equilibrium in many ways: in beliefs, in likes and dislikes, and in relations between attitudes and behaviors. We have seen that people use attitudes to give structure and meaning to reality; people and situations that we have not encountered before are interpreted in terms

Balance Models

One of the major frameworks in which attitudes have been studied is in cognitive consistency theory. There are a number of similar theories associated with Osgood, Lewin, Heider, Festinger, Ableson, and others. Although they differ in some important respects, the basic idea behind them is the same. Essentially "balance models" are concerned with the way an individual deals with beliefs or attitudes which are dissonant or consonant. An individual who has several beliefs or values that are inconsistent with one another strives, according to these theories, to make them more consistent. Similarly, if his cognitive views are consistent and he is faced with a new cognition that would produce inconsistency, he strives to minimize the inconsistency.

In balance models the dynamics of the system consist of two objects (one of which is often another person), the relationships between them, and an individual's evaluation of them. In the system there are three evaluations—the individual's evolution of each of the objects and the relationship of the objects to each other. Assuming that each evolution can only be positive or negative and the magnitude of strength is constant, the four possibilities are shown in Fig. 15.1.

Cognitive consistency theory is particularly effective in the study of attitude formation and change, because it can deal with the basic situation of one person receiving information from a second person about some object. However, research has also been conducted in situations among three people and the cognitive structure of one person thinking about two objects.

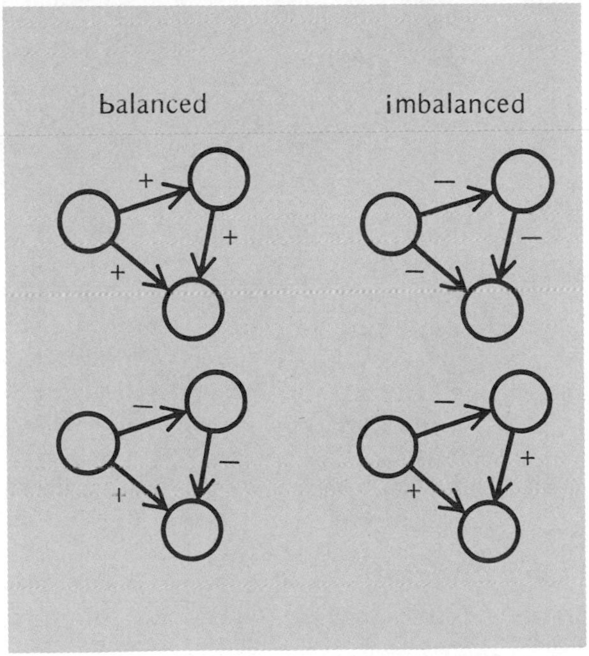

Fig. 15.1 Balanced and imbalanced cognitive structures. Plus and minus signs indicate positive and negative relationships; arrows indicate the direction of the relationships. The theory states that imbalanced structures tend to change to become balanced. (Freedman, Carlsmith, and Sears, 1970)

Attitude Averaging

attitude averaging

Norman H. Anderson

If the bits and pieces of information I glean about my new roommate as I get to know him are not extremely discordant, I will probably (and unconsciously) carry out an *attitude averaging,* in which the pluses and minuses of my information about my roommate are averaged out. The way this works was shown in an experiment by Anderson (1965). A large number of adjectives were rated on a scale from 0 to 6, 0 being very unfavorable and 6 being very favorable. The adjectives were then sorted into four categories: H (high), with values from 5.45 to 5.00; M+ (high medium), 3.74 to 3.45; M− (low medium), 2.54 to 2.22; and L (low), 1.00 to .72. Various combinations of four adjectives were then presented to the subjects, who were asked to indicate the degree of positive or negative feeling they would have toward a person with that collection of four characteristics; the subjects were instructed to grade the person on a scale in which 50 was neutral, high numbers indicated liking, and low numbers indicated disliking. The following average scores were obtained, confirming the averaging hypothesis:

Adjective Ratings	Average Liking Score
H, H, H, H	79
H, H, M+, M+	71
M+, M+, M+, M+	63
L, L, L, L	18

A somewhat similar theory was advanced by Osgood and Tannenbaum (1955), who suggested that when we are presented with an incongruous situation—as when a person we like does something we dislike—the more extreme of the two attitudes involved will determine what happens. If we like the person more than we dislike what he or she has done we will tend to overlook the misdeed. But if we dislike what he or she has done more than we like the person, we will tend to adopt a less favorable attitude toward the person.

of the attitudes we already have. My new next-door neighbor says he walked out after 5 minutes of a movie I liked. I assume the sex was too explicit for him and label him a conservative and a bore. But as I see him more, in spite of my desire to avoid him, the simplicity of my judgment (which is very near to prejudice) becomes increasingly uncomfortable for me. I learn a number of things about him that make me like him better or dislike him more. My attitude toward him becomes out of balance, and I must revise it.

Behavior and Cognitive Dissonance So far we have focused on the need of the individual to perceive an equilibrium among his different attitudes. Another important theory of consistency—Festinger's "cognitive dissonance" (see Chapter 14)—is concerned with the relationship between attitudes and behavior. Festinger (1957) distinguishes between the psychological process of decision-making and the perceived need to achieve equilibrium after the decision has been made. He draws a distinction between "decisions" that the individual perceives as imposed upon him or justified by some sufficient reward and those that he makes "voluntarily" (Festinger and Carlsmith, 1959). When subjects were paid $20 to tell a lie to the effect that a boring job was interesting they regarded the reward for lying as sufficient and they told the lie, but they did not change their attitudes toward the job—they still rated it as boring. When another group were paid only $1—an inadequate reward—for the lie, they perceived dissonance between the lie and their attitude toward the job; they subsequently judged the job as more interesting than they had before telling the lie. For the second group, evidently not changing their attitude toward the job would have meant that they lied without sufficient justification.

Decisions involve choice; for every yes there is a corresponding no. The individual who has made a decision needs to escape from the state of uncertainty in which he was before the decision; he wants to feel that his behavior is consonant with his attitude, or that his attitude is consonant with his behavior. He has hesitated between two makes of automobile; he chooses one; he then focuses his attention on the good features of his choice (he will probably tell all his friends what a fine model it is) and on the bad features of the other.

The effects of fear on attitude change can also be explained by the theory of cognitive dissonance. If the fear aroused is great, cognitive dissonance may impel the receiver of the message to ignore it or to contradict it (Janis and Terwilliger, 1962). Only by avoiding the message can he resolve the dissonance between the attitude engendered by the message and his actual behavior.

Evaluation of Cognitive Dissonance as an Attitude Theory   The theory of cognitive dissonance has probably led to more research than any other theory of social psychology. Its *explanatory* value—its ability to explain the psychological processes underlying a change of attitude or the lack of a change—has, however, been greater than its *predictive* value—its ability to forecast what will happen when someone is faced with conflicting information.

Freedman and Sears (1965) have pointed out that people do not always avoid information that is incompatible with their views. Adams (1961) found that mothers who listened to a speech opposing their own opinions were more likely to want additional information about *both* views than mothers who heard a speech they already agreed with. Apparently uncertainty or dissonance provokes information seeking, but the seeking is not necessarily confined to information supporting one's present views. At the same time, inconsistency may be tolerated, and even sought, if a person believes that some long-term benefit may accrue from it. This may be especially true of young people, particularly students, who may endorse one point of view now but may perceive that either they themselves or the situation relevant to that point of view may change sufficiently in the future to warrant a change of attitude. They may thus welcome exposure to information contradicting their point of view. Yet another situation in which dissonance may be not only tolerated but even welcomed is when our level of arousal or internal excitation is very low—when we are, in a word, bored. It is just such an explanation that probably accounts for our playing devil's advocate in some situations; if everyone present has the same attitude toward a particular object, we may find ourselves suddenly advancing arguments to support the other side. And not infrequently, the very act of arguing for the opposition will, if not reverse, at least modify our original attitude.

Chapanis and Chapanis (1964) have pointed out that most experimental situations based on cognitive dissonance involve many different forces and therefore are subject to different explanations. The $1-$20 experiment described above, for example, can also be explained in terms of incentive and rein-forcement—that is, in terms of learning theory (see Chapter 3) as well as by other parameters. But the existence of alternative explanations does not necessarily invalidate any of them.

Chapanis and Chapanis also point out that no one is completely conso-nant in his beliefs and behaviors. The possibility of cognitive dissonance is, to a greater or lesser extent, always with us. The extent to which dissonance is per-ceived and the psychological processes to which this perception gives rise would appear to be products of both the particular personality and the situation. A reflective, introspective person, in a situation in which he is free to act, will probably have a low "dissonance threshold"—he will be ready to perceive that he cannot believe, or have a favorable (or unfavorable) attitude toward, both A and B at the same time, and he will not feel comfortable until he has in some way eliminated or at least lessened the dissonance. But to the extent that he is not reflective, or perceives himself to be in a situation that he cannot control, his dissonance tolerance will rise.

WHAT ACCOUNTS FOR THE STABILITY OF ATTITUDES?

No one, we have seen, is completely consistent in his attitudes. But each person, as a part of his or her self-image, has constructed a network of perceptions and cognitions that satisfies him as consistent and "logical," as making sense of reality and of his position in reality. Attitudes, as part of this network, are inter-related in a complex way with each other and with many other aspects of the personality. They therefore tend to resist change, being, so to speak, anchored to many other parts of the psyche. This stability, or resistance to change, of attitudes has been implied in much of our previous discussion, but it will be useful to point out again a few of the factors that account for it.

What Is the Role of Cognitive Structure?

cognitive structure | One of the strongest supports of any individual attitude is the cognitive structure it is a part of. All our attitudes, or at least many of them, are so inexorably bound up with other attitudes that to change one of them can mean irreparable damage to the whole system. Your attitude toward any one course you are taking, for example, is probably closely related to your attitude toward college in general. This is not to say that if you have a favorable attitude toward college you will have a favorable attitude toward all your courses, but if you like being at college you will probably try to do well in all your courses—even those you don't like—so that you will be able to stay in school, and perhaps also so you may achieve a good grade record. You may also believe that the problem with a particular course lies with the instructor or the text, or with some other factor that is not really the same as the raw material of the course. At any rate, if you are in general an interested student, it would probably be difficult for you to decide that any particular course you have elected to take is just hogwash. Someone else, however, who has never liked school but recognizes the value of a college degree in the job market may think of all of his courses as hogwash. He'll do what is necessary to get through school but he won't like any of it. And it would be extremely upsetting to such a student to find that one day, in spite of himself, he was becoming really interested in one of his courses.

How Does Social Group Relatedness Influence Attitude Stability?

We know that many of our attitudes are learned from the groups we belong to or are acquired as "tickets of admission" to groups we want to be part of. Fear of expulsion from the group, or even of group disapproval, is an adequate rein-

© Henry S. Levy & Son, Inc.

Many of our attitudes are learned from the groups we belong to.

forcer of many attitudes. Although in such situations, it is theoretically possible to make an "invisible" change of attitude, people seldom do it—probably because the resulting dissonance is uncomfortable.

Groups, and particularly their leaders, recognize more or less consciously this reluctance to change attitudes. The most effective way to keep group members ideologically pure is not to brainwash them but to make group membership attractive, to sugarcoat the pill of ideology with rituals and celebrations. A hunt club does not maintain its membership by repeating that foxes are vermin, but by an elaborate paraphernalia of dress, hierarchies of officers, functions, and "extracurricular" activities, until the foxhunter acquires so great an identification with and enjoyment of the whole way of life that any change of attitude toward hunting foxes becomes unthinkable, no matter how "humane" the hunter's attitude to animals in general.

What Is the Role of Personality Factors?

Personality factors may also contribute to the stability of certain attitudes. In bullfighting, as in foxhunting, the slaughter of the bull is the culmination of a colorful and spectacular ceremony, bound up with rituals and traditions that carry significance beyond the killing of the animal. Most people who go to bullfights don't think of the spectacle as a slaughter at all but as a sport full of pageantry and color. But all students of the literature of bullfighting recognize that a certain personality type is typical of the *aficionado,* the devotee of bullfighting. In no sense is this element of the personality simple sadism. Ernest Hemingway, perhaps the greatest literary promoter of the bullfight, was no sadist —and whatever its ingredients, the tenacity with which this devotion to the bullfight is held is largely because of the way in which the attitude satisfies "logically irrelevant" aspects of the personality.

That personality factors contribute to the stability of attitudes was demonstrated experimentally by Katz and Stotland (1959). White college girls were measured for self-defensiveness and antiblack attitudes and then were exposed to various attempts to change their prejudice. The highly self-defensive girls resisted all influences designed to modify their attitudes toward blacks; their prejudice was an essential prop for their self-esteem, though "logically" completely unrelated to it. Our earlier discussion of the authoritarian personality provides another illustration of the contribution of personality factors to the stability of attitudes.

The effect of one's underlying personality structure on attitudes is inherent also in the notion of cognitive consistency, which plays so large a part in current social psychological thought. If, as dissonance theories would have us believe, the perception of incongruence among some of our behavior patterns, or predispositions to behave in certain ways, may cause us discomfort and lead to efforts to bring our behaviors and attitudes into better balance, then our attitudes are indeed closely related to our personality structures.

Daniel Katz

Of course, as we have already pointed out, neither our personalities nor our attitudes are perfectly consistent. All of us are quite capable of saying one thing and doing another, or of behaving one way today and another way tomorrow. Much of this inconsistency is due to our motivation in the particular situation. Our attitudes might be quite different according to whether in the psychology class today it is more important to us to let the instructor know we understand the cognitive dissonance theory or to impress our classmates that we are not show-offs, that we can give others an opportunity to show what they know.

Self-Esteem Our attitudes are also influenced by the amount of self-esteem we feel in a particular situation. Just as the consistently self-defensive person is likely to be consistently prejudiced against one or more minority groups, so the normally confident person may, in a situation that poses some fairly strong threat to his self-esteem, exhibit some prejudiced attitude or behavior, which he may later deeply regret.

Strength of Disposition Probably a good deal of such inconsistency can be attributed to the strength of the attitudinal or behavioral disposition in question. Campbell (1963) has suggested, for example, that an only mildly integrationist person might well demonstrate segregationist attitudes occasionally—where, perhaps, the news media have just reported the rape of a young white girl by a black classmate. But a strongly committed integrationist, even in this situation, would not express or support a segregationist argument. Similarly, we might expect a person whose self-esteem is normally high to exhibit considerably less vacillation in attitudes or behaviors than one whose self-esteem is normally low.

In What Ways Can We Insure against Attitudinal Change?

One of the best and simplest means of insuring against attitudinal change is to elicit some kind of commitment to the attitude we support. Freedman and Fraser (1966) had experimenters ask housewives to sign a petition urging their state senators to pass legislation promoting safe driving. Several weeks later 55 percent of the women who had signed the petition were willing to have an ungainly and unsightly sign reading "Drive Carefully" placed in their front yards. Of a group of women who had not been asked to sign the petition, only 17 percent agreed to display the sign.

Another means of insuring against attitudinal change is McGuire's (1969) *inoculation* method. Just as we inoculate children against diphtheria and other illnesses by introducing very small amounts of sera containing the germs into the body and thus stimulating the production of antisera that ultimately make the child immune to the disease, so we can, McGuire argues, immunize people against undesirable attitudes by exposing them to small doses at a time. Research to date has been confined to arguments of the cultural truism type—such as "It is good to brush your teeth three times a day" and "The effects of penicillin

inoculation

have been of great benefit to mankind"—and cannot be generalized to other sorts of attitudes or beliefs. Nonetheless, McGuire has found that

1. preexposure to weakened forms of counterarguments, with refutation of these arguments, is more effective in conferring resistance to strong subsequent attacks than is presentation of arguments supporting the truism;

2. resistance conferred in this manner is equally effective in combating strong counterarguments unrelated to those used to create resistance in the first place;

3. mention of the counterargument without refutation of it is even more effective in conferring resistance than when refutation is provided;

4. arguments supporting the truism confer resistance only if they are combined with forewarning of a subsequent attack.

What all this points to is that, at least in the case of truisms, which by definition do not generally meet much resistance, we can be better prepared to defend them by a warning of a forthcoming attack than by the presentation of arguments supporting them.

HOW ARE ATTITUDES DETECTED AND MEASURED?

Because attitudes, being theoretical constructs like perception, motivation, information, and personality, are not visible, we can only infer them from behaviors. But since it is impossible to observe all the behaviors that indicate attitudes, we usually limit our enquiry to verbal behavior. We ask a person a question about a particular attitude and then evelute the direction and strength of his response.

What Do Attitude Scales Measure?

attitude scale   Attitudes are measured for both direction and magnitude by means of *attitude scales,* collections of short, unambiguous statements of attitudes or opinions that are submitted to the subject and with which he expresses his agreement or disagreement.

The most difficult task of the attitude scale is to assess the magnitude as well as the strength of an attitude. For example, opinion polls that rely on yes-no or true-false responses fail to give the researcher any gauge of the degree of conviction behind the attitude expressed.

Thurstone's scale   **Thurstone's Scale**   One of the best-known attitude scales that measures both magnitude and direction of attitude was developed by Thurstone (Edwards, 1957; Thurstone, 1954; Thurstone and Chave, 1929). It is an example of what is known as *consensual location scaling* and is based on the assumption that items measuring an attribute can be ordered according to a dimension of magnitude.

Having chosen the attitude to be measured (toward wars, blacks, morality, inflation, and so on), an investigator developing this scale collects as many clear, simple, and unambiguous statements of *opinion* on the subject as he can. These can be of the "should" variety—"I think the country would be better off if the churches were closed and the ministers set to some useful work"—or less overtly attitudinal statements of opinion—"The church is needed to develop religion, which has always been concerned with man's deepest feelings and greatest values."

These statements are given to a group of judges—preferably more than a hundred—who are asked to react to the items along some specified dimension, from extremely pro to extremely anti. Then the *median* value assigned to each statement is computed, and that becomes its scale value. If there is widespread disagreement on the rating of an individual statement, that statement is eliminated.

The selection is then submitted to the subject, who checks those statements with which he agrees. From the values of the statements the subject accepts, a median value is calculated, which is assumed to measure the direction (1-5 is pro, 6 is neutral, 7-11 is anti) and the strength of the subject's attitude.

For example, in the two statements quoted above, which are from an actual Thurstone scale, the first was rated 10.5 (extremely anti) and the second 1.4 (extremely pro). We cannot imagine the same person choosing both of these statements, but if instead of the first he had checked "I like to go to church for I get something worthwhile to think about and it keeps my mind filled with right thoughts" (2.2) and "I believe in the church and its teachings because I have been accustomed to them since I was a child" (4.0), his score would be 2.2 (the mid value of the three).

In the following example, too, each item represents a level of magnitude distinct from that of other items:

Trait: Favorableness of attitude toward water fluoridation.
Least favorable: A. The use of fluoride in the water should be prohibited.
                      B. People should be allowed to use fluoride in their water by doctor's prescription only.
                      C. People should have the right to use or not use fluoridated water as they wish.
                      D. City water should be fluoridated but people should be able to use nonfluoridated sources if they wish.
Most favorable: E. The city should require all citizens to drink some fluoridated water each day.

Thurstone's scale items are considered noncumulative; acceptance of one does not imply acceptance of preceding items. We will look at a cumulative scale shortly.

Likert's Scale A second frequently used attitude scale, devised by Likert (1932), is a *summative* scale. It differs from the Thurstone scale in that the original list of statements is not rated by judges, but is simply submitted to subjects,

Likert's scale

who respond to a series of items according to whether they strongly approve (1), approve (2), are undecided (3), disapprove (4), or strongly disapprove (5). The direction and magnitude of the attitude is computed as the sum of item scores, which may range between k and $5k$, where k is the number of items. For example:

Direction: Circle one number on each scale.

1.	1	2	3	4	5
Fluoridation of water should be demanded of the city.				Fluoridation of water should be an individual decision.	

2.	1	2	3	4	5
Fluoridation of water is healthful.				Fluoridation of water is dangerous to health.	

3.	1	2	3	4	5
The city should publicize the benefits of fluoridation.				The city should publicize the dangers of fluoridation.	

The maximum positive score on this scale is 15, which should indicate strong advocacy of water fluoridation. A score of 3 is the minimum score, and it should indicate strong objection to water fluoridation.

Guttman's Scale The Guttman (1944, 1950) scale is based on the assumption that a set of items measuring a single, unidimensional trait can be ordered along a continuum of "difficulty" or magnitude representing the amount of the trait possessed by the person tested. For items of this "cumulative" type acceptance of one implies that the person would necessarily accept all items of lesser magnitude. For example:

Guttman's scale

Trait: Arithmetic ability.
Least difficult: A. What is $2 + 3$?
B. What is $25 + 30$?
C. What is $14 + (38 - 17)$?
D. What is $12 \div (7 + 4 - 5)$?
Most difficult: E. What is $43 (19 + 84) \div 17 (312 - 176)$?

Trait: Favorableness of attitude toward water fluoridation.
Least difficult: A. It is all right for people to drink fluoridated water if they wish.
B. If people want fluoride in their water but can't afford to pay for it, it is all right for the city to pay for it.
C. The city should publicize the availability of free fluoride for those who want it.
D. The city should add fluoride to the water so that everyone would get it automatically.
Most difficult: E. The city should require all citizens to drink some fluoridated water each day.

If the items are indeed ordered along a single dimension, only the following patterns should appear:

Accept no item .... Score 0
Accept item A .... Score 1
Accept items A and B .... Score 2
Accept items A, B, and C .... Score 3
Accept items A, B, C, and D .... Score 4
Accept items A, B, C, D, and E .... Score 5

Any other response pattern (for example, Accept B only) is taken to imply either that the subject is not responding according to the intended dimension or that he made an error in response.

Attitude scales and similar devices are able to bring to the surface and measure the strength of attitudes of which the subject may not even be aware. These techniques are useful primarily in research and in clinical settings. When the opinions of a large sample of the population are desired, briefer techniques must be used.

What Factors Cause Errors in Attitude Assessment Data?

The data obtained in attitude assessment may be contaminated by a variety of factors. Subjects may be momentarily distracted while making a response or they may misread a question, and so on. Such variables may be random. If a great deal of random intervention occurs, the ratings may not be reliable; that is, it becomes likely that the subject would respond differently in a quieter setting, or when he is more alert, or when he doesn't have a cold. No experi-

The public opinion poll is one of the best-known types of attitude assessment.

sampling methods

 Public Opinion Polls and Sampling Methods

Perhaps the best-known type of attitude assessment is the public opinion poll, which is often conducted by face-to-face questioning rather than by collecting written responses. Everyone is familiar with the polls that attempt to measure the popularity of political candidates, or even of the President at different points during his term in office. Magazines and newspapers frequently conduct polls designed to assess public opinion on some issue such as, during the sixties, the morality of the Vietnam war; during the Watergate scandal, confidence in President Nixon; or the people's attitude toward an energy crisis, a higher cost of living, and so on. Through the years research techniques have been repeatedly revised and refined in hopes of avoiding the embarrassment ensuing from the kinds of errors that predicted Dewey's victory over Truman in 1948.

Typically, public opinion polls confine themselves to narrow issues and seek to measure the direction of an attitude or opinion rather than both its direction and its force ("Do you approve of no-fault insurance?" rather than "How strongly do you approve of no-fault insurance?"). Those who construct these polls have three problems to solve: what to ask, whom to ask, and how to judge the response.

The phrasing of questions in an opinion poll is difficult, and two apparently similar questions may produce very different results. In June 1969, for example, the Gallup Poll asked: "[The President has] ordered the withdrawal of 25,000 troops from Vietnam in the next 3 months. [Do you think] troops should be withdrawn at a faster or slower rate?" The results were:

No opinion	13%
Slower	16%
Same as now	29%
Faster	42%

In September-October of the same year the Harris Poll asked, "In general, do you feel the pace at which the President is withdrawing troops is too fast, too slow, or about right?" The replies were

No opinion	16%
Too fast	6%
About right	49%
Too slow	29%

Notice that when *given* the opportunity of agreeing with the speed of withdrawal, approximately 10 percent of both the "too fast" and the "too slow" responses moved in the middle, which we suppose "had not occurred to them" when the possibility of that answer was not mentioned (Converse and Schuman, 1970).

Another problem has to do more directly with the nature of the scaling procedure used. Yes-no and true-false questions often fail to provide the assessor with a true indication of the conviction with which subjects respond and therefore make precise interpretation difficult.

This problem is sometimes circumvented by using *fixed alternatives,* in which the statement presented has alternative replies and the respondent chooses the reply he would be most likely to make himself.

A less satisfactory means of averting the problem is to offer an option like "no opinion" or "I don't know." This complicates matters considerably. For example in both the 1952 and the 1956 elections, it was found that people who made up their minds late, as opposed to those who made up their minds early, made decisions that could not have been predicted from their partisan attitudes.

Still another means of dealing with yes-no questionnaires entails supplementation with open or free answer questions in which the respondent formulates a reply in his own words. While this procedure is potentially the most valid of all, since it enables the researcher to obtain information he may have previously overlooked, it is time consuming for both the respondent and the researcher.

Once the poll questions have been formulated, the poll-takers must define an appropriate sample population, a representative portion of the whole—what in statistical terms is called a *sample of the universe.* Ideally, everyone should be represented, but this is unfeasible in terms of time, energy, and expense.

Respondents mailing in questionnaires may differ from the general population, which is probably made up of busier, and possibly less lonely or less compulsive people. Solicitation of opinions by telephone can eliminate the economically disadvantaged (who constituted a majority during the Depression and during the 1936 Presidential campaign). Solicitation on the street may tap out unemployed men, while door-to-door solicitation may result in an inflated representation of mothers with small children.

Thus sampling should be as random as possible: at the final stage of selection, and perhaps at other stages, all members of the group should stand an equal chance of being selected. The final group of respondents is selected by one of two methods: *area* sampling or *quota* sampling. In the first, the universe to be sampled is divided into geographical sections, preferably of approximately equal size, and one or a number of these groups are chosen randomly. These chosen sections are again broken down into subsections, and the procedure of random choice of the subsections follows. This continues until a manageable number of groups are left, and from the individuals that make up these groups a number are chosen as respondents—again by random choice.

area sampling
quota sampling

In the quota system the "universe" of individuals is divided into categories that have significance in relation to the opinion to be polled. Age, sex, income, educational level, and ethnic origin are frequent divisions. A selection is then made from these groups in proportion to the size of the group: if males under 25 make up 10 percent of the total population, approximately 10 percent of the final sample will be men younger than 25. (It is, of course, obvious that an individual person will belong to several categories at the same time: a black male aged 24 with a high school education and earning $10,000 a year would count in five different categories.)

We should note that these two methods of sample selection are frequently combined. In area sampling for a question regarding race prejudice the pollster would not allow chance to eliminate all southern areas. We should also note, as demonstrated by the example we have cited, that in neither of these methods is the pollster able to proceed mechanically; judgment inevitably enters into the selection at one stage or another.

Public opinion pollsters advise their clients to allow for a margin of error of about 6 percent, but unfortunately this is frequently forgotten. Actually a 6 percent margin of error, based on 1,000 to 1,500 respondents, which is the number usually interviewed in a Gallop Poll, is a reasonable estimate. With twice the number of respondents, the error rate would be substantially reduced. Of course, the margin of error is also dependent on the kind of sample taken.

menter can completely control random error, though its effects can presumably be balanced out. However when certain variables tend to affect all of a subject's responses in a similar way so that the total score is biased, the effect is said to be systematic and may constitute a form of what is referred to as *response bias*.

response bias

social desirability

Social Desirability   Notable among the many forms of response bias is "social desirability," the tendency of a subject to attempt to make a good impression, to place himself in a socially desirable light. This is the same response set we noted in Chapter 13; it affects performance on personality inventories as well as on opinion polls. A student who found the investigator sexually attractive might try to give the impression that she has far more dates than she really does, in the hope that he will seek her out socially. This tendency, of course, distorts the accuracy of attitude statements.

One means of reducing the effect of social desirability is to construct pairs of items that are equal in "desirability" or popularity and, through a forced-choice procedure, ask the subject to select the member of each pair that comes closest to representing his own opinion. ("Would you rather be a college professor or a doctor?") Supposedly if the two items are equally desirable socially from the subject's point of view (in practice this is often difficult to achieve), his choice should depend solely on the content of the items (Edwards, 1957).

Allen L. Edwards

Many tests have a "faking component"—that is, a number of items specifically designed to reveal social-desirability faking. Crowne and Marlowe (1966) devised a scale in which certain items have two distinct answer categories; one response that is presumably factually true for all subjects but socially undesirable is presented in conjunction with a second response that is presumed desirable for all subjects but probably contrary to fact. An example of the second kind of response would be, "I am always willing to admit it when I make a mistake."

As an alternative, the assessor can use filter questions, which are designed to avert conventional stereotyped responses: "Do you believe that only wealthy people should be candidates for the Presidency of the United States? If 'No,' do you believe that Presidential campaigns should be publicly financed?"

acquiescence

response style

Acquiescence and Response Style   Another form of response bias is "acquiescence." The acquiescence set (Cronbach, 1950) or style (Rorer, 1965) is manifest by the acceptance or rejection of all statements. It is especially likely to occur if items are ambiguously phrased ("Is it usually true that bookish students succeed later in the business world?"). Acceptance—always checking yes in a yes-no choice situation—may seem to indicate an interest or attitude the subject doesn't really have.

Another kind of response bias may be revealed in a respondent's consistent choice of an extreme answer. This is often more indicative of a respondent's style than of his actual attitude toward the issue of concern.

Subjects may also reply carelessly by giving overly brief responses, mis-checking, or random checking. This kind of response bias is especially likely to be a result of some difficulty in rapport between the subject and the assessor.

It is not always easy to eliminate data that the experimenter believes is contaminated by response bias, especially in tests that attempt to assess deviance. But sometimes experimenters find ways of detecting response biases other than the social-desirability one we have discussed. On the Minnesota Vocational Interest Inventory Campbell and Truckman (1963) developed a verification such that subjects accepting 13 or more of 58 items could be identified as careless. The cutoff point was established by comparison of subjects taking the test under ordinary conditions with subjects who filled out the answer sheet blindly.

We have not covered attitude assessment in great detail, although the processes are often quite complex in practice. Our purpose has been to suggest some of the general procedures and a few of the pitfalls.

SUMMARY

Attitudes are predispositions to respond favorably or unfavorably, to a more or less predictable degree, to particular situations on the basis of ideas and feelings we bring to these situations. Many attitudes never entail any action at all. Attitudes are measurable and, within limits, consistent. And attitudes usually have both cognitive and affective components. The cognitive component is likely to be a stereotype; this is difficult to justify but apparently necessary.

Attitudes serve three principal functions: they give our world some kind of cognitive structure; they are utilitarian, in that they may be instrumental in attaining some of our secondary goals; they are self-defensive, fulfilling some of the functions of the defense mechanisms discussed in Chapters 12 and 16.

Attitudes are related to each other in that there is a degree of consistency among those held by any one person. They are usually also fairly consistent among the members of a given social group.

One of the most distinct characteristics of attitudes is that we speak them virtually all the time. Speaking our attitudes serves the broad function of communication, and subsidiary to that, the functions of influencing others and expressing or confirming ourselves. Another important characteristic of attitudes is that we speak them *rather* than act them out; this is because their primary purpose is a cognitive one.

Attitudes are formed and changed in many ways. Some of them are the result of internalized norms (see Chapter 14), and some are formed from personal experience. A new attitude usually involves the change or relinquishment of an old one.

Just as attitudes may serve ego-defensive purposes, many of them are acquired as a response to an ego challenge or threat. Attitudes are also acquired in response to fear arousal; though there is some disagreement about the optimal level of fear arousal to effect attitude change, probably the greater the fear, the greater the attitude change, in most situations.

Another, quite different, means of effecting attitude change is to change the perception of the object of the attitude, as in changing the perception of "politician" to "statesman" rather than "ward-heeler."

Attitudes are also formed and changed as a response to uncomfortable levels of cognitive dissonance. When we have conflicting attitudes toward something, we usually find it necessary to modify some or all of them. Though we disapprove of lying, we may tell a lie without aversive consequences to our dissonance tolerance if we are given a sufficient reward for lying, but if the reward is insufficient and we still tell the lie, dissonance may cause us to believe the lie we told.

Contrary to what cognitive dissonance would seem to predict, however, people do not always avoid information that is incompatible with their views. In certain situations, they may even seek such information.

In spite of all the factors that have been shown to have an effect on attitudes, the fact is that, for most of us, they are remarkably stable, resistant to change. This is in part due to the intricate structure of our attitude networks; changing one attitude sometimes endangers the entire network. We also hesitate to change our attitudes because doing so may entail the threat of losing social sanction.

Certain personality factors also tend to support stability of attitudes. Self-defensiveness and authoritarianism tend to support highly stable minority-group prejudices. Inconsistency of attitudinal disposition can be due to motivational factors or to low self-esteem.

Two methods of insuring against attitudinal change are (1) eliciting a strong commitment to an attitude and (2) the inoculation method of exposing subjects to small amounts of counterarguments in order to evoke resistance to them.

Attitudes, being invisible, must be inferred from behavior. In practice, they are inferred and measured mostly from verbal behavior. The Thurstone attitude scale asks a subject to check the attitude statements he agrees with. The statements have been prerated, and the subject's score is the median of the values assigned to the statements he has checked. The Likert scale asks the subject to rate all the statements submitted from 1 to 5, according to the degree of his approval of them; his score, in this case, is the sum of his ratings. The Guttman scale presents attitudes toward something in order of difficulty; the score is the number of the last item checked. Attitude scales attempt to measure both the direction and the strength of an attitude.

The data that emerge from attitude assessment may be erroneous for a variety of reasons. When certain variables affect all of a subject's responses in a similar direction the result may constitute a response bias. One common form of response bias is "social desirability," the subject's attempt to show himself in a desirable light. Another is "acquiescence," or a subject's tendency to accept or reject all statements seeking to measure his attitudes. Various ways have been developed to detect test responses made on the basis of response bias.

Suggested Readings

Allport, Gordon, *The Nature of Prejudice.* Cambridge, Mass., Addison-Wesley, 1954.
An examination of the factors responsible for prejudice.

Baldwin, James, "Equal in Paris," in *Notes of a Native Son.* Boston, Beacon Press, 1955.
In this essay, as in much of his work, Baldwin is concerned with what it means to be black.

Bem, Daryl J., *Beliefs, Attitudes, and Human Affairs.* Monterey, Calif., Brooks-Cole, 1969.
A highly readable short book on attitudes and their significance.

Chisler, Phyllis, *Women and Madness.* New York, Doubleday, 1972.
Chisler contends that sex-role stereotypes are the basic cause of much of what we call mental illness in women.

Feldman, Saul D., and Gerald W. Thielbar, eds., *Life Styles: Diversity in American Society.* Boston, Little, Brown, 1972.
A discussion of the varied life syles of Americans.

Festinger, Leon, *A Theory of Cognitive Dissonance.* Stanford, Calif., Stanford University Press, 1967.
Festinger explains his cognitive dissonance theory in detail and describes some of his early experiments involving it.

Hartung, Frank E., *Crime, Law, and Society.* Detroit, Wayne State University Press, 1965.
One large question explored here is how the groups to which the criminal offender belongs influence whether he will pursue a criminal career.

Heinlein, Robert A., *Farnam's Freehold.* New York, New American Library, 1964.
The setting of this novel is a future world in which the roles of blacks and whites are reversed, with whites becoming the victims of discrimination.

Ibsen, Henrik, *A Doll's House,* in *Ghosts and 3 Other Plays by Henrik Ibsen,* trans. by Michael Meyer. New York, Doubleday, 1966.
First performed in 1879, Ibsen's famous play was one of the first pleas for the liberation of women.

Myrdal, Gunnar, *An American Dilemma.* New York, Harper & Row, 1944.
The classic study of the American black by the Swedish sociologist.

Schiller, Herbert I., "Polls Are Prostitutes for the Establishment," *Psychology Today,* July 1972.
The public opinion poll, Schiller argues, is really a choice-restricting mechanism, and as such can be "an instrument of potential oppression and coercion."

Selznick, Gertrude J., and Stephen Steinberg, *The Tenacity of Prejudice: Anti-Semitism in Contemporary America.* New York, Harper & Row, 1969.
From a 5-year study in the United States the authors conclude that while traditional negative stereotypes toward Jews and other minority groups are fading, they are being replaced by new stereotypes that are as unfounded as the old ones.

Terkel, Studs, *Working.* New York, Pantheon, 1974.
For this book Terkel interviewed hundreds of Americans at all socioeconomic levels to find out how they feel about their occupations and lives.

Credit lines for photographs on page 673: (A) Swedish Information Service; (B) German Information Center; (C) British Tourist Authority.

Chapter Sixteen

Maladjustment

What is disturbed behavior?
What are defense mechanisms?
What causes neurosis?
How many different kinds of neuroses can you name?
What is the difference between neurosis and psychosis?
What causes psychosis?
Are there other behavior disturbances besides the neuroses
    and psychoses?
What is psychopathy?

In the Middle Ages, there was no coming back from extended bouts of disturbed behavior. Those who were declared sufficiently "mad" were grouped together and sent off to sea on "ships of fools." These boats crisscrossed the European waters, unable to dock for more than supplies. Some of their passengers, we are told, "found pleasure and even a cure in their changing surroundings . . . while others withdrew further, became worse, or died alone. . . . The cities and villages which had thus rid themselves of their crazed and crazy could now take pleasure in watching the exciting sideshow when a shipfull of foreign lunatics would dock at their harbors" (Foucault, 1965). Behavior disturbance thus became a sport for the so-called adjusted, and a literal death sentence for many whose behavior was too incomprehensible to be accommodated within the culture.

Public reaction to disturbed behavior changes in time; now we institutionalize the dysfunctional, or subject them to therapy, or as the gray between* disturbed and normal becomes more and more a blur, we accept behavior that only recently we would have condemned. Einstein used his Princeton salary check as a bookmark, and we say that behavior reflects his genius; in anyone else, such behavior would be a symptom. Whatever the cause—mass civilization, industrialization, inefficient political and social systems—increasingly greater numbers of our population display behavior that, under some definitions, can be classified as maladaptive. In a famous survey of New Yorkers in 1962, 81.5 percent of those interviewed were found to be psychologically "less than well" and 23.4 percent were classified as "impaired" (Srole, Langner, Michael, Opler, and Rennie, 1962).

Now it is estimated that between 6 and 16 percent of all Americans will be treated professionally for definable behavior disorders at some point in their lives. But it is a measure of change that much we formerly labeled disturbed or abnormal is now accepted. The example of Jane Roberts, a writer in upstate New York, dramatizes the same shift in values that has encouraged some theorists to maintain that use of certain drugs may be normal and that homosexuality might not be universally a symptom of neurosis. Ms. Roberts was contracted to write a book on extrasensory perception, and knowing nothing about the subject, began her researches on the Ouija board. Soon a "spirit entity"—or a personality hidden deep in her subconscious—made contact. "Seth," as he called himself, helped her go into trances and, speaking through her, has since "dictated" 6,000 pages of manuscript—enough for two books. Far from committing Ms. Roberts to an asylum, today's society has avidly read her books.

The Granger Collection

In the Middle Ages the "mad" were considered to be possessed by demons, and there was little hope of recovery.

Arthur Tress   Mike Levins   Dick Swift

In today's urban society, there is much allowance for individual diversity and even eccentricity.

WHAT IS DISTURBANCE?

But though Ms. Roberts' somewhat unusual behavior has been encouraged and has apparently brought her considerable satisfaction, many other people are still seeking, or being sent to, a wide variety of mental health practitioners or asylums. We send others for help because we consider their behavior disturbed—disruptive or maladaptive; we seek help ourselves because we feel we cannot cope. But how does the psychologist or psychiatrist determine whether a disturbance really exists or not and, if so, what to do about it?

 Social Adjustment Rating Scale

Holmes and Rahe (1967) have developed a "life-event scale" which indicates the relative importance of stresses on mental health. They feel that an accumulation of 200 stress points in one year makes one vulnerable to mental illness.

Life Event	Mean Value
1. Death of spouse	100
2. Divorce	73
3. Marital separation	65
4. Jail term	63
5. Death of close family member	63
6. Personal injury or illness	53
7. Marriage	50
8. Fired at work	47
9. Marital reconciliation	45
10. Retirement	45
11. Change in health of family member	44
12. Pregnancy	40
13. Sex difficulties	39

14.	Gain of new family member	39
15.	Business readjustment	39
16.	Change in financial state	38
17.	Death of close friend	37
18.	Change to different line of work	36
19.	Change in number of arguments with spouse	35
20.	Mortgage over $10,000	31
21.	Foreclosure of mortgage or loan	30
22.	Change in responsibilities at work	29
23.	Son or daughter leaving home	29
24.	Trouble with in-laws	29
25.	Outstanding personal achievement	28
26.	Wife begins or stops work	26
27.	Begin or end school	26
28.	Change in living conditions	25
29.	Revision of personal habits	24
30.	Trouble with boss	23
31.	Change in work hours or conditions	20
32.	Change in residence	20
33.	Change in schools	20
34.	Change in recreation	19
35.	Change in church activities	19
36.	Change in social activities	18
37.	Mortgage or loan less than $10,000	17
38.	Change in sleeping habits	16
39.	Change in number of family get-togethers	15
40.	Change in eating habits	15
41.	Vacation	13
42.	Christmas	12
43.	Minor violations of the law	11

SOURCE: Holmes and Rahe (1967)

Points of View

The mental health practitioner evaluates a prospective patient from a number of points of view. At his most objective, he considers whether the symptoms reported are *statistically* abnormal—that is whether they occur in only a relatively small number of people or are, instead, fairly widespread. As psychology has become increasingly scientific, the statistical view of behavior has acquired considerable importance; it acts as a check against the natural tendency to judge others by one's own standards. But the statistical view unfortunately implies that what is abnormal is bad and should be changed and that what is normal is good or desirable. A student may turn up at the campus clinic complaining that it takes him twice as long as everyone else to write his Freshman English compositions; he gets good grades and encouragement from the instructor, but he thinks his work is good only because he gives more time to it than others do. Should this student be helped to work faster, or should he be reassured that his writing skill is real and that he needs more time for writing than others need because writing is more important to him?

The examiner also looks at his patient from a *cultural* point of view. He asks whether the reported symptoms are abnormal *within the patient's culture.* A man who reports difficulty getting along with a female employer may be treated differently if his ancestry is British or German than if he grew up in a Hispanic or Italian environment. This view, though valuable, has the same limitations as the statistical view—a behavior is not "bad" because it is culturally abnormal any more than because it is statistically abnormal in a broader sense.

Turning from these views of behavior that avoid value judgments, the examiner looks at the patient's symptoms from a *normative* view, asking whether they diverge from some standard of behavior. The patient reports that he doesn't desire sexual intercourse more than once a week. Is there anything wrong with that? This is obviously an important question, for according to his answer, the therapist may prescribe five sessions weekly with Masters and Johnson or nothing at all. But according to what, or whose, standards is a behavior to be judged?

The fourth point of view from which the examiner looks at the patient is the *subjective* view. He asks, "Does this person appear *to me* to be suffering from an emotional disturbance?" And if the answer is yes, he asks, "What do I think should be done about it?"

Today, however, the most important point of view from which symptoms are examined is that of the patient himself. If his behavior or his emotions are disturbing to him, then he can be said to be suffering from a disturbance. This way of viewing behavior is called the *clinical* view because it disregards notions of statistical normality and of external opinion to concentrate instead on what the person reports about his behavior and his reactions to it. From this point of view, it becomes possible to recognize disturbance in the person whose way of life appears efficient and well integrated to an outsider—but is unsatisfying to the person himself—and also to exclude from concern the person whose behavior is disturbing to others, but satisfying to himself. In the latter case, the person may be more appropriately treated by legal authorities. An important corollary of the clinical view of disturbance is the recognition that someone who does not want help probably cannot benefit from it.

An assessment of behavior, then, could take five points of view into account—statistical, cultural, normative, subjective, and clinical. Today, the clinical view seems by far the most valuable; it gives primary importance to the person's own view of his behavior and of himself.

Coping and Anxiety

Since it seems unlikely—and perhaps even undesirable—that we will arrive at any single definition of disturbed behavior, the emerging issue becomes that of *coping:* the ability to function in society and to live with oneself. From the

coping

stress   **Psychological Concomitants of Stress**

Irving Janis (1958) and his associates have pursued a systematic analysis of the psychological concomitants of stress. For Janis, a stressful environment is one in which most people experience a degree of emotional tension that interferes with normal functioning.

Under severe stress such as combat danger, the physiological manifestations resemble those of fear: tremor, sweaty hands, cold sweat, violent heart-pounding, and stomach disturbances. Such symptoms can result from innervation of striated muscles, or they may involve changes in the visceral organs innervated by the autonomic nervous system. These are also essentially the symptoms or somatic manifestations of anxiety, which characteristically follows exposure to some harrowing experience. Such symptoms, Janis has noted, can be experimentally induced in the laboratory.

In terms of motivation and learning, Janis notes an increased vigilance toward environmental cues and the acquisition of adaptive discriminations between the more and less dangerous features of the environment. Thus in one study he found that in time, infantrymen on the front lines learned to take cover when the sounds of projectiles were approaching them but to ignore the equally impressive sounds of projectiles that were traveling straight overhead. Green troops, in contrast, were aroused by both types of cues.

Such increased vigilance, discrimination, and use of safety precautions are positive adaptive reactions to stress. Maladaptive changes involving impairment of cognitive and judgmental processes occur typically after prolonged or unusually intense exposures to stress. In combat terminology this behavior is known as the "old sergeant syndrome" and is manifest by apathy, indifference, and depression resulting in an inefficiency in military and self-protective performance. At the other extreme, "trigger happy" behavior is a concomitant of hypervigilance.

Janis noted another form of hypervigilance among hospital patients who had gone through a preoperative period with relatively little fear but showed extreme stress reactions to the unfamiliar apparatus and activity of the operating room. They suspected far more drastic procedures than those that actually took place and sometimes even considered the surgeon a sadist.

Janis has described a model of "reflexive fear," which is defined as thoughtful or deliberate in the sense of reflecting the realities of a situation. It is distinguished from neurotic fear in terms of: (1) responsiveness to environmental cues—the environment plays the determining role in activating and perpetuating reflexive fear; (2) arousal of vigilance, in which the individual attends to his environment with greater readiness to take protective action; (3) arousal of a need for self-assurance in an attempt to alleviate emotional tension by obtaining convincing reassurances; and (4) development of compromise defenses involving discriminative vigilance and assurance.

Janis and Leventhal (1900) made a distinction between *reflexive emotion,* which is highly modifiable by informational inputs, and *internally aroused emotion,* which is relatively unmodifiable by the reception of new information. This distinction is applicable to other negative affects such as grief, guilt, and anger, as well as to fear.

They note that among antecedent conditions of a stress reaction is the content of the relevant threat cues. Thus with a mild warning evoking a low level of fear, blanket reassurance is a probable predominating response, leaving the person unmotivated to attend to subsequent threat cues or to prepare for action. This response can lead to serious maladjustment should the danger in fact be severe, but it is somewhat more appropriate than other responses under ambiguous environmental conditions. When the threat is unusually severe, the response may be a high degree of vigilance, which can also be maladaptive if high arousal interferes with appropriate functioning in the face of danger.

In terms of the above, Janis has evolved a curvilinear hypothesis describing responses as fear increases. At low levels of fear the probability of developing a compromise attitude is low because of the tendency to remain indifferent. As fear increases to moderate levels, vigilance is aroused, directing attention to available information bearing on the threat, which in turn leads to a reality-tested compromise. As fear mounts to a high level, the probability that the person will develop a compromise response decreases because of the disruptive effects of strong emotional stimulation, which results in indiscriminate vigilance, poor adjustment, and extreme forms of defensive avoidance. This series of reactions may be described as an inverted U-shaped function.

clinical point of view, what determines our ability to cope? That is, what determines our level of self-perceived adjustment?

Different theories of behavioral disturbance offer different explanations. Freud's theory, which we examined in Chapter 12, is by far the most developed. More recent explanations have pointed to the significance of specific learning experiences. But Freudians and learning theorists both suggest that we tend to adopt modes of behavior that work for us. And if they should fail after a while, then we adopt new behaviors to cope with new problems and situations. Freud calls coping behaviors defense mechanisms, or ways of dealing with anxiety. Although the defense mechanisms, as named and described by Freud, depend upon certain assumptions of psychoanalytic theory, they have counterparts in most other theories and so can be considered somewhat independent of theoretical orientation.

Hypnosis and Repression

For Freud repression was the process of unconscious forgetting or amnesia as a result of anxiety mobilized by the ego against the acting out of instinctual impulses and demands. Many attempts have been made to study repression in the laboratory, and several investigators have used hypnosis as a means of inducing conflict or repressions in their subjects.

Unfortunately the amount of information supplied by such studies is limited by the peculiar methodological constraints involved: the limited understanding of the hypnosis process itself; the necessity of differentiating between hypnosis and hypnotic state; and the fact that hypnosis is the means of inducing conflict in order to study behavioral manifestations of repression. One is in effect using one dependent variable to study another dependent variable. In addition, we cannot readily assume that hypnotically induced conflicts are greatly similar to the types of conflicts that theoretically occur spontaneously in life situations.

The fact that most of the physiological manifestations obtained under hypnotic trance can be obtained equally well in nonhypnotized simulating subjects (Barber, 1962; Orne, 1959; Sutcliffe, 1960) demonstrates a need for hypnotic experimentation to include a nonhypnotized control group given identical suggestions and instructions.

Williamsen, Johnson, and Eriksen (1964) made a study that included the proper controls. They used a group of hypnotizable and a group of nonhypnotizable subjects. Each group was subdivided into hypnotized, simulating, and control groups. Subjects in the hypnotized groups were given standard hypnotic induction and asked to learn a list of six words, which they were told they would be unable to remember after emerging from the trance until a cue was given by another experimenter. Simulating subjects, who had previously experienced a trance induction if they were hypnotizable and an attempt at trance induction if not, were asked to simulate posthypnotic amnesia for the six words. The control subjects learned the six words without hypnosis and with no amnesia instructions.

In a following session a second experimenter, who did not know what group each subject had been assigned to, administered various tests for recognition and recall of the six words. The hypnotically susceptible hypnotized group showed significant decrements over the control subjects and also differed from the simulating subjects, whose performance was characterized by exaggeration of posthypnotic amnesia.

Although the results of this experiment support the genuineness of posthypnotic amnesia, they also provide indications that this process should not be readily equated to clinical repression since posthypnotic amnesia was limited to direct measures of recall and recognition and did not affect performance on word-guessing tasks involving the amnesic words or word-association tests using these words. Such differences could be anticipated if posthypnotic amnesia were identical to clinical repression.

Martin T. Orne

MECHANISMS OF DEFENSE

Repression

Repression is a protective device by means of which forbidden impulses or painful memories are banished from consciousness. Freud claims that repression begins in early childhood, when we stifle our instinctual urges rather than face the disapproval of our parents. Later, these impulses constantly try to surface—and do, as Freud notes, in slips of the tongue, in dreams, and in forgetful behavior (see Chapter 12, the box on p. 550).

Repression is subconscious. We are only aware of it when our conscience troubles us, for conscience is the surface extension of repression. Thus, a man who has repressed a lifetime of resentment against his mother may say something unnecessarily harsh to her in a moment of anger; in the next moment, he is horror stricken and apologetic. This is a typical example, for the feelings most subject to repression are precisely those concerning sex and aggression.

Most, though probably not all, cultures seem to have subjected these two impulses to some forms of defense, though the particular forms may differ. In Western culture sexual and aggressive expressions are so heavily restricted and punished that defensive reactions to them are common. Are restrictions on sex and aggression necessary? Do people in some cultures have no defensiveness about lovemaking or warmaking? Presumably all human societies need rules to avoid *interpersonal* conflict, but do these rules have to engender *intrapersonal* conflict? We do not have answers to these questions because they are difficult to study. But given our present state of knowledge, it seems that society could find some means other than defensive reactions to control sex and aggression.

We can look at this matter in another way. Our culture seems to treat other motivational systems more openly. Competition, affiliation, and eating behaviors, for example, are controlled by values and norms, but except in extreme cases of pathology, they do not result in great defensiveness. But this is not so in all other cultures. In some competitiveness creates such levels of anxiety that all such feelings must be defended against. Therefore it is important to recognize that we are not talking about "human nature," but about specific experiences in specific time periods when we consider the importance of any motivational system.

Mechanisms of Escape or Flight

Regression Regression is an attempt to cope, but to cope as a past self, as a child confronting simpler situations in an easier time. Regression is a stage, therefore, beyond repression; it occurs when the threat is significant enough to force a response, but the response takes the form of behavior patterns that worked in childhood.

Regression in Play Behavior

Regression has been experimentally demonstrated in a study of the play behavior of children before, during, and after the introduction of a frustrating event (Barker, Dembo, and Lewin, 1941). Thirty children, aged 2 to 5, were given standardized toys, such as a truck and trailer, to play with and were individually rated on the "constructiveness," or imaginativeness, of their activities.

What the children did was closely correlated with their mental ages; those with higher mental ages created elaborate stories around the toys instead of merely manipulating them. Each child's play was therefore rated in terms of what were called "mental age units"—the greater the constructiveness was, the more units the child was awarded.

Subsequently, the children were introduced to new, much more interesting toys in a part of the room that had formerly been closed to them. They were allowed to play in this new situation for only a short time before being returned to the main part of the room and their original toys. The new toys were locked away behind a wire screen, where they were still visible but completely inaccessible.

A new assessment of the children's constructiveness of play with the original toys showed an overall average decrease of 1½ years in the mental age score. Moreover, some children demonstrated what was termed "barrier" and "escape" behavior: they poked their arms through the interstices of the screen or attempted to leave the room entirely. The play behavior of these children was found to have regressed most—an average of 2 years—whereas that of the other children had regressed only an average of four months and sometimes had even increased.

The experimenters felt that the regressive play behavior of the children in this study was like such regressive actions as stuttering, repetition, and restlessness in highly emotional situations. In particular, they discerned the same decreased level of performance and lack of ability to cope with reality.

Sometimes regression can play a constructive role, and it is then known as "regression in aid of the ego." The "stiff upper lip" that most men maintain, for example, or the calm, unaggressive behavior of the adult who has been conditioned to be polite under all circumstances may be much more damaging to the personality than a "relearned" ability to regress to tears or a harmless temper tantrum.

Fantasy In fantasy, we create private worlds, where our needs are satisfied and our own image of justice prevails. For children, fantasy is as much a preparation for adulthood as it is the creation of a playground that surpasses any the real world has to offer. For adults, fantasy is more often an escape from the known, from boredom, dullness, impotence and other frustrations of daily life. It is an egocentric creation of a world where inhibitions cannot trouble us because there is nothing to repress. Personality problems vanish and secret de-

Drive Reduction and Fantasy

Feshbach (1955) experimentally demonstrated a notion first introduced by Freud. Freud theorized that when a biological drive builds up in an infant, the energy associated with that drive may be dissipated in one of two ways: presentation of a real-life version of the satisfying object (for example, the mother's breast if the drive is hunger) or presentation of an imaginary version of the satisfying object. The latter possibility, which we ordinarily call "fantasizing," Freud called "primary process thinking."

Feshbach asked experimentally: Can primary process thinking about aggression toward an object release the tension associated with real-life hostility? Feshbach divided college-aged subjects into two groups. After being angered by the experimenter, the experimental group were asked to fantasize in response to TAT cards (see Chapter 13); then their level of aggressive tendencies was measured. The control group was asked to take part in a nonfantasizing task after their anger was instilled, and their aggressive tendencies were then assessed. Feshbach found that subjects in the experimental group showed a reduction in aggressive tendencies as compared to the control group subjects. In other words, primary process gratification did show drive-reducing properties.

Feshbach has utilized other fantasy techniques (1961). For example, he provided an experimental group of subjects, after he had angered them, with the opportunity to watch a movie of prizefighters hitting each other. It was assumed that subjects might in fantasy identify with the fighters and thereby reduce their aggresive drive. In fact, Feshbach did obtain results demonstrating a reduction in anger in subjects that watched the movie. These results are not without difficulty, however, since some investigators have shown results pointing in the opposite direction. Bandura, Ross, and Ross (1963a), in a well-known series of experiments, showed that children who watched a movie about aggression were more likely to behave aggressively themselves afterwards. This process Bandura called "modeling." Part of this difference may be due to whether an unacceptable (e.g., aggressive) drive is already present before the fantasy opportunity is presented.

sires are acted out. These fantasies are commonly romantic and sexual. In fantasy, unattainable lovers are delighted to be with us, and loneliness is replaced by the joys of an erotic and amatory union.

Death fantasies are also common, especially as the person ages. Approaching what seems to be the end, the mind tries to transcend death or simply make peace with it; in some fantasies death is more horrifying. As a kind of fantasy justice, revenge is often our reward for dying: those who don't appreciate us suffer, we fantasize, an inconsolable grief.

Denial To protect ourselves against a threatening situation, we may simply deny its existence. People suffering from incurable diseases often experience disbelief as the first stage of the adjustment process. The Nazi movement pro-

denial

duced similar symptoms among European Jews, who wanted to avoid the facts of their experience. Denial doesn't always take a passive form; promiscuous sexuality, compulsive spending, or any frenzied activity in the face of an unfavorable situation are signs that denial mechanisms are at work. Even fantasy may be enlisted in the effort to ignore the situation.

Mechanisms for Disguising the Source of Anxiety

displacement

Displacement In displacement, the person recognizes the existence of a threat but transfers his anxiety to something else. In a study of frustration (Miller and Bugelski, 1948), summer campers were given a series of boring tests that ran so long it took up the time normally allotted to a popular weekly outing to the movies. Both before and after the tests, the campers were asked their reactions to Mexicans and Japanese. Half gave their reactions to Japanese before the tests and to Mexicans afterwards; the other half rated the groups in reverse order. Both Mexicans and Japanese were more negatively rated after the testing session than before; the boys had transferred their aggressive impulses from the testers to the members of a more distant group.

Projection Projection entails the person's shifting of an entire conflict outside himself. He perceives others as experiencing difficulties that are actually his own. Several studies (Sarnoff and Katz, 1954; Katz, Sarnoff, and McClintock, 1956) showed the role projection plays in prejudice. Subjects were measured for such ego defenses as projection, denial, repression, and reaction formation and were then shown information that accurately described blacks and information about the relationship between ego-defensiveness and prejudice against blacks. The experimenters predicted that the amount of improvement in a subject's attitudes toward blacks as a result of this information would depend on the degree of his ego-defensiveness; that is, the greater his defensiveness, the more he would project that defensiveness onto others and the less his own attitudes would improve. The results indeed bore out their hypothesis; by far the most reliable predictor of resistance to change was defensiveness.

Another insight into projection is provided by a study of college women whose views on sexual morality were considered strict and conventional (Frenkel-Brunswik and Sanford, 1945). The subjects tended to project "immoral" sexual impulses, which they denied in themselves, onto the members of minority groups.

Rationalization In rationalization, the person disguises the source of his anxiety with semilogical arguments to convince himself—and anyone else who might listen—that his behavior is acceptably motivated when in fact it is not. Claiming to read magazines that feature nude women for their literary excellence is a common example, but others are equally familiar. Some people stay in undesirable situations because, they say, the effort to advance or attain what they want would cost too much. In truth, however, they are uncertain of their ability to conquer the demanding situation.

Prejudice and Projection

Studies such as those of Adorno (1950) and particularly Frenkel-Brunswik (1948, 1954) of prejudiced people indicate that aggressive feelings toward themselves and their parents are frequently denied by the ego, to which such feelings are alien, rather than integrated into a self-conceptualization. It seems that certain undesirable characteristics are not accepted as characteristics of the self or of the parents, but these characteristics nonetheless exist in the person, where they lead a kind of covert submerged life. Finally they are attributed to others, typically to minority groups. This pattern of behavior is identical to the mechanism Freud labeled projection.

The projection that lies behind prejudice appears to be revealed in such actual statements as the following: "I am not particularly sorry because of what the Germans did to the Jews. I think the Jews would do the same type of thing to me. I think the time will come when we will have to kill the bastards."

The aggressive impulses felt by a prejudiced person cannot be directed toward his in-group associates, with whom he identifies, but they can be directed at others whom he believes to be aggressive and to deserve attack. Prejudiced people typically have a low tolerance for ambiguity and manifest a comparatively rigid cognitive style. Although they typically are the products of strict, punitive environments, they seem compelled to see their parents as completely good; yet there are also indications that covertly they see their parents as far less faultless than their words would indicate. This profile is in marked contrast to the profiles of comparatively unprejudiced people, who appear to have been trained to accept and integrate feelings of love and hate toward their parents.

Pleading illness is another common form of rationalization. This excuse makes it possible to avoid activities in which one fears competition and failure or to explain away bad performances or unethical behavior. A bad cold or a "trick" knee both shields the ego from harsh criticism and elicits compassion from others.

Sublimation According to the psychoanalytic view, impulses that have been forbidden during childhood and therefore are repressed reappear in modified, socially acceptable forms later in life. This kind of expression of threatening impulses is called sublimation.

Aggression, for instance, when channeled into sports like football, is no longer dangerous to society because it is contained within a set of rules that limit its duration, area, and manner of expression. Likewise, sexual impulses arouse little anxiety if their energies are expressed through the arts. A finely sculpted nude or modern dance, though sensuous, is rarely deemed prurient. In fact, Freud attempted to account for many of man's greatest intellectual and artistic achievements through the idea of sublimation.

Reaction Formation In reaction formation a person expresses in his behavior something exactly the opposite of his true impulse. Thus, an antivivisec-

tionist may in fact harbor the unconscious desire to inflict hurt that he de-
nounces in others. It is important to understand, however, that the person's
underlying impulses are not conscious ones; his behavior, therefore, is not hyp-
ocritical but a sincere expression of his conscious beliefs.

Reaction formation is more commonly demonstrated in familial relationships where aggressive or negative feelings toward parent or child are perceived
as forbidden. In their place, excessive outpourings of affection and protec-
tiveness are manifested.

Is Cynicism a Reaction Formation?

Sarnoff (1960) has experimentally demonstrated that cynicism may be a reaction
formation against affectively warm tendencies that are consciously not acceptable.
He gave 81 male college students two questionnaires to complete, one measuring
cynicism and the other reaction formation. Then one group of men experienced
a high affection-arousal situation; they observed a live production of a moving
scene from a play in which the only character is a young man. A second group
(low affection arousal) heard the scene on a tape recorder.

After the presentation, the men once again answered the questions on
cynicism. All subjects, whether they had rated high or low in reaction formation,
tended to demonstrate less cynicism after the presentation in both the live and
taped forms than before. But those who had rated high on reaction formation
showed less attitude change than the others; the difference here was statistically
significant in the high arousal condition but not in the low arousal condition.
There was also a significant positive correlation between the ratings on cynicism
and on reaction formation, as measured before the presentation.

Although the results of this experiment would have been more impressive
if the men who scored high on reaction formation had shown greater cynicism
after the scene than before, Sarnoff was satisfied that the significant correlation
between resistance to affection and high reaction formation, combined with the
pretest correlation between cynicism and reaction formation, was good empirical
evidence that cynicism is sometimes a reaction formation to consciously rejected
affectionate tendencies.

Toward Neurosis

The defense mechanisms do not themselves necessarily constitute neurosis; they
signify, rather, the presence of threats and anxieties that we have learned to avoid
in various ways. Invoking defense mechanisms is, however, added work for the
psyche—work that is not a part of getting the job of life done. The person who
uses these mechanisms excessively spends so much time and energy avoiding
neurosis anxiety that he renders himself ineffective and finally, neurotic.

Sal Rovetto

A maladjusted person may spend so much time and energy avoiding anxiety that he becomes ineffective and finally, neurotic.

In some forms of neurosis anxiety becomes a symptom. In other forms, anxiety is not manifest at all. But the presence of anxiety, below or above the level of awareness, is considered the one common feature of all neuroses. It is therefore important to realize that the neurotic person is, from his point of view, behaving sensibly. He has found ways—his symptoms—of diminishing or even removing his burden of anxiety, and in his scale of values that must have first priority. He is in touch with reality, even though he may occasionally resort to the defense mechanism of denial. The neurotic is an unhappy person, eager to be rid of his condition.

The classification of the defense mechanisms has shown that in many cases they merge or change into each other, and the same will be found to be true of the neuroses and psychoses. They are not clearcut entities like chicken pox or measles, but convenient labels for kinds of behaviors that are considered disturbed. As you read the following pages it is important to remember that what is considered disturbed behavior is a product of the society, the person's place in the society, and most importantly, the person himself.

THEORIES OF NEUROSIS

The Psychoanalytic View: Sigmund Freud

We have seen, in the discussion of defense mechanisms in this chapter and in the earlier discussion of Freud's theory of personality (Chapter 12), that Freud attributed behavioral disturbances to inappropriate·methods of coping with anxiety-arousing instincts. The method of treating them he advocated, as we will see in more detail in Chapter 17, was to bring the cause of anxiety into consciousness so that it could be dealt with more rationally and effectively. The essence of this view is still very much alive today in psychoanalytic theory and practice. One outgrowth of it is the classification of neurotic behaviors that we will present later in this chapter.

Freud virtually introduced the neuroses to medical attention, and his theories about their causes and cures have long dominated the field. In recent years, however, rival theories of neurotic behavior have appeared, and today they form almost an embarrassment of riches. We will now look briefly at two of these rival theories.

Learning Theory: Joseph Wolpe

Townsend Wentz, Jr.

Joseph Wolpe

Like learning theorists in other areas of psychology, Joseph Wolpe (1958, 1969) has developed his theory from his work with animals, and like most learning theorists he is reluctant to erect large theoretical structures that are not buttressed by adequate scientific data. He is concerned only with the symptoms the patient complains of and not with their underlying causes. These symptoms, Wolpe believes, have been learned, and like any other habitual behavior, they can be unlearned. For learning psychologists "the symptom *is* the disorder"; for Freudians, treating the symptom is often worse than useless, for the disturbed inner dynamics of the patient will produce another symptom to take its place.

Accordingly, Wolpe and his colleagues take considerable pains to establish as precisely as possible what it is that is causing the patient distress. That he has a phobic neurosis is of no particular importance; that he is afraid of snakes, particularly black ones, and also of anything that remotely resembles a snake, is important.

This precise outlining of the problem facing the patient is not always as easy as it sounds. By the time the patient and the psychologist meet, the anxiety may have generalized to a number of objects or circumstances more or less similar to its original cause, and isolating the original cause may prove difficult and tedious.

Client-Centered Therapy: Carl Rogers

client-centered therapy

Carl Rogers' (1959) theory of the neuroses is based on attention to the patient's own perception of his experience, rather than the objective properties of that experience, and on Rogers' belief that the principal motivating force in man is the "inherent tendency of the organism to develop all its capacities in ways that serve to maintain or enhance the organism." This tendency is called an *actualizing tendency.*

actualizing tendency

As the child develops it needs *positive regard* (a broad synonym for "love"). From the frustrating or satisfying experiences he meets in seeking positive regard, he develops a corresponding self-regard. In seeking to maintain positive self-regard the person selects among experiences at the expense of the satisfaction of his actualizing drive, and he sometimes avoids experiences that he believes might not contribute to positive self-regard—enhance his feeling of worth. Having experienced something that was not self-enhancing, the person might remove it from awareness or distort it. This incongruence between aware- ness and experience is the source of psychopathology, leading to anxiety and *intensionality,* a tendency to "see experience in unconditional terms, to over- generalize, to be dominated by concept or belief, to fail to anchor . . . reactions in space and time, to confuse fact and evaluation, to rely upon abstractions rather than upon reality-testing."

Types of Neurosis

Of the three theories that we have discussed, the Freudian model is the least optimistic about the possibility of diagnosis and cure; too many layers of repres- sion interfere with the necessary revelation of early trauma. Learning theory has a more neutral outlook, and the view of Carl Rogers is quite hopeful. For all their disagreement about the ultimate possibilities of removing neurosis, how- ever, these three views share some common ground in their description of neu- rotic symptoms. The specific classifications we present here have grown more out of the Freudian tradition and not all psychologists and psychiatrists accept them unconditionally.

Anxiety Reactions Anxiety reactions are free-floating, nonspecific "panic episodes." They are more frightening than specific fear reactions because they occur seemingly without stimulus. The physical reactions—heart palpitations, rapid breathing, weakness, faintness, nausea, and perspiration—may be severe, although there is, of course, no organic cause for the body disturbances.

anxiety reaction

The anxiety attack typically strikes an anxiety-prone person—one who lives with high tension as a fact of life. When the unconscious source of conflict threatens to become conscious, usually because of its sexual or aggressive con- tent, it must be stifled. Repression proves inadequate to the task, and the anxiety reaction results.

Obsessive-Compulsive Reactions Obsessions are persistent, often unrea- sonable thoughts that cannot be banished, however aware the person is of their irrationality or impossibility. They are more than extensions of normal worries about home appliances left on or car keys left in the ignition; they are constant and haunting preoccupations with acts that the person typically regards as shameful, sinful, or violent. The person may devote all his time to his obsession, thereby depriving himself of the opportunity to resolve the actual problem the obsession has replaced.

obsessive-compulsive reaction

Compulsions are behaviors that occur repeatedly and without apparent purpose, usually with an element of ritual. Like obsessive thoughts, compulsive acts are often beyond the person's comprehension and control. If anything, he feels controlled by them. Compulsions are structured ways of dealing with

Arthur Tress

Being in a crowd or riding on an escalator may cause a phobic reaction in some individuals.

dangers the person both fears and desires; Lady Macbeth, for example, washed her hands as much to prolong guilt as to exorcise it. In other cases, compulsion is a way of structuring chaos, of imposing order on a world that is too threatening otherwise. In extreme forms, compulsive behavior is exhibited as kleptomania, the compulsion to steal, and pyromania, an uncontrollable desire to set fires.

phobic reaction   **Phobic Reactions** When harmless objects or situations take on frightening powers, they reflect a concern that we speak of as phobic. Though the phobic person is usually able to recognize the irrationality of his fear, he is unable to control it. Heights, close places, the dark, open spaces, animals: almost anything can be the object of a phobic reaction. The original cause frequently can be traced to early childhood, when something unpleasant was accidentally

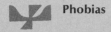 **Phobias**

Phobic reactions are persistent manifestations of fear of some object or situation that presents no actual danger to the subject, or in which the danger is magnified out of all proportion to its actual seriousness. Frequently the objects of phobias are things that most of us fear, such as darkness, fire, and disease, but sometimes they are such things as crowds or open places—situations that fail to elicit fear in most people. Here is a list of some common phobias:

acrophobia: fear of high places
agoraphobia: fear of open places
alophobia: fear of pain
astraphobia: fear of storms, thunder, and lightning
claustrophobia: fear of closed places
hematophobia: fear of blood
mysophobia: fear of contamination by germs
monophobia: fear of being alone
nyctophobia: fear of darkness
ocholophobia: fear of crowds
pathophobia: fear of disease
syphilophobia: fear of syphillis
zoophobia: fear of animals, or of some particular animal

Such phobias are essentially simple defensive reactions toward internal or external dangers that must be prevented or avoided. Should the phobic fail to utilize these defenses he must face the threat and with it the concomitant anxiety.

Phobias have been described and explained in terms of both psychoanalytic and social learning theory. The psychoanalyst considers the phobia as representing displacement of anxiety from some stress situation that elicited it onto some other object or situation. Freud has classically explicated the mechanism in the case history of Little Hans, who displayed a fear of horses—specifically of being bitten by horses. Freud saw this as a displaced fear of castration by the father. As in the Oedipus complex, the child, wanting to possess his mother sexually, found himself jealous and hostile toward his father, whom he also loved and who he feared would retaliate with castration in addition to withdrawal of love.

Many therapists, though they believe that a variety of stress situations may lead to phobic reactions, still base their explanations on the mechanism of displacement. Thus the behavior of a man with a morbid fear of syphillis has been explained as a displaced fear of his homosexual tendencies. The fear of syphillis enabled him to maintain sexually moral behavior and, in addition, prevented him from normal heterosexual behavior, which had never been enjoyable to him because his thoughts were dominated by homosexual fantasies. These fantasies aroused great anxiety and had on occasion terminated in impotence. The syphilophobia was a kind of reaction formation that enabled the man to control his threatening inner sexual impulses.

For social learning theorists, the phobias may be the result of some past trauma that is partially or wholly forgotten. The neurotic reaction can lead to secondary gains, such as increased attention and sympathy, assistance, and some control over others' behavior. Such phobias can be treated by means of a positive deconditioning procedure (Lazarus, 1960). For example, an 8-year-old boy who had developed an automobile phobia as a result of being in a car accident, was rewarded with a piece of candy (his favorite) whenever he made a comment about vehicles. In time he was able to observe simulated accidents with toy cars. The child was then seated in a nonmoving vehicle and was finally, with further chocolate reinforcement, able to enjoy motor travel without anxiety.

associated with the object or situation that becomes the trigger for a phobic reaction. The original cause is forgotten, but the fearful association remains.

hysterical neurosis
conversion reaction
dissociation reaction

Hysterical Neurosis Hysterical neurosis is usually manifested by one or the other of two symptoms—the *conversion reaction* or the *dissociative reaction*.

 How Phobias Are Conditioned

In phobic reactions, extreme and inexplicable fear becomes associated with a particular object or class of objects. Commonly observed forms of phobic reaction include fear of syphilis, dirt, closed spaces, high places, open spaces, or specific animals.

The phobic person attempts to control his anxiety by avoiding situations that cause him feelings of discomfort and anticipation of aversive consequences. By objective standards, however the person's fears are unfounded. In fact the person himself might report that his fears are irrational. However, if his reactions are not socially debilitating they are not considered phobic. For example, fear of snakes is relatively common; as many as 2 percent of college students may respond emotionally to snakes even when they are represented only symbolically, as in a film.

To be considered a phobia a fear must be socially evaluated as disproportional to the situation or disturbing to an observer or to the person himself. In this sociopsychological context, then, a behavior, if it is to be considered phobic, must deviate from what is expected in the culture and must also be disruptive.

Traditionally, the major reaction of phobics, as with other neurotics, is anxiety. Psychoanalytic theory views phobic anxiety as a danger signal that functions to alert the person, to put him on guard against the true and overwhelming cause of anxiety. The psychoanalytic viewpoint further assumes that there is an underlying cause and that the observed avoidance of a particular idea, object, or situation represents a displacement of anxiety from the true and more threatening cause to another, frequently symbolic cause.

Displacement is accomplished by the ego defense mechanisms, which redirect emotionally charged images and ideas to less dangerous objects.

In either case the hysterical person is emotional and unrealistic. He responds to feeling without consideration of the practical aspects of the situation.

A *conversion reaction* is a physical condition for which no organic basis can be found. The person may, for instance, suddenly be unable to move one of his limbs; he may become blind or deaf or lose feeling in a certain area of his body. Or he may cough continually or feel that he is choking.

That there is no physical cause for conversion reactions becomes apparent when the person is either asleep or under hypnosis. A facial tic that is a persistent affliction during the day disappears when one is sleeping. Similarly, one who, in a waking state, is unable to walk is readily supported by his legs when he is in a hypnotic trance.

 Eve White, Eve Black, and Jane

A famous case of multiple personality brought a 25-year-old woman known as Eve White to a therapist seeking relief from intense headaches and what she termed blackouts (Thigpen and Cleckley, 1954, 1957; Thigpen, 1961). Early in her treatment, Eve had the further complaint that she had been hearing voices. While reporting her new symptoms she underwent a sudden transformation in personality and began to call herself Eve Black.

The two Eve's turned out to be completely different from each other. Eve White was shy, a conservative dresser and a hard worker, whereas Eve Black was lively, outgoing and carefree, a provocative dresser. Eve White did not know about Eve Black, but Eve Black knew about Eve White and didn't in the least mind engaging in activities that Eve White disapproved of and leaving her to suffer for them. The existence of Eve Black explained Eve White's blackouts and the voices she heard as evidence that Eve Black was either in complete control or trying to assert control.

After the patient had been in therapy for several months, a third personality, named Jane, appeared. Jane, who was a good deal like, but stronger than, Eve White, came increasingly to be the dominant personality. Whereas the two Eves had existed since childhood, Jane was a newcomer, probably an improvement upon Eve White that therapy had helped make possible.

The therapist eventually learned that as a child Eve White had experienced poverty, stern discipline, and parental rejection in favor of her younger twin sisters, all of which possibly helped precipitate her psychological difficulties. The root of her disturbance, however, was discovered to be a terrifying incident that occurred when Eve was 6 years old: her mother had forced her to give her dead grandmother a farewell kiss as she lay in her coffin.

Once this incident was brought to light, Eve's personality quickly assumed its final form. This new integrated self, Evelyn, was the most complete personality of all and was eventually able to lead a normal life.

In a *dissociative reaction* the person abandons the sense of self-consistency that healthy people maintain, despite the different roles they play throughout life and the changes in behavior and outlook that the passage of time brings. This loss of personal unity and continuity may manifest itself in such forms as sleepwalking and amnesia, both involving loss of memory. However, while the somnambulist only intermittently suffers the inability to remember—he forgets what he has said and done during the night but otherwise seems normal on waking—the amnesiac's lapses of memory are far more serious and may occasionally last a lifetime. His conflicts seem so severe that he gives them up entirely, along with his identity and his past. In extreme cases he may move to another place and take up a completely new life. Except for his inability to remember who he is, he carries on, to all outward appearances, in a normal fashion.

In a dissociative reaction some people take on multiple personalities. Various aspects of the person control his consciousness at different times and fully repress all the other aspects. If the personalities house diametrically opposed impulses, then the split can attain a Dr. Jekyll/Mr. Hyde character—kindness versus cruelty, introversion versus extroversion, and so on—and the separate personalities may even use different names.

depressive neurosis   **Depressive Neurosis** The simplest of the depressive neuroses is typically manifested by a prolonged and exaggerated reaction to the death of a close

 Depression and Suicide

The three main factors that may cause suicide appear to be intolerable anxiety generated by responsibility that has been thrust upon one, depression, and alienation, a sense of loneliness. The fact that suicide is sometimes the result of increased responsibility reminds us that depression is often the sequel to achievement or promotion. Perhaps this is the reason why in unliberated cultures, men have a higher suicide rate than women (Maris, 1969), whereas as women gain positions of more nearly equal responsibility, their suicide rates increase, and as blacks gain social equality, they too become more likely to commit suicide.

It is fairly obvious that depression would play a role in suicide. Wold (1970), reviewing suicide rates in Los Angeles, found that 92 percent of the people were "clinically depressed." However, this depression is typically not the lethargic depression of the manic-depressive psychosis (see p. 727), but the period between the depressive and the manic stage, or the agitated depression of the involutionary psychotic reaction (see p. 729).

That alienation or loneliness is a predisposing condition for suicide is shown by the increased number of suicides during festive occasions, such as Christmas and New Year's. The lonely person contrasts his condition with the real or imagined happiness of others. In addition, unmarried people are more likely to commit suicide than married ones (Peck, 1970).

friend or relative or some other unhappy event; it is, in other words, a "reality-oriented" overreaction. Sometimes, however, it appears in response to an' achievement, such as a promotion, as a reaction to feared added responsibility or to the loss of friends through their envy. The depressed person feels sad, discouraged, and sometimes worthless; his day-to-day functioning is somewhat impaired.

A depressed person sometimes suffers from depersonalization—a feeling of unreality and strangeness, either because he has changed (or is in the process of changing) or because the world around him has changed. His emotions become flattened and dreamlike.

MAJOR SYMPTOMS OF PSYCHOSIS

The symptoms of psychosis reflect the disorientation and disintegration of the entire personality. Unlike the neurotic, who constantly struggles to keep his anxiety at manageable levels and continues to relate to the world, the psychotic has lost touch with reality and ceases to carry on a normal life. Freud defined the psychotic state as a "loss of the reality-testing function."

psychosis

Learning theorists prefer to regard this loss of contact with reality in the psychotic as an effect rather than a cause. For some reason—which may be rooted in early experience, in abnormalities of body chemistry, in heredity, or in distorted mechanisms of perception—the psychotic develops an extreme and intolerable degree of pervasive anxiety. His behaviors are ways of reducing that anxiety, and their extreme disorientation is not a product of the loss of a specific "reality-testing function" but of the extremes to which his defense mechanisms must go.

In agreement with this point of view, several authorities, notably Szasz (1961) and Laing (1967), have made the point that all behaviors are "natural" in the sense that they are the person's natural responses to his unique set of circumstances. By appreciating this we begin to understand the behavior of the psychotic, rather than "explaining it away" by labeling it abnormal, sick, or unnatural.

The chief signs of psychotic disturbance, not all of which afflict every patient, are the following:

Disorientation. The person may appear completely disoriented; upon being questioned, he does not seem to know who he is, where he is, or when he is. The inability to orient himself in the time and space of the real world is often an indication that he is responding rather to an inner fantasy world.

Delusions. Delusions, or beliefs contrary to reality, often afflict the psychotic. They are usually, though not always, of the persecution type; that is, the person feels that others are watching, following, or trying to harm him in some way. Equally common are beliefs that one's mind and body are being controlled by hostile forces. Delusions range from isolated, unconnected notions to full-fledged, intricate systems, and each belief is tied to the others in an internally logical way.

Hallucinations. The psychotic frequently experiences hallucinations—perceptions of objects, persons, or events that are not really there. Hallucinations may involve any sense modality, but are most often auditory in nature—the patient complains of hearing voices.

Emotional disturbance. Signs of emotional disturbance are typically indicative of personality breakdown. This may be evidenced by highly exaggerated, impulsive emotional displays, or at the opposite extreme by a completely flat, apathetic demeanor. The patient often demonstrates emotions that are inappropriate to the situation at hand. He may, for example, laugh when hearing of a sad event.

Verbal disturbance. The psychotic may disregard linguistic conventions. He may express himself autistically, that is, in a highly personalized way that cannot be understood by others. The connections between one statement and another seem meaningless, and even the patient's vocabulary may be of his own invention, thus further increasing his isolation.

Disturbance of nonverbal communication. The psychotic's nonverbal communication may also indicate severe disturbance. He may make strange gestures and twist himself into bizarre postures, in which he may remain for hours at a time. Such movements are usually highly ritualized and tied to the patient's personal imaginings.

Some forms of behavior with the characteristics we have described are caused by more or less obvious physical injury or disease, such as severe neurological damage (head wounds), general paresis (the terminal stage of syphilis), encephalitis, or senile deterioration as a result of hardening of the cerebral arteries.

organic psychosis
functional
psychosis

These organic psychoses will not be our concern here. Rather, our interest lies in the so-called functional psychoses—that is, disturbances whose only observable component is the person's behavior. The possibility of physical change must always be considered, but in the functional psychotic, it must appear unlikely. Much research today is seeking organic bases for the functional psychoses, but though it has produced numerous hypotheses, no one of them has yet found wide acceptance. Even in the absence of definitive evidence, however, many so-called functional illnesses are treated as if they were psysiologically determined. Some psychiatists believe, for instance, that a chemical imbalance may be involved in schizophrenia and accordingly administer drugs or vitamins to their patients.

For the psychoses as for the neuroses, theorists with different orientations have proposed different systems of classification. In fact, the difficulties of explaining and classifying the psychoses are much greater. We will therefore not attempt to present theories about their causes and mechanisms but will simply describe them, for the most part in conventional terms. Completing that, we will look at some of the factors that have been thought to contribute to psychosis. A problem the reader should note, however, is that unlike most people suffering from the neurotic symptoms we have discussed, the psychotic person often cannot describe his condition. The neurotic usually knows all too well that he is unhappy; the psychotic, however, may be so disoriented that he doesn't know he is disoriented. And in some forms of psychosis, especially the extreme forms of psychopathy, the person may perceive himself as normal and sane, although the society has unequivocally decided that his tendencies are harmful and in need of correction. Here the society's definition of acceptable behavior complicates the problem of classification.

Affective Reactions

affective reaction

Affective reactions are characterized by exaggerated emotional states, fluctuations between excessive elation (a manic phase) and utter despondency (a depressive phase) or between normal and only one of the two extremes. Most affective reactions show only the partial cycle, and depression is the more frequently exhibited state. The mood swings commonly occur without warning and do not seem to be precipitated by any particular environmental factors. They sometimes occur at regular intervals and sometimes persist whether treated or not, for a few weeks or months.

In a manic phase the patient becomes hypermobile, somewhat like a film that is run at a higher rate of speed than usual. His thought, speech, and actions, along with certain physiological functions such as heart rate, become more rapid and intense. He explodes in great bursts of energy and manages to sustain his dizzying pace on little food and only a few hours of sleep each night. Often, with characteristically boundless optimism and self-confidence, the patient concocts elaborate schemes, but he rarely brings them to fruition—if he attempts them at all.

If the mania progresses, the patient generally requires hospitalization and must be calmed with drugs. In such severe cases he may remain in constant motion, break things or throw them about, and become generally violent. His verbal behavior is equally unrestrained; his speech becomes unintelligible and his ideas disconnected. Delusions, hallucinations, and overt sexuality are not uncommon.

In the depressive phase, thought and action is slowed. The psychotically depressed lose the will to live and as a result, cease to function; they may stop eating, speaking, and moving and must in that case be hospitalized.

Schizophrenic Reactions

The most severe of the psychoses, schizophrenic reactions are also the most prevalent, accounting for some 50 percent of hospitalized mental patients. Though schizophrenia is commonly called "split personality," it is different from the multiple personality neurosis. The split that characterizes the psychosis is the separation of thought from feeling.

Though different types of schizophrenia are distinguished, the symptoms overlap considerably. What is called *simple schizophrenia* is a gradually developing psychosis that often begins in adolescence. The outward signs are mild—lack of interest and involvement in daily activities—and hospitalization is not normally required. The person withdraws from his social relationships, suffers occasional delusions, loses interest in his appearance, and retreats into dependence on alcohol, sexual stimulation, or drugs.

Hebephrenic schizophrenics show high personality disorganization, and are therefore the easiest for the layman to recognize as insane. The name is derived from Hebe, the Greek goddess of youth, who was considered quite silly and foolish. Disorientation and both auditory and visual hallucinations characterize this type, as does severe regression to childhood behavior. Speech becomes a verbal game.

Catatonic Schizophrenics also suffer hallucinations, but the characteristic symptoms are motor disturbances varying from stupor to excitation. The stupor, which is more frequently seen, is often expressed as physical rigidity, muteness, and unresponsiveness. In the excited state, the patient is sleepless and hyperactive; he may be destructive without provocation. Despite its severity, catatonia is more likely than other forms of schizophrenia to clear up spontaneously.

Paranoid schizophrenics tend to intellectualize, building up a logical set of beliefs based on wrong assumptions. Suspiciousness and hostility are followed by self-aggrandizement, which gradually leads to the certain knowledge that one is personally involved in everything that happens. At this point, delusions of grandeur may occur, but more frequently the ideas are of persecution.

Infantile autistic schizophrenia (sometimes called "childhood schizophrenia") often appears in the first years of life. Here the child seems incapable of responding to his environment. He displays no emotion, is highly withdrawn, and if he speaks, tends to use a language of his own. If there are several forms of stimulation, the child cannot respond; if given a single verbal command, he cannot translate it into action.

Etiology of the Psychoses

Whereas the majority of theories about the origins of neurosis stem from Freud's ideas about psychopathology (the principal variant element is the importance attributed to learning), the picture is somewhat different when we approach the psychoses. Because psychotic conditions have been recognized, though variously defined, for centuries, the body of literature concerned with them is very much larger and more diverse. Although a lot of ancient theories have been discarded, the early idea that some organic disturbance is involved in psychosis is still very much alive. Most current theories lean toward some kind of interaction between organic and environmental factors.

Some Other Psychoses

Some other psychotic conditions differ from the general characteristics of the affective psychoses and schizophrenia. Their existence as separate entities is sometimes questioned, but they are diagnosed rather frequently.

Involuntionary melancholia is a form of depression manifested by some men and women during the "change of life" (the menopause in women—about 45 to 55 years of age; the climacteric in men—about 55 to 65 years of age). The name given to this psychosis represents a compromise between the physical component ("involuntionary"—pertaining to the period of physical decline) and the psychological ("psychotic reaction"), and the relative importance that should be given to these two components is still unclear.

One possible bridge between the physical and the psychological in this condition is the importance attached to youth in our culture. The woman who perceives her sexual attractiveness—indeed, by her loss of menstruation, her whole sexual role—diminished is naturally placed under considerable psychological strain. When to this is added the mood swings caused by the hormonal disturbance of menopause a foundation has been laid for a "psychotic reaction" to an anxiety-creating situation. Because of the combination of physiological, psychological, and social factors that underlie involuntionary psychotic reaction, some authorities (Cameron, 1963) believe that this condition does not merit a separate category; they use the term for any psychosis that occurs in middle age.

The symptoms of this condition include worry, anxiety, agitation, and severe insomnia, frequently accompanied by guilt and hypochondria. The distinctive feature, as contrasted with neurotic depression and depressive psychosis, is the agitation, with pacing, hand-wringing, and self-reproach. Paranoid symptoms may appear.

Another psychotic condition whose existence as a separate category has been questioned is the *paranoid reaction*. As with the paranoid form of schizophrenia, the distinctive feature is the development of persecutory or grandiose delusions. However, in the paranoid reaction most of the patient's personality remains intact, and the delusion remains separate from the rest of his life. Because of the logical development of the delusion, the difficulty of penetrating to its core, and the relative normality of the individual's way of life, recognition of this condition is sometimes very difficult.

Psychological Factors Poor familial interaction in early childhood is the seedbed of mental disturbance for psychoanalytic theorists. They point out that mothers of disturbed children sometimes are overbearing and protective. But while there may be a relationship between schizophrenic children and mothers who are overbearing or do not provide proper care and support, it is also possible that the mother's behavior is the result of having a disturbed child rather than the cause of that disturbance. Klebanoff (1959) found that mothers of brain-in-

Parental emotional support in early childhood is important for mental health.

jured, retarded, and schizophrenic children held child-rearing attitudes in common. All tended to be more protective and controlling than mothers of normal children. Thus, such traits can be regarded as typical maternal reactions to behavioral disturbance in general—to schizophrenia as well as to other disorders.

double-bind   **Double-Bind** Another theory based on purely psychological factors explains psychosis as the result of a double-bind situation in childhood. Such a situation exists when incompatible or inconsistent demands are made of the child (Bateson, 1956). The father may punish or subtly disdain any signs of emotional dependence, while the mother encourages them. Or the mother may elicit the child's affections, and then communicate nonverbal disgust when he tries to kiss her; finally she may make him feel guilty when he pulls back.

When constantly faced with the conflicting messages in such situations as these, the child no longer knows whom or what to trust. Conforming to his father's demands entails the risk of losing his mother's affections, and vice-versa; he is, in effect, being forced to choose between them. In the case of the contradictory mother, if the child believes in his own perceptions, he must mistrust his mother's professed love for him. If, on the other hand, he accepts her inconsistent communications, then he loses all faith in himself. Rather than make a painful choice the child escapes his dilemma by gradually withdrawing from reality.

Organic Factors As in other studies of the significance of heredity, twins have provided a fertile experimental basis for determining the role of heredity in psychosis. Kallman (1959) concluded that if one twin develops schizophrenia, the possibility of the other twin's also developing it is six times greater when the twins are identical than when they are fraternal. For affective psychosis, the concordance rates were even higher (Kallman, 1954).

Gottesman and Shields Twin Study

Gottesman and Shields (1966) undertook a study of the incidence of schizophrenia in a sample of 57 pairs of twins, in which one twin had already been diagnosed schizophrenic. Ten of 24 pairs of identical twins (42 percent) were found to be concordant for schizophrenia, whereas only three of 33 pairs (9 percent) of fraternal pairs were diagnosed schizophrenics.

Gottesman and Shields also analyzed the pairs in terms of different gradients of concordance. They divided the known schizophrenic identical twins into two classes of severity: those who had been hospitalized for more than 52 weeks and those who had been hospitalized for less than 52 weeks. The concordance rate for the severe cases was 67 percent, but for those hospitalized less than 52 weeks it was only 20 percent.

In summary, Gottesman and Shields found:

1. The concordance rate for identical twins was considerably less than 100 percent, indicating that nongenetic factors play an important role in schizophrenia.
2. The concordance rate is much greater for identical than for fraternal twins, clearly indicating a genetic factor.
3. A polygenic theory, in which many genes acting autonomously are involved, is a likely explanation in the etiology of schizophrenia. This is suggested by the relationships found between concordance rates and severity of illness.
4. Also likely is a diathesis (or constitutional) stress model in which a large proportion of predisposing genes lower threshold for coping with stress. This heredity—environment interaction model accounts for the fact that the incidence even in identical twins is far less than it would be for a trait inherited in a strictly Mendelian fashion.

In a more recent theory, both a genetic predisposition to mental disturbance and a combination of special environmental circumstances are seen as essential for precipitating the psychotic breakdown (Laing, 1965). The predisposition, while necessary, is not by itself enough to trigger the disturbance.

Genetic Factors The attempt to determine what organic factors may be involved in psychosis is beset with problems. One cannot, for instance, work with hospitalized patients since they (even those who are not mentally disturbed) exhibit some neurological or neurochemical differences from an unhospitalized population. Hospitalization itself is sometimes the source of such differences. Investigators once thought they had isolated a chemical compound that produced schizophrenia when they discovered large amounts of it in the urine of schizophrenic patients. Subsequently, however, they traced the compound to the hospital diet.

It is also possible that compounds actually found to be unique to the body chemistries of schizophrenics and manic-depressives may be side effects, not causes, of the disorders. It is known, for example, that psychotics have peculiar eating habits and sleep patterns. Prolonged periods of such regimens could well be responsible for differences noted in the chemical analyses of their blood.

For the most part, then, the etiology of the affective and schizophrenic psychoses remains largely unknown. While the search for organic factors goes on, it may ultimately prove futile: Investigators may decide after all, with Szasz and Laing, that a person simply responds to his singular situation in the best way he knows.

OTHER FORMS OF MENTAL DISORDER

psychosomatic
disorder

Psychosomatic Disorders

It has been estimated that approximately one-third of the patients in any doctor's waiting room are suffering from symptoms for which the physician can find no organic cause. Their illnesses, from which they truly suffer and which are real to them, are the result of the interaction of the mind and the body: they are psychosomatic.

Freud's work with conversion hysteria (p. 554) was the first effort of the medical profession to understand this interaction. But while Freud's followers were concerned with hysterical conversion symptoms (for example, hysterical blindness or paralysis), specialists in internal medicine discerned other examples of the interaction. The general characteristic of psychosomatic illness is a change in the intensity or coordination of bodily functions under the influence of emotion. Simple examples of this are the increase in heartbeat or in depth of breathing that accompanies emotional arousal. When such a condition becomes chronic, the abnormality of function may produce pathological changes in an organ: continual hypersecretion of acid in the stomach, for example, may lead to a peptic ulcer.

Cannon's work (1929) on the autonomic nervous system, in which he described the bodily changes that occur in fear, pain, hunger, and rage, led to further investigations into the emotional components of many diseases, and into the reasons why certain people are prone to physical reaction to emotional crises.

Freud's followers considered all psychosomatic disorders as examples of a conversion reaction, but other theorists have tended to discredit this view. They have been seen as the expression of specific personality types (Dunbar, 1935, 1943) and as reactions to specific conflicts: executives who work in stress situations are prone to heart attacks, for example (Alexander, 1950). Still another view (Szasz, 1952) has drawn attention to the characteristic disturbances of organic balance in infancy and has suggested that a regression to this state in

Executive Monkeys

The distinction between functional causes (psychogenic in origin) and organic causes (associated with lesions of the nervous system) of mental illness have become increasingly less clearcut. What seems quite clear, however, is that there is an interaction between bodily states and mental states. Moreover, functional psychological illness may be associated with organic physical changes in parts of the body other than the nervous system. These are the illnesses commonly called psychosomatic. A lucid example of this interaction is provided by experiments with monkeys in whom duodenal ulcers were induced experimentally through a conditioning process (Brady, 1958). In this research design, monkeys were paired in groups of two, and each monkey was confined by a restraining device. An electric shock was then delivered at intervals. One of the monkeys of each pair was designated the "executive monkey" because he had the option of learning to press a lever which could turn off the shocks for both monkeys.

Since identical shocks were delivered to the two animals, equal physiological damage would be predicted, if no other (psychological) factors intervened.

What happened was that only the executive monkeys developed ulcers, which were apparently a reaction to the stress state produced by the constant alertness required to prevent the shock. The helpless monkey, who could only endure the shocks as they came, was somewhat less reactive and less disturbed. While a functional origin of symptoms in neurotic reactions has been rather firmly established, the causative factors in the psychotic reactions are still under intensive investigation.

emotional conflict is responsible for placing abnormal demands on particular organs.

The Personality Neuroses

personality
neurosis

Two themes, closely related, have been apparent in our discussion of disturbed behavior. The first has been that of continuity: the disturbed merges into the normal and the different forms of disturbance merge into each other. The second has been the important role of society in defining disturbance. These themes become evident again when we look at a quite recent development in psychology—interest in the more-or-less permanent individual character or personality, especially where it is deemed disturbed or unwholesome.

Wilhelm Reich (1949), a follower of Freud, has distinguished two types of neurosis, the symptomatic and the character. The former manifests the classic neurotic symptoms, which cause distress and which the patient is eager to be rid of. These symptoms have usually developed during adulthood and have caused a noticeable change in the personality. The character neurosis, in contrast, develops very early and is usually manifest by adolescence. The patient regards the symptoms as a part of him, has little or no insight into their disturbed nature, and rationalizes them as a "natural" way of responding to the world around him. Consequently he resists any attempt to change them as an attack upon his essential character.

Character neurosis may manifest any of the symptoms of symptomatic neurosis and, in addition, inadequacy, passive aggressiveness, and explosiveness. *Inadequacy* is an inability to meet the demands of reality—physical, emotional, social, or intellectual—in the absence of physical or intellectual handicap. *Passive aggressiveness* is the combination of strong dependency needs with anger that the needs are not gratified. Either the dependency or the anger may be repressed, or the two behaviors may alternate. *Explosiveness* is characterized by gross outbursts of rage, expressed both verbally and physically. Sometimes these outbursts are accompanied by amnesia.

psychopath   **Psychopathy**   The psychopath is a willful, impulsive, self-centered person who cannot tolerate delay or frustration. He frequently seems pleasant and well-mannered on first acquaintance, but it soon becomes apparent that he has no concern for others and is incapable of forming close relationships. He seems

✄ Assassins

"He was a loner. Never talked much with anybody. Just kept to himself. Sort of faded into the wallpaper."

Those words could be used to describe any one of the four political assassins in the United States in the past decade or so: Lee Harvey Oswald, James Earl Ray, Sirhan Bishara Sirhan, and Arthur Bremer. These men accused or convicted of shooting John F. Kennedy, Martin Luther King, Jr., Robert F. Kennedy, and George Wallace had many things in common.

Products of unstable, economically depressed families, they experienced difficulties in establishing identities. An absent father and a domineering mother interfered with the development of self-concepts when they were young boys. Oswald's father died before he was born, and his mother struggled to support her family. When Ray was in his teens, his father deserted his large family of 11

Lee Harvey Oswald, James Earl Ray, Sirhan Bishara Sirhan, and Arthur Bremer had many things in common.

children, whom he had often beat. Sirhan's family fled war-torn Palestine when he was very young; then his father abandoned his children to a very rigid mother and returned to his homeland. The fourth child in a "dysfunctional family" (according to Milwaukee social workers), Bremer sporadically fought with his father and was overprotected by his mother, who wouldn't allow him to go out for football.

These socially isolated human beings were incapable of developing genuine relationships with others. All four were unsuccessful in relating to women—perhaps because of the lack of a stable male figure in the formative years. Sirhan shunned girls throughout his life. A teen-ager who dated Bremer for a short time stopped seeing him because he did not trust her. The only women in Ray's life seem to have been prostitutes. Oswald married a Russian woman whom he commanded and abused.

Possibly the ultimate failure of these men was in setting ambitions and goals beyond the range of their intellectual or emotional abilities. Although a poor student, Oswald read a lot and became interested in Marxism. Following a stormy career in the U.S. Marine Corps, he went to Russia, announced his defection, and expected to be treated as a hero. After a 33-month stay, he was unsuccessful in obtaining Soviet citizenship and returned to Texas. Ray was discharged from the U.S. Army for "ineptness and lack of adaptability for military service"; he became a drifter. In and out of prisons on robbery charges, he thought of himself as a jailhouse lawyer, but every time he spoke he damaged his case. After flunking out of college, Sirhan pursued his burning desire to become a jockey. He was licensed as a "hot-walker" and exercise boy at a race track, but when he mounted a horse, he was thrown. Bremer hoped to become a great writer or photographer. Although he studied both at a technical college, he could obtain only janitorial or busboy jobs.

In their frustration and increasing alienation, these men concentrated their inner efforts on extreme political ideas. Fidel Castro was Oswald's idol, and Oswald killed the liberal president denounced by his hero. The man who shot civil rights leader King had inquired about gaining entry into segregationist Rhodesia. Sirhan, a Christian Arab, blamed the Jews for the suffering of his people and struck down Robert Kennedy, whom he considered the archenemy of Arabic hopes and dreams. Not known to be political-minded (except for cryptic notes in his diary), Bremer developed an unexplained interest in George Wallace and made an obsession of following him around until he finally attacked the politician.

to have no conscience at all and exhibits no anxiety about his often violently antisocial behavior. The absence of guilt and the absence of love are the two distinctive hallmarks of the psychopath.

No generally accepted theory of the origin of psychopathy exists. Nevertheless, the extreme and socially harmful nature of the disturbance and the absence of any exterior cause for the behavior legitimizes its inclusion among the personality neuroses. As Cleckley (1941) points out, perhaps the majority of psychopaths come into conflict with the law. But a complete lack of conscience and a quality of superficial charm and plausibility are not necessarily handicaps in all parts of society. He suggests that many recognizable psychopaths may be found outside of prison, sometimes in highly respected positions.

Alcohol Addiction

There appears to be a much larger psychological component in alcoholism, for which physiological addiction has not been demonstrated, than in drug addiction. The drug addict is physically dependent on his drug to the extent that withdrawal from it causes severely painful, sometimes potentially fatal symptoms. Of course the drug addict is also psychologically dependent on the tension relief his drug offers, but the physiological component is evidently the more dangerous: initial experiences with an addictive drug frequently lead to addiction, whereas only about 1 percent of drinkers become alcoholic. In neither form of addiction is there any identifiable personality configuration. The only characteristic that all addicts seem to share is a compelling search for relief from tension. For additional discussion of the use of drugs other than alcohol, see Chapter 9.

Probably because of its more ascertainable psychological component—and perhaps also because of its greater frequency in the middle classes—alcoholism has been the subject of many more theories than drug addiction. Though both physiological and psychological determinants have been suggested, little solid evidence has been produced for any of the physiological theories.

Early psychoanalytic views (Rado, 1933) regarded alcoholism as a characteristic behavior in people who resolved their conflicts by denial and flight from reality, probably caused by an overindulgent mother-child relationship. Menninger (1938) believed that a self-destructive motivation was important in alcoholics, springing from intense frustration and rage combined with fear and guilt. This in turn he ascribed to disappointment with the parents, who promised more than they could provide. Lolli (1956) agreed that a poor relationship with the mother is the cause of alcoholism but suggested that the result is a regressive need for comfort and security. Learning theorists, such as Dollard and Miller (1950), suggest that a flight from painful reality and depressive tendencies are crucial, but consider use of alcohol as a classically conditioned—that is, learned—behavior.

Perhaps the most generally acceptable psychological theory of alcoholism is Ullmann's (1952), which might almost be described as a nontheory. Ullmann, regards alcoholism as a symptom of the need to reduce the tensions of ordinary living. He does not believe that any benefit will come from attempts to identify a particular personality type that would experience a high degree of tension; all that needs to be recognized is that drinking is a form of self-therapy for tension and anxiety. Treatment, then, is not concerned with the development

Leonard P. Ullmann

of insight, but with the development of alternate and more adaptive forms of tension reduction, together with help in reorganizing the alcoholic's life situation to remove or reduce the sources of tension.

In this chapter, we have attempted to define generally what disturbed behavior is and, after a very quick look at some of the many equally valuable and equally unproved theories of its causation, to describe the most widely recognized categories of disturbance. If more were known about causes of disturbance the plan of this chapter would be quite different, but in view of the present state of knowledge, the most we can do is describe and add the warning that descriptions are of limited usefulness. Today what is said about causes depends on the speaker's theoretical orientation rather than upon the evidence before him. It thus becomes extremely difficult to classify particular behaviors, let alone to know what to do about them when someone says he wants help. In fact, as we have seen, in a few instances we don't wait for the person to say he wants help but decide instead, on a normative or even subjective basis, that he needs it whether he wants it or not. Is it possible to treat a condition without knowing its cause? The reader is doubtless aware that disturbed behavior is widely treated, and this chapter has, we hope, made clear that its causes are no clearer—indeed less clear—than ever. In the next chapter we will look at some of the ways in which mental health practitioners attempt to deal with the kinds of disturbance we have described here.

SUMMARY

Many meanings can be given to the term "disturbed" in psychology. Statistically it means "not average"; culturally it means "not conforming to the mores of the culture"; normatively it means "too far from standard"; subjectively it means "I think it's disturbed"; clinically it means that the person's way of life, which he feels unable to change, causes him distress and limits his ability to cope. These concepts, taken together, indicate that psychological impairment is defined by both the patient and his environment, but today the patient himself is most important.

And just as normal and disturbed are two ends of a continuum, so all people have anxieties and unhappiness. We counteract these anxieties with unconscious processes of the mind, *defense mechanisms,* that distort or deny the source of the anxiety. Of these the most important are *repression,* which banishes the forbidden impulses or painful memories from consciousness; *regression,* a return to primitive coping behaviors; *rationalization,* the attempt to convince oneself and others that one's behavior is acceptably motivated; and *sublimation,* in which the repressed impulses, such as sexual desires and aggression, reappear in modified and acceptable forms.

All of us use defense mechanisms, but when coping is hindered by unconscious preoccupation with defense mechanisms, and when these mechanisms nevertheless fail to provide a complete defense against anxiety, the person is said to be neurotic.

Freud's account of the nature and origin of the neuroses for a long time dominated the field, but in recent years alternate explanations have appeared. The most important is *learning theory,* which attributes neurotic symptoms to specific reactions to noxious events, which have become engrained as habitual reactions to similar circumstances and persist despite their inappropriateness. Rather than regarding these behaviors as symptoms of an underlying condition, the learning theorist believes that they themselves are the disease and attempts to eliminate them by extinction and reconditioning.

Carl Rogers and his followers pay attention to the patient's perception of his experience rather than to the objective characteristics of that experience. Treatment in *client-centered therapy* is based on developing unconditional self-regard, freed from the limitations that the client has imposed upon his experiences because of his perceptions of the demands of others.

The simplest form of neurosis is the *anxiety neurosis,* in which free-floating anxiety—sometimes of panic proportions—is the only symptom. In the *obsessive-compulsive neurosis,* persistent obsessive thoughts or compulsive behaviors interfere with the usual activities of life. *Phobias* are fears of harmless objects or circumstances.

Hysterical neuroses are of two types, the conversion reaction and the dissociative reaction. In the first physical symptoms—usually paralyses or anesthesias—express needs to escape from anxiety-creating symptoms; in the second, a whole part of a person's life is blocked from consciousness, leading to sleepwalking, amnesia, or multiple personalities. The *depressive neurosis,* as the name implies, is a period of depression, exaggerated in length or intensity, following some unhappy event. The neurasthenic depressive is chronically tired, and the depersonalized depressive feels unreal and alien.

The *psychoses* are distinguished from the neuroses by greater loss of contact with reality. The neurotic is unhappy and ineffectual but remains aware of and responsive to his circumstances; for the psychotic the only defense left is to shut out reality. In *affective* psychosis, this retreat takes the form of exaggerated emotional states of depression and euphoria, in which the *manic-depressive* patient either swings from one state to the other or remains more or less constantly in one. In the *schizophrenias,* which are the severest, the least understood, and the commonest of the psychoses, the distinctive behavior is a dissociation of thought from emotion. In *simple schizophrenia* the patient's behavior and social contacts steadily deteriorate, and there is an overall state of apathy. In *hebephrenic schizophrenia,* bizarre emotional reactions, hallucinations, and delusions are conspicuous, while in *catatonic schizophrenia* a stupor and rigid unresponsiveness are prominent. *Paranoid schizophrenia* is distinguished by suspiciousness, accompanied by delusions and a general disorganization of the personality.

The etiology of psychosis is still far from settled. Most authorities believe that purely psychological, genetic, organic, and environmental factors probably coexist.

The neuroses and psychoses are the most prominent psychological dysfunctions, but other classifications are receiving increasing attention. *Psychosomatic disorders* are genuine bodily dysfunctions for which the physician can find no organic cause. The general characteristic of psychosomatic illness is a change in the intensity or coordination of bodily functions under the influence of emotion.

The *personality neuroses* have symptoms that parallel many of the neuroses and psychoses, but they develop earlier and are generally not recognized by the person who has them. The most troublesome of them to society is psychopathy. Addiction is another recently recognized psychological disturbance; of which the greatest attention has been given to the psychological component of alcoholism.

SUGGESTED READINGS

Chesler, Phyllis, "Patient and Patriarch: Women in the Psycho-Therapeutic Relationship," in *Woman in Sexist Society*. New York, Basic Books, 1971.
    A sharp indictment of contemporary psychiatric theories and practices for their failure to recognize female psychology.

Fitzgerald, F. Scott, *Tender Is the Night*. New York, Scribner, Contemporary Classics ed., 1960.
    The story of a deteriorating marriage and its interrelationship with both partners' mental health.

Green, Hannah, *I Never Promised You a Rose Garden*. New York, Holt, Rinehart and Winston, 1964.
    A young girl's 3 years in a mental hospital and her route back from madness, as recounted by her psychiatrist.

Harris, Thomas A., M.D., *I'm OK—You're OK*. New York, Avon, 1967.
    From his work in transactional analysis the author has put together a system to help people develop healthy relationships with other people and to see themselves in a better light.

Horney, Karen, *Our Inner Conflicts*. New York, Norton, 1954.
    Horney's ideas concerning the sources of neurotic conflict.

Laing, R. D., *The Divided Self*. New York, Pantheon, 1970.
    Laing in this book seeks to explain madness and the process of going mad to persons who know little about the phenomenon, and he traces the lives of a number of schizoid and schizophrenic individuals.

Melville, Herman, *Moby Dick*. New York, Modern Library.
    The epic saga of Captain Ahab's fanatic quest to wreak revenge on the white whale that had crippled him.

Milford, Nancy, *Zelda: A Biography*. New York, Avon, 1972.
    An in-depth study of Zelda Fitzgerald and her painful descent into insanity.

Plath, Sylvia, *The Bell Jar*. New York, Bantam, 1972.
    Plath's autobiographical account of 6 tormented months in her twentieth year, ending as she leaves a mental hospital after a nervous breakdown.

Schreiber, Flora R., *Sybil*. New York, Warner, 1974.
    A look into the unconscious mind of a real woman who had 16 different personalities.

Snyder, Solomon H., *Madness and the Brain*. New York, McGraw-Hill, 1974.
    A popular book that presents the evidence for a biologically based theory of schizophrenia.

Szasz, Thomas P., *The Myth of Mental Illness*. New York, Hoeber, 1961.
    A leading psychiatrist believes that the entire concept of mental disorder is nonexistent, contending that so-called sick persons are merely individuals who use defective strategies for handling problems of living.

Ward, Mary J., *The Snake Pit*. New York, New American Library, 1973 (originally published in 1946).
    The classic novel of life in an insane asylum in the forties.

Chapter Seventeen

Maintaining Mental Health

What is the incidence of psychological disturbances in the
   United States?
What is the relationship of socioeconomic status to
   disturbance?
What is the major significance of diagnosis?
Is electroshock therapy harmful?
What is the goal of psychoanalysis?
What is client-centered therapy?
How is a neurosis "learned"? How can it be "unlearned"?
What is the focal point of preventive psychology?
Who are paraprofessionals?

In Chapter 16, it was pointed out that many people are in some way psychologically disturbed. Though the precise number would depend on the criterion of disturbance used, by any definition, there is alarming evidence that we are not in the best of mental health.

One out of ten people in the United States today will be hospitalized for psychiatric reasons at some time in his life (Goldhamer and Marshall, 1953). Over half of the country's hospital beds are now occupied by "mental patients," and the rate of new admissions is climbing steadily (Kisker, 1972), although modern methods of treatment are shortening the length of stay. An estimated fifty thousand people commit suicide each year; there are five million known alcoholics, and we do not know exactly how many persons are addicted to drug usage. Clearly, psychological impairment is one of the most critical public health problems of our time.

Since of the three topics we want to discuss in this chapter—detection, treatment, and prevention—detection seems to be both the most immediately pressing problem and the area of clinical psychology in which progress is most evident at the moment, we will talk about it first. Then we will move on to treatment, which now has a somewhat venerable tradition as well as a challenging future. Finally we will talk about the newest aspect of mental health— prevention of mental disturbance.

DETECTION

Detection involves the study of patterns of disturbed behavior, especially in populations that may be unaware of the sources of their problems or their need for help. For example, people in lower-class neighborhoods are usually unaware that some of their difficulties stem from the environment and not from personal shortcomings, and that counseling might make it easier for them to cope.

Perhaps the best-known investigation of the extent of psychological impairment in a population is the Midtown-Manhattan project (Srole, Langner, Michael, Opler, and Rennie, 1962). Only 18.5 percent of people investigated in this study were found to be relatively free of symptoms of emotional impairment. New York City is a notoriously difficult place to live, with its motley population, but similar results were found in a survey of a small town in Nova Scotia (Leighton, 1964): according to both surveys, only about 15–20 percent of the population did not need professional help (Table 17.1).

Whether such findings indicate a developing epidemic of disturbed behavior or a contemporary recognition of a long-term problem is difficult to say. As we have pointed out, the most consistent trend in the psychology of disturbance has been the broadening of its scope from a narrow interest in psychotic behavior to the inclusion of any behavior that is deemed disturbed. This change in the criteria for psychological attention has not been a purely conceptual one.

Bradford Hess

Self-understanding and acceptance is essential to the maintenance of mental health.

Table 17.1 Results of Studies in Midtown Manhattan and in Nova Scotia

Midtown-Manhattan Study	
Category of Symptom Formation	Percent
Well	18.5
Mild symptoms	36.3
Moderate symptoms	21.8
Marked symptoms	13.2
Severe symptoms	7.5
Incapacitated	2.7

N = 100 percent (1,660)
SOURCE: Srole et al., (1962)

Nova Scotia Study	
Symptoms of Psychiatric Disorder	Percent
No evidence of any symptoms of psychotic significance	14
Might be indicative, but respondent gave no other indication, and no doctor's substantiation was given	21
Probably indicative (e.g., asthma, ulcers, hypertension) but were too vague to warrant inclusion under category below	21
Almost certainly indicative (e.g., previous or current hospitalization or described anxiety attacks)	44

SOURCE: Leighton (1964)

It has accompanied a dramatic improvement in living standards (at least for some) and an increase in leisure time. Reiff (1959) has suggested that the trend of modern civilization has been a development from political man through the stages of religious man and economic man to, finally, psychological man, who "lives by the ideal of insight . . . leading to the mastery of his own personality." Certainly, those in the educated middle and upper classes would tend to include in a list of necessities of life psychological services that might assist them in their search for fulfillment.

But those who perceive a need for psychological services are as yet untypical. The greatest levels of disturbance are found in the less educated classes. Generally speaking, the indications are that the lower the socioeconomic status (SES), the greater the need. In the two surveys we have mentioned—the Midtown-Manhattan and the Nova Scotia—among lower SES members of the sample the figures were, in Midtown Manhattan, 47 percent significantly impaired, 10 percent completely incapacitated; in Nova Scotia, 50 percent significantly impaired. These figures are not unique; in a review of nine surveys, Mishler

Social Class and Mental Illness

In 1958, Hollingshead and Redlich published what became a famous study of social class and mental illness. They asked: "Is the presence of mental illness in the population related to class status?" And: "Is the treatment received by a mentally ill member of our society an effect of his class position?" The social classes recognized by the study were:

Class I: wealthy, high-prestige professionals
Class II: managers and lesser ranking professionals
Class III: small business proprietors, skilled laborers
Class IV: semiskilled workers
Class V: factory and unskilled laborers

The investigators took a "psychiatric census" that categorized persons receiving psychiatric care on a given day in the city of New Haven, Connecticut. Then they compared the distribution of psychiatric patients in each category to the overall population distribution among the five classes. The overall (control) distribution was established by categorizing a random sample of persons chosen from the New Haven Directory. Now, if the proportions of persons in each category were different for the mental patient population as compared to the overall population, the investigators could conclude that there was a relation between class status and recognized mental illness. In fact, this result did obtain. As compared to its overall representation in the community, Class I showed a much smaller percentage of persons under mental care. On the other hand, Class V showed a much greater percentage of persons in the psychiatric care units (36.8 percent) than should have been expected on the basis of its representation in the overall population (17.8 percent). Further, upper-class persons who were under care were most often diagnosed as neurotic whereas lower-class persons were more often considered psychotic.

In Class I: 53 percent neurotic classifications, 47 percent psychotic classifications
In Class V: 8 percent neurotic classifications, 92 percent psychotic classifications

When the same kinds of comparisons were made for patients in terms of kinds of therapy received, it was found that Class I patients more often received psychotherapy than did Class V patients, who were more likely to receive physical (shock or drug) treatments. Whether this is because upper-class patients are automatically given psychotherapy preference, or because upper-class patients suffer from disorders amenable to psychotherapy in the first place, we do not know.

and Scotch (1963) reported that in all but one, lower SES groups had demonstrably higher hospitalization rates for disturbed behavior.

However, we must be careful about the conclusions we draw from such studies. First, we have to realize that judgments of normal or disturbed are made by middle-class professionals. Second, the higher rates of hospitalization among the poor may merely indicate that confinement to a mental hospital is almost the only form of therapy available for them. If the surveys included all people receiving any form of therapy—private or institutional—the disproportion between different SES's would probably not be nearly as great. And finally, a variant of the self-fulfilling prophecy may be operating. To the professional who accepts the generalization that "the poor are sicker than the well-to-do," the gray area between normal and disturbed may look considerably darker for the poor than for the wealthy. In a study of examiner bias, Haase (1964) showed a single Rorschach inkblot test protocol (see Chapter 13) to trained psychologists. Half received the protocol with a preliminary background description of the patient as a middle-class, suburban accountant; the other half were told he was a vegetable vendor who lived in a fourth-floor walk-up tenement apartment in Brooklyn. On 15 of the 16 measures used to evaluate these protocols, significantly more favorable diagnoses were made for the "middle-class patient." Perhaps all we can say, then, is that while the need for help is great among all segments, there is a tendency to judge the poor as needing it more.

Demand for treatment either for oneself or others, based on the detection of need, also differs according to social level. The Midtown-Manhattan study showed that in the "significantly impaired" group, almost 20 percent of those in the middle and upper classes were currently receiving outpatient treatment and another 33 percent had previously received treatment. But among the low-income "significantly impaired," only 1 percent were receiving outpatient treatment.

There are several reasons for the differences between socioeconomic classes in the ratio of need to demand for psychological services. Among many middle-class urbanites therapy is almost a status symbol. In contrast, when the poor are in psychological distress, they turn to such sources of help as friends, relatives, the church, or the emergency ward of a general hospital, rather than to a mental health agency. Reiff (1966) describes the attitude of the poor very well:

> To the worker, emotional disability or impairment is either related to a physical illness, and should be treated as such by the doctor, or it is the result of undue distress or strains in the environment; or it is related to a moral weakness and should be treated by a minister or priest or conquered by oneself or accepted and lived with. If one attempts to treat what is considered to be a moral weakness, the worker, with his present view, considers it a tremendous invasion of his privacy. (p. 541)

Thus, members of lower socioeconomic classes do not define disturbance in psychological terms, and more often than not, the emergency ward, church, or friend they turn to for help does not encourage them to consult a mental health agency.

Diagnosis

We have been concerned up to this point with the problem of detecting that a behavior disturbance exists and with some of the obstacles in the path of detecting disturbance—or for that matter the absence of it. But once a disturbance has been detected, what is the next step? For many, it is diagnosis, which if it is attempted at all is extremely significant because it determines what kind of treatment, if any, will be given.

Diagnosis uses most of the basic assessment procedures that have been discussed in Chapter 13. Intelligence tests, personality tests, both objective and projective, and interviews allow the psychologist to classify the psychological problems facing the patient. First, it is necessary to establish that the patient is indeed a candidate for *psychological* therapy. If his behavioral and emotional problems are the result of a brain tumor, paresis (the terminal stage of syphilis), or other physical defect, treatment will obviously be very different than that for neurosis or one of the functional psychoses.

But even if an organic cause of disturbance is ruled out, the fact is that none of our diagnostic tools or classificatory systems are very reliable, beyond the point of indicating that *something* is wrong. In a recent study (Nathan, Andberg, Behan, and Patch, 1969), 32 mental health professionals observed an extensive diagnostic examination of a patient and, at the end, gave their own evaluations. The results produced 14 different diagnoses, ranging from depression to epilepsy to paranoid schizophrenia. In fact, the patient was suffering from chronic alcoholism.

 The Perils of Diagnosis: The Kemper Case

The issue of *Newsweek* dated June 4, 1973, reported a story that shocked the public because of the unusually horrendous consequences it associated with a not terribly unusual diagnostic mistake.

A 15-year-old boy had committed two psychopathic murders. Psychopathy was not difficult to diagnose, for the boy had said, "I just wanted to know how it would feel to shoot Grandma and Grandpa," with a minimum of emotion. In a state mental hospital, the boy proved to be a model inmate according to the standards of the institution's administrators. At the age of 21, he was released with court-appointed psychiatrists reporting, "He has made an excellent response to treatment," and, "I see no psychiatric reason to consider him a threat to himself or any other member of society."

In the next year the young man murdered and dismembered six young girls, killed his mother with a hammer, and strangled one of his mother's friends. One of the murders occurred only a few days before one of the follow-up psychiatric interviews that resulted in a "mentally well" conclusion.

Not only do individual mental health workers disagree about diagnoses. Institutions and cultures also tend to lean toward certain diagnoses. One Illinois hospital diagnosed 75 percent of its patients as hebephrenic schizophrenic; another considered that only 11 percent of its patients suffered from that disorder (Boisen, 1938) (Table 17.2). American psychiatrists classified their patients as schizophrenic 15 times more frequently than did their Dutch colleagues (Mosher and Finesilver, 1970).

Aside from such problems of diagnostic bias, there is the question of which of many classificatory systems, each with its own implications about cause and treatment, to use. The most common system is the one we used in Chapter 16 to describe categories of neurosis, psychosis, and other disturbances. But that system leans heavily on psychoanalytic, and especially Freudian, ideas of the causes of disturbance, and it therefore strongly indicates a psychoanalytically oriented therapy. Many psychologists, and some psychiatrists, today are not happy with Freudian notions of the causes of disturbance, and they are even less happy with the treatment procedures those notions indicate. Some investigators have even demonstrated a lack of congruence between symptoms of disturbance and the categories to which they are assigned by the traditional psychoanalytic classificatory system. Zigler and Phillips (1961), for example, investigated the frequency of 35 common presenting symptoms among 793 hospitalized psychiatric patients. All 35 symptoms were found among both psychotics and neurotics; 34 were found among character disorders, and 30 in manic-depressives. Thus, none seemed to be capable by itself of distinguishing the groups.

Psychologists following the behavioral (learning theory) model of disturbance (Chapter 16) find little use for most categorizing methods. Their interest is in identification of the antecedent conditions, the situation, and consequent events in terms of negative or positive reinforcements of behaviors rather than in the identification of such traits as anxiety, hostility, and dependency. Behaviorism "solves" the problem of diagnostic classification by ignoring it. For therapists of this school, the problem is to find out how the patient's disturbed behavior was conditioned. For them, as we have noted, "the symptom is the

Table 17.2 Types of Dementia Praecox

| Hospital | Percent in Each Classification of Schizophrenia | | | | |
	Catatonic	Simple	Hebephrenic	Paranoid	Undetermined
A	2	3	11	46	38
B	2	2	60	36	0
C	1	3	76	20	0
D	1	2	50	47	0
E	0	2	53	45	0
F	1	1	55	40	3
G	4	4	30	40	22
H	1	2	50	47	0

Being Sane in Insane Places

David Rosenhan

A study by Rosenhan (1973) in California has led many people to conclude that discharge from a mental hospital may be overly difficult to achieve, that a label of "sick" may be too hard to get rid of once it is applied.

Rosenhan's study, which he titled "Being Sane in Insane Places," rests on the reports of 12 confederates, mostly graduate students, who voluntarily entered various mental hospitals in California. Each of them lied to the admissions staff, claiming to have experienced perceptually clear and affectively disturbing auditory hallucinations, a symptom that is common to certain kinds of schizophrenia and that may occur in a few other mental disorders. From the moment of admission on, however, the confederates acted as normal as possible and no longer pretended to have symptoms. Yet they reported that even after they ceased feigning disturbance the hospital staff members continued to treat them like sick persons solely on the basis of the initial diagnosis. For example, when a confederate attempted to carry on an ordinary conversation with the staff members, he was talked to in a condescending or patronizing manner. In general, nothing the patients did could win recognition of their sanity. When they were finally released, which usually was at least two weeks after admission, they were discharged with the label, "schizophrenia with remission." Rosenhan concluded that neither the diagnosticians nor the rest of the hospital staff were sensitive to the real behaviors of the patients around them; staff members responded to the diagnostic label rather than to the real person.

Rosenhan's study has been attacked by many of the country's leading clinicians. One has pointed out that the diagnosis "in remission" means that the diagnosticians were in fact aware that these patients demonstrated normal behaviors; the diagnosis thus, he says, cannot be flatly rejected as "wrong." Other doctors have claimed that the diagnosticians were in fact in error, but that error is not typical of most institutions, where such transient symptoms would be attributed not to schizophrenia but rather to some acute physiological problems (for example, drug intoxication or cerebrovascular disease). The fact that the sampled institutions did not make such considerations, we are told, makes them atypical. Nevertheless, as Neisser (1970) has pointed out, "Rosenhan has dealt the scientific pretension of psychiatry a serious blow" simply because he has demonstrated that diagnosticians refuse to admit error.

disease." (Behaviorist, or learning, theories are discussed more thoroughly in Chapters 3, 12, and 16.)

NON-PSYCHOLOGICAL TREATMENT PROCEDURES

Whatever may be the reasons that lead a person to find or fail to find psychological help, upon presenting himself or being presented by friends, relatives, or the forces of society, the process of assessment and diagnosis begins. Is he or she sufficiently disturbed to need therapy?

We have discussed in Chapter 16 the ambiguities of the concept of disturbance and have pointed out that, at least for the neuroses and personality disorders, perhaps the only valid criterion is the potential patient's unhappiness and desire to change. The perception of another's behavior as neurotic—however valid that perception might be—does not make him a candidate for therapy; he must experience and admit to experiencing, a genuine desire to ease the discomfort his behavior causes him. A psychopath, for example, is immune to psychological treatment so long as he is satisfied with his behavior and its effects. We must make a preliminary distinction, then, between a candidate for therapy and a candidate for institutionalization—which does not necessarily entail therapy, even if the institution is a mental hospital rather than a jail.

Early man attempted to exorcise evil spirits from the body of a person afflicted with a behavior disorder through the use of prayer, magic, herbal potions, and the like.

Later, the Greek physician Hippocrates (c. 460-377 B.C.) believed that mental disturbances were the result of an imbalance of bodily fluids—not of invasion by evil spirits. He advocated special diets, baths, and potions. But in the Middle Ages starving, beating, and stoning became the common forms of treatment. Thousands of people were sentenced to death or mercilessly tortured in the belief that the demons that possessed them could bring disaster to the

Du folt nit laßen das glid an dir
So yedes Zaichen fein aber nur

Klarhayt der zeit beffert alle Laß tag

In the Middle Ages phlebotomy (bleeding) was a common treatment for almost all illnesses, although the mentally ill were frequently starved, beaten, and stoned as well.

entire community. Eventually "insane" people were chained in filthy cells in asylums.

Toward the end of the 18th century, Philippe Pinel assumed charge of an asylum in Paris and, as an experiment, replaced filthy cells and chains with clean, airy rooms and kind treatment. The results of his innovations were encouraging. But, it was not until the second half of the 19th century that public fear and horror of what was thought of as insanity were replaced by an attempt to understand, and torture treatment gradually gave way to more humane rehabilitative methods.

Even with our more enlightened attitudes, some modern treatment methods have been criticized as no less cruel than the punishment therapies of the Middle Ages. Electroshock therapy, for example, has no more scientific basis than the exorcist techniques of an earlier age, and it is nearly as unpleasant.

Physiological Therapy

Physiological therapy involves treating the body to get at the mind. Medical treatments take many forms, from special diets to radical types of brain surgery. Here we will deal with the two that are probably the most widely used: electroshock therapy (EST) and drug therapy. Since the discovery of new and more effective tranquilizers in the early 1950s drug therapy has gradually replaced electroshock therapy as a medical treatment. But EST is still often used, primarily because of its quicker action in cases of severe depression. Both EST and drug therapy are capable of causing damage that may well outweigh any benefits they bestow. Physiological therapy should be used as cautiously as if it were stamped "RADIOACTIVE."

electroshock therapy   **Electroshock Therapy** The most widely used form of EST induces a convulsion by sending an electric current of from 70 to 130 volts through the brain. EST usually alleviates severe depression immediately, though not necessarily permanently. Many people who undergo this type of therapy develop a strong fear of the treatment after hearing the screams and seeing the convulsions of other patients in treatment.

Those who favor EST argue that it is simple, effective, and free of noxious aftereffects. But evidence shows that the electroconvulsive shocks may interfere with learning and retention (Lenkel, 1957). EST is like common aspirin in that in some cases it works, but nobody is sure exactly how, and the technique is slowly being abandoned.

Drug Therapy The primary purpose of current drug therapies is to temporarily allay severe symptoms so that the patient may benefit from other forms of treatment, such as psychotherapy. The most commonly used drugs are tranquilizers, which have a calming effect. They are given in varying strengths, depending on the patient's symptoms. Mild tranquilizers such as meprobamate are prescribed for neurotics to reduce tension and anxiety. Stronger ones, notably reserpine and chlorpromazine, are often administered to psychotics, making them calmer, less inhibited, and more open to therapy. A serious objection to drugs is that they are often used for the benefit of the hospital staff to make patients more manageable rather than to aid them toward recovery. All too often, tranquilizers are prescribed without an accompanying therapy. The worth of the drugs, in such cases, is minimal; drug therapy controls symptoms, but it doesn't cure disturbance.

The best known group of drugs used to treat depression are called "tricyclics" or "energizers." A number of studies have found these drugs more than 80 percent effective (Klein and Davis, 1969) in enabling depressed people to carry on their daily lives during therapy.

Ultimately, however, psychological disturbances must be dealt with on their own terms. Physiological therapy, if it is useful at all, can only be a short-term accompaniment to more specific treatment of the complaint. In the section that follows, we will discuss the major schools of psychotherapy and the theories on which they are based.

PSYCHOTHERAPY

Psychotherapy can be defined as any treatment of disturbed behavior that is not applied by the person himself and is not primarily physical in nature. By this definition, all of us have received treatment at one time or another; we have sought the advice and sympathy of our parents, our teachers, and other authority figures, as well as of our friends. But in general usage, psychotherapy is some structured form of outside help in coping with life and with frustrations associated with the failure to cope with specific situations adequately. In most instances the need for help is more or less prolonged.

psychotherapy

The treatment of disturbance by psychological means is largely a 20th century phenomenon. In the late 1800s, Sigmund Freud began to suspect that unconscious motivations were responsible for disturbed behavior, and the era of modern psychology was born. Freud's method of treatment, *psychoanalysis,* has had a dramatic impact on modern therapeutic techniques. Neo-Freudians (see Chapter 12) have modified Freud's theories in the direction of attributing a larger role to social factors in the development of disturbance. But no matter how far from Freud, or from each other, they may sometimes be on theoretical issues, they all agree that psychoanalysis is the best way to treat mental and emotional distress.

Psychologists of other schools have challenged Freud's time-consuming psychoanalytic techniques, and some of the newer methods are credited with impressive successes. But it is still too soon to make any kind of definitive evaluation of any of the psychotherapeutic methods in use. The leading alternative, and the treatment most opposed in theory, to psychoanalysis is *behavior therapy.* Both psychoanalysis and behavior therapy come under the broad heading of psychotherapy. But the two methods diverge quite markedly.

behavior therapy

Psychoanalysis

Psychoanalysis rests on the belief that disturbed behavior is a symptom of frustrated impulses that lie beyond conscious perception. These impulses have been repressed from consciousness because they are in some way unacceptable. To modify the disturbed behavior, it is necessary to bring the repressed or buried impulses into consciousness, where they can be dealt with and understood. Once the conflicts are out in the open, the patient can begin to understand and accept the reasons for his behavior. With self-acceptance and awareness, the disturbed personality structure can be reorganized. Impulses that were expressed in troublesome ways may now find more satisfactory expression.

Psychoanalysis is a long and costly process. An orthodox analyst may treat only about one hundred patients during his entire career. The patient must delve deep into his memory and his consciousness to root out the complex causes of his disturbance. Moreover, he must find a way to accept the drives that have been causing him so much difficulty. Self-acceptance is never an easy matter. Several techniques are used to bring repressed memories and wishes into consciousness. Free association and dream analysis help the patient and the analyst explore unconscious conflicts; abreaction and insight are processes by which the conflicts are resolved.

Free Association In this technique, the patient is instructed to talk spontaneously about whatever comes into his head; he is encouraged to express every thought and feeling, and especially his fantasies.

The random thoughts expressed in free association are subject to symbolic interpretation. No matter how uninhibited a person tries to be, he still inhibits himself. Let us say, for example, that a young man finds it very difficult to express anger, or any negative emotion, to superiors, and that this stems from a repressed hostility to his father. As he explores his childhood in free association he may repress all criticism of his father and instead vent his repressed hostility on substitutes. One such substitute may be the analyst himself, an authority figure toward whom the patient may experience violent swings of attitude, similar to the love-hate ambivalence he felt for his father.

The psychoanalyst tries to help a patient overcome his resistance to thoughts and feelings he doesn't want to face. A sudden loss of memory is believed to be due to a significant incident that the person has found it necessary to block or repress. Once a patient becomes unblocked and is able to associate freely, his associations can be interpreted by the analyst. The complex root systems responsible for the disturbance can then be accepted and altered.

dream analysis | **Dream Analysis** While free association aims to remove, or at least recognize, subconsciously erected blocks, dream analysis attempts to deal directly with the subconscious itself. In sleep, the ego supposedly lets its guard down. Unconscious motives that never see the light of day often find expression in dreams, though even then, they are not expressed overtly but only symbolically. A dream is thus said to have two parts. One is the manifest part of the dream

Dream Analysis

Here is a dream that Freud includes in his major work, *The Interpretation of Dreams.* Freud's strictly sexual point of view is demonstrated by the interpretations he provides in footnotes. He tells us that "this is the dream of a woman of the lower class, whose husband is a policeman."

... Then someone broke into the house and she anxiously called for a policeman. But he went peacefully with two tramps into a church,[1] to which a great many steps led up.[2] Behind the church there was a mountain[3] on top of which there was a dense forest.[4] The policeman was provided with a helmet, a gorget, and a cloak.[5] The two vagrants, who went along with the policeman quite peaceably, had sacklike aprons tied round their loins.[6] A road led from the church to the mountain. This road was overgrown on each side with grasss and brushwood, which became thicker and thicker as it reached the top of the mountain, where it spread out into quite a forest. (p. 366–IV)

[1] Or chapel = vagina.
[2] Symbol of coitus.
[3] Mons veneris.
[4] Crines pubis.
[5] Demons in cloaks and hoods are, according to the explanation of a specialist, of a phallic character.
[6] The two halves of the scrotum. (p. 366–V)

An infantile dream, recalled many years later, points for Freud to the deep-seatedness and long-lastingness of psychosexual experiences in the infant years.

A man, now thirty-five, relates a clearly remembered dream which he claims to have had when he was four years of age: The notary with whom his father's will was deposited—he had lost his father at the age of three—brought two large emperor pears, of which he was given one to eat. The other lay on the windowsill of the living room. He woke with the conviction of the reality of what he had dreamt, and obstinately asked his mother to give him the second pear; it was, he said, still lying on the windowsill. His mother laughed at this.

Freud says:

The dreamer's inability to furnish associations justifies the attempt to interpret it by the substitution of symbols. The two pears ... are the breasts of the mother who nursed him; the windowsill is the projection of the bosom, analogous to the balconies in the dream of houses. His sensation of reality after waking is justified, for his mother had actually suckled him for much longer than the customary term, and her breast was still available. The dream is to be translated: "Mother, give (show) me the breast again at which I once used to drink." The "once" is represented by the eating of the one pear, the "again" by the desire for the other. (pp. 312–313)

we remember the next day. The other is the latent, or hidden, content that can only be reached by symbolic interpretation of the manifest content.

The unconscious process by which an unacceptable impulse is transformed into the dream we remember on waking is called "dream work." With the patient's help, the analyst can often read into the dream to perceive the distortion and reveal a conflict the patient has been repressing. The primary way the patient helps is once again to freely associate anything that comes to mind about the dream material.

Abreaction, Insight, and Working Through In analysis three experiences are generally believed to have high therapeutic value: (1) abreaction, (2) insight, and (3) working through.

catharsis
abreaction

insight

When a person is able to relieve tension by expressing an emotion or reliving a painful memory, he is said to be experiencing catharsis, or purgation of unpleasant emotion. In therapy, the catharsis is called *abreaction*. But if the abreaction is to be valuable, the patient must have a clear understanding of the conflict involved. He has "insight" when he begins to relate his cathartic experiences to present behavioral disturbances. Insight rarely comes from one divine revelation, except in the movies. Let's assume a man is afraid of airplanes. During a course of psychoanalytic treatment, he relives a traumatic event that took place when he was 8 years old; his older brother took him on a ferris wheel and scared the daylights out of him. He has repressed this memory because he loves his brother, but deep down, he thinks his elder sibling was trying to push him out of the seat. He has managed to repress his dark suspicions all these years; then in a cathartic experience, he dredges up this memory from the past. And as therapy progresses, he gains insight into the reasons why the event was pushed back into the far reaches of his unconscious. But many complex unconscious forces have manifested themselves in his fear of flying. Other memories, other conflicts must be verbalized and explored. And, once they are understood, the patient must "work through" the conflict in all its manifestations—a lengthy process.

Psychoanalysis aims at tearing down the distorted personality structure and rebuilding a stable foundation in its place. Through self-acceptance and understanding, it is hoped that the patient will be able to cope with future conflicts realistically. But many professionals feel it is possible to change behavior without probing the reasons for the disturbance. They are critical of conventional psychoanalysis on a number of counts. To begin with, they question the validity of the Freudian concepts on which it rests. And his emphasis on unconscious sexual conflicts as one of the prime causes of mental disturbance seems outmoded in an age of topless bars and legal abortions. In addition, Freud assumed that there was a "normal" reaction to each situation and any deviance from the assumed norm was caused by underlying, unconscious psychosexual causes. Unfortunately, a normative criterion is not an accurate guideline for mental illness, as we pointed out in Chapter 16.

Psychoanalysis is also vulnerable from a practical standpoint. Individual therapy sessions frequently cost from $25 to $50 an hour, and from one to five sessions a week may be prescribed. They are thus beyond the means of people with low or moderate incomes who do not have access to a psychoanalytic clinic. Among those who start psychoanalysis, more than 60 percent never complete the treatment (Kirtner and Cartwright, 1958). But is it in fact necessary for a patient to spend several hours a week with an analyst for months or even years? For a growing number of mental health professionals, the answer is an emphatic "no!"

Several modifications of psychoanalytic therapy have been developed that aim at reeducating the patient to live with himself rather than reorganizing his entire personality structure. One of the most popular of the reeducative techniques is known as "client-centered therapy."

Client-Centered Therapy

Psychologist Carl Rogers (b. 1902) has been largely responsible for developing this technique. As the name implies, in client-centered therapy the client is expected to arrive at solutions to his problems out of his own understanding of his needs rather than from conclusions drawn by the therapist. The assumption, here, is that each person has the inner potential to make a mature emotional adjustment to life.

The therapist makes no effort to interpret the patient's behavior or to impose judgments on anything that is said in therapy sessions. The patient defines his own problems and assumes the responsibility for guiding the course of treatment. The therapist acts as a mirror, reflecting the patient's train of thought so that the patient may understand himself better. But through his passiveness, the therapist is also creating an atmosphere of unconditional regard, which, as we saw in Chapter 12, is central to this kind of therapy. An open and tolerant atmosphere permits the patient to develop the strength to face his inner emotions and handle them effectively.

Although Rogers considers client-centered therapy applicable to all kinds of disturbed behavior, in fact psychotics and people who tend to blame others for their difficulties are rarely helped by it. People who cannot verbalize thoughts and feelings or who are unwilling to face problems also are generally poor choices for client-centered therapy. But they aren't very much better suited to psychoanalysis.

Both psychoanalysis and client-centered therapy seek to alter overt behavior by altering an underlying (covert) mental state. The next form of therapy we will consider does not presume to know anything about mental states. It is called behavior therapy because it concerns itself only with what is observable, and that in the case of psychological disturbance is behavior. Emotions and the mind may or may not be real, but in any event they cannot be observed. The vehaviorists—or learning theorists—therefore do not attempt to theorize about them.

Behavior Therapy

behavior therapy

Behaviorists see disturbed behavior as a series of inappropriate responses that have been learned through experience. Since these inappropriate responses have been learned, the theory goes, they can be unlearned as well.

Early Behavior Theories The behavior therapies used today have little relation to psychoanalytic techniques or theory. Yet the first learning theory of human behavior evolved out of the fundamental Freudian concept that disturbed behavior stems from frustrated impulses. John Dollard and Neal Miller, in the 1940s, proposed that many impulses are learned. In a now famous experiment, they demonstrated that rats placed in a half-white and half-black compartment could be conditioned to fear the white side (Miller, 1948b). The rats could avoid electric shocks in the white compartment only by scurrying over to the black side. Eventually, they displayed fear of the white compartment, and the fear remained long after the shocks had stopped. The animals learned all kinds of new responses—pressing bars and turning wheels, for example—to escape from the white compartment even when it was harmless. The process of acquiring a response in order to reduce a learned anxiety is called "avoidance conditioning" (see Chapter 5). The rats were conditioned to fear the white area, and they subsequently learned certain responses in order to avoid that area. The responses, in human terms, were neurotic. They made no sense once the white side was rendered harmless.

Miller (1959) later demonstrated that anxiety responses could be heightened when there was a conflict of goals. Hungry rats learned to run down an alley through a maze in order to get food. While they were eating, the animals were given an electric shock. Later, they began to run for the food, but hesitated before reaching their goals. These and other experiments laid the groundwork for many of the conditioning techniques used today in the treatment of disturbed behavior.

Desensitization On the assumption that anxiety is a conditioned response, Joseph Wolpe developed a theory of "reciprocal inhibition": one response can inhibit another (Wolpe, 1958). A patient can't be anxious and calm at the same time. If a neurotic person can be counterconditioned to relax in an anxiety-producing situation, Wolpe reasoned, the anxiety response can be eliminated or at least greatly weakened.

reciprocal
inhibition

Therapy begins by asking the patient to rank stimulus situations in order of severity from weakest to strongest. Then the therapist trains the patient in a method of deep-muscle relaxation. Hypnosis and tranquilizers are sometimes used, too. Once the patient can achieve total relaxation, the actual counterconditioning (desensitization) begins.

desensitization

The patient is asked to confront the least anxiety-producing situation on the list. If he can maintain his relaxed state, he goes on to confront the next situation. In this manner, the patient gradually works his way up the list. Anxiety cannot occur because it is incompatible with relaxation. The anxiety is said to be "inhibited." As the severity of the fearful situation increases, the relaxation response becomes strengthened until the patient can finally confront the strongest stimulus without anxiety. When this happens, the inhibition is said to be "generalized."

Take a fairly common example: a woman comes to therapy because she is claustrophobic. She has an anxiety attack every time she rides up and down the elevator to her 19th floor apartment. In addition she cannot bring herself to enter her tiny pantry, where she keeps most of her cleaning supplies. Through systematic desensitization, the strength of her anxiety response to the pantry is gradually replaced by the stronger relaxation response. And the inhibition eventually becomes generalized so that she can ride in an elevator confidently.

A psychoanalyst might cast a cynical eye on her improvement. He might contend that when the claustrophobia disappears, another symptom will take its place. However, objections to behavior therapy on the grounds of symptom substitution have not been substantiated, even in patients who have been examined as much as 2 years after treatment (Paul, 1967) (Table 17.3). And several controlled experiments have confirmed the effects of desensitization in eliminating anxiety responses.

Positive Reinforcement Many behavior therapists, drawing on B. F. Skinner's ideas (see Chapter 3), use principles of reinforcement to modify behavior. Positive reinforcement or rewards are given to strengthen desired behavior patterns, thus inhibiting disturbed responses.

Many attempts have been made to reinforce communicative speech habits in autistic children. The therapist typically makes the correct sounds and then requires the child to repeat them. At first, the child is rewarded with candy for making even the vaguest sound. As therapy progresses, more difficult verbal units are presented, in keeping with the child's progress. With this technique, some severely disturbed children have made great progress in learning to talk (Lovaas, 1968).

Table 17.3 Percentage of Cases Showing Significant Change
from Pretreatment to 2-Year Follow-up

Treatment	Significantly Improved	No Change	Significantly Worse
Focal Treatment (Speech Composite)[a]			
Desensitization	85	15	—
Insight	50	50	—
Attention-Placebo	50	50	—
Control	22	78	—
All Other Comparisons (six scales)[b]			
Desensitization	36	64	—
Insight	25	71	4
Attention-Placebo	25	70	5
Control	18	74	8

Note—N = 13, 12, 14, and 18, respectively, for desensitization, insight, attention-placebo, and control. Classifications derived by two-tailed .05 cut-offs on each individual change score.
[a]χ^2 = 11.64, $p < .01$.
[b]χ^2 = 8.11, $p < .05$.
SOURCE: Paul (1967)

A type of positive reinforcement that is frequently used in mental hospitals is known as the "token economy." Ayllon and Azrin (1965) gave psychiatric ward patients tokens that could be exchanged for cigarettes, candy, food, and TV privileges, but to receive tokens, the patients had to behave in socially acceptable ways such as maintaining clean living quarters and participating in activities. Morale on the ward increased, and similar programs have since been adopted in many mental institutions.

Positive reinforcement isn't really new. Mothers have been telling children for years, "If you want your dessert, you must eat your vegetables." What is new, though, is the widescale application of this type of approach to behavior disturbances. Token economy programs are used to motivate culturally deprived children to greater achievement. So far, evaluations of such programs have been encouraging (Krasner and Ullman, 1973).

Leonard Krasner

Negative Reinforcement Just as a reward for a specific behavior tends to increase the frequency of that behavior, so a punishment (a negative reinforcement) tends to decrease it. Aversive conditioning, another term for negative reinforcement, has been applied, for example, in the behavioral modification of homosexuality; an electric shock or induced aversive stimulus such as nausea is paired with the elicitation of homosexual fantasies (Rachman and Teasdale, 1969; Cantela and Wisocki, 1969). It has also been used to extinguish self-destructive behaviors in autistic children. A shock is applied that is stopped as soon as the child ceases the behavior.

Evaluation of Behavior Therapy Behavior modification has proved effective in treating a variety of problems, including fear of flying and addiction to cigarettes. And empirical evidence seems to indicate that it is by far the best way to treat specific anxiety responses and fears (phobias). The behavioral movement gained considerable impetus when Eysenck (1952) published his negative evaluation of conventional psychotherapy. Eysenck investigated 19 studies of more than 7,000 patients who had received either psychoanalysis, other treatment, or no psychotherapy. When he grouped them according to their assessed degree of improvement, he found that 72 percent of the patients who had received no therapy had improved, while only 44 percent of those who had been in analysis had improved.

But a consideration of the value of behavior therapy must include certain ethical and philosophical considerations. Many psychologists take issue with a reward system that is capable of programing out unwanted behavior and programing in "appropriate" responses. Critics of behavior therapy warn that desirable behavior may become whatever the therapist says it is and that this presents the danger of equating satisfactory behavior with conformity. In reply, it can be pointed out that psychoanalytic techniques can also promote conformity and that responsible therapists of whatever school attempt to avoid imposing their own values on the patient. A more philosophical objection to behavior therapy is that it is contingent upon a view of human beings as extremely passive creatures.

Evolution of Behavior Therapy

As psychotherapy grew in prestige and public acceptance, it joined the long list of panaceas for man's ills. Freud, Sullivan, Rodgers, and others developed therapeutic techniques that have since been challenged on the grounds that they are derived from scientifically unsound theories, and that their efficiency is questionable.

This attack began with the Eysenck critique (1952), which called into question the effectiveness of evocative (insight) therapies. In reviewing the literature on the effectiveness of evocative therapies, Eysenck arrived at a spontaneous recovery rate from neurosis of 72.5 percent and a cure rate for psychoanalytically oriented therapies of only 44 percent. Eysenck concluded that psychoanalysis was ineffective.

Although Eysenck's data were in fact quite biased, they turned clinical psychologists' attention to the so-called "objective" behavior therapies that drew on classical and operant conditioning techniques (see Chapter 3).

The term *behavior therapy* was coined by Skinner and Lindsley to describe an approach to psychotherapy allegedly based on behavioristic learning therapy.

According to Eysenck (1959), one of the foremost exponents of behavior therapy, "Behavior therapy consists of the direct application of experimentally derived principles of learning theory to the treatment of pathological disorders. . . . Once we are agreed that learning and conditioning are instrumental in determining the different kinds of reactions we make to environmental stimuli we will find it very difficult to deny that neurotic reactions, like all others, are learned reactions and must obey the laws of learning."

The natural science bent in American psychology, in trying to put psychology on an equal standing with the physical sciences, has tried to shape and absorb psychoanalysis and replace it with behavioristic therapies. While it is beyond the scope of this book to present a critique of behavior therapy, it can be said that behavior therapy itself only metaphorically resembles scientifically derived learning principles. It is unfortunate that the techniques used by behavior therapists have tended to become dogmatic and bent on attacking psychoanalytic theory, instead of taking an objective look at what can be learned from it.

In the controversy over therapeutic approach, one conclusion can be drawn: mild disturbances, as a rule, respond better to therapy than severe ones. The resistance of the more severe disturbances to most forms of therapy has unfortunately caused some psychologists to become disenchanted with all therapeutic approaches. More psychologists, however, have expanded their repertoire of therapies to include as many methods as possible. There is also a growing realization that any treatment method that is based on a one-to-one patient-therapist basis is limited—by both the patient and the therapist.

Masters and Johnson Research

According to Masters and Johnson (1966), half the marriages in this country are sexually dysfunctional or will be so in the future, and yet few real facts were known about human sexual behavior before their 11-year study in 1954. At that point, every other area of the human body had been studied in detail by the medical profession—the physiology of the human sexual response, about which a paucity of misinformation still existed, remained the last unexplored territory.

In their research at the Reproductive Biological Research foundation in St. Louis, Dr. Masters and Mrs. Johnson worked on the physiological aspects of sexual behavior. About 750 men and women performed various sexual acts while behavioral and physiological measures were obtained. Their research findings resulted in the publication of their first book, *The Human Sexual Response*. Although one may question the appropriateness of generalizing Masters and Johnson's results to the total population from the people who volunteered and were accepted in the program, it is the only scientific data of its kind.

Masters and Johnson's second book, *Human Sexual Inadequacy* (1970), reported the clinical findings from an 11-year-old study of sexual dysfunction. The sexual disorders which were most commonly observed were: (1) impotency in the male, which is an inability to attain sexual gratification because of loss of erection or *ejaculatis praecox* in which orgasm is reached immediately prior to or soon after insertion or an inability to attain erection at all; (2) frigidity, which is the failure on the part of the woman to achieve orgasm.

Rather than recommending that a couple receive intensive psychotherapy, a practical program was instituted, in which much of the therapy was focused on reeducation and practice of sexual techniques to maximize sexual gratification. Masters and Johnson found that the average couple with sexual problems has a 75 to 80 percent chance of having the sexual dysfunctions cured.

Play Therapy

Play therapy is most often used with young children, but it can be employed with psychotic patients who are uncommunicative. Toys, paint, dolls, clay, blocks, pillows, and so on are used as means of aiding communication. The patient may draw pictures or create toy settings that suggest family situations. Here the dolls or painted pictures play various roles. Through play, the patient conveys conflicts and emotions that he is unable to verbalize or is perhaps unaware of. Play therapy gives the therapist a strong tool to use when other methods elicit little information.

Group Therapy

group therapy   The private one-to-one setting is increasingly supplemented by group therapy. The members of a group, which may vary in number according to the wishes of the therapist, take on an important role in relation to each other, becoming therapists themselves in the sense that they comment on and sometimes clarify other members' problems. The relationship between the members is a strong bond of the group, and, at times, the therapist can remain on the sidelines as the group runs itself.

In "family therapy," the therapist attempts to guide an entire family unit into more satisfactory patterns of living without focusing on a particular member.

Group and individual therapy can work hand in hand; insight derived from one form of therapy may aid in getting insight from the other. Group therapy offers an opportunity to use some techniques not generally available in individual therapy. For example, a psychodrama might be enacted, where one member of the group plays a role that is significant to another member's problem. One person might act out the role of a member's sister, another may be the mother, and the patient plays himself. They may enact situations that have actually happened or that the patient would have liked to occur. Afterwards, the patient gives his reactions to the enactment, and then the group as a whole discusses its reactions to the psychodrama. This often helps many of the group members to derive insights into similar problems of their own.

Games are another group technique. For example, the group may form a tight circle around one member. That member has to break out of the circle as the members forcibly try to keep him in. The feeling of being enclosed or of forcibly enclosing someone is then discussed.

Another technique involves acting out verbal expressions. For example, a person who says he would like to wipe a thought out of his mind might be instructed by the therapist to wipe his brow as if he were wiping the thought out of his mind. Body exercises may also be employed to elicit various feelings. Marathon group sessions are meetings that continue for as long as 30 hours, in the belief that true feelings show themselves when people become very tired.

Halfway Houses Group therapy is an important part of the treatment in the halfway houses that serve as a buffer between the person released from hospital or prison and the society that fostered the illness.

Groups such as Synanon and Odyssey House provide housing and treatment within the community for drug addicts who seek to "kick the habit." Former drug users and newly admitted addicts live together as a family in a structured home environment. Peer pressure to stay off drugs is strong, and is usually reinforced during group therapy sessions. Those who remain with the program for an extended period of time are generally successful in conquering their addiction permanently.

Fairweather (1969) and his associates have demonstrated that patient-run halfway houses are effective in bridging the gap between hospital and community life. They established a lodge that was run entirely by newly released mental patients. The patients were responsible for setting up and enforcing "house rules" and meeting all operational expenses. To finance the lodge, they developed a service business that eventually brought in a good profit.

Confrontation group at Marathon House, a therapeutic community for drug addicts and others located at Coventry, Rhode Island, and six other locations in New England.

A follow-up study showed that patients who had participated in the lodge made a much better adjustment to community life than a comparable group of patients released directly from the hospital. Patients from the experimental group were holding better jobs and showing a higher level of emotional stability than those who had not participated in the lodge.

Photographs by Marvin Coe, reproduced from *Daytop Village: A Therapeutic Community,* by Barry Sugarman. (Holt, Rinehart and Winston, Inc., 1974)

PREVENTION

As great as the need for detection and treatment of mental disturbance is the need for prevention of it. Preventive techniques aim primarily at identifying life patterns and situations that foster disturbance, and also at recognizing situations that promote contentment and well-being. Effort can then be made to remove or reduce causes of anxiety and frustration, once they have been identified. The influence of the preventive approach can be seen, for example, in the open admissions policies and remedial programs designed to reduce pressures created by competitive school systems and to make available to a broader segment of society the kind of education essential for job advancement.

Community health programs at present do not often function as truly preventive instruments. They have been able to detect mental disturbance early, though usually in adults, and to make treatment available very quickly. If disturbance is really to be prevented, however, more attention must be paid to childhood and to faulty child-raising procedures and environments. As many studies

 Mednick's "High-Risk" Study of Schizophrenia

Since treatment of schizophrenia is virtually ineffective, fruitful research must be aimed at understanding the etiology (cause) of the disorder so that we may learn how to prevent it. One way of going about this is to attempt to predict who will break down.

Predictive studies have examined the proposition that people who eventually become schizophrenic show certain personality characteristics, physiological indicators, or behavioral patterns early in life. If some distinguishing traits can be found that may be related to subsequent breakdown, these early signs may tell us what makes people vulnerable to schizophrenia.

Methodologically the most sophisticated study of this type was carried out by Mednick and Schulzinger (1968) in Denmark. Using a "high risk" design, Mednick (1962) began with children of parents whose mothers were schizophrenic and who were therefore designated "high risk." A matched group of children of the same sex, age, and socioeconomic class, but who had two nonschizophrenic parents, served as a control group.

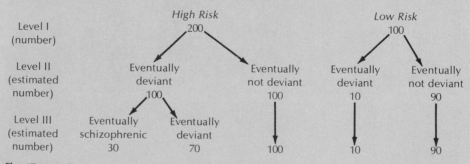

Fig. 17.1 Mednick high-risk design. (Mednick, 1962)

Fig. 17.1 shows us that at the first level we can study the distinguishing characteristics of children with schizophrenic mothers in comparison with chil-

dren having no familial psychiatric background. At the second level, we can estimate that 50 percent of the high-risk children will become seriously socially deviant. And finally, at the third level we can estimate that perhaps 30 of the 100
high-risk deviants will eventually be diagnosed schizophrenic (Mednick and
Schulzinger, 1968).

An "alarm network system" was set up to trace any one of the 300 subjects
in the study who was admitted to a psychiatric facility.

In 1962, six years earlier, a complete personality assessment of all 300 subjects was made to find possible factors associated with subsequent breakdown. The
tests included physiological measures, Wechsler IQ, MMPI word association test,
and an adjective checklist. In addition, each subject had a psychiatric interview,
reports of general adjustment were submitted by a teacher and a social worker,
and pregnancy and delivery reports were examined for indications of
complication.

Results showed very few differences between high- and low-risk children.
However, the GSR measure (a measure of resistance in the finger to passage of
an electric current; if a subject is nervous, sweat in the finger acts as a conductor
of the current) provided some very interesting data:

1. *Basal level.* A high basal level suggests a calm subject; a low basal level
suggests a nervous subject. No significant difference was found between high-
and low-risk subjects.

2. *Latency.* The time taken to respond to stimulation is latency. High-risk
subjects had a lower latency than low-risk subjects, indicating less evaluation of
the stimulus than in normal subjects.

3. *Recovery rate.* High-risk subjects exhibited a quick recovery rate, indicating that anxiety dissipated very quickly. This suggests an aptitude for avoidance
responses, which presumably have received great reinforcement.

4. *Amplitude.* The magnitude of response made to a stimulus is response
amplitude. High-risk subjects showed a larger response than low-risk subjects to
the same noxious stimulus.

Based on these findings, Mednick developed an anxiety generalization
theory, which states that schizophrenics begin with high anxiety that habituates
(extinguishes) slowly, a trait that could be hereditarily predisposed. When anxiety
is high, stimulus generalization occurs so that more stimuli are able to potentiate
the slowly habituating anxiety. The increased potentiation leads to increasingly
high anxiety levels, which in turn lead to increased stimulus generalization. This
anxiety generalization spiral culminates in a schizophrenic break, which initiates
an attempt to find remote cognitive associates that serve to avoid or reduce anxiety. Thus, the symptoms of cognitive and affective dissociation seen in chronic
schizophrenics develop.

have indicated, psychotic symptoms first appear early in childhood and relationships between discordant family life and aberrant behavior have been demonstrated time and again. Preventive psychology is a very young area of study
in a very broad field. It requires extensive study of the relationship between the

physical environment and individual behavior in order to identify the precise factors in an environment, even in an entire society, that contribute to or detract from psychological well-being. It needs to recognize that most systems do not have the same effect on all of their members, and to determine how systems and individuals interact. On the basis of naturalistic observation, it must introduce experimental social innovation that can be longitudinally and objectively evaluated.

School Programs

Most preventive studies have used the school setting because it makes available a larger number of children. Hallister (1965, 1967) emphasized the need for a positive approach—inculcating the mentally healthy response rather than rooting out the disturbed one. He introduced the term "stren" as an antonym for *trauma* and thus meaning a health-building, psychologically strengthening experience. One of the most promising results of this concept has been the development of behavioral-science and psychology curricula for use in the primary schools— curricula aimed at teaching children about themselves, how to cope with their problems, how to interact effectively with others (Roen, 1967; Long, 1968).

Emory L. Cowen

The Rochester Primary Mental Health Project is typical of efforts being undertaken to prevent mental illness (Zax and Cowen, 1972). All first-grade children in a selected school were extensively tested and their mothers were interviewed by social workers. The results, along with teachers' reports, were used to "tag" potentially disturbed children. The parents, teachers, and mental health professionals closely followed each child's classroom progress. Together, they worked out flexible programs for helping children who were having classroom or personal difficulties. An evaluation of the program at the end of 3 years compared the children in third grade at the experimental school with those in two control schools where similar information-gathering was done, but no preventive measures were taken. On nearly every measure of school performance, children from the experimental school excelled. They had better attendance records, higher grades, lower anxiety, and so on. The "tagged" children in the control schools, in contrast, showed a dramatic downward trend in the 3-year period. This evaluation demonstrates, once again, that early detection and help for potentially disturbed children can militate against a poor emotional adjustment later, and at the same time, can increase both the classroom learning and the interpersonal effectiveness of all the children in the program—"tagged" and non-"tagged."

Inner-City Programs

The problem of dealing with disturbed schoolchildren in severely depressed inner-city areas is more complex. Many of these children come from substandard home environments. As babies, they were left unattended in their cribs for hours on end, and as toddlers, they were seldom provided with toys and games. In such homes, adults rarely help small children to develop linguistic skills. Often, the language spoken in the home is foreign or is considered a substandard dialect. By the time these children reach first grade, they are often so far behind in basic language skills that learning to read presents insurmountable problems, and behavior becomes maladaptive.

Early learning programs such as Project Head Start aim at building up social and cognitive skills in preschoolers. While the immediate results are encouraging, studies indicate that there is substantial backslide once the children leave the program (Gordon, 1969). It is not enough, evidently, to give a child a "head start" before he enters school if his home and social environment are going to undo all the gains he made in preschool years.

Job help programs and facilities for unemployed high school dropouts are being established in many inner-city communities. The assumption here is that idleness can lead to disordered behavior, and statistics bear this out.

The elderly, too, are a major target group for preventive approaches. As medical science continues to discover new ways to prolong life expectancy, the mental health field must find new ways to keep the mind healthy. Nearly a quarter of all first admissions to state mental institutions are over 65 years of age, yet this age group accounts for only $\frac{1}{10}$ of the population (NIMH, 1970). In today's society, elderly people, like the unemployed, are left lonely and restless. Rejection, either by the vocational world or the family, can lead to emotional disturbance. Thus, vocational programs are being initiated for all age-groups. Businessmen are being recruited to help fledgling entrepreneurs; mature housewives are working as paraprofessionals; high school dropouts are entering career rehabilitation programs.

The impact of preventive techniques on inner-city areas has been slight so far. Slum housing can be bulldozed down in a matter of weeks. Pervasive attitudes of defeatism and suspicion fall less easily.

Crisis Intervention

Everyone meets crises in life, but some people meet them more successfully than others. The difference may be either in the kind of crisis faced or in the person's readiness at different times in his life to face crisis. Many crises can be anticipated—we know that an aged parent in failing health will soon die—and many crises, such as those that accompany each stage of psychosocial development in Erikson's view of personality (see Chapter 12), are even inherent to the developmental process. Nevertheless, we are frequently unable to deal with them satisfactorily. To prepare people to deal with real crises, Cumming and Cumming (1966) propose giving them a graded series of hypothetical crisis experiences to work through—a condition that favors constructive resolution because the crises are not real ones. They suggest that, after such an exercise, people may be better equipped to handle the real crises of life when they occur.

One way of dealing with actual crises is known as crisis intervention. This method is practiced by such groups as Alcoholics Anonymous, Synanon, and Gamblers Anonymous. Anyone who affiliates with such a group knows that he can, at any time of the day or night, get understanding help in a crisis. Similarly, there are suicide prevention centers and emergency telephone numbers that a suicidal person can call. As such services become increasingly known, a growing number of people use and benefit from them.

Paraprofessionals

Many of the preventive programs we have been talking about are staffed, in whole or in part, by people with very little, and sometimes no, training in the mental health professions. Such people, once called nonprofessionals, are now more frequently and more correctly known as paraprofessionals.

paraprofessional

In the Rochester Primary Mental Health Project mentioned earlier, for example, paraprofessional child-aides were used to work with "tagged" children outside of the classroom. These people, in the beginning, were housewives who, having raised their own children, were thought to have a better potential to function well in this role than people with intellectual training for the role but no experience with children. The housewives were indeed effective, and eventually paraprofessionals were selected from other groups as well.

We should note too that such groups as Alcoholics Anonymous and Synanon are staffed not by professionals but by reformed alcoholics and addicts. Both programs are based on the theory that the best help comes from others who have faced and conquered, even if only temporarily, the same problem.

In many ways the most helpful of all the paraprofessionals is the indigenous worker in an inner city mental health program. Because of his intimacy with the mores, the values, the members, and the language of the community, he can act as an ideal intermediary between the mental health professional and the community.

Current mental health programs draw paraprofessionals from among college and high school students, occasionally even younger students, mature housewives, indigenous neighborhood workers, retired people, ex-offenders and ex-delinquents, hospital attendants, parents, teachers, and welfare or enforcement workers. These people are working with institutionalized mental patients; clinic, agency, and court clientele; schoolchildren; residents of inner-city neighborhoods; and women in pregnancy and well-baby clinics. Their training ranges from none to two years of intensive, nearly full-time preparation.

SUMMARY

Phychological impairment is one of the most critical public health problems of our time. The three factors in curbing mental disturbance involve detecting and diagnosing it, treating it, and preventing it from occurring whenever possible.

An area of mental health in which good progress is currently being made is the detection of disturbance in groups of people who would otherwise be unaware that they are in need of help. It has been found that, in general, lower-class people are unaware of a need for psychological counseling; they turn instead to the church, family, friends, and even medical facilities for help in solving psychological problems. The Midtown-Manhattan urban project and the Nova Scotia rural study both showed that about 80 percent of the population surveyed was in need of psychological help.

For part of the middle class, psychotherapy has become a status symbol, and they readily present themselves for help. It seems that the lower the socioeconomic class, the greater the need for outside detection, though this statement is somewhat mitigated by the fact that the bias of the examiner seems to affect diagnoses. When therapists believe a patient is from a lower class, they are more likely to diagnose him as mentally ill than if they are told the patient is from the middle or upper class.

Once a disturbance has been detected, it may be diagnosed. Diagnosis is an extremely significant procedure because it makes strong implications about causes and methods of treatment. None of the existing diagnostic tools or classificatory systems is very reliable. They are subject both to rater and cultural bias, and there is much overlap of symptoms among the categories of disturbance they include. Therapists of the behavioral school completely disregard diagnosis; they attempt to treat the disturbance directly, without presuming to know what causes it.

Treatments of mental illness have varied from prayer and magic to torture and death. Pinel in the 18th century replaced cruelty with more humane treatment, but, even today, some methods, such as shock therapy, might seem as cruel as those used in early days.

Physiological therapy tries to alter the mind by changing the body. Its methods can vary from slight changes in the diet to severe brain surgery. The two major techniques used are drug therapy and electroshock therapy. Each of these techniques aims at making the patient more susceptible to conventional therapies rather than at introducing any permanent change in its own right.

Psychotherapy is a structured form of outside help in coping with life. Psychoanalysis, devised by Freud in the late 1800s, is a form of psychotherapy in which impulses that once caused disturbed behavior find acceptable expression with a therapist's help. This is accomplished through the use of such techniques as free association, dream analysis, abreaction, insight, and working through—which together are aimed at bringing repressed wishes and impulses into consciousness and understanding them.

Carl Rogers' client-centered therapy aims at establishing an environment in which the client experiences unconditional positive regard, enabling him to reflect on his feelings and come to his own conclusions. The therapist reflects back the feelings the client expresses.

Behavior therapy views disturbed behavior as behavior acquired through poor or improper learning and seeks to change the behavior by desensitization, negative reinforcement of the unwanted behavior, and positive reinforcement of a replacement behavior. When the disturbed behavior is changed, the patient is "cured."

Play therapy is a technique used with small children and psychotics to enable the therapist to get information from a patient who can't communicate his feelings verbally.

Group therapy uses a group setting and such techniques as psychodramas, games, and marathons as means of making a participant aware of the feelings he is experiencing. When the group is a family unit, it is called family therapy.

Halfway houses have become an answer to the treatment of drug addiction and other problems, and, in addition, serve as a means for mental patients to make a gradual transition from a mental institution to the outside world.

Preventive programs aim at early detection of situations likely to cause disturbance and at substitution of health-promoting experiences. The primary effort here is to reach the very young.

Preventive programs such as the Rochester Project reach the young before their problems become serious. Inner-city programs such as Project Head Start deal with children who have had poor learning experiences and attempt to overcome the detrimental environment the child lives in daily. Job help programs for teen-agers and elderly are ways of preventing disturbances caused by boredom and rejection.

Crisis intervention programs attempt, basically through good publicity, to reach people such as alcoholics and addicts and also potentially suicidal people.

Preventive programs increasingly are staffed, in whole or in part, by such paraprofessionals as housewives, students, retired persons, indigenous neighborhood workers, and ex-offenders and ex-delinquents. Because through helping others we help ourselves, the use of paraprofessionals seems to complete the detection-treatment-prevention cycle.

SUGGESTED READINGS

Braginsky, Benjamin M., Dorothea D. Braginsky, and Kenneth Ring, *Methods of Madness: The Mental Hospital as a Last Resort.* New York: Holt, Rinehart and Winston, 1969.
  On the basis of nine interrelated studies conducted at a large state mental hospital, the authors challenge the validity of current psychiatric practices and present an alternative approach to treating persons whom we call mentally ill.
Burgess, Anthony, *A Clockwork Orange.* New York, Ballantine, 1971.
  In this novel operant conditioning techniques are used to change the behavior of prisoners.
Ennis, Bruce J., *Prisoners of Psychiatry: Mental Patients, Psychiatrists, and the Law.* New York, Avon, 1974.
  An ACLU lawyer discusses the medical injustices and the judicial neglect connected with mental institutions today.
Freud, Sigmund, *Civilization and Its Discontents.* New York, Norton, 1962.
  In one of his last books Freud probes the large question of man's place in the world.
Janov, Arthur, *The Primal Scream.* New York, Putnam, 1970.
  Janov explains how primal therapy, which forces the patient to relive core experiences, has been successfully used to treat neuroses.
Krasner, L., and L. Ullman, *Research in Behavior Modification.* New York, Holt, Rinehart and Winston, 1968.
  A thorough coverage of the work that has been done in the area.
London, Perry, and David Rosenhan, *The Modes and Morals of Psychotherapy.* New York, Holt, Rinehart and Winston, 1973.
  A look at the uses and abuses of psychotherapy.
Rogers, Carl, *Carl Rogers on Encounter Groups.* New York, Harper & Row, 1971.
  Rogers discusses the history of the encounter movement and his own experiences with different groups.

Appendix

Statistical Methods

Statistical methods are mathematical ways of manipulating masses of numerical information in order to reduce these masses to convenient proportions and enable us to draw inferences from the information. One such statistical reduction is the familiar notion of *average*, which can be used to describe some characteristic of a particular group, for example, the average height of police officers in a certain city. Such a description enables us to compare two or more different groups, for example, the average height of officers in two different cities.

Statistical analysis has an important place in present-day psychological research, even though there is much variation in the necessity of statistics within different branches of psychology. One of the areas most dependent on statistics is psychological measurement.

To understand the necessity of statistical procedures in psychological measurement, consider the following problem with which an astronomer might be faced. He is required to measure with the greatest possible accuracy the distance between two close objects viewed in his telescope, and the measurements must be made during one particular hour of one particular night. Unfortunately, the viewing conditions at that time are imperfect; there are tiny fluctuations in the image of the objects due to atmospheric currents. Furthermore, his measuring instruments are somewhat cruder than might be desired for the task at hand, and he realizes that the limitations of his own eyes may lead to small misalignments of those instruments. Under these circumstances, the astronomer is likely to resort to the following stratagem: he will make a large number of measurements of the critical distance and then statistically average them, in the expectancy that the errors in each individual reading will tend to cancel each other out. In addition, when comparing his averaged readings to other sets of averaged readings he may well employ statistical techniques to determine if differences he observes are likely to be products of the imperfections of his measurements. In this way, he will attempt to compensate for various uncontrollable error-producing factors that may be influencing his data.

Although he would like it to be otherwise, the psychologist is compelled to admit that his measuring techniques are likely to be a good deal cruder than those of the

771

astronomer, and the objects he is likely to be observing far more subject to random fluctuations than the images of stars. Numerous variations in the mood, character, attitudes, and beliefs of his subjects are beyond his control and are likely to introduce errors into his measurements. Given this fact, the psychologist probably will become tremendously dependent on statistical techniques for the resolution and clarification of the underlying significance of his data: far more so than the physical scientist.

It is necessary to note that statistical methods cannot be employed on data that have resulted from haphazard experiment. Data must be appropriately collected by suitable methods of research, using the proper design for a given study. Experimental designs, in addition to rendering possible the statistical analysis of their data, should also permit the maximum possible reduction of known sources of error, and should make possible the checking of several different hypotheses from the same set of data.

population

sample

When considering the meaning of data, we must distinguish between its use in the description of a *sample* as opposed to a *population*. A population is the entire group of individuals or events having some common observable characteristic; for example, all individuals attending college or all individuals between the ages of 11 and 19. A sample is a subgroup of a population generally picked to be *representative* of that population. Psychologists normally study samples, since studying populations is not feasible. From data derived by studying a sample, sample descriptive measures are computable, whereas corresponding population measures are only estimatable from the sample statistics. Thus we are forced to draw inferences about a population from statistical measures of samples, and these inferences must be tested for their statistical significance—that is, the likelihood that they truly reflect a population characteristic.

The first section of this chapter deals with the various kinds of data which are appropriate for statistical analysis; the second section discusses the descriptions of data; and the last section is concerned with the inferences made from data and how they are tested.

Statistical Information

observation

Many kinds of information can be analyzed statistically, but the same statistical techniques do not apply to all kinds. One requisite for the statistical analysis of any kind of data is that it must be from more than one observation. In a word, statistical techniques can be applied to "data" but not to "a datum." More than one observation is required so that any one observation or set of observations can be viewed within a larger context.

Since data may be of several essentially different kinds, and the type of data determines what statistical techniques are appropriate for its analysis, this appendix begins with descriptions of each characteristic type.

categorical data

Categorical Data

In this kind of data, instances, or "frequencies" of events are simply counted. Events are counted as falling into categories that are described only qualitatively (nominally). The various categories bear no ordered mathematical relationship to one another. In the statement, "There are 4 men and 8 women on this jury," "men" and "women" are the two categories, "4" and "8" are the frequencies associated with each. In the statement, "This week I watched 6 programs on Channel 7," "7" names the category, "6" counts the instances. Most polling information is of this type; in a political poll persons are counted as supporting this or that candidate, each candidate representing a discrete category. In technical language, the categorical scheme is a rule for arranging observations into *equivalence* classes that are *mutually exclusive* and *exhaustive*. This means that within each category all observations carry equal weight, that no observation may be contained within more than one category, and that no observation is not within one of the categories. If each person polled were asked to rate his support for whichever candidate he chose (from "very supportive" to "slightly supportive"), the data would no longer be categorical, because each person's weight, within one category, would not be the same. If such a rating (scale) were utilized, that aspect of the data would be called *ordinal,* which is the next kind of mathematical scale we consider. Before going on to mathematically more sophisticated scales, however, remember that the simplicity of categorical frequency counts does not render them inferior except in terms of the extent to which refined mathematical manipulations can be applied to them. Often such manipulations are not appropriate until proper categories have been established. Biology's beginnings rest on categorical data, and taxonomy originally involved nothing more than assigning frequencies to classes (phyla, genera).

Ordinal Data

In contrast to categorical countings operations, ordinal scales employ classes that do bear an ordered relation to one another; specifically, the classes are ranked as *greater* or *less* than each other. Remember only equivalences and nonequivalences are involved in categorical classes. Ordinal scales represent rank position. The results of races are almost always expressed ordinally. When we speak of "finishing first, second, or third," in the Preakness, the categories, "first," "second," and "third," name positions that bear mathematical relations to each other specified in the names themselves. That mathematical information is limited, though, because there is no indication about the *amount* of difference between various rank positions. The winning horse in a race may have beat the runner-up by a 1-second or a 30-second interval, but in either case the runner-up would be ranked second. While in the case of races information as to difference intervals could be obtained if we wanted to, we cannot always do so. In a baking contest a judge may be able to say that Mrs. Foster's pie is better than Mrs. Brown's, but he may not be able to specify (quantify) the amount by which it is better, since we have no yardstick marked off in the units, "goodness of taste." It is true that people often say, "This pie is twice as good as that one," but this is probably an instance of an arithmetic term being used colloquially and thereby losing its arithmetic meaning.

Interval and Ratio Data

Although the numbers standing for ordinal measurements may be manipulated by arithmetic, the outcomes of these arithmetic operations cannot be interpreted as necessary statements about the true magnitudes or amounts of the measured quantities. When measurement is given by an *interval scale,* statements about amounts are made possible. In order to obtain interval data there must exist some standard, or measuring stick, that is marked off in units (intervals) all of which are equal to each other in magnitude. In the horserace mentioned above, the equal intervals would have been seconds of time. These units would have allowed us to go beyond rank, because we could have measured how many of them separated "first" from "second," "second" from "third," and so forth. Interval scales allow one to make statements regarding the relative differences between different observations. In addition to being an interval scale, the measurement of time in seconds is characterized as a *ratio scale.* All ratio scales are interval scales, but not vice versa. In ratio scales there must exist a *zero* value for the quantity being measured, which is in turn designated by the 0-point on the scale. In the example here, there is conceptually such a thing as no time at all, and it is represented by 0 on the scale of seconds.

The everyday temperature scale is an example of an interval scale that is *not* a ratio scale, because the scale's 0-point (whether the scale is Centigrade or Fahrenheit) does not represent the idea of no temperature at all. The existence of a designated zero allows for statements not only about equal intervals but also about equal ratios. Using a Fahrenheit temperature scale, you can say that the difference between 1 degree and 5 degrees is the same as the difference between 50 degrees and 55 degrees. That is to say, the intervals are equal, and an interval of 5 degrees maintains the same meaning anywhere along the scale. However, you cannot say that −1 degree is twice as warm as −2 degrees and mean the same thing as you would mean when you say that 80 degrees is twice as warm as 40 degrees. That is to say, a ratio does not maintain its meaning anywhere along the temperature scale, and the ratio is therefore useless.

Now consider the time scale again. Here just as in the temperature scale a 5-point difference (interval) is the same all over the scale. But, in addition, ratios are equal all along the scale; that is, 20 seconds is twice as long as 10 seconds, just as 100 seconds is twice as long as 50 seconds, with *twice* retaining a constant meaning. The "Kelvin" temperature scale, unlike the Farenheit, does have a true zero temperature, "absolute zero," making the Kelvin scale a ratio scale as well as an interval scale.

Some psychological tests, including all intelligence tests, are interval but not ratio scales. This is because we cannot conceptualize, and therefore cannot designate with a 0-point on the scale, an absolute absence of many psychological traits. We could not describe any living human being as being absolutely devoid of intelligence; the 0-point on IQ scales is really quite arbitrary, and therefore ratios are impossible.

parametric data

While the differences between the interval and ratio scales are important, psychological statisticians do not devise strictly separate and appropriate tests for each. Instead, a common group of statistical testing procedures, called *parametric,* are applied to both, taking advantage of the equal interval aspect in common. Parametric tests, which are powerful tools for the analysis of statistical information, are not appropriate for categorical or ordinal data. Some of these tests will be described later. In the following paragraphs, interval and ratio data will be referred to as "parametric data."

Descriptive Techniques

descriptive technique

Once we have collected our data, it is necessary to put the data into a usable form. The techniques for doing this are called descriptive techniques, and they refer to descriptions, tabular, graphic, and numerical, that convey information about a certain aspect of data. Some descriptive techniques are appropriate to all kinds of data while others are not. The foremost reason for utilizing the techniques discussed is *economy.* It would be laborious, time-consuming, and often confusing to have to enumerate, one by one, a group of individual scores that a researcher has collected. In addition to their economical benefits, statistical descriptive techniques often act to *clarify* data, rendering obvious trends and relationships that would otherwise be hidden by the complexity of masses of raw and unordered scores. Finally, statistical techniques can render data into forms which facilitate the *comparison* of disparate kinds of information. More will be said about this later when "correlation" is discussed.

For an illustration of the economizing and clarifying functions of statistical descriptive techniques, consider Fig. A2 (p. 776). Fig. A2(a) presents a set of data in raw form, (b) the same data ordered and tabulated, and (c) the same data presented as a "bar graph." Compare the ease with which information is obtained in the three cases.

Visual Description: Graphing

Visual descriptive techniques are often used for summarily describing an entire set of data when other techniques are not possible. However, even when other techniques are available these visual techniques are extremely useful, since the visual mode seems to allow for immediate simultaneous grasp of a whole set of data. *Graphing* is the word applied to the technique of visual representation of data. Graphing may be applied to all kinds of data, but it is particularly important for nonparametric data, since it is the only means available for describing the whole *distribution* of the data. Some categorical data and its visual presentation is given in Fig. A1; the graph shown is called a *bar graph*.

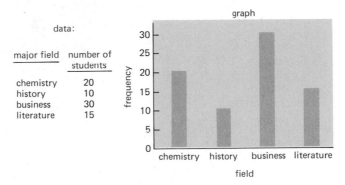

data:

major field	number of students
chemistry	20
history	10
business	30
literature	15

Fig. A1 Distribution of student majors.

Notice that on the horizontal axis of the graph, called the *abscissa*, there are names only, and there exists no mathematical relation between them as you move from left to right. The vertical axis, called the *ordinate*, does give mathematical information in terms of frequency (in this case the number of students in a particular category).

abscissa

ordinate

Let us look at the difference when the same type of graphing is applied to parametric data, in Fig. A2.

Notice the abscissa as well as the ordinate conveys some mathematical information, since more information is contained in parametric than nonparametric data. As you move from left to right the mathematical level of the variable, height, goes up in a regular way. The ordinate, as before, contains information about frequencies. This kind of bar graph, because it is applied to parametric data, is called a *histogram*. Histograms appear to be as simple as bar graphs, but the former involve more complex mathematical notions, specifically those concepts of *continuous variables* and *real limits*. On the histogram shown the variable presented on the abscissa is termed a *continuous variable*, because theoretically the heights of persons could be anywhere along the scale. Said another way, persons could score anywhere along the scale: relatively few people probably are in fact *exactly* 6'3", 6'4", 6'5", etc. However, when the scale is graphed, we cannot mark every theoretically possible height along the abscissa. Instead, each number on the abscissa names an *interval* of possible heights. The number 6'1" really is a name for the interval, 6'.5"–6'1.5. The numbers defining the edges of the interval are called

histogram

continuous variable
real limits

raw data		
height of players on squad		
6'3''	6'1''	6'3''
6'5''	6'3''	6'0''
6'6''	6'4''	6'4''
6'4''	6'1''	6'3''
6'2''	6'5''	
6'0''	6'4''	
6'7''	6'5''	

(a)

data	
height	# players
6'0''	2
6'1''	2
6'2''	2
6'3''	4
6'4''	4
6'5''	3
6'6''	1
6'7''	1

(b)

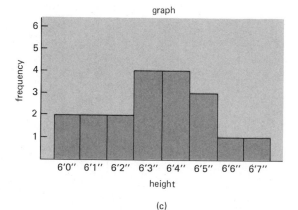

(c)

Fig. A2 Distribution of heights on basketball squad.

the *real limits* of the interval, and any number contained in those limits is *rounded off* to 6'1''. No matter how fine the measurements are made on a continuous variable, the scores on the abscissa necessarily represent just class intervals.

frequency polygon   Another common kind of graph is the *frequency polygon*. It can be used only when the abscissa variable may be ordered from left to right. Instead of using bars, a frequency polygon represents the frequency for any particular class interval by a point exactly above the *midpoint* of the interval, then adjacent points are connected by straight lines. The data given for Fig. A2 is recast in the form of a frequency polygon in Fig. A3.

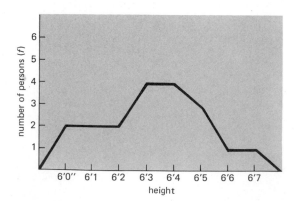

Fig. A3 Frequency polygon.

To put it succinctly, a histogram portrays a frequency distribution as if all scores in each interval were uniformly distributed throughout the interval, while a frequency polygon portrays the distribution as though all scores were concentrated at the midpoints of the intervals. With continuous variables neither assumption is exactly correct, but one of the two is almost always required in practice.

Histograms and frequency polygons usually exhibit irregularities. Assuming that these irregularities are due to the operation of chance, we can replace the frequency polygon by a smooth curve through the points of the polygon. This curve may give a more general picture of a frequency distribution under consideration than the original polygon. Such a curve is called a *frequency curve*. See Fig. A4.

frequency curve

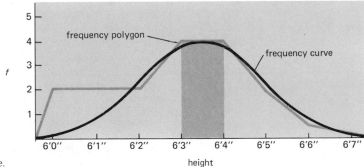

Fig. A4 Frequency curve.

In a histogram the height of each bar over a particular score represents the frequency of that score. By arbitrarily making the width of each bar equal to one unit (as we did in our example of the distribution of heights on a basketball team), the area under the bar over a particular score then also represents the frequency of that score. The total sum of the areas under all the bars of the histogram represents the total number of scores (in our example, the total number of basketball team members).

It is easy to show that the total area under a particular frequency polygon is the same as the area under the corresponding histogram. The same is true for the area under a frequency curve. Given the notion that area, and not height, represents frequency we can speak of the area under a certain portion of the frequency curve between two vertical lines drawn up from any two scores as the number of scores between the two particular points. Further, one can speak of the total area to the left or right of any vertical line drawn through the curve as representing the total frequency of scores less than or greater than the score defined by the line.

At this point a small but important step can be taken. If one envisions a frequency curve as describing the distribution of a set of scores of some unspecified total size, then the ratio of the area between any two vertical lines drawn up from the abscissa of the curve to the total area can be thought of as describing the *probability* that any score, picked at random from that distribution of scores, will fall between the values designated by those lines.

Frequency and Probability   The topic of probability is a mathematically complex one which is intertwined with the topic of statistics. For our purposes the probability of a particular event (score, opinion, value, etc.) may be regarded as its *expected relative frequency* of occurrence, when events are being randomly drawn from some population. The *relative frequency* of a class of events within some distribution is the frequency

probability

with which that class of events occurs, expressed as the *proportion* of the total number of scores in the distribution. If in a distribution of 100 exam grades 40 of those grades are "B's," then the relative frequency of B grades within that distribution of grades is 40 percent or .4.

To compute the relative frequency of any event, one divides the number of times it has occurred by the number of chances it has had to occur. (In the above example, since there were 100 exam grades, there were 100 chances for a B grade.) If one reaches into a bag of marbles 100 times and 25 times pulls out a red marble, then a marble of the class "red" has been drawn with a relative frequency of 25/100 = .25. If one drew a red marble 100 times in 100 draws, its relative frequency would be 100/100 = 1. If in 100 draws one never drew a red marble, its relative frequency would be 0/100 = 0. Probabilities, like relative frequencies, are expressed as values between 0 and 1 with 1 designating certainty and 0 impossibility.

Returning to the topic of frequency curves, assume the curve shown in Fig. A5 represents the smoothed frequency curve for a distribution of numerical exam grades. Instead of labeling the ordinate in terms of actual frequencies, relative frequencies are given. This will in no way change the form of the distribution.

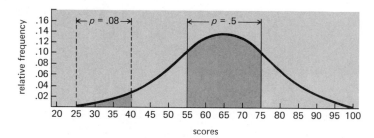

Fig. A5 Smoothed frequency curve.

On this curve, the vertical lines passing through the scores 55 and 75 define a region that contains 50 percent of the area under the total curve; it can therefore be said that 50 percent of the total number of exam scores fell between these two values, and the total relative frequency of exams falling within this class interval would be

$$\frac{.5 \text{ total}}{\text{total}} = .5$$

random   If the entire set of these exams was sitting on a table in front of you in a giant unarranged pile, and you drew one from the pile at random (*at random* signifying that each exam had an equal chance of being picked), your odds of picking an exam with a score between 55 and 75 would clearly be 50 percent, since 50 percent of the exams would be within this range. If you were to draw a sample of several exams from the pile, you would therefore expect 50 percent of the exams in your sample to be within this class range, so that you would expect the relative frequency of exams in the class interval 55-75 in your sample to be .5, which is their probability of being drawn.

An important special case is represented by the area falling between any score value and one end of the distribution. In the present example, the area between a line passing through the score of 40 on the abscissa and the lower (left) end of the distribution represents 8 percent of the total area under the curve. It can therefore be said that 8 percent of the total number of exams have scores which fall below 40, and that the probability of randomly picking an exam with a score of less than 40 is .08. Conversely, the probability of picking an exam with a score greater than 40 would be .92—better than 9 to 1.

    The Normal Curve   As a consequence of Darwin's insistence on the importance of individual differences between members of the same species, scientists have gone about measuring the distribution of those differences on many biological dimensions (variables). They have found that a surprising number of dimensions, when plotted on a frequency polygon, distribute themselves in a similar fashion that can be described visually as "bell-shaped." These bell-shaped curves approximate a set of ideal theoretical curves which are referred to as *normal curves*. Ideal normal curves are characterized   normal curve by a symmetrical diminishing of frequencies around a midpoint with the greatest frequency. The rate of frequency decline around the midpoint is at first accelerated, then decelerated as you move toward either extreme. A typical ideal normal curve is shown in Fig. A6.

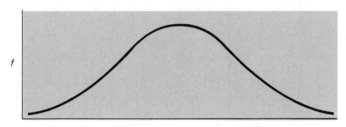

Fig. A6 The normal curve.

    The fact that biological traits are distributed so as to fit this ideal mathematical function (the *normal function*) is an important empirical discovery, that is, a discovery that was arrived at by observation of the real world, rather than conceptually. Subsequently psychologists have found that many mental traits plot normally too. In fact, psychologists have been so influenced by the concept that they now often construct tests so that they will yield results that plot normally. Standard IQ tests are constructed in this way. Such imposed normality may seem arbitrary, but defendants of the practice point up two arguments: (1) since many dimensions of individual differences distribute normally, there may be reason to believe that all dimensions do so, and (2) since the statistical possibilities afforded by a "normal distribution" of scores so outstrip all other possibilities now open to the statistician, it should be used whenever possible. These possibilities will be discussed in detail as we move on to descriptive and inferential statistical techniques. Nonnormal distributions do, of course, occur, and may be of any shape, some of which have been given specific names. An illustration of a *bimodal*   bimodal distribution distribution, which contains *two* values of the abscissa characterized by a peak frequency, is shown in Fig. A7.

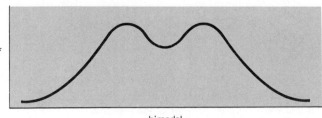

bimodal

Fig. A7 A bimodal distribution.

skewed curve

More common than symmetrical nonnormal curves are curves of distributions only slightly departing from normality by virtue of their asymmetricality. These curves, looking like normal ones that are slightly lopsided, are called *skewed curves* (Fig. A8). Notice that the *positively skewed* curve has more scores that deviate to the right of the point of greatest frequency, while the *negatively skewed* curve has more such extreme scores to the left of the point of greatest frequency.

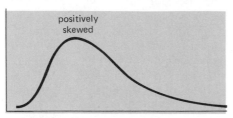
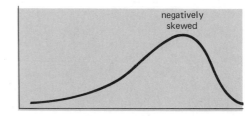

Fig. A8 Skewed curves.

Mathematical Description: Central Tendency

Scientists usually are interested in mathematical as well as visual summaries of data, in part because mathematical statements may allow them to *make inferences,* according to specified mathematical rules, to cases other than those specified by the data. But more obviously, mathematical summaries can distill a whole group of information to a concentrated point in a way that graphing cannot.

central tendency

One way to summarize a set of data is by describing the *central tendency* of the set. In the normal curve shown in Fig. A6, the centerpoint is intuitively obvious. No matter how you look at it, the central point is always that highest middle point representing greatest frequency of occurrence. The central point could be named by locating the number on the abscissa corresponding to that highest point. However, when data are not distributed normally, different definitions of central tendency may yield different estimates of the center point for a given set of data. Three different measures of central tendency are the mode, the median, and the mean.

mode

The *mode* is the most frequently occurring score. Visually this would be the highest point on a graph where the ordinate represents frequency, as it does in all our examples. The mode can be used to describe groups of scores measured on any kind of scale, but it is the *only* measure appropriate for categorical data. In Fig. A1, "business" is the *modal category*. The mode has two major disadvantages. First, a group of scores can have more than one mode, so that no single number designates the "most frequently occurring score." In Fig. A2, 6'3" and 6'4" both have the modal value. A distribution with two separated modes is shown in Fig. A7. Second, the mode is too sensitive to the size of the class intervals when the variable is a continuous one. "Too sensitive" here means that, for the same data, the estimate of mode could jump around depending on the size of the intervals the investigator has chosen.

median

The *median* is defined as the score that would divide the total number of scores in half, if the scores were arranged in order of magnitiude. When the total number of scores is odd, the median is the middle score. When there is an even number of total scores, median is defined as the calculated midpoint between the two real middle scores. Since the median takes advantage of the ordered aspect of the scores, it is appropriate only to ordinal or parametric data but never to categorical. One difficulty with the median is its insensitivity to extreme scores. (On the other hand, this can be an advantage when the distribution is very skewed.) When the mode was criticized for sensitivity, that sensitivity was to arbitrary aspects of the data. We do want sensitivity to substantive aspects of the data, one of which is the position (value or magnitude) of extreme scores. The median's insensitivity to this aspect is demonstrated by the fact that both of the following groups of numbers would be described by the same median, namely "8."

Group A: 4, 5, 8, 10, 11
Group B: 4, 5, 8, 10, 35

To repeat, the median is basically an ordinal statistic responding only to number of scores on each side, not to the real values of those scores. Hopefully the student will anticipate that what is needed for sensitivity to real values is a parametric statistic.

The *mean* is the parametric estimate of central tendency and therefore is appropriate only to interval or ratio data. In everyday language the mean is called an average; in fact, all three of the central tendency measures discussed here are referred to as "averages" at times. One calculates the mean of a set of scores by summing together the values of all the scores and then dividing by the number of scores added. The mean can be conceived as the balance-point (fulcrum) of a set of scores positioned along an equal interval scale. Instead of balancing number of scores on either side as the median does, though, the mean balances the additive magnitude of the values of all scores on either side. Fig. A9 schematizes the idea as if all scores were represented by equal-sized weights placed on the spot of the scale corresponding to their values.

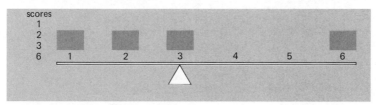

Fig. A9

The mean of the scores shown in Fig. A9 is 3 [(1 + 2 + 3 + 6)/4)], the median is 2.5 (the value midway between 2 and 3), and there is no mode (since no category has a greatest frequency—all have a frequency of 1.). Fig. A10 shows how the three measures of central tendency fall in a continuously distributed, positively skewed distribution. The mode falls at the highest point of the curve, the median divides the area under the curve exactly in half, and the mean is "pulled" away from the median point by the magnitude of the relatively few extreme scores to the right. Notice also in Fig. A9 how the extreme score, 6, pulled the mean away from the median.

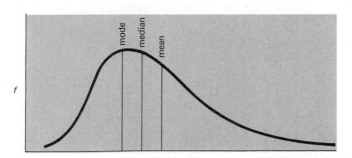

Fig. A10

Calculation of the Mean   The symbol, *M*, is often used to represent the mean. An alternative is to put a "bar" over the letter used to represent individual scores in the group. If you call every score a *Y*, then the mean of all *Y* scores would be written $\overline{Y}$. Another symbol, called the *summation sign,* is used in formulas for computation of the mean and for many other statistics; it is written, Σ. If a formula reads, ΣY, it instructs us to "sum together every *Y* score." Since the mean is calculated by summing all scores and then dividing the sum by the total number of scores involved, symbolized *N*, the equation for the mean can be written

$$\overline{Y} = \frac{\Sigma Y_i}{N}$$

The mean has a number of important properties. If a constant value is added to or subtracted from every score in a set of data, the mean of the new set of scores will be equal to the mean of the original set plus or minus this constant value. Likewise, if every score in a set is multiplied or divided by a constant value, the mean of the transformed distribution will be the original mean multiplied or divided by that constant. It should further be noted that if one subtracts the mean of a distribution of scores from every score in the distribution and sums the resulting differences, these differences will necessarily sum to equal 0. This is illustrated below.

Scores	$X - \overline{X}$
$X_1 = 1$	$1 - 3 = -2$
$X_2 = 1$	$1 - 3 = -2$
$X_3 = 2$	$2 - 3 = -1$
$X_4 = 7$	$4 - 3 = +1$
$X_5 = 4$	$7 - 3 = +4$

$$\text{Mean } X_i = \overline{X} = \frac{\Sigma X_i}{N} = \frac{15}{5} = 3 \qquad \Sigma(X - \overline{X}) = (-2) + (-2) + (-1) + (+1) + (+4) = 0$$

Why this is so should be clarified if one thinks back again to the notion of the mean as the balance point of a set of scores, as shown in Fig. A9. For all the scores to balance across the mean, it is necessary for the "weight" of the scores less than the mean to be equal to the "weight" of the scores greater than the mean. Since these two balanced sets of scores yield values with opposite signs when the mean is subtracted from them, those differences cancel to 0.

The concept of the dispersal of scores around the mean leads us to a second important set of statistics, the measures of variability.

Mathematical Description: Variation

Dispersion is a matter of distances (differences) between single scores and the mean. Therefore, it might seem that one way to get a single number to describe the characteristic (average) dispersion of some group would be to find the average amount by which all scores differ from their mean. To obtain such a measure it might at first seem logical to find the difference between each score and the mean and take the mean of these differences. But it was already demonstrated that the numerator of this operation, $\Sigma(X_i - \overline{X})$, necessarily equals 0. Thus, no information about differences in amounts of dispersion could be communicated.

What is needed is to disallow the possibility of the negative deviation scores cancelling out the positive ones. Statisticians have determined that the most sensible way to achieve this is not simply to drop the minus signs from the negative deviation scores, since such an operation has the arbitrary character of affecting some scores but not others. Instead, the same operation is applied to all difference scores; they are *squared,* an operation that eliminates negative values. When all squared difference scores are summed together, for any single group, the result is called the *sum of the squares* and is symbolized *SS*. It is represented by the equation, $SS = \Sigma(X - \overline{X})^2$, which instructs us to find each difference score, square each one separately, and then add those squared difference scores together.

When the sum of squares is divided by N, making it the *average squared deviation score*, it is called the *variance* and is symbolized σ^2, lower case Greek sigma, squared. The variance is calculated for some simple data.

variance

$$\sigma^2 = \frac{SS}{N} = \frac{\Sigma(X_i - \overline{X})^2}{N}$$

	$X - \overline{X}$	$(X - \overline{X})^2$
$X_1 = 2$	$2 - 5 = -3$	$-3^2 = 9$
$X_2 = 3$	$3 - 5 = -2$	$-2^2 = 4$
$X_3 = 3$	$3 - 5 = -2$	$-2^2 = 4$
$X_4 = 7$	$7 - 5 = +2$	$2^2 = 4$
$X_5 = 10$	$10 - 5 = +5$	$5^2 = 25$
		$= 46$
$\overline{X} = \dfrac{\Sigma X_i}{N} = \dfrac{25}{5} = 5$		$= \Sigma(X_i - \overline{X})^2$

$$\sigma^2 = \frac{SS}{N} = \frac{46}{5} = 9\frac{1}{5} = 9.2$$

While the variance is perfectly adequate, mathematically, for describing dispersion, it has the drawback of not being on the same level as the original units of raw data, since squaring was involved in the transition from raw scores to variance estimate. Therefore, to get back down to a noninflated measure, the final variance estimate is usually *square-rooted*. The result is called the *standard deviation*, symbolized σ or *SD* It is represented by the equation,

standard deviation

$$\sigma = \sqrt{\frac{\Sigma(x_i - x)^2}{N}}.$$

In the above example, the standard deviation of these scores is $\sqrt{9.2} = 3.02$.

Characteristics of the Standard Deviation Let us consider the changes in the standard deviation as a result of constant transformations just as we did for changes in the mean. When a constant is added to all members of a group, the standard deviation of the transformed group remains the same as it was for the original group; the same holds for constant subtractive transformations. This may seem confusing at first, but it should become clear when you remember that the mean, too, is increased or decreased with addition or subtraction of a constant. Since standard deviation is a measure of variability *relative* to the mean, these relative differences do not change when the individual scores are transformed additively.

In contrast to additive transformations, when all scores are multiplied or divided by a constant, the standard deviation does *not* remain unchanged. This is because, while the new mean is multiplied by the same amount, so are the *differences* between the new mean and each new score. The result is that the new standard deviation can be found simply by multiplying or dividing the old one by the same constant that was applied to the original scores. Thinking about these relations—that standard deviation does not change when a constant is added to scores but does change when scores are multiplied by a constant—should help the student understand the essence of this variability measure.

In order to exemplify the usefulness of the concept of the standard deviation, let us once again consider the normal curve. Assume that the shape of the frequency curve for a set of parametric scores closely approaches the form of a normal curve. As noted earlier, the total area under the curve will represent the total number of scores, designated *N*. Furthermore, the area under any portion of the curve lying between two particular scores, or a score and one end of the curve, will represent the total number of scores within that region, and thus the probability of any particular score falling within that region of the curve. The midpoint of the curve will represent the mean of this distribution of scores.

A critical feature of the normal curve is the following. It can be shown mathematically by means of the complex equation that specifies the form of an ideal normal curve that for any normally distributed distribution of scores, irrespective of its mean or standard deviation, 34.13 percent of the area under the curve and thus 34.14 percent of the scores will occur within *exactly one standard deviation of the mean* on either side of the mean. Thus, between a score value 1 *SD* above the mean and a score value 1 *SD*·below the mean, 68.26 percent of the total number of scores will occur. Similarly, 95.45 percent of the total number of scores will fall between −2 *SD* and +2 *SD* of the mean and 99.9936 percent will fall between +3 *SD* and −3 *SD* of the mean. This is illustrated in Fig. A11.

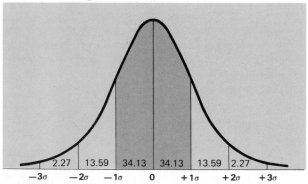

| 2.27 | 13.59 | 34.13 | 34.13 | 13.59 | 2.27 |

-3σ $\quad$ -2σ $\quad$ -1σ $\quad$ 0 $\quad$ $+1\sigma$ $\quad$ $+2\sigma$ $\quad$ $+3\sigma$

Fig. A11

Thus, given the *mean* and *standard deviation* of a set of scores *and the fact that that set of scores is normally distributed,* one can readily determine the *probability* that a score exceeding any specified value will occur within that distribution. One can say, for example, that a score more than 3 *SD* from the mean will have a probability of .000064 and therefore less than one chance in 10,000 of occurring (since only .0064 percent of the area of the curve falls outside these limits). This fact is of great importance to statistical procedures which involve making inferences and predictions.

Mathematical Description: The Position of Individual Members

The two major descriptive statistics, mean and standard deviation, are often used to describe a whole group summarily. In addition, a researcher may be interested in describing the position of an individual score within the group.

Percentile Ranks An elementary nonparametric measure of a score's relative standing is the *percentile rank*. When statisticians use percentile rank scores they are not referring to the percentage of items correct, but to the percentage of scores falling below a score with that percentile rank. Statisticians would say, "Henry falls at the 60th percentile on the math SAT exam," to mean that Henry scored better than exactly 60 percent of the whole group of persons who took the test.

percentile rank

Percentile ranks are computed by going through the following steps.

1. Make a *cumulative frequency count* of each possible score. This is done by listing all scores in their order of magnitude, beginning with the lowest, and summing the frequencies of each score as you move upward; the additive total associated with every score is its *cumulative frequency*.
2. Adjust the cumulative frequency count for each score to the midpoint level. This is achieved by subtracting the number of persons getting the particular score, divided by 2, from the cumulative frequency associated with that score, e.g., if three persons were to obtain a particular score, 3/2 would be subtracted from the cumulative frequency.
3. Make the cumulative frequency count for each score *relative* to the whole. This is accomplished by dividing the adjusted cumulative frequency by the total frequency for the whole group, which is N. Note that N is also equal to the unadjusted cumulative frequency of the uppermost score.
4. Put the ratio of cumulative to whole frequency, called *relative cumulative frequency*, on a *centile* level. This is simply done by multiplying the whole rate by *100*.

Below, these procedures are carried out for a group of five persons. Note that since only one person obtains any particular score, the adjustment of cumulative frequency is always a matter of subtracting 1/2.

	Raw Score	f	Cumu- lative Frequency	Adjustment	Relative Cumulative Frequency (RCF)	Centile RCF $\times$ 100	% Rank
John	70	1	5	5 − 1/2 = 4.5	4.5/5 = .9	.9 × 100 = 90th	
Marcia	65	1	4	4 − 1/2 = 3.5	3.5/5 = .7	.7 × 100 = 70th	
Carl	60	1	3	3 − 1/2 = 2.5	2.5/5 = .5	.5 × 100 = 50th	
Bill	31	1	2	2 − 1/2 = 1.5	1.5/5 = .3	.3 × 100 = 30th	
Joan	30	1	1	1 − 1/2 = 0.5	.5/5 = .1	.1 × 100 = 10th	

It should be clear that cumulative frequency counts according to the order of the scores, with no account taken of magnitude differences between ranks. Thus, percentiles are ordinal statistics. One result of using an ordinal system for describing originally parametric data is that the *shape* of the original distribution of scores is lost in the transformation. Look at the raw score difference around Bill's score. There is only one point of difference between Bill's and Joan's raw scores, but a 29-point jump upward between Bill's and Carl's scores. But when transformed into percentile ranks this interval difference has been lost—Bill's percentile score is 20 percentile points away from both Carl's and Joan's. What was originally a nonsymetrical interval around Bill's score has become a symmetrical one—the shape of the interval has been lost.

z score   **z Scores**   Another method of describing relative standing is the z *score*. Unlike percentile ranks, transforming a distribution into z *scores* does not alter the form of the distribution. Consequently z scores, unlike percentile ranks, do convey information about the relative standing of different scores and also about the magnitudes of the differences between them. If the difference between scores A and B is 5 times as great as the differences between scores C and D, the respective differences between their z scores will convey this fact. Z scores are appropriate only for parametric data because they are based on the statistics of the mean and standard deviation. The z score for any score in a distribution tells how many standard deviation units separate that score from the mean of the distribution. To convert any score in a z score you subtract the mean of its distribution from it and divide the difference by the standard deviation of the distribution. The equation representing this procedure is

$$z = \frac{X - \overline{X}}{SD}$$

where X is the score value, $\overline{X}$ the mean, and SD the standard deviation. Raw scores below the mean will produce negative z scores and raw scores greater than the mean, positive z scores.

Below an illustrative set of z scores is computed.

Raw Data		$\dfrac{X - \overline{X}}{SD} = Z_y$
X_1	2	$\dfrac{2-5}{2} = -\dfrac{3}{2} = -1.5$
X_2	4	$\dfrac{4-5}{2} = -\dfrac{1}{2} = -.5$
X_3	4	$\dfrac{4-5}{2} = -\dfrac{1}{2} = -.5$
X_4	5	$\dfrac{5-5}{2} = \dfrac{0}{2} = 0$
X_5	7	$\dfrac{7-5}{2} = +\dfrac{2}{2} = +1.0$
X_6	8	$\dfrac{8-5}{2} = +\dfrac{3}{2} = +1.5$

$\overline{X} = 5$

$\sigma^2 = \dfrac{SS}{N} = \dfrac{24}{6} = 4$

$\sigma = \sqrt{4} = 2$

The mean score of a distribution of raw scores will, when those scores are converted into z scores, necessarily be the mean of the new distribution, too, but it will now have a numerical value of 0. This fact results from the relational aspect of z scores—they define distance away from their midpoint, and the mean is 0 distance from that midpoint.

        Normally Distributed z Scores   A set of z scores will be normally distributed if and only if the raw scores from which they came were normally distributed. A normally distributed set of z scores, called *standard normal distribution,* has properties that render it very useful to statisticians.

It was pointed out earlier that z distributions and percentile distributions hold no necessary correspondence to one another, because percentiles are ordinal and center about the median while z scores are parametric and center about the mean. However, in normal distributions the mean and median happen to coincide; this fact allows for the possibility of conversion from z scores to percentile scores for normal populations. A z score states the position of a score in terms of its distance from the mean in standard deviation units. As was previously discussed, in a normally distributed set of scores the number of scores occurring within a region a specified number of standard deviations from the mean can be exactly determined. Furthermore, since the normal distribution is symmetrical about its mean, exactly 50 percent of its scores will fall below the mean and 50 percent above the mean. Thus, with a normally distributed set of z scores, all one need do to determine the percentile rank of any particular score is: (1) observe if it is above or below the mean, as indicated by its sign; (2) determine from a table designed for that purpose (see p. 800) the percentage of scores between a z score of that value and the mean; and (3) add 50 percent to this percentage if the z score is above the mean or subtract this percentage from 50 percent if the z score is below the mean.

The z table supplies information in terms of "areas under the normal curve" between various z scores and the mean z score of 0. These areas may be thought of directly as percentages of scores. For example, referring to the table one finds a z score of 1.645 corresponds to the value .45. This tells us that 45 percent of the total area of the curve, that is, 45 percent of the total population which the curve represents, falls between the mean and a z score of 1.645. To turn this value into a traditional percentile rank, expressing the total number of scores below this score, one notes that since the z score had a positive sign it was above the mean, and therefore we must add 50 percent to the 45 percent to include all the scores below the mean in our percentile rank. Thus, a z score of + 1.645 in a normal distribution corresponds to a percentile rank of .95 (see Fig. A12).

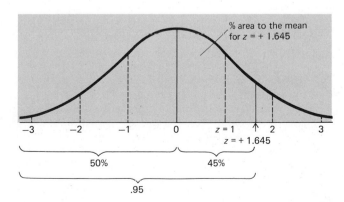

Fig. A12

Just as the percentile rank for any z score from a standard normal distribution can be determined from a z table, so can the probability of obtaining z scores greater or less than any specified value be determined. For example, we learn from the table that for any normally distributed set of scores 47.5 percent of the scores will fall between the mean and a score which, when transformed to a z score, will have an absolute value of 1.96. If the sign of that z score is +, then we will know that 47.5 percent + 50 percent or 97.5 percent of the scores in that distribution will be lower than that particular score. Therefore, the percentage of scores as *high or higher* than that score is 2.5 percent, so that the relative frequency of such scores is .025 and the probability of randomly picking such a score from the distribution .025. If the sign of the z score is −, then we will know that the percentage of scores in the distribution as *low or lower* than that score is 50 percent −47.5 percent or 2.5 percent and again the probability of picking such a score is .025.

It may be noted at this point that since the normal distribution is symmetrical, a z table presents a single set of z values to represent both + and − z scores. The user takes the sign of the z score being considered into account when interpreting the table.

Before proceeding to the next topic, the student might stop to consider for a moment how much information is provided by the various descriptive statistics we have dealt with. Suppose you are told that your grade on an exam is 73. How much information does this provide you with regarding how well you are doing in a class? Does the picture change if you learn the mean of the distribution of exam grades was 61, that the form of the grade distribution was normal, and your z score was 2.00?

Mathematical Description: Correlation

Pearson product moment correlation

So far we have discussed statistics that describe, summarily, either a whole set of data or the position of a single score within the whole set. Next we will consider a statistic called the *Pearson product moment correlation,* symbolized r, which goes further, to describe how one whole set of scores relates to another whole set, when the same individuals have contributed one score to each set. Note the structure of the word: co-relation. There are several ways in which two sets of scores might co-relate. Individuals might score similarly in both sets; for example, someone might score high on test A and high on test B, someone else might score low on both tests, and so forth. On the other hand, people might score dissimilarly on the two tests, but in a regular fashion; for example, persons scoring high on A might score consistently low on B, and persons scoring low on A might score consistently high on B. However there may also be no regularity existing at all; for example, some people scoring high on A score low on B while others scoring high on A score high on B.

Can we compare two sets of scores, directly, if they are idiosyncratically scored in the first place, for example, if one is graded from 1 to 10, the other from 1 to 50? The answer is, we cannot. Therefore, comparison of two groups can ensue only after they have been converted to standard, similar, comparable distributions. In other words, we must transform both sets of scores into standard scores. By using z scores for both sets, *correlation* will answer the question, do individuals' scores on A relate to the mean, $\overline{A}$, in any way that regularly corresponds to the way their scores on B relate to the mean, $\overline{B}$?

If all persons' scores on test A relate to the mean, $\overline{A}$, in exactly the same way their scores on B relate to its mean, then each person would have identical z scores, in number and in sign, for the two tests. If this were the case, we would say that there exists a *perfect positive correlation* between the two tests, and the *correlation coefficient, r,* would equal +1, which is the highest positive correlation possible.

The other possible "perfect" case would be if every time an individual scored low on test A he were to score correspondingly high, in relation to the mean, on test B. In this case each person would have the same numerical z value on the two tests, but the two would always be opposite in sign. This *perfect negative correlation* would have a value of −1.

If there is no relationship between the scores on two sets of data—that is, if high scores on one set do not tend to any degree to be regularly associated with either high or low scores on the other set, then a correlation of 0 or "no correlation" is said to exist between the sets of data. Between 0 correlation and "perfect" positive and negative correlations of +1 and −1 (perfect correlations which, it may be noted, virtually never occur in real-life psychological studies), there exists a continuous range of possible correlations, which are expressed as positive or negative fractions between 0 and 1 : e.g., + .82 or −.35. The *strength* of the correlation is reflected by how large this fraction is—that is, by how closely it approaches a value of 1, regardless of whether its sign is positive or negative. The sign of r tells only the direction of the relationship, whether the variables are positively or negatively correlated. An r of −.8 describes a more regular relationship between two variables than does an r of +.6, even though the former is arithmetically smaller.

To clarify the nature of correlations, it is useful to consider *scattergrams* of some hypothetical sets of data. Each dot represents one subject's score on two sets of measures; one (x) is plotted on the abscissa of the scattergram and the other (y) on the ordinate. If someone scores high on x and high on y, his dot would appear on the upper right-hand corner of the scattergram; if low on x and high on y, in the upper left-hand corner; if high on x and low on y, in the lower right-hand corner; if low on x and on y, in the bottom left-hand corner.

scattergram

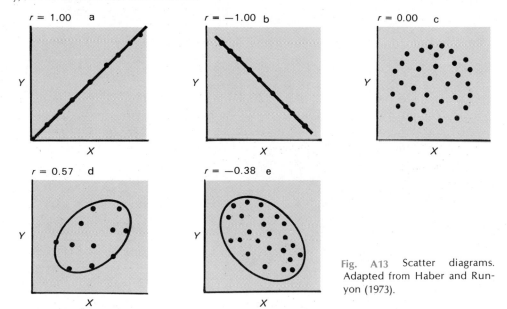

Fig. A13 Scatter diagrams. Adapted from Haber and Runyon (1973).

A scattergram for a set of scores with a perfect correlation of $+1$ is shown in Fig. A13(a), p. 789, and the scattergram for a set of scores with a perfect negative correlation in Fig. A13(b). Fig. A13(c) shows a scatterplot for a set of scores with a correlation of 0. Fig. A13(d) and (e) show scattergrams for sets of scores with correlations of .57 and $-.38$ respectively.

Considering (a) and (b), you will notice that in these cases the score on one variable is *perfectly predictable* from the score on the other. In (d) and (e), it is imperfectly or partially predictable from one score to the other; due to the correlation between the sets of scores, one is likely to be able to guess closer to an individual's score on one variable by considering the other variable. Finally, in the case of (c), knowing the value of one of an individual's scores will tell you absolutely nothing about the other set.

One equation by which the correlation coefficent can be computed is the following:

$$r = \frac{\Sigma(z_x \times z_y)}{N}$$

This instructs us to take an individual's z score for each of the two variables being correlated, multiply one times the other, sum the cross products for all individuals, and divide by the total number of individuals. (To gain some insight into how this equation functions in cases of perfect correlation, consider that in such cases z_x will be equal to $+$ or $-z_y$, and that it can be demonstrated that for any set of z scores, if all the z scores in the set are squared and the squares summed they will sum to equal $N : \Sigma z_1^2 = N.$)

Below, this formula is used to compute the correlation coefficient, r, for a set of imperfectly correlated scores.

	Raw Score	$Z_x = \dfrac{X-\overline{X}}{\sigma}$		Raw Score	$Z_y = \dfrac{Y-\overline{Y}}{\sigma}$	Cross Products $z_x z_y$
X_1	1	$-\dfrac{4}{3}$	Y_1	2	$-\dfrac{3}{2}$	$-\dfrac{4}{3} \times -\dfrac{3}{2} = 2.0$
X_2	2	$-\dfrac{3}{3}$	Y_2	3	$-\dfrac{2}{2}$	$-\dfrac{3}{3} \times -\dfrac{2}{2} = 1.0$
X_3	2	$-\dfrac{3}{3}$	Y_3	2	$-\dfrac{3}{2}$	$-\dfrac{3}{3} \times -\dfrac{3}{2} = 1.5$
X_4	3	$-\dfrac{2}{3}$	Y_4	5	$\dfrac{0}{2}$	$-\dfrac{2}{3} \times \dfrac{0}{2} = 0$
X_5	4	$-\dfrac{1}{3}$	Y_5	5	$\dfrac{0}{2}$	$-\dfrac{1}{3} \times \dfrac{0}{2} = 0$
X_6	5	$\dfrac{0}{3}$	Y_6	7	$\dfrac{2}{2}$	$\dfrac{0}{3} \times \dfrac{2}{2} = 0$
X_7	6	$\dfrac{1}{3}$	Y_7	5	$\dfrac{0}{2}$	$\dfrac{1}{3} \times \dfrac{0}{2} = 0$
X_8	8	$\dfrac{3}{3}$	Y_8	6	$\dfrac{1}{2}$	$\dfrac{3}{3} \times \dfrac{1}{2} = 0.5$

	Raw Score	$Z_x = \dfrac{X-\overline{X}}{\sigma}$		Raw Score	$Z_y = \dfrac{Y-\overline{Y}}{\sigma}$		Cross Products	$z_x z_y$
X_9	9	$\dfrac{4}{3}$	Y_9	7	$\dfrac{2}{2}$		$\dfrac{4}{3} \times \dfrac{2}{2} = 1.33$	
X_{10}	10	$\dfrac{5}{3}$	Y_{10}	8	$\dfrac{3}{2}$		$\dfrac{5}{3} \times \dfrac{3}{2} = 2.5$	

$$\overline{X} = 5 \qquad\qquad \overline{Y} = 5 \qquad\qquad \Sigma z_x z_y = 8.83$$

$$\sigma^2 = \frac{90}{10} = 9 \qquad \sigma^2 = \frac{40}{10} = 4 \qquad r = \frac{\Sigma z_x z_y}{N} = \frac{8.83}{10} = (+).883$$

$$\sigma = \sqrt{9} = 3 \qquad\qquad \sigma = \sqrt{4} = 2$$

Formulas for computing *r*, other than the one given here, are available, some of which allow computation directly from raw scores without the intervening transformation to standard scores. Nevertheless, the transformation is actually implicit in these *computational formulas*, otherwise comparisons across groups could make no sense.

Making Inferences from Data

Inferential techniques are made necessary by the practical impossibility of actually collecting data on all events about which the scientist might want to make statements. If, for example, a researcher has developed a parametric "scale of happiness" and he wants to determine whether rural or urban American residents score happier, he would require immense time and energy to administer the test to the whole populations of rural and urban residents. Therefore, he would be forced to *draw a sample* of persons from each whole population, samples that would be meant to *represent* the populations from which they came. Usually such a procedure is acceptable, though, only if the samples are chosen *randomly*. Random selection requires that every object, event, or person in the whole population has an equal and independent chance of being chosen (drawn). Therefore, sampling must begin with an inclusive listing of the whole population and must proceed with unbiased (blind) choices from that inclusive list. In the example here, the happiness researcher would have to have at his disposal two population lists, one of rural residents and one of urban residents, and he would randomly select a sample group from each. We now consider those special techniques developed to permit making such inferences.

Testing for Differences between Two Means

The researcher could simply describe each sample group using the descriptive methods we have already outlined; he might summarily describe each group by calculating its means and standard deviations. However, if the researcher is interested in ultimately describing the whole populations from which his samples came (if he wants to eventually be able to say, "rural residents are happier than urban ones," rather than just "this sample of rural residents is happier than this sample of urban ones"), he must take into account the systematic statistical errors that are inherent in the sampling procedure. For one, the description of *variability* of the sample consistently errs, if it is meant to describe the variability of the population from which the sample came. The sample's variability is consistently *smaller* than the "true" variability of the population. Usually there are few extreme values in a parent population; therefore, odds are against those extreme members being included in a sample, particularly if it is a small one. Since extreme members inflate variance (and standard deviation) estimates, the sample's variance will be too small if meant as an estimate of population variance. To "correct" the sample's variance, 1 is subtracted from N in the denominator of the variance equation, which will make the computed variance slightly larger. A sample variance is often symbolized s^2 and a sample standard deviation indicated by the symbol s.

A crucial problem that confronts the researcher, however, is determining whether differences in the means of the samples he obtains truly reflect differences in the means of the populations from which they were drawn. Suppose our "happiness" researcher finds that on the 1 to 10 happiness scale he has developed (where 10 is "very happy" and 1 is "very sad"), his rural sample has a mean score of 6 and his urban sample a mean score of 4. Is the rural population happier than the urban population—or does

sampling error this difference represent a chance *sampling error?* Since the means of his samples are not likely to be the *exact* means of his populations, it is conceivable that the mean of his rural sample is higher than the rural population mean by 1 point (because by chance his sample contained a few too many "very happy" people) and that his urban sample mean is 1 point lower than the real urban population mean (because he picked, by chance, a few too many "very sad" people.) If this were the case, the real mean of both populations would be 5, and there would be no difference between them. How sure can the experimenter be that this has not happened? Intuitively (and mathematically) it is clear that the larger the sample that he uses, the less likely he is to be led astray, but very large samples may simply not be practical for him—and even with large samples, some doubt as to the accuracy of his findings would remain—especially if the differences he found were not large.

hypothesis testing The procedures developed to resolve such problems are collectively called *hypothesis testing* procedures. For ratio and interval data, *parametric hypothesis tests,* such as the *t test* about to be described can be employed. These tests are more *powerful* than the *nonparametric* tests which must be used with category and ordinal data. By *more powerful* what is meant is that a parametric test will allow one to conclude on the basis of smaller samples, and smaller differences between sample means, that real population differences exist.

A hypothesis test asks how probable it is that an obtained sample difference is due to chance factors. The more *improbable* it is that the difference between two samples is due to chance, the more likely it is that the difference is due to a *systematic* factor,

independent variable called the *independent variable*. In the example here, place of residence is the independent variable.

There is a technical language associated with hypothesis testing. First, the possibility of the difference between two groups being due to chance alone is represented by

null hypothesis the *null hypothesis*. The null states that there is no real (systematic) difference, that whatever difference was found represents only random fluctuations of samples taken

alternate hypothesis from essentially the *same* population. The *alternate hypothesis* states the possibility that the two means are from samples that represent two initially distinct populations, distinct by virtue of their differences on the independent variable. The alternate hypothesis can either specify the direction in which the two samples are expected to differ; that is, it can specify which mean score will be larger, or it can hypothesize simply *some* real difference, in either direction. The alternate hypothesis, whichever kind it is, can never be directly "proved." It wins only by default; you can accept the alternate hypothesis as correct only if your test demonstrates that it is sufficiently *im*probable that the null hypothesis is correct. If the required level of improbability is not reached, the "null is retained." If it is reached, the "null is rejected."

The Standard Deviation of the Difference between Means   An experimenter must know, then, by how much two sample means would be expected to differ by chance alone, so that he can compare his obtained difference to see if it exceeds this expected one. He must have a yardstick of possible (hypothetical) differences between sample means that is marked off according to the probability of finding those differences by chance sampling errors alone. Such a yardstick is available, because it turns out that, for samples drawn from normal populations or samples that are large, *the differences between the means of samples drawn from the same parent population are normally distributed.* That is to say, if we draw a large number of pairs of samples from some population, subtract the mean of one sample in each pair from the mean of the other, and look at the frequency distribution of the set of difference values which we have thereby obtained, we will find that frequency distribution is a normal distribution, so long as the parent population was itself approximately normal in form *or* the size of our samples was sufficiently large. In the illustration we are using, it can be assumed that "happiness" is normally distributed among the total population of subjects sampled. In real studies of variables with unknown population distributions, approximate normality of the sample distributions can be taken as an indicator of population normality. However, with sample sizes over 30, substantial amounts of nonnormality in the parent population can be tolerated. The mean of this *sampling distribution of the difference between means* will be 0.

Now we have already seen that the probability of any range of values in a normally distributed set of values occurring can be determined if the mean and standard deviation of the distribution are known. If one has this information, then it is a simple matter to transform the distributed values into z scores (that is, turn the distribution into a standard normal distribution) and determine the likelihood that a score exceeding some specified distance from the mean will be encountered by referring to a z table and determining the total percentage of the area under the normal curve that lies beyond that distance from the mean.

In the present case then, if the investigator could determine the standard deviation of the sampling distribution of the difference between means for the population of subjects sampled, he could determine the probability of an observed difference between sample means occurring which was at least as great as the one which he obtained. If it turned out that the obtained difference in the sample means, in our example 2 points on the "happiness scale," was so great that the probability of this difference occurring by chance alone was very small, the researcher could happily conclude that the null hypothesis of "no difference" between the urban and rural populations was probably incorrect and that mean differences on the happiness scale existed between the urban and rural populations.

The t Test   The standard deviation of the sampling distribution of the difference between means is termed the *standard error of the difference between means* and is symbolized $\sigma_{\bar{x}-\bar{x}}$. It is not a value that an investigator is likely to know. However, an *estimate* of it may be derived from the pooled standard deviations of the experimental samples. This estimated standard error of the difference between means, symbolized $s_{\bar{x}-\bar{x}}$, may be used to obtain a "z score" for the obtained difference between means.

Unfortunately, unless the sample sizes are quite large, the standardized score obtained in this way will not distribute quite normally, and when the sample sizes are small, this non-normality is pronounced. A normal distribution can therefore not be used to evaluate this score. Fortunately, a distribution family similar to the normal distribution, referred to as the t distribution has been developed, which allows one to compensate for the estimation of $\sigma_{\bar{x}-\bar{x}}$ by $s_{\bar{x}-\bar{x}}$ for samples of various sizes. Thus, in most hypothesis testing, one does not compute a z score but a t *value* and refers to it in a t *table*. With large samples, the t distribution and normal distribution are virtually identical. The relationship of the normal distribution to t distributions for a number of different sample sizes is shown in Fig. A14. A z score represents the size of a score in terms of its distance, expressed in standard deviation units, from the mean of its distribution. The t value we are considering here similarly represents the size of an observed difference between two sample means in terms of its distance, expressed in standard error units, from the mean of its hypothetical sampling distribution. The equation for a z score, you will recall, was

$$z = \frac{X - \overline{X}}{SD}$$

where X is a score, $\overline{X}$ the mean of its distribution, and SD the standard deviation of that distribution. A t value is computed in a completely analogous manner, with the score, X, substituted for by an obtained difference between two sample means $(\overline{X} - \overline{X})$, and the standard deviation of the distribution of scores substituted for by the estimated standard error of the difference between means, $s_{\bar{x}-\bar{x}}$. Since the mean of the sampling distribution of the difference between means is 0, the equation for t can be shown

$$t = \frac{(\overline{X}_1 - \overline{X}_2) - 0}{s_{\bar{x} - \bar{x}}}$$

Just as one could refer to a z table to determine the total area under a normal curve beyond a specified z value, and thus the probability of obtaining a z score equal to

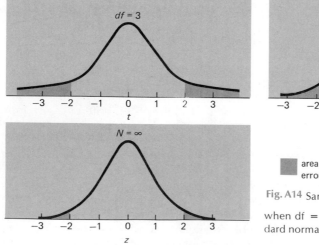

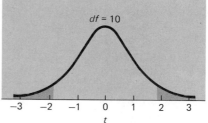

area beyond $\pm$ 1.96 standard errors of the mean

Fig. A14 Sampling distributions of $t = \dfrac{\overline{X} - \mu 0}{s_x}$ when df = 3, and 10, compared to the standard normal curve. (Haber and Runyon, 1973)

a greater than that value, so one refers to a t table to determine the probability of obtaining a t value equal or greater than some specified size.

Computation of t Values Given two samples with similar variances drawn from the same hypothetical population, a t for the difference between their means can be computed from the following equation.
as:

$$t = \frac{\overline{X}_1 - \overline{X}_2}{\sqrt{\left(\dfrac{(N_1 - 1)s_1^2 + (N_2 - 1)s_2^2}{N_1 + N_2 - 2}\right)\left(\dfrac{1}{N_1} + \dfrac{1}{N_2}\right)}}$$

In this equation, $\overline{X}_1$ is the mean of the first sample and $\overline{X}_2$ is the mean of the second, N_1 the number of persons in the first sample and N_2 the number of persons in the second, s_1 the standard deviation of the first sample and s_2 the standard deviation of the second. (The imposing denominator of this fraction is simply a computation for s_{x-x}.)

Returning to our "happiness" investigator, let us assign some values to the features of his data that are required for the computational equation for t. We have already observed that the mean for his rural sample was 6 ($\overline{X}_1$ = 6) and that the mean of his urban sample was 4 ($\overline{X}_2$ = 4). In addition, let us assume that his rural sample consisted of 10 individuals (N_1 = 10) and his urban sample consisted of 12 (N_2 = 12). Finally, let us assume that the corrected standard deviation of his rural sample was 2 (s_1 = 2) and the corrected standard deviation for his urban sample was 3 (s_2 = 3). We may now calculate a t value for his observed difference in sample means.

$$t = \frac{(\overline{X})_{\text{rural}} - (\overline{X})_{\text{urban}} - 0}{s_{\overline{x} - \overline{x}}}$$

$$= \frac{6 - 4}{\sqrt{\left(\dfrac{(6 - 1)(2)^2 + (5 - 1)(3)^2}{10 + 12 - 2}\right)\left(\dfrac{1}{10} + \dfrac{1}{12}\right)}}$$

$$= \frac{2}{.716}$$

$$= 2.79$$

How improbable must the difference between two sample means be before a researcher can conclude that that difference is not due to chance? The decision is to some extent arbitrary. In hypothesis testing, the probability chosen as the decision line is referred to as the *significance level*. If one decides on a significance level of 10 percent, this means that if the difference in sample means obtained has only a 10 percent probability of occurring by chance alone, one will conclude chance was not its cause and reject the null hypothesis of "no significant difference between the means." In psychology, the most commonly used significance levels are the 5 percent

significance level

level and the 1 percent level. In accord with mathematical conventions for expressing probabilities, these values are generally expressed as decimals; thus, one reads references to the .05 and .01 levels of significance.

one-tailed test
two-tailed test

One- and Two-tailed Tests   It was noted earlier that an experimenter may take as the alternate hypothesis he wishes to accept the assumption of either "some difference" between his sample means or a "difference in a particular direction." Let us think back a moment to the normal distribution. Assume one wished to show that a particular score was improbably smaller than the mean of a distribution of scores. One would be interested in the total area under the normal distribution representing scores equal to or smaller than that particular score. Since values smaller than the mean are conventionally shown on the left-hand of a normal distribution, one would be interested in that distribution's far left region or *left-tail*. Similarly, if one was interested in showing that a particular score was improbably larger than the mean, one would be interested in the *right-tail* of the distribution. Since scores below the mean have a negative sign in a *z* distribution and scores above the mean a positive sign, the left tail of a *z* distribution is characterized by high negative *z* scores and the right side by high positive *z* scores. But if one was interested simply in showing that a particular *z* score was improbable in some direction, one would be interested in *both tails* of the distribution, and therefore high *z* scores irrespective of their sign.

These relationships also apply to the *t* distribution. If an investigator is interested in showing that one mean is specifically greater than another, he will be interested only in the negative (left) or positive (right) tails of the *t* distribution, and thus high negative or positive *t* values only. If he wishes to show simply that *some* difference exists between two means, he is concerned with both tails and not the sign of his *t*. The difference is not trivial. To obtain a significance level of .05 on a one-tailed test, it is necessary to show that the proper tail of the *t* distribution "cut off" by the *t* value one has obtained contains less than 5 percent of the total area under the curve. With a two-tailed test, however, the .05 level will be obtained only when a *t* value is obtained such that when it is symmetrically applied so as to cut off both tails of the distribution, the combined total area cut off is less than 5 percent of the area under the curve. This means that each tail must contain less than 2.5 percent (not 5 percent) of the area under the curve. Therefore, in a given experiment, a *t* value that yields significance at the .05 level on a one-tailed test will only yield significance at the .1 level on a two-tailed test. T values must be higher on two-tailed tests than on one-tailed tests to achieve a specified significance. It is important when specifying one's experimental hypothesis to determine in advance whether a one-tailed or two-tailed test is to be used. Using a two-tailed test is always more "conservative."

The t Table   The form of the *t* curve changes for experimental samples of different sizes. Most *t* tables show the *critical values of t* for a specified set of one- and two-tailed significance levels for a series of possible sample sizes. Turn to the *t* table on page 801 of this book. The *df* heading on the column on the left stands for *degrees of freedom;* when two sample means are being compared. When comparing sample means, the degrees of freedom equals the total number of subjects in the two samples combined minus 2. Thus;

$$df = N_1 + N_2 - 2$$

Since the *t* distribution, like the normal distribution, is symmetrical, *t* tables like *z* tables do not give separate listings for $+$ and $-$ values of *t*. The person using the table simply takes into account the sign of the *t* he has obtained when interpreting his results. For one-tailed tests, the obtained *t* must be of the desired sign for significance to be found. (When computing a *t* value for the difference between means in a one-tailed test, one must be sure that the *mean hypothesized to be smaller is subtracted from the mean hypothesized to be larger* irrespective of which is actually larger, if the sign of the obtained *t* is to be correct.) When computing a *t* in a two-tailed test, the sign of the obtained *t* has no bearing on its significance or lack of significance.

Below, critical *t*'s are given for various kinds of tests at various degrees of freedom for various levels of significance. It is suggested that students try to locate these critical *t*'s for themselves on the *t* table, to get practice in using this table, which is a constant companion to psychological researchers.

df	Level of Significance	Kind of Test	Critical
6	.05	2-tailed	2.447
9	.05	1-tailed	1.833
9	.05	2-tailed	2.262
25	.01	1-tailed	2.485

Now, at last, we may see how our "happiness" investigator has fared. He wishes to obtain significance at the .05 level. Since he did not hypothesize in advance that either his urban or rural population would be the happier of the two, he conducts a two-tailed test. One of his sample groups contained 10 subjects, the other 12, so there are 10 + 12 − 2 = 20 degrees of freedom. Consulting our *t* table, we find that the critical *t* at the .05 level for a two-tailed test with 20 degrees of freedom is 2.09. Since the obtained *t*, 2.79, exceeds this value, the investigator can conclude that a real difference does exist between the means on the happiness scale of urban and rural populations.

Chi Square   We have dealt with some statistical methods for testing hypotheses when sample data is parametric. Now it is time to take a step backward and consider the problem of hypothesis testing when data is in more elementary, nonparametric, form. It is possible to test hypotheses about *frequencies* (categorical data), and the appropriate test is called the *chi-square test,* symbolized, "χ^2."

chi-square test

There are two kinds of chi-square tests, one called the test for *goodness of fit,* the other called the test for *independence*. Here we will deal with only the first kind, but the general principle to be outlined below applies to both kinds, the principle of comparing *expected* frequencies with *obtained* frequencies. The student should note that the principle is generally the same as that involved in all hypothesis testing. We always compare expected with obtained, only in parametric tests we compare obtained differences between means with expected ones, while in the chi-square test no such means are available. What is "expected" is, as always, determined by the null hypothesis, which specifies what should happen if only chance factors are at work. Often, but not always, what is expected by chance alone in the chi square is equal frequencies in all groups (in all categories).

Let us say a researcher is interested in a political race. He might select a random sample of 18 persons from a town, and ask them which of three mayoral candidates they support. Let us say that the following *distribution of frequencies* is found.

Candidate A: 1 supporter
Candidate B: 12 supporters
Candidate C: 5 supporters

These are the *obtained frequencies*. Now to determine what frequencies would be expected by chance alone, the researcher would simply multiply the total frequency, N, by the reciprocal of the number of candidates involved, the reciprocal in this case being 1/3. So, *expected frequency* for each cell (*cell* is the technical word for category) would be 18 × 1/3 = 6.

The chi-square table is traditionally set up in the following manner, with expected frequencies entered in small boxes under each category.

A		B		C
	6		6		6
1	———	12	———	5	———

Calculation of Chi Square   The equation for computing this statistic is:

$$\chi^2 = \Sigma \frac{(O_j - E_j)^2}{E_j}$$

This instructs the statistician to:

1. Subtract every expected score from its corresponding obtained score; in the example here that would result in the following calculations,

$$(A)\ 1 - 6 = -5 \quad (B)\ 12 - 6 = 6 \quad (C)\ 5 - 6 = -1$$

2. Square each difference score, and divide each squared difference by the expected frequency associated with it; for the data above,

$$(A)\frac{-5^2}{6} = \frac{25}{6} = 4.17 \quad (B)\frac{6^2}{6} = \frac{36}{6} = 6 \quad (C)\frac{-1^2}{6} = 0.17$$

3. Add each $\frac{(O - E)^2}{E}$ for each cell together; for the example data,

$$4.17 + 6 + 0.17 = 10.34$$

The obtained χ^2-score then must be compared to the one "required" for significance at the predetermined significance level. As usual, an index of degrees of freedom adjusting for number of categories must enter into this comparison. Degrees of freedom for the goodness-of-fit chi-square is computed by subtracting one from the number of categories, symbolized J, in the data. In the example here, $d.f. = J - 1 = 3 - 1 = 2$.

If the researcher has chosen the .01 level of significance, in this example, he would look up required χ^2 under .01, coordinated with 2 degrees of freedom, and he would find that a χ^2 of 9.21 is required. Since his obtained χ^2 is equal to a number exceeding the listed one, the researcher can conclude that the distribution of frequencies he found is significantly different from the distribution that would be expected by chance alone, at the .01 level. This means that if only chance factors are at work, the obtained distribution could have occurred only .01 of the time or less. Thus, the three candidates are not equally preferred.

Sampling Methods

There are three common ways in which a random sample can be drawn.

1. Ordinal selection. With this technique the experimenter lists all members of the population in which he is interested, ordering them on some arbitrary aspect. For example, if he is sampling students from a particular class, he might list all those students alphabetically. Random selection would then proceed by choosing members that fall at certain ordinal positions (which position is chosen depends on how many persons the experimenter wants in the final sample). For example, if the experimenter has a class of 50 and wants 10 subjects in his sample, he might choose every fifth person on the list; if he wants 5 subjects, he might choose every tenth person. This procedure is assumed to comply with the requirements of randomness, because the ordering of the population and decision as to which ordinal positions will be chosen are understood as being completely independent of (unrelated to) the dependent variable being measured.

2. Mechanical randomization. This is the common method of putting all names, physically, on slips of paper placed in a bin, and mechanically drawing out the number of slips corresponding to sample, N. This technique is fine when the population is small, because good mixing of the slips is possible. However, when the population is too large, good mixing is impossible, and systematic advantage might be given to those persons whose slips were dropped in last. This is a purely practical difficulty; if proper mixture can be accomplished, mechanical randomization is perfectly adequate.

3. Utilization of random number table. Tables have been developed, generated by computers, which list randomly selected digits, usually in rows of four or five digits. A portion of such a table appears on p. 803. To use this table the experimenter must make an ordered list of his population members, along any arbitrary variable, just as in the first technique listed here. Then the experimenter opens the random table, and blindly (with eyes closed) points to some point thereon. The experimenter now goes through his population list and assigns one four (or five) digit number to each member, going down the random number list, consecutively, from where he began. Now, if the experimenter wants a sample of 20, he can simply choose the 20 population members whose corresponding random numbers are the largest in comparison to the entire population. In the same way, he could choose the 20 members whose corresponding numbers are smallest. This technique is the best for insuring random selection. It is possible that every tenth person would be chosen; it is possible that the first ten members would be chosen; it is also possible that the last ten members would be chosen. In other words, *any* relation between position on the population list and magnitude of the random number is possible, because *no* relation between the two exists.

Table A1 Areas and Ordinates of the Normal Curve

(1) Z	(2) A Area from Mean to Z	(1) Z	(2) A Area from Mean to Z
0.00	.0000	1.55	.4394
0.05	.0199	1.60	.4452
0.10	.0398	1.65	.4505
0.15	.0596	1.70	.4554
0.20	.0793	1.75	.4599
0.25	.0987	1.80	.4641
0.30	.1179	1.85	.4678
0.35	.1368	1.90	.4713
0.40	.1554	1.95	.4744
0.45	.1736	2.00	.4772
0.50	.1915	2.05	.4798
0.55	.2088	2.10	.4821
0.60	.2257	2.15	.4842
0.65	.2422	2.20	.4861
0.70	.2580	2.25	.4878
0.75	.2734	2.30	.4893
0.80	.2881	2.35	.4906
0.85	.3023	2.40	.4918
0.90	.3159	2.45	.4929
0.95	.3289	2.50	.4938
1.00	.3413	2.55	.4946
1.05	.3531	2.60	.4953
1.10	.3643	2.65	.4960
1.15	.3749	2.70	.4965
1.20	.3849	2.75	.4970
1.25	.3944	2.80	.4974
1.30	.4032	2.85	.4978
1.35	.4115	2.90	.4981
1.40	.4192	2.95	.4984
1.45	.4265	3.00	.4987
1.50	.4332	3.05	.4989

Area under normal curve table as a function of Z. If you know the value of Z (column 1), column 2 indicates the area (or the percentage of scores, if multiplied by 100) that falls between the mean of the distribution and that particular Z score.

Table A2 Table of <u>t</u> Showing Two-tailed Values for Four Levels of Significance

df	.10	.05	.025	.01
1	6.314	12.706	31.821	63.657
2	2.920	4.303	6.965	9.925
3	2.353	3.182	4.541	5.841
4	2.132	2.776	3.747	4.604
5	2.015	2.571	3.365	4.032
6	1.943	2.447	3.143	3.707
7	1.895	2.365	2.998	3.499
8	1.860	2.306	2.896	3.355
9	1.833	2.262	2.821	3.250
10	1.812	2.228	2.764	3.169
11	1.796	2.201	2.718	3.106
12	1.782	2.179	2.681	3.055
13	1.771	2.160	2.650	3.012
14	1.761	2.145	2.624	2.977
15	1.753	2.131	2.602	2.947
16	1.746	2.120	2.583	2.921
17	1.740	2.110	2.567	2.898
18	1.734	2.101	2.552	2.878
19	1.729	2.093	2.539	2.861
20	1.725	2.086	2.528	2.845
21	1.721	2.080	2.518	2.831
22	1.717	2.074	2.508	2.819
23	1.714	2.069	2.500	2.807
24	1.711	2.064	2.492	2.797
25	1.708	2.060	2.485	2.787
26	1.706	2.056	2.479	2.779
27	1.703	2.052	2.473	2.771
28	1.701	2.048	2.467	2.763
29	1.699	2.045	2.462	2.756
30	1.697	2.042	2.457	2.750
∞	1.645	1.960	2.326	2.576

Table A3 Table of χ^2

DEGREES OF FREEDOM df	$P = .99$	.98	.95	.90	.80	.70	.50	.30	.20	.10	.05	.02	.01
1	.000157	.000628	.00393	.0158	.0642	.148	.455	1.074	1.642	2.706	3.841	5.412	6.635
2	.0201	.0404	.103	.211	.446	.713	1.386	2.408	3.219	4.605	5.991	7.824	9.210
3	.115	.185	.352	.584	1.005	1.424	2.366	3.665	4.642	6.251	7.815	9.837	11.341
4	.297	.429	.711	1.064	1.649	2.195	3.357	4.878	5.989	7.779	9.488	11.668	13.277
5	.554	.752	1.145	1.610	2.343	3.000	4.351	6.064	7.289	9.236	11.070	13.388	15.086
6	.872	1.134	1.635	2.204	3.070	3.828	5.348	7.231	8.558	10.645	12.592	15.033	16.812
7	1.239	1.564	2.167	2.833	3.822	4.671	6.346	8.383	9.803	12.017	14.067	16.622	18.475
8	1.646	2.032	2.733	3.490	4.594	5.527	7.344	9.524	11.030	13.362	15.507	18.168	20.090
9	2.088	2.532	3.325	4.168	5.380	6.393	8.343	10.656	12.242	14.684	16.919	19.679	21.666
10	2.558	3.059	3.940	4.865	6.179	7.267	9.342	11.781	13.442	15.987	18.307	21.161	23.209
11	3.053	3.609	4.575	5.578	6.989	8.148	10.341	12.899	14.631	17.275	19.675	22.618	24.725
12	3.571	4.178	5.226	6.304	7.807	9.034	11.340	14.011	15.812	18.549	21.026	24.054	26.217
13	4.107	4.765	5.892	7.042	8.634	9.926	12.340	15.119	16.985	19.812	22.362	25.472	27.688
14	4.660	5.368	6.571	7.790	9.467	10.821	13.339	16.222	18.151	21.064	23.685	26.873	29.141
15	5.229	5.985	7.261	8.547	10.307	11.721	14.339	17.322	19.311	22.307	24.996	28.259	30.578
16	5.812	6.614	7.962	9.312	11.152	12.624	15.338	18.418	20.465	23.542	26.296	29.633	32.000
17	6.408	7.255	8.672	10.085	12.002	13.531	16.338	19.511	21.615	24.769	27.587	30.995	33.409
18	7.015	7.906	9.390	10.865	12.857	14.440	17.338	20.601	22.760	25.989	28.869	32.346	34.805
19	7.633	8.567	10.117	11.651	13.716	15.352	18.338	21.689	23.900	27.204	30.144	33.687	36.191
20	8.260	9.237	10.851	12.443	14.578	16.266	19.337	22.775	25.038	28.412	31.410	35.020	37.566
21	8.897	9.915	11.591	13.240	15.445	17.182	20.337	23.858	26.171	29.615	32.671	36.343	38.932
22	9.542	10.600	12.338	14.041	16.314	18.101	21.337	24.939	27.301	30.813	33.924	37.659	40.289
23	10.196	11.293	13.091	14.848	17.187	19.021	22.337	26.018	28.429	32.007	35.172	38.968	41.638
24	10.856	11.992	13.848	15.659	18.062	19.943	23.337	27.096	29.553	33.196	36.415	40.270	42.980
25	11.524	12.697	14.611	16.473	18.940	20.867	24.337	28.172	30.675	34.382	37.652	41.566	44.314
26	12.198	13.409	15.379	17.292	19.820	21.792	25.336	29.246	31.795	35.563	38.885	42.856	45.642
27	12.879	14.125	16.151	18.114	20.703	22.719	26.336	30.319	32.912	36.741	40.113	44.140	46.963
28	13.565	14.847	16.928	18.939	21.588	23.647	27.336	31.391	34.027	37.916	41.337	45.419	48.278
29	14.256	15.574	17.708	19.768	22.475	24.577	28.336	32.461	35.139	39.087	42.557	46.693	49.588
30	14.953	16.306	18.493	20.599	23.364	25.508	29.336	33.530	36.250	40.256	43.773	47.962	50.892

SOURCE: Table A3 is reprinted from Table III of Fisher: *Statistical Methods for Research Workers*, Oliver & Boyd Ltd., Edinburgh, by permission of the author and publishers.

The degrees of freedom are listed on the left and the levels of significance across the top. The entries are the values of χ^2 that must be exceeded for those degrees of freedom to achieve that level of significance.

Table A4 Table of Random Numbers

	COLUMN NUMBER							
Row	00000 01234	00000 56789	11111 01234	11111 56789	22222 01234	22222 56789	33333 01234	33333 56789
				1st Thousand				
00	23157	54859	01837	25993	76249	70886	95230	36744
01	05545	55043	10537	43508	90611	83744	10962	21343
02	14871	60350	32404	36223	50051	00322	11543	80834
03	38976	74951	94051	75853	78805	90194	32428	71695
04	97312	61718	99755	30870	94251	25841	54882	10513
05	11742	69381	44339	30872	32797	33118	22647	06850
06	43361	28859	11016	45623	93009	00499	43640	74036
07	93806	20478	38268	04491	55751	18932	58475	52571
08	49540	13181	08429	84187	69538	29661	77738	09527
09	36768	72633	37948	21569	41959	68670	45274	83880
10	07092	52392	24627	12067	06558	45344	67338	45320
11	43310	01081	44863	80307	52555	16148	89742	94647
12	61570	06360	06173	63775	63148	95123	35017	46993
13	31352	83799	10779	18941	31579	76448	62584	86919
14	57048	86526	27795	93692	90529	56546	35065	32254
15	09243	44200	68721	07137	30729	75756	09298	27650
16	97957	35018	40894	88329	52230	82521	22532	61587
17	93732	59570	43781	98885	56671	66826	95996	44569
18	72621	11225	00922	68264	35666	59434	71687	58167
19	61020	74418	45371	20794	95917	37866	99536	19378
20	97839	85474	33055	91718	45473	54144	22034	23000
21	89160	97192	22232	90637	35055	45489	88438	16361
22	25966	88220	62871	79265	02823	52862	84919	54883
23	81443	31719	05049	54806	74690	07567	65017	16543
24	11322	54931	42362	34386	08624	97687	46245	23245

SOURCE: Table A4 is reproduced from M. G. Kendall and B. B. Smith. Randomness and random sampling numbers. J. R. statist. Soc., 101 (1938), 147–166, by permission of the Royal Statistical Society.

All the numbers in the table are in random sequence. Therefore, selecting a number anywhere in the table assures you that the next number is independent. Similarly, if you select a two-digit number, the next two-digit number is equally likely to be any number from 00 to 99, and so on.

References

Ackerman, R. C. 1971. *Approaches to beginning reading.* New York: Wiley.

Adams, I. S. 1961. Reduction of cognitive dissonance by evoking consonant information. *Journal of Abnormal and Social Psychology, 62, 74–78.*

Adams, J. A. 1967. *Human memory.* New York: McGraw-Hill.

Adams, J. A., and Montague, W. W. 1967. Retroactive inhibition and natural language mediation. *Journal of Verbal Learning and Verbal Behavior, 6, 528–535.*

Adamson, R. E. 1952. Functional fixedness as related to problem solving: A repetition of three experiments. *Journal of Experimental Psychology, 44, 288–291.*

Ader, R., and Conklin, P. M. 1963. Handling of pregnant rats: Effects on emotionality of their offspring. *Science,* whole no. 3590, 411–412.

Adler, A. 1930. *Praxis and Theorie des Individual Psychologie (Practice and theory of individual psychology),* 4th edition. Munich: Bergmann.

Adolph, E. F. 1941. The internal environment and behavior: Water content. *American Journal of Physiology, 125, 75–86.*

Adorno, T. W., Frenkel-Brunswik, E., Levinson, D. J., and Sanford, R. N. 1950. *The authoritarian personality.* New York: Harper & Row.

Adrian, E. D. 1953. The mechanism of olfactory stimulation in the mammal. *Advances in Science, 9, 417–420.*

Adrian, E. D. 1954. Basis of sensation: Some recent studies of olfaction (Banting memorial lecture). *British Medical Journal, 1, 287–290.*

Alexander, F. 1950. *Psychosomatic medicine.* New York: Norton.

Allport, G. W. 1961. *Pattern and growth in personality.* New York: Holt, Rinehart and Winston.

Allport, G. W., and Odbert, H. J. 1936. Traitnames: A psycho-lexical study. *Psychological Monographs: General and Applied, 47,* (1), whole no. 211.

Allport, G. W., Vernon, P. E., and Lindzey, G. 1960. *Study of values,* 3rd edition. Cambridge, Mass.: Riverside.

Alpert, R., and Haber, R. N. 1960. Anxiety in academic achievement situations. *Journal of Abnormal and Social Psychology, 61, 207–215.*

Amoore, J. E. 1962a. The stereochemical theory of olfaction, I: Identification of the seven primary odours. *Proceedings of the Science Section of the Toilet Goods Association, 37* (suppl.), 1–12.

Amoore, J. E. 1962b. The stereochemical theory of olfaction, II: Elucidation of the stereochemical properties of the olfactory receptor sites. *Proceedings of the Science Section of the Toilet Goods Association.*

Anderson, N. H. 1965. Averaging versus adding as a stimulus combination rule in impression formation. *Journal of Experimental Psychology, 70, 394–400.*

Andersson, B. 1951. The effect and localization of electrical stimulation of certain parts of the brainstem in sheep and goats. *Acta Physiologica Scandinavica, 23, 1–16.*

Andersson, B., and McCann, S. M. 1955. Drinking, antidiuresis and milk ejection from electrical stimulation within the hypothalamus of the goat. *Acta Physiologica Scandinavica, 35, 191–201.*

Archer, E. J. 1960. Re-evaluation of the meaningfulness of all possible CVC trigrams. *Psychological Monographs, 74,* No. 497.

Argyle, M., and Dean, J. 1965. Eye-contact, distance, and affiliation. *Sociometry, 28*(3), 289–304.

Aronson, E. 1969. Some antecedents of personal attraction. In W. J. Arnold and D. Levine (eds.), *Nebraska symposium on motivation,* Vol. 17. Lincoln: University of Nebraska Press, 1970.

Aronson, E., and Linder, D. 1965. Gain and loss of esteem as determinants of interpersonal attractiveness. *Journal of Experimental and Social Psychology, 1* (2), 156–171.

Aronson, E., Willerman, B., and Floyd, J. 1966. The effect of a pratfall on increasing interpersonal attractiveness. *Psychonomic Science, 4* (6), 227–228.

Asch, S. E. 1946. Forming impressions of personality. *Journal of Abnormal and Social Psychology, 41, 258–290.*

Asch, S. E. 1956. Studies of independence and submission to group pressure. I. A minority of one against a unanimous majority. *Psychological Monographs,* Vol. 7, Series No. 416.

Asch, S. E., Black, H., and Hertzman, M. 1940. Studies in the principles of judgments and attitudes. II. Determination of judgments by group and by ego standards. *Journal of Social Psychology,* 12, 433–465.

Aserinsky, E., and Kleitman, N. 1953. Regularly occurring periods of eye mobility and concomitant phenomena during sleep. *Science,* 118, 273–274.

Atkinson, J. W. 1958. *Motives in fantasy, action, and society.* New York: Van Nostrand.

Atkinson, J. W. 1964. *An introduction to motivation.* New York: American Book.

Atkinson, J. W., Heyns, R. W., and Veroff, J. 1954. The effect of experimental arousal of the affiliation motive on thematic apperception. *Journal of Abnormal and Social Psychology,* 49, 405–410.

Atkinson, R. C., and Shiffrin, R. M. 1968. Human memory, a proposed system and its control processes. In K. W. Spence and J. T. Spence (eds.), *The psychology of learning and motivation: Advances in research and theory,* Vol. 2. New York: Academic Press.

Atkinson, R. C., and Shiffrin, R. M. 1971. The control of short-term memory. *Scientific American,* 225 (2), 82–90.

Attneave, F. 1954. Some informational aspects of visual perception. *Psychological Review,* 61, 183–193.

Ayllon, T., and Azrin, N. H. 1965. The measurement and reinforcement of behaviors of psychotics. *Journal of the Experimental Analysis of Behavior,* 8, 357–383.

Ball, J. 1937. The effect of male hormone on the sex behavior of female rats. *Psychological Bulletin,* 34, 725.

Ball, S., and Bogatz, G. 1970. *A summary of the major findings in "The first year of Sesame Street: An evaluation."* Princeton, N.J.: Educational Testing Service.

Ball, W., and Tronick, E. 1971. Infant responses to impending collision: Optical and real. *Science,* 171, 818–820.

Bandt, P. L., Meara, N. M., and Schmidt, L. D. 1974. *A time to learn.* New York: Holt, Rinehart and Winston.

Bandura, A. 1965a. Influence of model's reinforcement contingencies on the acquisition of imitative responses. *Journal of Personality and Social Psychology,* 1, 589–595.

Bandura, A. 1965b. Vicarious processes: A case of no-trial learning. In L. Berkowitz (ed.), *Advances in experimental social psychology,* Vol. II. New York: Academic Press.

Bandura, A. 1969. *Principles of behavior modification.* New York: Holt, Rinehart and Winston.

Bandura, A., Grusec, J. E., and Menlove, F. L. 1967. Vicarious extinction of avoidance behavior. *Journal of Personality and Social Psychology,* 5, 16–23.

Bandura, A., and Menlove, F. L. 1968. Factors determining vicarious extinction of avoidance behavior through symbolic modeling. *Journal of Personality and Social Psychology,* 8, 99–108.

Bandura, A., Ross, D., and Ross, S. A. 1963a. Imitation of film-mediated aggressive models. *Journal of Abnormal and Social Psychology,* 66, 3–11.

Bandura, A., Ross, D., and Ross, S. A. 1963b. Vicarious reinforcement and imitative learning. *Journal of Abnormal and Social Psychology,* 67, 601–607.

Bandura, A., and Walters, R. H. 1963. *Social learning and personality development.* New York: Holt, Rinehart and Winston.

Barber, T. X. 1962. Experimental controls and the phenomenon of "hypnosis." *Journal of Nervous and Mental Diseases,* 134, 493–505.

Barker, R., Dembo, T., and Lewin, K. 1941. Frustration and regression: An experiment with young children. *University of Iowa Studies in Child Welfare,* 18 (1).

Barron, F. 1955. The disposition toward originality. *Journal of Abnormal and Social Psychology,* 31, 478–485.

Bateson, G., Jackson, D. D., Haley, J., and Weakland, J. 1956. Toward a theory of schizophrenia. *Behavioral Science,* 1, 251–264.

Beach, F. A. 1956. Characteristics of masculine "sex drive." *Nebraska symposium on motivation.* Lincoln: University of Nebraska Press.

Beauvoir, S. de. 1949. *The second sex.* New York: Knopf.

Beck, J. 1972. Similarity grouping and peripheral discriminability under uncertainty. *American Journal of Psychology,* 85, 1–20.

Békésy, G. von. 1964. Sweetness produced electrically on the tongue and its relation to taste theories. *Journal of Applied Physiology,* 19, 1105–1113.

Békésy, G. von. 1966. Taste theories and the chemical stimulation of single papillae. *Journal of Applied Physiology,* 21, 1–9.

Belbin, E. 1956. The effects of propaganda on recall, recognition and behavior. *British Journal of Psychology,* 47, 259–270.

Bell, R. Q. 1968. A reinterpretation of the direction of effects in studies of socialization. *Psychological Review,* 75 (2), 81–95.

Bennett, E. L., Diamond, M. C., Krech, D., and Rosenzweig, M. R. 1964. Chemical and anatomical plasticity of the brain. *Science,* 146, 610–619.

Berkeley, G. 1709. An essay toward a new

theory of vision. In C. M. Turbnyne (ed.), *Berkeley's work on vision.* New York: Bobbs-Merrill, 1963.

Berko, J. 1958. The child's learning of English morphology. *Word,* 14, 150–177.

Berkowitz, L., and Cottingham, D. R. 1960. The interest value and relevance of fear-arousing communications. *Journal of Abnormal and Social Psychology,* 60, 37–43.

Berlyne, D. E. 1960. *Conflict, arousal, and curiosity.* New York: McGraw-Hill.

Berlyne, D. E. 1966. Curiosity and exploration. *Science,* 153, 25–33.

Berlyne, D. E., and Slater, J. 1957. Perceptual curiosity, exploratory behavior, and maze learning. *Journal of Comparative and Physiological Psychology,* 50, 228–232.

Bexton, W. H., Heron, W., and Scott, T. H. 1954. Effects of decreased variation in the sensory environment. *Canadian Journal of Psychology,* 8, 70–76.

Birch, H. G. 1945. The relation of previous experience to insightful problem solving. *Journal of Comparative Psychology,* 38, 362–383.

Blaine, G. B. 1967. Sex and the adolescent. *New York State Journal of Medicine,* 67 (14), 1967–1975.

Blodgett, H. C. 1929. The effect of the introduction of reward upon the maze performance of rats. *University of California Publications in Psychology,* 4(8), 113–134.

Boisen, A. T. 1938. Types of Dementia Praecox —a study in psychiatric classification. *Psychiatry,* 1, 233–236.

Boring, E. G. 1942. *Sensation and perception in the history of experimental psychology.* New York: Appleton.

Borke, H. 1971. Interpersonal perception of young children: Egocentrism or empathy? *Developmental Psychology,* 5.

Borko, H. (ed.). 1962. *Computer Applications in the Behavioral Sciences.* Englewood Cliffs, N.J.: Prentice-Hall.

Bourne, L. E., and Archer, E. J. 1956. Time continuously on target as a function of distribution of practice. *Journal of Experimental Psychology,* 51, 25–33.

Bourne, L. E., and Ekstrand, B. 1973. *Psychology: Its principles and meanings.* New York: Dryden.

Bousfield, W. A. 1953. The occurrence of clustering in the recall of randomly arranged associates. *Journal of Genetic Psychology,* 49, 229–240.

Bousfield, W. A., Cohen, B. H., and Whitmarsh, G. A. 1958. Associative clustering in the recall of different taxonomic frequencies of occurrence. *Psychological Report,* 4, 39–44.

Bower, G. H. 1969. Mental imagery and associative learning. *Fifth Annual Symposium on Cognition.* Pittsburgh, Pa.: Carnegie-Mellon University.

Bower, G. H. 1970. Organizational factors in memory. *Journal of Cognitive Psychology,* 1, 18–46.

Bower, T. G. R. 1965. Stimulus variables determining space perception in infants. *Science,* 149, 88–89.

Bower, T. G. R., Broughton, J. M., and Moore, M. K. 1970. Infant responses to approaching objects: An indicator of response to distal variables. *Perception and Psychophysics,* 9, 193–196.

Bowlby, J. 1958. The nature of the child's tie to his mother. *International Journal of Psychoanalysis,* 39, 350–373.

Bowlby, J. 1960. Separation anxiety. *International Journal of Psychoanalysis,* 41, 89–113.

Bradway, K. P., and Thompson, C. W. 1962. Intelligence at adulthood: A twenty-five year follow-up. *Journal of Education Psychology,* 53, 1–14.

Braine, M. D. S. 1963. The ontogeny of English phrase structure: The first phase. *Language,* 39, 1–13.

Brehm, J. W. 1960. A dissonance analysis of attitude-discrepant behavior. In M. J. Rosenberg *et al.: Attitude organization and change.* Yale Studies in Attitude Communication, Volume III. New Haven: Yale University Press. Pp. 164–197.

Brennan, W. M., Ames, E. W., and Moore, E. W. 1966. Age differences in infants' attention to patterns of different complexities. *Science,* 151, 354–356.

Brindley, G. S., and Merton, P. A. 1960. The absence of position sense in the human eye. *Journal of Physiology,* 153, 127–130.

Broadbent, D. E. 1958. *Perception and communication.* London: Pergamon.

Brody, N. 1972. *Personality: Research and theory.* New York: Academic Press.

Bronfenbrenner, U. 1958. The study of identification through interpersonal perception. In R. Taguiri and L. Petrullo (eds.), *Person perception and interpersonal behavior.* Stanford, Calif.: Stanford University Press. Pp. 110–130.

Bronfenbrenner, U. 1970. Reaction to social pressure from adults versus peers among Soviet day school and boarding school pupils in the perspective of an American sample. *Journal of Personality and Social Psychology,* 15 (3), 179–189.

Brown, F. A., Jr. 1972. The "clocks" timing biological rhythms. *American Scientist,* 60, 756–766.

Brown, J. S. 1948. Gradients of approach and avoidance responses and their relation to level of motivation. *Journal of Comparative and Physiological Psychology*, 41, 450–465.

Brown, R. 1970. The first sentences of child and chimpanzee. In R. Brown (ed.), *Psycholinguistics*. New York: Macmillan.

Brown, R. W., and McNeill, D. 1966. The "tip-of-the-tongue" phenomenon. *Journal of Verbal Learning and Verbal Behavior*, 5, 325–327.

Brown, R., and Bellugi, U. 1964. Three processes in the child's acquisition of syntax. In M. E. Lenacherg (ed.), *New directions in the study of language*. Cambridge, Mass.: MIT Press.

Brown, R., and Hanlon, C. 1970. Derivational complexity and order of acquisition in child speech. In M. J. R. Hayes (ed.), *Cognition and the development of language*. New York: Wiley.

Bruce, R. W. 1933. Conditions of transfer of training. *Journal of Experimental Psychology*, 16, 343–361.

Bruner, J. 1968. *Processes of cognitive growth: Infancy*. Worcester, Mass.: Clark University Press.

Bugelski, B. R. 1962. Presentation time, total time, and mediation in paired-associate learning. *Journal of Experimental Psychology*, 63, 409–412.

Bugelski, R. 1938. Extinction with and without subgoal reinforcement. *Journal of Comparative Physiological Psychology*, 26, 121–134.

Burtt, H. E. 1941. An experimental study of early childhood memory. *Journal of Genetic Psychology*, 58, 435–439.

Butler, R. A. 1954. Curiosity in monkeys. *Scientific American*, 190 (2), 70–75.

Byrne, D. 1965. Parental antecedents of authoritarianism. *Journal of Personality and Social Psychology*, 1, 369–373.

Campbell, B. A., and Sheffield, F. D. 1953. Relation of random activity to food deprivation. *Journal of Comparative and Physiological Psychology*, 46, 320–322.

Campbell, D. P. 1963. A cross-sectional and longitudinal study of scholastic abilities over twenty-five years. *Journal of Counseling Psychology*, 12, 55–61.

Cannon, W. B. 1927. The James-Lange theory of emotions: A critical examination and an alternative theory. *American Journal of Psychology*, 39, 106–124.

Cannon, W. B. 1929. *Bodily changes in pain, hunger, fear and rage*, 2nd edition. New York: Appleton.

Cantril, H. 1944. *Gauging public opinion*. Princeton, N.J.: Princeton University Press.

Carmichael, L., Hogen, H. P., and Walter, A. A. 1932. An experimental study of the effect of language on the reproduction of visually perceived form. *Journal of Experimental Psychology*, 15, 73–86.

Cattell, R. B. 1950. *Personality: A systematic theoretical and factual study*. New York: McGraw-Hill.

Cattell, R. B. 1946. Description and measurement of personality. Yonkers, N.Y.: World Book Company.

Cattell, R. B. 1965. *The scientific analysis of personality*. Baltimore: Penguin.

Cermak, L. S. 1972. *Human memory*. New York: Ronald.

Chapanis, N. P., and Chapanis, A. 1964. Cognitive dissonance: Five years later. *Psychological Bulletin*, 61, 1–22.

Chaplin, J. P., and Krawiec, T. S. 1968. *Systems and theories of psychology*. New York: Holt, Rinehart and Winston.

Cherry, E. C. 1953. Some experiments on the recognition of speech with one and with two ears. *Journal of the Acoustical Society of America*, 25, 975–979.

Cherry, R., and Cherry, L. 1974. Showing the clock of age. *New York Times Magazine*.

Chomsky, N. 1957. *Syntactic structures*. The Hague: Mouton.

Chomsky, N. 1964. Current issues in linguistic theory. In J. A. Fodor and J. J. Katz (eds.), *The structure of language: Reading in the philosophy of language*. Englewood Cliffs, N.J.: Prentice-Hall.

Chomsky, N., and Halle, M. 1968. *The sound pattern of English*. New York: Harper & Row.

Chomsky, C. S. 1969. *The acquisition of syntax in children from five to ten*. Cambridge, Mass.: MIT Press.

Christie, R., and Geis, F. L. (eds.). 1970. *Studies in Machiavellianism*. New York: Academic Press.

Cleckley, H. 1941. *The mask of sanity*. St. Louis: Mosby.

Cohen, A. R. 1961. Cognitive tuning as a factor affecting impression formation. *Journal of Personality*, 29, 235–245.

Cohen, P., Whitmyre, J. W., and Funk, W. H. 1960. Effect of group cohesion and training upon creative thinking. *Journal of Applied Psychology*, 44, 319–322.

Cohen, S. I., Silverman, A. J., and Shmavonian, B. 1961. Problems in isolation studies. In P. Solomon et al. (eds.), *Sensory deprivation*. Cambridge, Mass.: Harvard University Press. Pp. 114–129.

Coleman, J. S. 1961. *The adolescent society*. New York: Free Press.

Collins, A., and Quillian, M. R. 1969. Retrieval time from semantic memory. *Journal of Verbal Learning and Verbal Behavior, 8,* 240–247.

Conrad, R. 1962. An association between memory errors due to acoustic masking of speech. *Nature, 193,* 1314–1315.

Conrad, R. 1964. Acoustic confusions in immediate memory. *British Journal of Psychology, 55,* 75–84.

Converse, P. E., and Schuman, H. 1970. "Silent majorities" and the Vietnam war. *Scientific American, 222,* 17–25.

Cooper, R., and Zubek, J. 1958. Effects of enriched and restricted early environments on the learning ability of bright and dull rats. *Canadian Journal of Psychology, 12,* 159–164.

Cornsweet, T. N. 1970. *Visual perception.* New York: Academic Press.

Corso, J. F. 1967. *The experimental psychology of sensory behavior.* New York: Holt, Rinehart and Winston.

Cowles, J. T. 1937. Food tokens as incentives for learning by chimpanzees. *Comparative Psychological Monographs,* 14(71).

Cox, C. M. 1926. *Genetic studies of genius. Vol. II. The early mental traits of three hundred geniuses.* Stanford, Calif.: Stanford University Press.

Crespi, L. P. 1942. Quantitative variation of incentive and performance in the white rat. *American Journal of Psychology, 55,* 467–517.

Crocker, E. C. 1947. Odor in flavor. *American Perfumer, 50,* 164–165.

Cronbach, L. J. 1950. Further evaluation on response sets and test design. *Educational and Psychological Measurements, 10,* 3–31.

Cronbach, L. J. 1970. *Essentials of psychological testing,* 3rd edition. New York: Harper & Row.

Crowne, D. P., and Marlowe, D. 1966. A new scale of social desirability independent of psychopathology. *Journal of Consulting Psychology, 24,* 349–354.

Cumming, J., and Cumming, E. 1966. *Ego and milieu: Theory and practice of environmental therapy.* New York: Atherton.

Dallman, M., Rouch, R., Chang, L. Y. C., and De Boer, J. J. 1974. *The teaching of reading,* 4th edition. New York: Holt, Rinehart and Winston.

Davidson, H. H., and Lang, G. 1960. Children's perceptions of their teacher's feelings towards them related to self-perception, school achievement, and behavior. *Journal of Experimental Education, 29,* 107–118.

Davis, H. 1957. In C. M. Harris (ed.), *Handbook of noise control.* New York: McGraw-Hill. Chap. 4.

Davis, H. 1962. The problem of consciousness. In K. E. Schaefer (ed.), *Environmental effects on consciousness.* Proceedings of the First International Symposium on Submarine and Space Medicine. New York: Macmillan. Pp. 61–63.

Davis, H. et al. 1953. Acoustic trauma in the guinea pig. *Journal of the Acoustic Society of America, 25,* 1180.

Davis, H., and Silverman, S. R. 1960. *Hearing and deafness.* New York: Holt, Rinehart and Winston.

Deese, H., and Hulse, S. H. 1967. *The psychology of learning,* 3rd edition. New York: McGraw-Hill.

Deikman, A. J. 1963. Experimental meditation. *Journal of Nervous and Mental Diseases, 136,* 329–373.

Deikman, A. J. 1966. A de-automatization and the mystic experience. *Psychiatry, 29,* 329–343.

Dellas, M., and Gaier, E. L. 1970. Identification of creativity: The individual. *Psychological Bulletin, 73* (1), 55–73.

Dement, W. C. 1969. A new look at the third state of existence. *Stanford Medical Digest, 8,* 2–8.

Dement, W. 1960. The effect of dream deprivation. *Science, 131,* 1705–1707.

Dement, W. C., Greenberg, S. and Klein, R. 1966. The effect of partial REM sleep deprivation and delayed recovery. *Journal of Psychiatric Research, 4,* 141–152.

Dement, W., and Kleitman, N. 1957. The relation of eye movements during sleep to dream activity: An objective method for the study of dreaming. *Journal of Experimental Psychology, 53,* 339–346.

Dennis, W. 1942. The performance of Hopi children on the Goodenough Draw-a-Man test. *Journal of Comparative Psychology, 34,* 341–348.

Dennis, W. 1960. Causes of retardation among institutional children: Iran. *Journal of Genetic Psychology, 96,* 47–59.

Dennis, W., and Najarian, P. 1957. Infant development under environmental handicap. *Psychological Monographs, 71,* whole no. 436.

Deutsch, M. 1969. Happenings on the way back to the forum: Social science, I.Q., and race differences revisited. *Harvard Education Review, 39,* 1–35.

Di Cara, L. V., and Miller, N. E. 1968. Changes in heart rate instrumentally learned by curarized rats as avoidance responses. *Journal of Comparative and Physiological Psychology, 65,* 8–12.

Digman, J. M. 1959. Growth of a motor skill as a function of distribution of practice. *Journal of Experimental Psychology,* 57, 310–316.

Ditchburn, R. W. 1955. Eye movements in relation to retinal action. *Optica acta,* 1.

Dollard, J., and Miller, N. E. 1950. *Personality and psychotherapy.* New York: McGraw-Hill.

Doob, A. N. 1964. Eidetic images among the Ibo. *Ethnology,* 3, 357–363.

Douvan, E., and Gold, M. 1966. Modal patterns in American adolescence. In M. L. Hoffman and L. W. Hoffman (eds.), *Review of child development research,* Vol. II. New York: Russell Sage.

Dowling, J. E., and Boycott, B. B. 1966. Organization of the primate retina: Electron microscopy. *Proceedings of the Royal Society,* Series B, 166.

Dunbar, H. F. 1935. *Emotions and bodily changes.* New York: Columbia University Press.

Dunbar, H. F. 1943. *Psychosomatic diagnosis.* New York: Hoeber-Harper.

Düncker, K. 1945. On problem-solving. Trans. by L. S. Lees. *Psychological Monographs,* 58 (5).

Dunnette, M. D., Campbell, J., and Jaastadt, K. 1963. The effects of group participation on brainstorming effectiveness for two industrial samples. *Journal of Applied Psychology,* 47, 30–37.

Ebbinghaus, H. 1885. *Über das Gedachtnis: Untersuchungen zur experimentalen Psychologie.* Leipzig: Duncker und Humbolt.

Ebert, J. D., Loewy, A. G., Miller, R. S., and Schneiderman, H. A. 1973. *Biology.* New York: Holt, Rinehart and Winston.

Edfelt, A. W. 1960. *Silent speech and silent reading.* Chicago: University of Chicago Press.

Edwards, A. L. 1957. *The social desirability variable in personality assessment and research.* New York: Dryden.

Eibl-Eibesfeldt, I. 1961. The fighting behavior of animals. *Scientific American,* 205 (6), 112–122.

Elkind, D. 1967–8. Cognitive structure and adolescent experience. *Adolescence,* 2 (8), 427–434.

Elliot, J. M. 1964. Measuring creative ability in public relations and in advertising work. In C. Taylor (ed.), *Widening horizons in creativity.* New York: Wiley. Pp. 396–400.

Elliott, M. H. 1929. The effect of appropriateness of reward and of complex incentives on maze performance. *University of California Publications in Psychology,* 4, 91–98.

Engel, B. T. 1973. Clinical applications of operant conditioning techniques in the control of cardiac arrhythmias. Part 1. *Seminars in Psychiatry,* 5 (4).

Engen, T. 1960. Effect of practice and instruction on olfactory threshold. *Perceptual and Motor Skills,* 10, 195–198.

Engen, T. 1961. Direct scaling of odor intensity. *Reports from the psychological laboratories, The University of Stockholm,* 106.

Engen, T. 1962. The psychological similarity of the odors of the aliphatic alcohols. *Reports from the psychological laboratories, The University of Stockholm,* 127.

Engen, T. 1964. Psychophysical scaling of odor intensity and quality. *Annual of the New York Academy of Science,* 116, 504–516.

Epstein, W., Rock, I., and Zuckerman, C. B. 1960. Meaning and familiarity in verbal learning. *Psychological Monographs,* 74 (491).

Erdelyi, M. H. 1974. A new look at the new look: Perceptual defense and vigilance. *Psychological Review,* 81 (1), 1–25.

Eriksen, C. W. 1958. Unconscious processes. In M. R. Jones (ed.), *Nebraska symposium on motivation.* Lincoln: University of Nebraska Press.

Erikson, E. H. 1950. *Childhood and society.* New York: Norton.

Erikson, E. H. 1963. *Childhood and society,* 2nd edition. New York: Norton.

Erikson, M. 1956. Deep hypnosis and its induction. In Le Cron (ed.), *Experimental hypnosis.* New York: Macmillan. Pp. 71–112.

Ervin, S. 1964. Imitation and structural change in children's language. In E. Lenneberg (ed.), *New directions in the study of language.* Cambridge, Mass.: MIT Press.

Exline, R. V. 1963. Explorations in the process of person perception: Visual interaction in relation to competition, sex and need for affiliation. *Journal of Personality,* 31 (1), 1–20.

Eysenck, H. J. 1952. The effects of psychotherapy: An evaluation. *Journal of Consulting Psychology,* 16, 319–324.

Eysenck, H. J. 1957. *The dynamics of anxiety and hysteria.* London: Routledge.

Eysenck, H. J. 1960. *Behavior therapy and the neuroses.* Elmsford, N.Y.: Pergamon.

Eysenck, H. J. 1960. The effects of psychotherapy. In H. J. Eysenck (ed.), *Handbook of abnormal psychology.* London: Pitman Medical Publishing Co.

Eysenck, H. J. 1967. *The biological basis of personality.* Springfield, Ill.: Charles C Thomas.

Eysenck, H. J., and Rachman, S. 1965. *The causes and cures of neurosis: An intoduction to modern behavior therapy based on learning theory and the principles of conditioning.* San Diego: Knapp.

Fairweather, G. W., Sanders, D. H., Maynard, R. F., and Corssler, D. L. 1969. *Community life for the mentally ill: Alternative to institutional care.* Chicago: Aldine.

Feather, N. T. 1959. Subjective probability and decision under uncertainty. *Psychological Review,* 66, 150–164.

Feshbach, S. 1955. The drive-reducing function of fantasy behavior. *Journal of Abnormal and Social Psychology,* 50, 3–11.

Feshbach, S. 1961. The stimulating versus cathartic effects of a vicarious aggressive activity. *Journal of Abnormal and Social Psychology,* 63, 381–385.

Festinger, L. 1954. A theory of social comparison processes. *Human Relations,* 7, 117–140.

Festinger, L. 1957. *A theory of cognitive dissonance.* New York: Harper & Row.

Festinger, L., and Carlsmith, J. M. 1959. Cognitive consequences of forced compliance. *Journal of Abnormal and Social Psychology,* 58, 203–210.

Festinger, L., Riecken, H. W., and Schachter, S. 1956. *When prophecy fails.* Minneapolis: University of Minnesota Press.

Festinger, L., Schachter, S., and Back, K. 1950. *Social pressure in informal groups.* New York: Harper & Row.

Fitts, P. M. 1962. Factors in complex skill training. In R. Glaser (ed.), *Training research and education.* Pittsburgh: University of Pittsburgh Press.

Fitts, P. M. 1964. Perceptual-motor skill learning. In A. W. Melton (ed.), *Categories of human learning.* New York: Academic Press.

Flanagan, J. L. 1965. *Speech analysis, synthesis and perception.* New York: Academic Press.

Flanders, J. P. 1968. A review of research on imitative behavior. *Psychological Bulletin,* 69, 316–337.

Flavell, J. H. 1963. *The developmental psychology of Jean Piaget.* Princeton, N.J.: Van Nostrand.

Flavell, J. H., Beach, D. R., and Chinsky, J. M. 1966. Spontaneous verbal rehearsal in a memory task as a function of age. *Child Development,* 37.

Fleishman, E. 1962. The description and prediction of perceptual-motor learning. In R. Glaser (ed.), *Training Research and Education.* Pittsburgh: University of Pittsburgh Press.

Fleishman, E. A., and Parker, J. F. 1962. Factors in the retention and relearning of perceptual-motor skill. *Journal of Experimental Psychology,* 64, 215–226.

Ford, C. S., and Beach, F. A. 1951. *Patterns of sexual behavior.* New York: Harper & Row.

Foucault, M. 1965. *Madness and civilization.* New York: Pantheon.

Fraisse, P., Siffre, M., Oleron, G., and Zuili, N. 1968. Le rhythme veille-sommeil et l'estimation du tempo, in *Cycles biologiques et psychiatriques,* Symposium Bel Air. Paris: Mosson & Co. Pp. 257–265.

Freedman, J. L. 1965. Long-term behavioral effects of cognitive dissonance. *Journal of Experimental Social Psychology,* 1, 145–155.

Freedman, J. L., Carlsmith, J. M., and Sears, D. O. 1970. *Social psychology.* Englewood Cliffs, N.J.: Prentice-Hall.

Freedman, J. L., and Fraser, S. C. 1966. Compliance without pressure: The foot-in-the-door technique. *Journal of Personality and Social Psychology,* 4, 195–202.

Freedman, J. L., and Sears, D. 1965. Selective exposure. In L. Berkowitz (ed.), *Advances in experimental social psychology,* Vol. 2. New York: Academic Press.

Frenkel-Brunswik, E. 1948. Intolerance of ambiguity as an emotional and perceptual personality variable. *Journal of Personality,* 18, 108–143.

Frenkel-Brunswik, E. 1954. Further explorations by a contributor to *The authoritarian personality.* In C. Jahoda, and M. Jahoda (eds.), *Studies in the scope and method of the authoritarian personality.* New York: Free Press.

Frenkel-Brunswik, E., and Sanford, R. N. 1945. Some personality factors in anti-Semitism. *Journal of Psychology,* 20, 271–291.

Freud, S. 1915. *The psychopathology of everyday life.* Trans. from the 4th edition. New York: Macmillan.

Freud, S. 1923. *The interpretation of dreams.* Trans. from the 3rd edition. New York: Macmillan.

Freud, S. 1949. *Collected papers.* New York: Basic Books.

Frey, M. von, and Kiesow, F. 1899. Über die function der Tastkörperchen. *Zeitschrift fuer Psychologie,* 20, 126–263.

Fromm, E. 1956. *The art of loving.* New York: Harper & Row.

Furth, H. G. 1971. Linguistic deficiency and thinking: Research with deaf subjects, 1964–1969. *Psychological Bulletin,* 76(1).

Galanter, E. 1962. Contemporary psychophysics. In R. Brown, E. Galanter, E. H. Hess, and G. Mandler (eds.), *New Directions in Psychology.* New York: Holt, Rinehart and Winston.

Galton, F. 1869. *Hereditary genius.* New York: Harcourt (published in 1964).

Gardner, R. A., and Gardner, B. T. 1969. Teaching sign language to a chimpanzee. *Science,* 165, 644–672.

Gergen, K. J. 1972. Multiple identity: The healthy, happy human being wears many masks. *Psychology Today, 5*, 31–35, 64–66.

Gesell, A. L. 1928. *Infancy and human growth.* New York: Macmillan.

Gesell, A. L. 1940. *The first five years of life.* New York: Harper & Row.

Getzels, J. W., and Jackson, P. W. 1962. *Creativity and intelligence: Explorations with gifted children.* New York: Wiley.

Ghiselin, B. 1952. *The creative process: A symposium.* Berkeley, Calif.: University of California Press.

Gibson, E. J. 1969. *Principles of perceptual learning and development.* New York: Appleton.

Gibson, J. J. 1950. *The perception of the visual world.* Boston: Houghton Mifflin.

Gibson, J. J. 1966. *The senses considered as perceptual systems.* Boston: Houghton Mifflin.

Ginott, H. 1965. *Between parent and child.* New York: Macmillan.

Glucksberg, S., and King, J. 1967. Motivated forgetting mediated by implicit verbal chaining: A laboratory analog of repression. *Science, 158*, 517–519.

Goldberger, L., and Holt, R. 1961. Studies on the effects of perceptual alteration. *USAF ASD Technical Report,* No. 61–416.

Goldhamer, H., and Marshall, A. W. 1953. *Psychosis and civilization.* New York: Free Press.

Goldstein, K. 1939. *The organism.* New York: American Book.

Gollin, E. S. 1954. Forming impressions of personality. *Journal of Personality, 23*, 65–76.

Goltz, K. 1892. Der Hund ohne Grosshirn Pfug. *Archiv. Ges. Physiol., 51*, 570–614. In S. P. Grossman (ed.), *A Textbook of Physiological Psychology.* New York: Wiley, 1967. p. 518.

Gordon, E. W. 1969. Introduction. In J. Hellmuth (ed.), *Disadvantaged child,* Vol. II. New York: Brunner-Mazel. Pp. 8–14.

Gordon, W. J. J. 1961. *Synetics: The development of creative capacity.* New York: Harper & Row.

Gottesman, I. J. 1963. Heritability of personality. *Psychological Monographs, 77*, 1–21.

Gottesman, I. J., and Shields, J. 1966. Contributions of twin studies to perspectives on schizophrenia. In B. Maher (ed.), *Progress in experimental personality research,* Vol. 3. New York: Academic Press.

Gough, H. G. 1962. Clinical versus statistical prediction in psychology. In L. Postman (ed.), *Psychology in the making.* New York: Knopf.

Greenstein, F. I. 1960. The benevolent leader: Children's images of political authority. *American Political Science Review, 54*, 934–943.

Greenstein, J. M. 1966. Father characteristics and sex typing. *Journal of Personality and Social Psychology, 3*, 271–277.

Grey, J. A., and Wedderburn, A. A. I. 1960. Grouping strategies with simultaneous stimuli. *Quarterly Journal of Experimental Psychology, 12*, 180–184.

Guilford, J. P. 1957. Creative abilities in the arts. *Psychological Review, 64*, 110–118.

Guilford, J. P. 1967. *Nature of human intelligence.* New York: McGraw-Hill.

Guthrie, E. R. 1952. *The psychology of learning,* rev. ed. New York: Harper & Row.

Guthrie, G. 1970. The shuttlebox of subsistence attitudes. Paper delivered at the ONR-Maryland Symposium on Attitudes, Conflict, and Social Change, May.

Guttman, L. 1944. A basis for scaling qualitative data. *American Sociological Review, 9*, 139–150.

Haaf, R. A., and Bell, R. Q. 1967. A facial dimension in visual discrimination by human infants. *Child Development, 38*, 893–899.

Haan, N., Smith, M., and Block, J. 1968. Moral reasoning of young adults: Political-social behavior, family background, and personality correlates. *Journal of Personality and Social Psychology, 10*, 183–201.

Haan, N., and Block, J. 1969. *Further studies in the relationship between activism and morality: I. The protest of pure and mixed moral stages.* Berkeley, Calif.: Institute of Human Development.

Haase, W. 1964. The role of socioeconomic class and examiner class in examiner bias. In F. Riessman, J. Cohen, and A. Pearl (eds.), *Mental health of the poor.* New York: Free Press. Pp. 241–247.

Haber, R. N., and Erdelyi, M. H. 1967. Emergence and recovery of initially unavailable perceptual material. *Journal of Verbal Learning and Verbal Behavior, 6*, 618–628.

Haber, R. N., and Haber, R. B. 1964. Eidetic imagery: I. Frequency. *Perceptual and Motor Skills, 19*, 131–138.

Haber, R. N., and Standing, L. G. 1970. Direct measures of short-term visual storage. *Quarterly Journal of Experimental Psychology,* 43–54.

Haber, R. N., and Hershenson, M. 1973. *The psychology of visual perception.* New York: Holt, Rinehart and Winston.

Haimowitz, M. L., and Haimowitz, R. H. 1960. *Human development: Selected readings.* New York: Crowell.

Halberg, F. 1959. Physiologic 24-hour periodicity, general and procedural conditions with reference to the adrenal cycle. *Z. f. Vitomin-Hormon-and Ferment-forschung,* 10, 225–296.

Hall, J. F. 1954. Learning as a function of word-frequency. *American Journal of Psychology,* 67, 138–140.

Hall, J. F. 1971. *Verbal learning and retention,* Philadelphia: Lippincott.

Hanson, N. R. 1958. *Patterns of discovery.* New York: Cambridge University Press.

Harlow, H., and Harlow, M. K. 1966. Learning to love. *American Scientist,* 54(3), 244–272.

Harlow, H., and Zimmermann, R. R. 1959. Affectional responses in the infant monkey. *Science,* 130, 421–432.

Harlow, J. F., Harlow, M. K., and Meyer, D. R. 1950. Learning motivated by a manipulation drive. *Journal of Experimental Psychology,* 40, 228–234.

Harper, R. 1966. On odour classification. *Journal of Food Technology,* 1, 167–176.

Hartline, H. K., and Ratliff, F. 1957. Inhibitory interaction of receptor units in the eye of Limulus. *Journal of General Physiology,* 40, 357–376.

Heber, R. (ed.). 1959. A manual on terminology and classification in mental retardation. Monograph, *American Journal of Mental Deficiency,* 64 (2).

Hecht, S. 1934. Vision: II. The nature of the photoreceptor process. In C. Murchison (ed.), *A handbook of general experimental psychology.* Worcester, Mass.: Clark University Press. Pp. 704–828.

Heidbreder, E. 1947. The attainment of concepts: III. The process. *Journal of Psychology,* 24, 93–138.

Heist, P. 1965. Intellect and commitment: The faces of discontent. In O. W. Knorr and J. W. Minter (eds.), *Order and freedom on the campus: The rights and responsibilities of faculty and students.* Boulder, Colo.: Western Interstate Commission for Higher Education.

Held, R. 1965. Plasticity in sensory-motor systems. *Scientific American,* 211, 84–94.

Held, R. and Freedman, S. 1963. Plasticity in human sensorimotor control. *Science,* 142, 455–462.

Heron, W. 1961. Cognitive and physiological effects of perceptual isolation. In P. Solomon *et al.* (eds.), *Sensory deprivation.* Cambridge, Mass.: Harvard University Press. Pp. 6–33.

Hick, W. E. 1952. On the rate of gain of information. *Quarterly Journal of Experimental Psychology,* 4, 11–26.

Hilgard, E. R. 1965. *Hypnotic susceptibility.* New York: Harcourt.

Hilgard, E. R., Atkinson, R. C., and Atkinson, R. L. 1971. *Introduction to psychology,* 5th edition. New York: Harcourt.

Hilgard, E. R., Sait, E. M., and Magret, G. A. 1940. Level of aspiration as affected by relative standing in an experimental social group. *Journal of Experimental Psychology,* 27, 411–421.

Hill, W. F. 1956. Activity as an autonomous drive. *Journal of Comparative and Physiological Psychology,* 49, 15–19.

Hillman, B., Hunter, W. S., and Kimble, G. H. 1953. The effect of drive level on the maze performance of the white rat. *Journal of Comparative and Physiological Psychology,* 46, 87–89.

Hochberg, J. 1964. *Perception.* Englewood Cliffs, N.J.: Prentice-Hall.

Hochberg, J. 1968. In the mind's eye. In R. N. Haber (ed.), *Contemporary theory and research in visual perception.* New York: Holt, Rinehart and Winston. Pp. 303–331.

Hochberg, J. 1970. Attention, organization, and consciousness. In D. I. Mostofsky (ed.), *Attention: Contemporary theory and analysis.* New York: Appleton. Pp. 99–124.

Hochberg, J., and McAlister, E. 1953. A quantitative approach to figural "goodness." *Journal of Experimental Psychology,* 46, 361–364.

Hochberg, J., Triebel, W., and Seaman, G. 1951. Color adaptation under conditions of homogenous stimulation (Ganzfeld). *Journal of Experimental Psychology,* 41, 153–159.

Hoffman, M. L. 1954. Moral development. In L. Carmichael (ed.), *Manual of child psychology,* 2nd edition. New York: Wiley.

Hoffman, M. L. 1970. Moral development. In P. H. Mussen (ed.), *Carmichael's manual of child psychology,* Vol. II. New York: Wiley. Pp. 261–359.

Hoffman, M. L., and Saltzstein, H. D. 1967. Parent discipline and the child's moral development. *Journal of Personality and Social Psychology,* 5, 45–57.

Holmes, T. H., and Rahe, R. H. 1967. The social readjustment rating scale. *Journal of Psychosomatic Research,* 11, 213–218.

Holst, E. von. 1954. Relations between the central nervous system and the peripheral organs. *British Journal of Animal Behavior,* 2, 89–94.

Hood, W. R., and Sherif, M. 1962. Verbal report and judgment of an unstructured stimulus. *Journal of Psychology,* 54 (1), 121–130.

Horney, K. 1937. *The neurotic personality of our time.* London: Routledge.

Housman, A. E. 1933. *The name and nature of poetry.* New York: Macmillan.

Hovland, C. I. 1937. The generalization of conditioned responses: I. The sensory generalization of conditioned responses with varying frequencies of tone. *Journal of General Psychology,* 17, 125–148.

Howes, D. H., and Solomon, R. L. 1950. A note on McGinnies' "Emotionality and perceptual defense." *Psychological Review,* 57, 229–240.

Hsia, Y., and Graham, C. H. 1957. Spectral luminosity curves of protanopic, deutanopic, and normal subjects. *Proceedings of the National Academy of Science,* 43, 1011–1019.

Hubel, D. H., and Wiesel, T. N. 1962. Receptive fields, binocular interaction and functional architecture in the cat's visual cortex. *Journal of Physiology,* 160, 106–154.

Hunt, J. McV. 1969. Has compensatory education failed? Has it been attempted? *Harvard Educational Review,* Reprint Series 2, 130–152.

Jackson, C. M. (ed.). 1925. *Morris' Human Anatomy.* New York: McGraw-Hill.

Jacobson, E. 1932. Electrophysiology of mental activities. *American Journal of Psychology,* 44, 677–694.

Jakobson, R. 1968. *Child language, aphasia, and general sound laws.* Trans. by A. Keiler. The Hague: Mouton.

James, W. 1884. What is an emotion? *Mind,* 9, 188–205.

James, W. 1890. *Principles of psychology.* New York: Holt.

James, W. 1929. *The varieties of religious experience.* New York: Modern Library.

Janis, I. L. 1958. *Psychological stress.* New York: Wiley.

Janis, I. L., and Feshbach, S. 1953. Effects of fear-arousing communications. *Journal of Abnormal and Social Psychology,* 48, 78–92.

Janis, I. L. 1963. *Psychological stress.* New York: Wiley.

Janis, I. L., and Terwilliger, R. F. 1962. An experimetal study of psychological resistances to fear-arousing communications. *Journal of Abnormal and Social Psychology,* 65, 403–410.

Jarvik, M. E. 1967. The psychopharmalogical revolution. *Psychology Today,* 1 (1), 51–59.

Jenkins, J. G., and Dallenbach, K. M. 1924. Oblivescence during sleep and waking. *American Journal of Psychology,* 35, 605–612.

Jenkins, J. J. 1963. Mediated associates, paradigms and situations. In C. N. Cofer and B. S. Musgrove (eds.), *Verbal behavior and learning.* New York: McGraw-Hill.

Jensen, A. R. 1969. How much can we boost I.Q. and scholastic achievement? *Harvard Educational Review,* 31, 1–123.

Johnson, W. H., Delanney, L. E., Cole, T. A., and Brooks, A. C. 1972. *Biology,* 4th edition. New York: Holt, Rinehart and Winston.

Jouvet, M., and Delorme, F. 1965. Locus coeruleus et sommeil paradoxal. *Comptes-rendus de La Société Biologique,* p. 895.

Julesz, B. 1960. Binocular depth perception of computer-generated patterns. *The Bell System Technological Journal,* 39, 1125–1162.

Julesz, B. 1964. Binocular depth perception without familiarity cues. *Science,* 145, 356–362.

Kallman, F. J. 1952. Comparative twin study of genetic aspects of male homosexuality. *Journal of Nervous and Mental Disorders,* 115, 283–298.

Kallman, F. J. 1959. The genetics of mental illness. In S. Arieti (ed.), *American handbook of psychiatry.* New York: Basic Books.

Kallman, F. J., and Sander, G. 1949. Twin studies on senescence. *American Journal of Psychiatry,* 106, 29–36.

Kamiya, J. 1969. Operant control of EEG alpha rhythm and some of its reported effects on consciousness. In C. T. Tart (ed.), *Altered states of consciousness: A book of readings.* New York: Wiley. Pp. 507–517.

Katcher, A. 1955. The discrimination of sex differences by young children. *Journal of Genetic Psychology,* 87, 131–143.

Katz, D., Sarnoff, I., and McClintock, C. 1956. Ego defense and attitude change. *Human Relations,* 9, 27–45.

Katz, D., and Stotland, E. 1959. A preliminary statement to a theory of attitude structure and change. In S. Koch (ed.), *Psychology: A study of a science,* Vol. 3. New York: McGraw-Hill.

Kaufmann, H. 1973. *Social psychology: The study of human interaction.* New York: Holt, Rinehart and Winston.

Kellogg, R. 1967. Understanding children's art. In P. Cramer (ed.), *Readings in developmental psychology today.* Del Mar, Calif.: CRM Books.

Kellogg, W. N., and Kellogg, L. A. 1933. *The ape and the child.* New York: McGraw-Hill.

Kendon, A. 1967. Some functions of gaze-direction in social interaction. *Acta Psychologica,* Amsterdam, 26(1), 22–63.

Keniston, K. 1969. Notes on young radicals. *Change,* 1(6).

Keniston, K. 1970. Student activism, moral development, and morality. *American Journal of Orthopsychiatry,* 40.

Kessen, W., Salapatek, P., and Haith, M. M. 1972. The visual response of the human newborn to linear contour. *Journal of Experimental Child Psychology,* 13, 9–20.

Kinsey, A. C., Pomeroy, W. B., and Martin, C. E. 1948. *Sexual behavior in the human male.* Philadelphia: Saunders.

Kinsey, A. C., Pomeroy, W. B., Martin, C. E., and Gebhard, P. H. 1953. *Sexual behavior in the human female.* Philadelphia: Saunders.

Kirtner, W. L., and Cartwright, D. S. 1958. Success and failure in client-centered therapy as a function of client personality variables. *Journal of Consulting Psychology, 22,* 259–269.

Kisker, W. 1972. *The disorganized personality.* New York: McGraw-Hill.

Klebanoff, L. B. 1959. Parental attitudes of mothers of schizophrenics, brain-injured and retarded, and normal children. *American Journal of Orthopsychiatry, 29,* 445–454.

Klectman, N. 1939. *Sleep and wakefulness.* Chicago: University of Chicago Press.

Klein, D. F., and Davis, J. M. 1969. *Diagnosis and drug treatment of psychiatric disorders.* Baltimore: Williams & Wilkins.

Kling, J. W., and Riggs, A. G. 1971. *Woodworth and Schlosberg's experimental psychology.* New York: Holt, Rinehart and Winston.

Koffka, K. 1935. *Principles of Gestalt psychology.* New York: Harcourt.

Kogan, N. 1956. Authoritarianism and repression. *Journal of Abnormal and Social Psychology, 53,* 34–37.

Kohlberg, L. 1963. The development of children's orientations toward a moral order. I. Sequence in the development of moral thought. *Vita Humana, 6,* 11–33.

Kohlberg, L. A. 1966. A cognitive-developmental analysis of children's sex-role concepts and attitudes. *General Psychological Monographs, 75,* 128.

Kohlberg, L. 1967. Moral and religious education and the public schools: A developmental view. In T. Sizer (ed.), *Religion and public education.* Boston: Houghton Mifflin.

Kohlberg, L. 1968. The child as a moral philosopher. *Psychology Today,* Sept., 25–30.

Kohlberg, L. 1969. Stage and sequence: The cognitive-developmental approach to socialization. In D. A. Goslin (ed.), *The handbook of socialization theory and research.* Chicago: Rand-McNally. Pp. 347–380.

Kohlberg, L. 1970. *Stages in the development of moral thought and action.* New York: Holt, Rinehart and Winston.

Kohler, I. 1951. *The formation and transformation of the perceptual world.* Trans. by H. Fiss. New York: International Universities. 1964. Originally *Über Aufbau and Wandlungen der Wahrnehmungswelt.* Vienna: R. M. Rohrer.

Kohler, W. 1925. *The mentality of apes.* New York: Harcourt.

Kolers, P. A. 1970. Three stages of reading. In A. Levin, and J. P. Williams (eds.), *Basic studies in reading.* New York: Basic Books. Pp. 90–118.

Kolers, P. A. 1972. Reading pictures: Some cognitive aspects of visual perception. In T. S. Huang, and O. S. Tretaik (eds.), *Picture bandointh compression.* New York: Gordon Beach.

Koppitz, E. M. 1968. *Psychological evolution of children's human figure drawings.* New York: Grune & Stratton.

Krasner, L., and Ullman, L. P. 1973. *Behavior influence and personality: The social matrix of human action.* New York: Holt, Rinehart and Winston.

Krech, D., Crutchfield, R. S., and Ballachey, E. L. 1962. *Individual in society.* New York: McGraw-Hill.

Krech, D., Crutchfield, R. S., and Livson, N. 1974. *Elements of psychology,* 3rd edition. New York: Knopf.

Kretschmer, E. 1936. *Physique and character.* New York: Harcourt. Originally published in German, 1921.

Krueger, W. C. F. 1929. The effect of overlearning on retention. *Journal of Experimental Psychology, 12,* 71–78.

Kuehn, J. L. 1970. The student drug user and his family. *Journal of College Student Personnel, 11,* 409–413.

Laing, R. D. 1967. *The politics of experience.* New York: Pantheon.

Lang, P. J., and Lazovik, A. D., 1963. Experimental desensitization of a phobia. *Journal of Abnormal Social Psychology, 66* (6), 519–525.

Landauer, T. K., and Whiting, J. W. M. 1963. Infantile stimulation and adult stature of human males. *American Anthropologist, 66,* 1007–1028.

Lashley, K. S. 1942. The problem of cerebral organization in vision. In H. Kluver (ed.), *Visual mechanisms and biological symposium,* Vol. 7.

Latané, B., and Darley, J. M. 1970. *The unresponsive bystander; Why doesn't he help?* New York: Appleton.

Latour, P. 1962. Visual threshold during eye movements. *Vision Research,* 2.

Lazarus, A. D. 1960. The elimination of children's phobias by deconditioning. In H. G. Eysenck (ed.), *Behavior and the neuroses.* Oxford, England: Pergamon. Pp. 114–122.

Lazarus, R. S., and McCleary, R. A. 1951. Autonomic discrimination without awareness: A study of subception. *Psychological Review, 58,* 113–122.

Leighton, D. C. 1964. Distribution of psychiatric symptoms in a small town. *American Journal of Psychiatry,* 112, 716–723.

Lemere, F., and Voegtlin, W. L. 1950. An evaluation of the aversion treatment of alcoholism. *Quarterly Journal of Studies on Alcohol,* 11, 199–204.

Lenkel, F. 1957. A comparison of the effects of ECS and anesthesia on acquisition of the maze habit. *Journal of Comparative and Physiological Psychology,* 60, 300–306.

Lenneberg, E. H. 1969. On explaining language. *Science,* 164, 635–643.

Lewin, K., Lippitt, R., and White, R. K. 1939. Patterns of aggressive behavior in experimentally created social climates. *Journal of Social Psychology,* X, 271–299.

Lewis, M. 1972. Parents and children: Sex-role development. *School Review,* 80(2).

Lidz, T., Cornelison, A. R., Fleck, S., and Terry, D. 1957. The intrafamilial environment of schizophrenic patients: II. Marital schism and marital skew. *American Journal of Psychiatry,* 114, 241–248.

Likert, R. 1932. A technique for the measurement of attitude. *Archives of Psychology,* 22, whole number 140.

Lindsay, P. H., and Norman, D. A. 1972. *Human information processing: An introduction to psychology.* New York: Academic Press.

Livingston, R. B. 1962. Neurophysiology and psychology. In S. Koch (ed.), *Psychology: A study of a science,* Vol. 4. New York: McGraw-Hill.

Lolli, G. 1956. Alcoholism as a disorder of the love disposition. *Quarterly Journal of Studies on Alcohol,* 17, 96–107.

Long, B. E. 1968. Teaching psychology to children. *American Psychologist,* 23, 691–692.

Lovaas, O. I. 1968. Some studies on the treatment of childhood schizophrenia. In J. M. Schlien (ed.), *Research in psychotherapy,* Vol. III. Washington, D.C.: American Psychological Association.

Lowenthal, H., and Niles, P. 1964. A field experiment on fear arousal with data on the validity of questionnaire measures. *Journal of Personality,* 32, 459–479.

Luchins, A. S. 1957. Primacy-recency in impression formation. In C. I. Hovland *et al.* (eds.), *The order of presentation in persuasion,* Vol. 1. New Haven: Yale University Press.

Luria, A. R. 1957. The role of language in the formation of temporary connections. In B. Simon (ed.), *Psychology in the Soviet Union.* London: Routledge.

Luria, A. R. 1968. *The mind of a mnemonist.* Trans. by L. Solotaroff. New York: Basic Books.

MacDonald, A. P., Jr. 1970. Anxiety affiliation and social isolation. *Developmental Psychology,* 3(2), 242–254.

MacKinnon, D. W. 1938. Violation of prohibitions. In H. A. Murray (ed.), *Explorations in personality.* New York: Oxford.

McCarthy, D. A. 1946. Language development in children. In L. Carmichael (ed.), *Manual of child psychology.* New York: Wiley. Pp. 476–581.

McClelland, D. C. 1958. Risk taking in children with high and low need for achievement. In J. W. Atkinson (ed.), *Motives in fantasy, action, and society.* New York: Van Nostrand.

McClelland, D. C. 1965a. Achievement and entrepreneurship: A longitudinal study. *Journal of Personality and Social Psychology,* 1, 380–391.

McClelland, D. C. 1965b. Toward a theory of motive acquisition. *American Psychologist,* 20, 321–333.

McClelland, D. C., Atkinson, J. A., Clark, R. A., and Lowell, E. 1953. *The achievement motive.* New York: Appleton.

McClelland, D. C. and Winter, D. 1969. *Motivating economic achievement.* New York: Free Press.

McConnell, J. V., Cutler, R. L., and McNeil, E. B. 1958. Subliminal stimulation: An overview. *American Psychologist,* 13, 229–242.

McGeoch, J. A. 1930. The influence of associative value upon the difficulty of nonsense syllable lists. *Journal of Genetic Psychology,* 37, 421–426.

McGinnies, E. 1949. Emotionality and perceptual defense. *Psychological Review,* 56, 244–251.

McGuigon, F. J. 1970. Covert oral behavior during the silent performance of language tasks. *Psychological Bulletin,* 74, 309–326.

McGuire, W. J. 1966. Attitudes and opinions. *Annual Review of Psychology,* 17, 475–514.

McGuire, W. C. 1969. The nature of attitudes and attitude change. In G. Lindzey and E. Aronson (eds.), *The handbook of social psychology,* Vol. III. Reading, Mass.: Addison-Wesley.

McNeill, D. 1966. Developmental psycholinguistics. In F. Smith and G. A. Miller (eds.), *The genesis of language: A psycholinguistic approach.* Cambridge, Mass.: M.I.T. Press.

McNeill, D. 1970. *The acquisition of language: The study of developmental linguistics.* New York: Harper & Row.

Mackworth, N. H. 1950. Researches on the measurement of human performance. Medical Research Council Special Report Series, No. 268. England.

Mackworth, N. H. 1965. Visual noise causes tunnel vision. *Psychonomic Science, 3*, 67–68.

Mackworth, N. H., and Morandi, A. J. 1967. The gaze selects informative details within pictures. *Perception and Psychophysics, 2*, 547–552.

Madigan, F. C. (ed.). 1967. *Human factors in Philippine rural development.* Cagayan de Oro City: Xavier University Press.

Mandler, G. 1967. Organization and memory. In K. W. Spence and J. T. Spence (eds.), *The psychology of learning and maturation.* New York: Academic Press.

Mandler, G., and Sarason, S. B. 1952. A study of anxiety and learning. *Journal of Abnormal and Social Psychology, 47*, 166–173.

Mann, R. D. 1959. A review of the relationships between personality and performance in small groups. *Psychological Bulletin, 56*, 241–270.

Maranon, G. 1924. Contribution à l'étude de l'action emotive de l'adrenaline. *Revue Fr. Endocrinal., 2*, 301–325.

Maris, R. W. 1969. *Forces in urban suicide.* Homewood, Ill.: Dorsey.

Martin, C. J. 1965. Association and differentiation variables in all-or-none learning. *Journal of Experimental Psychology, 69*, 308–311.

Maslow, A. 1954. *Motivation and personality,* 2nd edition. New York: Harper & Row.

Masters, W. H., and Johnson, V. E. 1966. *Human sexual response.* Boston: Little, Brown.

Masters, W. H., and Johnson, V. E. 1970. *Human sexual inadequacy.* Boston: Little, Brown.

Maupin, E. W. 1972. On meditation. In C. T. Tart, *Altered states of consciousness.* New York: Doubleday. Pp. 181–190.

Mayhew, L. B. 1965. Non-test predictors of academic achievement. *Educational and Psychological Measurement, 25*, 39–46.

Mednick, S. A. 1962. The associative basis of the creative process. *Psychological Review, 69*, 220–232.

Mednick, S. A., and Schulzinger, F. 1968. Some premorbid characteristics related to breakdown in children with schizophrenic mothers. In D. Rosenthal and S. S. Kety (eds.), *The transmission of schizophrenia.* London: Pergamon. P. 268.

Meer, S. J. 1955. Authoritarian attitudes and dreams. *Journal of Abnormal and Social Psychology, 51*, 74–78.

Mehler, J. 1963. Some effects of grammatical transformations on the recall of English sentences. *Journal of Verbal Learning and Verbal Behavior, 2*, 346–351.

Mehler, J., and Carey, P. 1967. Role of surface and base structure in the perception of sentences. *Journal of Verbal Learning and Verbal Behavior, 6*, 335–338.

Meissner, G. 1859. Untersuchungen über en Tastsinn. *Zeitschrift für Rationelle Medicin, 7*, 92–118.

Menninger, K. 1938. *Man against himself.* New York: Harcourt.

Meryman, J. J. 1952. Magnitude of startle responses as a function of hunger and fear. Unpublished master's thesis, State University of Iowa.

Mewhort, D. J. K. 1967. Familiarity of letter sequences, response uncertainty, and tachistoscopic recognition experiment. *Canadian Journal of Psychology, 21*, 309–321.

Milgram, S. 1963. Behavioral study of obedience. *Journal of Abnormal and Social Psychology, 67*, 371–378.

Milgram, S. 1964. Group pressure and action against a person. *Journal of Abnormal and Social Psychology, 69*, 137–143.

Milgram, S. 1965. Some conditions of obedience and disobedience to authority. *Human Relations, 18*, 57–75.

Miller, G. A. 1956. The magical number seven plus or minus two: Some limits on our capacity for processing information. *Psychological Review, 63*, 81–97.

Miller, G. A., Bruner, J. S., and Postman, L. 1954. Familiarity of letter sequences, response uncertainty, and tachistoscopic identification. *Journal of General Psychology, 50*, 129–139.

Miller, G. A., and Selfridge, J. A. 1950. Verbal context and the recall of meaningful material. *American Journal of Psychology, 63*, 176–185.

Miller, N. E. 1944. Experimental studies in conflict. In J. McV. Hunt (ed.), *Personality and behavior disorders.* New York: Ronald.

Miller, N. E. 1948a. Fear as an acquireable drive: I. Fear as motivation and fear-reduction as reinforcement in the learning of new responses. *Journal of Experimental Psychology, 38*, 89–101.

Miller, N. E. 1948b. Theory and experiment relating psychoanalytic displacement to stimulus-response generalization. *Journal of Abnormal and Social Psychology, 43*, 155–178.

Miller, N. E. 1958. Central stimulation and other new approaches to motivation and reward. *American Psychologist, 13*, 100–108.

Miller, N. E. 1959. Liberalization of basic S-R concepts: Extensions to conflict behavior, motivation, and social learning. In S. Koch (ed.), *Psychology: The study of a science.* New York: McGraw-Hill.

Miller, N. E. 1961. Analytic studies of drive and reward. *American Psychologist, 16*, 739–754.

Miller, N. E. 1969. Learning of visceral and glandular responses. *Science,* 163, 434–445.

Miller, N. E., and Bugelski, R. 1948. Minor studies of aggression: II. The influence of frustrations imposed by the in-group on attitudes expressed toward out-groups. *Journal of Psychology,* 25, 437–452.

Miller, N. E. and Di Cara, L. 1967. Instrumental learning of heart rate change in curarized rats: Shaping, and specificity to discriminative stimulus. *Journal of Comparative and Physiological Psychology,* 63, 12–19.

Mills, J., and Aronson, E. 1965. Opinion change as a function of the communicator's attractiveness and desire to influence. *Journal of Experimental and Social Psychology,* 1(2), 173–177.

Milner, B., Corkins, S., and Teuber, H. L. 1968. Further analysis of the hippocampal amnesia syndrome: 14-year followups study of H. M. *Neuropsychalogia,* 6, 215–234.

Mischel, W. 1958. Preference for delayed reinforcement: An experimental study of a cultural observation. *Journal of Abnormal and Social Psychology,* 56, 57–61.

Mishel, W. 1968. *Personality and assessment.* New York: Wiley.

Mishler, E. G., and Scotch, N. A. 1963. Sociological factors in the epidemiology of schizophrenia. *Psychiatry,* 35, 500–508.

Mogar, R. E. 1965. Current status and future trends in psychedelic (LSD) research. *Journal of Human Psychology,* 2, 147–166.

Moncrieff, R. W. 1967. *The chemical senses.* Cleveland: CRC Press.

Montague, W. E., Adams, J. A., and Kriess, H. O. 1966. Forgetting and natural language mediation. *Journal of Experimental Psychology,* 72, 829–833.

Moore, O. K., and Anderson, A. R. 1968. The responsive environments project. In R. D. Hess and R. M. Beor (eds.), *Early education.* Chicago: Aldine.

Morgan, C. D., and Murray, H. A. 1935. A method for investigating fantasies: The Thematic Apperception Test. *Archives of Neurological Psychiatry,* 34, 289–306.

Morgan, C. T., and King, R. A. 1971. *Introduction to psychology,* 4th edition. New York: McGraw-Hill.

Moscovici, S. E., Lage, E., and Naffrechoux, M. 1969. Influence of a consistent minority on the responses of a majority in a color perception test. *Sociometry,* 32, 365–380.

Mosher, L. R., and Finesilver, D. 1970. *Special report on schizophrenia.* Chevy Chase, Md.: National Institute of Mental Health.

Murdock, B. B., Jr. 1962. The serial position effect of free recall. *Journal of Experimental Psychology,* 64, 482–488.

Murray, F. 1972. Acquisition of conservation through social interaction. *Developmental Psychology,* 6.

Murray, H. A. 1938. *Explorations in personality.* New York: Oxford.

Mussen, P. H. 1961. Some antecedents and consequences of masculine sex-typing in adolescent boys. *Psychological Monographs,* 75.

Mussen, P. H. 1962. Long-term consequences of masculinity of interests in adolescents. *Journal of Consulting Psychology,* 26.

Mussen, P. H., and Rosenzweig, M. R. 1973. *Psychology: An introduction.* Lexington, Mass.: Heath.

Nash, J. 1965. The father in contemporary culture and current psychological literature. *Child Development,* 36 (1), 261–297.

Nash, M. 1958. Machine age Maya: The industrialization of a Guatemalan community. *American Anthropologist,* 60(2), Pt. 2, Memoir No. 87.

Nathan, P. E., Andberg, M. M., Behan, P. O., and Patch, V. D. 1969. Thirty-two observers and one patient: A study of diagnostic reliability. *Journal of Clinical Psychology,* 25, 9–15.

Neisser, U. 1963. Decision-time without reaction time: Experiments in visual scanning. *American Journal of Psychology,* 76, 376–385.

Neisser, U. 1967. *Cognitive psychology.* New York: Appleton.

Neisser, U., and Beller, H. K. 1965. Searching through word lists. *British Journal of Psychology,* 56, 349–358.

Neisser, U., and Lazar, R. 1964. Searching for novel targets. *Perceptual and Motor Skills,* 19, 427–432.

Newell, A., Shaw, J. C., and Simon, H. A. 1960. Report on a general problem-solving program. *Proceedings of the International Conference on Information Processing,* W. R. Reitman (ed.). Paris: UNESCO. Pp. 256–264.

Newell, A., and Simon, H. A. 1963. GPS, a program that stimulates human thought. In E. A. Feigenbaum and J. Feldman (eds.), *Computers and thought.* New York: McGraw-Hill.

Neymann, C. A., and Yacorzynski, G. K. 1942. Studies of introversion-extroversion and conflict of motives in the psychoses. *Journal of General Psychology,* 27, 241–255.

Noble, C. E., and McNeely, D. A. 1957. The role of meaningfulness in paired-associate verbal learning. *Journal of Experimental Psychology,* 53, 16–22.

Oden, M. H. 1968. The fulfillment of promise: 40 year follow-up of the Terman gifted group. *Genetic Psychology Monographs.* 77, 3–93.

Ogle, K. N. 1962. The optical space sense. In H. Davidson (ed.), *The eye.* New York: Academic Press. Pp. 211–417.

Olds, J., and Milner, P. 1954. Positive reinforcement produced by electrical stimulation of septal area and other regions of the rat brain. *Journal of Comparative and Physiological Psychology,* 47, 419–427.

Oleron, G., Fraisse, P., Siffre, M., and Zuili, N. 1970. Les variations circodiennes du temps de reaction et du temps spontane au cours d'une expérience "hors du temps." *L'Annee Psychologique,* 70, 347–356.

Orne, M. T. 1959. The nature of hypnosis: Artifact and essence. *Journal of Abnormal and Social Psychology,* 58, 277–299.

Osborn, A. F. 1963. *Applied imagination, 3rd edition.* New York: Scribner.

Osgoood, C. E., and Tannenbaum, P. H. 1955. The principle of congruity in the prediction of attitude change. *Psychological Review,* 62, 42–55.

Pahnke, W. N., and Richards, W. A. 1966. Implications of LSD and experimental mysticism. *Journal of Religion & Health,* 5, 175–208.

Paivio, A. 1969. Mental imagery in associative learning and memory. *Psychological Review,* 76, 241–263.

Paivio, A. 1971. *Imagery and verbal process.* New York: Holt, Rinehart and Winston.

Paivio, A., and Csapo, K. 1969. Concrete-image and verbal memory codes. *Journal of Experimental Psychology,* 80, 279–285.

Paivio, A., and Foth, D. 1970. Imaginal and verbal mediators and noun concreteness in paired-associate learning: The elusive interaction. *Journal of Verbal Learning and Verbal Behavior,* 9, 384–390.

Paivio, A., Yuille, J. C., and Madigan, S. A. 1968. Concreteness, imagery, and meaningfulness values for 925 nouns. *Journal of Experimental Psychology, Monograph Supplement,* 76, 1–25.

Parke, R. D., and Walters, R. H. 1967. Some factors influencing the efficacy of punishment training for inducing response inhibition. *Monographs of Social Research in Child Development,* 32 (1).

Pasamanick, B., and Lilienfeld, A. M. 1955. Association of maternal and fetal factors with development of mental deficiency: 1. Abnormalities in the prenatal and paranatal periods. *Journal of the American Medical Association,* 159, 155–160.

Pasnau, R. O., et al. 1968. The psychological effects of 205 hours of sleep deprivation. *Archives of General Psychiatry,* 18, 496.

Paul, G. L. 1967. Insight versus desensitization in psychotherapy two years after termination. *Journal of Consulting Psychology,* 31, 333–348.

Pavlov, I. P. 1927. *Conditioned reflexes.* Oxford, England: Clarendon.

Peck, M. L. 1970. Paper presented at the Third Annual American Association of Suicidologists Convention, San Francisco.

Penfield, W. 1951. Memory mechanisms. *Transactions of the American Neurological Association,* 76, 15–31.

Penfield, W., and Jasper, H. H. 1954. *Epilepsy and the functional anatomy of the human brain.* Boston: Little, Brown.

Penfield, W., and Roberts, L. 1959. *Speech and brain-mechanisms.* Princeton, N.J.: Princeton University Press.

Peskin, H. 1967. Pubertal onset and ego functioning. *Journal of Abnormal Psychology,* 72 (1), 1–15.

Peterson, L. R., and Peterson, M. J. 1959. Short-term retention of individual items. *Journal of Experimental Psychology,* 58, 193–198.

Pfaffman, C. 1941. Gustatory afferent impulses. *Journal of Cellular and Comparative Physiology,* 17, 243–258.

Pfaffman, C. 1955. Gustatory nerve impulses in rat, cat and rabbit. *Journal of Neurophysiology,* 18, 429–440.

Pfaffman, C. 1960. The pleasures of sensation. *Psychological Review,* 67, 253–268.

Piaget, J. 1932. *The moral development of the child.* New York: Harcourt.

Piaget, J. 1950. *The psychology of intelligence.* Trans. by M. Piercy and D. E. Berlyne. London: Routledge.

Piaget, J. 1951. *Play, dreams, and imitation in childhood.* Trans. by C. Gattegno and F. M. Hodgson. New York: Norton.

Piaget, J. 1952. *The child's conception of number.* London: Routledge.

Piaget, J., and Inhelder, B. 1941. *Le developpement des quantiles chez l'enfant.* Neuchatel, Switzerland: Delacheux et Niestle.

Piaget, J. 1957. *Logic and psychology.* New York: Basic Books.

Posner, M. I., and Keele, S. W. 1967. Decay of visual information from a single letter. *Science,* 158, 137–139.

Posner, M. I., and Mitchell, R. F. 1967. Chronometric analysis of classification. *Psychological Reviews,* 74, 392–409.

Posner, M. I., and Taylor, R. L. 1969. Subtractive method applied to separation of visual and name components of multiletter arrays. *Acta Psychologica,* 30, 104–114.

Postman, L., and Rau, L. 1957. Retention as a function of the method of measurement.

University of California Publications in Psychology, 8(3).

Prytulak, L. S. 1971. Natural language mediation. *Cognitive Psychology,* 2, 1–56.

Rado, S. 1933. Psychoanalysis of pharmacotheymia. *Psychoanalytic Quarterly.* 2, 1–23.

Raphelson, A. C. 1957. The relationship between imaginative, direct, verbal, and physiological measures of anxiety in an achievement situation. *Journal of Abnormal and Social Psychology,* 54, 13–18.

Reich, W. 1949. *Character analysis,* 3rd edition. New York: Noonday.

Reiff, R. 1959. *Freud: The mind of the moralist.* New York: Viking.

Reiff, R. 1966. Mental health manpower and institutional change. *American Psychologist,* 21, 540–548.

Reitman, J. S. 1971. Mechanisms of forgetting in short-term memory. *Cognitive Psychology,* 2, 185–195.

Reitman, W. R. 1965. *Cognition and thought: An information processing approach.* New York: Wiley.

Rock, I. 1957. The role of repetition in associative learning. *American Journal of Psychology,* 70, 186–193.

Roen, S. R. 1967. Primary prevention in the classroom through a teaching program in the behavioral sciences. In E. L. Cowen, E. A. Gardner, and M. Zax (eds.), *Emergent approaches to mental health problems.* New York: Appleton. Pp. 252–270.

Roffwarg, H. P., Muzio, J. N., and Dement, W. C. 1966. Ontogenic development of the human sleep-dream cycle. *Science,* 604–619.

Rogers, C. R. 1959. A theory of therapy, personality and interpersonal relationships all developed in the client-centered framework. In S. Koch (ed.), *Psychology: A study of a science,* Vol. 3. New York: McGraw-Hill. Pp. 184–256.

Rogers, C. R. 1963. The actualizing tendency in relation to "motives" and to consciousness. In M. R. Jones (ed.), *Nebraska symposium on motivation.* Lincoln: University of Nebraska Press. Pp. 1–24.

Rorer, L. G. 1965. The great response style myth. *Psychological Bulletin,* 63, 129–156.

Rosen, B., and D'Andrade, R. C. 1959. The psychosocial origins of achievement motivation. *Sociometry,* 22, 185–218.

Rosenhan, D. L. 1973. On being sane in insane places. *Science,* 179, 250–258.

Rosenzweig, M. R., and Bennett, E. L. 1970. Effects of differential environments on brain weights and enzyme activities in gerbils, rats, and mice. *Developmental Psychology.*

Rosenzweig, M. R., Bennett, E. L., Diamond,

M. C., Wu, S., Stagle, R. W., and Saffran, E. 1969. Influences of environmental complicity and visual stimulation on development of occipital cortex in rats. *Brain Research,* 14, 427–445.

Rosenzweig, N. 1959. Sensory deprivation and schizophrenia: Some clinical and theoretical similarities. *American Journal of Psychiatry,* 116, 326–329.

Rubin, E. 1915. *Synoplevede Figurer.* Copenhagen: Gyldendalske.

Rubin, Z. 1973. *Liking and loving: An invitation to social psychology.* New York: Holt, Rinehart and Winston.

Ruch, F. L., and Zimbardo, P. G. 1971. *Psychology and life,* 8th edition. Glenview, Ill.: Scott, Foresman.

Rundus, D., and Atkinson, R. C. 1970. Rehearsal processes in free recall: A procedure for direct observation. *Journal of Verbal Learning and Verbal Behavior,* 9, 99–105.

Russell, W. A., and Storms, L. H. 1955. Implicit verbal chaining in paired-associate learning. *Journal of Experimental Psychology,* 49, 287–293.

Sacerdote, P. 1966. The use of hypnosis in cancer patients. *Annals of the New York Academy of Science,* 125 (3), 1011–1019.

Salapatek, P. 1969. The visual investigation of geometric patterns by the one- and two-month old infant. Paper presented at the meeting of the American Association for the Advancement of Science, Boston, December.

Salapatek, P., and Kessen, W. 1966. Visual scanning of triangles by the human newborn. *Journal of Experimental Child Psychology,* 3, 113–122.

Salk, L. 1972. *What every child would like his parents to know.* New York: MacKay.

Sarason, S. B., and Mandler, G. 1952. Some correlates of test anxiety. *Journal of Abnormal and Social Psychology,* 47, 810–817.

Sarason, S. B., Mandler, G., and Craighill, P. G. 1952. The effect of differential instructions on anxiety and learning. *Journal of Abnormal and Social Psychology,* 47, 561–565.

Sarnoff, I. 1960. Reaction formation and cynicism. *Journal of Personality,* 28, 129–143.

Sarnoff, I., and Katz, D. 1954. The motivational bases of attitude change. *Journal of Abnormal and Social Psychology,* 49, 115–124.

Savin, H. B., and Perchonock, E. 1965. Grammatical structure and the immediate recall of English sentences. *Journal of Verbal Learning and Verbal Behavior,* 4, 348–353.

Schachter, S. 1959. *The psychology of affiliation.* Stanford, Calif.: Stanford University Press.

Schachter, S., and Singer, J. E. 1962. Cognitive,

social and physiological determinants of emotional state. *Psychological Review, 39,* 379–399.

Schaie, K. W., and Strother, C. R. 1968. A cross-sequential study of age changes in cognitive behavior. *Psychological Bulletin, 70,* 671–680.

Scott, J. P. 1968. *Early experience and the organization of behavior.* Belmont, Calif.: Brooks-Cole.

Scott, J. P. 1970. Biology and human aggression. *American Journal of Orthopsychiatry, 40*(4), 568–576.

Scoville, W. B. 1968. Amnesia after bilateral mesial temporal lobe excision: Introduction to Case H. M. *Neuropsychologia, 6,* 211–213.

Sears, P. S. 1940. Levels of aspiration in academically successful and unsuccessful children. *Journal of Abnormal and Social Psychology, 35,* 498–536.

Sears, R. R., Maccoby, E. E., and Levin, H. 1957. *Patterns of child rearing.* Evanston, Ill.: Row, Peterson.

Seay, B., Alexander, B. K., and Harlow, H. F. 1964. Maternal behavior of socially deprived Rhesus monkeys. *Journal of Abnormal and Social Psychology, 69* (4), 345–354.

Sekular, R. W., and Ganz, L. 1963. Aftereffect of seen motion with a stabilized retinal image. *Science, 139,* 419–420.

Selfridge, O. 1959. Pandemonium: A paradigm for learning. In *The mechanism of thought processes.* London: H. M. Stationery Office.

Shannon, C. C. 1949. *Mathematical theory of communication.* Urbana: University of Illinois.

Sheldon, W. H. (with the collaboration of S. S. Stevens). 1942. *The varieties of temperament: A psychology of constitutional differences.* New York: Harper & Row.

Shields, J. 1962. *Monozygotic twins brought up apart and brought up together.* London: Oxford.

Shipley, T. E., and Veroff, J. 1952. A projective measure of need affiliation. *Journal of Experimental Psychology, 43,* 349–356.

Silverman, L. H. 1959. A Q-sort study of the validity of evaluations made from projective techniques. *Psychological Monographs, 73,* whole no. 477.

Silverman, R. E. 1971. *Psychology.* New York: Appleton.

Simmons, R. 1924. Relative effectiveness of certain incentives in animal learning. *Comparative Psychology Monographs, 2,* no. 7.

Simon, H. A., and Newell, A. 1964. Information processing in computer and man. *American Scientist, 52,* 281–300.

Singh, J. A. L., and Zingg, R. M. 1942. *Wolf children and feral man.* New York: Harper & Row.

Skinner, B. F. 1938. *The behavior of organisms.* New York: Appleton.

Skinner, B. F. 1953. *Science and human behavior.* New York: Macmillan.

Skinner, B. F. 1957. *Verbal behavior.* New York: Appleton.

Skodak, M., and Skeels, H. M. 1949. A final follow-up study of one hundred adopted children. *Journal of Genetic Psychology, 75,* 85–125.

Smedslund, J. 1959. Learning and equilibration: A study of the acquisition of concrete logical structures. Prepublication draft. Oslo.

Smedslund, J. 1966. Les origines sociales de la centration. In F. Bresson and M. de Montmalin (eds.), *Psychologie et épistemologie génetiques.* Paris: Dunod.

Smith, S. M., Brown, H. O., Tomon, J. E. P., and Goodman, L. S. 1947. The lack of cerebral effects of *d*-tubocurarine. *Anesthesiology, 8,* 1–14.

Solomon, R. L., and Howes, D. H. 1951. Word probability, personal values, and visual duration thresholds. *Psychological Review, 58,* 256–270.

Solomon, R. L., and Turner, L. H. 1962. Discriminative classical conditioning in dogs paralyzed by curare can later control discriminative avoidance responses in the normal state. *Psychological Review, 69,* 202–219.

Somers, R. H. 1965. The mainsprings of the rebellion: A survey of Berkeley students in November 1964. In S. M. Lipset and S. S. Wilin (eds.), *The Berkeley student revolt: Facts and interpretations.* Garden City, N.Y.: Doubleday.

Spearman, C. 1904. "General intelligence" objectively determined and measured. *American Journal of Psychology, 15,* 201–293.

Spelt, D. K. 1948. The conditioning of the human fetus *in utero. Journal of Experimental Psychology, 78,* 375–376.

Sperling, G. 1960. The information available in brief visual presentations. *Psychological Monographs, 74* (11), whole no. 498.

Sperling, G. 1963. A model for visual memory tasks. *Human Factors,* 19–31.

Sperling, G. 1967. Successive approximation to a model for short-term memory. *Acta Psychologica, 27,* 285–292.

Sperry, R. W., and Gazzaniga, M. S. 1967. Language following surgical disconnection of the hemispheres. In F. L. Darley (ed.), *Brain mechanisms underlying speech and language.* New York: Grune & Stratton. Pp. 108–121.

Spitz, R. A. 1945. Hospitalism: An inquiry into the genesis of psychiatric conditions in early childhood. *Psychoanalytic Study of the Child,* 1, 53–74.

Spitz, R. A. 1949. Hospitalisme: une enquête sur la genèse des états psychopathiques de la première enfance. (The effects of institution residence: an inquiry into the genesis of psychopathic states in early childhood). *Rev. franc Psychoanal,* 13, 397–425.

Spitz, R. A. 1945. Diacritic and coesnesthetic organizations: The psychiatric significance of a functional division of the nervous system into a sensitive and emotive part. *Psychoanalytic Review,* 32, 146–162.

Spock, B. M. 1946. *The common sense book of baby and child care.* New York: Duell, Sloan & Pearce.

Spranger, E. 1928. *Types of men.* New York: Stechert.

Srole, L., Langner, T. S., Michael, S. T., Opler, M. K., and Rennie, T. A. C. 1962. *Mental health in the metropolis: The midtown Manhattan study.* New York: McGraw-Hill.

Staats, A. W., and Staats, C. K. 1958. Attitudes established by classical conditioning. *Journal of Abnormal Social Psychology,* 57, 37–40.

Standing, L., Conezio, J., and Haber, R. N. 1970. Perception and memory for pictures: Simple-trial learning of 2500 visual stimuli. *Psychonomic Science,* 19 (2), 73–74.

Stott, L. H. 1957. Persisting effects of early family experience upon personality development. *Merril-Palmer Quarterly,* 3, 145–159.

Strongman, K. T., and Champness, B. G. 1968. Dominance hierarchies and conflict in eye contact. *Acta Psychologica,* Amsterdam, 28 (4), 376–386.

Sultz, E. 1971. *The cognitive bases of human learning.* Homewood, Ill.: Dorsey.

Sutcliffe, J. P. 1960. "Credulous" and "skeptical" views of hypnotic phenomena. *International Journal of Clinical and Experimental Hypnosis,* 8, 73–101.

Sutton-Smith, B. 1967. The role of play in cognitive development. *Young Children,* 22.

Szasz, T. S. 1952. Psychoanalysis and the autonomous nervous system. *Psychoanalytic Review,* 39, 115–151.

Szasz, T. S. 1961. *The myth of mental illness.* New York: Harper & Row.

Tart, C. E. 1971. *On being stoned.* New York: Science and Behavior Books.

Taylor, D. W., Berry, P. C., and Block, C. H. 1958. Does group participation when using brainstorming facilitate or inhibit creative thinking? *Administrative Science Quarterly,* 3, 23–47.

Terman, L. M. 1916. *The measurement of intelligence.* Boston: Houghton Mifflin.

Terman, L. M., et al. 1925. *Genetic studies of genius.* Vol. II, *Mental and physical traits of a thousand gifted children.* Stanford, Calif.: Stanford University Press.

Terman, L. M., and Merrill, M. A. 1937. *Measuring intelligence.* Boston: Houghton Mifflin.

Terman, L. M., and Merrill, M. A. 1960. *Stanford-Binet intelligence scale: Manual for the third revision, form L-M.* Boston: Houghton Mifflin.

Terman, L. M., and Oden, M. H. 1947. *The gifted child grows up.* Stanford, Calif: Stanford University Press.

Terman, L. M., and Oden, M. H. 1959. *The gifted group at mid-life.* Stanford, Calif.: Stanford University Press.

Teuber, H. L., Milner, B., and Vaughan, H. G., Jr. 1968. Persistent anterograde amnesia after stale wound of the basal brain. *Neuropsychologia,* 6, 267–282.

Thiessen, D. D., and McGaugh, J. L. 1958. Conflict and curiosity in the rat. Paper presented at the meeting of the Western Psychological Association, Monterey, Calif.

Thigpen, C. H., and Cleckley, H. A. 1954. A case of multiple personality. *Journal of Abnormal and Social Psychology,* 49(1), 135–144.

Thigpen, C. H., and Cleckley, H. A. 1957. *The three faces of Eve.* New York: McGraw-Hill.

Thompson, R., and McConnell, J. V. 1955. Classical conditioning in the Planarian, Dugesia dorotocephala. *Journal of Comparative and Physiological Psychology,* 48, 65–68.

Thorndike, R. L. 1948. Growth of intelligence during adolescence. *Journal of Genetic Psychology,* 72, 11–15.

Thurstone, L. L. 1954. The measurement of values. *Psychological Review,* 61, 47–58.

Thurstone, L. L. 1935. *Vectors of mind.* Chicago: University of Chicago Press.

Thurstone, L. L., and Chave, E. J. 1929. *The measurement of attitudes.* Chicago: University of Chicago Press.

Titchener, E. B. 1899. *An outline of psychology.* New York: Macmillan.

Tolman, E. C. 1932. *Purposive behavior in animals and men.* New York: Appleton.

Tolman, E. C., and Honzig, C. H. 1930a. Degrees of hunger, reward and nonreward, and maze learning in rats. *University of California Publications in Psychology,* 4(16), 246.

Tolman, E. C., and Honzig, C. H. 1930b. Introduction and removal of reward, and maze performance in rats. *University of California Publications in Psychology,* 4, 257–275.

Torrance, E. P. 1962. Non-test ways of identifying the creatively gifted. *Gifted Child Quarterly,* 6 (3), 71–75.

Treisman, A. M. 1961. Verbal cues, language and meaning in selective attention. *American Journal of Psychology,* 27, 206–219.

Tronick, E. and Clanton, C. 1971. Infant looking patterns. *Vision Research,* 11, 1479–1486.

Tulving, E., and Patkau, J. E. 1962. Concurrent effects of contextual constraint and word frequency on immediate recall and learning of verbal material. *Canadian Journal of Psychology,* 16, 83–95.

Tyler, L. E. 1965. *The psychology of human differences,* 3rd edition. New York: Appleton.

Ullman, A. D. 1952. The psychological mechanism of alcohol addiction. *Quarterly Journal of Studies on Alcohol,* 13, 602–608.

Underwood, B. J. 1957. Interference and forgetting. *Psychological Review,* 64, 49–60.

Underwood, B. J. and Good, D. 1951. Studies of distributed practice: I. The influence of introlist similarity in serial learning. *Journal of Experimental Psychology,* 42, 125–134.

Underwood, B. J., and Keppel, G. 1962. Coding processes in verbal learning. *Journal of Verbal Learning and Verbal Behavior,* 1, 250–257.

Underwood, B. J., and Postman, L. 1960. Extra experimental sources of interference in forgetting. *Psychological Review,* 67, 73–95.

Underwood, B. J., Rebula, R., and Keppel, G. 1962. Item selection in paired-associate learning. *American Journal of Psychology,* 75, 353–371.

Underwood, B. J. and Schultz, R. W. 1959. Studies of distributed practice: XIX. The influence of introlist similarity with lists of low meaningfulness. *Journal of Experimetal Psychology,* 58, 106–110.

Veroff, J. 1957. Development and validation of a projective measure of power motivation. *Journal of Abnormal and Social Psychology,* 54, 1–8.

Voegtlin, W. L. 1940. The treatment of alcoholism by establishing a conditioned reflex. *American Journal of Medical Science,* 199, 802–810.

Volkmann, F. C., Schick, A. M., and Riggs, L. A. 1968. Time course of visual inhibition during voluntary saccades. *Journal of the Optical Society of America,* 58 (4), 562–569.

Walk, R. D., and Gibson, E. J. 1961. A comparative and analytical study of visual depth perception. *Psychological Monographs,* 75, Series No. 519.

Walker, E. L. 1964. Psychological complexity as a basis for a theory of motivation and choice. *Nebraska symposium on motivation.* Lincoln: University of Nebraska Press.

Wallach, M. A., and Kogan, N. 1965. *Modes of thinking in young children.* New York: Holt, Rinehart and Winston.

Walster, E., Aronson, V., Abrahams, D., and Rottman, L. 1966. Importance of physical attractiveness in dating behavior. *Journal of Personality and Social Psychology,* 4 (5), 508–516.

Walters, R. H., Bowen, N. V., and Parke, R. D. 1963. Experimentally induced disinhibition of sexual responses. Unpublished manuscript, University of Waterloo.

Walters, R. H., Parke, R. D., and Cane, V. A. 1965. Timing of punishment and the observation of consequences to others as determinants of response inhibition. *Journal of Experimental Child Psychology,* 2 (1), 10–30.

Wang, G. H. 1923. The relation between "spontaneous" activity and oestrous cycle in the white rat. *Comparative Psychological Monographs,* 2(6).

Watson, J. B. 1930. *Behaviorism.* New York: Norton.

Watts, W. A., and Whittaker, D. N. 1966. Some sociopsychological differences between highly committed members of the Free Speech Movement and the student population at Berkeley. *Journal of Applied Behavioral Science,* 2, 41–62.

Webb, W. B. 1965. Stages of sleep across a night. From *Sleep characteristics of human subjects, Bulletin of the British Psychological Society,* 18, 1–10.

Wechsler, D. 1949. *Wechsler intelligence scale for children.* New York: Psychological Corporation.

Wechsler, D. 1955. *Wechsler adult intelligence scale.* New York: Psychological Corporation.

Wechsler, D. 1958. *The measurement and appraisal of adult intelligence.* Baltimore: Williams & Wilkins.

Weiner, N. 1948. *Cybernetics.* Cambridge, Mass.: MIT Press.

Weitzenhoffer, A. M., and Hilgard, E. R. 1959. *Stanford hypnotic susceptibility scales.* Palo Alto, Calif.: Consulting Psychologists Press.

Welch, L. 1946. Recombination of ideas in creative thinking. *Journal of Applied Psychology,* 30, 638–643.

Wenger, M. A., and Bagchi, B. K. 1961. Studies of autonomic functions in practitioners of yoga in India. *Behavioral Science,* 6, 312–323.

Werner, H. 1957. The concept of development from a comparative and organismic point of view. In D. B. Harris (ed.), *The concept of development.* Minneapolis: University of Minnesota Press.

Werner, H., and Kaplan, E. 1950. Development

of word meaning through verbal context: An experimental study. *Journal of Psychology,* 29, 251–257.

Wertheimer, M. 1945. *Productive thinking.* New York: Harper & Row.

Wertheimer, M. 1959. *Productive thinking,* exp. edition. New York: Harper & Row.

Wexler, D., Mendelson, J., Leiderman, P. H., and Solomon, P. 1958. Sensory deprivation: A technique for studying psychiatric aspects of stress. *AMA Archives of Neurological Psychiatry,* 79, 225–233.

White, R. W. 1959. Motivation reconsidered: The concept of competence. *Psychological Review,* 66, 297–333.

Whitehead, A. N., and Russell, B. 1925. *Principia mathematica,* 2nd edition. Cambridge, England: Cambridge University Press.

Whiting, J. W. M., and Child, I. L. 1953. *Child training and personality.* New Haven, Conn.: Yale University Press.

Whorf, B. L. 1956. *Language, thought, and reality.* New York: Wiley.

Williams, H. L. 1967. The problem of defining depth of sleep. In S. S. Kety, E. V. Evarts, and H. L. Williams (eds.), *Sleep and altered states of consciousness.* Baltimore: Williams & Wilkins.

Williams, R. L., Agnew, H. W., and Webb, W. B. 1964. Sleep patterns in young adults: An EEG study. *Electroencephalograph and Clinical Neurophysiology,* 17, 376–381.

Williamson, J. A., Johnson, H. A., and Eriksen, C. W. 1965. Some characteristics of post hypnotic amnesia. *Journal of Abnormal Psychology,* 70, 123–131.

Winterbottom, M. R. 1958. The relation of need for achievement to learning experience in independence and mastery. In J. W. Atkinson (ed.), *Motives in fantasy, action and society.* Princeton, N.J.: Van Nostrand. Pp. 453–478.

Wold, C. I. 1970. Characteristics of 26,000 suicide prevention center patients. *Bulletin of Suicidology,* 6, 24–28.

Wolpe, J. 1958. *Psychotherapy by reciprocal inhibition.* Stanford, Calif.: Stanford University Press.

Wolpe, J. 1969. *The practice of behavior therapy.* New York: Pergamon.

Wood, G., and Bolt, M. 1968. Mediation and mediation time in paired-associate learning. *Journal of Experimental Psychology,* 78, 15–20.

Woodruff, D. S., and Birren, J. E. 1972. Biofeedback conditioning of the EEG alpha rhythm in young and old subjects. *Proceedings of the Annual Convention of the American Psychological Association,* 7, 673–674.

Wundt, W. 1902. *Outlines of psychology,* 4th German ed. Trans. by C. H. Judd. Leipzig: Englemann.

Yarbus, A. L. 1967. *Eye movements and vision.* New York: Plenum Press.

Yarrow, M. R. 1963. Problems of methods in parent-child research. *Child Development,* 34(1), 215–226.

Yerkes, R. M., and Dodson, J. D. 1908. The relation of strength of stimulus to rapidity of habit-formation. *Journal of Comparative Neurological Psychology,* 18, 459–482.

Zax, M., and Cowen, L. 1972. *Abnormal psychology: Changing concepts.* New York: Holt, Rinehart and Winston.

Zigler, E., and Phillips, L. 1960. Social effectiveness and symptomation behavior. *Journal of Abnormal and Social Psychology,* 61, 231–238.

Zigler, E., and Phillips, L. 1961. Psychiatric diagnosis: A critique. *Journal of Abnormal and Social Psychology.*

Zimbardo, P. G. 1969. *The human choice. Nebraska Symposium on Motivation.* Vol. 17. Lincoln: University of Nebraska Press.

Zimbardo, P. G., Rapaport, C., and Baron, J. 1969. Pain control by hypnotic induction of motivational states. In P. Zimbardo (ed.), *The cognitive control of motivation.* Glenview, Ill.: Scott, Foresman.

Zobrist, A. L., and Carlson, F. R. 1973. An advice-taking chess computer. *Scientific American,* 228, 92–105.

Zubeck, J. P., Pushkar, D., Sansom, W., and Gowing, J. 1961. Perceptual changes after prolonged sensory isolation (darkness and silence). *Canadian Journal of Psychology,* 15, 83–100.

Subject Index and Glossary

Page numbers in italics refer to tables or illustrations.

Hallucinations, sensory perception (visual, auditory, etc.) not corresponding to reality (see also **Delusions**), 422–423, 726

Hallucinogens, 299–301

Halo effect, a source of error in **rating scales** of personality assessment, in which an unusually low or high score in one trait results in similar scores in other traits, 600, 636

Handbook of Social Psychology, 675

Handwriting analysis, 578–579

Harmavoidance, 249

Head Start Program, 594, 767

Hearing, 62–68
  influences on, 66–68
  sensitivity of, 66–67

Hebephrenic schizophrenia, 728

Heredity, 447–450
  determination of, 292
  and environment, 7–12
  mechanisms of, 451
  and personality, 526–528
  and psychosis, 730–732

Heuristics, shortcuts or rules of thumb that often simplify or shorten the time required to solve a problem, 390–391

Higher-order conditioning, in **classical conditioning,** the development of the ability on the part of a **conditioned stimulus** to serve as an **unconditioned stimulus;** similar to **secondary reinforcement** in **operant conditioning,** 147–148, 155, 225

Hindbrain, 272–274

Hippocampus, 279, 280

Histogram, in statistics, a diagram consisting of a set of bars, with the height of each bar indicating the number of cases that are observed to occur within a certain interval of a **continuous variable,** 775–777, 776

Homosexuality, 294–295

Hormones, chemical agents that transfer information from one set of cells to another, generally via the bloodstream, 255–256
  definition, 286
  information-transferring and permissive, 286

How to study, 172–173

Hue, the perceived dimension of color (usually what we mean by color names such as red, green, etc); determined primarily by the wavelength of the light, 58

Human Sexual Inadequacy, 760

The Human Sexual Response, 760

Hunger, 277–278

Hyperthyroidism, 528

Hypnosis, the induction of changed states of consciousness, behavior, or perception at the "suggestion" of a hypnotist, 235, 424–428
  of Aldous Huxley, 425–426
  applications of, 428
  hypnotic state, 427
  induction, 424–427
  and repression, 710

Hypothalamus, a small organ between the forebrain and midbrain, involved in holding the internal environment constant and determin-

ing the use made of the resources of the body, 270, 275, 277, 279

Hypothesis testing, a general term for the tests that explore the probability that experimental results are caused by chance in the **sample,** 790

Hypothetico-deductive method, in Piaget's theory of cognitive development, a characteristic ability learned during the **stage of formal operations;** the child can imagine hypothetical situations, deduce their consequences, and devise a test to see if the consequences hold true, 500

Hysterical neurosis, a form of **neurosis,** usually either manifested in either the **conversion reaction** or the **dissociative reaction,** 722–724

Icon, 353–354

Iconic storage, the first stage of visual **information processing,** brief visual storage; the briefly held internal representation of the information received from the eye (see also **Visual image representation, Short-term memory,** and **Long-term memory**), 318, 320–326
  duration of, 322–326

Iconic store, information extraction from, 321–322
  studying, 321

Id, the reservoir of instinctual energy in Freud's theory of the development of the personality (see also **Ego** and **Superego**), 236, 550–551

Identification, the act of placing a stimulus in a category, 36; in developmental psychology, the process whereby the child seeks to become like a significant adult (see also **Sex role**), 464–465, 510–511; in Freudian theory, a **defense mechanism** whereby anxiety-arousing or practically unrealizable desires are satisfied by imagining oneself in another's place, 554

Identity crisis, 513

Identity theory, 399

Idiots, 297–298

Imagery, kinetic, 503
  kinetic and transformational, 498
  and play, 508–510
  and verbal learning, 185–186
  visual, 497

Image, stored representation of sensory information, 353–355
  and memory, 354–355

Imagining, 503–504

Imbeciles, 297–298

Imitation, 162
  deferred, 493–494
  in learning, 567–568
  See also Modeling

Implicit speech, the theory of J. B. Watson that thought was "silent" speech, with similar but reduced use of the same muscles, 398–399

Impressions, personal, 631–636

Inadequacy, 734

Incus (anvil), the second of the three **ossicles** connecting the **ear drum** to the **oval window,** 64

Independent variable, in research design, the fac-

how to improve, 204–208
See also Memory

Retroactive inhibition, a form of **interference** with **retrieval;** the interference of new learning in the **retrieval** of old learning, 200–201, *201*

Retrograde amnesia, 296

Reversal-shift problems, 502

Reversible figures, *88*

Rhodopsin, the chemical in the **rods** of the **retina** which absorbs **photons** and thereby creates a neural impulse, 42

Ribonucleic acid (RNA), 295

Ribosomes, 257

Rochester Primary Mental Health Project, 766, 768

Rod, of eye, one of the two light-sensitive photochemical receptive elements of the **retina** (see **cone**), which are mainly responsible for perception under low light levels, 42, 43, 48

Rorschach Inkblot Test, a **projection technique** in personality assessment, developed by Herman Rorschach, in which the subject is asked to respond to a set of 12 symmetrical inkblots, 609, 611

Saccadic movement, of eyes, rapid movement of the eyes to a new point of fixation, as in reading, 50, 51, 318

Sample of the universe, 697

Sample population, a representative subgroup of a **population,** 772

Sampling error, an error introduced into research results by the lack of representativeness of the **sample** drawn from the **population,** 790

Sampling methods, a general term for the techniques employed to select a portion of a large group that will be representative of the whole (see **Area sampling** and **Quota sampling**), 696–698, 799–800

Sander parallelogram, 88

Saturation, of color, the richness of a **hue,** measured by the amount of white mixed with a single wavelength, 60

Saving score, a measure of verbal learning: S = 100 × (original trials to criterion—relearning trials to criterion)/original trials, 197

Scaling, placing different stimuli in order along some dimension, such as brightness or loudness, 36–38

Scanning, the systematic investigation of all parts of an information field in turn; serial **information processing,** 316, 326

Scapegoat, a victim of blame and aggression, chosen not for his own qualities but as a means of venting feelings of frustration, guilt, or anger, 676–677

Scattergram, a way of describing the relationship of two frequency distributions of scores by the same set of individuals: the two frequency distributions are made the **abscissa** and **ordinate** of the graph; each individual's pair of scores is plotted as a single point, 789–790

Schema, in Piaget's theory of cognitive development, an organized pattern of thought and activity that mediates the child's interaction with his world, 374, 487, 491–492

Schemata, in developmental psychology, the infant's mental representations, his organized patterns of thought and action, 458

Schizophrenia, and dementia praecox, *747*
  "high-risk" study, 764–765
  and parents, 537

Schizophrenic reactions, 727–728

Scholastic Aptitude Test, 598

School, and personality, 538–540

Scientific method, 12–16

Sclera, the white protective covering of the eyeball, 41

Scoring consistency, 580

Scotopic vision, vision resulting from stimulation of the retinal **rods;** responding to low levels of light intensity but not to color, 48, *49*

Secondary circular reactions, in Piaget's theory of cognitive development, the third stage of the **sensorimotor period,** from 4 to 8 months; the infant amalgamates **schemata** developed earlier, repeating interesting events; a concept of objects as distinct from self develops, 490–491

Secondary reinforcement, the term applied to **higher-order conditioning** in **operant conditioning,** 155, 224–226

Selective attention, the ability to pay attention to certain sensory data in the total environment and to screen out others, depending on **motivation,** past experience, or instruction, 272, 314, 340–348, 401–402
  See also Attention

Self-actualization, a concept of phenomenological theories of personality: the highest need of man, to fulfill and extend his potentialities, 570–571
  characteristics of, 571

Self-concept, the view the individual has of himself, particularly of whether he is weak or strong, 569–570
  in adolescence, 513–514
  in adulthood, 514
  in childhood, 465
  development of, 510–514
  and teacher, 539–540

Self-esteem, 691

Self-knowledge, 640

Self-ratings, 600–601

Semantic differential, 601

Semantic memory, 202

Semantics, the study of the relation of meaning to **surface structure** of a language, 371–373

Senile psychosis, 298

Sensation, 29–84
  aspects of, 30–38
  compared to perception, 86
  summary, 81–83

Sensorimotor period, in Piaget's theory of cognitive development, the first 2 years, during which the child learns to integrate sensory information and adapt his motor behavior to that information, 374–375, 489, 490–495
  overview, 493–495

Name Index

Page numbers in italics refer to tables or illustrations.